# The
# Blackwell Encyclopedia
# of
# Social Psychology

# The Blackwell Encyclopedia of Social Psychology

*Edited by*

## Antony S. R. Manstead

### and

## Miles Hewstone

*Advisory Editors*

Susan T. Fiske
Michael A. Hogg
Harry T. Reis
Gün R. Semin

First published 1995
First published in paperback 1996

Blackwell Publishers Ltd
108 Cowley Road
Oxford OX4 1JF, UK

Blackwell Publishers Inc.
238 Main Street
Cambridge, Massachusetts 02142, USA

*British Library Cataloguing in Publication Data*
A CIP catalogue record for this book is available from the British Library

*Library of Congress Cataloging in Publication Data*
The Blackwell encyclopedia of social psychology / edited by Antony S. R. Manstead
and Miles Hewstone : advisory editors, Susan T. Fiske . . . [et al.].
p.   cm.
Includes bibliographical references and index.
ISBN  0–631–18146–6 (Hbk)  —  ISBN  0–631–20289–7 (Pbk)
1. Social psychology–Encyclopedias. I. Manstead, A. S. R. II. Hewstone, Miles.
HM251.B476   1995                                        93–51074
302'.03—dc20                                                 CIP

Typeset in 9.5 on 11pt by Pure Tech Corporation, Pondicherry, India
Printed and bound in Great Britain by Hartnolls Ltd, Bodmin, Cornwall

This book is printed on acid-free paper

To Our Parents

# Contents

# Contributors

Dominic Abrams
*University of Kent*

Icek Ajzen
*University of Massachusetts at Amherst*

Irwin Altman
*University of Utah*

Teresa M. Amabile
*Brandeis University*

Nalini Ambady
*Harvard University*

John Archer
*University of Central Lancashire*

Albert Bandura
*Stanford University*

C. Daniel Batson
*University of Kansas*

Roy F. Baumeister
*Case Western Reserve University*

Gary G. Berntson
*Ohio State University*

Michael Billig
*Loughborough University*

Hart Blanton
*Princeton University*

Herbert Bless
*University of Heidelberg*

Gerd Bohner
*University of Mannheim*

Susan D. Boon
*University of Calgary*

Robert F. Bornstein
*Gettysburg College*

James Bradac
*University of California, Santa Barbara*

Veronika Brandstätter
*University of Munich*

Jack W. Brehm
*University of Kansas*

Rupert Brown
*University of Kent*

Christopher T. Burris
*University of Kansas*

Bram P. Buunk
*University of Groningen*

Wayne H. Bylsma
*Pennsylvania State University*

John T. Cacioppo
*Ohio State University*

Charles S. Carver
*University of Miami*

Mary Ann Collins
*Brandeis University*

Richard J. Contrada
*Rutgers University*

Thomas D. Cook
*Northwestern University*

Joel Cooper
*Princeton University*

William D. Crano
*University of Arizona*

Jennifer Crocker
*SUNY at Buffalo*

W. Ray Crozier
*University of Wales, College of Cardiff*

Nanne de Vries
*University of Amsterdam*

F. M. J. Dehue
*University of Groningen*

Bella M. DePaulo
*University of Virginia*

David A. DeSteno
*Yale University*

Michael Diehl
*University of Mannheim*

Edward Donnerstein
*University of California, Santa Barbara*

John F. Dovidio
*Colgate University*

Stephen Drigotas
*Southern Methodist University*

Kevin Durkin
*University of Western Australia*

Nancy Eisenberg
*Arizona State University*

J. Richard Eiser
*University of Exeter*

Nicholas Emler
*University of Oxford*

Leandre R. Fabrigar
*Ohio State University*

Klaus Fiedler
*University of Heidelberg*

Frank D. Fincham
*University of Wales, College of Cardiff*

Alan Page Fiske
*Bryn Mawr College, Pennsylvania*

Susan T. Fiske
*University of Massachusetts at Amherst*

Joseph P. Forgas
*University of New South Wales*

Friedrich Försterling
*University of Erfurt*

Donelson R. Forsyth
*Virginia Commonwealth University*

Adrian F. Furnham
*University College London*

Russell G. Geen
*University of Missouri*

Thomas R. Geen
*University of California, Davis*

Seth Geiger
*University of California, Santa Barbara*

G. P. Ginsburg
*University of Nevada, Reno*

Faith Gleicher
*University of California, Santa Barbara*

Peter M. Gollwitzer
*University of Konstanz*

Carl F. Graumann
*University of Heidelberg*

Sarah E. Hampson
*Oregon Research Institute*

Andrea Harvan
*State University of New York at Albany*

John H. Harvey
*University of Iowa*

Jutta Heckhausen
*Max-Planck-Institut für Bildungsforschung, Berlin*

Miles Hewstone
*University of Wales, College of Cardiff*

E. Tory Higgins
*Columbia University*

Michael A. Hogg
*University of Queensland*

Christopher E. Houston
*University of Virginia*

William Ickes
*University of Texas at Arlington*

Craig Johnson
*Syracuse University*

Charles M. Judd
*University of Colorado at Boulder*

Lee Jussim
*Rutgers University*

Birgit Kaufmann-Bryant
*Syracuse University*

Kathryn Kelley
*State University of New York at Albany*

Norbert L. Kerr
*Michigan State University*

Barbara Krahé
*University of Potsdam*

Jon A. Krosnick
*Ohio State University*

Arie W. Kruglanski
*University of Maryland*

Ellen J. Langer
*Harvard University*

Bibb Latané
*Florida Atlantic University*

Lorella Lepore
*University of Kent*

Howard Leventhal
*Rutgers University*

Wim B. G. Liebrand
*University of Groningen*

Neil Macrae
*University of Wales, College of Cardiff*

Antony S. R. Manstead
*University of Amsterdam*

Pam Maras
*University of Kent*

Kerry L. Marsh
*University of Notre Dame*

Carol Lynn Martin
*Arizona State University*

René Martin
*University of Iowa*

Christina Maslach
*University of California, Berkeley*

David M. Messick
*Northwestern University*

Michael J. Migdal
*Syracuse University*

Robert M. Milardo
*University of Maine*

Arthur G. Miller
*Miami University, Ohio*

Dale T. Miller
*Princeton University*

Beth A. Morling
*University of Massachusetts at Amherst*

Brian Mullen
*Syracuse University*

Sik Hung Ng
*Victoria University of Wellington*

Stuart Oskamp
*Claremont Graduate School*

Bernadette Park
*University of Colorado at Boulder*

Brian Parkinson
*University of Leicester*

W. Gerrod Parrott
*Georgetown University*

Miles L. Patterson
*University of Missouri-St Louis*

Daniel Perlman
*University of British Columbia*

Anthony R. Pratkanis
*University of California, Santa Cruz*

Dean G. Pruitt
*SUNY at Buffalo*

Harry T. Reis
*University of Rochester*

Robert Rosenthal
*Harvard University*

Caryl E. Rusbult
*University of North Carolina*

James A. Russell
*University of British Columbia*

Peter Salovey
*Yale University*

Barry R. Schlenker
*University of Florida*

Jeanette Schmid
*University of Heidelberg*

Richard Schulz
*University of Pittsburgh*

Henk Schut
*University of Utrecht*

Shalom H. Schwartz
*The Hebrew University of Jerusalem*

Norbert Schwarz
*University of Michigan*

Gün R. Semin
*Free University, Amsterdam*

Kelly G. Shaver
*College of William & Mary*

John J. Skowronski
*Ohio State University*

Charles P. Smith
*City University of New York, Graduate School*

Peter B. Smith
*University of Sussex*

Philip M. Smith
*Warlpole Ltd*

Mark Snyder
*University of Minnesota*

Russell Spears
*University of Amsterdam*

Geoffrey M. Stephenson
*University of Kent*

Fritz Strack
*University of Trier*

Charles G. Stangor
*University of Maryland*

Margaret Stroebe
*University of Utrecht*

Wolfgang Stroebe
*University of Utrecht*

Sheldon Stryker
*Indiana University*

Jerry Suls
*University of Iowa*

Stephen Sutton
*Institute of Psychiatry, London*

Abraham Tesser
*University of Georgia*

Philip E. Tetlock
*University of California, Berkeley*

Charles W. Tolman
*University of Victoria*

Harry C. Triandis
*University of Illinois at Urbana-Champaign*

John C. Turner
*Australian National University*

Tom R. Tyler
*University of California, Berkeley*

Eddy Van Avermaet
*Catholic University of Leuven*

Joop van der Pligt
*University of Amsterdam*

Paul A. M. Van Lange
*Free University, Amsterdam*

Peter Warr
*University of Sheffield*

Gifford Weary
*Ohio State University*

Paul Webley
*University of Exeter*

Daniel M. Wegner
*University of Virginia*

Toni G. Wegner
*University of Virginia*

Bernard Weiner
*University of California, Los Angeles*

Tracy R. Wellens
*ZUMA, Mannheim*

Carol M. Werner
*University of Utah*

Robert A. Wicklund
*University of Bielefeld*

Gail M. Williamson
*University of Georgia*

Leslie A. Zebrowitz
*Brandeis University*

# Preface

Neither of us ever aspired to edit an encyclopedia, but when we were approached independently by two separate publishers, we began to think there was real merit in the idea. Our commitment to social psychology, and our belief in the important contributions made by our discipline, quickly led us to take up the challenge. After all, social psychology is now taught, studied, and researched throughout the world, and is an accepted core subject in every serious degree course in psychology, as well as being a discipline with spheres of interest in sociology, anthropology, and other behavioral sciences. We hope that this book will be a standard resource for all social psychologists: a volume to which students, instructors, researchers, and practitioners can turn when they want to discover more about a particular phenomenon, concept, or theory.

Every step has been taken to ensure that all key topics in social psychology are addressed, and the entries themselves have been written by a large but carefully selected team of authors. The principal criterion used to select authors was that they should be internationally recognized authorities on the topic(s) in question. The book is therefore comprehensive in coverage and authoritative in content. In short, this *Encyclopedia* can be used by introductory students as a comprehensive introduction to the field of social psychology, by more advanced students and instructors as a way of checking or extending their knowledge of a particular topic, and by researchers as an informed and informative guide to the research literature.

Talking to colleagues we realized that there is a broad consensus about what the key sources of literature are in our field: we agree on a selection of top journals, for example. But there is no existing encyclopedia or dictionary which is accepted as a standard work of reference. We have aspired to provide such a volume. To this end, we have been ably supported by four superb Advisory Editors, who helped us generate the initial list of entry titles and then each contributed several key entries. They also emphasize something we wanted to highlight, namely, the international profile of social psychology – Susan Fiske (University of Massachusetts at Amherst, USA), Michael Hogg (University of Queensland, Australia), Harry Reis (Rochester University, USA), and Gün Semin (Free University, Amsterdam, The Netherlands). Our task was then made immeasurably easier by the overwhelmingly positive reactions to our first wave of invitations, which ensured that the entries in this book are written by leading scholars, and indeed its list of contributors reads like a "Who's Who" of social psychology. We take this opportunity of thanking them all for their scholarly and impartial contributions, which it has been our pleasure to read and edit.

We envisage that the target audiences of this volume will use the *Encyclopedia* differently. For example, instructors will be able to use entries to update lectures, react quickly to the challenging questions of students which fall outside their areas of expertise, and to keep themselves abreast of recent developments in the field as a whole. Students should find the book particularly useful when searching for definitions of a key term, and for directing their own writing assignments to the core of an area. Various aspects of the structure of the book should help both audiences. There are four levels of entry, appropriate to the importance of an area within the field – 3,000 word feature items (of which there are 93), 1,000 word *major items* (101), 200 word *glossary items with brief explanation* (64), and 50 word *glossary items* (90). The three main levels of entry have a bibliography of commensurate length (10, 5, and 2 references, respectively), which guide the reader to more detailed literature, focusing on classic as well as contemporary sources. Page numbers of all book chapters are given, to facilitate library searches. Finally, all entries (with a few reasonable exceptions) provide a definition in the first paragraph, and make clear cross-references to other relevant entries (these are printed in uppercase on first mention in the text, and feature and major items are relisted alphabetically at the end of each entry).

The structure of the entries allows readers to use the book in a "top-down" or "bottom-up" fashion. Top-down, a complete newcomer to the field might start with the feature entry on SOCIAL PSYCHOLOGY, which includes cross-references to areas recognized as part of the core of the discipline. These include ATTITUDE THEORY AND RESEARCH, ATTRIBUTION THEORIES, RESEARCH METHODS, SOCIAL COGNITION, STATISTICS, SOCIAL INFLUENCE, and INTERGROUP RELATIONS. If intrigued by the topic of social influence, say, the reader can proceed from the entry on this topic (3,000 words), to more specific entries on MAJORITY SOCIAL INFLUENCE (200 words) and glossary items (50 words), including NORMATIVE INFLUENCE and INFORMATIONAL INFLUENCE. Alternatively, one might work from the bottom up, beginning with a key term such as ADJUSTMENT AND ANCHORING (50 words), working up to HEURISTICS (3,000 words), and cross-checking the entry on REASONING (1,000 words). Entries are arranged in alphabetical order, but if you cannot immediately locate material on a desired topic, consult the extensive index. Even where we have decided that a topic did not merit a separate entry of its own, it is often covered extensively in more than one other entry.

When we began work on this book, we came across two quotations which neatly illustrate the roles of contributors to, and editors of, this volume. Goethe wrote that "In der Beschränkung zeigt sich der Meister" (which might be rendered as "Mastery lies in brevity,"!). We believe our set of entries shows that to be the case, and thank our contributors once again for prostrating themselves on our Procrustean bed of editorial guidelines. Regarding our own role as editors, Dr Johnson defined a lexicographer as "a harmless drudge"! We certainly do not recognize this as a description of our work on this volume, perhaps because the objective of this book is to go well beyond the task of merely defining key terms and concepts. Instead, the goal is to provide accurate, up-to-date, and lively explications of key topics in social psychology. Our decision that we should both read, and where necessary re-read, all the entries has been vindicated. We have been students of social psychology again, we have benefited enormously from our journey through the field, and we have both gained from our discussions *en route*. We have also enjoyed each other's "company" tremendously (often at the end of a telephone or email node, but sometimes over a bottle or two of Barolo). Last, but not least, as a challenge to the hegemony of alphabetical order, the order of our names was determined by height in centimetres.

TONY MANSTEAD, AMSTERDAM

MILES HEWSTONE, CARDIFF

# A

**accessibility** This refers to how easily a construct is retrieved. Knowledge is accessible when it is recently, frequently, or chronically available. PRIMING makes categories temporarily accessible before a stimulus is perceived. In addition, individuals have categories that are chronically accessible; they are regularly and readily usable. For example, some people may chronically perceive everyone in terms of how intelligent they are. When a person's chronic and temporary primes conflict, contextual priming initially dominates individual differences in accessibility, but a person's chronic constructs dominate contextual priming after a delay (Bargh et al., 1986).

Accessible constructs significantly influence the ENCODING of relevant stimuli, affecting how they are perceived and judged; this is especially true of stimuli that are moderate or ambiguous (Bruner, 1957). For example, if a person's construct for friendliness is accessible, the person would interpret an ambiguously described other person to be more friendly than otherwise.

BIBLIOGRAPHY
Bruner, J. S. (1957). On perceptual readiness. *Psychological Review*, *64*, 811–24.
Bargh, J. S., Bond, R. N., Lombardi, W. L., & Tota, M. E. (1986). The additive nature of chronic and temporary sources of construct accessibility. *Journal of Personality and Social Psychology*, *50*, 869–79.

SUSAN T. FISKE
BETH A. MORLING

**accountability** This refers to social pressures to justify one's views or decisions to others. As such, accountability plays a key part in most proposed solutions of the classic Hobbesian riddle: How is society possible? (*see* Semin & Manstead, 1983). Organized social life cannot exist without some regularity. This regularity is provided by shared rules, norms, and social practices. Accountability is a critical rule and norm-enforcement mechanism – the social psychological link between individual decision makers on the one hand and social systems on the other. Expectations of accountability are an implicit or explicit constraint on virtually everything people do ("If I do this, how will others react?"). Failure to act in ways for which one can construct acceptable accounts leads to varying degrees of censure, depending on the gravity of the offence and the norms of the society (Tetlock, 1992).

Although one can make a powerful case for the universality of accountability (Semin & Manstead, 1983), the specific NORMS and values to which people are held accountable vary dramatically from one culture or time to another. When people leave groups and join new ones, they must often learn new vocabularies of motives – new rules for generating acceptable explanations of behavior. Vocabularies of motives vary as a function of both the micro and macro contexts. The micro context includes IDEOLOGIES and VALUES that characterize distinctive organizations within society and rules within organizations. The macro context refers to cultural ideologies and values. An important research task is systematic ethnographic work to characterize the normative beliefs and values that define standards of accountability in particular decision-making settings.

Accountability researchers generally assume that people seek the approval and respect of those to whom they are accountable. Researchers do, however, characterize the approval motive in quite distinctive ways. Some trace it to the desire to protect and enhance one's social image or identity, some trace it to the desire to protect and enhance one's self-image, and still others (most notably, SOCIAL EXCHANGE theorists) trace it to the desire to acquire power and wealth. Researchers also diverge over the degree to which people are motivated more by fear of loss of approval or by the quest to enhance their standing in the eyes of others (defensive versus expansive SELF-PRESENTATION).

Research on accountability has proceeded at the micro and macro levels. At the micro level, numerous experimental studies have manipulated whether people feel accountable for their judgments and decisions, to whom people feel accountable, whether people learn that they are accountable prior to or only after exposure to the evidence on which they base their decisions, and the importance of the audience to whom people feel accountable. This research reveals that accountability can have a wide range of cognitive, emotional, and behavioral effects. When people learn that they must justify their opinions to an audience whose own views are known, and people have not yet taken a position themselves, accountability motivates people to shift their views to the anticipated audience (ingratiation, CONFORMITY, and strategic attitude shifts). When people are asked to justify their opinions to an audience whose own views are unknown, and people have not yet taken a stand themselves, accountability motivates preemptive self-criticism in which people attempt to anticipate objections the audience might raise to their positions (increased INTEGRATIVE COMPLEXITY). When people are asked to justify their opinions on an issue where they have already taken a difficult-to-reverse stand, accountability motivates defensive bolstering in which people try to generate as many justifications as they can for their initial position. When people are accountable to multiple audiences with conflicting policy preferences, they often cope by buckpassing (trying to transfer responsibility for the decision to others) and by procrastination (delaying the decision until further evidence is in hand).

Experimental research has also shown that the effects of accountability are not limited to shifts in public response thresholds (e.g., making people reluctant to take any kind of controversial stand). This point can be most conclusively made by manipulating whether people learn of being accountable prior to or only after exposure to the evidence on which they base judgments. If accountability reduces judgmental biases such as primacy effects or overconfidence simply by transforming people into fence-sitters who never stray from the midpoints of attitude scales, then it should not matter when they learn of being accountable. If accountability reduces judgmental biases by motivating people to think in more nuanced, self-critical, and differentiated ways about the stimulus evidence, it should matter a great deal whether they learn of being accountable prior to exposure to the stimulus evidence. Research indicates that the latter position is correct (Tetlock & Boettger, 1989; Tetlock & Kim, 1987; Tetlock, Skitka, & Boettger, 1989).

Research on the macro level focuses on the role that accountability plays in facilitating or impeding the functioning of social systems. Economists, for example, stress the role of market accountability in motivating providers of goods and services to do so in the most efficient way possible. Political scientists have devoted much attention to the incentives that different accountability arrangements create for both leaders and followers (e.g., constitutional democracy, oligarchy, tyranny). Sociologists and anthropologists have documented enormous variation in accountability ground rules across both institutions and cultures.

One important theme running through the voluminous macro literature on accountability is the frequency with which "perverse effects" arise in the functioning of real-life accountability systems. Corporate Boards of Directors are supposed to hold top management accountable to shareholders, but instead often become allies and accomplices of the Chief Executive Officer. Government regulatory agencies are supposed to hold the regulated industry accountable to the public interest but instead are often "captured" by the regulated interests. Politicians in democracies are accountable to the mass public but often give greater weight to highly cohesive special interests. This macro literature has numerous implications for micro researchers who are interested both in diffusion of responsibility and the logic of collective action.

In sum, accountability is a construct that links levels of analysis. Researchers have appropriately approached accountability from a variety of perspectives. Some have focused on both individual and situational variation in the social motives underlying responses to accountability demands; some focus on the cognitive and political strategies people use to cope with accountability demands; and still others focus on how accountability systems function or malfunction in complex real-world settings. *See also*: IDEOLOGY; INTEGRATIVE COMPLEXITY; NORMS; VALUES.

BIBLIOGRAPHY

Semin, G. R., & Manstead, A. S. R. (1983). *The accountability of conduct: A social psychological analysis*. London: Academic Press.

Tetlock, P. E. (1992). The impact of accountability on judgment and choice: Toward a social contingency model. In M. Zanna (Ed.), *Advances in experimental social psychology* (Vol. 25, pp. 331–76). New York: Academic Press.

—— & Boettger, R. (1989). Accountability: A social magnifier of the dilution effect. *Journal of Personality and Social Psychology: Attitudes and Social Cognition, 57*, 388–98.

—— & Kim, J. (1987). Accountability and overconfidence in a personality prediction task. *Journal of Personality and Social Psychology: Attitudes and Social Cognition, 52*, 700–9.

—— Skitka, L., & Boettger, R. (1989). Social and cognitive strategies of coping with accountability: Conformity, complexity, and bolstering. *Journal of Personality and Social Psychology: Interpersonal Relations and Group Dynamics, 57*, 632–41.

PHILIP E. TETLOCK

**accounts** Storylike constructions containing description, interpretation, emotion, expectation, and related material (*see* ATTRIBUTION OF RESPONSIBILITY). This concept has two heritages:

(1) research in sociology that emphasizes people's need to save face and present to others acceptable excuses and justifications for their behavior that is potentially blameworthy (e.g., Scott & Lyman, 1968). These scholars gave the term account a relatively narrow definition, focusing on "valuative inquiry" – meaning, principally, ascription of responsibility for some type of problematic event or predicament.

(2) research in social psychology on attribution that emphasizes the processes by which people interpret and understand aspects of their world such as interpersonal event (e.g., ATTRIBUTION THEORIES). This work led to the broader definition of account stated above, in which attribution or interpretation is a central part of the overall storylike presentation (*see* Harvey, Weber, & Orbuch, 1990, for a summary of theory and research embracing this broader conception); this latter line of theory subsumes situations involving valuative inquiries and those which are relatively nonevaluative. The extension of attribution ideas to the accounts paradigm was developed in order to provide a sensitive way to examine explanation within naturally occurring contexts, such as written stories and oral presentations (*see* DISCOURSE ANALYSIS). In developing this extension, it was assumed that the meaning conveyed by these storylike constructions is different from that supplied by the individual attributions that form part of the story. A concept highly related to the concept of account is that of narrative (Shotter, 1984). Similar to work on accounts, this area of investigation focuses on people's stories and story-telling orally and in writing, and the effects of these stories on aspects of their lives.

Why do people offer accounts? In general, they do so in order to achieve a greater sense of control (Schönbach, 1992). More specifically, accounts are offered for the following reasons: to maintain or enhance self-esteem; to engage in catharsis or emotional purging regarding some highly grievous matter; simply to achieve completion in understanding of some complex state of affairs; and to stimulate enlightenment, hope, and will (e.g., the instance of stories written by persons who have suffered through great loss or anguish and who wish to enlighten and give strength to those who read their stories).

Thus far, research on accounts has attempted to reveal different conditions leading to and consequences of account-making, and to how people's accounts affect the way they are perceived by others (*see* PERSON PERCEPTION). One prominent line of research involves asking individuals to provide an autobiographical micronarrative – or a very short story – pertaining to some highly memorable event in their life. Baumeister and colleagues (e.g., Baumeister, Stillwell, & Wotman, 1990) have used this approach to investigate the different perceptions and attributions made by people remembering such events as when they were victims or perpetrators of wrong-doing, or when they had unrequited love for another, or were the object of such unrequited love. While the possibility of memory distortion and comparability of accounts across people are daunting issues for this program of research, work to date shows the merit of the technique in eliciting stories about various human dilemmas. A general type of evidence emerging is that people either remember events, or color their accounts of these events, in ways that present themselves to others in relatively positive lights (*see* IMPRESSION FORMATION, SELF-PRESENTATION).

The most active research domain for work on accounts pertains to their role in helping people cope with stressful events. One such event that has received considerable attention to date is that of divorce and separation, or dissolution of CLOSE RELATIONSHIPS. When a major stressor such as divorce or unexpected death of a spouse occurs (*see* BEREAVEMENT, STRESS AND COPING), account-making and the related activity of confiding in close others (which presumably involves part, but not all, of an individual's account of an event) are conceived to contribute to positive coping. On the other hand, suppression of the account-making and/or confiding activities are posited to contribute to negative coping, or psychological and physical health problems. Evidence tends to support this model of the role of accounts as related to health outcomes. Account-making and confiding research also has been extended to situations involving sexual abuse and incest, again with the findings showing more positive coping for persons who are able to engage in account-making activities and confiding versus those who are not about to engage in such activities.

Overall, research on accounts and confiding in dealing with major stressors and relationship loss is quite promising because of its focus on:

(1) the context, as perceived by the individual, surrounding the stressful event; and

(2) a relatively broad and full analysis of the individual's own words, thoughts, and feelings associated with the stressor.

In order to make substantial further gains, however, this line of research must address such imposing issues as: how to code accounts reliably; how to delineate more precisely health and behavioral outcomes associated with accounts and confiding activities; and how to establish causal links among accounts, confiding, and health and behavioral outcomes.

*See also*: ATTRIBUTION OF RESPONSIBILITY; ATTRIBUTION THEORIES; DISCOURSE ANALYSIS; IMPRESSION FORMATION; STRESS AND COPING.

BIBLIOGRAPHY

Baumeister, R. F., Stillwell, A. M., & Wotman, S. R. (1990). Victim and perpetrator accounts of interpersonal conflict: Autobiographical narratives about anger. *Journal of Personality and Social Psychology*, *59*, 994–1005.

Harvey, J. H., Weber, A. L., & Orbuch, T. L. (1990). *Interpersonal accounts: A social psychological perspective*. Oxford: Basil Blackwell.

Schönbach, P. (1992). Interactions of process and moderator variables in account episodes. In J. H. Harvey, T. L. Orbuch, & A. L. Weber (Eds.), *Attributions, accounts, and close relationships* (pp. 40–51). New York: Springer-Verlag.

Scott, M. B., & Lyman, S. M. (1988). Accounts. *American Sociological Review, 33,* 46–62.

Shotter, J. (1984). *Social accountability and selfhood.* Oxford: Basil Blackwell.

JOHN H. HARVEY

**accuracy in impression formation** With no single criterion for assessing accuracy, it may be inferred from consensus among those judging a target's attributes, from agreement between judges' impressions and the target's self-reports, or from concordance between judges' impressions and objective measures, such as target behaviors or test scores.

LESLIE A. ZEBROWITZ

**achievement motivation** The need for achievement, or achievement motivation, has been defined as "the desire or tendency to do things as rapidly and/or as well as possible . . . to accomplish something difficult . . . and attain a high standard . . . to excel" (Murray, 1938, p. 164). The study of achievement motivation, which was a minor issue in the experimental analysis of motivation during the Murray era, subsequently ascended to become *the* central topic in human motivation (*see* Atkinson, 1964; Weiner, 1992).

THE INDIVIDUAL DIFFERENCE
APPROACH
Following Murray, the next person of importance in the study of achievement motivation was David McClelland, for he refined the Thematic Apperception Test (TAT), a projective technique developed by Murray and used primarily in clinical settings, so that it would be applicable for the measurement of human needs in research settings. Individuals were classified as high or low in achievement needs based on their scores on the TAT, and their achievement strivings (e.g., intensity of performance, persistence at achievement tasks) were anticipated based on these need scores.

In addition, McClelland (1961) related achievement needs to the economic development of countries, using various sources of written material to classify cultures as high or low in achievement needs.

The first attempt to place the study of achievement strivings within a broader conceptual framework was then undertaken by Atkinson (1964). Rather than predicting behavior knowing only one's intrapsychic need state, Atkinson contended that achievement strivings could be understood within a decision theory framework in which behavior was conceptualized as determined by what one values and the expectancy of attaining that valued goal. The incentive VALUE of an achievement goal was assumed to be pride in accomplishment. Furthermore, pride was postulated to be inversely related to the expectancy of success (the more difficult the goal, the greater the pride in accomplishment). Guided by Murray and McClelland, Atkinson also specified that the motivation to undertake achievement behavior is influenced by the need for achievement. According to his theory, achievement strivings are a product of: Need for Achievement × Expectancy of Success × Incentive Value. Thus, Atkinson was able to predict that positive achievement strivings are most aroused at tasks of intermediate difficulty, where incentive and expectancy both are given numerical values of 0.50. In addition, individuals high in achievement needs are predicted to be more motivated by intermediate difficulty tasks, and thus are more likely to select those tasks, than are persons low in achievement needs.

Difficulties with TAT assessment, and with the implicit assumption that an individual's need for achievement is constant across different content domains, in part resulted in the relative demise of this approach. Consistent with the emerging emphasis on cognitions in psychology, the study of achievement strivings turned to the thoughts that mediate between an achievement-related stimulus and achievement behaviors.

THE ATTRIBUTIONAL APPROACH
The thought process that attracted most attention related to attributions of causality, or

the perceived reasons why one succeeded or failed (Weiner, 1986). Attribution theorists documented that causal thinking influences performance, affective reactions, and the responses of others to those who are succeeding or failing. For example, an ascription of failure to low ability impedes subsequent performance as compared with an attribution to low effort or bad luck (*see* HELPLESSNESS). Further, an individual failing because of low ability experiences humiliation and shame, whereas poor performance due to lack of effort evokes guilt. In addition, failure due to low effort is more severely punished by others than is failure ascribed to lack of ability, which tends to give rise to sympathy from others (*see* ATTRIBUTION OF RESPONSIBILITY). Thus, ATTRIBUTION THEORIES incorporated a variety of AFFECTS that were neglected by need theorists, as well as broadening the cognitive determinants of performance.

Other variables have also been identified that exert an influence on achievement strivings. These are linked with the structure of the environment which, in turn, shapes particular achievement-related thoughts.

THE ACHIEVEMENT CONTEXT
The structural characteristics of the school system have been argued to have negative motivational consequences for school children. The general contention is that in competitive environments, success is defined as doing better than others. Thus, SOCIAL COMPARISON is involved, there are few winners but many losers, and failure indicates that one is not as good as others (*see* COOPERATION AND COMPETITION). In this setting, the goal of the students therefore is to demonstrate superior capacity (high ability). Hence, ability is equated with value and students may protect their self-worth by not trying (*see* SELF HANDICAPPING) or by telling their peers that they are not trying. Student goals are therefore egoistic (self-focused) or directed toward peer acceptance, rather than directed toward environmental mastery (task-focused). Ego-versus task-orientation and self-versus mastery-focus relate to a variety of achievement behaviors.

Another important environmental influence on achievement strivings is whether the situation is perceived as self-regulated or as controlled by others, and whether the reward is intrinsic to the learner or is imposed from the environment. INTRINSIC MOTIVATION and self-responsibility for achievement strivings tend to enhance learning, persistence, and achievement-related actions (*see* CONTROL MOTIVATION, LOCUS OF CONTROL).

CONCLUDING COMMENTS
In the past 50 years, there has been much empirical and theoretical process in the study of achievement motivation. What began as a search for the qualities of a person that produce achievement-related behavior has now extended to include the thoughts, emotions, and contextual factors that can enhance or inhibit achievement strivings.

*See also*: ATTRIBUTION OF RESPONSIBILITY; ATTRIBUTION THEORIES; COOPERATION AND COMPETITION; CONTROL MOTIVATION; SOCIAL COMPARISON; VALUES.

BIBLIOGRAPHY
Atkinson, J. W. (1964). *An introduction to motivation*. Princeton, NJ: Van Nostrand.
McClelland, D. C. (1961). *The achieving society*. Princeton, NJ: Van Nostrand.
Murray, H. A. (1938). *Explorations in personality*. New York: Oxford University Press.
Weiner, B. (1986). *An attributional theory of motivation and emotion*. New York: Springer-Verlag.
——(1992). *Human motivation: Metaphors, theories, and research*. Newbury Park, CA: Sage.

BERNARD WEINER

**activation** The generalized innervation of the cerebral cortex associated with either external stimulation or emotional states and mediated by various structures in the midbrain and limbic system. The term is sometimes used outside the context of physiology to describe undifferentiated excitation (*see* AROUSAL, DRIVE).

*See also*: AROUSAL; DRIVE.

RUSSELL G. GEEN

**actor–observer differences** Research on AT-TRIBUTIONAL BIAS proposed that actors attributed their actions to situational factors, whereas observers tended to attribute the same actions to stable personal dispositions. The effect is confined to a difference in situational attribution, and appears due to differences in information, perceptual focus, and linguistic factors.

*See also*: ATTRIBUTIONAL BIAS.

MILES HEWSTONE

**adaptation-level** In perceptual or SOCIAL JUDGMENT, the subjective average of a series of stimuli along some continuum; claimed by Helson (1964), to reflect the combined effect of all prior and current experience and to account for wherever stimuli are contrasted from their context, background, or some comparison standard. Thus, swimming-pool water feels cool after sun-bathing because its temperature is lower than the heat to which one has adapted. Other authors dispute Helson's reliance on physiological homeostatic mechanisms, stressing more cognitive factors, e.g., changes in how people define the response scale. In size judgments, a large standard could lead to smaller judgments (contrast) simply by requiring "large" to be redefined to refer to even bigger objects than before. Parducci (1963) argued that adaptation-level reflects a compromise between two tendencies to use response categories:

(1) to cover similar proportions of the stimulus range; and
(2) with similar frequencies.

Relevant recent work concerns the activation of judgmental norms appropriate to the context or class of objects (*see* NORM THEORY).

*See also*: NORM THEORY; SOCIAL JUDGMENT.

BIBLIOGRAPHY
Helson, H. (1964). *Adaptation-level theory*. New York: Harper & Row.
Parducci, A. (1963). Range-frequency compromise in judgment. *Psychological Monographs 77* (2, Whole No. 565).

J. RICHARD EISER

**addiction** The term addiction (and its near-synonym, dependence) is used in many different ways; there is no single accepted scientific definition (*see* Oxford, 1985). It is perhaps most frequently used as a rubric for certain behaviors that have important characteristics in common – particularly, but not exclusively, behaviors that involve the use of psychoactive (mood-altering) DRUGS. Among the criteria that may be used to group particular activities together under the heading "addictive behaviors" are the following:

(1) the behavior becomes established rapidly;
(2) the behavior is frequent, regular, and stereotyped;
(3) the behavior is done to excess and/or occupies a large part of the individual's time;
(4) the behavior causes health, financial, marital, or other problems for the individual concerned;
(5) the behavior has a compulsive quality;
(6) the behavior is difficult to relinquish completely and permanently;
(7) the behavior is associated with recurrent urges or cravings; and
(8) (drug use only) there is physiological adaptation (*physical dependence*) in the form of *tolerance* (decreased sensitivity to the same dose) and a withdrawal syndrome.

This is not a formal definition of addiction; it is merely an attempt to illustrate how the word is used as a label for a category of behaviors. The list of criteria is not exhaustive. Emphasizing a particular set of characteristics implies a particular definition of addiction and results in a particular set of addictive behaviors. For example, criterion (2) excludes occasional drug use and criterion (8) excludes regular use of cocaine (which does not produce physical dependence) as well as behaviors that do not involve the intake of drugs (e.g., compulsive gambling, obsessive exercising, addiction to computer games). Different definitions are likely to reflect different explanatory and ideological perspectives. Addiction – or the activity described as addictive – may be seen variously as a problem behavior, a physical disease, a mental disorder, an overlearned habit, a psychological tool, an excessive appetite, or a subjectively rational choice.

Diverse aspects of addiction have been studied from a social–psychological viewpoint. Here, three important areas of work will be briefly described.

## SOCIAL FACTORS IN THE INITIATION OF DRUG USE

Experimentation with drugs is typically a phenomenon of adolescence. Social factors, in particular PEER PRESSURE, are frequently invoked to explain the onset of drug use. It is a common finding that children who use drugs or engage in other "problem behaviors" are more likely than those who do not to have friends who do likewise. This is sometimes interpreted as evidence for the powerful role of peer pressure. However, this interpretation has been criticized as oversimplistic. Rather than being passive victims of coercion from the "bad company" into which they have fallen, they may have actively sought out friends who use drugs (or who do other things but who also just happen to be drug users). Based on a more careful analysis of adolescents' REFERENCE GROUPS, future work should investigate the onset of drug use in relation to the processes of friendship choice and peer group influence.

## ADDICTIVE BEHAVIORS AS REASONED ACTIONS

There have been a number of attempts to apply attitude–behavior and DECISION-MAKING models such as the SUBJECTIVE EXPECTED UTILITY model and the THEORY OF REASONED ACTION to addictive behaviors (Eiser & van der Pligt, 1988; Sutton, 1987). This domain of behaviors poses a special problem for such theoretical approaches. Unlike many behaviors to which such models have been applied, the decision to quit smoking, drugs, or gambling may be regarded as being outside "volitional control" and hence outside the scope of such models. One way around this is to reconceptualize the decision as one of *trying* to quit: "Trying to do X," it can be argued, *is* under volitional control even if "doing X" is not. The attempt to do X can end in success or failure. The subjective probability of succeeding given that an attempt is made has been termed *confidence* and is related to the concept of self-efficacy. Studies applying this approach to smoking cessation have confirmed the utility of behavioral intentions in predicting the attempt to quit and the role of confidence, motivation (defined in terms of perceived costs and benefits), and past behavior in the prediction of intentions.

Those who continue to smoke, drink, or gamble to excess in the face of actual or potential harm are sometimes regarded as behaving irrationally. The application of decision-making models offers an alternative perspective. According to such approaches, a decision may be influenced by many different outcomes of personal relevance and not simply by those that seem salient to an observer. Thus a smoker who continues to smoke despite the widely accepted risks to health may do so because they are concerned about gaining weight or because they know they are unable to tolerate the withdrawal symptoms or because they remain unconvinced that stopping smoking will materially reduce their personal risk of serious illness. On this approach, continuing to engage in the addictive behavior is a subjectively rational choice.

## THE ATTRIBUTION OF ADDICTION

Drawing on the sociological theory of the sick role and on ATTRIBUTION and COGNITIVE DISSONANCE theories, Eiser and colleagues (e.g., Eiser, Sutton & Wober, 1978) developed the notion that it may be functional for users of drugs, alcohol, or tobacco to label themselves as "addicted" – as helpless victims of their habit. By this means, they can reduce the dissonance engendered through continuing to engage in a behavior that has potentially harmful consequences and they can explain and justify their continued use both to themselves and to others. This view has recently been popularized by Davies (1992). Although the ideas are provocative and there is some indirect supportive data, the theory needs to be more tightly specified and more direct tests conducted.

See also: ATTRIBUTION THEORIES; COGNITIVE DISSONANCE THEORY; DECISION MAKING.

BIBLIOGRAPHY
Davies, J. B. (1992). *The myth of addiction: An application of the psychological theory of attribution to illicit drug use*. Reading: Harwood Academic Publishers.
Eiser, J. R., Sutton, S. R., & Wober, M. (1978). "Consonant" and "dissonant" smokers and the self-attribution of addiction. *Addictive Behaviors, 3*, 99–106.
——— & van der Pligt, J. (1988). *Attitudes and decisions*. London: Routledge.
Oxford, J. (1985). *Excessive appetites: A psychological view of addictions*. Chichester: Wiley.
Sutton, S. R. (1987). Social-psychological approaches to understanding addictive behaviours: Attitude-behaviour and decision-making models. *British Journal of Addiction, 82*, 355–70.

STEPHEN SUTTON

**adjustment and anchoring** Quantitative estimation judgments under uncertainty often have to rely on a HEURISTIC called anchoring and adjustment. A starting value or anchor, which may be chosen arbitrarily, is repeatedly updated or adjusted in the light of relevant information until a final estimate is reached. Since the adjustment process is often incomplete, the resulting judgments tend to be biased toward the starting value.
See also: HEURISTICS.

KLAUS FIEDLER

**adolescence** The definition of adolescence as the period of transition from childhood to maturity (Coleman & Hendry, 1990) draws attention to the extended character of the transition but also raises questions about its content – what are the essential differences between children and adults? The most obvious transitions are in morphology and physiology: in the second decade of life humans become capable of sexual reproduction, while changes in size and strength extend the capacity for physical effort. Less obvious, but also of importance, the second decade sees significant growth in intellectual capacity.

Beyond the fact of these changes, almost everything else is a function of the social ecology in which they occur. This includes the extent and content of intellectual change, individuals' reactions to their own bodily changes, and even to some degree the precise timing of the physical changes themselves. Social ecology here includes the immediate family environment, the community, social structure, and geography, as well as the political, cultural, and historical context. But, within the social ecology, economy assumes a special importance because of its influence upon the period over which the transition to adulthood occurs.

In brief and to simplify somewhat, in agrarian and other pastoral economies the transition is normally brief, relatively early in the second decade and quite closely linked to the physical changes of puberty. Industrialized economies, in which employment relations predominate, are characterized by a much more extended transition, with a significant interval between the development of adult physical capacity and the opportunity to behave completely as an adult. A longer period will be spent in full-time education and training, acquiring the cognitive and technical skills required by an advanced industrial economy.

ADOLESCENCE AS A PERIOD OF CRISIS
Early theorizing about adolescence concentrated on the supposed problems entailed in negotiating the transition from child to adult. Moreover, the difficulties experienced or displayed by some individual adolescents were taken to be characteristic of adolescence as such and accounts were constructed in which problems of behavior and adjustment became normal and virtually definitive of the transitional phase. G. Stanley Hall, who provided the first systematic psychological treatment of adolescence (*see* Petersen, 1988), did much to establish this view of adolescence as a natural and inevitable period of inner conflict and behavioral turmoil. He also argued that

adolescence involves a recapitulation of human social evolution from the precivilized to the civilized state. Mead's (1939) research on puberty in Samoa and New Guinea revealed a much more tranquil transition. Nonetheless, Hall's memorable image of adolescence as a decade of storm and stress reappears in other theoretical perspectives.

For psychoanalysis the adjustment difficulties of adolescence arise from the reawakening of libidinal or sexual drives at puberty. These reenergize the individual's search for "love objects," but the prior internalization of an incest taboo forces this search outside the family. In psychoanalytic thinking the fundamental developmental task of adolescence is emotional disengagement from childhood caretakers and the achievement of autonomy of the PERSONALITY. The demands of this task produce the moodiness, emotional ambivalence and confusion, the occasionally infantile behavior, preoccupation with SELF, rebelliousness, and nonconformity that psychoanalytic writers have taken to be intrinsic features of adolescence (see Blos, 1962).

Erikson (1968) characterized this separation process as a crisis of identity. The crisis, precipitated by the coincidence of a number of changes, some requiring major decisions on the part of the individual, carries the threat that identity will fail to coalesce in any coherent way. Thus adolescents are regarded as experimenting with different lifestyles – delinquent, DRUG user, rebel – as a process of trying out different identities. Research arising from Erikson's theory has been further stimulated by Marcia's (1980) analysis of the progress of this crisis in terms of four distinct identity statuses: diffusion, foreclosure, moratorium, and achievement. Despite these conceptual innovations, however, there is still no convincing evidence that serious identity crises are commonplace, let alone invariable features of adolescence (Coleman & Hendry, 1990).

Sociological approaches have also tended to treat interpersonal conflict and inner turmoil as natural features of adolescence but have attributed these entirely to factors in the adolescent's social environment. Significant among these environmental factors are changes in the roles others expect adolescents to play (see ROLE THEORY). Thus teenagers may experience on the one hand conflicting expectations from parents and peers, and on the other rapidly changing role expectations associated, for example, with the move from school to the labor market. Another theme in sociological treatments is the idea of adolescence as involving entry to a relatively self-contained "teenage culture" based on the peer group, with its own distinctive VALUES, lifestyles, patterns of consumption, and leisure activities, and independent of, if not in active conflict with, adult culture. Associated with this has been the idea that adolescence entails more extensive exposure to agents of SOCIALIZATION other than parents.

The research picture now suggests that emotional difficulties and behavior problems are neither universal and natural in the second decade nor a healthy and normal part of the process of adjustment to new roles and statuses (Petersen, 1988). There are also indications that psychopathologies manifested in adolescence often continue into adulthood. Coleman (see Coleman & Hendry, 1990) has offered an interesting resolution of the apparent contradiction between, on the one hand, clinicians' experience of adolescents with serious emotional problems, eating disorders, behavioral disturbances, depression, and other psychological difficulties and, on the other, evidence from representative samples of adolescents indicating that such problems afflict only a minority. Coleman found that adolescents experience a number of concerns, in particular anxiety over heterosexual relations, fears of rejection from the peer group, and conflict with parents. Normally, however, each concern becomes "focal" at a different point in adolescence. Coleman argues that if each issue can be dealt with in turn adjustment will be relatively successful. The kinds of difficulty which bring teenagers to the attention of clinicians occur when these various concerns and the potentially stressful adjustments they require occur close together in time. Simmons and Blyth (1987) have provided support for this argument, showing that the co-occurrence of more than two life-transitions has a significant negative impact on such outcomes as SELF-ESTEEM and educational performance.

## THE PRIMACY OF PEER RELATIONS

Another issue which requires reassessment in the light of more recent research is the traditional contrast between family and peer group. According to the traditional view, adolescence involves a shift to new forms of social relationship focused upon similar aged peers, and a corresponding decline in the significance of parent–child relations. For psychoanalysis, peer-group involvement represents a transitional phase in the separation process, a substitute for parent–child relations. For sociologists the peer group reflects a temporary society and semiautonomous culture associated with the marginal status of the adolescent, as compared to the more clearly defined roles of child and adult. Moreover, peers are assumed to be a source of role expectations in conflict with those of parents and other adults. And generally adolescence is represented as a period in which the individual is peculiarly vulnerable to PEER PRESSURE, with negative effects on conduct.

Again the traditional view exaggerates the discontinuities. First, peer relations are certainly important to adolescents but so are they to children and adults; the desire to be liked and accepted by one's peers is not peculiar to this period of life. Second, peer relations are neither a substitute for, nor in conflict with, good relationships with parents. On the contrary, the two kinds of relationship appear if anything to complement one another, while relations with parents remain highly important in the second decade (Petersen, 1988). There is also very little evidence that parent–adolescent conflict over values is commonplace; adolescents are rather more likely to share basic values with their parents.

Third, peer relations are not in themselves responsible for problem behaviors. Drug use and delinquency are social activities and young people who are delinquent or who experiment with drugs associate with others who are similarly inclined. But teenagers who are not significantly involved in these activities are equally likely to be involved in a peer group; the crucial difference is rather in the composition of the group. On the other hand, it is the case that certain forms of DEVIANCE peak in adolescence and it may generally be true that behavior which is hazardous, which involves some kind of personal or social RISK, such as experimenting with drugs, driving dangerously, or having unprotected sex, is more common in adolescence than at other times of life (see SEXUAL BEHAVIOR). The reasons for this are likely to be a complex mix of changes in capacity, skills, and foresight in combination with a changing structure of opportunities.

Fourth, the concentration of teenage social participation within an age-homogeneous group may reflect the societal structuring of adolescent life rather than any affiliative inclinations intrinsic to adolescence. In highly urbanized and industrialized societies the organization of education tends to create an immediate social environment in which individuals of similar age predominate.

Fifth, although the capacity for sexual reproduction emerges in the second decade of life, changes in social behavior are partly a function of the manner in which the culture manages this emerging capacity. In some cultures it is managed by physically segregating the sexes prior to puberty and through parental control of mate selection. In contemporary Western society adolescents are less closely supervised by adults than are children, and an ideology of choice prevails in mate selection. But it remains common for adolescent girls to be more extensively supervised than adolescent boys, and consequently the home is a more significant setting for social interaction among the former than among the latter.

Sixth, changes in the content of peer social relations, for example a greater inclination to INTIMACY and SELF-DISCLOSURE, will reflect the effects of changes in intellectual capacity as well as, for example, desires to make sense of bodily changes.

## PUBERTY AND THE SELF CONCEPT

Puberty as such includes a number of related physical changes, including a growth spurt lasting three to four years. For girls it also involves the appearance of pubic hair, breast and pelvic girdle growth, and menarche. For boys it also involves penis growth, testes development, pubic and facial hair growth, breaking of the voice, and more dramatic changes in musculature. The physical development of females is on average one to two years in advance of that of males. Additionally there has been a secular trend over the last one hundred years toward earlier onset; for girls the changes are now beginning, on average at between 10 and 11 years. The secular trend has also been towards faster and greater change, probably reflecting improvements in diet.

Puberty has both direct effects on subjective experience (boys, for example, experience pubertal eroticism, girls experience menarche) and indirect effects of morphological changes on the self concept, mediated both by SOCIAL COMPARISON and by the reactions of others. However, research has focused rather more on effects of the considerable interindividual variations in the timing of these changes. Broadly speaking, early maturation has advantages for males but disadvantages for females. One argument attributes these effects to the social meaning of deviation from the average. Because height and muscularity are valued male attributes late maturation is the less desirable form of deviation among males, and late-maturing males are less popular with adults and peers. Negative effects may also arise, however, insofar as late maturation overlaps with other significant transitions, thereby placing a greater a burden on coping resources.

Cultural standards for female attractiveness which emphasize thinness make early maturation with its associated weight gain the less desirable deviation. It would be interesting to know what the effects of different cultural standards for attractiveness might be on female reactions to the timing of their own pubertal changes. There is now evidence from various quarters that individuals, particularly girls, may modify the timetable for their own maturation, most probably through diet (see Coleman & Hendry, 1990).

SOCIO-COGNITIVE DEVELOPMENT
Cognitive developmental theory has emphasized the intellectual rather than physical, emotional, or role transitions which occur in the second decade. Inhelder and Piaget (1958) argued that adolescence sees a qualitative change in intellectual strategies, a change which makes available to the individual abstract thinking, based on propositional logic, and a hypothetico–deductive approach to problem solving. Subsequent research has supported the conclusion that this intellectual change is virtually unique to the second decade but also that it is not universal in this decade; many young people do not fully develop formally operational thought.

These intellectual changes are of interest to social psychology because they potentially transform the capacities of the individual as a social actor. Thus, the social dimensions of cognitive development have become an important focus for research in the last two decades (see Coleman & Hendry, 1990). Numerous studies have now revealed that there is, over the course of adolescence, significant growth in intellectual insight into almost every aspect of the social environment. This includes developments in understanding of organizational roles and structures, of commercial and employment relations, and of law and politics. Other research has linked intellectual growth to transformations of social competence, arising for instance from more complex role-taking skills. Finally, there is the argument that adolescence is an important period of MORAL DEVELOPMENT, and that this can largely be attributed to underlying intellectual changes (Kohlberg, 1984). The work of Kohlberg and others suggests that the most significant change in adolescence is likely to be the emergence of an understanding of moral obligations in terms of shared standards of rights, duties, and values. Adolescents come to adopt what Kohlberg called a "member of society" perspective on moral questions.

Despite wider recognition that socio-cognitive development proceeds at different rates in different individuals, and terminates at different levels, the cognitive developmental approach is still substantially concerned with the manner in which all individuals acquire the basic intellectual equipment to function socially as adults. A question for future research is the extent to which the second decade sees differentiation in the intellectual resources of individuals as a function of the different social environments they inhabit.

## ECONOMIC SOCIALIZATION

In contemporary Western society adolescence has become an important transitional period with respect to ECONOMIC BEHAVIOR. The child's economic role is almost entirely confined to consumption, although development of the intellectual equipment for participation in other kinds of economic role is already well advanced by the beginning of the second decade. Adolescents, as consumers, participate far more extensively and directly than most children in commercial exchanges. But the major economic role shifts are in the contribution of labor to the domestic economy and entry into the employment market. In these areas adolescence is also a significant period of GENDER differentiation; males and females perform increasingly divergent economic functions.

Psychological research on WORK socialization in adolescence has tended to emphasize processes of vocational choice, stressing the effects of cognitive development and the influence of personal values and interests. Sociologically inspired work has given more weight to the operation of opportunity structures and social selection processes. These are held to direct the career trajectories of young people to a variety of different destinations within a stratified economy, reproducing gender and class differences in economic status. Researchers in this area are now much more sensitive to the impact of labor market conditions on adolescence (Banks et al., 1992), and some arguments have linked the extended transition to adult status, which now characterizes many Western societies, to changes in which the market for unskilled labor is rapidly declining.

Whether individually motivated choice or socially structured opportunity is emphasized in the process of economic socialization, it is clear that events in the second decade of life influence socio-economic position in adulthood (Banks et al., 1992). One of the single most important events of this kind occurs at the end of compulsory schooling. At this point some individuals leave full-time education either to enter directly into the labor market or to enter some form of training. Others stay on voluntarily in academic education. This dividing point is highly predictive of later employment status but also has repercussions for political participation, social network characteristics, and mate selection. What is not clear is whether the direction taken at this dividing point can be predicted from individual characteristics already present at the end of childhood. However, amount of schooling is strongly associated with an adolescent's orientation to formal authority; it is not a function of intellectual ability or social background alone. Finally, research on adolescent "careers" through education and into adult economic roles provides very little support for the idea that adolescence is a period in which the individual can experiment with different identities; commitments are more often than not irreversible.

## CONCLUSIONS

The transition from childhood to adulthood entails some obvious and major physical changes which have repercussions for the relationship between individuals and their social environments. Likewise, intellectual changes alter the ways in which individuals are able to think about the social environment and participate in social relations. But many and perhaps most of the changes in social identity and self concept, and in patterns of social and sexual behavior, are also shaped by the structured response that cultures and social systems make to puberty.

*See also*: DEVIANCE; ECONOMIC BEHAVIOR; GENDER; INTIMACY; MORAL DEVELOPMENT; PERSONALITY; RISK; ROLE-THEORY; SELF; SELF-ESTEEM; SEXUAL BEHAVIOR; SOCIAL COMPARISON; SOCIALIZATION; VALUES; WORK.

BIBLIOGRAPHY

Banks, M., Bates, I., Breakwell, G., Bynner, J., Emler, N., Jamieson, L., & Roberts, K. (1992). *Careers and identities*. Milton Keynes: Open University Press.

Blos, P. (1962). *On adolescence: A psychoanalytic interpretation*. Glencoe, IL: Free Press. London: Macmillan.

Coleman, J. C., & Hendry, L. (1990). *The nature of adolescence*. London: Routledge.

Erikson, E. (1968). *Identity: Youth and crisis*. New York: Norton.

Inhelder, B., & Piaget, J. (1958). *The growth of logical thinking from childhood to adolescence.* London: Routledge.

Kohlberg, L. (1984). *Essays on moral development: The psychology of moral development.* San Francisco: Harper & Row.

Marcia, J. E. (1980). Identity in adolescence. In J. Adelson (Ed.) *Handbook of adolescent psychology* (pp. 159–187). New York: Wiley.

Mead, M. (1939). *From the South Seas: Studies of adolescence and sex in primitive societies.* New York: William Morrow.

Petersen, A. C. (1988). Adolescent development. *Annual Review of Psychology, 39,* 358–67.

Simmons, R., & Blyth, D. A. (1987). *Moving into adolescence.* New York: Aldine.

NICHOLAS EMLER

**advertising**   Advertising is any paid form of nonpersonal, mass-media presentation with the primary purpose of informing or persuading people about ideas, goods, or services. The first recorded advertisement appeared on a 3000 B.C. Babylonian clay tablet and announced the services of an ointment dealer, a scribe, and a shoemaker. Advertising emerged on a mass scale in mid-nineteenth century England and the United States as a result of the increased productivity of the industrial revolution and the rise of mass-market periodicals (*see* Fox, 1984; MASS MEDIA). Today advertising is big business. For example, in 1991, advertisers spent $126.6 billion in the United States alone. Advertising is also an ubiquitous aspect of Western culture. The typical North American receives 200 to 400 advertisements per day or 7 million advertisements in an average lifetime.

ADVERTISING MANAGEMENT
From a business perspective, the goal of advertising is to sell the product (*see* Aaker & Myers, 1987; Kleepner, 1973). This objective is difficult to measure and advertisers frequently establish more specific communication goals. For example, one approach called DAGMAR (Defining Advertising Goals for Measured Advertising Results) lists 52 possible communication goals including creating brand awareness, creating a brand image, reminding the consumer to buy, and stimulating impulse sales. One important aspect of specifying a communication goal is to identify the target market. Markets can be segmented on a number of attributes including product-related factors (e.g., benefits-sought by the consumer, past usage rates, brand loyalty) and general consumer characteristics (e.g., demographics and psychographics).

Businesses and other advertisers often hire advertising agencies to help in the preparation of a communications campaign. One of the most important functions of an advertising agency is the creative process – the translation of communication objectives into a specific campaign with theme, copy (content), and visual elements. Advertising agencies also help with the execution of the campaign including creating the actual physical advertisement, purchasing media space, and setting the media schedule (when and where the advertisement will be placed). The media schedule is important for determining who sees an advertisement and for thus reaching the target market.

HOW DOES ADVERTISING WORK?
In the message-dense environment of advertising, recipients often lack the time and the ability to process critically every communication. Much of advertising is what Herbert Krugman describes as "low-involvement learning"; message recipients find advertising of little interest and thus pay little attention to it (*see* ELABORATION LIKELIHOOD MODEL). Ironically, this lack of interest can result in effective advertising because recipients often fail to counterargue a communication. Through repetition of simple slogans and images, advertising alters the structure of perceptions about a product and shifts the relative SALIENCE of product attributes. With few other sources of information, the consumer acts on these perceptions at the time of purchase. Repetition of brand name and image can also create accessible brand attitudes that lead to attitude-consistent behavior (*see* ATTITUDES AND BEHAVIOR).

Given that recipients allocate limited attention to an advertisement advertisers often use simplistic PERSUASION devices (as opposed to elaborate arguments). Some of the most common persuasion tactics used in advertising include: repetition of advertisement, attractive or credible sources, MODELING the use of a product, vivid images, brand positioning, decoys and phantoms, glittering generalities and purr words, distraction, and playing on emotions such as fear, guilt, commitment, and self-regard (*see* Pratkanis & Aronson, 1992; ATTITUDE CHANGE, ATTITUDE FORMATION).

HOW EFFECTIVE IS ADVERTISING?
There is a widespread belief by the general public that advertising has powerful effects. This belief sometimes results in demands for the governmental regulation of advertising, especially regulations designed to protect certain groups (in particular, children) and to outlaw deceptive practices. Despite this belief in the power of advertising, economic time-series studies have found small or no effects of the amount a firm spends on advertising on either growth in market share or total product-category sales. Similarly, experimental investigations of single exposures to advertisements find that few people pay attention to any specific advertisement exposure and what little effects are created usually dissipate quickly. However, given the pervasiveness of the mass media, even small effects can be socially significant.

Although the perception that advertising always produces strong effects is probably untrue, there are numerous examples of advertising effectiveness under specific conditions. For example, great advertising campaigns – Ogilvy's Hathaway shirt man, Leo Burnett's Marlboro man, Doyle Dane Bernbach's Volkswagen advertisements, and Chiat/Day's 1984 Macintosh advertisement – all produced measurable results. Political advertising is especially effective when the candidates are relatively unknown. Econometric studies find that advertising is effective when a brand has hidden qualities or a relative differential advantage. Copy-testing of specific advertisements indicates that communication

objectives are often obtained. Advertisers have attempted to specify what makes an effective advertisement (*see* Ogilvy, 1983). For example, Rosser Reeves argues that an advertisement should have a "Unique Selling Proposition"; Leo Burnett believes an advertisement should portray the inherent drama of the product; John Caples and David Ogilvy have developed guidelines for creating effective advertisements.

Social critics also point out that advertising can have indirect effects including: maintaining social stereotypes (*see* STEREOTYPING), creating a consumer culture, producing a nation of conformists (*see* SOCIAL INFLUENCE), and specifying false choices (i.e., Chevy versus Ford as opposed to cars versus mass transportation). As with direct effects, it is difficult to state how many of these social effects are attributable to advertising versus other aspects of a mass-market society. However, both correlational and experimental research lend support to the argument that advertising does create pictures in our heads of what the world is and should be.

*See also*: ATTITUDES AND BEHAVIOR; ATTITUDE CHANGE; ATTITUDE FORMATION; MASS MEDIA; SOCIAL INFLUENCE; STEREOTYPING.

BIBLIOGRAPHY
Aaker, D. A., & Myers, J. G. (1987). *Advertising management*. Englewood Cliffs, NJ: Prentice Hall.
Fox, S. (1984). *The mirror makers*. New York: William Morrow.
Kleepner, O. (1973). *Advertising procedure*. Englewood Cliffs, NJ: Prentice Hall.
Ogilvy, D. (1983). *Ogilvy on advertising*. New York: Crown.
Pratkanis, A. R., & Aronson, E. (1992). *Age of propaganda: The everyday use and abuse of persuasion*. New York: W. H. Freeman.
ANTHONY R. PRATKANIS

**affect** A general term which describes mental processes that involve feeling, such as EMOTIONAL EXPERIENCE or MOOD. Affect is contrasted with cognition, motivation, and action. Whether affect should be reified as a distinct mental entity or rather be conceived

abstractly as an aspect of mental states is controversial.
*See also*: EMOTIONAL EXPERIENCE; MOOD IMPACT ON COGNITION AND BEHAVIOR.

W. GERROD PARROTT

**affective–cognitive consistency**  A model of attitude structure and change. Attitudes are comprised of an affective or emotional component and a BELIEF about the probability that the attitude object will facilitate or hinder a valued goal. Inconsistency between the affective and the cognitive yields unstable attitudes and leads to ATTITUDE CHANGE that restores consistency.
*See also*: ATTITUDE CHANGE; COGNITIVE CONSISTENCY.

JOEL COOPER

**affordances**  Opportunities for acting or being acted upon that persons or objects provide. Emergent properties, affordances reflect both target characteristics and the perceptual experience, goals, and action capabilities of the perceiver. Specified in the target's perceptible characteristics, affordances can be detected by appropriately attuned, active perceivers.

LESLIE A. ZEBROWITZ

**aggression**  The deliberate and intentional infliction of harm upon another person who is motivated to avoid such treatment. Aggression is often classified into two basic types of behavior. In affective aggression, which is accompanied by the experience of strong affective arousal and anger, the motive of the aggressor is to punish the victim. In instrumental aggression, in which strong affective arousal and anger typically do not occur, the motive is to attain some goal at the victim's expense. Affective aggression has been the subject of more research and theorizing than instrumental aggression. Affective aggression is elicited by some condition in the environment that provokes the aggressor. Among the most commonly studied antece-

dent conditions for aggression are frustration, physical attack, and verbal insult.

ANTECEDENTS OF AGGRESSION
An early attempt at a unitary theory of aggression was the FRUSTRATION–AGGRESSION HYPOTHESIS. In its simplest form the hypothesis states that frustration, defined as the arbitrary blocking of goal-directed behavior by another person or persons, creates a state of readiness to aggress, and that aggression is always preceded by some form of frustration. The hypothesis also outlines various corollary behaviors associated with frustration and aggression: inhibition of aggression by fear of punishment, displacement of aggression to substitute targets, indirect aggression, and aggression CATHARSIS. Although few investigators would now accept the idea that all aggression is the result of frustration, the other premise of the hypothesis – that frustration creates a readiness to aggress – is still debated. The evidence shows that the relationship is not a simple one. Whether frustration leads to aggression or some other response depends to some extent on the person's SOCIAL LEARNING history. Frustration may elicit many types of instrumental behavior designed to remove the source of blocking, of which aggression may only be one. The reaction to being frustrated can also depend on whether the frustrated person believes that he or she has an aggressive response available; if this is not perceived, the result of being frustrated may be helpless resignation. Finally, aggression may not be a response to frustration as much as a reaction to the victim's perception of the frustrator's intent.

Several theoretical explanations for the link between frustration and aggression have been proposed. Possibly aggression is an innate, unlearned reaction to being thwarted. Studies of lower animals have shown that when a reward is abruptly terminated, animals often respond by attacking a cagemate. Little attention has been given to the study of an innate frustration–aggression connection in humans, however. Another possibility is that frustration does not instigate aggressive behavior, as the frustration–aggression hypothesis stipulates, but instead that it creates an increased level of general arousal or activation that energizes whatever behavior happens to be predominant at the time. If persons find themselves in a situation in which aggression is likely, possibly because of prior reinforcement for aggression in that setting or the presence of an aggressive model, and if the people are then frustrated, the likelihood of their responding with aggression should be relatively high (Geen, 1968).

Frustration may also be linked to aggression through an associative network of cognitive, affective, and behavioral elements (Berkowitz, 1989). The starting point in the process is an immediate experience of negative affect in response to an aversive condition. Following the suggestion of certain cognitive theorists, Berkowitz considers negative affective states to be encoded in hypothetical central connecting points, or *nodes*, in memory. Linked to affect in these nodes are related thoughts, emotions, and expressive motor patterns, so that activation of an affective condition in turn activates these other processes along directional pathways. The immediate affective reaction to aversive stimulation sets in motion a complex of emotions and thoughts related to either agression or to escape from the aversive situation along with what may appear to be related reflexive behaviors usually described as "fight or flight." Frustration activates this process by eliciting an immediate state of negative affect. Thus frustration may lead to either aggression or behavioral withdrawal; the nature of the response depends on other factors such as the person's social learning history, sociocultural values regarding aggression, and cognitive judgments of the circumstances of the frustration itself.

Interpersonal attacks, such as physical assaults and verbal insults, are more obvious antecedents of aggression than frustration, and considerably greater consensus exists regarding their effects. Whether attack elicits negative affect or a desire to retaliate depends to some extent on the way in which the attack is perceived by the victim. Research by Zillmann and his associates has shown that when the victim recognizes the existence of mitigating circumstances that help to rationalize the attack, the initial impact of the attack is less than it would have been without recognition of the mitigation (e.g., Zillmann, 1983). Personality variables also have an influence on attack-elicited aggression. Strong personal dispositions to become irritable and then to ruminate over attacks from others have both been shown to moderate aggressiveness in response to interpersonal provocations. Developmental variables may also have a moderating function. Very young children are relatively unable to differentiate among attacks on the basis of the attacker's motives, and then consequently to retaliate indiscriminately. With increasing maturity, children acquire the ability to adjust their retaliation to cognitive attributions regarding the nature and intent of the attack (Geen, 1990, Chap. 6).

In recent years, interest has been growing in the possible role of environmental stressors in aggression. These stressors have been shown to have several effects relevant to aggression. They evoke negative affect, which, as already noted, may initiate hostile thoughts and feelings as well as aggressive behavior. In addition, environmental stressors may cause stimulus overload and interfere with behavior, thereby frustrating the person. Furthermore, by increasing the person's level of general arousal, stressors may also intensify whatever aggression does occur. Several stressors in the environment are related to aggressive behavior. High ambient temperatures have been shown to produce increases in aggressive motivation and tendencies in studies of behavior in natural settings. Hotter regions of the world have more aggression than cooler regions, and hotter years, seasons, months, and days are more likely than cooler ones to yield such behaviors as murders, rapes, assaults, riots, and spouse abuse (Anderson, 1989). Laboratory studies of the relation between temperature and aggression under controlled conditions sometimes yield a different finding, however: a curvilinear relation of temperature to aggression such that maximum aggression is elicited by moderate temperatures. It has been suggested that this effect results from the simultaneous evocation of two motives by ambient temperature. Over low-to-moderate temperature ranges, the motive to aggress increases as negative affect mounts. Over moderate-to-high ranges, the motive to escape the situation displaces the motive to aggress, so that aggression becomes less intense as flight becomes the dominant response.

Intense noise may also be an antecedent of aggression. Noise may reduce subsequent ability to cope with frustration, especially if the person must invest considerable effort in adjusting to the noise. In addition, noise may influence aggression by raising the person's level of arousal and thereby energizing ongoing behavior, including aggression. This is especially likely if the noise is administered after the person has become ready to aggress as a consequence of a prior provocation, and if the noise is outside the person's control. Whereas uncontrollable noise leads to high levels of retaliatory aggression in provoked people, noise that can be terminated by the victim produces no more aggression than is observed in unstimulated controls. Controllable noise also elicits less physiological arousal than uncontrollable noise of the same intensity and duration, suggesting that the influence of noise on aggression is mediated by arousal.

A role for spatial variables such as CROWDING and population density in aggression has been proposed, but the evidence is not strong. There is some evidence that aggression may be elicited by crowding, especially when the person is helpless to control the density of people, and by violations of personal space (Geen, 1990, pp. 68–73). Likewise, some evidence points to air pollution (e.g., smoke, noxious odors, and airborne pollutants) as a possible cause of aggression. Evidence has also indicated that increasing the concentration of negative-charged molecules (ions) in the air can have effects on emotion, behavior, and physiological activation that could serve as mediators of aggression.

## EFFECTS OF OBSERVING AGGRESSION

Observing aggression committed by others, either in natural settings or through the communications and entertainment media, can initiate processes that lead to aggressive behavior. Studies of observational learning in children have shown that a child can acquire novel aggressive behaviors by observing an adult model enact them. Whether the newly acquired behaviors are subsequently carried out by the child depends upon certain additional factors, notably some provocation that motivates the child to aggress, and the presence of suitable incentives for behaving aggressively. The observation of aggressive models may also facilitate the expression of previously acquired aggressive behaviors, by reducing restraints against aggressing and by providing information that aggressive behavior is acceptable. Observed acts of aggression are stored in memory as scenarios within larger behavioral scripts that are strengthened and elaborated through repetition and rehearsal. Conditions similar to those in which the script is encoded lead to the retrieval of the script, which is then likely to serve as a guide to behavior.

Observation of aggression may also activate ("prime") associative networks related to aggressive thoughts and actions in long-term memory. Witnessed acts of aggression may elicit memories of other violent acts which, because they are associated in memory with related emotions and behavioral tendencies, are capable of eliciting these emotions and expressive motor behaviors. They therefore serve to activate in a preliminary way the same networks that are involved in responses to provocations. The end result is that aggressive responses to provocation, as well as the related emotion of anger and aggression-related thoughts, are facilitated by prior exposure to the aggressive acts of others (Berkowitz, 1984).

A third way in which observation of aggression may facilitate aggression is by increasing the viewer's level of arousal. Zillmann (1983) has suggested that arousal evoked in this way may be in part misattributed to subsequent provocations (see MISATTRIBUTION OF AROUSAL) and as a consequence may exacerbate anger and instigation to retaliate.

A relationship between observation of aggression in the mass media and subsequent aggression by the viewer has been demonstrated in both experimental and naturalistic investigations (Friedrich-Cofer & Huston, 1986; Geen & Thomas, 1986). The relationship is influenced by several variables. When observed violence is thought to be real behavior it elicits more aggression than when it is thought to be fictitious. When observers identify with an aggressor they tend to be more aggressive afterwards than when they do not identify. Aggression that is described as motivated by a desire for revenge elicits more aggression in viewers than the same activity when it is said to be instrumental to the attainment of other goals. Aggression that is regarded as being justified in its context elicits more aggression than that which is regarded as unjust. The observation of unsuccessful aggression, in which the aggressor is punished, does not promote aggressive behavior, but instead inhibits it (Geen, 1990, Chap. 4).

Considerable attention has also been paid to a possible link between observation of PORNOGRAPHY and sexual violence against women. Research has shown that whereas watching erotic but nonviolent movies leads to no more aggression by males against female victims than does nonerotic material, a violent RAPE scene is associated with significantly greater aggression. This effect is even stronger when the male aggressors have been told beforehand that the female victim in the movie actually enjoys being the victim of her attacker. The belief that women enjoy being sexually abused, called the "rape myth," is also fostered among men by exposure to pornography, as is a general attitude of acceptance of violence toward women. Among women viewers, exposure to pornography decreases both of these variables (Malamuth & Donnerstein, 1984).

## VIOLATION OF NORMS AND AGGRESSION

Several theorists, most of them coming out of European social psychology, have taken the position that aggression must be understood within the larger context of the violation and restitution of NORMS that govern social behavior. In most instances aggression is not an isolated act. It arises in the context of an ongoing relationship between two persons in which both persons have certain expectations regarding how the two of them should be-

have. It is proposed that one norm that is implicit in such settings prescribes that each person will cause only as much discomfort to others as is necessary for attaining his or her goals. Should either person exceed the normative level, that person's behavior will be considered by the other to be excessive and motivated by intent to hurt. It will, in other words, be regarded as a malicious act of aggression that calls for retaliation. If the retaliation is exact and in kind, the normative state that existed before the malicious transgression will be restored. Thus, according to this viewpoint, the major provocation for aggression is not frustration, attack, or some other form of interpersonal provocation as such, but rather the violation of a behavioral norm (DaGloria, 1984).

It should be noted that this approach to aggression emphasizes the instrumental nature of the aggressive act. This does not rule out the possibility that retaliation may be accompanied by negative affect, emotion, and hostile thoughts even when its principal purpose is restoration of a normative condition. Such an interpretation therefore obscures the commonly accepted viewpoint that aggression may be either affective or instrumental.

A closely related viewpoint is that of ATTRIBUTION THEORY, according to which interpersonal provocations are analyzed by the victim in order that the underlying structure of the aggressor's motives are understood. In general, a provocation should elicit aggression only when it is regarded as intentional and malicious. It must, in other words, violate the norm that one cannot behave maliciously toward others without being at risk for retaliation or punishment. Attribution theorists ask three questions about an act of provocation: Was it intentional? If so, was it guided by malice? If not, were its consequences still seen as avoidable? Under two conditions provocative acts are typically judged to be worthy of blame and thus counter-normative: when they are intended and malicious and when they are not intended but have aversive consequences that the actor can foresee. In the latter case the provocateur is judged guilty for not having done anything to inhibit the unintentional act.

CONCLUSION

As is the case with all topic areas in social psychology, conceptions of human aggression have changed greatly since systematic study began in the late 1930s. The original models, under the influence of then-dominant theories of drive, arousal, and affect, placed heavy emphasis on the role of intervening emotional variables, particularly anger, in mediating responses to provocation. With the onset of the cognitive domination of social psychology, explanations during the 1970s turned more toward attributional mediators and cognitive control. More recently the emergence of explanatory models that combine affective and emotional variables with cognitive processes (e.g., Berkowitz, 1989) brings the promise of a new and more complex integration. In addition, the analysis of aggression in terms of normative behavior in response to violations of standards, which has been largely dominated by sociologists, is beginning to attract attention among psychologists as well. A still higher level of integration, in which traditional distinctions between affective and instrumental aggression are supplanted by an approach that subsumes the two, may be the next major development. Such developments will no doubt be facilitated by the increasing reliance on research in natural settings, including longitudinal designs.

*See also*: ATTRIBUTION THEORIES; CROWDING; NORMS; PORNOGRAPHY; RAPE; SOCIAL LEARNING.

BIBLIOGRAPHY

Anderson, C. A. (1989). Temperature and aggression: The ubiquitous effects of heat on the occurrence of human violence. *Psychological Bulletin, 106,* 74–96.

Berkowitz, L. (1984). Some effects of thoughts on anti- and prosocial influences of media events: A cognitive neoassociationist analysis. *Psychological Bulletin, 95,* 410–27.

—— (1989). The frustration–aggression hypothesis: An examination and reformulation. *Psychological Bulletin, 106,* 59–73.

DaGloria, J. (1984). Frustration, aggression, and the sense of justice. In A. Mummendey (Ed.), *Social psychology of aggression: From individual behavior to social interaction* (pp. 127–41). New York: Springer-Verlag.

Friedrich-Cofer, L., & Huston, A. C. (1986). Television violence and aggression: The debate continues. *Psychological Bulletin, 100,* 364–71.

Geen, R. G. (1968). Effects of frustration, attack, and prior training in aggressiveness upon aggressive behavior. *Journal of Personality and Social Psychology, 9,* 316–21.

—— (1990). *Human aggression.* Milton Keynes: Open University Press.

—— & Thomas, S. L. (1986). The immediate effects of media violence on behavior. *Journal of Social Issues, 42,* 7–27.

Malamuth, N., & Donnerstein, E. (Eds.) (1984). *Pornography and sexual aggression.* New York: Academic Press.

Zillmann, D. (1983). Arousal and aggression. In R. G. Geen & E. Donnerstein (Eds.), *Aggression: Theoretical and empirical reviews* (Vol. 1): *Theoretical and methodological issues* (pp. 75–101). New York: Academic Press.

RUSSELL G. GEEN

**aging** The normative changes that occur within individuals throughout the life course. These changes are thought to be universal and inevitable. Aging differs from illnesses and diseases, which are avoidable, may have external causes, and may be cured, or alleviated. *Gerontologists* are scientists interested in the study of aging who focus on changes within the individual throughout adulthood (*Intra-individual Changes*), the extent to which such changes occur at different rates among different adults (*Inter-individual Differences*) and how individuals adapt to those changes. *Geriatricians* are interested primarily in the diseases and debilities associated with old age, and the provision of health care to the elderly.

Interest in the study of adult development and aging is in part the result of dramatic increases in the number of elderly persons in developing countries around the world. Because of increased life expectancy, a high birth rate after World War II, and relatively low birth rates in the last three decades, the proportion of persons aged 65 and older has increased to well over 10 percent of the total population in most western European countries and the United States and Canada. As the "baby boomers" age, the growth of the elderly population will accelerate, particularly those aged 85 and older. Because of worldwide advances in medical care and birth control, the proportion of elderly in developing countries such as China, India, and Mexico will also grow rapidly. Thus, aging will become a worldwide phenomenon that poses important challenges and opportunities for researchers and policy makers (Schulz & Ewen, 1993).

A second impetus to the study of aging was the recognition that relatively little is known about the development of the human organism beyond early adulthood. The scientific community has spent more than 100 years studying the biological, cognitive, and social development of persons from infancy through adolescence but virtually no research was carried out on development in middle and old age until the 1950s. With the support of government agencies and private foundations, the study of aging became a mainstay on most university campuses in the 1970s and 1980s. Research programs on aging can be found within all of the health and social science disciplines.

BIOLOGICAL AND SOCIOSTRUCTURAL ASPECTS OF AGING

The development of the human organism is shaped by both biological and sociostructural constraints and opportunities. The overall biological resources across the life span resemble an inverted U-function. During childhood and adolescence, cognitive abilities and physical maturity increase and provide the basis for the development of complex motor and cognitive skills. During adulthood, physical development plateaus and then declines. When persons are pushed to their limits, age-related declines in physical and cognitive abilities can be detected beginning in the late twenties and continuing throughout middle age, although the functional consequences of these declines are minor. In addition to the clearly visible external changes associated with old age, import-

ant, less visible biological changes occur as well. With increasing age, muscle tissue slowly declines in strength, tone, and flexibility. The cardiovascular, pulmonary, digestive, and excretory systems become less efficient. Stamina decreases. Joints and bones become more brittle and less flexible. The brain loses from 5 to 10 percent of its weight over the life span and at the same time accumulates inter- and intracellular garbage in the form of neuritic plaques, neurofibrillary tangles and lipofuscin. Communication among neurons is affected by decreases in essential neurotransmitters such as dopamine, acetylcholine, and norepinephrine (Schulz & Ewen, 1993).

The combined functional consequence of these changes is that the elderly are less resilient to stress, less physiologically adaptable, less immunologically competent and have less efficient homeostatic regulatory mechanisms. Perhaps the most compelling evidence for the consequences of these changes is the covariation of aging with disease, disability, and death.

Sociostructural constraints on development can be characterized at two levels: at the level of social institutions and in individuals' normative conceptions about development and the life course. Life-course sociologists emphasize that all societies can be characterized as having age-graded systems which constrain and provide a scaffold for life-course patterns, yielding predictability and structure at both individual and societal levels (Riley, 1985). The magnitude of constraint imposed by age graded systems varies across societies as well as historical time.

A recent debate among life-course sociologists focuses on changing trends in industrialized societies toward the elimination or softening of age graded NORMS (e.g., Dannefer, 1989). For example, Riley argues that because of significant increases in life-expectancy in the last few decades, elderly individuals are rendered in a state of role-lessness because of the lack of age-graded norms after retirement. As a result, old people are condemned to spend a large portion of their lives unconnected to social institutions, having to fill their lives with hobbies and other individually initiated activities. Under such conditions of increased reliance on personal resources in old age, the impact of socio-economic differences on everyday life becomes very pronounced.

Individual conceptions about development are reflected in three basic types of constraints:

(1) constraints imposed by lifetime remaining until death;
(2) constraints associated with chronological age; and
(3) constraints resulting from age-sequential patterns.

First, time left to live restricts the future time extension of developmental goals and life plans. Whatever is to be accomplished in life must be done within a specific and relatively finite period of time. A case in point is career planning near retirement age. There is a point in the life course beyond which one has to settle for what one has, rather than entertain ideas about possible career changes. Second, the human life course is an age-graded structure which defines normative ages for important life events and transitions. The prototypical case is fertility in women, which is shaped both by social institutions and biological limits. Finally, age-sequential constraints result from a channeling of developmental and life-course processes into biographical tracks. Life-course sociology has identified such tracks as segregated paths in a given society which give rise to intracohort heterogeneity. A typical case is professional specialization, which yields ever-increasing levels of expertise in the chosen field, while giving up on nonchosen alternatives. Along such developmental tracks, functioning is optimized, while crossovers to alternative life tracks become increasingly difficult.

## A SOCIAL PSYCHOLOGICAL PERSPECTIVE ON AGING

Social psychological theories and research methods have been a guiding influence on the study of aging for over four decades. The early development of the field is characterized by an emphasis on the sociological as opposed to the psychological components of this approach. The works of Cumming and Henry, and Rosow are representative of this perspective, which relies heavily on structural–functionalist theories, survey research methods, and the use of correlational analytic techniques. More recently, this perspective has been augmented by another view emphasizing the psychological half of the equation. This perspective is characterized by the use of experimental methods and its attempt to generate explanations based ultimately on an understanding of the phenomenology of the individual. The contributions of persons such as Rodin (1987) and Schulz (Schulz, Heckhausen, & Locher, 1991) are representative of this approach.

If one had to identify a central theoretical idea of the recent contributions to the social psychology of aging, it would be the concept of POWER and CONTROL. Dowd developed a view of aging as SOCIAL EXCHANGE, drawing on the work of sociologists such as Homans and Blau, and argued that the problems of aging are the consequences of decreasing power resources among the aged. Schulz and colleagues (Schulz, Heckhausen, & Locher, 1991) identified perceived choice and a sense of personal control as the critical determinants of the aged individual's physical and psychological well-being. This idea, which had its origins in the work of Janis, Glass and Singer, and Seligman, has evolved into a general life-span theory of control (Heckhausen and Schulz, in press).

Most individuals come to terms with the biological declines and socio-cultural constraints associated with aging. This is accomplished through a shift from control strategies that emphasize direct action on the environment to strategies relying on cognitive adjustment. In order to articulate more fully how and why this shift is achieved, it will be useful first to examine in greater detail the concept of control as it has evolved in the past two decades.

Despite the extensive empirical literature and theoretical rationale extolling the positive effects of increased control, there also exist both theory and research suggesting some important caveats to this general belief. Most people prefer and benefit from control most of the time: however, the exceptions to this rule raise important theoretical, practical and sometimes ethical questions concerning the general conclusion, the more control the better, particularly when applied to the elderly. For example, in his popular book, *Escape from Freedom*, Erich Fromm argued that people may not wish to be masters of their own fate. In a similar vein, it has been suggested that the desire for control may vary with age. The sense of control may erode gradually during the later years, but along with this comes the wisdom to "shuck off" some of the sense of responsibility over matters clearly outside the span of control.

Weisz and colleagues (Weisz, Rothbaum, & Blackburn, 1984) reiterate this theme, suggesting that the desire for control varies substantially among different cultural groups. Using Rothbaum's distinction between *primary* and *secondary control*, Weisz et al. point out that while most Westerners are concerned with shaping existing physical and social realities to fit their perceptions, goals or wishes (i.e., exerting primary control), other cultural groups such as the Japanese place a much greater emphasis on accommodating to existing realities (i.e., exerting secondary control) (*see* CROSS-CULTURAL SOCIAL PSYCHOLOGY; INDIVIDUALISM–COLLECTIVISM). Secondary control is achieved by predicting events to control their impact on oneself, aligning oneself with powerful others and gaining control through them, accepting fate, or construing existing realities so as to derive a sense of meaning or purpose from them.

The availability of primary control varies not only by cultural group and historical time, but also as a function of age in the life course of the individual. Early development is characterized by an increased ability to exert primary control over the environment. One of the hallmarks of biological and social development in early childhood is the increased ability to produce behavior–event contingencies. The action–outcome experiences of the child provide the basis for the development of self-competence, including generalized expectancies of control and perceptions of self-efficacy. As development progresses, children attain the capacity to differentiate competence into ability and effort and develop domain-specific expectations for control. Early adulthood is characterized

by increased selectivity with respect to the domain-specificity of control as well as overly optimistic perceptions of one's competencies. It has been suggested that a positive bias in control expectations at this stage in life may be conducive to persistence when faced with difficulties and to active attempts at attaining and maintaining high levels of control. On the other hand, excessive tenaciousness in striving for inaccessible goals means wasting effort and exposing oneself to frustration and failure. Thus, the peak potential of the individual is achieved by walking a fine line between attainable and unrealistic goals.

Middle age is characterized by increased selectivity with respect to the domain-specificity of control. Individuals increasingly invest time and energy resources into those domains where they are relatively good and relinquish goals that cannot be achieved.

During late middle age and old age, the strategy of choice leans more toward the elaboration and increased use of secondary control strategies. Increasing age-related constraints on primary control make it difficult to enhance or maintain primary control without incurring high costs in wasted effort, frustration, and failure. In addition, because of the changing ratio between years lived and years left to live, it may be advantageous to focus on interpretation of the past rather than changing the future. Tracking personal consistencies (Ross, 1989), discovering meaning and connectedness in one's personal past, and interpreting successes and failures are primary tasks of old age.

It is important to note that this view of control through the life course emphasizes the primacy of primary control. Individuals prefer primary to secondary control. When threatened with a loss of primary control, individuals have the option of taking direct action on the environment to maintain control or making cognitive adjustments through mental representations of the situation (secondary control). Both of these strategies serve to minimize losses, or maintain and expand prior levels of control. Since the ratio of gains to losses in primary control becomes less and less favorable in the later periods of the life span, the individual increasingly resorts to secondary control processes. Evidence supporting this life-span view of control is found in four research areas:

(1) age differences in self-reports of perceived control;
(2) age differences in control-related behavior and health;
(3) perceptions of life-span development; and
(4) theories about adult personality development (*see* Schulz, Heckhausen, & Locher, 1991; Heckhausen & Schulz, 1993, for reviews of this literature).

FUTURE DEVELOPMENTS

Research on diseases that co-vary with age will remain a high priority on the research agenda of many gerontologists and geriatricians. A prototypical case is Alzheimer's disease. The incidence of this disease increases dramatically with age such that approximately half of those over the age of 85 are thought to suffer from it. It exacts a high price not only from the patient who experiences it, but also from family members who are involved in the patients' care, and from society as whole. On the biological front, investigators will continue to search for clear markers of the disease, along with possible cures. On the social front, researchers are investigating ways in which the patient can be managed with psychosocial interventions and identifying the types of assistance needed by family members to cope with patient behavior problems. At the societal level, policy makers grapple with the immense health and long-term care costs associated with this disease.

In contrast to the focus on illness and disability, other researchers have turned their attention to what has been called aging well, successful aging, or optimal aging (Baltes & Baltes, 1990). Here, the goal is to understand how some individuals remain both biologically and psychologically robust well into old age. According to this view, by identifying what is possible, we will be better able to set appropriate goals and achieve desired outcomes for future generations of the elderly.
*See also*: CONTROL; CROSS-CULTURAL SOCIAL PSYCHOLOGY; INDIVIDUALISM–COLLECTIVISM; NORMS; POWER.

BIBLIOGRAPHY
Baltes, P. B., & Baltes, M. M. (1990). *Successful aging: Perspectives from the behavioral sciences.* New York: Cambridge University Press.
Dannefer, D. (1989). Human action and its place in theories of aging. *Journal of Aging Studies, 3,* 1–20.
Heckhausen, J., & Schulz, R. (in press). A life-span theory of control. *Psychological Review.*
Riley, M. W. (1985). Age strata in social systems. In R. H. Binstock & E. Shanas (Eds.), *Handbook of aging and the social sciences* (pp. 369–411). New York: Van Nostrand.
Rodin, J. (1987). Personal control through the life course. In R. P. Abeles (Ed.), *Lifespan perspectives and social psychology* (pp. 103–20). Hillsdale, NJ: Lawrence Erlbaum.
Ross, M. (1989). Relation of implicit theories to the construction of personal histories. *Psychological Review, 89,* 341–7.
Schulz, R., & Ewen, R. (1993). *Adult development and aging* (2nd ed.). New York: Macmillan.
——Heckhausen, J., & Locher, J. (1991). Adult development, control, and adaptive functioning. *Journal of Social Issues, 47,* 177–96.
Weisz, J. R., Rothbaum, F. M., & Blackburn, T. C. (1984). Standing out and standing in. The psychology of control in America and Japan. *American Psychologist, 39,* 955–69.

RICHARD SCHULZ
JUTTA HECKHAUSEN
GAIL M. WILLIAMSON

**alcohol** Often described as "our favorite DRUG," alcohol is widely used as a social lubricant because of its disinhibiting effects. Social psychologists have studied a number of aspects of alcohol use, including underage drinking as a "problem behavior" and the role of expectancies in mediating the effects of alcohol.
*See also*: ADDICTION.

STEPHEN SUTTON

**altruism** A type of HELPING BEHAVIOR that is generally defined in terms of:

(1) relative costs and benefits; and
(2) the helper's motives.

Sociobiologists, economists, and game theorists typically focus on a cost–benefit analysis and refer to altruism as helping that provides more material benefit to the recipient than to the helper. Social psychologists often consider motivation as the distinguishing characteristic and define altruism as voluntary and intentional helping with the primary goal of reducing another person's distress.
*See also*: HELPING BEHAVIOR.

JOHN F. DOVIDIO

**androgyny**  A term that refers to individuals having both masculine (e.g., instrumental) and feminine (e.g., expressive) personality characteristics. Although the correlates of androgyny are unclear, some researchers argue that androgynous individuals are capable of a wider range of behaviors than sex-typed individuals and, as such, are assumed to be better adjusted.
*See also*: GENDER.

CAROL LYNN MARTIN

**anger**  An emotion that results from displeasure at an undesired event, particularly one that is perceived as having resulted from someone's blameworthy action. Anger's relevance to social psychology includes its roles in AGGRESSION and VIOLENCE. Anger also has roles in regulating interpersonal relations and CONFLICT by expressing disapproval and by threatening and justifying retaliation (Averill, 1982). As a social emotion, anger has interested social psychologists studying AFFECT and EMOTIONAL EXPERIENCE.

The nature of anger has been explored from a variety of perspectives. Some researchers have investigated anger's FACIAL EXPRESSION; others, the effect of EXCITATION TRANSFER on anger's intensity. Behaviorists, notably Berkowitz, consider anger a primitive response to aversive events such as frustration and PAIN; they postulate that anger automatically motivates aggression, thus mediating the hypothesized linkage FRUSTRATION–AGGRESSION. Those taking more cognitive or social constructivist perspectives focus on the importance of perceived blameworthiness and the factors that influence its perception and social consequences, e.g., ATTRIBUTION OF RESPONSIBILITY, self-control, SELF-ESTEEM, SOCIAL SKILLS, and MORAL DEVELOPMENT (Wyer & Srull, 1993).
*See also*: AGGRESSION; ATTRIBUTION OF RESPONSIBILITY; CONFLICT; EMOTIONAL EXPERIENCE; MORAL DEVELOPMENT; PAIN; SELF-ESTEEM; SOCIAL SKILLS.

BIBLIOGRAPHY
Averill, J. R. (1982). *Anger and aggression.* New York: Springer-Verlag.
Wyer, R. S., & Srull, T. (Eds.) (1993). *Perspectives on anger and emotion: Advances in social cognition* (Vol. 6). Hillsdale, NJ: Lawrence Erlbaum.

W. GERROD PARROTT

**anxiety**  An emotion characterized by apprehension about potentially unpleasant or harmful future events. Its EMOTIONAL EXPERIENCE typically entails worry about the upcoming event and a desire to avoid it, often with hopelessness about avoiding it; it therefore often produces inhibition. Anxiety is sometimes distinguished from fear based on greater uncertainty or intangibility of the perceived threat, or a greater role of personal inadequacy in causing the threat. Anxiety may motivate affiliation with others for SOCIAL SUPPORT.

Many causes of anxiety are inherently social because the anxiety concerns interaction with others. The fear that others will gain an unfavorable impression of oneself is a frequent source of social anxiety. Social anxiety may be especially acute when a person is being closely observed or evaluated by others, but nearly any social situation can produce it if others' perceptions might contradict the desired SELF-PRESENTATION. Thus, social anxiety is often linked to public SELF-AWARENESS (Buss, 1980). Social anxiety has been described as a component of SHYNESS and EMBARRASSMENT (Crozier, 1990).

*See also*: EMBARRASSMENT; EMOTIONAL EX-
PERIENCE; SELF-AWARENESS; SHYNESS; SOCIAL
SUPPORT.

BIBLIOGRAPHY
Buss, A. H. (1980). *Self-consciousness and social anxiety*. San Francisco, CA: Freeman.
Crozier, W. R. (Ed.) (1990). *Shyness and
embarrassment: Perspectives from social psychology*. New York: Cambridge University
Press.

W. GERROD PARROTT

**applied social psychology** This can be
broadly defined as application of social psychological methods, theories, principles, or
research findings to the understanding or
solution of social problems (Oskamp, 1984).
This area of work has been growing rapidly
in recent years, but its roots go back as far as
Munsterberg's analysis of courtroom psychology in 1908, the Hawthorne plant studies of
WORK conditions and worker behavior in the
1930s, and Lewin's (1948) concept of "action
research" aimed at helping to resolve social
conflicts. Currently, many social psychologists engage in both traditional laboratory or
field research and in applied work aimed at
influencing people's "real world" experiences
and outcomes (Rodin, 1985).

Applied social psychology has several characteristics which distinguish it from more
traditional research approaches, which gather
"knowledge for knowledge's sake." First, it
begins with a problem orientation, that is, a
focus on some problem in society, such as
ethnic prejudice and discrimination, or the
rate of infant mortality. Second, rather than
claiming to be value-free, it adopts a value
orientation, positing that a problem needs to
be corrected or improved, and a utilitarian
approach aimed at achieving that social purpose. To accomplish that, it often uses a
broad perspective, adapting or combining
relevant theoretical ideas and research findings from many sources. Finally, it carries
out most of its research and application
work in field settings – that is, in naturally
occurring situations rather than in laboratories.

When conducting research, applied social
psychologists utilize many different research
methods. Among them are SURVEY research,
which gathers descriptive information about
people's knowledge, attitudes, and/or reported behavior regarding salient local topics
or broader political issues such as national
health insurance. In other studies, OBSERVA-
TIONAL METHODS may be used to determine
people's actual behavior in complex social
situations. Frequently in applied research,
variables measured through observations, interviews, questionnaires, tests, or performance tasks are correlated to specify their
pattern of relationships. EXPERIMENTATION
AND QUASI-EXPERIMENTAL DESIGNS may also
be used to try to tease apart the multiple
causal factors that contribute to a problem,
such as drunken driving. Finally, when a
program to alleviate some social problem has
been established, PROGRAM EVALUATION research is often conducted to assess the degree
of impact and effectiveness of the program.
Examples of applications of many of these
research methods to a wide variety of social
problems are presented in a volume by Edwards, Tindale, Heath, and Posavac (1990).

Among the other professional roles of applied social psychologists are consultation
with organizations or agencies to help them
accomplish desired changes in their operational methods or results. Such change
agents may work intensively with individual
members, or meet with groups to try to
modify group processes and norms, or give
expert analyses of the organization's activities
to top administrators (Hornstein, 1975). Sometimes applied social psychologists become organizational managers themselves, and often
they offer policy advice to government agencies or businesses on desirable changes in
their goals and programs. Alternatively, they
may work from the outside to try to influence
organizations, taking the role of social activists.

Major substantive areas where social psychology has been widely applied in recent years
are summarized in the sections that follow.

SOCIAL INDICATORS
Social indicators are measures of the subjective, psychological aspects of people's lives,

such as their satisfaction with their family life, health, job, standard of living, or other domains of life. Many of these indicators tap dimensions of personal life that are important in psychological theory, such as satisfaction and happiness versus DEPRESSION, perceived stress, self-efficacy, and feelings of control. Since the 1960s there has been a growing movement to collect such data from representative national samples through careful quantitative measurements, in order to determine typical levels of these important variables and to study trends in the way they change over time.

Use of these social indicators can be a valuable counterbalance to the past overemphasis on economic indicators of national life such as the gross national product and the consumer price index. For example, a trend analysis of responses to a survey question asking people what they think is "the most important problem facing this country today" showed that economic problems have frequently been overshadowed in U.S. public opinion by international problems of war and peace, and occasionally by domestic social problems such as race relations, the energy crisis, drug abuse, or crime.

A trend analysis of Americans' responses concerning satisfaction with their personal life displayed unusually high levels from 1988 to 1991. However, an index measuring respondents' satisfaction with "the way things are going in the United States' has always been substantially lower than people's satisfaction with their personal lives. Another time series of survey data concerning U.S. residents' trust in their national government documented a sharp downward trend in this important index from 1958 to an all-time low point in 1980, when well over twice as many citizens had a "low" level of trust as a "high" level, followed by only a small recovery in the subsequent years (Oskamp, 1991).

HEALTH PSYCHOLOGY

One of the fastest growing subareas of psychology is health psychology, which deals with people's beliefs, attitudes, and behavior that affect their HEALTH, and with behavioral aspects of prevention, diagnosis, and treatment programs. Central to this field is the biopsychosocial model, which posits that health and illness conditions result from the interaction of biological, psychological, and social factors (*see* Taylor, 1991). Health psychology aims not just at prolonging people's lives but also at improving their quality of life. Pursuing this approach, many studies have been devoted to changing health-related aspects of people's lifestyles (e.g., diet, exercise, SMOKING), or to training of health personnel to be more sensitive to patients and better at communicating with them, or to developing more effective programs to deal with specific health conditions.

Among the major topics addressed by health psychologists are stress management, PAIN control, patient compliance with treatment regimens, and understanding and controlling high-risk behaviors. For example, programs have been developed to improve the treatment of heart disease, cancer, substance abuse, and AGING. Currently, much research is focused on social psychological techniques aimed at influencing people to avoid behavior that increases their risk of contracting AIDS (*see* Edwards et al., 1990).

Within the health area, several social psychological variables have been found to be useful in understanding and modifying people's behavior (Taylor, 1991). For instance, a sense of perceived CONTROL over the conditions of life is typically linked to better psychological and physical health, whereas a lack or loss of control can contribute to illness and even death. Likewise, SOCIAL SUPPORT from friends and relatives is an important factor in maintaining people's mental and physical health and in buffering them against the effects of various stress conditions. Psychological stress has been found to be an important contributing factor in disorders such as heart disease, ulcers, and immune disorders, among others, and different patterns of coping with stress can have either beneficial or detrimental effects on health (*see* STRESS AND COPING). As a final example, PEER PRESSURE and low SELF-ESTEEM are frequently involved in various high-risk behaviors, such as beginning to smoke or use DRUGS; and successful social psychological programs to combat these risky behaviors have been developed.

## ENVIRONMENTAL PROBLEMS

Applied social psychologists have stressed that environmental conditions such as noise, CROWDING, pollution, and crime rates sharply affect people's behavior; and most of them, in turn, are *caused by* people's behavior. Thus it is important both to reduce these problems and to understand their effects.

Environmental researchers have also studied the area termed human factors, which concerns how humans perform when operating complex mechanical systems (e.g., automated assembly lines, or military weapon systems). Others have contributed to advance planning and subsequent evaluation of the built environment, such as office buildings, schools, hospitals, and urban settings.

Much of the research on noise has been done in laboratory settings, where the immediate and delayed effects of this kind of psychological stress have been precisely determined. Studies of long-continued noise in everyday settings, such as noisy factories or homes near jet airports, have confirmed that it can produce many negative effects, including anxiety, sleep disturbances, reduced scholastic performance, low tolerance for frustration, and increased blood pressure. Research on another psychological stressor, crowding, has found rather similar negative effects, both immediate and delayed, on people's task performance, emotional reactions, aggressiveness, and coping mechanisms. In studies of both noise and crowding, giving people perceived control over the stressor has been found to reduce its negative effects somewhat.

Even more serious environmental problems involve damage to earth's life-sustaining resources. These problems include air pollution; toxic contamination of water supplies; pesticides on foodstuffs; dangers from toxic wastes; acid rain destroying aquatic life and forests; chemical damage to the life-protective ozone layer; the threat of worldwide climatic changes and resulting famine due to the "greenhouse effect," which is caused by excessive burning of oil, gas, and wood; and the destruction of tropical rainforests with its accompanying mass extinction of plant and animal species. Though each of these problems has technological aspects, they are all also psychological in nature, for they are caused by human behavior. Applied social scientists have made contributions toward solving a number of these problems, most notably in encouraging reduced use of fossil fuels through energy conservation, and in recycling and reuse of solid waste materials such as paper, aluminum, glass, and plastics (*see* Edwards et al., 1990; Oskamp, 1984). In doing so, they have often been able to translate their findings into useful policy advice for government officials and business leaders.

## ORGANIZATIONAL PSYCHOLOGY

ORGANIZATIONS, in both the public and private sectors, have often benefited from the work of applied social psychologists. Applied research has contributed to analysis and design of jobs, training of personnel, understanding and improving LEADERSHIP methods, increasing organizational effectiveness, and providing advice for management decisions. One popular approach to overcoming problems in organizations, termed *organization development*, involves working with small groups of members and attempting to change their GROUP PROCESSES, NORMS, attitudes, and/or behaviors, in order to make the organization function more smoothly and with less conflict.

In working with organizations as well as with individuals, processes of PERSUASION are important in producing ATTITUDE CHANGE and desired alterations in group norms and behavior. The social psychological principles behind such influence processes include people's learned tendencies toward RECIPROCITY, commitment and consistency, imitation, liking for others, deference to authority, and attraction to scarce items (Cialdini, 1988). Concrete examples of the application of influence processes in a variety of organizational settings have been offered by Edwards et al. (1990).

A key variable in organizational life is the *job satisfaction* of workers. Research studies have found that it is complexly related to many other factors, including the nature of the work itself (e.g., the importance, variety, autonomy, and challenge of the job), impersonal working conditions (including pay, job security, working conditions, and role ambiguity), and interpersonal relations with co-workers and supervisors. Low job satisfaction has been shown to contribute to employee turnover, absenteeism, grievances and complaints, and poor physical and mental health. However, high job satisfaction does not necessarily lead to higher worker productivity, which is more likely to be an antecedent than a consequence of job satisfaction (*see* Oskamp, 1984).

EDUCATIONAL ISSUES
In educational settings, applied social psychologists have contributed to planning innovative educational programs, such as the use of computers in instruction, developing techniques for strengthening student motivation and performance, improving measurement of educational achievement, and evaluating specialized educational programs such as Head Start.

A unique challenge came to the field when the U.S. Supreme Court ruled in 1954 that racially segregated education was unconstitutional. Social psychologists had long been studying the social problems of ethnic PREJUDICE and discrimination, and some of their research findings were cited in that Supreme Court ruling. Unfortunately, however, when school systems began to desegregate, they generally ignored social psychological knowledge about how to improve INTERGROUP RELATIONS and to create constructive social change. As a result, the conditions necessary for desegregation to have its desired effects were rarely present; and consequently the self-esteem of minority students and the favorability of interracial attitudes among both majority and minority students often decreased rather than increased after schools were desegregated.

A number of applied social scientists rose to this challenge by proposing educational formats designed to improve the effects of racially integrated education (*see* INTEGRATION). Past research had clearly established that INTERGROUP CONTACT alone was not sufficient to create better interracial relationships, so later studies generally concentrated on three additional factors: creation of equal-status relationships, *cooperative learning* situations, and support by administrative authorities. One example of such programs is Aronson et al.'s (1978) "jigsaw classroom," in which each student is responsible for teaching his or her small interracial group part of the lesson material, and all students have to learn that material in order to be prepared for the next test. Studies of such cooperative learning programs have generally shown their success in improving liking for classmates and for school, cooperativeness, and minority students' self-esteem and school performance. As a result of such research, social scientists have been able to offer important policy advice about ways to make desegregation work better.

LEGAL ISSUES
In the legal field, social psychologists have studied the accuracy of EYEWITNESS TESTIMONY, jury selection procedures, jury decision making processes, factors in judges' and parole boards' decisions, people's attitudes about dispute resolution procedures such as mediation and arbitration, public attitudes about crime, and the effectiveness of various crime reduction programs (*see* LAW). Though U.S. courts have generally ignored social science evidence, a few court cases have cited relevant scientific findings, such as the effects of jury size on the adequacy of their deliberations and verdicts.

The most thoroughly studied legal topic has been the myriad factors affecting JURIES' decision processes. However, because U.S. laws forbid the study of actual juries during their deliberations, all of this research has used simulated "mock juries" made up of participants who were conveniently available and willing to be studied. In addition, many other research conditions have markedly departed from actual courtroom procedures (e.g., very brief time periods, presentation of information about the trial in written form, lack of group deliberation, etc.), so the generalizability of these research findings to actual courtroom conditions is highly questionable.

Bearing on this issue, there has been some very useful research on factors influencing judges' and parole boards' DECISION-MAKING processes. These studies compared the predictors of actual, everyday decisions in the legal system with predictors of decisions in simulated studies in which judges or parole board members were asked to make sentencing or probation decisions exactly as they would if the cases were real ones. The findings showed quite different patterns of predictors that were used in the real cases than in the simulations, so these results emphasize that the environmental conditions under which decisions are made are crucial in determining which factors will be considered in the decisions. In addition to casting great doubt on the value of simulation research, these findings have led to empirically based guidelines for legal decision makers, specifying the factors and weights that they have implicitly been using in previous decisions.

POLICY ADVICE

As a number of the sections above have indicated, applied social psychology findings are beginning to be used as the basis for advice to policy makers in various institutional settings. However, there is controversy concerning the degree of certainty necessary in research findings before policy advice should be based on them, and concerning how much attention policy makers actually pay to advice based on social science research. Applied researchers have studied these issues empirically and demonstrated particular characteristics of social science research that increase the chances of its being used by policy makers. In addition, they have shown that government and business leaders more often use research findings as a conceptual background to broaden their thinking than as a direct determinant of policy decisions (*see* Edwards et al., 1990; Oskamp, 1984).

A final issue that has been gaining increased attention is the cultural relativity of many social psychological findings (*see* CROSS-CULTURAL SOCIAL PSYCHOLOGY). That is, because of variations in cultural patterns, some psychological research findings may differ for different ethnic, national, racial, social class, or gender groups (*see* Moghaddam, Taylor, &

Wright, 1993). Consequently, additional studies are necessary before research conclusions or policy advice can be safely generalized to people from other cultural groups or nations.

*See also*: AGING; ATTITUDE CHANGE; CONTROL; CROSS-CULTURAL SOCIAL PSYCHOLOGY; CROWDING; DECISION MAKING; DEPRESSION; EXPERIMENTATION; EYEWITNESS TESTIMONY; GROUP PROCESSES; HEALTH PSYCHOLOGY; INTEGRATION; INTERGROUP RELATIONS; JURIES; LAW; LEADERSHIP; NORMS; OBSERVATIONAL METHODS; ORGANIZATIONS; PAIN; PREJUDICE; PROGRAM EVALUATION; SELF-ESTEEM; SOCIAL SUPPORT; STRESS AND COPING; SURVEY METHODS; WORK.

BIBLIOGRAPHY

Aronson, E., Blaney, N., Stephan, C., Sikes, J., & Snapp, M. (1978). *The jigsaw classroom*. Beverly Hills, CA: Sage.

Cialdini, R. B. (1988). *Influence: Science and practice* (2nd ed.). Glenview, IL: Scott, Foresman.

Edwards, J., Tindale, R. S., Heath, L., & Posavac, E. J. (Eds.) (1990). *Social influence processes and prevention*. New York: Plenum.

Hornstein, H. A. (1975). Social psychology as social intervention. In M. Deutsch & H. A. Hornstein (Eds.), *Applying social psychology: Implications for research, practice, and training* (pp. 211–34). Hillsdale, NJ: Erlbaum.

Lewin, K. (1948). *Resolving social conflicts*. New York: Harper.

Moghaddam, F. M., Taylor, D. M., & Wright, S. C. (1993). *Social psychology in cross-cultural perspective*. New York: Freeman.

Oskamp, S. (1984). *Applied social psychology*. Englewood Cliffs, NJ: Prentice Hall.

—— (1991). *Attitudes and opinions* (2nd ed.). Englewood Cliffs, NJ: Prentice Hall.

Rodin, J. (1985). The application of social psychology. In G. Lindzey & E. Aronson (Eds.), *The handbook of social psychology* (3rd ed., Vol. 2, pp. 805–81). New York: Random House.

Taylor, S. E. (1991). *Health psychology*. New York: McGraw-Hill.

STUART OSKAMP

arousal   Minimally defined as an organism's level of physiological activation or excitation. The earliest modern version of this construct came from Cannon's idea of the emergency "fight or flight" response. Cannon's research during the early decades of this century suggested that the sympathetic division of the autonomic nervous system (ANS) was the primary physiological mechanism for responding to situations involving a threat to one's well-being, or vigorous or prolonged physical activity. Because the sympathetic ganglia tend to be closely linked, they generally function together as a single system, and this fact has encouraged what is commonly referred to as the "undifferentiated" or "unidimensional" arousal construct. In the 1950s a broader general theory of activation emerged in the work of Lindsley, Hebb, Malmo, Duffy, and others, linking cortical, skeletal motor, and autonomic indicants via a single continuum ranging from deep sleep to strong excitement. Cortical arousal is prominent in certain theories of personality, but social psychologists have tended to describe the physiological basis of arousal primarily in terms of autonomic indices such as heart rate, blood pressure, and electrodermal activity.

The impact of the arousal construct in social psychology can be roughly outlined in terms of three developments. The first was the appearance of Schachter and Singer's (1962) experiment combining arousal with self-perception and attribution processes. Although this study has generated a great deal of critical discussion and research on the nature of emotion (see EMOTIONAL EXPERIENCE), it also signaled an important change in the status of arousal as an independently manipulated variable. Many studies subsequently were built on the dualistic notion that bodily arousal represents a source of information to be interpreted or "labeled" by higher-level mental processes. Some researchers, such as Valins, went further and suggested that actual physiological arousal was relatively less important than the mere belief that one is aroused.

The second development was the rapid growth during the 1960s and 1970s of arousal-based theories in a variety of other topic areas such as AGGRESSION, SOCIAL FACILITATION, COGNITIVE DISSONANCE, interpersonal ATTRACTION, and PERSUASION. Arousal was usually posited as a component in these phenomena, sometimes in connection with DRIVE (e.g., social facilitation), but more often as part of a presumed affective or emotional state. Some researchers have sought indicants of the different arousal levels predicted by a given theory under different conditions; another strategy has been to manipulate subjects' attributions of the causes of their feelings of arousal. The effects of dissonance, for example, can be reduced by providing subjects with a plausible – but untrue – explanation for their feelings of unpleasant tension. Such experiments on the MISATTRIBUTION OF AROUSAL were conceptually similar to those on EXCITATION TRANSFER, which also suggested that the perception of arousal and of its cause could be dissociated under certain conditions.

The third important event in social psychology's relationship with the arousal construct was Lacey's critical review of activation theory in 1967, which Fowles (1984) has described as "the death knell of the arousal concept." Although psychophysiologists had known for decades that multiple indicants of autonomic activity rarely correlate perfectly, Lacey made a critical conceptual break with general activation theory by suggesting that such anomalies did not represent sampling errors or reliability problems, but were instead evidence for different *kinds* of arousal, or different arousal systems. Lacey proposed three forms of arousal – electroencephalographic, autonomic, and behavioral – each complex in itself and only imperfectly related to the others. This implies that any single index of arousal, such as heart rate, cannot be assumed to reflect all forms of arousal equally well. Also, it becomes more difficult to design appropriate arousal manipulations for the laboratory if different psychological processes are associated with different forms of physiological arousal. In response, Zillmann (1983) has argued that instances of emotional arousal have in common some degree of undifferentiated sympathetic arousal, implying that a unidimensional arousal concept might still be functional even if not strictly accurate.

Lacey's (1967) concept of multiple arousal systems can be seen underlying present day calls for abandoning the arousal construct altogether in favor of examining discrete "psychobiological states" (Neiss, 1988). Unfortunately, there does not yet appear to be a genuine consensus on issues such as how many patterns or systems of arousal there are, the physiological specifications of those arousal patterns, and their interactions with other variables. As a result, the multiple-arousal concept is often advocated by describing what it is not (namely, the older general activation theory), rather than by describing in detail what it is.

This state of affairs may have led many in social psychology to take a "wait and see" attitude with respect to changes in arousal theory. It would appear, however, that many social psychologists, perhaps the majority, are relatively less interested in the physiological details of arousal than in having an easily manipulated variable which interacts predictably with a variety of other constructs. Despite widespread acknowledgement of the failures of the unidimensional arousal construct, there appears to be little enthusiasm at present for abandoning or even reworking the large body of theory and research which has made use of it.

*See also*: AGGRESSION; ATTRACTION; COGNITIVE DISSONANCE THEORY; DRIVE; EMOTIONAL EXPERIENCE; SOCIAL FACILITATION.

BIBLIOGRAPHY
Fowles, D. C. (1984). Arousal: Implications of behavioral theories of motivation. In M. G. H. Coles, J. R. Jennings, & J. A. Stern (Eds.), *Psychophysiological perspectives: Festschrift for Beatrice and John Lacey* (pp. 143–56). New York: Van Nostrand.
Lacey, J. I. (1967). Somatic response patterning and stress: Some revisions of activation theory. In M. H. Appley & R. Trumbull (Eds.), *Psychological stress: Issues in research* (pp. 14–37). New York: Appleton-Century-Crofts.
Neiss, R. (1988). Reconceptualizing arousal: Psychobiological states in motor performance. *Psychological Bulletin, 103*, 345–66.
Schachter, S., & Singer, J. E. (1962). Cognitive, social, and physiological determinants of emotional state. *Psychological Review, 69*, 379–99.

Zillmann, D. (1983). Transfer of excitation in emotional behavior. In J. T. Cacioppo & R. E. Petty (Eds.), *Handbook of social psychophysiology* (pp. 215–30). New York: Guilford Press.

THOMAS R. GEEN
RUSSELL G. GEEN

**assimilation-contrast** A theory of SOCIAL JUDGMENT predicting that individuals' attitudes will affect their ratings of the viewpoints expressed by different statements, rejected statements being rated as even more distant, accepted statements as closer. Also predicts less persuasion in response to communications advocating positions highly discrepant from one's own.
*See also*: SOCIAL JUDGMENT.

J. RICHARD EISER.

**associative network** An associative network models human MEMORY as the connections among isolated items of stored knowledge. Stored ideas are connected by links of meaning, strengthened through rehearsal and elaboration. Multiple links to a given concept in memory make it easier to retrieve because of many alternative routes to locate it.
*See also*: MEMORY.

SUSAN T. FISKE
BETH A. MORLING

**attachment** The emotional bond between infants and their caregivers, and the impact of these bonds on the developing self-concept and capacity for RELATIONSHIPS, is the central focus of attachment theory. Postulated by Bowlby (1969, 1973, 1980), the attachment system was designed by evolutionary processes to maintain proximity between infants and caregivers. Accordingly, infants who kept in close proximity with adult caregivers, and who displayed appropriate protest behaviors when separated or threatened, were more likely to survive into adulthood. A key advantage of attachment theory is its synthesis of evolutionary accounts and EMOTION concepts. At its core, attachment is a theory of how children experience and internalize such emotions as security, LOVE, ANXIETY, ANGER, sadness, and loss.

Attachment relationships are said to be secure or insecure. When the bond between infant and caregiver is secure, the child's expressions of FEAR or anxiety usually result in appropriate, sensitive responses from the caregiver. As a consequence, the developing child feels safe and secure, and begins to use the attachment relationship as a "secure base" from which to explore the environment. Gradually, he/she also internalizes a positive "internal working model" of SELF as love-worthy and valued, and of relationships as desirable and self-satisfying.

In contrast, insecure attachment relationships arise when the caregivers' response is chronically inadequate to the infants' needs. Research has identified two general forms of insecure attachment. Anxious-avoidance may result when caregivers consistently ignore the infants' requests for comfort. These children tend to avoid social contact with peers and adults. Anxious-ambivalent relationships tend to develop when caregivers are inconsistent, intrusive at one moment and unresponsive at the next moment. These children are often preoccupied with relationships, clinging to caregivers, but also easily angered with them.

Attachment theory posits stability of inner working models over the lifespan, so that experiences in early infant–caregiver relationships may exert profound influence over adult behavior and self-concept. Researchers have recently established a role for attachment in such diverse phenomena as SELF-ESTEEM and mental health; adult romantic love; friendship during childhood, ADOLESCENCE and adulthood; coping with divorce, BEREAVEMENT, and stress; personal beliefs about relationships; parental behavior toward their children; and school performance and work attitudes.

*See also*: ADOLESCENCE; EMOTIONAL EXPERIENCE; RELATIONSHIPS; SELF; SELF-ESTEEM.

BIBLIOGRAPHY

Bowlby, J. (1969). *Attachment*. New York: Basic Books.

—— (1973). *Separation: Anxiety and anger*. New York: Basic Books.

—— (1980). *Loss: Sadness and depression*. New York: Basic Books.

HARRY T. REIS

**attention** Whatever occupies consciousness, thus, a person's mental focus at a particular time. People pay attention to external stimuli, such as objects in the environment, and to internal stimuli, such as retrieved long-term memories that currently occupy consciousness. Attention is often equated with working or short-term memory. People are attending to the stimuli that are in conscious focal awareness.

Attention is important in ENCODING, which transforms an external stimulus into a meaningful, internal representation. Encoding is viewed as having four steps. First, a stimulus is noticed. Then it comes into focal attention to be identified and categorized. Then it is given semantic meaning and, finally, it is linked to other knowledge for complex inferences. As part of encoding, attention is a vital step in social information processing.

Attention has two dimensions: direction (those objects to which people selectively attend) and intensity (how effortfully people attend). Because social environments and people are complex and attentional capacity is limited, people are unable to attend to many of the available stimuli. The focus and intensity of people's attention is directed toward particular features of external stimuli in context and toward internal processes as well (Kahneman, 1973; Posner, 1982).

STIMULUS AND CONTEXT FACTORS IN ATTENTION

Two stimulus factors that determine direction of attention are SALIENCE and VIVIDNESS (*see* Fiske & Taylor, 1991). Salience refers to how noticeable a stimulus is in its context. People are salient in the context of other people or the surrounding environment, such as when they are the solo person of their gender or ethnicity in a group, or when they stand out because they are visually different. Salience also occurs in the context of people's prior knowledge or expectations, such as when people behave in ways that are unusual for them as individuals (e.g., behaving in unexpected ways), for their social category (e.g., behaving in out-of-role ways), or for people in general (e.g., behaving negatively or extremely). People who dominate a perceiver's visual field also attract attention because of salience.

The quality of vividness is inherent in a stimulus itself, regardless of context. Intuitively, it seems that like salient stimuli, vivid stimuli attract significant attention. However, unlike salient stimuli, vivid stimuli do not necessarily have greater impact on people's judgments. People are entertained by vivid stimuli and recall them more easily than less graphic stimuli. But though vividly presented arguments capture attention, people are not necessarily persuaded by them.

People's goals in context can also affect attention. People who are goal-relevant are salient, so they attract attention. For example, when people are dependent on another person for an outcome (such as an incentive for work done together), they attend more to their partner, especially to the most informative information (i.e., information inconsistent with their initial impressions). The increased attention can cause people's impressions of their partners to change.

Another factor that influences attention is ACCESSIBILITY, the effect of prior context or constructs in memory. People's accessible categories can filter what they heed in the social environment. In general, accessibility refers to the ease with which a category is retrieved. A category is more accessible if it has been recently or frequently used. PRIMING will make a category temporarily accessible; individuals also have categories that they use frequently and which are termed *chronically accessible*. People's accessible categories influence their impressions, especially when the target is moderate or ambiguous. Thus, attention is directed by accessible categories.

EFFECTS OF ATTENTION ON SOCIAL JUDGMENTS

When people are the focus of attention, other people are more likely to see them as espe-

cially influential and to make dispositional attributions about them (*see* Fiske & Taylor, 1991). As more attention is paid to a person, impressions of that person tend to be more exaggerated, structured, and internally consistent. As they pay more attention, people tend to emphasize features that create a coherent impression, and they may reinterpret inconsistent features to fit it.

People's differential recall of information may be the one factor mediating why increased attention leads to exaggerated evaluations and causal attributions. Perhaps attention causes people to recall different kinds of information. Two theories of differential recall have received some empirical support. One relates to the accessibility, or ease of recall, of the behaviors of people who attract attention. Noticeable people may later be evaluated as more causal or extreme because information about them is recalled more easily. A second theory predicts that people recall in particular the causally relevant information about people to whom they have attended. Diagnostic data about people, such as how long they talk or how dramatically they behave, should be especially important in impression formation. When people pay a lot of attention to a target, they are more likely to witness such causally relevant behaviors and to recall them later when forming an impression.

INTERNAL PROCESSES AND ATTENTION

Attention can be focused on internal processes as well as external ones (*see* Wegner & Pennebaker, 1993). Consciousness has been variously defined, but some social psychologists have described its content as attention to internal thoughts, emotions, and body sensations that compete for attention with the external world.

Ruminations are thoughts that intrude on attention apparently because people's goals have been interrupted. Although people consciously attend to ruminations, they may not be able to control them short of completing the relevant goal. Like the external stimuli to which people attend, attention to these internal thoughts over time can polarize people's attitudes.

Relatedly, people have difficulty suppressing thoughts to which they do not want to attend. People who try not to attend to something are usually unsuccessful. Later, when people cease trying to suppress it, the formerly unwanted thought can show rebound effects. Effortfully attending to a specific substitute thought prevents rebound effects.

BIBLIOGRAPHY
Fiske, S. T., & Taylor, S. E. (1991). *Social cognition* (2nd ed., chapter 7). New York: McGraw-Hill.
Kahneman, D. (1973). *Attention and effort.* Englewood Cliffs, NJ: Prentice Hall.
Posner, M. I. (1982). Cumulative development of attentional theory. *American Psychologist, 37*, 168–79.
Wegner, D. M., & Pennebaker, J. W. (Eds.). (1993). *Handbook of mental control.* Englewood Cliffs, NJ: Prentice Hall.

SUSAN T. FISKE<br>BETH A. MORLING

**attitude change** An attitude is "a psychological tendency that is expressed by evaluating a particular entity with some degree of favor or disfavor" (Eagly & Chaiken, 1993, p. 1). Thus attitude change refers to a noticeable and therefore measurable change in this evaluative tendency. Understanding when and why such change occurs has been a key topic in social psychological research on attitudes. A major reason for this enduring concern with attitude change is the applied relevance of such change. Because attitudes are thought to exercise a directive influence on behavior (*see* ATTITUDES AND BEHAVIOR), those who have an interest in changing other people's behavior, for political, commercial, or public health and safety reasons, have been and continue to be keen to know more about the dynamics of attitude change. The present entry will focus on three approaches to the study of attitude change:

(1) the message-learning approach;
(2) the cognitive response approach; and
(3) the so-called "dual process" models.

Other approaches to the study of attitude change, notably those with a more motivational flavor (e.g., COGNITIVE CONSISTENCY THEORIES – especially COGNITIVE DISSONANCE THEORY, IMPRESSION MANAGEMENT theory, and REACTANCE theory) are dealt with elsewhere in this volume, as are SELF-PERCEPTION THEORY and approaches that emphasise the importance of SOCIAL JUDGMENT processes. The best single source for learning more about any of these approaches to the study of attitude change is the recent book by Eagly and Chaiken (1993).

THE MESSAGE-LEARNING APPROACH
One of the earliest and most influential lines of research on attitude change was developed in the 1940s and 1950s by Carl Hovland and his colleagues (*see* Hovland, Janis & Kelley, 1953). These researchers adopted an approach to the study of attitude change that was influenced by the then-current learning theory principles of how people acquire verbal and motor skills. Just as someone learns how to ride a bicycle or to speak a foreign language, so (it was reasoned) people can "learn" a new attitudinal position, given the right conditions. This approach has been dubbed the "message-learning approach" (Petty & Cacioppo, 1981), and focused on the impact on attitude change of four classes of independent variable: source, message, receiver, and channel.

*Source Factors*
These refer to attributes of the source of a persuasive message. The source may be an individual, a group, or an institution. For example, it was reasoned that recipients of a message should find it more rewarding to agree with a source who is high in perceived expertise, trustworthiness, or similarity to the audience. Some of the research evidence collected by Hovland and his team was consistent with the view that source factors, such as the credibility of a communicator, would influence attitude change, but later research has shown that the effects of source variables such as credibility are greatest when the message is one that the recipients do not find personally involving.

*Message Factors*

These refer to the contents of a persuasive message, and especially to what is said or written. Variables studied by Hovland and his colleagues included message comprehensibility, the number of arguments contained in a message, whether the message was one-sided or recognised both sides of an issue, and the emotional quality of the message. Unsurprisingly, perhaps, there is support for the prediction that a message that is comprehended will be more effective in changing attitudes. Less obviously, the number of arguments presented was not found to have a consistent effect: more arguments are not always more persuasive than fewer arguments. The effects of a two-sided message, which acknowledges and tries to address some of the arguments for the opposite side of the issue to the one being advocated, are most apparent when it comes to resisting "counter-propaganda." Being exposed to a two-sided message helps people to resist future attempts to undermine the impact of the persuasive message.

More research has been conducted on the emotional quality of messages than on any other type of message factor (*see* FEAR APPEALS). Specifically, researchers have compared the effectiveness of high-fear messages, which deliberately try to evoke fear in recipients, with that of moderate- or low-fear messages. Early findings gave rise to inconsistent findings. Later research helped to resolve these inconsistencies by showing that high-fear appeals tend to be effective under specific conditions, namely when the message convincingly argues that negative consequences for the audience will occur unless the audience accepts the advocacy, and when the recommendations contained in the message are perceived as an effective and achievable means of avoiding those negative outcomes. Such findings gave rise to the dominant theoretical framework for present-day research on fear appeals, namely Rogers' (1983) protection motivation theory.

*Receiver Factors*

Hovland and his colleagues tried to identify INDIVIDUAL DIFFERENCES associated with persuasibility. One factor that was identified early in their research program was education: It was found that more highly educated recipients were more persuaded by a message than their less-educated counterparts. Hovland and his colleagues reasoned that such findings were due to the fact that more education led recipients to be better able to attend to the message, and to understand and remember its contents. However, subsequent research examining the relationship between intelligence and persuasibility sometimes found that persons of higher intelligence were less persuasible than persons with average or low intelligence. McGuire (1968) helped to resolve this apparent inconsistency by arguing that attitude change is determined not only by amount of attention to, comprehension of and retention of the message (which together comprise what McGuire calls "reception of the message"), but also by the extent to which the audience yields to the advocacy. As intelligence increases, one might expect the quality of the reception of the message to *increase*, but the amount of yielding to the message to *diminish* – because more intelligent recipients will be better able to attend to, understand, and remember a message, and will also be more confident of their initial position on the issue and more critical of the contents of the message. Thus the consensus among researchers in this field is that the relationship between attitude change and receiver factors often takes the form of an inverted-U curve, with attributes that enhance message reception helping to boost attitude change until the point at which the decrease in yielding to the message takes over, when attitude change begins to decline.

*Channel Factors*

Research on channel factors considers whether the effectiveness of persuasive communications is influenced by the medium through which they are delivered (e.g., television, radio, telephone, newspaper, face-to-face). A common finding in early research on the impact of channel factors was that face-to-face communications have a greater impact than mediated communications. However, the lesser impact of mediated communications is more than offset by their potentially tremendous cost-effectiveness: Changing the attitudes of even a tiny proportion of a prime-time television audience is clearly much more efficient than achieving attitude change with the vast majority of those people who can be reached in face-to-face communications. Which of the various channels of mediated communication is most effective appears to depend on the content of the message. There are grounds for thinking that simple messages are more effective in audiovisual than in written form; however, more complex messages are more effective when in written form than in audiovisual form, presumably because the written version allows the audience to reread difficult passages and reflect on the message content.

THE COGNITIVE RESPONSE APPROACH

The cognitive response approach to studying persuasion also stresses the importance of learning in attitude change, but differs from the message-learning approach in that it emphasizes the importance of the role played by the thoughts that are elicited in recipients by a message, both during and after the reception of that message. Greenwald (1968) suggested that learning the content of one's cognitive responses might be more important in persuasion than learning the content of the message itself, partly on the grounds that previous research failed to find strong relationships between attitude change and memory for message content. The cognitive response model proposed by Greenwald regards recipients as active processors of information, who relate the content of a message to their existing beliefs and feelings about the topic at issue. Cognitive responses are the self-generated thoughts and ideas that emerge from this inner dialogue between message content and preexisting attitudes. These cognitive responses are presumed to mediate the impact of the message on attitude change.

The methodological hallmark of the cognitive response approach is, naturally enough, the measurement of cognitive responses. This is achieved using the "thought-listing technique," a simple but effective means of tapping subjects' thoughts during or immediately after exposure to a persuasive communication (an example of PROCESS TRACING). Subjects are simply asked to list all the thoughts and ideas that occur to them that are relevant to the topic of the message. These listed thoughts are then coded by judges (or by the subjects themselves), typically into one of two (positive or negative) or three (positive, neutral or negative) categories, where positive means that the thought is consistent with or favorable to the position advocated in the message and negative means thoughts that are inconsistent with or unfavorable to that position.

Messages that evoke predominantly positive thoughts in respondents should be effective in changing attitudes in the direction advocated by the message, whereas those that evoke predominantly negative thoughts will either fail to change attitudes or even have an effect contrary to that advocated by the message. Furthermore, the amount of attitude change effected by a message is deemed to be a function of the amount of cognitive responding of a particular type: Messages that evoke more cognitive responses will tend to have a greater impact on attitude change.

There is by now a great deal of empirical evidence that is consistent with the cognitive response model (for reviews, see Eagly & Chaiken, 1993; Petty & Cacioppo, 1981). Two representative lines of investigation are those concerned with the impact on attitude change of (1) distraction and (2) involvement.

*Distraction*

Distraction reduces a persons' ability to think about the arguments contained in a message. Thus if the dominant cognitive response to a given message would be negative, distraction should enhance the effectiveness of the message in changing attitudes, because the opportunity to engage in those negative thoughts would be restricted. However, if the dominant cognitive response to the message is positive, distraction should reduce the impact of the message on attitude change. In an influential paper, Petty, Wells, and Brock (1976) reported two experiments with findings that are consistent with this reasoning.

*Involvement*

Involvement refers to the extent to which recipients of a message regard the topic of the message as personally relevant or important. It is argued by cognitive response theorists that recipients who are personally involved in an issue are more highly motivated to engage in thinking that is relevant to the message and/or the issue. It follows that involvement should enhance the effectiveness of messages containing strong arguments but decrease the effectiveness of messages containing weak arguments. Several studies have produced findings consistent with these predictions, especially that part of the prediction concerning the beneficial effect of involvement on responses to strong messages; support for the corresponding prediction concerning the negative effect of involvement on reactions to weak messages is more uneven (*see* Johnson & Eagly, 1989, for a meta-analytic review).

THE DUAL-PROCESS APPROACH

The dual-process approach to attitude change is closely related to the cognitive response approach, in that one of the two processes believed to be responsible for attitude change is based on perception of and responses to the arguments contained in the message. What this approach adds is the notion that under some conditions attitude change may result from factors other than the arguments themselves. There are two theories that adopt this dual-process approach: the ELABORATION LIKELIHOOD MODEL developed by Petty and Cacioppo (e.g., 1986) and the HEURISTIC-SYSTEMATIC MODEL developed by Chaiken (e.g., Chaiken, Liberman & Eagly, 1989).

*Elaboration Likelihood Model (ELM)*

The ELM assumes that people want to hold "correct" attitudes, but that how carefully they process attitude-relevant information will be a function of situational and individual difference factors. When recipients are motivated and able to process message-content carefully, they will be more likely to elaborate (i.e., think about) issue-relevant arguments, and to follow the so-called *central route* to persuasion. This route is based on the cognitive responses generated by the arguments contained in the message, or what Petty and Cacioppo refer to as message-relevant thinking. Numerous variables are thought to affect motivation and ability to process message-content carefully. Classic examples

are involvement (which affects motivation) and distraction (which affects ability). How attitudes are affected by this processing of message-content is said to depend on argument quality, in the same way as predicted by the cognitive response approach, and is not dependent on factors external to these arguments. Attitude change via this central route is predicted to be longer-lasting, more resistant to counter-persuasion, and more predictive of subsequent behavior.

When ability or motivation to process message-content is low, it is likely that recipients will follow the so-called *peripheral route* to persuasion. Any attitude change resulting from factors external to the arguments contained in the message must by definition occur via this peripheral route. These factors are referred to as peripheral cues. A classic example of a peripheral cue is source attractiveness (i.e., the attractiveness of the source of the message). Such cues may have a positive (e.g., high attractiveness) or a negative (e.g., low attractiveness) effect on attitude change, but this effect will be independent of argument quality. Attitude change via the peripheral route to persuasion is likely to be short-lived, vulnerable to counter-persuasion and a poor predictor of future behavior.

Much current attitude change research is designed to test predictions derived from the ELM (for a review, *see* Eagly & Chaiken, 1993). There is a good deal of evidence to support the hypothesis that manipulations of ability and/or motivation to process message-content interact with argument quality to determine attitude change. There is also a good measure of support for the hypothesis that peripheral cues are relatively unimportant determinants of attitude change when ability and/or motivation to process message-content are high, but that they are influential when ability and/or motivation are low. Finally, there is some support for the prediction that attitude change elicited under conditions promoting elaboration of the message-content is more durable and predictive of behavior or behavioral intentions.

*Heuristic-Systematic Model (HSM)*

The HSM also specifies two routes to persuasion: *systematic processing*, which is an analytic orientation to information processing, and *heuristic processing*, which is a more restricted mode of information processing that makes fewer demands on cognitive resources. Both types of processing, it is argued, can serve each of a number of motivations that message recipients might have. One key motive is referred to as "validity seeking," which is a concern to hold attitudes that are accurate in the sense that they are consistent with the relevant facts.

Although the language used to describe the central route to persuasion within the ELM and systematic processing mode in the HSM is different, the rationale underlying these two conceptions of attitude change is quite similar: Systematic processing is also thought to be determined by ability and motivation. However, heuristic processing is not the same as the peripheral route to attitude change, in the sense that heuristic processing is more narrowly defined. Whereas the peripheral route to persuasion embraces *any* nonargument-based influence on attitudes, in heuristic processing recipients are seen as using cognitive HEURISTICS to form judgments and decisions, and as focusing on that subset of the available information that enables them to use such heuristics. An example of such a heuristic is "experts can be trusted," which would lead recipients using this processing mode to agree more with positions advocated by experts, without careful scrutiny of the content of the arguments used in support of that advocacy.

The HSM assumes that both modes of processing can occur simultaneously, such that when weak arguments are presented by expert sources, systematic processing will attenuate any heuristic tendency to agree with positions espoused by experts. Likewise, systematic processing can be biased by heuristic processing, in that the perceived expertise of a source may establish expectations about the validity of the arguments from this source which may then bias the evaluation of those arguments.

Insofar as the predictions derived from the HSM overlap with those of the ELM, the supportive evidence alluded to in connection with the ELM also supports the HSM. More distinctive are the HSM hypotheses concerning heuristic processing, such as the prediction that heuristic cues influence attitude change only when the associated heuristics are highly accessible to recipients. There are several studies examining such hypotheses, and the evidence is generally supportive of the theory (see Eagly & Chaiken, 1993).

CONCLUSION
The study of attitude change has been an important theme in social psychological research on attitudes. The three approaches considered here, namely the message-learning, cognitive response, and dual-process approaches, constitute the mainstream of theoretical activity in this domain and it can be seen how each approach stands on the shoulders of its predecessor. What is missing from this mainstream theorizing about attitude change is what could be called "social context." Both theory and experimentation in the field of attitude change are typically concerned with the impact of persuasive messages, usually verbal in nature, delivered by one communicator to a number of persons who are conceptualized as individuals. It is remarkable that there is as yet relatively little formal connection between the fields of attitude change and SOCIAL INFLUENCE. In the latter field careful consideration is given to norms, roles, identities and relationships. The markedly cognitive flavor of attitude change research has tended to ignore these social factors in favor of trying to understand the intra-individual processes involved in attitude change.

*See also*: ATTITUDES AND BEHAVIOR; COGNITIVE CONSISTENCY; COGNITIVE DISSONANCE THEORY; HEURISTICS; IMPRESSION MANAGEMENT; REACTANCE; SELF-PERCEPTION THEORY; SOCIAL INFLUENCE; SOCIAL JUDGMENT.

BIBLIOGRAPHY
Chaiken, S., Liberman, A., & Eagly, A. H. (1989). Heuristic and systematic processing within and beyond the persuasion context. In J. S. Uleman & J. A. Bargh (Eds.), *Unintended thought* (pp. 212–52). New York: Guilford Press.
Eagly, A. H., & Chaiken, S. (1993). *The psychology of attitudes*. Forth Worth, TX: Harcourt Brace Jovanovich.

Greenwald, A. G. (1968). Cognitive learning, cognitive response to persuasion, and attitude change. In A. G. Greenwald, T. C. Brock, & T. M. Ostrom (Eds.), *Psychological foundations of attitudes* (pp. 147–70). New York: Academic Press.

Hovland, C. I., Janis, I. L., & Kelley, H. H. (1953). *Communication and persuasion: Psychological studies of opinion change*. New Haven, CT: Yale University Press.

Johnson, B. T., & Eagly, A. H. (1989). The effects of involvement on persuasion: A meta-analysis. *Psychological Bulletin, 106*, 290–314.

McGuire, W. J. (1968). Personality and susceptibility to social influence. In E. F. Borgatta & W. W. Lambert (Eds.), *Handbook of personality theory and research* (pp. 1130–87). Chicago, IL: Rand McNally.

Petty, R. E., & Cacioppo, J. T. (1981). *Attitudes and persuasion: Classic and contemporary approaches*. Dubuque, IL: William C. Brown.

——(1986). The elaboration likelihood model of persuasion. In L. Berkowitz (Ed.), *Advances in experimental social psychology* (Vol. 19, pp. 123–205). San Diego, CA: Academic Press.

—— Wells, G. L., & Brock, T. C. (1976). Distraction can enhance or reduce yielding to propaganda: Thought disruption versus effort justification. *Journal of Personality and Social Psychology, 34*, 874–84.

Rogers, R. W. (1983). Cognitive and physiological processes in fear appeals and attitude change: A revised theory of protection motivation. In J. T. Cacioppo & R. E. Petty (Eds.), *Social psychophysiology: A sourcebook* (pp. 153–76). New York: Guilford Press.

ANTONY S.R. MANSTEAD

**attitude formation** The distinction between *attitude formation* and *attitude change* is a fine one. If people change their attitudes, they can be said to be forming new attitudes. Thus much of the theorizing and research considered under ATTITUDE CHANGE can be regarded as relevant to the issue of attitude formation. Attitude change theorists tend to share the view that attitudes are modified by the provision or acquisition of new information. The general assumption in such an approach is that the new information will modify an individual's BELIEFS about the attributes of the attitude object. To the extent that these attributes are positively or negatively evaluated by the individual, his or her attitude should change. However, this approach does not directly address the issue of why the individual values some attributes positively and others negatively. What is the origin of such evaluative preferences? This is the question that will be addressed in the present entry.

Most attitude theorists regard attitudes as learned predispositions. As noted by Eagly and Chaiken (1993, p. 392), "Consensus on this point has been so widespread that very little empirical attention has been paid to the possible genetic or biological basis of some attitudes' (but *see* GENETIC INFLUENCES). Since learning is widely assumed to be deeply implicated in the formation of attitudes, it is not surprising to find that the bulk of the relatively small research effort investigating attitude formation has had a learning theory orientation (but for an alternative approach to the study of attitude formation, *see* MERE EXPOSURE).

The role played by classical conditioning in attitude formation has been investigated by several researchers, among whom Staats (e.g., 1983) has been one of the most influential. The essential idea is that people acquire new attitudes because unconditioned stimuli, i.e., inherently rewarding or punishing stimuli such as food or physical punishment, are repeatedly paired with conditioned stimuli, i.e. stimuli that have no intrinsic reward value but which come to be able to elicit the same pleasurable affective response as the unconditioned stimuli. Thus words such as "good" and "bad," which have no intrinsic power to elicit affective responses, may acquire such power through repeated pairing with unconditioned stimuli. This is referred to as *first-order conditioning*, and creates the potential for these words to serve as unconditioned stimuli in order to establish new affective reactions to yet other stimuli. Thus words such as *good* and *bad* can be paired repeatedly with new stimuli; to the extent that these new stimuli come to elicit the same affective reactions as the words, there is evidence of what is referred to in the literature as *second-order conditioning*.

An example of the use of the first-order conditioning procedure to study attitude formation is the experiment reported by Zanna, Kiesler, and Pilkonis (1970). They repeatedly paired the words *light* and *dark* with the onset or offset of electric shock. The prediction was that the word paired with shock onset would come to be evaluated more negatively, and that the word paired with shock offset would be evaluated more positively. This prediction was tested by having a second experimenter (apparently as part of a separate investigation) administer a questionnaire measuring attitudes to the words light and dark, their synonyms (e.g., *white, black*) and control words. The word paired with shock onset was indeed evaluated more negatively, and the word paired with shock offset more positively, than control words. This conditioning effect also generalized to the synonyms.

An example of the use of the second-order conditioning procedure to study attitude formation is a well-known investigation by Staats and Staats (1958, Expt. 1). They gave their subjects two lists of words to learn, one of which was presented visually and the other orally. The visually-presented list consisted of six nationality names; the orally-presented list consisted of words with a positive evaluative connotation, words with a negative evaluative connotation, and neutral words. In each of a series of conditioning trials, one of the nationality names appeared on a screen, then after a one second interval the experimenter read one of the words from the list of positive, negative, or neutral words. Four of the nationalities were always paired with neutral words, but the remaining two (Swedish and Dutch) were always paired with either positive or negative words. Subsequently, each nationality name had to be evaluated for pleasantness. As predicted, Swedish and Dutch were rated as more pleasant if they had been paired with positive words than if they had been paired with negative words. These results suggest one way in which prejudiced attitudes might be acquired.

It seems clear, then, that attitudes can be acquired through classical conditioning procedures. What is less clear is *why* such procedures have an effect on attitudes. Specifically, there is a dispute in the literature concerning whether or not these effects are mediated by cognitive processes. A noncognitive account of these effects argues that the affective responses elicited by the unconditioned stimulus become conditioned to any stimulus that is repeatedly paired with that stimulus. This implies no conscious awareness or deliberation on the part of the subject. However, critics of this reasoning argue that for conditioning to occur, subjects need to be aware of the contingency between the conditioned and unconditioned stimuli; the effects of their repeated pairing on attitude to the conditioned stimulus may therefore depend on cognitive processes. Page (1969) showed that significant conditioning effects were only obtained when subjects reported having been aware of the contingency between the conditioned and unconditioned stimuli, and that manipulations intended to increase awareness of this contingency enhanced the classical conditioning effects. He interpreted such evidence in terms of the operation of DEMAND CHARACTERISTICS. The idea is that awareness of the contingency creates "demand awareness," or awareness of the hypothesis that the contingency is designed to influence attitudes to the conditioned stimulus. For an illuminating discussion of the relationship between contingency awareness and classical conditioning effects, readers are referred to Eagly and Chaiken (1993, pp. 403–12).

Classical conditioning is not the only learning process that may be involved in the acquisition of new attitudes. There is also evidence that operant conditioning (i.e., directly rewarding or punishing a person for expressing certain attitudes) and observational learning (*see* SOCIAL LEARNING) can influence attitude formation. However, classical conditioning effects (whether or not they are cognitively mediated) are likely to provide an especially important basis for the formation of attitudes. This is because such principles can influence the value attached to a stimulus either more-or-less directly (as in the Zanna et al. experiment cited above) or less directly, by providing a means by which people evaluate stimulus attributes (e.g., one might learn via classical conditioning procedures that a particular nationality is "good" and subsequently be inclined to have a positive attitude towards anyone who has this nationality).

See also: ATTITUDE CHANGE; GENETIC INFLUENCES; MERE EXPOSURE; SOCIAL LEARNING.

BIBLIOGRAPHY

Eagly, A. H., & Chaiken, S. (1993). The psychology of attitudes. Forth Worth, TX: Harcourt Brace Jovanovich.

Page, M. M. (1969). Social psychology of a classical conditioning of attitudes experiment. Journal of Personality and Social Psychology, 11, 177–186.

Staats, A. W. (1983). Paradigmatic behaviorism: Unified theory for social-personality psychology. In L. Berkowitz (Ed.), Advances in experimental social psychology (Vol. 16, pp. 125–79). New York: Academic Press.

—— & Staats, C. K. (1958). Attitudes established by classical conditioning. Journal of Abnormal and Social Psychology, 57, 37–40.

Zanna, M. P., Kiesler, C. A., & Pilkonis, P. A. (1970). Positive and negative attitudinal affect established by classical conditioning. Journal of Personality and Social Psychology, 14, 321–28.

ANTONY S. R. MANSTEAD

**attitude measurement and questionnaire design**  A great deal of research has examined methods of designing questionnaires to measure attitudes and other subjective psychological constructs effectively (see also ATTITUDE THEORY AND RESEARCH, SURVEY METHODS), and this research provides a basis for a number of recommendations. We shall begin below by reviewing some of the original attitude measurement techniques, which involved elaborate procedures and multiple items. Then we will review the more recent literature on single-item measurement and the many decisions one must make in designing such measures.

EARLY ATTITUDE MEASUREMENT METHODS: MULTIPLE ITEM INDICES

A number of elaborate attitude measurement techniques were developed beginning in the 1920s (for reviews, see Dawes & Smith, 1985; Mueller, 1986; Summers, 1970). One such technique was developed by L. L. Thurstone. In his classic paper, "Attitudes can be measured," Thurstone (1928) argued that attitudes toward objects could be gauged in ways similar to those used to assess perceptions of sensory stimuli such as light and sound. Although this idea does not seem to be particularly revolutionary today, it marked a bold departure from the dominant behaviorist tradition of the time, which held that latent psychological constructs were not legitimate topics of scientific inquiry or assessment.

Thurstone developed several techniques for measuring attitudes, the most popular of which was the method of equally appearing intervals (EAI). EAI scales are developed by generating a large pool of statements, each of which expresses some degree of positivity or negativity toward a target object. A group of judges then classifies each statement into one of eleven categories according to how much positivity or negativity the statement reflects toward the object. The categories are then numbered from 1 to 11, representing increasing positivity, and a scale value is assigned to each statement by computing the median or mean rating of the statement (on the 1 to 11 scale) across the judges. A final item set is then constructed by selecting one statement to best represent each of the 11 intervals. This final set of items can then be administered to respondents, instructing them to indicate with which statements they agree. The median or mean scale value of the statments with which each respondent agrees serves as the index of the respondent's attitude.

Although the EAI method is highly reliable, the extensive preparation necessary to construct EAI scales spurred researchers to investigate other, simpler methods. One popular one proposed by Rensis Likert is the method of summated ratings. This method begins by generating a large number of statements reflecting positivity or negativity toward the target object. Respondents then indicate the extent of their agreement or disagreement with the statements using 5-point agree/disagree scales. Next, responses to these items are summed to create an overall score for each respondent, and the correlation of each item with the total score is computed. Items that correlate poorly with the total score are deleted, and the remaining items are used to yield a final index of the attitude. Thus, the method of summated ratings does not require a separate group of judges to rate items prior to administering the final scale to the sample of interest.

Another measurement method traditionally used to assess attitudes towards ethnic groups is the method of social distance. According to this method, respondents are given a series of statements reflecting increasingly proximal degrees of social contact with members of a target social group (e.g., shopping in a store where members of the target group shop versus having a member of the target group over for dinner). The respondent's attitude is assessed by determining the most proximal behavior the respondent is comfortable with.

Another method of measuring attitudes is the semantic differential, developed by Charles Osgood and his colleagues. These investigators argued that attitudes can be measured by asking respondents to rate an object on bipolar scales anchored by pairs of adjectives reflecting an evaluative, positive–negative dimension (e.g., good–bad, wise–foolish). Responses to these scales can then be summed to arrive at an overall attitude score for each respondent. Because the same adjective pairs can be used for nearly any attitude object with little if any pretesting, this method has been quite popular among social scientists.

CONTEMPORARY ATTITUDE MEASUREMENT: DESIGNING SINGLE ITEM MEASURES

Unfortunately, it is often not practical to measure attitudes using one of the above methods, because they involve multiple items per attitude and sometimes involve elaborate pretesting. Especially in surveys in which attitudes towards dozens of objects are assessed, it is not feasible to obtain multiple measures of each attitude. Consequently, re-searchers have turned increasingly often to single item measurement approaches that they believe best reflect the underlying attitude.

An advantage of the multiple item approach is that the particular characteristics of any particular item are unlikely to have a substantial impact on the results of an assessment procedure. But when one relies on only a single item, its characteristics can potentially have tremendous impact on one's conclusions. Therefore, one must design single item measures very carefully in light of one's research goals. Below, we will review the existing literature on designing single items and summarize some of the recommendations supported by these studies (for more details, see Himmelfarb, 1993; Krosnick & Fabrigar, in press; Schuman & Presser, 1981).

OPEN VERSUS CLOSED QUESTIONS

One of the first issues that a researcher must confront when constructing an item is whether to use an open-ended or a closed-ended question. Closed questions provide a list of response options among which a respondent must choose, whereas open questions allow respondents to answer in their own words. Although researchers have typically used closed questions due to the ease of administering and coding them, recent research has suggested that this may sometimes be at a cost to data quality.

One drawback of closed questions is that respondents usually limit their responses to the offered alternatives, even if their optimal answers are ones not mentioned in the question. For example, if asked "What is the most important problem facing the country today: unemployment, inflation, the government's budget deficit, or some other problem?", nearly all respondents will choose one of the first three options rather than generating alternatives. Yet when these same individuals are asked an open-ended question, they are likely to generate a much larger set of important problems. It is possible to avoid this problem, however, if one builds lists of closed question response alternatives based upon pretesting with open-ended questions.

One concern about open-ended questions is that they may disproportionately reflect concerns or feelings that happen to be on the minds of respondents at the time a question is asked, rather than tapping deeper, more considered beliefs or attitudes. According to a number of studies, momentary SALIENCE of considerations does indeed influence responses to open questions, but salience does so to about the same extent with closed questions. Therefore, this concern does not seem to be a basis for shying away from open questions.

Finally, some research in this area has investigated whether closed questions are more likely than open questions to elicit vacuous responses from respondents who actually have no opinion toward an object. This work has indeed found that respondents are more likely to give answers to closed questions than to open questions when the target is a fictitious object, toward which respondents could not have an opinion. Presumably, the ease of responding to closed questions encourages respondents to provide answers even when these answers are not meaningful. Taken together, then, this literature suggests a number of advantages to open-ended questions, so they may be particularly useful for some attitude measurement tasks.

## RATING VERSUS RANKING

When one uses a closed question format, one must choose between a rating format and a ranking format. Rating formats require respondents to report the absolute magnitude of a psychological construct along a continuum (e.g., ranging from "like a great deal" to "dislike a great deal"). Rankings require respondents to order a set of objects according to some criterion (e.g., most preferred to least preferred).

Rating formats are more common in attitude research, presumably because rankings have a number of inherent disadvantages. For example, they yield ordinal and ipsative data, which are less informative and harder to analyze than the interval level data provided by ratings. Furthermore, rankings are a great deal more time consuming and difficult for respondents to complete. Nonetheless, there is some evidence that rankings yield more valid data. Specifically, rankings yield more reliable data than ratings, produce more interpretable factor solutions, and have greater

criterion validity. Furthermore, ratings appear to be more susceptible than rankings to response set biases, due to a failure of some respondents to make fine distinctions among objects in rating tasks. Therefore, rankings have a number of psychometric advantages when one is interested in comparisons of attitudes across sets of objects.

## NUMBER OF SCALE POINTS

When using rating scales, one must decide how many scale points to use for each item. Popular single-item attitude measures have ranged from as small as 2-point yes/no or agree/disagree scales to ones as large as 101 points. On one hand, using scales with more points may allow for greater precision. On the other hand, there may be limits to respondents' ability to make fine discriminations, so increasing the number of scale points beyond a certain point may enhance random error rather than enhancing information acquisition. In fact, the various empirical studies on this matter indicate that scales with 5 to 7 points seem to be both more reliable and valid than scales with more or fewer points (*see* Krosnick & Fabrigar, in press).

A related issue is the question of whether one should use rating scales with odd numbers of points (i.e., including a clear midpoint) or whether to use an even number of scale points. Including a midpoint allows respondents with neutral opinions to report them rather than arbitrarily indicating either a positive or a negative attitude. It is also possible, however, that offering the midpoint may reduce validity by providing a response alternative that is easy to select without much thought and therefore discourages respondents from expending the cognitive effort to report a more substantive view based upon their beliefs about an object.

Empirical research on these matters currently supports four conclusions (*see* Bishop, 1987; Krosnick & Fabrigar, in press; Schuman & Presser, 1981). First, respondents are unlikely to report neutral opinions if a midpoint is not explicitly provided, and they are much more likely to report such opinions when a midpoint is offered. Second, the distribution of positive and negative attitudes expressed can sometimes be very different depending upon whether a response scale includes a midpoint or not. Therefore, the decision regarding whether or not to offer a midpoint may well have a significant effect on substantive research conclusions. Third, a couple of initial studies suggest that the validity of attitude reports is enhanced when a middle alternative is provided. However, additional evidence suggests that middle alternative selection may in fact reflect a desire on the part of some respondents to avoid the cognitive work necessary to formulate and report substantive opinions. Consequently, it is difficult to say at this point whether including a midpoint is desirable.

BRANCHING

Nearly all single-item attitude measures ask respondents to place themselves on a scale ranging from favorable to unfavorable, thus reporting attitude direction and extremity in one step. However, the difficulty of administering long scales during survey interviews over the telephone has led some researchers to employ a branching approach. Accordingly, respondents are first asked whether their attitude is positive or negative or neutral (i.e., direction only). Then, in a follow-up question, respondents expressing positive or negative attitudes are asked how extreme those attitudes are. Respondents who express a neutral attitude initially can be asked a follow-up about whether they would lean in a positive or negative direction. This is called branching because the wording of the follow-up question varies depending upon which initial answer a respondent provides. A number of recent studies indicate that this decomposing of the reporting process into 2 steps enhances the speed and ease with which respondents can report their attitudes as well as the reliability and predictive validity of those reports (Krosnick & Berent, 1993).

VERBAL VERSUS NUMERIC LABELS

It is quite common for researchers to design long rating scales with verbal labels only on the endpoints (e.g., "like a great deal" versus "dislike a great deal") and perhaps also at the

midpoint (e.g., "neither like nor dislike"). Thus, the precise meaning of the other scale points is left implicit. However, a great many scaling studies have been done in recent years to quantify the meaning that people attach to such modifiers as "a great deal," "somewhat," "a little," and so on, so it is conceivable that consensually interpreted and evenly spaced verbal labels can be attached to all points on ratings scales (except, of course, very long ones). A number of studies suggest that this reduces ambiguity in the meanings of those scale points and thereby enhances reliability (see Krosnick & Berent, 1993).

NO-OPINION FILTERS

Regardless of whether open or closed questions are used, a researcher must decide whether to include a no-opinion filter. Such filters sometimes involve asking respondents if they have an opinion toward an object and then only asking what that opinion is if they say they do in fact have one. Alternatively, filtering sometimes involves simply including a "don't know" or "no opinion" category as one of the response options in a single attitude question. Not surprisingly, many more respondents indicate that they have no opinion when a filter is included than when no filter is offered. Again, however, it is not clear whether respondents select a "no opinion" response because they truly have no opinion or because they simply want to avoid the cognitive work necessary to formulate and report an opinion. Because including a no-opinion filter can dramatically alter the proportions of favorable and unfavorable attitudes expressed, the decision about whether or not to include a filter can have important substantive implications.

One set of relevant research has examined whether no-opinion filters enhance validity in the sense of detecting more true non-opin-ions. This work has focused on the fact that many respondents offer attitudes toward objects that are completely fictitious when asked unfiltered questions. Not surprisingly, including a no-opinion filter does dramatically reduce the number of respondents reporting such attitudes, though filters do not completely eliminate them. This suggests that filtering may enhance validity.

However, other evidence suggests that filtered questions are not superior to unfiltered questions in terms of data quality. First, studies examining test–retest response consistency indicate that reliability does not increase notably when filters are included. Second, associations between attitude reports and other variables do not seem to increase when filters are included. Third, it appears that respondents are especially attracted to no-opinion responses when selecting a substantive response would be especially cognitively burdensome. Therefore, it seems that no-opinion filters may not be desirable in attitude questions.

RESPONSE SETS AND RESPONSE STYLES
Response sets refer to the tendency for an individual to respond to questions in a particular fashion as a result of the structural features of the questions or the data-gathering situation, independent of the content of the questions. In contrast, response styles are response tendencies independent of content that are a function of dispositions of individual respondents, rather than a function of situational factors. A vast literature has invest-igated response styles and sets, most notably acquiescence and social desirability bias (see Paulhus, 1991).

Acquiescence refers to a tendency to agree with any item, irrespective of its content. This bias often occurs in items using "agree/disagree" or "yes/no" formats. This tendency appears to be a result of both situational demands (e.g., the difference in social status between interviewers and respondents) and PERSONALITY characteristics (e.g., deferential personality). Some researchers believe that acquiescence can be eliminated by administering a large number of items, half of which express positive attitudes and half of which express negative attitudes. Combining across such a set of items may unconfound acquiescence with substantive responses in some cases. However, recent research suggests that this approach may often be unsuccessful, because different items can stimulate different levels of acquiescence, so counterbalancing these levels may be difficult. Fortunately, though, it appears that acquiescence bias can be eliminated by abandoning agree/disagree or yes/no questions and instead using forced choice formats that ask respondents to select one of two opposing substantive points of view.

Social desirability bias refers to a tendency to respond to questions in a way that is socially desirable. This bias can take two forms. In some cases, self-deception is involved, where people are inclined to perceive themselves in inaccurate and socially desirable ways. Alternatively, IMPRESSION MANAGEMENT motives can lead people to distort their presentations of themselves to others in socially desirable directions. Social desirability bias does indeed appear frequently in studies that have looked for it, and its magnitude appears to be a function of both situational and dispositional factors. The impact of social desirability bias may be reduced by conducting pretests to equate response alternatives in terms of their social desirability or to select items that are relatively unaffected by desirability. Additionally, scales measuring social desirability can be used to statistically remove the influence of this bias from other scales. In the case of impression management, assuring anonymity of responses can reduce social desirability biases.

CONCLUSION
Although elaborate procedures for attitude measurement were the norm in the early stages of empirical research in this area, practical considerations have led current researchers to adopt simpler, single-item approaches. However, this move has increased the significance of the structural characteristics of the items used in terms of their potential impact on substantive findings. Fortunately, however, the accumulating body of literature we have reviewed provides numerous insights that aid researchers in designing their measures to tap attitudes as effectively as possible. With continued work in this area will come even clearer recommendations for optimal procedures.
See also: ATTITUDE THEORY AND RESEARCH; IMPRESSION MANAGEMENT; PERSONALITY; SURVEY METHODS.

BIBLIOGRAPHY
Bishop, G. F. (1987). Experiments with the middle response alternative in survey questions. *Public Opinion Quarterly*, *51*, 220–32.

Dawes, R. M., & Smith, T. L. (1985). *Attitude and opinion measurement*. In G. Lindzey & E. Aronson (Eds.), *The handbook of social psychology* (Vol. I; pp. 509–66). New York: Random House.

Himmelfarb, S. (1993). *The measurement of attitudes*. In A. Eagly & S. Chaiken, *The psychology of attitudes* (pp. 23–87). Fort Worth, TX: Harcourt Brace Jovanovich.

Krosnick, J. A., & Berent, M. K. (1993). Comparisons of party identification and policy preferences: The impact of survey question format. *American Journal of Political Science*, 37, 941–64.

—— & Fabrigar, L. R. (in press). *Questionnaire design for attitude measurement in social and psychological research*. New York: Oxford University Press.

Mueller, D. J. (1986). *Measuring social attitudes: A handbook for researchers and practitioners*. New York: Teacher's College Press.

Paulhus, D. L. (1991). *Measurement and control of response bias*. In J. P. Robinson, P. R. Shaver, & L. S. Wrightsman (Eds.), *Measures of personality and social psychological attitudes* (pp. 17–59). San Diego: Academic Press.

Schuman, H., & Presser, S. (1981). *Questions and answers in attitude surveys*. New York: Academic Press.

Summers, G. F. (1970). *Attitude measurement*. Chicago, IL: Rand McNally.

Thurstone, L. L. (1928). Attitudes can be measured. *American Journal of Sociology*, 33, 529–44.

LEANDRE R. FABRIGAR
JON A. KROSNICK

**attitude theory and research**  In an often-quoted passage, Gordon Allport (1935, p. 198) asserted that "the concept of attitude is probably the most distinctive and indispensable concept in contemporary American social psychology." Few (if any) statements this extreme about social psychology could reasonably be expected to remain valid over a period of nearly 60 years; yet it is arguably true that attitude is still at least one of the most indispensable concepts in social psychology, if not the most indispensable. Despite its prominent status over such an extended

period of time, there is no single definition of attitude that is universally accepted. As noted by Olson and Zanna (1993), attitudes are variously defined in terms of evaluation, affect, cognition, or behavioral dispositions. These different approaches tend to emphasize, respectively, the *evaluation* of attitude objects with respect to their positivity or negativity, the *feelings* of pleasantness or unpleasantness associated with attitude objects, *knowledge* about attitude objects, or predis-positions to *behave* positively or negatively towards attitude objects. However, if there is one core feature of attitudes that distinguishes this concept from others, it is that they are evaluative in nature. As Eagly and Chaiken (1993) put it, "Attitude is a psychological tendency that is expressed by evaluating a particular entity with some degree of favor or disfavor" (p. 1). Evaluation here can refer to different classes of response, be they affective, cognitive, or behavioral.

Thus the kernel of the definition of attitude is the notion of *evaluative responding* to some entity. Evaluative responses can vary with respect to response category (affective, cognitive, and behavioral) and response mode (verbal or nonverbal), as shown in Table 1 (*see* Ajzen, 1988). Which category or mode is deemed to be most important in a given research context will of course have implications for ATTITUDE MEASUREMENT.

*Table 1.*  Different types of evaluative response

| Response mode | Response category | | |
| --- | --- | --- | --- |
| | Affect | Cognition | Behavior |
| Verbal | Expressions of feelings towards attitude object | Expressions of beliefs about attitude object | Expressions of behavioral intentions towards attitude object |
| Nonverbal | Physiological responses to attitude object | Perceptual responses (e.g. reaction time) to attitude object | Overt behavioral responses to attitude object |

Broadly speaking, the large quantity of theory and research on attitudes that has accumulated over the decades can be divided into five general domains:

(1) attitude structure;
(2) attitude function;
(3) the formation of attitudes;
(4) the relationship between attitudes and behavior; and
(5) attitude change and persuasion.

The last three of these domains are dealt with in separate entries in the present volume, and the reader is referred to those entries for further information (*see* ATTITUDE FORMATION; ATTITUDES AND BEHAVIOR; and ATTITUDE CHANGE, respectively). Furthermore, theory and research relating to interattitudinal structure are also addressed elsewhere, under COGNITIVE CONSISTENCY theories (*see also* BALANCE THEORY, COGNITIVE DISSONANCE THEORY, and REACTANCE). Accordingly, the present entry focuses principally on issues concerning (1) intra-attitudinal structure, and (2) the functions of attitudes.

## INTRA-ATTITUDINAL STRUCTURE

### *Three-component model*

Just as there is no single accepted definition of attitude, so there is as yet no single model of the internal structure of attitudes. However, the most widely cited model of attitude structure is undoubtedly the *tripartite* or *three-component* model. This view of attitudes has been influential from the beginnings of attitude research; indeed, the tripartite distinction into feeling, thought and action has been pervasive inside and outside psychology (*see* McGuire, 1985). At the very least, it provides a useful heuristic for thinking about attitudes although, as we shall see, there is surprisingly little direct evidence in support of this three-component view.

According to this model of attitude structure, attitudes consist of affective, cognitive, and behavioral elements, or components. Thus a person might *feel* anxious whenever he or she thinks about flying (affective component), *believe* that flying is a dangerous activity (cognitive component), and *avoid flying* if at all possible (behavioral component). The affective component can include feelings, moods, emotions, and the expressive and physiological changes associated with such states. The cognitive component is usually conceptualized as consisting of BELIEFS, or perceived associations between the attitude object and attributes. These attributes are qualities that can be evaluated with respect to positivity or negativity. The behavioral component can include both intentions to behave in a certain way and actual behaviors.

In principle, there should be some degree of consistency among these three components. Thus someone who believes that flying is a dangerous activity is more likely to feel anxious about flying and to avoid traveling by plane than someone who believes that flying is a safe activity. However, the correlations among these three components should not be so great as to make the distinctions between them worthless. As Ajzen (1988) has argued, there should not be complete overlap among the three components. However, research examining the convergent and discriminant validity of these three components is not entirely conclusive.

Kothandapani conducted a study of the convergent validity of the three-component model, using the multitrait–multimethod matrix. Each of the three components (or "traits") of attitude was assessed by four different kinds of method. The attitudes concerned were those of low-income women towards birth control. Kothandapani found that when a given component was measured in two different ways, the resulting measurements correlated more highly with each other than they did with the corresponding measures of other components. This suggests that the three components are sufficiently different for the distinction between them to be regarded as valid. According to Breckler (1984), possible weaknesses of Kothandapani's approach to this issue are that the four different methods of measuring the components were all verbally based, and were made in relation to a symbolic representation of the attitude object. Accordingly, in his own research (Breckler, 1984, Expt. 1) examining the discriminant validity of the three-component model, Breckler took both verbal and nonverbal measures of the three components of subjects" attitudes to a live snake that was physically present, and made use of STRUCTURAL EQUATION MODELING to test the adequacy of 1-factor versus 3-factor accounts of the findings. He found that the 3-factor model fitted the data much better than the 1-factor model. The use of both verbal and nonverbal measures and a physically present attitude object appeared to make an important contribution to this finding, because a second study in which subjects simply provided verbal responses to the symbolically presented stimulus "snake" provided less clear support for the 3-factor model. This seems reasonable, in that we might expect the degree of overlap between the affective, cognitive, and behavioral components to be weaker where people have had relatively little direct exposure to or experience with the attitude object (which is likely in the case of a live snake). Readers interested in this issue should also consult the discussion of "affective-cognitive consistency" in the cognitive consistency entry.

Eagly and Chaiken (1993) provide a balanced assessment of the research evidence on consistency between attitude components: "Because cognitive, affective and behavioral responses are often not empirically distinguishable as three classes, the three-component terminology is overly strong and is inappropriate in its implication that the three types of responses are . . . distinguishable in most people most of the time. . . . Nonetheless, the tripartite distinction provides an important conceptual framework, one that allows psychologists to express the fact that evaluation can be manifested through responses of all three types, regardless of whether the types prove separable in appropriate statistical analyses" (pp. 13–14). Consistent with this analysis, Zanna and Rempel (1988) argue that attitudes (in the sense of evaluations) can be based on affective information (as in conditioning); on cognitive information (as in much persuasion research); or on behavioral information (as when people infer their attitudes from their own actions; *see* SELF-PERCEPTION THEORY).

*Expectancy-value models*

Another approach to the internal structure of attitudes is represented by *expectancy-value* models, which focus on the relationship between a person's attitudes and the evaluative significance of his or her beliefs. In Zanna and Rempel's (1988) terms, this is an approach that regards attitudes as being based primarily on cognitive information. The idea is that one's attitude to something or someone is a function of one's evaluative beliefs about the attributes of that thing or person. These evaluative beliefs have an expectancy component (usually conceptualized as the perceived likelihood that the attitude object possesses an attribute) and a value component (i.e., the evaluation of that attribute). The expectancy-value principle is well established in psychology (*see* SUBJECTIVE EXPECTED UTILITY). In one of the best-known applications of this principle to attitudes, Fishbein (e.g., Fishbein & Ajzen, 1975) regards attitudes as the outcome of beliefs about the attitude object. The sum of the products of the expectancies (beliefs) and values (evaluations) is taken to be a measure of attitude to the object in question, as shown in the following formula:

$$\text{Attitude} = \sum_{i=1}^{n} b_i e_i$$

where $b_i$ is the belief $i$ about the attitude object, $e_i$ is the evaluation of attribute $i$, and $n$ is the number of salient attributes of the object. Thus people are seen as having positive attitudes toward objects that they believe to have positive attributes and negative attitudes towards objects that they believe to have negative attributes. Baldly stated this sounds a little trite, but this approach does point to ways in which attitudes should be measured and also to ways in which they can be changed. This expectancy-value approach has also been influential in theorizing the attitude–behavior relationship.

An obvious question that arises in connection with this approach is whether it can be reconciled with the three-component approach discussed above. The most obvious similarity is that the summed products of expectancies and values are equivalent to the cognitive component in the three-component model. The most obvious difference is that the expectancy-value approach does not include a behavioral component, preferring to see intention as an outcome of an attitude rather than an integral part of it. Another apparent difference is that the expectancy-value approach seems to overlook the role of affect. However, some expectancy-value theorists (e.g., Ajzen, 1988) equate affect with attitude. Thus one strength of the expectancy-value approach is that it adds specificity to the conceptualization of how beliefs relate to attitudes. It also to some extent side-steps the issue of the degree to which affective, cognitive, and behavioral measures of attitude relate to each other, by treating affect, cognitive, and behavior as separate constructs, rather than different facets of the same underlying construct. Thus affect (i.e., attitude) is seen as an outcome of cognition (i.e., expected values) and behavior (i.e., intention) as an outcome of attitude. A potential weakness of the expectancy-value approach is that it appears to preclude the possibility that affect (in the sense of moods, feelings, and emotions, together with their physical accompaniments) and behavior can provide direct input into an attitude, independently of beliefs.

## THE FUNCTIONS OF ATTITUDES

It is widely observed that attitudes are pervasive. As Greenwald (1989) notes, the pervasiveness of attitudes is evident from the ease with which people report evaluative reactions to a wide range of objects, including those with which they have had little or no experience, the difficulty of finding categories of objects in which evaluative discriminations are not made, and the apparent ubiquity of the evaluative component in judgments of meaning. This pervasiveness suggests that attitudes serve one or more psychological functions. In fact virtually all attitude research includes some notion that attitudes serve a function. However, this function often remains implicit, and in much attitude research the function has to do with presumed needs to adopt a "correct" attitude to the external environment. Thus much of the research on attitude change tends to assume

that individuals are motivated to hold valid attitudes, and that they will change their attitudes if a different attitudinal position can be shown to be more valid. In fact, there is both theory and research suggesting that attitudes serve a much broader range of functions than this.

Katz (1960) argued that attitudes can serve at least four types of function: *knowledge, utilitarian, ego-defensive,* and *value-expressive.* The *knowledge* function (sometimes referred to as the object-appraisal function) concerns the organization and simplification of experience. The idea is that reality is too complex to be dealt with in every detailed aspect. Attitudes can serve as summary tags or labels that group together stimuli that have the same evaluative connotation (*see also* CATEGORIZATION, SCHEMAS, SOCIAL CATEGORIZATION). This function assumes that people are motivated to have a meaningful and stable view of the world, and that attitudes help to satisfy this need by providing an organizing frame of reference into which both existing and new stimulus information can be accommodated.

The *utilitarian* function (also referred to in the literature as the instrumental or adjustment function) concerns rewards and punishments. The idea is that people seek to maximize rewards and to minimize punishments, and that attitudes will be formed in a way that helps to attain rewards or to avoid punishments. This function assumes that people are motivated by self-interest and that attitudes can help to serve those interests, by being instrumental in securing the desired outcomes.

The *ego-defensive* function concerns the management of emotional conflicts. The idea is that people cope with threats to their self-concept or SELF-ESTEEM by adopting attitudes that negate or minimize such threats. This function assumes that individuals are motivated to protect their self-concepts from threats emanating either from their own unconscious or from the external world. Attitudes can be adopted in a way that helps to meet this need. For example, people can cope with hostile feelings towards themselves or towards close others by displacing these feelings onto convenient others (e.g., members of ethnic minorities).

The *value-expressive* function also concerns the individual's sense of SELF. The idea is that individuals adopt attitudes as a means of expressing their personal values or identities. This function assumes that an individual is motivated by a need to clarify and affirm his or her sense of self, and that adopting a particular attitude can help to achieve this goal. For example, the person who wishes to see him- or herself as someone who is "environmentally sound" is motivated to adopt attitudes towards issues like public transport, energy, waste management, and road-building that reflect this core value.

A more strategic version of the value-expressive function is sometimes referred to as the *social adjustment* function (*see* Eagly & Chaiken, 1993, Chap. 10). Here the expression of certain attitudes is more for the benefit of others than oneself. By expressing attitudes perceived to be acceptable to others, one can maintain or enhance one's social acceptability (*see also* IMPRESSION MANAGEMENT; NORMATIVE INFLUENCE; SELF-PRESENTATION).

One of the difficulties posed by a functional approach to attitudes is knowing how to operationalize this concept of function on anything other than a post hoc basis, and this has limited the influence of the functional approach. However, as Olson and Zanna (1993) have noted, recent years have seen renewed interest in this approach, as researchers have begun to identify strategies for operationalizing attitude functions. One strategy has been to argue that different PERSONALITY types are characterized by differing motivations. For example, there are theoretical grounds for thinking that people high in SELF-MONITORING (a dispositional concern with the situational appropriateness of one's behavior) will have higher social-adjustive needs. As a result, their attitudes will be more likely to meet these needs, and they should be more influenced than low self-monitors by persuasive communications that play on these social-adjustive concerns. A second strategy noted by Olson and Zanna uses the nature of the attitude object as a basis for predictions concerning which function it fulfils. Thus attitudes towards "luxury" products like perfume are more likely to serve value-expressive functions than utilitarian ones, and attitudes towards such objects should be more influenced by appeals to value-expressive functions. Finally, some types of situation are more likely than others to cue certain types of motive. For example, very novel situations characterized by high levels of uncertainty are likely to increase most people's need for certainty and clarity, and thereby to enhance the likelihood that attitudes expressed under these conditions will serve the knowledge or object-appraisal function.

CONCLUSION

The study of attitudes has been one of the constants in social psychology, seemingly less subject to the whims of scientific fashion than other research topics. Because theory and research on attitude measurement, inter-attitudinal structure, attitude formation, and attitude change are covered elsewhere in this volume, the present entry has focused on issues relating to the internal structure of attitudes and the functions served by attitudes. Even within these relatively restricted boundaries, the literature involved is huge. Although there is no single, accepted definition of attitude, there is a consensus among researchers that attitudes are best regarded as evaluative responses. Much of the theorizing concerning the internal structure of attitudes has taken as its starting-point the idea that attitudes have three components: affect, cognition, and behavior. Another influential approach to the study of attitude structure is based on the expectancy-value model. However, it is generally accepted that no one source of "information" has primacy in shaping evaluative responses, which can be based on one or more of the three traditional "components" of attitude: affect, cognition, and behavior. Finally, the functional approach to attitudes is currently enjoying something of a revival of fortunes, helped by new ways of operationalizing attitude function.

*See also*: ATTITUDES AND BEHAVIOR; ATTITUDE CHANGE; ATTITUDE FORMATION; ATTITUDE MEASUREMENT AND QUESTIONAIRE DESIGN; CATEGORIZATION; COGNITIVE CONSISTENCY; COGNITIVE DISSONANCE THEORY; IMPRESSION MANAGEMENT; PERSONALITY; REACTANCE;

SCHEMAS; SELF; SELF-ESTEEM; SELF-MONIT-
ORING; SELF-PERCEPTION THEORY; SOCIAL
CATEGORIZATION; STRUCTURAL EQUATION
MODELING.

BIBLIOGRAPHY
Ajzen, I. (1988). *Attitudes, personality, and
behavior.* Chicago, IL: Dorsey; Milton
Keynes: Open University Press.
Allport, G. W. (1935). Attitudes. In C. Murchison (Ed.), *Handbook of social psychology*
(pp. 798–1124). Worcester, MA: Clark
University Press.
Breckler, S. J. (1984). Empirical validation of
affect, behavior, and cognition as distinct
components of attitude. *Journal of Personality and Social Psychology, 47,* 1191–205.
Eagly, A. H., & Chaiken, S. (1993). *The
psychology of attitudes.* Forth Worth, TX:
Harcourt Brace Jovanovich.
Fishbein, M., & Ajzen, I. (1975). *Belief, attitude, intention and behavior: An introduction
to theory and research.* Reading, MA: Addison-Wesley.
Greenwald, A. G. (1989). Why are attitudes
important? In A. R. Pratkanis, S. J. Breckler, & A.G. Greenwald (Eds.), *Attitude
structure and function* (pp. 1–10). Hillsdale,
NJ: Lawrence Erlbaum.
Katz, D. (1960). The functional approach to
the study of attitudes. *Public Opinion Quarterly, 24,* 163–204.
McGuire, W. J. (1985). Attitudes and attitude change. In G. Lindzey & E. Aronson
(Eds.), *Handbook of Social Psychology* (Vol.
2, pp. 233–346). New York: Random
House.
Olson, J. M., & Zanna, M. P. (1993). Attitudes and attitude change. *Annual Review
of Psychology, 43,* 117–54.
Zanna, M. P., & Rempel, J. K. (1988). Atti-
tudes: A new look at an old problem. In D.
Bar-Tal & A. W. Kruglanski (Eds.), *The
social psychology of knowledge* (pp. 315–34).
New York: Cambridge University Press.
                        ANTONY S. R. MANSTEAD

**attitudes and behavior**  Defined as evaluative response tendencies, attitudes exert a
dynamic and directive influence on behavior.

As a general rule, positive attitudes predispose behaviors that support or enhance the
attitude object, while negative attitudes predispose unfavorable behaviors toward the attitude object. Casual observation supports the
idea that attitudes motivate and guide our
actions: We tend to associate with people we
like and avoid people we dislike, we mainly
eat foods that are to our tastes, we speak out
in opposition to policies we consider undesirable, and we generally seem to behave in ways
that are consistent with our attitudes.

Social psychologists rely extensively on the
attitude construct to predict and explain
human behavior, to the extent that attitude
has been called the most distinctive and indispensable concept in social psychology (Allport, 1968). Thus, discriminatory behavior is
attributed to PREJUDICE (negative attitudes
toward racial or ethnic groups); opposition to
family plannng or abortion is explained by
reference to religiosity; behavior in the political domain is ascribed to liberal or conservative attitudes; and educational decisions and
achievements are traced to favorable or unfavorable attitudes toward education.

To discern the effects of attitudes on behavior is, however, not as easy as it may appear
at first glance. Indeed, empirical research
conduced between 1935 and 1970 revealed for
the most part only weak and inconsistent
relations between verbal attitudes and nonverbal behavior with respect to the attitude
object (Wicker, 1969). Social psychological
studies failed to find significant relations between racial attitudes and such behaviors as
extending an invitation to members of the
racial group, accepting them in a hotel or
restaurant, or conforming with their views or
behaviors. Similarly, attitudes toward cheating failed to predict actual cheating behavior,
attitudes toward another person were unrelated to cooperation with that person, attitudes toward one's job seemed to have little
to do with absenteeism, tardiness, or turnover, and so forth.

Critical analyses of the literature produced
several possible explanations for the poor
predictive validity that attitudes were found
to exhibit in empirical investigations (*see*
Eagly & Chaiken, 1993 for a review). Initial
accounts tended to question the adequacy of

verbal responses as indicators of a person's true attitude. However, the most widely accepted explanation today rests on the realization that investigators often misinterpret the nature and meaning of the attitude construct. Attitudes are dispositions or tendencies to behave in a *generally* favorable or unfavorable manner toward the object of the attitude. Attitudes can thus find expression in a variety of responses, verbal as well as nonverbal, but to observe the general response tendency we must rely on a broad and representative sample of behaviors in the domain to which the attitude applies (*see* Fishbein & Ajzen, 1975). This idea was clearly appreciated when investigators constructed attitude scales that relied on broad samples of verbal responses to the attitude object. Not equally well understood was the fact that if we want to see attitudes expressed in nonverbal behavior we have to observe an equally broad and representative sample of nonverbal responses to the attitude object.

To illustrate, many investigators assessed racial attitudes by means of a standard multi-item verbal attitude scale and then proceeded to observe a single behavior, such as inviting a member of the group in question for a cup of coffee. Whereas the verbal attitude scale captures a broad range of responses reflective of racial prejudice, the decision to extend or not extend an invitation for a cup of coffee is clearly not a representative sample of discriminatory behavior. To obtain a valid measure of racial discrimination, one would have to observe a broad sample of nonverbal behaviors directed at members of the racial group and then aggregate these observations into a total score.

Laboratory as well as field studies have clearly and consistently substantiated these ideas. For example, broad measures of religious behavior are found to be well predicted from verbal expressions of religiosity, samples of different behaviors protective of the environment are closely linked to environmental attitudes, and representative sets of activities relevant to the abortion issue correlate highly with pro- or antiabortion attitudes. Findings of this kind have allayed the concerns that were expressed in the wake of earlier failures, and it is now widely accepted that attitudes do in fact exert a dynamic and directive influence on behavior.

MODERATING VARIABLES

The reason that global attitudes are often unrelated or only weakly related to specific actions has to do with the fact that any given attitude-relevant behavior is influenced by a multitude of additional factors that vary from one behavior to another and from one situation to another. Aggregation across many different behaviors and situations tends to cancel out the varying influences of these other factors, while leaving intact the consistent impact of the attitude. As a result, broad attitudes tend to correlate well only with aggregated behavioral scores.

Nevertheless, these considerations suggested that it should be possible to find strong relations between general attitudes and specific actions in some behavioral domains, or that strong relations may be found under certain conditions or for certain types of people. Sometimes, few factors of importance are present in the situation to overshadow or obscure the impact of the general attitude. A good case in point are the strong relations between attitudes toward political candidates and voting choice typically found in empirical studies of voting behavior. The privacy of the voting context is deliberately designed to prevent interference from other factors.

Much research in recent years has focused on the conditions under which we can expect relatively strong correlations between global attitudes and specific actions, that is, on variables that *moderate* the effect of general attitudes on behavior. One line of work has attempted to identify types of individuals who would tend to behave in accordance with their attitudes. Most interest has been generated by the SELF-MONITORING construct. A personality scale developed to assess people's tendencies toward self-monitoring identifies individuals who are chronically aware of their attitudes and who tend to see their attitudes as relevant to their actions (Snyder, 1982). Some support for the moderating role of the self-monitoring tendency has been obtained in research on the relation between attitudes toward affirmative action and verdicts rendered in a mock court case involving a sex discrimination suit. Although still of only moderate magnitude, the attitude–behavior correlation was significantly stronger for people whose scores on the self-monitoring scale identified them as highly sensitive to the behavioral relevance of their attitudes. However, other studies have not been able to replicate this finding (*see* Ajzen, 1988).

A different personality characteristic of potential importance as a moderating variable is the need for cognition, identified by Petty and Cacioppo (1986). People with a high need for cognition are likely to process information carefully and thus to develop well-founded, strong attitudes that are predictive of their behavior. Consistent with this expectation, attitudinal preferences for political candidates have been found to predict actual voting choice better for individuals who are high in need for cognition than for individuals who score low on this personality characteristic.

A second line of research concerned with moderating variables has focused on the nature of a particular attitude and the way in which it is acquired. Of greatest interest is the role of direct experience in the process of attitude formation. Favorable or unfavorable attitudes toward other people, for example, can arise as a consequence of interacting with them (direct experience) or as a result of reading or hearing about them. In comparison to attitudes based on second-hand information, attitudes based on direct experience with the attitude object are found to be relatively strong: they are held with greater confidence, they can be brought to mind more easily, and they are more resistant to change. As a result, they also tend to predict subsequent behavior more accurately.

Another characteristic related to an attitude's ability to predict behavior is the importance of the attitudinal domain to the person. Individuals differ in their degree of involvement with a given attitude object or have varying degrees of vested interest in a particular behavior. When the object or issue under consideration is highly involving, people are motivated to think more about it and they tend to have more information relevant to it. As a result, individuals who are highly involved are more likely to act on their attitudes than are those who are less involved. Evidence of this effect has been reported in the political domain where it has been shown that people who are highly committed to a position on an issue or who have a vested interest are more likely to take action in accordance with their attitudes than are people who have no vested interest.

THE ATTITUDE-TO-BEHAVIOR PROCESS
The search for moderating variables has confirmed that the relation between general attitudes and specific actions is influenced by a variety of factors, but consideration of moderating variables can provide no more than a partial solution to the prediction of specific action tendencies. Even under conditions that tend to promote prediction of behavior from attitudes, the relations obtained are usually of only moderate magnitude. Moreover, as we discover personal or situational factors that enhance the prediction of behavior from attitudes, we also identify types of individuals whose tendencies to engage in specific behaviors cannot be predicted from general attitudes, and conditions under which only very low attitude–behavior correlations can be expected. For example, although it is true that general attitudes based on direct experience tend to predict specific action tendencies quite well, it is also true that attitudes based on second-hand information tend to have little effect on behavior. Similarly, we can predict specific behaviors reasonably well for people who have a high need for cognition or who have a vested interest in the issue at hand. This also means, however, that we cannot predict behavior for other individuals who have a low need for cognition or who have no vested interest. From a theoretical point of view, identification of moderating factors enhances our understanding of the processes involved in going from attitudes to behavior, but from a practical point of view, it is of only limited value.

To predict specific action tendencies more consistently and with greater accuracy, it is necessary to examine the processes whereby attitudes guide behavior in greater detail. Two alternative and complementary models have been suggested, involving a deliberative mode and a spontaneous or automatic mode. Relatively little is known at this time about the automatic processing mode in relation to the guiding influence of attitudes on behavior. It is argued that strongly held attitudes can be activated automatically, without any conscious effort, by the mere presence of the attitude object; that the automatically activated attitude biases perception of the situation in an attitude-consistent manner; and that in this fashion, the attitude guides subsequent behavior (Fazio, 1990). The most controversial aspect of this model is the assumption that only strongly held attitudes are automatically activated, an assumption that has been challenged in recent research.

Most theory and empirical research have focused on the deliberative processing mode. Here, individuals carefully appraise the information they have about the behavior, form BELIEFS and attitudes on the basis of this information, and then act in ways that are consistent with their considerations. The best-known model of this process is the THEORY OF REASONED ACTION (Fishbein & Ajzen, 1975). It focuses on the prediction of volitional behavior and, consistent with this concern, it postulates that the tendency to engage in a particular behavior is determined by the person's intention to do so. This behavioral intention mediates the effect of attitudes on behavior. Unlike previous work that was concerned with general attitudes toward the target of a behavior, the attitude in the theory of reasoned action is directly compatible with the behavior itself. For example, to predict parents' willingness to have their children bused to racially integrated schools, past research might have assessed general racial attitudes, i.e., prejudice. In the theory of reasoned action, the attitude of interest would be the attitude toward having your children bused to a racially integrated school. Just as a general attitude is compatible with a broad aggregated measure of different behaviors, attitude toward a behavior is compatible with the tendency to perform the specific behavior in question. Because of this high level of compatibility, attitudes toward behaviors correlate much better with specific behaviors than do the more general attitudes toward the target of the behavior.

The theory of reasoned action postulates a second factor – subjective norm – which, in combination with attitude toward the behavior, determines intention and thus actual behavior. The subjective norm is the perception of what important others think the individual should do. At the most basic level of analysis, the theory of reasoned action postulates that attitudes and subjective norms rely on information about the behavior that is available to the individual. This information provides the basis for beliefs about the likely consequences of the behavior, producing a positive or negative attitude toward the behavior; and it leads to the formation of normative beliefs or perceptions that certain individuals favor or oppose performance of the behavior, producing a positive or negative subjective norm.

A great deal of empirical research has provided support for the theory of reasoned action in a variety of experimental and naturalistic settings (see Eagly & Chaiken, 1993). The behaviors involved have ranged from very simple strategy choices in laboratory games to actions of appreciable personal or social significance, such as having an abortion, smoking marijuana, reenlisting in the military, using generic prescription drugs, conserving energy, and choosing among candidates in an election. Intentions to perform behaviors of this kind can be predicted from attitudes toward the behaviors and from subjective norms, and the intentions in turn correlate well with observed actions.

Although the theory of reasoned action permits prediction of specific action tendencies and enables exploration of the underlying determinants, it is explicitly limited to behaviors under volitional control. Several modifications of the theory have been suggested, incorporating additional predictors designed to overcome this limitation. Some investigators have proposed adding habit to deal with nonvolitional aspects of human behavior, while others have included a direct link from attitudes to behavior, bypassing intentions. The most influential extension, however, can be found in the THEORY OF PLANNED BEHAVIOR (Ajzen, 1988). This theory acknowledges that intentions can be carried out only to the extent that people have sufficient control over the behavior in question. To deal with this issue, the theory of planned behavior adds the concept of perceived behavioral control as a predictor of intentions and behavior. This factor refers to the perceived ease or difficulty of performing the behavior and it is assumed to reflect past experience as well as anticipated impediments and obstacles. Given relatively favorable attitudes and subjective norms with respect to a behavior, an individual's intention to perform the behavior increases with perceived behavioral control. Moreover, to the extent that perceptions of behavioral control are accurate, they can help predict the likelihood that people will carry out their intentions.

The importance of perceived behavioral control in the attitude-to-behavior process has been demonstrated repeatedly in empirical investigations (see Ajzen, 1991). Perceived behavioral control has been found to improve prediction of intentions and behaviors in such areas as problem drinking, leisure choice, losing weight, dishonest conduct, exercising, looking for a job, and using condoms. In comparison to people who perceive themselves as having little behavioral control, people with a high degree of perceived control form stronger intentions to engage in these types of behaviors and are more likely to actually carry out their intentions under appropriate circumstances.

CONCLUSIONS

Our understanding of the relation between verbal attitudes and nonverbal behavior has greatly expanded in the past three decades. We have gained insight into the nature of attitudes and into the ways in which attitudes can be inferred from verbal and nonverbal behaviors. As a result, theory and research have reaffirmed the central position of the attitude construct in social psychology by showing it to be an extremely useful tool for the prediction and explanation of human social behavior. In addition, we have learned a great deal about the ways in which attitudes guide behavior by looking at the conditions that promote strong attitude–behavior correlations and by examining the variables that mediate between attitudes and behavior.

Recent work on the attitude–behavior relation has begun to shift from the focus on prediction of behavior to a consideration of the motivational properties of attitudes. Human behavior is largely goal-directed, even if the goal is far removed in the individual's hierarchy of goals, and even if the same behavior can serve more than one goal. The dynamic and directive influence of attitudes on behavior can be seen most clearly in the selection of goals and the choice of means to attain those goals.

See also: PREJUDICE; SELF-MONITORING.

BIBLIOGRAPHY

Ajzen, I. (1988). *Attitudes, personality, and behavior*. Chicago, IL: Dorsey; Milton Keynes: Open University Press.

—— (1991). The theory of planned behavior. *Organizational Behavior and Human Decision Processes*, 50, 179–211.

Allport, G. W. (1968). The historical background of modern social psychology. In G. Lindzey & E. Aronson (Eds.), *The handbook of social psychology* (2nd ed., Vol. 1, pp. 1–80). Reading, MA: Addison-Wesley.

Eagly, A. H., & Chaiken, S. (1993). *The psychology of attitudes*. Fort Worth, TX: Harcourt Brace Javanovich.

Fazio, R. H. (1990). Multiple processes by which attitudes guide behavior: The MODE model as an integrative framework. In M. P. Zanna (Ed.), *Advances in experimental social psychology*, (Vol. 23, pp. 75–109). San Diego, CA: Academic Press.

Fishbein, M., & Ajzen, I. (1975). *Belief, attitude, intention, and behavior: An introduction to theory and research*. Reading, MA: Addison-Wesley.

Petty, R. E., & Cacioppo, J. T. (1986). *Communication and persuasion*. New York: Springer- Verlag.

Snyder, M. (1982). When believing means doing: Creating links between attitudes and behavior. In M. P. Zanna, E. T. Higgins, & C. P. Herman (Eds.), *Consistency in social behavior: The Ontario symposium* (Vol. 2, pp. 105–30). Hillsdale, NJ: Lawrence Erlbaum.

Wicker, A. W. (1969). Attitudes versus actions: The relationship of verbal and overt behavioral responses to attitude objects. *Journal of Social Issues*, 25, 41–78.

ICEK AJZEN

**attraction** Among the most durable topics in the past half century of social psychological research is interpersonal attraction. Begun in the 1930s, this research concerns the general question of who is attracted to whom, and for what reasons. Interest in interpersonal attraction can be traced to the influence of two researchers. J. L. Moreno originated the field of sociometry, which was intended to provide objective techniques for assessing attraction and repulsion between individuals. During roughly the same period, Theodore Newcomb began his studies of attraction and acquaintance at Bennington College and the University of Michigan, which demonstrated unequivocally that matters as subjective as liking and FRIENDSHIP could yield to systematic empirical scrutiny. Although attraction may have entered the purview of modern research methods through this work, by no means is its allure novel. Fascination with questions about attraction and liking is evident throughout written history, and even casual examination of modern popular media illustrates how pervasive this interest remains. (Dale Carnegie's *How to Win Friends and Influence People*, first published in 1937, is one of the 50 best-selling books of the twentieth century.) Perhaps it is not surprising, then, that interpersonal attraction is one of social psychology's enduring research interests.

The attention devoted to the phenomena of attraction has generated an extensive, diverse, and informative treasury of empirical findings. Nevertheless, when one compares the landscape of attraction experiences with the published literature, it becomes apparent that certain domains have received considerably more attention than others. Particularly pervasive are studies of initial encounters between unacquainted persons, and studies of romantic attraction, during both courtship and marriage. Less common, but nonetheless influential, are studies of friendship development, especially among children and college students. These emphases reflect both conceptual and pragmatic concerns. Conceptually, these are among the most important human relationships, and they intrinsically warrant concerted attention. Moreover, most researchers see no particular reason to expect that principles derived from studies of students, friends, and lovers will not generalize to other RELATIONSHIPS or other contexts. The experimental and conceptual rigor inherent in studying the acquaintance process from its inception, either in laboratory experiments or longitudinal field studies, provides distinct and indispensable advantages. Benefits of this sort make the social psychological approach to these timeless questions unique. Of course pragmatic advantages, notably the ready availability of unacquainted college student research participants, have also contributed to the predominant slant, but they should not obscure the theoretical rationale for this focus.

Attraction is commonly conceptualized as an attitude directed at a particular person (Berscheid, 1985), lending it the three traditional components of attitudes: cognition (beliefs about the person); affection (feelings about the person); and behavioral predisposition (tendencies to act in a particular way to the person; *see* ATTITUDE THEORY AND RESEARCH). Most studies rarely differentiate these components, so that the statement "I like X," a common measure of attraction, is presumed to reflect all three elements. The interplay of AFFECT, cognition, and behavioral predisposition was particularly evident in early theories that applied cognitive consistency principles to attraction. These theories emphasized people's natural desire for symmetry, balance, and consistency among all three components. For example, BALANCE THEORY asserts that people should favorably evaluate others whom they like, and that people should like their friends' friends, and their enemies' enemies (Heider, 1958). Although consistency theories have lost much of their popularity, perhaps because their simplicity minimizes their ability to explain complex human relationships, many of their core principles remain useful, especially as first-pass approximations (*see* COGNITIVE CONSISTENCY).

Despite the attention that interpersonal attraction has received, no comprehensive theories have emerged that can account for the broad range of observed attraction phenomena. Nevertheless, the notion of "rewards others provide" offers a useful heuristic for characterizing and summarizing existing research. This principle asserts that people are attracted to others to the extent that they find interactions with them rewarding. Thus, positive outcomes that a person experiences, or expects to experience, from interaction with another person will enhance attraction, whereas costs that are incurred, or expected to be incurred, will decrease attraction. It is important to note that this principle embodies considerable depth, and is not merely a superficial accounting of personal gains and losses. For example, the rewards that a relationship may provide include INTIMACY, sharing, long-term security, opportunities to be helpful to others, intellectual stimulation, and vicarious experiences of a partner's joy. Also, the notion of rewards and costs, as utilized within this framework, is intended to be highly personal: Interactive behavior is rewarding only if it fulfills personal needs and goals (which are often idiosyncratic). For these and other reasons, the construct of "rewards others provide" has proven to be a useful means of conceptualizing attraction phenomena (see INTERDEPENDENCE THEORY, SOCIAL EXCHANGE).

As noted earlier, most research has sought to determine the specifics of attraction: who is attracted to whom, and for what reasons. Four general principles can be extracted from the existing literature (Hendrick & Hendrick, 1992). These four principles are discussed next, along with the underlying processes that they represent.

PEOPLE ARE ATTRACTED TO SIMILAR OTHERS
*Ceteris paribus*, people tend to be attracted to others who are similar to themselves. Many different dimensions have been studied, with the strongest and most consistent evidence obtaining for SIMILARITY of attitudes, values, and activity preferences. For example, questionnaire studies have shown that friends and romantic partners tend to be more similar to each other than are acquaintances or randomly

paired strangers. In laboratory studies, randomly paired, unacquainted subjects tend to like each other more to the degree that they are attitudinally similar. Some of the most compelling evidence comes from longitudinal studies, in which the degree of pre-acquaintance similarity predicts how well college roommates eventually come to like each other. Interestingly, the impact of similarity on attraction is not limited to particular attitudes, values, or activities. The list of dimensions for which similarity effects have been documented is lengthy and diverse. Perhaps the only qualification to the pervasiveness of similarity effects is that similarity matters only to the extent that the particular dimensions are important to the individuals involved. For example, similarity of religious values may not matter to an agnostic, but would be very important to a fundamentalist.

Somewhat less robustly, the literature also documents the influence of personality similarity in friendship and marriage. That is, people tend to develop relationships with others whose personalities are similar to their own. The principle of COMPLEMENTARITY – that relationships function best when partners' traits are dissimilar in ways that mesh well – has long been offered as an alternative model. However, despite the intuitive plausibility of this notion, empirical support has been at best weak and inconsistent. Thus, a dominant person seems more likely to be attracted to another dominant person than to a submissive person.

Particularly notable is the evidence for similarity in the physical attractiveness of romantic partners. Much research supports the "matching hypothesis" – i.e., the tendency for dating partners and spouses to possess similar levels of physical attractiveness (Hatfield & Sprecher, 1986). In some studies, attractiveness levels of long-term spouses have correlated above 0.50, a value equivalent to the correlation between IQ tests and school achievement, for example. There is less consensus about the mechanism underlying attractiveness matching, however. Some researchers believe that people prefer partners of roughly the same attractiveness, presumably to maintain equity. On the other hand, others have noted that even if everyone preferred the most attractive partners, *de facto* matching would result from selection pressures such as assortative mating (i.e., the most attractive persons choose to pair off with each other). Although not all couples are matched in attractiveness, as a generalization the matching hypothesis seems remarkably accurate.

Why does similarity influence attraction so pervasively? Several mechanisms have been supported in empirical research, suggesting that multiple processes are involved. Prominent among them is the notion that similar others are more likely than dissimilar others to validate our self-concept and personal world view. People often rely upon feedback from others to evaluate their opinions, abilities, and personal characteristics. Because similar others possess views and traits relatively closer to our own, they are more likely to provide positive, affirming feedback. Such feedback is of course gratifying, and hence fosters attraction (*see* SELF-VERIFICATION, SOCIAL COMPARISON). Prior contact with a particular person may not even be necessary. People may expect similar others to be more validating by virtue of past interpersonal experience, which would be sufficient to encourage attraction.

Other, somewhat more parsimonious explanations have also been supported. One is that interaction with similar others is more likely to be enjoyable, since similar others are relatively likely to share our interests and activity preferences. Even simpler is the potential role of serendipity. All other things being equal, people are more likely to encounter similar than dissimilar others, given that personal values and traits influence the activities in which people participate. (For example, an avid skydiver comes into contact with other skydivers more often than a non-skydiver does.) Because social contacts are enjoyable more often than not, attraction often develops from chance encounters.

All of this evidence does not argue that similarity among friends is ubiquitous or inevitable, or that people are most attracted to others who are functionally identical to themselves. Needs for individuation and UNIQUENESS also influence friendship choices, especially given the importance of establishing individual identities in the context of a relationship. Furthermore, not all dimensions of similarity matter equally. To many persons, for example, similarity of educational background is critical in choosing a spouse, whereas similarity of movie preferences is considerably less important. Context also plays a part. Similarity between spouses and best friends is probably more consequential than similarity between co-workers. Finally, it must be remembered that perceptions of similarity are relative. Two California college student Psychology majors may readily perceive important differences between themselves, but from a broader perspective they are likely to be much more similar to each other than to non-Californians, non-college students, and non-Psychology majors. In short, whereas people clearly seem to be attracted to similar others, this preference must be viewed in relative terms.

## PEOPLE ARE ATTRACTED TO OTHERS IN CLOSE PROXIMITY

The more often people come into contact with each other, the more likely they are to become friends. Many studies have supported this simple proposition. In some of this research, proximity takes the form of distance between residences or workplaces – roommates are more likely to become close friends, for example, than people who live across the hall or in different dormitories. In other studies, proximity is represented by opportunities for contact rather than sheer distance. Of course, mere contact does not always produce attraction, leading some researchers to suggest that proximity functions as an intensifier, magnifying the prevailing qualities of a relationship. In other words, people in close proximity who are favorably predisposed may come to like each other even more. On the other hand, proximity may make people prone to dislike each other more antagonistic. Factors that may predispose people to dislike each other include competition, status differentials, conflicts of interest, and personality and value differences. But because people usually socialize pleasantly, and are positive with each other more often than not, proximity tends to promote attraction.

One explanation for the impact of proximity relies on the principle of reward. Proximity provides opportunities for people to reward each other – chatting with a neighbour allows one to compliment the other, for example. These rewards may be explicit, or they may be subtle or indirect; even enjoying a shared activity, like sports or quilting, may engender attraction to coparticipants. As will be discussed under the next heading, people are generally attracted to those with whom they feel rewarded. Hence it is not really proximity that produces attraction. Rather, proximity creates opportunities for people to reward one another, and rewarding experiences beget attraction.

Proximity effects are sometimes considered as a special case of familiarity. Research has shown that MERE EXPOSURE breeds preference; that is, the more familiar a stimulus, the more that people tend to like it (Bornstein, 1989). For example, subjects shown unknown faces or Chinese characters with varying frequency tended to like best the ones they had seen most frequently. Increased attraction to others in close proximity might therefore be a function of their increased familiarity. Although this explanation cannot account for the intensification of negative affect that proximity occasionally produces, it seems likely that the mere exposure effect enhances our comfort with proximate others and hence our attraction to them.

Several processes contribute to this phenomenon. Predominant among them is the reinforcement value of being liked by others. Social approval is a potent source of positive emotions, such as love, joy, and pride, and social disapproval often engenders negative emotions, such as fear, rejection, anger, and guilt. These feelings, which may have acquired their significance through evolutionary forces, play a substantial role in motivating thought and action. Being accepted by others also has instrumental value, inasmuch as attainment of many personal goals inherently requires, or is facilitated by, coordinated activity. Finally, approval by others may help validate one's sense of SELF and bolster SELF-ESTEEM, as symbolic interaction theories assert. (see SYMBOLIC INTERACTIONISM)

The value of being liked by others is not hedonically one-sided, however. Several theories, notably EQUITY THEORY posit that people feel most comfortable in relationships that are balanced; that is, in which both persons receive outcomes proportional to their contributions, and to the other's outcomes. Equity research has shown that under-benefitted persons tend to feel angry and resentful, whereas over-benefitted persons may feel guilty, and that both of these feelings inhibit attraction. The preference for equitable relationships can help account for the finding that in on-going relationships, liking is typically mutual.

### PEOPLE ARE ATTRACTED TO OTHERS WHOM THEY BELIEVE LIKE THEM

In most relationships, liking is mutual: People like others who like them, and they dislike others who dislike them. Laboratory experiments and field studies have shown that people typically respond positively when they believe that another person likes them. Even anticipating that someone will like oneself can be sufficient to produce attraction. This principle may in part underlie the similarity effect, described above. Because people generally expect others with similar views and traits to appreciate their own views and traits, they expect to be liked, and to like the other in return.

### ATTRACTION IS HEIGHTENED UNDER ANXIETY-PROVOKING CIRCUMSTANCES

Attraction research is usually concerned with the question of who is attracted to whom. However, researchers are also interested in understanding the conditions under which forces of attraction are heightened or diminished. One circumstance that has received considerable attention is ANXIETY (or stress). This research was pioneered by Schachter (1959), who demonstrated that subjects about to participate in an anxiety-provoking experiment preferred to wait with others rather than alone. (One important qualification was the role of similarity: People preferred waiting with someone undergoing a similar fate, but not with someone in different circumstances. Apparently, misery only loves miserable company.) Since this early work, other research has sought to determine why anxiety enhances attraction. These experiments dovetail nicely with field studies conducted in natural disasters and emergencies, which also show augmented desires for social contact.

Several mechanisms have been proposed to account for this phenomenon. Schachter himself favored a social comparison explanation: that the reactions of others help people evaluate their own anxious thoughts and feelings. Other processes are also relevant (Shaver & Klinnert, 1982). For example, in stressful circumstances, the mere presence of supportive others may help lessen anxious feelings. That the ability of social contact to reduce anxiety need not involve self-evaluation is demonstrated by studies of animals and human infants (see ATTACHMENT, SOCIAL SUPPORT). Furthermore, other people can provide useful clues about the nature of the anxiety-producing situation, and how to cope best with it.

These studies notwithstanding, in terms of their appeal for social psychological researchers, the "who" questions of attraction considerably outpace the "when" questions. Nevertheless, studies of the circumstances under which people are more or less likely to seek social contact add substantially to our understanding of the functional significance of social relations in human activity and well-being.

CONCLUSION

Interpersonal attraction has over time been one of the most robust areas of social psychological inquiry. Much has been learned, yet translation of this knowledge to useful predictions about whether person X will be attracted to person Y remains a promissory note at best. Indeed, at present we may be limited to describing who will *not* be attracted to whom. That is, it seems clear that people are unlikely to be attracted to dissimilar others with whom they have had little contact, and who do not like them. As the next generation of attraction research un-

folds, this fascinating and uniquely human experience should reveal more of itself to our understanding. The theoretical and practical significance of such advances may be great.

*See also*: ATTITUDE THEORY AND RESEARCH; COGNITIVE CONSISTENCY; FRIENDSHIP; INTERDEPENDENCE THEORY; INTIMACY; MERE EXPOSURE; RELATIONSHIPS; SELF; SELF-ESTEEM; SOCIAL COMPARISON; SOCIAL SUPPORT; SYMBOLIC INTERACTIONISM; UNIQUENESS.

BIBLIOGRAPHY

Berscheid, E. (1985). Interpersonal attraction. In G. Lindzey & E. Aronson (Eds.), *Handbook of Social Psychology* (pp. 413–84). New York: Random House.

Bornstein, R. F. (1989). Exposure and affect: Overview and meta-analysis of research, 1968–87. *Psychological Bulletin, 106*, 265–89.

Hatfield, E., & Sprecher, S. (1986). *Mirror, mirror: The importance of looks in everyday life*. Albany, NY: SUNY Press.

Heider, F. (1958). *The psychology of interpersonal relations*. New York: Wiley.

Hendrick, S., & Hendrick, C. 1992. *Liking, loving, and relating* (2nd ed.). Pacific Grove, CA: Sage.

Schachter, S. (1959). *The psychology of affiliation*. Stanford, CA: Stanford University Press.

Shaver, P., & Klinnert, M. (1982). Schachter's theories of affiliation and emotion: Implications of developmental research. In L. Wheeler (Ed.), *Review of Personality and Social Psychology* (Vol. 3, pp. 37–72). Beverly Hills, CA: Sage.

HARRY T. REIS.

attribution of responsibility This is the specific name for a process of SOCIAL COGNITION by which moral accountability is assigned to a person believed to have produced a socially disapproved behavior or effect. Although in everyday language "responsibility" can refer to liability for either praise or condemnation, in social psychology the term is used almost exclusively to mean liability for condemnation.

## SENSES OF RESPONSIBILITY

Four different senses of the term, "responsibility," have been identified by the philosopher H. L. A. Hart (1968). The first of these, *role responsibility*, requires that people be bound to perform whatever duties are attached to their "distinctive place or office in a social organization" (Hart, 1968, p. 212). This is the sense in which parents are responsible for the behavior of their children or the president of a company is responsible for illegal activities of employees. The second sense, *causal responsibility*, refers merely to the production of effects. Not only human beings, but also physical forces, can be causally responsible. This is the sense in which a devastating storm or flood is responsible for destroying a town. A third sense, *capacity responsibility*, refers to the person's ability to understand and behave according to the dictates of law or morality. This is the sense presumed to be lacking in an individual found not guilty by reason of insanity. Finally, there is *liability responsibility*, the moral or legal accountability of a person judged to possess capacity responsibility. Hart actually distinguished legal liability from moral liability, but for present purposes the two may be regarded as "not essentially different" (Fincham & Jaspars, 1980, p. 97). Liability responsibility is the sense in which a person capable of self-control is held to account for harm produced negligently or intentionally. This is the sense typically meant in social psychological discussions of responsibility. The amount of responsibility assigned depends on the actor's intentions (Anscombe, 1957) and on whether the actor offers persuasive excuses or justifications (*see* ACCOUNTS). The psychological consequences of (liability) responsibility for the creation of a problem differ from those of (role) responsibility for finding the solution.

## FREE WILL: THE BASIS FOR RESPONSIBILITY

The concept of responsibility, in either the legal liability sense or the moral liability sense, rests on a fundamental philosophical assumption: The person being judged freely chose the behavior being considered for sanc-tion. Thus the concept of moral responsibility is inextricably linked with the philosophical notion of free will (*see* Ryle, 1949). Discussions of freedom of will – and its alternative, *determinism* – have a long history in philosophy, including the writings of Laplace, Spinoza, Hume, and Reid. Among modern writers, one of the most convincing defenses of free will was offered by Campbell (1957), who asks the reader to imagine a person confronted by a difficult moral decision. Passing inclinations and external inducements lead the individual to do something "wrong," whereas internalized moral principles lead the individual to resist. Campbell's question for us is whether it is possible to *dis*believe that an individual who elects to "do the right thing" is not making a real choice. We as perceivers, and the law as an instrument of social control, certainly act as though free choice is possible.

Each side of the debate has its defenders among major psychological theories. The deterministic view is represented, for example, in Freud's biological determinism and Skinner's radical behaviorism. Freud placed the source of behavior in unconscious processes, Skinner placed it outside the person, but both argued against the idea of freely chosen actions. Needless to say, neither Freudian theory nor radical behaviorism places much stock in individual responsibility for action.

The free will view is represented, for example, in much of cognitive psychology, especially theories concerning choice under uncertainty, and in most of the humanistic or existential theories of personality. For example, existential theories of psychotherapy argue that the "authenticity" for which we search as human beings can *only* be achieved if we take full responsibility for our actions. In general, the midrange theories so prevalent in social psychology also take free will as a given. People whose actions are determined by forces beyond their control cannot legitimately be held accountable (*see* ACCOUNTABILITY).

Building on philosophy, social psychology considers the term "responsibility" to incorporate five different elements (Shaver, 1985). First, there must be some connection between the actor and the event. Usually, but not always, this connection will be a causal one. Second, there must be a shared system of morality by which the event is judged to be harmful. Note that such a system of morality is not presumed to be universal – people may differ in their moral beliefs, and consequently in the way they assign responsibility. Third, human beings must be seen as capable of free choice. Fourth, perceivers must believe that the person being held to account acted voluntarily. A specific voluntary act (either the choice to engage in behavior that produces harm or the choice to refrain from behavior that prevents it) is different from being capable of freedom of action in principle. Harmful outcomes may occur by accident or through coercion; in either case the actor's responsibility is diminished. Finally, responsibility for intentional actions may be reduced if the perceiver believes that there were extenuating circumstances. We recognize, for example, that creating harm to one person may occasionally be necessary in order to prevent the occurrence of greater harm to many people.

## THE LEGAL ANALOGY

Responsibility attribution is one of the few processes in social psychology that has an explicit, systematized parallel in the social world. In any society governed by laws, legal principles provide just such a parallel. Whether its procedures are inquisitorial, investigative, or adversarial (see PROCEDURAL JUSTICE), one of a criminal justice system's primary objectives is to assign legal responsibility for prohibited actions. On the assumption that the criminal law embodies a society's moral values and codifies its language for determining guilt, social psychologists have considered the law's potential as a model for determining moral accountability (see Fincham & Jaspars, 1980). The current consensus of opinion is that legal culpability and moral responsibility are comparable, but not identical.

In many industrialized countries a legal finding of guilt usually requires two separate elements. The first element, called the *actus reus*, is an offending behavior that is willfully performed, occurs in legally specified circumstances, and produces certain harmful consequences. The circumstances are important, because an act (such as getting married) that is usually socially desirable may be illegal in some instances (such as when one of the partners is already married to someone else). The second element, called *mens rea*, is the criminal state of mind with which the act was performed. Such a "guilty mind" is attributed to a person who acts "negligently," "recklessly," "knowingly," or "purposely."

Explicit separation of criminal guilt into act and mental state has two consequences for the attribution of moral accountability. First, it suggests that perceivers may attribute responsibility for bad intentions that are never expressed in behavior and for harm produced inadvertently, as well as for intentional evil. Second, it clearly implies that causality should be distinguished from responsibility and liability for punishment. A version of an example used by Fincham and Jaspars (1980) makes this point quite well: Suppose that X intends to murder a child Y, replaces Y's medicine with poison and gives the bottle to Y's nurse. The nurse decides that Y does not need the medicine, and so places it in the medicine cabinet. From there, it is retrieved by the nurse's 10-year-old child, who administers it to Y, who dies. The originator of the intent, X, should be (and is) held responsible for the death of Y, despite the fact that this result actually followed the intervening actions of two other people, neither of whom intended the outcome.

Despite the law's heuristic value in helping us understand the assignment of moral accountability, legal processes are not identical to everyday judgments of responsibility. Specifically, there are important differences in both content and process between legal culpability and moral accountability. As regards content, for example, murder committed by a 13-year-old is – in the eyes of the law – different from murder committed by an adult. It is unlikely that everyday moral judgment would follow this precedent. As regards process, legal systems have procedures designed to ensure that the accused receives a fair hearing. This is so because a legal system can impose powerful sanctions on an offender, over that person's strenuous objections.

Because everyday moral judgments normally do not carry similar penalties for the offender, extensive procedural safeguards are unnecessary.

Even in the legal arena, a moral judgment process can sometimes be substituted for a legal judgment process. An example is "jury nullification," the jury acquittal of a defendant who is legally guilty (see Kalven & Zeisel, 1966; JURIES). For example, a jury might decide to acquit a defendant charged with manslaughter in the accidental death of a lifelong companion, because the defendant, whose prior record is spotless, is so obviously devastated at the loss (and by his or her culpability for the event) that adding a jail sentence would serve no useful purpose. Despite the law's value as a guide, the process of responsibility attribution will ultimately be illuminated by psychological, not legal, theories (see EYEWITNESS TESTIMONY for other ways in which the legal and the psychological do not necessarily correspond).

LEVELS OF RESPONSIBILITY

Although Piaget's writings contained important insights about the moral judgment of the child (see MORAL DEVELOPMENT), the first social psychological explanation of responsibility attribution was outlined by Heider (1958). Heider's book on interpersonal relations is regarded as having established attribution theory as a separate area of study within social perception. After carefully examining commonsense language, Heider proposed the now familiar idea that behavior is the product of a combination of personal forces – ability, intention, effort – and environmental forces – opportunity, task difficulty, luck. These stable and variable causes of action are discussed in more detail under ATTRIBUTION THEORIES.

Given that action involves both personal and environmental forces, with the latter often being obstacles, then the responsibility attributed will increase directly with the amount of personal force. Heider's discussion included five different levels of responsibility. At the most primitive level, *association*, responsibility is attributed in the absence of any causal connection between the actor and the event. At the second level, *causality*, anything caused by a person is ascribed to the person, although neither intention nor motivation may be present. At the third level, *foreseeability*, there is still no intention, but observers would readily agree that the actor should have anticipated that the harm might occur. This level represents the "reasonable person" standard in many legal systems, a standard used to determine whether someone has acted negligently. At the fourth level, *intentionality*, the actor is presumed to have foreseen the outcome and intended to bring it about. At the last level, *justifiability*, intentional actions are excused to some degree because of coercion from legitimate authority or illegitimate force. In effect, the responsibility attributed to the actor is discounted (see DISCOUNTING) because his or her motivation is seen as having its source in the environment.

The levels model predicts that responsibility will increase from association to intentionality, and then will drop off slightly at justifiability. This attributional pattern has been confirmed in such a wide variety of subject groups that it is beyond serious question. Despite the consistency of the empirical pattern, there is less than unanimity regarding the conceptual issues involved. For example, some writers argue that Heider's levels represent a unidimensional scale, others claim the levels are a multidimensional scale. Some writers assert that the levels are true developmental stages, others disagree. Some writers argue that the levels are irrelevant to the real issue, namely the increase in subjective probability of the outcome that occurs when the actor is present in the setting, others believe the levels are only part of the whole story (see Jaspars, Fincham, & Hewstone, 1983, and Shaver, 1985 for a thorough discussion of these issues). As of this writing, it is only clear that Heider's levels have framed the context for subsequent discussions of responsibility attribution.

MODELS OF RESPONSIBILITY ATTRIBUTION

When asked to account for an occurrence of harm in everyday parlance, it is common for perceivers to say that the perpetrator "caused" or "was responsible for" or "was to blame for" the harm. In short, without reflection on their judgments, perceivers may use these three constructions interchangeably. Indeed, a surprisingly large amount of research on the assignment of culpability will use one of these terms as a dependent variable and discuss the results using one of the others.

Yet it is clear, both empirically and theoretically, that the attribution of causality is different from the attribution of responsibility, which, in turn, is different from the attribution of blame (Fincham & Jaspars, 1980; Shaver, 1985). The difference begins in the intellectual history of the terms. Inquiry into the causes of events owes its primary allegiance to epistemology or philosophy of science; inquiry into responsibility owes its allegiance to moral philosophy. The difference between causality and responsibility is continued in the law. As we have seen above, full criminal responsibility requires *intent*; causing harm is not by itself sufficient. Indeed, even the research literature that confounds the terms does so asymmetrically: a dependent variable of "causality" is more likely to be described as indicating responsibility or blame than a dependent variable of "blameworthiness" is likely to be described as indicating causality.

The distinction between causality and moral accountability is an important feature of two leading models of the attribution of culpability. The first of these is an "entailment model" of responsibility attribution introduced by Shultz, Schleifer, and Altman (described by Fincham & Jaspars, 1980; and Shultz & Schleifer, 1983). This model asserts that an attribution of responsibility necessarily implies, or entails, an accompanying attribution of causality. Indeed, the model makes the even stronger claim that the causal attribution precedes the attribution of responsibility in time.

The second model is a detailed theory of the attribution of blame described by Shaver (1985). According to this theory, the *process* of blame attribution begins with a morally disapproved action for which there is a single personal cause. If the actor did not intend the consequences but should have anticipated them, then negligence will be attributed, but not blame. If the actor intended the consequences but was coerced by powerful external forces, or did not have the capacity to appreciate the wrongfulness of the action, responsibility will be attributed, but not blame. When called to account, the actor may offer either an excuse or a justification. If either is accepted, then responsibility will be attributed, but not blame. According to the theory, blame is attributed only for those intentional actions, performed voluntarily, for which no excuse or justification is accepted. Thus blame is a perceiver's social judgment that would be disputed by the actor.

The two models agree that the term "causality" should be restricted to the production of events or actions. Causes must precede events, and must be sufficient to produce those events. Similarly, in both models, "responsibility" refers to the moral evaluation of a person thought to have produced an effect. In terms used by the entailment model, responsibility normally *presupposes* causality. Both models note that by requiring causality as a precondition for responsibility they depart from the legal principle of "vicarious responsibility," according to which a person may be held legally accountable for the actions of those under his or her control. They assert, however, that instances of vicarious responsibility are so rare in everyday moral judgments that the departure from legal principles is justified.

Where the two models part company is in their third major term. For the entailment model, the third term is *punishment*, the social sanctions applied following a judgment of responsibility. Application of such sanctions presupposes an attribution of responsibility in the same way that responsibility presupposes causality. For the theory of blame attribution, the third term is *blame*, a moral judgment that presupposes responsibility, but goes beyond it. Where responsibility can be assigned for negligence, blame should be reserved for intentionally produced harm; where responsibility may be mitigated by excuses, blame follows the perceiver's rejection of those very excuses. A more detailed description of account episodes is provided by Schönbach (1990); this and other information on excuse making is discussed in the section on AC-COUNTS.

## CONCLUSION

The attribution of responsibility is a social judgment that presupposes causality, involves examination of intent, and may end in sanctions if the excuses offered are not accepted. Moreover, because of its inherently social nature, the attribution of responsibility may be compromised by the perceivers' own motives such as self-serving biases and the need to believe in a just world (*see* JUST WORLD PHENOMENON).

*See also*: ACCOUNTABILITY; ACCOUNTS; ATTRIBUTION THEORIES; EYEWITNESS TESTIMONY; JURIES; MORAL DEVELOPMENT; SOCIAL COGNITION.

BIBLIOGRAPHY

Anscombe, G. E. M. (1957). *Intention*. Oxford: Basil Blackwell.

Campbell, C. A. (1957). *On selfhood and godhood*. London: Allen & Unwin.

Fincham, F. D., & Jaspars, J. M. (1980). Attribution of responsibility: From man the scientist to man as lawyer. In L. Berkowitz (Ed.), *Advances in experimental social psychology* (Vol. 13, pp. 81–138). New York: Academic Press.

Hart, H. L. A. (1968). *Punishment and responsibility*. New York: Oxford University Press.

Heider, F. (1958). *The psychology of interpersonal relations*. New York: Wiley.

Jaspars, J., Fincham, F. D., & Hewstone, M. (Eds.). (1983). *Attribution theory and research: Conceptual, developmental and social dimensions*. London: Academic Press.

Kalven, H. Jr, & Zeisel, H. (1966). *The American jury*. Boston: Little, Brown.

Ryle, G. (1949). *The concept of mind*. London: Hutchinson.

Schönbach, P. (1990). *Account episodes: The management and escalation of conflict*. Cambridge: Cambridge University Press.

Shaver, K. G. (1985). *The attribution of blame: Causality, responsibility, and blameworthiness*. New York: Springer-Verlag.

Shultz, T. R., & Schleifer, M. (1983). Towards a refinement of attribution concepts. In J. Jaspars, F. D. Fincham, & M. Hewstone (Eds.), *Attribution theory and research: Conceptual, developmental and social dimensions* (pp. 37-62). London: Academic Press.

K. G. SHAVER

**attribution theories** The study of how people explain human behavior – their causal attributions or commonsense explanations – is the focus of a group of approaches termed "attribution theory." Research on this topic exploded during the 1970s and 1980s, but the major conceptual advances were made by four main theories, three of which were developed quite early. The four theories are summarized below, together with critical issues pertaining to each, followed by an overview of the contemporary field of research on causal attributions (*see* Hewstone, 1989; Weary, Stanley & Harvey, 1989; *see also* ACCOUNTS).

### "PHENOMENAL CAUSALITY" AND THE "NAIVE ANALYSIS OF ACTION"

Fritz Heider's (1958) "naive psychology" attempted to formulate the processes by which an untrained observer, or *naive psychologist*, makes sense of the physical and social world. It is impossible to summarize his "theory," because his writings are rich yet arcane; they have nonetheless laid the foundations for all the subsequent attribution theories. As Ross and Fletcher (1985) argued, there are four central ideas in Heider's naive psychology. First, Heider proposed that invariant dispositional properties were needed to explain the behavior of others and render the perceiver's world stable, predictable, and controllable. Second, Heider introduced a focal distinction between personal and situational causes, and he referred to the ATTRIBUTIONAL BIAS whereby perceivers tend to underemphasize situational factors and overemphasize personal factors when explaining behavior (the FUNDAMENTAL ATTRIBUTION ERROR). Third, Heider refined the personal-situational dichotomy, and suggested that personal dispositions were more readily inferred for intentional than unintentional actions. Fourth, Heider proposed J. S. Mill's "method of difference" (which he called the COVARIATION principle) as a canon for "naive scientists" making causal attributions based on multiple attributional information. These ideas, although expressed in a somewhat arcane style, were the building blocks for the three theories developed later, each of which proved eminently testable.

*Critical issues*
It can be argued that Heider's insights into social perception, rather than his theory *per se*, had the greater impact on subsequent empirical research (but *see* ATTRIBUTION OF RESPONSIBILITY). His distinction between internal and external attribution, although central to all the subsequent theories, has since been strongly criticized for four main reasons:

(1) there is no clear evidence of the implied inverse relation between the two kinds of attributions;
(2) the categories are so broad that they risk being meaningless;
(3) statements that seem to imply external attributions can be rephrased as statements implying internal attributions (and vice versa); and
(4) there is low convergent validity among measures of internal and external causality.

CORRESPONDENT INFERENCE THEORY
According to Jones and Davis' (1965) theory, the goal of the attribution process is to infer that observed behavior and the intention that produced it *correspond* to some underlying stable quality in the person, or actor. The central concept of the theory, the CORRESPONDENT INFERENCE, refers to the perceiver's judgment that the actor's behavior is caused by, or corresponds to, a particular trait (e.g., someone's hostile behavior is ascribed to the trait "hostility"). There are two main stages in the process of inferring personal dispositions: the attribution of intention, and the attribution of dispositions.

To infer that any of the effects of an action were intended, the perceiver must believe that the actor *knew* the consequences of his/her action, and that s/he had the *ability* to perform the action. According to the theory, the perceiver processes information backwards from effects, through action, to inferences about knowledge and ability. To infer dispositions, the perceiver compares the consequences of chosen and nonchosen actions, using the "noncommon effects principle." According to this principle, a correspondent inference is made when the chosen action has a few relatively unique or noncommon consequences. For example, pushing someone over backwards has little in common with some other possible actions (politely disagreeing, or shouting at someone), because it has the consequence of physically hurting someone. Correspondent inferences are stronger when the consequences of the chosen behaviour are socially *unde*sirable. More generally, only behaviors that disconfirm expectancies are truly informative about the actor.

Jones and Davis anticipated later work by distinguishing two kinds of attributional bias – motivational and cognitive. Motivational biases were triggered by the personal involvement of the perceiver in another person's actions: perceivers were more likely to make a correspondent inference when the actor's choice had positive or negative effects for the perceiver ("hedonic relevance"), and when the actor's behavior was seen as aimed at the perceiver personally ("personalism"). The main cognitive bias identified was the underestimation of situational factors (a key component of the fundamental attribution error).

*Critical issues*
Although experimental studies have yielded some support for correspondent inference theory, there are four main limitations:

(1) Although the theory argues that attribution of intention must precede a dispositional inference, some dispositions are defined in terms of unintentional behaviors (e.g., clumsiness). Thus the theory is applicable only to "actions," which have some element of choice, and not to "occurrences" which may be involuntary.
(2) The theory does not provide an accurate description of the way people actually

make attributions. Subsequent research has indicated that perceivers tend to attend to instances, not noninstances of an event.

(3) Although behavior that disconfirms expectancies is obviously informative, expectancy-confirming behavior can also be so (e.g., behavior that confirms stereotypes).

(4) Most of the studies generated by the theory did not include causal attributions among their dependent measures. Processes of dispositional and causal attribution should be kept conceptually distinct.

The theory has declined as a primary focus of research, but was influential in stimulating research on biases in the attribution process.

COVARIATION AND CONFIGURATION
Kelley's (1967, 1972) attribution theory outlined two different processes that depend on the amount of information available to the perceiver. In the first case the perceiver has information from multiple observations and can perceive the covariation of an observed effect and its possible causes. In the second case, the perceiver is faced with a single observation and must take account of the configuration of factors that are plausible causes of the observed effect.

*Covariation*
Kelley presented the covariation principle as a naive version of J. S. Mill's method of difference: "The effect is attributed to that condition which is present when the effect is present and which is absent when the effect is absent" (Kelley, 1967, p. 194). He based his model on the analysis of variance (ANOVA) statistical technique, which examines changes in a dependent variable (the "effect") when the independent variables (the "conditions") are manipulated. According to Kelley, the perceiver's purpose, like the scientist's, is to separate out which effects are to be attributed to which of several possible factors.

To make causal attributions in this way, Kelley argued, the perceiver needed to have three kinds of information: CONSENSUS (variation of an effect over persons), CONSISTENCY (variation of an effect over time/modalities), and DISTINCTIVENESS (variation of an effect over stimuli). Thus if only John laughs at the

comedian (low consensus), he has done so in the past (high consistency), and he also laughs at all other comedians (low distinctiveness), then the effect is seen as caused by something in the person (John).

*Critical issues*
A large number of studies have produced results apparently consistent with the model, confirming that consensus, distinctiveness, and consistency do indeed affect the attribution of causality in the way predicted by Kelley and in line with the covariation principle. However, later work indicated four limitations relating to this theory:

(1) The covariation principle is limited as a basis for scientific inferences of causality, because it actually allows causal relationships that are spurious (i.e., based on mere correlation).

(2) In the type of experiment used to collect the relevant data, subjects are provided with prepackaged covariation information that, under normal circumstances, they might neither seek out, nor use.

(3) People are not always very skilled at assessing covariation between events; their performance can depend on their existing causal preconceptions.

(4) Although subjects' attributions may appear *as if* they use the covariation principle, their actual information-processing may be completely different from Kelley's model. The cognitive processes underlying causal attribution are currently receiving detailed attention.

Although competing models exist, it does seem that when subjects are presented with a full set of causal information they are capable of producing inferences that correspond very closely to those that would be predicted by a normative analysis of variance (*see* Hilton, 1991).

*Configuration*
When a perceiver lacked the information, time, or motivation to examine multiple observations and detect covariation, Kelley proposed that attributions would be made instead using "causal schemata." These schemata, or SCHEMAS, are beliefs or preconcep-

tions, built up from experience, about how certain kinds of causes interact to produce a specific kind of effect. Kelley outlined two main types of causal schema from which others could be generated, and put forward two attributional "principles" that accompany the causal schemata. One of the simplest causal schemata is the multiple sufficient cause (MSC) schema. It conveys the idea that an effect occurs if *either* cause A *or* cause B is present, or when *both* are present. The MSC schema is associated with the "DISCOUNTING principle": given that different causes can produce the same effect, the role of a given cause in producing the effect is discounted if other plausible causes are present. According to the more complex multiple necessary cause (MNC) schema, several causes must operate together to produce the effect. The "AUGMEN-TATION principle" applies to both MSC and MNC schemata and proposes that the role of a given cause is augmented if an effect occurs in the presence of an inhibitory cause.

Causal schemata are important for three main reasons: they help the perceiver to make attributions when information is incomplete; they are general conceptions about causes and effect which may apply across content areas; and they provide the perceiver with a "causal shorthand" for carrying out complex inferences quickly and easily.

*Critical issues*
Despite the apparent advantages of causal schemata, there are two main weaknesses associated with their conception:

(1) the existence and functioning of causal schemata, although intuitively plausible, have not been directly demonstrated; and
(2) the abstract, content-free conception of schema is limited.

A schema represents organized knowledge, based on cultural experience and not just an abstract relation between cause and effect.

## ATTRIBUTION, AFFECT AND MOTIVATION

Weiner (1986) has developed a more recent theory of achievement and emotion that is based on a multidimensional approach to the structure of perceived causality. His theory is *attributional* (dealing with the sequence from attributions to responses, especially behavior), whereas the previous *attribution* theories are concerned with the link between stimuli, or information, and causal attributions. Weiner's taxonomy of causes specifies their underlying properties in terms of three dimensions. *Locus* refers to the location of a cause internal or external to the person; *stability* refers to the temporal nature of a cause, varying from stable (invariant) to unstable (variant); and *controllability* refers to the degree of volitional influence that can be exerted over a cause. This conception has obvious value in taking us beyond the simplicity of the internal–external distinction. For example, ability and effort might both be seen as internal causes of achievement, but ability is further classified as stable/uncontrollable, and effort as unstable/controllable. As a result, the attribution of a failure to lack of effort has implications different from those of an attribution to lack of ability. Lower future expectancies of success arise from lack-of-ability attributions which are stable, but the unstable lack-of-effort implies that exerting greater effort will result in success.

Weiner has specified the roles of each of the three underlying dimensions for his general theory of MOTIVATION and EMOTIONAL EXPERIENCE:

(1) *Locus*: The main hypothesis is that success attributed internally (e.g., to personality, ability, or effort) results in greater SELF-ESTEEM (pride) than success attributed externally (e.g., to task ease, or good luck). Weiner also predicted that failure attributed internally will result in lower self-esteem than failure attributed externally.
(2) *Stability*: The major importance of this dimension is in relation to (changes in) the *expectancy* of success and failure in the future. Weiner has also suggested that stability may be linked to affective reactions such as "hopelessness", when failure is attributed to internal and stable causes.
(3) *Controllability*: This dimension relates to sentiment and evaluations of others. The main hypothesis is that if personal failure is due to causes perceived as controllable

by others, then ANGER is elicited. If negative outcomes for other people are due to causes perceived as uncontrollable, then *pity* is elicited.

Weiner has argued for a distinction between two kinds of achievement-related affects: "outcome-dependent" and "attribution-linked" affects. Outcome-dependent affects refer to the very general, even "primitive" emotions that are experienced following success (e.g., happy) and failure (e.g., sad) outcomes. These emotions are labeled outcome-dependent because they depend on (non)attainment of a desired goal, not on causal attributions given for the outcome. Attribution-linked affects, in contrast, are influenced by the specific causal attribution for the outcome. Especially if an outcome is negative, unexpected or particularly important, we are likely to seek causal attributions in order to make sense of it. According to Weiner, both causal attributions and their underlying causal properties generate more differentiated affects (e.g., if personal failure is attributed to causes perceived as controllable by others, then anger is elicited).

*Critical issues*
Notwithstanding the supportive evidence for this theory, here too critical issues remain to be resolved:

(1) It is debatable whether controllability is, strictly speaking, a causal dimension. It is, rather, a function of the interaction between a person and a cause.
(2) There is evidence to support the existence of other general dimensions, such as globality, which has proved important in attributional research on both clinical DE-PRESSION and marital RELATIONSHIPS but finds no place in Weiner's theory.
(3) The distinction between outcome-dependent and attribution-linked emotions remains tentative, due to mixed empirical results.

THE CONTEMPORARY FIELD OF
ATTRIBUTION RESEARCH
Although the high-water mark of attribution theory has now passed, research continues apace at virtually every level of social–psychological

analysis: intrapersonal, interpersonal, intergroup and societal (Hewstone, 1989).

At the intrapersonal level, attribution theory has merged into SOCIAL COGNITION and pursued research on the logic, process, and content of causal attributions. Developments have included more detailed logical models of how perceivers might analyze multiple sources of information; process models relating SALIENCE of information, MEMORY and causal attribution; and a knowledge-structure approach to attribution based on SCRIPTS.

Attribution research at the interpersonal level has contributed to our understanding of social interaction, where attributions play a role in BEHAVIORAL CONFIRMATION/DISCONFIRMATION. Attributions are also central to analyses of interpersonal conflict, close relationships and MARRIAGE. In particular, there is now a large body of research, much of it highly sophisticated, showing that patterns of attribution distinguish between distressed and nondistressed couples, serve to maintain marital distress, and may actually determine marital satisfaction (*see* Fletcher & Fincham, 1991).

Belatedly, theorists of INTERGROUP RELATIONS have also acknowledged the importance of attributions, given a tendency of group members to make more favorable attributions for own-group than outgroup behavior. This bias can be seen as a core phenomenon of PREJUDICE and STEREOTYPING, which helps the perceiver to maintain negative outgroup beliefs in the face of disconfirming information. Intergroup attributions therefore also have implications for the reduction of intergroup conflict.

At a societal level, attributions have been seen as a component of SOCIAL REPRESENTATIONS, referring to widely shared beliefs about the causes of social events (e.g., poverty and unemployment). Cross-cultural research has shown that members of different cultures sometimes make different attributions for similar events. Comparing the developmental course of attributions across cultures may help us better to understand attributional biases.

Finally, attributional analyses have illuminated our understanding of a wide variety of basic social-psychological phenomena, ranging from ATTITUDE CHANGE to OBEDIENCE. At the same time attribution thories, although sometimes seemingly artificial and even contrived, have made enormous contributions to APPLIED SOCIAL PSYCHOLOGY (*see* Weary, Stanley, & Harvey, 1989). These include research on physical and mental HEALTH, LONELINESS, the development of attributional therapies for depression, and achievement-motivation programmes in educational psychology.

CONCLUSION

Although some scholars have attempted theoretical integrations of the distinct attribution theories, these are at such an abstract level that they have had little impact. It is perhaps better to acknowledge that each theory has made a unique contribution, and each seems to offer insights about specific attributional phenomena. It can, however, be said that the four theories converge on a few general and specific themes. Generally, they highlight mediation between stimulus and response, active and constructive causal interpretation, and the perspective of the naive scientist or layperson. Specifically, the theories all address the kinds of information that people use to determine perceived causality, the kinds of causes that they distinguish, and the rules they use for going from information to inferred cause. Most important, all share a concern with commonsense explanations and answers to the question "why?" Their contribution to social psychology has been fundamental, widespread, and enduring.

*See also*: ACCOUNTS; APPLIED SOCIAL PSYCHOLOGY; ATTITUDE CHANGE; ATTRIBUTION OF RESPONSIBILITY; ATTRIBUTIONAL BIAS; BEHAVIORAL CONFIRMATION/DISCONFIRMATION; DEPRESSION; EMOTIONAL EXPERIENCE; HEALTH PSYCHOLOGY; INTERGROUP RELATIONS; LONELINESS; MARRIAGE; MEMORY; MOTIVATION; OBEDIENCE; PREJUDICE; RELATIONSHIPS; SCHEMAS/SCHEMATA; SCRIPTS; SELF-ESTEEM; SOCIAL COGNITION; SOCIAL REPRESENTATIONS; STEREOTYPING.

BIBLIOGRAPHY

Fletcher, G. J. O., & Fincham, F. D. (Eds.). (1991). *Cognition in close relationships.* Hillsdale, NJ: Lawrence Erlbaum.

Heider, F. (1958). *The psychology of interpersonal relations.* New York: Wiley.

Hewstone, M. (1989). *Causal attribution: From cognitive processes to collective beliefs.* Oxford, UK & Cambridge, MA: Basil Blackwell.

Hilton, D. J. (1991). A conversational model of causal attribution. In W. Stroebe & M. Hewstone (Eds.), *European review of social psychology* (Vol. 2, pp. 51–82). Chichester: J. Wiley.

Jones, E. E., & Davis, K. E. (1965). From acts to dispositions: The attribution process in person perception. In L. Berkowitz (Ed.), *Advances in experimental social psychology* (Vol. 2, pp. 219–66). New York: Academic Press.

Kelley, H. H. (1967). Attribution theory in social psychology. In D. Levine (Ed.), *Nebraska symposium on motivation* (Vol. 15, pp. 192–238). Lincoln, NE: University of Nebraska Press.

——(1972). Causal schemata and the attribution process. In E. E. Jones, D. E. Kanouse, H. H. Kelley, R. E. Nisbett, S. Valins, & B. Weiner, *Attribution: Perceiving the causes of behaviour* (pp. 151–74). Morristown, NJ: General Learning Press.

Ross, M., & Fletcher, G. J. O. (1985). Attribution and social perception. In G. Lindzey & E. Aronson (Eds.), *Handbook of social psychology* (3rd ed., Vol. 2, pp. 73–122). New York: Random House.

Weary, G., Stanley, M. A., & Harvey, J. H. (1989). *Attribution.* New York: Springer-Verlag.

Weiner, B. (1986). *An attributional theory of motivation and emotion.* New York: Springer-Verlag.

MILES HEWSTONE

**attributional bias** A BIAS occurs if the social perceiver systematically distorts (e.g., over- or under-uses) some otherwise correct procedure, or indeed if the result of the procedure itself is distorted. Early models of the attribution process tended to view the perceiver as a fairly rational person, and Kelley's ANOVA model was even given the status of a normative model that indicated how perceivers *should* make attributions (using CONSENSUS, CONSISTENCY, and DISTINCTIVENESS, according to the COVARIATION principle; *see* ATTRIBUTION THEORIES). These models also identified several "errors" or biases in attribution, defined by their departures from the models. These biases have generated an enormous amount of research and seem to provide a better descriptive analysis of causal attribution than do complex normative models.

Although the original terms for these deviations have stuck, they should not be termed errors, but *biases*. The term error should be reserved for "deviations from a normative model" or "departures from some accepted criterion of validity," and such models or criteria are not normally available for attribution research. Funder (1987) has put forward a rather different view, that what have been termed errors are largely a function of the laboratory context and might not result in "mistakes" in the real world. Funder defines an error as above, but he defines a mistake as "an incorrect judgment in the real world" (p. 76), which must be determined by different criteria and, indeed, is much more difficult to determine. The term *bias* has a wide currency throughout SOCIAL COGNITION and makes fewer assumptions than the alternatives. The following sections review the evidence and explanations for the four main attributional biases, and contrast cognitive (information-processing) and motivational (need-based) accounts (*see* Hewstone, 1989).

UNDERUTILIZATION OF CONSENSUS INFORMATION
The first experimental studies to test Kelley's ANOVA model concluded that consensus information was a relatively unimportant determinant of causal attributions. This "underutilization of consensus" quickly became established as a pervasive attributional bias. Because the extent to which an effect was shared across persons could be taken as a measure of BASE RATES, the phenomenon was seen as an instance of the base-rate fallacy in social judgement (*see* Nisbett & Ross, 1980).

This finding led researchers to question how faithfully the layperson followed the

scientific rules of the analysis of variance model. As it turned out, however, the appropriate question to ask was not whether consensus has an effect on attribution, but under what conditions. These conditions have now been carefully delineated (Borgida & Brekke, 1981) and should qualify any statements concerning a pervasive bias. The conditions under which consensus has been used or sought include the following: when subjects are told that the sample on which consensus is based is a random sample; when the social-group membership of the consensus sample is specified; when the information variables are presented in counterbalanced order; when social norms are not known; and when expectancies are neutralized. To the extent that consensus, or other base-rate information, is ignored, it is often due to the pallid manner of its presentation.

THE FUNDAMENTAL ATTRIBUTION ERROR
Building on the work of pioneers such as Heider and Ichheiser, Ross (*see* Nisbett & Ross, 1980) identified a tendency for perceivers to underestimate the impact of situational factors and to overestimate the role of dispositional factors in controlling behaviour. He called this the FUNDAMENTAL ATTRIBUTION ERROR.

Initial evidence for this bias was gleaned from studies on attitude attribution (where perceivers attach too little weight to the situation and too much to the person when trying to attribute someone's true position on an issue). Studies have also shown that perceivers tend to make inadequate allowance for the effects of social roles on behavior, and instead over-attribute to personal factors. There are, however, criticisms of the way in which information is presented to subjects in these studies, and how this may mislead them when they consider how to respond (Funder, 1987).

The major accounts of this bias are cognitive, invoking the use of HEURISTICS. One explanation is that the actor's behavior is often more salient than the situation. Actor and act form a "causal unit"; the perceiver focuses on the other person, not the situation, and he or she comes to be overrated as causally important. This account involves the AVAILABILITY heuristic, whereby actor-linked causes may assume prominence in explanations over time. A salience explanation is also supported by evidence that increasing the ACCESSIBILITY of situational constructs (by priming) increased the likelihood that situational factors would be considered in explaining a target's behavior. The structure of LANGUAGE also determines the salience of causes. It has been noted that both an action and an actor can be described using near-identical terms, thus linking them psychologically as well as linguistically (e.g., we speak of generous/hostile actions or actors). In contrast, the English language rarely allows us to label situations succinctly, using synonyms for action (e.g., there is no word to describe the kind of situations that typically elicit generous/hostile behavior). Linguistic factors in causal attribution are currently receiving belated attention, as part of the burgeoning interest in social psychology and language.

Alternative accounts implicate REPRESENTATIVENESS and anchoring heuristics: since people's implict theories give too much weight to dispositional causes of behavior, dispositional causes will be seen as "representative" in explaining behavior; attributions can also be seen as strongly "anchored" to person attribution, with insufficient adjustment for situational causality.

There is also relevant evidence for cross-cultural differences in attribution. For example, there is a developmental increase in reference to dispositional factors among Americans, but an increase in reference to contextual factors among Indian Hindus. Studies have also shown that as children in a Western culture develop, they come to hold an increasingly dispositional view of the causes of behavior. Other scholars have proposed a societal norm for internality, so that internal attributions are viewed more favorably than external attributions.

Questions remain about how "fundamental" this bias really is, and three main areas of contention have arisen. First, there are now extensive criticisms of the dichotomy between situational and dispositional attribution

(*see* ATTRIBUTION THEORIES). Second, there are no criteria to justify the term error. Third, under some circumstances people will overattribute another person's behavior to situational factors: most notably, when behavior is inconsistent with prior expectations and when attention is focused on situational factors that could have produced a person's behavior. In view of these considerations, a more modest label ("correspondence bias") should be assigned to this bias.

## ACTOR–OBSERVER DIFFERENCES

Jones and Nisbett (1972) proposed that actors attributed their actions to situational factors, whereas observers tended to attribute the same actions to stable personal dispositions. Watson (1982) has provided a comprehensive review of subsequent research, although he prefers the terms *self* and *other*, rather than ACTOR–OBSERVER DIFFERENCES, because in many studies there is not, in fact, one person acting while another observes. His review confined the effect to a difference in situational attribution: self-attributions to situations are higher than other-attributions to situations.

There are three main explanations for this bias. First, self–other differences may arise from the greater amount of *information* available to the actors or self-raters. We should, after all, know more about our own past behavior, and its variability across situations, than we know about the behavior of others; equally, we should know more about our own behavior than others do. Thus observers may assume more consistency of others' behavior and infer dispositional causes. Several studies have shown that actors perceive more cross-situational variability in their behavior and that observers make more trait attributions.

Second, actor–observer differences might be explained by differences in *perceptual focus*: self and other have, quite literally, different "points of view." There is, however, only mixed evidence for the claim that showing subjects a new orientation (e.g., a videotape of the other person's perspective) makes actors' attributions less situational, and observers' more situational. There is, however, some evidence for salience effects: the participant in the center of the visual field is rated as more causally important, but this weighting does not always have a clear effect on dispositional and situational attributions. Observers' attributions can also be made more situational through instructions to empathize with the actor, and vary as a function of which perspective (e.g., husband's, wife's or counsellor's in a marital conflict) they are instructed to adopt.

Third, Jones and Nisbett (1972) also predicted that *motivational* factors might limit, eliminate or even reverse their proposed effect. But evidence for this explanation is limited to studies using competitive experimental games. A motivational explanation is, in any case, circumscribed, because the actor–observer bias occurs for neutral as well as valenced behaviors.

Finally, linguistic factors are again significant. Recent research has shown that actors and observers use different linguistic devices. Actor–attributors typically avoid statements about themselves in general and abstract terms which ascribe dispositional attributes to themselves in particular. In contrast, observer–attributors typically tend to describe actors with relatively more abstract terms that imply enduring, dispositional properties. Thus what is generally regarded as the result of causal thinking or intra-individual cognitive processes may, in fact, be determined by the social rules of language use. There is also evidence that the actor–observer bias may be due to, and attenuated by changes in, the implicit focus of causal questions.

The psychology of the processes that underlie self–other differences in attribution is fascinating and their identification is of obvious significance to our everyday understanding of each other's actions. For example, self–other attribution differences have been shown to vary as a function of marital distress. The bias may be best understood in terms of perceptual salience and linguistic factors. It would appear incautious to assert, as has sometimes been done, that the attributions of actors are more accurate than those of observers. First, there are no criteria for accuracy. Second, even if actors are in a better position to know their own reasons for behaving as they do, because of motivational

distortions they may be in a worse position than an impartial observer to know other causes. Such motivational distortions are likely to become more important as research moves away from laboratory interactions between strangers to conflicts in CLOSE RELATIONSHIPS or INTERGROUP RELATIONS.

## SELF-SERVING BIASES

Research has shown that people are more likely to attribute their successes to internal causes such as ability, whereas they tend to attribute their failures to external causes such as task difficulty; this is the SELF-SERVING BIAS. Especially when relations between social groups are poor, group members also tend to make group-serving attributions for ingroup members and group-derogating attributions for outgroup members.

Although the self-serving bias has been widely researched, its exact nature and explanation have aroused controversy, primarily between cognitive and motivational accounts. There are, in fact, two biases – a "self-enhancing bias" (attributing success to internal, relative to external, causes) and a "self-protecting bias" (attributing failure to external, relative to internal, causes). Miller and Ross (1975) claimed support only for the self-enhancing bias and argued that it could be explained by cognitive factors, without recourse to motivational explanations. According to their cognitive, information-processing account, people:

(1) intend and expect to succeed rather than fail, and are more likely to make self-attributions for expected than unexpected outcomes;
(2) are more likely to perceive covariation between response and outcome if they are experiencing a pattern of increasing success, rather than constant failure; and
(3) erroneously base their judgments of the contingency between response and outcome on the occurrence of the desired outcome, rather than the true pattern of contingencies.

Zuckerman (1979), however, concluded a systematic review of the literature in favor of motivational explanations of this bias, arguing that the need to maintain SELF-ESTEEM directly affected the attribution of task outcomes. But he also pointed out that the strength of this effect depended on factors including the extent to which self-esteem concerns were aroused in experimental subjects.

Self-serving attributions can also be viewed from a wider perspective, which goes beyond biased attributions for success and failure (egotism) to include self-presentational and egocentric biases. Although there is clear evidence of self-serving, egotistic biases in interpersonal attribution, the bias is by no means ubiquitous. Instead, performance attributions are influenced by the setting and seem tailored to fit the needs of specific social situations. This more strategic conception of interpersonal attribution is best seen in work that relates attributions to IMPRESSION MANAGEMENT or SELF-PRESENTATION.

If self-serving biases in attribution are viewed as public self-presentations, then the MOTIVATION to maximize public esteem, rather than to maintain or increase one's private self-esteem, could explain counter-defensive attributions. According to this view, public-esteem needs might sometimes be best served by making self-attributions for negative, rather than positive, outcomes. For example, people might not want to accept undeserved credit for positive outcomes and to avoid credit for negative outcomes if they were aware that an unrealistically positive self-presentation could be invalidated by their own subsequent behavior or by observers' present or future assessment of their behavior. The potential embarrassment resulting from such public invalidation would probably threaten their public image. This perspective required that attributions be compared in public and private settings. Under public conditions, people tend to make more internal attributions for negative outcomes than they do when their performance outcomes and attributions are more private.

Whereas attributional egotism refers to self-serving attributions for success and failure, the egocentric, or "contribution," bias refers to the tendency for people to accept more credit or responsibility for a joint product than other contributors ascribe to them. One explanation for this finding is that biased attributions are due to an egocentric bias in availability of information in memory. There is evidence of egocentric bias in the attributions made by partners in MARRIAGE.

There is, then, overwhelming evidence for self-serving biases, when that term is used loosely to encompass evidence of egotism, self-presentation and egocentrism. Broadly speaking, egotism is especially likely in competitive interpersonal contexts; self-presentation is typical of evaluative public settings; and egocentrism is most likely to occur when responses are memory-based. Viewed more narrowly as egotism, the self-serving bias is likely to extend beyond causal attributions to the selection of hypotheses for testing, the generation of inference rules, the search for attribution-relevant information, the evaluation of accessed information, and the amount of evidence (confirmatory and disconfirmatory) that is required before an inference is made. As such it is surely one of the most pervasive biases in social cognition, although exceptions (e.g., patients suffering from DEPRESSION) do exist.

## COGNITIVE AND MOTIVATIONAL EXPLANATIONS OF BIAS

An important issue raised by self-serving biases, but of relevance more generally, is whether, in fact, it is possible to distinguish between cognitive and motivational explanations (*see* Tetlock & Levi, 1982). Various arguments have been raised against purely cognitive accounts. Some of the cognitive explanations for self-serving bias actually contain motivational aspects; and the cognitive research programme has been described as so flexible that it could generate the predictions of virtually any motivational theory. On the other hand, the most powerful argument against a purely motivational explanation is that motivational factors can have an effect on, and possibly via, information processing. It appears impossible to choose between the cognitive and motivational perspectives; both are surely correct.

Because it is practically impossible to separate motivational-functional and cognitive-information-processing explanations of bias, one should be wary of invoking functions for causal attributions. However, there is agreement that attributions may fulfill three general functions – CONTROL, self-esteem and self-presentation – and a fascination with bias should not lead us to ignore this fact, which may help us to make sense of people's otherwise seemingly bizarre (but adaptive) explanations for events in their lives.

CONCLUSIONS

Although there is a considerable body of evidence for these four main attributional biases and others, statements about how pervasive their effects really are should be qualified by careful reading of the available systematic literature reviews. The study of biases has been most influential in amassing evidence that people do not use the kinds of formal, quasi-scientific processes laid down in the classic attribution theories. Instead, they often make judgments quickly, on the basis of quite minimal information, and show clear tendencies to over-use some kinds of information and under-use others. A fascinating "new look" at biases suggests, however, that it is not the laypersons, but the scientists, who make mistakes; even well-established biases can be overturned by reframing problems or by subtle changes in the information presented (see Cheng & Novick, 1992).

See also: ATTRIBUTION THEORIES; CONTROL; DEPRESSION; HEURISTICS; IMPRESSION MANAGEMENT; INTERGROUP RELATIONS; LANGUAGE; MARRIAGE; MOTIVATION; SELF-ESTEEM; SOCIAL COGNITION.

BIBLIOGRAPHY

Borgida, E., & Brekke, N. (1981). The base rate fallacy in attribution and prediction. In J. H. Harvey, W. J. Ickes, & R. F. Kidd (Eds.), New directions in attribution research (Vol. 3, pp. 63–95). Hillsdale, NJ: Lawrence Erlbaum.

Cheng, P. W., & Novick, L. R. (1992). Covariation in natural causal induction. Psychological Review, 99, 365–82.

Funder, D. C. (1987). Errors and mistakes: Evaluating the accuracy of social judgment. Psychological Bulletin, 101, 75–90.

Hewstone, M. (1989). Causal attribution: From cognitive processes to collective beliefs. Oxford, UK & Cambridge, MA: Basil Blackwell.

Jones, E. E., & Nisbett, R. E. (1972). The actor and the observer: Divergent perceptions of the causes of behaviour. In E. E. Jones, D. E. Kanouse, H. H. Kelley, R. E. Nisbett, S. Valins, & B. Weiner (Eds.), Attribution: Perceiving the causes of behaviour (pp. 79–94). Morristown, NJ: General Learning Press.

Miller, D. T., & Ross, M. (1975). Self-serving biases in the attribution of causality: Fact or fiction? Psychological Bulletin, 82, 213–25.

Nisbett, R. E., & Ross, L. (1980). Human inference: Strategies and shortcomings of social judgment. Englewood Cliffs, NJ: Prentice Hall.

Tetlock, P. E., & Levi, A. (1982). Attribution bias: On the inconclusiveness of the cognition-moivation debate. Journal of Experimental Social Psychology, 18, 68–88.

Watson, D. (1982). The actor and the observer: How are their perceptions of causality divergent? Psychological Bulletin, 92, 682–700.

Zuckerman, M. (1979). Attribution of success and failure revisited, or: The motivational bias is alive and well in attribution theory. Journal of Personality, 47, 245–87.

MILES HEWSTONE

augmentation The augmentation principle (originally invoked in relation to causal schemata) implies that the role of a given cause is increased if an effect occurs in the presence of an inhibitory cause. This idea has also been used to explain the SOCIAL INFLUENCE exerted by minorities.

See also: ATTRIBUTION THEORIES; SOCIAL INFLUENCE.

MILES HEWSTONE

authoritarianism An orientation which is overly deferential to those in authority whilst simultaneously adopting an overbearing and hostile attitude towards those perceived as inferior. It is also commonly associated with a very conventional value system in which "right" and "wrong" are unambiguously demarcated and deviant or minority groups are openly derogated.

The most well-known analysis of authoritarianism was undertaken by Adorno, Frenkel-Brunswik, Levinson, and Sanford (1950). They hypothesized that the psychological origins of authoritarianism lay in a particular pattern of childhood socialization. They characterized this as one in which the parents – and especially the father – adopted a very harsh disciplinary approach towards their children. All transgressions, however minor, were severely punished. Drawing on psychoanalytic theory, Adorno et al. argued that such an upbringing would lead to a child's "natural" aggressive tendencies towards its parents being repressed, only to be later displaced onto alternative and "safer" targets (e.g., outgroups, or anyone who deviated from the societal norm). At the same time, an anxious and deferential attitude towards authority figures would be developed since these symbolize the parents. Adorno et al. further hypothesized that the strict moralistic atmosphere which prevailed in such families would foster a cognitive style which is marked by the consistent use of clearly defined categories and an intolerance of any overlap between them. Such a style was thought to facilitate the adoption and use of rigid stereotypes in the person's social judgments.

Adorno et al. conceived of authoritarianism as a personality syndrome in which certain individuals would be more susceptible than others to fascist or racist ideas, especially if these emanated from prestigious authority sources. They conducted a large research project which combined quantitative methodologies with individual clinical interviews. The former resulted in the development of an inventory (the F-scale) which became widely used as a measure of PREJUDICE. In parallel with the construction of the F-scale, small numbers of very high and very low scorers on it were selected for intensive interviews which consisted of questioning of the respondents' recollection of their childhood, perceptions of their parents, and their current social attitudes. Consistent with the original hypothesis, high scorers did portray their childhood as a time of strict obedience to parental authority and often manifested openly prejudiced views.

Initially Adorno et al.'s theory excited considerable interest among social psychologists. The concept of authoritarianism was employed in the investigation of such diverse phenomena as LEADERSHIP, IMPRESSION FORMATION, problem solving, psychopathology and, of course, prejudice. This research did much to substantiate the theory's validity since reliable differences in the cognitive style, social behavior, and intergroup attitudes of high and low authoritarians were often observed (Brown, 1965). For example, it was observed that high and low authoritarians solved mental puzzles in different ways, the former being less able or willing to change their problem-solving strategy once they had embarked on it. Prejudice was also reliably correlated with authoritarianism, a relationship which is still observable in more recent studies.

However, subsequent research has identified a number of limitations of this work on authoritarianism (*see* Brown, 1965). Methodologically the F-scale has been extensively criticized for having been developed on unrepresentative samples and for not employing routine safeguards against response set biases. Authoritarianism was found to correlate with such variables as educational level and social class, suggesting that it may reflect socialized attitudes of societal subgroups rather than a particular personality type. Furthermore, its utility as an explanation for the occurrence of ethnic prejudice has been questioned by studies which showed variations in socio-cultural levels of prejudice with no corresponding variations in levels of prejudice (Pettigrew, 1958). Adorno et al. also tended to neglect the impact of situational factors and group norms on authoritarianism; reliable changes in authoritarianism have been observed after immersion in a group which espouses particularly progressive (i.e., nonauthoritarian) attitudes (Siegel & Siegel, 1957). Finally, some have argued that the syndrome identified by Adorno et al. should more properly be called *right wing* authoritarianism and that another term should be employed for authoritarianism in general (*see* DOGMATISM). Another criticism is that conceiving of authoritarianism as an *individual* personality type rooted in particular family dynamics creates insuperable difficulties when explaining societal phenomena like prejudice which are usually manifested more or less uniformly across large numbers of individuals.

Despite these limitations, authoritarianism continues to be studied. One current approach seeks the origins of authoritarianism in the social hardships imposed by economic recession (Doty, Paterson, and Winter, 1991). Reliable correlations have been observed in these studies between economic indicators (e.g., per capita income, unemployment rates) and cultural indices of authoritarianism (e.g., membership in authoritarian churches, ownership of "aggressive" breeds of dogs). The significance of these findings is that they suggest that it may be more appropriate to regard authoritarianism as a social psychological reaction to wider socio-cultural changes rather than as a consequence of a particular individual socialization experience.

*See also:* DOGMATISM; IMPRESSION FORMATION; LEADERSHIP; PREJUDICE.

BIBLIOGRAPHY

Adorno, T. W., Frenkel-Brunswik, E., Levinson, D. J., & Sanford, R. N. (1950), *The Authoritarian Personality*. New York: Harper & Row.

Brown, R. W. (1965), *Social Psychology*. New York: Macmillan.

Doty, R. M., Peterson, B. E., & Winter, D. G. (1991). Threat and authoritarianism in the United States, 1978–87. *Journal of Personality and Social Psychology*, 61, 629–40.

Pettigrew, T. F. (1958). Personality and sociocultural factors in intergroup attitudes: a cross-national comparison. *Journal of Conflict Resolution*, 2, 29–42.

Siegel, A. E., & Siegel, S. (1957). Reference groups, membership groups and attitude change. *Journal of Abnormal and Social Psychology*, 55, 360–4.

RUPERT BROWN

**automaticity** Information processing (e.g., ENCODING and ATTENTION) that occurs without conscious control. Automatic processing can develop in response to stimuli and environments that people habitually encounter, as a way to save cognitive effort. Automatic responses can be defined with several criteria (Bargh, 1984). First, automatic processes are unintentional; they do not require a goal to be activated. Second, they are involuntary, always occurring in the presence of the relevant cue. Third, they are effortless, using no cognitive capacity. Fourth, they are autonomous, running to completion without any conscious monitoring. Finally, they are outside awareness, meaning they are activated and operated without consciousness.

Mental processes fall on a continuum from more automatic to more controllable (Bargh, 1989). At the most automatic end is preconscious automaticity, followed by postconscious automaticity and goal-directed automaticity. Next are spontaneous processes, which are activated without consciousness but processed only with effort. Ruminative processes are slightly more controlled; they are conscious but not deliberately directed by goals. At the most controlled end, intentional thoughts are characterized by people having choices, especially if they make the hard (more effortful) choice, and paying attention to that choice to enact it.

TYPES OF AUTOMATICITY

Varying degrees of automaticity adhere more or less to the above criteria (Bargh, 1989). The purest kind of automaticity, fitting all of the criteria, is preconscious automaticity. When people process social information preconsciously, they react immediately and effortlessly. An example is people's impressions based on categories that are chronically or subliminally accessible (*see* ACCESSIBILITY).

A less pure form of automaticity, fitting fewer of the criteria, is postconscious automaticity. This form occurs when people are conscious of an environmental stimulus, but not the processing it activates. For example, when people are primed by the environment, they are aware of the priming stimulus, but they are not aware that the prime affects their later judgments (*see* PRIMING). Another example of postconscious automaticity is mood effects. People are usually aware of their moods, but they are unaware of the influence moods have on later processing. Postconscious automaticity is also at work when people respond with schema-triggered affect, an immediate emotional judgment or response that results from activated SCHEMAS. Other category-based responses can be post-conscious as well. People's judgments that are based on physical characteristics or SALIENCE are postconscious.

The last form, goal-dependent automaticity, fits only some of the criteria for automaticity. Some ways of processing information depend on people's conscious goals to initiate them, but the processing itself is often automatic. For example, a deliberate goal to form an accurate impression of someone can initiate a search for schema-inconsistent information. The goal may be conscious, but the process of searching may occur without awareness. People's conscious goals in impression formation can also automatically influence their MEMORY for features of a person.

## PROCEDURALIZATION: PRACTICE AFFECTS AUTOMATICITY
Automatic processes require practice to develop. Just as extensive practice makes activities such as driving or typing become automatic, practice can influence processes of social inference. If people regularly judge others in a particular way (e.g., if they regularly make inferences about their honesty), the judgments are likely to become proceduralized (Smith, 1984). A process becomes proceduralized when an appropriate stimulus (e.g., a person's behavior) automatically sets the process (e.g., an honesty judgment) into action. Repeated practice of the exact process is important to proceduralization, but the content of the process can change. For example, as honesty judgments become proceduralized, it does not matter if the specifically practiced behaviors (e.g., admitting a mistake, cheating a waiter) differ.

Judgments that are proceduralized are faster and easier, and a well-practiced judgment will be used before a less-practiced one. The speed and priority of proceduralized judgments may be responsible for some instances of STEREOTYPING. People's well-practiced judgments on the basis of race, sex, or age may cause them to prefer these judgments over less practiced ones. For example, people who regularly make judgments based on femininity will be more likely to judge an ambiguous behavior in feminine terms rather than, for example, in helpfulness terms.

## FIRST STEPS IN IMPRESSION FORMATION ARE AUTOMATIC
Automaticity may explain why people process information about new people in regular ways. People from Western cultures, for example, tend to make dispositional inferences about people rather than situational inferences. These tendencies appear to be automatic first steps in impression formation. People first categorize a person according to personality dispositions. Later, they may correct a dispositional attribution with situational factors, but only if they have time and capacity. The dispositional categorization is an automatic step, but the correction is effortful. The categorization step is not easily interrupted, but the correction step can be.

As a broader principle, the first and automatic step in comprehending any premise (such as an opinion or a dispositional attribution) may involve accepting the premise as true. Rejecting the premise requires additional effort. Thus, if people do not have time to think about a judgment, they may accept it as true automatically (Gilbert, 1991). This principle can be adaptive. In person perception, people often do behave as their personalities predict, so an automatic dispositional inference makes sense.

## OTHER AUTOMATIC PROCESSES
Information may be automatically encoded for some combinations of people and particular traits. Depressed people may automatically encode negative information. For people in general, threatening and otherwise negative cues are encoded automatically. Other stimuli relevant to people's needs, goals, and interests may also be processed automatically (see Fiske & Taylor, 1991).
See also: ATTENTION; MEMORY; SCHEMAS/ SCHEMATA; STEREOTYPING.

BIBLIOGRAPHY

Bargh, J. A. (1984). Automatic and conscious processing of social information. In R. S. Wyer, Jr & T. K. Srull (Eds.), *Handbook of social cognition* (Vol. 3, pp. 1–44). Hillsdale, NJ: Lawrence Erlbaum.

——(1989). Conditional automaticity: Varieties of automatic influence in social perception and cognition. In J. S. Uleman & J. A. Bargh (Eds.), *Unintended thought* (pp. 3–51). New York: Guilford Press.

Fiske, S. T., & Taylor, S. E. (1991). *Social cognition* (2nd ed., chapter 8). New York: McGraw-Hill.

Gilbert, D. T. (1991). How mental systems believe. *American Psychologist, 46*, 107–19.

Smith, E. R. (1984). Model of social inference processes. *Psychological Review, 91*, 392–413.

SUSAN T. FISKE
BETH A. MORLING

**availability**  The distinction between availability of information in memory (i.e., whether traces are available at all) and its temporal ACCESSIBILITY is not applied consistently. The most frequent use of the term is with reference to the availability HEURISTIC which affords a means of making statistical judgments under uncertainty. Accordingly, subjective estimates of the frequency or probability of events are based on the ease with which relevant examples or experiences come to the judge's mind.
*See also*: HEURISTICS.

KLAUS FIEDLER

**averaging model**  IMPRESSION FORMATION model holding that information about a person is averaged to yield an overall impression, such as likability. According to the *Weighted Average* model, an impression reflects the average *scale value* of attributes – how positively they are evaluated – weighted according to their importance to the perceiver.
*See also*: IMPRESSION FORMATION.

LESLIE A. ZEBROWITZ

# B

**balance theory** Heider formulated balance theory on the basis of GESTALT principles to account for people's preferences in social perception. Balance theory holds that people have an innate preference for harmonious and consistent relationships among their cognitions. A balanced relationship is one in which things or persons perceived as belonging together are evaluated similarly.

JOEL COOPER

**bargaining** The process of moving toward agreement when there is a conflict of interest among two or more parties. Verbal bargaining, which is also called negotiation, can be distinguished from tacit bargaining (Schelling, 1960), in which the parties exchange signals or take nonverbal actions. Most of the literature in this field concerns either two-party verbal bargaining or mediation, which is third-party assistance to bargainers.

Bargaining is found in all realms of society, from interactions on the playground to relations between nations; hence it is studied by all fields of social science. Psychological research on bargaining is mainly done with EXPERIMENTAL GAMES methodology, but case studies and questionnaire research are common outside psychology.

Bargaining can lead to one of four kinds of outcomes: Victory for one party; compromise, involving an agreement that is part way between the parties' initial preferences; win–win (also called "integrative") agreement, in which both parties achieve much of what they want; and failure to reach agreement. A win–win agreement is not always possible, as when there is only a single issue such as the price of an antique. Such situations are said to lack integrative potential.

## PROMINENT SOLUTIONS

Sometimes a single alternative stands out in a negotiator's thinking as the fairest or most likely solution, for example, a 50–50 division of money earned, a mediator's suggestion about an appropriate wage, or a mountain range in a border dispute. If the same alternative stands out in the other party's thinking, and each party knows that this is true of the other, a "prominent solution" is said to exist (Schelling, 1960). This solution is likely to be the point of agreement, because each party can anticipate that the other will concede no further than the prominent solution, making it pointless to try to achieve a more favorable agreement. When there is a prominent solution, compared to when there is not, negotiation moves faster and other determinants of behavior have a reduced effect. By contrast, if *different* alternatives stand out in the two parties' thinking, concessions are likely to be slower than otherwise, and there is a stronger possibility of failure to reach agreement.

## DEMANDS, CONCESSIONS, AND CONTENTIOUS TACTICS

A large number of tactics are available in bargaining. The most common of these involve one or another level of initial demand or pattern of concessions. Demands are statements about preferred outcomes; concessions are changes in demands in the direction of the other party's preferences. Negotiators who make larger initial demands and slower concessions usually achieve higher outcomes if agreement is reached, but their agreements are reached more slowly and they are less certain to reach agreement. This implies that the most effective approach is usually one of moderation; demanding a lot, but not so much as to make it hard to reach agreement in a reasonable period of time. Many bargainers employ a tit-for-tat tactic, in which they reward the other party for conceding by making a reciprocal concession of comparable magnitude. This encourages the other to make further concessions, and hence tends to produce agreement on favorable terms. However, implementation of the tit-for-tat tactic is often undermined by reactive devaluation (Ross & Stillinger, 1991), a commonly found tendency to underestimate the size of the other's concessions, which leads to meager reciprocation.

Demands are often backed up by contentious (also called "competitive" or "distributive") tactics, such as persuasive arguments, threats, harassment, putting time pressure on the other party, and positional commitments ("here I stand and I will not move"). Though they are frequently successful, contentious tactics other than persuasive arguments tend to be resented and to be answered in kind, risking the start of a conflict spiral (*see* CONFLICT). When contentious tactics are the main ones used, win–win agreements are unlikely to be developed and there is often no agreement at all.

PROBLEM SOLVING

Another set of tactics, referred to as problem solving, is aimed at finding mutually acceptable solutions. Problem solving is the most common route to win–win solutions in situations with integrative potential. It is often a solitary pursuit, but it is more likely to be successful if both parties work together.

Successful problem solving requires an understanding of the structure of win–win solutions. Such solutions take three forms: expanding the pie, exchanging concessions on different issues, and finding new options that satisfy the underlying interests of both parties (Pruitt & Carnevale, 1993). Problem solving tactics include seeking and providing information about interests and priorities among issues, reframing the issues, and trying to devise new options. Effective problem solving is encouraged by informal discussions between the parties in private settings that encourage good moods. Personal attacks should

be avoided, and empathic listening is useful provided that the listener does not act so warmly as to encourage an impression of weakness. Bargainers need to focus on the future (which can be difficult when there are past grievances) and to state their proposed solutions in a tentative fashion that seeks the other's feedback (Fisher, Ury, & Patton, 1991). When there are many complex issues, agendas that prioritize the discussion should be formed; and it is often useful to agree on broad preliminary formulas before filling in the details. Problem solving is most successful when bargainers take a firm but concerned and flexible stance: firm about one's basic interests, but also concerned about the other's interests, and flexible enough to seek and adopt new solutions.

Good problem solving tactics tend to be incompatible with good contentious tactics. It is hard to be flexible while committing oneself to a particular demand, to devise new ideas while thinking up arguments for old ones, or to put the other party in a good mood while making threats. Yet both problem solving and contentious tactics serve legitimate goals; and limited contentious tactics can enhance the effectiveness of problem solving, by clarifying the issues and revealing what is important to the parties and where they are rigid and flexible. This means that bargainers constantly face a dilemma between these two sets of tactics. There are many ways of bridging the horns of this dilemma, including moving from one set of tactics to the other or (when groups are involved) putting these two sets of tactics into the hands of different personnel.

DETERMINANTS OF CHOICE AMONG TACTICS

Rubin, Pruitt, and Kim (1994) have proposed a Dual Concern Model, which helps organize many of the findings on the antecedents of choices among tactics. Two intervening variables are postulated: concern about own outcomes (own-concern), which is the extent to which one seeks high benefit for oneself, and concern about the other party's outcomes (other-concern), which is the extent to which one seeks high benefit for the other. When other-concern is low, high own-concern produces rigid, contentious behavior – one tries hard to win. When own-concern is low, high other-concern produces concession making – one lets the other win. When both concerns are high, the result is problem solving – one seeks a mutually beneficial solution.

Many of the conditions that encourage high demands, a low concession rate, and the use of contentious tactics may be viewed as sources of own-concern. These include having ambitious goals; seeing attractive alternatives to agreement; expecting low costs if agreement is not reached; having strong principles underlying one's demands, such as religious beliefs or a conviction that DISTRIBUTIVE JUSTICE or PROCEDURAL JUSTICE is at issue; being an accountable representative; and framing issues negatively. Issues are framed negatively when the available options are seen as involving various degrees of loss, and positively when they are seen as involving various degrees of gain. Negative framing, in contrast to positive framing, makes bargainers reluctant to concede and reduces the likelihood that agreement will be reached (Neale & Bazerman, 1991).

Many of the conditions that encourage concession making or problem solving may be viewed as sources of either genuine or strategic other-concern. These include warm feelings toward the other party, positive moods, future dependence on the other, and having a stake in the other's success. Several studies have shown that problem solving is especially likely to occur under conditions that encourage high other-concern in conjunction with high own-concern, as predicted by the Dual Concern Model (Pruitt & Carnevale, 1993).

The Dual Concern Model is by no means a comprehensive theory of the determinants of tactical choice. Other determinants include the following: Time pressure encourages both concession making and contentious behavior, perhaps because both are alternatives to inaction. TRUST encourages problem solving, perhaps because it increases the perceived likelihood that the other party will join in. Relative POWER in comparison with the other party is also important in tactical choice. For example, bargainers with high threat capacity tend to use contentious tactics, while those with low threat capacity are more partial to problem solving and concession making. Tenacious behavior can substitute, in part, for high power.

Stages are also prevalent in tactical choice, the most common being the progression from mutually contentious behavior to joint problem solving (Morley & Stephenson, 1977). This progression can usually be explained by a sense of stalemate that often develops on both sides after a period of mutually contentious behavior. Neither party is getting anywhere, so they seek a new approach.

## MEDIATION

Mediators are third parties who try to help bargainers reach agreement. They must be distinguished from arbitrators, who actually impose a settlement. There are arguments for both mediation and arbitration: The advantages of mediation are that the parties (the "disputants") are more likely to identify with the final decision, since they have made it themselves, and that this decision is more likely to reflect their true interests. The advantages of arbitration are that it ensures that a decision will be made, allows the introduction of community norms that might be ignored by the disputants, and often saves time.

Mediators usually intervene only after a stalemate has been reached or it has become clear that the disputants are unable or unwilling to talk with each other. Mediators sometimes come in as professionals from the outside, but they more often emerge from the social milieu surrounding the conflict, as a result of discomfort with the conflict or a desire to help the parties. They may meet with the parties jointly or deal with each of them separately, the latter being more likely the greater the antagonism between the parties.

Research suggests that mediation is ordinarily quite effective in producing agreements that satisfy the disputants and to which they later comply (Kressel, Pruitt, & Associates, 1989). However, mediation is no panacea, and it tends to fail when antagonism between the parties is quite high or integrative potential quite low. Furthermore, mediation is not particularly useful for repairing RELATION-SHIPS. If dysfunctional patterns of relating are the problem, deeper therapies are indicated. Conditions that are favorable to the success of mediation include disputant motivation to reach agreement, disputant commitment to mediation, the absence of issues of principle, relatively equal power between the parties, and (if they are groups) the absence of severe discord within the parties.

A large number of tactics are available to mediators, including interpreting the parties to one another, identifying the true issues, suggesting agendas, keeping order in joint sessions, pressing the parties to make concessions, challenging the parties to devise new ideas, devising new ideas themselves, advising representatives about relations with their constituents, providing compensation for concession making, and providing incentives for complying with the eventual agreement. Mediators can counteract reactive devaluation by offering as their own proposal a position that is endorsed by the other party but would be rejected if the other party made it. Some mediator tactics appear to be universally effective, such as building rapport with the disputants, identifying the issues, and constructing an agenda; but the effectiveness of most tactics depends on the circumstances (Carnevale & Pruitt, 1992). In general, the more intense the conflict, the more active and forceful must mediators be.

Carnevale (Carnevale & Pruitt, 1992) has found support for a Concern Likelihood Model which predicts mediator behavior. It postulates two antecedent variables that interact:

(1) level of concern, which is the mediator's sympathy with the parties' interests; and
(2) perceived common ground, which is the mediator's estimate of the availability of win–win agreements.

When both variables are high, mediators are predicted to emphasize a problem-solving strategy aimed at devising win–win solutions. When level of concern is high and perceived common ground is low, mediators are predicted to use compensation to entice the parties into making concessions. When level of concern is low and perceived common ground is high, mediators are predicted to use pressure tactics to push down the parties' aspirations. When both variables are low, mediators are predicted to be inactive, letting the parties handle the dispute themselves.

Two common beliefs have come under recent criticism (Kressel et al., 1989): that mediators should have no power over the parties and that biased mediators cannot be effective. One basis for this criticism is that mediation–arbitration ("med–arb"), in which the mediator has the power to make a binding decision if agreement is not reached, has been shown to encourage more serious disputant attention to the issues than straight mediation. In addition, it has been observed that emergent mediators (those who come from the surrounding milieu) are often quite effective, despite the fact that they are usually closer to one side than the other and tend to be quite powerful.

CONCLUSIONS

The study of bargaining began with mathematical models developed by economists and game theorists, and the history and present character of this field have been heavily influenced by these disciplines. This accounts for the emphasis on experimental games methodology. It also accounts for the traditional assumption that bargainers are only interested in their own welfare, which has been recently challenged by the Dual Concern Model. While much progress has been made within this initial framework, the framework has also produced blinders which need to be removed. More attention needs to be paid to the impact of preexisting relationships between the bargainers, and the effect of decision processes in the organizations that are so often involved in bargaining. Bargaining that involves three or more parties also needs to be studied. Much more research is needed on the prebargaining period, in which decisions are made about whether to enter bargaining and which issues, parties, and procedures will be involved. Another important but neglected topic is the impact of social NORMS, especially the principles of fairness. There can be little doubt that concerns about fairness have a major effect on the demands people make and the agreements they reach, but little attention has been paid to this topic. Cultural differences in bargaining behavior also need to be addressed, and somebody needs to straighten out the large but inconclusive literature about individual differences.

On a more radical plane, it is possible that students of bargaining are mistaken in their nearly universal effort to build a linear theory that links prior conditions to tactics and tactics to outcomes. Morley (1992) has questioned this orientation, arguing that bargaining should be understood instead as a collective effort to make sense of the situation in light of "what has happened in the past and what needs to happen in the future" (p. 206). Empirical data must be the arbitrator of this controversy.

*See also*: CONFLICT; EXPERIMENTAL GAMES; NORMS; POWER; RELATIONSHIPS; TRUST.

BIBLIOGRAPHY

Carnevale, P. J., & Pruitt, D. G. (1992). Negotiation and mediation. *Annual Review of Psychology, 43*, 531–82.

Fisher, R., Ury, W. L., & Patton, B. M. (1991). *Getting to yes: Negotiating agreement without giving in* (2nd ed.). Boston: Houghton Mifflin.

Kressel, K., Pruitt, D. G., & Associates. (1989). *Mediation research: The process and effectiveness of third-party intervention*. San Francisco: Jossey–Bass.

Morley, I. E. (1992). Intra-organizational bargaining. In J. F. Hartley & G. M. Stephenson (Eds.), *Employment relations*. Cambridge, MA: Blackwell Publishers.

—— & Stephenson, G. M. (1977). *The social psychology of bargaining*. London: Allen & Unwin.

Neale, M. A., & Bazerman, M. H. (1991). *Cognition and rationality in negotiation*. New York: Free Press.

Pruitt, D. G., & Carnevale, P. J. (1993). *Negotiation in social conflict*. Buckingham: Open University Press.

Rubin, J. Z. Pruit, D. G., & Kim, S. H. (1994). *Social conflict: Escalation, stalemate, and settlement* (2nd edn.). New York: McGraw-Hill.

Ross, L., & Stillinger, C. (1991). Barriers to conflict resolution. *Negotiation Journal, 7*, 389–404.

Schelling, T. (1960). *The strategy of conflict*. Cambridge, MA: Harvard University Press.

DEAN G. PRUITT

**base rates** In making probabilistic inferences perceivers ought to take account of general, broadly based information about population characteristics, and more specifically the prior probability of an event occurring. The tendency to under-use, sometimes even ignore, such information is called the base-rate fallacy (e.g., under-use of CONSENSUS information as an ATTRIBUTIONAL BIAS). *See also*: ATTRIBUTIONAL BIAS.

MILES HEWSTONE

**Bayes' theorem** This theorem deals with the impact of new information on the revision of probability estimates, and provides a normative model to assess how well people use empirical information to update the probability that a hypothesis is true. Bayes' theorem states that

$$P(H_i \mid D) = \frac{P(D \mid H_i)\, P(H_i)}{P(D)}$$

$P(H_i D)$ refers to the posterior probability that $H_i$ is true, taking into account the new datum $D$, and all previous data (base-rate probability). $P(D \mid H_i)$ is the conditional probability that the datum $D$ would be observed if hypothesis $H_i$ were true. The value $P(H_i)$ refers to the prior or base-rate probability of hypothesis $H_i$. $P(D)$ is a conditional probability and is, among other things, dependent on the hypotheses being considered $P(D) = \sum_i P(D \mid H_i)\, P(H_i)$. This denominator serves as a normalizing constant.

A standard test is to present subjects with two bookbags, one containing 80 blue poker chips and 20 red poker chips, the other containing 80 red chips and 20 blue chips. One of the bags is selected and the experimenter begins to draw chips from the selected bag (with replacement). After each chip, the subject is asked to estimate the probability that a specific hypothesis is true (referring to which bag is being sampled). Generally, subjects' estimates are conservative, in the sense that their assessment tends to be significantly lower than the optimal posterior probability $P(H_i D)$ as calculated with Bayes' theorem. The major finding in these experiments is that human INFERENCE is routinely conservative; i.e., people do not revise their opinions as much as the optimal Baysian rule requires.

This finding encountered substantial criticism in the 1970s. The crux of these criticisms was that the standard task was too complex for unaided human performance, and that the task was rather contrived and of a type that rarely occurs outside the laboratory. Bayes' theorem specifies that proper inference from fallible evidence ought to combine that evidence with prior probabilities. A large number of experiments have questioned the use of prior probabilities (*see* BASE RATES). Conservatism and the neglect of base rates have also been applied to social perception and stereotyping (*see* Fiske & Taylor, 1991)

BIBLIOGRAPHY
Fiske, S. T., & Taylor, S. E. (1991). *Social Cognition*. New York: McGraw-Hill.
                                    JOOP VAN DER PLIGT

**behavioral confirmation/disconfirmation**
When people interact with other people, they often use their preconceived beliefs and expectations as guides to action. Their actions, in turn, may prompt their interaction partners to behave in ways that confirm these initial beliefs. This phenomenon, in which belief creates reality, is known by several names – the SELF-FULFILLING PROPHECY, EXPECTANCY CONFIRMATION, and behavioral confirmation (terminology which emphasizes that it is the target's actual behavior that confirms the perceiver's initial beliefs; Snyder, 1984).

THE PHENOMENON OF BEHAVIORAL CONFIRMATION
The behavioral confirmation interactional scenario has been demonstrated in a series of empirical investigations in which a person (the perceiver), having adopted erroneous beliefs about another person (the target), acts in ways that cause the behavior of the target to confirm these beliefs.

In one experiment, Snyder, Tanke, and Berscheid (1977) examined the effects on interactions between college-aged men and women of the stereotyped assumption that physically attractive people have socially appealing personalities. Before a telephone conversation with a female partner, each man was randomly assigned a snapshot (ostensibly of his partner) of a physically attractive or a physically unattractive woman. Men who believed their partners to be attractive treated them with more warmth and friendliness than men who believed their partners to be unattractive. As a result, women thought to be attractive (regardless of their actual looks) reciprocated these overtures and actually came to behave in a friendly and sociable manner; in contrast, women assumed by their partners to be unattractive became cool and aloof during the conversations.

Such behavioral confirmation scenarios have been demonstrated in a wide variety of laboratory and nonlaboratory contexts and for a wide range of beliefs and expectations, including STEREOTYPES about sex, assumptions about race, beliefs about age, self-images, beliefs about personality, expectations of being liked or disliked, hypotheses about other people, imputations of STIGMA, and arbitrary designations of ability (for reviews of the literature, *see* Jussim, 1986; Snyder, 1984, 1992).

THE MECHANISMS OF BEHAVIORAL CONFIRMATION
With numerous demonstrations of behavioral confirmation, investigators have turned to the mechanisms of these phenomena. Discussions have focused on four steps in behavioral confirmation sequences:

(1) perceivers adopt beliefs about targets;
(2) perceivers act as if these beliefs were true and treat targets accordingly;
(3) targets assimilate their behavior to perceivers' overtures; and

(4) perceivers interpret targets' behavior as confirming their beliefs.

Such step-wise analyses of behavioral confirmation provide a useful heuristic for organizing and systematizing the research literature. Moreover, by segmenting behavioral confirmation into components that are familiar building blocks of social interaction (i.e., thoughts and behaviors of perceivers and targets), they make it easier to comprehend the frequent occurrence of behavioral confirmation.

## THE MATTER OF BEHAVIORAL DISCONFIRMATION

In addition, by delineating links in the chain of interaction between perceiver and target, researchers have been able to identify points in the interaction sequence at which actions by perceivers and targets might produce interactions culminating in the target behaving contrary to the perceiver's anticipations. In fact, the literature contains several demonstrations of such behavioral disconfirmation outcomes (for reviews, *see* Snyder, 1984, 1992). It should be noted that, in some of these studies, perceivers clung to their initial expectations, thus demonstrating perceptual confirmation in the face of behavioral disconfirmation.

## MOTIVATIONAL FOUNDATIONS OF BEHAVIORAL CONFIRMATION AND DISCONFIRMATION

In recent years, researchers have begun to probe the psychological processes that underlie and motivate behavioral confirmation and disconfirmation. That is, they have been seeking to understand why perceivers act on their beliefs in ways that initiate confirmation and disconfirmation scenarios, and why targets come to behave in ways that confirm or disconfirm expectations. To do so, students of social interaction have turned increasingly to theoretical and empirical research on the motivational foundations of behavioral confirmation and disconfirmation.

Thus, some theories of self-fulfilling prophecies in the classroom have emphasized the role that teachers' and students' motivations play in determining educational outcomes (e.g., Jussim, 1986). Similarly, some accounts of behavioral confirmation and disconfirmation have examined the goals that perceivers and targets bring to their interactions, and how these interaction goals influence the dynamics and outcomes of the ensuing interactions (e.g., Hilton & Darley, 1991). Other theoretical analyses have focused on the social and psychological functions served by the activities of perceivers and targets in behavioral confirmation and disconfirmation sequences; research based on such analyses has revealed that, when behavioral confirmation occurs in the context of the acquaintance process, the activities of the perceiver serve the function of acquiring knowledge and the activities of the target serve the function of facilitating interaction (for elaboration, *see* Snyder, 1992).

## CONCLUSIONS

For social scientists, behavioral confirmation and disconfirmation sequences are of special concern. They represent a particularly complex intertwining of cognitive activities and behavioral processes in the context of ongoing social interaction and interpersonal relationships, with intriguing implications for the reciprocal influences of "subjective" reality (the perceiver's beliefs) and "objective" reality (the target's behavior) in a wide range of interaction contexts of considerable theoretical and practical significance.

*See also*: SELF-FULFILLING PROPHECIES; STEREOTYPING; STIGMA.

### BIBLIOGRAPHY

Hilton, J. L., & Darley, J. M. (1991). The effects of interaction goals on person perception. In M. P. Zanna (Ed.), *Advances in experimental social psychology* (Vol. 24, pp. 236–67). Orlando, FL: Academic Press.

Jussim, L. (1986). Self-fulfilling prophecies: A theoretical and integrative review. *Psychological Review*, 93, 429–45.

Snyder, M. (1984). When belief creates reality. In L. Berkowitz (Ed.), *Advances in experimental social psychology* (Vol. 18, pp. 248–305). Orlando, FL: Academic Press.

—— (1992). Motivational foundations of behavioral confirmation. In M. P. Zanna (Ed.), *Advances in experimental social psychology* (Vol. 25, pp. 67–114). Orlando, FL: Academic Press.

—— Tanke, E. D., & Berschied, E. (1977). Social perception and interpersonal behavior: On the self-fulfilling nature of social stereotypes. *Journal of Personality and Social Psychology*, *35*, 656–66.

MARK SNYDER

**belief congruence theory** A 'theory of PREJUDICE which proposes that the most important determinant of one person's attitude toward another is the similarity or "congruence" between the two people's belief systems. Where there is high similarity mutual attraction is thought to ensue; dissimilarity is presumed to lead to rejection. The rationale for this idea is similar to that derived from SOCIAL COMPARISON theory: that the perception of similarity of opinion is assumed to provide consensual validation for one's own beliefs, and hence is socially attractive.

The theory was proposed by Rokeach (1960). What lent controversy to the theory was Rokeach's hypothesis that belief similarity (or dissimilarity) was a more important factor in determining people's attitudes toward outgroups than the ingroup–outgroup category difference itself. That is, he suggested that members of ethnic minorities are discriminated against not because they belong to a particular group but because they are assumed to have different beliefs from the discriminators. In the final analysis, he proposed, an outgroup member who agreed with us would be preferred to an ingroup member who disagreed. A common empirical test of this theory has been to present people with target persons, who may be hypothetical "others" or experimental confederates, who are seen to endorse similar or dissimilar opinion statements to the subject. The group membership of the target person is also varied so as to be the same as or different from the subject's own. The subject's liking for these different target persons is then measured. In a large number of studies, in both laboratory and field variants of this basic paradigm, a consistent finding has indeed been that the "similar" target is preferred to group membership. Group membership effects – that ingroup members are preferred to outgroup members – have also been observed, but the magnitude of these effects has usually been smaller than those due to belief congruence (Insko, Nacoste, & Moe, 1983).

Despite this seemingly impressive support, two problems have inhibited the wider acceptance of Belief Congruence Theory as a general explanation of prejudice. The first concerns the evidence from a number of studies where there was strong normative pressure for the display of prejudice. In such studies the importance of belief congruence has often been dwarfed by categorical effects. A second difficulty has stemmed from those studies which have sought to vary the interpersonal or intergroup nature of the basic paradigm (*see* CONTACT HYPOTHESIS). In conditions under which group memberships are highly salient, then similarity or difference of category membership, rather than belief system, becomes the deciding factor in controlling discrimination. Moreover, it has even proved possible to observe the reverse of the usual belief congruence effects in some strongly intergroup situations (Diehl, 1990). *See also*: CONTACT HYPOTHESIS; PREJUDICE; SOCIAL COMPARISON.

BIBLIOGRAPHY

Diehl, M. (1990). The Minimal Group Paradigm: Theoretical explanations and empirical findings. In W. Stroebe, & M. Hewstone (Eds.) *European review of social psychology* (Vol. 1, pp. 263–92) Chichestar: J. Wiley.

Insko, C. A., Nacoste, R. W., & Moe, J. L. (1983). Belief congruence and racial discrimination: Review of the evidence and critical evaluation. *European Journal of Social Psychology*, *13*, 153–74.

Rokeach, M. (1960). *The Open and Closed Mind*. New York: Basic Books.

RUPERT BROWN

**beliefs** As used by social psychologists, beliefs represent people's information about themselves and about their social and nonsocial environment, be that information accurate or inaccurate. A belief associates an object with a certain attribute. In the belief statement, "nuclear power stations generate radioactive waste," the object *nuclear power stations* is linked to the attribute *radioactive waste*. The srength of this association is given by the subjective probability or certainty that the object has the attribute in question. Beliefs are formed as a result of direct experience, on the basis of second-hand information received from various sources, and by means of logical or quasi-logical inference from other information about the object (Fishbein & Ajzen, 1975).

Although people can form a large number of beliefs about any object, they can attend to only relatively few at any given moment. These *salient* beliefs are thought to be the immediate determinants of a person's attitude toward the object. When most beliefs associate the object with favorable attributes, a positive attitude is formed, but when unfavorable beliefs predominate, the attitude is negative.

BIBLIOGRAPHY
Fishbein, M., & Ajzen, I. (1975). *Belief, attitude, intention, and behavior: An introduction to theory and research.* Reading, MA: Addison-Wesley.

ICEK AJZEN

**bereavement** The situation of a person who has recently lost a loved one through death. Bereavement is the cause of GRIEF, the emotional (affective) reaction to the death of a significant person. It is associated with *mourning*, the practices of societies (e.g., funeral rites) serving as guidelines for how bereaved people are expected to behave.
*See also*: GRIEF.

MARGARET STROEBE<br>HENK SCHUT

**bias** The term bias has a wide currency throughout SOCIAL COGNITION and ATTRIBUTION THEORIES and refers to the social perceiver systematically distorting (e.g., over- or under-using) some otherwise correct procedure, or to the distorted outcomes of such a procedure. The study of ATTRIBUTIONAL BIAS, in particular, has generated a large literature including the underutilization of CONSENSUS information, the FUNDAMENTAL ATTRIBUTION ERROR, ACTOR–OBSERVER DIFFERENCES, and SELF-SERVING BIAS. These biases seem to provide a better descriptive analysis of causal attribution than do complex normative models. Attempts to distinguish between cognitive and motivational explanations of various bias have stimulated much research, but have ultimately been frustrating. It appears impossible to choose between the cognitive and motivational perspectives, not least because motivational factors can have an effect on, and possibly via, information processing.

It is generally more accurate to speak of biases than errors, because the latter imply deviations from a normative model or departures from some accepted criterion of validity (*see* Kruglanski & Ajzen, 1983). Such models or criteria are not usually available for social–psychological research (an exception being research on the use of BASE RATES, in cases where the correct probability can be calculated according to BAYES' THEOREM). Current research is challenging some well-established biases, by showing that they can be overturned by subtle reframing of instructions or changes to stimulus materials (Gigerenzer, 1992). Thus it may have been the scientists, not the laypersons, who have made the mistakes.
*See also*: ATTRIBUTION THEORIES; ATTRIBUTIONAL BIAS; SOCIAL COGNITION.

BIBLIOGRAPHY
Gigerenzer, G. (1992). How to make cognitive illusions disappear: Beyond "heuristics and biases". In W. Stroebe & M. Hewstone (Eds.), *European review of social psychology* (Vol. 2, pp. 83–115). Chichester: J. Wiley.
Kruglanski, A. W., & Ajzen, I. (1983). Bias and error in human judgment. *European Journal of Social Psychology, 13*, 1–44.

MILES HEWSTONE

**bogus pipeline** The bogus pipeline is a procedure intended to reduce distortions in self-report measures (*see* ATTITUDE MEASURE-MENT AND QUESTIONNAIRE DESIGN). It involves convincing respondents that the researcher has a reliable and valid means of knowing what their true responses are, typically by means of bogus psychophysiological apparatus. The assumption is that the motivation to distort responses is reduced if respondents believe in the efficacy of the bogus pipeline. The effectiveness of the procedure is controversial.

*See also*: ATTITUDE MEASUREMENT AND QUESTIONNAIRE DESIGN.

ANTONY S. R. MANSTEAD

**brainstorming** A technique developed by Osborn (1953, 1957, 1963), an advertising executive, to increase the effectiveness of group sessions at his advertising agency. He called the sessions conducted according to this technique "brainstorming sessions," because "brainstorming means using the brain to storm a problem" (Osborn, 1963). Brainstorming is based on two principles, called "deferment of judgment" and "quantity breeds quality." Deferment of judgment means a strict separation of idea generation and idea evaluation. This can be done by having different people or at least different group sessions for generating and evaluating ideas. This principle should enhance the quantity of idea production and thus, according to the second principle, also the quality of the ideas produced. In line with these considerations, Osborn (1957) divided the problem solving process into three successive phases:

(1) fact-finding;
(2) idea-finding; and
(3) solution-finding.

In the first phase, the problem in question is to be defined and information relevant to the solution of the problem is to be gathered. In order to collect suggestions for solving the problem the second phase should be used to generate new ideas and to combine ideas already mentioned or to elaborate on earlier suggestions. Finally, in the third phase, all the ideas should be evaluated in order to

select the idea that offers the best solution to the problem.

From the two principles of brainstorming, Osborn derived four rules for idea-finding:

(1) criticism is ruled out;
(2) "free-wheeling" is welcomed;
(3) quantity is wanted; and
(4) combination and improvement are sought.

Adhering to the four brainstorming rules should enhance quantity and quality of ideas in individual as well as in group brainstorming. However, because of mutual inspiration, brainstorming should be especially successful for group problem solving compared to individual problem solving. Osborn (1957) assumed that "the average person can think up twice as many ideas when working with a group than when working alone" (p. 229).

Osborn's claims were soon disproved by studies that compared real groups with so-called nominal groups. Nominal groups are control groups of people working alone. The performance of a nominal group of $n$ persons is the quantity and/or quality of all nonredundant ideas produced by the $n$ persons (nonredundant means that ideas that were mentioned twice or more were counted only once). Numerous experiments comparing individual with group brainstorming have consistently found real groups to be significantly *less* productive than nominal groups both in terms of quantity and quality of ideas (for a review, *see* Diehl & Stroebe, 1987; *see also* GROUP PRODUCTIVITY).

Three explanations have been offered for the relative inferiority of brainstorming groups:

(1) *Evaluation apprehension.* Whereas individual brainstorming should lead to concerns about the quantity of idea production, the lower identifiability of individual performance in groups should make group members less apprehensive with regard to the quantity of ideas produced. On the other hand the presence of other group members might evoke evaluation apprehension concerning the quality of ideas. This might lead to a self-censoring of ideas and thus to a reduction of both quantity and quality of idea production.

(2) *Free riding*. Due to the lower identifiability and the higher dispensability of individual contributions in groups, individuals might be less motivated when working with a group than when working alone. Because generating ideas depends on effort as well as on ability, the productivity loss of brainstorming groups might be due to a motivational loss of individual group members.

(3) *Mutual production blocking*. Mutual production blocking results from the constraint on groups that members of real groups can only talk in turns whereas members of nominal groups can talk simultaneously. Mutual production blocking reduces individual speaking time and due to repeated interruptions, might decrease ability and motivation to generate ideas.

All three explanations were tested experimentally by Diehl and Stroebe (1987). These experiments showed that although evaluation apprehension and free riding affect individual performance, their joint influence in brainstorming groups can only account for a marginal proportion of the productivity loss in group brainstorming. Mutual production blocking was manipulated in an experiment that compared brainstorming performance of real groups and nominal groups with an experimental condition in which members of nominal groups were working alone but were only allowed to speak in turns controlled by red and green signal lights which simulated turn taking. Whereas nominal groups without production blocking produced nearly twice as many ideas as real groups, the performance of nominal groups with production blocking equaled that of real groups.

Further studies showed that the effect of mutual production blocking on brainstorming productivity is not due to a reduction of individual speaking time, but is presumably caused by an impairment of the cognitive processes of idea generation (Diehl & Stroebe, 1991). Thus interpersonal communication in groups decreases instead of increases brainstorming performance. However, this does not preclude the possibility that there is mutual inspiration due to interpersonal communication (*see* CREATIVITY). It may merely reflect the fact that the positive effects of inspiration are typically much smaller than the negative effects of production blocking. Therefore communicating in small groups without mutual production blocking, as is possible in computer networks, might overcome the disadvantages of group brainstorming (*see* COMPUTER-MEDIATED COMMUNICATION).

Experiments on electronic brainstorming (e.g., Gallupe, Bastianutti, & Cooper, 1991) suggest that at some point members of brainstorming groups will enjoy the advantages of inspiration by others, without having the disadvantages of mutual production blocking. Until then, there is nothing else members of problem-solving groups can do but to generate ideas alone and to discuss and evaluate possible solutions in the group: a procedure recommended by the so-called nominal group techniques (e.g., Fox, 1987).

*See also:* COMPUTER-MEDIATED COMMUNICATION; CREATIVITY; GROUP PRODUCTIVITY.

BIBILIOGRAPHY
Diehl, M., & Stroebe, W. (1987). Productivity loss in brainstorming groups: Toward the solution of a riddle. *Journal of Personality and Social Psychology*, 53, 497–509.
—— (1991). Productivity loss in idea-generating groups: Tracking down the blocking effect. *Journal of Personality and Social Psychology*, 61, 392–403.
Fox, W. M. (1987). *Effective group problem solving*. San Francisco, CA: Jossey-Bass.
Gallupe, R. B., Bastianutti, L. M., & Cooper, W. H. (1991). Unblocking brainstorms. *Journal of Applied Psychology*, 76, 137–42.
Osborn, A. F. (1953, 1957, 1963). *Applied imagination*. New York: Scribner.

MICHAEL DIEHL<br>WOLFGANG STROEBE

**buffering hypothesis**  Buffering is the idea that having a particular resource or positive personality quality can serve to protect a person against the adverse impact of a stressful event. An example is the hypothesis that a high level of SOCIAL SUPPORT acts as a buffer against negative effects of STRESS (Cohen &

Wills, 1985). This hypothesis has two parts, which are both important: First, the hypothesis predicts that people who have little social support will have negative reactions (psychological distress, susceptibility to illness, etc.) when they experience high levels of difficult life events, compared to what they experience in the absence of the events. Second, the hypothesis predicts that people who have high levels of social support will *not* have as much negative reaction to the difficult life events (their reaction will not differ so much from what they experience in the absence of the events). The buffering hypothesis is one example of the broader principle of statistical interaction (*see* STATISTICS). As a result, evidence used to support the hypothesis must also take the form of an interaction. In the absence of an interaction, one cannot be sure that buffering is actually taking place (*see* Cohen & Wills, 1985).

*See also*: SOCIAL SUPPORT; STATISTICS; STRESS AND COPING.

BIBLIOGRAPHY
Cohen, S., & Wills, T. A. (1985). Stress, social support, and the buffering hypothesis. *Psychological Bulletin, 98*, 310–57.

CHARLES S. CARVER

**burnout** A type of prolonged response to chronic emotional and interpersonal stressors on the job (*see* STRESS AND COPING). As such, burnout has been an issue of particular concern for human services occupations where:

(1) the relationship between providers and recipients is central to the job; and
(2) the provision of service, care, treatment, or education can be a highly EMOTIONAL EXPERIENCE.

The operational definition (and the corresponding research measure) that is most widely used in burnout research is a three-component model in which burnout is conceptualized in terms of emotional exhaustion, depersonalization, and reduced personal accomplishment (Maslach & Jackson, 1981/1986). Emotional exhaustion refers to feelings of being emotionally overextended and de-

pleted of one's emotional resources. Depersonalization refers to a negative, callous, or excessively detached response to other people, who are usually the recipients of one's service or care. Reduced personal accomplishment refers to a decline in one's feelings of competence and successful achievement in one's work. Thus, burnout can be conceptualized as an individual stress experience embedded in a context of complex social RELATIONSHIPS, and it involves the person's conception of both self and others.

Burnout first emerged as a social problem, rather than a scholarly construct, and so the research that has been done in this area is an example of APPLIED SOCIAL PSYCHOLOGY. The earliest articles, which appeared in the latter half of the 1970s in the United States, presented descriptive information about burnout in a wide variety of human service professions, including health care, social services, mental health, criminal justice, and education. Interviews, observations, and case studies were the primary data sources, and these descriptions were often supplemented by recommendations for coping and preventive strategies. Building on this descriptive base, subsequent theoretical analyses of burnout utilized concepts from both social and clinical psychology (e.g., Cherniss, 1980; Maslach, 1982).

In the next decade, the emphasis shifted to systematic empirical research on burnout, and in particular to the assessment of this phenomenon. Much of this work consisted of self-report data from cross-sectional surveys of large samples, although there were a few longitudinal studies. As burnout became more clearly identified as a form of job stress, with significance for the functioning of ORGANIZATIONS, it received increasing attention from researchers in the field of industrial-organizational psychology (*see* WORK). In addition, burnout began to be noticed by researchers outside the United States. Articles, books, and assessment measures were translated into many languages, and cross-cultural studies were begun. Thus, the burnout literature in the 1990s has outstripped its original American borders, and contains contributions from many European, Canadian, and Israeli researchers (*see* Schaufeli,

Maslach, & Marek, 1993; Kleiber & Enzmann, 1990).

Consistent with the social framework of the major conceptual models, the empirical research on burnout has focused primarily on situational factors. Thus, studies have included such variables as relationships on the job (clients, colleagues, supervisors) and at home (family), job satisfaction, role conflict and role ambiguity, job withdrawal (turnover, absenteeism), expectations, workload, institutional policy, and so forth. Although some demographic and personality variables have also been studied, they appear to be less strongly related to burnout than the situational factors. In terms of antecedents of burnout, role conflict and lack of SOCIAL SUPPORT on the job seem to be important. The effects of burnout are seen most consistently in various forms of job withdrawal and dissatisfaction, and in problems with HEALTH. The level of burnout seems fairly stable over time, underscoring the notion that its nature is more chronic than acute.

In addition to further exploration of these general findings, current research is addressing several new issues. One of these concerns the relationship between the three components of burnout and how they develop over time. Alternative models have been proposed, and the initial empirical evidence suggests that there is a sequential relationship between emotional exhaustion and depersonalization, with reduced personal accomplishment developing separately in response to different factors in the work environment. Another issue concerns diagnostic criteria for burnout. Proposals have been made about possible distinctive symptoms of burnout, with the implication that burnout could be diagnosed and treated at the individual level.

Although most burnout studies continue to focus on human service professionals, some researchers have extended the concept to other types of occupations in the business world and even to nonoccupational spheres of life (such as sports, marriage, and parenting). There is considerable debate about whether or not burnout is a viable construct in these other domains. On the one hand, burnout seems to be specific to the job situation, which would argue against its transfer to other nonjob contexts. On the other hand, the centrality of relationships to burnout would suggest that the concept is more relevant to other interpersonal domains than it is to jobs that have a nonsocial focus.

There is a growing tendency to view burnout as a dynamic process, rather than a static state, and this has important implications for the proposal of developmental models and process measures. These research gains should yield increasingly sophisticated knowledge about the experience of burnout, and will enable both individuals and institutions to deal with this social problem more effectively. *See also*: APPLIED SOCIAL PSYCHOLOGY; EMOTIONAL EXPERIENCE; HEALTH PSYCHOLOGY; ORGANIZATIONS; RELATIONSHIPS; SOCIAL SUPPORT; STRESS AND COPING; WORK.

BIBLIOGRAPHY

Cherniss, C. (1980). *Professional burnout in human service organizations*. New York: Praeger.

Kleiber, D., & Enzmann, D. (1990). *Burnout: 15 years of research: An international bibliography*. Gottingen: Hogrefe.

Maslach, C. (1982). *Burnout: The cost of caring*. Englewood Cliffs, NJ: Prentice Hall.

—— & Jackson, S. E. (1981/1986). *The Maslach Burnout Inventory*. Palo Alto, CA: Consulting Psychologists Press.

Schaufeli, W. B., Maslach, C., & Marek, T. (Eds.) (1993). *Professional burnout: Recent developments in theory and research*. Washington, DC: Taylor & Francis.

CHRISTINA MASLACH

# C

**categorization** The process of classifying things or people as members of a group or category, similar to other members of that category and different from members of other categories. The principles of categorization were first explored by cognitive psychologists for classifying nonsocial information, but many of the same principles can apply, with some modification, to the categorization of social information (for a review, *see* Fiske & Taylor, 1991).

## TWO FUNCTIONS OF CATEGORIES

People categorize a vast range of social and nonsocial objects. Categories can contain examples of birds, professional athletes, emotions, jobs, or friends. People's categories (interchangeably called concepts) help to simplify the world. To consider each new piece of information as unique would require improbably extensive cognitive capacity. Therefore, classifying two or more instances as essentially the same under a category makes sense economically. The more general categories are, the more instances they cover, so fewer categories are needed to classify the world, and the more economical categorization becomes.

But categories also function to provide information. Once a single instance is categorized, people can go beyond the information given about the particular instance, and infer its qualities from its category. For example, once told that a particular animal is a type of horse, a person could infer, from its similarity to other members of the category, that it sleeps standing up. Smaller and more homogeneous categories are more informative because their members reliably share more attributes.

Categories vary inversely in their economy and their informativeness. In general, using fewer, more inclusive categories is more economical, but it is less informative. Depending on people's situational goals, they may favor one of these functions over the other (*see* Komatsu, 1992).

## BASIC ISSUES

The classical view of categorization was that categories had strict boundaries and that membership in the category required necessary and sufficient features. If an instance possessed these necessary and sufficient features, it was in the category. If it did not, it was not. The classical view also implied that category membership is discrete. In this view, items were clearly in or out of a category, and there was no possibility of being more or less of a member (Smith & Medin, 1981).

Psychologists abandoned the classical view as work on categorization indicated that natural categories do not seem to have necessary and sufficient defining features, and their boundaries are much looser than implied by the classical view. For example, one might describe the category "chair" as a piece of furniture on which people sit; it has legs, a back, and a seat. But people would still recognize as a chair the less typical instances: a stool (with no back), a doll's chair (on which people cannot sit), or a beanbag chair (with no back or legs). Therefore, categories are said to have fuzzy boundaries, and no one feature is necessary for membership in a category. More typical members of a category fall clearly within the boundaries (such as a desk chair), but other, less typical, instances may be less clear category members (such as a tree stump that might serve as a place to sit while camping). People are more likely to disagree on category membership for cases that are less typical or not clearly within the boundaries.

Prototype models (also called family resemblance or probabilistic models), were developed to accommodate these shortcomings of the classical view. A PROTOTYPE is the central tendency or average of a variety of category members, and it is the most typical member of a category. Prototypes are abstract conceptions that may not exist in the world. In the prototype view category membership is assessed by its "family resemblance." In this view, all members of a category share at least one, and usually several, features with others, and yet no single feature is common to all category members (Rosch & Mervis, 1975). The instance (perhaps hypothetical) with the most features in common with all category members is the prototype.

Under the family resemblance view, a new instance is classified by the features it shares with other category members. Features that are shared by many of the category members are given more weight in judging family resemblance. The more features a new instance shares, the more typical it is judged to be, and the more quickly and consistently it will be classified as belonging to that category. Strict rules of inclusion into a category do not apply here, and some instances will be harder to categorize, especially if they share few features with the prototype. Under prototype models, then, categories can be defined as fuzzy sets centering on a prototype.

Categories are thought to be organized hierarchically (Rosch, 1978). A broad category (vehicles) may include subcategories (such as cars, buses, and trucks). These subcategories might include smaller categories (e.g., four-door cars, city buses, pickup trucks). Different levels of categorization are useful for different purposes, but people commonly refer to basic, intermediate levels in everyday conversation. For example, people would be more likely to refer to a "car" than to a "vehicle" or a "four-door car." These basic-level categories are assumed to provide an optimum balance between the functions of economy and informativeness: They are large enough to save effort, and small enough to be informative.

## SOCIAL CATEGORIES

People categorize other people just as they might classify an object. Categories for social information include, for example, categories of social roles, personality traits, and social situations. Social categories, like nonsocial categories, may also be viewed as fuzzy sets centering on a prototype, where people's social prototypes are the average of many behavioral and personality features (Cantor & Mischel, 1979). For example, a prototypic extrovert may possess such features as talking to strangers, being energetic, or acting outgoing.

Like their nonsocial counterparts, social categories may also be seen as hierarchically organized, with broader categories including more instances and attributes. For example, under the broad category "athletes," one might have the subcategories "tennis pro" and "football player." In a strict hierarchy, lower-level, specific categories inherit defining attributes from upper-level, general categories, but not vice versa. For example, the upper-level category "athlete" may contribute the attributes "strong" and "hard-working" to the lower-level category "tennis pro," but the tennis player may have attributes, such as "quickness" and "carries a racket," that may not be true of athletes in general.

Just as people tend to use intermediate, basic-level categories when referring to objects, there may be a common, basic level of social categorization as well. For example, "nun" may be a basic level category under the higher-level category of "religious devotee." Basic level categories tend to be differentiated from other similar categories, quite detailed in content, and concrete in application. Thus, they are more commonly used in everyday conversation. Talking about a "nun" is more concrete than mentioning a "religious devotee," but not so specific as referring to a "Benedictine nun." People choose an intermediate level that maximizes both economy and informativeness.

Social situations, such as weddings or birthday parties, tend to be categorized the same way as information about people. They are centered around prototypes and embedded in hierarchies. A person might have a category centered around a prototypical wedding, and this category might be subsumed by the broader category of "celebrations." One of the most useful ways to categorize people may be a person–situation compound episode (Cantor & Kihlstrom, 1987). It is easier to imagine certain kinds of people in their most common situations, such as a tennis pro at a country club or a nun in a worship service.

Negative traits or traits on which people are extreme seem to be more diagnostic in social categorization. For example, learning that a person earned four PhDs in three years or that someone refused a two-million-dollar bribe would make relevant categorization (as intelligent or honest, respectively) more likely. Like extreme behaviors, negative behaviors (such as lying or being irritable) also tend to stand out and are more diagnostic (*see* NEGATIVITY EFFECTS).

CRITICISMS AND EXTENSIONS OF THE PROTOTYPE MODEL
As prototype models of social categories have been increasingly widely cited and studied, many criticisms have been raised. First, people may not always use prototypes to decide membership. Sometimes people see extremes or ideals as the best representatives of a category. For example, the best example of a tennis pro may not be the most typical one, but instead may be the Wimbledon champion.

Critics have also questioned a number of claims about the hierarchical nature of social categories. Although the hierarchical model posits that a basic, intermediate level is most commonly used in categorization, it may be true that people's use of hierarchical levels depends on their specific goals, knowledge, or context. For example, a woman looking for a date may have a specific, low-level category in mind (nice-looking, good dancer, tall).

Social categories also do not seem to be as cleanly organized as nonsocial information, with subcategories fitting neatly under higher levels. Hierarchies predict that attributes at upper levels will be passed on to subcategories, but not vice versa, and that upper levels of the hierarchy provide richer information. But data on social categories do not always support these predictions. Social ca-

tegories probably do not follow hierarchies at all. Instead, the arrangement of categories may be better described as a tangled web of associations, with overlapping features, idiosyncratic sharing of attributes, and fuzzy boundaries (Cantor & Kihlstrom, 1987).

EXEMPLAR MODELS
The exemplar approach to categorization was developed in response to the shortcomings of the prototype model (*see* Smith & Medin, 1981, for a review). Instead of defining category membership in relation to an average of typical features, the exemplar model states that people remember specific instances of category members. A new instance is compared to several remembered instances to verify category membership. If the new instance is similar to remembered instances, it will be included in the category.

The exemplar model has some explanatory advantages over the prototype model. First, it describes how people can answer new questions about or demonstrate specific knowledge of their categories. For example, when asked if restaurants usually have cashiers, one might review several different examples of restaurants to find the answer.

Another theoretical advantage of the exemplar model is that it accounts for variability within a category. People can consult the exemplars of their categories to determine how much variance a category has. A single prototype cannot account for such knowledge of variation. Because it explains people's knowledge of variance, the exemplar view also allows for people's knowledge about correlations among attributes in a category. For example, people may know that the traits "ambitious" and "hardworking" go together, while "ambitious" and "kind" do not necessarily covary. A prototype alone could not contain such information about covariation.

Exemplar models also allow more easily for changes in categories. Adding a new instance to one's collection of exemplars can change the category, and thus change future category judgments. In contrast, it is not clear how prototype models account for change in categories.

## EXEMPLARS AND PROTOTYPES: A RESOLUTION?

Although research on both exemplars and prototypes has been successful, it is unlikely that either of them alone will be able to account for all categorization processes. People probably use both kinds of representations when they consider their categories. New or unusual instances are likely to be stored as exemplars, but people can also make abstractions about general category membership, so they use both, often depending on the situation (Cantor & Kihlstrom, 1987).

Exemplars and prototypes may be used to different extents, depending on people's goals and circumstances. An exemplar representation may be a more basic or automatic process, because people tend to use it when they are under cognitive load. Exemplars are also used more by children. People are more likely to use exemplars and prototypes to represent their own groups, but to use only prototypes to represent groups to which they do not belong. Thus, when people know less about something (such as an outgroup), they may rely more on an abstract category prototype.

Recognizing that both prototypes and exemplars are probably used at different times reflects the complexity of social cognition. People need both a fuzzy, core concept and a knowledge of the variability within a category in order to have the flexibility to operate in a social world.

## EXPLANATION-BASED VIEWS OF CATEGORIZATION

Recently, psychologists have begun to explore an explanation-based view of categorization. The models described above (classical, prototype, and exemplar) describe categorization in terms of the perceived similarity of instances to each other or to an abstract prototype. These models could be grouped as similarity-based models. The newer explanation-based view adds that people's knowledge of categories specifies how they are related to other categories and how members within a category are related to each other. The relationships within and among categories can be causal, narrative, or explanatory. For a non-social example, members of the category "bird" share in common a causal relationship: an underlying genetic code that causes them, under normal circumstances, to develop feathers, wings, and hollow bones.

Explanation-based views account for instances that have no important features in common with other category members, yet are nonetheless categorized with them. For example, a bird that accidentally loses its wings and feathers is still categorized as a bird by most people, even though it shares few important features with other birds. What this bird does share is a genetic code for wings and feathers. This causal explanation, not its current features, is the basis for its categorization as a bird (*see* Komatsu, 1992, for a review).

Social psychology has incorporated explanation-based views mainly by emphasizing the role of narrative and causal explanation (Lalljee, Lamb, & Abelson, 1992) (*see* SCRIPTS). People can make sense of the features of a stimulus by creating a story that connects them. People on JURIES connect evidence by constructing stories. Victims of traumatic life events also use narrative to interpret and cope with the experience. And people use prototypical event sequences to explain common events. By its focus on relationships, the narrative view is similar to the SCHEMA concept. But while schemas emphasize the relationships among particular features of a schematic stimulus, explanation-based views deal more with underlying theories that unite the members of a category.

## EFFECTS OF CATEGORIES ON SOCIAL COGNITION

Whether categorization occurs through comparison to a prototype, similarity to exemplars, or fit to a theory, category membership can be important in people's thinking about social events. Categorization of social information cues the use of schemas. Categorization is a first step: before applying a schema, people must decide if a person or situation fits a category. As it is usually studied, the contents of a category are members of the class. In contrast, as usually studied, the contents of a schema center more on describing the various attributes shared by class members. The concept of categorization emphasizes initial classification, whereas the concept of schema emphasizes the application of prior knowledge to understand and elaborate the information given. The two concepts and the resulting research do however overlap to a great extent.

Because categories can cue schemas, they also serve to cue varied stereotypes. People categorize easily on the basis of ingroups and outgroups (ethnicity, gender, age, and the like). Simply being told that they are a member of a group causes people to emphasize the homogeneity of the outgroup and emphasize the variability in the ingroup (*see* OUTGROUP HOMOGENEITY). People also polarize judgments about people in an outgroup (*see* STEREOTYPING).

Much social cognition research has explored the circumstances under which people rely more on categories or more on the perceived data as provided by a stimulus. Current models state that the more motivated people are to make an accurate impression of another person, the more they look at the data and the less they rely on category-based generalizations (Brewer, 1988; Fiske & Neuberg, 1990). This does not guarantee accuracy, but it does encourage attribute-based impressions.

Finally, the prototypes people have may help in everyday decision making. For example, when people decide whether or not they would be happy in a certain job, they might compare their prototypic selves to the prototypic person in that job category. This decision-making strategy is especially likely among people who are attuned to their inner selves, called low self-monitors (*see* SELF-MONITORING).

*See also*: JURIES; NEGATIVITY EFFECTS; OUTGROUP HOMOGENEITY; SCHEMAS/SCHEMATA; SCRIPTS; SELF-MONITORING; STEREOTYPING.

BIBLIOGRAPHY

Brewer, M. B. (1988). A dual process model of impression formation. In T. K. Srull & R. S. Wyer, Jr. (Eds.), *Advances in social cognition* (Vol. 1, pp. 1–36). Hillsdale, NJ: Lawrence Erlbaum.

Cantor, N., & Kihlstrom, J. F. (1987). *Personality and social intelligence*. Englewood Cliffs, NJ: Prentice Hall.

——— & Mischel, W. (1979). Prototypes in person perception. In L. Berkowitz (Ed.), *Advances in experimental social psychology* (Vol. 12, pp. 3–52). New York: Academic Press.

Fiske, S. T., & Neuberg, S. L. (1990). A continuum of impression formation, from category-based to individuating processes: Influences of information and motivation on attention and interpretation. In M. P. Zanna (Ed.), *Advances in experimental social psychology* (Vol. 23, pp. 1–74). New York: Academic Press.

——— & Taylor, S. E. (1991). *Social cognition* (2nd ed., chapter 4). New York: McGraw-Hill.

Komatsu, L. K. (1992). Recent views of conceptual structure. *Psychological Bulletin, 112*, 500–26.

Lalljee, M., Lamb, R., & Abelson, R. P. (1992). The role of event prototypes in categorization and explanation. In W. Stroebe & M. Hewstone (Eds.), *European review of social psychology* (Vol. 3, pp. 153–82). Chichester: J. Wiley.

Rosch, E. H. (1978). Principles of categorization. In E. Rosch & B. B. Lloyd (Eds.), *Cognition and categorization* (pp. 27–48). Hillsdale, NJ: Lawrence Erlbaum.

——— & Mervis, C. B. (1975). Family resemblances: Studies in the internal structure of categories. *Cognitive Psychology, 7*, 573–605.

Smith, E. E., & Medin, D. L. (1981). *Categories and concepts*. Cambridge, MA: Harvard University Press.

SUSAN T. FISKE
BETH A. MORLING

**catharsis** The reduction or elimination of emotionality through either direct or vicarious acting out of emotionally relevant behavior. Although the concept is often invoked in popular psychology, little empirical evidence for it has been reported.
*See also*: AGGRESSION; AROUSAL.

RUSSELL G. GEEN

**causality** A goal of many studies in social psychology is to demonstrate the causal impact of the independent variable on the dependent one. In a formal sense, arguments for causality must make three claims: time precedence of the independent variable to the dependent one, covariation between the two, and the demonstration that the covariation is not due to some other variable that is a common cause of both the independent and dependent variables (Kenny, 1979). Only randomized experimental designs or EXPERIMENTATION permit the researcher to make all three claims, assuming that a reliable relationship between the independent and dependent variables is observed (*see* METHODOLOGY).

Claims of causality must be considerably more circumspect if designs other than experimental ones are used. Often researchers construct "causal models" based on purely correlational data. Such descriptions are misnomers, however. Although the models may represent the causal sequence of effects that the researcher believes to exist, no model or analysis can be used to argue for causality with purely correlational data. Arguments for causality must be based on research design considerations, not data analytic procedures.
*See also*: EXPERIMENTATION; METHODOLOGY.

BIBLIOGRAPHY
Kenny, D. A. (1979). *Correlation and causality*. New York: Wiley.

CHARLES M. JUDD

**close relationships** Those relationships in which participants are highly involved with each other are generally termed "close." The dimensions of involvement may vary widely, so that the literature reveals many different operational definitions of closeness. Some theories rely on high levels of particular interpersonal processes, such as INTIMACY, emotional impact, mutual caring and concern, love, or mutual knowledge. Another approach defines closeness in terms of partners' degree of INTERDEPENDENCE. For example, Kelley et al. (1983) proposed that relationships are close to the extent that partners exert causal influence over each other. They specified four markers of causal influence: frequency, intensity,

diversity, and duration. Thus, relationships are considered close if the participants interact often, influence each other strongly across many different activities, and have done so for a relatively long time. A third, more descriptive account is based on lay conceptions of closeness, such as affection, mutual understanding, and frequency of conversation or shared activity. Common to all these approaches is the notion that closeness involves intensification of the various interpersonal processes that generally characterize RELATIONSHIPS.
*See also*: INTERDEPENDENCE; INTIMACY; RELATIONSHIPS.

BIBLIOGRAPHY
Kelley, H. H., Berscheid, E., Christensen, A., Harvey, J. H., Huston, T. L., Levinger, G., McClintock, E., Peplau, L. A., & Peterson, D. R. (1983). *Close relationships*. New York: W. H. Freeman.

HARRY T. REIS

**coalition formation** The process by which three or more parties decide on alliances among themselves. Research on this process usually involves EXPERIMENTAL GAMES methodology. Most studies examine how the distribution of resources across the parties affects the composition of the coalitions that form and the division of gains within these coalitions.
*See also*: EXPERIMENTAL GAMES.

DEAN G. PRUITT

**cognitive consistency** The general notion that people prefer congruence or consistency among their various cognitions, especially among their BELIEFS, VALUES, and attitudes. When consistency does not occur, people experience discomfort, strain, or tension and are motivated to restore consistency. A variety of cognitive consistency theories exist that deal with inconsistency in slightly different ways. While all sharing the common assumption that people dislike inconsistency, they differ about either the source of the inconsistency, the nature of the motivational state that inconsistency creates, or the consequences of the inconsistency.

## BALANCE THEORY

BALANCE THEORY (Heider, 1946) was perhaps the first of the consistency theories. Heider was influenced by the GESTALT tradition in the field of perception and sought to show the influence of perceptual gestalts in the field of SOCIAL PERCEPTION. He argued that people perceive the social world in terms of perceptual units of belongingness and referred to such belongingness as "unit" relations. In addition, people have "sentiment" relationships to stimulus objects in their social environments – which, of course, include other people. They can feel positively toward others with verbs such as like, love, approve, and so forth, or negatively with relationships such as dislike and disapprove. These sentiments can be described symbolically such that when someone likes or feels positively about another person, then pLo or, alternatively when someone feels negatively, the expression may be written as pDLo, where p stands for the perceiver, o another person, and L or DL represents the liking or disliking relationship. Similarly, the relationship to objects in the environment, including inanimate objects or abstract ideas, may be expressed as pLx or pDLx, where x represents the object in the environment.

Heider posits that people prefer relationships that fit well with each other. When perceivers survey their social worlds, they prefer sentiments that fit together, especially with regard to stimuli to which they are related. Thus, assuming that p feels a connection to o (expressed as pUo), then it is important that their sentiments be consistent. Schematically, if pLo, p prefers o to reciprocate the positivity, oLp. This is also true with regard to p's and o's feeling about an attitude object, x. If pLo and pLx, then p prefers a situation in which oLx. That is, if the perceiver likes another person(o) and feels positively about an issue (x), the perceiver will prefer it if the other person also feels positively about that issue (oLx).

If consistency or balance does not obtain, then there is a "strain toward balance." People are motivated to alter their sentiments or reorganize their social perceptual units in order to restore balance. Most of the research following Heider's model has been based on an analysis of the sentiments with little attention paid to unit relationships. Many investigators have found it useful to use a simple algebraic rule to determine if a set of relationships is balanced. It is possible to multiply algebraically the signs connecting the people and objects in the relationship. If the algebraic multiplication is positive, the relationship is balanced. If negative, the relationship is imbalanced. As an example, if a set of relationships consists of pLo, pLx, and oLx, there are three positive relationships. Algebraically, the multiplication of three (+) signs is positive. Thus, the set of relationships is balanced. If the set contains a negative sign such as pLo, pLx, but oDLx, then the result of the multiplication of these three signs is negative and is indicative of an imbalanced state. In an imbalanced relationship, the strain toward balance causes people to feel uncomfortable and motivates them to change one of more of the sentiments so that balance is restored.

Figure 1 depicts an example of a balanced and an imbalanced relationship.

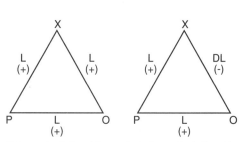

| Balanced relationship | Imbalanced relationship |

Figure 1. Representations of balanced and imbalanced relationships.

Heider's balance theory is known for the power of its ideas and the interest that it spawned in the problem of consistency. It did not lead to an abundance of studies designed to test it. Jordan's (1953) work is perhaps the most influential of the early empirical research. Jordan described 64 triadic relationships to subjects that consisted of all of the possible unit and sentiment relationships. He asked them to rate the degree of pleasantness or unpleasantness in each relationship. Subjects rated the triads consistently with the predictions of balance theory. Those that were conceptually imbalanced were rated as more unpleasant than those that were balanced.

In later years, researchers (e.g, Insko, 1981) examined some of the implicit assumptions of balance theory. For example, should it be assumed that if a person likes another, that they necessarily feel they are in a unit relationship? And, if they do not experience the unit relationship, do the gestalt rules of balance apply? Insko has shown that such issues as the probability of future interaction may cause the dyad to be perceived as a unit or not to be so perceived. The rules of balance, which generally operate on the affective sign of the sentiment relation, may require the appropriate unit assumptions in order for them to operate on attitudes and interpersonal perceptions.

## SYMMETRY

A model of cognitive consistency that is similar in many respects to Heider's is Newcomb's symmetry model. A "strain toward symmetry" exists when people perceive that their attitudes toward people and/or objects are inconsistent. The strain causes activity on the part of the perceiver to restore symmetry. Newcomb's consistency model, unlike Heider's, is based on a principle of learned instrumentality. It is useful to have one's cognitions in symmetrical relations. It helps people negotiate their social world and is also useful in helping people validate their opinions.

In his seminal study, Newcomb (1956) studied friendship patterns among a group of previously unacquainted students in a university dormitory. Newcomb examined the degree of interpersonal ATTRACTION among the students over time. He found that liking for a particular person was predicted by two primary factors. First was the degree of assumed liking of the individual by the other student. In short, if a student believed he was liked by another student, he tended to reciprocate the liking. Second was the similarity of each student's attitudes toward issues, people, and objects. The more similar the

attitudes, the more positive were students' attitudes toward each other. Looked at as a dyadic relationship, people preferred symmetry within the dyad. If a particular student was liked by a peer and if both students had similar attitudes toward an issue, then symmetry existed. To the extent that symmetry did not exist, there was pressure to communicate (i.e., convince, cajole) to achieve that symmetry.

## SYMBOLIC PSYCHO-LOGIC

A variation of the balance and symmetry models of consistency was provided by Abelson and Rosenberg (1958) in their model of Symbolic Psycho-logic. Like balance theory, it focuses on the strain that exists for people to restore consistency among their cognitions or cognitive categories. Psycho-Logic uses the concept of "relationship" to refer to a combination of Heider's sentiment and unit notions. Verbs such as liking, possessing, and favoring all connote positive relationships while terms of negation such as opposes, dislikes, and prevents connote negative relationships. Cognitive relations are seen as balanced whenever two positively valued concepts are positively related, two negatively valued concepts are positively related or whenever a positively and a negatively valued concept are negatively related. The Psycho-Logic model of cognitive consistency allows for greater complexity in people's responses to imbalance. As in the previous models, if relationships are not in balance, the balance can be restored by changing the direction of the relationship. Disliking can become liking; opposing can become favoring. But there are other, more subtle, possibilities as well. Faced with imbalance, a person can redefine the cognitive categories to make them unrelated or ignore the imbalanced categories by not thinking about one of them when confronted with the other. A person who likes a favorite dessert, believes that dessert will cause weight gain and who also believes that weight gain is bad has the potential for imbalanced cognitive categories. As with other models, balance can be restored directly by changing the sign of one of the relationships. Alternatively, the imbalance can be dealt with by deciding that ice cream is one of those desserts that do not cause weight gain, thus rendering those two cognitive categories irrelevant. Or, one can make certain never to think about gaining weight when downing one's favorite flavor of ice cream.

## AFFECTIVE–COGNITIVE CONSISTENCY

While balance and symmetry theories addressed consistency across attitudes in dyadic and triadic relationships, Rosenberg (1960) proposed a theory of AFFECTIVE–COGNITIVE CONSISTENCY to account for consistency within attitudes. This theory of attitude structure holds that attitudes are comprised of an affective and a cognitive component. The affective component is the pattern of feeling that is aroused by the attitude object while the cognitive component is the set of beliefs about the degree to which an attitude object helps or hinders the attainment of those values. In Rosenberg's view, the affective and cognitive components of an attitude must be congruent with each other. ATTITUDE CHANGE occurs when an attitude becomes unstable – i.e., when there is inconsistency between the affective and cognitive components. For example, if there is a change in the belief structure that links the attitude object to a value, there will be a change in the attitude toward the object to restore consistency.

## CONGRUITY PRINCIPLE

The Congruity Principle of Osgood and Tannenbaum (1955) is a further step in the development of consistency theories. It deals with the consistency between the evaluation of an attitude object and the evaluation of a source of communication. Osgood had developed a method known as the SEMANTIC DIFFERENTIAL by which concepts or objects could be placed in semantic space on a number of dimensions, including potency, evaluation, and activity. The most robust of those dimensions was the *evaluative* dimension, accounting for most of variance in the early research. The evaluative dimension is what is usually thought of as the attitude.

The congruity principle asserts that people seek consistency or congruity in their evaluations of concepts and sources. Congruity differs from other consistency models in at least two ways. First, it emphasizes evaluation of the source of communication and considers that factor to be as important as the evaluation of the concept itself. Thus, a positively evaluated source who espouses a negatively evaluated position may be the stimulus that undergoes change in the eye of the evaluator just as much as, if not more than, the position. Second, congruity emphasizes the concept of intensity. The congruity principle holds that evaluative changes to restore congruity will occur inversely to the intensity of evaluation. A communicator who is held in high esteem with great intensity will be less likely to have her or his evaluation lowered as a function of espousing a position which an audience evaluates negatively but with much less strength.

The mediating mechanism for the congruity principle was not based on gestalt preferences as in balance theory or on internal tension states postulated by dissonance theory. Instead, congruity is based on the presumption that people learn to make cognitive representations of stimulus objects and that these representations are associated with hedonic evaluations. The result of two simultaneous but incongruous representations – e.g., a source of communication and an attitude object – is a compromise that ultimately results in congruity.

## DISSONANCE THEORY

The theory that probably took the broadest perspective on consistency and produced more data as well as controversy is Festinger's (1957) COGNITIVE DISSONANCE THEORY. According to dissonance theory, people experience unpleasant psychological tension if they perceive that their cognitions are psychologically inconsistent. Cognitions are thought to be any knowledge about one's own attitudes, beliefs, values, and so forth, or about the physical and social world. In this theory, then, attitudes are only one source – albeit an important one – of grist for the consistency mill. To the extent that a person holds a pair of cognitions such that one follows from the obverse of the other, then the person experiences cognitive dissonance. Unlike the balance and symmetry models, dissonance theory allowed for predictions of different magnitudes of tension. The greater the discrepancy between and among cognitions, and the more important the cognitions involved in the discrepancy, then the greater the dissonance. The more cognitions that are consonant with a given cognition, the less the dissonance. Dissonance, then, is directly proportional to the magnitude and importance of discrepant cognitions and inversely proportional to the magnitude and importance of a person's consonant cognitions.

Dissonance, being physiologically arousing and psychologically uncomfortable, motivates a person to find ways to reduce it. The greater the magnitude of dissonance, the greater the magnitude of change. People typically reduce dissonance by changing the cognition that is least resistant to change, or by adding consonant cognitions.

Dissonance theory is a general model of MOTIVATION based on the consequences of inconsistency. It is also thought of as a theory of attitude change because an attitudinal cognition often serves as the dependent variable in dissonance studies. For example, if a person is induced to act in a way that is inconsistent with his or her attitudes, dissonance is aroused. The uncomfortable tension state can be reduced by a change in cognition. Since it is considerably easier to change a cognition about one's private attitude than it is about a publicly committed behavior, changes of attitudes are what typically result from attitude–behavior inconsistency.

Festinger and Carlsmith established the basic paradigm of research involving counterattitudinal behavior in a procedure they referred to as FORCED COMPLIANCE. Experimental subjects were induced to say something publicly that was contrary to their attitudes. In addition, they were offered either a small or a large incentive for making the counterattitudinal statement. Their attitudes were then assessed. It was predicted and found that people changed their attitudes to make them consistent with their behavior, but only if their statement was made for the small rather than the large inducement. Other research in dissonance has demonstrated that

people change their attitudes following a choice between two alternative products or courses of action, that people come to like that for which they suffer, that they come to dislike an activity that they had insufficient reason to refrain from engaging in, and that they seek social support following the disconfirmation of an important belief (see Wicklund and Brehm, 1976, for a review.)

VALUES–ATTITUDES–BEHAVIOR MODEL
Rokeach (1980) argued for theoretical approaches to consistency that use the concept of value. While most of the consistency theories examine consistency of attitudes with one another, or consistency of attitudes and behaviors, Rokeach argues that values play a more fundamental role than either attitudes or behaviors. He views attitudes as relatively enduring evaluative predispositions to favor or oppose a particular object or situation. However, he defined values as "shared prescriptive or proscriptive beliefs about ideal modes of behavior and end-states of existence that are activated by, yet transcend object and situation" (1980, p. 262). Thus, beliefs about goodness and evil, about salvation or about equality are exemplars of the concept of values. Rokeach holds that people strive toward cognitive consistency within a hierarchically structured system that places values at the top of the hierarchy. In the empirical work conducted on his Values–Attitudes–Behavior model, Rokeach and his colleagues have shown impressive degrees of value–attitude and value–behavior consistency across a broad array of specific issues and domains.

CONCLUSION
Theories of cognitive consistency were among the first systematic attempts to examine the relationships among people's cognitions. On the one hand, they are theories of cognitive structure because they examine the "fit" among different types of cognitions. For some theories, the fit between different types of elements – such as the fit between values and attitudes or attitudes and behaviors – took center stage. For other theories, the structure of a complex cognition

such as an attitude in terms of the consistency of its elements was the focus. On the other hand, cognitive consistency theories also function as theories of attitude change because they posited hypothetical mechanisms to deal with the consequences of the failure to achieve consistency. Whether the mechanism functioned on drive-like arousal, gestalt preferences, learning, or strains, the search to achieve consistency is the hallmark and defining characteristic of the cognitive consistency approach to attitude change.

See also: ATTITUDE CHANGE; ATTRACTION; COGNITIVE DISSONANCE THEORY; MOTIVATION; SOCIAL PERCEPTION; VALUES.

BIBLIOGRAPHY

Abelson, R. P., & Rosenberg, M. J. (1958). Symbolic psycho-logic: A model of attitudinal cognition. *Behavioral Science, 3*, 1–13.

Festinger, L. (1957). *A theory of cognitive dissonance.* Stanford, CA: Stanford University Press.

Heider, F. (1946). Attitudes and cognitive organization. *Journal of Psychology, 21*, 107–12.

Insko, C. A. (1981). Balance theory and phenomenology. In R. E. Petty, T. M. Ostrom, & T. C. Brock (Eds.), *Cognitive responses in persuasion* (pp. 309–38). Hillsdale, NJ: Lawrence Erlbaum.

Jordan, N. (1953). Behavioral forces that are a function of attitudes and cognitive organization. *Human Relations, 6*, 273–88.

Newcomb, T. M. (1956). The prediction of interpersonal attraction. *American Psychologist, 11*, 575–86.

Osgood, C. E., & Tannenbaum, P. H. (1955). The principle of congruity in the prediction of attitude change. *Psychological Review, 62*, 42–55.

Rokeach, M. (1980). Some unresolved issues in theories of beliefs, attitudes, and values. *Nebraska symposium on motivation, 1979* (Vol. 27, pp. 261–304). Lincoln, NE: University of Nebraska Press.

Rosenberg, M. J. (1960). An analysis of affective-cognitive consistency. In C. I. Hovland & M. J. Rosenberg (Eds.), *Attitude organization and change: An analysis of consistency among attitude components* (pp. 15–64). New Haven, CT: Yale University Press.

Wicklund, R. A., & Brehm, J. W. (1976). *Perspectives on cognitive dissonance.* Hillsdale, NJ: Lawrence Erlbaum.

JOEL COOPER

**cognitive dissonance theory**  When people perceive that two or more of their cognitions are inconsistent, the internal state of cognitive dissonance arises. Festinger (1957) proposed his theory of cognitive dissonance to account for the consequences of such inconsistency. He held that people experience dissonance as a state of psychological tension which, like the drive states of hunger and thirst, needs to be reduced.

In the terms of the original theory, a cognition was defined as any knowledge, opinion, or belief about the environment, about oneself, or about one's behavior (Festinger, 1957, p. 3). Thus, anything a person knows can serve as a cognition. People have a myriad of cognitions. Most of those cognitions, considered in pairwise comparisons, are not logically or psychologically related to one another and thus can be said to be in irrelevant relationships with each other. Alternatively, many cognitions are consistent in the sense that one member of the pair follows from the other. A person who knows it is cold outside and perceives that she is wearing a coat has a pair of consonant cognitions. Finally, Festinger defined the dissonant relationship between a pair of cognitions: The "two elements are in a dissonant relation if, considering these two alone, the obverse of one element would follow from the other" (p. 13). A person who perceives she is wearing a bathing suit while standing in the cold holds dissonant cognitions. Recognition of the dissonant cognitions would place a person in the psychologically uncomfortable state of cognitive dissonance. Like other psychologically uncomfortable states, people are motivated to reduce the discomfort.

Cognitive dissonance shares much in common with other BALANCE or COGNITIVE CONSISTENCY theories. One hallmark of the dissonance formulation, however, is that dissonance is conceived to have a magnitude. Considering a pair of inconsistent cognitions that a person may hold, the magnitude of dissonance is a function of the importance of the cognitions. More dissonance is experienced when the cognitions are important than when they are trivial. Thus, a person may experience a great deal of psychological tension by advocating a position on abortion that he or she does not agree with than by advocating a preference for a bar of candy that is actually contrary to the person's attitudes.

The magnitude of dissonance is conceived in the total context of cognitions relating to a particular cognitive element. Dissonance varies as a function of the proportion of cognitive elements that are consonant with a given cognition compared to the proportion of elements that are discrepant from that cognition. The higher the proportion of elements that are discrepant, the greater the dissonance. The higher the proportion of consistent elements, the smaller the dissonance. A person who advocates an increase in the income tax rates will experience dissonance the more elements he or she has that are inconsistent with that position. For example, he or she may think about the loss of personal income that will ensue from the advocated increase. On the other hand, the person may think of reasons that are consistent with the advocacy: Programs that he/she agrees with can be supported.

Putting the features together, we can offer a more formal definition of the magnitude of dissonance: The magnitude of dissonance relevant to a particular cognition is directly proportional to the number of cognitive elements discrepant with that cognition and inversely proportional to the number of cognitions consonant with that cognition, each weighted by its importance. A person is motivated to reduce cognitive dissonance as a function of the total magnitude of the dissonance. How this can be accomplished will now be addressed by examining some of the typical research patterns, or paradigms, that have proved to be useful and informative in dissonance research.

RESEARCH IN THE FREE CHOICE PARADIGM

Cognitive dissonance is an ubiquitous, post-decisional phenomenon. It occurs whenever we make decisions. Much of the early research in dissonance theory considered the situation of people who were permitted to make free choices among alternative course of action. Whenever such choices are made, dissonance exists as a natural consequence. Consider a person who wishes to make a decision between two automobiles – e.g., a full-size Saab and a small Fiat. Prior to making the decision, the person considers all of the elements as dispassionately and as objectively as possible. After talking to people and reading the consumer magazines, the person concludes that Saabs are reliable, well built, and contain many state-of-the-art safety features, all elements that are positive reasons to purchase that car. On the other hand, they are too conservative for this person's taste and their repair costs are high. The small Fiat, on the other hand, has the attractive feature of being fuel efficient and comes in colors that the person finds very attractive. On the other hand, the small Fiat is difficult for the whole family to fit into and is not as safe as the larger sedan. The person makes the choice to purchase the Saab.

With the decision made, cognitive dissonance follows. All of the attractive features of the Fiat have been foreclosed by the choice and all of the unattractive features of the Saab now have to be lived with. Each of those cognitions is discrepant from the cognition that the person has purchased the Saab and thus helps to create the unpleasant tension state of dissonance. How can the dissonance be reduced? In general, dissonance can be reduced by changing cognitions, adding cognitions, or altering the importance of the already existing cognitions.

Consider the individual experiencing dissonance from freely choosing to buy the Saab. The individual can change his or her position from disliking the conservative image of the Saab to one in which its conservative flair is actually liked and appreciated. Alternatively, the person can add new cognitions that would support the purchase, perhaps by reading magazines devoted to Saab's qualities. Finally, he or she can change the importance of the existing cognitive elements, perhaps by deciding that safety is the most significant feature to consider when purchasing a new car. Any one of these strategies would lower the dissonance and allow this individual to enjoy the new purchase.

The seminal research supporting dissonance reduction in the free choice paradigm was provided by Brehm (1956). He predicted that the conclusion of the cognitive changes, additions, and alterations that followed a choice would lead the chosen alternative to become even more attractive following a decision than it had been prior to the choice, and that the rejected alternative would decrease in attractiveness. He had research subjects make choices between two consumer products that they could take home as a gift. Brehm obtained attractiveness ratings of the items before and after the decisions had been made and found, as predicted, that the items were perceived to be further apart after the decision than they had been prior to the decision. Brehm also found that the spreading apart of the alternatives was significantly greater if the choice was between two items that had been perceived nearly equally attractive prior to the choice than for items whose choice was easy to begin with. This finding offered strong support for the predictions of dissonance theory. A difficult choice between nearly equally attractive items meant that there were necessarily more cognitions discrepant with the choice than when the items were clearly different in their prechoice attractiveness. The difficult choice aroused more dissonance, and people engaged in more cognitive changes to reduce the magnitude of tension.

## THE PSYCHOLOGY OF FORCED COMPLIANCE

The paradigm of research that has come to be known as the forced compliance paradigm has been perhaps been the most widely studied situation in dissonance theory. Festinger and Carlsmith (1959) set the original scenario: They had subjects participate in a very tedious experimental task. Then, they requested the subjects to tell a person in the waiting room that the task was actually fun and exciting. Subjects complied, working hard to convince the person waiting for the study that an exciting experience could be

anticipated. Subjects' cognitions that the task was dull were discrepant from their public statement that it was fun and interesting. Counterattitudinal behavior can be expected to create dissonance. How can the dissonance be reduced? Festinger and Carlsmith reasoned that the most straightforward possibility was for the subject to change the attitudinal cognition and decide that the task was, in fact, fun and exciting. That way, the statement would no longer be discrepant from the subject's attitude.

Festinger and Carlsmith went further by offering the subjects a financial incentive for making the counterattitudinal statement. Half of the subjects were offered a large incentive and half were offered a trivial sum of money. Since the incentive served as a cognition consonant with the counterattitudinal behavior and its importance varies with its magnitude, it was predicted that subjects would be more motivated to change their attitude if they had been offered only a small incentive rather than a large incentive. The small incentive would not serve as an important consonant cognition, thus the magnitude of dissonance would be higher and more ATTITUDE CHANGE would be obtained. This is precisely what Festinger and Carlsmith found. Attitudes changed following counterattitudinal behavior as an inverse function of incentive magnitude. This inverse function has become the hallmark prediction of research in the induced compliance paradigm.

## THE PSYCHOLOGY OF EFFORT JUSTIFICATION

Dissonance theory predicts that people are motivated to justify expenditures of unpleasant effort by believing that they love that for which they suffered. Imagine a person who works hard, expends considerable effort and possibly some humiliation in order to join a club. The negative aspects of the initiation are discrepant from an overriding cognition that people like hedonically pleasing events rather than negative ones. Imagine, too, the possibility that the club is only moderate in its attractiveness. The person suffers considerable dissonance. All of the negative features of the initiation are dissonant with the person's desire to engage in pleasant activities. One way to reduce the magnitude of dissonance is to change his or her cognition about the attractiveness of the club. The more attractive the club – i.e., the goal for whose attainment the person suffered – the more it can serve as a consonant cognition.

Aronson and Mills (1959) had subjects attempt to join a sexual discussion club. In order to achieve entry, they needed to pass a "screening test'. That tests differed in their level of embarrassment depending on the condition to which subjects were assigned. In a Low Effort condition, the test was very easy, requiring subjects to read some words with mild sexual innuendo. However, subjects in a High Effort condition found themselves in a situation in which they had to read aloud some sexually explicit words and passages. After subjects passed the tests, they overheard a discussion being held by the group they had just suffered in order to join. The group discussion was boring, tedious, and unattractive. Consequently, subjects who suffered – i.e., who expended a great deal of effort in order to join – were theoretically in a state of considerable dissonance. In order to reduce their dissonance, subjects in the High Effort condition changed their opinion of the group, finding the members and the discussion to be much more attractive than did subjects in the Low Effort condition. In general, then, suffering leads to liking because a change in the level of attractiveness of a goal is at the service of reducing the tension of cognitive dissonance.

## INSUFFICIENT JUSTIFICATION

Cognitive dissonance also applies to people who choose to refrain from an activity. Consider a child who refrains from playing with an attractive toy or who refrains from taking a biscuit when left unguarded by its parent. Refraining from the attractive activity is discrepant with the desire to engage in the activity. These two cognitions, considered alone, create dissonance. Aronson and Carlsmith (1963) asked children to refrain from playing with an attractive robot toy. Some of the children were given a firm admonition with a strong threat against playing with the

robot. Other children were given a mild threat to refrain from playing. Dissonance theory predicts that children who had only a mild threat did not have sufficient justification to refrain from playing. They needed to change their opinion about the attractiveness of the toy, thereby reducing their dissonance. Children in the High Threat condition already knew why they were not playing with the attractive toy: The adults had provided ample threat. Aronson and Carlsmith found that children who refrained from playing with only a mild threat devalued the toy more than subjects in the High Threat condition. Having insufficient justification for refraining from engaging in the activity, they reduced their dissonance by changing their attitude about the activity.

## QUALIFICATIONS AND MODIFICATIONS TO THE FORMULATION

Dissonance theory is easiest to understand in its original version. When people act in ways that provide inconsistent cognitions, the arousal state of dissonance ensues. However, research has demonstrated that the simple version of dissonance needs amplification. For example, it is now clear that counterattitudinal advocacy does not always lead to dissonance. It requires the provision that people freely choose to engage in the behaviors and that the consequences of those behaviors be foreseeable. It is also true that people must feel committed to their counterattitudinal advocacy and that the advocacy must have some discernible unwanted or aversive consequence (see Cooper & Fazio, 1984, for a review.)

## TENSION AND DISSONANCE

Dissonance theory posits that people engage in changes of cognitions in order to reduce unpleasant tension. Several alternative theories were spawned to account for the same phenomena that dissonance theory had predicted, but without the need to posit an internal motivational state. Among these were SELF-PERCEPTION THEORY which holds that people's attitudes are often a function of their behavior and the environmental pressures that gave rise to that behavior. Bem applied self-perception to counterattitudinal behavior and demonstrated the plausibility that dissonance results – particularly, those in the induced compliance paradigm – may be a function of self-perception processes (*see* Cooper and Fazio, 1984, for a review). In a different vein, Tedeschi, Schlenker, and Bonoma made a compelling case that the results of dissonance research may be due to people's desire to present themselves in a positive light to others. Called IMPRESSION MANAGEMENT, this theory also eschewed any need to posit tension or psychological discomfort on the part of an actor in a dissonance situation (*see* Schlenker, 1980, for a review).

Subsequent research has shown that dissonance does indeed have psychological and physiological arousal properties. Zanna and Cooper (1974) used a misattribution approach to demonstrate that arousal occurs in the dissonance process and that it is necessary to motivate attitude change. Croyle and Cooper were able to measure the physiological consequences of dissonance through changes in skin conductance responses (*see* Cooper & Fazio, 1984).

## MODERN VERSIONS OF DISSONANCE

Cognitive dissonance theory has undergone a number of revisions. Three will be mentioned here. The first was introduced by Aronson (1969). His version of dissonance theory posits that the SELF is always involved in dissonance arousal. Counterattitudinal advocacy is dissonant not just because a position a person espouses is contrary to his or her attitude. It leads to dissonance because a person with generally high SELF-ESTEEM finds him or herself doing something that has negative implications for the self. Do moral and worthy people do something that is in opposition to their attitudes? Since the answer to that is negative, Aronson's self-esteem view is that people will change their attitudes in order to restore their positive view of themselves.

A different view was taken by Cooper and Fazio (1984) in their theory of dissonance motivation. Cooper and Fazio's theory was presented as a way to incorporate the importance of such variables as choice, foreseeability, and aversive consequences that several decades of empirical research had shown to be important in the dissonance process. They hold that dissonance is created whenever people accept responsibility for bringing about an aversive event. They take the position that counterattitudinal advocacy creates dissonance because such advocacy often results in an aversive consequence. However, it is the consequence – and the acceptance of personal responsibility for bringing about that consequence – that causes dissonance to be aroused.

In a variation of Aronson's and Fazio and Cooper's notion, Steele (1988) suggested the theory of self-affirmation. This theory takes as its premise that people feel unworthy after having brought about an aversive consequence or after having engaged in counterattitudinal advocacy. What they seek is affirmation of their own goodness as human beings. Changing one's attitudes to bring them in line with one's behaviors is a way of affirming oneself. Steele has demonstrated that if other affirmations are available, people may use them and forego attitude change because it is affirmation, not consistency, they seek.

## CONCLUSIONS

Cognitive dissonance theory has generated thousands of research studies since its introduction in 1957. It holds that people are aroused when they perceive that they hold inconsistent cognitions and that they will take measures to reduce that arousal. Several alternative positions have been offered to explain the source of the motivation. Nonetheless, the theory has generated provocative hypotheses in a number of areas including induced compliance and effort justification.

*See also*: ATTITUDE CHANGE; COGNITIVE CONSISTENCY; IMPRESSION MANAGEMENT; SELF; SELF-ESTEEM; SELF-PERCEPTION THEORY.

BIBLIOGRAPHY

Aronson, E. (1969). The theory of cognitive dissonance: A current perspective. In L. Berkowitz (Ed.), *Advances in experimental social psychology* (Vol. 4, pp. 1–34). New York: Academic Press.

Aronson, E., & Mills, J. M. (1959). The effect of severity of initiation on liking for a group. *Journal of Abnormal and Social Psychology, 12,* 16–27.

Aronson, E., & Carlsmith, J. M. (1963). Effect of the severity of threat on the devaluation of forbidden behavior. *Journal of Abnormal and Social Psychology, 66,* 583–8.

Brehm, J. W. (1956). Post-decision changes in desirability of alternatives. *Journal of Abnormal and Social Psychology, 52,* 384–9.

Cooper, J., & Fazio, R. H. (1984). A new look at dissonance theory. In L. Berkowitz (Ed.), *Advances in experimental social psychology* (Vol. 17, pp. 229–62). New York: Academic Press.

Festinger, L. (1957). *A theory of cognitive dissonance.* Evanston, IL: Row Peterson.

—— & Carlsmith, J. M. (1959). Cognitive consequences of forced compliance. *Journal of Abnormal and Social Psychology, 58,* 203–10.

Schlenker, B. R. (1980). *Impression management: The self-concept, social identity and interpersonal relations.* Monterey, CA: Brooks/Cole.

Steele, C. M. (1988). The pschology of self affirmation: Sustaining the integrity of the self. In L. Berkowitz (Ed.) *Advances in experimental social psychology* (Vol. 21; pp. 261–302). Orlando, FL: Academic Press.

Zanna, M. P., & Cooper, J. (1974). Dissonance and the pill: An attribution approach to studying the arousal properties of dissonance. *Journal of Personality and Social Psychology, 29,* 703–9.

JOEL COOPER

**commitment** Diverse literatures define commitment as the binding of an individual to a specific line of activity. RELATIONSHIPS researchers discuss commitment in terms of cohesiveness, desire to maintain a relationship, feelings of attachment, and continuance decisions; organizational researchers adopt similar definitions of commitment in WORK settings (*see* Rusbult & Buunk, 1993). In addition to orienting individuals toward the future, commitment stands as an enduring, internalized macromotive that promotes a relationship's long-term well-being by motivating a variety of maintenance behaviors (e.g., accommodation, derogation of alternatives). Existing theories emphasize four classes of variable that strengthen commitment:

(1) greater satisfaction – degree to which a relationship gratifies important needs and exceeds one's generalized expectations;

(2) poorer alternatives – perceived attractiveness of specific alternatives or the option of noninvolvement;

(3) greater investments – importance of resources that are directly invested in a relationship (e.g., time, effort), or become indirectly linked to it (e.g., identity, material goods); and

(4) greater prescriptive support – strength of personal or normative obligations that dictate persisting.

Importantly, commitment can lead individuals to persist at a relationship in the absence of positive feelings: Voluntary commitment involves dedication to persist at a desirable line of behavior; nonvoluntary commitment involves obligation to persist at an undesirable line of behavior (*see* Thibaut & Kelley, 1959).

*See also*: INTERDEPENDENCE THEORY; RELATIONSHIPS; WORK.

BIBLIOGRAPHY

Rusbult, C. E., & Buunk, B. P. (1993). Commitment processes in close relationships: An interdependence analysis. *Journal of Social and Personal Relationships, 10,* 175–204.

Thibaut, J. W., & Kelley, H. H. (1959). *The social psychology of groups.* New York: Wiley.

CARYL E. RUSBULT

**communication** A process of exchanging messages in a social environment entailing cognitive activity, affective states, and behavioral outcomes. This process is one of the fundamental components of social behavior; through NONVERBAL COMMUNICATION, LANGUAGE, SOCIAL EXCHANGE, and the MASS

MEDIA, communication is the central mechanism for social organization.

Two broad and to some extent opposing conceptions of human communication have guided scholarly inquiry in this century. From one perspective communication entails transmission of information from a source to a receiver; thus, there is "information flow" through a channel or medium which can result in receiver "knowledge gain." Information is a physical entity that can be subdivided into discrete "chunks" or "bits," which are potentially quantifiable. The concern here is with how much information can be imparted and with what degree of efficiency or effectiveness.

The second perspective suggests that communication is a process of symbolic exchange serving to stimulate or generate meanings. The emphasis here is upon symbols (arbitrary, conventional elements that refer to things, ideas, actions, etc.) and upon meanings (inferences about symbols and their referents). Although it is quite possible to conduct quantitative studies of the uses and effects of symbols, referential meanings are not easily broken into discrete "bits." Moreover, the meanings of a single word can be highly variable from person to person and from context to context. Messages do not transmit information; rather they confirm or disconfirm receivers' hypotheses about a source's intended meaning.

APPROACHES TO COMMUNICATION

There are two general approaches to the study of communication. The empirical paradigm emphasizes the scientific method for assessing the effects of messages that are transmitted from an encoder to a decoder over some channel or medium. The critical paradigm focuses on the production and exchange of meanings that occur in a sociocultural context. Historically, the empirical approach to communication has developed alongside social psychology, specifically in the work of Hovland, Lewin, Festinger, and Newcomb. Consequently, our focus will be on the empirical approach.

Within the broad field of empirical communication research, there are meta-theoretical orientations that characterize and distinguish the pursuits of different groups of scholars. Thus, some researchers examine "microscopic" communication variables, while others examine communication variables that are "macroscopic." This distinction refers to the level of analysis undertaken in research. For example, a number of studies have examined the details of eye-gaze behavior in same- and mixed-sex interaction; others have scrutinized lexical choices in the creation of newspaper headlines. On the other hand, researchers have studied social network patterns at a general level, ignoring the details of interpersonal messages; and they have analyzed the forms and functions of mass media institutions, attending to large-scale structures and processes.

Another orientational difference can be labeled "mediated versus nonmediated communication." This suggests that some entities (messages) that transmit information or generate meaning are produced by multiple parties and flow in one direction across considerable stretches of time and space, while others are produced spontaneously and on-the-spot in face-to-face contexts. The nature and qualities of messages produced in these different types of situations will typically differ; there are highly stylized advertisements on the one hand and rambling, unedited tirades on the other. The effects of mediated and nonmediated messages may differ also. For example, observers will usually attribute high levels of intentionality to mediated messages, whereas they may not make this sort of attribution for particular nonmediated messages − as in the case of an inebriated person shouting obscenities. Finally, mediated messages are characterized by the inability of the source to monitor and adjust for immediate audience response, the limited opportunities for the receiver to respond with feedback, the fact that an organization within an industry is producing these messages, and of course the large size of the audience. Certain characteristics of both mediated and nonmediated messages can be found in COMPUTER-MEDIATED COMMUNICATION where messages transcend time and space and allow for spontaneity among multiple sources and receivers.

Still another difference is: message analysis versus message effects. Thus, one can examine a series of advertisements or conversations for recurrent themes. Persons who conduct CONTENT ANALYSIS of messages are often interested in making inferences about the intention or purpose of message sources. In the absence of supportive extra-message data, such inferences may be hazardous. More hazardous still are inferences about the effects of messages based upon message content. The content of a message is not represented isomorphically in receivers' memories or beliefs; the fact that a violent world is depicted on television does not ensure that viewers will believe in the ubiquity of violence. On the other hand, the effects of message substance and style can be studied directly. Typically, this is done by conducting experiments in which message features are manipulated and their effects (e.g., on ATTITUDE CHANGE) observed. Examples of *substantive features* include: number and strength of arguments, ratio of violent to nonviolent acts depicted, types of persuasive appeals, emotional content, and use or nonuse of evidence to support claims. Examples of *stylistic features* include: image intensity, language intensity, lexical diversity, formality of presentation, the visual pacing of images, and message complexity.

## INTERPERSONAL COMMUNICATION

In the realm of interpersonal or nonmediated communication, important topics of inquiry include: the nature and consequences of messages designed to gain compliance, message-based IMPRESSION FORMATION, and DECEPTION. Thus, some communicators attempt to create an impression of authoritativeness by exaggerating or falsifying their expertise in order to get others to behave in particular ways. With regard to compliance gaining, many studies have examined the strategies that people use when attempting to get their way (Burgoon, 1990). For example, communicators may use promises (indicating rewards contingent upon performance of the desired behavior), threats (indicating punishments), or appeals to the respondent's personal or moral obligation. Other studies have examined subjectively salient features of situations in which COMPLIANCE-gaining attempts occur, such as "intimacy" and "dominance" and their effect on a compliance gainer's choice of strategies. Still other studies have investigated the effectiveness of particular strategic choices, e.g., the "FOOT-IN-THE DOOR" technique (a small initial request followed by a larger one) and the "DOOR-IN-THE-FACE" technique (a large initial request followed by a smaller one). Comparatively little research has been done on the effects of specific lexical choices in the production of compliance-gainiang strategies (Ng & Bradac, 1993).

A large number of studies have explored the effects of communicators' lexical choices (and other linguistic features) upon impressions formed by message recipients. (Of course impression formation and lexical choice are linked – creating a favorable impression may enhance one's chances of getting one's way.) There appear to be two major social dimensions underlying impressions of communicators: status and solidarity; the former term refers to social position, whereas the latter refers to approachability or social distance. A focus upon communicator personality leads to impressions of high or low competence and warmth. Several language variables have been shown to affect judgments of status, competence, etc. (Ng & Bradac, 1993). For example, nonstandard dialects (e.g., Black English vernacular) typically lead to lower status and competence ratings than do standard dialects, but may lead to higher ratings of solidarity and warmth, especially in informal contexts. Status and competence ratings will also be enhanced by use of a high level of lexical diversity; in this case there is no evidence that a low level of diversity will enhance solidarity ratings.

When planning a message designed to gain compliance or create a particular impression, a communicator may be truthful or deceive the mesage recipient. Deceptive messages may be constructed by omitting crucial information, falsifying information, and by using ambiguity to obscure the communicator's intent. Much of the research on deceptive communication has focused upon the problem of detection: what communicative behaviors lead to accurate receiver inferences about deceptive or nondeceptive intent? For example, de Turck and Miller (1985) found that increased hand gestures, speech errors, pauses, and response latency were objective indicators of deception under a condition of high communicator arousal. A later study (de Turck and Miller, 1990) showed that knowledge of these indicators enabled naive respondents to detect deception with considerable accuracy. Apart from the question of accurate detection, there are a number of communicative behaviors that naive respondents *believe* to be linked to deceptive intent: averted gaze, rapid speech, postural shifting, and a slow response rate (Friedman & Tucker, 1990).

These communication processes, i.e., compliance gaining, impression formation, and deception, along with other processes, are explained (tentatively and incompletely) by various theories. For example, SELF-PERCEPTION THEORY indicates that a person who complies with a large request after complying with a smaller one does so because of a change in self-perception induced by the initial act of compliance. On the other hand, communication accommodation theory specifies that a speaker who converges to another speaker's style will create an impression of relatively high attractiveness or solidarity because this communicative act will typically be seen as an attempt to highlight similarities between the two speakers. According to uncertainty reduction theory the formation of an impression in this case (and others) emerges from a basic human drive to explain and predict the behavior of other persons. Finally, politeness theory explains some deceptive acts as attempts to protect the message recipient's "positive face," e.g., the desire to be perceived as skilled and competent (even if one is not).

## MASS COMMUNICATION

Research in mediated communication is characterized by an assessment of the influence of mass media messages on audiences' cognition, attitudes, and behaviors. The mass media play an important role, alongside everyday experience and interpersonal contact, in how individuals form beliefs about their social reality. Research on social reality and the mass media has sought to demonstrate an association between the amount of cumulative television viewing, and predictable biases and beliefs about the real world (Gerbner et al., 1986). The notion that television viewing cultivates a particular social reality is based on two premises: first, that there is a consistent systematic bias in television messages over-representing the likelihood of violence and emphasizing traditional gender roles, racial stereotypes, and depictions of family life; and second, that this content is learned and applied to beliefs about the real world.

Social reality is a more specific case of a larger process of SOCIALIZATION, wherein individuals learn social norms, expectations, and ways of interpreting meaning, and behaving socially. Research in mass media and socialization dates back to the Payne Fund studies of movies and youth conducted in the 1930s, and continues to focus primarily on children and adolescents who are seen as a unique and vulnerable audience because of their lack of experience, less developed cognitive capacities, and their basic trust and curiosity (Roberts & Maccoby, 1985).

The mass media have been viewed as both positive and negative socialization agents in society. Antisocial effects of the mass media on individuals are the result of unintentional consequences of exposure to messages containing portrayals of VIOLENCE, GENDER roles, and social STEREOTYPES. By far the bulk of the research has focused on the effects of violent television on AGGRESSION, and a wide array of measures and controls indicate that there is a correlation between exposure to violent media, and aggressive attitudes and behaviors. Experimental research using short film clips, entire films and television programs has demonstrated that young children can learn and acquire novel and complex behaviors from media messages. In addition violent messages may result in the disinhibition of previously learned behaviors and the desensitization to violent fare. Finally, the SOCIAL LEARNING perspective indicates the likelihood that a learned act will be performed is often determined by the perceived rewards and/or costs that are likely to accrue from the act. Among the potential prosocial benefits of mass media exposure that have begun to be researched are educational achievement and development, the learning of altruistic and cooperative behavior, and CREATIVITY.

PERSUASION and information campaigns have a long and eventful history in social psychology and communication, beginning with Hovland's message-effects framework. This research employed four categories of factors: characteristics of the source of a message, attributes of the message itself, receiver characteristics, and channel or medium attributes. Source characteristics such as credibility, expertise, trustworthiness, POWER, and attractiveness have been found to be significant predictors of attitude change, independent of the attributes of a particular message. Among the message factors promoting attitude change are the complexity or comprehensibility of a message, the number of arguments contained, FEAR APPEALS, the repetitiveness of a message, the inclusion of one-sided or two-sided arguments, the style of presentation, including verbal and nonverbal message factors, and the salience of a message. In addition to message factors, attributes of the medium or channel are important, with the focus on differences between nonmediated and mediated communication, or between print and audio-visual media such as film and television. The conceptualization of the audience has shifted from a concern with demographic variables such as gender, education, and intelligence, to include more cognitive concepts, including involvement, individual goals, AVAILABILITY, AUTOMATICITY, and ATTENTION. These concepts are central to the ELABORATION LIKELIHOOD MODEL of persuasion, which focuses on central and peripheral processing goals and strategies as indicators of the message attributes individuals attend to and of subsequent attitude change.

A number of the effects of the mass media on social psychological processes may be explained in part by the following theories. The *theory of agenda setting* addresses how ideas and issues receiving the greatest prominence in the mass media come to be the issues and problems with which the public is most concerned. Both the frequency and placement of news stories are significantly related to the issues the public deems to be the most important issues and problems facing the nation (Iyengar & Kinder, 1987). Consequently, agenda setting may influence both what people think about, and the importance they ascribe to a particular social problem.

The *spiral-of-silence theory* focuses on how the popularity of an issue as represented by the media influences individuals' attitudes, and ultimately, their own issue orientations. This theory is based on the assumptions that people shun isolation, and therefore tend to express their own opinions only when they see their views as being consonant with those in the majority (Noelle-Neumann, 1984). Consequently, how the media report public opinion on an issue will lead to the predominance of the majority view. This is because those in the minority will tend to be less vocal, decreasing their social influence and culminating in a spiral process leading to the acceptance of one opinion and the rejection of dissenting opinions.

Finally, the *third-person effect* addresses how individuals overestimate the effects that a media message will have on others by comparison with themselves (Davison, 1983). In this process individuals mistakenly presume the media to have a powerful effect on others in society. As a result the media may have an impact on individuals' judgments, even when they regard themselves as uninfluenced. This phenomenon has been demonstrated in studies of media libel, election campaigns, and attitudes toward social issues such as pornography and apartheid.

While the majority of communication research falls into the domain of either interpersonal or mass communication, the comparative influence of these communication modes has a long research tradition. These date to the early Lazarsfeld studies of political campaigns and voting behavior which concluded that media influence is mediated by interpersonal networks of exchange dominated by opinion leaders. Interpersonal communication has also been viewed as a complement to or a reinforcement of mass media effects, with media messages serving as a source of information that people talk about, potentially increasing their effect.

Differences in impact between the two communication modes may be dependent upon the issues and judgments being affected. Interpersonal channels have the greatest impact on personal-level decisions where there are real-world consequences for a person, while the mass media are more influential for more abstract, societal-level phenomena. The distinction between interpersonal and mass communication is therefore in some respects an artificial one that fails to capture communication as a rich process involving a number of information sources, a distinction that ultimately serves to inhibit theory construction about communication.

*See also*: AGGRESSION; ATTENTION; ATTITUDE CHANGE; ATTITUDES AND BEHAVIOR; AUTOMATICITY; COMPUTER-MEDIATED COMMUNICATION; CONTENT ANALYSIS; CREATIVITY; DECEPTION; GENDER; IMPRESSION FORMATION; LANGUAGE; MASS MEDIA; NONVERBAL COMMUNICATION; POWER; SELF-PERCEPTION THEORY; SOCIAL LEARNING; SOCIALIZATION; STEREOTYPING.

BIBLIOGRAPHY

Burgoon, M. (1990). Language and social influence. In H. Giles & W. P. Robinson (Eds.), *Handbook of language and social psychology* (pp. 51–72). Chichester: J. Wiley.

Davison, W. (1983). The third-person effect in communication. *Public Opinion Quarterly, 47*, 1–15.

deTurck, M. A., & Miller, G. R. (1985). Deception and arousal: Isolating the behavioral correlates of deception. *Human Communication Research, 12*, 181–201.

—— (1990). Training observers to detect deception: Effects of self-monitoring and rehearsal. *Human Communication Research, 12*, 181–201.

Friedman, H. S., & Tucker, J. S. (1990). Language and deception. In H. Giles & W. P. Robinson (Eds.), *Handbook of language and social psychology*, (pp. 257–70). Chichester: J. Wiley.

Gerbner, G., Gross, L., Morgan, M., & Signorielli, N. (1986). Living with television: The dynamics of the cultivation process. In J. Bryant & D. Zillmann (Eds.), *Perspectives on media effects* (pp. 17–40). Hillsdale, NJ: Lawrence Erlbaum.

Iyengar, S., & Kinder, D. R. (1987). *News that matters*. Chicago, IL: University of Chicago Press.

Ng, S. H., & Bradac, J. J. (1993). *Power in language*. Newbury Park, CA: Sage.

Noelle-Neumann, E. (1984). *The spiral of silence: Public opinion – our social skin*. Chicago, IL: University of Chicago Press.

Roberts, D. F., & Maccoby, N. (1985). Effects of mass communication. In G. Lindzey & E. Aronson (Eds.), *Handbook of social psychology* (Vol. 2, pp. 539–98). New York: Random House.

SETH GEIGER
JAMES BRADAC

**communication game** In the "communication game" approach to interpersonal communication, communication is conceptualized as a "game" – an organized system of social actions and interactions involving social roles, rules, and goals (Higgins, 1981). This approach views interpersonal communication as a "social" action that is pursued to achieve social goals, involves taking other people into account, and requires following social conventions of language use within social settings. This approach contrasts with an "information transmission" approach, inspired by mathematical models of communication, that emphasized the transmission of information from a sender (as the message encoder) to a recipient (as the message decoder). The "communication game" approach presented a perspective that integrated the insights and findings on language by sociologists, anthropologists, and other social scientists and philosophers (e.g., Grice, 1975; Gumperz & Hymes, 1972).

Historically, "game"-like perspectives on interpersonal communication have described communication in terms of four general characteristics:

(1) shared patterns of expectations, rules, or conventions concerning the participants' social roles and appropriate language use, which require that both the linguistic and extralinguistic context be taken into account;

(2) coorientation and monitoring between the participants, with each participant taking the others' characteristics into account;

(3) functions that include, in addition to information transmission, creating and defining relationships among the participants; and

(4) social interaction processes in which the participants collaboratively determine the purpose and social reality of the interchange.

The communication game literature has also proposed general rules of the game for message communicators and recipients. For communicators the general rules are:

(1) take the recipient's (or the audience's) characteristics into account;
(2) convey the truth as you see it;
(3) try to be understood (coherent and comprehensible);
(4) give neither too much nor too little information;
(5) be relevant (stick to the point);
(6) be appropriate to the communication context and circumstances; and
(7) be appropriate to your communicative intent or purpose

For recipients the general rules are:

(1) take the communicator's (or the source's) characteristics into account;
(2) determine the communicator's communicative intent or purpose;
(3) take the communicative context or circumstances into account;
(4) pay attention to the message and be prepared for receiving it;
(5) try to understand the message and;
(6) provide feedback to the communicator (when possible) concerning your interpretation or understanding of the message.

In addition to these general rules, there are general social interaction goals pursued in the communication game. These include initiating and maintaining social bonds (social relationship goals), achieving a common or shared definition of social reality (social or shared reality goals), maintaining and managing one's own and others' esteem for oneself (IMPRESSION MANAGEMENT goals), accomplishing specific tasks (task goals), and enjoying the intrinsic pleasures of communication (entertainment goals).

The "communication game" provides a framework for relating interpersonal language use and SOCIAL COGNITION (*see* Higgins, 1981, 1993). Early research taking this perspective focused on how communicators' goals and sensitivity to their recipient's characteristics influenced their description of another person (the message topic), and how this description, in turn, later influenced their own memory, impression, and evaluation of the person they had described. More generally, researchers with a communication game perspective study how the characteristics of both the communicator and the recipient, including their interpersonal relations, influence message formulation and production. They also examine how social cognition influences, and is influenced by, interpersonal communication (*see* Schwarz & Strack, 1991).

*See also*: CATEGORIZATION; IMPRESSION MANAGEMENT; SOCIAL COGNITION.

BIBLIOGRAPHY

Grice, H. P. (1975). Logic and conversation. In P. Cole and J. L. Morgan (Eds.), *Syntax and semantics* (Vol. 3): *Speech acts* (pp. 365–72). New York: Seminar Press.

Gumperz, J. J., & Hymes, D. (Eds.), (1972). *Directions in sociolinguistics: The ethnography of communication.* New York: Holt, Rinehart & Winston.

Higgins, E. T. (1981). The "communication game": Implications for social cognition and persuasion. In E. T. Higgins, C. P. Herman, & M. P. Zanna (Eds.), *Social cognition: The Ontario symposium* (pp. 343–92). Hillsdale, NJ: Lawrence Erlbaum.

—— (1992). Achieving "shared reality" in the communication game: A social action that creates meaning. *Journal of Language and Social Psychology, 11,* 107–132

Schwarz, N., & Strack, F. (Eds.) (1991). *Social cognition and communication: Human judgment in its social context.* Special Issue in *Social Cognition, 9.* New York: Guilford Press.

E. TORY HIGGINS

**comparison levels**   *see*   INTERDEPENDENCE THEORY.

**complementarity** The complementarity hypothesis proposes that persons with dissimilar but compatible traits will be attracted to each other. For example, people with dominant personalities should complement, and therefore be attracted to, partners who are submissive. Despite the plausibility of this notion, evidence for its applicability in close relationships is limited.

*See also*: ATTRACTION.

HARRY T. REIS

**compliance** SOCIAL INFLUENCE that leads to changes in the recipient's overt behavior in the direction intended by the source (but may or may not lead to private ATTITUDE CHANGE) is defined as producing public compliance. Compliance results when the source controls desired outcomes and can monitor the recipient's behavior.

*See also*: ATTITUDE CHANGE; SOCIAL INFLUENCE.

JOHN C. TURNER

**computer-mediated communication** This term covers a range of systems and software which use computer networks to facilitate communication among individuals, groups, and organizations (e.g., electronic mail, computer conferencing, and groupware). Developments in this technology and in its scope and degree of penetration are transforming the structure and functioning of ORGANIZATIONS and thus the very nature of organization itself (Fulk & Steinfield, 1990; Kiesler, Siegel, & McGuire, 1984; Lea, 1992; Sproull & Kiesler, 1991). Computer-mediated communication (CMC) opens up global access to people and information (e.g., via electronic bulletin boards), frees group decision making from the constraints of time and space (via asynchronous electronic mail), and provides new technologies of collaboration (e.g., computer-supported cooperative work). It has been applied in the office, the classroom and the home, or as a way of linking between these environments. The impact of CMC systems on individual and organization need

not necessarily be beneficial or consistent with expectations, of course (*see* Lea, 1992; Sproull & Kiesler, 1991), and although they have necessarily lagged behind technical developments, social psychological analyses of this medium undoubtedly have a critical role to play in helping us understand its social effects.

An analysis of the social effects and uses of COMMUNICATION via computer begins with an understanding of its distinctive properties as compared to other media, and typically face-to-face interaction. Most approaches converge on the idea that the channel of communication is more restricted in CMC compared to other media, being characterized by reduced "bandwidth," reduced "information richness," reduced "social presence," fewer "social context cues," and so forth. Despite some degree of consensus about the properties of CMC, views diverge as to their consequences for the communication process and with respect to their social effects. On the one hand, what might loosely be termed the rationalist perspective (*see* Lea, 1991) tends to emphasize those properties of CMC that define it as a fast and efficient communications medium that eliminates extraneous and even biasing social "noise," allowing for a more productive, task-oriented focus. On the other hand, this filtering of information can also be seen to have deleterious consequences by cutting out those very social and normative cues which regulate and moderate social interaction (e.g., Kiesler et al., 1984). According to this view CMC is in certain respects quite an inefficient, and even clumsy communications medium, in which feedback delays, lack of feedback cues, and the limited scope for expression in the medium cause frustration and "flaming" – the display of uninhibited language and behavior in CMC.

Research by Kiesler and her associates has drawn on both of these themes to help explain another important social psychological effect of CMC, namely that decision making in CMC tends to result in more GROUP POLARIZATION compared to face-to-face interaction (*see*, e.g., Kiesler et al., 1984). Reducing social cues is argued to have two general effects which result in the exchange of more extreme arguments in line with the persuasive arguments explanation of group polarization. First, it is thought to reduce normative constraints on the articulation of extreme arguments by removing cues to LEADERSHIP, status, and POWER, and by inducing a state of DEINDIVIDUATION, associated with the expression of antinormative behavior. Second, the absence of social cues, and the protection of anonymity afforded by CMC, are associated with more equal participation, again facilitating the exchange of views. Although early studies were consistent with this analysis, subsequent research has questioned whether CMC really is so devoid of social context cues and has argued for more normative explanation of group polarization in CMC (*see* Lea, 1992). According to this line of argument, although CMC may reduce individual or interpersonal cues, the isolation and anonymity associated with CMC may actually accentuate the salience of social identities thought to underlie more normative explanations of group polarization (*see* SELF-CATEGORIZATION THEORY). This would suggest that CMC is a much more social and socially sensitive medium than hitherto supposed.

A number of studies do, however, confirm that CMC results in greater equality of participation in CMC (*see* Sproull & Kiesler, 1991) although it is less clear whether this means that CMC actually undermines hierarchical power structures or power differentials in organizational and decision-making terms. Researchers also have to be wary of generalizing from laboratory studies in which operationalizations of status and power are likely to be weaker and have less long-term consequences than in the organizational settings (Sproull & Kiesler, 1991). The effects produced by CMC are likely to be complex and grounded in organizational culture and practices, especially if the influence of normative context is stronger than is implied by the reduced social cues perspective (Lea, 1992).

Meanwhile, the reduced social cues tradition has prompted a more differentiated and task-specific approach to the suitability of CMC as a communications medium (Lea, 1991). Research has explored those organizational contexts and domains that might be particularly well-tailored to the distinctive features of CMC and those considerations that influence media choice (see, e.g., Fulk & Steinfield, 1990). It has thus been argued that CMC is more geared to formal and routine "cognitive" tasks with other "information-rich" media (e.g., telephone, face-to-face) being more suitable for issues that have social and emotional content (*see* Lea, 1991). However, this verdict is again partly a product of the rationalist/restrictive perspective on CMC; field studies suggest that there may often be a gap between the tasks for which CMC is (pre)defined as being best suited and the manner and the domains in which it is actually used. The popularity of CMC as a means of informal exchange, as a means for creating on-line identities, and as a channel for expressing criticism and organizing protest, suggest that it is a flexible medium capable of being put to social and recreational use. Such findings suggest that it is important to be wary of formalist and rationalist assumptions concerning the properties of media such as CMC and rather that one should to see how they are used (or abused) in practice as a function of social context and social relations.

*See also*: COMMUNICATION; DEINDIVIDUATION; LEADERSHIP; ORGANIZATIONS; POWER; SELF-CATEGORIZATION THEORY.

BIBLIOGRAPHY

Fulk, J., & Steinfield, C. (Eds.) (1990). *Organizations and communication technology.* Newbury Park, CA: Sage.

Kiesler, S., Siegel, J., & McGuire, T. W. (1984). Social psychological aspects of computer-mediated communication. *American Psychologist, 39,* 1123–34.

Lea, M. (1991). Rationalist assumptions in cross-media comparisons of computer-mediated communication. *Behavior and Information Technology, 10,* 153–72.

—— (Ed.). (1992). *Contexts of computer-mediated communication.* Hemel Hempstead: Harvester.

Sproull, L., & Kiesler, S. (1991). *Connections: New ways of working in the networked organization.* Cambridge, MA: MIT Press.

RUSSELL SPEARS

**conflict** This term has two meanings. One ("overt conflict") places conflict out in the open, as a physical or symbolic confrontation in which one party's words or actions are opposed by another (Deutsch, 1973). The other ("conflict of interest") places conflict inside the head, as a situation in which two parties' goals cannot be simultaneously achieved (Rubin, Pruitt, & Kim, 1994). (More than two parties may be involved, but two-party conflict is the most commonly studied.) These two kinds of conflict are related, in that conflict of interest often produces overt conflict, as postulated by REALISTIC CONFLICT THEORY. But conflict of interest can produce other reactions as well, including yielding, conciliation, and inaction; and overt conflict has other antecedents, including perceived value dissimilarity and ANGER.

Conflict, in both meanings, occurs at all levels of society, from individuals to nation states. Above the level of the individual, conflict of interest often involves collective goals, shared by group members, that result from a perception of collective rights, collective deprivation, or collective jeopardy. Conflict between groups is often more intense than that between individuals because of SOCIAL IDENTITY, DEINDIVIDUATION, ILLUSORY CORRELATION, and GROUP POLARIZATION effects (*see* Stroebe, Kruglanski, Bar-Tal, & Hewstone, 1988).

There are three basic procedures for dealing with conflict of interest: struggle, in which one or both parties try to win by means of political or physical actions; BARGAINING, in which they seek a verbal agreement; and arbitration, in which they seek a binding decision by a third party. Other procedures are variants of these three: mediation is negotiation assisted by a third party, adjudication is arbitration by a judge. All three can be considered forms of overt conflict.

Of the three basic procedures, bargaining is least likely to injure the parties or their relationship and most likely to resolve an underlying conflict of interest. Hence, disputants often start with this procedure; and concerned third parties often encourage it, either directly or by designing dispute management systems that make it more likely (Ury, Brett, & Goldberg, 1988).

Escalation, the use of increasingly harsh tactics, is common when conflicts take the form of struggle. Escalation is sometimes a unidirectional process, in which one party puts increasing pressure for change on the other and the other resists. But it is more often a bidirectional process, involving a conflict spiral, in which each party reacts angrily or defensively to the other's most recent actions, provoking further reactions from the other. Conflict spirals take on a life of their own, in which the original issues may be all but forgotten.

Escalation is the main reason for the bad reputation associated with conflict; it often leads to the disintegration of RELATIONSHIPS and can produce VIOLENCE. However, most conflicts are much milder than this and can be quite beneficial. Mild conflict often helps to clarify issues, and it motivates the parties to find better solutions to the problems that provoked it. Conflict is so essential that organizations and societies are likely to stagnate if they try to prevent it.

Conflict needs to be managed rather than prevented. The main challenges in conflict management are to avoid or reverse heavy escalation and to encourage productive discussion. A number of procedures for reversing escalation have been devised. Simple *contact* between the parties (*see* CONTACT HYPOTHESIS) was once thought to be useful but has come into disrepute. *Cooperation* on SUPERORDINATE GOALS has proven to be a much more powerful approach. *Unilateral conciliatory initiatives* are sometimes helpful in starting a deescalation process, the most famous example being Egyptian President Sadat's surprise trip to Jerusalem in 1977, which paved the way to peace between Egypt and Israel. *Bargaining*, though a type of overt conflict, often helps to combat escalation; and *mediation* often improves the chances of success in bargaining.

When conflict is severely escalated, it is sometimes necessary for third parties to provide *relationship therapy*, with the goal of reversing dysfunctional patterns of interaction between the parties. The best-known form of this is marital therapy, a province of clinical psychology; but social psychologists have been pioneers in the development of problem solving workshops, which provide therapy for interethnic and international conflicts.

All of the procedures just described are more likely to be adopted and to be successful at moments of "ripeness," when both parties recognize their dependence on each other, see themselves as in a hurting stalemate, and/or perceive that they are moving toward mutual disaster. If a moment of ripeness is not at hand and escalation is extremely severe, third parties may have to engage in *peace keeping*, first stopping the parties from using violence or other harsh tactics before moving on to mediation or therapy (Fisher, 1990).

Conflict is studied in all fields of the social sciences. Social psychologists have made particularly heavy use of EXPERIMENTAL GAMES methodology in their research on this topic, but other methods are becoming increasingly popular.

*See also*: BARGAINING; CONTACT HYPOTHESIS; DEINDIVIDUATION; EXPERIMENTAL GAMES; RELATIONSHIPS; SOCIAL IDENTITY THEORY.

BIBLIOGRAPHY
Deutsch, M. (1973). *The resolution of conflict.* New Haven, CT: Yale University Press.
Fisher, R. J. (1990). *The social psychology of intergroup and international conflict resolution.* New York: Springer-Verlag.
Rubin, J. Z., Pruitt, D. G., & Kim, S. H. (1994). *Social conflict: Escalation, stalemate and settlement* (2nd edn.). New York: McGraw-Hill.
Stroebe, W., Kruglanski, A. W., Bar-Tal, D., & Hewstone, M. (1988). *The social psychology of intergroup conflict.* Berlin: Springer-Verlag.
Ury, W. L., Brett, J. M., & Goldberg, S. B. (1988). *Getting disputes resolved.* San Francisco, CA: Jossey-Bass.

DEAN G. PRUITT

**conformity** A major area/paradigm/effect of SOCIAL INFLUENCE, conformity is typically defined as movement on the part of a deviant person or subgroup towards the group NORM (the majority position) as a result of group pressures to restore uniformity. Its opposite may be either independence or anticonformity.

*See also*: NORMS; SOCIAL INFLUENCE.

JOHN C. TURNER

**consensus** In Kelley's covariation theory of causal attribution, consensus information refers to whether an effect varies over persons. Using such covariation information is said to help the perceiver to arrive at a causal attribution.

*See also*: ATTRIBUTION THEORIES.

MILES HEWSTONE

**consensus estimation** Whether real, judged, or assumed, consensus is fundamental to our being as social animals; consensus about social convention, and even about human nature, are arguably prerequisities for mutual comprehension, communication, and interaction. The importance of perceived consensus is reflected in a number of theories and models within social psychology. For example, beliefs about consensus or consensus information play an important role in attitude theory, ATTRIBUTION THEORIES, SOCIAL INFLUENCE and CONFORMITY, GROUP PROCESSES, and perceived ATTRACTION. Consensus is important in defining the social nature of stereotypes and in SOCIAL REPRESENTATIONS, and it bonds people together as individuals and as groups, providing a basis for common identity. In short, it gives social being and behavior its characteristically social form. Rather than examining the role of consensus in these various domains, the present focus is primarily on processes that determine, influence, and bias consensus estimation.

Interest in the process of consensus estimation as a research topic in its own right really took off in social psychology under the umbrella of the HEURISTICS and biases approach to SOCIAL JUDGMENT which developed in the 1970s. Indeed the study of consensus estimation and how this could be biased contributed in no small part to the character of this approach in SOCIAL COGNITION. Central in this development was research by Ross and associates who showed that people had a tendency to overestimate the consensus for their own opinions, attributes, or behaviors, and to see these as relatively normal and situationally appropriate (*see* Ross, Greene, & House, 1977). So was born the term "FALSE CONSENSUS," although in fact evidence of this overestimation phenomenon has been available in a number of guises within psychology, sociology, and related disciplines for a number of decades (e.g., the psychoanalytic concept of "projection"). It is important to be clear from the start about how false consensus is measured and thus defined. In estimating the consensus of preference for two alternative options, estimated consensus for the perceiver's own preference is compared with estimates of that same option made by people preferring the alternative option (Ross et al., 1977). False consensus is therefore defined as a relative or between-subjects effect. Estimates are referred to as false or biased because both groups of people cannot be right simultaneously. However, this method of measurement indicates that the relation of such judgments to the actual distribution of consensus is a separate issue. In a meta-analysis Mullen and Hu (1988) have shown that although subscribers to a minority position tend to show absolute false consensus (or overestimation of actual consensus) for their choice, subscribers to majority positions tend in fact to underestimate actual consensus for their position. The fact that the former effect is typically stronger than the latter results in a net false consensus effect. Meanwhile evidence that people sometimes underestimate the absolute consensus for their attributes, especially when these are positive or desirable, has been advanced as evidence of a FALSE UNIQUENESS effect (e.g., Suls & Wan, 1987). However, evidence for a genuine false uniqueness effect, defined in relative terms as the inverse of false consensus, has been difficult to find whereas the false consensus effect has proved to be an extremely reliable and robust phenomenon (Mullen & Hu, 1988).

The great bulk of research on consensus estimation has focused on determining the mechanisms underlying the false consensus effect, and especially on the issue of whether these are cognitive or more motivational in nature. Four main explanations have been identified, namely selective exposure and cognitive AVAILABILITY, SALIENCE and focus of attention, logical information processing, and motivational factors. The first explanation holds that instances congruent with one's own position are more available in memory because of our tendency to associate with similar or like-minded others (or become similar to our friends). The salience argument asserts that our own preferences and choices will be more perceptually and cognitively salient than nonchosen alternatives, again enhancing availability and thereby frequency judgments. The logical information processing explanation derives from attribution theory, with perceivers seeing their own choices or behaviors as caused by the situation and therefore typical of people in general. The motivational argument refers to the functional support that derives from the perception of one's own views or attributes as shared, rather than as indosyncratic or deviant. The reason why people might display false uniqueness for desirable attributes could also have a motivational basis (Suls & Wan, 1987); presumably exclusivity contributes to the worth of positive characteristics. We can also add a fifth, more cognitive explanation for false consensus, namely the idea that false consensus reflects differential "construal" of the judgment issue (Gilovich, 1990). Here the idea is that people who have a preference for a certain option may overestimate consensus for their position because they define their option in broader and more positive terms than other options. The wealth of research on these mechanisms has not definitively identified the cause of false consensus. Although Mullen and Hu (1988) nominate salience and focus of attention as the most likely candidate, their meta-analysis predates the construal explanation and Marks and Miller suggest that motivational factors may also be important. It seems likely that the false consensus effect is overdetermined, or at least determined by different factors as a function of specific perceiver, item, and population characteristics. Identifying which factors produce false consensus under what conditions would seem to be the most profitable course for research.

The bulk of existing research has tended to concentrate on the individual causes and functions of consensus estimation and to neglect the social functions they may serve, and the social differences they may reflect (Spears & Manstead, 1990). For example, exploring consensus estimation in the intergroup context raises a number of issues not relevant to consensus estimation for general target populations, such as whether consensus estimation is similar for outgroup and ingroup populations. One prediction here is that people may be more inclined to display contrast rather than assimilation in estimating consensus for outgroups, for a range of cognitive and motivational reasons (*see* ASSIMILATION-CONTRAST). This prediction was confirmed in a recent study by Mullen et al. (1992), who found what is probably the first evidence of a genuine false uniqueness effect for consensus estimation of an outgroup.

*See also*: ATTRACTION; ATTRIBUTION THEORIES; GROUP PROCESSES; HEURISTICS; SOCIAL COGNITION; SOCIAL INFLUENCE; SOCIAL JUDGMENT; SOCIAL REPRESENTATIONS.

BIBLIOGRAPHY
Gilovich, T. (1990). Differential construal and the false consensus effect. *Journal of Personality and Social Psychology*, 59, 623–34.
Mullen, B., Dovidio, J. F., Johnson, C., & Copper, C. (1992). Ingroup–outgroup differences in social projection. *Journal of Experimental Social Psychology*, 28, 422–40.
—— & Hu, L. (1988). Social projection as a function of cognitive mechanisms: Two meta-analytic integrations. *British Journal of Social Psychology*, 27, 333–56.
Ross, L., Greene, D., & House, P. (1977). The false consensus phenomenon: An attributional bias in self perception and social perception processes. *Journal of Experimental Social Psychology*, 13, 279–301.
Spears, R., & Manstead, A. S. R. (1990). Consensus estimation in social context. In W. Stroebe & M. Hewstone (Eds.), *European review of social psychology* (Vol. 1, pp. 81–109). Chichester: J. Wiley.
Suls, J. M., & Wan, C. K. (1987). In search of the false uniqueness phenomenon: Fear and estimates of social consensus. *Journal of Personality and Social Psychology*, 52, 211–17.

RUSSELL SPEARS

**consistency** In Kelley's covariation theory of causal attribution, consistency information refers to whether an effect varies over time and/or modalities. Using such covariation information is said to help the perceiver to arrive at a causal attribution.
*See also*: ATTRIBUTION THEORIES.

MILES HEWSTONE

**consumer behavior** Those activities directly involved in selecting, obtaining, using, and disposing of products, services, and ideas to satisfy needs and desires, including the decision processes that precede and follow these actions. The study of consumer behavior combines theories and ideas from sociology, anthropology, marketing, economics, and psychology (for a treatment of the psychological approach, *see* Mullen and Johnson, 1990). As the above definition illustrates, the focus of most research on consumer behavior is on the decision processes of the individual consumer or the consuming organization. Several handbooks on consumer behavior (e.g., Engel, Blackwell, & Miniard, 1993; Schiffman & Kanuk, 1994) offer models of the decision process. These models normally include most or all of the following components:

MOTIVES/NEEDS
In general, consumer behavior models assume that behavior is motivated by needs people have. The consumer is conceived as a goal-directed, purposeful, free actor. Needs vary according to all kinds of stratifications, group memberships, and REFERENCE GROUP.

INTERNAL AND EXTERNAL
INFORMATION SEARCH
Consumers will search their MEMORY for information already stored about possible solutions/products that satisfy their needs.

Spreading activation models are frequently used to describe this process (*see* ASSOCIATIVE NETWORK). Brand awareness is measured by Top-Of-Mind-Awareness (the brand that first comes to mind), free or aided recall. When further information is needed, consumers will engage in more or less extensive external search.

INFORMATION PROCESSING

Usually McGuire's or related models are used to describe the processing of relevant external information, specifying different stages, e.g., exposure – attention – comprehension – acceptance – retention. In McGuire's PERSUASION matrix these are combined with communication variables (source, channel, recipient, and message) to classify effects of persuasion attempts relevant in external search.

EVALUATION

Subsequently, knowing the characteristics of alternatives, either compensatory (described in, e.g., belief x evaluation attitude models, *see* THEORY OF REASONED ACTION, or multiattribute utility models, *see* SUBJECTIVE EXPECTED UTILITY) or noncompensatory (e.g., disjunctive, Elimination By Aspects) decision rules are used to compare products (*see* DECISION MAKING). In research, the evaluation strategy is often studied using an information board that presents alternatives or brands (in rows) and attributes (in columns) (*see* PROCESS TRACING). The final evaluation may be conceived of as an attitude (*see* ATTITUDE MEASUREMENT, ATTITUDE THEORY AND RESEARCH).

INTENTION AND ACTION

Attitudes are not seen as the sole determinants of intention and behavior. Other factors, especially SOCIAL INFLUENCE, peer group pressures (*see* PEER PRESSURE), and reference group influence may intervene. Social psychological models of attitude-behavior relations are applied (*see* ATTITUDES AND BEHAVIOR).

EXPERIENCE

Having direct experience with a certain product feeds back into subsequent decision processes: the consumer learns about and stores new information in memory. As has been documented in attitude research, direct experience also affects attitudes. In consumer research, some attention has been given to habitual decision making or repetitive choice.

(DIS)SATISFACTION

The final result of the decision process is need fulfillment or the recognition of new needs.

Models comprising the components described above portray the consumer as rational, goal-oriented, and with enough energy and time to engage in careful and elaborated decision making. Of course this extensive decision process will not always take place. A continuum is suggested that runs from routine problem solving (e.g., buying what you bought yesterday) via limited problem solving (using HEURISTICS in decision making and in the processing of advertisements and other information) to extensive problem solving (as described above). The amount of effort invested in a choice problem varies as a function of time pressures, personal involvement, importance of the choice problem, processing capacity, and an estimation of the extent to which alternatives differ from each other (for related ideas, *see* the ELABORATION LIKELIHOOD MODEL).

One of the main goals of studying consumer behavior is to be able to influence the consumer. Therefore theories and research about attitude change, persuasion, and social influence are applied in this field. Research in the tradition of the Elaboration Likelihood Model and the Yale school has been used to understand consumer persuasion. ADVERTISING has become more and more important (*see* Burke & Edell, 1986). On the theoretical level this has led to the introduction of the concept of attitude toward the advertisement in an attempt to model affective influencing of consumers.

Marketing and social influence are of special importance at the introduction of new products. In diffusion theory (Rogers, 1983) the acceptance of innovations is described as a function of characteristics of the product (such as relative advantage, compatibility, complexity, trialability, observability, divisibility, etc.) and of receivers. Different segments of the market will adopt innovations at different moments in time. According to the idea of the two-step flow of communication, innovators and opinion leaders influence the majority of consumers to use a product.

Market segmentation can be used to tailor campaigns to the target group. Recently, instead of stratifying the market according to geographic, socio-economic, or demographic variables, the concepts of "user behavior categories" and "life styles" have been introduced. These segmentation criteria have a much closer relation to consumer behavior. Instead of marketing a product to "all single men under forty," products are introduced using strategies aiming at "yuppies," "dinkies", etcetera.

Nevertheless, the power of advertising should not be overrated. Word-of-mouth influence, CONFORMITY, the influence of opinion leaders, and other personal influence processes are at least as important. Advertising is therefore regarded as just one of the four Ps of marketing (product, price, place, and promotion), indicating that other factors also determine the eventual success of a product.

New trends in this field are studying consumer behavior from an intercultural perspective, as the behavior of groups (organizations and families; see GROUP DECISION MAKING), and to devote more attention to emotional and affective factors in persuasion. See also: ADVERTISING; ATTITUDE MEASUREMENT AND QUESTIONNAIRE DESIGN; ATTITUDE THEORY AND RESEARCH; ATTITUDES AND BEHAVIOR; DECISION MAKING; ECONOMIC BEHAVIOR; GROUP DECISION MAKING; HEURISTICS; MEMORY; SOCIAL INFLUENCE; VALUES.

BIBLIOGRAPHY

Burke, M. C. & Edell, J. A. (1986). Ad reactions over time: Capturing changes in the real world. *Journal of Consumer Research*, 13, 114–18.

Engel, J. F., Blackwell, R. D., & Miniard, P. W. (1993). *Consumer behavior* (7th ed.). Hinsdale, IL.: Dryden Press.

Mullen, B., & Johnson, C. (1990) *The psychology of consumer behavior*. Hillsdale, NJ: Lawrence Erlbaum.

Rogers, E. M. (1983). *Diffusion of innovations* (3rd ed.). New York: Free Press.

Schiffman, L. G., & Kanuk, L. L. (1994). *Consumer behavior* (5th ed.). Englewood Cliffs, NJ: Prentice Hall.

NANNE DE VRIES

**Contact Hypothesis** In its simplest form this proposes that bringing members of different groups into contact with one another will reduce any preexisting PREJUDICE between them and result in more positive intergroup attitudes and STEREOTYPES.

This idea has a long history in social psychology but it was first properly systematized by Gordon Allport (1954). He recognized that contact alone would bring about little positive attitude change and would often worsen relations between groups. Instead he proposed a number of conditions that should be met before contact could be expected to effect positive change. Of these, the most important were that interactions in the contact situation should involve equal status participants cooperating over common goals in a social climate in which there was clear institutional support for INTEGRATION policies. These ideas were later refined, most notably by Stuart Cook (see Miller & Brewer, 1984; Stephan & Brigham, 1985), who also emphasized the importance of contact facilitating the development of close interpersonal relationships between members of different groups.

The rationale for these delimiting conditions is several fold. Equal status contact is important to permit the possibility of stereotype-disconfirming information (that minority group members are of equal ability and worth to those in the dominant group) to be processed by the (prejudiced) participants. Cooperation between groups has long been observed to bring about positive changes, presumably for instrumental reasons (see INTERGROUP RELATIONS). The presence of institutional support for contact helps to promote social norms which prescribe and delimit the ranges of acceptable behaviors. The role of closer acquaintanceship is thought to permit the discovery of similarities of values between the groups, thus encouraging still more interpersonal ATTRACTION.

The Contact Hypothesis has been one of the most extensively researched ideas in social psychology. Many of the central ideas are contained in three publications: Miller & Brewer (1984), Hewstone & Brown (1986), and Stephan & Brigham (1985). Much of this research has supported the tenets of the Allport hypothesis although in some of the studies the direction of causality is difficult to establish: does contact lead to more favorable attitudes or vice versa? (Hewstone & Brown, 1986). A further problem has been to assess how far the positive change engendered by the contact experience has generalized beyond those outgroup members actually encountered. It is not difficult to find proximal attitude change; more distal effects are often harder to detect.

In an attempt to deal with this problem of lack of generalization three revisions to the traditional Contact Hypothesis have been proposed. In one the importance of reducing the salience of all cues to category membership is emphasized (Miller & Brewer, 1984). The rationale behind this is that social categorizations can, in themselves, create the conditions for the arousal of intergroup discrimination. Thus their removal, by techniques designed to focus people's attention on individual characteristics rather than group memberships, should lessen the risk of such biases emerging. Multiple interactions with such "individuated" persons are hypothesized to lead to generalized positive attitude change. There is some laboratory evidence which supports this model since experimental inductions designed to encourage interpersonal awareness rather than a task orientation have led to more positive attitudes and less behavioral discrimination toward both outgroup co-workers and outgroup members not yet encountered.

A second model proposes that the contact situation should be so structured that previous outgroup members can be recategorized as members of the ingroup (Gaertner et al., 1993). In this way, more positive attitudes towards them should follow. Evidence from both laboratory and field studies supports this model since those outgroup members

seen as sharing membership with the ingroup in a larger superordinate group are more positively evaluated than those who continue to be seen as members of a different group.

A third model addresses the generalization issue by drawing on a theoretical distinction between interpersonal and intergroup situations. In the former case group memberships are not salient and the interaction is assumed to be governed mainly by idiosyncratic features of the participants and their particular interpersonal relationships. In the latter case group memberships are significant and the interaction is thought to be controlled mostly by features of the *intergroup* relationship. Interactions with "typical" or representative outgroup members are often intergroup affairs. According to the third model such interactions offer the best prospect of the positive attitude change generated in the contact situation spreading to unknown outgroup members (Hewstone & Brown, 1986). This is because the inference from the particular case to the general category is easier to make if that case is seen as prototypical of the category in question. In contrast, interpersonal encounters make such an inference harder to draw since the person in question is, by definition, not perceived as being linked to any particular group. Supportive evidence for this model has come from studies where an encounter with (or information about) "typical" category exemplars has evoked more attitudinal or stereotype change.

The potential of each of these three models to promote lasting and generalized change remains controversial. A direct comparison of their competing predictions remains to be made. *See also*: ATTRACTION; INTEGRATION; INTERGROUP RELATIONS; PREJUDICE; STEREOTYPING.

BIBLIOGRAPHY

Allport, G. W. (1954/1979 ed.). *The nature of prejudice*. Cambridge & Reading, MA: Addison-Wesley.

Gaertner, S., Dovidio, J., Anastasio, P. A., Bachman, B. A., & Rust, M. C. (1993). The common ingroup identity model: Recategorization and the reduction of intergroup bias. In W. Stroebe & M. Hewstone (Eds.), *European review of social psychology* (Vol. 4, pp. 1–26). Chichester: J. Wiley.

Hewstone, M., & Brown, R. (Eds.) (1986). *Contact & conflict in intergroup encounters.* Oxford: Basil Blackwell

Miller, N., & Brewer, M. B. (Eds.) (1984). *Groups in contact: The psychology of desegregation.* Orlando, FL: Academic Press.

Stephan, W. B., & Brigham, J. C. (Eds.) (1985). Intergroup contact;. *Journal of Social Issues, 41*, No. 3.

RUPERT BROWN
MILES HEWSTONE

**contagion** Originally thought to involve hypnosis, contagion is now thought to involve a process in which people gain confidence in the appropriateness of their behavior because others who imitate them are behaving in the same way. This produces the amplification and rapid transmission of feelings, ideas, and behaviors associated with crowd behavior and other collective phenomena (*see* CROWD PSYCHOLOGY).

*See also*: CROWD PSYCHOLOGY.

MICHAEL A. HOGG

**content analysis** A research technique used to extract desired information from symbolic (primarily verbal) materials by systematically and objectively classifying or rating specified characteristics (*see* Stone, Dunphy, Smith, & Ogilvie, 1966). The impartial and consistent application to all selected material of explicitly defined procedures is intended to be objective in the sense of yielding results that are reproducible by other qualified investigators.

A related term, *coding*, is used interchangeably with content analysis by some authorities. For others, coding denotes either a classification system (coding manual) or the application of such a system. In a more restricted sense, the term coding sometimes refers to the assignment, for each category, of a number to be entered into a computer for data storage and analysis.

Although nonverbal materials, such as gestures, facial expressions, films, and melodies may be studied by this technique, its main use is for the analysis of either the content or the formal properties (e.g., style) of verbal material. Although spoken expressions can be categorized as they occur, content analysis usually employs recorded text. Whether the text was originally in written form, or was spoken and then transcribed, its contents are used *verbatim*, preserving misstatements, omissions, errors of spelling and grammar, etc. Words or phrases (or errors) in a text may be interpreted in terms of their "manifest" or ordinary meaning, or in terms of their "latent" or inferred underlying meaning (e.g., symbols in Freudian dream research).

The technique may be used for description or for inference. For example, language patterns characteristic of different socio-economic levels may be analyzed in order to describe social class differences or to make inferences about the influence of social structure on language use.

The typical product of a content analysis is a set of categories containing frequencies or ratings of intensity that are amenable to quantitative analysis. However, the method is also employed in qualitative research in which systematic classification procedures are used to obtain a descriptive characterization of a body of verbal material, such as themes in popular magazines concerning the effect on marital relationships of a husband's retirement (*see* Gilgun, Daly, & Handel, 1992).

SCOPE AND APPLICABILITY

Content analysis is employed in the behavioral and social sciences and in the humanities to obtain information about individuals, groups, cultures, and historical periods. In anthropology the technique has been used to describe and compare cultures, to study cultural change, and to study relations among different aspects of cultures (e.g., childrearing and adult PERSONALITY). In political science, analyses have been made of PROPAGANDA, media coverage of political campaigns, and factors affecting VOTING BEHAVIOR. In sociology, the range of topics studied includes family dynamics, media analyses of the stock market, and the decision making of corporate executives. Content analysis has also been used in economics, education, geography, history, and psychiatry.

Within psychology extensive use has been made of content analysis in many subfields as indicated by the illustrative topics listed below:

Clinical psychology: suicide, DEPRESSION, effects of psychotherapy, personality assessment through projective techniques.

Developmental psychology, educational psychology, and psycholinguistics: ego development, moral reasoning, language acquisition, readability of text, writing skills.

Personality and SOCIAL PSYCHOLOGY: AUTHORITARIANISM, CREATIVITY, dreams, everyday explanations (see ACCOUNTS, ATTRIBUTION THEORIES), moods and emotions, VALUES, personological approaches to narrative, identity, and biography (see Holsti, 1968; Winter, 1992). Detailed coding systems have been developed to measure INDIVIDUAL DIFFERENCES in personal characteristics such as explanatory styles, human motives, and conceptual complexity (see Smith, 1992). Quantitative archival studies have dealt extensively with AGGRESSION and VIOLENCE, attitudes and BELIEFS, and LEADERSHIP (Simonton, 1981).

Some topics have been approached from the perspective of several disciplines. For example, political leadership has been studied by historians, political scientists, sociologists, and social psychologists, and researchers in different disciplines have employed both quantitative and qualitative content analysis in different approaches to DISCOURSE ANALYSIS.

Most extensively studied by means of content analysis is the cross-disciplinary field of COMMUNICATION. Holsti (1968) reviews the contributions from the 1930s to the 1950s of Berelson, Lasswell, Lazarsfeld, Osgood, Pool, White, and others who introduced many of the conventions used in contemporary studies. This body of research concerns the content of communications, the sources or initiating circumstances of communications, and the characteristics of the recipients of communications or their responses. Areas of study include: trends in communication content, differences between materials produced by different sources, techniques of PERSUASION, changes that occur as messages are transmitted, communication networks, and inferences about communication sources (e.g., the motives, values, or psychological state of an author, or the IDEOLOGY or intentions of a group or government).

Another cross-disciplinary area that entails a form of content analysis is the study of interaction (see OBSERVATIONAL METHODS). In addition to categorizing verbalizations, an observer may record who expresses them, to whom they are addressed, and the responses made, thereby preserving information about the sequence of events over time (see Bakeman & Gottman, 1986). Research on group dynamics also deals with changes over time in the types and directions of communications that occur, and with the functions that statements fulfill rather than their content (e.g., the category "gives suggestion" disregards the content of the suggestion; see INTERACTION PROCESS ANALYSIS).

The cross-disciplinary method of SURVEY RESEARCH primarily employs fixed response questions that require no content analysis, but may also employ free response questions which do. Such questions may also be used in preliminary research to ascertain the range of answers concerning a subject. The categories thus established may be used subsequently as fixed alternative questions.

SELECTION OF VERBAL MATERIALS

The use of content analysis entails decisions about the type and amount of material to be analyzed, and about the sampling of both sources and materials. These decisions affect the reliability, validity, and generalizability of the conclusions.

The material selected should appropriately reflect the phenomenon being studied. For example, to learn about the values transmitted by a culture, one might select such cultural products as children's readers, traditional dramas, or songs. The quantity of material analyzed will affect the reliability (internal consistency and/or stability) of the results. Too little material does not provide enough information on which to make a sound estimate of whatever is being assessed.

Content analysis may be used with naturally occurring (archival or everyday) verbal materials or with materials obtained specifically for research purposes. Archival materials include symbolic cultural products, personal documents, publications, records and official documents, broadcast media transcriptions, and so on. Everyday materials, such as recorded conversations, or reported dreams, may be of value for their spontaneity and external validity and, like archival materials, they provide unobtrusive measures. The selection and use of archival and everyday materials is discussed by Simonton (1981) and Winter (1992). With materials elicited for research, the investigator has control over who will participate, on what topic, under what conditions, and at what length.

It is necessary to sample sources (e.g., persons, cultures) as well as the content of their verbal productions. For example, survey respondents are selected by one sampling process, and their views are sampled by another (the questions asked). A cross-cultural analysis of folktales requires consideration of:

(1) whether cultures are to be sampled from each major geographical area;
(2) whether all types of folktales are equally appropriate;
(3) how many folktales are needed to provide a sufficient sample of the thought of each culture; and
(4) whether that number of folktales is recorded for each selected culture (see Stone et al., 1966).

Quantitative research tends to employ probability sampling to insure representativeness, although purposive sampling may be used instead. Qualitative research tends to deal in depth with smaller samples selected purposefully. The type of sampling procedure selected will affect the kinds of bias that can occur and the generalizability of the conclusions. Different rationales for sample selection, and pitfalls to avoid, are discussed in Gilgun et al. (1992), Holsti (1968), and Weber (1990).

## NATURE AND DEVELOPMENT OF CLASSIFICATION SYSTEMS

Coding systems consist of rules for assigning specified units of verbal material into specified categories. Categories reflecting variables to be assessed can be defined either by an exhaustive list of what is to be included, or by a statement of the meaning of the category together with illustrative examples.

Normally, categories are intended to be unidimensional, mutually exclusive, exhaustive, and independent (the value of an entry in one category does not affect the value of an entry in another). These properties of categories have important implications for the analysis and reporting of data. However, some authors intentionally employ categories that are not fully independent, exclusive, or exhaustive (see Bakeman & Gottman, 1986; Smith, 1992; Weber, 1990, pp. 23ff, 32ff). Categories can also differ in inclusiveness, abstractness, and degree of inference required.

Each system will specify the unit of text (recording unit or unit of analysis) that is to be categorized. Such units may be defined by linguistic properties (words, sentences, paragraphs), physical or temporal properties (inches of column space, amount of time spent on a broadcast topic), or conceptual properties such as themes ("a single assertion about some subject" Holsti, 1968, p. 647; for definitions of thematic analysis, see also Smith, 1992). Characters in a story, or answers to individual survey questions may also be recording units.

Also specified are units of enumeration: whether an entry is recorded in terms of its presence or absence, frequency of occurrence, degree of intensity, or physical units such as time, length, or weight. For further discussion of categories, rules, and units, see Bakeman and Gottman (1986) and Holsti (1968).

The development of a new coding system is affected by the problem to be studied, the conceptual framework of the investigator, and an examination of the type of verbal material to be used. Categories can be developed a priori on the basis of a theory, or be derived inductively, ad hoc, using whatever distinctions are suggested by the obtained material. Typically, a combination of these approaches is employed – theory suggests what to look for and text suggests modifications and additions. A third approach, used to develop various motive scoring systems, identifies as coding categories those aspects of thematic material that occur more frequently under motivationally aroused conditions than under neutral conditions (see Smith, 1992).

The advent of computerized content analysis has affected the conception and implementation of the method. This innovation is described in a landmark volume by Stone et al. (1966). In brief, text entered into the computer is analyzed in terms of programmed categories. These may be specific to the research problem or all purpose categories (dictionaries) that may be used with many types of verbal material. Programming requires that research ideas be made explicit.

Advantages of computerized content analysis include accuracy (perfect intercoder reliability), speed, and lack of fatigue, which together enable the processing of large amounts of material in great detail. Among other things, the computer can look for internal contingencies, note the context in which keywords appear, and call up for inspection all sentences in which keywords are used. Analyses that were not previously feasible are made possible. However, some complex conceptual scoring systems, such as that for ACHIEVEMENT MOTIVATION, have not yet been programmed satisfactorily. For recent developments in this field see Weber (1990).

## RELIABILITY AND VALIDITY

It is important to determine the reliability of: (1) coders; and (2) their categorizations. Intercoder reliability reflects the extent to which different persons (blind to identifying characteristics of the material) can apply the coding system with the same results. Coding reliability provides information about the objectivity and accuracy of the assessment procedure, and is *prerequisite* to the reliability of the classifications themselves. (*See*, however, the discussion of generalizability theory by Bakeman & Gottman, 1986.)

The second kind of reliability provides information about the repeatability, unidimensionality, and stability over time of the categorizations or ratings derived from the analysis. For example, using scores assigned to thematic apperceptive stories, one may obtain measures of repeatability (from alternate forms), homogeneity (internal consistency among scores from different stories) and stability (test–interval–retest).

Indexes of reliability, coder training, and factors affecting inter- and intra-coder agreement are reviewed in Bakeman and Gottman (1986), Holsti (1968), and Smith (1992). Steps to take to maximize the reliability of thematic measures are discussed in Smith (1992).

Regarding the validity of content analysis, a researcher needs to know whether the results reflect what they are intended to assess, and whether interpretations or conclusions are correct. The validation of content analytic assessments is similar to that of other forms of assessment except that it may be difficult to obtain an appropriate independent criterion. For example, a measure obtained from content analysis (e.g., values) can be correlated with a previously validated measure, if one exists (congruent validity). A conclusion about verbal differences between two groups can be confirmed by determining whether the findings can discriminate between existing groups, such as normals and schizophrenics, or between existing materials, such as the works of two different authors (concurrent validity). Interpretations that lend themselves to predictions (e.g., about changes in purchasing behavior) may be tested by determining whether the expected behavior occurs (predictive validity). The results possess construct validity if a set of theoretically expected relationships exist. For example, as compared with persons with low need for achievement scores, those with high scores are expected more often to set goals of intermediate difficulty, and to remember more unfinished tasks under ego-involving conditions. One form of validity that does not require an independent measure is content validity which depends on whether the selected material adequately represents the domain under investigation.

An unbiased sample and a reliable (i.e., repeatable) assessment are necessary, but not sufficient, conditions for validity. Interestingly, high internal consistency is not necessary for validity (*see* Smith, 1992). Validity issues are examined in greater detail by Holsti (1968), and Weber (1990). McClelland et al. (1989) consider the validity of self-report and thematic apperceptive measures of motives, and Simonton (1981) discusses the internal and external validity of content analytic measures derived from archival materials.

## ADVANTAGES AND LIMITATIONS
A major reason for employing content analysis is that it provides a way of transforming and reducing large amounts of qualitative material into a manageable number of ordered and meaningful units for quantitative analysis. In addition, the technique guards against bias in the form of selectivity in interpreting a text. Less obvious is the fact that systematic analysis may reveal information in a text that is not apparent even to a careful reader. Studies of disputed authorship, themes in literary works, and suicide notes, for example, have revealed unanticipated substantive and stylistic characteristics, such as adjective–adverb use, that distinguish a particular text or type of material (see Holsti, 1968; Stone, 1966; Weber, 1990).

Content analysis may be used in both hypothesis-testing and exploratory research. For example, analysis of unstructured interviews may provide information about the adequacy of a researcher's conceptualizations and also suggest entirely new possibilities and hypotheses.

Materials used for content analysis, such as expressive documents, elicited stories, or responses to open-ended interview questions, tend to be stated in terms meaningful to the author, whereas fixed response questions may not capture the respondent's frame of reference and may, therefore, fail to obtain an accurate or relevant response.

On a related point, McClelland et al. (1989) show that self-report inventories and projective tests are not simply alternative ways of assessing the same personality variables. Although many attempts have been made to find an easier way to assess human motives than by means of content analysis, self-report measures tend to be uncorrelated with measures obtained from samples of imaginative thought, possibly because "imaginative stories . . . reflect motivational and emotional themes in the person's life, unevaluated as to their appropriateness in terms of concepts of the self, others, and what is important" (p. 698).

Finally, content analysis may be the only feasible way to study:

(1) persons who are dead, unavailable, or uncooperative;
(2) past historical periods, or trends over long periods of time; or
(3) entire cultures.

Although it is a broadly applicable technique, content analysis has its limitations. First, it may be prohibitively time-consuming and costly to obtain and prepare verbal materials, develop a classification system, train coders, and code the material. Second, some researchers may be concerned that the trade-off for quantification is a reductionistic loss of richness and meaning. In such instances, however, it may be possible to use content analysis in conjunction with qualitative research methods. Third, conclusions may be misleading if the wrong categories of analysis are employed. For example, the use of an "all purpose" general system of categories, such as a dictionary developed for computerized content analysis, may fail to detect information of interest that would be identified by a conceptually based system particular to the problem under investigation. And, finally, it may not be possible to obtain verbal materials that adequately reflect the variables of interest to the researcher. For example, secret documents may have been destroyed, archival documents may underrepresent persons who are poorly educated, and secondary sources (e.g., biographies) may introduce bias.

*See also*: ACCOUNTS; ACHIEVEMENT MOTIVATION; AGGRESSION; ATTRIBUTION THEORIES; AUTHORITARIANISM; COMMUNICATION; CREATIVITY; DEPRESSION; DISCOURSE ANALYSIS; IDEOLOGY; LEADERSHIP; OBSERVATIONAL METHODS; PERSONALITY; PROPAGANDA; SOCIAL PSYCHOLOGY; SURVEY METHODS; VALUES.

BIBLIOGRAPHY
Bakeman, R., & Gottman, J. M. (1986). *Observing interaction: An introduction to sequential analysis*. New York: Cambridge University Press.
Gilgun, J. F., Daly, K., & Handel, G. (Eds.) (1992). *Qualitative methods in family research*. Newbury Park, CA: Sage.

Holsti, O. R. (1968). Content analysis. In G. Lindzey & E. Aronson (Eds.), *The handbook of social psychology* (2nd ed., Vol. 2, pp. 596–692). Reading, MA: Addison-Wesley.

McClelland, D. C., Koestner, R., & Weinberger, J. (1989). How do self-attributed and implicit motives differ? *Psychological Review*, 96, 690–702.

Simonton, D. K. (1981). The library laboratory: Archival data in personality and social psychology. In L. Wheeler (Ed.), *Review of personality and social psychology* (Vol. 2, pp. 217–44). Beverly Hills, CA: Sage.

Smith, C. P. (Ed.). (1992). *Motivation and personality: Handbook of thematic content analysis*. New York: Cambridge University Press.

Stone, P. J., Dunphy, D. C., Smith, M. S., & Ogilvie, D. M. (1966). *The general inquirer: A computer approach to content analysis*. Cambridge, MA: MIT Press.

Weber, R. P. (1990). *Basic content analysis* (2nd ed.). Newbury Park, CA: Sage.

Winter, D. (1992). Content analysis of archival materials, personal documents, and everyday verbal productions. In C. P. Smith (Ed.), *Motivation and personality: Handbook of thematic content analysis* (pp. 110–25). New York: Cambridge University Press.

CHARLES P. SMITH

**control** A concept that plays an important role in several psychological theories. It is central to Rotter's (1954) SOCIAL LEARNING Theory (locus of control), Weiner's (1986) attributional analysis of motivation and emotion (causal controllability), Bandura's (1977) Self-efficacy theory, and it is the key concept in Seligman's (1975) theoretical analysis of learned HELPLESSNESS and DEPRESSION.

Seligman (1975) has defined this concept most explicitly. He defines an event as controllable when the voluntary responses that an organism emits have an impact on the consequences of that event. By contrast, an event is considered to be uncontrollable when no voluntary response has an impact on the event. For instance, when an organism receives electric shocks regardless of what responses it shows, the electric shocks are uncontrollable for the organism. However, when the organism can terminate the electric shock by, e.g., pressing a button, the shock is considered to be controllable.

Voluntary responses are those that can be modified by reward and punishment and differ from involuntary responses, which are, by contrast, unmodifiable by rewards and punishments. For instance, individuals can be induced to press a button by rewarding them (e.g., with money or by terminating an electric shock). By contrast, most individuals will not be able to alter their reflexes (involuntary responses), even if rewards are presented.

According to Seligman (1975) the controllability of an event is a function of two parameters (probabilities). The first parameter concerns the probability that an event (e.g., the termination of a shock) will occur when a certain voluntary behavior (e.g., pressing a button) is performed. This probability can range from "0" (i.e., the shock is never terminated when the button is pressed), through "0.5" (the shock is terminated in 50 percent of the cases when the button is pressed), to "1" (the shock is always terminated whenever the individual presses the button).

The second parameter concerns the probability that the event (e.g., the termination of the shock) will occur in the absence of the respective action (i.e., pressing a button). Again, these probabilities can range from "0" (the shock is never terminated when the button is not pressed), through "0.5" (the shock is terminated in about 50 percent of the cases when the button is not pressed) to "1" (the shock is always terminated when the button is not pressed).

Referring to these two parameters, Seligman defines an event as uncontrollable when the probability of its occurrence in the presence and in the absence of the response under consideration are equal. For instance, when the shock is terminated in 50 percent of the cases when the organism presses the button and in 50 percent of the cases when the organism does not press the button, the reactions of the organism "do not make a difference." However, when the shock never terminates when the button is not pressed and it terminates in about 50 percent (intermittent reinforcement) or 100 percent (continuous reinforcement) of the cases when the button is pressed, the organism has (varying degrees of) control over the event.

Several research programs have studied the impact of loss of control. Seligman assumes that lack of control can lead to an expectancy that there is lack of contingency between behaviors and outcomes (uncontrollability expectation) which, in turn, can lead to motivational, emotional, and cognitive deficits. For instance, Seligman has demonstrated that exposure to uncontrollability often results in learned helplessness and depression. This finding has been demonstrated both for animal and for human subjects (*see* Seligman, 1975).

However, under certain circumstances, lack of control can lead to a different psychological state – i.e., REACTANCE (*see* Wortman & Brehm, 1975). Wortman and Brehm argue that the initial response to uncontrollable outcomes is an increase in motivation and performance (the organism is reactant and attempts to regain control). It is only when uncontrollability experiences continue that the state of helplessness emerges. Note, however, that according to Wortman and Brehm the organism still believes in controllability when in the state of reactance.

Research within the framework of Rotter's (1954) social learning theory is not primarily concerned with the conditions that lead to uncontrollability expectations. Instead, the psychological consequences of the belief that one can or cannot control the causes of events is the focus of social learning theorists. Nonetheless, Rotter defines "control" quite similarly to Seligman (1975). He states that an individual has an internal LOCUS OF CONTROL if he/she perceives that the event is contingent upon his/her own behavior or relatively permanent characteristics, whereas external locus of control is characterized by the belief that reinforcement is perceived as not being contingent upon action.

Both experimentally induced locus of control and the relatively stable personality disposition of internal versus external locus of control (that can be assessed via questionnaires) have been shown to be connected to several central psychological variables. Most importantly, internal locus of control leads to typical shifts in expectations of success following success or failure (i.e., increased expectancies following success and decreased expectancies following failure), whereas an external locus of control leads, by comparison, more often to atypical expectancy shifts (i.e., decreased expectancies of success following success and increased expectations of success following failure). (*See also* Weiner, 1986, for a critical analysis of this relationship.)

In Weiner's (1986) attributional analysis of motivation and emotion, the concept of controllability plays a central role in evaluative interpersonal actions. Weiner postulates that individuals' (observers') reactions to others (actors) who experience failure, sickness, or need for help, are largely determined by the perceived controllability of the causes of these events. Attributions (of, e.g., failure) to controllable causes (e.g., lack of effort) lead to anger, punishment, and reduced willingness to help, whereas the belief that the actor has no control over the cause of the negative event (e.g., failure attributed to lack of ability) leads to pity, help-giving, and to lesser or no punishment.

*See also*: DEPRESSION; REACTANCE; SOCIAL LEARNING.

BIBLIOGRAPHY

Bandura, A. (1977). Self-efficacy: Toward a unifying theory of behavioral change. *Psychological Review*, 2, 191–215.

Rotter, J. B. (1954). *Social learning and clinical psychology*. Englewood Cliffs, NJ: Prentice Hall.

Seligman, M. E. P. (1975). *Helplessness: On depression, development, and death*. San Francisco, CA: W. H. Freeman.

Weiner, B. (1986). *An attributional theory of motivation and emotion*. New York: Springer-Verlag.

Wortman, C. B., & Brehm, J. W. (1975). Responses to uncontrollable outcomes: An integration of reactance theory and the learned helplessness model. In L. Berkowitz (Ed.), *Advances in experimental social psychology* (Vol. 8, pp. 277–336). New York: Academic Press.

FRIEDRICH FÖRSTERLING

**control motivation** Theorists of CONTROL have generally assumed that individuals want control; they have assumed that individuals are motivated to gain or maintain the ability to influence events (e.g., Pittman & D'Agostino, 1989). This proposed desire does not seem misplaced. An ability to effect control appears to lead to a large number of positive consequences: greater INTRINSIC MOTIVATION, interest, CREATIVITY, cognitive flexibility, TRUST, and persistence at achieving behavioral change; less pressure and tension; and improved AFFECT, SELF-ESTEEM, and physical health (Deci & Ryan, 1987).

Interestingly, what seems to drive the positive effects of having control is not so much the actual use of control, but the perception that such use is possible. Furthermore, efforts to gain control, in and of themselves, may have important psychological effects. Control motivation has been proposed to influence social cognition (e.g., PERSON PERCEPTION and attribution) and social behavior (e.g., learned HELPLESSNESS and RISK-taking behaviors).

## THE NATURE OF CONTROL MOTIVATION

The most general conceptualization of control motivation, as stated above, is as a desire, or need, on the part of individuals to perceive that they have the ability to influence events. Control motivation also has been described as a desire to maintain freedom of behavior or opinion, and as a desire to influence the aversiveness of an event. Questions regarding the nature of control motivation concern its globality and its relationships to prediction, to perceptions of contingency and control, and to self-esteem.

## GLOBALITY

Most references to a "motivation to control" (e.g., Heider, 1958; Strube & Yost, 1993; Swann, Stein-Seroussi, & Geisler, 1992) reflect global interpretations of control motivation that follow from notions of "effectance motivation." White (1959) proposed that people are motivated to interact in an effective, competent way with the world, and that they engage in behaviors that facilitate the development of such efficacy.

Often intertwined with this notion of control motivation as a motivation toward general competence is an emphasis on prediction: individuals seek to predict and control events in their environments because such prediction and control indicates competent interaction with the environment. One interpretation of the role of prediction is that the ability to predict is a precursor and facilitator of the ability to control. An alternative interpretation suggests the inverse: that control motivation really satisfies "prediction motivation." In other words, this approach suggests that people seek control because control allows for prediction. This might be because being able to predict when negative events will occur releases an individual from constantly searching the environment for signs of imminent threat, or because it allows the person to relax when threat is not expected (see Thompson, 1981, for review). In either case, prediction and control are relatively globally defined.

Whereas most theoretical approaches either actively or by default adopt a general interpretation of control motivation, Brehm's RE-ACTANCE theory (e.g., Brehm, 1993) points to the usefulness of considering more specific forms of control. Reactance theory was proposed to explain individuals' efforts at achieving specific forms of control (conceptualized as the freedom to behave in a desired manner or hold desired attitudes). According to reactance theory, individuals believe that they have specific behavioral freedoms, and they become motivated to reinstate any of those freedoms that are threatened or eliminated in any way.

The consideration of specific freedoms suggests that freedoms may not necessarily be additive. It also suggests that a given freedom may be considered more important than another, and so can arouse greater reactance if it is threatened. It also suggests that the magnitude of reactance experienced when a freedom is threatened can be predicted based on the presence of other freedoms and on the relationship of the lost freedom with the remaining freedoms. For example, one study found that subjects' reactance to a threat to their freedom to choose to watch a given movie was determined by how many other movies were available (*see* Brehm, 1993, for review).

Although reactance theory's conceptualization of specific freedoms, or specific forms of control, facilitates comparisons among freedoms, this conceptualization is problematic in that the only way to resolve the reactance aroused by a threat to a given freedom is to restore that particular freedom. In contrast, research on learned helplessness suggests that although an individual may initially try harder to restore the lost freedom, this reactance may eventually be supplanted by giving up. In addition, other research (*see* Pittman & D'Agostino, 1989) suggests that reactance aroused by a threat to control in one domain may be resolved by increases in control in another domain. Conceptualizations of control as relatively global and nondomain-specific allow for these apparent "cross-domain" restorations of control. In addition, although a global control construct does not, in itself, predict learned helplessness effects, it does allow for the generalization of helplessness once it has been learned.

*Arousal of Control Motivation*
White (1959) proposed that the motivation for competent interaction with the environment was a constant, low-level motivation. Control motivation can be thought of similarly, as a motivation that always exists at some level. However, it also appears to vary in the extent to which it is both chronically and temporarily aroused. Burger (1992) suggests that individuals differ in the extent to which they desire and seek control (*see* INDIVIDUAL DIFFERENCES). Experiments that examined this individual difference found that subjects high in desire for control appeared to seek more control than did subjects low in desire for control: they tended to perform better in achievement situations, were less susceptible to conformity pressures, paid greater attention to control-relevant information, and were more likely to succumb to the ILLUSION OF CONTROL (*see* Burger, 1992, for review). As we will see below, other individual differences may also influence the level of control that people prefer to maintain.

Control motivation may also be aroused by situational factors that result in lowered or threatened perceptions of control. Experimental manipulations of control motivation have relied on this relationship in that they are actually manipulations of control deprivation. It has been assumed that subjects who are deprived of control experience a consequent increase in control motivation (e.g., Pittman & D'Agostino, 1989).

*Relationship to Self-Esteem*
Although it seems clear that motivations for control and for positive self-regard are intertwined, the exact nature of the relationship between the two is the subject of some debate. Practically, the nature of the relationship varies as a function of how control and self-esteem are defined. The more that control is conceptualized as general effectance and self-esteem is conceptualized as a perception that the self is effective, competent, and good, the greater is the equivalence between the two concepts. They diverge, however, when self-esteem is conceptualized more as positive affect regarding the self, and when control is conceptualized as referring to relatively specific, multiple freedoms. In their most divergent forms, we can think of control as a component of self-esteem, and infer that people seek control as one means of achieving self-esteem.

EFFECTS OF CONTROL MOTIVATION
Control motivation may influence psychological processing both proactively and reactively. By "proactively," we mean that certain psychological processes may be instigated because the outcome of the process, or the process itself, provides individuals with the perception that they can predict and control their outcomes. For example, individuals have been hypothesized to engage in attributional processing because it increases, in some way, their certainty that they can understand, predict, and influence future events. By "reactively," we mean that threats to individuals' perceptions of control may influence their motivation to engage in psychological processing. As we will see below, threats to control have been demonstrated to lead to both increased and decreased effort on subsequent tasks. It may be that the effects of

heightened control motivation on psychological processing are influenced by the type of processing that is involved. The greater the relationship between a psychological process and perceptions of control, the greater may be the effect on that process of heightened motivation to control.

Attribution, self-verification, the formation of positive illusions, and self-appraisal are psychological processes that are hypothesized to increase, in some way, individuals' certainty that they can understand, predict, and influence events. Let us consider how each of these processes might provide individuals with a perception that they can predict and control.

## Attribution

Heider (1958) and subsequent attribution theorists have assumed that individuals form attributions in order to increase their ability to predict and control (see ATTRIBUTION THEORIES). According to this assumption, to the extent that individuals can understand the causes for others' behavior, they will be better able to predict and influence those others' future behavior and ultimately, their own outcomes.

Although the assumptions of classic attribution theory mostly focus on the significance of forming attributions for others' behavior, subsequent theory and research has pointed also to the importance of attributions for one's own behavior. Hypotheses regarding the influence of control motivation on self-related processes are intriguingly contradictory. Control motivation has been claimed to instigate the following potentially contradictory processes:

(1) the development of unrealistically positive illusions about the self;
(2) SELF-VERIFICATION, in which individuals seek information consistent with their own self-views, even when that information is negative; and
(3) impartial self-appraisal.

Under different conditions, each of these effects of control motivation on the search for and incorporation of information about the self may occur.

## Positive Illusions

The formation of positive illusions, or unrealistic assessments about one's abilities (among them the ability to control) may provide one means of satisfying control motivation. Although these illusions can prove detrimental if they are "put to the test," they can provide individuals, at least temporarily, with the perception that they are capable of exerting desired influence on events.

## Self-Verification

Notions of positive illusions are based on the assumption that people like to think well of themselves, and that sometimes such thoughts are adaptive. Self-verification theory focuses, in contrast, on the adaptiveness of thinking accurately about the self (see Swann, Stein-Seroussi, & Geisler, 1992). This theory predicts that individuals are motivated to maintain a stable self-concept because they are aware of the importance of a stable self-concept in negotiating social reality. To this end, they are proposed to selectively seek assessments of themselves that confirm their self-concepts, even if those assessments are unflattering, and to avoid assessments that contradict their self-concepts.

These predictions have been supported in studies that have compared subjects with negative and positive views of themselves. Compared to people with positive self-views, people with negative self-views tended to seek unfavorable evaluations, to prefer interaction partners who evaluate them negatively to partners who evaluate them positively, and to withdraw from personal relationships in which their partner appraises them favorably (see Swann, Stein-Seroussi, & Geisler, 1992, for review).

## Self-Appraisal

Individuals engage in self-verification processes when they have a relatively stable self-concept that they feel the need to maintain. What happens when they don't have such a stable self-concept? Strube and his colleagues suggest that when people are unsure of how to assess their abilities, the motivation for control leads them to seek, in a relatively impartial manner, information that facilitates accurate assessment (*see* Strube & Yost, 1993). Their research points to two individual differences related to concern with accurate self-appraisal, and thus indirectly with control motivation. The first is a relatively straightforward individual difference in desire for accurate self-appraisal. The second is less intuitive, and refers to the Type A/Type B distinction that was defined to identify individuals at risk for coronary disease (*see* TYPE A BEHAVIOR PATTERN). Type A individuals, who are at risk, exhibit a behavior pattern that can be described as achieving, competitive, hard-driving, impatient, and time-urgent, whereas Type B individuals do not exhibit this behavior. Strube and his colleagues suggest that Type A individuals have a high desire for accurate self-appraisal (which leads to greater control), and it is this desire for accurate self-appraisal that leads to the hard-driving, competitive behaviors that compose the Type A behavior pattern.

*Effects of Threats to Control*
To the extent that a psychological process does increase individuals' perceptions of control, individuals may be expected to engage in that process to a greater extent, or more effortfully, when their perception of control is threatened (Pittman & D'Agostino, 1989). This notion is adapted from the prediction made by reactance theory, that a threat to control induces efforts to regain control. It relies on the assumption, however, that threats to control in one domain can be made up for by gains in other domains.

Research based on the notion that people form attributions for the purpose of prediction and control demonstrated that increases in control motivation can lead to more effortful attributional processing. Pittman and his colleagues aroused control motivation in some of their subjects by depriving them of control (i.e., by providing them with noncontingent feedback on a task). Subjects who experienced this experimentally induced control motivation appeared to try harder on subsequent attribution tasks: compared to subjects who were not deprived of control, in one study their attributions were more influenced by available information, and in a second study they sought more diagnostic

information about a target individual (*see* Pittman & D'Agostino, 1989).

We noted earlier that the individual difference in desire for control is related to the arousal of control motivation. Research on this individual difference variable also offers further support for the notion that increased control motivation leads to increases in attributional processing (*see* Burger, 1992, for review). In several studies, subjects who scored relatively high in the desire for control were more likely to be influenced by available attributional information, sought more attributional information, and tended to score higher on a measure of attributional complexity than did subjects low in desire for control.

Interestingly, subjects who experience extreme deprivation of control, although their motivation to gain control may be as high or higher than that of subjects who experience moderate deprivation of control, appear to withdraw effort from subsequent tasks. It is possible that such withdrawal reflects an accurate assessment of the implausibility of actually achieving control; and/or it may reflect efforts on the part of the individual to protect her self-esteem by withdrawing effort (*see* Burger, 1989; Pittman & D'Agostino, 1989; Strube & Yost, 1993).

DO PEOPLE ALWAYS WANT CONTROL?
Most researchers and theorists have assumed that people generally seek to gain control, and research has tended to support this perspective. However, it also is likely that under certain conditions the possession of control becomes less desirable. These may be conditions in which the possession of control raises self-presentation concerns to an uncomfortably high level, decreases the likelihood that the person will be able to achieve desired outcomes, or leads to an increase in predictability that draws the person's attention to aversive aspects of the situation (Burger, 1989). Under these conditions, individuals might be expected to relinquish control or to feel discomfort if they are unable to relinquish control.

The existence of conditions that limit when control will be perceived as desirable suggests that although individuals often desire the influence conveyed by a position of control, they also can recognize the responsibility that accompanies this influence. This suggests that the motivation to control is therefore not necessarily unidirectional, but rather may be influenced by a variety of situational and dispositional factors.

See also: ATTRIBUTION THEORIES; CONTROL; CREATIVITY; REACTANCE; RISK; SELF-ESTEEM; TRUST.

BIBLIOGRAPHY
Brehm, J. W. (1993). Control, its loss, and psychological reactance. In G. Weary, F. Gleicher, & K. L. Marsh (Eds.), *Control motivation and social cognition* (pp. 3–30). New York: Springer-Verlag.
Burger, J. M. (1989). Negative reactions to increases in perceived personal control. *Journal of Personality and Social Psychology, 56*, 246–56.
——(1992). *Desire for control: Personality, social, and clinical perspectives.* New York: Plenum.
Deci, E. L., & Ryan, R. M. (1987). The support of autonomy and the control of behavior. *Journal of Personality and Social Psychology, 53*, 1024–37.
Heider, F. (1958). *The psychology of interpersonal relations.* New York: Wiley.
Pittman, T. S., & D'Agostino, P. R. (1989). Motivation and cognition: Control deprivation and the nature of subsequent information processing. *Journal of Experimental Social Psychology, 25*, 465–80.
Strube, M. J., & Yost, J. H. (1993). Control motivation and self-appraisal. In G. Weary, F. Gleicher, & K. L. Marsh (Eds.), *Control motivation and social cognition* (pp. 220–54). New York: Springer-Verlag.
Swann, W. B., Stein-Seroussi, A., & Geisler, R. B. (1992). Why people self-verify. *Journal of Personality and Social Psychology, 62*, 392–401.
Thompson, S. C. (1981). Will it hurt less if I can control it? A complex answer to a simple question? *Psychological Bulletin, 90*, 89–101.
White, R. W. (1959). Motivation reconsidered: The concept of competence. *Psychological Review, 66*, 297–333.

FAITH GLEICHER
GIFFORD WEARY

**conversion** In contemporary research, conversion refers to a process of SOCIAL INFLUENCE-induced ATTITUDE CHANGE which is delayed and long-lasting rather than immediate and temporary, indirect rather than direct, and represents private acceptance rather than public COMPLIANCE. An "indirect" effect is one which appears on more general, indirectly relevant measures reflecting core VALUES in the source's position rather than more limited, directly relevant measures focusing on the issue raised in the influence attempt. Conversion may be contrasted with compliance in that it embodies a private, latent, informational impact of influence which leads one to see things from the source's point of view rather than being a public, immediately manifest, unthinking yielding (i.e., involving no active cognitive elaboration) which does not affect one's understanding of the issues. Moscovici (1980) proposes that MAJORITY SOCIAL INFLUENCE tends to produce compliance rather than conversion (one *compares* with the majority and conforms), whereas MINORITY SOCIAL INFLUENCE tends to produce conversion rather than compliance (one cognitively *validates* the minority's views and comes to accept them). The basis of conversion is being actively researched (e.g., Nemeth, 1986).

See also: ATTITUDE CHANGE; SOCIAL INFLUENCE; VALUES.

BIBLIOGRAPHY
Moscovici, S. (1980). Towards a theory of conversion behavior. In L. Berkowitz (Ed.), *Advances in experimental social psychology* (Vol. 13, pp. 209–39). New York: Academic Press.
Nemeth, C. J. (1986). Differential contributions of majority and minority influence. *Psychological Review, 93*, 1–10.

JOHN C. TURNER

**cooperation and competition** Central to defining cooperation and competition is the concept of INTERDEPENDENCE of outcomes. A state of interdependence of outcomes exists whenever two or more individuals' outcomes are jointly determined by their own and the others' actions. Situations of interdependence vary along a continuum of degree of correspondence between the outcomes (or interests) of the parties involved. One end of this continuum refers to situations of positive outcome correspondence (actions promoting my gain always promote your gain and vice versa), while the other pole defines situations of negative outcome correspondence (actions leading to gains for one party produce losses for the other party and vice versa). In between these poles, one finds the more frequently occurring case of mixtures of partly corresponding and partly noncorresponding outcomes (*see* CONFLICT).

The concepts of cooperation and competition are used by researchers to refer to the interdependence structures themselves, the behaviors emitted in these settings, the orientations that people bring to these settings or that are elicited by them, or a combination of the above. The basic distinction however is between a definition based on the structure of the interaction setting and a definition based on the motivational orientations or goals of the persons involved in the interaction, as they also lead to partly different research questions.

When cooperation and competition are equated with strictly positively and negatively correspondent structures of outcome interdependence, the key questions concern the effects of these structures on the behaviors and attitudes of the parties involved. A number of authors view the behavioral and attitudinal effects of these structures themselves as also a part of their definition of cooperation and competition (Deutsch, 1973). Alternatively, when cooperation and competition are viewed as motivational orientations or goals they constitute but two of a larger variety of social motivations that may underlie people's behavior in settings of outcome interdependence. Here the key questions concern:

(1) the determinants of these goals; and
(2) the effects of these goals on behavioral choices (strategies), as these goals interact with characteristics of the interdependence structure and the expected or observed behaviors of others.

Relating these two definitions, the first perspective departs from the assumption that people strive towards the goal of maximizing their own absolute gains and that they will therefore use the strategy of cooperation or competition dependent on which strategy best serves this goal. The second perspective views an own gain orientation as conceptually distinct from a cooperative and a competitive orientation. A cooperative orientation implies a striving towards the maximization of joint gain and a competitive orientation implies a tendency to maximize the difference between own and others' gain in one's own favor, independent of whether actions towards these goals do or do not yield the highest personal profit (Kelley & Thibaut, 1978). This distinction makes it understandable that research in the first tradition has paid more attention to behavior in situations of perfect positive or negative outcome correspondence, whereas research in the second tradition has devoted more attention to behavior in situations of partial correspondence. A setting of only partial correspondence becomes an essential research tool if one wants to discriminate between multiple goals, their respective determinants and their impact on behavior.

There is of course a good deal of overlap between these two approaches, shown most explicitly in their shared search for interventions which could increase people's motivation to behave cooperatively rather than competitively.

Researchers have used both laboratory and field methodologies to study cooperation and competition in settings differing in the number of parties involved in an interdependence relationship, namely:

(1) in 2-person interpersonal (dyadic) relationships;
(2) in $n$-person intragroup relationships; and
(3) in intergroup relationships.

Although the fundamental questions to be asked across these settings are in part conceptually identical, it is worthwhile to look also at each setting in its own right. Some questions and their answers take on a specific form precisely as a function of the level of analysis.

## COOPERATION AND COMPETITION IN INTERPERSONAL (DYADIC) SETTINGS

Mixed motive EXPERIMENTAL GAMES have constituted the most prominent research paradigm for studying factors that influence the likelihood of cooperative and competitive behavior in two-person or dyadic situations. In spite of criticisms which can be leveled against their unqualified use, this paradigm has proven to be a valuable tool in assessing the role of theory-relevant factors which influence cooperative versus competitive choice behavior. Most notable amongst them is the PRISONER'S DILEMMA. It has two persons choose between cooperation (at the risk of being exploited by other) and competition, which – if reciprocated – leads to lower joint outcomes than does joint cooperation. Variants of this paradigm, most notably decomposed games, permit a more fine-grained analysis of the specific motives that may underlie cooperative or competitive choices in dyadic interactions.

Structural, individual difference, and situational variables have all been found relevant in understanding behavior in the prisoner's dilemma game and its variants. For example, as the payoff for cooperative responding increases relative to the payoff for competition, so too does the extent of observed cooperation. With increasing age children in most cultures become more competitive. Members of some cultures behave more competitively than those of other cultures. Together with the age-related findings the latter results reveal the impact of the value society attaches to the one or the other orientation (see VALUES).

Independent of the role of the above factors, research using decomposed games finds that some people are more cooperatively oriented than others. At the same time behavior is also strongly determined by characteristics of the opponent (friend versus stranger) and by his or her behavior. In this latter regard a tit-for-tat strategy, defined by an initial cooperative move followed by a strategy which matches the other person's choice on the previous trial, is most efficient in inducing cooperation. Similarly, the opportunity to communicate and the expectation that the other person will cooperate strongly affect one's own tendency to cooperate (see TRUST, TRIANGLE HYPOTHESIS). These latter findings indicate that the appearance of cooperative behavior depends not only on an actor's own orientation or goal, but equally on his or her expectation that the other will reciprocate, thereby revealing the importance of the theoretical distinction between behavioral strategies and interaction goals (see McClintock & Van Avermaet, 1982; Pruitt & Kimmel, 1977).

Although repetitively played experimental games are sometimes conceived of as instances of BARGAINING, more typically bargaining refers to mixed interest interdependence settings where a particular joint outcome is not decided upon until both parties, following a series of communicated offers and counter-offers, agree on it. The level of cooperation and competition in these situations has been observed to vary as a function of variables conceptually similar to those influencing choices in experimental games. The same holds with respect to settings which involve three or more people, and which allow for a subset of them to join their resources in a cooperative fashion in competition against others (see COALITION FORMATION).

## COOPERATION AND COMPETITION IN INTRAGROUP SETTINGS

The basic interdependence structure of the 2-person prisoner's dilemma is also present in its n-person extension. This extension has proven particularly appealing to researchers as it captures the essence of many problems contemporary societies face, such as overpopulation, the depletion of energy sources, the creation and maintenance of public goods and the like (see SOCIAL DILEMMAS). Members of (large) groups often have to choose between seeking their own absolute or relative gain (competition) and showing concern for the needs and interests of the collectivity (cooperation). The first alternative entails the risk that, given that everybody acts this way, all stand to gain less or lose more than if all cooperate. The second entails the risk that, if one's cooperation is not reciprocated by others, exploitation will be the undesired outcome. For example, if I turn my thermostat down to save energy but others do not, then I am suckered into suffering from the cold while the others reap the benefits of my cooperative behavior. If they show restraint and I do not, I get to free ride on their efforts. But if we all restrict our use of energy, in the long run we are all better off than if nobody does.

Although the interdependence structure of the *n*-person case is similar to that of the 2-person case, it also differs in a number of important respects, which reduce the likelihood of cooperation. One's own impact on the joint outcome becomes smaller as *n* increases, one has less control over the behaviors of others, there is a greater degree of anonymity in one's behavior, and often the negative consequences of one's own or others' competitive behavior are not apparent until after a time delay.

These differences make it more difficult to achieve cooperative behavior in *n*-person than 2-person relationships, and therefore the former require additional means to promote cooperation. More specifically, as studies have shown, cooperation is created by installing a sense of "we-ness," by increasing the perceived effectiveness of one's behavior, reducing the size of the group, rendering one's choice behavior more visible to other group members and by making the negative long-term consequences of noncooperative behavior more salient.

Generally speaking, in attempting to solve social dilemmas, the choice of the social engineer is between psychological and structural alternatives. Psychological solutions attempt to influence members of groups to be more cooperative (joint gain oriented) by:

(1) appeals to norms;
(2) the use of social influence;
(3) the induction of trust; and
(4) the promotion of insight into the structure of the interdependence setting.

Structural solutions attempt to modify overt behavior in the direction of cooperation, by making it more profitable – in own gain terms – to cooperate than to compete or to behave individualistically. Providing positive rewards for cooperation, imposing negative sanctions for competition, and removing the individual freedom to act as one wants are examples of such structural solutions. It appears obvious that the larger the group, the greater the probability that structural solutions are more effective than psychological ones (*see* Liebrand & Messick, 1992).

A somewhat different line of research, emanating more from a structural definition of cooperation and competition, has looked into the effects of cooperative and competitive reward structures on GROUP PRODUCTIVITY, and on intragroup behaviors and attitudes. Moreover, whereas in the *n*-person extensions of 2-person games groups are often no more than mere aggregates of interdependent individuals, here they are conceived of as psychological groups, characterized by entitativity. This research tradition, initiated by Deutsch (*see* Deutsch, 1973) and carried further by many others (*see* Johnson & Johnson, 1989), typically has subjects work on a group task (e.g., solving a puzzle or a human relations problem) where performance is evaluated in terms of meeting a goal set for the group as a whole (cooperative interdependence), or in terms of doing better or worse than the other individual group members (competitive interdependence).

The standard observation in the great majority of these studies is that a cooperative structure leads to higher productivity, more positive intragroup attitudes and less aggressiveness than a competitive structure. A crucial factor that contributes to this higher productivity is that cooperative group members are not only positively interdependent with respect to outcomes, but also are interdependent with regard to the means required to achieve these outcomes. Given independence of means (each performs his or her own tasks), productivity tends to be higher under a competitive reward structure, albeit at the cost of reducing the quality of interpersonal relations (*see* GROUP COHESIVENESS, GROUP STRUCTURE). It should also be observed that the productivity comparisons made here are between cooperatively or competitively structured group tasks and not between a group and an individual task (*see* SOCIAL FACILITATION, SOCIAL LOAFING).

An interesting and dramatic example of the negative behavioral effects of a competitive interdependence structure can be found in situations in which people exhibit panic behavior, as is the case in a theatre fire. Although most if not all people could escape if they coordinate their behaviors (cooperate), it is often observed that the fear of not being able to get out in time causes deadly jams of individuals who are all trying to get to safety first (competition).

## COOPERATION AND COMPETITION IN INTERGROUP SETTINGS

The effects of cooperative and competitive reward structures have also been studied at the level of INTERGROUP RELATIONS. In line with Deutsch's arguments (Deutsch, 1973), Sherif's REALISTIC CONFLICT THEORY (Sherif, Harvey, White, Hood, & Sherif, 1961) posits that a reward structure in which one's own group's interests are negatively correspondent with those of another group will yield competitive intergroup attitudes and behaviors. As Sherif's famous Robber Cave's experiment showed, this form of structure produces strong feelings and behaviors of intergroup discrimination, fosters the development of PREJUDICE, leads to a overevaluation of one's own group's products and increases intergroup aggressiveness. At the same time, however, it also promotes strong feelings and behaviors of intragroup cooperation and cohesion. When, on the other hand, own and other group's interests are positively correspondent, as is the case when both groups depend on each other to achieve a goal they jointly want, friendly and cooperative attitudes and behaviors dominate (*see* SUPERORDINATE GOALS).

Recently it has been shown that:

(1) an intergroup reward structure as such need not necessarily be competitive for the above prejudicial effects to be observed; and
(2) it is not essential that groups have a history of prior cooperation and/or intergroup antagonism (Rabbie, 1982; Tajfel & Turner, 1986).

In the MINIMAL GROUP PARADIGM subjects are divided into two groups on the basis of a relatively arbitrary criterion, and are then asked to allocate points between anonymous members of the ingroup and the outgroup. Although the reward structure permits them to allocate these points in a noncompetitive manner, the standard observation is that they favor the ingroup. Moreover, favoritism observed in an intergroup setting is often more pronounced than self-favoritism in 2-person situations.

Ingroup favoritism sometimes takes on the form of a purely competitive allocation of resources where absolute own group gain is sacrificed for the sake of maximizing the difference between the ingroup and the outgroup members. Sometimes it is expressed in terms of holding more positive attitudes towards the anonymous ingroup than the anonymous outgroup members. At present there is still theoretical uncertainty with respect to the exact causes of these competitive and prejudicial behaviors and attitudes (SOCIAL IDENTITY THEORY versus instrumentality explanations). Further, the competitive orientation is often partly tempered by fairness considerations. Still it remains most striking that even minimal SOCIAL CATEGORIZATION conditions can produce these attitudes and behaviors.

It should come as no surprise that considerable attention has been paid to the question of how these strong tendencies towards competitive and antagonistic intergroup attitudes and behaviors can be reduced. Macro-societal problems, associated with the relations between different racial, religious, and ethnic groups, have played a major part in stimulating concerns. Most prominent in understanding these problems is a set of theoretical and empirical contributions related to the contact hypothesis. Basically, this hypothesis states that direct interpersonal contact between members of antagonistic groups will result in a reduction of competitiveness and prejudice in intergroup attitudes, but only if this contact is realized under a number of specific conditions. As reviews of this literature have shown (*see* Messick & Mackie, 1989), it is one thing to prescribe what these conditions should be, but it is quite another to realize them. Moreover, theorists vary in their prescription as to the overall format that intergroup contact should take. Some propose that intergroup contact should take place in settings where category membership is minimized (by personalizing intergroup contact and by having people differentiate among outgroup members). Others, who emphasize the positive and enriching value of maintaining different categories and groups in society, focus on creating positive experiences when interacting with typical representatives of other groups.

Recently, various programs have been designed which attempt to induce a cooperative process and higher overall achievement in school classes composed of pupils who belonged initially to different groups (e.g., racial), with differing resources and with initially antagonistic competitive attitudes. These programs partially rely on the above contact perspective (*see* Messick & Mackie, 1989). In addition, they also incorporate elements which draw on Deutsch's (1973) premise that the probability of cooperation is greatly enhanced when making group members positively interdependent with respect to the achievement of desired outcomes. Contact combined with common fate appears indeed to be a most powerful determinant of the future course of intergroup relationships and behaviors.

CONCLUSION

At first glance the questions and answers regarding cooperation and competition appear to be somewhat different depending on whether one defines these concepts in terms of the interdependence structures (with a focus on their effects) or in terms of interparty goals and strategies (with a focus on their determinants). The differences may be more apparent than real, however, as was most keenly observed by Deutsch when he formulated his "crude law of social relations: the characteristic processes and effects elicited by a given type of social relationship (cooperative or competitive) tend also to elicit that type of relationship" (Deutsch, 1973, p. 365).

*See also:* BARGAINING; CONFLICT; EXPERIMENTAL GAMES; GROUP COHESIVENESS; GROUP PRODUCTIVITY; GROUP STRUCTURE; INTERDEPENDENCE THEORY; INTERGROUP RELATIONS; PREJUDICE; SOCIAL CATEGORIZATION; SOCIAL DILEMMAS; SOCIAL FACILITATION; SOCIAL IDENTITY THEORY; SOCIAL LOAFING; TRUST; VALUES.

BIBLIOGRAPHY
Deutsch, M. (1973). *The resolution of conflict: Constructive and destructive processes.* New Haven, CT: Yale University Press.
Johnson, D. W., & Johnson, R. T. (1989). *Cooperation and competition: Theory and research.* Edina, MN: Interaction Book.
Kelley, H. H., & Thibaut, J. W. (1978). *Interpersonal relations: A theory of interdependence.* New York: Wiley.
Liebrand, W. B., & Messick, D. M. (1992). *Social dilemmas: Theoretical issues and research findings.* Oxford: Pergamon Press.
McClintock, C. G., & Van Avermaet, E. F. (1982). Social values and rules of fairness. In V. J. Derlega & J. L. Grzelak (Eds.), *Cooperation and helping behavior: Theory and research* (pp. 43–71). New York: Academic Press.
Messick, D. M., & Mackie, D. M. (1989). Intergroup relations. *Annual Review of Psychology, 40,* 45–81.
Pruitt, D. G. & Kimmel, M. J. (1977). Twenty years of experimental gaming: Critique, synthesis, and suggestions for the future. *Annual Review of Psychology, 28,* 363–92.
Rabbie, J. M. (1982). The effects of intergroup competition and cooperation on intragroup and intergroup relations. In V. J. Derlega & J. L. Grzelak (Eds.), *Cooperation and helping behavior: theory and research* (pp. 123–49). New York: Academic Press.
Sherif, M., Harvey, O. J., White, B. J., Hood, W. R., & Sherif, C. W. (1961). *Intergroup conflict and cooperation: The Robber Cave's experiment.* Norman, OK: University of Oklahoma.
Tajfel, H., & Turner, J. C. (1986). The social identity theory of intergroup behavior. In S. Worchel & W. G. Austin (Eds.), *Psychology of intergroup relations* (pp. 7–24). Chicago, IL: Nelson-Hall.

EDDY VAN AVERMAET

**correspondent inference** In Jones and Davis' correspondent inference theory, a correspondent inference refers to the perceiver's judgment that the actor's behavior is caused by, or corresponds to, a particular trait. Thus the actor's behavior reflects an underlying disposition.

*See also*: ATTRIBUTION THEORIES.

MILES HEWSTONE

**counterattitudinal behavior** Behavior that is inconsistent with attitudes is known as counterattitudinal. It is a feature of research in the FORCED COMPLIANCE paradigm of COGNITIVE DISSONANCE THEORY to create dissonance by having someone engage in counterattitudinal advocacy – usually, advocating a position that is at variance with his or her attitudes.

*See also*: COGNITIVE DISSONANCE THEORY.

JOEL COOPER

**counterfactual thinking** The thoughts people have about the alternative ways in which an event could have occurred. The counterfactual thoughts that an event brings to a perceiver's mind affect the perceiver's judgments of that event as well as his or her emotional reactions to it (*see* NORM THEORY).

*See also*: NORM THEORY.

DALE T. MILLER

**covariation** In Kelley's theory of causal attribution, a perceiver with sufficient time and motivation can make attributions by perceiving the covariation of an observed effect and its possible causes. The effect is attributed to the condition that is present when the effect is present, and that is absent when the effect is absent.

*See also*: ATTRIBUTION THEORIES.

MILES HEWSTONE

**creativity** The generation of ideas or products that are both novel and appropriate (correct, useful, valuable, or meaningful). Psychologists have a long history of disagreement over the definition of creativity (*see* Runco & Albert, 1990; Sternberg, 1988). Gestalt psychologists and, more recently, cognitive psychologists have focused on the creative process (the thought processes and stages involved in creative activity). Other theorists have argued that creativity is best conceptualized in terms of the person (the distinguishing characteristics of creative individuals). Although many contemporary theorists think of creativity as a process and look for evidence of it in persons, current definitions most frequently use characteristics of the product as the distinguishing signs of creativity. Most product definitions stipulate that a creative product or response must be both novel and appropriate. An additional criterion used by some researchers is that the task should be heuristic (open-ended) rather than algorithmic (having a clear path to solution). Although many researchers operationally define creativity as performance on creativity tests, most social psychologists working in the field consider consensual product assessment by experts as more appropriate; a product or response is deemed creative to the extent that appropriate observers agree it is creative.

Until the late 1970s a social psychological approach to creativity did not really exist. For most of the century, creativity research has been dominated by a TRAIT approach, an attempt to identify precisely the PERSONALITY differences between creative and noncreative individuals (Guilford, 1950). As a result, some potentially important areas of inquiry were virtually ignored. There was a concentration on the creative person to the neglect of creative situations; there was a narrow focus on intrapersonal determinants of creativity to the neglect of external determinants; and, within studies of intrapersonal determinants, there was an implicit concern with genetic influences to the neglect of contributions from learning and the social environment. Contemporary theorists have begun to argue that creativity is best conceptualized not as a personality trait or a general ability but as a behavior resulting from particular constellations of personal characteristics, cognitive abilities, and environmental factors (e.g., Amabile, 1983).

PERSONAL CHARACTERISTICS

A cluster of personal characteristics has been repeatedly identified as important to high-level creative behavior:

(1) self-discipline in matters concerning work;
(2) an ability to delay gratification;
(3) perseverance in the face of frustration;
(4) independence of judgment;
(5) a tolerance for ambiguity;
(6) a high degree of autonomy;
(7) an absence of sex-role STEREOTYPING;
(8) an internal LOCUS OF CONTROL;
(9) a willingness to take RISKS; and
(10) a high level of self-initiated, task-oriented striving for excellence.

Recently, creativity theorists and researchers have also shown an interest in the role of motivational variables in creativity. Research suggests that INTRINSIC MOTIVATION (engaging in an activity for its own sake) is conducive to creativity while extrinsic motivation (engaging in an activity to achieve some external goal) is detrimental to creativity.

COGNITIVE ABILITIES

While it is important for creative individuals to be skilled in their particular domain, several domain-independent features of cognitive style appear to be relevant to creativity:

(1) breaking perceptual set;
(2) breaking cognitive set;
(3) understanding complexities;
(4) keeping response options open as long as possible;
(5) suspending judgment;
(6) using "wide" categories;
(7) remembering accurately;
(8) breaking out of performance SCRIPTS; and
(9) perceiving creatively.

SOCIAL ENVIRONMENTAL INFLUENCES

Social psychologists interested in creativity have primarily investigated the impact of the social environment, both at the micro- and the macro-levels. Using controlled experimental paradigms, Amabile (1983) has provided evidence that situations characterized by evaluative pressures, surveillance, contracted-for reward, competition, or restricted choice undermine intrinsic motivation and creativity by focusing the person on external reasons for doing the task. OBSERVATIONAL METHODS have been used to explore the effect of classrooms, families, and work environments on creativity. Classroom environments that provide individualized instruction, models of creative activity, and opportunities for exercising autonomy are generally conducive to creativity. Children's creativity may also be enhanced when they have a special position in the family, when parents are relatively unconcerned about CONFORMITY, and when the family is characterized by a low level of AUTHORITARIANISM and restrictiveness, an encouragement of independence, and a moderate interpersonal distance between parents and children. Work environments most conducive to the fulfillment of creative potential appear to be characterized by: a high level of worker autonomy in carrying out the work, encouragement to take risks from administrative superiors, work groups that are both diversely skilled and cooperative, COMMUNICATION and collaboration across work groups, and a substantial degree of challenge in the work. Research in work environments has also led psychologists to look not only at individual levels of creativity but also at INNOVATION produced by groups using techniques such as BRAINSTORMING.

Using sophisticated historiometric techniques and archival data, Simonton (1984) has generated an extensive body of research on societal, cultural, and political influences on creativity. He suggests that a person's creative success is positively influenced by the amount of formal education, up to a certain point where higher education becomes negatively related to eminence. Also, the more available role models in a field during an individual's developmental period, the more likely that individual is to show early creative achievement in that field, provided he does not adhere too strictly to the models provided. Political fragmentation and civil disturbance in an individual's youth, possibly indicating cultural diversity, are positively related to adult productivity. However, political instability in an individual's youth contributes negatively to creative productivity.

In order to gain a more comprehensive understanding of creativity, contemporary theorists are attempting to integrate personality, cognitive, and social-environmental factors.

*See also*: AUTHORITARIANISM; BRAINSTORM-ING; COMMUNICATION; COOPERATION AND COMPETITION; OBSERVATIONAL METHODS; PER-SONALITY; RISK; SCRIPTS; STEREOTYPING.

BIBLIOGRAPHY

Amabile, T. M. (1983). *The social psychology of creativity*. New York: Springer-Verlag.

Guilford, J. P. (1950). Creativity. *American Psychologist, 5*, 444-54.

Runco, M. A., & Albert, R. S. (Eds.) (1990). *Theories of creativity*. Newbury Park, CA: Sage.

Simonton, D. K. (1984). *Genius, creativity, and leadership: Historiometric inquiries*. Cambridge, MA: Harvard University Press.

Sternberg, R. J. (Ed.) (1988). *The nature of creativity*. New York: Cambridge University Press.

TERESA M. AMABILE<br>MARY ANN COLLINS

**critical social psychology** Any one of a number of social psychologies that trace their roots to the student movements of the late 1960s and the "crisis of relevance" in social psychology of the same period. While critical social psychologies count among the many dissenting psychologies that appeared around that time, they are distinguished by their espousal of Marxism, usually, in the beginning stages at least, that of the Frankfurt School's Critical Theory, whence the label "critical." Some psychologies to which this label is attached have in the meantime distanced themselves in varying degrees from strict allegiance to the Frankfurt School in favor of more traditional forms of Marxist analysis.

Critical social psychologies pass through three stages of development: dissent, critique, and reconstruction. At the first stage they agree with all dissenting psychologies that much of what passes for knowledge in social psychology is irrelevant to the real needs of the subjects it studies. Critique is usually directed at revealing the ways in which this irrelevance is produced by capitalist relations of production, and establishing that the felt irrelevance is often the reverse side of social psychology's real relevance for the dominant classes or elites, which is that it serves to legitimate the reproduction of dominant societal relations in the minds and actions of subordinated individuals and groups. Mainstream social psychology is thus shown to be an essential component of and support for bourgeois IDEOLOGY and its hegemony. A typical target of critique is SOCIAL EXCHANGE THEORY (Archibald, 1978; Billig, 1982; Wexler, 1983) owing to its transparent reproduction – and consequent legitimation – of the interpersonal aspects of capitalist relations of production. Critiques of this kind, however, are accepted by many who would otherwise oppose the project of critical social psychology as simply more evidence of the obvious thesis that all societal practices, science included, are part and parcel of the social–historical fabric of society (*see* Billig, 1982, pp. 203ff). Such revelation in itself says nothing about why social psychology should be judged wrong or reactionary.

At the level of reconstruction, two general strategies are found. The first, largely identified with Anglophone authors and leaning more toward Critical Theory, adopts its basic categories directly from Marx's political economy. The second, working within the framework of traditional Marxism, seeks to develop its own specifically psychological categories.

The title of Archibald's book, *Social Psychology as Political Economy* (1978), epitomizes the Anglophone approach. The author develops a view of social psychology seen through the political economic categories of exchange, COOPERATION AND COMPETITION, class, status, and POWER, to which he adds race, ethnicity, sex, and nationality. The result is less to alter the prevailing social psychology than to provide it with a more radical framework intended to facilitate the actions of social movements in bringing about social change.

Wexler (1983) adopts the categories of alienation, commodification, and exploitation, bringing these ultimately to bear on the social psychological categories of interaction, SELF, and INTIMACY. A class analysis (pp. 91 ff) identifies the emergence of a new revolutionary class made up of intellectuals who posses the "symbolic competence" required to produce an alternative psychology that "can comprehend and facilitate social change movements" (p. 167). An important aim of such a psychology is to overcome the denial of the social and subsequent isolation of individuals brought about and reinforced by the ultraindividualism of traditional social psychology.

German critical psychology represents a larger-scale and more concerted effort than its Anglophone counterparts. Although under the intellectual leadership of a single individual, Klaus Holzkamp of the Free University of Berlin, its programme has been formulated and carried out by a large number of people over a period of more than twenty years. These efforts have produced a monograph series, *Texte zur Kritischen Psychologie* (since 1973); a journal, *Forum Kritische Psychologie* (since 1975); many books and articles on a wide range of topics; and numerous workshops and conferences at German and Austrian universities.

This critical social psychology moves beyond attempts to deduce a psychology from the "Marxist anatomy of bourgeois society" (Tolman & Maiers, 1991, p. 51). The point of a critical, social–historical psychology is to gain an adequate account of individual subjectivity, and such an account cannot be found ready-made in the categories of political economy, despite their overall importance for theory building. What is needed, then, is to reconstruct the psychological categories themselves. The results of this reconstruction are presented in a number of works (e.g., Holzkamp, 1983).

Reconstruction is carried out in two broad phases. The first focuses on phylogenesis. Using a wide range of ethological and paleoanthropological evidence, three major qualitative shifts in the evolution of psyche are identified: its emergence from prepsychical life forms, emergence of the capacity for individual learning and development, and, finally, the emergence of human consciousness. The major categorial dimensions traced

through these shifts are orientation and meaning, emotionality and need, and communication and social structure.

The second phase focuses on the specifically human. Most important here is the emergence of a *societal* mode of existence from one that is merely social. This new mode is characterized by a division of labor aimed at collective provision for future needs. It is this new societal agency that becomes reflected in individuals as subjectivity, a conscious relating to societal meanings as possibilities for action. Subjectivity grows out of participation in societal production on the basis of a commonality of societal and individual needs. Problems develop when these needs diverge, as in modern capitalist society. Individuals become restricted in or excluded from participation in societal production, and this is felt as distortion in their subjective states and effective capacities as agents. Psychological practice, accordingly, is aimed at empowering individuals through understanding of societal dynamics (*see* Tolman & Maiers, 1991).

*See also*: COOPERATION AND COMPETITION; IDEOLOGY; INTIMACY; POWER; SELF.

BIBLIOGRAPHY

Archibald, W. P. (1978). *Social psychology as political economy*. Toronto: McGraw-Hill Ryerson.

Billig, M. (1982). *Ideology and social psychology*. Oxford: Basil Blackwell.

Holzkamp, K. (1983). *Grundlegung der Psychologie*. Frankfurt am Main: Campus Verlag.

Tolman, C. W., & Maiers, W. (Eds.) (1991). *Critical psychology*. New York: Cambridge University Press.

Wexler, P. (1983). *Critical social psychology*. Boston, MA: Routledge & Kegan Paul.

CHARLES W. TOLMAN

**cross-cultural social psychology** This field of research is concerned with establishing the effects of CULTURE upon social behavior and SOCIAL COGNITION. It became well-established during the 1980s, as researchers sought to test how general was the applicability of social psychological theories and findings which had mostly originated in North America (*see* Berry et al., 1992; Bond, 1988; Smith & Bond, 1993). Its growth reflects the increasing importance of cross-cultural communication, both within multicultural societies and for those who live in, work in, study in, or visit cultures other than their own.

The first stage in the development of the field involved attempts to replicate classic North American studies in other countries. These rather frequently showed that the effects obtained were not the same as in the original studies. This gave way to a second stage in which studies were mounted concurrently in two or more countries and increasingly to a third stage in which the locations of the populations selected for study are determined by reasons based on relevant theory, rather than by convenience.

SOME REQUIRED CONCEPTS

A prerequisite for worthwhile cross-cultural studies in social psychology is an adequate definition of culture, and a means of classifying different national cultures. The most influential attempt to provide these has been that of Hofstede (1980). He defined culture as "the collective programming of the mind," and proposed that cultures could be classified according to the similarity of VALUES prevailing within them. His study was based upon 117,000 responses to a questionnaire distributed to the employees of an American-owned multinational firm. He analyzed this databank not at the level of individual responses, but by examining the mean scores obtained on each question for each of the 53 countries and regions for which he had sufficient data. Factor analysis of these means enabled him to classify national cultures along four dimensions, which he named as INDIVIDUALISM–COLLECTIVISM, power distance, uncertainty avoidance, and femininity–masculinity.

It has often been pointed out that the heterogeneity of values within particular nations renders hazardous the assumption of the Hofstede study that one could classify national cultures in this way, particularly when all his data came from employees of one firm.

However, later studies using different samples have confirmed the importance of his dimensions, while suggesting one or two additional important dimensions of variance. Hofstede himself cautioned against the "ecological fallacy," namely the assumption that because a population as a whole scores high on some dimension, individuals and subgroups within that population must necessarily also be high.

Of Hofstede's dimensions, the one which has attracted greatest attention is individualism–collectivism. Individualist cultures are those in which one's identity and affiliations are seen largely as a matter of personal choice; collectivist cultures are those in which one's identity is more strongly determined by one's existing group memberships, usually in terms of the family into which one is born, or the organization for which one works. The particular significance of this dimension to cross-cultural social psychology is that the countries in which most social psychology has been done turn out to be the most individualist cultures of all. According to Hofstede, the most individualist nations are USA, Australia, Britain, Netherlands, and Canada, in that order. These same countries also scored rather low on another of Hofstede's dimensions, namely power distance. In other words, in these countries relations between those in superior and subordinate positions were relatively informal and not so deferential.

There is therefore a substantial risk that results obtained in these locations will prove a poor guide to social behavior in other countries. Equally, it might be the case that subgroups within these predominantly individualist cultures would also show different behavior patterns. This risk applies not just to the findings which may be obtained from nonindividualist cultures, but also to the very concepts themselves. Concepts such as individualism have arisen from within Western cultures and to attempt to derive measures from them and use these measures within non-Western cultures may lead us to misunderstand the responses we obtain. Social anthropologists have given these issues fuller attention, and the proponents of "indigenous psychology" argue that we should do better to study each society in its own terms and later see whether our findings do or do not converge.

A study by a group of researchers naming themselves the Chinese Culture Connection (1987) suggests that this problem may not be too severe. Starting with traditional Chinese sayings, they constructed a VALUES questionnaire which was administered to students in 22 countries. Using methods similar to those of Hofstede, they identified four dimensions of variation, three of them similar to those obtained in Hofstede's study, and an additional one which they termed Confucian Work Dynamism. The overlapping dimensions included individualism–collectivism. Thus a study starting with traditional Chinese sayings and a study derived from a Western business organization yielded convergent results.

Within collectivist societies we may expect that people will think about themselves and others in different ways. The fact that one's destiny is inextricably linked with a particular group is likely to mean that one is more concerned to preserve harmony in the group. Within the group this should lead to greater deference to the leader, more equal sharing with others, more cooperative behavior, less aggression, less direct styles of communication, longer time perspective, and stronger social influence. However, in relating to those outside one's own group few of these effects are to be expected. Thus we may see that Western researchers' predilection for using previously unacquainted subjects in their experiments is likely to give misleading results in collectivist cultures.

The great majority of published cross-cultural studies involve comparisons between North Americans, Europeans, or Australians, on the one hand, and Japanese, Chinese, or Indians, on the other. The findings summarized below refer primarily to these groups. Although the individualism–collectivism concept is frequently invoked to generate predictions and interpret findings of these studies, only in a few cases were measures actually obtained of the values endorsed by subjects in each study. Individual researchers are therefore vulnerable to the ecological fallacy against which Hofstede cautioned, although the consistency of the findings obtained does enhance their validity.

## DIFFERENCES IN SOCIAL BEHAVIORS

Effective LEADERSHIP in collectivist cultures proves to be that in which both task and maintenance roles are concurrently provided by the leader. There is little support for Western-type situational contingency theories. The OBEDIENCE effects reported by Milgram have also been found in eight other countries, most of them Western. As was found in the USA, obedience levels are greatly reduced if others who are present refuse to cooperate with the experimenter. CONFORMITY, as studied in Asch-type experiments, is on average higher than that reported from individualist cultures. However, the findings are rather variable, probably because whether or not subjects were strangers to one another would be crucial in a collectivist setting and some researchers failed to make clear what had been the subjects' relation to one another. MINORITY SOCIAL INFLUENCE has proved replicable within some collectivist cultures, though it may be accomplished less through consistency than through greater willingness of the majority to compromise. SOCIAL LOAFING does occur in collectivist cultures where the experimental task is a trivial one, such as clapping or shouting. However, when more meaningful tasks have been employed, the social loafing effect is totally reversed. Where groups work together individual performance is enhanced rather than reduced.

In the matter of DISTRIBUTIVE JUSTICE, it is crucial whether resource distribution is to be made within or outside one's own group. Within the group, greater priority is given in collectivist cultures to equality and need than to equity. Outside one's own group the pattern is reversed, and the preference for distribution based on equity is stronger than that found in Western samples. Similarly, the level of COOPERATION AND COMPETITION will depend upon who is the other party. In many of the EXPERIMENTAL GAMES employed, such as the PRISONER'S DILEMMA, it is not clear who is one's opponent, so that the results are sometimes confusing. In most cases, prisoner's dilemma responses from subjects in more collectivist cultures have initially been more competitive than those shown by North American subjects. However, in circumstances where the payoffs have been adjusted by experimenters, subjects from more collectivist countries became more cooperative, thus showing themselves to be more sensitive to their environmental context than those from more individualist countries. In BARGAINING situations, where one's opponent is visible and more readily categorizable, subjects from more collectivist cultures showed more cooperation. Similarly, children from collectivist cultures have been shown to be more cooperative in experimental games.

Face-to-face bargaining is itself likely to be a procedure for the resolution of CONFLICT which is more attractive to those from individualist cultures. Other procedures such as arbitration or mediation are preferred in collectivist cultures, since they are thought more likely to enhance harmony. Western preferences are for procedures thought likely to maximize equity or justice. The types of conflict resolution preferred by members of collectivist cultures are consistent with their preferred modes of COMMUNICATION. Verbal communication will be less direct, less urgent, and less focused upon immediate tasks, since this will permit the covert accumulation of information as to the other's trustworthiness and an assessment of the risks of conflict or loss of face. NONVERBAL COMMUNICATION in many collectivist cultures (though not East Asian societies) involves greater proximity, more touching, and more eye contact than found in most Western cultures. These behaviors also yield information as to the state of relations between the parties. Effective cross-cultural communication thus requires not only mastery of relevant languages, but also of the meanings placed upon different styles of verbal and nonverbal communication.

Where it is clear to a member of a collectivist culture that they are dealing with someone who is not in any way affiliated to their own group, we might expect that INTERGROUP RELATIONS will show similar effects to those found in Western studies. The MINIMAL GROUP PARADIGM, for instance, has proved replicable in Japan, though not with Maori or Samoan children. In more naturalistic settings, existing power differentials between groups will also affect the way in which they perceive one another's behavior. For instance, studies of how members of Malay and Chinese groups perceive one another show different results in Malaysia, where Malays are the majority, to those from Singapore where Chinese are in the majority.

UNDERLYING COGNITIONS
These reported cultural differences in the frequency of different types of social behavior raise the more fundamental question of the processes of social cognition which generate them. Markus and Kitayama (1991) propose that those of us who are socialized within an individualist culture are likely to develop a self-concept which they define as independent. Such a person may be expected to scan the environment in a manner which emphasizes one's independence from it. In contrast, those socialized within a collectivist culture will learn to scan their social environment in such a manner as to maintain harmony with it. Their self-concept will be an "interdependent" one. For the independent actor, COGNITIVE CONSISTENCY with one's self-concept will be a high priority. For the interdependent actor, it will be more important to be in harmony with one's group, even if this requires tolerance for internal inconsistencies. Studies of self-concept (e.g., Cousins, 1989) have shown that Americans readily attributed traits to themselves, while Japanese were more likely to qualify traits by specifying situations to which they apply. Conversely, when subjects were asked to describe themselves within specific settings, the Japanese readily did so, but Americans added qualifications indicating that the "real" me was not necessarily encompassed by the traits relevant to that particular situation.

These differences in self-concept have numerous ramifications. For instance, American measures of SELF-MONITORING have proved to be invalid in Japan, since the personal attributes of SELF which someone with an independent self-concept would monitor are not the same as the attributes of self-in-relation-to-others which are found to be monitored by someone with an interdependent self-concept. Similarly, the so-called SELF-SERVING BIAS, whereby successes are attributed to oneself, but failures are blamed on other factors, proves not to be replicable. In collectivist cultures a "modesty bias" is frequently found, whereby one's success on a specific task is attributed to luck or environmental factors and failure is put down to one's personal shortcomings. Such a bias is of course much more helpful to the preservation of group harmony than would be self-attributions for success.

The differences found in social cognition affect not only self-perception but also PERSON PERCEPTION. Independent subjects are found to be much more likely to attribute others' actions to their personal qualities, whereas interdependent subjects give more weight to the situation within which the other party's actions occur. One way of summarizing the manner in which members of collectivist cultures process information is to say that they treat their multiple obligations to others concurrently, whereas members of individualist cultures tend to order their priorities and hence their attention in a more linear fashion. A particular instance of this is in differing time perspectives. While Western societies value promptness and the setting of short-term task deadlines, the priorities elsewhere lie with establishing and maintaining one's long-term obligations to others.

However, the differences in information-processing found in all these instances are differences of degree, rather than absolute ones. The basic processes of social cognition appear to be present in all cultures. The difference lies in the ways in which these processes are channelled.

POSSIBLE UNIVERSALS
In addition to the many differences which have been identified between social behaviors in individualist and collectivist cultures, other researchers have been interested in how far one can identify universals of social behavior. The answer appears to depend upon how precisely one specifies the behavior under study. For instance, in the study of interpersonal ATTRACTION, Buss (1989) has found consistency over 37 cultures in male preferences for partners who are young, attractive, and healthy, while female preferences were stronger for partners who are ambitious, industrious, and of high earning capacity. However, these consistencies accounted for no more than 2 percent of the variance, and the qualities valued most highly of all were the same for men as for women – both favored partners who were dependable, stable, mature, and mutually attracted.

Preference for such generalizable character traits does appear to be widespread if not universal. However the specific behaviors a partner might need to enact in order to be judged mature or dependable certainly vary greatly from one culture to another. Very large differences were found, for example, in evaluations of premarital chastity. In some cultures, chastity might be seen as an indication of dependability, whereas in other cultures quite other behaviors would form the basis for such a judgment.

Another area in which universals have been proposed is that of FACIAL EXPRESSION OF EMOTION. Portrayals of anger, happiness, disgust, and sadness can be reliably identified by groups as diverse as Americans and New Guineans. However there is some suggestion that research in this field has focused only on emotions salient in Western cultures and has failed to note that other, more distinctive emotions may occur within non-Western cultures. Furthermore, although there may be universals as to how certain emotions are portrayed facially, there prove to be wide cultural differences in the rules as to when and where it is appropriate to express emotions. Reported frequencies of emotion also vary by culture. For instance, fear is less often reported from cultures rated high by Hofstede's study on Uncertainty Avoidance, presumably because unexpected events occur less frequently there.

Recent research has also suggested that the "Big Five" dimensions of PERSONALITY identified by McCrae and John (1992), may summarize the range of ways in which personality varies in many cultures. The dimensions they specify, namely agreeableness, extroversion, openness to experience, will to achieve, and emotional stability may well be expressed in different specific ways in particular cultures. However, studies show that five personality factors frequently emerge when studies using locally constructed test items are employed, and that these dimensions show strong resemblance to the Big Five dimensions.

## PROSPECTS FOR THE FUTURE

Cross-cultural researchers face formidable methodological problems. Valid conclusions will only be achieved when tests and materials have been adequately translated, and where research procedures are plausible to participating subjects (Brislin, Lonner and Thorndike, 1973). Western researchers in search of universally valid conclusions have frequently assumed that their designs and measures will prove valid in settings where subjects place quite other meanings upon them. Such procedures, usually referred to as "imposed etic" (Berry et al., 1992) must be replaced by locally valid "emic" studies. Only where a series of emic studies show convergent conclusions may we infer a valid "derived-etic" generalization about universal aspects of social behavior. Several such emergent generalizations have been touched upon above, but in all cases it appears that they are valid only at a rather broad and abstract level. For many practical purposes it is more fruitful to focus upon the manner in which these generalizations are expressed in their culturally specific ways.

Several writers have considered whether there is evidence for a contemporary convergence of world cultures, toward a more individualist value system induced by industrialization. Although there is evidence of increasing individualism in many parts of the world, it is also clear that modernity continues to take culturally different forms. Studies of immigrants' adaptation indicates substantial selectivity in response to the host culture. Some communities seek integration, while others preserve their distinctive values and yet others accommodate in some aspects of their behavior but not in others. If social psychological theories are to claim universal validity, they will need to take increasing account of this continuing diversity in the world's cultural values.

*See also*: ATTRACTION; BARGAINING; COGNITIVE CONSISTENCY; COMMUNICATION; CONFLICT; COOPERATION AND COMPETITION; CULTURE; EXPERIMENTAL GAMES; FACIAL EXPRESSION OF EMOTION; INDIVIDUALISM–COLLECTIVISM; INTERGROUP RELATIONS; LEADERSHIP; NONVERBAL COMMUNICATION; OBEDIENCE; PERSONALITY; SELF; SELF-MONITORING; SOCIAL COGNITION; SOCIAL LOAFING; VALUES.

BIBLIOGRAPHY
Berry, J. W., Poortinga, Y. H., Segall, M. H., & Dasen, P. R. (1992). *Cross-cultural psychology*. Cambridge: Cambridge University Press.
Bond, M. H. (Ed.) (1988). *The cross-cultural challenge to social psychology*. Newbury Park, CA: Sage.
Brislin, R. W., Lonner, W., & Thorndike, R. M. (1973). *Cross-cultural research methods*. New York: Wiley.
Buss, D. M. (1989). Sex differences in human mate preference: Evolutionary hypotheses tested in 37 cultures. *Behavioral and Brain Sciences, 12*, 1–49.
Chinese Culture Connection (1987). Chinese values and the search for culture-free dimensions of culture. *Journal of Cross-Cultural Psychology, 18*, 143–64.
Cousins, S. (1989). Culture and selfhood in Japan and the US. *Journal of Personality and Social Psychology, 56*, 124–31.
Hofstede, G. (1980). *Culture's consequences: International differences in work-related values*. Newbury Park, CA: Sage.
Markus, H., & Kitayama, S. (1991). Culture and the self: Implications for cognition, emotion and motivation. *Psychological Review, 98*, 224–53.
McCrae, R. R., & John, O. P. (1992). An introduction to the five factor model and its applications. *Journal of Personality, 60*, 175–215.
Smith, P. B., & Bond, M. H. (1993). *Social psychology across cultures: Analysis and perspectives*. Hemel Hempstead: Harvester-Wheatsheaf.

PETER B. SMITH

**cross-lagged panel correlation** With two variables, each measured at two points in time, one can compute six correlations: two synchronous correlations between the two variables at a given time; two lagged correlations between the same variables over time; and two correlations between different variables at different time points, i.e., cross-lagged panel correlations. If the relationship between the two variables is a spurious one (i.e., their association is due to some underlying third variable that is a cause of them both), then the cross-lagged correlations should be equal to each other, assuming equal stabilities of the underlying two constructs. Thus, unequal cross-lagged correlations can be used to argue against spuriousness (Kenny, 1975).

Although one can argue against spuriousness with unequal cross-lagged correlations, they do not permit the estimation of casual effects. It is a misuse of such correlations to argue that their relative magnitude indicates the "causal predominance" of one variable over the other (Rogosa, 1980). CAUSALITY cannot be established by particular patterns of correlations.

*See also*: METHODOLOGY.

BIBLIOGRAPHY
Kenny, D. A. (1975). Cross-lagged panel correlation: A test for spuriousness. *Psychological Bulletin, 82*, 887–903.
Rogosa, D. (1980). A critique of cross-lagged correlation. *Psychological Bulletin, 88*, 245–58.

CHARLES M. JUDD.

**cross-racial facial identification**
Cross-racial facial identification refers to the general tendency for people to exhibit superior memory for faces belonging to members of their own ethnic or racial group than for faces belonging to another group. Plausible accounts for this phenomenon, such as greater actual similarity among faces in one race than in another or differential contact or experience with the ingroup than with the outgroup, have generally not been supported by the evidence (*see* Brigham & Malpass, 1985). In a recent integration of this research, Anthony, Copper, and Mullen (1992) documented that the cross-racial facial identification effect, similar to the OUTGROUP HOMOGENEITY effect, represents a specific operationalization of the general tendency to fail to distinguish among members of the outgroup. This tendency seems to be due to different cognitive representations employed for the ingroup and the outgroup.

*See also*: OUTGROUP HOMOGENEITY.

BIBLIOGRAPHY
Anthony, T., Copper, C., & Mullen, B. (1992). Cross-racial facial identification: A social cognitive integration. *Personality and Social Psychology Bulletin, 18*, 296–301.
Brigham, J. C., & Malpass, R. S. (1985). The role of experience and contact in the recognition of own- and other-race faces. *Journal of Social Issues, 41*, 139–55.

BRIAN MULLEN

**crowd psychology** The study of collective behavior in which large numbers of people who are in the same place at the same time behave in a uniform manner which is volatile, appears relatively unorganized, is characterized by strong emotions, and is often in violation of social norms (Graumann & Moscovici, 1986; Milgram & Toch, 1969; Moscovici, 1985; Reicher, 1987). Crowds include mobs, panics, demonstrations, rallies, and audiences. Social psychologists often treat crowd behavior as a major part of the wider phenomenon of collective behavior, which also includes RUMORS, crazes, fads and fashions, social movements and cults, and contagions of expression, enthusiasm, anxiety, fear, and hostility. The study of the crowd is often a part of the study of GROUP PROCESSES or INTERGROUP RELATIONS (Hogg & Abrams, 1988), but is distinct from the study of CROWDING – the latter emphasizes the effect of contextual or enduring population density on individual behavior, while crowd psychology focuses on the collective aspect of behavior in a gathering.

The crowd is a vivid social phenomenon both for those who are involved and for those who witness the events first hand or through literature and the media. Consider the Tian'anmen Square protest in 1989, the Los Angeles riots of 1992, the Nazi rallies of the 1930s, the celebrations at the removal of the

Berlin wall in 1990, the huge antiwar demonstrations of the late 1960s, the enormous rock festivals of the 1970s, and the crowd scenes in Richard Attenborough's movie *Gandhi*. Not surprisingly, crowd behavior, in its full manifestation, can be difficult to research in the laboratory.

### GUSTAVE LEBON

One of the earliest theories of crowd behavior was proposed by Gustave LeBon (1896/1908). LeBon observed and read accounts of the great revolutionary crowds of the French revolution of 1848 and the Paris Commune of 1871 – accounts such as those to be found in Zola's novels *Germinal* and *La Débâcle*, and Hugo's *Les Misérables*. He was appalled by the "primitive, base, and ghastly" behavior of the crowd, and the way in which people's civilized conscious personality seemed to vanish and be replaced by savage animal instincts. He believed that "by the mere fact that he forms part of an organized crowd, a man descends several rungs in the ladder of civilization. Isolated, he may be a cultivated individual; in a crowd he is a barbarian – that is, a creature acting by instinct" (1908, p. 12). LeBon believed that crowds produce primitive and homogeneous behavior because:

(1) members are anonymous and thus lose personal responsibility for their actions;
(2) ideas and sentiments spread rapidly and unpredictably through a process of CONTAGION (a process whereby the expression of emotions by one person instinctively evokes the same emotion in another); and
(3) unconscious antisocial motives ("ancestral savagery") are released through suggestion (a process akin to hypnosis).

Although criticized, largely for being unscientific, LeBon's ideas are still important today. This is mainly due to the enormous influence of his perspective, in which crowd behavior is considered abnormal/pathological, on later theories of collective behavior.

### PSYCHOANALYTIC VIEWS

Sigmund Freud, for example, argued that the crowd "unlocks" the unconscious. Society's moral standards maintain civilized behavior because they are installed in the human psyche as the super-ego. However, in crowds, the super-ego is supplanted by the leader of the crowd who now acts as the hypnotist who controls unconscious and uncivilized id-impulses. Crowd leaders have this effect because of a deep and primitive instinct in all of us to regress, in crowds, to the "primal horde" – the original brutal human group at the dawn of existence. Civilization is only able to evolve and thrive to the extent that the leader of the primal horde, the "primal father," is rebelled against.

Psychoanalytic principles led also to the development of the FRUSTRATION–AGGRESSION hypothesis. Although not a theory of the crowd, the frustration–aggression hypothesis is an explanation of collective VIOLENCE in which people (e.g., poor whites) who are frustrated (e.g., by economic disadvantage) repress their anger against the source of frustration (e.g., the politico-economic system) and displace it as aggression onto weaker others who act as a scapegoat (e.g., a racial outgroup).

### WILLIAM MCDOUGALL

Another important early theorist was William McDougall (1921). He characterized the crowd as: "excessively emotional, impulsive, violent, fickle, inconsistent, irresolute, and extreme in action, displaying only the coarser emotions and the less refined sentiments; extremely suggestible, careless in deliberation, hasty in judgement, incapable of any but the simpler and imperfect forms of reasoning, easily swayed and led, lacking in self-consciousness, devoid of self-respect and of a sense of responsibility, and apt to be carried away by the consciousness of its own force, so that it tends to produce all the manifestations we have learnt to expect of any irresponsible and absolute power" (1921, p. 45). McDougall believed that the most widespread instinctive emotions are the simple primitive ones (e.g., fear, anger), and that therefore these would be the most common and widely shared emotions in any human aggregate. More complex emotions would be rare and less widely shared. Stimuli eliciting the primitive simple emotions would therefore cause a strong consensual reaction, while those eliciting more complex emotions would not. Primary emotions spread and strengthen very rapidly in a crowd as each member's expression of the emotion acts as a further stimulus to others – a snowball effect dubbed "primitive sympathy." This effect is not easily modulated, as individuals feel depersonalized and have a lowered sense of personal responsibility.

## DEINDIVIDUATION AND SELF-AWARENESS

More recent explanations of collective behavior discard some of the specifics of earlier approaches (e.g., the emphasis on instinctive emotions, the psychodynamic framework), but retain the overall perspective. People usually refrain from indulging their basically impulsive, aggressive, and selfish nature, because of their identifiability as unique individuals in societies that have strong norms against "uncivilized" conduct. In crowds these restraints are relaxed and people can revert to type, and embark upon an orgy of aggressive, selfish, antisocial behavior. The mediating mechanism is DEINDIVIDUATION (e.g., Prentice-Dunn & Rogers, 1989). Large groups provide people with a cloak of anonymity that diffuses people's personal responsibility for the consequences of their actions. This leads to a loss of identity and a reduced concern for social evaluation – there exists a state of deindividuation that causes behavior to become impulsive, irrational, regressive, and disinhibited because it is not under the usual social and personal controls.

Research on deindividuation focuses upon the effects of anonymity on behavior in groups. In one study, subjects who were dressed in grey laboratory coats and seated in a poorly lit room for a group discussion of their parents made more negative comments about their parents than did subjects in a control condition. Similarly, subjects dressed in laboratory coats used more obscene language when discussing erotic literature, and subjects dressed in cloaks and hoods (reminiscent of the Ku Klux Klan) gave larger electric shocks to a confederate in a paired associate learning task. In another classic study, a simulated prison was constructed in the psychology department of Stanford University – student subjects who were deindividuated by being dressed as guards were extremely brutal to other students who were deindividuated as prisoners. There is also evidence that people are more willing to lynch someone or bait a disturbed person to jump from a building if it is dark, and they are in a larger group.

Although in general, anonymity seems to increase the incidence of aggressive antisocial behavior there are problematic findings. For instance, Belgian soldiers were found to give smaller electric shocks when deindividuated by being dressed in cloaks and hoods. It has been suggested that perhaps this happened because the soldiers were an intact group (i.e., already deindividuated), and the "cloak and hood" procedure had the paradoxical effect of decreasing deindividuation. However, other studies have also found a reduction in aggression as a consequence of anonymity or group membership. For instance, in one study, subjects administered shocks to confederate "learners" in a paired-associates learning task. Subjects were deindividuated by either wearing a robe resembling a Ku Klux Klan outfit or a robe resembling a nurse's uniform – the experimenter highlighted the situational norms by explicitly commenting on the resemblance. Although all subjects wore the special clothing, half also wore a large badge displaying their name in order to individuate them (or to reduce deindividuation). Deindividuation failed to increase aggression, even among those dressed as Ku Klux Klan members. Those dressed as nurses were significantly less aggressive than those dressed as Ku Klux Klan members, and deindividuated nurses were the least aggressive of all. These studies tell us two important things:

(1) aggression and antisocial behavior are not automatic and inevitable consequences of anonymity; and
(2) normative expectations surrounding situations of deindividuation may influence behavior.

Regarding this second point, simply note the similarity between the "hood and robe" method of deindividuation, and the wearing of the *chadoor*, or full-length veil, by women in certain Islamic countries. Far from setting free antisocial impulses, the chadoor very precisely specifies one's social obligations.

Recent perspectives on deindividuation have assigned objective self-awareness (awareness of oneself as an object of attention) a central role (Prentice-Dunn & Rogers, 1989). A deindividuated person is someone who is prevented by situational factors present in a group from becoming aware of him/herself as a separate individual, and is unable to monitor his/her own behavior. Factors present in crowds (i.e. anonymity, arousal, group unity, and external focus of attention) reduce self-awareness and create a psychological state of deindividuation that has specific consequences for behavior. These consequences include weakened restraints against impulsive behavior, increased sensitivity to immediate cues or current emotional states, inability to monitor or regulate own behavior, lessened concern about evaluations by others, and reduced ability to engage in rational planning. Although these consequences do not inevitably include aggression, they tend to facilitate the emergence of antisocial behavior.

Another perspective on deindividuation distinguishes between public and private self-awareness. Reduced attention to one's private self (feelings, thoughts, attitudes, and other private aspects of self) is equated with deindividuation, but does not necessarily produce antisocial behavior unless the appropriate norms are in place. It is reduced attention to one's public self (how one wishes others to view one's conduct) that causes behavior to be independent of social norms and thus to become antisocial.

RELATIVE DEPRIVATION AND SOCIAL UNREST
The role of frustration in collective behavior, divorced from the psychoanalytic framework of the frustration–aggression hypothesis, re-emerges in a variety of theories of RELATIVE DEPRIVATION (*see* Walker & Pettigrew, 1984). When people feel that their attainments or achievements fall short of their expectations or their perceived entitlements, a psychological state of relative deprivation exists.

Relative deprivation can be egoistic (based on comparison with similar others) or fraternalistic (based on intergroup comparisons between one's own group and other groups). Fraternalistic relative deprivation may provide a basis for social unrest, which can be manifested as crowd behavior if other conditions are met – for instance:

(1) aggregation;
(2) aversive environmental conditions (e.g., excessive heat);
(3) violent stimuli (e.g., armed police); and
(4) appropriate norms (e.g., norms legitimating violence).

The collective nature of the phenomenon is sometimes attributed to a process of SOCIAL FACILITATION in which people's habitual or customary behavior patterns are instinctively intensified by the physical presence of other people.

EMERGENT NORM THEORY
Emergent norm theory takes a different approach to the explanation of collective behavior (Turner & Killian, 1987). Rather than treating collective behavior as pathological or instinctual behavior, it focuses on collective action as norm-governed behavior, much like any other group behavior. Turner believes that what is distinct about the crowd is that it has no formal organization or tradition of established NORMS to regulate behavior, and so the problem of explaining crowd behavior is to explain how a norm emerges from within the crowd (hence, "emergent norm theory"). People in a crowd find themselves together under circumstances in which there are no clear norms to indicate how to behave – they are essentially an ad hoc collection of people with no history of association and therefore no existent norms. Their attention is attracted by distinctive behaviors (or the behavior of distinctive individuals). These behaviors imply a norm and consequently there is pressure against nonconformity. Inaction on the part of the majority is interpreted as tacit confirmation of the norm, which consequently amplifies pressures against nonconformity.

By focusing on norms, emergent norm theory acknowledges that members of a crowd may communicate with one another in the elaboration of appropriate norms of action. However, the general nature of crowd behavior is influenced by the role of "distinctive" behaviors, which are presumably behaviors that are relatively rare in most people's daily lives – for instance, antisocial behaviors. Two other critical observations have been made:

(1) a norm-regulated crowd would have to be a self-aware crowd (there is no need for people to comply with norms unless they are identifiable and thus individuated and self-aware), and yet evidence indicates that self-awareness is very low in crowds; and

(2) crowds rarely come together in a normative vacuum.

More often than not, members of a crowd congregate for a specific purpose and thus bring with them a clear set of shared norms to regulate their behavior as members of a specific group – for example a crowd of people welcoming the Queen, watching a rugby match, or protesting on campus. The lack of tradition of established norms referred to by Turner may be more myth than reality. There is a logic to the crowd, Reicher (1987) argues, that is not adequately captured by emergent norm theory.

## SOCIAL IDENTITY THEORY

An important feature of crowd behavior that is usually ignored is that it is actually very much an *intergroup* phenomenon. Many crowd instances involve, for instance, a direct collective confrontation between police and rioters, or rival gangs or team supporters, and even where no direct confrontation occurs there is symbolic confrontation in that the crowd event symbolizes a confrontation between, for instance, the crowd, or the wider group it represents, and the state. A second point is that far from losing identity, people in the crowd actually assume the identity provided by the crowd: there is a change from idiosyncratic personal identity to shared social identity as a crowd member. These points have been made by Reicher (1987),

who applies SOCIAL IDENTITY THEORY and SELF-CATEGORIZATION THEORY to collective behavior and the crowd.

From this perspective, individuals come together, or find themselves together, as members of a specific social group for a specific purpose (e.g. conservationists protesting environmental destruction). There is a high degree of shared social identity that promotes social categorization of self and others in terms of that group membership. It is this wider social identity that provides the limits for crowd behavior – for example, for certain groups violence may be legitimate (e.g., neo-Nazi groups in Germany) while for others it may not (e.g., supporters at a sportsgame). While these general group norms provide the limits for acceptable crowd behavior, there are often few norms to indicate how to behave in the specific context of the crowd event. Crowd members look to the identity-consistent behavior of others, usually central group members, for guidance. Self-categorization produces conformity to these context-specific norms of conduct. This explains why different groups in a crowd event often behave differently – for example, the police act in one way while the protesters act in a different way because, despite being exposed to the same environmental stimuli, their behaviors are being controlled by different group memberships.

This analysis does appear to be consistent with what actually goes on in the crowd. For example, analyses of American race riots of the 1960s show that the violence was not arbitrary and directionless, and that participants reported a sense of positive social identity (e.g., Milgram & Toch, 1969). Reicher (1987) provides a detailed analysis of a riot which occurred in the Spring of 1980 in the St Pauls district of the British city of Bristol. Three important findings emerged:

(1) The violence, burning, and looting was not unconstrained – the crowd was "orderly" and the rioters were selective. Aggression was directed only at symbols of the state – the bank, the police, and entrepreneurial merchants in the community.

(2) The crowd remained within the bounds of its own community – St Pauls.

(3) During, and as a consequence of, the riot, rioters felt a strong sense of positive social identity as members of the St Pauls community.

All this makes sense when it is recognized that the riot was an antigovernment protest on the part of the St Pauls community – an economically depressed area of Bristol with very high unemployment during a time of severe national unemployment.

## CONCLUSION

Crowd behavior is rarely unbounded, irrational, and instinctive – usually it has clear limits which legitimize some forms of action and not others. These limits may be furnished by the specific context and purpose of the crowd event, but also by the wider cultural and socio-historical context. Above all, crowd behavior is collective behavior. The challenge for social psychology is to be able to account for these features in such a way that individual psychological processes are explicitly articulated with wider social processes. Finally, the political sensitivity of much crowd behavior makes it important to be able to distinguish between the objective science and the political rhetoric of explanations.

See also: CROWDING; DEINDIVIDUATION; GROUP PROCESSES; INTERGROUP RELATIONS; NORMS; RELATIVE DEPRIVATION; SELF-CATEGORIZATION THEORY; SOCIAL FACILITATION; SOCIAL IDENTITY THEORY.

## BIBLIOGRAPHY

Graumann, C. F., & Moscovici, S. (Eds.) (1986). *Changing conceptions of crowd mind and behavior.* New York: Springer-Verlag.

Hogg, M. A., & Abrams, D. (1988). *Social identifications: A social psychology of intergroup relations and group processes.* London & New York: Routledge.

LeBon, G. (1908). *The crowd: A study of the popular mind.* London: Unwin. (First published in French in 1896).

McDougall, W. (1921). *The group mind.* London: Cambridge University Press.

Milgram, S., & Toch, H. (1969). Collective behavior: Crowds and social movements. In G. Lindzey & E. Aronson (Eds.), *The handbook of social psychology* (2nd ed., vol. 4, pp. 507–610). Reading, MA: Addison-Wesley.

Moscovici, S. (1985). *The age of the crowd.* Cambridge: Cambridge University Press.

Prentice-Dunn, S., & Rogers, R. W. (1989). Deindividuation and the self-regulation of behavior. In P. B. Paulus (Ed.), *Psychology of group influence* (2nd ed. pp. 87–109). Hillsdale, NJ: Lawrence Erlbaum.

Reicher, S. D. (1987). Crowd behavior as social action. In J. C. Turner, M. A. Hogg, P. J. Oakes, S. D. Reicher, & M. S. Wetherell (Eds.), *Rediscovering the social group: A self- categorization theory* (pp. 171–202). Oxford: Basil Blackwell.

Turner, R. H., & Killian, L. (1987). *Collective behavior* (3rd ed.). Englewood Cliffs, NJ: Prentice Hall.

Walker, I., & Pettigrew, T. F. (1984). Relative deprivation theory: An overview and conceptual critique. *British Journal of Social Psychology, 23,* 301–10.

MICHAEL A. HOGG

**crowding** A process involving negative psychological reactions, coping responses, and short- and long-term consequences associated with population density; it is one of several possible consequences of inadequate management of interpersonal contact. Crowding is not necessarily limited to very densely populated situations but rather occurs when individuals experience more contact with others than they desire. Thus, although the presence of others is necessary, it is not a sufficient condition for crowding.

Density and crowding are distinct concepts. Density refers to the number of people per unit of space and does not imply any affective response; in contrast, crowding involves affectively negative feelings, coping responses, and psychological consequences. Two kinds of density have been studied extensively: in *social density*, the number of people is increased while space remains constant; in *spatial density*, the number of people remains constant but the amount of space per person is decreased (Bell, Fisher, Baum, & Greene, 1990).

## GENERAL CROWDING MODEL

Descriptions of how and when crowding occurs typically contain five broad categories of variables as well as additional descriptions of the processes by which these variables are interconnected (Baum & Paulus, 1987; Evans & LePore, 1992). There is considerable variety in explanations of crowding processes, especially with respect to details such as which particular variables are included and how and when they contribute to crowding processes. The simplest models posit that undesired density leads to a perceived loss of CONTROL which in turn leads to a feeling of being crowded and a variety of negative outcomes, including stress, illness, performance decrements, and AGGRESSION, among other things. Below is a more complex general crowding model that illustrates five aspects of crowding:

(1) preexisting circumstances and expectations;
(2) density-related experiences that represent a loss of control;
(3) appraisals of the loss of control;
(4) coping mechanisms; and
(5) consequences.

A central idea is that crowding results from inadequate regulation of interpersonal boundaries. Another assumption is that crowding can involve a great deal of cycling through expectations, appraisal, coping, and experienced consequences as individuals appraise, cope, reappraise, and so on (Baum & Epstein, 1978; Baum, Singer & Valins, 1978).

1. In crowding, the stage is set by four classes of *preexisting circumstances and related expectations*:

(a) characteristics of the physical setting;
(b) cultural, demographic, and PERSONALITY characteristics of the people involved and their interpersonal and role relationships;
(c) descriptions of the ongoing tasks or goals; and
(d) social or spatial density.

These circumstances often lead the individual to decide what level of social contact is needed or desired before entering a setting, they can enable the individual to anticipate what a setting will be like, and they can also influence how the individual appraises a situation after being immersed in it.

2. The preexisting circumstances and the individual's expectations provide the context in which *density-related experiences* will be interpreted. Often, high spatial and social density result in a variety of restrictions on behavioral freedom, such as:

(a) interference with desired activities or goals;
(b) restricted access to needed or desired resources (including space); and
(c) unexpected and uncontrollable violations of NORMS.

And (d) sometimes high density simply results in uncontrolled and unwanted interactions and the inability to control the sheer amount of ongoing social and nonsocial stimulation. When these two kinds of experiences, *behavioral constraints* and *stimulus overload*, are so intense that they represent a threat to *personal* control, the result is *physiological AROUSAL*.

3. These experiences lead the individual to interpret or *appraise* the situation, comparing it to his or her goals and desired level of contact. Most research emphasizes cognitive appraisals of controllability and constraint, or the attributions made about the situation (*see* ATTRIBUTION THEORIES). These labels are influenced by such preexisting conditions as personal and group characteristics and the importance of individual and group goals.

4. A subsequent aspect of the process is coping mechanisms, or attempts to regain control such as through deliberate avoidance of interaction, leaving the situation, or confronting (sometimes aggressively) others in the setting; group members may attempt to coordinate their interactions so as to reduce disruptions. These coping mechanisms are often followed by additional appraisals as the individual reassesses the situation to see whether goals are being met and the desired level of contact has been achieved, further coping is necessary, or the situation should be abandoned (*see* STRESS AND COPING).

5. An array of consequences follow from successful and unsuccessful coping and reappraisal. Often the focus is on short-term experiences, such as psychological state,

immediate stress reactions, feelings of efficacy or frustration, GROUP COHESIVENESS, task performance, and other outcomes. Long-term consequences of ineffective coping with density can be more severe, such as illness, emotional problems, aggression, and learned HELPLESSNESS.

## CROWDING RESEARCH

### Animal Crowding Research

Research on human crowding was stimulated by observations and research with animals which indicated that crowding disrupted normal social, territorial, reproductive, and maternal behaviors and resulted in behavioral pathologies and physiological symptoms of stress. These early findings raised alarms because the human population worldwide was growing at a rapid rate, especially in large urban areas as migration, high birth rates, and low death rates intensified urban density.

### Human Crowding Research

Human crowding research includes an array of methodologies, purposes, and psychological and behavioral processes. This overview provides examples of research in each of the five categories described above.

*Preexisting circumstances*

*Urban density.* Early studies in the 1920s through 1940s found little relationship among high urban density and indices of stress and pathology such as crime rates, mental illness, health and mortality. Many of these studies did not take into consideration factors such as UNEMPLOYMENT, discrimination, and poverty which could also account for negative outcomes. Furthermore, many of these studies depended on archival data such as citywide census and crime data which do not provide fine-grained, sensitive indices of either density or negative outcomes.

*Interior density.* Recent analyses distinguish between density inside and outside of the dwelling. These studies indicate that high densities inside of the dwelling may be associated with stress and its associated problems. High density inside homes is associated with marital and parental stress, poor school performance, disciplinary problems, and other interpersonal and social problems. Studies also show that people in dense living arrangements may be unable to benefit from the stress-buffering benefits of their friends and social networks (*see* BUFFERING HYPOTHESIS).

*Personal factors.* Individual factors such as desires for sociability and the ability to screen out others can enable people to function effectively in and even prefer dense environments.

*Cultural factors.* Whether a setting is defined as having too many people varies greatly from one cultural group to the next, and mechanisms for adjusting to a desired level of contact also vary with cultural norms and VALUES. Different groups develop levels of openness and ways of functioning but they simultaneously devise mechanisms for avoiding contact with others when desired. Many groups experience extensive contact with others both inside of and outside of their homes, but each group adopts ways of gaining control over this situation, perhaps by not looking at others, not entering others' areas in communal living arrangements, not gossiping about others, and so on (*see* Altman & Chemers, 1980). Poverty-related high density may exceed culturally controllable levels, and is usually not a chosen alternative.

*Architectural and design features.* Extensive studies of prison conditions document associations between long-term spatial and social density and a variety of negative outcomes including illness, mortality, aggression, and stress symptoms (Paulus, 1988). Large, open dormitories have been associated with numerous problems; providing privacy control by installing low-cost, individual cubicles reduces the negative outcomes. These findings are consistent with simulation studies which showed that rooms and buildings can hold a larger number of people comfortably when the space has architectural features which provide barriers or increase perceptions of spaciousness (e.g., high ceilings).

Extensive studies of student dormitory residents compared various aspects of the built environment and examined psychological adjustment, social relations, coping mechanisms, and academic performance. Consistent with the idea that the inability to control interactions with others is stressful, the data indicated that dormitory rooms arranged along long corridors resulted in more negative outcomes than those on short corridors or arranged in clusters or suites. Housing three people in rooms designed for two was also stressful, especially for women who attempted to cope by staying in the room and interacting more, whereas men coped by withdrawing from the setting (*see* Aiello & Baum, 1979).

*Density-related experiences*

Density can be associated with a host of interpersonal experiences that disrupt ongoing goals or in other ways interfere with intra- and interpersonal boundary regulation processes. The inability to control interactions is usually more intense in high social than in high spatial density settings.

*Behavioral constraints.* These include goal blockage, resource competition, and norm violations. A number of studies indicate that people report more negative AFFECT, like their colleagues less, and perceive the environment as more crowded when their own goal attainment is interrupted or blocked by others or when they have to compete with others for scarce resources. Other studies show that people who sit or stand closer than is appropriate for the situation and room size are viewed as inappropriate and the situation is rated as being more competitive, aggressive, and crowded, especially by male participants. In some studies, behavioral constraints have greater impact on perceptions of crowding than does the objective social density, suggesting that interference from others is more important than the sheer number of people.

*Stimulus overload.* Sometimes social and spatial density have their impact because individuals are unable to control and discriminate among all of the incoming stimulus information. People may withdraw physically or they may withdraw psychologically and narrow their attention to selected topics. Research guided by this concern examines such consequences of cognitive overload as the withdrawn and impersonal behavior of strangers on city streets, lowered helpfulness (*see* HELPING BEHAVIOR), and confusion and disorder in densely populated settings and microsettings.

*Boundary regulation.* In a model that includes both behavioral constraints and stimulus overload, Altman (1975) described privacy regulation as selectively controlling access to the self or group, and proposed a dynamic privacy model in which people attempted to match their desired and achieved levels of contact with others. The desired level changes with time, circumstances, and the social opportunities available, and people engage in a variety of privacy regulation mechanisms (including PERSONAL SPACE, TERRITORIALITY, and other verbal, nonverbal, and environmental behaviors) to avoid being lonely or crowded. In this model, LONELINESS and crowding are seen as aspects of a total social regulation process; crowding occurs when actual interaction exceeds a desired level of exchange. Research on perceived crowding in offices indicates that dissatisfaction and perceived crowding are high when individuals cannot control noises and visual distractions, and when they feel compelled to moderate their own behaviors to accommodate others.

*Perceived control.* Both behavioral constraints and stimulus overload have been linked to crowding and stress. Crowding stress shares three qualities with other environmental stressors:

(1) reactions to spatial and social density depend on the task or goal in the situation (e.g., consistent with SOCIAL FACILITATION research, high density is related to enhanced performance on simple and reduced performance on complex tasks);
(2) perceived crowding and crowding stress are more likely when contact with others is unpredictable and uncontrollable; and
(3) long-term exposure has more effects than does short-term exposure.

Providing a sense of control can often ameliorate the effects of density. Studies show that people who have a choice over where to sit or who can control where they sit or stand report less stress, less crowding, and have lower physiological indicators of stress. Other work indicates that people who have *decision* control (e.g., leaders of spatially dense groups) feel more positively about the group and report less crowding and stress than do other group members. And telling people that they have *termination* control (the freedom to leave a spatially dense room) can also reduce crowding stress, especially residual effects.

*Appraisals and attributions*

The experiences of behavioral constraint and stimulus overload and their associated loss of perceived control often result in physiological arousal. As people scan the high density situation, trying to understand what is occurring and trying to interpret their own physiological arousal, they may focus on density or other features, and that focus can determine how they interpret the situation. One view is that density simply intensifies whatever affect is preexisting or anticipated in a situation, so whether a crowd is interpreted positively (e.g., crowd enthusiasm), or negatively (e.g., crowding interference) depends on what people want or expect.

In general, research on attributions shows that – if density is made salient – high density is interpreted negatively as crowding unless alternative attributions are made available. Researchers have successfully reduced perceptions of crowding by redirecting participants' attention to art work on the walls, a film, anticipated subliminal noise, and by reducing perceived group size by suggesting (through different uniforms) that the large group was actually composed of subgroups. This line of research indicates the importance – and malleability – of cognitive interpretations and misinterpretations, but may overestimate the extent to which people can ignore or reinterpret long-term, highly dense, low-control conditions.

*Coping*

*Individual responses.* Coping with density is a dynamic process that can occur in anticipation of crowding or at any point thereafter. People can take a proactive stance and select a location that provides them with optimum control, or they can control exposure to crowds temporally by arriving before or after other people, such as by shopping midweek or by commuting at off-peak times. Once in the dense situation, people can attempt to control others' actions verbally, they can withdraw physically – a common response in studies of dormitory crowding – or they can withdraw psychologically and avoid eye contact, reduce their level of interaction, or only focus on their immediate situation. Coping by withdrawing can be effective, especially when

people are successful at both avoiding unwanted and achieving wanted contacts with others. Coping often entails cycling through appraisals and behavioral coping strategies, as people make repeated efforts to establish or reestablish control.

*Situational interventions.* Changes in the design or configuration of space can help to ameliorate crowding stress. Breaking groups up into smaller subunits, providing physical barriers to enhance privacy regulation, using queue control devices such as rope barriers, providing an adequate number of supplies or better organizing the work environment, and structuring a task can all reduce the problems associated with a lack of control. Stimulus overload can be brought under control with the use of signs or verbal information that give instructions, allow people to anticipate high density effects, and bring a sense of order to the situation.

Behavioral opportunities are also lost in high density settings. Extensive research in schools indicates that students fill more important roles and have more satisfactory experiences when they are in small rather than extremely large schools. In large schools, on the other hand, skilled individuals compete for scarce opportunities, and students tend to demand more of themselves and achieve more in extracurricular domains. By increasing the number of school clubs, large schools may compensate for sheer size and provide a greater variety of significant and important opportunities (Wicker, 1979).

*Consequences*

If coping efforts are successful, there should be few or no negative effects of high density, depending on how long a time and how much effort and psychological energy were expended on the coping. On the other hand, unsuccessful coping can result in short- and/or long-term consequences.

*Short-term.* Short-term negative consequences include decrements in task performance, psychophysiological indicators of stress, negative affect, and disrupted social interaction. Often, people are able to manage and be successful while in the crowded situation, but afterwards they may show residual stress effects, such as interpersonal hostility, lowered task performance, or less tolerance for frustration. Prison research indicates that rapid changes in density (severe, short-term lack of control) can also result in negative consequences.

*Long-term.* Prison, dormitory, and household crowding studies all indicate that in long-term, high and uncontrollable density situations, people show MOOD changes, interpersonal withdrawal, or interpersonal competition and aggression indicative of ongoing stress. In some cases, pathologies such as VIOLENCE, physical and mental illness, and even severe illness and death can occur. Research on residential crowding shows that young children and college students may exhibit motivational deficits and signs of learned helplessness.

CONCLUSION

Major strides have been made in studies of density and crowding. Improved methodologies include more research in naturalistic situations, a broader array of behavioral processes and outcome variables, and greater specificity in conceptual and statistical analyses. These have combined to give a comprehensive understanding of crowding, mediating and coping processes, short- and long-term consequences, and architectural and other mechanisms for alleviating negative effects of high spatial and social density.

*See also:* AGGRESSION; AROUSAL; ATTRIBUTION THEORIES; CONTROL; GROUP COHESIVENESS; HELPING BEHAVIOR; LONELINESS; MOOD IMPACT ON COGNITION AND BEHAVIOR; NORMS; PERSONALITY; SOCIAL FACILITATION; STRESS AND COPING; TERRITORIALITY; UNEMPLOYMENT; VALUES.

BIBLIOGRAPHY
Aiello, J., & Baum, A. (1979). *Residential crowding and design.* New York: Plenum.
Altman, I. (1975). *Environment and social behavior: Privacy, personal space, territory and crowding.* Monterey, CA: Brooks/Cole.
—— & Chemers, M. M. (1980). *Culture and environment.* Monterey, CA: Brooks/Cole.
Baum, A., & Epstein, Y. M. (Eds.) (1978). *Human response to crowding.* Hillsdale, NJ: Lawrence Erlbaum.
—— & Paulus, P. B. (1987). Crowding. In D. Stokols & I. Altman (Eds.), *Handbook of environmental psychology*, (Vol. 1, pp. 533–70). New York: Wiley.
—— Singer, J. E., & Valins, S. (Eds.) (1978). *Advances in environmental psychology* (Vol. 1): *The urban environment.* Hillsdale, NJ: Lawrence Erlbaum.
Bell, P. A., Fisher, J. D., Baum, A., & Greene, T. E. (1990). *Environmental psychology* (3rd ed.). Chicago, IL: Holt, Rinehart & Winston.
Evans, G. W., & Lepore, S. J. (1992). Conceptual and analytic issues in crowding research. *Journal of Environmental Psychology*, *12*, 163–73.
Paulus, P. B. (1988). *Prison crowding: A psychological perspective.* New York: Springer-Verlag.
Wicker, A. W. (1979). *An introduction to ecological psychology.* Monterey, CA: Brooks/Cole.

CAROL M. WERNER
IRWIN ALTMAN

**culture**   The more or less systematically related set of constructions that people share as members of an enduring, communicatively interacting social group. Culture is what people learn and use by virtue of participating in a social system and what links people together so as to constitute that social system. This means that culture includes the patterns of action, ideations, and things with which a group of people collectively generate, coordinate, understand, and evaluate their worlds.

Culture encompasses everything socially constructed, as well as the uses and relations of these constructions (*see* SOCIAL CONSTRUCTIONISM). Consider, for example, cultural constructions of sex, which encompass taboos, romantic myths (*see* INTIMACY and LOVE), body ideals, GENDER definitions and NORMS, forms of prostitution and RAPE, clothing, plastic surgery, and contraception. Cultural patterns of action include sexual practices, forms of relationship, and techniques (*see* SEXUAL BEHAVIOR). Cultural ideations about sex include sets of symbols, meanings, concepts, PROTOTYPES, SCHEMAS, BELIEFS, and AFFECTS; all of these are connected to many cultural things, including objects, structures, modifications of the environment, and spatiotemporal arrangements. Cultural constructions of sex encompass features of action, thought, emotion, persons, other beings, RELATIONSHIPS, and representations of "nature" (see SOCIAL REPRESENTATIONS) and causality (see ATTRIBUTION THEORIES).

Anthropologists have found that along with LANGUAGE and other channels of COMMUNICATION, people understand and coordinate with each other through diverse mixtures of ritual, RELIGION, art, mythology, kinship and MARRIAGE systems, material exchange, and VIOLENCE. More generally, sociality is mediated by systems of meaning and the universes of signs (icons, indexes, and symbols) by which these meanings are formulated, conveyed, and negotiated. Cultural representations are models both *of* and *for* entities, so there are referential, constitutive (e.g., performative), affective, motivational, and evaluative (e.g., moral and ideological) aspects of meaning (see SUBJECTIVE CULTURE; see also Geertz, 1973; Shweder & LeVine, 1984). For example, cultures shape judgments, emotions, motives, and interpretations concerning sex and death.

In contrast to the broader definition of culture in the social sciences, cultural approaches in the humanities focus on intentional expressive communications. Under the influence of the humanities, some anthropological researchers in the 1970s and 1980s adopted the methods of literary criticism, interpreting cultures as expressive "texts" – and sometimes deconstructing the power relations behind them. Following this came a postmodern concern with the subjectivity of cultural interpretation and the question of interpretive authority. This led to attempts to reverse the postcolonial power relations between researchers and the people they study by giving "them" a direct voice as authors of their own cultures (see Ortner, 1984; Skinner, 1985). Throughout these changes, however, there has always been a consensus that cultural analysis should begin from the subjective point of view of the people who make the culture (see Geertz, 1973).

The term culture is often used in a contrastive sense to mark the distinctive constructions shared within each respective group that potentially differentiate it from other groups. Thus, culture is often defined in terms of the constructions that tend to be transmitted to and acquired by social descendants and that – for the observer or the people concerned – are important factors in defining collective identity. However, the boundaries of cultures are almost always fuzzily overlapping, and people tend to use any given culture identifier (e.g., "Pakistani") in many different, contextually dependent ways – whether using it in the first, second, or third person (see OUTGROUP HOMOGENEITY, REFERENCE GROUP, SOCIAL IDENTITY THEORY, STEREOTYPING). Furthermore cultures (e.g., ethnicities, or the Amish) are often nested units within other cultures, and every culture today participates to some degree in the world culture – at least by withdrawal or opposition. So the actual degree and precision of sharing within and across cultures is variable and difficult to determine in practice (see INTERGROUP RELATIONS). This creates complex problems for systematic comparison and sampling.

When treating culture as an independent variable, social scientists sometimes use the term loosely as a synonym for "society," or to refer to geographic (or temporal) variations in experience and environment. Indeed, culture is often characterized by its spatiotemporal continuity, since it is transmitted and diffused largely through language, material exchange, social interaction, and direct observation. This most important form of face-to-face enculturation results from the relative lability of young children, who are capable of acquiring and participating in any culture. During the course of subsequent development, people usually become committed to the culture they acquired in childhood and perceive it as uniquely natural, inviolable, and good. Adolescents and adults tend to perceive other cultures as less valid and their participants as morally inferior (ethnocentrism).

In addition to this lineal transmission, cultural diffusion occurs through many lateral channels. MASS MEDIA and modern transportation facilitate the reproduction of cultures and cultural constructions which extend far beyond face-to-face communities. People who attend to the same communicative media (e.g., books, radio networks, electronic news groups, arcade games) or models (e.g., religious texts, spiritual leaders, media stars) may share cultures without ever coming together in each other's presence.

Especially in oral communities with little or no writing, participants often perceive their culture as immutable and more or less inviolable. In fact, however, the stability of constructions varies across different periods of history within and between cultures. Consequently, researchers today are increasingly attending to processes of cultural transformation and recombination. Along with this has come a recognition that culture is not simply a rigid track that mechanically channels action or thought. Individuals are more or less constrained by the constructions that they collectively produce; for example, if everyone defines hair length as marking gender or mourning, your haircut has practical consequences. But in the process of actively reproducing their culture from models of prior constructions, people may (intentionally or unintentionally) generate novel constructions that can become models for transforming the preexisting conditions. However, choice and control over cultures are not equally or randomly distributed. Some individuals and groups tend to exercise hegemony over cultural communications, meanings, and standards – including those for hair.

Cultures are collective subjective constructions, but people perceive and experience them as objective, external facts (*see* Sahlins, 1976). For example, witches are cultural constructions, but people may die because they believe that a witch is attacking them, and witches may be executed. Polyandry (marriage to multiple husbands) is a cultural construction, but it determines how people live, love, and reproduce. Furthermore, people perceive cultures as inherent in the "nature" of social groups, so there is a danger of

essentializing culture in a racial manner (*see* PREJUDICE). Hence it is important to note that the concept of culture has nothing intrinsically to do with biological inheritance or population genetics, let alone physical appearance.

Culture is probably universal to the genus *Homo*, and on this planet all but the simplest forms are limited to *Homo sapiens*. However, empirical research must determine whether – and why – any specific construction is unique to a particular individual, shared by a group, common to a number of societies, universal among humans, typical of a number of primates, or common among many social species. More generally, the nature of the intentional, social, cultural, historical, psychological, neurophysiological, ecological, and evolutionary mechanisms that result in any cultural construction are unresolved empirical questions (*see* Ortner, 1984; Skinner, 1985).

*See also*: ATTRIBUTION THEORIES; COMMUNICATION; GENDER; INTERGROUP RELATIONS; INTIMACY; LANGUAGE; MARRIAGE; MASS MEDIA; NORMS; OUTGROUP HOMOGENEITY, PREJUDICE; RAPE; RELATIONSHIPS; RELIGION; SCHEMAS; SEXUAL BEHAVIOR; SOCIAL CONSTRUCTIONISM; SOCIAL IDENTITY THEORY; SOCIAL REPRESENTATIONS; STEREOTYPING; SUBJECTIVE CULTURE.

BIBLIOGRAPHY

Geertz, C. (1973). *The interpretation of cultures*. New York: Basic Books.

Ortner, S. B. (1984). Theory in anthropology since the sixties. *Comparative Studies in Society and History, 26*, 126–66.

Sahlins, M. (1976). *Culture and practical reason*. Chicago, IL: University of Chicago Press.

Shweder, R. A. & LeVine, R. A. (Eds.) (1984). *Culture theory: Essays on mind, self, and emotion*. Cambridge & New York: Cambridge University Press.

Skinner, Q. (Ed.) (1985). *The return of grand theory in the human sciences*. Cambridge & New York: Cambridge University Press.

ALAN PAGE FISKE

# D

**deception** When a person purposefully tries to foster in others an understanding or belief which he or she considers to be false, that person is engaging in deception (Krauss, 1981). Deception, then, can occur when not a word has been spoken, as long as one person is intentionally trying to mislead another. The social psychology of deception has focused primarily on the verbal and nonverbal communication of deception (*see* COMMUNICATION and NONVERBAL COMMUNICATION). Questions include, how successful are people at deceiving, and how successful are they at detecting deceit, when they must rely solely on verbal and nonverbal cues? The two questions are reverse sides of the same coin, for when one person has been successful at deceiving another, the other person has been unsuccessful at detecting the deceit.

In the paradigms typically used to study the communication of deception, speakers ("senders") are videotaped as they tell their truths and their lies, and then another group of subjects (alternatively called judges, detectors, or perceivers) is recruited to observe the tapes and try to distinguish the truths from the lies. In other studies, the liars and their targets interact face-to-face. In many studies, the participants have been college students who might lie and tell the truth about their liking for people they know, their opinions on controversial issues, factual matters, or their responses to items on personality tests (DePaulo, Stone, & Lassiter, 1985). But many other kinds of people have been studied as well. Much of Ekman's research on lying is based on films of nurses who watched either a pleasant film or an extremely gory one, but who always tried to convince the interviewer (who could not see the film that they were watching) that the film they were watching was pleasant (Ekman, 1992). In Feldman's research, children of different ages sip sweetened or unsweetened drinks while trying to dissemble about the kind of drink they are sampling (Feldman, 1982). Other participants have included salespersons, police officers, customs inspectors, polygraphers, and other special groups who might have especially extensive experience at lying or at attempting to detect lies.

If detectors are to have any hope of distinguishing truths from lies, there must be systematic, observable ways in which lies differ from truths. That is, there must be reliable clues to deceit. Research has not uncovered a single verbal or nonverbal behavior that is a *perfect* indicator of deception (i.e., one that always occurs when people are lying and never occurs when they are telling the truth), and probably never will. However, dozens of studies indicate that there are numerous cues that have a probabilistic association with deception – they correlate with deception, but not perfectly (DePaulo et al., 1985). For example, when people are lying, compared to when they are telling the truth, they hesitate more and speak more disfluently and in a higher pitch. Their communications are shorter and more negative; more irrelevant, overgeneralized, and inconsistent; and more emotionally distancing. They also sound more rehearsed. Liars blink more and have more dilated pupils than do truth-tellers, and they also use more "adaptors" (nervous-seeming gestures such as rubbing or scratching). These kinds of behaviors probably occur because lying is more cognitively challenging than truth-telling and people have less confidence in their ability to convey a convincing lie than a convincing truth; because liars often feel guilty about their lies or about their untoward behaviors, and they might also feel apprehensive about the possibility of being caught in their lies; and because lying can be more arousing than telling the truth (*see* AROUSAL).

The cues uncovered by averaging across studies are slippery indices to deceit, however, because they do not equally characterize all kinds of lies told by all kinds of liars. For instance, people lie differently when they are highly motivated to get away with their lies than when they are less highly motivated. The motivated liars appear more expressively inhibited, as though, in an attempt to control their own behavior, they *over*control it. Also, the cues that might reveal deceit are most likely to be useful when considered in light of the sender's usual style of communicating. People who characteristically stutter and stammer when they talk are unlikely to be lying unless their rate of doing so is especially high *for them*. Finally, cues that are associated with deceit can be associated with other states as well. Most dangerously, people who are upset about being falsely accused of lying can sometimes look and sound very similar to people who really are lying.

## PREDICTORS OF SUCCESS AT DETECTING DECEIT

Do perceivers succeed in using these observable behavioral cues to deceit, along with their own intuitions, to distinguish lies from truths? In one sense, yes (*see* ACCURACY IN IMPRESSION FORMATION). When rating truths and lies on, say, 9-point scales of deceptiveness, people generally rate the lies as somewhat more deceptive than the truths. However, their ratings are systematically biased toward the truthful end of the scale. Similarly, if they are simply asked to categorize each message as either a truth or a lie, they reliably judge many more of the messages to be truths than lies, even when they have in fact seen equal numbers of each. They tend to read the overt message that the speaker is trying to convey rather than the covert message that the speaker is trying to hide (*see* CORRESPONDENT INFERENCES and FUNDAMENTAL ATTRIBUTION ERROR).

Perhaps, then, people are simply too trusting (*see* TRUST). If they were urged to be more suspicious, would they be more accurate at

distinguishing truths from lies? Research has shown that there is a hazard to telling perceivers that the people with whom they are interacting might lie to them – such primed perceivers tend to see everyone as more deceptive than they would otherwise, but they do not necessarily see the liars as especially more deceptive than the truth-tellers. They become more cynical, but not more insightful.

Where should people look, or how should they listen, in order to distinguish truths from lies more effectively? The answer comes from many studies in which perceivers were given limited information – for example, they might be shown only the faces of the senders (with no sound) or only their bodies (from the neck down), or they might hear only the audio portion of the tape (with no picture). These studies showed that words, tone of voice cues, and body cues all provide useful information. Facial expressions, however, generally do not.

The question of whether on-the-job experience at trying to detect deception could be predictive of lie-detection success has motivated studies of customs inspectors, law enforcement officers, judges, police officers, psychiatrists, polygraphers, and members of the US Secret Service (DePaulo & Pfeifer, 1986; Ekman, 1992). Of all of these groups, only the Secret Service performed notably well at distinguishing truths from lies solely on the basis of expressive cues.

Would experience at interacting with a particular other person over a long period of time predict skill at distinguishing that person's truths from his or her lies? This question has been addressed in studies in which friends, spouses, and dating partners try to read each other's truths and lies. Typically, these studies show that people in CLOSE RELATIONSHIPS are *not* any more accurate than are strangers at detecting each other's deceit. Instead, they tend to be more biased toward seeing their partner's communications as truthful. If they can overcome this truthfulness bias, though, as when the experimenter warns them that their partner may in fact be lying to them during parts of the study, then partners in close relationships sometimes can show some special sensitivity to the differences between each other's truths and lies (McCornack & Levine, 1990).

Although people with professional experience at detecting lies (such as law enforcement officers) and those with experience with particular other people in close personal relationships do not – without any extra help – show any special skill at distinguishing truths from lies, they *think* that they do. That is, they are more confident. However, study after study has shown that the correlation between confidence in one's judgments of deceptiveness and the accuracy of those judgments is essentially zero.

Another kind of experience that might predict success at detecting deceit is experience with particular kinds of lies or particular kinds of liars. For example, might attractive people be especially sensitive to the kinds of lies that are characteristically told *to* attractive people? Apparently so. When watching speakers on videotape talking to attractive or unattractive listeners who could not be seen on the tape, perceivers who were themselves attractive were especially skilled at detecting the lies told to the attractive listeners; unattractive perceivers, in contrast, were relatively more adept at spotting the lies told to the unattractive listeners (*see* PHYSICAL ATTRACTIVENESS).

That skill at detecting deceit might be specific to specific liars was also the implication of research reporting attempts to train people to detect deceit more successfully (Zuckerman, Koestner, & Alton, 1984). In these studies, subjects watch a series of truthful and deceptive messages. After each one, they record their truth/lie judgment, then are given feedback about the accuracy of that judgment. This training improves people's accuracy at detecting the deceit of the person they were trained to read, but it does not generalize to skill at detecting the deceit of other liars.

There are also specificity effects at the cultural level (*see* CROSS-CULTURAL SOCIAL PSYCHOLOGY). For example, Americans can distinguish lies from truths when observing Americans and Jordanians can do the same when observing Jordanians, but neither can successfully detect the lies told by people from the other culture (Bond, Omar, Mahmoud, & Bonser, 1990).

The effectiveness of training people to detect deception also depends on the kinds of information made available to the trainees. The paradigm in which subjects are given feedback each time about the accuracy of their judgments improves their rate of learning more if they have access to the senders' speech (alone or in combination with the senders' faces) than if they can only see the senders' faces. It may be that when left to their own devices, untrained human lie detectors rely too much on facial expressions. For when they are given the very simple hint to pay special attention to the tone of voice of the sender, they do better at detecting deception than when they are given no hint. The alternate suggestion to pay special attention to the senders' faces does *not* help their lie-detection success.

Another approach to training is to educate perceivers as to the kinds of cues that have been found to be associated with deception in past research. Although there have been some reports of success with this method, it is likely to be limited by the fact that cues to deception can be different for different kinds of liars and different kinds of lies.

Another potential approach to improving lie-detection skill is even more "micro" in its focus. It would involve training people to look for very precise nonverbal behaviors, such as specific muscle movements, that they might not ordinarily notice or know how to interpret. For example, Ekman has shown that smiles of genuine enjoyment differ from false smiles in the particular muscle movements that occur during each (Ekman, 1992). Whether training in the identification of such behaviors can in fact enhance lie-detection success remains to be seen.

There is one limitation that applies to training techniques of all kinds and that is that some people are such skillful liars, and some lies are so well executed, that there simply will be no observable cues that will render the lies identifiable.

In the absence of any special training, there are important individual differences in people's readings of truths and lies. People who are socially anxious, for example, do not see lies as any more deceptive than truths; those who are not so anxious or shy, in contrast, can tell that the lies are more deceptive (*see* SHYNESS).

Sex differences may well be among the most important of all individual differences in perceptions of truths and lies. Women, more than men, tend to read what other people seem to want them to read, and to overlook what others want them to miss. For example, when senders are pretending to like people they really detest, women rate the senders as actually liking the people more than men do. They act as if they believe the fond feelings that the senders are faking. Similarly, when senders are pretending to dislike people they really like, women report perceiving more genuine antipathy in the descriptions than do men. It is not yet clear whether women really do read the communications as the senders want them to, or whether women actually see through to how the senders really do feel, but politely report seeing only what the senders want them to see. The possibility that women might be less sensitive to other people's true feelings when those people are lying is especially interesting because women perform better than men on other interpersonal perception tasks. For example, in tests of skill at reading facial expressions when deception is not an issue (because no one is lying), women routinely outperform men (*see* SEX DIFFERENCES and NONVERBAL COMMUNICATION).

## PREDICTORS OF SUCCESS AT DECEIVING

From the senders' point of view, "success" means getting away with their lies. It means that others see their lies as no more deceptive than their truths, and that they take the senders' words or behaviors at face value. What could augment this kind of success? Intuitively, it would seem that people who have an opportunity to plan their strategy – compared to those who have to perform without warning – would tell more successful lies. Although planning can in fact be useful to people who are skilled at regulating their behavior for self-presentational purposes (*see* SELF-MONITORING), it can also backfire. Sometimes, when people plan their performances (lies *and* truths), perceivers can tell that the performances were rehearsed and they also think they seem more deceptive than performances that were not planned.

Senders' motivation to succeed at getting away with their lies can also, ironically, have undermining effects. When senders care about telling an effective lie – as when they are talking to members of the opposite sex, or when they are telling ingratiating lies that it would be embarrassing to be caught telling – their lies are actually more obvious to perceivers than when they care less about success. When motivated liars fail, it is typically their nonverbal cues that betray them. Even their facial expressions, which can usually be controlled effectively when the stakes are not too high, can give away the lies when liars are trying too hard to keep that from happening (*see* FACIAL EXPRESSION OF EMOTION). However, not all liars are equally vulnerable to this "motivational impairment effect." Senders who have high expectations for success, and those who are physically attractive can instead rise to the challenge and tell effective lies when the pressure is on.

Does experience at deceiving predict skill at telling effective lies? Research on experienced salespersons suggests that it might. When people with years of experience in sales pitch products they like and products they dislike, perceivers see no differences whatsoever in the apparent truthfulness of the two kinds of communications. Even when given a hint that is useful in detecting the lies of senders with no notable experience at lying (i.e., pay special attention to tone of voice), perceivers still cannot tell that the salespersons are being less honest about certain products (the ones they really do not like). Experienced salespersons seem to control successfully the kind of cues that betray other less experienced liars.

Although the behaviors of liars have sometimes – for good methodological reasons – been studied apart from the behaviors of perceivers, the process of telling and detecting lies is usually interactive. Liars can, for instance, sense that the perceiver is becoming suspicious, and modify their behavior accordingly (Buller, Strzyzewski, & Comstock, 1991). And indeed, there is evidence that when senders are probed by their targets, they regulate their behavior more carefully and appear more truthful than when they are not probed. Further, the mere fact of being probed makes senders *appear* more truthful, even when their behavior has not actually changed, perhaps because they seem to hold their own even when challenged by a skeptic. *See also*: AROUSAL; COMMUNICATION; CROSS-CULTURAL SOCIAL PSYCHOLOGY; FACIAL EXPRESSION OF EMOTION; NONVERBAL COMMUNICATION; SELF-MONITORING; SEX DIFFERENCES; SHYNESS; TRUST.

BIBLIOGRAPHY

Bond, C. F. Jr, Omar, A., Mahmoud, A., & Bonser, R. N. (1990). Lie detection across cultures. *Journal of Nonverbal Behavior, 14,* 189–204.

Buller, D. B., Strzyzewski, K. D., & Comstock, J. (1991). Interpersonal deception: I. Deceivers' reactions to receivers' suspicions and probing. *Communication Monographs, 58,* 1–24.

Ekman, P. (1992). *Telling lies: Clues to deceit in the marketplace, politics, and marriage.* New York: Norton.

Feldman, R. S. (Ed.) (1982). *Development of nonverbal behavior in children.* New York: Springer-Verlag.

Krauss, R. M. (1981). Impression formation, impression management, and nonverbal behaviors. In E. T. Higgins, C. P. Herman, & M. P. Zanna (Eds.), *Social cognition: The Ontario symposium* (Vol. 1, pp. 323–41). Hillsdale, NJ: Lawrence Erlbaum.

McCornack, S. A., & Levine, T. R. (1990). When lovers become leery: The relationship between suspicion and accuracy in detecting deception. *Communication Monographs, 57,* 219–30.

Paulo, B. M. & Pfeifer, R. L. (1986). On-the-job experience and skill at detecting deception. *Journal of Applied Social Psychology, 16,* 249–67.

—— Stone, J. I., & Lassiter, G. D. (1985). Deceiving and detecting deceit. In B. R. Schlenker (Ed.), *The self and social life* (pp. 323–70). New York: McGraw-Hill.

Zuckerman, M., Koestner, R., & Alton, A. O. (1984). Learning to detect deception. *Journal of Personality and Social Psychology, 46,* 519–28.

BELLA M. DEPAULO

**decision making** Judgment and decision making have been studied by philosophers, economists, and statisticians for centuries, but this field of research has a relatively short history in psychology. A judgment or decision-making task is characterized by uncertainty of information or outcome(s), or by a concern for a person's preferences (values), or both. Generally, tasks therefore have a probability component or a "value" component, or both. For many judgment and decision tasks there may not exist an objective criterion to determine whether a specific judgment or choice is correct, since the response is (partly) based on personal opinions about probabilities and/or values.

Ward Edwards provided the first major review of research on judgment and decision making. He argued that normative and prescriptive models based on economic and statistical theory could be important to psychologists interested in human judgment and decision making. Edwards (1954) introduced SUBJECTIVELY EXPECTED UTILITY theory (SEU), which decomposes decisions or choices in probabilities and preferences, and provides a set of rules for combining beliefs (probabilities) and preferences ("values" or utilities). The theory is normative or prescriptive because it specifies how decisions should be made. If one accepts the axioms upon which it is based, then the most rational choice or decision is the one specified by the theory as having the highest subjectively expected utility. A basic assumption is that people's primary choice criterion is the maximization of subjectively expected utility. Thus, the theory provides rules to reach rational and consistent decisions on the basis of subjective, personal assessments of probabilities and values or utilities. Bayesian decision theory is a related, normative theory of choice based on a combination of probability theory (*see also* BAYES' THEOREM) and expected utility principles. The validity of these prescriptive, normative theories as adequate descriptions of human choice and decision making has been a dominant theme in this research area for some decades. This is partly based on the idea that the study of human decision making requires an approach that focuses on the perceptual and cognitive factors that cause human choice and decision making to deviate from the predictions of normative models. Normative models such as SEU theory assume extensive information processing capabilities and adopt a rational "homo economicus" model of human decision making. Simon (1957) argued that the limited computational capabilities of decision makers are likely to produce "bounded" rationality, especially in the context of highly complex task environments.

Thus research on judgment and decision making tends to be strongly influenced by formal prescriptive approaches and algebraic representations of information integration processes. Prescriptive or normative decision theory provides a set of principles and rules for combining beliefs (perceived likelihoods or probabilities) and preferences (values or utilities) in order to select an alternative. The distinction between beliefs and preferences is probably the most significant contribution of this research field to the study of human behaviour. Initially SEU models of judgment and decision making dominated research on decision making. However, not all axioms of SEU theory have been accepted, sometimes the theory is applied inappropriately, and sometimes it leads to constraints which make it difficult to represent real-life decision making. A broader approach is to adopt a multidimensional definition of utility. Multi-Attribute Utility (MAU) theory has significantly increased the scope of application of formal decision theory (Von Winterfeldt & Edwards, 1986). It puts more emphasis on the clarification of the preference structure of the individual decision maker. Several models for preference among multi-attribute objects disregard uncertainty about the state of the world and about individual preferences. MAU theory helped to decrease the gap between prescriptive theories and individual decision making. Both SEU theory and MAU theory have had a major impact on ATTITUDE THEORY AND RESEARCH. Theories in this area such as the THEORY of REASONED ACTION essentially employ a model based on SEU theory and MAU theory, assuming that attitudes are based on the assessment of a variety of positive and negative attributes associated with a specific behavioral alternative or choice.

A number of algebraic models of judgment and decision have been advanced to account for judgments based on multiple sources of information. Anderson's (1981) information integration theory is an example of such a model. Hammond's social judgment theory (based on Brunswik's LENS MODEL) relates judgments to environmental cues by means of correlational analyses (Hammond, Stewart, Brehmer & Steinmann, 1975). Both these models and SEU and MAU models rely on linear combination rules. The central issue is to find a rule (e.g., adding, multiplying, or averaging) that adequately describes judgments based on multiple sources of information. The most commonly observed integration rule is an averaging rule. Averaging could also explain the so-called subadditivity effect, by which the simultaneous offer of two valuable objects is perceived as less valuable than what is predicted on the basis of their individual values.

Theoretically, the most interesting findings in studies using normative models of information integration are the departures from the models' predictions. People do not always behave as normative theories such as SEU theory claim they should. More then three decades of research in cognitive psychology cast serious doubt on the descriptive validity of SEU theory. The theory assumes that people are capable of combining substantial quantities of information. However, when there are many cues or unusual relationships between the cues, people tend to violate decision rules such as those of SEU. Moreover, people find it difficult to learn and use the weighted sum decision rule of SEU theory. An added difficulty is that people find it difficult to think probabilistically. Research has also shown that context effects such as how the options are presented, the number of options presented, and even the presentation of irrelevant information have a significant impact on judgment and decision making. These findings also point to the limitations of normative theories and suggest that the conscious thought preceding a decision may be of a rather simple nature given the difficulty of processing complex information. People seem to rely on simple heuristics for making probability judgments, and seem to use different decision-making strategies for different situations. As a consequence psychologists became more interested in understanding how people actually make decisions in the real world. This research field tends to develop descriptive models of judgment and decision making, and puts more emphasis on information processing aspects. PROSPECT THEORY attempts to provide a more general theory of decision making under uncertainty and is probably the most comprehensive attempt to meet the various objections to normative theories such as SEU theory. Two lines of research focus on the discrepancies between normative models and actual decision behavior: research on heuristics and biases, and process-oriented research. The first tradition deals primarily with probabilistic thinking, the second puts more emphasis on information search, information integration and decision rules.

HEURISTICS AND BIASES

The study of heuristics and biases tends to be dominated by attempts to expose systematic errors and inferential biases in human judgment and decision making. These errors and biases can improve our insight into the psychological processes that govern judgment and decision making and suggest ways of improving the quality of our thinking (*see also* the entry on REASONING).

Three HEURISTICS that deal with probabilistic thinking have received considerable attention: (1) AVAILABILITY; (2) REPRESENTATIVENESS; and (3) ANCHORING AND ADJUSTMENT. The availability heuristic refers to the tendency to assess the probability of an event based on the ease with which instances of that event come to mind. This heuristic has been investigated in a variety of domains and relates probability estimates to memory access. Generally people overestimate the probability of an event if concrete instances of that event are easily accessible in memory. The representativeness heuristic refers to the tendency to assess the probability that a stimulus belongs to a particular class by judging the degree to which that event corresponds to an appropriate mental model. This heuristic can be associated with a number of

cognitive errors such as insensitivity to prior probabilities and misconceptions about conjunctive probabilities. A well-known example of how ignoring prior probabilities can affect judgment was reported by Kahneman and Tversky (1973). In their study subjects were provided with brief personality sketches, supposedly of engineers and lawyers. Subjects were asked to assess the probability that each sketch described a member of one profession or the other. Half the respondents were told the population from which the sketches were drawn consisted of 30 engineers and 70 lawyers, the remaining respondents were told that there were 70 engineers and 30 lawyers. The findings showed that the prior probabilities were essentially ignored, and that subjects estimated the probability of class membership by judging how similar each personality sketch was to their mental model of an engineer or a lawyer. Anchoring and adjustment refers to a general judgment process in which an initially given or generated response serves as an anchor, and other information is unsufficiently used to adjust that response. All three heuristics can lead to the neglect of potentially relevant information. It needs to be added that the adaptive use of heuristics, even though leading to a neglect of some information, can save considerable cognitive effort, and still result in adequate or even good solutions to decision problems. In many situations, however, people do make systematic errors in assessing probabilities. Most of the heuristics seem to operate across a wide range of stimulus materials. Some, however, seem to depend on a combination of judgmental vulnerabilty and rather clever stimulus designs highlighting this vulnerability. While people may seem to use informal decision rules and simplifying heuristics rather than normative principles, it is far from obvious that it is maladaptive to do so. Cognitive heuristics may not only be functional, but may even be a valid basis for decision making in real-life contexts. An important shortcoming of the existing literature is that many studies of heuristics involve discrete judgmental tasks at a single point in time. In more natural contexts, however, judgments and actions evolve and influence each other continuously over time. Judgments and decisions in everyday life are typically made on a data base that is redundant rather than randomly generated, and that can constantly be updated. Moreover, correction through feedback may give rise to contingent decision making, resulting in adequate decisions (*see*, e.g., Hogarth, 1990). This is less likely in tasks that require once-and-for-all judgments.

As argued by Payne, Bettman, & Johnson (1992) the question is no longer *whether* biases exist, but *under what conditions* relevant information will or will not be used to arrive at a probability judgment. Payne et al. (1992) review research on the use of prior probabilities or base-rate information and conclude that research should not focus on the question of whether people are good or bad statisticians but on understanding the cognitive factors that determine the type of inference rule being employed. Generally, people seem to use a variety of approaches in their attempts to solve probabilistic reasoning tasks. How individuals use these methods contingently has hardly been investigated.

The heuristics discussed in this section deal primarily with the assessment of probabilities. In many tasks, subjective perceptions of probabilities can often be compared with an objective standard. As argued before, decisions also have a value component. Questions of value, however, are typically subjective. Abelson and Levi (1985) rightly point out that research on the judgment of values has not led to a list of distorting factors as is the case for probability judgment. They list several ways in which values might be inadequately considered. For instance, relevant values may be overlooked, one may not really know one's values, and the context or frame of the decision problem may affect the perception and weighting of values.

## DECISION RULES

Other research on decision making has paid attention to the decision rules people use when they are confronted with complex decisions. Since cognitive overload provokes a need for simplification, especially when combining relevant information about probabilities and values, it can be expected that people also use decision rules that require less cog-

nitive effort than normative theories such as SEU theory. PROCESS TRACING is one of the methods that provided insight into the use of decision rules that serve a simplifying function, and help to avoid complicated trade-offs between good and bad features of decision options. When confronted with a choice between alternatives that can be described in terms of several attributes, people can use a variety of decision rules. Most of these require less cognitive effort than a complete cost–benefit analysis of the available alternatives. Five simplifying decision-rules are discussed below, all of which apply to decision problems with certain outcomes.

*The dominance rule* states that alternative $A_1$ should be chosen over $A_2$ if $A_1$ is better on at least one attribute and not worse than $A_2$ on all remaining attributes.

*The conjunctive decision rule* requires the decision maker to specify a criterion value for each attribute. If an alternative does not meet this minimally required value on one or more attributes the alternative is dropped from the list of remaining possible alternatives.

*The disjunctive decision rule* is the mirror image of the conjunctive rule, and also requires a set of criterion values of the attributes. In this case, a chosen alternative must have at least one attribute that meets the criterion while all remaining alternatives do not meet any of the criterion values.

*The lexicographic decision rule* prescribes a choice of the alternative which is most attractive on the most important attribute. If two alternatives are equally attractive in terms of the most important attribute the decision will be based on the next most important attribute, etc.

*The elimination by aspects rule* is often interpreted as a combination of the lexicographic rule and the conjunctive rule. First, the most important attribute is selected. All alternatives that fail to meet the criterion on this attribute are eliminated. This procedure is repeated for each of the remaining attributes.

Especially the last four decision rules require less cognitive effort than the decision rule required by SEU and MAU models, i.e., the maximization of expected value or utility. This latter principle requires a compensatory decision rule (negative scores on one attribute can be compensated by positive scores on another attribute). The simplifying rules discussed in this section are used quite often in everyday decision making and can provide adequate short-cuts in complex decision environments.

## FORMULAS VERSUS INTUITIVE DECISION MAKING

One of the aims of decision-making research is to improve our understanding of how a decision maker searches for information and of how this information is combined or processed. The process of information integration "in the head" is often called clinical judgment, and compared with the use of a formula or model. The latter can be based on experts' decision rules, or empirically assessed relationships between predictors (e.g., the presence of symptoms, scores on tests) and outcomes (e.g., having a specific disease or the ability of a job candidate). A substantial amount of research has shown that judgments are generally better if they are made using a formula (Dawes, 1988). This applies especially to diagnostic judgments in which a limited number of indicators can lead to adequate prediction. Some organizations use formulas instead of clinical judgment for specific decision problems. The use of statistical judgment based on formulas as opposed to clinical decision making is, however, more the exception than the rule.

Payne et al. (1992) note that two questions are of importance in this context. First, what factors influence the use of a statistical, automated decision procedure? Second, how can we reach a situation in which clinical and automated decision making complement one other, rather than compete? The modest use of automated decision procedures could be related to limited knowledge about their benefits, experienced difficulties in applying the rules to individual decisions, and overly optimistic beliefs in the accuracy of clinical judgment. Integration of the two decision procedures could also enhance the use of formulas.

For instance, one could aggregate the judgment by formula and the judgment in the head to reach an overall solution.

## CONCLUSIONS

Some four decades after the seminal work of Edwards, decision-making research is becoming more prominent in psychology textbooks and a clear and separate research area has emerged, generally referred to as Behavioral Decision Research. An important characteristic of this field of inquiry is that it adopts an interdisciplinary approach. Concepts, models and methods from economics, statistics and social and cognitive psychology can all be found in decision-making research. A second characteristic of this field of inquiry is that it often proceeds by testing the descriptive quality of normative theories of judgment and decision making. Unlike research on many social psychological issues such as aggression, helping behavior, conformity and personal relationships, research on decision making pays considerable attention to the discrepancies between normative models and actual behavior. Most of the research attempting to account for these discrepancies has focused on the information processing strategies, or heuristics, that people use when making judgments or decisions. A final and third characteristic of this field of research is that many concepts and methods are being widely adopted in applied areas. Payne et al. (1992) mention applied areas such as environmental research, accounting, marketing, consumer behavior, finance, law, medicine, and policy decision making.

See also: ATTITUDE THEORY AND RESEARCH; HEURISTICS; PROSPECT THEORY; REASONING.

BIBLIOGRAPHY
Abelson, R. P., & Levi, A. (1985). Decision making and decision theory. In G. Lindzey & E. Aronson (Eds.), *The handbook of social psychology*. New York: Random House.

Anderson, N. H. (1981). *Founations of information integration theory*. New York: Academic Press.

Dawes, R. M. (1988). *Rational choice in an uncertain world*. San Diego, CA: Harcourt Brace Jovanovich.

Edwards, W. (1954). The theory of decision making. *Psychological Bulletin, 51*, 380–417.

Hammond, K. R., Stewart, T. R., Brehmer, B., & Steinmann, D. O. (1975). Social judgment theory. In M. Kaplan & S. Schwartz (Eds.). *Human judgments and decision processes*. New York: Academic Press.

Hogarth, R. M. (Ed.). (1990). *Insights in decision making: A tribute to Hillel J. Einhorn*. Chicago, IL: Chicago University Press.

Kahneman, D., & Tversky, A. (1973). On the psychology of prediction. *Psychological Review, 80*, 237–51.

Payne, J. W., Bettman, J. R., & Johnson, E. J. (1992). Behavioral decision research: A constructive processing perspective. *Annual Review of Psychology, 43*, 87–132.

Simon, H. A. (1957). *Models of man: Social and rational*. New York: Wiley.

Von Winterfeldt, D., & Edwards, W. (1986). *Decision analysis and behavioral research*. Cambridge: Cambridge University Press.

JOOP VAN DER PLIGT

**deindividuation** Classically defined, deindividuation describes a state of reduced SELF-AWARENESS or even "loss of self" associated with immersion and anonymity within a group. This state results in deregulated and disinhibited behavior prey to the vagaries of immediate environmental cues and unresponsive to social NORMS and standards (*see* Diener, 1980; Zimbardo, 1969). It has been employed to explain aspects of mass behavior, and has long been associated with negative psychological and social consequences of the crowd (e.g., suggestibility, disinhibition, AGGRESSION, etc.; *see* CROWD PSYCHOLOGY). Recent definitions try to separate the effects of anonymity from reduced awareness as well as further delineating the effects of different dimensions of self-awareness (Prentice-Dunn & Rogers, 1989). However, these "refinements" also reveal the slippery nature of the phenomenon if not the whole concept of deindividuation. Although it has sometimes struggled to meet the challenge of empirical test, developments in social psychological theory have been used to rejuvenate as well as question its status as a predictive and explanatory concept.

The idea underlying deindividuation can be traced back to the theorizing of LeBon in the last century and has its roots in pioneering work in social psychology. According to LeBon, in the crowd the otherwise "rational" individual becomes taken over by the collective racial unconscious, and returns to a primitive state (*see* CONTAGION). Although metaphysical notions of group mind were rejected on the grounds of their unscientific basis by Floyd Allport and subsequent deindividuation theorists, these later psychologists shared the idea that the crowd had the effect of stripping away the veneer of social constraint, revealing the individual's "natural" instincts. The result was largely the same: a basic irrational response which was atavistic and asocial in nature (Reicher, 1987). If not a blueprint, then, these early writings certainly helped to steer the direction of subsequent theorizing and research.

Within contemorary social psychology, the classic study by Festinger, Pepitone, and Newcomb (1952) gave deindividuation its name, and marked the first in a long line of empirical studies of this phenomenon. Following the legacy of LeBon, Festinger et al. reasoned that "submergence in the group" could produce a state of deindividuation defined in terms of reduced identifiability, with the consequence that behavior becomes less inhibited. The concept of deindividuation was further refined in subsequent work, notably by Zimbardo (1969) and Diener (1980). In this line of research the theme of anonymity in the group became emphasized and was usually operationalized by disguising participants in masks and overalls, with the prediction that subjects so deindividuated would display more antisocial or antinormative behavior (such as delivering electric shocks to a confederate). Although much early evidence was supportive, some studies also showed evidence of more prosocial behavior under deindividuating conditions (*see* Diener, 1980; Zimbardo, 1969). By the early 1980s theorizing began to reflect new developments in self-awareness theory. Specifically, Prentice-Dunn & Rogers (1989) applied the distinction between private and public self-awareness to the deindividuation paradigm. They argued that anonymity was associated with reduced public self-awareness, and immersion and arousal within the group with reduced private self-awareness. Although both could produce more disinhibited and antinormative behavior, they argued that it was reduced private self-awareness caused by submergence and increased arousal in the group that defines deindividuation.

Deindividuation theory has not been without its problems, as demonstrated by the need for regular theoretical adjustment. From its inception the concept has been plagued by a lack of operational precision, and a lack of specificity about its defining attributes and antecedents. For example, researchers have often failed to distinguish between the effects of anonymity of others to oneself, and oneself to others, and whether identifiability is with respect to the ingroup or an outgroup (e.g., other subjects, the experimenter). This point also raises the more general question of external validity, and whether anonymity among the (in)group reflects the reality of many crowd situations. Such problems are exacerbated by difficulties in measuring the state of deindividuation directly or independently of the outcomes used to characterize it. Although measuring arousal and behavioral outcomes can be used to infer the state, the link between these two is not always clear-cut, and behavioral outcomes have often been open to alternative interpretations. More generally, it is a moot point whether submergence in the group necessarily reduces self-awareness or undermines identity (*see* Reicher, 1987). Although research has tended to become more rigorous and explicit in operational definition, it is questionable whether we have got closer to the state and whether such a generalized state that can result in such diverse outcomes has great explanatory or predictive utility.

A more general theoretical criticism concerns the basic individualism characteristic of the deindividuation approach (in its model of group phenomena and the SELF) and thus whether it constitutes an appropriate level of explanation for distinctively social behavior. It should be remembered that the deindividuation perspective argues that submergence in the group undermines the influence of social norms, whereas research on GROUP PROCESSES has consistently demonstrated the normative hold of the group on the individual. This underlines a basic failure of the deindividuation approach to distinguish between general social standards assumed to be operational in the research, and the role of more context-specific (and thus variable) group norms. In many deindividuation experiments the situational requirement (e.g., to deliver shocks) might be considered as implying a local group norm or "demand," in contrast to a generic prosocial norm. In these terms much deindividuation might actually be seen as group-normative. Attempts to manipulate this context suggest that this may be the case, which could help to explain many apparently contradictory findings (*see* Diener, 1980; Zimbardo, 1969). More generally, deindividuation theory tends to ignore important aspects of the social context of crowd behavior and particularly its intergroup character (Reicher, 1987). The distinction between public and private self-awareness also does little to change the individualistic model of the self which pervades this paradigm. Social identity theorists have argued that immersion in a group may produce a switch from individual to group identity, rather than a loss of identity per se (Reicher, 1987). This approach is more consistent with a normative interpretation of deindividuation phenomena, allows for self-awareness in the group, and does not privilege the rationality of the individual over the collective.

*See also*: AGGRESSION; CROWD PSYCHOLOGY; GROUP PROCESSES; NORMS; SELF; SELF-AWARENESS.

BIBLIOGRAPHY

Diener, E. (1980). Deindividuation: The absence of self-awareness and self-regulation in group members. In P. Paulus (Ed.), *The psychology of group influence* (pp. 209–42). Hillsdale, NJ: Lawrence Erlbaum.

Festinger, L., Pepitone, A., & Newcomb, T. (1952). Some consequences of deindividuation in a group. *Journal of Abnormal and Social Psychology*, *47*, 382–9.

Prentice-Dunn, S., & Rogers, R. W. (1989). Deindividuation and the self-regulation of behaviour. In P. Paulus (Ed.), *The psycho-*

*logy of group influence* (2nd ed., pp. 87–109). Hillsdale, NJ: Lawrence Erlbaum.

Reicher, S. D. (1987). Crowd behaviour as social action. In J. C. Turner, M. A. Hogg, P. J. Oakes, S. D. Reicher, & M. S. Wetherell (Eds.), *Rediscovering the social group: A self- categorization theory* (pp. 171–202). Oxford: Basil Blackwell.

Zimbardo, P. G. (1969). The human choice: Individuation, reason and order versus deindividuation, impulse, and chaos. In W. J. Arnold & D. Levine (Eds.), *Nebraska symposium on motivation* (pp. 237–307). Lincoln, NE: University of Nebraska Press.

RUSSELL SPEARS

**depression** The state of depression is a clinical syndrome that includes affective, cognitive, behavioral, and vegetative components. Due to the salience of the sad and depressed affect, this disorder is classified as a mood disorder (*see Diagnostic and Statistical Manual*, third revised edition; *DSM* 111-R, 1987).

In clinical psychological and psychiatric textbooks one can find (historically) many differentiations of depression including endogenous and exogenous, neurotic or psychotic, agitated and retarded, and autonomous versus reactive depression. However, most of these categories have now been abandoned, due to difficulties of making reliable diagnoses on the bases of these labels.

The *DSM* 111-R, currently the most influential diagnostic system, differentiates whether the mood disorder is unipolar or bipolar. In unipolar depression, only the depressed syndrome is present, whereas bipolar depression (formerly labeled manic depressive illness) is characterized by one or more manic episodes in addition to the depressed syndrome. Manic episodes are characterized by inflated SELF-ESTEEM, grandiosity, irritability, and psychomotor agitation that may harm the person or others. As social psychological theories have not yet been applied to bipolar depression (which may be due to its possible genetic, biological bases), the present discussion is limited to unipolar depression.

A Major Depressive Syndrome is defined as depressed mood or loss of interest of at least two weeks' duration, accompanied by several associated symptoms such as weight loss, concentration difficulty, sleep disturbances (difficulty falling asleep and/or returning to sleep), feelings of worthlessness, hopelessness, guilt, indecisiveness, and suicidal thoughts. In addition, social and occupational activities are impaired.

Unipolar depression is a widespread and frequent affective disorder accounting for 75 percent of all psychiatric hospitalizations (*see* Gotlib & Hooley, 1988), and females appear to be more prone to it than males: Estimations of the proportion of the adult population currently afflicted with the disorder range from 4.5 percent to 9.3 percent for females and from 2.3 percent to 3.2 percent for males (*see DSM* 111-R, 1987). In addition, depression is among the most important precipitating factors of suicide.

CLINICAL THEORIES
Probably more than for any other psychological disorder, social psychological theories have been used to explain and to guide research on depression as well as to suggest treatment techniques. Before describing social psychological analyses of depression, a brief summary of the dominant clinical theories is useful.

Until the 1970s, the most influential psychological theories of depression were based on psychoanalysis and learning theory. Psychoanalysts assumed that a predisposition for depression results from disturbances in the oral stage. This may lead to the development of an (orally) dependent personality. When these personalities experience a loss (such as that of a loved one), they fail to show the normal reactions to loss (uncomplicated BEREAVEMENT; e.g., sadness) and tend instead to introject the loved person (i.e., to assume that the lost person has become part of the self). Furthermore, it is assumed that the potentially depressed individual also feels hate toward the lost one (for presenting them with the loss), however, this hate is not socially acceptable. In order to prevent the (unacceptable) hate becoming conscious, defence mechanisms prevent the potentially depressed person from becoming angry; instead the anger is turned inward, resulting in depression (aggression turned inward).

Classical learning theory, by contrast, conceptualizes depression as a vicious cycle due to lack of reinforcement. It is assumed that following a loss (e.g., of a loved one) behaviors that used to be reinforced (e.g., having dinner together) are no longer reinforcing. Instead of being reinforced for activities, the individual is now reinforced for passivity (others feel sorry for the person and offer assistance). Hence, learning theorists conceptualize the symptoms of depression as a result of altered reinforcement contingencies.

The most influential contemporary clinical theory of depression was presented by Beck (1967, 1976). (This theory also shares important similarities with the social psychological analyses of depression that are discussed later.) Beck postulates that it is the particular way in which potentially depressed persons process, explain, and evaluate events that predisposes them to depression. His cognitive theory of depression assumes that depressed individuals might have experienced traumatic events that predispose them to react depressively later. For instance, a child whose parents had a prolonged stay in hospital may misinterpret the absence of the parents as eternal loss, and hence (understandably) conclude that he or she is unable to survive, or to support him- or herself. As a consequence, a loss SCHEMA is formed (e.g., in childhood) that is characterized by the definition of a loss as catastrophic.

When the traumatic negative event has lost its impact (e.g., the parents return from the hospital) this schema ("loss is awful") can become dormant. However, under certain circumstances (e.g., the person loses a spouse in adulthood), the schema becomes reactivated (e.g., the person explains the loss in adulthood as awful as well), and, as a result of the reactivation of a ("childish") schema, depression occurs.

The contents of the thoughts that are guided by depressive schemata can, according to Beck, be characterized by the cognitive triad. By cognitive triad he means the tendency of depressives to carry out unrealistically negative observations of the self, the situation, and the future. The self is regarded to be inadequate (e.g., "I am a failure"), the current situation is thought to be bad and unfair (e.g., "everything is terrible"), and the future is interpreted as unalterably negative (e.g., "I do not expect it to get any better").

In addition to being negative, depressive cognitions, according to Beck, are characterized by their unrealistic nature. Beck assumes that the depressed person unrealistically evaluates the self, the situation, and the future as bad. For instance, he gives the examples of "a wealthy man [who] moans that he doesn't have the financial resources to feed his children, and a widely acclaimed beauty [who] begs for plastic surgery in the belief that she is ugly" (Beck, 1967, p. 3).

The fact that the unrealistically negative view of the self is maintained despite contradictory (positive) information is explained through the observation that depressives "systematically misconstrue specific kinds of experiences" (Beck, 1976, p. 90). Examples for such misconstructions include "overgeneralization" (e.g., "because the dinner was so expensive, the whole evening was terrible"), minimization of positive experiences (e.g., "my success was due to luck") and maximizing negative events (e.g., "my failure was due to lack of intelligence"). As a consequence, depressive schemata (e.g., "I am a failure") are maintained in spite of contradictory information (success) through distorted thinking (e.g., "I was lucky").

SOCIAL PSYCHOLOGICAL THEORIES
The most important social psychological analyses of depression have been guided by attribution theory (e.g., Abramson, Seligman, & Teasdale, 1978), social comparison theory (see Swallow & Kuiper, 1988, for a summary), self-awareness theory (e.g., Pyszczynski & Greenberg, 1987), and interpersonal approaches (see Gotlib & Hooley, 1988).

LEARNED HELPLESSNESS AND DEPRESSION
The application of social psychological theories to the analysis of depression can be

traced back to the discovery that loss of CONTROL leads to learned HELPLESSNESS, a state similar to depression. Seligman (1975) assumes that experiences of uncontrollability (e.g., the loss of a loved one) can lead to the expectancy that future events will also be uncontrollable; and this expectancy, in turn, leads to learned helplessness and depression. According to this theory, depressed individuals should differ from nondepressed persons in that they tend to expect to be unable to control events.

### ATTRIBUTION THEORY

Abramson, Seligman, and Teasdale (1978) have pointed to several weaknesses in Seligman's theory: First, the model does not permit predictions about the conditions under which uncontrollability leads to long-term and/or broadly generalized helplessness symptoms, and about when such experiences result in temporary and/or specific helplessness that only concerns a few areas of behavior. Second, the model has difficulties explaining the observation that feelings of guilt and taking responsibility for negative events are a characteristic symptom of depression: responsibility and guilt imply that one could have avoided a negative event, which, in turn, implies controllability. However, according to the model, depressives should be characterized by perceived *lack* of control.

In order to rectify the weaknesses of the original model, Abramson et al. (1978) applied ATTRIBUTION THEORY to the question of the relationship between uncontrollability, helplessness, and depression. Attribution theorists assume that individuals not only notice events (e.g., "I lost a loved one"), but are also motivated to gain an understanding of their causes (e.g., "Why did she leave?", "Did I do anything wrong?"). According to Abramson et al. (1978), individuals who experience uncontrollability also ask why they failed to control an event. The answer to this "why question" (the causal attribution) determines important psychological reactions to the experience of uncontrollability, including whether or not and to what extent the individual reacts to uncontrollability depressively or with feelings of guilt.

Abramson et al. (1978) classify causal attributions along three dimensions: locus of control, stability, and generality. Each of these dimensions is supposed to be responsible for different aspects of depression. Locus of control (i.e., whether the perceived cause resides within or outside the attributor) determines whether the individual experiences reduced self-esteem in connection with the negative event. For instance, if the husband explains the loss of his spouse in terms of his unattractive personality (an internal cause), he may develop self-doubts, and so-called personal helplessness results. However, if he identifies an external cause (she was killed in an accident), the negative event is less likely to trigger esteem-related emotions; the resultant state is labeled "universal helplessness."

The dimension "stability over time" determines the temporal duration of helplessness. If one assumes that the cause for the bad event (e.g., the loss of a close friend) is stable (e.g., she died), helplessness should be prolonged, because the individual does not expect any change in the unfortunate situation (and "chronic helplessness" evolves). However, if the perceived cause is variable (e.g., "she went away to do a temporary job"), changes in the negative situation are anticipated and the resulting helplessness should be only transient (i.e., temporary helplessness). Finally, the dimension of "generality" determines the breadth of areas to which helplessness deficits generalize. If the negative event is attributed to a specific cause (e.g., "she left because I work too much"), helplessness deficits will not generalize to other areas of life (specific helplessness). However, if the bad event is attributed to a global cause ("she left because of my unattractive personality"), helplessness deficits will generalize to a greater variety of situations (e.g., to relationships with many persons) and "global helplessness" will occur.

Abramson et al. (1978) assume that there are interindividual differences in how persons causally explain events and that individuals with an "attributional style" of making internal, stable, and global attributions for negative events are especially at risk of becoming depressed. As a consequence, therapy for this disorder should consist of changing internal, stable, and global attributions for negative events to more external, variable, and specific ones.

The attributional approach to learned helplessness has stimulated hundreds of research studies, criticisms, and also a recent revision (*see* Abramson, Metalsky & Alloy, 1989). These activities clearly demonstrate the usefulness of an attributional approach to depression.

## THE ATTRIBUTIONAL APPROACH TO DEPRESSION AND BECK'S THEORY

Several authors have pointed out that there are striking similarities between Beck's cognitive theory of depression and the attributional approach (*see* Försterling, 1988). The cognitive triad, which Beck considers to be responsible for reactive depression (i.e., the tendency of the depressive to judge the self, the environment, and the future as bad), corresponds to the tendency to make internal, stable, and global attributions for negative events. The tendency to make internal attributions corresponds to the negative view of the self, the stability of the attribution is in line with the negative view of the future, and the tendency to make global attributions for negative events reflects the negative view of the environment.

In addition, both Beck's and the attributional model suggest that therapy for this disorder should consist of changing the dysfunctional beliefs, and both approaches suggest that this change can be accomplished by gathering data with regard to these beliefs, just as in a scientific test of an hypothesis (*see* Försterling, 1988, for a summary).

Hence, the attributional analysis of depression has revealed a framework for the comprehensive understanding of depression including its prevention and therapy. In addition, this experimentally based theory is quite consistent with the independently developed clinical theory (Beck, 1976). None of the other social psychological approaches has provided such a comprehensive framework.

## SOCIAL COMPARISON APPROACHES TO DEPRESSION

A series of social psychological studies on depression that is closely related to the attributional approach was guided by SOCIAL COMPARISON theory (*see*, for a summary, Swallow & Kuiper, 1988). The theory postulates a basic need for self-evaluation, that is, a need to evaluate one's opinions and abilities. Under certain circumstances, the self can be evaluated by comparing one's own achievements or opinions to those of other individuals. One of the central questions of social comparison research is "with whom will individuals seek to compare themselves?" Several studies have investigated with whom depressives – as opposed to non-depressives – compare themselves. For instance, it has been found that depressed subjects tend to ignore information about other persons who have failed and to compare themselves instead with successful others.

## SELF-FOCUSED ATTENTION

Self-focused attention is a cognitive concept that has been related to numerous social psychological variables. When individuals direct attention toward themselves, internal perceptual processes or changes in bodily activity may become salient and/or a heightened awareness of one's present or past behavior or attributes may result (*see also* SELF-AWARENESS).

It is assumed that shifting away the attention from the environment and focusing it on the self also results in self-evaluative processes. For instance, individuals in a state of self-focused attention may wonder whether their performances are in line with their personal standards. Furthermore, self-focused attention has been shown to intensify affective states: Focusing attention toward the self intensifies positive affects following success and negative affects following failure.

Some of the components of self-focused attention are similar to aspects of the state of depression (*see*, for a summary, Pyszczynski & Greenberg, 1987). For instance, depression is characterized by self-criticism as well as a lack of positive and an increase in negative affect. Therefore, social psychological studies have been conducted that relate these two variables. Several studies have revealed significant correlations among measures of depression and dispositional measures of self-focused attention. In addition, it has been found that depressives and nondepressives differentially focus attention on the self following success and failure. Depressives preferentially focus on themselves following failure, whereas nondepressives, by comparison, tend to focus on the self to a greater extent following success. Hence, the self-critical outlook as well as the lack of positive and excess of negative emotions of depressives are compatible with a self-directed attention perspective.

## AN INTERPERSONAL PERSPECTIVE ON DEPRESSION

An interpersonal (social psychological) perspective on depression has also been developed (see, for a summary, Gotlib & Hooley, 1988). Numerous studies in the early 1970s revealed a relationship between depression and disturbances in interpersonal relationships and interactions. For instance, married women were found to be more prone to depression than unmarried women, and there was a correlation between self-report measures of marital distress and depressive symptomatology. Furthermore, it was found that depressed patients reported greater conflicts in their marriages than did nondepressed controls. Findings of this type triggered studies of the interpersonal RELATIONSHIPS of depressed persons.

Of course, correlations between interpersonal distress and depression do not allow one to draw causal conclusions regarding, for instance, whether depression has a negative impact on interpersonal interaction or whether interpersonal distress leads to depression. Studies have revealed findings compatible with both of these possible causal paths. For instance, when communicating with strangers, depressives are less socially skilled, maintain less eye contact with the person with whom they interact, and exhibit a self-focused conversational style. Hence, it is not surprising that depressives – more so than nondepressives – induce tension as well as negative behaviors in strangers. Furthermore, it was found that conversations of depressed persons with their spouses are more disrupted than conversations in nondepressed couples.

However, there is also evidence that disrupted interpersonal relationships might be causes rather than consequences of depression: disturbances in marital relationships precede the onset of a depression, criticism of formerly depressed clients is correlated with relapse, and marital therapy has been found to be effective in alleviating depression (see, for a summary, Gotlib & Hooley, 1988).

Thus depression has a strong interpersonal component, although it is not yet clear whether or to what extent depression causes interpersonal disturbances, or vice versa, or both. However, although research has clearly pointed to the importance of an interpersonal perspective on depression, social psychological theories and methods have not yet been applied to the understanding of the role of interpersonal relationships for depression.

## TREATMENT OF DEPRESSION AND OUTCOME STUDIES

Without treatment, depressed episodes last on average about six months or longer (*DSM* 111-3R, 1987, p. 220). However, dozens of research studies have indicated that therapies based on clinical theories of depression (cognitive and behavioral therapies) are highly effective in the alleviation of this disorder. Unfortunately, outcome studies of therapies derived from social psychological theories have not yet been conducted on clinical populations. However, there are therapeutic analog studies derived from attributional approaches (i.e., attributional retraining studies) that have shown with nonclinical subjects that central components of a depressed reaction (e.g., low expectations and lack of persistence following failure) can be altered successfully with methods derived from social psychological theories (see, for a summary, Försterling, 1988).

*See also* ATTRIBUTION THEORIES; CONTROL; RELATIONSHIPS; SCHEMAS/SCHEMATA SELF-AWARENESS; SELF-ESTEEM; SOCIAL COMPARISON.

BIBLIOGRAPHY

Abramson, L. Y., Metalsky, G. I., & Alloy, L. B. (1989). Hopelessness depression: A theory-based subtype of depression. *Psychological Review*, *96*, 358–72.

Abramson, L. Y., Seligman, M. E. P., & Teasdale, J. D. (1978). Learned helplessness in humans. *Journal of Abnormal Psychology*, *87*, 49–74.

Beck, A. T. (1967). *Depression: Clinical, experimental, and theoretical aspects*. New York: Harper & Row.

—— (1976). *Cognitive therapy and the emotional disorders*. New York: International Universities Press.

*DSM* 111-R (1987). *Diagnostic and statistical manual of mental disorders*. Washington DC: American Psychiatric Association.

Försterling, F. (1988). *Attribution theory in clinical psychology*. Chichester: J. Wiley.

Gotlib, I. H., & Hooley, J. M. (1988). Depression and marital distress: Current status and future directions. In S. W. Duck (Ed.), *Handbook of personal relationships* (pp. 543–80), New York: Wiley.

Pyszczynski, T., & Greenberg, J. (1987). Self-regulatory perseveration and the depressive self-focusing style: A self-awareness theory of reactive depression. *Psychological Bulletin*, *102*, 122–38.

Seligman, M. E. P. (1975). *Helplessness: On depression, development, and death*. San Francisco, CA: W. H. Freeman.

Swallow, S. R., & Kuiper, N. A. (1988). Social comparison and negative self-evaluations: An application to depression. *Clinical Psychology Review*, *8*, 55–76.

FRIEDRICH FÖRSTERLING

**deviance** How social entities are organized to ensure the commitment of their members to shared NORMS is a central issue in social psychology. If deviance is defined as a departure from normative standards, then theories of normative behavior are by definition also theories of deviance and vice versa. One difficulty faced by all theories of deviance, however, is the sheer breadth of the behavioral category they seek to explain. The scope of this category is also historically and culturally relative; thus in the West tobacco smokers are increasingly treated as deviant, homosexuals decreasingly so. Two kinds of theoretical response have emerged in response to these difficulties.

SOCIAL CONSTRUCTIVIST VERSUS
AETIOLOGICAL APPROACHES

One response has been to examine how and why certain forms of behavior, but not others which pose objectively similar degrees of danger to individuals or collectives, come to be defined as deviant, that is, how deviance as a category is socially constructed. The "how" has been addressed by conflict theorists in terms of the distribution of economic and political POWER among interest groups within a society; for example, large corporations may influence legislation to ensure that only some kinds of DRUGS use are treated as criminally deviant (Chambliss, 1974). Social movements often have the objective of redefining normative boundaries, for example, the Temperance and Pro-Life movements. Moscovici's (1976) analysis of MINORITY SOCIAL INFLUENCE highlights the the conflicts that may arise around the definition of deviance. The "why" has been addressed in terms of the latent functions of deviance; deviant acts, or rather the collective responses of condemnation and punishment which they attract, serve to sustain the solidarity and coherence of the community, providing a fundamental source of moral instruction (Archer, 1985).

The other, and in psychology so far the more common, response been to develop general theories of the etiology of deviance, but to test them only against a limited range of deviant behaviors. Thus it has been common for theories to be tested largely in terms of their capacity to predict various kinds of dishonesty, property crime, crimes against the person, and antisocial conduct. The same theories may exclude serious crimes such as murder and RAPE as special cases or even as a range of special cases each with their own unique etiology (Hollin, 1989). The etiology of deviance in SEXUAL BEHAVIOR is rarely addressed in mainstream theorizing.

One problem in defining the scope of deviance is that the category has included at one extreme forms of behavior such as predatory crime which appear to be elective or voluntary and, at the other, manifestly involuntary conditions such as physical or mental handicap. A justification for subsuming such diverse phenomena under a single heading is the similarity of the interpersonal reactions they elicit. STIGMA may attach to being blind, left-handed, or schizophrenic, just as it may to being pregnant out of wedlock, overweight, a child molester, an alcoholic, or a convicted felon. A justification for distinguishing between the elective and the involuntary, even though the precise location of the dividing line is a matter of both ideological and scientific dispute, is that the causes of the former are likely to be quite different from those of the latter.

If normative behavior is thought of as arising from the combined effects of a socialized capacity for self-control and socialized susceptibility to social control, deviance could arise from the breakdown of one or both of these forms of behavioral control. Theories differ with respect to:

(1) the emphasis given respectively to self- and social control; and
(2) hypothesized processes and effects of SOCIALIZATION.

## SOCIALIZATION FAILURE IN THE ETIOLOGY OF DEVIANCE

Theories of deviance emphasizing socialization failure have been linked by a set of more or less implicit assumptions:

(1) humans are naturally inclined to deviate from normative standards because the proscribed alternatives are inherently rewarding;
(2) social controls are sufficient to suppress overt deviance and indeed so effective as to be theoretically uninteresting;
(3) self-control operates as a back-up when social controls cannot function effectively; hence self-control is particularly important when conditions put the actor beyond the reach of social controls; and
(4) such conditions – particularly of anonymity and social isolation – are in fact widespread in contemporary mass societies; they are the chronic conditions of modern life.

Thus social order in contemporary society depends to a far greater degree than is the case in folk societies upon self-control, and deviance occurs to the extent that this self-control fails.

Three kinds of explanation for such failure attribute it, respectively, to the process of socialization, the content of socialization, and conditions which undermine or neutralize the effects of socialization.

Social disorganization theories (Box, 1981) emphasize the social conditions under which the socialization process may fail, without being precise about the nature of the process. Thus it has been argued that socialization is less likely to be accomplished effectively under conditions of family instability and breakdown, poverty, overcrowded housing, and population transience.

Psychological theories focus on the nature of the process rather than the social conditions which support it. Psychoanalytic thinking holds that internalized control over conduct is a function of early parent–child relations. Freud located the crucial events in early childhood; infantile fantasies about castration create a crisis in parent–child relations which is successfully resolved if the child internalizes parental VALUES and parental disapproval of proscribed conduct. Other theorists have given particular emphasis to ATTACHMENT, or the strength of the emotional bond formed between infants and their caretakers; yet others have focused upon the content of parents' disciplinary practices. An empirical link between features of parent–child relations on the one hand and deviant, particularly antisocial, conduct on the other is well established. Uncertainty remains as to whether this link is mediated by an internalized structure such as conscience or the superego, or whether it is direct, as suggested by Control theorists (Hirschi, 1969).

Learning theorists offer a different view of the discipline process: parents shape children's moral habits through processes of reward and punishment. Eysenck (1977) has argued that the relevant socialization process is one of conditioning anxiety but also that effectiveness of the process depends on inherited characteristics. However, the PERSONALITY TRAITS which Eysenck claims index these characteristics have not proved to be reliably related to criminal deviance.

Cognitive developmental theory takes the internal control mechanism to be moral reasoning; normal MORAL DEVELOPMENT involves emergence of progressively more sophisticated systems of moral reasoning. However, no direct link has yet been unequivocally established between individuals' levels of moral reasoning and their proneness to deviance; research has frequently confounded possible causes of deviance with its consequences, such as incarceration. A further difficulty faced by this and other theories of socialization failure is that they do not predict SEX DIFFERENCES in failure rates, yet the greater prevalence of criminal deviance among males is one of its most conspicuous features.

## SOCIALIZATION INTO DEVIANT STANDARDS

Another group of theories raise no questions about the success or otherwise of the socialization process but propose that inappropriate content is internalized. Deviance is not a failure of self-control but failure to internalize the appropriate values or habits. This is the position of Sutherland's theory of cultural diversity and differential association (*see* Archer, 1985): modern societies contain diverse CULTURES and the values an individual internalizes depend on the cultural origins of those others with whom he or she has most contact. Similarly, SOCIAL LEARNING theories assume that individuals can acquire deviant habits of behavior as readily as normative habits; what matters is the nature of the behavioral models to which they are exposed. It has also been argued that males and females experience systematically different patterns of association and are rewarded for imitation of quite different behavioral models. On the other hand these approaches are less well equipped to account for another salient feature of criminal deviance, its correlation with age.

Such theories have also been criticized as overly deterministic. Thus Matza (*see* Box, 1981) argues that adolescents in particular drift in and out of deviance and retain a degree of commitment to conventional values. They cope with the threats to identity entailed in their occasional deviance through "techniques of neutralization," accounts of their own behavior which exonerate them from guilt or responsibility.

## PROXIMATE CAUSES OF DEVIANCE

A range of other explanations for deviance invoke the effects of particular social conditions in weakening or temporarily undermining self-control. In general, social psychology has emphasized the immediate effects of the group while sociology has given more attention to the cumulative effects of conditions experienced in ADOLESCENCE, a strategy intended to address the observed age distribution of criminal deviance. Thus a number of analyses (reviewed by Box, 1981) assume that childhood socialization is unproblematic but that its effects are undermined by difficulties of adjustment in adolescence. Almost all such theories begin from the now well-documented link between adolescent delinquency and educational career and from a claimed link between crime and class background. Analyses of adjustment difficulties are then built upon the association between class and educational attainment.

According to Merton's Anomie theory (*see* Box, 1981), working class adolescents experience particular strains in trying to reconcile the core values of the culture which they have internalized, such as the pursuit of material wealth, with their lack of access, by virtue of poor educational credentials, to legitimate means such as well-paid jobs for realizing these values. Feelings of RELATIVE DEPRIVATION are relieved through the use of deviant means to achieve normative ends.

Cohen (*see* Box, 1981) argued that insofar as a society settles competitions for status in terms of educational attainment then working-class adolescents will be disproportionate losers. They will resolve the emotional discomfort of failure by reaction formation, ostentatiously rejecting those values and standards conspicuously supported by the winners, namely the middle class. Cloward and Ohlin (*see* Box, 1981) argued that adolescents become alienated from the system when they find they are illegitimately denied status. (Tyler, 1990, also invokes the concept of perceived legitimacy to explain criminal deviance, but the legitimacy of law-enforcement procedures rather than status ascription procedures.)

Box (1981) criticizes "strain" theories for attempting to explain a feature of juvenile deviance which has proved at best elusive, namely its concentration within the working class. Self-report evidence indicates smaller class differences than do official statistics, leading some theorists to focus on societal reactions to deviance and in particular the processes by which individuals become offically labeled as deviant.

LABELING theory has assumed that all adolescents are prone to occasional misbehavior or "primary deviance" but that a few are singled out and publicly labeled as deviant. This labeling traps them in a deviant identity which becomes a SELF-FULFILLING PROPHECY, amplifying and solidifying a commitment to norm-violation, or "secondary deviance." A related approach implicates low SELF-ESTEEM; according to this view the crucial experiences involve devaluing social feedback generating feelings of personal failure. Deviance is likely subsequently either because depressed feelings of self-worth fail to contain it (deviance is no longer inconsistent with self-concept) or insofar as deviant actions offer a means of restoring self-esteem.

## DEVIANCE-ENHANCING EFFECTS OF THE GROUP

Social psychology has had more to say about the immediate situations in which acts of deviance are likely. According to LeBon's CROWD PSYCHOLOGY, individuals are more likely to be criminally deviant when gathered together in a mob because this condition both renders them suggestible and weakens socialized inhibitions against violence. This theme has been taken up in a number of other analyses. One attributes deviance to DEINDIVIDUATION; the group context increases the individual's sense of anonymity. A similar argument is that the presence of others has the effect of diffusing moral RESPONSIBILITY. Janis argued that the group context can induce a form of moral blindness or GROUPTHINK.

The successful experimental manipulations of conditions influencing the occurrence of deviance led some social psychologists to question whether PERSONALITY has any role at all in the generation of deviant conduct. "Situationism" is the argument that conduct is a function of the situation alone; in effect, anyone, irrespective of personal characteristics is capable of deviance under the right conditions. Crowd- and group-influence interpretations of deviance, however, are more accurately represented as interactionist positions. If the effect of the group is to undermine or weaken internalized control, not everyone is assumed to be equally vulnerable. The working class, the masses, the weak-willed or those in whom intellectual or moral autonomy is not sufficiently robust are most at risk.

The extreme situationist position is also contradicted by evidence that many forms of deviance are relatively stable characteristics of an individual's conduct. Thus, for example, involvement in violence, delinquency, and illegal drug use have been shown to be quite stable across time. Moreover, involvement in one kind of delinquency, such as vandalism, is highly correlated with involvement in other kinds such as theft and aggression (Emler & Reicher, 1994). What remains at issue is whether such consistencies arise from the internal psychological characteristics of individuals or from enacting the public identities negotiated with or imposed by their social environments.

## THE SOCIAL CONTROL OF CONDUCT

An empirical observation raising difficulties for the assumptions underpinning several theories is that much deviant behavior is neither solitary nor covert. One implication which flows from this observation is that anonymity is not a necessary condition for deviance. Indeed, particular kinds of deviant act may actually be more likely if the actor is identifiable to certain audiences. Second, deviant levels of antisocial and criminal conduct, drug abuse, and alcohol consumption are all strongly associated with having friends who are similarly deviant. It may be that elective deviance cannot be sustained in the absence of this kind of social support.

A third implication is that social controls do not invariably inhibit public deviance. The strong pressures against deviance and towards uniformity in face-to-face groups have been extensively demonstrated under laboratory conditions (Moscovici, 1976; *see also* COMPLIANCE). What is less clear is what determines the effectiveness of those pressures under more natural conditions. Hirschi's (1969) Control theory provides one of the few systematic accounts here. He argued that individuals are restrained from deviance to the extent that they have:

(1) strong emotional attachments to other people;
(2) commitments to the conventional order, such as investments in career goals; and
(3) beliefs about the importance of obeying the law and the probability of punishment if one does not.

Hirschi also argues that these are qualities of an individual's current circumstances and relationships, not enduring traits of his or her personality.

Hirschi allows a role for one personality characteristic, intelligence, but argues that its effect is mediated by its impact on educational performance; low intelligence leads to educational failure which in turn both reduces investment in the conventional system and weakens attachment to significant others. Despite widespread claims of an association between low intelligence and criminal deviance, however, the evidence for this link remains equivocal (Emler & Reicher, 1994).

## SOCIAL ORGANIZATION AND OPPORTUNITY

The psychology of ORGANIZATIONS offers an interactionist perspective on deviance (Emler & Hogan, 1991). In essence organizational theories assume that development equips individuals to differing degrees with attributes that are relevant to their functioning as organizational members. These theories also assume that social organization entails a variety of mechanisms for the coordination and control of behavior. Thus behavior is an interactive function of the effectiveness with which controls are organized and of the individuals to whom these controls are applied.

Four key ideas inform this as an interpretation of deviance:

(1) Much behavior, including deviance, depends on the cooperation of others. This draws attention to the availability of co-operators and the impact of individuals' reputations on the cooperation they can secure.
(2) A common procedure for organizing and coordinating action is through a hierarchy of authority and supervision. This draws attention to variability in the extent of direct supervision, OBEDIENCE to authority, and individual differences in attitudes to authority.
(3) Organized activity also depends on the explication of standardized procedures or rules. Deviance is more likely to the extent that patterns of social interaction do not involve regular reminders of rules and disapproval of departures from rules. Research on GROUP DECISION MAKING and compliance in face-to-face interaction has illuminated the mechanics of these processes.
(4) Organized activity involves selective access to behavioral opportunities, including opportunities for deviance. Systematic selection which is sensitive to individual attributes operates as a mechanism to limit deviance by limiting access to opportunities for deviance.

An organizational perspectice on deviance appears to bring us back to the position of early social disorganization theories (Archer, 1985). Unlike the latter, however, this perspective allows that social organization can facilitate as well as contain deviance and that deviance is not confined to low status members of society. Indeed, organizational selection procedures may be systematically insensitive to certain kinds of personality flaw, putting into positions of power and responsibility individuals who are likely to use the opportunities these provide to engage in particularly damaging deviations from normative standards (Emler & Hogan, 1991).

CONCLUSIONS

The study of deviance has been dominated, and probably hindered, by the pursuit of "single cause" models. Attention to processes by which deviance is defined has encouraged a more interactionist view, while the adoption of multifactor models which seek to integrate the effects of socialization and those of social control processes is likely to produce more progress and to shed more light on both normative and deviant behavior.

*See also*: ADOLESCENCE; CROWD PSYCHOLOGY; CULTURE; DEINDIVIDUATION; GROUP DECISION MAKING; GROUPTHINK; MORAL DEVELOPMENT; NORMS; OBEDIENCE; ORGANIZATIONS; PERSONALITY; POWER; RAPE; RELATIVE DEPRIVATION; SELF-ESTEEM; SELF-FULFILLING PROPHECIES; SEX DIFFERENCES; SEXUAL BEHAVIOR; SOCIAL LEARNING; SOCIALIZATION; STIGMA; VALUES.

BIBLIOGRAPHY

Archer, D. (1985). Social deviance. In G. Lindzey & E. Aronson (Eds.), *Handbook of social psychology* (3rd ed., Vol. 2, pp. 743–804). New York: Random House.

Box, S. (1981). *Deviance, reality and society* (2nd ed.). London: Holt, Rinehart & Winston.

Chambliss, W. J. (1974). The state, the law, and the definition of behavior as criminal or delinquent. In D. Glaser (Ed.), *Handbook of criminology* (pp. 7–43). Chicago, IL: Rand McNally.

Emler, N., & Hogan, R. (1991). Moral psychology and public policy (Vol. 3). In W. Kurtines & J. Gewirtz (Eds.), *Handbook of moral development and behavior* (pp. 69–93). Hillsdale, NJ: Lawrence Erbaum.

Emler, N., & Reicher, S. (1994). *A social psychology of adolescent delinquency*. Oxford: Blackwell Publishers.

Eysenck, H. J. (1977). *Crime and personality*. St Albans: Paladin.

Hirschi, T. (1969). *Causes of delinquency*. Berkeley, California: University of California Press.

Hollin, C. R. (1989). *Psychology and crime*. London: Routledge.

Moscovici, S. (1976). *Social influence and social change*. London: Academic Press.

Tyler, T. (1990). *Why people obey the law*. New Haven, CT: Yale University Press.

NICHOLAS EMLER

**discounting** The discounting principle (originally invoked in relation to causal schemata) implies that the role of a given cause in producing an effect is decreased if other plausible causes are present.
*See also*: ATTRIBUTION THEORIES.

MILES HEWSTONE

**discourse analysis** A field and form of study which has grown in popularity over the last decade, particularly as a result of developments in the United Kingdom. Although its forebears and influences lie largely outside or on the margins of social psychology it has increasingly begun to address similar interests and has as a consequence attempted to challenge the traditional concepts, meta-theories, and methods of the mainstream in the process. Not surprisingly then it is a somewhat controversial area for social psychology, and it is not clear whether it should be viewed as trying to join the club or usurp it (or whether this matters). Controversy is not restricted to its relation to social psychology; internally, views differ as to precisely what discourse is and what discourse analysis entails (e.g., Parker, 1990; Potter et al., 1990).

Most advocates and practitioners are probably agreed that discourse analysis runs deeper than simply a defining method. It also prescribes a particular approach to language and language use that forms the basis of its critique of traditional theory and methodology. Above all, language is regarded critically, not as reflecting reality or providing a "window on the world," but as a "reality constituting practice" (Edwards & Potter, 1992, p. 27). Thus the constructive, performative, and reflexive aspects of language use are emphasized along with its nature as a symbolic system or structure, a level of reality in itself, rather than a neutral referential medium. As such discourse analysis has important roots in speech act theory, semiology and poststructuralism (notably in the writings of Barthes, Derrida, Foucault), and ethnomethodology and conversation analysis, although again views differ as to where the accent lies or should lie in these influences (*see*, e.g., Potter & Wetherell, 1987; Potter et al., 1990; Parker, 1990). Within social psychology, discourse analysis is motivated by some similar concerns to earlier and other attempts to provoke a "crisis" through critiques of positivism, mechanistic and mentalistic models of person and mind, and the experimental method (e.g., in the ETHOGENICS of Harré, the hermeneutics of Shotter, and the SOCIAL CONSTRUCTIONISM of Gergen; see also CRITICAL SOCIAL PSYCHOLOGY).

Discourse is not simply language but includes "all forms of spoken interaction, formal and informal, and written texts of all kinds" (Potter & Wetherell, 1987, p. 7). Parker defines discourse as "a system of statements which constructs an object" (1990; p. 191), although Potter et al. (1990) have argued that this definition reifies discourse, and splits it from its context-specific instantiation. The latter group have emphasized the functional aspects of discourse and its deployment, defining discourse analysis as "a functionally oriented approach to the analysis of talk and text" (Edwards & Potter, 1992, p. 27). This orientation to action and the goal-directed use of language underline the critique of language as purely referential or descriptive. Moreover, because the orientation and interest of the speaker will vary the construction or deployment of discourses (or "linguistic repertoires") will be chosen to suit functions or aims. Ostensibly "factual" discourse can even (or especially) be regarded in this light, namely as fulfilling aims and interests (Edwards & Potter, 1992). These factors ensure that discourse is characterized by variablity; discourses will vary not just across but also within persons along with occasion, context, and functional orientation (Edwards & Potter, 1992; Potter et al., 1990; Potter & Wetherell, 1987).

This focus on situated and variable use of discourses lies at the heart of a criticism of basic concepts in social psychology such as "attitudes" (Potter & Wetherell, 1987) and "attributions" (Edwards & Potter, 1992) as grounded in its cognitivistic and perceptualist meta-theory. The variety and contradictions in discourse are seen as undermining the case for stable or consistent attitudes so that they are regarded as redundant abstractions from the discursive realm. It is claimed that classical experimental approaches to attribution miss out on how people actually account for themselves or others in natural discourse because experimental control removes their "interestedness." More generally it has been proposed that the interconnected nature of language, the reflexivity of discourse and the fact that language and discourses both transcend individuals and are contained within them mean that experimental closure in social psychology is likely to be problematic or to distort the nature of that which it is designed to measure (e.g., Parker, 1992).

The emphasis by some researchers on discourse as a resource of linguistic repertoires available for individual use arguably tends to underplay the constraining and coercive nature of discourses (see Althusser, Foucault), and that discourses "interpellate" and deploy individuals as well as vice versa (Parker, 1990; 1992). In emphasizing their role in supporting institutions, reproducing POWER relations, Parker (1992) suggests that discourse analysis can be regarded as "implicit ideology critique." This realist approach to discourse provides a counter to the dominant relativist tendencies in discourse analysis. The idea that there is no escape from the text has led some to argue that there is nothing beyond it, so that claims that discourse analysis supersedes the idealism–materialism debate and the epistemology–ontology dualism, often result in practice in the reduction of material to ideal, and ontology to epistemology. Like some radical forms of social constructionism, discourse analysis runs the danger of becoming a free floating epistemology without any connections to ontology beyond the linguistic realm.

When mainstream social psychologists have taken notice of discourse analysis, a persistent criticism has been that the method is obscure or intuitive, and that there is no guarantee of reliability, representativeness or replicability – in short that it is "unscientific." Discourse analysts have in return emphasized the rhetorical nature of scientific practice. Because of the rejection of the Cartesian subject and the very notion of discrete individuals entailed in its metathory and critique, discourse analysis is not committed to regarding the individual as its unit of analysis and sides consciously with the hermeneutic tradition. The only problem is (in common with much poststructuralist antihumanism) the absence of a theorized subject to be interpreted – both to act as an intentional agent of discourse, and to provide an explanatory footing at the individual level. If we are to understand the impetus and motives behind the much vaunted functional deployment of discourse, discourse analysis misses and arguably requires a psychology of the social individual.

*See also*: CRITICAL SOCIAL PSYCHOLOGY; ETHOGENICS; POWER; SOCIAL CONSTRUCTIONISM.

BIBLIOGRAPHY

Edwards, D., & Potter, J. (1992). *Discursive psychology*. London: Sage.

Parker, I. (1990). Discourse: Definitions and contradictions. *Philosophical Psychology*, *3*, 189–204.

—— (1992). *Discourse dynamics: A critical analysis for social and individual psychology*. London: Routledge.

Potter, J., & Wetherell, M. (1987). *Discourse and social psychology: Beyond attitudes and behaviour*. London: Sage.

—— Wetherell, M., Gill, R., & Edwards, D. (1990). Discourse – noun, verb, or social practice. *Philosophical Psychology*, *3*, 205–17.

RUSSEL SPEARS

**distinctiveness** In Kelley's covariation theory of causal attribution, distinctiveness information refers to whether an effect varies over stimuli or entities. Using such covariation information is said to help the perceiver to arrive at a causal attribution.

*See also*: ATTRIBUTION THEORIES.

MILES HEWSTONE

**distributive justice** People evaluate the outcomes they receive from others not by their absolute favorability, but by their consistency with principles of outcome fairness. Distributive justice research examines these justice effects and explores the justice principles people use to evaluate outcomes, including the principles of equity, equality, and need.

*See also*: SOCIAL JUSTICE.

TOM R. TYLER

**dogmatism** A personality syndrome marked by a cognitive style in which different belief systems are well insulated from one another so that mutually contradictory opinions can be tolerated. Such belief systems are resistant to change in the light of new information and are often characterized by the use of appeals to authority to justify their correctness. A final characteristic of a dogmatic personality is intolerance, whether towards those who hold different beliefs or those that are seen as different or deviant in some way.

In modern social psychology the concept of dogmatism originated with the work of Rokeach (1960), who developed his theory of dogmatism as a critique of Adorno et al.'s (1950) *The Authoritarian Personality* (*see* AUTHORITARIANISM). Rokeach argued that authoritarianism as traditionally conceived applied only to those with conservative political beliefs and prejudice toward conventional targets such as communists, Jews, and other minority groups. Challenging this restricted conception, Rokeach hypothesized that it was possible to observe authoritarian-like tendencies amongst people of all political persuasions and parallel examples of outgroup rejection, albeit towards different targets. He labeled this personality "dogmatic" or, to illustrate its typical cognitive style, The Closed Mind (Rokeach, 1960). Apart from this important difference, Rokeach followed others in believing that the origins of dogmatism lay in early family socialization experiences and particularly relationships with the child's parents. He thus predicted that dogmatic people would display the same glorification of their parents and manifest other symptoms of repressed hostility and anxiety that had been described in the earlier analysis of authoritarianism. Similarly dogmatism was also expected to be correlated with PREJUDICE toward outgroups although it should be noted that Rokeach is better known for a theory of prejudice which relies less on individual differences in personality than on interpersonal differences in beliefs as its main explanatory tool (*see* BELIEF CONGRUENCE THEORY).

To substantiate his theory of dogmatism Rokeach devised scales of Opinionation and Dogmatism. The former consisted of a series of rather extreme attitude statements worded in both a left- and a right-wing direction and was designed to measure intolerance. The Dogmatism scale, while related to Opinionation, was designed to tap general authoritarianism in more content-free manner than others had done. Using these scales Rokeach (1960) compared the dogmatism of extant groups which, on a priori grounds, might be considered more dogmatic than average (e.g., certain religious and extreme political groups) with those generally regarded as more open-minded (e.g., nonbelievers, political liberals). At the same time he also measured their authoritarianism. Some of these comparisons supported his contention that dogmatism was a more general measure than authoritarianism. For instance, a group of Communists scored the same as some Conservatives on dogmatism but considerably lower on authoritarianism. On the other hand, Communists were less authoritarian than Liberals but more dogmatic. However, dogmatism did not always differentiate so successfully amongst religious groups. Tracing the developmental origins of dogmatism, Rokeach (1960) found the expected evidence of an exaggerated glorification of parents and some symptoms of repressed anxiety amongst dogmatic individuals, although there was some evidence that it was those "intermediate" rather than extreme in dogmatism who showed these tendencies most strongly.

As an explanation of ethnic prejudice Rokeach's theory of dogmatism has attracted rather less interest than the earlier *Authoritarian Personality*. Some studies have found dogmatism to be reliably correlated with various kinds of outgroup prejudice although such correlations are not always very robust and sometimes disappear when other variables (e.g., concern for social status) are controlled for (Hoge & Carroll, 1973). However, more supportive evidence for the idea that

ideologues of left and right share similar psychological characteristics has come from content analysis of the political rhetoric of conservative and socialist politicians. This shows the arguments used by such people tend to be less complex and circumspect than their centrist counterparts (*see* INTEGRATIVE COMPLEXITY).

Many of the criticisms made of *The Authoritarian Personality* as an explanation of social phenomena like prejudice apply equally to Rokeach's theory. For instance, the latter, like its predecessor, tends to down-play the importance of socio-cultural and situational determinants of intolerant attitudes. Yet much evidence exists that such factors are often important (*see* authoritarianism). There are some similarities between Rokeach's theory of dogmatism and Eysenck's (1954) personality theory of political attitudes since both propose psychological similarities between politically disparate groups. The extent of the similarities between the two accounts has, however, been the subject of some controversy (Brown, 1965). A further criticism of such attempts to equate extremists of different political persuasions is that the instruments designed to achieve this may not be politically neutral but may contain items which are ideologically heavily laden. Thus, any differences – or similarities – observed between groups may be attributable more to the aggregation of political attitudes elicited by the particular mix of items on a given scale than to any underlying similarity of personality (Billig, 1976).

*See also*: AUTHORITARIANISM; INTEGRATIVE COMPLEXITY; PREJUDICE.

BIBLIOGRAPHY
Adorno, T. W., Frenkel-Brunswik, E., Levinson, D. J., & Sanford, R. N. (1950), *The Authoritarian Personality*. New York: Harper & Row.
Billig, M. (1976). *Social psychology and intergroup relations*. New York: Academic Press.
Brown, R. W. (1965). *Social psychology*. New York: Macmillan.
Eysenck, H. J. (1954). *The psychology of politics*. London: Routledge & Kegan Paul.
Hoge, D. R., & Carroll, J. W (1973). Religiosity and prejudice in Northern and South-

ern churches. *Journal for the Scientific Study of Religion*, 12, 181–97.

Rokeach, M. (Ed.). (1960). *The open and closed mind*. New York: Basic Books.

RUPERT BROWN

**door-in-the-face**   The door-in-the-face technique obtains COMPLIANCE to the target request by first obtaining noncompliance to a larger request (Cialdini et al., 1975). For example, a salesperson who wants someone to buy a moderately priced car will first attempt to sell that person an expensive car. Upon being turned down, the salesperson will offer the moderately priced car as an alternative. There are two explanations for this effect. By offering the moderately priced car as an alternative, the salesperson has made a concession. When the consumer makes a concession, such as buying the moderately priced car, he or she has reestablished equity with the salesperson (*see* EQUITY THEORY). Alternately, if someone is friendly to you, it is normative to be friendly in return (*see* RECIPROCITY). Thus, when the salesperson makes a concession, it is normative for the consumer to accept this concession (Gouldner, 1960).

BIBLIOGRAPHY

Cialdini, R. B., Vincent, J. E., Lewis, S. K., Catalan, J., Wheeler, D., & Danby, B. L. (1975). Reciprocal concessions procedure for inducing compliance: The door-in-the-face technique. *Journal of Personality and Social Psychology*, 31, 206–15.

Gouldner, A. W. (1960). The norm of reciprocity: A preliminary statement. *American Sociological Review*, 25, 161–78.

BIRGIT KAUFMANN-BRYANT
BRIAN MULLEN

**drive**   An internal state of the person that energizes and maintains behavior. The term was introduced by Woodworth (1918) to account for the intensive component of action. As an intervening state that is aroused by stimuli and to which the person in turn responds, it took the place previously held by some conceptions of instinct, such as that of McDougall. The early studies of drive, conducted during the 1920s and 1930s, were largely empirical and atheoretical, and were addressed to the problem of delineating antecedent conditions. Typical of such research was that of Richter, in which the activity level of rats was found to increase gradually prior to feeding and to drop quickly after feeding. From this finding, Richter concluded that conditions of deprivation are the principal contributor to drive.

The high point in the study of drive was the publication of Hull's *Principles of Behavior* (1943), in which the major variables of drive theory were described. Hull built on the findings of Richter by proposing that drive is a unitary condition produced by deprivation of commodities or conditions necessary for adaptation and survival. It accumulates as a direct function of the amount of deprivation that is experienced. Drive is a nonspecific energizer of all behaviors in a given situation, but it does not activate or direct any specific activities. The directive control of behavior Hull assigned to internal cues called *drive stimuli*, which are also produced by deprivations. Drive energizes all potential responses in the situation differentially as a function of their relative dominance, or habit strength. Drive and habit strength multiply to produce response potential (called excitatory potential), hence the formula $E = D \times H$. By multiplying with the habit strength of each response, drive energizes the dominant responses more than the subordinate ones. One result of this multiplicative effect is that under conditions of high drive, performance on simple or well-learned tasks is facilitated whereas the performance of complex behaviors or the acquisition of new responses is inhibited.

Drive is an aversive condition that is reduced in intensity by responses that mitigate or terminate the deprivation conditions. Such responses are thereby reinforced by drive reduction and gain in habit strength as a consequence. Thus drive enters into both the establishment of habit strength for responses and the energization of these responses in behavior. Hull's drive theory is therefore both a theory of motivation and a theory of learning.

The extension of drive theory to personality and social psychology has been mainly through the construct of learned, or *secondary* drive. This state is elicited by stimuli that have been associated with the activation of primary drive and, like primary drive, is an aversive condition that energizes responses. It has been studied primarily in the context of research on fear and anxiety. During the 1950s, learned fear was the basis for most human motivation in drive theoretical accounts (Brown, 1961). An example was the two-factor theory of avoidance behavior, which explained avoidance as an instrumental response to a signal for fear that is reinforced by termination of that signal.

A major extension of the study of learned fear was the experimental research on ANXIETY conducted by Taylor and her colleagues. The Manifest Anxiety Scale (Taylor, 1953) defines anxiety operationally in terms of individual differences in drive level. The theory of anxiety that subsumes the scale treats the person's level of anxiety as a response energizer that functions identically to drive evoked by other primary or secondary sources. High drive therefore enhances performance on relatively easy tasks, such as classical conditioning or simple verbal learning, but retards performance on more complicated cognitive tasks.

Drive theory was also used by Zajonc (1965) to explain the variable effects of coactors or audiences on performance in the SO-CIAL FACILITATION paradigm. By assuming that the physical presence of other people increases the drive level of the performer, Zajonc explained the common finding that such presence facilitates perfomance of easy tasks but hinders the performance of more difficult ones. From 1965 until the late 1970s,

drive theory provided the most coherent explanation for such effects.

In other contexts, drive has been invoked by social psychologists in a more limited way to describe nonspecific increases in excitement in connection with such processes as COGNITIVE DISSONANCE, ATTITUDE CHANGE, and interpersonal ATTRACTION. In these instances the term tends to be synonymous with other descriptors of nonspecific effects, such as ACTIVATION and AROUSAL.

*See also*: AROUSAL; ATTITUDE CHANGE; ATTRACTION; COGNITIVE DISSONANCE THEORY; SOCIAL FACILITATION.

BIBLIOGRAPHY

Brown, J. S. (1961). *The motivation of behavior*. New York: McGraw-Hill.

Hull, C. L. (1943). *Principles of behavior*. New Haven; CT: Yale University Press.

Taylor, J. A. (1953). A personality scale of manifest anxiety. *Journal of Abnormal and Social Psychology*, 48, 285–90.

Woodworth, R. S. (1918). *Dynamic psychology*. New York: Columbia University Press.

Zajonc, R. B. (1965). Social facilitation. *Science*, 149, 269–74.

RUSSELL G. GEEN
THOMAS R. GEEN

**drugs**  This term refers both to medicines (e.g., antibiotics) and to substances used for their psychoactive (mood-altering) effects which may be addictive (*see* ADDICTION). The latter includes licit drugs such as ALCOHOL, nicotine, and domestic solvents as well as illicit ones such as heroin, cocaine, and Ecstasy.

*See also*: ADDICTION.

STEPHEN SUTTON

# E

**ecological validity** A study is said to possess ecological validity when its operationalizations, particularly of the independent variables, resemble everyday or mundane reality. Thus, a more ecologically valid study is one in which subjects seem to be doing things that they normally do outside of the laboratory.

*See also*: METHODOLOGY.

CHARLES M. JUDD

**economic behavior** Generally considered to be that part of the social world concerned with the acquisition, management, and distribution of wealth. Thus working and spending, borrowing and lending, investing and saving, gambling and giving are all economic behaviors. But although anything that involves the exchange of goods or services for money is usually seen as clearly economic, so too are a wide range of other behaviors; good examples would be housework (part of the domestic economy) and swopping at school (part of the "playground economy"). The defining characteristics of all these behaviors is that they involve exchange and optimization. The study of economic behavior has leant heavily on social psychological theory (especially the THEORY OF REASONED ACTION, PROSPECT THEORY, ATTRIBUTION THEORIES) to help identify the underlying processes but is also notable for its openness to theory and data from economics (*see* Furnham & Lewis, 1986; Lea, Webley, & Young, 1992).

Although there has been marked increase in interest among social psychologists in economic behavior in recent years, such an interest is not new. The notion of an "economic psychology" dates back at least to the beginning of the century and the writings of the French social theorist Gabriel Tarde and there have been intermittent attempts over the past 90 years to produce a fruitful fusion of economics and social psychology, though only the work of George Katona (1975) has been successful and become widely known. These failed interactions between psychology and economics are partly a result of the fact that economics is dominated by a single theory and psychology is not and partly as psychologists have got bogged down in trying to demonstrate to economists that the assumption of human rationality (crucial to nearly all theories in economics) is misguided. Lea, Tarpy, and Webley (1987) argue that this preoccupation with rationality is sterile, since it can be shown that any behavior that is consistent can be described as maximizing something (*see* SUBJECTIVE EXPECTED UTILITY and DECISION MAKING). Even if people do behave in ways that very obviously maximize their utility, we would still need to understand the psychological mechanisms underlying their behavior.

Thus psychologists interested in economic behavior have two major concerns:

(1) What psychological processes underlie individuals' economic behavior?
(2) What effect does the economy have on individuals?

## INDIVIDUAL ECONOMIC BEHAVIOR

Individuals WORK, invest, borrow, and become entrepreneurs to get money (among other things) which they then spend (on goods or leisure for themselves and others) or save. A wide range of processes are implicated here. The key question in each case is usually why people do it. For example, while earning money may be the main "manifest" reason for working, there are a large number of other "latent" functions (*see* UNEMPLOYMENT), such as the provision of regularly shared experiences and the structuring of time. Here two kinds of individual behavior will be discussed; buying and saving.

*Buying*
Why do people buy what they do? We can identify two main kinds of answers to this question; one that is based on economic notions of utility maximization, the other on the expressive functions of consumption. The heart of the economic approach is the derivation from a few assumptions about choice behavior of a complex theory of the relationship between prices, incomes, and the quantities of different goods that people will buy. These assumptions, in the main, do not stand up to experimental investigation (Lea, Tarpy, & Webley, 1987) but the predicted relationships (e.g., that people buy less when prices increase) do. In particular, the more sophisticated versions of micro-economic theory, which recognize that people do not demand goods as such but the characteristics that goods possess (which is rather similar to the Fishbein and Azjen multiattribute approach to ATTITUDES), account for the data quite well. However, people regularly refuse to buy products because the prices are too low (presumably because this acts as a quality cue) and may buy products precisely because they are very expensive just to display their wealth (Veblen's notion of "conspicuous consumption"). This notion that goods can be used as a form of communication has been extended by Mary Douglas. She argues that the satisfaction of needs and competitive display are not the core of consumption; on the contrary goods are essential for their expressive and ritual functions and are a vital part of culture. This approach has been ably applied to modern consumer society by Lunt and Livingstone (1992).

The research discussed so far deals only with individual buying; the best-known economic psychologist, George Katona, explored the aggregate tendency to buy. Katona's major achievement was the development of the Index of Consumer Sentiment (ICS), a simple measure of people's confidence in the economy. This consists of questions such as "Do you expect the state of the economy to improve/stay the same/get worse during the coming year?", questions which are rather crude but which do give an indication of general consumer confidence and how likely consumers are to spend their discretionary income. Katona was interested in predicting aggregate expenditure. He claimed that the ICS showed a time-lagged correlation with economic indicators so one could predict the behavior of the whole economy from a measure which gave an indication of average attitudes. He scored a major success when, in 1946, he was able to predict that the US economy was about to enter a consumer-led boom when conventional economic indicators were predicting a recession (Katona, 1975).

It is now widely accepted that crude attitude data can predict the behavior of the economy. There is more debate over Katona's claim that attitudes give us information that cannot be obtained from conventional economic indicators. Surveys of consumer sentiment have been regularly conducted now for 45 years in America and since 1972 in the European Community, and analyses of this vast store of data suggest that consumer attitudes often add nothing to the usual predictors of economic trends (*see* van Raaij, van Veldhoven, & Wärneryd, 1988) and they have been derided by some as mere "intervening variables" in an economic analysis.

However, dismissing the index would be premature on two grounds: first, there have been recent efforts to understand the origins of consumer confidence (the coverage of the economy in newspapers and the pessimism found in pop song lyrics have been found to predict, with a time lag, the ICS and movements in the economy) and second, psychometric studies of the ICS have identified separate components which do add considerably to the predictions based solely on economic variables of, for example, the demand for home loans.

*Saving*
Saving is, in some sense, the opposite of buying; whatever we do not spend, we must

save. We can differentiate between contractual, discretionary, and involuntary saving (Katona, 1975). Contractual saving involves an earlier decision which commits us to save (e.g., a pension plan); discretionary saving involves an active decision to save during the current period; and involuntary saving is saving we do by accident.

The dominant economic theory of saving is the life-cycle hypothesis, which proposes that people use saving to smooth out their income across their life span. This predicts that people will borrow when young adults, save in middle age (when income is at its highest) and dissave (spend out of savings) when they are old. Though neat, this theory does not correspond with the data; most households save less than they intend and those in retirement often add to their savings. A new version of the life-cycle model (the behavioral life-cycle hypothesis of Shefrin and Thaler) goes some way to overcoming these problems by incorporating the notions of self-control, mental accounting, and framing. The traditional life-cycle model assumes that people work out an optimum consumption plan and then stick to it. However, it is known that people have great difficulty in delaying gratification and if offered a choice between a small reward now or a larger one later are likely to take the small immediate reward. Hence, Thaler and Shefrin have incorporated the idea of self-control by treating the individual as an organization containing a far-sighted planner and a myopic doer, both of whom operate rationally but with different preference functions. They also propose that people have a number of mental accounts at their disposal which operate fairly independently of each other. These accounts are hierarchically organized according to the source of income: current disposable income, assets, and future income. Individuals are predisposed to spend money from these different accounts (a psychological equivalent of the piggy-bank on the mantelpiece) differently; they will spend most of their current income and almost none of their future income with the propensity to spend assets falling somewhere between these two. This theory does quite a good job of accounting for the data (although few of its predictions have

so far been directly tested), but whatever its merits it is an interesting example of the fusion of psychological and economic theories.

THE EFFECTS OF THE ECONOMY ON INDIVIDUALS

The study of individual behavior is only one half of the study of economic behavior, although it is, in terms of published research, far and away the larger half. It is just as important, however, to explore the way in which the economy affects individuals. The economic environment may primarily affect economic behavior but also has other effects; it is well established that indicators of mental disorders increase in times of economic recession; (though milder economic adversity may actually benefit people) and threatening economic conditions have also been shown to lead to an increase in astrology and mysticism. Similarly, although ADVERTISING has obvious economic effects (in persuading us to buy goods and services) it also has unintended noncommercial side effects. There is evidence that higher levels of exposure to advertising are associated with greater materialism and some have claimed that advertisements define us and reinforce social stereotypes, particularly of women.

*The economic system*

One way to look at the effects of the economic environment is to compare economies with different forms of organization. One could contrast the market economies of the West with the command economies that operated in Eastern Europe from 1945 to 1990 or with the planned market economies of the Far East. One has to recognize that this effectively involves the comparison of CULTURES; it is not possible to disentangle economic factors from social and political conditions. It is evident that the dominant management culture of Japan, for example, with its concern for quality and gradual improvement in all aspects of a company's functioning and its emphasis on the need for employees to identify with the company, has striking economic and psychological effects. The economic success of this management culture has been such that, in the guise of "Total Quality Management," it is now being imported into Western companies.

A very different example comes from the field of economic SOCIALIZATION. Leiser, Sevón and Lévy (1990) summarize the results of an extensive cross-cultural investigation into economic understanding. Children were interviewed about their understanding of who decides what and why with regard to prices, salaries, savings, and investment. They were asked about the consequences of particular economic events and asked to account for the economic fate of individuals. The same basic interview was used in all countries. As in previous research, the growth in children's knowledge could be characterized as progress through a set of stages; a typical finding in this area is that children younger than seven explain the value of an object by referring to its physical size, 7- and 8-year-olds by reference to its usefulness, and older children shift to understanding value from the point of view of production. More interesting in this case were the differences between countries. Different institutional arrangements (e.g., the size of the public sector) were reflected in the children's answers. When cultures differ, then so do explanations of economic behavior. So some cultures emphasize individualistic interpretations of poverty and wealth whereas others favor more societal explanations (*see* SOCIAL REPRESENTATIONS). This can be related to Hofstede's dimension of uncertainty-avoidance. A society high in uncertainty-avoidance feels threatened by uncertain and ambiguous situations and tries to avoid these by providing for career stability and by establishing formal rules. It is also characterized by anxiety which, among other things, creates an inner urge to work hard.

*Money*
Most cultures that have ever existed have done without money and our Western money (coins and notes) is only one of many forms that money has taken. The question is then, what difference does it make to live in an economy that has money compared to one that does not?

The traditional answer, most eloquently articulated by Marx, is that money has com-

modified or monetized relationships, that the exact calculation of what goods and services are worth which money makes possible is extended to people and social interaction. But the evidence for this is slight (*see* Lane, 1991); on the contrary it looks as if the possibility of exact calculation may be one reason why, in a modern economy, money is often unacceptable as a gift or as a return for neighborly help (Lea, Tarpy, & Webley, 1987). Nonetheless, there are some costs of having a precise value system like money; when we are paid for some task we are given an exact reason for doing the job, rather than vague feelings of enjoyment and this may undermine the intrinsic satisfaction the task may have given (*see* INTRINSIC MOTIVATION).

On a lower level the forms that money takes also have an important influence on behaviour. There is a U-shaped relationship between the value of a currency unit and how long it spends in people's possession, with low-value coins and high-value bank notes being held onto the longest. In addition, coins are spent quicker than notes and so when the £1 note was replaced with a £1 coin in Britain in 1983, the £1 coin was spent more quickly (Lea, Tarpy, & Webley, 1987). The size-value effect (that the larger the coin, the greater its value – *see* SOCIAL JUDGMENT) also implies that reducing the size of a coin will reduce its perceived value. In 1992 the British government introduced a new 5p coin, much smaller than the old one and, as expected, a simple field experiment showed that people who noticed apparently lost coins were more likely to pick up the old 5p than the new 5p coins. This suggests that the new coins were indeed seen as less valuable.

*Taxation and tax evasion*
The tax system is one of the most obvious ways in which the wider economy impinges on individuals; for example, if public expenditure rises to cope with growing unemployment the government may respond by raising taxes. The individual, who is in a real-life SOCIAL DILEMMA where the benefits from government expenditure may be obtained without paying for them in taxes, may respond by evading part of his or her taxes.

One study, which is unique in combining self-report data and official data, sheds particular light on this issue. Hessing, Elffers, and Weigel (1988) studied two carefully audited groups of individuals: one group who had made accurate tax returns for 2 years, the other who had evaded tax for 2 years. The anonymity of the respondents was carefully protected. Despite the safeguarding of anonymity (which should have minimized the effects of SELF-PRESENTATION) the results showed that official and self-reported tax evasion did not correspond at all. More significantly core attitude variables (alienation, competitiveness, tolerance of deviance) predicted officially documented evasion whereas attitudes towards the act of evasion and subjective norms correlated with self-reported evasion. These results suggest that relatively enduring dispositions may guide some part of our economic behavior and cast doubt on the logic underlying Fishbein and Azjen's attitude–behavior model, since, in this domain self-reports do not provide a useful approximation to behavior (*see* ATTITUDES AND BEHAVIOR).

CONCLUSIONS

The study of economic behavior is a separate domain of inquiry within social psychology that draws heavily on neighboring disciplines, most notably economics, social anthropology, and sociology. The advantage of this interdisciplinary approach is that the intellectual traffic is two-way; thus notions from economics may shed light on the more obvious areas such as SOCIAL EXCHANGE and SOCIAL DILEMMAS but also on SOCIAL COGNITION and the SELF. The behavioral life-cycle hypothesis, for example, is clearly relevant to the latter two areas. Conversely social psychological ideas, such as EQUITY THEORY, may be incorporated into economic theory, as by Cowell (1992). One problem with this interdisciplinary approach is that economics is very individualistic and positivistic and thus ensuring that future interactions are fruitful will be a real challenge.

*See also*: ADVERTISING; ATTITUDES AND BEHAVIOR; ATTRIBUTION THEORIES; CULTURE; DECISION MAKING; PROSPECT THEORY; SELF; SOCIAL COGNITION; SOCIAL DILEMMAS, SOCIAL JUDGMENT; SOCIAL REPRESENTATIONS; SOCIALIZATION; UNEMPLOYMENT; WORK.

BIBLIOGRAPHY

Cowell, F. A. (1992). Tax evasion and inequity. *Journal of Economic Psychology*, *13*, 521–45.

Furnham, A., & Lewis, A. (1986). *The economic mind: The social psychology of economic behaviour*. Brighton: Harvester Wheatsheaf.

Hessing, D. J., Ellfers, H., & Weigel, R. H. (1988). Exploring the limits of self-reports and reasoned action: An investigation of the psychology of tax evasion behaviour. *Journal of Personality and Social Psychology*, *54*, 405–13.

Katona, G. (1975). *Psychological economics*. New York: Elsevier.

Lane, R. E. (1991). *The market experience*. Cambridge: Cambridge University Press.

Lea, S. E. G., Tarpy, R. M., & Webley, P. (1987). *The individual in the economy*. Cambridge: Cambridge University Press.

—— Webley, P., & Young, B. M. (1992). *New directions in economic psychology*. Cheltenham: Edward Elgar.

Leiser, D., Sevón, G., & Lévy, D. (1990). Children's economic socialization: Summarizing the cross-cultural comparisons of ten countries. *Journal of Economic Psychology*, *11*, 591–614.

Lunt, P. K., & Livingstone, S. M. (1992). *Mass consumption and personal identity*. Buckingham: Open University Press.

van Raaij, W. F., van Veldhoven, G. M., & Wärneryd, K-E. (1988). *Handbook of economic psychology*. Dordrecht: Kluwer.

PAUL WEBLEY

**ego-involvement** The extent to which a task or issue is personally significant or motivating to an individual, and hence carries implications for that individual's self-concept and SELF-ESTEEM. Closely related to SALIENCE. According to Sherif and Hovland (1961), it mediates SOCIAL JUDGMENT by leading to biased reinterpretation of attitude statements and messages. Individuals high in ego-involvement on some issue are assumed to find fewer viewpoints discrepant from their own as still acceptable, i.e., they have narrower "latitudes" of acceptance and non-commitment and wider latitudes of rejection. This is hypothesized to lead to ASSIMILATION–CONTRAST effects in judgments of attitude statements, and to "boomerang effects" in reactions to communications advocating rejected viewpoints. Empirical support is patchy, with effects of ego-involvement and attitude extremity often indistinguishable. According to the ELABORATION LIKELIHOOD MODEL, involvement leads to more thorough processing of persuasive messages, and to strong arguments producing more ATTITUDE CHANGE.

*See also*: ATTITUDE CHANGE; SELF-ESTEEM; SOCIAL JUDGMENT.

BIBLIOGRAPHY
Sherif, M., & Hovland, C. I. (1961). *Social judgment: Assimilation and contrast effects in communication and attitude change*. New Haven, CT: Yale. University Press.

J. RICHARD EISER

**elaboration likelihood model (ELM)** Proposed by Petty and Cacioppo (1981) as a model of PERSUASION. Like the HEURISTIC–SYSTEMATIC MODEL, it argues that there are two "routes" to persuasion. When respondents are motivated and able to process message content carefully, they are likely to follow the *central route*, which involves elaboration of (i.e., thinking about) issue-relevant arguments. Persuasion via this route is based on thoughts generated by the arguments contained in the message. How attitudes are influenced by careful processing of message content is said to depend on argument quality: given strong arguments, careful processing will result in ATTITUDE CHANGE in the direction of the message; given weak arguments, there may be attitude change in the reverse direction. Attitude change via the central route is predicted to be relatively enduring and more predictive of subsequent behavior. When ability or motivation to process message content is low, recipients are likely to follow the *peripheral route* to persuasion. Any attitude change resulting from factors other than the arguments contained in

the message must by definition occur via this peripheral route. A classic example of such a factor is the attractiveness of the source of the message. Attitude change via the peripheral route is likely to be relatively short-lived and a poor predictor of future behavior. Much current attitude change research is designed to test predictions derived from the ELM, and there is a good measure of support for the model (for a review, *see* Eagly & Chaiken, 1993).

*See also*: ATTITUDE CHANGE.

BIBLIOGRAPHY
Eagly, A. H., & Chaiken, S. (1993). *The psychology of attitudes*. Forth Worth, TX: Harcourt Brace Jovanovich.
Petty, R. E., & Cacioppo, J. T. (1981). *Attitudes and persuasion: Classic and contemporary approaches*. Dubuque, IL: William C. Brown.

ANTONY S. R. MANSTEAD

**embarrassment** An uncomfortable emotional state that occurs in awkward social situations. It is perhaps the most social of all emotions. It always occurs in response to social situations, real or imagined. It requires knowledge of social conventions. It requires mental representation of others' beliefs and evaluations. It is an emotion that stems as much from one's social roles and appearances as from one's private sense of SELF.

Embarrassment plays important roles in social life. Despite its reputation as a minor unpleasantness, people's actions suggest that they consider embarrassment quite aversive. People often go to extremes to avoid this emotion and, when it occurs, they struggle, often cooperatively, to eliminate it. Many aspects of social interaction appear motivated to reduce the possibility of embarrassment (Goffman, 1959). For this reason it may be said that actual episodes of acute embarrassment are fairly infrequent, whereas the fear of embarrassment is nearly ubiquitous.

Avoidance of embarrassment may underlie many of the phenomena studied by social psychologists, including CONFORMITY, PEER PRESSURE, inhibited HELPING BEHAVIOR in bystanders, and OBEDIENCE to authority. Avoiding the social awkwardness of deviance, confrontation, moral reproach, or falsely declaring an emergency appears to be a central motive producing these phenomena, even to the point of preventing people from following their moral convictions. That these phenomena are often considered counterintuitive illustrates the underappreciation of the power of embarrassment.

The subjective EMOTIONAL EXPERIENCE of embarrassment is characterized by several reactions (Parrott & Smith, 1991). Its hallmark is a feeling of social awkwardness, often accompanied by flustering, surprise, or feelings of foolishness. The embarrassed person typically feels self-conscious and the focus of attention. There is a strong motivation to mend or escape the situation. Behaviorally, embarrassment is often accompanied by blushing, nervous laughter or smiling, reduced eye contact, and signs of nervousness and autonomic arousal.

## THEORIES OF EMBARRASSMENT

Because emotional experience in embarrassing situations is frequently complex, theorists focusing on different aspects have produced a variety of theories of the causes and nature of embarrassment. The theories may be classified into three groups: decreased others' esteem theories, decreased SELF-ESTEEM theories, and dramaturgic theories.

Decreased others' esteem theories focus on one of the most common themes in embarrassment: looking bad in the eyes of others (see IMPRESSION MANAGEMENT). Such theories assert that embarrassment occurs when one is concerned that one has made an undesirable impression on others, or when there is a discrepancy between one's self-image and a more negative image projected to others (Edelman, 1987). Such theories often depict the subjective experience of embarrassment as social ANXIETY. They may also postulate negative affect of a nonanxious type, stemming from acute awareness of a negative public image (Crozier, 1990).

Decreased self-esteem theories claim that the emotional feelings of embarrassment originate in a loss of one's self-esteem, not in the loss of others' esteem. In one theory of this type, it is claimed that embarrassment begins with decreases in others' esteem, but that the emotional intensity of embarrassment is caused by a subsequent decrease in one's own self-esteem (Modigliani, 1971). Other theories of this type conceive of embarrassment as a mild form of shame, or as a reaction to a violation of one's personal standards.

In contrast, dramaturgic theories deny that either others' or one's own esteem for oneself need decrease in embarrassment. Dramaturgic theories instead claim that embarrassment arises from the disruption of the assumptions necessary for social interaction. Drawing on Goffman's (1959) analysis of social interaction as self-presentation, embarrassment is said to result when there is a disruption in the working consensus of identities in a social interaction. Although such a disruption may result from appearing worse than desired, it need not, because embarrassment can result from being publicly praised or from being in the same situation with someone who commits a *faux pas*. Dramaturgic theories therefore characterize the subjective experience of embarrassment as flustering and social awkwardness that stem from lacking a coherent or acceptable way to behave.

One way to reconcile such different characterizations of embarrassment is to realize that all three accurately describe some of the emotions occurring in prototypical cases of intense embarrassment. For example, a person who is publicly disgraced may well experience all three types of emotion. If one were to adopt a PROTOTYPE approach to the definition of embarrassment, one might consider such actuely embarrassing episodes to be prototypical, and use similarity to this prototype as the basis for deciding whether other situations contained embarrassment. With this approach, embarrassment would be conceived as a multifaceted phenomenon that can appear in a variety of forms, and all three theories could be said to capture aspects of it.

On the other hand, inspection of a wide assortment of cases of embarrassment suggests that a narrower conception of embarrassment is warranted (Parrott & Smith, 1991). In particular, there appear to be many cases in which decreased self-esteem is not salient. Laboratory experiments generally fail to find evidence of decreased self-esteem in embarrassment, and there is increasing evidence that embarrassment can be distinguished from shame. In contrast, both decreased others' esteem theories and dramaturgic theories have generally proved quite helpful in explaining embarrassment. Dramaturgic difficulties are the most consistent markers of embarrassing situations, and they best predict its symptoms. Concern about the decreased esteem of others is also very common, and it is often implicit in everyday usage of the word "embarrassment." There is no consensus at present as to which of these two approaches is to be preferred.

See also: EMOTIONAL EXPERIENCE; HELPING BEHAVIOR; IMPRESSION MANAGEMENT; OBEDIENCE; SELF; SELF-ESTEEM.

BIBLIOGRAPHY
Crozier, W. R. (Ed.) (1990). *Shyness and embarrassment: Perspectives from social psychology*. New York: Cambridge University Press.
Edelman, R. J. (1987). *The psychology of embarrassment*. New York: Wiley.
Goffman, E. (1959). *The presentation of self in everyday life*. Garden City, NY: Doubleday.
Parrott, W. G., & Smith, S. F. (1991). Embarrassment: Actual vs. typical cases, classical vs. prototypical representations. *Cognition and Emotion*, 5, 467–88.
Modigliani, A. (1971). Embarrassment, facework, and eye contact: Testing a theory of embarrassment. *Journal of Personality and Social Psychology*, 17, 15–24.

W. GERROD PARROTT

**emotional experience**  Central to most conceptions of emotion is the idea that emotions are characterized by subjective experiences of certain types. Despite emotion's complexity and the considerable disagreement among theorists about its nature, there is remarkable consensus that subjective experience ("feeling") is an important aspect of emotion, at least in humans. Many areas of psychology have contributed to our understanding of emotion, and social psychology has been among the most influential, especially in addressing emotional experience. This article surveys the major theories of emotional experience; it emphasizes social psychology's contributions but includes other perspectives as well.

An adequate understanding of emotional experience must address two fundamental questions. First, what is an emotion? Then, what is it about emotions that produces their characteristic subjective experiences?

DEFINITION OF EMOTION
It is easy to name examples of emotion: this concept includes such states as fear, anger, happiness, and sadness. There is disagreement, however, about what these states have in common and how they can be distinguished from nonemotional states. In everyday usage the term "emotion" refers to a wide range of phenomena that may have little in common. Some researchers have proposed that the concept of emotion is therefore intrinsically "fuzzy" and will never be defined more precisely than by describing what seem to be good examples of emotion; similarity to these PROTOTYPES would be the only basis for distinguishing emotion from nonemotion. Other authors maintain that researchers must strive for more precise definitions, either by theoretical fiat or by empirical discoveries that will clarify the natural category of emotion or will suggest that this category can be divided into more precise subcategories.

Whatever the ultimate outcome, it can be said that most researchers at present are content to use a somewhat loose, working definition such as the following: *Emotions are valenced reactions to personally significant events, including physiological reactions, behavioral reactions, cognitive reactions, and subjective feelings of pleasure or displeasure.*

Such an answer to the question of definition foreshadows answers to the second question about emotional experience. The definition depicts emotion as a multifaceted phenomenon, and three of the facets – physiology, behavior, and cognition – form the material from which theorists have tried to explain the fourth facet – subjective feelings. Emotional feelings have been proposed to originate in physiological processes, in emotional behavior, and in cognitive activity. Some theorists have emphasized just one of these constituents, whereas others have combined several.

It may seem puzzling that such disparate entities as physiology, behavior, and cognition could be proposed to explain the same phenomenon, but it seems that feelings can result from all such sources. We speak of feeling cold, feeling sleepy, feeling like screaming, and feeling confused. Whether some or all such sources contribute to emotional feelings is a central issue in the theory of emotional experience. The following sections survey these theories, organizing them according to how they address this issue.

## SOURCES OF EMOTIONAL EXPERIENCE

### Emotional Experience from Physiological Activity

Physiological approaches to emotion may be divided into two types. The first type emphasizes the bodily symptoms of emotions – the pounding heart, dry mouth, sweaty palms, and butterflies in the stomach that are characteristic of many powerful emotions. This approach emphasizes regions of the body that lie beyond the brain and spinal cord in the periphery of the nervous system. The second physiological approach to emotion has the opposite emphasis, on activities of the central nervous system that appear to be responsible for emotions.

*Peripheral physiological activity*. The most influential statement of the peripheral approach was made a century ago by William James (1884). James proposed that emotional experience results from the awareness of various bodily changes, especially those occurring in the autonomic nervous system such as autonomic AROUSAL. James' theory is appealing in that it postulates a source of feelings that is fairly concrete and easily understood, but in this simple form it encounters formidable problems. Evidence suggests that autonomic arousal is unnecessary for emotional experiences to occur. Investigations of people with spinal cord injuries that block feedback from the autonomic nervous system reveal

that their emotional experiences are just as intense as those of uninjured people (Chwalisz, Diener, & Gallagher, 1988). Furthermore, autonomic arousal alone is insufficient for emotional experiences to occur. Artificial activation of the sympathetic nervous system (such as by injection of epinephrine) does not usually produce emotional experience; nor does there appear to be enough differentiation in the patterning of autonomic nervous system activity to account for subjective differences between emotional states (Cannon, 1927). At best, it seems that peripheral physiological activity can make a contribution to the intensity and quality of emotional experiences.

*Central physiological activity*. Following Cannon's (1927) critique of James, Cannon and others proposed that emotional experiences were produced by structures in the brain that control many aspects of emotions, including autonomic arousal. Papez (1937) proposed that an interconnected set of structures located near the middle of the brain – called the *limbic system* – produced emotional feelings and responses. Subsequent research investigated the effects of stimulus, inhibition, and trauma to these regions. The findings suggested that activity of regions in the hypothalamus and limbic system was associated with a number of emotional experiences. Electrical or chemical stimulation or inhibition of these regions produced subjective experiences of pleasure, displeasure, sexual pleasure, anxiety, and rage. Damage to these regions produced a variety of emotional disorders. Such evidence suggests to some theorists that activity of certain brain structures directly gives rise to the subjective experience of emotion. These experiences, it is argued, occur without obvious involvement of peripheral feedback or cognition (Buck, 1988).

### Emotional Experience from Action

William James' (1884) account of emotion can be read as basing emotional experience on more than just autonomic arousal; James often wrote as if actions also gave rise to emotional feelings. Discovery of the limitations of the early emphasis on autonomic activity has led to a reemphasis in recent decades on the role of action in producing emotional feelings. This approach can be divided into two types: feelings resulting from fully produced action and feelings resulting from unrealized tendencies toward action.

*Action.* A variety of actions have been claimed to contribute to emotional experience. The most frequently cited of these are actions that are expressive of emotion, such as FACIAL EXPRESSIONS OF EMOTION, posture, and gaze patterns. One hypothesis is that proprioceptive feedback from these actions produces emotional feelings. A variety of experiments have shown that manipulating subjects' expressive actions produces corresponding changes in subjects' emotional experiences – subjects who are induced to contract their brows feel more sad than do those who do not; those induced to grin experience more humor than do those whose grins are inhibited; subjects who sit upright feel more pride than do those who slump (Laird & Bresler, 1992; Stepper & Strack, 1993). There is controversy concerning the reliability, magnitude, and mechanism of these effects, but the evidence is adequate to conclude that expressive actions can contribute to emotional experience.

Other types of action may contribute to emotional experience as well. William James claimed that flight increased the experience of panic, that muscular tension increased rage, and that sobbing increased sorrow. The effects of such actions have not been subject to as much empirical scrutiny, however.

*Action tendency.* Tendencies to act may also contribute to emotional experience, even if the actions are not actually carried out. Emotions involve inclinations to act in certain ways, along with preparations for such actions (Frijda, 1986). One is ready to attack, to withdraw, to block another's action or, in the case of joy, just to do *something*. We speak of feeling moved or frozen, as wanting to leap or run or hug. Awareness of one's readiness for action could contribute to emotional experience.

### Cognition

Cognition may enter into emotional experience in a variety of ways. Best known are

ways in which cognition might combine with one of the noncognitive sources already discussed. Less well known are the ways in which cognition alone could produce emotional experience, so we shall begin with these.

*Cognitive actions and cognitive tendencies.* The noncognitive sources described above – physiology and action – are compatible with the notion that feelings are sensory in nature. Thumping heartbeats, facial grimaces, tensed muscles – all these elements of emotional experience are feelings of a fairly straightforward sensory kind. Yet, as was pointed out previously, not all feelings are of this type. Confusion, for example, is subjectively experienced as a feeling, yet does not appear to be based on a sensory process; rather, it appears to arise from a pattern of cognitive activity in which one's framework for understanding events is contradicted and no new framework can be found. *Déjà vu*, to take another example, appears to result from a partial recollection in which a situation seems familiar but the basis for that familiarity is not recognized. Such states might be called "cognitive feelings," and their existence suggests the possibility of a cognitive basis for subjective experience. Some emotional experiences may be of this cognitive type (Parrott, 1988).

In emotional situations people may feel confused, or certain, or unable to solve a problem, or mentally sharp, or preoccupied, or unable to concentrate. Furthermore, just as there are behavioral action tendencies, there may also be cognitive action tendencies. People may consciously experience effort to find fault, vigilance for possible threats, tendency toward pessimistic conclusions, or bias toward optimistic interpretations. Such cognitive actions and tendencies might contribute to feelings of anger, fear, sadness, happiness, or other emotions.

*Cognitive appraisals.* One well-known feature of cognitive theories of emotion is the claim that emotions can be distinguished by the appraisals that are associated with them. Thus, fear is said to entail an appraisal of threat, sadness an appraisal of irrevocable loss, pride an appraisal of deserving credit for a positive attribute, and so forth. Less well known is the claim that such appraisals color the phenomenology of one's experience. It could be that the distinctive subjective experience of these emotions results from the awareness of these appraisals and their implications. What distinguishes emotional appraisals is the fact that they relate a situation to one's concerns, values, and goals. Such appraisals may produce an emotional subjective experience because of the personal importance of what they signify, because they refer to future pleasures or pains, and because they suggest that certain actions ought to be attempted (Frijda, 1986). Appraisal of the potential for coping with the current situation can modify the emotional experience (*see* STRESS AND COPING).

*Cognitive interpretation of physiology and action.* Aside from producing emotional experience on its own, cognition has also been proposed to produce emotional experience in conjunction with physiology or behavior. The most famous statement of this approach is the "two-factor" theory proposed by Schachter (*see* Reisenzein, 1983). Two-factor theory depicts emotional experience as involving both physiological arousal and a cognitive interpretation of a situation as being "emotional." The theory postulates that neither can produce emotion alone; only when they are joined is an emotional experience produced, with arousal providing the emotional intensity and the cognitive interpretation providing the emotional quality. The means by which these two are joined is a second cognitive process, described variously as "labeling" or as "causal attribution," that construes the arousal as being caused by the emotional situation.

One of the theory's predictions is that MISATTRIBUTION OF AROUSAL from an irrelevant source to an emotional source will increase the intensity of that emotion. This prediction has been reliably confirmed, suggesting that EXCITATION TRANSFER is one means of increasing the intensity of such emotional experiences as anger, anxiety, and romantic attraction. In other respects the theory has not fared well, however. The theory's prediction that decreasing arousal will decrease emotional intensity has received little empirical support (Reisenzein, 1983). The same evidence that suggested that arousal is

not necessary for emotion (discussed previously) also suggests that the two-factor theory cannot account for all emotional experiences. Misattribution of arousal appears to account for only a small proportion of emotional experiences.

## HOW ARE NONCOGNITIVE SOURCES REGISTERED IN CONSCIOUSNESS?

Aside from determining the sources of emotional experience, theorists have debated the means by which these sources come to be experienced as emotional. Three general approaches may be discerned, differing primarily with respect to the need for cognition in producing emotional experience.

### Direct, Noncognitive Registration

One approach maintains that cognition is unnecessary; physiological activity and action can directly produce emotional experiences. We have already encountered the argument that activity of certain brain regions produces emotional experiences without intervening interpretation (Buck, 1988). It has also been argued that peripheral physiological activity and action can directly produce emotional experiences. Since emotional feelings are affected even by very unobtrusive manipulations of facial expressions, some theorists conclude that emotional feelings are caused by peripheral sensory input which has a distinct phenomenal quality that is intrinsically emotional (Stepper & Strack, 1993).

### Explicit, Conscious Cognitive Registration

The theorists who propose the previous arguments often direct them against the alternative hypothesis that sensory information must be subjected to inferences, judgments, or semantic interpretations before producing emotional experiences. Certain statements of SELF-PERCEPTION THEORY or ATTRIBUTION THEORIES do seem to advance this hypothesis, and the data certainly seem to suggest that it is wrong. Oddly, however, there do not appear to be any contemporary theorists who actually advocate this alternative hypothesis. Those to whom it has been attributed disavow it, and instead propose a more plausible alternative.

*Implicit, Perception-like Cognitive Registration*
It can instead be argued that emotional experience is based on cognitive processes that tend to be "unconscious inferences," like those leading to the perception of depth. For example, self-perception theory depicts emotional experience as a form of self-knowledge based on observation and interpretation of one's emotional behaviors. Behaviors such as facial expressions, other expressive actions, autonomic arousal, and action are interpreted along with contextual information to produce a perception of one's emotional state (Laird & Bresler, 1992). These self-perceptions, however, need not be conscious or reasoned; rather, they are automatic, unavailable to awareness, and give rise to a perception-like conscious experience.

Other theories focus less on behavior and more on cognitive appraisal, yet retain the assertion that experience results from perception-like cognition. Frijda (1986), following Sartre and other phenomenologists, depicts emotional experience as awareness of the world as having certain properties that relate it to oneself and to one's goals and values. The situation is perceived as if it objectively contained these implications for oneself. The experience is perception-like in that it typically lacks consciousness of itself; the feeling arises simply from the emotional meaning perceived in the object or event.

The cognitive position also claims some empirical support. Subjects whose emotions are most affected by their facial expression also tend to be most affected by their posture, gaze, or autonomic arousal, suggesting there exist reliable INDIVIDUAL DIFFERENCES in using internal cues to perceive emotions. Furthermore, the literature on the misattribution of arousal suggests that identical sensations can result in very different emotional experiences, suggesting perceptual inference, not an immutable phenomenal quality, underlies emotional experiences.

CONCLUSIONS
Given the variety of sources and mechanisms postulated to produce emotional experiences, it is reassuring to note that these perspectives may not conflict as much as it may seem.

First, the numerous potential sources of emotional feelings are not mutually exclusive; all of them – central and peripheral physiology, action and action tendencies, cognitive tendencies and appraisals – may contribute to emotional experience. In fact, it seems quite plausible that they do, although few may be *necessary* for emotional experiences to occur.

Second, the length of the list of sources may be deceptive. It is unclear, for example, what occurs when sites in the limbic system are stimulated. We know that emotional experiences may occur, but we do not know why. It may be that limbic system activity gives rise to emotional appraisals, or to behavioral or cognitive action tendencies. Likewise, actions (e.g., facial expressions) may generate emotional experience not via proprioceptive feedback but rather by confirming an appraisal or an action tendency (Frijda, 1986). So some of the listed sources of emotional experience may turn out to overlap.

Finally, it is important to emphasize that the many elements entering into emotional experience are not haphazard; they cohere when the purpose of the emotion is appreciated. If one adopts a functionalist perspective, emotions are seen as responses that modify one's relation to the environment in response to significant events. Changes in physiological activity and in readiness to act make sense in terms of the appraisal that has been made and of the future possibilities that have been anticipated. The adaptiveness of emotions becomes apparent from this perspective; the reasons for the many aspects of their subjective experience become apparent as well.

*See also*: AROUSAL; ATTRIBUTION THEORIES; FACIAL EXPRESSIONS OF EMOTION; SELF-PERCEPTION THEORY; STRESS AND COPING.

BIBLIOGRAPHY
Buck, R. (1988). *Human motivation and emotion* (2nd ed.). New York: Wiley.
Cannon, W. B. (1927). The James-Lange theory of emotions: A critical examination and an alternative theory. *American Journal of Psychology*, *39*, 106–24.
Chwalisz, K., Diener, E., & Gallagher, D. (1988). Autonomic arousal feedback and

emotional experience: Evidence from the spinal cord injured. *Journal of Personality and Social Psychology*, *54*, 820–8.

Frijda, N. H. (1986). *The emotions*. Cambridge: Cambridge University Press.

James, W. (1884). What is an emotion? *Mind*, *9*, 188–205.

Laird, J. D., & Bresler, C. (1992). The process of emotional experience: A self-perception theory. In M. S. Clark (Ed.), *Review of personality and social psychology* (Vol. 13, pp. 213–34). Beverly Hills, CA: Sage.

Papez, J. (1937). A proposed mechanism of emotion. *Archives of Neurology and Psychology*, *38*, 725–44.

Parrott, W. G. (1988). The role of cognition in emotional experience. In W. J. Baker, L. P. Mos, H. V. Rappard, & H. J. Stam (Eds.), *Recent trends in theoretical psychology* (pp. 327–37). New York: Springer-Verlag.

Reisenzein, R. (1983). The Schachter theory of emotion: Two decades later. *Psychological Bulletin*, *94*, 239–64.

Stepper, S., & Strack, F. (1993). Proprioceptive determinants of emotional and nonemotional feelings. *Journal of Personality and Social Psychology*, *64*, 211–20.

W. GERROD PARROTT

**empathy** In the last two decades, empathy and related emotional reactions have received increasing attention from social and developmental psychologists. This is probably because of the strong theoretical link between empathy (and related constructs such as sympathy) and both positive social behavior and social competence (*see* Batson, 1991; Eisenberg & Miller, 1987).

The term *empathy* has been defined in many ways in the psychological literature (*see* Batson, 1991; Eisenberg & Miller, 1987). Although there is still disagreement regarding its definition, many social and developmental psychologists currently differentiate between various vicarious emotional responses to others' emotions or state – which are generally viewed as empathy or related to empathy – and cognitive and affective perspective taking. Perspective taking involves the cognitive comprehension of another's internal psychological processes such as thoughts and feelings. Whereas perspective taking often may result in empathy and related emotional responses (Batson, 1991), it is not the same as *feeling* something as a result of exposure to another's emotions or condition.

Many theorists and researchers now use the term empathy to mean feeling an emotional response consistent with the emotions or situation of another. Some also use it to refer to related other-oriented reactions such as sympathy and compassion (Batson, 1991). However, it is useful to differentiate among *empathy*, *sympathy*, and *personal distress*. Specifically, empathy is defined as an emotional reaction to another's emotional state or condition that is consistent with the other's state or condition (e.g., feeling sad when viewing a sad person). *Sympathy*, which frequently may stem from empathy (Eisenberg & Fabes, 1990), is defined as a vicarious emotional reaction based on the apprehension of another's emotional state or condition, which involves feelings of sorrow, compassion, or concern for the other (Batson, 1991, labels our definition of sympathy as empathy). Conceptually, sympathy involves an other-orientation whereas empathy does not.

Another vicariously induced emotional reaction that is frequently confused with empathy and sympathy is *personal distress* (Batson, 1991). Personal distress is an aversive vicariously induced emotional reaction such as anxiety or worry which is coupled with self-oriented, egoistic concerns. Batson (1991) has argued that experiencing personal distress leads to the motive of alleviating one's own distress.

Empathy and related emotional reactions have received increasing attention from social and developmental psychologists in the last two decades. This is probably because of the strong theoretical link between empathy (and related constructs such as sympathy) and both positive social behavior and social competence (*see* Batson, 1991; Eisenberg & Miller, 1987). Indeed, much of the recent research on empathy and sympathy has concerned a few topics:

(1) gender differences in empathy;
(2) the relation of empathy and sympathy to prosocial behavior (voluntary behavior intended to benefit another);

(3) whether empathy or sympathy is associated with altruistic motives (i.e., whether empathy is associated with the motivation to benefit another rather than self-interest; *see* ALTRUISM);

(4) the relation of empathy to aggression; and

(5) the development and socialization of empathy and related vicarious emotions.

Each of these topics is now briefly reviewed.

## GENDER DIFFERENCES IN EMPATHY AND RELATED RESPONSES

In reviews of gender differences in empathy, Eisenberg and her colleagues (Eisenberg, Fabes, Schaller, & Miller, 1989) found that gender differences in empathy and related vicarious emotional responses varied as a function of the method of assessing empathy. There were large differences favoring females for self-report measures of empathy, especially questionnaire indices. However, no gender differences were found when the measure of empathy was either physiological or unobtrusive observations of nonverbal behavior. Eisenberg has suggested that this pattern of results was due to differences among measures in the degree to which the intent of the measure was obvious and respondents could control their responses. Gender differences were greatest when demand characteristics were high (i.e., it was clear what was being assessed) and respondents had conscious control over their responses (i.e., self-report indices were used). In contrast, gender differences were virtually nonexistent when demand characteristics were subtle *and* respondents were unlikely to exercise much conscious control over their responding (i.e., physiological responses). When gender stereotypes are activated and people can easily control their responses, they may try to project a socially desirable image to others or to themselves.

In recent work investigators have attempted to differentiate between sympathy and personal distress using physiological and facial reactions, as well self reports. They generally have found modest self-reported gender differences in sympathy and personal distress in reaction to empathy-inducing stimuli (females tend to report more), occasional differences in facial reactions (generally favoring females), and virtually no gender differences in heart rate findings (*see* Eisenberg, Fabes, Schaller, & Miller, 1989). Findings for skin conductance are mixed. Overall the pattern of findings suggests that females are slightly more likely than males to evidence both sympathy and personal distress, but that the differences are quite weak (except for questionnaire measures) and dependent on method of measurement and context. Whether these slight gender differences are due to biological factors or socialization (or both) is not clear, although socialization clearly influences empathic responding (e.g., Eisenberg, Fabes, Carlo, & Karbon, 1992).

## THE RELATION OF EMPATHY AND RELATED REACTIONS TO PROSOCIAL BEHAVIOR

Philosophers and psychologists frequently have hypothesized that empathy and sympathy are associated with prosocial behavior or altruism (nonegoistically motivated prosocial behavior). People who experience another's distress or sadness and feel concern for the distressed or needy person are expected to be motivated to alleviate the cause of the other person's sadness or distress.

Generally, this hypothesis has been supported, although results vary as a function of the index of empathy and prosocial behavior (Batson, 1991). Eisenberg and Miller (1987) found that children's self-reports of vicarious emotion in experimental contexts and in response to hypothetical stories about other people in emotionally evocative situations were unrelated to their prosocial behavior. In contrast, nearly all other indexes of empathy (e.g., questionnaire measures, facial indexes, experimental inductions of empathy) were positively related to prosocial behavior. In experimental studies, the relation between sympathy and prosocial behavior has been especially clear when researchers have differentiated between sympathy and personal distress and have examined helping in contexts in which it is easy to escape from dealing with the empathy-inducing cues (*see*

Batson, 1991). Moreover, in recent studies, children's sympathy, as assessed with facial and physiological reactions, has been associated with their helping and sharing whereas personal distress reactions to others' need or distress have been correlated with low levels of prosocial behavior (particularly for boys; Eisenberg & Fabes, 1990). Thus, the research indicates that empathy and sympathy are positively associated with prosocial behavior, at least in some contexts. In contrast, personal distress reactions tend to be unrelated or negatively correlated with prosocial behavior (Batson, 1991; Eisenberg & Fabes, 1990).

## EMPATHY/SYMPATHY AND ALTRUISTIC MOTIVATION

An ongoing debate in social psychology is whether empathy (or sympathy) is associated with true altruism or whether all prosocial behavior, even that engendered by sympathy, is egoistically motivated (see Batson, 1991; Cialdini & Fultz, 1990). Batson (1991) has argued that empathy (sympathy, in our terminology) is associated with the selfless desire to benefit another and that empathically motivated altruistic behavior is not due to the desire for external rewards, the goal of avoiding guilt, or the desire to feel good due to vicarious sharing of a distressed or needy person's joy when their condition is improved. In contrast, people experiencing personal distress are expected to assist only when assisting is the easiest way to make themselves feel less distressed, that is, when it is difficult to escape contact with the needy or distressed other who is causing them to feel distressed and when assisting is not highly costly. Thus, according to Batson, people experiencing personal distress are expected to leave rather than help if it is easy to escape from the distressed person and the aversive cues emitted by that person.

Although Batson (1991) and others have gathered much experimental data consistent with Batson's arguments, there also are findings suggesting that people experiencing empathy sometimes help to experience empathic joy. However, data on this issue are still scarce and can be interpreted in conflicting ways (see Batson, 1991). In addition, Cialdini and his colleagues have argued that people frequently assist in empathy producing contexts to alleviate their own negative mood state (Cialdini & Fultz, 1990) – that is, to make themselves feel better. Cialdini has suggested that helping can be used to lift one's mood because helping behaviors become associated with internal rewards due to reinforcements for helping during the socialization process. If Cialdini is correct, much of what has been viewed as helping due to empathy may in reality be egoistically motivated behavior. However, there is much debate regarding the validity of Cialdini's negative state relief model (see Batson, 1991; Cialdini & Fultz, 1990). Thus, debate regarding the motivational status of empathy and sympathy is likely to continue in the future.

A related issue is whether there is an altruistic personality based, at least in part, on sustained dispositional differences in empathy or sympathy. Many theorists and researchers have assumed that this is the case – that individuals differ in their tendency to experience empathy or sympathy and that such differences underlie personality differences in the tendency to be altruistic (see Eisenberg & Miller, 1987). However, Batson (1991) has questioned the validity of such an assumption; he argues that people who appear to be altruistic may be helping as an instrumental means of enhancing their own welfare by receiving self-rewards or avoiding self-punishment. Although it is not unusual for researchers to find correlations between measures of dispositional sympathy or empathy and instances of prosocial behavior (Eisenberg & Miller, 1987), it generally is very difficult to determine for certain the nature of individuals' motivation for their prosocial tendencies (see Batson, 1991). However, if individuals sometimes assist for altruistic reasons (an issue for which the research is more convincing; see Batson, 1991), it is reasonable to assume that some people do so more than do others. This association likely holds more in some situations (e.g., those in which sympathy inducing cues are relevant) than others. Nonetheless, this is an issue of continuing debate.

## EMPATHY, AGGRESSION, AND SOCIAL COMPETENCE

Empathy has been considered as relevant to an understanding of AGGRESSION as well as prosocial behavior. Theorists have suggested that people who experience another's pain or distress are likely to restrain from aggression or cease their aggression because of their empathic reactions to the victim's emotional reactions (or imagined reactions; *see* Miller & Eisenberg, 1988). Conversely, it has been argued that individuals high in empathy and sympathy are likely to be socially competent (Eisenberg & Miller, 1987).

There is some empirical support for the link between empathy and aggression, although the link appears to be modest. Moreover, the association between the two varies with the method of measuring empathy. When empathy is assessed by using picture-story measures with children (in which children are told stories about hypothetical children in emotion-eliciting situations and the subjects are then asked how they themselves feel), empathy is related to children's aggression, but only for children older than preschool age. There also is an association between empathy and aggression/acting out behaviors when empathy is assessed with questionnaire measures; however, the relation of aggression to report of empathy in experimental settings and to facial indexes of children's empathy is very weak (Miller & Eisenberg, 1988). Perhaps most compelling is the link between maternal empathy and both child abuse and offspring's empathy. However, findings in this regard must be viewed as tentative due to the small number of relevant studies (*see* Miller & Eisenberg, 1988, for a review of these issues).

The notion that emotional empathy is associated with socially competent behavior has received modest support. However, research on this issue is relatively scarce and generally involves children and indexes of global empathy (Eisenberg & Miller, 1987). It is quite possible that the relation between sympathy and measures of social competence will prove to be more robust than that for global emotional empathy.

## THE DEVELOPMENT AND SOCIALIZATION OF EMPATHY AND SYMPATHY

Empathy and sympathy appear to develop early in life. In the first days of life, infants cry in reaction to the cries of other infants — a behavior that, it has been suggested, is a precursor to empathic responding (although others question whether this is true). Although 6- to 12-month-olds show little reaction to the distress of others, between 12 to 18 months of age many children react with agitation or sustained attention (e.g., Radke-Yarrow & Zahn-Waxler, 1984). By 18 months of age, children sometimes try to comfort others in distress, and it appears that some children's prosocial actions are based on empathic reactions (*see* Radke-Yarrow & Zahn-Waxler, 1984). With increasing age, as children can better differentiate their own internal states from those of others, children appear to be capable of experiencing sympathy *for* another person rather than merely vicariously sharing another's negative emotion. Thus, by 2 to 3 years of age, it is not uncommon for a child to demonstrate behaviors that seem to reflect genuine sympathy. However, it is, of course, difficult to ascertain whether young children's vicarious emotional responding is sympathy, personal distress, or emotional contagion. Nonetheless, by age 4 to 5, it appears that children experience both sympathy and personal distress, and that the former, but not the latter, is positively associated with children's willingness to assist others (e.g., *see* Eisenberg & Fabes, 1990).

There is debate regarding the degree to which biological versus environmental factors influence individual differences in children's and adults' empathy and sympathy. In studies of twins' self-reports of empathy, there is some evidence that genetic factors may account for a considerable degree of variance in empathy (e.g., Rushton et al., 1986; *see* GENETIC INFLUENCES). Nonetheless, socialization clearly influences individual differences in vicarious emotional responding.

Research on the socialization of empathy and sympathy clearly suggests an association between children's vicarious responding and both parental empathy/sympathy and parents' child-rearing practices. Children's empathy has been associated with quality of the mother–child attachment early in life and supportive parenting (*see* Eisenberg et al., 1992), although the findings are not always consistent. In addition, parents' reported sympathy and perspective taking have been positively correlated with same-sex elementary school children's sympathy and negatively correlated with their personal distress reactions (Eisenberg et al., 1992). Supportive, empathic caretakers are likely to model and encourage the capacity for empathy in children, although parental warmth by itself may be insufficient to foster empathy in children (Janssens & Gerris, 1992). Indeed, practices that involve some discipline or restrictiveness may facilitate the development of empathy (Janssens & Gerris, 1992).

Parents may also subtly model or communicate acceptance of a variety of emotional responses through their own expressivity or their acceptance of others' emotional responses in everyday life. In homes where submissive (i.e., nonassertive) negative emotions such as sympathy and apologizing are expressed frequently, children would be expected to learn to express empathy and sympathy and to be relatively uninhibited in doing so. Consistent with this argument, Eisenberg and her colleagues have found that women (but not men) who reported growing up in homes high in positive emotion and submissive negative emotions were particularly likely to report responding emotionally to sympathy inducing and distressing films. In contrast, expression of hostile or aggressive (i.e., dominant negative) emotions (e.g., anger) in the home was unrelated to women's vicarious responding. In addition, for boys, parental emphasis on controlling emotion seems to be associated with high levels of personal distress and low levels of sympathy whereas an emphasis on instrumentally dealing with situations that cause the child's negative emotions has been associated with sympathy in response to another's distress (*see* Eisenberg et al., 1992, for a review).

In summary, it appears that individual differences in empathy and related vicarious emotional responses are likely to be due to both biological and environmental factors.

Recently it has been argued that sympathetic individuals tend to be relatively emotionally reactive but are able to regulate their vicariously induced emotion; in contrast, individuals prone to personal distress may be both emotionally reactive and relatively unable to regulate their emotional responses (Eisenberg & Fabes, 1990). Both emotionality and regulation appear to have temperamental bases; however, both, especially the latter, can be modified by interaction with the environment. Thus, attention to both the contributions of temperament to vicarious emotional responding and socializers' role in shaping individuals' regulatory processes may improve our understanding of the origins of empathy. *See also*: AGGRESSION; GENETIC INFLUENCES.

BIBLIOGRAPHY

Batson, C. D. (1991). *The altruism question: Toward a social-psychological answer*. Hillsdale, NJ: Lawrence Erlbaum.

Cialdini, R. B., & Fultz, J. (1990). Interpreting the negative mood/helping literature via mega-analysis: A contrary view. *Psychological Bulletin, 107*, 210–14.

Eisenberg, N., & Fabes, R. A. (1990). Empathy: Conceptualization, assessment, and relation to prosocial behavior. *Motivation and Emotion, 14*, 131–49.

—— Carlo, G., & Karbon, M. (1992). Emotional responsivity to others: Behavioral correlates and socialization antecedents. *New Directions in Child Development, 55*, 57–73.

—— Schaller, M., & Miller, P. A. (1989). Sympathy and personal distress: Development, gender differences, and interrelations of indexes. *New Directions in Child Development, 44*, 107–26.

—— & Miller, P. A. (1987). The relation of empathy to prosocial and related behavior. *Psychological Bulletin, 101*, 91–119.

Janssens, J. M. A. M., & Gerris, J. R. M. (1992). Child rearing, empathy and prosocial behavior. In J. M. A. M. Janssens & J. R. M. Gerris (Eds.), *Child rearing: Influence of prosocial and moral development* (pp. 57–75). Amsterdam: Swets & Zeitlinger.

Miller, P., & Eisenberg, N. (1988). The relation of empathy to aggression and externalizing/antisocial behavior. *Psychological Bulletin, 103*, 324–44.

Radke-Yarrow, M., & Zahn-Waxler, C. (1984). Roots, motives, and patterns in children's prosocial behavior. In E. Staub, D. Bar-Tal, J. Karylowski, & J. Reykowski (Eds.), *Development and maintenance of prosocial behavior: International perspectives on positive behavior* (pp. 81–99). New York: Plenum.

Rushton, J. P., Fulker, D. W., Neal, M. C., Nias, D. K. B., & Eysenck, H. J. (1986). Altruism and aggression: The heritability of individual differences. *Journal of Personality and Social Psychology, 50*, 1192–8.

NANCY EISENBERG

**encoding**  This transforms a perceived external stimulus into an internal representation. Encoding may be viewed as having four steps: preattentive analysis (combining features into recognizable objects), focal ATTENTION (conscious representation of the stimulus), comprehension (giving meaning to the stimulus), and elaborative reasoning (making inferences by linking the stimulus with other knowledge).

*See also*: ATTENTION.

SUSAN T. FISKE
BETH A. MORLING

**environmental psychology**  This is concerned with the mutual relationship between people and the physical environment; that is, environmental psychologists study how people use, influence, and are influenced by both the built (such as homes, offices, airports, and cities) and natural environments (such as wilderness areas, seashores, parks, and gardens). Environmental psychology emerged as a field in the 1960s, stimulated in part by environmental problems of the period and in part by changing values in the field of psychology which supported studying phenomena in their physical/social context.

PHILOSOPHICAL ORIENTATION
Over the years, environmental psychology has developed in the following ways.

(1) *A holistic molar perspective* in which researchers study complex networks of psychological processes and environmental factors.

(2) *An applied, problem-solving perspective* based in the action research tradition so that research is simultaneously designed to uncover basic principles of behavior and to contribute to the solution of social problems involving the physical environment.

(3) *A broad and eclectic methodology* that encourages the use of laboratory experiments, field experiments, surveys, qualitative analyses, and naturalistic observations, because the problems of the field are diverse and not amenable to study by a single procedure.

(4) *A range of levels of analysis*: from micro-levels of study (such as the impact of noise on task performance), to moderate scale analyses (such as home design and use), to large-scale units of study (such as community and city design), and to cross-cultural analyses.

(5) *A range of approaches to concepts and theory*: environmental psychologists draw freely from emerging theoretical developments in psychology and related disciplines such as the application of SCHEMA theory to environmental cognition and MEMORY, use of stress models in the analysis of noise and crowding, use of community psychology and social change principles in studying environmental conservation, and so on. Environmental theorizing and research is also enriched by collaboration with members of other disciplines, such as anthropology, geography, sociology, family studies, architecture, design, and planning (*see*, for example, Altman et al., 1976–1994; Baum et al., 1978–1986; Stokols & Altman, 1987; Zube & Moore, 1987–1994); and finally (6) environmental psychologists have developed *unique theoretical perspectives*. For many years, ecological psychology and "behavior setting theory" have been based on the assumption that behavior and psychological processes are grounded in the physical and social milieu; emerging contextual and transac-

tional orientations share this view. So, in contrast to more linear, cause–effect models, these approaches assume mutual dependency and multiple forms of influence between people and their physical environments. Furthermore, these perspectives hold that time and change are integral to psychological phenomena so that phenomena are expected to change and events are studied as they unfold naturally over time. Thus, in contrast to the traditional views that psychological phenomena are context free, can be subdivided into component parts, and should generalize across time, setting, and circumstances, these approaches assume that phenomena are integral wholes that are largely time- and place-specific.

## RESEARCH: PROCESSES, PLACES, AND PEOPLE

Research in environmental psychology encompasses a broad spectrum of psychological processes, a few of which are reviewed below. In some lines of research, a single process is studied in multiple settings, whereas in others a single setting is the focus of analysis, and researchers study how multiple processes unfold, are supported, or go awry in that setting. Analyses of processes and places are often accompanied by a focus on particular groups such as those defined by age, culture, or special environmental needs. In accord with a holistic approach, researchers often study processes, places, and people as totalities, such as wayfinding among hospital patients, social relationships among school children, territorial defense in inner-city neighborhoods, and so on. The present overview illustrates both research on core psychological processes across places and research on places across multiple processes.

### Processes

*Perception and aesthetic preference.* Large-scale environments contain a myriad of information that the perceiver must notice, organize, interpret, and evaluate. Perceptual judgments allow people to decide whether areas are safe and comfortable, and whether they provide needed amenities. In addi-

tion, perception is often linked to aesthetic preference for and affective responses to environments. Some researchers encourage respondents to consider the total array of stimuli when evaluating an environment – auditory, visual, olfactory, and ambient factors such as wind and rain – although most research on environmental preference focuses exclusively on visual information. There appears to be a general preference for environments whose visual elements are balanced and whose organization can be grasped by the viewer, but which also contain some degree of mystery, novelty, and complexity. Consistent with the premise that perception involves interpretation, these elements are not the sole determinants of preference; there is considerable variability in the kinds of environments that people choose to visit or inhabit.

*Cognitive maps and wayfinding.* An important skill is learning where things are and how to get from one location to another. Research on cities and buildings suggests that people are most likely to develop accurate "cognitive maps" in settings that have: simple path structures (well-traveled central paths with perpendicular intersections rather than Y, O, or X layouts); clear nodes, or places where paths intersect, which help to organize the path structure; landmarks that allow individuals to locate themselves (such as tall structures, or distinctive multimodal elements that allow one to "fix" a spot in memory); districts and subdistricts that have a uniform physical or social character; and edges that give boundaries and define the shape of an area (Lynch, 1960). In buildings or cities that lack these characteristics, people often get confused and lost, and tend to be dissatisfied with the environment. At the same time, a highly regular environment may be boring, especially to frequent users or people seeking adventure or opportunities for exploration.

*Meanings of and attachment to places.* Analyses of place ATTACHMENT include studies of environmental meaning, the feelings and memories people have about places, and their preferences for various settings. This work indicates that places with cultural meanings (such as historic monuments, religious settings, and archeological sites) provide concrete representations of group history and particular settings in which to memorialize the group, thereby becoming integral to group identity. Research on places with primarily individual or family meaning (such as homes, favorite vacation spots) suggest that places become integral parts of and contribute to individual and family identity (*see* TERRITORIALITY).

*Social relationships.* Another aspect of environmental psychology concerns social processes such as the regulation of privacy, PERSONAL SPACE and territoriality (Altman, 1975). Interpersonal distance, physical orientation, and symbolic and physical barriers can all contribute to perceived and actual CONTROL over who has access to the group or individual. For example, in office buildings where numerous people must coordinate their use of space, regulate access to each other, and get along socially in order to work productively, research examines how environmental factors such as open-space designs, forms of personalization of offices, and the organization of space and equipment relate to such consequences as worker productivity, satisfaction with the environment, and employee cohesiveness.

*Environmental problems: hazards, stressors, and disasters.* Environmental problems and stresses, such as crowding, noise, pollution, extreme temperatures, and commuting have been studied extensively. High density is not always negative, but when it is – especially in interpersonal, face-to-face situations – the consequences can be quite severe (*see* CROWDING). Laboratory studies of noise (unwanted sounds) indicate that unpredictable and uncontrollable noise is stressful and has negative impacts on physiology, task performance, tolerance for frustration, and social behavior. Naturalistic studies of the psychological, interpersonal, and physiological consequences of living close to noisy freeways, subways, trains, and airports reveal similar findings (e.g., decrements in intellectual development and scholastic performance among children). Studies of automobile commuting indicate that time, distance, and route interference are related to elevated blood pressure, negative mood changes, and relationship problems (*see* STRESS AND COPING).

Environmental psychologists have had a long-term interest in natural and technological disasters. Studies of differing perceptions of the dangers of living close to hazards such as flood plains, tornado- or hurricane-prone areas, and earthquake faults suggest that the closer one lives to a potential hazard, the less concerned one is about a real disaster occurring. Research on risk assessments (such as the risks of nuclear power plants) show that experts and lay public often differ in values and interpretations of potential hazards rather than differing in their understanding of factual risk evidence.

Another line of work examines how people behave during the disaster itself, such as during earthquakes and building fires, and shows that clear signs and even auditory cues increase safety behaviors and reduce casualties. A great deal of research has examined immediate and long-term psychological and social consequences of large-scale disasters, such as the disruption of home, family, and community, and coping with personal GRIEF and loss. Researchers suggest that it is important to keep neighborhoods and SOCIAL SUPPORT systems intact after disasters in order to enhance psychological recovery. Recent large-scale technological disasters such as accidents at nuclear power plants or nuclear waste facilities, discoveries of toxic waste sites near homes and schools, and so on, indicate that these are particularly stressful when the effects are long term and uncontrollable, when friends and relatives outside the area withdraw their socioemotional support, and when victim-residents feel as though their concerns are being ignored. Research also examines how residents organize themselves to effect change in government plans and policies, and how they work together as a community to provide socioemotional support for one another.

*Conservation attitudes and behavior change.* Considerable attention has been paid to resource utilization and reuse, such as through recycling, home or automobile energy conservation, and water conservation. Early work showed that while rewards and incentives were effective at inducing behavior change, these programs were not cost effective and did not produce long-term, self-sustaining changes in behavior. Social normative approaches – public praise or recognition, social MODELING, intergroup competition, and group pressure – often lead to internalized changes in attitudes and behavior. Other effective approaches begin with the literature on ATTITUDE FORMATION and ATTITUDE CHANGE, such as the relationship between psychological commitment and behavior, attitude-behavior consistency, and PERSUASION. Simply asking individuals for commitment can lead to long-term behavioral change. Other analyses of resource utilization have treated it as an example of a common dilemma in which individual and social goals are in conflict; overuse may be mitigated by emphasizing the value of sustainable use (*see* SOCIAL DILEMMAS).

*People and Places*
*Children's environments.* Children's environments – daycare centers, preschools, play areas, schools, and classrooms – have received extensive study as researchers attempt to understand how the physical environment supports or interferes with different aspects of intellectual, social, and physiological growth and development (Weinstein & David, 1987). For example, some researchers study children's play in home and near-home areas, noting increases in autonomy and freedom to explore as children mature. Others study classroom environments, observing such behaviors as learning, task performance, comportment, disruptions, and social relations, especially with respect to whether the physical building is designed as an open, modified open, or closed classroom environment. Researchers note that the physical environment and educational philosophy are often linked, so any differences cannot be attributed exclusively to the physical structure. Modified open plans are currently more popular than totally open because of the noise and distraction in open environments; but many features of open classrooms are valued because they provide flexibility and multiple options for group and individual activities. Other research examines learning, comportment, and social relations with respect to the density of the classroom, the sheer number of children present, and the amounts of certain kinds of space (e.g., play space, hideaway space), and seeks to define optimum sizes as a function of educational goals and children's age.

*Work environments.* Offices and factories have also received a great deal of research interest, either in actual WORK settings or in laboratory simulations. A central focus of this work is, of course, on the relationship between environmental factors and the quality and quantity of performance. Researchers study office layout, work flow and work-team proximity, lighting, ambient conditions, and so on, as they relate to accomplishment. Other research examines socioemotional aspects such as job satisfaction, worker morale, safety practices, and group cohesion as these relate to such physical environmental factors as ambient temperature, noise, music, artificial and natural lighting, color schemes, and office features such as location, size, windows and degree of closure. Much of the focus has been on private offices compared to open offices or modified open plans (e.g., small work groups sharing a single large office; offices with short walls or barriers that provide some privacy). For many types of jobs, modified open plans provide less expensive work space without reducing productivity or job satisfaction. Private offices are often preferred because they provide more status but also may provide needed protection from distractions and interruptions.

*Hospitals and care centers.* Research on settings for individuals with physical impairments has examined staff behaviors, efficiency, and job satisfaction as a function of such environmental features as the layout of patient wards, location and design of the nursing station, and whether the staff participated in the design process. A common finding is that when wards are laid out in a wheel style (multiple short halls around a central nursing area), patients are more accessible and nurses are able to get to them more quickly and visit them more frequently, compared to traditional long hallway arrangements. With respect to hospital patients, of primary concern has been the relationship between the physical environment (windows, pleasant views, furniture arrangements, number of beds per ward) and patient health. A typical finding is that – all other factors being equal – recovery is facilitated in the more attractive environments. A great deal of research has focused on wayfinding in hospital and care centers. These are often large and confusing buildings with few environmental cues to differentiate one subarea from another. Patients (and their visitors) often complain of being lost or of restricting their activities for fear of getting lost. Improved designs include clearly written and well-placed signs; colored stripes on walls or floors that guide visitors to particular subareas; and separate entrances for different units (Carpman, Grant, & Simmons, 1986).

Care centers for the elderly are faced with difficult challenges because of the variety of problems experienced by their residents, coupled with an overriding goal to maintain and enhance residents" competence (*see* AGING). Some residents have auditory, visual, and mobility impairments, and others are quite competent physically but have psychological or cognitive dysfunctions that require special constraining environments. A common finding is that physical features that enhance residents' perception of control contribute to their autonomy, satisfaction, and continued effective functioning; these can often allow them to remain in their own homes instead of moving to a care center. Sturdy, well-placed bars in bathrooms and along hallways, and lowered countertops and shelves enable individuals to remain independent. Well-placed day rooms can serve as behavioral focal points and allow people to gather for casual interaction or independent activities. Another body of research examines how the elderly manage the transition from their home to the care center, and shows that perceiving a choice in the move and bringing significant objects to the center contribute to short- and long-term viability.

*Urban settings.* An enduring interest of environmental psychologists and others is the life and vitality of large-scale urban environments. One interest has been in the design, location, and social opportunities of parks and public plazas and how these relate to when and how the setting is used, by how many people, in what age groups, and for what purposes (Whyte, 1980). A large body of work examines urban problems such as homelessness, deteriorating neighborhoods, and the anonymity of large-scale public housing in order to understand how to restore the viability of these areas, and to empower the residents to take territorial control of their homes and their neighborhood.

CONCLUSION

Research in environmental psychology has been designed to develop a body of scientific knowledge regarding various aspects of human functioning in relation to various aspects of the physical environment. In the coming decades environmental psychologists around the world will probably work on newly emerging social problems that relate to the environment, they will continue to cooperate with other fields to explore emerging methods and theories, and they will facilitate innovative approaches to the study of psychological phenomena.

*See also*: AGING; ATTITUDE CHANGE; ATTITUDE FORMATION; CONTROL; CROWDING; GRIEF; MEMORY; SCHEMAS; SOCIAL DILEMMAS; SOCIAL SUPPORT; STRESS AND COPING; TERRITORIALITY; WORK.

BIBLIOGRAPHY

Altman, I. (1975). *Environment and social behavior*. Monterey, CA: Brooks-Cole.

—— & individual editors (Eds.) (1976–1994). *Human behavior and the environment: Advances in theory and research* (Vols. 1–13). New York: Plenum.

Baum, A., & individual editors (Eds.) (1978–86). *Advances in environmental psychology* (Vols. 1–6). Hillsdale, NJ: Lawrence Erlbaum.

Carpman, J. R., Grant, M. A., & Simmons, D. A. (1986). *Design that cares: Planning health facilities for patients and visitors*. Chicago, IL: American Hospital Publishers.

Lynch, K. (1960). *The image of the city*. Cambridge, MA: MIT Press.

Stokols, D., & Altman, I. (Eds.) (1987). *Handbook of environmental psychology* (Vols. 1 & 2). New York: Wiley.

Weinstein, C. S., & David, T. G. (Eds.) (1987). *Spaces for children: The built environment and child development*. New York: Plenum.

Whyte, W. H. (1980). *The social life of small urban spaces*. Washington, DC: Conservation Foundation.

Zube, E. H., & Moore, G. T. (Eds.) (1987–1994). *Advances in environment, behavior and design* (Vols. 1–4). New York: Plenum.

CAROL M. WERNER
IRWIN ALTMAN

**episodes, perception and evaluation of** Social episodes may be defined as basic units of social interaction, with temporal and often physical boundaries, and with a culturally accepted scheme of appropriate behaviors about which members of a subculture share consensual cognitive representations (Forgas, 1979). Everyday life largely consists of such recurring, patterned activities, and most of our interactions occur within the confines of a limited number of social episodes. Research on social episodes first emerged in the late 1970s, drawing on a rich tradition of theorizing about situational regularities in interpersonal behavior in social, cognitive, personality and developmental psychology, as well as in sociology.

## CONCEPTUAL AND HISTORICAL BACKGROUND

Within psychology, interest in the study of situations has its roots in early behaviorist theories, which emphasized an external, objective, and atomistic conception of situations as determinants of behavior. Brunswik's arguments for a "representative design" in psychology highlighted the need for a reliable classification of realistic situations, a task never properly addressed by behaviorists. In contrast, cognitive-phenomenological and Gestalt theorists such as Lewin, Koffka, and Murray focused on the "molar" situation as interpreted by the actor. Within PERSONALITY research, Mischel's criticisms of traditional "trait" theories of personality in the late 1960s stimulated intense new interest in the study of social situations (Argyle, Furnham, & Graham, 1982). Within cognitive psychology, the information processing consequences of SCRIPTS, or event SCHEMAS about common

interaction routines, have also received growing attention over the past few decades.

There also exists a rich tradition within sociology concerned with the situational analysis of behavior, linked to the work of Max Weber, W. I. Thomas, F. Znaniecki, and A. Schutz. The SYMBOLIC INTERACTIONIST approach of G. H. Mead in particular was among the first to highlight the dual nature of social episodes, as both preexisting, culturally determined structures that regulate individual behavior, and at the same time, creative, constructive interactions that generate shared cognitive representations about an ordered social world. More recent microsociological models developed by Goffman, Garfinkel, and others drew heavily on the concept of "episodes" and the work of Mead, Thomas, and others.

## EPISODES IN SOCIAL PSYCHOLOGY

Within social psychology, the study of episodes probably originates with the work of Lewin and his students. Roger Barker implemented an ingenious ecological approach to the study of "behavior settings" as meaningful, molar units of behavior-in-situation. More recently, within a SOCIAL COGNITION framework, episodes came to be defined as shared cognitive representations about typical interaction routines within a specified cultural milieu (Forgas, 1982). With the advent of descriptive techniques such as MULTI-DIMENSIONAL SCALING (MDS) allowing the structural analysis of complex cognitive representations, the empirical study of social episodes took a major step forward. Numerous studies explored the structure of episode representations, and their links with a range of other psychological and cultural variables.

## RESEARCH ON SOCIAL EPISODES

Most recent research on episode perception employs a two-stage procedure. Stage 1 is usually designed to elicit a representative sample of typical interaction episodes within a defined cultural milieu. Stage 2 seeks to construct a structural model or "map" of people's implicit cognitive representations about episode domains, allowing an exploration of the empirical links between episode representations and other individual and social variables.

*Elicitation*
Several techniques have been used to elicit interaction episodes. The *diary method* asks subjects to record recurring interactions for a set period. The *recollection method* asks subjects to list their interactions retrospectively, while participant or nonparticipant *observation* of a group's activities may also be used to record typical interactions. One remarkable finding is the surprisingly small number of typical interactions generally reported. Usually, no more than 15–25 prototypical episodes appear sufficient to adequately capture most people's recurring interactions.

The level of abstraction of reported interactions is also of interest. There appears to be a "basic" level of CATEGORIZATION of social episodes that optimizes inclusiveness and concreteness, referring to events that are common, yet specify a great deal of scripted behavioral and situational details. Such episodes correspond to "basic level categories" as defined by Rosch, carrying the most information, possessing the highest cue validity, yet most easily discriminated from each other.

*Structural analysis*
Episodes may thus be regarded as the building blocks of social life, part of the consensual, social domain. On the other hand, episodes are also idiosyncratic, as every person has unique, private cognitive representations about the interaction routines practised within their milieu. Empirical studies of perceived episode structures seek to capture this duality, constructing consensual episode spaces, while simultaneously evaluating individual differences in cognitive representations of episode domains. For a detailed description of the applicable research strategies, and the use of MDS methods in particular, *see* Forgas (1979, 1982).

Structural analyses of episode domains using MDS techniques found subtle cultural, subcultural, and individual differences in representations that could be readily quantified and related to a broad range of predictor variables (Argyle et al., 1982; Forgas, 1982). Analyses of episode representations have so far been carried out in student milieus, among housewives, sports teams, and academics, and in a variety of countries such as the USA, Britain, Australia, and Hong Kong. Results consistently show that:

(1) AFFECT, and connotative features play a determining role in cognitive representations of social episodes;
(2) there is a high degree of consensuality in episode representations across individuals; and
(3) individual differences in terms of personality characteristics, attitudes, social skills, social status, and cultural background are significantly related to a person's idiosyncratic way of perceiving social encounters.

*Applications*
Research on social episodes has also been applied in a number of fields. Research has focused on questions such as:

(1) the kind of features people use to construe AGGRESSION and even criminal incidents (Forgas, 1982);
(2) the role of distorted episode representations in social skill deficits; and
(3) the links between personality characteristics and episode representations (Forgas & VanHeck, 1991).

Current research tends to focus on:

(1) the role of affect in the perception of social episodes (Forgas, 1992);
(2) the influence of episode schemata on social judgments and decisions; and
(3) the links between personality characteristics and habitual episode perception style (Forgas & VanHeck, 1991).

*See also*: AGGRESSION; CATEGORIZATION; PERSONALITY; SCHEMAS; SCRIPTS; SOCIAL COGNITION; SYMBOLIC INTERACTIONISM.

BIBLIOGRAPHY
Argyle, M., Furnham, A., & Graham, J. (1982). *Social situations*. Cambridge: Cambridge University Press.

Forgas, J. P. (1979). *Social episodes: The study of interaction routines*. London: Academic Press.

—— (1982). Episode cognition: Internal representations of interaction routines. In L. Berkowitz (Ed.), *Advances in experimental social psychology* (Vol. 15, pp. 59–104). New York: Academic Press.

—— (1992). Affect in social judgments: A multi-process model. In M. Zanna (Ed.), *Advances in experimental social psychology* (Vol. 25, pp. 227–75). New York: Academic Press.

—— & VanHeck, G. (1991). The psychology of situations. In G. Caprara & G. VanHeck (Eds.), *Modern personality psychology*. Hemel Hempstead: Harvester.

JOSEPH P. FORGAS

**equity theory**  A theory of social justice developed by Adams (1965), to outline the conditions that make individuals perceive a situation as inequitable, and to specify the various ways in which individuals will respond to such a situation *see* Greenberg & Cohen, 1982. Following SOCIAL COMPARISON and RELATIVE DEPRIVATION theorists, Adams stated that individuals compare their inputs and outcomes with a reference person. Two types of reference persons were proposed:

(1) someone with whom one has an exchange relationship to which both participants make certain contributions, and from which both obtain certain outcomes; and
(2) someone who has, as oneself has, an exchange relationship with a third party and obtains certain outcomes from this party (e.g., employer).

In line with earlier work on DISTRIBUTIVE JUSTICE, the central assumption in equity theory is that individuals will perceive a situation as fair when their own ratio of outcomes to inputs is the same as that of the comparison other. "Inputs" are the contributions *perceived* by an individual as relevant to an exchange, and can consist of factors such as seniority, education, skills, and effort. "Outcomes" are described as the *perceived* receipts from the exchange, including status, intrinsic rewards, and pay. Although there has been an extensive statistical discussion of the appropriate way to calculate equity, in recent years researchers have been less concerned with the mathematical aspects of the theory than with its theoretical implications and heuristic value.

Equity theory is a strongly motivational theory and, due to its theoretical link to COGNITIVE DISSONANCE THEORY, also a drive reduction theory. Adams suggested that inequity is a type of cognitive dissonance, a hedonically aversive state, that individuals aim to reduce. According to Adams, advantageous as well as disadvantageous inequity is felt as unpleasant, and both types of inequity will generate a desire for equity restoration. This can be done in various ways, by

(1) altering one's inputs;
(2) altering one's outcomes;
(3) cognitively distorting one's inputs and outcomes;
(4) leaving the field;
(5) acting on the other (i.e., alter or cognitively distort outcomes and inputs of the other); and
(6) changing the comparison other.

A substantial amount of research has supported the hypothesis that both undercompensation and overcompensation are aversive, and that both foster behaviors aimed at restoring equity. Research has focused especially upon the nonobvious effects of *over*compensation. In the original experiments on the effects of overpayment by Adams and his co-workers, subjects were hired to do interviews, and overcompensation was induced by suggesting to subjects that they were underqualified for the pay they would receive (e.g., "You don't have any experience"). These experiments were criticized, particularly because the manipulation might primarily have threatened the subjects' self-esteem rather than inducing inequity. Nevertheless, later research avoiding this problem has also provided support for the effects of overpayment. As predicted, underpaid hourly workers reduce their inputs by becoming less productive, while underpaid piece-rate workers increase their outcomes without raising their inputs by producing more, lower-quality products. By contrast, overpaid workers on an hourly basis tend to raise their performance level, and overpaid piece-rate workers tend to become less productive, but to produce higher-quality work.

Although a considerable amount of research now supports these predictions, there are a number of qualifications to these statements. First, in some studies, overcompensated subjects have been found to reduce their inequity by quitting, by changing their perceptions of what is fair, or by emphasizing the difficulty of the task (thus cognitively enhancing the inputs). Second, equitable behavior may at least be engaged in for reasons of SELF-PRESENTATION rather than for intrinsic motives. Third, applying equity theory to "real life" employment situations is not without its problems. For example, there is evidence that overpayment has only temporarily motivating effects.

While equity theory started as a theory focusing upon business relationships, over the years the theory has been expanded to various other types of RELATIONSHIPS. Indeed, although Adams focused primarily upon employee–employer relationships, he noted that the theory should have a wider generalizability. A first expansion came from Walster, Walster, and Berscheid (1978) who integrated *post hoc* a number of studies on harmdoer–victim relationships, including the work on the JUST WORLD PHENOMENON, within an equity theoretical perspective. They argued that harmdoing, for example giving electric shocks to another individual, results in distress due to fear of retaliation and threat to self-esteem. Harmdoers can reduce this distress by compensation, by self-deprivation, or by justification, i.e., by derogating the victim, by minimizing his or her suffering, or by denying the act. Various studies have outlined some of the conditions under which these different techniques will occur. For instance, derogation of the victim has been found to be more likely when the exploiter does not anticipate future interaction with the victim, and when the exploiter knows that the victim will not be able to retaliate. A second expansion of the theory was to the domain of helping relationships. In general, it has been argued that in this type of relationships con-

siderations of equity will also prevail, and there is evidence supporting this assumption. For example, benefactors are liked more when the benefits they provide can be reciprocated than when they cannot, people prefer gifts that can be reciprocated over those that cannot, and if one cannot repay the donor, one will be more likely to benefit a third party (Hatfield & Sprecher, 1983).

The third, and in recent years most important expansion of equity theory has been to the realm of intimate relationships. In general, research in this area has focused upon the relationship between inequity and satisfaction, showing that with different operationalizations of equity, those experiencing equity are indeed the most satisfied, followed by the overbenefited, with the underbenefited expressing the lowest satisfaction (Walster et al., 1978). There is also some evidence that individuals perceiving equity in their relationship are less likely to engage in extramarital affairs, and are more confident of staying together. Nevertheless, other factors such as the level of rewards may be more important for satisfaction, and some individuals may be more concerned with equity than others. Moreover, contrary to what equity theory would predict, relationships do not become more equitable over time, and there is little evidence for the power of equity theory in predicting the quality and stability of close relationships over time *see* VanYperen & Buunk, 1990. Finally, there is evidence that it is not especially equity, but rather *equality* that is the central issue in close relationships.

Equity theory has been criticized on a number of points. First, the meaning of the concept of "equity" is somewhat ambiguous. Adams (1965) equated equity more or less with "justice," but preferred the term "equity" to avoid the confusion of the many connotative meanings associated with the term justice. However, some authors consider equity to be one specific type of justice *rule*, in addition to other rules such as the equality rule (all participants should get the same rewards), and the needs rule (participants ought to receive rewards in congruence with their needs). Second, while for Adams (1965) the preference for a proportional distribution was primarily *reactive* behavior, a sort of dissonance-reducing response to perceived inequity, other authors have emphasized that behaving equitably constitutes *proactive* behavior. According to these authors, equity is a valued goal in itself, and individuals derive intrinsic satisfaction from an equitable division of inputs and outcomes. Third, the theory has been criticized for being not specific enough in outlining what constitute inputs and outcomes, what factors govern the choice of comparison others, and what conditions determine the use of the various equity restoration techniques.

*See also*: COGNITIVE DISSONANCE THEORY; RELATIONSHIPS; RELATIVE DEPRIVATION; SOCIAL COMPARISON.

BIBLIOGRAPHY
Adams, J. S. (1965). Inequity in social exchange. In L. Berkowitz (Ed.). *Advances in experimental social psychology* (Vol. 2, pp. 267–99). New York: Academic Press.
Greenberg, J., & Cohen, R. L. (Eds.) (1982). *Equity and justice in social behavior*. New York: Academic Press.
Hatfield, E., & Sprecher, S. (1983). Equity theory and recipient reactions to aid. In J. D. Fisher, A. Nadler, & B. M. DePaulo (Eds.), *New directions in helping behavior* (Vol. 1): *Recipients" reactions to aid* (pp. 113–43). New York: Academic Press.
VanYperen, N. W., & Buunk, B. P. (1990). A longitudinal study of equity and satisfaction in intimate relationships. *European Journal of Social Psychology*, 20, 287–309.
Walster, E., Walster, G. W., & Berscheid, E. (1978). *Equity: Theory and research*. Boston, MA: Allyn and Bacon.

BRAM P. BUUNK

**ethogenics**  An approach to the study of social interaction which emphasizes DISCOURSE and SOCIAL CONSTRUCTIONISM and which treats the meanings of actions, as perceived by interacting persons, as crucial for the scientific understanding of those actions. The objects of analysis – the phenomena to be explained – typically are episodes of action occurring within specifiable, culturally meaningful contexts, and have ranged from the use of nicknames and forms of address to the occurrence of aggressive behavior in classrooms and at soccer games. The explanations of such empirically investigated actions have focused largely on the meanings of the acts to the various participants, particularly those meanings which had a bearing on reputation or status, and on the act–action structure – that is, the relationship between actions and the larger act which successful performance of the component actions will accomplish. The meanings are extracted from the ACCOUNTS that various participants offer of their actions, although the accounts are not presumed to be accurate depictions of the reasons or causes of the actions at the time the actions were performed. Instead, the accounts are used to reveal the reputational concerns and belief systems (*see* BELIEFS) of the participants, which imply the social relationships among them, and the knowledge and skill resources they have available for action.

This approach has superficial similarity to the study of IMPRESSION MANAGEMENT and SELF-PRESENTATION in experimental social psychology, but actually differs both in method and in metatheory. Ethogenics views the controlled experiment in social psychological research as having serious flaws, primarily in:

(1) constraining the participants from using the resources typically at the disposal of persons, such as negotiating the identity and meaning of the actions under way;
(2) unrealistically treating the participants as passive "subjects" whose behaviors occur as responses to causal pushes or pulls, rather than as active agents; and
(3) ignoring the special nature of the experiment as a situated social episode.

From this perspective, the controlled experiment in social psychology usually has questionable ECOLOGICAL VALIDITY and may also face problems of internal validity (*see also* EXPERIMENTATION, EXPERIMENTER EFFECTS, and METHODOLOGY).

Much of the published material in ethogenics has been theoretical and metatheoretical, and its primary contribution to the discipline has been to spur the growth of alternatives to the positivist emphasis that its proponents claim still characterizes experimental social psychology (*see also* CRITICAL SOCIAL PSYCHO-LOGY). Both the theory and the metatheory have been articulated in a series of books over the last 20 years, beginning with *The Explanation of Social Behaviour* (Harré & Secord, 1972) and followed by treatments of the social construction of social identity, of personal identity, and of the body and bodily experiences (Harré, 1979, 1984, 1991, comprising a series of "Ways of Being"). The philosophy of science within which ethogenics is grounded is presented by Harré (1986) as a modest realism; it emphasizes the practices of scientists through which they search the real world for objects or relations that are denoted by substantive terms in the theoretical discourse of their disciplines. A science, then, is specified by the practices of its practitioners and not by a certain form of logical relations among its terms. There are three types of scientific theories, according to this view: one which refers to observables; a second which refers to physical systems, and their behaviors, which are currently unobserved but are representable in pictures or diagrams; and a third which refers to systems which in principle cannot be pictured and can never be observed directly but which are represented mathematically (e.g., special theory of relativity). Evaluation of theory statements rests not upon the application of truth conditions but upon assessment of the plausibility of the theory statements, as specified both by their empirical adequacy and their compatibility with the framework of current, communally accepted ontology. Theories provide explanations of the behavior of a system in terms of causal powers and causal mechanisms, but require the clear identification (or "critical description," as in Harré & Secord, 1972) of the nature of the system and behavior of interest. The discovery of causal powers, causal mechanisms, and conditions which enable the exercise of powers, are major objectives of any science. The modest realism of ethogenics, then, differs considerably from the more positivistic philosophy of science of experimental social psychology, particularly with the emphasis of the latter on Humean notions of causality. But it also is noteworthy that ethogenics shares a commitment to causal explanations and causal modelling.

A major role is given in ethogenics to discourse on the argument that reality is both created and reflected by discourse. Human discourse is seen as "the fundamental reality" (Harré, 1991, p. 67). Discourse is part of the material world, meanings are features of situated talk, and talk entails status distinctions (e.g., use of pronouns, forms of address), implications of cause and responsibility (e.g., in different verb forms and nouns), and accomplishments (e.g., speech acts such as promises and requests which obligate oneself or another). Physical reality is instantiated similarly, since a hammer or a disease is each pointed to by the referential function of discourse and is each given functional utility by the pragmatic meanings of its label within the culture.

Ethogenics emerged during the "crisis" in social psychology during the 1970s, and carried an emphasis which reflected both the concerns of that time and the philosophical roots of its major proponents. The direct impact of ethogenics on mainstream social psychology is difficult to trace, since it shared with other dissident schools of that time a dissatisfaction with the controlled and often deceptive experiment and a promotion of social constructionism. But ethogenics has probably had an important indirect influence on the discipline through the progressive maturation of its metatheory and through its very active promulgation.

*See also*: ACCOUNTS; CRITICAL SOCIAL PSYCHOLOGY; EXPERIMENTATION; EXPERIMENTER EFFECTS; IMPRESSION MANAGEMENT; METHODOLOGY; SOCIAL CONSTRUCTIONISM.

BIBLIOGRAPHY
Harré, R. (1979). *Social being*. Oxford: Basil Blackwell.
——(1984). *Personal being*. Cambridge, MA: Harvard University Press.
——(1986). *Varieties of realism*. Oxford: Basil Blackwell.
——(1991). *Physical being*. Oxford: Blackwell Publishers.
——& Secord, P. F. (1972). *The explanation of social behaviour*. Oxford: Basil Blackwell.

G. P. GINSBURG

**ethology** The study of animal behavior from a naturalistic and evolutionary perspective. Although it had a number of important forerunners in the nineteenth and early twentieth centuries, Niko Tinbergen and Konrad Lorenz were the two researchers who established it as an important sub-branch of zoology in the 1930s and after World War II. Lorenz studied animals by surrounding himself with them. His early contributions included setting out the characteristics of imprinting, and using cross-species comparisons to trace the evolutionary history of courtship displays in birds. He also theorized about the causation of stereotyped behavior. Tinbergen combined being a field naturalist with experimentation, meticulous observations, pictorial records, and theoretical analyses. He studied a wide range of animals and topics, including the role of external stimuli in controlling behavior, the motivational bases of social displays, social organization, and the survival value and evolution of behavior.

Since its beginnings, ethology has progressed in varied and often conflicting directions in different countries, has formed extensive links with comparative psychology, and has influenced other areas of psychology and the social sciences (Archer, 1992; Hinde, 1982). The early emphasis on the innate control of behavior, and its rigid control by specific stimuli, was criticized by a number of researchers in the 1950s, and this led the way to a more flexible and theoretically sophisticated form of ethology. Tinbergen himself contributed to this reexamination. In contrast, many of the original features of Lorenz's ethology have been maintained by "classical ethologists" such as Eibl-Eibesfeldt (1989).

A further important development was the emergence of social ethology (Crook, 1970). In contrast to the original emphasis on behavior at the individual or dyadic level, social ethology was concerned with social organization and its relation to ecology. It was based partly on an older tradition of studying animal societies from a sociological viewpoint and partly on an ecological approach to behavior. It played an important role in the development of sociobiology in the 1970s.

Ethology has influenced social psychology in several ways. First, its emphasis on the use of OBSERVATIONAL METHODS was transferred to the study of NONVERBAL COMMUNICATION (Archer, 1992). Ethologists who observed human expressions and gestures produced detailed descriptive categories, paralleling those derived by psychologists such as Ekman (see FACIAL EXPRESSION OF EMOTION). Second, there have been a limited number of experimental assessments of ethological hypotheses about social behavior, for example concerning appeasement postures in children's AGGRESSION. Thirdly, there has been discussion about the nature of human nonverbal communication, and the extent to which it is related to the displays and gestures of animals. Some social psychologists, such as Birdwhistell, took the view that the human case is too complex to be understood in terms of animal displays, whereas Eibl-Eibesfeldt (see above) saw most gestures as pancultural and minimally influenced by culture (Hinde, 1982).

Ethological studies of animal displays have concentrated on their COMMUNICATION function, rather than being primarily concerned with the expression of emotions, as social psychologists such as Ekman have been. The ethological approach to displays has also concerned questions of evolutionary history and current motivational significance, which can usefully be applied to human facial expressions of emotion, such as smiling and laughing, although this has only been carried out to a limited extent at present (Archer, 1992).

In analyzing animal communication, an important distinction was made by W. J. Smith between the message, the motivational state of the signaller, and the meaning, how this is interpreted in the light of other information by the recipient. This analysis enabled researchers to go beyond the view that specific signals automatically "released" particular responses, which was inherent in classical ethological theory.

The information accompanying a message includes what has gone before in the interaction: this realization led to more complex analyses of longer behavioral sequences. More recent studies of animal communication have introduced theoretical analyses from game theory applied to the evolution of behavior (*see* SOCIOBIOLOGY): their main conclusion is that communication has evolved not to transfer accurate information about another individual but to manipulate the reactor to behave in the interests of the signaller.

In addition to these specific topics of mutual interest to ethologists and social psychologists, the general orientation of ethology is reflected in the work of some researchers seeking new ways of approaching SOCIAL PSYCHOLOGY. Ethology helped to inspire the alternative to EXPERIMENTATION advocated by Rom Harré and Paul Secord in the form of ETHOGENICS. When the ethologist Robert Hinde examined studies of human RELATIONSHIPS, he found no systematic descriptive base. Since this is the starting point in an ethological analysis, he set out to provide one in the form of descriptive categories on which relationships might differ (Hinde, 1979); he also highlighted the theoretical importance of relationships in terms of mediating between GROUP PROCESSES and INDIVIDUAL DIFFERENCES.

We can conclude that although the existing impact of ethology on social psychology has been slight, there is the potential for more extensive links in the future, particularly if the impact of experimentation as a method, and SOCIAL LEARNING as a theoretical approach, diminish.

*See also*: AGGRESSION; COMMUNICATION; ETHNOGENICS; EXPERIMENTATION; FACIAL EXPRESSION OF EMOTION; GROUP PROCESSES; NONVERBAL COMMUNICATION; OBSERVATIONAL METHODS; RELATIONSHIPS; SOCIAL LEARNING; SOCIAL PSYCHOLOGY; SOCIOBIOLOGY.

BIBLIOGRAPHY
Archer, J. (1992). *Ethology and human development*. Hemel Hempstead: Harvester; Savage, MD: Barnes & Noble.
Crook, J. H. (1970). Social organization and the environment: Aspects of contemporary social ethology. *Animal Behaviour, 18*, 197–209.
Eibl-Eibesfeldt, I. (1989). *Human ethology*. New York: Aldine de Gruyter.
Hinde, R. A. (1979). *Towards understanding relationships*. London & New York: Academic Press.
—— (1982). *Ethology: Its nature and relations with other sciences*. Oxford: Oxford University Press.

JOHN ARCHER

**even a penny helps**   A SOCIAL INFLUENCE strategy in which COMPLIANCE is achieved by making the request appear trivial. In Cialdini and Schroeder (1976), experimenters went door-to-door asking adults for donations to the American Cancer Society. Those who received the request followed by the words, "even a penny helps" had a higher rate of compliance than those receiving the generic request. This technique is thought to be effective because individuals have difficulty arguing against requests that are of negligible cost. They therefore quickly and easily comply to the request.
*See also*: SOCIAL INFLUENCE.

BIBLIOGRAPHY
Cialdini, R. B., & Schroeder, D. A. (1976). Increasing compliance by legitimizing paltry contributions: When even a penny helps. *Journal of Personality and Social Psychology, 34* 599–604.

MICHAEL MIGDAL
BRIAN MULLEN

**evolutionary psychology**   This has been defined as the study of human psychological processes from the viewpoint of the principle of natural selection that produced them. It is similar in aims to SOCIOBIOLOGY but more specifically focused on psychological dispositions.
*See also*: SOCIOBIOLOGY.

JOHN ARCHER

**excitation transfer**   When AROUSAL elicited by one stimulus is mistakenly attributed to another, it may summate with arousal evoked by the latter. This summation exacerbates the EMOTIONAL EXPERIENCE produced by the second stimulus.

*See also*: AROUSAL; EMOTIONAL EXPERIENCE.

RUSSELL G. GEEN

**expectancy effects** A general term for the influence of preconceived beliefs and expectations on thought, behavior, and interaction. When people form beliefs and expectations about themselves and other people, these preconceptions can and do guide subsequent cognitive, behavioral, and interpersonal activities in ways that confirm or disconfirm those beliefs and expectations.

MARK SNYDER

**experimental demand** Procedural cues inherent in experimental (laboratory) research may give rise to respondent behaviors unrelated to the experimental manipulation(s). Such behaviors are attributed to the *demand effects* of the research context. Orne (1962) called explicit attention to experimental demand, which he viewed as an important threat to internal validity (*see* EXPERIMENTATION). Demand effects are the result of participants' choices of the roles they assume in an experimental investigation. Will they explicitly follow the directions provided? Will they attempt to discern the hypotheses under study and, having done so, strive to confirm, or infirm, them? Cook and his colleagues (1970) suggest that participants' prior experience in experimentation, their past histories of deception and debriefing, and similar experiment-relevant behaviors affect attitudes toward research, levels of suspicion, and the likelihood that behaviors will be influenced by (demand) factors external to the independent variable.
*See also*: EXPERIMENTATION.

BIBLIOGRAPHY
Cook, T. D., Bean, J. R., Calder, B. J., Frey, R., Krovetz, M. L., & Reisman, S. R. (1970). Demand characteristics and three conceptions of the frequently deceived subject. *Journal of Personality and Social Psychology, 14*, 185–94.

Orne, M. (1962). On the social psychology of the psychological experiment: With particular reference to demand characteristics and their implications. *American Psychologist, 17*, 776–83.

WILLIAM D. CRANO

**experimental games** A laboratory method for studying decisions and outcomes in settings where two or more parties are interdependent. These settings are called "games," a technical term that has little in common with its everyday meaning. A game consists of a set of options that are available to the parties, a set of rules governing decisions among these options, and a reward structure. Reward structures are sets of numbers that indicate the value for all parties of every possible decision or combination of decisions, and thus precisely specify the nature of the INTERDEPENDENCE among the parties.

Experimental gaming was developed simultaneously by Deutsch (1958) and Siegel and Fouraker (1960), who borrowed the concept of game from the Theory of Games (Luce & Raiffa, 1957), a branch of mathematics that seeks to determine the most rational approach for each game and the logical outcome of employing this approach. Psychologists, by contrast, seek to understand how people actually behave in these games and how environmental and organismic variables affect this behavior.

Most experimental gaming has focused on mixed-motive games. These involve reward structures that evoke both competitive and cooperative motives, because the parties have differing preferences among some options but similar preferences among others. Social CONFLICT often entails such reward structures; hence, it is frequently studied by means of experimental games.

TYPES OF EXPERIMENTAL GAMES
Most of the research in this tradition has employed four types of games: matrix games, social dilemmas, bargaining games, and coalition games. The first two types are games of moves, in which the parties make separate

decisions. The second two types are games of agreement, in which some or all of the parties try to coordinate on a single option.

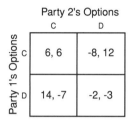

Figure 1. Example of the prisoner's dilemma.

A two-party matrix game is shown in figure 1. Party 1 must choose between the rows and party 2 between the columns. The outcomes (often called "payoffs") for each combination of choices are shown at the intersection of these choices, with party 1's outcome before the comma and party 2's outcome after the comma. In the laboratory versions of these games, the numbers may refer to money or points. The reward structure shown in this figure is the famous PRISONER'S DILEMMA (PD), whose outcomes must conform to the following rule for both parties (*see* figure 2): $Y > W > Z > X$. In the PD, C is called the "cooperative" option, because it benefits the other party, and D is called the "noncooperative" or "competitive" option. The PD is a mixed-motive game because the parties differ in their preferences between two of the options (party 1 prefers DC over CD and party 2 prefers CD over DC) but have similar preferences between the other two (both parties prefer CC over DD). Hence, they have incentives for both COOPERATION AND COMPETITION.

Party 2's Options

| | D | D |
|---|---|---|
| C | $w_1, w_2$ | $x_1, y_2$ |
| D | $y_1, x_2$ | $z_1, z_2$ |

Party 1's Options

Figure 2. Abstract form of the 2 × 2 matrix game.

The PD embodies a paradox: For an individual making a decision, noncooperation seems preferable to cooperation, because D provides higher rewards than C regardless of what the other party does ($Y > W$ and $Z > X$). Yet if this reasoning is followed on both sides, the result will be mutual noncooperation, which is worse for both parties than mutual cooperation ($Z < W$). In other words, individual rationality leads to collective irrationality.

Situations with a PD reward structure are very common in interpersonal relations, and many social NORMS (including ethical codes) appear to be rules that ensure mutual cooperation in PDs despite the temptation to be selfish. For example, consider the case of two workers doing the same kind of task, both of whom are periodically overloaded. Each has a choice between helping the other when overloaded (option C) or not helping the other (option D). Looking at each party's choices separately, it is better not to be helpful, because helping takes time and effort. Yet looking at their choices jointly, they are better off if both are helpful than if neither is helpful. As is often true of PDs, a norm of being helpful tends to develop in such settings, to counteract the lure of individual advantage.

Another matrix game that has received some attention is chicken. Its outcomes conform to a slightly different rule: $Y > W > X > Z$. Again C is the cooperative and D the noncooperative option; but in chicken, unlike the PD, a party can win by committing itself to noncooperation. For example, if party 1 signals a commitment to choose D, it is in party 2's interest to cooperate (choose C rather than D), because $X$ is larger than $Z$. Again there are many real-life analogies, for example, the interaction of two motorists at an intersection, who must decide whether to move ahead (C) or wait (D). If both move ahead, they will crash, with outcome $Z$. Victory often goes to the first party who signals a firm commitment to move, e.g., by driving steadily into the intersection while pretending not to see the other. The danger is that both parties will simultaneously adopt a commitment strategy or that one party will resent the other's commitment strategy enough to challenge it. Norms are also available in chicken to reduce the likelihood of mutual noncooperation, for example the norm that the car on the left (or the right) goes first.

The PD and chicken are two of the many games that can be produced by different orders of the outcomes in a $2 \times 2$ matrix. Matrix games involving more than two parties and more than two options per party are also possible.

SOCIAL DILEMMAS (also called "resource dilemmas") involve a common pool of resources, which either may be periodically removed by the parties (in the case of *harvesting dilemmas*) or must be periodically renewed (in the case of *public goods dilemmas*). Two-party versions are sometimes found, but social dilemmas usually involve larger groups. Social dilemmas have features in common with the (multiparty) PD (Messick & Brewer, 1983). As with the PD, each party is tempted to behave noncooperatively, to overharvest or fail to renew the common resource; but if all behave this way, the resource will be destroyed and all will be worse off than if they had cooperated.

An example of a harvesting dilemma is the famous tragedy of the commons, in which the farmers in a region have the option of grazing their animals on public land. The situation is a dilemma because each farmer is tempted to use the common land; but if all of them do so, the grass there will die and all of them will suffer. An example of a public goods dilemma involves paying dues to a club. Each club member is tempted to avoid payment; but if all members do so, the club will fail, hurting them all. Experimental gaming analogs of both types of dilemma are available.

In BARGAINING games, two or more parties communicate in an effort to reach agreement on one of a number of possible options. Bargaining is almost always a mixed-motive game. It involves both incentives for competition, in that the parties have differing preferences among many of the options, and incentives for cooperation, in that some options (e.g., reaching agreement) are favored by all parties over others (e.g., not reaching agreement). Like social dilemmas, bargaining has features in common with the PD (Rubin & Brown, 1975). Each party is tempted to hold firm to its demands, in an effort to incline the agreement in its favor; but if all parties do so, agreement will not be reached, hurting them all.

In coalition games (*see* COALITION FORMATION), three or more parties communicate in an effort to decide which of them shall be allied with which others. There are two main versions of these games (*see* Kahan & Rapoport, 1984): In the "resource" version, each party has a set of resources (e.g., a number of votes in a simulated parliament) which can be added to those of other parties in an effort to get a large enough total to win some contest. In the "characteristic function" version, each possible coalition has a specified value to its members, some coalitions being more valuable than others. In both versions, an important topic of communication is how the proceeds should be divided among coalition members. A common sequence of events is that a tentative coalition is formed with a provisional agreement about how to divide the proceeds, and then parties outside this coalition try to lure away some of its members with offers of better outcomes for joining with them.

RESEARCH FINDINGS

Because of their common reward structure, there are similar findings for cooperation in three of the games just described: the PD, the social dilemmas, and negotiation (Pruitt & Carnevale, 1993). By "cooperation" is meant the percentage of C choices over a series of trials in the PD, the amount of resource conservation or contribution over a period of time in a social dilemma, and the extent of concession making over a period of time in negotiation. Findings for at least two of these types of games show that cooperation is a direct function of the following variables: the size of incentives for cooperation (e.g., $W$ or $X$ in the PD), the size of disincentives for noncooperation (e.g., the cost of no agreement in negotiation), concern about the other party's (or parties') outcomes, TRUST in the other party(ies) or in people as a whole, future dependence on the other party(ies), and common group identity with the other party(ies).

In two-party settings, there is a tendency to reciprocate both the other party's cooperation and noncooperation. However, reciprocation of noncooperation is the stronger of these tendencies, because there is also a temptation to exploit a cooperative other. Cooperation is especially likely when the other party employs a tit-for-tat strategy or, in multiparty settings, when a large proportion of the other parties employ tit-for-tat. Tit-for-tat means replying cooperatively to cooperation and noncooperatively to noncooperation.

The more parties are involved in a game, the less cooperation is likely to ensue. This is mainly because group size diminishes trust that others will reciprocate one's cooperation (Yamagishi & Sato, 1986). In games of moves, communication often leads to markedly increased cooperation, because it contributes to an understanding of the situation, encourages trust, and allows the parties to coordinate their actions. (Communication turns games of moves into coordination games.) Enforcement procedures, involving penalties for noncooperation, are sometimes necessary to achieve high levels of cooperation, especially when there are many actors. People tend to favor such procedures when distrust is low.

Coalition games have a different structure from those just discussed, and different research problems have been addressed. Research suggests that there is a tendency toward the formation of minimal winning coalitions, involving the smallest number of members with the least resources needed to form a successful coalition (Komorita, 1984). If the purpose of the coalition is an ideological or political one, coalition members tend to be adjacent to each other on the ideological or political spectrum. Within a coalition, it is common for a larger share of the proceeds to go to members with the larger resources and to those who are more avidly sought for membership in other coalitions. Women, in comparison to men, tend to form larger coalitions that are less exclusionary and to divide the proceeds more equally among coalition members. This may reflect their greater concern about social solidarity.

## CONCLUSIONS

Mixed-motive settings are clearly among the most important in the human experience, and experimental gaming has the virtue of studying these settings. Another virtue of this methodology is that it looks at actual social behavior rather than marks made on questionnaires. However, experimental games have often been criticized for their artificiality and questionable generality (Pruitt & Kimmel, 1977). People do not usually receive their values in the form of numbers or make choices between rows or columns. Hence, their normal responses to mixed-motive settings may not fully transfer into these laboratory analogues. One indication of the validity of this criticism is that emotion tends to be muted in the laboratory, in contrast to real-life mixed-motive settings, where anger and fear are common. An additional criticism is that some experimental games are not very involving, allowing the subject wander. Despite these defects, many of the findings from this research make theoretical sense and have been accepted as contributions to knowledge.

*See also*: BARGAINING; CONFLICT; COOPERATION AND COMPETITION; INTERDEPENDENCE THEORY; NORMS; SOCIAL DILEMMAS; TRUST.

BIBLIOGRAPHY

Deutsch, M. (1958). Trust and suspicion. *Journal of Conflict Resolution*, 2, 265–79.

Kahan, J. P., & Rapoport, A. (1984). *Theories of coalition formation*. Hillsdale, NJ: Lawrence Erlbaum.

Komorita, S. S. (1984). Coalition bargaining. In L. Berkowitz (Ed.), *Advances in experimental social psychology* (Vol. 18, pp. 183–245). New York: Academic Press.

Luce, R. D., & Raiffa, H. (1957). *Games and decisions: Introduction and critical survey*. New York: Wiley.

Messick, D. M., & Brewer, M. B. (1983). Solving social dilemmas: A review. In L. Wheeler & P. Shaver (Eds.), *Review of personality and social psychology* (Vol. 4, pp. 11–44). Beverly Hills, CA: Sage.

Pruitt, D. G., & Carnevale, P. J. (1993). *Negotiation in social conflict*. Buckingham: Open University Press.

——& Kimmel, M. J. (1977). Twenty years of experimental gaming: Critique, synthesis and suggestions for the future. *Annual Review of Psychology*, 28, 363–92.

Rubin, J. Z., & Brown, B. R. (1975). *The social psychology of bargaining and negotiation*. New York: Academic Press.

Siegel, S., & Fouraker, L. E. (1960). *Bargaining and group decision making: Experiments in bilateral monopoly*. New York: McGraw-Hill.

Yamagishi, T., & Sato, K. (1986). Motivational bases of the public goods problem. *Journal of Personality and Social Psychology*, 50, 67–73.

DEAN G. PRUITT

**experimentation** An empirical research strategy used to examine the causal relationships among a set of selected variables. All experimentation involves application of rules that govern research operations. These rules of procedure, or METHODOLOGY, include precise control over the application of experimental treatments to participants, random assignment of participants to conditions (at a minimum, "conditions" involve treatment and comparison groups), and consistency of measures used to assess effects – all receive the same measure regardless of assignment. In its simplest form, experimentation entails controlled application of a treatment to one group of participants (be they planaria, pigeons, or people), while simultaneously withholding the treatment from a comparable group. Groups are rendered comparable through random assignment of participants to treatment and control conditions. Differences that arise between randomly assigned groups, exhibited on a common measure, are attributed to the one factor that differentiates them systematically, the presence, absence, or level of the treatment. The treatment is said to have *caused* the observed differences. Without randomization, the research is QUASI-EXPERIMENTAL, and causal interpretation of results is nearly impossible (*see also* CAUSALITY).

Temporal order is the foundation on which the inference of causation is built. If an event (say, Event A) consistently precedes another (Event B), Event A is said either to be a cause of B, or Events A and B are viewed as the common effects of some undetermined prior cause. This latter possibility is termed the "hidden third variable" explanation (Crano & Brewer, 1986), and it is this prospect that gives rise to the aphorism "correlation does not necessarily imply causation." In the hidden third variable case, Events A and B are correlated, but they are not involved causally. The application or appearance of the treatment variable(s) is controlled in experimentation, and thus, explanations appealing to a hidden third variable are rendered implausible. Precise control over the appearance or nonappearance of variables logically precludes explanations based on naturally co-occurring events.

Variables whose appearance or level of intensity are under experimental control are termed *independent*. They are independent of the natural forces that affect their presence, absence, and intensity. The instrument that measures the impact of the independent variable (or treatment) is the *dependent* variable. It is termed dependent because variation on such measures is regarded as dependent on variations on the independent variable(s).

Ideally, all experimentation begins with theory, a collection of abstract propositions that link a set of conceptual variables, and from which a series of concrete and testable expectations (hypotheses) may be deduced. The translation of conceptual variables to researchable (observable) variables occurs in two stages. In the first, an abstract, theory-based expectation is redefined in empirical terms; abstract variables are specified so that they are potentially observable or manipulable. The second stage of concept translation entails specification of the treatments, procedures, and instruments used to represent the critical independent and dependent variables. This is the *operationalization* stage. An operationalization must be detailed sufficiently that other scientists with comparable instruments and training can replicate it. Because direct observation of the causal factors thought to underlie a relationship is typically beyond measurement capabilities, theory-based conceptualizations may be poorly embodied by the variables generated to represent them. This lack of fit between abstract conception and observable variable is the cause of considerable difficulty. Consider the following example:

The research director of a major agency was ordered to prepare a study about fleas. He put a flea on his desk and trained it to jump over his finger at his command. Then he pulled off two of the flea's six legs. "Jump," he ordered, and the flea still jumped. Two more legs came off. Again the flea jumped. Finally, he pulled off the last two. "Jump," he commanded. The flea did not move. With that, the research director wrote his report: "When a flea loses all six legs, it becomes deaf" (*Time*, Nov. 25, 1957, p. 112).

Although our leaps of inference are seldom so far off the mark, the moral of this example is important – a test of theory is impaired to the extent that operationalized variables fail to represent adequately the theoretical conceptualizations on which they are based.

The proper role of *replication* in experimentation is highlighted by this example, for if the study were to be repeated exactly, the resulting findings would not address the central inferential problem. By changing one aspect of the study – e.g., if the flea were taught to bite on command – then the continued performance of this trick after the removal of all six legs would call the original (deafness) interpretation into question. Ideally, experimental replications vary as many theoretically irrelevant features as possible. If these variations do not affect the central findings, then confidence in theory-based explanation is bolstered. This approach implicitly recognizes that any observation is inevitably imperfect, colored by many factors – measurement error, instrumentation error, context-specific events – which may have nothing whatever to do with the phenomenon of interest. Research that replicates central findings under a broad set of widely varying (and theoretically irrelevant) conditions serves to demonstrate the independence of results from factors not germane to the theory, and to bolster the plausibility of the theory.

Theoretical conceptions are never perfectly embodied in any single observation. For this reason, considerable work in social psychology is guided by the concept of *multiple operationism*, a perspective that acknowledges that no single operation can "define" a concept completely and unambiguously. Accordingly, multiple related (or convergent) operations are employed to delineate, or triangulate upon, the theoretical concept of interest. The goal of multiple operationism is to design convergent operations that are as different as possible on theoretically irrelevant features, and thus susceptible to different sources of error. Such errors, being random, will tend to cancel. The resulting conglomerate or convergent operationalization provides a more valid, more trustworthy, realization of the theoretical conception than any measure taken in isolation.

Theory-testing in social psychology follows the general logic of multi-operationism. The intent of most research programs is to test an hypothesis or set of hypotheses under maximally heterogeneous conditions. Comparing the *pattern* of observed results with theory-based predictions lies at the heart of the theory-testing process. Successive failure to *dis*confirm the theory creates greater confidence in its validity, although validity is never unambiguously established in the inductive model that characterizes the scientific method. In this framework, the purpose of good research design is to conduct empirical observations so as to minimize the plausibility of explanations that are contrary to those derived from the theory under study. Successive falsification of rival alternative explanations (based on competing theories or hunches), developed under conditions of maximal contextual heterogeneity, bolsters confidence in the plausibility of the (unfalsified) theory.

## INTERNAL VALIDITY

Experiments can be constructed in many ways, but the designs of all *true experiments* (Campbell & Stanley, 1963) are oriented toward the common goal of enhancing *internal validity*, which is concerned with the extent to which the independent variable may be judged responsible for all *systematic* post-treatment differences observed between experimental and control participants. Proper experimental design is meant to render implausible any explanation of differences between groups that is not conditional or contingent upon the treatment itself. Some of the more common of these rival alternative explanations are history, maturation, testing, instrumentation, statistical regression, selection, experimental mortality, and the interaction of selection with the other threats noted. Each of these alternatives represents a threat to internal validity, and hence, to proper inference. To facilitate their exposition, let us consider these alternative explanations in the context of one or two *preexperimental designs*, which are diagrammed in figure 1. Like the true experimental designs to be discussed,

(a)  Pretest ------► Treatment ------► Posttest

(b)
  Pretest ------► Treatment ------► Posttest

  Pretest ------► No Treatment ------► Posttest

Figure 1. Examples of (a) one- and (b) two-group preexperimental designs (Random assignment to conditions IS NOT assumed).

preexperimental designs expose participants to treatment(s), the effects of which are subsequently assessed on a posttest. Unlike true experiments, preexperimental designs do not employ randomization to assign participants to conditions. This deficiency gives rise to a host of problems, as will be shown.

*Threats to Internal Validity*
*History.* The rival alternative hypothesis of history refers to the possibility that differences observed between pretest and posttest are attributable to events that have occurred over the passage of time, rather than to the experimental treatment. The preexperimental designs of figure 1 do not allow an unambiguous assessment of the cause of pre-to-posttest differences.
*Maturation.* Changes in the internal state of participants – growing older, becoming more tired, less interested – which are unrelated to the treatment, can occur between pre- and posttreatment measurements. In preexperimental designs, these changes are not unambiguously attributable to the treatment, and hence may serve as a rival alternative explanation of observed differences.
*Testing.* Scores may be affected as a consequence of prior experience with the dependent measure. For example, participants' scores on

a test of achievement may increase because of their prior exposure to the test. If such performance enhancement were found in the context of the designs of figure 1, it could not be attributed unambiguously to the treatment.
*Instrumentation.* Changes from pre- to posttreatment may occur because the instrument employed to measure effects has itself changed – observers may become fatigued, their attention may wane, an instrument may overheat, etc. If human observers' judgments serve as dependent measures, care must be taken to insure that these human "instruments" maintain fidelity over the course of observation.
*Statistical regression.* If participants are selected on the basis of extreme pretest scores, they will inevitably demonstrate change between pretest and posttest that is independent of treatment effects, if the tests on which the selection is based are not completely free from error. Since few such tests exist, use of extreme groups must be contemplated with extreme caution.
*Selection.* Dependent measures for two or more groups of participants will be prone to misinterpretation if special (nonrandom) selection procedures are implemented to constitute the groups (figure 1(b) ). Discrepancies between groups may reflect initial discontinuites, or differences in susceptibility to the treatment, rather than true treatment effects.
*Experimental mortality.* When one group exhibits an appreciably greater drop-out rate than others in an experiment, differences on the dependent measure may be attributable to this differential mortality rather than the treatment itself. The preexperimental design of figure 1b cannot unambiguously disentangle these competing possibilities.
*Interactions with selection.* If participants are assigned to different comparison groups on the basis of nonrandom criteria, the specially selected groups may experience different maturation rates, different histories, different mortality rates, etc. These selection-based interactions may be wholly unrelated to the independent variable, but as before, the preexperimental design (figure 1(b) ) does not allow an unambiguous assessment of their viability.

Figure 2. Pretest-posttest-control group experimental design (Random assignment to conditions IS assumed).

## True Experimental Designs

These alternative explanations may be rendered implausible by the use of true experimental designs. Such designs involve the utilization of a minimum of two groups of randomly assigned participants, who are exposed to different *levels* of one or more independent variables. Effects of the independent variable are assessed on a common dependent measure. Levels of an independent variable may be categorical (high versus low induced stress, high versus low shock) or continuous (10/20/30 g). To meet the criteria of a true experimental design, participants must be assigned *randomly* to conditions. Randomization requires that all participants be available for any condition of the study, and that the ultimate condition assignment is determined by chance alone. Random assignment is undertaken to insure initial comparability of the groups under study. Its effectiveness depends upon the availability of large numbers of participants. When a large pool of participants is employed, randomization assures the cancellation of systematic initial differences between groups. When large numbers are unavailable, randomization does not necessarily create comparable groups, and the fundamental logic of the experimental approach is compromised. The effectiveness of randomization may be augmented by a process of *blocking*, in which participants are sorted into categories before assignment to conditions. Procedurally, the pool of potential participants is categorized according to some theoretically relevant variable (e.g., gender, IQ, marital status, race, religiosity, etc.). Then, from within the categories (or blocks), participants are assigned randomly to experimental conditions. Random assignment of preclassified participants reduces the possibility that differences between groups are attributable to effects of the classification variable, since such effects have been randomized across all conditions.

One common true experimental design is the pretest–posttest–control group design, summarized in figure 2. This design requires pretesting a group of participants, and then randomly assigning them to either the experimental or the control condition. Experimental participants are exposed to the treatment, and afterwards are tested again. Participants assigned to the control condition do not receive the treatment, but receive the posttest contemporaneously with experimental group. Differences that occur between the two groups cannot plausibly be attributed to any of the threats to internal validity presented earlier. It may be assumed that no systematic differences set the two groups apart initially, owing to their random assignment to conditions. Randomization offsets the rival alternative hypothesis of selection. In combination with randomization, the contemporaneous timing of pretest and posttest in the experimental and control groups renders implausible any explanations based on differential history, maturation, testing, instrumentation, or their interaction with selection. This is not to suggest that these extraneous effects cannot affect participants over the course of the study, but rather that they should not affect experimental and control participants differently. Accordingly, posttest differences between experimental and control participants are attributed to the one factor that systematically differentiates them, the independent variable. Differential experimental mortality is not offset by the true experimental design, but its existence can be determined. Obviously, if many more participants drop out of the experimental than the control conditions, internal validity is compromised. In most social psychological research, however, the threat of experimental mortality is slight.

To this point, the experimental process has been described as a procedure in which the impact of a treatment on one group is assessed by comparison with a nontreated (control) group. This one-variable-at-a-time approach has been employed for purposes of exposition, but it is not characteristic of experimentation in contemporary social psychology. Generally, more than one factor is manipulated, and their combined effects assessed. In such multifactorial experimental research, every level of each variable is paired with every level of all other experimental variables. When every experimental variable (or factor) is crossed with every other, the design is termed a *factorial* design. The logic of the true experiment is maintained in the factorial design. The design-based rationale that renders threats to internal validity implausible in the simple pretest–posttest–control group study is operative as well in the factorial experiment. In addition to providing a more efficient vehicle for investigating effects of treatment variables, factorial designs allow determination of whether one variable has an impact on participants' responses to other manipulated variables. Such *interaction effects*, as they are termed, form the basis of many theoretical advances in social psychology.

## EXTERNAL VALIDITY

The strong emphasis on internal validity as the "gold standard" in experimentation is intentional, for if a study, univariate or otherwise, is susceptible to any of the threats outlined earlier, its interpretation is rendered problematic. However, in addition to internal validity, researchers are increasingly concerned with *external validity*, the extent to which study results may be generalized to other populations and other contexts. The question of external validity is never definitively answerable in the abstract – whether a result will generalize to contexts removed from the strict confines of the experimental laboratory is an empirical issue. However, strategies have evolved to enhance generality (*see* Aronson, Brewer, & Carlsmith, 1985).

One strategy involves conducting experiments with diverse subject populations. Such studies are more likely than experiments on highly restricted populations to produce results that generalize across a wide spectrum of persons. Research arrangements that limit the impact of EXPERIMENTER EFFECTS, participants' perceptions of the hypotheses under investigation, or that enhance the ECOLOGICAL VALIDITY, or realism, of the experimental context, attenuate demand effects, and thereby enhance generalizability. Another means of diminishing participants' awareness of experimental hypotheses involves use of the "*posttest-only design*," a true experimental design that mimics the pretest–posttest–control group design of figure 2 with one exception – it forgoes the use of the pretest. In this design, participants are randomly assigned to treatment or control conditions, the treatment is employed where appropriate, and the dependent measures administered. Given random assignment, the initial comparability of groups is assumed, and differences between groups on the dependent measure are attributed to treatment variations. Because no pretest is employed, external validity is enhanced – obviously, the pretest cannot have sensitized participants to the treatment.

A variation that combines the two true experimental designs discussed to this point has also been employed. This design, labeled the Solomon four-group design after its originator, is a factorial design in which one treatment factor is the presence or absence of the pretest. This factor is factorially combined with all the others in the study to provide information about the extent to which the pretest affects participants' reactions to the other treatment(s). Creative design variations of this type maintain the vitality of the experimental approach in social psychology, and are largely responsible for its continued progress.

*See also*: EXPERIMENTER EFFECTS; METHODOLOGY.

BIBLIOGRAPHY

Aronson, E., Brewer, M. B., & Carlsmith, J. M. (1985). Experimentation in social psychology. In G. Lindzey & E. Aronson (Eds.), *The handbook of social psychology*

(3rd ed., Vol. 1, pp. 441–86). New York: Random House.

Campbell, D. T., & Stanley, J. C. (1963). Experimental and quasiexperimental designs for research on teaching. In N. L. Gage (Ed.), *Handbook of research on teaching* (pp. 171–246). Chicago, IL: Rand-McNally. Reprinted as *Experimental and quasi-experimental designs for research*. Chicago, IL: Rand-McNally, 1966.

Crano, W. D., & Brewer, M. B. (1986). *Principles and methods of social research*. Boston, MA: Allyn & Bacon.

WILLIAM D. CRANO

**experimenter effects** The term experimenter effect refers to the effect of the experimenter on the results of the research. Experimenter effects are *artifacts* or threats to the validity of the study.

Certain experimenter effects such as observer, interpreter, and intentional effects occur without investigators actually affecting their subjects' responses to the experimental task. These effects occur in the mind, the eye, or the hand of the investigator. Other effects such as biosocial, psychosocial, situational, MODELING, and EXPECTANCY EFFECTS are interactional. These effects occur when some attributes or behavior of the experimenter actually affect subjects' responses to the experimental task.

OBSERVER EFFECTS

Observer effects, unintentional inaccuracies in the observation and recording of the events being studied, were first detected by astronomers. Early in the nineteenth century, Bessel, an astronomer at Konigsberg studied the observations of stellar transits made by senior astronomers. He found that differences in observation occurred surprisingly often (Boring, 1950).

Things do not seem to have changed much in the present century: in an analysis of 21 studies involving 314 observers and 139,000 observations, about 1 percent of the observations were found to be in error. Further, approximately 66 percent of these errors were found to occur in the direction of the experimenter's hypothesis (Rosenthal, 1991). Observer effects can be reduced by exercising great care in data collection. Such effects might also be reduced by the use of multiple independent observers so that observers' errors cancel each other.

INTERPRETER EFFECTS

Interpreter effects occur when data are inaccurately interpreted. Interpreter effects, however, might be less serious than observer effects because the former are public whereas the latter are private. Researchers can agree or disagree on the interpretation of observations (and they often do, as can be seen from the debates in technical journals) but they generally do not have access to the observations themselves.

Some common interpreter effects in the social sciences can be reduced by improved research and data-analytic methodology. For example, many people doubted the effectiveness of psychotherapy until Smith and Glass (1977) demonstrated on the basis of a quantitative, comprehensive analysis of the literature on psychotherapy that there is strong, convincing evidence for the effectiveness of psychotherapy. Until recently, researchers could impose a wide range of interpretations on vast bodies of literature depending on their own personally preferred theory. But now a variety of meta-analytic procedures allow for systematic and quantitative summaries of vast research domains that tend to increase the objectivity of the conclusions drawn (Rosenthal, 1991; *see* META-ANALYSIS).

INTENTIONAL EFFECTS

Intentional effects include dishonest reporting and fabrication of data. Although instances of fraud and dishonesty are probably relatively rare, intentional effects should nevertheless be regarded as effects of the investigators themselves. Self-serving errors in citations of the literature also fall under the category of intentional effects.

Intentional effects have been demonstrated in many of the sciences (Broad & Wade, 1982). Perhaps the most notorious example of intentional effects in the behavioral sciences is the case of the late Cyril Burt. In three separate reports of over 20, over 30, and over 50 pairs of twins, he reported a correlation of exactly 0.771 for all three studies: statistically, a virtually impossible finding! But we cannot be entirely sure whether Burt fabricated his data or whether he was just careless in recording the data (an observer error).

Intentional errors are hard to prevent precisely because they are planned. Careful implementation of ethical codes of conduct and ethical training of researchers might help to prevent such errors.

### BIOSOCIAL EFFECTS

Biosocial effects are associated with such attributes as the age, gender, and race of the investigator. It is difficult to disentangle the direct effect of the biosocial attributes of the investigator on subjects from the influence of these attributes on the behavior of the investigator. Thus, because of their biosocial characteristics, researchers might be *perceived* in a certain manner by their subjects, or as a result of their biosocial characteristics, researchers might *actually behave* differently toward their subjects. For example, there is evidence that male and female experimenters conduct the "same" experiment quite differently and therefore might obtain different results. Moreover, biosocial attributes of the subject can affect the experimenter's behavior which might in turn affect the responses of the subject. Researchers should be alert to possible biosocial effects when they plan their studies and conduct the research. A good strategy might be to compare results obtained from different experimenters to check for biosocial effects.

### PSYCHOSOCIAL EFFECTS

Psychosocial effects result from the personality of the experimenter. Experimenters' characteristics such as their level of ANXIETY, need for approval, their status, and their warmth all influence the results of studies in different, unpredictable ways. Thus, experimenters who are higher in status tend to obtain more conforming responses from sub-

jects and warmer examiners tend to obtain better intellectual performance on standardized tests of intelligence than do cooler examiners (Rosenthal, 1969). As in the case of biosocial effects, psychosocial effects should be considered when studies are being planned and should be checked for by comparing the results obtained from different experimenters when data are being analyzed.

### SITUATIONAL EFFECTS

Many situational effects are possible, e.g., effects of the level of experience of the investigator or effects of the degree of acquaintance between the subject and the experimenter. Thus, experienced experimenters may get different results from inexperienced ones. Similarly, experimenters who know their subjects sometimes get different responses from experimenters who do not know their subjects. Further, events that happen during the course of the experiment can lead to changes in subjects' responses. Researchers should be alert to the possibility of situational effects when they plan their studies and should also examine their data for possible situational effects (e.g., by comparing results obtained from experimenters with different levels of experience).

### MODELING EFFECTS

There is some evidence that in a variety of research contexts research subjects tend to respond to a task in the same way their experimenter would respond to it. As in the case of biosocial, psychosocial, and situational effects, investigators should consider possible modeling effects in planning their research and, to minimize such effects, should, if possible, use multiple experimenters.

### EXPECTANCY EFFECTS

Last, experimenter expectancy effects occur when investigators' hypotheses and expectations regarding how the research will turn out influence the way in which the research does turn out. The hypothesis held by the experimenter leads unintentionally to behavior toward the subjects which, in turn, increases the likelihood that the hypothesis will be confirmed. This phenomenon is also called a SELF-FULFILLING PROPHECY (Rosenthal, 1966).

*A classic case*
One of the earliest demonstrations of experimenter effects occurred in the case of Clever Hans (Pfungst, 1911). Hans was the horse of Mr Von Osten, a German mathematics teacher. By tapping his foot, Hans could add, subtract, multiply, divide, spell, read, and solve problems of musical harmony. Unlike other performing animals, Hans had not been trained to perform by his owner. And unlike other performing animals, he was able to perform consistently well even in the absence of his owner. Intrigued by Hans' skills, Pfungst and his colleague Stumpf undertook a program of systematic research to discover the secret of Hans' talent. They discovered that Hans could not answer questions that his questioners could not answer. Further, Hans could not answer questions if he could not see the questioner. Based on these observations, Pfungst and Stumpf reasoned that Hans must be picking up cues from the questioner as to when to begin and when to stop tapping his foot. Indeed, a forward inclination of the head would start Hans tapping and as the questioner straightened up Hans would stop tapping – even a slight motion of the eyebrows or nostrils was sufficient to stop Hans from tapping. Clearly, Hans was able to pick up the expectations of his questioners and thereby fulfill their prophecies.

*Experiments with human subjects*
In the first demonstration of experimenter expectancy effects in the laboratory, ten advanced undergraduate and graduate students of psychology served as the experimenters. Each experimenter was assigned 20 introductory psychology students as his or her subjects. The experimenter showed a series of ten photographs of people's faces to each subject individually and asked the subject to rate the degree of success or failure shown in the face of each person pictured in the photograph. The photos had been selected so that on the average they were quite neutral. All ten experimenters were given identical instructions regarding the task and identical

instructions to read to their subjects. They were told not to deviate from these instructions. They were also told that the purpose of the experiment was to see how well they could duplicate well-established experimental results. Half the experimenters were told that the "well-established" finding was that their subjects should rate the photos as being of successful people and half the experimenters were told that the finding was that the subjects should rate the photos as being of unsuccessful people. Results showed that experimenters expecting "successful" photo ratings did obtain higher photo ratings than did the subjects expecting unsuccessful photo ratings (Rosenthal & Fode, described in Rosenthal, 1966). Because all the experimenters read the same instructions to the subjects it was not clear how exactly the experimenters were able to influence their subjects. But an ingenious experiment provided an explanation for this subtle influence process.

Adair and Epstein (described in Rosenthal, 1969) replicated the basic photo rating experiment on the self-fulfilling effects of experimenters' hypotheses. But during the replication experiment, they tape-recorded experimenters' instructions to their subjects. They then conducted a second experiment using the tape-recordings of experimenters' voices instead of real experimenters. They found that when the tape-recorded instructions had originally been read by experimenters expecting failure perception by their subjects, the tape-recordings evoked greater failure perceptions from the subjects. Apparently the experimenters' tone of voice influenced subjects to perceive success or failure in correspondence with the experimenters' own expectations.

*Experiments with animal subjects*
Experimenter expectancy effects have also been found with infra-human subjects. For example, Rosenthal and Fode (described in Rosenthal, 1966) told 12 students in an experimental psychology class that studies had shown that maze-brightness and maze-dullness could be developed in strains of rats by successive inbreeding of well performing and poorly performing maze runners. Half the experimenters were told that their rats were

maze-bright and the other half were told that their rats were maze-dull. Each student was assigned five rats. The animals had to learn to run to the darker of two arms of an elevated T-maze. The two arms were interchangeable and the rewarded arm was located equally often on the right as on the left. The results revealed that animals believed to be better performers actually became better performers. After the experiment, experimenters' ratings of their animals indicated that experimenters who had been led to expect better performance rated their animals as brighter, more pleasant, and more likeable than experimenters who had been led to expect worse performance. Further, experimenters expecting better performance reported that they had handled their rats in a more gentle manner than did experimenters expecting poor performance.

*Expectancy effects beyond the laboratory.*
The majority of studies on interpersonal expectancy effects have been conducted in the laboratory. But a number of studies have revealed that the phenomenon exists in the real world as well. For example, in one of the earliest field experiments, the "Pygmalion" experiment, all of the children in an elementary school were administered a test of intelligence disguised as a test to predict "blooming." Approximately 20 percent of the children from each of 18 classrooms were chosen at random to be in the experimental condition and their names were given to their teachers. The teacher was told that these childrens' performance on a test of "intellectual blooming" indicated that they would make significant gains in intellectual performance in the next 8 months of school. After 8 months, at the end of the school year, all the children were retested with the same IQ test and the children whom the teachers believed to be "bloomers" showed significantly greater gain in performance than did the children in the control group (Rosenthal & Jacobson, 1968).

The cumulative results of over 450 studies provide unequivocal evidence for the existence of interpersonal expectancy effects (e.g., Rosenthal & Rubin, 1978). These findings have important substantive implications for

*Table 1*

---

*Strategies for the Control of Experimenter Effects*

---

1. Increasing the number of experimenters
   decreases learning of influence techniques
   helps to maintain blindness
   minimizes effects of early data returns
   increases generality of results
   randomizes expectancies
   permits the method of collaborative disagreement
   permits statistical correction of expectancy effects
   decreases the likelihood of biosocial, psychosocial, situational, and modeling effects
2. Observing the behavior of the experimenter
   sometimes reduces expectancy effects
   permits correction for unprogrammed behavior
   facilitates grater standardization of experimenter behavior
3. Maintaining blind contact (see table 2)
   minimizes expectancy effects
4. Minimizing experimenter–subject contact (see table 3)
   minimizes biosocial, expectancy, modeling, psychosocial, and situational effects
5. Employing expectancy control groups
   permits assessment of expectancy effects
6. Analyzing experiments for order effects
   permits inferences about changes in experimenter behavior
7. Analyzing experiments for computational errors
   reduces effects of interpreter effects
   permits inference about expectancy effects
8. Developing selection procedures
   permits prediction of expectancy effects
   minimizes biosocial, psychosocial effects
9. Developing training procedures
   permits prediction of expectancy effects
   minimizes situational and modeling effects
10. Developing a new profession of psychological experimenter
    maximizes applicability of controls for all experimenter effects
11. Conducting meta-analyses
    minimizes interpreter, observer, and intentional effects.

investigators. Perhaps the most striking implication is that we engage in highly influential unintended COMMUNICATION with one another and that this process of unintentional influence can affect our experimental results. Consequently, individuals who conduct experiments, such as research assistants, should be kept blind to the hypotheses under investigation so that their expectations will not influence the results of the research.

A number of strategies to prevent experimenter effects including expectancy effects are presented in table 1. Table 2 suggests methods to promote blind contact in order to control for experimenter expectancy effects. Table 3 suggests methods to minimize contact between experimenters and subjects.

*Table 2*

*Blind Contact as a Control for Expectancy Effects*

A. Sources of breakdown of blindness
1. Principal investigator
2. Subject.
B. Procedures for facilitating maintenance of blindness
1. The "total blind" procedure
2. Avoiding feedback from the principal investigator
3. Avoiding feedback from the subject

*Table 3*

*Minimized Contact as a Control for Expectancy Effects*

A. Automated data collection systems
1. Written instructions
2. Tape-recorded instructions
3. Filmed instructions
4. Televised instructions
5. Telephoned instructions
6. Computerized instructions
B. Restricting unintended cues to subjects and experimenters
1. Interposing screen between subject and experimenter
2. Contacting fewer subjects per experimenter
3. Having subjects or machines record data

CONCLUSION

It has been our task to describe the nature of experimenter effects as a source of artifacts in behavioral research. The recognition of these sources of artifact should not result in readers feeling discouraged. We agree with Herbert Hyman's comment that the demonstration of systematic error may well mark an advanced state of science.

All scientific inquiry is subject to error, and it is far better to be aware of this, to study the sources in an attempt to reduce it, and to estimate the magnitude of such errors in our findings, than to be ignorant of the errors concealed in the data. One must not equate ignorance of error with the lack of error. The lack of demonstration of error in certain fields of inquiry often derives from the nonexistence of methodological research into the problem and merely denotes a less advanced stage of that profession (Hyman, 1954, p. 4).

*See also*: COMMUNICATION; META-ANALYSIS; SELF-FULFILLING PROPHECIES.

BIBLIOGRAPHY

Boring, E. G. (1950). *A history of experimental psychology* (2nd ed.). New York: Appleton-Century-Crofts.

Broad, W., & Wade, N. (1982). *Betrayers of the truth*. New York: Simon & Schuster.

Hyman, H. H. (1954). *Interviewing in social research*. Chicago; IL: University of Chicago Press.

Pfungst, O. (1911). *Clever Hans (The horse of Mr. Von Osten)*. New York: Henry Holt. (Reissued 1965).

Rosenthal, R. (1966). *Experimenter effects in behavioral research*. New York: Appleton-Century-Crofts.

——(1969). Interpersonal expectations. In R. Rosenthal & R. L. Rosnow (Eds.), *Artifact in behavioral research* (pp. 181–277). New York: Academic Press.

——(1991). *Meta-analytic procedures for social research* (rev. ed.). Newbury Park, CA: Sage.

——& Jacobson, L. (1968). *Pygmalion in the classroom*. New York: Holt, Rinehart & Winston.

——& Rubin, D. B. (1978). Interpersonal expectancy effects: The first 345 studies. *Behavioral and Brain Sciences*, 3, 377–86.

Smith, M. L., & Glass, G. V. (1977). Meta-analysis of psychotherapy outcome studies. *American Psychologist, 32,* 752–60.

NALINI AMBADY
ROBERT ROSENTHAL

**eyewitness testimony**  Research into the reliability of eyewitnesses has been one of the "pillars" of legal psychology for almost a century (*see* Lösel, Bender, & Bliesener, 1992; Wells & Loftus, 1984; Wrightsman, Willis, & Kassin, 1987). Following a first peak of notable contributions in the early decades of the century, the late sixties brought renewed interest in the field. The turning point came with the application of experimental methods and the first tentative theories and integrative efforts.

If an eyewitness report acquires legal status and becomes trial evidence, jurors and judges have to come to a decision concerning the reliability as well as the veracity of the testimony. Experimental psychologists on the one hand have for the main part investigated perceptual and memory processes that relate to the accuracy and completeness of a report. Applied legal psychologists on the other hand have been more interested in the improvement of interrogation techniques. Both groups have been and are still concerned with the problem of deception. The present entry follows that division. First it will focus on memory processes, then discuss facilitation of recall and finally it will converge on some aspects of lie detection.

PERCEPTION
An accurate witness report requires in the first instance reliability of perception. Evaluating an eyewitness account therefore has to attend to the interaction of situational factors at the actual time of the episode (e.g., light, distance of target) with the limitations inherent in the sensory equipment, be they general (e.g., sensory thresholds, adaptation time) or differential (e.g., nearsightedness, hearing impairment). An example of a perceptual law entailing an error is the tendency to overestimate the duration of an observed sequence.

Constructive processes can also play an important part. For instance a spatial and temporal coincidence of stimulus events can lead to the inference of causality and the attribution of intention.

MEMORY
Analyses of MEMORY processes in eyewitness research usually employ the tripartite system of an acquisition, retention and retrieval stage.

ACQUISITION/ENCODING
Witness factors such as prior knowledge or special encoding strategies (e.g., depth of processing, giving verbal labels to actions or persons) have instigated considerable research. Among the event characteristics that are most likely to improve encoding accuracy are long exposure time and familiarity with the situation, complexity of the situation and frequency of the observed act. Some hold that a high stress level and/or a high level of crime seriousness are detrimental to accuracy, due to a reduced attention span (as in a state of "weapon focus," in which the witness fails to perceive the offender's face or other relevant information, because his or her attention is constricted to a threatening object). Among the significant characteristics of the target person are attractiveness, sex and race (CROSS-RACIAL FACIAL IDENTIFICATION being more difficult).

RETENTION/STORAGE
An assumption of memory decay obviously entails an emphasis on storage time. It has consistently been shown that witnesses remember more details when interrogated immediately than after a delay. Another research focus has been the effect of memory stemming from postevent information. If it originates in an external source, such postevent information amounts to leading questions or suggestive communications. Loftus (1979) was among the first to investigate such influences on memory during the storing phase. She used a series of coloured slides depicting an accident. In different experimental conditions one group of subjects saw a yield sign,

the other a stop sign. Immediately after presentation a series of questions was asked, including one with a misleading presupposition, implying the existence of a sign different from the one actually shown. Based on the rate of mistaken identifications in a subsequent forced choice recognition task, Loftus concluded that verbal–semantic information is translated into and confused with visual memory for the original events. This conclusion was criticized by McCloskey and Zaragoza (1985) on methodological grounds. They held that Loftus' results could be alternatively explained by the assumption that some of the subjects had forgotten the correct answer by the time the distraction was introduced and merely utilized the postevent information for guessing in the forced choice test. In a series of follow-up studies using various materials, Loftus and collegues were able to show that not only memory for the presence or absence of objects but also memory for continous attributes such as speed and even color could be influenced by adequately worded questions (for an overview, *see* Loftus, Miller, & Burns, 1987). A related case with practical applications is reconstructive recall, as for instance when original memory is misled by the witness' active memory constructions (e.g., construction of a composite drawing or search of mug shots).

Detrimental postevent information can also stem from internal sources as a witness tends to adjust the memorized event to expectations. These expectations can be related to stereotypes, especially regarding "criminal" appearance and personality characteristics. Thus memory for a sequence can be modified by personal prejudices as well as by prior information about events. The need for consistency can result in confabulation of details and in doubts concerning true but unusual details (*see* Clifford & Bull, 1978).

## RETRIEVAL/COMMUNICATION

A willing witness is of course a prerequisite for an accurate report. Social pressure influences what and how much people will report and social desirability and self-presentation concerns must be kept in mind when evaluating a testimony.

The question structure in witness interrogation has received considerable interest. There seems to be an inverse relationship between accuracy and the quality of a testimony, both variables reflecting the specifity of the questions. Free recall produces less complete but also less erroneous reports than cued recall. Identification of a suspect is improved if the context in the retrieval situation resembles the encoding context; a change in clothing or (even worse) a disguise in the appearance of the offender decreasing accuracy of recognition dramatically.

## APPLIED SOCIAL PSYCHOLOGY

The APPLIED SOCIAL PSYCHOLOGY angle on eyewitness testimony mainly deals with the criminal justice system. The aim is to generate scientific knowledge that will maximize the chances that a guilty defendant will be justly convicted while minimizing the chances that an innocent defendant will be mistakenly convicted (Wells, 1987, p. 140). Whereas the processes that govern acquisition and storage are usually beyond the criminal investigator's reach, retrieval and communication of information can be helped or hindered by the manner in which answers are elicited from the witness. Among the techniques employed to facilitate recall are hypnosis and the cognitive interview (*see* Wrightsman, Willis, & Kassin, 1987). The latter technique seems quite successful in increasing the number of correct details. The number of incorrect details is not reduced, however (Geiselman, Fisher, MacKinnon, & Holland, 1986).

Whereas indirect methods in a criminal investigation (e.g., fingerprints) can merely indicate the presence of the subject at the scene of a crime, eyewitness testimony is direct evidence and therefore of greatest importance for the identification of an offender. The stimulus material presented to a witness during an interrogation can be either unspecific (e.g., composite drawings, mug shots) or consist of a lineup (e.g., life parade, video, or photo array) including a definite suspect. The rationale is that there is only a negligible probability that the suspect is chosen by chance. The instructions for this recognition task are crucial. If they lead the witness to expect a definite inclusion of the perpetrator of the crime, the likelihood of a false identification increases. An adequate lineup requires that the description of the offender applies to the suspect as well as to the foils, so that only the actual memory of the witness differentiates between the guilty and the innocent. Contrary to the routine lineup with all persons simultaneously present, a sequential lineup (without telling the witness how many persons to expect) seems to decrease incorrect identifications (false alarms) (Wells, 1984).

The last two decades of eyewitness research have seen a definite shift of interest from the credibility of the witness to the credibility of the testimony. The general memory competence of certain groups of people has nevertheless remained a debatable question up to now, with those groups including rape victims, children and juveniles, or very old witnesses (for a comprehensive treatment of children in court, see Lösel, Bender, & Bliesener, 1992).

DETECTION OF DECEPTION

Since very often the verdict hinges solely on the testimony of a single witness, accuracy in determining the credibility of the testimony is of utmost importance and has therefore been the subject of much research over the years. A false testimony can be given intentionally to hide incriminating information or to defame another person. The relationship of veracity of statement, cues, and attribution of credibility can be conceptualized in an adapted LENS MODEL framework, which represents the relationship between the objective truth of the report on the one side and subjective judgments of truth and credibility on the other side. Since the objective truth is not directly observable, this relationship is mediated by a set of observable cues or symptoms, from which the veracity of the testimony can be inferred subjectively.

This assumption of behavioral cues to DECEPTION can be retraced to at least four different theoretical approaches:

(1) A person who knowingly lies might experience greater AROUSAL, with increased sympathic activity reflecting inner turmoil. Such arousal may reflect a conditioned reaction to questions tapping into guilty knowledge (e.g., incriminating knowledge that the witness intends to conceal). A second explanation postulates a conflict between the tendency to lie and to tell the truth. Thirdly the increased physiological activity can be a consequence of anticipation of punishment pending discovery, and finally the cognitive dissonance due to a counter-attitudinal communication might also enhance physiological activity.

(2) The self-control approach expects that the liar uses a stereotype about behavioral cues that indicate a lie and tries to counterbalance them. This is only possible for cues which can be intentionally controlled. As a consequence, the liar's efforts lead to channel discrepancies, for instance response incongruities in several behavioral areas which in their turn act as deception cues.

(3) The AFFECT approach suggests that lying is associated with fear of discovery and/or feelings of guilt because of the immoral and reprehensible act. Affects are seen as direct instigators of certain observable behaviours, by which the liar dissociates himself/herself from the testimony.

(4) From a cognitive point of view, the lying person is faced with a dual task: to conceal incriminating evidence and at the same time to appear credible. This puts a strain on the information processing system and results in a drain of cognitive resources from other operations. According to this limited capacity approach, the cognitive strain or overload should be manifested in disfluencies, pauses, decreased speed rate, and reduced response quality.

Of course, experts as well as lay persons have their idiosyncratic theories about which cues are of diagnostic value. Several META-ANALYSES have so far been conducted, all with mixed results. Cue validity varies with factors like type of crime, age of person, and context of interrogation. The observable variation between lying witnesses owes partially to idiosyncratic differences in the baselines of behavioral cues.

An examination of statement cues on the one hand and behavioral cues on the other hand reveals two distinct research traditions, associated with the following compilation of diagnostic cues:

(1) Semantic and stylistic analyses of statements intend to provide checklists for practitioners. Such lists include the following cues for deceptive statements: Increase of negative statements, overgeneralization, and less detailed descriptions. Unusual details and spontaneous corrections seem to indicate truthfulness.

(2) Among the behavioral cues associated with deception are increased pupil dilation, decreased blinking, reduced head movements. Shrugging increases whereas overall body movements decrease. With respect to speaking behavior, lying is associated with an increased voice pitch, increased latency, reduced speech rate, and reduced statement length.

These particular cues are not perfectly congruent, but overlap with the cues that have been identified in laboratory experiments on lie detection.

The polygraph technique has attained a special importance in the physiological measurement of autonomic cues which are not directly observable. The physiological reactions (generally relating to the galvanic skin reaction) are usually elicited with the Control Question Technique (CQT), though recently the Guilty Knowledge Test (GKT) has received some support.

Considering the fact that credibility of a witness is usually assessed by jurors and judges who do not employ scientific methods, two questions immediately suggest themselves: How do they do it and how accurate are they? In experimental settings, accuracy has been found to be medium or low, occasioning a pessimistic view of the matter. The observers' confidence is grossly out of proportion to their skill. The observers utilize more body than facial cues. Extralinguistic factors and the contents of the statement seem to be of highest diagnostic relevance.

METHODOLOGY

With the exception of a few cases in which an objective criterion of truth is available (e.g., a video-recording of a bank robbery), field studies have to cope with the problem of the uncertainty of guilt. Other testimonies or even a confession serve as corroborating evidence. Whether these can be sufficient is arguable, for witnesses can be influenced by knowledge of others' testimonies, and an innocent defendant might plead guilty in order to get a lenient punishment in a case given up for lost.

The bulk of studies so far have used a simulated event (mock crime studies), along with experimental variation of situational factors. There has been a marked shift of research interest from testimony relating to an incident to the identification of a target person. The motivation of deceivers in these studies is typically based on a promised gain or mere cooperation, rather than fear of detection. Therefore these studies do not allow for the realistic investigation of affect and arousal influences.

Further problems inherent in laboratory experiments on eyewitness accuracy include the following (Wells, 1987):

(1) Usually the questioning of the experimental eyewitnesses is conducted in a way that makes them aware of having been exposed to a mock crime. This encourages risk taking in identification of the "criminal," because the costs of a wrong identification are rather low.

(2) Controlled experiments involve asking every potential witness for a testimony. This may lead to lesser accuracy, because it forces the subjects to deliver a testimony, whereas real eyewitnesses may choose not to volunteer, if they doubt their memory.

(3) A further problem stems from the fact that in real life the victim is often the only witness to a crime aside from the perpetrator. This unique perspective is usually not reproduced in laboratory experiments.

CONCLUSIONS

The study of eyewitness testimony has clearly profited from the interest devoted to this subject by researchers from different areas. The intermediate position between basic and applied research as well as the joint approach of experimental, social, and legal psychology have proven fruitful and promising for the field.

*See also*: APPLIED SOCIAL PSYCHOLOGY; AROUSAL; DECEPTION; MEMORY; META-ANALYSIS.

BIBLIOGRAPHY

Clifford, B. R., & Bull, R. (1978). *The psychology of person identification*. London: Routledge & Kegan Paul.

Geiselman, R. E., Fisher, R. P., MacKinnon, D. P., & Holland, H. L. (1986). Enhancement of eyewitness memory with the cognitive interview. *American Journal of Psychology, 99 (3)*, 385–401.

Loftus, E. (1979). *Eyewitness testimony*. Cambridge, MA: Harvard University Press.

——Miller, D. G., & Burns, H. J. (1987). *Semantic integration of verbal information into a visual memory*. In L. S. Wrightsman, C. E. Willis, & S. M. Kassin (Eds.), *On the witness stand: Controversies in the courtroom* (pp. 157–77). Newbury Park, CA: Sage.

Lösel, F., Bender, D., & Bliesener, Th. (Eds.) (1992). *Psychology and the Law. International perspectives*. Berlin: De Gruyter.

McCloskey, M., & Zaragoza, M. (1985). Misleading postevent information and memory for events: Arguments and evidence against memory impairment hypotheses. *Journal of Experimental Psychology: General, 114 (1)*, 1–16.

Wells, G. L. (1984). The psychology of lineup identifications. *Journal of Applied Social Psychology, 14*, 89–103.

——(1987), Applied eyewitness-testimony research. System variables and estimator variables. In L.S. Wrightsman, C. E. Willis, & S. M. Kassin (Eds.), *On the witness stand: Controversies in the courtroom* (pp. 139–56). Newbury Park, CA: Sage.

——& Loftus, E. F. (1984). *Eyewitness testimony: Psychological perspectives*. New York: Cambridge University Press.

Wrightsman, L. S., Willis, C. E., & Kassin, S. M. (Eds.) (1987). *On the witness stand: Controversies in the courtroom*. Newbury Park, CA: Sage.

JEANNETTE SCHMID
KLAUS FIEDLER

# F

**facial expressions of emotion** The phrase is not a neutral description of a class of behavior, but a premise: The premise is that our faces express our emotions; our faces are windows to our souls. Put in more modern terms, certain facial actions are assumed to signal basic emotions.

The premise may be common sense, but it has turned out to be the single most important idea in the psychology of emotion (*see* AFFECT and EMOTIONAL EXPERIENCE). Facial expression is taken to be a visible outcropping of an otherwise hidden process. It is central to a research program (or what might be considered in Kuhn's terms a paradigm) that claims Charles Darwin as its originator, Silvan Tomkins as its modern theorist, and Carroll Izard, Paul Ekman, Wallace Friesen, and dozens of other scientists as its practitioners. The research program offers to make of emotion something measurable and understandable within an evolutionary framework.

This program has generated more research than any other in the psychology of emotion (*see* Fridlund, Ekman, & Oster, 1987). According to its proponents, the evidence is conclusive: Happiness, surprise, fear, anger, disgust, contempt, and sadness have been established as basic emotions by showing that members of cultures isolated from each other recognize these seven emotions from each other's facial expressions. The best-known cross-cultural studies ever conducted were designed to demonstrate the universality of facial expressions of emotion (*see* CROSS-CULTURAL SOCIAL PSYCHOLOGY). Observers in literate cultures around the world were reported to recognize the same specific emotions from the same facial expressions with the same high degree of accuracy. Ekman and Friesen went to New Guinea to study the South Fore, a recently discovered, nearly Stone Age culture relatively isolated from Western influence. Ekman and Friesen reported that the South Fore recognized the emotions of Americans from their facial expressions, and Americans in turn recognized the emotions posed by the South Fore. The universality of facial expressions is now asserted without debate in journal articles, chapters, and textbooks. It has been called an "axiom of behavioral science" and a "fact," the implications of which must be considered by any emotion theorist.

## THE RESEARCH PROGRAM

The "facial expressions of emotion" program consists of a network of assumptions, theories, and methods. Each investigator presents a somewhat different version of the program, but it may be useful to make explicit a prototypical version. Some of its key assumptions, premises, and implications would be as follows:

(a) Facial action is a part of the complex that constitutes each emotion. As Izard (1971) put it, "at *one* level, emotion *is* facial action" (p. 188). The other parts of any emotion are its distinctive conscious experience (its subjective feeling), its physiological underpinnings, and other expressive and instrumental actions characteristic of that emotion. Note that on this definition, emotion has no necessary cognitive component. Rather, emotions are said to be *triggered* by environmental or other conditions.

(b) Any state lacking a recognizable facial signal is not an emotion.

(c) The production (encoding) and recognition (decoding) of distinct facial expressions constitute a signaling system, which is an evolutionary adaptation to some of life's major problems. This premise predicts and relies upon similarity in facial configurations across species (*see* EVOLUTIONARY PSYCHOLOGY);

(d) Manipulating the face into the appropriate configuration creates (the rest of) the corresponding emotion. For instance, wrinkling the nose creates the experience and physiology of disgust. The "fact" that facial manipulation can produce the corresponding emotion can then be used as a method in the laboratory to study, for example, the physiological correlates of each emotion. Systematic research has begun using this technique to identify the autonomic pattern unique to each of the basic emotions.

(e) Emotional state is revealed by facial measurement. Thus the emotions of newborns and of others unable or unwilling to speak truthfully become accessible. Verbal report can be bypassed. Great effort has gone into the development of scoring systems for facial movements. These systems objectively describe and quantify all visually discriminable units of facial action seen in adults or in babies. Scoring keys are available to translate the observed facial action units into emotion categories. Subtle or inhibited emotions can be revealed through facial electromyography. Expressions too brief to be seen by the unaided eye can be detected through high-speed photography.

(f) The feelings associated with an emotion are due to feedback from facial movements. This "facial feedback hypothesis" has been offered as the means by which an individual "knows" which emotion he or she is feeling (and thus answers a question that has been central in the psychology of emotion since William James). The existence of these highly differentiated internal "cues" to an ongoing emotion would refute Schachter and Singer's theory that emotion consists of cognition plus undifferentiated arousal (*see* MISATTRIBUTION OF AROUSAL).

(g) Seven, plus or minus two, facial signals exist that are easily recognized by all human beings regardless of their culture.

The seven emotions signaled are happiness, surprise, fear, anger, contempt, disgust, and sadness. There is some uncertainty over contempt and over the distinction between surprise and fear. Izard (1971) adds interest and shame to the list.

(h) The number and identity of basic emotions is revealed by discovering which facial expressions signal the same emotion universally. Thus, evidence that a unique facial expression, a unilateral lip curl, is panculturally interpreted as contempt was taken as evidence that contempt is the seventh basic (genetically determined, universal, discrete, elemental) emotion.

(i) All emotions other than the basic ones are subcategories or blends of the basic emotions. For example, ANGER includes fury and annoyance as subcategories. ANXIETY is a blend of fear, sadness, anger, shame, and interest.

(j) Because facial expressions are discrete, the emotions they convey are discrete.

(k) The ability to recognize the emotion in a facial expression is innate rather than culturally determined (*see* GENETIC INFLUENCES).

(l) The ability to recognize emotions from facial expressions is present very early, possibly at birth. In "social referencing," for example, young children use the emotion in their caregiver's face to decide how to handle ambiguous and potentially dangerous situations. The information obtained from the face is more specific than simply whether the caregiver feels positively or negatively about the situation. For instance, anger and fear expressions send very different messages to the child.

(m) The categories by means of which recognition occurs (in the self as facial feedback or in others through facial signaling) are genetically rather than culturally determined. The words *happiness, surprise, fear, anger, disgust, contempt*, and *sadness* thus designate innate and therefore universal categories. Other languages may use other names, but the categories named are the same. These categories are natural kinds and semantic primitives. Like the emotions themselves, additional emotion labels designate blends or sub-categories of the basic categories.

(n) The meaning ("signal value") of the facial expression for each basic emotion is fixed by nature, and is thus invariant across changes in the context in which it occurs. Observers can recognize the emotion in another's facial expression, even when the other's context and behavior provide conflicting information. Observers can recognize the same emotion in the same facial expression across a range of modes of presenting the facial expression.

(o) Voluntary facial expressions can simulate spontaneous ones. Voluntary expressions are deceptive in nature, and culturally conditioned. Different cultures establish different display rules, which dictate when an expression can be displayed freely, and when it must be inhibited, exaggerated, or even masked with a different expression. Great effort has gone into techniques of reading through individuals' attempts to inhibit, mask, or exaggerate (*see* DECEPTION). The true emotion "leaks" through the camouflage, and can be detected through facial measurement.

(p) Spontaneous and voluntary facial expressions originate in different regions of the brain.

(q) The ontogeny of emotion is revealed by the emergence of distinct facial expressions.

EMERGING QUESTIONS

Of course, no-one advocates the full program, especially when it is stated so starkly. All of the corollaries (*a*) through (*q*) are debatable, and no writer advocates all of them without qualification. Thus, there are arguments about whether the unilateral lip curl really signals contempt, about whether children actually engage in social referencing, and about whether newborns can recognize emotions from facial expressions. Five rather than seven emotion words might be the semantic primitives. The ability to recognize facial

expressions might not be innate. Conceivably, they might be so common and so obviously associated with the corresponding emotion that they are easily learned. Such arguments are *within* the program.

Evidence supporting any one corollary supports the program, but no one pillar of support is necessary for the program to survive. Of course, if enough difficulties surface in enough domains, they may constitute the kind of anomalies that Kuhn found attract the attention of young scientists and eventually stimulate the questioning of the program itself. And this kind of questioning may be beginning.

The first question concerns the missing evidence. Reading that the universality of facial expressions of emotion has been established as a fact, readers could be forgiven if they assumed that, across a reasonable sample of the world's cultures, each so-called basic emotion had been found to produce the same recognizable facial expression. That evidence is missing. The most direct evidence for the premise is so far limited to American subjects and to a correlation between self-reported happiness and certain smiles. Even this evidence has been questioned by Fridlund (1991).

New questions have also surfaced about the evidentiary base that has been provided for many of the other corollaries. The facial feedback hypothesis has generated much debate. Facial electromyography has not yet been able to detect discrete emotions (Tassinary & Cacioppo, 1992). Biologists have questioned whether "emotion signals" in nonhuman species actually signal emotions (Fridlund, 1991). Zajonc and McIntosh (1992) questioned whether each so-called basic emotion is associated with a separate autonomic pattern. Camras (1991) now doubts whether the facial expressions of infants actually correspond to the specific emotions hypothesized. Fridlund (1991) now doubts the evidence for the role of display rules.

The well-known cross-cultural studies did not address the question of which facial expression results from a given emotion but rather which emotion observers *attribute* to a particular facial expression. Even on the question of attribution, the evidence is questionable. The "signal values" of the hypothesized universal facial expressions were determined with a limited range of questionable methods: Observers, in a within-subjects design, were typically shown still photographs of posed facial expressions and were given a list of the hypothesized emotion terms. The task was to match each expression with one term. Observers were given no information about the person whose face was to be judged or the context in which the expression was supposed to have occured. Results obtained with this method have been taken to show recognition of specific emotions in all cultures. However, the recognition scores were not uniformly high across either cultures or types of facial expression, and when the method is altered, recognition scores decline or disappear (Russell, 1994). For example, when spontaneous rather than posed expressions are studied, nothing more than a discrimination between positive and negative states has been found. When the experimenter does not provide a list of emotions to choose from, "recognition" declines for some facial expressions, dramatically so in some cases. Common sense suggests that if recognition of emotion from facial expression is indeed a universal, biologically based ability, then posed expressions, a list of emotion terms, a within-subjects design, and other such typically used features of method should not be necessary for recognition to occur. Certain questions thus remain open: For example, is recognition invariant across modes of presenting the facial stimulus and across differences in the expresser's context and behavior? Do observers spontaneously recognize specific emotions from spontaneous facial expressions?

The concepts of *happiness, surprise, anger, fear,* and the like – and indeed of *emotion* itself – are to some extent culture-specific rather than universal (Russell, 1991). The way in which the English language carves up the emotion domain is in some ways similar to but in some ways different from the way it is done in other languages. Even in English, a semantic analysis does not suggest that all emotion words are subcategories or blends of seven plus or minus two semantic primitives that denote basic emotions.

The assumption that some emotions are basic has been questioned on a number of grounds by Ortony and Turner (1990). The number and identity of the basic emotions has not been agreed upon. Different criteria as to what constitues a basic emotion do not converge on the same list.

EMERGING ALTERNATIVES

The "facial expressions of emotion" program today stands as the dominant approach to facial action. Two alternatives have recently been suggested. Fridlund (1991) argued that facial movements do not signal emotions, but contingent action. On this account, a smile is not an expression of happiness but an invitation to engage in or to continue in friendly interaction. The smiler might be happy, but could be lonely or sad or fearful. The smiler could be acting deceptively, having no intention of keeping the interaction friendly. An "anger" expression is interpreted as a threat; the expresser might be angry, but could be frightened, or bluffing, or asserting dominance over a subordinate. Fridlund's approach is based on modern theory in biology, in which it is thought that any animal that invariably signals its true internal state to a potential adversary ahead of time would be at a disadvantage. In a competition, fear is better hidden than signaled. Ordinarily, social context and emotion are confounded, but Fridlund has offered evidence that, in accord with his theory, facial actions vary more with the person's social context than with his or her emotional state. For example, as social signals, facial expressions vary with the signaler's audience more than with his or her emotion. Even when alone, a person's facial actions vary with the audience imagined.

Another, and perhaps complementary, alternative is that components of facial expressions are what carry meaning (Scherer, 1992). Thus, the "anger expression" is composed of dissociable parts (such as the furrowed brow, the widened eyes, the compressed lips). Each component is produced and interpreted separately (Ortony & Turner, 1990). The furrowed brow may accompany the discovery that a goal is blocked. Widened eyes may accompany visual attention. Compressed lips may accompany determination to do something. Anger often, but not necessarily, accompanies a blocked goal, visual attention, and determination. What would be telling is what happens when anger happens to occur without, say, visual attention. In this case, the widened eyes should be absent. If anger happens to occur without the determination to do something, then the compressed lips should be absent. The componential approach awaits validation.

*See also*: CROSS-CULTURAL SOCIAL PSYCHOLOGY; DECEPTION; EMOTIONAL EXPERIENCE; GENETIC INFLUENCES.

BIBLIOGRAPHY

Camras, L. (1991). A dynamic systems perspective on expressive development. In K. Strongman (Ed.), *International review of studies on emotion* (Vol. 1, pp. 16–28. New York: Wiley.

Fridlund, A. J. (1991). Evolution and facial action in reflex, social motive, and paralanguage. *Biological Psychology*, *32*, 3–100.

—— Ekman, P., & Oster, H. (1987). Facial expressions of emotion. In A. Siegman & S. Feldstein (Eds.), *Nonverbal behavior and communications* (2nd ed., pp. 143–224). Hillsdale, NJ: Lawrence Erlbaum.

Izard, C. E. (1971). *The face of emotion*. New York: Appleton-Century-Crofts.

Ortony, A., & Turner, T. J. (1990). What's basic about basic emotions? *Psychological Review*, *74*, 315–41.

Russell, J. A. (1991). Culture and the categorization of emotion. *Psychological Bulletin*, *110*, 426–50.

—— (1994). Is there universal recognition of emotion from facial expression? A review of the cross-cultural studies. *Psychological Bulletin*, *115*, 102–41.

Scherer, K. (1992). What does a facial expression express? In K. Strongman (Ed.), *International review of studies on emotion* (Vol. 2, pp. 138–65. New York: Wiley.

Tassinary, L. G., & Cacioppo, J. T. (1992). Unobservable facial actions and emotion. *Psychological Science*, *3*, 28–33.

Zajonc, R. B., & McIntosh, D. N. (1992). Emotions research: Some promising questions and some questionable promises. *Psychological Science*, *3*, 70–4.

JAMES A. RUSSELL

**false consensus**  The tendency for people to perceive their own preferences, attributes or behavior as relatively common and situationally appropriate compared to those displaying alternative preferences, attributes or behaviors (*see* CONSENSUS ESTIMATION). It is not to be confused with the absolute overestimation of consensus, determined according to some objective criterion.

*See also*: CONSENSUS ESTIMATION.

RUSSELL SPEARS

**false uniqueness**  A tendency for people to underestimate consensus for their own attributes or behaviors that appears to be particularly associated with positive attributes (*see also* CONSENSUS ESTIMATION). Some controversy exists as to whether false uniqueness should be assessed in absolute or relative terms like FALSE CONSENSUS.

*See also*: CONSENSUS ESTIMATION.

RUSSELL SPEARS

**family relations**  The social psychology of family relations is largely concerned with the initiation, development, and deterioration of CLOSE RELATIONSHIPS. The nature of these relationships may take many forms but typically involves individuals who view themselves as a unit with a long-term commitment to continue their relationship. Traditionally, at least in Western societies, families are defined in terms of two parents living together with responsibility for rearing their children. In fact, these so-called nuclear families are unique in many respects. For instance, in the United States the Bureau of the Census reported in 1991 that married couples living together with one or more children represented only 26 percent of all American families. Single-parent families, childless couples, lesbian or gay male couples with or without children are all represented in the broad mix of relations we may usefully refer to as families.

RELATIONSHIP INITIATION

What kinds of events and processes influence the choice of a long-term partner? Social psychologists have long sought an answer to this question and at times have provided contradictory answers. In this section we are concerned with how casual relations develop into enduring relationships, and how people move from courtship to marriage or marriage-like relationships. Generally, we can distinguish four sets of factors that influence the initiation and growth of a close relationship: background characteristics, characteristics of individuals-in-relationship, relationship qualities, and contextual factors.

Background factors refer to qualities of people that are manifested prior to and independent of the initiation of a relationship. Much of the early work on mate selection and interpersonal ATTRACTION focused on the homogamy or similarity of partners on background characteristics, and indeed marital partners tend to be similar on characteristics such as age, education, race, residential propinquity, and attitudes. Homogamous selections probably occur for a number of reasons. For one, similar others are predictable and understandable because of our familiarity with their ways of living, and because we often share common associates, beliefs, VALUES, and attitudes. Homogamy in mate selection is not universal, however, and is principally observed among first marriages of young couples (see Cate & Lloyd, 1992).

Characteristics of individuals-in-relationship include features that result from the interaction of partners. For example, based on a series of social encounters, two people may form some evaluation of each other such as the degree of LOVE or TRUST.

Romantic love has been especially well studied. Rubin defined romantic love in terms of three components: attachment, caring, and intimacy (see Hendrick & Hendrick, 1992). Taken together, these components do indeed predict relationship stability as one would expect. Sternberg developed a more general "triangular theory of love" based on the dimensions of intimacy, passion, and commitment (see Hendrick & Hendrick, 1992). Although this model shares some similarity with Rubin's, it is a broader conceptualization that may be applied to a variety of relationships. Many family relationships, for instance between siblings or parent and child, are intim-

ate, but only certain relationships are expected to be passionate, and family relationships will certainly vary in their commitment. People vary as well in their preferences for expressing their love and several prototypical love styles have been identified (see Hendrick & Hendrick, 1992).

Analyses of attitude SIMILARITY and need COMPLEMENTARITY also figured prominently in the early work on mate selection. Comparisons of partners' attitudes and needs formed the basis of the so-called "filter models" of mate selection. Although popular, they are unsupported by research. Essentially these models suggest that as couples pass through various filters (e.g., by first establishing some degree of attitude similarity) they move closer to a more enduring relationship.

Levinger and his co-workers (1970) attempted to replicate some of the earlier findings on filter models. Although they were unable to find any evidence for filtering, they made several critical distinctions that were to have a far-reaching effect on the field. In summarizing their analyses, Levinger et al. suggested two processes that operate during the initiation and advancement of a close relationship. The first involves a mutual discovery of personal conditions, like PHYSICAL ATTRACTIVENESS, basic attitudes, and needs. The second concerns the development of the relationship per se in terms of the build-up of a common pool of shared experiences, NORMS that guide interaction, regular patterns of interaction and a unique knowledge of the other.

In a series of inquiries directed at identifying unique relational properties, Cate, Surra, Huston and their colleagues required newly weds to recall key features of their courtships. This permitted the authors to depict graphically the movement of couples from first meeting to eventual marriage (see Cate & Lloyd, 1992). Couples differed in the length of their courtships, but also in terms of the trajectory by which they reached certainty of marriage. Some trajectories were rapid, some extended, some smooth, and others turbulent with many upturns and rapid downturns where couples reported conflicts. Essentially this procedure permits a detailed examination of how relational events and properties, rather than individual conditions, influence development.

Of course family relationships do not develop or endure independent of ties with kin, friends, and other personal associates. Research on the context of relationship development has largely focused on how network members influence the initiation of pair relationships and their ongoing character, as well as the changes which occur in the constellation of network members, such as the development of a joint network of mutual friends, as couples become more or less intimate (*see* Milardo, 1988).

MARITAL INTERACTION

With the exception of some early work by Lewis Terman, Kurt Lewin, and somewhat later, George Levinger, a social psychology of MARRIAGE and family relations developed only recently. Previously, family studies was the province of clinicians, sociologists, and scholars in interdisciplinary programs in human development. The unique contribution of social psychology is in the merging of relatively broad analyses of social structural influences on family relationships and relatively molecular analyses of interaction, including the underlying behaviors, emotions, and cognitions. Four major developments stimulated research in family relations. Social psychologists in the late 1970s began to recognize the distinction between relational and individual properties and to anticipate the development of a science of relationships. Kelley and Thibaut's SOCIAL EXCHANGE theory, as well as Kelley et al.'s (1983) general INTERDEPENDENCE model were central in providing conceptual frameworks for addressing relationship issues. Highly reliable techniques were developed in the laboratories of Gottman, Weiss, and Markman, among others, for encoding the actual interactions of family members. And finally concurrent developments were made in the statistical analysis of behavioral data.

As is true of much of the research in family sociology, psychologists share a fascination with the prediction of marital quality, satisfaction, and stability. The typical research design compares the interaction of distressed couples (those low in marital satisfaction scores) with nondistressed couples (those with higher marital satisfaction scores) as spouses discuss an issue over which they have experienced conflict. Interactions are recorded and later coded by highly trained technicians.

Lag-sequential and time series analyses of behavioral sequences permit researchers to examine patterns of interaction and describe the likely sequence of responses, given a particular behavior by one spouse. For instance, in an argument distressed and nondistressed spouses are equally likely to complain but the pattern of events is distinct. In nondistressed couples, one spouse's complaint is apt to be followed by some validation of that complaint by the partner before another reciprocal or cross-complaint is issued. In distressed couples, validation of the other's position is absent and couples quickly lock into parallel cross-complaining (*see* Gottman, 1979).

Two coding schemes are most frequently used, although others are available. The Marital Interaction Coding System, developed by Weiss and his colleagues, provides a means to identify specific categories of behaviors, or blends of behavior and AFFECT, and thereby retains the emotional tone of the interaction. The Couples Interaction Scoring System developed by Gottman encodes behaviors and affect separately, and additional physiological and self-report data are often generated. Self-reports of the affect corresponding to particular behaviors is generated by having spouses sit across from one another at a "talk-table" and, using an electronic panel, rate the speaker's intent and the listener's reception of each statement made in a problem-solving discussion. In general, distressed spouses are distinct in both their actual behaviors, issuing more negative statements, and in their reception and decoding of their partner's statements, inferring more negative affect than was intended (*see* Fincham & Bradbury, 1990).

In a more recent series of studies, Levenson and Gottman monitored physiological states (e.g., heart rate) of spouses during an interaction, and later as spouses observed a replay of their interaction on video, while simultaneously rating their affect at a "talk-table." These studies were important in several respects. First, the correspondence of spouses' physiological states accounted for a substantial 59 percent of the variance in marital satisfaction. The self-report measures of affect added an additional 16 percent above that accounted for by the physiological measures of affect. Given the rather contrived nature of these interactions, which occurred in a laboratory setting, and their relative brevity, it is remarkable that such a microlevel analysis is such a robust predictor of a global index of marital satisfaction (*see* Gottman, 1990).

Comparisons of husbands and wives in distressed and nondistressed marriages are consistent with clinical observation: depressive behaviors and coercive sequences (i.e., depressive behaviors, like sadness, followed by ANGER) are associated with the long-term decline of a marriage; wives are the "emotional barometers" of marriage in that their self-reported affect is predictive of their future satisfaction; and deteriorating marriages are typified by a comparatively unresponsive husband and a wife's unsuccessful attempts to engage him (*see* Gottman, 1990).

Additional analyses by a variety of research teams have yielded a consistent portrait of dissatisfied and satisfying marriages in the overall rates of behaviors and in the pattern or sequencing of behaviors. Satisfied couples use more positive verbal and nonverbal behaviors, approval and caring, EMPATHY, and agreement. They smile, laugh, and touch more often and engage in more problem description and suggest solutions. While dissatisfied couples are more negative, critical, hostile, and nonresponsive. They are apt to deny responsibility for problems and make more personal complaints joined with negative affect. Dissatisfied couples differ in the sequence of their actions, for example, in sequences punctuated by confrontation, complaint, and defensiveness (*see* Fincham & Bradbury, 1990). Future advances will undoubtedly emerge from longitudinal studies that combine direct observation with contemporary self-report measures.

Recent advances have been made in the development of structured diaries as a method for gathering observational data on personal events. These procedures include Weiss's Spouse Observation Checklist (SOC), a compendium of actions common to a marriage. With the SOC spouses provide a daily record of their affectional and instrumental behaviors. Although not yet widely used, initial findings are compelling both in understanding relationship processes and in the design of treatment strategies. For example, in Wills et al.'s now classic study, events rated as "displeasing" have a stronger effect on marital satisfaction than "pleasing" events; in Huston et al.'s longitudinal study of newlyweds, the early years of marriage were characterized by substantial declines in affectional behaviors but relatively stable levels of negative behaviors; and in Margolin's study of families, substantial declines in the ratio of pleasing to displeasing behaviors were reported by distressed and nondistressed couples across four stages of the childbearing years (*see* Fincham & Bradbury, 1990). Additional methods have been developed by Larson for generating momentary ratings of mood states through the use of electronic paging devices, and by Milardo for gathering daily records of spouses' leisure activity with one another and with members of their social networks (*see* Milardo, 1988).

SOCIAL COGNITION in marriage is yet another emerging area that examines spouses' BELIEFS and ATTRIBUTIONS. Unrealistic beliefs about relationships are linked to lower marital satisfaction, and beliefs regarding self-efficacy to successful conflict resolution. Research on attributions in marriage, or spouses' understanding and evaluation of partners' behavior, indicates distressed spouses, relative to their nondistressed counterparts, view the cause of negative marital events as stable, global, and the responsibility of the partner whose actions are selfishly motivated. Among distressed couples, attributions are made that minimize the importance of positive behaviors and highlight negative actions (*see* Fincham & Bradbury, 1990).

The influence of other family members, including children and to a certain extent kin, has engendered considerable research. Children inhibit marital dissolution while at the same time contributing to a decline in the time spouses have for one another, and increasing the strain on available resources. Marital satisfaction and personal well-being decline with the entry of the first child and continue to decline until children mature and become independent, after which satisfaction increases. However, some of these effects may also occur in childless couples and certain aspects of marriage may in fact improve with the arrival of children (e.g., when husbands increase their participation in household labor).

Families are influenced by the kin and other personal relationships spouses and their children maintain. Kin are important because they typically have a dual nature, being significant sources of both support and criticism. A large proportion of kin in one's network, and a substantial volume of contacts with them may introduce significant benefits, but not without costs. Women, being largely responsible for maintaining ties with kin, are both the primary beneficiaries of their support and the primary target of their criticism. Consequently, for wives the number of kin and the amount of interaction with them has ambiguous effects on marital interdependence, effects that are dependent on the relative proportion of support and interference. On the other hand, friends are less apt to be critical, lest they cease to be friends, and involvement with them has largely beneficial effects (*see* Milardo, 1988). Finally, parents and children can have reciprocal effects on each other's social participation. School-aged children may integrate parents into their community and the social activity of parents can spill over to their children, leading to improvements in their self-regard, SOCIAL SKILLS, and school achievement (*see* Cochran et al., 1990).

MARITAL DISSOLUTION

Life-time divorce rates in the USA have increased from approximately 10 percent to over 50 percent in this century with similar increases for northwestern Europe. Research has focused on the factors that influence marital dissolution and the effects of dissolution on adults and children. At .the macrostructural level, economic downturns, a rise in the organization of extrafamilial institutions that provide alternative sources of financial security and personal services, a rise in the economic independence of women, and increased social mobility have all been linked to a higher probability of divorce.

The literature on interpersonal processes is less well developed and typically is based on some form of cost/benefit analysis. For example, the reconciliation of partners is more likely when the costs of divorce are high (e.g., children are present) and alternatives are low (e.g., older partners, lower income; *see* COMPARISON LEVEL FOR ALTERNATIVES).

The consequences of divorce are usually organized in terms of adjustment in the areas of personal health, and economic and social well being. Unquestionably the divorced, relative to the married or widowed, show heightened levels of mortality, and psychological or physiological morbidity. Economic consequences are more severe for women, especially women with custody of children, and consequently limit the potential for the development of new relationships. The relationships of spouses with kin and friends undergo considerable change during the entire dissolution process and perhaps prior to actual separation and divorce. Preliminary evidence suggests that these declines in social participation that are concurrent with separation continue for an extended period. Nonetheless, friendships can serve an important function in moderating the deleterious effects of divorce, whereas relations with kin are often marked by interference or disapproval as well as support (*see* White, 1990).

For children, the effects of divorce are equivocal: They do not have any clear or single impact, nor are the effects necessarily long term. Economic factors, relations between parents, contact with the noncustodial parent (usually fathers), age of the children, and a variety of additional factors have been examined with mixed results. Social psychological theory will become critical to the extent that it centers on how the internal character of relationships between family members trouble children or enrich their development.

CONCLUSIONS

Our review of the social psychology of family relations has been brief, highlighting key findings as well as areas where recent advances in theory and methodology have been most impressive. Over the last decade the field has developed rapidly and undoubtedly will continue to do so. The most promising areas of future research are varied but include longitudinal studies of marriage – it's initiation, ongoing character, and eventual dissolution, inquiries that detail the social context of family relationships – such as the mutual influence of work and family environments or the influence of kin and friends, and inquiries that broaden our focus to alternate forms of families. The field of social psychology offers a unique perspective in an area of human activity that is singularly important, often complex, and always fascinating.

See also: ATTRACTION; ATTRIBUTION THEORIES; EMPATHY; INTERDEPENDENCE THEORY; MARRIAGE; NORMS; SOCIAL COGNITION; SOCIAL SKILLS; TRUST; VALUES.

BIBLIOGRAPHY

Cate, R., & Lloyd, S. (1992). *Courtship*. Newbury Park, CA: Sage.

Cochran, M., Larner, M., Riley, D., Gunnarsson, L., & Henderson, C. (1990). *Extending families*. New York: Oxford University Press.

Fincham, F., & Bradbury, T. (Eds.) (1990). *The psychology of marriage: Basic issues and applications*. New York: Guilford Press.

Gottman, J. (1979). *Marital interaction: Empirical investigations*. New York: Academic Press.

——(1990). How marriages change. In G. Patterson (Ed.), *Depression and aggression in family interaction* (pp. 75–101). Hillsdale, NJ: Lawrence Erlbaum.

Hendrick, S., & Hendrick, C. (1992). *Romantic love*. Newbury Park, CA: Sage.

Kelley, H., Berscheid, E., Christensen, A., Harvey, J., Huston, T., Levinger, G., McClintock, E., Peplau, L., & Peterson, D. (1983). *Close relationships*. New York: W. H. Freeman.

Levinger, G., Senn, D., & Jorgensen, B. (1970). Progress toward permanence in courtship: A test of the Kerckhoff–Davis hypothesis. *Sociometry, 33*, 427–43.

Milardo, R. (Ed.) (1988). *Families and social networks*. Newbury Park, CA: Sage.

White, L. (1990). Determinants of divorce: A review of research in the eighties. *Journal of Marriage and the Family, 52*, 904–12. [NB: The entire issue of this journal is devoted to a decade review of family research.]

ROBERT M. MILARDO

**fear appeals** This term refers to persuasive communications that are deliberately designed to elicit fear or ANXIETY in the respondent, with the aim of increasing the effectiveness of the message (*see* ATTITUDE CHANGE). Communications designed to change health behaviors have been a common testing ground for research on fear appeals. In an early experiment, Janis and Feshbach (1953) examined the impact of different levels of fear arousal on reactions to communications about dental hygiene. They found that conformity to the recommendations of the message was *inversely* related to the level of fear, which they explained in terms of defensive avoidance. However, subsequent studies (*see* Rogers, 1983) have found that high-fear messages can be more effective than low-fear messages. Such apparent inconsistencies can be explained by theoretical models in which the respondent is seen as someone who wishes to avoid danger, and who will adopt recommendations to the extent that they are seen as effective in averting personally relevant dangers. However, if the recommendations are seen as ineffective, fear appeals may have no influence – or even a negative influence – on adoption of the recommendations. Rogers' (1983) protection motivation theory is the most comprehensive of these models. It proposes that high-fear messages will be effective if they convince respondents that the problem is a *serious* one, that they are *vulnerable* to the problem, that the recommended action will be *effective* in avoiding the problem, and that they are *capable of executing* this recommendation. The main role played by fear in this model is to influence perceptions of the severity of the threat and of personal vulnerability to the threat.

See also: ATTITUDE CHANGE.

BIBLIOGRAPHY

Janis, I. L., & Feshbach, S. (1953). Effects of fear-arousing communications. *Journal of Abnormal and Social Psychology*, *48*, 78–92.

Rogers, R. W. (1983). Cognitive and physiological processes in fear appeals and attitude change: A revised theory of protection motivation. In J. T. Cacioppo & R. E. Petty (Eds.), *Social psychophysiology: A sourcebook* (pp. 153–76). New York: Guilford Press.

ANTONY S. R. MANSTEAD

**foot-in-the-door** This technique predisposes people to comply to a critical request by first obtaining COMPLIANCE to a minor request (Freedman & Fraser, 1966). For example, an automobile salesperson may ask a potential buyer to test drive a car. Compliance to the critical request (buying the car) will be enhanced as a result of obtaining compliance to the initial, smaller request. One explanation for this phenomenon is in terms of SELF-PERCEPTION THEORY. By complying to the minor request, the individual may infer from that behavior that he or she is the kind of person who, in this case, drives that sort of car.

*See also*: SELF-PERCEPTION THEORY.

BIBLIOGRAPHY

Freedman, J. L., & Fraser, S. C. (1966). Compliance without pressure: The foot-in-the-door technique. *Journal of Personality and Social Psychology*, *4*, 195–202.

BIRGIT KAUFMANN-BRYANT
BRIAN MULLEN

**forced compliance** When a person is induced to advocate publicly a position that is contrary to his or her attitudes, it is known as forced compliance (sometimes called induced compliance.) The forced compliance paradigm has been useful in studying predictions of COGNITIVE DISSONANCE THEORY that COUNTER-ATTITUDINAL BEHAVIOR results in attitude change. Research on forced compliance has shown an inverse relationship between incentive magnitude and attitude change.

*See also*: COGNITIVE DISSONANCE THEORY.

JOEL COOPER

**friendship** A special, familiar, and highly valued type of human social RELATIONSHIP. Researchers typically distinguish three kinds of relationships: kinship, instrumental relationships, and friendships. Kinship refers to family relationships (including MARRIAGE), and instrumental relationships are those that are mandated by life activities (e.g., co-workers or neighbors). In contrast, the term friendship describes voluntary, ongoing associations between two persons that facilitates attainment of socioemotional goals (Hays, 1988). These aims may be diverse, incorporating any number of endeavors, commonly including companionship, shared activities, INTIMACY, affection, helpfulness, and a sense of loyalty or security.

Friendships may be based on numerous and highly varied factors. Psychological models generally assert that friendship develops out of compatibility in the participants' personal dispositions (which include PERSONALITY traits, VALUES, opinions, interests, and activity preferences; *see* COMPLEMENTARITY; SIMILARITY). Other researchers are more interested in the impact of social roles and structures on friendship development (e.g., of being neighbors or workmates, or of having friends in common). These two approaches are not contradictory, of course. Social structures provide opportunities to discover and experience another person's dispositions.

Regardless of perspective, a central idea inherent in most theoretical models is that friends, in contrast to most other types of relationships, choose to associate with each other. (One may feel friendly toward other kinds of associates. Presumably this indicates that the features of a voluntary, affectionate relationship are added onto a relationship established for other reasons.) Such choices need not be conscious or deliberate. Often, friendships develop incidentally out of coincidences or shared experiences. The interpersonal attraction literature, for example, indicates that mere proximity usually facilitates the development of friendships. In fact, only rarely do people actively set out to find new friends. Rather, friendship is more likely to develop when two people who have come into contact incidentally or for instrumental reasons discover that their association is mutually gratifying, and that they would like it to continue. This is the sense in which friendships are chosen.

Researchers who study friendship tend to take one of two general approaches (Blieszner & Adams, 1992). The process approach seeks to identify and characterize the interpersonal processes that regulate interaction among friends. Many such processes have been studied, including affection, attraction, cohesiveness, COMMITMENT, COMMUNICATION (both verbal and nonverbal), COOPERATION AND COMPETITION, EQUITY, INTERDEPENDENCE, INTIMACY, liking and loving, POWER, RECIPROCITY, SELF-DISCLOSURE, SOCIAL SUPPORT, and TRUST. Of course, these processes may also operate in other types of relationships, allowing theories and empirical findings to be generalized from one sort of relationship to another. Nevertheless, the manner in which these processes function in friendships, particularly close friendships, may differ substantially from their operation in nonvoluntary or less committed relationships. For example, interdependence may differ in long-term friendships and newly formed relationships. In the former, the balance of rewards and costs tends to be flexible, spanning relatively long time periods, multiple exchanges, and anticipated future outcomes. In the latter, more immediate reciprocity is usually mandated.

Structural approaches to studying friendship are more directly concerned with describing the nature of friendship, and assessing the impact of personal and social-structural variables on interaction among friends (Fischer, 1982). Regarding the nature of friendship, researchers typically attempt to characterize friendships along conceptually or pragmatically significant dimensions. Common examples are solidarity, status and power differentials, and homogeneity of interests or traits. Many studies of differences among the various phases of friendship development have also been conducted; for example, initiation, acquaintance, maintenance, and dissolution. Other researchers are concerned with personal variables that influence the nature of friendships. Two very popular examples are SEX DIFFERENCES and age differences. At least on their surface, men's friendships tend to be relatively more activity focused, whereas women's friendships tend to be more emotion focused. As for age differences, the basis for children's friendships appears to move through several stages, beginning with proximity and shared play in early childhood, and developing to the adult characteristics of mutuality, sharing, affection, and support, usually during adolescence (see Asher & Gottman, 1981). More recently, researchers have begun to consider how the features of friendships might continue to evolve during adulthood and into old age.

Finally, social network researchers (see Wellman & Berkowitz, 1988) have long been interested in the structural features of friendships and friendship networks, including such basic characteristics as network size, density (the degree to which one person's friends are also friends of each other), and centrality (which persons are central to a social group and which are peripheral). Typically, this perspective goes beyond the immediate friendship dyad to consider the impact of the larger social network in which the dyad is embedded.

Like all relationships, friendships are complex, multiply determined phenomena. No single study or theoretical approach is likely to provide a complete description understanding of the phenomenon. When integrated, however, the various theories and empirical findings paint a rich, enlightening portrait of this most important component of human social life.

*See also*: COMMUNICATION; COOPERATION AND COMPETITION; INTERDEPENDENCE THEORY; INTIMACY; MARRIAGE; NONVERBAL COMMUNICATION; PERSONALITY; POWER; RELATIONSHIPS; SEX DIFFERENCES; SOCIAL SUPPORT; TRUST VALUES.

BIBLIOGRAPHY

Asher, S. R., & Gottman, J. (1981). *The development of children's friendships*. New York: Cambridge University Press.

Blieszner, R., & Adams, R. G. (1992). *Friendship*. Newbury Park, CA: Sage.

Fischer, C. (1982). *To dwell among friends*. Chicago, IL: University of Chicago Press.

Hays, R. B. (1988). Friendship. In S. Duck (Ed.), *Handbook of personal relationships* (pp. 391–408). Chichester: J. Wiley.

Wellman, B., & Berkowitz, S. D. (1988). *Social structures: A network approach*. Cambridge: Cambridge University Press.

HARRY T. REIS

**frustration–aggression** The interruption of goal-directed behavior arising from either the arbitrary interference of other persons or personal inability. Frustration evokes negative AFFECT, which instigates aggressive thoughts, ANGER, and aggressive behavioral tendencies. *See also*: AGGRESSION.

RUSSELL G. GEEN

**fundamental attribution error** Research on ATTRIBUTIONAL BIAS identified a tendency for perceivers to underestimate the impact of situational factors and to overestimate the role of dispositional factors in controlling behavior. This bias can be explained in terms of cognitive, cultural, and linguistic factors. *See also*: ATTRIBUTIONAL BIAS.

MILES HEWSTONE

# G

gender The term "gender" was originally used by linguists to refer to the rules associated with grammatical categories of words with masculine and feminine designations (Unger & Crawford, 1993). The term has now taken on much broader meaning, and controversies about its meaning, especially versus the term "sex," abound in psychological literature. The controversy centers on issues of causality, that is, the roles that nature and nurture play in differences found between males and females, and whether causality should be reflected in terminology. Some researchers argue that causality should be explicit in the terms chosen to describe findings, with "sex" being used for biologically-based differences and "gender" used for sociocultural-based differences. Others argue that the causes of differences include both biological and sociocultural factors, thus it is inappropriate to presuppose a single cause. A popular resolution is to use "sex" to refer to the categories of male and female, "gender" when making judgments about masculinity and femininity, and "sex-related" or "gender" to refer to differences between females and males (Unger & Crawford, 1993).

An important advance has been the increasing recognition that sex and gender are multidimensional. The literature has been divided into a number of different content areas, including biological gender, activities and interests, personal–social attributes, gender-based social relationships, and stylistic and symbolic content. Different approaches can be used to assess content, including assessing concepts and beliefs; self-perceptions; preferences, attitudes, and VALUES; and behavioral enactment and adoption (Huston, 1983). The multidimensional approach has been important because it has encouraged researchers to examine the relations among the many different aspects, rather than simply assuming that all aspects are interrelated.

## GENDER DIFFERENCES

The study of the differences between females and males has a long and controversial history. Research on gender differences has been controversial because of the implications that findings about ability, PERSONALITY, and social differences have on educational and career opportunities, RELATIONSHIPS, and social institutions. Furthermore, the proposed explanations of these differences are often linked to assumptions about whether differences are inevitable.

Within psychology, the study of gender differences was triggered by the publication of Maccoby and Jacklin's (1974) classic book, *The psychology of sex differences*. After reviewing the available literature, Maccoby and Jacklin concluded that only a few consistent differences exist, namely, males perform better than females on mathematical and visual–spatial tasks, females perform better than males on verbal tasks, and males tend to be more aggressive than females. Males and females were not found to differ on most tasks, including measures of intelligence, SELF-ESTEEM, analytic abilities, and sociability.

Since then, there has been an explosion in the number of studies on gender differences and our understanding of such differences. The sexes can differ in many different ways: in their average scores on some measure, in how variable they are, and in the patterns of relations among outcome measures. Furthermore, care must be taken in interpreting differences. When a difference is found, no assumption should be made that it is biologically based, or that one sex is inferior to the other. Most differences appear to be multiply determined by both biological and sociocultural factors. Furthermore, it is inappropriate to conclude that if differences have a strong biological component, they are more difficult to change than differences having a strong sociocultural component.

From the research on gender differences, a number of general conclusions can be drawn. First, some of the originally identified gender differences seem to be disappearing. In analyses of numerous studies of mathematical abilities, the magnitude of difference between the sexes has declined since 1974, and now no differences are found for many types of mathematical skills. Similarly, although the largest gender differences have been found for visual–spatial tasks, the differences are declining, and the extent of difference depends on the type of visual–spatial task used (Basow, 1992).

The second conclusion is that differences have been found in other domains that were not originally identified by Maccoby and Jacklin. For instance, females conform more than males in group pressure situations, they are more susceptible to PERSUASION, and they are better able to decode nonverbal messages than males (Deaux, 1984). Men and women communicate differently: men use more assertive verbal styles, the sexes tend to use different vocabulary, and women tend to have less control over conversations than men. Women and men differ in the POWER strategies they tend to use. Furthermore, males and females tend to develop different mental disorders at different times in their lives (see Basow, 1992 for a review).

The third conclusion is that sex is a weak predictor. Even when gender differences are found, they typically explain only a small fraction of the variance for any given outcome (1–5 percent). Because of the large amount of variability within each sex and the small differences between the sexes, sex fails to be a strong predictor of behavior.

## EXPLANATIONS FOR GENDER DIFFERENCES

The study of gender differences and explanations concerning the origins of differences span many different areas, including anthropology, sociology, and psychology. Anthropologists explain present day gender differences as having resulted from early divisions of labor, and they examine cross-cultural differences in the social status of various masculine and feminine roles. Sociologists tend to use a role perspective in that they examine the kinds of activities that males and females perform in families and the types of role strain they experience. Furthermore, sociological explanations of difference are often based on institutional barriers that produce role inequalities (Basow, 1992).

Within psychology, there are three general approaches to the study of gender differences and gender-related behavior (see Eisenberg, Martin, & Fabes, in press). Learning-based approaches emphasize the role of the environment. There are several variations of learning theories but each shares the assumption that individuals change in response to changes in the environment. SOCIAL LEARNING theories are based on the idea that gender-related behavior is shaped by environmental contingencies and by observational learning. More recent cognitive social learning theories include the idea that individuals' expectancies about the consequences of behaviors also influence their actions.

Cognitive approaches assume that individuals take an active role in perceiving and interpreting information from their environments and, as such, the locus of change is within the individual. There are several influential cognitive approaches. The earliest was cognitive developmental theory based on the idea that children's cognitive abilities influence their understanding and adherence to gender roles. More recent cognitive approaches include gender schema theories which are based on the idea that gender knowledge is represented as SCHEMAS, and that these schemas act similarly to other social schemas in influencing attention, encoding, and retrieval of information.

Psychoanalytic approaches have changed their focus recently. Traditional psychoanalytic theory was based on the notion of children's identification with same-sex parent, thereby resulting in learning of gender-related roles. Boys identify with their fathers due to fear of castration in retaliation from boys' desires for their mothers. Girls identify with their mothers as a way of symbolically possessing their fathers. These notions have been criticized extensively and reformulations of psychoanalytic ideas have become very popular. Neopsychoanalytic theories are based on ideas about males and females differing in their ways of knowing about the world. For instance, women are assumed to emphasize caring and interconnectedness whereas men are assumed to emphasize autonomy and independence.

Biological approaches are also used. These researchers examine a broad array of factors concerning gender including sexual differentiation, chromosomal and hormonal differences, and gender differences in the brain (Huston, 1983). Research using clinical samples suggests that hormones, particularly androgens, influence the adoption of masculine gender roles. Proposals of gender differences in brain structure and function have been controversial. Some investigators have examined very specific areas for differences, whereas others focus on global differences, such as brain laterality. Overall, males and females have brains that are more alike than different.

## GENDER IDENTITY

Gender identity is a term used to describe individuals' subjective feelings of themselves as males or females. Gender identity is not dependent on conforming to particular ROLES or to having specific PERSONALITY characteristics. Developmental researchers have studied normative patterns of how children acquire a sense of being male or female. Medical researchers have studied atypical patterns concerning the development of gender identity.

## GENDER ROLES

The term "gender roles" is sometimes used to represent gender stereotypes or gender differences. More specifically, however, it refers to the socially assigned roles traditionally associated with each sex. For women, MARRIAGE and motherhood are considered to be traditional roles; for men, being the head of the household and provider are considered to be traditional roles.

## SELF-PERCEPTIONS OF MASCULINITTY AND FEMININITY

One of the most popular areas of study within psychology has been investigating individual differences in MASCULINITY AND FEMININITY. In early psychological research, masculinity and femininity were assumed to represent ends of a single dimension. More recent research suggests that femininity and masculinity are independent dimensions, and that each dimension has multiple domains within it, including appearance, behavior, personality, and interests (Huston, 1983).

Many instruments have been developed to assess femininity and masculinity, although the most popular measures are self-reports of personality characteristics. Individuals are asked to rate the extent to which they believe they have masculine traits (e.g., assertive, independent) and feminine traits (e.g., sympathetic, understanding).

One of the major controversies concerning masculinity and femininity is the degree to which the many domains associated with each concept relate to one another. Bem (1974) proposed that the domains are highly related and that it is therefore possible to use masculinity personality scores to predict many other aspects of behavior such as interests, attitudes, etc. In contrast, Spence and Helmreich (1978) proposed a narrower approach. They argued and provided empirical evidence that the domains are not highly related. Specifically, the measures commonly used do not assess the full range of either masculinity or femininity. Instead, measures of masculinity assess only instrumentality, and relate to other aspects of instrumentality, whereas measures of femininity assess only expressivity, and relate to other aspects of expressivity.

## ANDROGYNY

The concept of psychological ANDROGYNY, which refers to individuals having the combination of both feminine and masculine characteristics, was proposed simultaneously by several gender researchers. The idea became immensely popular because of the theoretical framework Bem (1974) developed concerning androgyny (Deaux, 1984) and, because of the appeal of the idea that individuals could embrace both kinds of characteristics rather than being limited to just one kind.

According to Bem (1974), androgynous individuals, because they possess both masculine and feminine characteristics, have a wide array of behaviors available to them, allowing them to engage in whatever behavior is most effective depending on the situation. Thus, androgynous individuals were assumed to be interpersonally flexible. In contrast, sex-typed individuals have a restricted range of available behaviors (either masculine or feminine) and are limited in their interpersonal flexibility. Because of their greater flexibility, androgynous individuals are assumed to be more psychologically well adjusted.

A number of controversies have ensued concerning androgyny (Deaux, 1984). One concern is the lack of congruence between the way androgyny is measured and the way it has been conceptualized. The typical method of assessing androgyny is to identify individuals who report high levels of masculine personality characteristics and high levels of feminine personality characteristics. Because the masculine characteristics represent only one aspect of masculinity, namely, instrumentality, and the feminine characteristics represent only one aspect of femininity, namely, expressiveness, these measures fail to assess the full range of masculine and feminine characteristics.

Another concern is whether the unique combination of masculinity and femininity predicts aspects of behavior and mental health above the contributions of each dimension individually. Most of the empirical evidence indicates that "masculinity" and "femininity" relate to self-esteem and adjustment, although masculinity shares the stronger relationship. Furthermore, the effects are additive, not interactive, suggesting that androgyny does not have any unique properties to predict above the individual dimensions used to determine androgyny.

GENDER STEREOTYPES

Gender stereotypes are beliefs about the behaviors and characteristics of each sex. Specifically, gender stereotypes are hierarchically organized knowledge structures containing category labels (i.e., males, females) and gen-der-related attributes, such as appearance and occupations. This information is associatively linked such that individuals are able to make judgments based on only limited knowledge about others (see STEREOTYPING). Gender stereotypes are commonly considered to be schemas (i.e., gender schemas), sharing the functions and liabilities associated with other types of schemas.

Cultural gender stereotypes are distinct from the personal stereotypes individuals hold about the sexes. As a group, most Americans share the view that females are warm, expressive, and nurturant, whereas males are considered to be dominant, active, and rational (Basow, 1992). Individuals vary, however, in the extent to which they believe that differences exist between females and males on these characteristics.

Researchers have examined the functions and liabilities associated with using gender stereotypes from a social cognitive perspective (see SOCIAL COGNITION). Studies have been conducted to assess how gender stereotypes influence MEMORY, judgments, and behavior (see Martin, 1991). Researchers generally agree that gender stereotypes are useful because they reduce the complexity of the social environment, yet they are detrimental because they bias what individuals pay attention to, and remember, and they can lead to PREJUDICE and discrimination.

Adults and even young children have extensive gender stereotypes (see Huston, 1983). Given their widespread existence, it is important to analyze how often stereotypes are used to make inferences about others' behavior, particularly if some other kind of information is known about the individual. When individuals only have information about someone's sex, they use it to make a wide variety of judgments. When additional relevant information is available, adults tend to rely mainly on the additional information. In contrast, young children pay more attention to sex than to other kinds of information (see Martin, 1991).

ORIGINS OF GENDER STEREOTYPES

Social psychologists and developmental psychologists have investigated the possible sources of stereotypes using a variety of research methods. One approach is to assess the extent to which stereotypes are accurate reflections of real differences between the sexes. Although it is very difficult to assess their accuracy, evidence suggests that gender stereotypes are not very accurate because they are more extensive than actual sex differences, and they contain information based on exaggerations of minor differences between the sexes (Martin, 1991). Gender stereotypes reflect real differences but also go beyond real differences.

Another proposal is that gender stereotypes arise from the different social roles that women and men fulfill in society (*see* Basow, 1992 for a review). Because women more than men fill domestic roles, based on knowledge of the requirements of this role, individuals assume that women are more likely to be communal. Because men more than women work full-time outside the home, individuals assume that men are more likely to have agentic qualities.

Social and developmental psychologists have investigated the cognitive bases of gender stereotypes (*see* Hamilton, 1981; Martin, 1991). According to a social cognitive approach, the ways in which individuals process information about groups provides a basis for stereotyping. For instance, when groups are labeled, differences between group members are exaggerated, whereas similarities between group members are minimized. Furthermore, membership in a group leads to ingroup/outgroup processes, such as assigning more positive evaluations to ingroup members than to outgroup members, beliefs that ingroup members are more diverse as a group than outgroup members, and a tendency to provide more rewards for ingroup members (*see* INTERGROUP RELATIONS, SOCIAL CATEGORIZATION).

Developmental psychologists have investigated the origins of gender stereotypes from the perspective of SOCIALIZATION within the family, schools, and peer groups (*see* Huston, 1983). Gender information is transmitted by social agents who label the sexes and describe the characteristics associated with each sex. Television, in particular, is considered to be a powerful socialization force because of its popularity and because it often presents exaggerated gender stereotypes. Peers also play a

role in the development of gender differences and in gender stereotypes. Children tend to gender segregate, that is, prefer same-sex playmates. Because play in male groups is qualitatively different from play in female groups, girls and boys are socialized in different worlds.

Families are also considered powerful socializing forces for learning about gender (*see* FAMILY RELATIONS). Parents provide different environments for sons versus daughters. Although research has demonstrated that parents do not consistently encourage different types of personality characteristics or social behaviors in their children, they do encourage traditional roles by assignment of chores and by their expectations about their children's competencies (Eisenberg et al., in press).

CONCLUSIONS

The topics of sex and gender are popular within psychology and related fields. There are many distinct areas embraced under these topics as well as many different theoretical and methodological approaches. Some topics generate controversy because of their political and social implications. Moreover, issues concerning sex and gender have relevance for our daily lives.

*See also*: FAMILY RELATIONS; INTERGROUP RELATIONS; MARRIAGE; MEMORY; PERSONALITY; POWER; PREJUDICE; RELATIONSHIPS; ROLE THEORY; SCHEMAS; SELF-ESTEEM; SOCIAL CATEGORIZATION; SOCIAL COGNITION; SOCIAL LEARNING; SOCIALIZATION; STEREOTYPING; VALUES.

BIBLIOGRAPHY

Basow, S. A. (1992). *Gender stereotypes and roles* (3rd ed.). Belmont, CA: Brooks/Cole.

Bem, S. L. (1974). The measurement of psychological androgyny. *Journal of Consulting and Clinical Psychology, 42,* 155–62.

Deaux, K. (1984). From individual differences to social categories. *American Psychologist, 39,* 105–16.

Eisenberg, N., Martin, C. L., & Fabes, R. A. (in press). Gender development and gender effects. In D. C. Berliner & R. C. Calfee (Eds.), *The handbook of educational psychology.* New York: Macmillan.

Hamilton, D. L. (Ed.) (1981). *Cognitive processes in stereotyping and intergroup behavior.* Hillsdale, NJ: Lawrence Erlbaum.

Huston, A. C. (1983). Sex-typing. In E. M. Hetherington (Ed.), *Handbook of child psychology* (Vol. 4, pp. 388–467). New York: Wiley.

Maccoby, E. E., & Jacklin, C. N. (1974). *The psychology of sex differences.* Stanford, CA: Standford University Press.

Martin, C. L. (1991). The role of cognition in understanding gender effects. In H. Reese (Ed.), *Advances in child development and behavior* (Vol. 23, pp. 113–49). San Diego, CA: Academic Press.

Spence, J. T., & Helmreich, R. L. (1978). *Masculinity and femininity: Their psychological dimensions, correlates, and antecedents.* Austin, TX: University of Texas Press.

Unger, R. K., & Crawford, M. (1993). Commentary: Sex and gender – the troubled relationship between terms and concepts. *Psychological Science, 4,* 122–4.

CAROL LYNN MARTIN

**genetic influences** People differ on a variety of dimensions: Some are aggressive, others meek; some are liberal, others conservative; some are smart, others dull. How are we to understand these differences? The science of behavioral genetics approaches the problem by assuming that there are two sources of influence for all dimensions of variability among people: Each individual has an inherited or biologically transmitted genetic endowment and each individual develops in a set of environmental circumstances. Thus, observed differences between people, i.e., differences in phenotype, are due to differences in their genetic makeup, i.e., differences in genotype, or differences in their environment, or both. Psychological entitites such as personality and attitudes are subject to this same analysis.

ESTIMATING GENETIC INFLUENCE

The most common index of the importance of genetic influence is known as heritability. It is defined as the proportion of variance in phenotype that is due to variance in genotype in a particular population. Heritability has no absolute biological meaning and fluctuates with the population sampled. If both genetic and environmental influences are important then populations with restricted environments will produce greater heritability estimates than populations with large environmental differences; heritability estimates will be lower in genetically homogeneous populations then in genetically diverse populations.

Heritability is not directly observable but can be inferred. In adoption designs relatives reared in different environments are studied. If we assume that the environments are uncorrelated then any correlation between relatives in their behavior must be due to genetic influences. Since identical twins have 100 percent of their genes in common the correlation is a direct estimate of heritability. (Identical twins reared apart are rare but a number of such cases have been studied.) Since siblings (or parent–child pairs) have only 50 percent of their genes in common the correlation must be multiplied by 2 to estimate heritability, and so on for different levels of genetic similarity. The major potential problem with adoption designs is the assumption of independent environments.

The twin method for estimating heritability is based on the difference between correlations for identical (monozygotic) and fraternal (dizygotic) twins reared together. The correlation for both identical and fraternal twins reflects the influence of their shared environment and the influence of their shared genes. Identical twins share 100 percent of their genes but fraternal twins, like ordinary siblings, share only 50 percent of their genes. Thus, the correlation for fraternal twins includes only 50 percent of the genetic influence. If the correlation among fraternal twins is subtracted from the correlation for identical twins the effects of the shared environmental influence and half the genetic influence will be removed. The remainder will estimate half the heritability. A full estimate can be had by multiplying by 2. The major potential problem in this design is the assumption of equivalent environments for identical and fraternal twins.

ADDITIONAL ASSUMPTIONS

These rather simple designs for studying genetic influence make several additional assumptions. They assume that the behavior of interest is affected by many specific genetic influences and these influences combine in an additive way, i.e., the more similar the genotype the more similar the behavior regardless of the particular elements. However, genetic influences can interact, i.e., specific combinations of these influences may be necessary for the behavior to be expressed. Where such specific combinations are necessary, identical twins will exhibit similar behavior (they have the same combinations of genetic influences) but siblings will show disproportionately less similarity in behavior. (Although they have 50 percent common genetic influences, they don't have 50 percent of the same combinations of influences.) Assortative mating, the tendency for persons to select mates who are similar to themselves, provides additional complexity by inflating the level of genetic similarity among their offspring and themselves and by increasing variability in behaviors that are based on additive gene influences. Finally, the genotype and the environment may not be independent but correlated or their effects on behavior may not be additive – violent movies may trigger violence only among people with certain genetic predispositions. See Plomin, DeFries, and McClearn (1990) for a readable introduction to these designs, their assumptions and how they might be used to make realistic estimates of heritability.

GENETIC INFLUENCE ON SELECTED BEHAVIORS

The nature/nurture controversy played itself out most visibly with respect to questions of race and intelligence, but most social scientists now believe that intelligence test scores are significantly affected by genetics. There is also evidence of genetic influence in psychopathology, e.g., schizophrenia, affective disorders, alcoholism, antisocial personality, anorexia nervosa, infantile autism, Tourette's syndrome, and Alzheimer's disease (see Loehlin, Willerman, & Horn, 1988 for a review). Perhaps the area which is getting the most current attention is PERSONALITY. Dramatic reports of genetic influence in this domain are coming from the Minnesota Twins Project (e.g., Tellegen, Lykken, Bouchard, Wilcox, Segal, & Rich,

1988), from developmental studies, and from large-scale American, Soviet, and Anglo studies.

For social psychologists the ATTITUDE construct is central and attitude researchers have generally assumed that there is little if any genetic influence on attitudes. Nevertheless there is evidence that at least some attitudes do have sizeable heritabilities. For example, there are sizeable heritabilities associated with vocational attitudes, religious attitudes, and attitudes toward alcohol (Tesser, 1993).

Some political attitudes also have substantial heritabilities. For example, Eaves, Eysenck, & Martin (1989) studied 50 items from a conservatism scale with such heterogeneous items as Death Penalty, Divorce, and Jazz and found a range of heritabilities over the 50 items from 8 percent to 51 percent. They also report a similar range of heritabilities (from 1 percent to 63 percent) from the analysis of 40 items from a different inventory and a different sample.

Attitudes with high heritabilities function differently than attitudes with low heritabilities. Tesser (1993) reports that high heritability attitudes are responded to faster and are more difficult to change than low heritability attitudes. Further, the relationship between attitude similarity and interpersonal attraction is stronger for high than for low heritable attitudes.

A SURPRISING ROLE OF THE ENVIRONMENT

Behavioral genetic designs can also be used to estimate environmental effects. For example, the correlation between unrelated children adopted into the same environment or the correlation between adopted child and (biologically) unrelated adoptive parents estimates the effect of the shared environment on behavior. Although there are substantial environmental effects on most behavioral systems, these effects seem to be due to nonshared environments or environments that persons in the same family do not have in common.

See also: ATTITUDE THEORY AND RESEARCH; PERSONALITY.

BIBLIOGRAPHY
Eaves, L. J., Eysenck, H. J., & Martin, N. G. (1989). *Genes, culture and personality: An empirical approach*. London: Academic Press.
Loehlin, J. C., Willerman, L., & Horn, J. M. (1988). Human behavior genetics. *Annual Review of Psychology, 39*, 101–33.
Plomin, R., DeFries, J. C., & McClearn, G. E. (1990). *Behavioral genetics: A primer* (2nd ed.). New York: W. H. Freeman.
Tellegen, A., Lykken, D. T., Bouchard, T. J., Wilcox, K., Segal, N. L., & Rich, S. (1988). Personality similarity in twins reared apart and together. *Journal of Personality and Social Psychology, 54*, 1031–9.
Tesser, A. (1993). The importance of heritability in psychological research: The case of attitudes. *Psychological Review, 100*, 129–42.

ABRAHAM TESSER

**gestalt** A whole which is more than the sum or average of individual elements. Gestalt models of IMPRESSION FORMATION hold that each of a person's attributes affects the meaning of others such that the positivity of the final impression is not algebraically predicted from the individual attributes.
*See also*: IMPRESSION FORMATION.

LESLIE A. ZEBROWITZ

**gossip** Scholarly interest in gossip largely begins with Gluckman's (1963) functionalist argument that gossip is, contrary to popular wisdom, a rule-governed activity serving group-defining and social control functions. Insofar as gossip presupposes shared acquaintances who may be the subject of gossiping it serves to mark the boundaries of a social group; outsiders cannot participate. Gossip also sustains collective VALUES by drawing attention to instances of their violation (thus making them concrete) and subjecting offenders to criticism and censure. Its social control function derives additionally from its role in evaluating the character of group members and thus their suitability for positions of trust, responsibility, or LEADERSHIP.

Paine (1967) criticized this view, arguing that gossip serves firstly as informal COMMUNICATION and secondly as a means to promote individual interests. Other arguments are that gossip serves the same interpersonal bonding function for humans that social grooming serves for apes, and that it is the basic means by which humans monitor the reputations of others and manage their own. As yet there has been little systematic research which might shed light on these various interpretations or indeed on the truth of one of the most widespread of popular beliefs about gossip, namely that it is largely a female activity.
*See also*: COMMUNICATION; LEADERSHIP; VALUES.

BIBLIOGRAPHY
Gluckman, M. (1963). Gossip and scandal. *Current Anthropology, 4*, 307–15.
Paine, R. (1967). What is gossip about? An alternative hypothesis. *Man, 2*, 278–85.

NICHOLAS EMLER

**grief** This is primarily an *emotional reaction* to the loss of a loved one, usually following a death (although grief-like reactions can follow other types of loss). It is typified by intense personal anguish, not limited to negative affects or expressions, such as sadness, distress, and crying, but comprising a complex emotional syndrome. Manifestations of grief extend to physiological changes and bodily complaints. Recent studies are beginnng to identify a variety of *cognitive and behavioral coping processes and strategies* used by bereaved people for coming to terms with grief. Thus, grief has come to be regarded as a multidimensional phenomenon.

In everyday language the term grief has been used interchangeably with mourning and BEREAVEMENT. Conceptual distinctions have, however, been made in the bereavement and emotion literatures to differentiate these terms (Parkes, 1986; Stroebe & Stroebe, 1987; Stroebe, Stroebe, & Hansson, 1993). Thus, bereavement refers to the situation of an individual who has recently experienced the loss of someone significant through that person's death, mourning refers to the social expressions or acts expressive of grief, which are shaped by the practices of a given society or cultural group (e.g., mourning rituals). (Note that these definitions differ from those of the psychoanalytic school.)

SYMPTOMATOLOGY

Patterns of normal grief responses have been extensively studied, and assessment instruments have been developed. Frequent affective symptoms include distress and DEPRESSION, ANXIETY, guilt, ANGER and HOSTILITY, anhedonia and LONELINESS. Behavioral manifestations include agitation, fatigue, and crying. Grief is often accompanied by changes in attitudes toward the SELF (e.g., self-reproach, low SELF-ESTEEM) and RELATIONSHIPS with others. Not all symptoms appear in every bereaved person, nor at any one time across the duration of bereavement. Symptomatology also differs from culture to culture. While grief is most frequently identified with prevailing negative affect, not all "symptoms" of grief have negative connotations (relief can be felt alongside sadness; creative activity can be increased).

While most people recover from their grief and its accompanying symptoms over the course of time, for a few, mental and physical suffering is extreme and persistent. Bereaved persons are at greater risk than the non-bereaved from a variety of mental and physical ailments and disorders, including depression, anxiety disorders, somatic complaints, and infections. The relative risk of mortality from many causes, notably suicide, is also excessive (Stroebe, Stroebe, & Hansson, 1993).

PHASES

The close relationship between manifestations of grief and time since death has led some investigators to suggest "phases" or "stages" of grief (Bowlby, 1981). Most have postulated a succession from an initial stage of *shock*, with associated symptoms of numbness and denial, through *yearning and protest* as realization of the loss develops, to *despair*, accompanied by somatic and emotional upset

and social withdrawal, until gradual *recovery*, which is marked by increasing well-being and acceptance of the loss. Durations vary, but generally the first two phases are suggested to last up to a number of weeks, and the third, intense grieving phase may last several months or even years.

Such phasal descriptions have been understood too literally. Almost without exception they have been introduced as descriptive guidelines, yet they have frequently been regarded as set rules or "prescriptions" regarding where the bereaved ought to be in the "normal" grieving process. Recently developed "task models" take more account of the richness of idiosyncratic manifestations of grief than do phasal models. Well known is Worden's (1991) task model, in which the grief process is taken to encompass four tasks (accepting the reality of loss; experiencing the pain of grief; adjusting to an environment without the deceased; and "relocating" the deceased emotionally and moving on with life). It should be emphasized that not all grieving individuals work through these tasks.

COMPLICATING AND MITIGATING FACTORS

Grief does not affect all people equally and much effort has been invested in identifying so-called "risk factors." High risk subgroups of bereaved persons can be classified according to:

(1) *sociodemographic variables* (e.g., younger bereaved, widowers);
(2) *personal history factors* (e.g., ambivalent and dependent marital relationships; previous losses);
(3) *causes and circumstances of death* (e.g., sudden death; child loss); and
(4) *circumstances after loss* (e.g., absense of support; additional stresses).

However, further methodologically sophisticated research on these aspects and, particularly, on mediating processes is needed. Perhaps the most striking feature to emerge consistently from empirical research is that high levels of distress in the course of bereavement are best predicted by a high level of distress early after loss.

## NORMAL VERSUS PATHOLOGICAL GRIEF

Grief is a normal reaction to the death of a loved one and as such does not usually require the help of professional therapists. However, a minority of bereaved people suffer so intensely that intervention is called for. Yet distinctions between normal and complicated grief are difficult to make, first of all, due to lack of clarity with regard to the definition of complicated grief. Time course and intensity of symptoms are dimensions on which complicated grief can primarily be assessed. Delayed, chronic, absent, and prolonged grief, as well as unresolved, maladaptive, conflicted, distorted, neurotic, and dysfunctional grief frequently reflect these dimensions (they last too long or too short, have too little or too great an intensity). It is frequently the case that complications of grief manifest themselves with regard to certain symptoms, while others remain at an unproblematic level or duration.

Given the variety and richness of individual manifestations of grief, and the problem of defining the parameters of normal grief, at the present state of knowledge the following definition appears to be useful: Pathological grief is a deviation from the norm in the time course or intensity of specific or general symptoms of grief.

Grief has only recently begun to receive attention from social psychologists. This is surprising in view of the fact that bereavement typically involves the disruption of significant interpersonal relationships.

*See also*: DEPRESSION; LONELINESS; RELATIONSHIPS; SELF; SELF-ESTEEM.

BIBLIOGRAPHY
Bowlby, J. (1981). *Attachment and loss* (Vol. 3): *Loss: Sadness and depression*. Harmondsworth: Penguin.
Parkes, C. M. (1986). *Bereavement: Studies of grief in adult life*. Harmondsworth: Penguin. (Originally published 1972.)
Stroebe, M., Stroebe, W., & Hansson, R. O. (Eds.) (1993). *Handbook of bereavement: Theory, research and intervention*. New York: Cambridge University Press.
Stroebe, W., & Stroebe, M. (1987). *Bereavement and Health*. New York: Cambridge University Press.
Worden, J. W. (1991). *Grief counseling and grief therapy: A handbook for the mental health practitioner*. New York: Springer-Verlag. (Originally published 1982.)

MARGARET STROEBE
HENK SCHUT

**group cohesiveness**   One of the most basic properties of a group is its cohesiveness (solidarity, esprit de corps, team spirit, morale) – the way it "hangs together" as a tightly knit self-contained entity, characterized by uniformity of conduct and belief and by mutual support among members. Cohesiveness is a variable property: some groups are more cohesive than others, and the same group can be more or less cohesive in different contexts and at different times. Groups with extremely low levels of cohesiveness appear hardly to be groups at all, and so the term may also capture the very essence of being a group – the psychological process that transforms an aggregate of unrelated individuals into a social group. Cohesiveness is, therefore, a descriptive term used to describe a property of the group as a whole. But it is also a psychological term to describe the individual psychological process underlying the cohesiveness of groups and the psychology of group membership. Herein lies a problem – it makes sense to say that a group is cohesive, but not that an individual is cohesive.

### THEORY AND RESEARCH

After almost a decade of informal usage, cohesiveness was first formally defined by Festinger, Schachter, and Back (1950). They believed that a psychological field of forces, deriving from the attractiveness of the group and its members and the degree to which the group helps to achieve individual goals, acts upon the individual. The resultant valence of these forces produces cohesiveness that is responsible for group membership continuity and adherence to group standards. Because concepts such as "field of forces" are difficult to operationalize, and also because the theory was not very precise about exactly how to define cohesiveness operationally (i.e., in terms of specific measures or experimental manipulations), social psychologists almost immediately simplified their conception of cohesiveness. For instance, in their own research into the cohesiveness of postwar student housing projects at the Massachusetts Institute of Technology, Festinger, Schachter and Back simply asked students "What three people. . . . do you see most of socially?" (1950, p. 37).

Major reviews (e.g., Evans & Jarvis, 1980; Hogg, 1992; Lott & Lott, 1965; Mudrack, 1989) tend to agree that the bulk of research conceptualizes cohesiveness in terms of attraction to group or interpersonal attraction, derives the cohesiveness of the group as a whole from summing across members (or some other arithmetical procedure), and operationalizes cohesiveness accordingly. Not surprisingly, this research reveals that factors which increase interpersonal attraction (e.g., similarity, cooperation, interpersonal acceptance, shared threat) generally elevate cohesiveness, and elevated cohesiveness produces, for example, conformity to group standards, accentuated similarity, improved intragroup communication, and enhanced liking (see ATTRACTION).

It has been suggested (e.g., Hogg, 1992) that this perspective on group cohesiveness represents a much wider *social cohesion* or *interpersonal interdependence* model of the social group (*see* INTERDEPENDENCE THEORY). Unrelated individuals come together to satisfy shared goals that cannot be satisfied individually. Mutual interdependence and cooperative interaction produce mutual goal satisfaction, mutual positive regard, and thus interpersonal attraction and cohesion. Researchers tend to differ principally with respect to which components of the model they emphasize.

Because social psychologists have not really resolved the problem of knowing unambiguously how to operationalize cohesiveness, more recent research on cohesiveness, particularly since the mid-1960s, has tended to be in APPLIED SOCIAL PSYCHOLOGY, and in particular, in sports psychology, where a number of quite rigorous scales has been devised – for example, the seven- or eight-item *sports cohesiveness questionnaire*, the 22-item *multidimensional group cohesion instrument*, and the 18-item *group environment questionnaire*. Such scales tend to be broad-spectrum instruments. They access cohesiveness on a range of dimensions reflecting task and socio-emotional aspects of group membership as well as perceptions and evaluations of, and feelings about, the group, its members, and membership in the group.

CRITICISMS AND ALTERNATIVE
FORMULATIONS
Critics of the attraction formulation of cohesiveness feel that there may be more to cohesiveness than attraction, or that attraction may actually be either a consequence or an epiphenomenon of a more basic process responsible for group membership and solidarity. These concerns have spawned a number of attempts to reconceptualize cohesiveness in terms of, for instance, commitment and shared representations of the group.

Perhaps the most systematic of these recent attempts is an application and extension of SOCIAL IDENTITY THEORY and SELF-CATEGORIZATION THEORY (Hogg, 1992). Social identity researchers ask to what extent an analysis of group cohesiveness in terms of aggregation (or some other arithmetic integration) of interpersonal attraction really captures a *group* process at all (*see* GROUP PROCESSES). To all intents and purposes the group has disappeared entirely from the analysis and we are left simply with interpersonal attraction – about which we already know a great deal. To resolve this problem, a distinction is made between *personal attraction* (true interpersonal attraction based on close relationships and idiosyncratic preferences) and *social attraction* (interindividual liking based on perceptions of self and others in terms not of individuality but group normativeness or prototypicality). Personal attraction has nothing to do with groups, while social attraction is the "liking" component of group membership. Social attraction is merely one of a constellation of effects (ethnocentrism, CONFORMITY, intergroup differentiation, STEREOTYPING, ingroup solidarity) produced by the process of self-categorization specified in self-categorization theory. This analysis has at least two major advantages over the traditional model:

(1) it does not reduce group solidarity and cohesiveness to interpersonal attraction; and

(2) it is as applicable to small interactive groups (the only valid focus of traditional models) as large-scale social categories such as an ethnic group or a nation (people can feel attracted to one another on the basis of ethnic or national norms).

*See also*: APPLIED SOCIAL PSYCHOLOGY; AT-TRACTION; GROUP PROCESSES; INTERDEPEND-ENCE THEORY; SELF-CATEGORIZATION THEORY; SOCIAL IDENTITY THEORY; STEREOTYPING.

BIBLIOGRAPHY

Evans, N. J., & Jarvis, P. M. (1980). Group cohesion: A review and re-evaluation. *Small Group Behavior, 11*, 359–70.

Festinger, L., Schachter, S., & Back, K. (1950). *Social pressures in informal groups.* New York: Harper & Row.

Hogg, M. A. (1992). *The social psychology of group cohesiveness: From attraction to social identity.* Hemel Hempstead: Harvester Wheatsheaf, New York: New York University Press.

Lott, A. J., & Lott, B. E. (1965). Group cohesiveness as interpersonal attraction. *Psychological Bulletin, 64*, 259–309.

Mudrack, P. E. (1989). Defining group cohesiveness: A legacy of confusion. *Small Group Behavior, 20*, 37–49.

MICHAEL A. HOGG

**group decision making**  Groups perform a wide range of tasks, of which decision making is probably one of the most significant. The course of our lives is largely determined by decisions made by groups: for example, selection committes, juries, parliaments, committees of examiners, groups of friends. In addition, many of us spend a significant portion of our working lives actually engaged in group decision making.

Social psychologists have long been interested in the sorts of social processes involved in group decision making, and whether groups make better or different decisions than do individuals. There are many different ways to approach the analysis of group decision making (e.g., social communication approaches, social combination models, social influence perspectives), there are many different facets of group decision making (e.g., PERSUASION, CONFORMITY, negotiation), and there are many different group decision making phenomena (e.g., juries, GROUPTHINK, GROUP POLARIZATION). Group decision making almost always involves psychological movement of group members from a relative diversity of positions to a more consensual position or to agreement on a group position – group decision making reduces opinion differences within groups. Group decision making can therefore be considered a SOCIAL INFLUENCE phenomenon (sometimes even a conformity phenomenon) that often also involves discussion, argument, persuasion, POWER, and LEADERSHIP (*see* GROUP PROCESSES – Brown, 1988; Moreland & Levine, 1994).

SOCIAL COMBINATION MODELS
Social combination models have been developed to relate the distribution of initial opinions in a decision-making group to the final group decision (Stasser, Kerr, & Davis, 1989). These models, unlike social communication models, are not primarily concerned with the intragroup communication processes that transform individual positions into a group decision, but rather with the way in which group members combine their preferences (initial positions, opinions) into a group decision – the focus is on group preferences and their change over time. There is now an array of social combination models (Baron, Kerr, & Miller, 1992). Some are complex computer simulation models, while others, although expressed in a rather formalized mathematical style, are more immediately related to real groups.

Davis's (1973; Stasser, Kerr, & Davis, 1989) *social decision schemes* model identifies a small number of explicit or implicit decision-making rules that groups can adopt. Knowledge of the initial distribution of individual opinions in the group, and what rule the group is operating under allows prediction, with a high degree of certainty, of the final group decision. These rules include:

(1) unanimity – discussion serves to pressurize deviants to conform;

(2) majority wins – discussion simply confirms the majority position, which is then adopted as the group position;

(3) truth wins – discussion reveals the position that is demonstrably correct;

(4) two-thirds majority – unless there is a two-thirds majority the group is unable to reach a decision; and

(5) first-shift – the group ultimately adopts a decision consistent with the direction of the first shift in opinion shown by any member of the group.

For intellective tasks (ones where there is a demonstrably correct solution – e.g., a mathematical puzzle) groups tend to adopt the truth wins rule, and for judgmental tasks (no demonstrably correct solution – e.g., aesthetic preference) the majority wins rule.

Rules differ in

(1) their strictness – i.e., the degree of agreement required by the rule (unanimity is extremely strict and majority less strict); and

(2) the distribution of power among members – i.e., authoritarian rules concentrate power in one member, while egalitarian rules spread power among all members.

In general, the stricter the rule the less the power concentration – unanimity is very strict but very low in power concentration, while two-thirds majority is less strict but has greater power concentration. The type of rule adopted can have an effect, largely as a function of its strictness, not only on the group's decision itself, but also on members' preferences, their satisfaction with the group decision, the perception and nature of group discussion, and members' feelings for one another (Miller, 1989). For example, stricter decision rules can make final agreement in the group slower, and more exhaustive and difficult to attain, but can enhance liking for fellow members, and satisfaction with the quality of the decision.

Kerr's (Stasser, Kerr, & Davis, 1989) *social transition scheme* model focuses attention on the actual pattern of member positions that a group, operating under a particular decision rule, moves through en route to its final decision. In order to do this member opinions have to be monitored during the process of discussion, either by periodically asking the discussants, or by getting them to note any and every change in their opinion. These procedures can be rather intrusive, and therefore one issue concerns the extent to which they affect the natural ongoing process of discussion.

JURY DECISION MAKING

Social combination models have often been tested with simulated juries, as the laboratory analogue can have very similar features to an actual jury (e.g., ad hoc collection of people who initially do not know one another). JURIES are, of course, important decision-making groups in their own right (Pennington & Hastie, 1990). They may even represent one of the most significant decision-making groups, not only because they are held up as a symbol of all that is democratic, fair and just in a society, but also because of the consequences of their decisions for defendants, victims, and the community. For instance, the 1992 Los Angeles riots were sparked by an unexpected "not guilty" verdict delivered by an all-White jury in the case of the police beating of a Black suspect. Juries are groups and thus potentially prey to all the consequences of group processes involved in group decision making.

Research on juries indicates that the initial majority position usually prevails in determining the final verdict. Close cases, which are, by definition, generally associated with an even split of initial juror positions, tend to produce a hung jury. Hung juries, which are considered a relatively favorable outcome from the perspective of the defendant (financial considerations can lead to dismissal of the case), are less likely as jury size decreases from 12 to 6 persons, and if the decision rule changes from unanimity to some form of majority. Because jurors are instructed to presume the defendant innocent while reasonable doubt remains, juries tend to have a leniency bias. This bias tends to surface (in the form of acquittal) in close cases where there is an initial even split of opinions.

Juries are rather special decision-making groups in so far as they are making a group decision about a person (but *see* appointment committees). Thus, characteristics of the defendant and of the victim can affect the jury. Physically attractive defendants are more likely to be acquitted or to receive a lighter sentence, though biases can be reduced by furnishing sufficient factual evidence, presenting the jury with written rather than in vivo testimony, or explicitly directing the jury to consider the evidence alone. In the United States (and possibly elsewhere, as well) race can also affect the jury. Blacks are more likely to receive prison sentences, and people who murder a Black are less likely than those who murder a White to receive the death penalty (11.1 percent versus 4.5 percent – according to one set of figures). Another issue is the influence of laws and penalties on the jury. Harsh laws with stiff penalties (e.g., the death penalty) tend to discourage juries from convicting – quite the reverse of the intention of legislators who introduce such laws. The jury foreperson is important in guiding the jury to its verdict, because he/she occupies the role of leader. Research suggests that the foreperson is most likely to be someone of higher socioeconomic status, someone who has had previous experience as a juror, or simply occupies the seat at the head of the table at the first sitting of the jury.

Research indicates that older, less educated, and lower socioeconomic status jurors are more likely to vote to convict, but that males and females do not differ, except that females are more likely to convict defendants in rape trials. Jurors who score high on authoritarianism favor conviction when the victim is an authority figure (e.g., police officer) while jurors who are more egalitarian have the opposite bias of favoring conviction when the defendant is a police officer.

## RISKY SHIFT AND GROUP POLARIZATION

Folk wisdom has it that groups are inherently more conservative in their decisions than individuals. Individuals are likely to take risks, while group decision making is regarded very much as involving a tedious averaging process

that errs towards caution. This is consistent with traditional social psychological perspectives on conformity and group influence processes – through mutual influence in groups, people's attitudes tend to converge on the group mean (*see* Turner, 1991). Under some circumstances, however, groups can make more risky decisions than individuals. The phenomenon is one in which a group which already favors risk to some extent (i.e., the mean of the members' prediscussion opinions favors the risky pole of a decision-making dimension) reaches, through group discussion, a group decision that is even more risky. This has been called *risky shift*. Later research has shown that if the group initially favors caution then there is a cautious shift. Furthermore, group decisions can be more extreme than the mean of the members' prediscussion opinions on a whole range of decision-making dimensions that do not involve risk or caution, provided that the group initially tends towards one direction. In recognition of this wider applicability, the phenomenon was renamed group polarization. It is defined as a tendency for groups, as a consequence of discussion, to make decisions that are more extreme than the mean of individual members' initial positions, in the direction already favored by that mean.

Thirty years of research has produced many different theories to explain polarization, but they can be simplified to three major perspectives: persuasive arguments, social comparison/cultural values, and self-categorization.

(1) *PERSUASIVE ARGUMENTS THEORY* focuses on the persuasive impact of novel information in changing people's opinions. A group which already leans in one direction will throw up, during discussion, more novel arguments favoring that direction than the opposing direction, and so will cause members to become more committed to their original position and thus the group to shift more in that direction.

(2) *SOCIAL COMPARISON*/*cultural values* focuses on people's motivation to avoid social censure and to seek social approval. Group discussion reveals the group's

views, which are assumed by members to reflect what is socially desirable or culturally valued, and so group members shift in the direction of the group in order to gain approval and avoid disapproval.

(3) *SELF-CATEGORIZATION THEORY* argues that people in decision-making groups identify with the group and construct a contextually appropriate and identity-consistent group norm (cognitively represented as a group prototype) to which they conform through self-categorization (*see* SOCIAL IDENTITY THEORY).

Because group norms not only minimize variability within the group (i.e., among ingroup members) but also distinguish the ingroup from outgroups, they are not necessarily the mean ingroup position – they can be polarized away from an explicit or implicit outgroup. A polarized norm will arise if the group occupies a relatively extreme position, and thus conformity will produce group polarization.

## GROUPTHINK

Groups can sometimes employ suboptimal decision-making procedures that produce poor decisions that can have disastrous consequences. Janis (Janis & Mann, 1977) coined the term *groupthink* to define a mode of thinking in cohesive groups in which the desire to reach unanimous agreement overrides the motivation to adopt proper rational group decision-making procedures. The principal cause of groupthink is excessive GROUP COHESIVENESS but there are other antecedents that relate to basic structural faults in the group (e.g., lack of impartial leadership) and to the immediate decision-making context (e.g., high stress). Together these factors generate a range of symptoms that are associated with defective decision-making procedures. For example, there is inadeqate and biased discussion and consideration of objectives and alternative solutions, and a failure to seek the advice of experts outside the group. A number of major American foreign policy decisions that had unfavorable outcomes (e.g., the 1961 Bay of Pigs fiasco, the unsuccessful defence of Pearl Harbor in 1941) have been attributed to groupthink in Presidential decision-making committees. Groupthink is probably a lot more common than we would like to think (for instance, the 1985 space shuttle *Challenger* tragedy may have been partly due to groupthink). It is a serious pitfall of group decision making, and groups need to be particularly vigilant in order to avoid it. A special decision-making procedure called the "nominal group technique" is available to help groups avoid the pitfalls of groupthink.

## GROUP REMEMBERING

Group decision making usually involves collaborative recall of information – i.e., group remembering. Group remembering is not simply a retrieval activity in the pursuit of veridical recall, rather it is a constructive process in which social comparisons among group members shape the resultant group memory. As such, group remembering may not be more accurate than individual remembering, but may be subject to implicit or even intentional bias (*see* SOCIAL REMEMBERING).

## INTERGROUP DECISION MAKING

Decision-making groups can often contain deep factional rifts. In fact, many decision-making groups can be considered to be interactive decision-making contexts in which representatives from different groups are brought together in order to reach a mutually satisfactory agreement. In this sense, the group is actually a context for intergroup decision making, often in order to reduce intergroup conflict (*see* INTERGROUP RELATIONS). Examples of intergroup decision making include negotiations between nations, hostage crises, union/management confrontations, and even parliament (*see* BARGAINING). The intergroup dimension introduces an additional dynamic into group decision making, because decision makers are charged with the responsibility to argue on behalf of their group, not themselves.

When people are bargaining on behalf of social groups to which they belong they tend to bargain much more fiercely and less compromisingly than if they were simply bargaining for themselves. The effect is enhanced when negotiators are aware that they are being observed by their constituents, either directly or through the media. This rather "bullish" strategy of relative intransigence is actually less likely to secure a satisfactory compromise than a more interpersonal orientation in which both parties make reciprocal concessions. Direct negotiation between group representatives is therefore quite likely to reach an impasse in which neither group feels it can compromise without losing face.

To break the deadlock a third party can be brought in to mediate between the groups (Pruitt & Carnevale, 1993). To be effective, mediators should have power, must be seen by both groups to be impartial, and the groups should already be fairly close in their positions. Biased mediators are ineffective because they are not trusted, and weak mediators are ineffective because there is little pressure for intransigent groups to be reasonable. Although mediators have no power to impose a settlement they can help in several important ways:

(1) they are able to reduce the emotional heat associated with deadlock;
(2) they can help reduce misperceptions, encourage understanding, and establish trust;
(3) they can propose novel compromises that allow both groups to appear to win – that is, change a zero-sum conflict (one in which one group's gains are precisely the other group's losses – the more one gains the more the other loses) into a nonzero-sum conflict (i.e., both group's can gain);
(4) they can help both parties make a graceful retreat, without losing face, from untenable positions;
(5) they can inhibit unreasonable claims and behaviors by threatening to publicly expose the group as being unreasonable; and
(6) they can reduce intragroup conflict and thus help a group clarify its consensual position.

Many intergroup conflicts are so intractable, the underlying interests so divergent, that mediation is ineffective. The last resort is arbitration, in which the mediator or some other third party is invited to impose a mutually binding settlement. Research shows that arbitration really is the very last resort for conflict resolution. The prospect of arbitration can backfire because both groups adopt outrageous final positions in the hope that arbitration will produce a more favorable compromise. One way to combat this is through "final-offer arbitration," where the third party chooses one of the final offers. This tends to encourage more reasonable final positions.

It should be noted, however, that although direct communication may help to improve intergroup relations, tensions and suspicions often run so high that getting opposing sides together in a group decision-making context in the first place is all but impossible. Instead, conflicting groups threaten, coerce or retaliate against one another, and if this behaviour is reciprocated there is an escalation of intergroup conflict.

*See also*: BARGAINING; GROUP COHESIVENESS; GROUP PROCESSES; GROUPTHINK; INTERGROUP RELATIONS; JURIES; LEADERSHIP; POWER; SELF-CATEGORIZATION THEORY; SOCIAL COMPARISON; SOCIAL IDENTITY THEORY; SOCIAL INFLUENCE; SOCIAL REMEMBERING.

BIBLIOGRAPHY

Baron, R. S., Kerr, N., & Miller, N. (1992). *Group process, group decision, group action*. Buckingham: Open University Press; Monterey, CA: Brooks/Cole.
Brown, R. (1988). *Group processes: Dynamics within and between groups*. Oxford: Basil Blackwell.
Davis, J. H. (1973). Group decision and social interaction: A theory of social decision schemes. *Psychological Review, 80*, 97–125.
Janis, I. L., & Mann, L. (1977). *Decision making*. New York: Free Press.
Miller, C. E. (1989). The social psychological effects of group decision rules. In P. B. Paulus (Ed.), *Psychology of group influence* (2nd ed., pp. 327–55). Hillsdale, NJ: Lawrence Erlbaum.
Moreland, R. L., & Levine, J. M. (1994). *Understanding small groups*. Boston, MA: Allyn & Bacon.
Pennington, N., & Hastie, R. (1990). Practical implications of psychological research

on juror and jury decision-making. *Personality and Social Psychology Bulletin, 16*, 90–105.

Pruitt, D. G., & Carnevale, P. (1993). *Negotiating and social conflict*. Buckingham: Open University Press; Monterey, CA: Brooks/Cole.

Stasser, G., Kerr, N. L., & Davis, J. H. (1989). Influence processes and consensus models in decision-making groups. In P. B. Paulus (Ed.), *Psychology of group influence* (2nd ed., pp. 279–326). Hillsdale, NJ: Lawrence Erlbaum.

Turner, J. C. (1991). *Social influence*. Milton Keynes: Open University Press; Monterey, CA: Brooks/Cole.

MICHAEL A. HOGG

**group polarization** A tendency for groups to make decisions that are more extreme than the mean of members' initial positions, in the direction already favoured by that mean (Isenberg, 1986). Furthermore, members' private opinions converge on this polarized decision. Group polarization challenges the more usual CONFORMITY perspective in social psychology that considers social pressure in groups to have an averaging, not extremitizing, effect. There are three major explanations, each of which has empirical support:

(1) PERSUASIVE ARGUMENTS THEORY (*see also* INFORMATIONAL INFLUENCE) – through discussion extreme groups produce a pool of novel extreme arguments that persuade members (novel information is intrinsically persuasive) to embrace even more extreme positions;

(2) cultural values theories (*see* NORMATIVE INFLUENCE) – people infer from the initial group position what is the culturally valued pole of an attitudinal dimension, and then publicly espouse that pole more strongly in order to gain social approval; and

(3) SELF-CATEGORIZATION THEORY (*see also* SOCIAL IDENTITY THEORY) – members of an initially extreme group generate and conform (through self-categorization) to an ingroup norm that is subjectively polarized to differentiate ingroup from non-ingroup (Turner, 1991).

*See also*: SELF-CATEGORIZATION THEORY; SOCIAL IDENTITY THEORY.

BIBLIOGRAPHY
Isenberg, D. J. (1986). Group polarization: A critical review and meta-analysis. *Journal of Personality and Social Psychology, 50*, 1141–51.

Turner, J. C. (1991). *Social influence*. Milton Keynes: Open University Press; Monterey, CA: Brooks/Cole.

MICHAEL A. HOGG

**group processes** The study of group processes is enormously wide ranging. It can focus on individual cognitive and motivational processes that produce group behaviors, interpersonal processes among more than two people, cognitive and social processes that cause people to conceive of themselves as group members and behave accordingly, intergroup relations that affect intragroup processes, the interrelationship of individual, interpersonal, and social processes, the behavior of specific groups or types of group, and so forth (Baron, Kerr, & Miller, 1992; Brown, 1988; Hogg & Abrams, 1988; Moreland & Levine, 1994). What unites this diversity is a focus on the group as a social psychological entity.

DEFINING THE GROUP
There is, however, little agreement on a social psychological definition of the group. The prevalent view (since Floyd Allport in the early 1920s) is that a group is a collection of individuals, and that group processes are actually individual or interpersonal processes among a number of people. For instance, Latané's SOCIAL IMPACT THEORY attributes differences between interpersonal and group behavior to, among other things, the effects of increasing the number of people. An alternative perspective is that groups and group behavior are qualitatively distinct from individuals and interpersonal behavior, and that

different or additional concepts are required to analyze groups. This perspective is represented by the work of, for example, William McDougall (in the 1920s), Muzafer Sherif, Henri Tajfel, and presently by social identity theory, self-categorization theory, and intergroup approaches. It is argued that the analysis of groups in terms only of interpersonal processes is reductionist – it does not adequately address questions to do with group processes, but instead deals only with interpersonal processes among more than two people.

The issue of "What is a group?" continues to fuel this important, and unresolved, metatheoretical debate in social psychology. Although many researchers adhere to one view or the other, a large number opt out of the formal controversy. This is particularly true of an increasing number of scholars who research group processes from more applied perspectives – e.g., sport psychology and organizational behavior.

STUDYING GROUP PROCESSES
Traditionally the study of group processes has been at the very heart of social psychology. It was in many ways the enormous explosion in the late 1940s and early 1950s of research into what was then called group dynamics that really set experimental social psychology off on its current expansion. Even now, early group dynamics researchers like Kurt Lewin and Leon Festinger still have significant impact on the discipline. Group processes research thrived until about the mid-1960s when it suffered a fairly rapid decline in popularity (replaced by ATTRIBUTION THEORIES, then SOCIAL COGNITION), from which it is only now showing signs of recovery (Moreland, Hogg, & Hains, in press), and then often in disciplines outside of mainstream social psychology (Levine & Moreland, 1990). The apparent demise of group processes may be due to a variety of factors (Steiner, 1974). For instance:

(1) it is time consuming and costly to conduct research with interactive groups;
(2) data from group research are rarely neat, tidy, and easily explained;
(3) the computer revolution shifted social psychological interest from the study of

groups to the development of theories of individual human behavior that resembled computer software; and
(4) the logical endpoint of reductionist perspectives on group processes is to focus exclusively on individual psychology.

GROUP FORMATION, COMMITMENT, AND IDENTITY
A pivotal concept in the study of group processes is GROUP COHESIVENESS. It addresses the overall solidarity of groups, their "groupness", and the process that transforms an aggregate of unrelated individuals into a psychological group. The core idea is that through cooperative interdependence in the pursuit of shared goals, individuals become attracted to one another, the group, and the group's goals. In this way a group forms, and its overall cohesiveness is some form of arithmetic combination of individual members' attraction to one another and the group. This attraction-to-group, or interpersonal attraction, analysis has not gone unchallenged, and recent perspectives place an emphasis on some form of commitment to group, or self-definition in terms of group membership (Hogg, 1992). For instance, social identity theory does not consider attraction-to-group to be the basic process of group formation, but rather one of a range of consequences of a process of identification with the group (i.e., self-categorization in terms of the group's defining features – see self-categorization theory). Moreland and Levine have developed a group socialization model to address what they consider to be a lack of diachronic perspective in many models of group formation and development. Commitment is considered the most basic process – it is produced as a consequence of ongoing cost–benefit analyses of membership (of the ingroup and possible outgroups) by both the group and its members, and it suffers qualitative discontinuities (called role transitions) during members' passage through the group.

GROUP INFLUENCE
Groups influence the attitudes and behaviors of their members (Paulus, 1989; Turner,

1991) – *see* SOCIAL INFLUENCE. One way in which this comes about is through direct influence attempts in which individuals, subgroups, or the group as a whole try to persuade (*see* PERSUASION) members (deviants, dissenters) to go along with or come into line with the group. Persuasion attempts may range from relatively polite requests all the way to direct orders (*see* OBEDIENCE) backed up by threats and ultimately force. Persuasion is generally more effective if the source of influence has a degree of legitimate authority and POWER within the group (*see* LEADERSHIP). Direct influence generally produces behavioral COMPLIANCE which is not necessarily matched by underlying cognitive or attitudinal change – people go along with the group for instrumental reasons which often include a desire to be evaluated favorably.

Groups can also influence members indirectly through the power of social NORMS that describe and prescribe appropriate behavior for group members in that context. In the absence of direct social pressure people conform to group norms (*see* CONFORMITY). This may happen through NORMATIVE INFLUENCE in which people simply publicly comply in order to obtain social approval or avoid disapproval from others – there is no underlying cognitive change. Another process is INFORMATIONAL INFLUENCE which produces true conformity – underlying cognitive change which goes along with behavioral change. Informational influence is effective where people are uncertain about the objective correctness of their beliefs, and in the absence of objective criteria they use group members' behaviors as social criteria (*see* SOCIAL COMPARISON). A third process is called "referent informational influence" (*see* SOCIAL IDENTITY THEORY) in which people who identify with a group construct a contextually appropriate norm that defines the ingroup in contrast to relevant outgroups, and then enact the norm as an automatic consequence of self-categorization (*see* SELF-CATEGORIZATION THEORY).

## GROUP STRUCTURE

While norms and social influence processes tend to produce uniformity within groups, other factors introduce unevenness and variability across the group – i.e., structure the group into different regions. Aspects of GROUP STRUCTURE can surface through intragroup patterns of who prefers or likes whom – called "sociometric choice." Groups usually embrace a number of different roles that can be occupied by different people, or by subgroups of people. Roles prescribe behavior, and they emerge to assist the group to function better as an integrated entity. Roles are rarely equal – some are more desirable than others, and have more power, prestige, and status attached to them. In this way, groups are often internally structured into role hierarchies. The most high status and prestigious role in a group is usually the leadership role. Another feature of group structure is the ease with which members or role occupants can communicate with one another. Depending on the group's task, different communication structures can emerge – highly centralized structures channel all communication through a single communication hub (often the leader), while less centralized networks allow freer communication among all members. The nature of the communication network affects group functioning, task performance, member satisfaction, and group solidarity. For instance, highly centralized networks can, under certain circumstances, reduce efficiency, cause peripheral members to feel excluded and dissatisfied, and even reduce group cohesion. Communication networks can be traced and described using Bales' INTERACTION PROCESS ANALYSIS method, which documents who communicates what with whom, and how often.

## GROUP PERFORMANCE

Since groups often exist to perform specific tasks, an important question to ask is whether groups perform better or worse than individuals. This is an extension of an even more fundamental question of how individual task performance is affected by the presence of others. Coactors or a passive audience tend to improve performance of a well-learned or easy task, but impede performance of a poorly learned or difficult task (*see* SOCIAL FACILITATION). In general, however, groups are interactive entities, and the question becomes one of whether the task is better accomplished by interaction in a group, or simply by individuals working alone. The answer to this question is that it depends on the specific nature of the task – for instance, more cars can be produced by a group effort based on a coordinated division of labor, than by individuals building them from scratch (*see* GROUP PRODUCTIVITY).

Groups can often perform less well than would be suggested by the sum of the abilities or performances of individual members. This can be because of coordination losses – i.e., interference between individuals trying to coordinate their actions within the group. Coordination losses may be one explanation of why BRAINSTORMING is often a suboptimal way to generate novel ideas in a group. Groups can also perform less well because of motivation losses – i.e., people in groups put in less effort because they are less motivated. This latter SOCIAL LOAFING effect seems to be partly due to a reduction in perceived personal identifiability and responsibility in the group (*see* DEINDIVIDUATION), and can be explained in terms of social impact theory. Social loafing can be reduced by, among other things, task importance, enjoyment, and relevance, and increased group cohesiveness and personal identifiability. Related to loafing is a tendency for individuals in a group confronted by a scarce resource to "free ride" – i.e., maximize their own short-term benefits with little regard for the group as a whole and thus their long-term benefits (*see* SOCIAL DILEMMAS). Many of the environmental problems faced by the world today are examples of social dilemmas.

### GROUP DECISION MAKING

One of the most common tasks that groups perform is decision making (Baron, Kerr, & Miller, 1992). GROUP DECISION MAKING is potentially superior to individual decision making because in a group there is a larger pool of expertise, viewpoints, and so forth. Groups may come to decisions slowly, but this may be a good thing, particularly for complex issues, because it indicates a proper consideration of all facets of the issue. However, groups are also subject to an array of

group processes that may impair decision making – e.g., factional conflict, biased leadership, and pressures to be obedient and compliant.

One potential problem is the tendency for highly cohesive decision-making groups, which are under stress and do not have impartial leadership, to fall prey to GROUP-THINK – a mode of thinking in which the desire to reach unanimous agreement overrides the motivation to adopt proper, rational group decision-making procedures. Groupthink involves suboptimal decision-making procedures, which generally produce very poor decisions that can have disastrous consequences. Many poor-quality crisis decisions made by governments have been attributed to groupthink–e.g., the 1961 Bay of Pigs fiasco. Another potential bias in group decision making is GROUP POLARIZATION. This is a tendency for group discussion to cause groups to come to a decision that is more extreme than the mean of the individual members' prediscussion opinions. Polarization occurs only when the prediscussion mean already tends to favor one pole of the decision-making dimension – the group decision is then more extreme in this direction.

A major focus of research on group decision-making concerns how one can predict a group decision from the initial distribution of members' views. A number of "social combination models" have been derived to relate the distribution of initial opinions in a decision-making group to the final group decision. The most enduring of these is Davis's "social decision schemes" model, which identifies at least five implicit (or explicit) decision rules that can exist in groups (e.g., unanimity, majority wins, truth wins). Different rules tend to prevail for tasks in which there is a demonstrably correct solution (called "intellective tasks") as opposed to tasks which are more a matter of taste and preference (called "judgemental tasks"). Rules also differ in terms of how strict they are (i.e., how much intragroup agreement is called for), and how much power concentration they have (i.e., how much power is located in one individual). Unanimity is very strict but low on power concentration, while two-thirds majority is less strict but has greater power concentration. Strictness and power concentration have effects on satisfaction within the group, and on the speed with which a group makes a decision. Social combination models are often tested using a simulated jury paradigm (*see* JURIES).

Group decision making usually involves collaborative recall of information – i.e., group remembering. Group remembering is not simply a retrieval activity in the pursuit of veridical recall, rather it is a constructive process in which social comparisons among group members shape the resultant group memory. As such, group remembering may be subject to implicit or even intentional bias (*see* SOCIAL REMEMBERING).

Decision-making groups can contain factional rifts, or can be considered to be interactive decision-making contexts in which opposing groups or their representatives come together to reach an agreement. Under these circumstances the group provides a context for intergroup decision making (*see* INTERGROUP RELATIONS). Because individuals are acting as group representatives rather than individuals, face-to-face intergroup BARGAINING has a relatively low probability of success – intransigence and stalemate is more likely. Third-party mediation can help, and as a last resort, so can arbitration (in which a settlement is imposed by a third party).

## THE INTERGROUP DIMENSION

The study of group processes has tended to focus on what occurs among members of small interactive groups, and does not really consider how relations between groups may influence these processes. There are, however, indications that an intergroup perspective may be useful in helping to understand intragroup processes (Hogg & Abrams, 1988). For instance, group polarization may be an intergroup phenomenon in which a relatively extreme ingroup differentiates itself from a less extreme outgroup by becoming even more extreme. We have already seen how group decision making may sometimes actually be intergroup decision making, and also how the commitment process that underlies group socialization involves an assessment not only of ingroup membership but

also outgroup memberships. There is also a whole array of group behaviors that are really more properly termed intergroup behaviors: these may include a more favorable evaluation of the ingroup, its members, and all it stands for, in relation to outgroups (i.e., ethnocentrism); discriminatory behavior against outgroups and in favor of the ingroup; and stereotypic perceptions and assumptions about ingroup and outgroup members (*see* OUTGROUP HOMOGENEITY, STEREOTYPING, PREJUDICE). Also, the extreme forms of collective behavior that occur in crowds are sometimes best explained in intergroup terms (*see* CROWD PSYCHOLOGY) – the crowd is a group with a passion that is guided and fueled by the group's opposition to an outgroup (e.g., football supporter groups, demonstrations against the state). Finally, group influence is not purely one-way, with the group bringing dissenters and deviates into line. It is often an intergroup affair with active minorities within the group trying to sway the majority to its own position (*see* MINORITY SOCIAL INFLUENCE).

## SPECIFIC GROUPS

The study of group processes has tended to have numerically small, face-to-face, demographically homogeneous, short-lived, task-oriented groups in mind. As such, a great deal of research has used 4- to 6-person laboratory groups of university (often psychology) students. In many cases, experimental studies of group processes have used the dyad as the prototypical group. This is based on an assumption that group processes are merely aggregated interpersonal processes. More naturalistic studies have dealt with a great variety of groups – gangs, housing programs, sports teams, summer camps, scout troops, school classes, military groups, therapy groups, juries, government and organizational decision-making groups, and so forth. Studies in the intergroup tradition have tended to be interested in cognitive processes and so have often, though not exclusively, used rather abstract laboratory experiments where groups are often only nominal and there is no interaction (*see* MINIMAL GROUP PARADIGM). Although the study of larger, naturally occurring groups in more naturalistic contexts is time consuming, methodologically problematic, and involves weaker experimental control, future developments in group processes may be assisted by more of this type of research.

*See also*: ATTRIBUTION THEORIES; BARGAINING; BRAINSTORMING; CROWD PSYCHOLOGY; DE-INDIVIDUATION; GROUP COHESIVENESS; GROUP DECISION MAKING; GROUP PRODUCTIVITY; GROUP STRUCTURE; GROUPTHINK; INTER-GROUP RELATIONS; JURIES; LEADERSHIP; NORMS; OBEDIENCE; OUTGROUP HOMOGENE-ITY; POWER; PREJUDICE; SELF-CATEGORIZATION THEORY; SOCIAL COGNITION; SOCIAL COMPARI-SON; SOCIAL DILEMMAS; SOCIAL FACILITATION; SOCIAL IDENTITY THEORY; SOCIAL IMPACT THE-ORY; SOCIAL INFLUENCE; SOCIAL LOAFING; SO-CIAL REMEMBERING; STEREOTYPING.

BIBLIOGRAPHY

Baron, R. S., Kerr, N. L., & Miller, N. (1992). *Group process, group decision, group action*. Buckingham: Open University Press; Monterey, CA: Brooks/Cole.

Brown, R. (1988). *Group processes: Dynamics within and between groups*. Oxford: Basil Blackwell.

Hogg, M. A. (1992). *The social psychology of group cohesiveness: From attraction to social identity*. Hemel Hempstead: Harvester Wheatsheaf, & New York: New York University Press.

—— & Abrams, D. (1988). *Social identifica-tions: A social psychology of intergroup rela-tions and group processes*. London & New York: Routledge.

Levine, J. M., & Moreland, R. L. (1990). Progress in small group research. *Annual Review of Psychology*, *41*, 585–634.

Moreland, R. L., Hogg, M. A., & Hains, S. C. (in press). Back to the future: Social psychological research on groups. *Journal of Experimental Social Psychology*.

—— & Levine, J. M. (1994). *Understanding small groups*. Boston, MA: Allyn & Bacon.

Paulus, P. B. (Ed.) (1989). *Psychology of group influence* (2nd ed.). Hillsdale, NJ: Law-rence Erlbaum.

Steiner, I. D. (1974). Whatever happened to the group in social psychology? *Journal of Experimental Social Psychology*, *10*, 94–108.

Turner, J. C. (1991). *Social influence*. Milton Keynes: Open University Press; Monterey, CA: Brooks/Cole.

MICHAEL A. HOGG

**group productivity** There was widespread consensus among early group researchers that individuals performed better when working in groups than when working on their own. In apparent support of this assumption, re-search on group problem solving published in 1928 by Watson showed that groups gener-ated twice as many solutions of an anagram task as the average individual. Similarly, the classic study by Shaw in 1932 indicated that a higher percentage of groups compared to individuals solved a given intellectual puzzle (*see* Steiner, 1972). However, a more adequate analysis of the findings of these and similar studies raised doubts as to whether such results could be taken as evidence for the superiority of groups over individual per-formance. Even Watson himself realized that a group generated significantly fewer respon-ses to the anagram tasks than the *same number of people working alone*. Similarly, Shaw's findings were later explained by Marquart (1955) without recourse to the assumption that the interaction process affected problem solving in groups. Marquart suggested that Shaw's groups were successful if, and only if, they happened to include *at least one member who could have solved the problem had he worked alone*. Marquart replicated Shaw's study and then compared the obtained pro-portion of group successes with the propor-tion which might have been expected on the basis of her own explanation. She created "nominal groups" of individuals who had worked singly on the problems and who were randomly assigned to be "members" of these purely statistical groups. She found that the proportion of nominal groups which con-tained at least one member who had solved the problem while working alone was quite similar to that of real groups.

It thus became apparent that evidence that groups outperform *single* individuals should not be taken as indications for the superiority of groups. Instead the productivity of a group has to be compared to the productivity of the same numbers of individuals who work on their own and whose individual contributions have been combined into a (nominal-) group product according to the same rules that determine the aggregation of individual contributions in interacting groups. The performance of such nominal groups indicates the level at which group members should perform if working in a group neither facilitated nor impaired individual performance.

## DETERMINANTS OF POTENTIAL PRODUCTIVITY

The performance of nominal groups allows one to estimate the "potential productivity" of groups, that is the *maximum* level of productivity which can be achieved by a group. According to Steiner (1972) potential productivity depends on two classes of variables, task demands and resources. Task demands include all the requirements imposed on the individual or group by the task itself, or by the rule under which the task must be performed. Resources include all the relevant knowledge, abilities, skills, or tools possessed by the individuals working on the task. Relevance of resources is determined by task demands.

Steiner (1972) developed a classification of tasks that allows for the prediction of potential group productivity for certain task types. If a task can be broken down into different subtasks, a group can accomplish it on the basis of a division of labor. That is to say, each subtask becomes an individual task and group productivity will depend on the assignment of persons to subtasks and the coordination of the subtasks (e.g., sequential versus parallel). A task that cannot be divided into subtasks is called a "unitary task." The productivity of groups working on unitary tasks depends on the way in which individual inputs are related to the group product. This relationship in turn depends on the specific task demands. For "additive tasks" such as generating as many responses as possible in an anagram task, collecting money for charity, pulling a rope or running a relay, the group product consists of the sum of individual inputs. Whereas for additive tasks potential contribu-

tion is determined by the individual contribution of *all* group members, there are other tasks where potential group productivity depends solely on the performance of the best or worst group member. For example, solving intellectual puzzles, or remembering certain facts are disjunctive tasks where group productivity depends on the best (most intelligent or most retentive) group member. On the other hand, going on a bicycle tour, eating a meal, or writing a book jointly with others are conjunctive tasks where the worst (usually the slowest) group member determines a group's potential productivity.

Thus, task type determines the rules according to which individual contributions are aggregated into group products to estimate potential productivity. According to the additive model, the individual contributions of the "members" of nominal groups are added together. For "disjunctive" (or "conjunctive") tasks, nominal groups will be credited with a solution if one member (or all members) have solved the task. Instead of nominal groups, simple mathematical models can be used to achieve the same purpose (e.g., Lorge & Solomon, 1955). Thus, for additive tasks potential group productivity should equal the average individual performance multiplied by the number of group members. For disjunctive (or conjunctive) tasks, the potential productivity of a group will be equal to the probability that at least one group member (or *all* group members) will be able to solve the tasks.

## DETERMINANTS OF ACTUAL PRODUCTIVITY

Whereas potential productivity depends solely on the adequacy with which member's resources meet task demands, actual performance depends in addition on the willingness of members to contribute their resources to the collective effort, and on the success with which members coordinate their individual contributions. Steiner postulated that actual group productivity should always be lower than potential group productivity because of process losses due to poor coordination and low motivation.

Theoretically, this assumption has to be correct, because Steiner defined potential productivity as the maximum level of productivity to be achieved by a group if members make optimal use of their resources and are maximally motivated. Empirically, however, this relationship may not always hold, since potential productivity is estimated on the basis of the performance of individuals working on their own. Although the mere aggregation of individual resources cannot result in coordination gains, situations seem feasible where the process of coordinating individual resources may result in gains at the group level. For example, a group discussion could increase the individual accessibility of ideas which would otherwise not have been retrieved. Whereas there is no evidence for such gains in groups to date, motivation gains have been documented (e.g., Köhler, 1927; Williams & Karau, 1991). These gains occur when group members are more motivated when working in groups rather than working alone. Below, we will discuss the role of coordination and motivation in the transformation of individual resources into group products.

## TRANSFORMING INDIVIDUAL CONTRIBUTIONS INTO GROUP PRODUCTS: THE ROLE OF COORDINATION

If individual contributions are optimally aggregated into a group product there will be no coordination loss. However, as Steiner argued, group members are rarely completely efficient in transforming their resources into a group product and thus coordination losses are likely to occur. Coordination losses are particularly important for tasks where all group members contribute to the group product. With an additive task like a tug-of-war, coordination losses will occur when the group members do not simultaneously pull with maximum effort in the same direction. Another example of a coordination loss in an additive task is the so-called "production blocking effect" in group brainstorming that results from the fact that only one group member can speak at any given time (see BRAINSTORMING). But even for disjunctive tasks where one correct answer should be sufficient (e.g. intellectual puzzles with only one correct solution) groups may suffer from

coordination losses. In cases where the other group members have to be convinced of a correct solution actual group productivity depends on the prevailing decision rules. With problem-solving or decision-making tasks which involve a definite objective criterion of success (i.e., intellectual tasks) "truth-supported wins" was observed as the most frequently used decision rule (Laughlin, 1980). Thus, correct solutions which were suggested by more than one group member had an excellent chance of being accepted by the group (see GROUP DECISION MAKING).

## MOTIVATIONAL INFLUENCE ON GROUP PERFORMANCE

The extent to which nominal groups outperform actual groups will not only depend on the efficiency with which individual resources are coordinated but also on how the work motivation of the members of the nominal group, who work on their own, compares to that of members of real groups who jointly work on a group product. In this section we will examine the influence which being in a group has on the motivation of individuals. We will distinguish three levels of influence: intrapersonal, interpersonal, and intragroup.

## MOTIVATIONAL INFLUENCE AT THE INTRAPERSONAL LEVEL

At the intrapersonal level, the presence of other individuals can affect group members' motivational state and thus result in an improvement of individual performance on well-learned or simple tasks and an impairment of individual performance on unfamiliar or complex tasks (for a review, see Baron, Kerr, & Miller, 1992). Zajonc's drive theory of SOCIAL FACILITATION attributes these changes in performance to the following chain of events: The mere presence of others increases individual drive levels. According to the learning theory of Hull and Spence, an increased drive level increases the speed, strength, and probability of the dominant response (i.e., the response most likely to be emitted in a given situation). Since the dominant response is likely to be the correct response for well-learned or simple tasks but an incorrect response for unfamiliar or complex tasks, this theory can account for both social facilitation and impairment in terms of the same principle.

The learned drive theory (formulated by Cottrell) attributes the elevated drive level to anticipatory excitement in the presence of others. This excitement results from the fact that we have learned to associate species mates with a variety of rewards and punishments (i.e., evaluation apprehension). Finally, the distraction/conflict theory of Baron and Sanders assumes that increased arousal in the presence of others results from a conflict: The performer, who needs to attend to the task, is distracted by the presence of others. The attempt to overcome the distraction leads to an increase in drive level, which in turn produces the social facilitation/impairment effects described earlier.

Other theories postulate that the impact of others on individual performance is due to cognitive rather than physiological processes. For example, Manstead and Semin account for social facilitation/impairment in terms of Shiffrin and Schneider's two-process (automatic versus controlled) theory of human information processing. According to Manstead and Semin, the presence of others demands attention and therefore might lead to an attentional overload and impaired performance on tasks requiring controlled information processing. On the other hand, Manstead and Semin make the assumption that tasks accomplished by automatic information processing generally suffer from suboptimal performance. However, performance might be *improved* by the presence of others because distraction from the task demands a more controlled information processing. Whatever the causes of intrapersonal influences on individual performance might be, they will occur when a person performs a task individually in the presence of others and thus will also be highly relevant for most group work situations.

## MOTIVATIONAL INFLUENCE AT THE INTERPERSONAL LEVEL

At the interpersonal level, influences on group productivity can occur because the performance of other individuals or groups serves as a frame of reference for the performance of individual group members. This can lead to changes in the motivation to increase or reduce performance. The minimal condition for interpersonal influences on individual performance is that at least two persons perform the same task independently but are able to compare their performance. Therefore these influences are to be expected in many group situations as well. For example, coacting on the same task might lead to a greater uniformity of individual performance due to the development of performance NORMS or uniformity pressures as a result of direct interpersonal comparisons.

According to Festinger's (1954) theory of SOCIAL COMPARISON, however, uniformity is only one of two motives operating in the comparison of evaluative personal attributes like ability or performance. The second motive is the so-called "unidirectional drive upward" which might lead to an improvement in performance due to interpersonal competition. Rijsman (1974) developed a quantitative model to predict changes in performance from the result of interpersonal comparisons. Considering uniformity, drive upward, performance differences and comparability, it postulates that there are no pressures to change one's performance if the performance is slightly superior to that of a comparison person, or if the performance of the comparison person is so much better or worse that one would no longer compare oneself with such a person. The pressure to increase performance should have its maximum strength if one is slightly inferior and the pressure to reduce performance should be most intense if one is clearly superior.

Furthermore, in cases where performance is instrumental for receiving a valued outcome, the interpersonal comparison of this relationship between input (performance) and output (e.g., payment) relation may lead to changes in individual performance and thus group productivity. According to EQUITY THEORY individuals who realize that their input/output relation is less favorable or more favorable than that of relevant comparison persons might increase or reduce their effort and thus their performance to restore equity (*see* Baron et al., 1992).

## MOTIVATIONAL INFLUENCE AT THE INTRAGROUP LEVEL

In contrast to intrapersonal and interpersonal influences on performance which occur even when people perform before an audience or are coacting, intragroup influence implies situations where at least two persons perform a common task interdependently. In groups working on disjunctive or conjunctive tasks, motivation losses are likely to occur because the contribution of only one of the group members determines group productivity and thus the other group members will not be motivated to contribute, since they will perceive their contributions as dispensable. However, if group members have agreed on whose contribution counts, motivation losses of noncontributors cannot impair the group's productivity. In contrast, for groups working on tasks where each individual contribution counts towards the group product (e.g., additive tasks), any reduction in individual effort will lower group productivity.

In many cases, group work on additive tasks is comparable to a social dilemma situation (see SOCIAL DILEMMAS). A social dilemma situation is characterized by a conflict between individual and collective interests. Whereas for each individual member it is better not to contribute to the group product, if he or she can share in the product regardless of own contribution, collectively it is better if all group members contribute their share. Members of groups who work on an additive task and who have agreed to share the group product equally regardless of individual contributions are confronted with such a social dilemma situation; they can maximize their outcome by minimizing their contributions to the group product (i.e., their costs) with the consequence of damaging the group's collective interests. The tendency of group members to reduce their effort will increase with increasing group size, due to lower identifiability and higher dispensability of individual contributions. In terms of expectancy value models of motivation, identifiability is a necessary precondition for comparing and evaluating individual contributions, whereas dispensability refers to the instrumentality of the individual contribution for the group product.

Motivation losses that are due to lack of identifiability are referred to as SOCIAL LOAFING, whereas motivation losses due to increases in perceived dispensability of individual contributions which might occur despite high identifiability are called "free-rider effects." Members of a group who realize that other group members are free riding will perceive inequity and thus will respond with a retaliatory demotivation to contribute to the group product. This is known as the "sucker effect" (see Baron et al., 1992). An integrative theoretical analysis of motivational losses in performance groups can be found in Shepperd (1993).

Working interdependently on a group product, however, will not always result in decreased motivation. Under certain circumstances, motivational *gains* might even occur. For groups of individuals who work under disjunctive or conjunctive task conditions, the perceived dispensability of an individual contribution depends on the relative performance of each group member. Under conjunctive task conditions, highly qualified group members will be demotivated whereas under disjunctive task conditions the less qualified group members will be demotivated. On the other hand, conjunctive group tasks should especially motivate the less qualified group members whereas disjunctive group tasks should especially motivate the highly qualified group members. Evidence for such motivational gains comes from studies by Williams and Karau (1991) and Köhler (1927). Williams and Karau showed that a person who worked together in a dyad with a less qualified partner under additive task conditions, and thus was virtually single-handedly responsible for the group product, worked harder than when working individually. This was obviously done to compensate for the partner's poor performance. This effect is therefore called the "social compensation effect." Köhler showed that with a dyad that is working on a conjunctive task, group performance depended on the relative performance of the two group members. Group performance was higher than the sum of individual performances if there was a moderate discrepancy, whereas group performance was lower than the sum of individual performance if individual performance was very similar or very dissimilar.

## CONCLUSIONS

Early research on group productivity appeared to support the then prevalent belief that individuals are more productive when working in groups than when working on their own. However, when proper baseline measures were developed, it was found that individual performance in interacting groups was frequently lower than their potential productivity due to coordination and motivation losses. Although coordination losses can often be reduced through organizational techniques (e.g. GROUP STRUCTURE, LEADERSHIP), there is no evidence for a gain in the transformation of individual resources into a group product. In contrast, motivation gains are possible. As the work of Köhler and Williams and Karau shows, individuals sometimes appear to be more motivated when working in groups rather than individually. Groups should therefore be most effective in all situations where gains in motivation outweigh potential losses due to faulty coordination.

*See also*: BRAINSTORMING; GROUP DECISION MAKING; GROUP STRUCTURE; LEADERSHIP; NORMS; SOCIAL COMPARISON; SOCIAL DILEMMAS; SOCIAL FACILITATION; SOCIAL LOAFING.

BIBLIOGRAPHY

Baron, R. S., Kerr, N., & Miller, N. (1992). *Group process, group decision, group action*. Buckingham: Open University Press; Monterey, CA: Brooks/Cole.

Festinger, I. (1954). A theory of social comparison processes. *Human Relations*, *7*, 117–40.

Köhler, O. (1927). Über den Gruppenwirkungsgrad der menschlichen Körperarbeit und die Bedingung optimaler Kollektivkraftreaktion [On group efficiency in human physical labor and the condition of optimal collective strength reaction]. *Industrielle Psychotechnik*, *4*, 209–26.

Laughlin, P. R. (1980). Social combination processes of cooperative problem-solving groups in verbal intellective tasks. In M. Fishbein (Ed.), *Progress in social psychology* (pp. 127–55). Hillsdale, NJ: Lawrence Erlbaum.

Lorge, I., & Solomon, H. (1955). Two models of group behavior in the solution of eureka-type problems. *Psychometrika*, *20*, 139–48.

Marquart, D. I. (1955). Group problem solving. *Journal of Social Psychology*, *41*, 103–13.

Rijsman, J. B. (1974). Factors in social comparison of performance influencing actual performance. *European Journal of Social Psychology*, *4*, 279–311.

Shepperd, J. (1993). Productivity loss in performance groups: A motivational analysis. *Psychological Bulletin*, *113*, 67–81.

Steiner, I. D. (1972). *Group Processes and Productivity*. New York: Academic Press.

Williams, K. D., & Karau, S. J. (1991). Social loafing and social compensation: The effects of expectations of co-worker performance. *Journal of Personality and Social Psychology*, *61*, 570–81.

MICHAEL DIEHL
WOLFGANG STROEBE

**group structure** A distinctive feature of groups is normative uniformity of attitude and conduct within groups, and normative discontinuity between groups (*see* GROUP PROCESSES, CONFORMITY, SOCIAL INFLUENCE). Against this background of intragroup uniformity there is, however, marked unevenness and asymmetry. In very few groups are all members equal, do all members perform identical activities, or do all members communicate freely with one another. Groups are structured with respect to people's roles, their status, and who can communicate with whom (Baron, Kerr, & Miller, 1992; Brown, 1988; Hogg & Abrams, 1988; Moreland & Levine, 1994). There is also sociometric structuring reflecting interpersonal preferences.

## NORMS

NORMS are emergent and transcendent properties of human interaction. They describe and prescribe the appropriate attitudes and conduct for group members in a particular context, and they furnish groups with their characteristic uniformity of attitudes and behavior. Strictly speaking, norms do not contribute to the internal structure of a group, though they do differentiate between groups and therefore contribute to the structure of INTERGROUP RELATIONS.

## ROLES

Roles, like norms, describe and prescribe behavior. However, while norms apply to the group as a whole, roles, which can be implicit or explicit, differentiate among functions within the group. Roles are not people, but behavioral prescriptions that are assigned to people to facilitate group functioning:

(1) they reflect a division of labor – only in the simplest groups is there no division of labor;
(2) they furnish unambiguous social expectations, and information about how members relate to one another; and
(3) they provide members with a self-definition and place within the group.

Although we often speak of people "acting" or "assuming" roles, the roles become very real aspects of behavior and identity. People often only see us in particular roles and so assume that that is how we really are: professional actors are easily "typecast" in this way. This tendency to attribute roles internally to dispositions of the role-player may be an example of the FUNDAMENTAL ATTRIBUTION ERROR.

## STATUS

All roles are not equal – some are consensually more valued and respected and thus confer greater status on the role occupant. Higher status roles or their occupants tend to:

(1) have consensual prestige; and
(2) initiate ideas and activities that are adopted by the group.

SOCIAL COMPARISON theory provides one explanation of why status hierarchies emerge so readily. Groups furnish a pool of "relevant others" with whom to compare oneself. Comparisons are particularly widespread on behavioral dimensions relating to roles that have more power and influence, and are therefore

more attractive and desirable. Since only a few people can occupy these roles, a majority of members will be unsuccessful and will, through social comparisons, come to the conclusion that they are less able than those who are successful. Thus arises a shared view that those occupying the attractive role are superior to the rest – i.e., consensual prestige and high status.

Status hierarchies often become institutionalized so that individuals do not engage in ongoing, systematic social comparisons. Instead, people simply assume that certain roles or role occupants automatically have higher or lower status. One consequence of this, particularly for newly formed groups, is that people who already have relatively high status in society (on the basis of occupation, sex, ethnicity, age, and so forth) generate favorable expectations and are automatically assigned high status roles in the group. Status hierarchies in groups, however, are not fixed: they can vary over time, and also from situation to situation.

## LEADERSHIP

The highest status role is usually the group leader. LEADERSHIP is a complex interaction of group task specifications and requirements, and individual behavioral styles. For well-structured and clearly specified tasks, and for badly structured and poorly specified tasks, autocratic task-oriented leadership styles are most effective. For tasks that fall between these extremes, a democratic relationship-oriented leadership style is more effective. Leadership is a dynamic process involving a continual transaction between leaders and followers, in which followers confer the trappings of leadership (power, prestige, status) on individuals who contribute most to the achievement of group goals. This restores equity (see EQUITY THEORY), but also provides leaders with the power to maintain their position even when followers call for a change in leadership. There is a paradox in that leaders are expected simultaneously to exemplify and conform to the group's norms, and to be innovative and steer the group in new directions. Innovation may be permitted because leaders acquire "idiosyncracy credits"

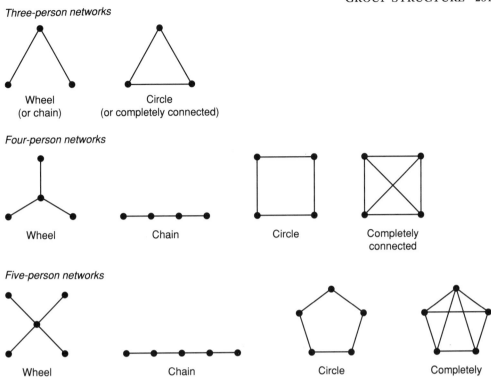

Figure 1. Communication networks for three-person, four-person and five-person networks.

as a consequence of previously having been competent and highly conformist, and having been democratically appointed (Hollander, 1958).

COMMUNICATION NETWORKS

People occupying different roles in a group coordinate their actions through COMMUNICATION. Thus, the role structure of a group entails an internal communication network that regulates who communicates with whom (*see* figure 1). Although such networks can be informal, we are probably more familiar with the rigidly formalized ones found in large organizations and bureaucracies. Communication networks vary in the number of communication links to be crossed for one person to communicate with another. As networks become more centralized it becomes increasingly difficult for people to communicate freely with all other members; instead all communication passes through a single "hub" person.

For simple tasks centralization improves group performance – the hub is able to receive, integrate, and pass on information efficiently, freeing peripheral members to concentrate on their roles. For complex tasks centralization impairs group performance – the hub is overwhelmed by the quantity and complexity of information requiring assimilation, integration and communication. Coordination is disrupted, delays and miscommunication occur, and efficiency suffers. However, centralization for complex tasks can pay off, in the long run, if appropriate procedures have been established and learned.

Because they are dependent on the hub for regulation and flow of information, peripheral members have less power in the group, and can feel restricted, dependent, and dissatisfied, while hub members, who are often the group leaders, are relatively autonomous and feel satisfied. Centralized communication networks can thus reduce group satisfaction, harmony, and solidarity, and instead produce internal conflict.

## SUBGROUPS

One final feature of group structure is the existence of subgroups and cliques. These can often be based on large-scale social category membership, like sex, age, or ethnicity, or on differing ideological or attitudinal positions. Subgroups relate to one another within the group in terms of their wider intergroup relations outside the group – as such, this aspect of group structure may be more appropriately analyzed as a case of intergroup relations (*see* SOCIAL IDENTITY THEORY).

*See also*: COMMUNICATION; GROUP PROCESSES; INTERGROUP RELATIONS; LEADERSHIP; NORMS; SOCIAL COMPARISON; SOCIAL IDENTITY THEORY; SOCIAL INFLUENCE.

BIBLIOGRAPHY

Baron, R. S., Kerr, N. L., & Miller, N. (1992). *Group process, group decision, group action*. Buckingham: Open University Press; Monterey, CA: Brooks/Cole.

Brown, R. (1988). *Group processes: Dynamics within and between groups*. Oxford: Basil Blackwell.

Hogg, M. A., & Abrams, D. (1988). *Social identifications: A social psychology of intergroup relations and group processes*. London & New York: Routledge.

—— & Vaughan, G. M. (1995). *Social psychology*: An introduction. Hemel Hempstead: Harvester Wheatsheaf.

Hollander, E. P. (1958). Conformity, status, and idiosyncrasy credit. *Psychological Review*, 65, 117–27.

Moreland, R. L., & Levine, J. M. (1994). *Understanding small groups*. Boston, MA: Allyn & Bacon.

                                    MICHAEL A. HOGG

**groupthink**    "A mode of thinking that people engage in when they are deeply involved in a cohesive ingroup, when members' strivings for unanimity override their motivation to realistically appraise alternative courses of action" (Janis, 1982, p. 9; Janis & Mann, 1977). The presence of a directive leader strengthens concurrence-seeking behavior. Groupthink is a deficient GROUP DECISION MAKING process that has a high probability of producing poor decisions with disastrous consequences.

## THEORY

The principal cause of groupthink is excessive GROUP COHESIVENESS, but there are other antecedents that relate to:

(1) basic structural faults in the group (i.e., insulation of the group, lack of a tradition of impartial leadership, lack of norms requiring proper decision-making procedures, and homogeneity of members' social background and ideology); and

(2) the immediate decision-making context (i.e., high stress from external threats, low hope of a better solution than that proposed by the leader, and low self-esteem induced by members' perceptions of recent failures, moral dilemmas, and excessive decision-making difficulties).

Together these factors encourage concurrence-seeking, and produce a set of eight symptoms of groupthink (i.e., illusion of invulnerability, collective efforts to rationalize, unquestioned belief in the group's inherent morality, stereotyped views of enemy leaders as weak or stupid, direct pressure on dissenters to comply with the group, self-censorship of deviations from group consensus, shared illusions of unanimity, and emergence of self-appointed "mind-guards" to screen the group from adverse information). These, in turn, generate seven symptoms that are associated with defective decision-making procedures (i.e., discussion is limited to few alternatives, originally preferred solutions are not reevaluated, initially discarded solutions are not reevaluated, advice of experts is not sought, advice which is presented is selectively attended to in a biased manner, objectives are incompletely surveyed, and the reactions of people and groups outside the decision-making group are not anticipated and so no contingency plans are developed).

## RESEARCH FINDINGS

The term groupthink was originally coined by Janis (1982 – first published in 1972).

Janis employed an archival method, relying on retrospective accounts and CONTENT ANALYSIS to compare American presidential decision-making groups which had been responsible for foreign policy decisions that had unfavorable or disastrous outcomes (e.g., the 1961 Bay of Pigs fiasco, the failure to anticipate the attack on Pearl Harbor in 1941) with others that had been responsible for decisions that had favorable outcomes (e.g., the 1962 Cuban missile crisis). The group decision-making process that produced the poor decisions with unfavorable outcomes was called groupthink, and was characterized by a mode of thinking in cohesive groups in which the desire to reach unanimous agreement overwhelmed and suppressed the motivation to adopt proper rational decision-making procedures.

Other descriptive studies of groupthink are relatively plentiful. In addition to decisions made by scientific, technological, business, and industrial groups, these studies have reanalyzed Janis's original presidential decision-making groups and have also investigated the Watergate cover-up, the bungled Iran hostage rescue attempt, and the 1985 space shuttle *Challenger* tragedy. The data are broadly supportive of the main features of the model, but they do not permit a conclusive examination of the important causal role of cohesiveness and concurrence-seeking. Experimental studies have been conducted to address this issue. Experiments are less numerous and are less supportive – particularly of the crucial causal role of cohesiveness. Experiments tend to establish background conditions for groupthink in four-person laboratory or quasi-naturalistic groups, and then manipulate cohesiveness (usually as strangers versus friends) and either a leadership variable (directiveness or need-for-power) or procedural directions for effective decision-making. Some experiments have found no relationship between cohesiveness and groupthink, some have found a positive relationship only under certain conditions (e.g., when there is an explicit groupthink norm), and some have found a negative relationship.

## CONCEPTUAL PROBLEMS AND ALTERNATIVE APPROACHES

These problems have encouraged people to suggest other ways to approach the explanation of groupthink (*see* Aldag & Fuller, 1993; Hogg, 1992; Longley & Pruitt, 1980).

(1) Group cohesiveness may need to be more precisely defined before its relationship to groupthink can be specified – presently it ranges from close friendship to group-based liking. At very least we need to know whether groupthink is due to overly close friendship in a small group (i.e., close interpersonal relationships rather than group solidarity), or due to lavish interindividual regard grounded in excessive group solidarity.

(2) It has been suggested that groupthink may be a specific instance of GROUP POLARIZATION in which a group that already tends towards making a risky decision polarizes through discussion to an even more risky decision (i.e., there is a "risky shift") – thus increasing the probability of the decision having disastrous negative consequences.

(3) Others have suggested that groupthink is not really a group process at all but an aggregation of individual coping-responses to excessive stress (*see* STRESS AND COPING). Group members are under decision-making stress and adopt defensive coping strategies to minimize stress. These strategies are behaviors that involve suboptimal decision-making procedures that are the symptoms of groupthink. The behaviors are mutually reinforced by members of the group and thus can produce defective group decisions.

## COMBATING GROUPTHINK

Conceptual problems notwithstanding, groupthink is a real group decision-making problem that can have disastrous consequences. It is, therefore, important for decision-making groups to be aware of ways to minimize groupthink. One such procedure, called the "nominal group technique," specifies a formal set of procedures for group decision-making that in effect establish a counter-groupthink norm. Individuals:

(1) identify the problem;
(2) write down solutions which are presented to the group for clarification and evaluation; and
(3) privately rank each solution.

The group then selects the highest ranking solution as the group decision.

*Also see*: CONTENT ANALYSIS; GROUP COHESIVENESS; GROUP DECISION MAKING; STRESS AND COPING.

BIBLIOGRAPHY
Aldag, R. J., & Fuller, S. R. (1993). Beyond fiasco: A reappraisal of the groupthink phenomenon and a new model of group decision processes. *Psychological Bulletin, 113*, 533–52.
Hogg, M. A. (1992). *The social psychology of group cohesiveness: From attraction to social identity*. London: Harvester Wheatsheaf; New York: New York University Press.
Janis, I. L. (1982). *Groupthink: Psychological studies of policy decisions and fiascos* (2nd ed.). Boston, MA: Houghton Mifflin.
——& Mann, L. (1977). *Decision making*. New York: Free Press.
Longley, J., & Pruitt, D. G. (1980). Groupthink: A critique of Janis's theory. In L. Wheeler (Ed.), *Review of personality and social psychology* (Vol. 1, pp. 74–93). Beverly Hills, CA: Sage.

MICHAEL A. HOGG

**guilt and shame**  These emotions are both characterized by self-reproach. There is considerable disagreement about what differences, if any, exist between these EMOTIONAL EXPERIENCES.

What little consensus there is has formed around a proposal by Lewis (1971) that guilt is focused on specific blameworthy actions that one has performed, whereas shame is focused on the inadequacy of the entire self. On this account, the negative evaluation of shame is more global and painful than that of guilt.

Shame may therefore produce an inward focus, a sense of helplessness, a fear of others' disapproval, and a desire to hide from interpersonal situations. These symptoms may motivate the shamed person to externalize blame to others and become angry.

In contrast, the very occurrence of guilt may be interpreted as proof that one's self is intrinsically good despite its transgressions. Guilt may therefore provide a sense of being able to rectify the situation; it may motivate one to make restitution, encouraging empathy and PROSOCIAL BEHAVIOR (Tangney, 1991).

*See also*: EMOTIONAL EXPERIENCE.

BIBLIOGRAPHY
Lewis, H. B. (1971). *Shame and guilt in neurosis*. New York: International Universities Press.
Tangney, J. P. (1991). Moral affect: The good, the bad, and the ugly. *Journal of Personality and Social Psychology, 61*, 598–607.

W. GERROD PARROTT

# H

**halo effect** The halo effect in IMPRESSION FORMATION occurs when one positive attribute increases the positivity of impressions of a person's other attributes. For example, a physically attractive person is perceived to have positive personality traits, and a warm person is perceived to have other positive traits.

*See also*: IMPRESSION FORMATION.

LESLIE A. ZEBROWITZ

**health psychology** This involves the study of cognitive, affective, behavioral, and interpersonal aspects of physical health. Its recent emergence reflects a larger trend toward increased integration of behavioral and biomedical science. The product of this trend is a broad, multidisciplinary field of scientific activity concerned with health, which has been referred to as behavioral medicine. Behavioral health is an interdisciplinary specialty within behavioral medicine that is concerned with health maintenance and disease prevention. Health psychology is a discipline-specific term for the role of psychology in behavioral medicine and behavioral health (Gatchel, Baum & Krantz, 1989).

METATHEORETICAL FOUNDATIONS:
THE BIO-PSYCHO-SOCIAL MODEL
The guiding premises of health psychology are embodied in the bio-psycho-social model, which stands in contrast to the biomedical model (Taylor, 1991). To draw very sharp distinctions between these two perspectives would be overly simplistic. Nonetheless, it is useful to consider how they differ in:

(1) defining disease;

(2) explaining health-related phenomena; and
(3) specifying factors whose manipulation can promote wellness, reduce disease, and optimize illness management.

The biomedical approach views disease as an aberrant somatic process triggered by a pathogenic entity such as a genetic defect or invading microorganism. By contrast, the bio-psycho-social model views disease as an organism-wide phenomenon: The organic disorder involves a thinking, feeling, behaving individual and his/her social–cultural surround. This implies a definition of health that includes a subjective state of wellness, satisfaction with physical capabilities, and ability to enact valued social roles, a set of variables often studied under the rubric of "quality of life" (*see* LIFE SATISFACTION).

A second facet of the contrasting definitional stances of the bio-psycho-social and biomedical views concerns the distinction between "health" and "illness". In the biomedical view, health is essentially an absence of physical disorder. The bio-psycho-social view places greater emphasis on factors that render individuals differentially resistant to disease, particulary social, psychological, and behavioral factors. Such a view is indicated by research demonstrating that longevity is in part a function of subjective health assessments, of behaviors such as eating habits and sleep patterns, and of social attributes such as being married and well educated.

The conceptual underpinnings of health psychology have direct implications for the nature of explanation and the specification of factors that control health and disease. Whereas explanation under the biomedical model favors a single-factor, biological reductionism, the bio-psycho-social model encourages a multilevel approach in which explanation entails distinct but interacting sociological, psychological, and biological factors. Thus, AIDS is seen not merely as a consequence of exposure to the HIV virus, but as the product of cultural forces favoring the occurrence of high-risk SEXUAL BEHAVIOR and intravenous DRUG use in certain segments of the population, individual SOCIALIZATION, and social–psychological processes activated when the individual is confronted by risky behavioral choices (*see* RISK). It follows that the bio–psycho-social model emphasizes the individual's ability to play an active role in maintaining good health, maximizing resistance to disease, and optimizing illness management. Health promotion and disease control become matters of individual and community knowledge, attitudes, and behavior, as much as they are matters for medical practitioners and the health-care system.

## SUBSTANTIVE THEORETICAL MODELS IN HEALTH PSYCHOLOGY

A number of specific theoretical models have been used to guide research in health psychology. Several have been drawn directly from traditional areas of social psychology. For example, the THEORY OF REASONED ACTION has been employed in research on the role of normative beliefs, attitudes, and intentions in determining health-related behaviors such as contraception and drug use. SOCIAL COMPARISON principles have been employed to describe processes whereby an individual preserves SELF-ESTEEM when threatened by a cancer diagnosis. ATTRIBUTION THEORY has had a number of applications in health psychology, including efforts to explain why some individuals respond to negative life events by experiencing HELPLESSNESS and undergoing health-damaging physiological changes (*see also* CONTROL, SELF-EFFICACY). Increasingly, it appears that processes involving the concepts of SELF and personal identity may have very important implications for understanding the social psychology of health and illness.

Some models have arisen from health psychological problems but have conceptual underpinnings that are quite familiar to social psychologists. For example, the Health Belief

Model employs the concept of SUBJECTIVE EXPECTED UTILITY in attempting to explain health-promoting behavior. The likelihood that a person will engage in a particular health-promoting action is seen as a function of factors such as the degree to which the person feels vulnerable to a health threat and the perception that the action in question will be effective threat-reduction.

The model of psychological STRESS AND COPING developed by Lazarus (Lazarus & Folkman, 1984), which has been very influential in health psychology, reflects a number of different traditions, including ego psychology, the study of EMOTIONAL EXPERIENCE, and the "New Look" in perception. This model emphasizes the cognitive evaluative process of appraisal, in which the individual judges whether his/her physical or psychological well-being is threatened in a particular environmental encounter and considers cognitive and behavioral strategies for dealing with the threat, and the coping process, which involves enacting cognitive and behavioral responses aimed at removing the source of the threat or at ameliorating its effects. Research on psychological stress has identified a number of individual attributes (e.g., PERSONALITY) and social-contextual factors (e.g., the availability of SOCIAL SUPPORT) that shape the appraisal process and guide coping responses in ways that have a significant effect on adaptation (Contrada, Leventhal & O'Leary, 1990; Gottlieb, 1988).

Still other theoretical perspectives in health psychology have drawn upon control-theoretical principles to provide a model of the person coping with illness threats. For example, Leventhal's (Leventhal, Myer, & Nerenz, 1980) Common Sense Illness model emphasizes the active role played by the person in developing a lay theory to explain an illness episode. Illness representations are based on both abstract information about the health threat and concrete bodily symptoms. These inputs lead the person to arrive at judgments regarding the identity of the condition, its best label, likely causes and consequences, temporal attributes (e.g., acute, chronic, cyclic), and potential cures. The illness representation generates coping procedures executed as a means of dealing with the condition. The individual then appraises the success of these efforts, and makes appropriate adjustments in subsequent coping actions. Problems arise when the illness representation is inaccurate and when criteria for appraising coping efforts are inappropriate. For example, if an individual holds the inaccurate belief that it is possible to know when his/her blood pressure is high because this produces headaches or dizziness, and erroneously views hypertension as an acute condition, that individual may take medicine only when symptomatic. This would lead to less than optimal blood pressure control and expose the individual to negative health outcomes such as heart disease, stroke, and kidney failure.

CAUSAL MECHANISMS LINKING
PSYCHOLOGICAL FACTORS AND
PHYSICAL HEALTH
Much research on psychology and health may be organized in terms of the causal mechanisms whereby these two domains interact. Most basic is the distinction between relationships in which psychological factors influence aspects of physical health/disease, and those in which causal direction is reversed. Both causal sequences represent active areas of research. It has become increasingly clear that psychosocial factors are among the most important determinants of diseases that represent major sources of sickness and death. At the same time, developing a physical disorder, being ill, and undergoing medical treatment and rehabilitation, may have a profound psychological impact.

*Psychological Influences on Health:*
*Physiological and Behavioral Pathways*
Turning first to the case where psychological factors represent the causal agent, and disease the outcome, it is possible to distinguish between two general types of causal mechanism: Direct, psychophysiological influences, and indirect, behaviorally mediated influences. Psychophysiological influences involve the psychological production of disease-promoting physiological activity. The construct of psychological stress is central to explanations involving this type of mechanism.

There is now considerable evidence indicating that stress emotions are associated with alterations in physiological activity that may facilitate the initiation and/or progression of physical disorders.

Behaviorally mediated influences involve overt actions (or inactions) that promote disease. Many of these entail behavioral exposure to health-damaging agents such as nicotine, ALCOHOL, dietary fat, and the HIV virus. Others involve failure to enact health-promoting behaviors such as physical exercise, regular check-ups, prompt health-care seeking, and adherence to medical regimens. Taken together, potentially modifiable behavioral influences account for a considerable portion of the enormous social and economic burden associated with poor health. That burden would be greatly reduced if it were possible to effect a substantial reduction in even a single behavior pattern, such as cigarette smoking, unsafe sexual practices, drug use, or failure to control conditions such as hypertension or diabetes (Schaie, Blater & House, 1991).

*The natural History of Physical Disorders*
Health-damaging effects of psychological factors may be further differentiated by locating their points of influence within the natural history of the disorder. There are many ways to distinguish transitions in disease processes, and these vary depending upon the particular disorder in question. Four general distinctions are worth noting:
*Primary etiological role.* Psychological factors may participate in the initiation of disease. It is suspected that psychological stress operates in this manner. Research conducted over the past several decades indicates that neuroendocrine and cardiovascular effects of psychological stress may reflect processes involved in the development of coronary heart disease (Krantz & Manuck, 1984). This mechanism may explain predictive associations linking hostile personality characteristics to cardiovascular disorders (*see* TYPE A BEHAVIOR PATTERN), and may also be relevant to findings suggesting that individuals who lack supportive interpersonal relationships may be at heightened cardiovascular risk.

More recent findings suggest that the immune system, like the cardiovascular system, may also be subject to psychological influences. The immune system serves to detect and combat pathogens, such as viruses, bacteria, and cancerous cells. Evidence indicating that immunity is influenced by social psychological factors such as stress, DEPRESSION, and LONELINESS has implications for understanding the development of infectious disease and cancer, and has given birth to a multidisciplinary research area known as psychoneuroimmunology (Herbert & Cohen, 1993).

A number of health-damaging behaviors are well established as initiators of various disorders. Two prominent examples are behaviors that increase the probability of exposure to the HIV virus, such as unprotected sexual intercourse and intravenous drug use, and cigarette smoking, which may increase risk for coronary heart disease, cancer, and cardiopulmonary disorders. Cigarette smoking represents a paradigm case for the biopsycho-social model. Factors that predispose young people to experiment with tobacco products include sociological attributes such as low socio-economic status, interpersonal influences associated with having parents and friends who smoke, and positive images of the smoker as portrayed in the MASS MEDIA. The transition from experimentation to habitual use is favored by both social psychological processes (e.g., being rewarded for conveying a certain image to one's peers) and physiological processes (e.g., ADDICTION to nicotine, effects of nicotine on affect and performance). Accordingly, efforts to reduce cigarette smoking range from interventions designed to enhance SOCIAL SKILLS to treatments that target nicotine addiction.

Whereas the foregoing illustrations emphasize behaviors that may promote the initiation of physical disorders, there is a considerable body of research on psychological/behavioral "immunity." Having a supportive social network and possessing personality traits such as optimism (positive expectations about the future) and hardiness (internal LOCUS OF CONTROL and a sense of commitment and challenge) have been examined as possible buffers against the health-damaging effects of psychological stress (*see* BUFFERING HYPOTHESIS). Specific preventive behaviors include self-directed actions, such as proper diet and aerobic exercise, and actions aimed at reducing exposure to environmental hazards, such as home-testing for radon gas and wearing seat belts.

*Course.* Psychological factors may influence the developmental course of a preexisting, subclinical condition. Associations between psychosocial factors and cancer may reflect this type of influence. Stressful life events, such as BEREAVEMENT, have been implicated in the reduction of immune competence and acceleration of cancer growth. Psychological stress also may contribute to acute flare-ups or progressive worsening of other disorders, such as rheumatoid arthritis, diabetes, and coronary disease.

With respect to behavioral influences, lifestyle modification is often critical for the optimal control of chronic disease. Dietary adjustments and exercise may produce benefits for individuals with hypertension, heart disease, diabetes, and other chronic disorders. In addition, behavioral interventions, including relaxation, biofeedback, and hypnosis, have been used with varied success as adjuncts to more traditional treatments.

*Reactions to disease.* Health-damaging psychological influences may begin specifically as a response to clinical disease. Although there is reason to suspect that physiological concomitants of emotional responses to illness may directly exacerbate certain conditions, of primary interest are cognitive-affective processes that influence efforts to identify and to manage medical problems. The efficiency with which an illness episode is resolved depends in large part upon the degree to which the person attends to symptoms, how symptoms are interpreted, and whether and when medical attention is sought. Detection of physical disorders and health-care utilization are influenced by a host of psychosocial factors, including sociological characteristics such as income and education, normative BELIEFS regarding health and the health-care system, features of the health-care system such as clinic accessibility and length of time spent waiting for appointments, and COMMUNICATION between patient and practitioner.

*Reactions to treatment.* Health-damaging psychological influences may also begin specifically as a response to some aspect of medical care, for example, medication, surgery, or hospitalization. Side-effects of pharmacological therapies, such as fatigue or reduced sexual function, may undermine motivation to take medicine. Effective control of diabetes involves a complex behavioral regimen that may include blood glucose monitoring, dietary restrictions, exercise, and medication. Adherence is especially problematic during ADOLESCENCE, a stage of psychosocial development in which the desire for autonomy from adults and acceptance by peers is psychologically incompatible with effective control of diabetes. At any stage of psychosocial development, family- and work-related role responsibilities, GENDER-related features of identity, and personality characteristics may run counter to the perceived or actual requirements of enacting the patient role, thereby undermining effective management of physical disorders.

*Effects of Disease and Treatment on Psychological Outcomes: Direct and Indirect effects*
Turning now to cases where disease/health influence psychological functioning, a somewhat different set of distinctions may be made. Disease or its treatment may have direct psychological consequences produced by effects on the brain and spinal cord, or indirect psychological consequences mediated by cognition and affect. In the latter case, psychological outcomes may reflect the individual's own appraisal of his/her medical condition and/or treatment regimen, or they may also involve the psychological reactions of others, including medical practitioners, family members, friends, and co-workers (Costa & VandenBos, 1990).

Few events produce more stress than receiving a serious medical diagnosis. To cope successfully with a serious health threat, the individual must engage in efforts to understand the experience, to maintain a sense of mastery over his/her life, to bolster self-esteem, and to manage emotional reactions – all in addition to the task of negotiating with the health-care system in a way that optimizes

treatment of the disorder itself. Compounding these demands are features of medical settings that may cause frustration, loss of privacy, depersonalization, and passivity.

An important moderator of the individual's ability to cope with a serious medical condition is the set of interpersonal relationships in which the patient is embedded. Support from close social network members, in the form of information, tangible assistance, and emotional comfort, may make a critical difference in the patient's reaction to the diagnosis, to medical and/or surgical treatment, and to the need to follow what may be a complex medical regimen and set of life-style adjustments involving changes in diet, exercise, cigarette smoking, and alcohol consumption. To the degree that social support is lacking, or that close network members become overinvolved, critical, and controlling in their efforts to help the patient, the goals of treatment and rehabilitation may be seriously undermined.

Many physical disorders have consequences that are particularly disruptive of the patient's interpersonal relationships. Treatment of breast cancer and other malignancies may involve surgical procedures whose effects on physical appearance pose a severe challenge to the marital relationship. Family members of individuals with Alzheimer's disease and other forms of severe dementia may develop a sense of loss when the patient appears to lose his/her identity as a consequence of cognitive deficits. Illness may strain FAMILY RELATIONS when it causes a member of the household to relinquish a major role commitment (e.g., breadwinner, homemaker) and thrusts others into a caretaker role which they may experience as unfamiliar and excessively demanding.

CONCLUDING COMMENT
The small sample of problem areas reviewed above, while by no means exhaustive, illustrates a number of theoretical themes worth emphasizing. One is a view of the person as an active, thinking problem solver, who appraises health threats and other stressors and formulates and evaluates strategies for coping with threat. Another is the importance of the

social–cultural context, whose demands, constraints, and resources shape the health threats likely to confront the person, the person's view of these threats, and the available courses of action. A third theme is the remarkable potential for interactions across three levels of analysis – individual, social, and biological – interactions that confirm the bio-psycho-social model underlying health psychology.

*See also*: ADDICTION; ADOLESCENCE; ATTRIBUTION THEORIES; COMMUNICATION; CONTROL; DEPRESSION; EMOTIONAL EXPERIENCE; FAMILY RELATIONS; GENDER; LIFE SATISFACTION; LONELINESS; MASS MEDIA; PERSONALITY; RISK; SELF; SELF-ESTEEM; SEXUAL BEHAVIOR; SOCIAL COMPARISON; SOCIAL SKILLS; SOCIAL SUPPORT; SOCIALIZATION; STRESS AND COPING; WORK.

BIBLIOGRAPHY
Contrada, R. J., Leventhal, H., & O'Leary, A. (1990). Personality and health. In L. Pervin (Ed.), *Handbook of personality* (pp. 638–69). New York: Guilford Press.
Costa, P. T., & VandenBos, G. R. (1990). *Psychological aspects of serious illness: Chronic conditions, fatal diseases, and clinical care*. Washington, DC: American Psychological Association.
Gatchel, R. J., Baum, A., & Krantz, D. S. (1989). *An introduction to health psychology* (2nd ed.). New York: Random House.
Gottlieb, B. H. (1988). *Marshalling social support; Format, processes, and effects*. Newbury Park, CA: Sage
Herbert, T. B., & Cohen, S. (1993). Depression and immunity: A meta-analytic review. *Psychological Bulletin, 113,* 472–86.
Krantz, D. S., & Manuck, S. B. (1984). Acute psychophysiologic reactivity and risk of cardiovascular disease: A review and methodological critique. *Psychological Bulletin, 96,* 435–64.
Lazarus, R. S., & Folkman, S. (1984). *Stress, appraisal, and coping*. New York: Springer–Verlag.
Leventhal, H., Meyer, D., & Nerenz, D. (1980). The common-sense representation of illness danger. In S. Rachman (Ed.), *Medical psychology* (Vol. 2, pp. 7–30). New York: Pergamon.
Schaie, K. W., Blazer, D. G., & House, J. S. (1991). *Aging, health behaviors, and health outcomes; Social stratification, age, and health*. Hillsdale, NJ: Lawrence Erlbaum.
Taylor, S. E. (1991). *Health psychology* (2nd ed.). New York: McGraw-Hill.
RICHARD J. CONTRADA

**helping behavior**  Voluntary acts performed with the intent of providing benefit to another person (Piliavin, Dovidio, Gaertner, & Clark, 1981). It is one example of the broader category of PROSOCIAL BEHAVIOR, behavior that is valued by the individual's society. The empirical work on helping has been relatively recent: Over 98 percent of the research on this topic has been published since 1962 (Dovidio, 1984).

Helping behavior research has developed in several stages. The research of the early and mid-1960s typically focused on NORMS, such as social RESPONSIBILITY and RECIPROCITY, that seemed to govern help giving. By the end of that decade and into the early 1970s, investigators, stimulated by public outrage at bystander apathy and guided by the pioneering work of Latané and Darley (1970), explored factors that reduced the likelihood of intervening in emergency situations. The focus of research in the mid-1970s was on identifying the factors that inhibit and promote helping. This period was also characterized by considerable interest in developmental influences in ALTRUISM and helping behavior.

In the 1980s, researchers' questions moved primarily from *when* people help to *why* people help. They frequently attempted to understand fundamental motivational processes, often distinguishing egoistic helping (with the primary goal of benefiting oneself ) from altruistic helping (with the main objective of improving the other person's welfare). The research of the 1990s promises to provide a clearer link between the motivational processes involved in helping with more general social motivations and behaviors. Thus, two of the most central questions that have been addressed in the literature on help giving are:

(1) When do people help?; and
(2) Why do people help?

## WHEN DO PEOPLE HELP?

Much of the research on when people help has been guided by Latané and Darley's (1970) *cognitive model of bystander intervention*, which was originally developed to account for bystander responses during emergencies. Latané and Darley proposed that whether a person helps depends upon the outcomes of a series of decisions. Before a person initiates a helping response, the person must:

(1) notice that something is wrong;
(2) define it as an emergency;
(3) decide whether to take personal responsibility;
(4) decide what type of help to give; and
(5) implement the decision.

A negative response at *any* step means that the victim will not be helped.

There is extensive evidence, not only from emergency situations but also from less serious circumstances, that is consistent with this framework. With respect to the first step of the model, bystanders are more likely to notice events that are inherently more vivid and attention getting. As a consequence, they are more likely to intervene. Aspects of the physical and social environment may also influence whether people notice an event. For example, one reason why people in urban environments tend to be less helpful than residents in rural settings is that, in order to cope with *stimulus overload*, urban residents restrict their ATTENTION mainly to personally relevant events. The needs of strangers may therefore go unnoticed.

One of the basic factors that can influence whether a situation, once noticed, is interpreted as a situation requiring assistance (Step 2 of the model) is the nature of the event. Across a range of studies, bystanders are more inclined to help victims who make their need clearer with overt signals of distress (Piliavin et al., 1981). The social environment can also influence whether an event is interpreted as requiring help. When bystanders notice an event but the nature of the event is unclear, the reactions of other witnesses may shape their assessment of the situation. This process is related to INFORMATIONAL INFLUENCE in other types of group behavior; when objective reality is ambiguous, people rely on social information. Consequently, particularly when the need for assistance is ambiguous, words or actions of others that suggest that help is needed increase intervention; responses of other bystanders that indicate that assistance is not needed reduce intervention.

According to Latané and Darley's model, once the need for assistance is determined, bystanders must decide who is responsible for helping. When a person is the only witness to an emergency, the decision is obvious. In contrast, when a bystander believes that other people are also witnessing the event and that these other people can help, *diffusion of responsibility* may occur. That is, the belief that others will take action can relieve a bystander from assuming *personal* responsibility for intervention. Diffusion of responsibility is more likely to occur when personal danger is involved in helping, when other witnesses are perceived as better able to help, and when norms permit or support it. Whereas the first three steps of the Latané and Darley model have received careful empirical scrutiny and support, the fourth and fifth steps, deciding what to do and implementing the chosen course of action, have not been the focus of substantial research. Nevertheless, the work that does exist is generally supportive. People with first aid training, for instance, are more likely to offer effective help than are people without relevant training.

Whereas the Latané and Darley model offers a broad framework concerning when people will help, a *cost-reward* perspective allows a more detailed analysis of how the nature of the situation and characteristics of the victim influence helping. A cost–reward analysis of helping assumes an economic view of human behavior – people are motivated to maximize rewards and minimize costs (e.g., Piliavin et al., 1981). Two general categories of costs and rewards include:

(1) costs (e.g., effort, danger) and rewards (e.g., fame, self-praise) *for helping*; and
(2) costs for *not helping* (e.g., feelings of discomfort due to another's distress).

Current research is consistent with the central tenet of this approach. Situational factors that decrease the net costs (costs minus rewards) for helping or increase the costs for not helping facilitate intervention (Dovidio et al., 1991).

The values associated with costs and rewards are subjective ones. Thus, characteristics of the person in need and PERSONALITY differences among potential benefactors may systematically influence perceptions of costs and rewards. For instance, more positive attitudes towards and feelings for a person in need (based on SIMILARITY, attraction, or social attitudes) may increase rewards for helping (e.g., more value associated with the recipient's gratitude), decrease costs for helping (e.g., less ANXIETY about how the person will respond to help), or increase costs for not helping (e.g., stronger feelings of shame) – and thereby increase helping. INDIVIDUAL DIFFERENCES and GENDER differences in helping also may occur, in part, as a function of differences in perceived costs and rewards. For example, women may be less likely than men to help in situations in which their potential costs are higher (e.g., involving greater danger for assisting a male hitch-hiker).

WHY DO PEOPLE HELP?

Although the Latané and Darley model and the cost–reward perspective are valuable frameworks for understanding *when* people will or will not intervene to help others, they do not focus primarily on *why* people would intervene on behalf of another, particularly a stranger. Recent research that has considered the motivation for helping examines more fully the issue of why people help. Approaches to this issue have focused on three types of mechanisms:

(1) learning;
(2) AROUSAL and AFFECT; and
(3) social and personal standards.

According to the learning approach, people are motivated to help others because they have been reinforced for helping in the past. SOCIAL LEARNING, through either direct PERSUASION or MODELING, can also be an effective way to facilitate helping. Consistent with more general research on attitudes and beha-

vior, the effectiveness of persuasion is related to the nature of the message and characteristics of the audience and the persuader. Social learning through observing models has both immediate and long-term effects on helping. Again consistent with general principles, the consequences to the model (e.g., positive, neutral, negative), characteristics of the model (e.g., status, PHYSICAL ATTRACTIVENESS, similarity), and relationship between the observer and the model (e.g., ATTACHMENT between a child and parent) influence the effectiveness of prosocial models. Furthermore, temporary states or MOODS, such as positive affect, that may increase the SALIENCE of positive, previously learned behaviors can increase the likelihood of helping (Salovey, Mayer, & Rosenhan, 1991).

The relationship between the nature of rewards and helpfulness, however, varies developmentally. Very young children are usually motivated by specific material rewards and punishments, older children are motivated by social approval, and adolescents are motivated by self-satisfaction and personal conviction. Furthermore, reliance on material rewards may undermine the internalization of helping tendencies for older children (Grusec, 1991). Children who help in order to receive material rewards may be less likely to assist others when these rewards are unlikely (e.g., for anonymous help) and may be less likely to develop INTRINSIC MOTIVATION for helping. In addition, punishment for not helping may be ineffective for the SOCIALIZATION of intrinsic motivations for helping because the negative emotions that punishment arouses (e.g. ANGER, hostility) are incompatible with a prosocial orientation.

The role of EMPATHY and EMOTIONAL EXPERIENCE in prosocial motivation is the focus of several arousal and affect models of helping. The *arousal: cost–reward model* (Dovidio et al., 1991; Piliavin et al., 1981) proposes that arousal is generated by witnessing the distress of another person. When the bystander's arousal is attributed to the other person's distress, it is emotionally experienced as unpleasant; the bystander is therefore motivated to reduce it. One normally efficient way of reducing this arousal is by helping to relieve the other's distress.

There is considerable empirical support for the hypothesis, which the Arousal:Cost–Reward Model shares with several other models of helping, that people are subjectively and physiologically aroused by the distress of others (*see* Eisenberg & Fabes, 1991). These affective reactions appear quite early developmentally and are sufficiently strong and universal that empathic arousal may be a biologically inherited capacity. There is also substantial support for the hypothesis that empathic arousal attributed to the other person's situation motivates helping. Personality and developmental differences may moderate this effect by influencing either the amount of arousal experienced or the association of one's own arousal with the other person's problem.

Although many researchers agree that empathic arousal motivates intervention, there is much less consensus about the affective nature of this arousal and its specific motivational qualities. Depending on the situation, arousal may sometimes be interpreted as one emotion, sometimes as a quite different emotion. In severe emergency situations, bystanders respond with upset and distress; in less critical, less intense problem situations, arousal may be interpreted as sadness (Cialdini et al., 1987) or empathic concern and compassion (Batson, 1991). Weiner (1986) proposes a general attributional framework in which another's need for help stimulates a search for causes. The perceived causes are then analyzed (with ATTRIBUTION OF RESPONSIBILITY and controllability being particularly important dimensions). These attributions, in turn, create an emotional experience that motivates action. Weiner suggests, for example, that attribution to uncontrollable causes (e.g., illness) produces sympathy that motivates helping. Attribution to controllable causes (e.g., lack of effort) generates anger, which inhibits helping.

Arousal that is interpreted as sadness can produce an egoistic motivation to help – that is, helping another person with the primary goal of improving one's own state. The *negative state relief model* (Cialdini et al., 1987) suggests that people experiencing negative states, such as sadness or GUILT, are motivated to alleviate this aversive condition through whatever means may be available. Through socialization and experience, people learn that helping may be personally rewarding and thus capable of eliminating the negative state. Helping, however, is just one way that the negative state can be relieved; other mood-improving events can also be effective. In support of the negative state relief model, potential benefactors are not particularly motivated to help if some other event that relieves the negative state (such as receiving praise or money) precedes the opportunity to help or if people do not believe that helping will improve their mood. Thus, according to the negative state relief model, the basis of the motivation to help appears egoistic, depending primarily on the anticipated *personal* emotional consequences.

In contrast to egoistic models of helping, Batson and his colleagues (*see* Batson, 1991) present an *empathy-altruism hypothesis*. Although they acknowledge that egoistically motivated helping occurs, Batson and his colleagues argue that true altruism also exists. Altruism is defined as helping with the primary goal of improving the other person's welfare. Specifically, according to the empathy-altruism hypothesis, witnessing another person in need can produce a range of emotional experiences. Whereas sadness and personal distress produce egoistic motivations to help, empathic concern (e.g., sympathy, compassion) creates altruistic motivation. Supportive of the hypothesis, subjects who experience relatively high levels of empathic concern (and who presumably are altruistically motivated) show high levels of helpfulness even when it is easy to avoid the other person's distress, when they can readily justify not helping, and when mood-improving events occur prior to the helping opportunity (see Batson, 1991). Thus, although the issue of altruistic motivation remains somewhat controversial, there is considerable empirical support for this position.

Both emotional and cognitive (learning) factors are likely involved in the third motivational perspective: social norms and personal standards. Normative theories of helping emphasize that people help others because they have expectations based on previous social learning or the current behavior of others that it is the socially appropriate response. Two types of social norms related to helping have generally been proposed. The first is the *social responsibility norm*, which states that people are supposed to help others who are dependent upon them. The second type of norm relates to feelings of fairness, and involves perceptions of reciprocity, EQUITY, and SOCIAL JUSTICE. People will help others who have helped them. Because it is often difficult to identify all of the relevant social norms in a situation and assess their relative impact, more recent research has focused on the role of personal standards in helping.

Whereas general norms of social responsibility provide only a vague guide for general behavior, personal norms and standards are valuable for explaining how a particular person will behave in a specific situation (Schwartz & Howard, 1982). Internalized moral VALUES and personal norms can motivate helping both cognitively and affectively. The cognitive component involves expectations of behavior that are based on personal standards; the affective component concerns the emotional reaction (e.g., pride, guilt) associated with meeting or not meeting one's standards. Personal norms typically predict helping better than do general social norms. Perhaps because of similar cognitive and affective mechanisms, people who are led to make dispositional self-attributions for their helpfulness and develop the self-concept that they are helpful people subsequently show relatively high levels of helpful behavior. Also, with respect to nonspontaneous helping such as volunteering, helping may be functional in fulfilling personal needs and motives. The consequences of action or inaction for one's self-concept, values, and needs may be directly related to cost–reward considerations and affective reactions to opportunities to help. The issues of when people help and why they help may therefore be closely interrelated.

CONCLUSION

In summary, answers to the questions concerning when people help and why people help involve both cognitive and affective influences. Cognitively, people learn that helping is a positively valued social behavior and

learn when it is appropriate to help. Individual, developmental, and cultural differences occur in this process. Aspects of the social situation or one's mood may affect the salience of prosocial behavior and internalized standards. In addition, Latané and Darley's cognitive model of intervention outlines a series of decisions that bystanders must make before helping occurs. Cost–reward considerations can alter the outcomes of the decision at any number of points in the process. Affectively, the distress of another person can elicit empathic arousal. Depending on how this arousal is interpreted, this arousal can inhibit intervention, facilitate egoistic helping, or produce altruistic motivation. As many models emphasize (e.g., Piliavin et al., 1981), the affective and cognitive components are not independent. Previous learning and current assessment of costs and rewards can influence the experience of arousal; arousal can influence the assessment of costs and rewards or the salience of previously learned associations.

Despite the extensive research on helping, a number of relatively unresolved issues and unexplored areas remain. In addition to clarifying more fully the potential interrelationships among cognitive and affective influences, emerging topics include long-term, nonspontaneous helping; helping among people involved in CLOSE RELATIONSHIPS; and institutional helping (Piliavin & Charng, 1990). Beyond understanding processes in help giving, future research may also examine more fully recipient reactions to aid. Helping is not always helpful: Receiving assistance may imply one's relative inferiority and vulnerability and thus may have negative consequences for the recipient's SELF-ESTEEM and self-image (Nadler, 1991). Similarly, at an institutional level, programs aimed at providing help to classes of individuals (e.g., affirmative action) can have unintended negative consequences. The central questions in this area may thus move from when and why people help spontaneously – issues that have received most of the empirical attention – to a consideration of longer-term motivations for and consequences of helping.

*See also*: AROUSAL; ATTENTION; ATTRIBUTION OF RESPONSIBILITY; EMOTIONAL EXPERIENCE;

EMPATHY; GENDER; MOOD: ITS IMPACT ON COGNITION AND BEHAVIOR; NORMS; PERSONALITY; SELF-ESTEEM; SOCIAL JUSTICE; SOCIAL LEARNING; SOCIALIZATION; VALUES.

BIBLIOGRAPHY

Batson, C. D. (1991). *The altruism question: Toward a social-psychological answer.* Hillsdale, NJ: Lawrence Erlbaum.

Cialdini, R. B., Schaller, M., Houlihan, D., Arps, K., Fultz, J., & Beaman, A. L. (1987). Empathy-based helping: Is it selflessly or selfishly motivated? *Journal of Personality and Social Psychology, 52,* 749–58.

Dovidio, J. F. (1984). Helping behavior and altruism: An empirical and conceptual overview. In L. Berkowitz (Ed.), *Advances in experimental social psychology* (Vol. 17, pp. 361–427). New York: Academic Press.

——Piliavin, J. A., Gaertner, S. L., Schroeder, D. A., & Clark, R. D., III (1991). The Arousal: Cost–Reward Model and the process of intervention: A review of the evidence. In M. S. Clark (Ed.), *Review of personality and social psychology: Prosocial behavior* (Vol. 12, pp. 86–118). Newbury Park, CA: Sage.

Eisenberg, N., & Fabes, R. A. (1991). Prosocial behavior and empathy: A multimethod perspective. In M. S. Clark (Ed.), *Review of personality and social psychology: Prosocial behavior* (Vol. 12, pp. 34–61). Newbury Park, CA: Sage.

Grusec, J. E. (1991). The socialization of altruism. In M. S. Clark (Ed.), *Review of personality and social psychology: Prosocial behavior* (Vol. 12, pp. 9–33). Newbury Park, CA: Sage.

Latané, B., & Darley, J. M. (1970). *The unresponsive bystander: Why doesn''t he help?* New York: Appleton-Century-Crofts.

Nadler, A. (1991). Help-seeking behavior: Psychological costs and instrumental benefits. In M. S. Clark (Ed.), *Review of personality and social psychology: Prosocial behavior* (Vol. 12, pp. 290–311). Newbury Park, CA: Sage.

Piliavin, J. A., & Charng, H. (1990). Altruism: A review of recent theory and research. *Annual Review of Sociology, 16,* 27–65.

——Dovidio, J. F., Gaertner, S. L., & Clark, R. D., III (1981). *Emergency intervention.* New York: Academic Press.

Salovey, P., Mayer, J. D., & Rosenhan, D. L. (1991). Mood and helping: Mood as a motivator of helping and helping as a regulator of mood. In M. S. Clark (Ed.), *Review of personality and social psychology: Prosocial behavior* (Vol. 12, pp. 215–37). Newbury Park, CA: Sage.

Schwartz, S. H., & Howard, J. A. (1982). Helping and cooperation: A self-based motivational model. In V. J. Derlega & J. Grzelak (Eds.), *Cooperation and helping behavior: Theories and research* (pp. 327–53). New York: Academic Press.

Weiner, B. (1986). *An attributional theory of motivation and emotion.* New York: Springer-Verlag.

JOHN F. DOVIDIO

**helplessness** This state is characterized by motivational, cognitive, and behavioral deficits, and hence shares similarities with the state of DEPRESSION. It was first discovered in experiments on avoidance learning (Overmier & Seligman, 1967); Dogs were placed in Pavlovian harnesses and therefore had no means of escaping shocks; none of their reactions had any influence on the cessation of the negative stimuli (i.e., the dogs were subjected to uncontrollability). In a second stage of the experiment, the animals were placed in a cage in which they could now avoid shocks by jumping over a barrier. It was discovered that these animals still continued to show unusual reactions (deficits) in the second phase. These deficits were labeled learned helplessness. The motivational deficits that constitute learned helplessness consisted of the apathetic tolerance of the shocks. The emotional deficit consisted of a lack of aggression and resigned affects in the animals. The cognitive (learning) deficits manifested themselves in the fact that an accidentally performed escape reaction was rarely repeated. The results of these laboratory experiments were replicated with different kinds of animals as well as with humans (*see* Seligman, 1975).

*See also:* DEPRESSION.

BIBLIOGRAPHY

Overmier, J. B., & Seligman, M. E. P. (1967). Effects of inescapable shock upon subsequent escape and avoidance learning. *Journal of Comparative and Physiological Psychology, 63,* 28–33.

Seligman, M. E. P. (1975). *Helplessness: On depression, development, and death.* San Francisco, CA: W. H. Freeman.

FRIEDRICH FÖRSTERLING

**heuristics** The term "heuristic" derives from the old Greek word "heureka" which cheerfully expresses that one has found the solution to a problem. By analogy, the notion of cognitive heuristics ought to refer to those cognitive structures or processes that serve the creative function of knowledge enrichment and productive thinking. While the term was actually used in this way by some scholars, a slightly different meaning has been established since the seminal publications of Daniel Kahneman and Amos Tversky (*see* Kahneman, Slovic & Tversky, 1982) on heuristics and cognitive BIASES. According to the now prevailing definition, heuristics are rather parsimonious and effortless, but often fallible and logically inadequate, ways of problem solving and information processing. A heuristic provides a simplifying routine or "rule of thumb" that leads to approximate solutions to many everyday problems. However, since the heuristic does not reflect a deeper understanding of the problem structure, it may lead to serious fallacies and shortcomings under certain conditions. Thus, in contrast to the positive connotations of the original term, the modern notion of cognitive heuristics has attained the negative quality of a mental shortcut that frees the individual of the necessity to process information completely and systematically.

OUTLINE OF MOST COMMON
HEURISTICS AND BIASES

The most prominent heuristics, in terms of the amount of empirical research, are REPRESENTATIVENESS, AVAILABILITY, ADJUSTMENT AND ANCHORING, and the SIMULATION HEUR-

ISTIC. While the domains and limiting conditions of these concepts are not clearly defined, there is sufficient experimental and anecdotal evidence to suggest that human judgments and decisions are at least sometimes guided by these heuristics.

Representativeness is mostly applicable to CATEGORIZATION judgments (Kahneman et al., 1982). Whether an object or instance belongs to a particular category is often decided quickly on the basis of some crude assessment of the similarity between object and category, rather than a logically sound comparison of the object with all the defining features of the category. For instance, the sequence 462315 is more likely to be considered an example of a random event than the sequence 123456, although some mathematical reflection shows that both sequences are equally likely; however, the lack of order in the former sequence is more representative of the random-event category than the latter, orderly sequence. Similarly, an unknown person who is characterized as aggressive and uninterested in computer technology is more likely to be identified as a professional boxer than a teacher, although the given information is not particularly diagnostic and despite the fact that the BASE RATE of teachers in the population is much higher than the base rate of professional boxers. Indeed, the relative insensitivity of human judges to statistical base-rate information is most often cited as evidence for the representativeness heuristic.

While representativeness pertains to relative judgments of objects with reference to categories, the availability heuristic is applicable to absolute estimates of frequency or probability (see Tversky & Kahneman, 1973). It can be considered a useful but logically illegitimate reversal of the valid law that frequently experienced events are easily recallable. Although this does not imply the inverse law that easily recallable events have to be frequent (because salient events can also be recallable for different reasons), people sometimes appear to follow this pseudological principle when they make statistical judgments under uncertainty. For instance, when judging the prevalence of different causes of death (Combs & Slovic, 1979), judgmental biases reflect the SALIENCE of newspaper reporting, such that highly spectacular causes (e.g., homicide) are overestimated relative to less spectacular causes of death (e.g., suicide). Likewise, human judges typically overestimate their own contribution to various social activities relative to others' contribution, and this egocentric bias is correlated with selective MEMORY of one's own contribution. Thus, empirical support for the availability heuristic mostly stems from correlations of judgment and memory biases.

The correlational nature of most research on the availability heuristic entails a serious source of criticism. First, explaining, say, high judgments of risk by the availability of risky episodes in memory may be a circular argument unless the former is measured independently of the latter. Second, a correlation between biased memory and biased judgment (of RISK) may not reflect a direct causal influence but the independent operation of a third variable (e.g., actual risk, learned expectations) on both memory and judgment. Third, the repeated demonstration that judgments can be influenced by deliberate manipulations of memory ACCESSIBILITY (e.g., through PRIMING of risks into consciousness) does not imply that naturally occurring judgments are also determined by the selective availability of information in memory. Indeed, a more systematic review shows that judgment tendencies are often detached from corresponding memory biases (Hastie & Park, 1986), because many judgments about attitude objects or familiar persons are already stored in memory as fixed reactions or utterances. Such preformed judgments do not have to be derived from accessible memory contents at the time when the judgment is called for.

Thus, although the availability heuristic provides a descriptive account of many statistical judgments under certain conditions, its domain or range of application is not perfectly clear, mainly because the correlation between judgment and memory is difficult to interpret and sometimes disappears altogether. A modified version of availability that has recently been proposed by Schwarz et al. (1991) may increase the scope of the heuristic markedly. Accordingly, the experienced ease with which relevant information is retrieved, rather than the number of recallable events, will determine judgmental biases. Thus, the subjective feeling of easiness experienced when recalling only a few instances of assertive behavior may lead to higher assertiveness judgments than when difficulty is experienced in recalling many instances. This refined interpretation of availability (in terms of experienced ease) may actually come closer to the original formulation by Tversky and Kahneman (1973) than the usual operational definition (in terms of the number of recallable items) which has guided the greatest part of past research.

Adjustment and anchoring (Kahneman et al., 1982) provides a supplementary heuristic that can be employed for the updating and revision of quantitative judgments, although its range of application is not confined to numerical estimates. Judgment biases in the direction of an initial anchor or starting point are especially prominent in financial calculations, unrealistic temporal commitments, or comparative statistical judgments. For example, when calculating the costs of a three-week vacation, one would typically start from the basic costs for traveling and accommodation as an anchor and then adjust the sum according to all additional expenses one can think of. However, this adjustment process is typically incomplete because many expenses cannot be anticipated or imagined in advance, resulting in too low a prediction of the actual costs. Had the same person started from a high anchor (e.g., an upper limit of available money) and subtracted any expense that can be omitted, then the downward adjustment process would have resulted in too high a calculation of the total costs. However, the prediction of a primacy effect (i.e., judgments biased towards an initial value) is again restricted by certain limiting conditions. Evidence by Hogarth and Einhorn (1992) suggests that primacy effects are less likely to occur when the task is of the evaluation mode (updating the positive versus negative value of an object) than when the judgment task is of the estimation mode (calculating a quantitative value).

The theory underlying the simulation heuristic assumes that judgments are biased towards information that can be readily imagined or simulated mentally. It therefore comes rather close to the availability principle, except that the emphasis is on self-generated rather than remembered information. While the simulation heuristic may also apply to any kind of likelihood or frequency judgment, another interesting application is in the area of COUNTERFACTUAL REASONING. For instance, if an affectively negative experience such as a fatal car accident was brought about by an extraordinary event (e.g., if someone who usually goes by train has taken the car only on this occasion), the simulation heuristic should produce an emotional reaction of regret. This emotional reaction is due to the fact that the exceptional event is easy to mentally undo and replace by a more common event that would not have caused the accident (e.g., the person might reason that nothing would have happened if he or she had gone by train). Counterfactual thinking can be facilitated if a causal model is available to support the mental simulation. For instance, many medical students who have rich causal knowledge about the mechanisms by which diseases give rise to bodily symptoms would often observe some of these (otherwise harmless) symptoms in themselves and infer, through mental simulation, that they have contracted a serious disease.

Apart from the aforementioned applications, cognitive heuristics have been postulated to account for a number of other biases and fallacies. The so-called conjunction fallacy (Tversky & Kahneman, 1983) refers to the fact that the conjunction of two events is sometimes judged to be more probable than the singular component events, which is logically impossible of course. Thus, the likelihood that somebody who is over 55 years old will have a heart attack is judged to be higher than the likelihood that somebody will have a heart attack, simply because a heart attack is more imaginable in somebody over 55. According to normative probability calculus, of course, the conjunction of two events can never be more probable than one event alone. While this manifestation of a conjunction fallacy is obviously due to the simulation heuristic, other manifestations reflect the operation of representativeness or availability. For instance, if a six-sided die has four green

(G) and two red (R) faces, the sequence GRGRRR may appear more likely than the sequence RGRRR, just because the former sequence is more representative (or less unrepresentative) of the 4G:2R proportion than the latter sequence, although it is obvious that the latter RGRRR sequence is included in the former and must therefore be more likely. The latter example also demonstrates that the conjunction fallacy cannot be simply attributed to a misinterpretation of the conjunction as a conditional probability. Thus, while the task to rate the probability of getting a heart attack and being over 55 years could be misunderstood in terms of the conditional probability of getting a heart attack given somebody is over 55, such an account does not apply to the die problem.

Indeed, the different heuristics do not exclude each other but may blend into multiply determined biases. Thus, if a student's performance on a rather easy task is extremely bad, an explanation in terms of the conjunction of low ability and lack of effort is more likely than an explanation in terms of one single cause. Such a conjunction fallacy in causal attribution may be due to the fact that strong or multiple causes are representative of strong or severe effects or it may reflect the availability or mental simulation of relevant examples.

Analogical reasoning is also sometimes referred to as a case of heuristic thinking, as when historical analogies are utilized to make predictions about the future. Again, it is evident that such analogies may rest on more than one basic heuristic, such as the representativeness of the semantic or metaphoric relation used in the analogy, the availability of relevant memory traces, or the mental simulation of an analogical inference.

HEURISTICS AND COMMUNICATION
Less prominent examples of cognitive heuristics in social psychology include the "How-do-I-feel-about-it" heuristic in affective self-reports (Schwarz & Clore, 1988) or heuristic strategies in veracity judgment or DECEP-TION detection (Stiff et al., 1989). When people are asked to report their general life satisfaction or job satisfaction, they typically

do not engage in a systematic assessment of all relevant sources of satisfaction but simply rely on their current feeling as a source of information as if they were asking themselves "How do I feel about it?". Their momentary mood may then serve as a guideline for judging satisfaction with their entire life. In lie detection judgments, people sometimes lack the necessary authentic cues to make informed veracity judgments, especially when the communication is presented in written form. In these cases, lie detectors have to rely on simple heuristics based on intuitive expectations about the concomitants, or symptoms, of lying. Although these expectations may rest on stereotypes rather than valid rules, recent research has shown that such heuristic judgments may sometimes lead to lie detection performance that is as good as more accurate methods.

In the context of modern PERSUASION research (Chaiken, 1987), the notion of heuristic information processing has attained the status of an important theoretical concept. Complementary to the "central route" of persuasion where information is processed systematically, a "peripheral route" or heuristic processing mode is assumed that is activated whenever the individual is not sufficiently involved or motivated to engage in systematic and effortful processing. However, persuasion researchers differ in the breadth or restrictiveness with which the "peripheral route" is conceived, referring either to non-argumentative (affective or suggestive) influences in general or to heuristic processing in particular.

FUNCTIONS OF HEURISTICS
There is hardly any disagreement that heuristics serve the important function of simplification and economy in an extremely complex environment in which a systematic and exhaustive attempt at every routine task would cause a permanent overload of information and a breakdown of adaptive behavior. Heuristic processing helps the individual to save mental resources for the most important problems and enables him or her to cope with multiple affordances at the same time. Considered in this way, heuristics are not a symptom of malfunctioning but an essential aspect of human intelligence. The price for the cognitive economy gained from heuristic problem solving is the occurrence of biases and suboptimal performance resulting from the inappropriateness of heuristic tools for certain task situations.

Apart from the cognitive economy aspect, however, another useful function of heuristic processing is to prepare the organism for a changing environment. This aspect may be illustrated with reference to the so-called probability matching strategy, which may also be considered as a universal heuristic employed in many probability learning situations. In an operant learning task, when the reinforcement rates of two response options are 75 percent and 25 percent, the outcome can be maximized by choosing the first response option in 100 percent of the trials. By contrast, probability matching (i.e., response rates of 75 percent and 25 percent which match the success rates) leads to reduced outcomes but has the adaptive advantage of preparing the individual to deal with a changing environment. Someone who stereotypically chooses the optimal response option will not even notice when the environment changes and the formerly optimal response becomes worse or even lethal. Therefore, an intelligent function of heuristics in the long run is to maintain variability and to induce deviations from optimal behaviors that may prove extremely important for adaptive purposes.

Finally, it should be noted that even when heuristics are suboptimal from a normative point of view, they are often shared consensually and form the basis of social conventions. This conventional nature of everyday judgments may contribute to the overconfidence phenomenon as an undesirable concomitant of heuristic processing. Because of the lack of mental effort and the commonality of the underlying conventions, the subjective confidence experienced when decisions and predictions are made is often ill-calibrated. In many applied domains, subjective confidence increases much more strongly as a function of familiarity or expertise than does accuracy.
*See also*: CATEGORIZATION; DECEPTION; MEMORY; REASONING; RISK.

BIBLIOGRAPHY

Chaiken, S. (1987). The heuristic model of persuasion. In M. P. Zanna, J. M. Olson, & C. P. Herman (Eds.). *Social influence: The Ontario symposium* (Vol. 5, pp. 3–39). Hillsdale, NJ: Lawrence Erlbaum.

Combs, B., & Slovic, P. (1979). Newspaper coverage of causes of death. *Journalism Quarterly*, *56*, 837–43.

Hastie, R., & Park, B. (1986). The relationship between memory and judgment depends on whether the judgment task is memory-based or on-line. *Psychological Review*, *93*, 258–68.

Hogarth, R. M., & Einhorn, H. J. (1992). Order effects in belief updating: The belief-adjustment model. *Cognitive Psychology*, *24*, 1–55.

Kahneman, D., Slovic, P., & Tversky, A. (Eds.) (1982). *Judgment under uncertainty: Heuristics and biases*. Cambridge: Cambridge University Press.

Schwarz, N., Bless, H., Strack, F., Klumpp, G., Rittenauer-Schatka, H., & Simons, A. (1991). Ease of retrieval as information: Another look at the availability heuristic. *Journal of Personality and Social Psychology*, *61*, 195–202.

—— Clore, G. L. (1988). How do I feel about it? The informative functions of affective states. In K. Fiedler & J. P. Forgas (Eds.), *Affect, cognition and social behavior* (pp. 44–62). Toronto: Hogrefe.

Stiff, J. B., Miller, G. R., Slieght, C., Mongeau, P., Garlick, R., & Rogan, R. (1989). Explanations of visual cue primacy in judgments of honesty and deceit. *Journal of Personality and Social Psychology*, *56*, 555–64.

Tversky, A., & Kahneman, D. (1973). Availability: A heuristic for judging frequency and probability. *Cognitive psychology*, *5*, 207–32.

—— (1983). Extensional versus intuitive reasoning: The conjunction fallacy in probability judgment. *Psychological Review*, *90*, 293–315.

KLAUS FIEDLER
JEANNETTE SCHMID

**heuristic–systematic model (HSM)** The HSM is a model of ATTITUDE CHANGE proposed by Chaiken (1980) and later developed by Chaiken and her colleagues (*see* Eagly & Chaiken, 1993). It specifies two routes to PERSUASION: *systematic processing*, an analytic orientation to information processing, and *heuristic processing*, a more restricted mode of information processing that makes fewer demands on cognitive resources. Systematic processing is believed to be determined by the ability and motivation of respondents to process message content. Heuristic processing is triggered by features of the available information that enable the use of cognitive HEURISTICS to form judgments and decisions. An example of such a heuristic is "experts can be trusted," leading those using this processing mode to agree more with positions advocated by experts. The HSM assumes that both modes of processing can occur simultaneously, such that when weak arguments are presented by expert sources, systematic processing will attenuate the heuristic tendency to agree with positions espoused by experts. Likewise, systematic processing can be biased by heuristic processing, in that the perceived expertise of a source may establish expectations about the validity of the arguments from this source which then bias the evaluation of those arguments. The HSM predictions concerning systematic processing are similar to those made by the ELABORATION LIKELIHOOD MODEL in relation to the "central route" to persuasion. More distinctive are HSM hypotheses concerning heuristic processing. There are several studies examining such hypotheses, and the evidence is generally supportive of the theory (*see* Eagly & Chaiken, 1993).

*See also*: ATTITUDE CHANGE; HEURISTICS.

BIBLIOGRAPHY

Chaiken, S. (1980). Heuristic versus systematic information processing and the use of source versus message cues in persuasion. *Journal of Personality and Social Psychology*, *39*, 752–66.

Eagly, A. H., & Chaiken, S. (1993). *The psychology of attitudes*. Forth Worth, TX: Harcourt Brace Jovanovich.

ANTONY S. R. MANSTEAD

**history of social psychology** With the term "history" we mean to refer to what has happened in the past (of a people, or group, or institution). The implication is that such past events are either remembered or have been recorded. Hence, "history" comes to mean recorded events, i.e., their analysis and explanation. This systematic account of the past, usually presented in chronological order, may become an independent branch of knowledge. Although this branch is often called "historiography" it is less the writing down of past events than their reconstruction or construction from a given perspective, which increasingly comprises conceptions and methods of the sociology of science.

In histories of science as, for example, of social psychology, the construction of a discipline's past usually serves a present purpose. The past is constructed in such a way as to lead more or less directly, continuously, and with a cumulative growth of knowledge to the present "state of the art." Critics, however, have claimed that in disciplinary history unity and linear continuity tend to be overemphasized. For social psychology this critique gives rise to the double question: Is there a unitary field named SOCIAL PSYCHOLOGY? Is there one linear and continuous development of this field? Both questions have to be answered if a history of social psychology is addressed (*see* Graumann, 1988; Patnoe, 1988).

SOCIAL PSYCHOLOGY
At present "social psychology" is the name for:

(1) a subdiscipline of psychology, from which the major part of social psychological research and publications take their origin;
(2) a field of research in (micro)sociology;
(3) any of several other social science studies dealing with the individual in society; and
(4) all of social psychology, "including its two main subdivisions and its several areas of specialization" (Cartwright, 1979, p. 91), which is for some the future rather than the past or the present of social psychology (Stephan et al., 1991).

Both the preeminence of its psychological variant and the variety of social psychology across the social sciences are better understood if one looks at the history of the field.

EARLY FORMS OF SOCIAL PSYCHOLOGY
Following Ebbinghaus's dictum that psychology has a long past but only a brief history, many authors of books and comprehensive chapters on the history of social psychology present whatever may be called (prescientific) social thought from antiquity to the nineteenth century as social psychology's past (*see* Allport, 1985; Graumann, 1989; Sahakian, 1982). The justification for connecting 24 centuries of social philosophy with the last 100 years of social psychology may be found in fundamental problems shared, though treated differently, by philosophy and psychology.

Before social psychology in one of its modern conceptions came into being in the twentieth century there were in the second half of the nineteenth century two major starts towards a social branch of psychology: *Völkerpsychologie* and CROWD PSYCHOLOGY.

The former, whose name we leave untranslated (German as it was by origin and major distribution), was a comparative cultural psychology. According to Wundt (1916, p. 2), its main protagonist, it deals with "those mental products which are created by a community of human life and are, therefore, inexplicable in terms merely of individual consciousness since they presuppose the reciprocal action of many." The major sociocultural products brought about by reciprocal interaction are language, myth, customs, of which LANGUAGE deserves special psychological attention since it shapes all "higher mental functioning," i.e., cognition. Coupled with the belief that individual experimental psychology can only deal with elementary mental functions, Wundt considered *Völkerpsychologie*, to which he dedicated 10 sizable volumes, as the former's necessary and ultimately more important "social" complement.

Psychology owes to this early interest in a (nonexperimental) sociocultural approach its first professional journal (the *Zeitschrift für Völkerpsychologie und Sprachwissenschaft*, dedicated according to its charter issue of

1860, to a "psychology of societal man or of human society"). Nevertheless, this historical social psychology has not survived, at least not in psychology. Many of its topics and theorems have been absorbed by anthropology and linguistics and some had a kind of mediated reentry into cross-cultural and language psychology. But there was no continuity in social psychology, which, in its formative years during the first third of the twentieth century, became a primarily experimental discipline.

The other project for a social psychology was crowd psychology which, in its original form of assuming an "abnormal" crowd mind, different in kind from individual "normal" consciousness (as maintained, e.g., by LeBon & McDougall), was also discontinued under the impact of early social–psychological critique. Its major topics, however, namely phenomena of collective behavior, CONFORMITY, DEINDIVIDUATION, effects of CROWDING, social conditions, and forms of VIOLENCE have been preserved and dealt with in both sociology and social psychology. In the latter, many phenomena previously thought to be crowd-specific or "mass-psychological," such as suggestion, imitation, high conformity, deindividuation, and certain aspects of LEADERSHIP, are now being studied as interindividual or GROUP PROCESSES.

At least conceptually and certainly historically, the distinction between "crowd" and "group" has remained somewhat arbitrary. When Moede (1920) published his *Experimentelle Massenpsychologie* (Experimental crowd psychology) he subtitled it "Contributions to the experimental psychology of the group." His focus of research was on the "change of . . . mental functions under collective factors" (p. v). Explicitly borrowing from Wundt's conception of *Völkerpsychologie*, Moede defined the group as "a larger or smaller number of individuals in reciprocal interaction" (p. 4), which, in principle, includes the dyad and the small group, as well as larger collectives as far as reciprocal interaction obtains.

EXPERIMENTAL SOCIAL PSYCHOLOGY:
NORTH AMERICA
Moede's monograph of 1920 was, on the one hand, a deliberate break with the traditional, so-called "Latin" crowd psychology. On the other hand, it was a visible landmark of the new experimental social psychology gradually emerging from studies in which students of Wilhelm Wundt's investigated the influence of others or of a group upon an individual's attention and mental work. It was Hugo Münsterberg, another student of Wundt's, whom William James had brought to Harvard, who made Floyd H. Allport take up this research program which, under the title SOCIAL FACILITATION, became one of the enduring fields of experimental social psychology in the United States.

F. H. Allport (1924) was also influential in establishing social psychology as an experimental branch of science "which studies the behavior of the individual in so far as his behavior stimulates other individuals, or is itself a reaction to this behavior" (p. 12). If from then on social psychology has become "largely a North American phenomenon," as E. E. Jones (1985, p. 47) assesses the situation in the 1980s, at least two major European influences or imports have to be registered. The first one, leading from the Leipzig laboratory via Münsterberg to the American social facilitation program is behind Pepitone's (1981, p. 975) contention of the "German roots of the experimental tradition in social psychology." The second impact was that of the European refugees from Hitler (below).

The period from the 1920s to the 1940s may be called the formative years of social psychology (Sahakian, 1982). Almost exclusively in North America the new social branch of psychology was "mainly concerned with the problem of establishing itself as a legitimate field of empirical research" (Cartwright, 1979, p. 84). In Europe there were a few single individuals who without dubbing themselves "social psychologists," made significant contributions to the new field: Frederic Bartlett in 1932 in England, Marie Jahoda and Paul Lazarsfeld in Austria in 1933, or Erich Fromm and David Katz in the 1920s in Germany (*see* Graumann, 1989). The German-speaking psychologists among them became refugees after 1933 and in their later years contributed to social psychology abroad. But in prewar Europe there was neither a coherent social psychology nor a corresponding scientific community. The situation was different in North America since right after the first World War a societal interest in the enculturation of immigrants gave rise to the study of attitudes. In order to "scientize" this concern the first focus was on ATTITUDE MEASUREMENT. It was the proof of the measurability of attitudes that, together with F. H. Allport's emphasis on EXPERIMENTATION, gave social psychology its first credit as a scientific discipline (*see* McGuire, 1985). Yet, the first *Handbook of Social Psychology* (Murchison, 1935) contained only one chapter on experimental social psychology, the rest being chapters on observational and comparative studies, still reflecting the major topics of *Völkerpsychologie*.

But it was also in the 1930s that Muzafer Sherif, with his experimental studies of social factors in perception, of attitudes, and NORMS, ostensibly extended the range of the experimental procedures, only to be outbid by Kurt Lewin's experiments on group or LEADERSHIP "atmosphere." More than 50 years after Lewin's group experiments his contribution to the development of modern social psychology is unanimously acknowledged for several reasons. One is his boldness in manipulating complex situational variables in natural settings. Even more important was his use of a theory that generated experiments which, in turn, modified the theory. Although Lewin's own field theory, a perspective rather than a formal theory, has not survived, even within the Lewin tradition (Patnoe, 1988), it has spawned a rich variety of theory-guided experiments, mainly in the fields of SOCIAL COGNITION, social motivation, and on group processes. Lewin's lasting effect, however, is to be seen in his immediate and indirect influence on three generations of outstanding social psychologists, the first of whom, like Cartwright and Festinger, had worked with Lewin and helped him to establish and run the Research Center for Group Dynamics in 1945, which soon attracted students like K. Back, M. Deutsch, H. H. Kelley, A. Pepitone, S. Schachter, and J. Thibaut, who, in turn, trained E. E. Jones, R. Krauss, L. Ross, P. Schönbach, J. Singer, and P. Zimbardo. Even if we merely add a few names of the "third generation," such as

E. Aronson, R. Nisbett, and R. Zajonc (see Festinger, 1980), we have listed the majority of the most cited social psychologists of the postwar era through the 1980s, but also a set of scholars whose theories and research topics differ widely. Their major contributions have been to ATTRIBUTION THEORIES, COGNITIVE CONSISTENCY and dissonance theories, theories of and research on ATTITUDE CHANGE, COOPERATION AND COMPETITION; COMPLIANCE, CONFLICT, interdependence, SOCIAL COMPARISON, SOCIAL EXCHANGE, to name but a few of the topics that still help define the subject-matter of social psychology.

Finally, there is the ongoing influence of Lewin, the practitioner and social "field worker" whose conception of group dynamics also gave birth to "action research," a synthesis of empirical social research, social action, and its controlled evaluation, and to a practice that became a movement of group experience with its various centers of group or sensitivity training for educational, therapeutic, or self-actualizing purposes. Although representatives of the group dynamics movement keep invoking his name, Kurt Lewin cannot be held responsible for what happens in sensitivity and encounter groups.

Related to the Lewin influence is that of another European immigrant, Fritz Heider. His work on interpersonal relations (Heider, 1958) has become a point of departure for both the short-lived balance theory and the rather long-lived family of attribution models.

Altogether, it can be stated that from the early emphasis on attitudes to the present interest in information processing in HEURISTICS and SOCIAL JUDGMENT, a central interest of social psychology has been cognitive processes and structures. Whereas behaviorism has never had more than a rhetorical impact on social psychology, there have been theoretically and empirically significant contributions based on various learning theories. Perhaps the most salient, but controversial S-R theory (which contained psychoanalytical elements) was, in the late 1930s, the frustration-aggression theory which, with the (Freudian) inclusion of displacement, became instrumental in the explanation of "scapegoating," PREJUDICE and the so-called "authoritarian personality." Also early theories of AGGRESSION and of "imitation" (MODELING) grew out of S-R theories. But the theories of SOCIAL LEARNING (as well as of social facilitation) are historical examples for the gradual change from S–R to cognitive accounts of social behavior.

While the process of what has been called the "cognitivation" of (social) psychology is still going on, we have, since the 1980s, partly as an outcome of what, in the 1970s, was named the "crisis" of social psychology, various trends opposing the prevailing cognitivism. One of them is the (renewed) attempt to overcome the schism between psychological and sociological social psychology and their respective theoretical and methodological "preferences" (or biases). Whether these efforts toward unity or, at least, toward an interdisciplinary social psychology will lead anywhere, is presently an open question (Stephan, Stephan, & Pettigrew, 1991). A closer look at the reasons for this "unification" reveals that some of the goals Wundt had set for his (nonexperimental) *Völkerpsychologie* and which his temporary student, George H. Mead, had transformed into his conception of social psychology, are still considered worth pursuing.

SOCIAL PSYCHOLOGY IN EUROPE

Although it is historically correct to speak of a European background of American social psychology it is hardly possible to speak of a social psychology in prewar Europe. What we had was individual scholars, most of them psychologists, who occasionally did research or, at least, published on topics that were either then or very much later labeled "social psychology." The term itself was still very broad comprising everything from psychological studies of society through treatises rather than research on collective phenomena to experimental studies of the social behavior of chickens (*see* Graumann, 1989). The preference for an experimental social psychology of the individual as already developed in North America in the 1930s (*see* Murphy & Murphy, 1931/1937), was nonexistent in Europe. There was neither one social psychology, nor were there two (Pepitone, 1981).

There were as many as there were individual scholars. Even the fact that the 1920s and 1930s were the era of the "Schools" of psychological theorizing had no relevance for social psychology. And then there was Hitler and the war.

Not that the field had to start from zero after 1945. In most European countries there were cultural traditions from which social problems were articulated and a social psychology could be conceived. Hence, the situation was less homogeneous than in North America. This cultural variety must be considered as the baseline for the postwar development of social psychology in Europe which fell into the period of the "Cold War," i.e., the East–West split which inhibited or even prevented communication across the "Iron Curtain" for several decades.

Into this situation in which some West European social psychologists had already made their first contacts with centers of psychology in the United States, but had no relationships with their European colleagues, there came, in the 1950s and 1960s, the initiative of American psychologists (partly students of European refugees) to help their European colleagues to get to know each other and eventually to organize themselves into a scientific community. In the 1960s this became the European Association of Experimental Social Psychology (EAESP) whose public platform became the *European Journal of Social Psychology* in 1971. The 1960s were also the years in which social psychology became institutionalized in many European universities.

From the beginning, in the mid-1960s, it was the policy of the EAESP to bring together social psychologists from various cultural backgrounds, mainly from Eastern and Western Europe, without trying to "homogenize" this typically European variety. Also the fact that some of the major initiators of the association (Tajfel, Moscovici, Himmelweit, and G. Jahoda) were themselves refugees from various European countries reconfirms the cultural variability that is frequently associated with the usage of the attribute "European" in connection with social psychology.

While it may be difficult to distinguish the average contents of a volume of the *European*

*Journal of Social Psychology* from those of a leading American journal, like the *Journal of Personality and Social Psychology*, or to distinguish between the topics, methods, and citation habits of European and American textbooks and edited volumes, it is possible to outline some preferences and emphases that are characteristic of the recent development of social psychology in Europe. They all may have to do with the cultural diversity of the social climate in Europe. One such emphasis (an aspiration rather than an achievement) is on the social context, not only of cognition and interaction, but also – at the meta-level – of social psychology (*see*, e.g., CRITICAL SOCIAL PSYCHOLOGY). The recent debate between representatives of theories of individuals' social cognitions and of Moscovici's theory of SOCIAL REPRESENTATIONS may exemplify the difference of emphasis and the different interests in the role of the social or societal context in shaping individual cognition and action. In this respect one may note a stronger tendency among European social psychologists to come to terms with the more complex problems of SOCIAL IDENTITY and of INTERGROUP RELATIONS or, for that matter, of language use.

There may have been times when European ideas influenced American theorizing and research. There certainly was a time when the more established social psychology of North America helped organize and – at least methodologically – shape incipient social psychology in Europe. At the end of the first century of social psychology the relationship between its manifestation in America and Europe has begun to be transactional, i.e., truly interdependent.

*See also*: AGGRESSION; ATTITUDE CHANGE; ATTITUDE MEASUREMENT AND QUESTIONNAIRE DESIGN; ATTRIBUTION THEORIES; COGNITIVE CONSISTENCY; CONFLICT; COOPERATION AND COMPETITION; CRITICAL SOCIAL PSYCHOLOGY; CROWD PSYCHOLOGY; CROWDING; DEINDIVIDUATION; EXPERIMENTATION; GROUP PROCESSES; HEURISTICS; INTERGROUP RELATIONS; LANGUAGE; LEADERSHIP; NORMS; PREJUDICE; SOCIAL COGNITION; SOCIAL COMPARISON; SOCIAL FACILITATION; SOCIAL IDENTITY THEORY; SOCIAL JUDGMENT; SOCIAL LEARNING; SOCIAL PSYCHOLOGY; SOCIAL REPRESENTATIONS.

BIBLIOGRAPHY

Allport, F. H. (1924). *Social psychology*. Boston, MA: Houghton Mifflin.

Allport, G. W. (1985). The historical background of social psychology. In G. Lindzey & E. Aronson (Eds.), *The handbook of social psychology* (3rd ed., Vol. 1, pp. 1–46). New York: Random House.

Cartwright, D. (1979). Contemporary social psychology in historical perspective. *Social Psychology Quarterly, 42*, 82–93.

Festinger, L. (Ed.) (1980). *Retrospections on social psychology*. New York: Oxford University Press.

Graumann, C. F. (1988). Introduction to a history of social psychology. In M. Hewstone, W. Stroebe, J. P. Codol, & G. M. Stephenson (Eds.), *Introduction to social psychology: A European perspective* (pp. 3–19). Oxford: Basil Blackwell

——(1989). The origins of social psychology in German-speaking countries. In J. A. Keats, R. Taft, R. A. Heath, & S. H. Lovibond (Eds.), *Mathematical and theoretical systems* (pp. 333–43). Amsterdam: North-Holland.

Heider, F. (1958). *The psychology of interpersonal relations*. New York: Wiley.

Jones, E. E. (1985). Major developments in social psychology during the past five decades. In G. Lindzey & E. Aronson (Eds.), *The handbook of social psychology* (3rd ed., Vol. 1, pp. 47–107). New York: Random House.

McGuire, W. J. (1985). Toward social psychology's second century. In S. Koch & D. E. Leary (Eds.), *A century of psychology as a science* (pp. 558–90). New York: McGraw-Hill.

Moede, W. (1920). *Experimentelle Massenpsychologie*. Leipzig: Hirzel.

Murchison, C. (Ed.). (1935). *Handbook of social psychology*. Worcester, MA: Clark University Press.

Murphy, G., & Murphy, L. B. (1931). *Experimental social psychology*. New York: Harper. (Rev. ed. with T. M. Newcomb, 1937.)

Patnoe, S. (1988). *A narrative history of experimental social psychology: The Lewin tradition*. New York: Springer-Verlag.

Pepitone, A. (1981). Lessons from the history of social psychology. *American Psychologist, 36*, 972–85.

Sahakian, W. S. (1982). *History and systems of social psychology* (2nd ed.). Washington, DC: Hemisphere.

Stephan, C. W., Stephan, W. G., & Pettigrew, T. F. (Eds.) (1991). *The future of social psychology*. New York: Springer-Verlag.

Wundt, W. (1916). *Elements of folk-psychology*. London: Allen & Unwin.

CARL F. GRAUMANN

**hormones**  Chemical substances secreted by glands and circulated to other parts of the body by the bloodstream. Hormones regulate various functions in the body and play a role in emotion. They are given some attention in the study of certain social behaviors, such as ATTRACTION and AGGRESSION.

*See also*: AGGRESSION; ATTRACTION; EMOTIONAL EXPERIENCE.

RUSSELL G. GEEN

**hostility**  An interpersonal disposition characterized by negative affect, feelings of dislike and rejection of others (*see* Latin *hostis* = foreigner), and tendencies toward behavioral aggression. In the study of human AGGRESSION, hostility is usually treated as a trait that moderates aggressive responses to provoking situations.

*See also*: AGGRESSION.

RUSSELL G. GEEN

# I

**ideology** The concept of "ideology" has been used in various ways by different social scientists. As far as social psychologists are concerned, three principal uses can be distinguished. Ideology has been used to denote:

(1) rigid systems of belief, particularly the official doctrines of political or religious groups;
(2) unsystematic beliefs, which are shared within a given society and which perpetuate unequal power relations within that society; and
(3) political assumptions, which are expressed within academic work, including mainstream social psychology.

## IDEOLOGY AS A RIGID BELIEF SYSTEM

Often the beliefs of a group, which provides its adherents with a systematic and integrated view on the world, have been described as "ideology." Prime examples of such ideologies are the doctrines of religious sects or of extreme political groups such as Marxist or Fascist parties. These ideological groups typically demand total loyalty from their members, and this total commitment is itself justified by the ideology. One such ideology, which has been investigated by social psychologists, is the "conspiracy theory." This ideology, which is to be found in many extreme right-wing groups, "explains" the whole of politics in terms of the actions of a small group of conspirators, who are said to be plotting to dominate the world (Graumann & Moscovici, 1986).

Social psychologists have tended to ask two sorts of questions about rigid, group ideologies. First, they have asked whether a particular sort of personality-type is attracted to such ideologies. It has been claimed that ideological thinking appeals to those whose mental and personal psychology is characterized by DOGMATISM or AUTHORITARIANISM. Second, social psychologists have investigated the processes of conversion, by which recruits to extreme political parties or religious sects come to adopt their group's ideology.

## IDEOLOGY AS UNSYSTEMATIC BELIEFS.

The second conception does not view "ideology" as the systematic beliefs of an extreme group, but as the unsystematic, shared beliefs of the majority. Theorists, using the term in this way, are often interested in examining how commonsense values and everyday practices function to reproduce the unequal power relations of the society. Through ideology, the particular social order is experienced by its members as being the "natural" order. Thus, "ideology" refers to the processes – both social and psychological – by which the members come to accept the psychological relations of their society.

Mainstream social psychologists have typically not used the concept of "ideology" in this way. However, the concept has played an important part in CRITICAL SOCIAL PSYCHOLOGY, especially in the works of Marxist and feminist social psychologists. Theories which seek to expose the workings of ideology have often adapted psychoanalytic concepts to show how the dominated sections of society can unconsciously repress their own desires and accept the existing social order. For instance, some Marxist social psychologists have claimed that the ideology of capitalism has stunted the personality structures of contemporary Westerners. Erich Fromm provided a classic example of such an analysis. In *Fear of Freedom* (1942), he argued that capitalist individualism created an unfulfilled sense of aloneness. Combining insights from Marx and Freud, Fromm claimed that the social psychological relations to be found in capitalist society alienated people from their instincts for sociability.

Feminist social psychologists have also adapted psychoanalytic concepts in order to analyze critically the ideology of patriarchal society. Patriarchal ideology is assumed to comprise the gender stereotypes and values, whose acceptance ensures that men and women adopt their respective and unequal roles in society. A number of feminist theorists, whilst strongly criticizing the masculine bias of Freudian notions such as the Oedipus Complex and penis envy, have sought to construct a psychoanalytically influenced feminist psychology (Sayers, 1986). This sort of psychology, whose influence has stretched beyond the academic world, examines how the processes of psychological repression and identification lead to patriarchy being reproduced as an everyday ideology. One topic which has been particularly examined has been the psychological injuries suffered by women in male-dominated societies. In analyzing ideology in this way, feminist theorists are also exploring how gender identities are created by social forces.

POLITICAL ASSUMPTIONS OF PSYCHOLOGICAL THEORY

Critical social psychologists do not see ideology as operating only in the thinking of "ordinary" people: it also operates in academic theories. As Marx and Engels noted in *The German Ideology*, intellectual ideas can be ideological if they serve the conservative function of justifying the existing order of society. Academic theorists can present existing social relations as being "natural" and, thus, the order of society is intellectually legitimated. Critical social psychologists have claimed that mainstream social psychology is ideological in this sense.

This ideological critique of social psychology has a number of themes. According to the critics, the findings of social psychology reflect the times and conditions in which they are produced. For instance, it has been claimed

that the findings about personal relationships and individualist attributions of blame reflect Western (or capitalist) values (Parker & Shotter, 1990). However, social psychologists tend to write as if their theories were universal, rather than being bounded by times and place. In this way, the social psychological characteristics of contemporary Western society are presented as if they were universal characteristics of human beings in general.

Feminist thinking has also produced ideological critiques of social psychology. Some feminists have suggested that social psychological theories have typically described masculine patterns of response as if they were the universal norm. It is also claimed that the quantitative, experimental methodologies, which currently dominate orthodox social psychology, are themselves products of a masculine vision of science. For instance, the journal *Feminism and Psychology* (1991), in its initial issue, called for a thorough critique of "main/malestream psychology," in order to produce a social psychology which does not reflect patriarchal ideology. In consequence, ideological critiques of this sort entail a radical reexamination of both theory and practice in social psychology.

See also: AUTHORITARIANISM; CRITICAL SOCIAL PSYCHOLOGY; DOGMATISM; POLITICAL PSYCHOLOGY; PROPAGANDA; SOCIAL CONSTRUCTIONISM.

BIBLIOGRAPHY

*Feminism and Psychology* (1991), Volume 1, Number 1. London: Sage.
Fromm, E. (1942). *Fear of freedom*. London: Routledge & Kegan Paul.
Graumann, C. F., & Moscovici, S. (Eds.) (1986). *Changing conceptions of conspiracy*. New York: Springer-Verlag.
Parker, I., & Shotter, J. (Eds.) (1990). *Deconstructing social psychology*. London: Routledge.
Sayers, J. (1986). *Sexual contradictions: Psychology, psychoanalysis and feminism*. London: Tavistock.

MICHAEL BILLIG

**illusion of control** The incorrect perception that a person's actions can affect the

outcomes of chance events. In gambling situations involving purely chance outcomes, adults believe their chances of winning are higher if cues normally involved in skill tasks (e.g., an opportunity to practise, or a choice over a lottery ticket) are present (Langer, 1975). For young children such illusory contingency beliefs are especially common; almost all kindergartners predict older or smarter children will perform better than younger or less intelligent children on a wholly noncontingent task (e.g., drawing a card blindly). Although contingency reasoning reaches asymptote in adolescence, substantial errors in contingency judgments and behavior still occur, implying some residual perception of CONTROL over chance events. In part, such errors may reflect a CONTROL MOTIVATION essential for psychological health. For instance, persons who are depressed are less apt to make such errors. Such findings support the view that an illusion of control is often adaptive (Taylor & Brown, 1988).
*See also*: CONTROL; CONTROL MOTIVATION.

BIBLIOGRAPHY

Langer, E. J. (1975). The illusion of control. *Journal of Personality and Social Psychology*, *32*, 311–28.
Taylor, S. E., & Brown, J. D. (1988). Illusion and well-being: A social psychological perspective on mental health. *Psychological Bulletin*, *103*, 193–210.

KERRY L. MARSH<br>GIFFORD WEARY

**illusory correlation** The illusory correlation occurs when an individual perceives a correlation between two classes of events which in reality are not correlated or which are correlated to a lesser extent than perceived (Chapman & Chapman, 1967). Illusory correlations are frequently observed in everyday judgments of covariation.

There are two types of illusory correlations: *Expectancy-driven illusory correlations* occur when judgments of covariation are colored by preexisting expectations. For instance, observers may overestimate the number of lawyers who are wealthy and underestimate the number of nurses who are wealthy, based upon their stereotypes about these groups. *Data-driven illusory correlations* occur when the distribution of the two classes of events are skewed and thus frequencies in the contingency table are highly uneven. Because infrequent events are more easily remembered than are more frequent events, their frequency of occurrence is relatively overestimated and they have a disproportionate weight in judgment of covariation.

Illusory correlations may lead to erroneous STEREOTYPING of target individuals when one of the classes involves a social category and the other involves the occurrence of a negative behavior (Hamilton, 1981). Because negative behaviors are naturally less frequent in everyday life, the negative behaviors of minority groups may be overestimated.
*See also*: STEREOTYPING.

BIBLIOGRAPHY

Chapman, L. J., & Chapman, J. P. (1967). Genesis of popular but erroneous psychodiagnostic observations. *Journal of Abnormal Psychology*, *73*, 193–204.
Hamilton, D. L. (1981). Illusory correlation as a basis for stereotyping. In D. L. Hamilton (Ed.), *Cognitive processes in stereotyping and intergroup behavior* (pp. 115–44). Hillsdale, NJ: Lawrence Erlbaum.

CHARLES G. STANGOR

**implicit personality theory** Tacit assumptions regarding people's personality traits and the relationships among them. MULTIDIMENSIONAL SCALING plots traits according to psychological relatedness, and identifies dimensions that describe these relationships. Although controversial, the evidence suggests that perceived trait relationships reflect actual trait co-occurrences, not merely the perceivers' semantic associations.

LESLIE A. ZEBROWITZ

**impression formation** This is a major component of SOCIAL PERCEPTION, and is the process of forming evaluative and descriptive judgments about a target person. Most research has concerned the formation of *first* impressions of a person's traits or likeability. The process of forming impressions in ongoing relationships and impressions of contextual qualities, such as social roles, relationships, and AFFORDANCES, have been studied less frequently. Fundamental goals of impression formation research have been to determine the contributions of the perceiver's cognitive and affective processes and the target's physical and behavioral characteristics and to ascertain biases and accuracy.

THEORETICAL MODELS

A structuralist approach to impression formation is reflected in linear combination models which assume that the individual elements in information about a person will be summed or averaged to form an overall impression such as the person's likability (Anderson, 1981). A constructivist approach is reflected in the GESTALT model, which holds that traits are organized to form a whole which is not an algebraic combination of the individual traits. Rather, each trait affects the *meaning* of each of the others such that the final impression is not easily predicted from the individual traits. Focusing on the construction of an impression from a target person's traits, this model acknowledges that impressions are in part "data-driven." Schema theories, on the other hand, allow for purely theory-driven impressions, which may reflect the perceiver's SELF-SCHEMATA or group stereotypes (*see* STEREOTYPING).

Mixed models of impression formation incorporate both constructivist, theory-driven, processes and structuralist, data-driven, processes. Brewer (1988) proposes that information can be processed either way, depending on the perceiver's decisions. After an "automatic" perception of a target's demographic characteristics, impressions will be data-driven if the perceiver feels interdependent with the target or ego-involved in the judgment task. Otherwise, impressions will be theory-driven, determined by stereotypes of the category into which the target person is placed. Similarly, Fiske and Neuberg (1990) proposed a continuum model, which proceeds

from constructivist processes, in which impressions derive from preexisting concepts and theories about a particular category of people, to structuralist processes, in which impressions derive from some linear combination of the target person's actual attributes. According to this model, constructivist processes are most common, with structuralist processes engaged only when the target is interesting or personally relevant to the perceiver and the perceiver is unable to fit the target's attributes to an initial categorization. McArthur and Baron's (1983) ecological model emphasizes the joint effect on impressions of perceiver processes and target attributes. According to this model perceivers form impressions of a target person's affordances, which are opportunities for acting or being acted upon that a particular target provides the perceiver. The detection of certain affordances is postulated to depend not only on structured stimulus information provided by a target but also on the perceivers' *attunements* – the particular stimulus information to which they attend. Attunements, in turn, depend upon the perceiver's social goals, perceptual learning, and actions. Thus, according to the ecological model, "perceiving is for doing," and impressions emerge from data revealing the affordances of the target person for a particular perceiver.

PERCEIVER EFFECTS

Support for constructivist theories is provided by evidence that impressions of a target person are influenced by the perceiver's short-term mental states. PRIMING effects reveal that perceivers' impressions of a person reflect those descriptive terms that are most accessible because they have been recently and/or frequently activated. Such effects are not solely a constructive process, since they require some match between a target's behavior and the perceiver's most accessible descriptors. Descriptors that an individual most frequently uses, personal constructs, can influence impressions of others just as temporarily primed constructs do. Such constructs affect the information that is emphasized in impressions when a range of information is available. They also influence how ambiguous information is processed, increasing the likelihood of detecting traits that are central constructs for the perceiver.

Self-schemata may also influence impression formation by virtue of focusing attention on schema-relevant behavioral information. Perceivers weight information relevant to their self-schemas more heavily when forming evaluative impressions. They also seek out information about others that is related to their self-schemas. The desirability of traits in the self-schema affects their influence on impression formation, with highly desirable traits more central to impressions of others than less desirable ones. Although the foregoing evidence indicates that self-schemas influence the process of impression formation, they do not reliably affect the content of judgments about the target person that can be informed by the objective information available. However, self-schemas do affect more conjectural judgments. Schema-relevant traits seem to be embedded within an IMPLICIT PERSONALITY THEORY which causes the perceiver to go beyond the information given in forming impressions of targets who have such traits.

EXPECTANCY EFFECTS also reveal the constructive processes of the perceiver. Although impressions of a person are often assimilated to the perceiver's prior expectations, there is also evidence for a reverse, contrast effect (see ASSIMILATION-CONTRAST). When behaviors are not too discrepant from expectations, impressions show assimilation. When a target manifests behaviors extremely discrepant from expectations, the result is a "contrast" effect in which impressions move in a direction opposite to expectations. The ultimate influence of an unexpected behavior on impressions may be influenced by a variety of factors in addition to its degree of discrepancy. Assimilation to expectancy is diminished when situational forces can yield discounting of the unexpected behavior, when the expectancy derives from an unreliable source, when the perceiver's goals require accurate impressions, or when the disconfirming behavioral data are stronger than the expectancy. Like expectations about a person provided to us by informants or early information, those provided by stereotyping can also influence our impressions of a specific person's observed behaviors. As in the case of other expectancy effects, contrast rather than assimilation to the group stereotype may occur when the observed behavior strongly violates expectations.

One way in which expectancies may influence impressions is via their impact on the information recalled. Person memory research reveals preferential recall of expectancy congruent information given the conditions under which impressions are typically formed in the real world. Such effects tend to be greater for groups than for individuals and for well-established expectations. Thus, expectancy congruent recall effects should be more significant in the maintenance of pre-existing group stereotypes than in the creation or maintenance of expectancies about individuals (see Stangor & McMillan, 1992).

The role of constructive processes of the perceiver in impression formation is seen in the operation of HEURISTICS that simplify complex problem solving. The AVAILABILITY heuristic is manifested in a tendency to judge the probability of a trait according to the ease with which one can think of behavioral examples. For example, impressions of how irritable someone is may be influenced by how easily one can think of instances of that person losing his temper. The REPRESENTATIVENESS heuristic is manifested in a tendency to judge the category membership of people according to the extent to which they are similar to or "representative" of the average person in that category (see SOCIAL CATEGORIZATION). Thus, for example, impressions of someone's ethnicity may be influenced by the extent to which the person looks or sounds like others in that group.

Like cognitive processes, the perceiver's affective processes can also contribute to impression formation, at least when behaviors are somewhat ambiguous (see AFFECT). Such effects seem to be mediated by both attentional and interpretive responses to the target (Fiske & Neuberg, 1990). Ambiguous behaviors may be assimilated to the perceiver's values or construed as consistent with the perceiver's goals. These effects could reflect wishful thinking and/or selective attention to those behaviors that would in fact facilitate the perceiver's goals. Perceivers do pay more attention to people on whom their outcomes depend, and they form more positive impressions of their traits.

Sometimes perceivers' goals influence what information they accurately detect rather than creating biased impressions. Specifically, perceivers form impressions of those attributes which are pertinent to their social interaction goals. Also, biases in impression formation decrease when perceivers' goals are accuracy oriented rather than confirmatory or closure seeking. Evaluative as well as descriptive components of impressions may be influenced by the perceiver's goals. Thus, perceivers form more positive impressions of those who can fulfill their social interaction goals. Research on ATTRACTION provides additional evidence for the influence of perceiver goals on evaluative impressions.

Perceivers' moods, like their goals, can influence evaluative impressions (see MOOD: ITS IMPACT ON COGNITION AND BEHAVIOR). People are perceived as more attractive by those whose mood has been elevated and as less attractive by those whose mood has been depressed. Interestingly, the negative emotion of fear has been shown to increase attraction under certain circumstances. The high arousal characterizing fear narrows attention to the most salient cues and may thereby cause fearful perceivers to accentuate the attractiveness of a basically attractive target. The impact of other positive and negative emotions on impressions has also been attributed to selective attention, namely to mood congruent information. MISATTRIBUTION OF AROUSAL provides still another explanation for the impact of fear and other emotional states on attraction. Perceivers who are uncertain about the causes of their own emotional states may attribute a happy mood to liking for a target person or a sad mood to disliking for the target. They may also mistakenly attribute a highly aroused state to sexual attraction rather than to its true cause, such as a fear-arousing situation (see Forgas, 1991).

TARGET EFFECTS

Research in the structuralist tradition has supported an AVERAGING MODEL of impres-

sion formation (Anderson, 1981). The positivity of perceivers' overall impression reflects the average *scale value* of the target's individual traits – how positively each trait is evaluated – weighted according to the trait's importance to the perceiver. To accurately predict impressions from the weighted average model further requires factoring in the perceiver's initial impression. Thus, this data-driven model also incorporates perceiver characteristics. Context effects in impression formation can also be accounted for by the averaging model. These include the tendency for impressions to be most influenced by a single, central trait, the tendency for evaluations of a particular trait to be influenced by the context in which it appears (see HALO EFFECTS) and the tendency for impressions to be more influenced by early information (see PRIMARY–RECENCY EFFECTS). The weighted average model predicts these effects by assuming that later or peripheral traits are *weighted less* than earlier or central traits and that the context in which a trait occurs influences its *scale value*. However, an alternative interpretation is provided by the constructivist argument that the *meaning* of a person's later or peripheral traits is influenced by the earlier or central ones. Implicit personality theories provide another constructivist account of context effects, attributing them to trait associations. Regardless of whether change in meaning accounts for halo and primacy effects, the meaning of various traits nevertheless may be altered by the context in which they appear.

SALIENCE effects provide additional evidence consistent with the assumption that impression formation is data-driven. Negative or extreme behaviors draw more attention and are generally weighted more in impressions than less salient positive or moderate behaviors (see NEGATIVITY EFFECTS). These effects may reflect not only the greater novelty and intensity of extreme and negative behaviors, but also the adaptive value of attending to such behaviors, which may be threatening to the perceiver and/or particularly diagnostic of the target's internal dispositions (Skowronski & Carlston 1989). Perceivers also form more polarized impressions of targets who are physically salient, with the polarization occurring in the direction of the target's most salient behaviors. The tendency for increased attention to salient people to polarize impressions may be related to the MERE EXPOSURE EFFECT, whereby repeated, unreinforced exposure results in an increase in positive affect toward a person. Interestingly, this effect is not dependent on consciously knowing or perceiving that the person is familiar, and it is strongest when produced by subliminal exposure to photographs of a target person.

The tendency for evaluations of physically salient persons to be polarized in the direction of their most salient behaviors is related to ILLUSORY CORRELATION effects. When people observe behaviors by members of two groups, the perceived correlation between group membership and behavior is disproportionately influenced by the actor-behavior pairs that draw the most attention. The result is that impressions reflect an illusory correlation between salient people and their salient behaviors. Thus, people perceive an illusory correlation between people who are salient by virtue of being a member of a minority group and behaviors which are also salient by virtue of infrequency. When the infrequent behaviors are negative, illusory correlation yields more negative impressions of minority than majority group members, whereas the reverse is true when the infrequent behaviors are positive. The strength of the illusory correlation between minority group members and infrequent behaviors depends upon factors that influence the salience of the various behaviors apart from their relative frequency. Such an illusory correlation does not occur when it is the *frequent* behaviors which are more salient to perceivers either because they render the target similar to themselves or because they are already associated with the minority group members.

The influence of the target person's appearance provides additional evidence for data-driven impressions. There is an attractiveness halo effect, such that perceivers form more positive impressions of attractive people, particularly in the domain of social competence (Feingold, 1992) (*see* PHYSICAL ATTRACTIVENESS). There is also a babyface overgeneralization effect, such that people whose facial qualities resemble those of infants are perceived to have childlike traits. A variety of other appearance qualities also influence impressions as do vocal qualities, gait, and non-verbal behaviors (*see* Hall & Knapp, 1992; Zebrowitz, 1990).

Research demonstrating ACCURACY IN IMPRESSION FORMATION supports data-driven models, since accuracy presumes agreement between impressions of a person and the data provided by that person's attributes. There is high consensus regarding a target's attributes, even among strangers who have seen only facial photographs or videotapes of the target, an effect that is dubbed "consensus at zero acquaintance." Moreover, strangers' ratings have been corroborated by the target's self ratings, scores on personality tests, or actual behavior. When the "big five" personality traits are considered, strangers are best at detecting extraversion and conscientiousness, whereas agreeableness, emotional stability, and openness to experience are less accurately detected. Dominance and warmth are also accurately perceived. Efforts to determine what data drives these accurate impressions have revealed that some traits can be judged from visual cues, others from vocal cues, and still others from either one. This research provides evidence for a kernel of truth in some facial and vocal stereotypes. For example, consistent with the attractiveness halo effect, attractive individuals are in fact more popular and socially skilled (Feingold, 1992).

The evidence for accuracy in impression formation is not necessarily inconsistent with evidence for perceiver biases, such as expectancy effects. BIAS refers to a systematic overuse or underuse of some otherwise accurate information or appropriate procedure, and need not necessarily imply errors or mistakes which interfere with adaptive action. Indeed, because perceivers are often concerned only with *circumscribed accuracy* – the accuracy of impressions of targets when they are in the perceiver's pesence – they may achieve accuracy by eliciting the very behaviors that are anticipated (*see* SELF-FULFILLING PROPHECIES). Such effects may be mediated by nonverbal behaviors or conversational strategies that covary with the perceiver's expectations and elicit behavioral confirmation. However, in most situations highly diagnostic questions are preferred over hypothesis-confirming ones, thereby yielding accurate impressions via the target's SELF-VERIFICATION.

CONCLUSIONS

Research has provided support for both constructivist and structuralist models of impression formation, revealing an influence of both perceiver and target characteristics. It remains for future research to fulfill the promise of mixed models by more fully exploring the joint effects of the perceiver and the target. This endeavor will focus attention on the important but neglected question of what functions impressions serve.

*See also*: ATTRACTION; HEURISTICS; MERE EXPOSURE EFFECT; MOOD: ITS IMPACT ON COGNITION AND BEHAVIOR; NEGATIVITY EFFECTS; SELF-FULFILLING PROPHECIES; SOCIAL CATEGORIZATION; SOCIAL PERCEPTION; STEREOTYPING.

BIBLIOGRAPHY

Anderson, N. H. (1981). *Foundations of information integration theory*. New York: Academic Press.

Brewer, M. B. (1988). A dual process model of impression formation. In T. K. Srull & R. S. Wyer, Jr. (Eds.), *Advances in social cognition* (Vol. 1, pp. 1–36). Hillsdale, NJ: Lawrence Erlbaum.

Feingold, A. (1992). Good-looking people are not what we think. *Psychological Bulletin, 111*, 304–41.

Fiske, S. T., & Neuberg, S. L. (1990). A continuum of impression formation from category-based to individuating processes: Influences of information and motivation on attention and interpretation. In M. P. Zanna (Ed.), *Advances in experimental social psychology* (Vol. 23, pp. 1–74). New York: Academic Press.

Forgas, J. P. (Ed.) (1991). *Emotion and social judgments*. Oxford: Pergamon.

Hall, J., & Knapp, M. (1992). *Nonverbal communication in interpersonal interactions*. Holt, Rinehart & Winston.

McArthur, L. Z., & Baron, R. (1983). Toward an ecological theory of social perception. *Psychological Review, 90*, 215–47.

Skowronski, J. J., & Carlston, D. E. (1989). Negativity and extremity biases in impression formation: A review of explanations. *Psychological Bulletin, 105*, 131–42.

Stangor, C., & McMillan, D. (1992). Memory for expectancy-congruent and expectancy-incongruent information: A review of the social and social developmental literatures. *Psychological Bulletin, 111*, 42–61.

Zebrowitz, L. A. (1990). *Social perception*. Buckingham: Open University Press.

LESLIE A. ZEBROWITZ

**impression management**  The goal-directed activity of controlling or regulating information in order to influence the impressions formed by an audience. Through impression management, people try to shape an audience's impressions of a person (e.g., self, friends, enemies), object (e.g., a business organization, a gift), or event (e.g., a transgression, a task performance). When actors are trying to control impressions of themselves, as opposed to other people or entities, the activity is called SELF-PRESENTATION. The study of how information is regulated and controlled in social interactions provides insights into the strategic side of interpersonal behavior (*see* Cody & McLaughlin, 1990; De Paulo, 1992).

HISTORY

The concept of impression management has a rich history. An intellectual forbearer of current views was the idea that people are like actors on the stage of life, controlling the impressions they impart to audiences (Schlenker, 1980). Although glimpses of this dramaturgical analogy can be traced to antiquity (e.g., Plato spoke of the "great stage of human life"), it became a popular theme in the seventeenth century, exemplified by Shakespeare's credo, "All the world's a stage, and all the men and women merely players." Several social psychological concepts trace their roots to dramaturgical origins, including the concepts of person, from the Latin *persona*, which was a mask worn by an actor on stage; role, from the Latin *rotula*, which was a wooden roller containing the lines that an actor recited on stage; and attitude, which was the orientation and feeling an actor's character displayed on stage.

Goffman's (1959) seminal work, *The Presentation of Self in Everyday Life*, popularized among social scientists the concept of impression management. Endorsing the dramaturgical analogy, Goffman viewed interpersonal conduct as a performance by the participants. Goffman (1959, p. 4) argued that it is the very essence of social life that whenever "an individual appears in the presence of others, there will usually be some reason for him to mobilize his activity so that it will convey an impression to others which is in his interest to convey." Although Goffman's work has been criticized for deemphasizing the psychology of the individual (he emphasized social roles and rules) and focusing on what often seemed to be illicit behaviors designed to manipulate others, his insights provided a springboard.

## CONTEMPORARY PERSPECTIVES

The 1980s brought a torrent of conceptual analyses that treated impression management as a fundamental interpersonal process (Baumeister, 1982; Jones & Pittman, 1982; Leary & Kowalski, 1990; Schlenker, 1980; Schlenker & Weigold, 1992; Tedeschi, 1981; Tetlock & Manstead, 1985). Impression management approaches share the central idea that people communicate strategically and must, like politicians, take into account the varying perspectives and agendas of audiences. The witting or unwitting control of information about oneself, one's audience, and one's activities lies at the very heart of interpersonal relations. Further, the control of information not only takes place in initial encounters or superficial relationships but continues over the course of life-long relationships. Despite these core ideas, there is no single theory of impression management. Instead, there are several theories that have similar central cores but differ in many of their specifics. When discussing conceptual perspectives, it is more appropriate to regard impression management as an approach rather than a specific theory.

In general, theory and research on impression management has taken two directions. First, impression management approaches offer new insights into "old" phenomena that had been interpreted via alternative theoretical approaches, particularly ones that were intrapsychic in nature. These include reinterpretations of COGNITIVE DISSONANCE phenomena (e.g., justifying counterattitudinal behavior by changing one's attitudes), anticipatory ATTITUDE CHANGE, REACTANCE, SOCIAL FACILITATION, GROUP POLARIZATION, AGGRESSION, HELPING BEHAVIOR, eating behavior, and equitable behavior, to name a few. In some cases, impression management predictions were contrasted with the alternative predictions to determine which set of hypotheses provided the best fit to the data. Second, an impression management approach, conceived broadly, has been advanced as a major theoretical perspective in its own right, in the same sense that a SOCIAL COGNITION approach can be regarded as a major theoretical perspective. Each approach offers a set of core assumptions and ideas, along with different methodological implications, that can guide research on social behavior. Impression management analyses share the common idea that people attempt to control information that is presented to one or more salient audiences, and do so in ways that attempt to facilitate goal-achievement. This is a fundamental feature of human social behavior. In this context, impression management ideas have been applied not only within social psychology, but also to analyses of PERSONALITY, SOCIALIZATION, counseling, education and child-rearing practices, mental illness, and even criminal behavior. Many clinical problems, including social ANXIETY, SHYNESS, and DEPRESSION, have been examined from an impression management perspective, focusing on people's self-presentational difficulties as primary or contributing components of the problems.

## KEY QUESTIONS
Six key questions have stimulated research on impression management.

(1) Why do people engage in impression management?

(2) What images of self do people try to construct and protect?

(3) How do they go about doing so?

(4) What role do audiences play in the impression management process?

(5) Is impression management duplicitous, or can it be sincere?

(6) What individual differences exist in impression management behavior?

*Motivation*

Why do people engage in impression management? Goffman (1959) provided the most global answer. Although he recognized that impression management is instrumental in gaining approval and achieving valuable outcomes in life, he regarded it as a *condition* of interaction, one that is inherent in the very structure of social life. In order to interact, people must define the situation and the roles each will play. Impression management serves the necessary function of communicating definitions of each person's desired identity and their overt plans. Once identities are established, each participant has a moral obligation to behave congruently with the identity he or she has selected (the rule of self-respect: to maintain one's own face) and to accept and respect the identity selected by the others (the rule of considerateness: to help maintain the faces of others). Impression management activities thereby permit the participants to define who each will be and permit interactions to run smoothly and efficiently.

More specific answers about why people engage in impression management are derived from analyses of the functions it serves in social life. Impression management behavior is instrumental in acquiring social and material outcomes, including approval, respect, pay raises, and promotions. Success and status in everyday life are closely related to people's abilities to construct identities that are valued and rewarded by other members of society. Similarly, what people think and feel about themselves (self-esteem) varies, at least in part, with their successes in impressing others. As such, it has been suggested that people engage in impression management in order to gain approval, gain respect, optimize self-esteem, socially valid-

ate idealized images of self, socially verify existing self-beliefs, and gain material advantages. Further, impression management behavior has been cited as a vehicle through which people can exercise needs for power and control over their environments. Clearly, the motives underlying impression management are as varied as those proposed for any social behavior.

*Desired Self-Images*

Most research on impression management has focused on self-presentation. As such, researchers have addressed the question, "What images of self do people try to construct and protect?" Early research emphasized people's motivation to gain approval and be liked by others, and therefore suggested that people present themselves in socially desirable ways (i.e., ways valued in the social group) or ways known to be valued by the specific audience. More recent work has recognized a variety of desired images and effective self-presentational tactics (Jones & Pittman, 1982; Schlenker, 1980). These include intimidation, in which people present themselves as powerful or irrational in order to be feared by audiences; supplication, in which people present themselves as weak or irresponsible in order to receive nurturance from audiences; exemplification, in which people present themselves as morally worthy in order to make others feel guilty; self-promotion, in which people present themselves as competent and effective in order to gain respect; and ingratiation, in which people present themselves in ways they think will produce liking. These five tactics permit actors to exercise some control over the behavior of others (Jones & Pittman, 1982). Research indicates that people do not merely try to present themselves positively; people try to accomplish goals, and these goals may involve modest or even unflattering self-presentations (Schlenker & Weigold, 1992).

Two important determinants of how people present themselves are the extent to which a particular self-presentation is personally beneficial (the actor regards it as facilitating his or her goals and values) and believable (the actor perceives it as an accurate or defensible construal of reality). Self-presentations are more beneficial if they are more important to the actor's identity (e.g., they comprise central components of his or her self-concept) or are seen as producing valued outcomes from significant audiences. Yet, self-presentations produce obligations for actors to be what they say they are or risk social sanctions. For this reason, people's self-presentations are held in check by "reality" and tend to be consistent with publicly known information about them. The factors that have been found to influence self-presentations have been summarized (Schlenker & Weigold, 1992) by suggesting that a particular self-presentation is more likely to occur when:

(1) its beneficiality to the actor is greater (i.e., its expected value to the actor is greater, as when a significant audience highly values a particular attribute and will reward those who possess it); and

(2) it can be justified as a believable claim (e.g., supporting evidence is available and inconsistent evidence, if it exists, can be hidden from public view).

*Self-Presentation Modes*

How do people go about constructing and protecting desired images of self? Researchers have distinguished between direct and indirect modes of self-presentation. Direct modes are straightforward and involve making claims about oneself via either verbal or nonverbal communications. Indirect modes involve a more circuitous path; actors strategically associate (or dissociate) themselves with particular people or events so as to control how they will be evaluated by audiences. Basking-in-reflected-glory, as when people connect themselves to successful sports teams ("We won," when the local football team triumphs; but "they lost," when the local team falters) is an example of an indirect tactic.

*Accounting*

As people go about the business of constructing desired identities, they inevitably confront impediments and threats (e.g., accident and mistakes, failed task performances, unwelcome feedback from others). People then mobilize their activities to deal with the problem, and as part of this mobilization construct explanations for the difficulties. In everyday language, ACCOUNTS are explanations of an event that are proffered when its meaning is unclear or might be misconstrued. In the social psychology literature, accounts usually represent self-serving explanations that are proffered by actors who confront predicaments. Four general classes of accounts have been studied. Defenses of innocence claim either that no transgression occurred (e.g., the "murder victim" actually committed suicide) or the actor was not involved. Excuses attempt to minimize the actor's personal responsibility for the event, shifting responsibility from central facets of the actor's identity to peripheral or external causes. Justifications attempt to alter the audience's interpretation of the event itself, either by minimizing the importance of the prescriptions that were violated (e.g., "Marijuana laws are ill-conceived and antiquated"), minimizing the amount of harm that was done ("I did not hit him very hard and he was not hurt badly"), or appealing to an alternative set of prescriptions that might transform the act from bad to good (e.g., "I punished him for his own good; he'll thank me some day"). Apologies are admissions of blameworthiness and regret for undesirable events. They serve the important social functions of acknowledging that prescriptions have been violated, reaffirming the value of the prescriptions, recognizing interpersonal obligations, and extending a promise of better conduct in the future. Defenses of innocence, excuses, justifications, and apologies can all serve to protect identity when threatening conditions arise, provided the audience believes them to be truthful. All have been shown to minimize the damage to the actor's identity and the negative sanctions applied to the actor by audiences.

*Audiences*

What role do audiences play in the impression management process? By definition, impression management involves trying to create a particular impression on an audience. As such, the audience and its perceived reactions are presumed to play a central role in regulating the actors' behavior. Most research has emphasized the role of immediate audiences in influencing behavior. Audiences have greater impact on the actor's behavior if they are more powerful, more attractive, more expert, or higher in status. Recent work also has begun to explore other audiences for impression management, including imagined audiences who are not actually present but who are significant to the actor (e.g., parents, friends), and even the self-as-audience for one's own behavior (Schlenker & Weigold, 1992).

### Authenticity and Deceit

Is impression management duplicitous? Given that it involves controlling the information that is presented to audiences, it is sometimes regarded as dealing with matters of appearance rather than substance. In fact, some analyses of impression management have equated it with illicit, deceitful conduct. However, it is more accurate to say that impression management can involve behavior that falls all along the continuum of sincere versus deceitful conduct. People who want to communicate an accurate, sincere portrait of self to another person must distill and edit vast amounts of personal information, such that it is presented as a comprehensible package that leads the other to draw the desired conclusion. It takes just as much interpersonal skill to create a desired, sincere impression as a desired, false one. Research shows that people who have the smallest discrepancies between their own self-views and their friends' views of them, that is, people who seem to have done the best job of getting their friends to view them as they view themselves, have good acting skills.

Authenticity is based on the perceived relationship between private beliefs and public statements. There is a reciprocal relationship between the private and public sides of self, with each influencing the other. People's private self-conceptions will influence how they prefer to be viewed by others and hence will affect their public impression management behaviors. Self-images that are more central and important to the actor are more likely to be presented publicly. Further, people's public self-presentations can influence their private self-conceptions. Research has shown that people will change their self-beliefs and self-evaluations to bring them in line with

their prior strategic self-presentations. Self-presentations produce the greatest impact on private self-appraisals when the behavior can be justified as representative of self, as when it occurs under conditions of high decision freedom and the actor can choose the specific contents of the self-presentation. Thus, self-presentations that were initially shaped by situational inducements and role expectations may later be regarded by the actor as authentic representations of self.

### Individual Differences

There are individual differences in impression management proclivities and skills. The concept of SELF-MONITORING has stimulated more research on individual differences in impression management than any other personality variable. High self-monitoring reflects a senstivity to cues about the situational appropriateness of one's social behavior and a willingness and ability to use these cues as guidelines for regulating and controlling self-presentations. Research indicates that high self-monitors are effective social participants who adapt their behavior to social expectations but pay the price of cross-situational inconsistency.

Another important individual difference is people's inner versus outer social orientation. People who are outer-oriented (e.g., high in public self-consciousness), tend to use impression management strategies that involve conforming to audiences' preferences. They tend to present themselves as they think the audiences want them to be and to see themselves as cooperative, team players. In contrast, people who are inner-oriented (e.g., high in private self-consciousness), tend to see themselves as independent, tend to resist conforming to others' preferences, and want others to view them as autonomous, authentic individuals with characteristics that match those in their self-conceptions. If they discover that an audience is not viewing them in these ways, they will engage in more dramatic impression management tactics in order to insure that the impression they want to make is actually being made. Research thus indicates that both inner-oriented and outer-oriented people are concerned about how audiences view them, they simply have different objectives in mind. For outer-oriented people, the audience serves as a source for designating what type of identity they should project and as a source of feedback about whether they are coming across as that type of person; for inner-oriented people, the audience serves more as a source of social feedback about whether they are coming across in the way they prefer.

CONCLUSIONS

People's communications do not dispassionately express information without regard to their agendas. Impression management activities permit people to construct and protect meaningful social realities and represent strategic adaptations to the opportunities and threats encountered in their social environments.

See also: ACCOUNTS; AGGRESSION; ATTITUDE CHANGE; COGNITIVE DISSONANCE THEORY; DEPRESSION; HELPING BEHAVIOR; PERSONALITY; REACTANCE; SELF-MONITORING; SHYNESS; SOCIAL COGNITION; SOCIAL FACILITATION; SOCIAL INFLUENCE; SOCIALIZATION.

BIBLIOGRAPHY

Baumeister, R. F. (1982). A self-presentational view of social phenomena. *Psychological Bulletin, 91,* 3–26.

Cody, M. J., & McLaughlin, M. L. (Eds.) (1990). *The psychology of tactical communication.* Bristol, PA: Multilingual Matters Ltd.

DePaulo, B. M. (1992). Nonverbal behavior and self-presentation. *Psychological Bulletin, 111,* 203–43.

Goffman, E. (1959). *The presentation of self in everyday life.* Garden City, NY: Doubleday.

Jones, E. E., & Pittman, T. S. (1982). Toward a general theory of strategic self-presentation. In J. Suls (Ed.), *Psychological Perspectives on the Self* (Vol. 1, pp. 231–62). Hillsdale, NJ: Lawrence Erlbaum.

Leary, M. R., & Kowalski, R. M. (1990). Impression management: A literature review and two-component model. *Psychological Bulletin, 107,* 34–47.

Schlenker, B. R. (1980). *Impression management: The self concept, social identity, and interpersonal relations.* Monterey, CA: Brooks/Cole.

——— & Weigold, M. F. (1992). Interpersonal processes involving impression regulation and management. *Annual Review of Psychology, 43,* 133–68.

Tedeschi, J. T. (Ed.) (1981). *Impression management theory and social psychological research.* New York: Academic Press.

Tetlock, P. E., & Manstead, A. S. R. (1985). Impression management versus intrapsychic explanations in social psychology: A useful dichotomy? *Psychological Review, 92,* 59–77.

BARRY R. SCHLENKER

**inconsistency** This implies a lack of congruence between various aspects of a person's cognitions, attitudes, VALUES, or behaviors. Inconsistency exists when one cognition or attitude, etc., does not follow psychologically from another cognition, attitude, and so forth. A number of influential COGNITIVE CONSISTENCY THEORIES have been generated that take as their premise that people prefer consistency among their cognitions and work diligently to avoid and reduce inconsistency.

See also: COGNITIVE CONSISTENCY THEORIES; VALUES.

JOEL COOPER

**individual differences** Whereas the TRAIT concept is usually reserved for personality characteristics only, individual differences are conceptually much broader encompassing personality, intelligence, temperament, and any psychological process susceptible to individual variation in expression (*see* Gale & Eysenck, 1991). Central to the study of individual differences are the principles of psychological measurement, or psychometrics. The origins of the psychometric tradition can be traced to the nineteenth-century British biologist Sir Francis Galton who, in the course of his investigations into heredity, established the first large and systematic body of data on individual differences. In the twentieth century, the achievement of universal education in Western societies, and the need for selection procedures in both world wars, stimulated the study of individual differences and their measurement.

Individual differences are now studied in every branch of psychology. Individual variation can be studied at the level of discreet behaviors, but more usually conceptually related behaviors are aggregated to assess individuals on underlying constructs or factors. The statistical technique of factor analysis has been critical for the advancement of the study of individual differences because it assists in identifying meaningful patterns of individual differences from among the many possibilities.

BIBLIOGRAPHY

Gale, A., & Eysenck, M. W. (Eds.) (1991). *Handbook of individual differences: Biological perspectives*. Chichester: J. Wiley.

SARAH E. HAMPSON

**individualism–collectivism** In our everyday life, as well as in psychology, we treat the individual as a fundamental analytic unit. We regard the individual as a self-contained whole, whose cognitive, motivational and behavioral processes constitute the central focus of all and any type of psychological analysis. Recently, this assumption has been increasingly challenged in the social sciences in two different but related ways, with potentially radical implications for social psychology in particular, and psychology in general. One source of challenge is a family of increasingly influential metatheoretical orientations (e.g., SOCIAL CONSTRUCTIONISM, ETHOGENICS). The other and somewhat earlier challenge emerged from cross-cultural sociology, anthropology, social history, and literary and art history. In these disciplines there has accumulated converging evidence of the cultural formation of the person and in particular of the fact that our social and scientific treatment of the individual as an independent unit of analysis is from an historical and a cross-cultural perspective a somewhat peculiar one. It is within the framework of this latter develop-

ment that the terminology of individualism versus collectivism has been developed (Hofstede, 1980). Individualism refers to the peculiarly Western conception of the person and collectivism to a conception of the person, which is widespread in a range of cultures in our world, where to conceive of the person as a separate entity is, apart from some exceptional circumstances, an alien thought. In collectivistic societies the person is typically conceived of only in relation to others to whom s/he is bound by duties, role relations, and obligations.

Before going into the details of individualism–collectivism, the cultural/historical formation of the person and their implications for social psychology, we shall examine some transhistorical and transcultural aspects of the person, in order to distinguish those features of the person which are likely to vary from those that do not. It is certainly not the case that we are completely malleable and that the types of constructions that we have are utterly at the mercy of historical or cultural forces. Forms of human existence do not merely come about as the products of responses to sociocultural forces. To this extent, one has to consider what the minimal assumptions of invariance and consistency of an "individual" are. One of the central and obvious sources of evidence comes from the documentation of linguistic classifications that include personal pronouns as well as the term "I" across a wide range of cultures (*see* Mühlhäuser & Harré, 1991). Thus there is a linguistic marking of "self" which is distinct from nonself. By recognizing the self we necessarily also recognize the "nonself."

A corollary of this distinction is the awareness of the "continuity" of the self. That is, to be aware of what I am now presupposes the ability to know what I was in the past, and to project myself into the future. Furthermore, as some (e.g., Hallowell, 1971) argue, continuity means an orientation in relation to norms and the responsibility one carries towards upholding them. In sum, there are a number of fundamental distinctions that are assumed to be common to human kind: a sense of self; a sense of spatio-temporal location; a sense of willed action; and finally, a sense of responsibility for one's actions. The manner in which all these elements are culturally anchored can, however, vary considerably. What is traced in such universalistic reasoning is that there are some fundamental ways in which human existence is anchored in social and physical reality, because of the limiting biological conditions that are characteristic of our species (*see* Semin & Manstead, 1983). Nevertheless, this does not mean that they are manifested identically across cultures. Moreover, there is ample evidence that how the person is formed historically and culturally can vary substantially despite some potentially invariable features. It is to these that we now turn.

## THE CULTURAL FORMATION OF THE PERSON

The cultural and historical formation of the person becomes evident from even a cursory survey of etymological, social historical, and anthropological evidence, all of which suggests that there is considerable variation in the way in which identities are embedded in social relationships. This variation, which is *analytically* referred to as individualism versus collectivism, can also be found under other names in the literature (e.g., ego-centred versus socio-centred, Shweder & Bourne, 1982; independent versus interdependent, Markus & Kitayama, 1991). When reading about this distinction and its characteristics as well as consequences it is important not to lose sight of the fact that this is purely an *analytic distinction*. This means that there are numerous examples of collectivistic behavior within an individualistic culture or of individualistic behavior in a collectivistic culture. The distinction is primarily an intellectual tool.

## COLLECTIVISM

Across and *within* cultures one finds circumstances in which the meaning of a person and its realization is expressed predominantly in relationships. There are instances where the meaning of being a person is completely embedded in relationships that are formalized and contextualized within a social organiza-

tion. For collectivists there is a sharper distinction between ingroup and outgroup than for individualists as some research suggests. Cross-cultural work shows that in India, for instance, there are distinctly holistic and thus relational cultural conceptions of the person. In such cases, the social role rather than the "individual" is treated as the primary normative unit (*see* Shweder & Bourne, 1982). Another instance is traditional Japanese culture, formed under the strong influence of Confucianism, where the person is not individualistic. The status of the person is a dependent one, whereby s/he is identified in terms of his or her affiliations with a certain social group and where the person perceives him/herself as the sum total of several autonomous "areas of duties" such as "ko" (to one's parents), "giri" (to people to whom one is indebted socially), "jin" (humanity and loyalty), "ninjo" (duties to oneself), etc. Thus, the category of the person and its assessment are related to its area of action. Behavior is derived from the general rule, the norm, where personality, in our Western sense, is not valued. Instead, "personhood" is seen as duties and responsibilities resulting from being a part of a community, or a family, where the self is not separable from the role. This appears to be very similar to conceptions of the person which were prevalent in mediaeval Europe.

The main tenet of the person in collectivism is the fundamental connectedness of persons. The essential aspect of this is the normative interdependence, or relatedness of persons (Shweder & Bourne, 1982; Triandis, 1988). Thus, one of the important aspects of the person in this perspective is the interconnectedness of self to a variety of different social demands, roles, and contexts, the existence of obligations that regulate identity. This does not mean that properties of persons such as traits, abilities, and other personal attributes are not available, but rather that these are seen as less important or less central in regulating behavior. Furthermore, they are not seen as indicative of the person, in a diagnostic sense, to the same degree as they are in the individualistic cultural context, discussed below. More influential determinants of behavior are the relationships that are obtained in roles, social interdependences, etc.

Contrasting with this sketch of how the domain of the person is conceptualized in collectivistic cultures we have the Western mentality of individuality, which is a "modern form of self-conception" in which, in Cherry's words, "Man is now alone; he has lost personal identity and meaning in any permanent group and cannot find them in himself" (Cherry, 1967, p. 724). It is to this that we turn next.

## THE INDIVIDUALISTIC CONCEPTION OF THE PERSON

In the case of contemporary Western culture the person is predominantly represented independent of *permanent* groups. Rather, the person derives meaning in this type of cultural context from uniqueness and the realization of this uniqueness as is manifested in such highly valued goals as self-actualization, the felt need to develop one's abilities, fulfill one's potentials, and so on.

Obviously, this does not mean that the person in an individualistic culture is oblivious to the social environment. The role that the social environment plays in this culture is however mainly in terms of how best to express and realize one's qualities, abilities, and personality. In this sense the social environment sets conditions for strategic decisions, and serves as a set of markers by which one can measure and assess one's self. The self is perceived as independent of others and as a bounded, unique center of cognition, emotion, and action. Furthermore, the person is perceived to be relatively stable over time and characterized in terms of a number of stable personality and ability characteristics that are seen as enabling the prediction of the person's behaviors.

It is the more specific social psychological processes that we turn to next and the concern now is to examine how the broader analytic distinction that is made between individualism and collectivism influences fundamental social psychological processes. It should be noted that this research is very much in its infancy although the implications of the findings are far-reaching.

## THE SOCIAL PSYCHOLOGICAL IMPLICATIONS OF COLLECTIVISM–INDIVIDUALISM

As Triandis (1988) points out, identifying dimensions of cultural variation, such as collectivism versus individualism is one thing; to translate such a distinction into a psychological one and then show influence upon cognitive, affective, and behavioral processes is another. The distinction that we have examined analytically so far, namely collectivism versus individualism, translates itself in psychological terms with respect to the differences in the way the person relates to the group or in the way identities are embedded in social relationships. Triandis (1988) contrasts individualism with collectivism and suggests that in collectivism personal goals are subordinate to ingroup goals; greater emphasis is put on the social norms and duties; beliefs are consensual to the ingroup; there is a higher readiness towards ingroup co-operation; and emotional attachment to the ingroup is stronger. Other distinctions suggest that in cultures with a predominantly collectivist orientation activities are more "situation centred" rather than "individual centred"; there is a stronger "social orientation" rather than an "individual orientation." Such distinctions have to be translated into meaningful psychological constructs and most importantly, the distinction between the two cultural orientations has to be anchored in terms of operationalizable psychological variables.

In particular, one can argue and show that if the cultural construction of the person varies along the lines that have been suggested so far then there are fundamental implications for cognitive activities that involve the person (*see* Markus & Kitayama, 1991). This is evident in the types of issues that one can explore with respect to variations in cognitive activity that involve the self, whereby the self varies as a function of cultural background. Markus and Kitayama (1991) suggest three important implications. These are:

1. If persons construct themselves *interdependently* then they will be more sensitive and attentive to others than are *individualistic* persons. Thus, one may expect that the construal of the other will be more elaborated

cognitively and this will express itself in self–other differences in cognitive elaboration.

2. For interdependent persons the construction of the self in relation to the other will entail a relatively specific context in which self and other are related. Thus, knowledge about self and others will not be abstracted and generalized across contexts, but will be anchored in particularistic contexts. It may be noted that this should also express itself in different use of language, in that interdependent persons should use more concrete language than individualists when describing self and others.

3. Contextual representation and the reactions of others versus person-centered representation may also influence other cognitive activities such as categorization of events and persons and counterfactual thinking.

One of the important implications that Markus and Kitayama (1991) derive from these considerations is the following: "How a given object is culturally construed and represented in memory should importantly influence and even determine how one thinks about the object" (p. 231). This is an acknowledgement of content over process, which is quite remarkable in view of the general tenor of cognitive social psychology which to date has emphasized the reverse, namely the primacy of process over content.

IMPLICATIONS FOR SOCIAL COGNITION
There are a number of ways in which central social psychological findings are brought into question by a consideration of how differences in the cultural formation of persons may affect SOCIAL COGNITION (*see* Smith & Bond, 1993).

An early classic study is the one reported by Miller (1984). She examined different patterns of explanation used by Americans and Indian Hindus. The question she tried to answer was whether Americans, who have a more ego-centred conception of the person, explain the causes of social behavior in more dispositional terms than Hindu Indians, who have a socio-centred conception of the person. Subjects were asked to explain two prosocial and two deviant behaviors. On average 40 percent of the American subjects responded with general dispositions for the actor. Hindu respondents, in contrast, used dispositional language for only 20 percent of their answers, thereby apparently failing to display the FUNDAMENTAL ATTRIBUTION ERROR. Another type of cognitive difference that has been explored is sensitivity to others who are present in a social situation. If people in a collectivistic culture are more concerned about social relationships and the maintenance of harmony in such relationships, they should be more knowledgeable about how the others feel, think and are likely to act. The argument is that collectivistic people should have a denser and more informed store of knowledge about others and their self in relation to others. Typical studies show that in American students the self is seen to be more dissimilar to the other than the other is to self. This asymmetry has been interpreted as a result of the more elaborate self-representation in memory that Americans have than their representation of "others." Consequently, similarity is judged to be less when the question is posed about a more distinctive object (Is self similar to other?) than when the question is posed about a less distinctive object (Is other similar to self?). With Eastern subjects one finds the reverse pattern. This is seen as suggesting that knowledge about the other is more elaborated and distinctive than knowledge about the self.

Other studies have investigated SELF-SERVING BIAS in Japanese and American subjects by administering a series of "false uniqueness" items. Whereas American subjects display the false uniqueness tendency, Japanese subjects do not. They estimate about 50 percent of their fellow students to be better than themselves or to have more of a given trait or ability. Indeed, what studies with Japanese students seem to show is a "self-effacing bias" or a "modesty bias," as has been demonstrated by the causal attributions Japanese subjects make after success and failure.

The studies summarized here (*see* Markus & Kitayama, 1991, for detail) represent a selection of the various experiments that are now emerging within a framework of what one may term comparative experimental social psychology. The noteworthy element in these studies is that what were often regarded as stable experimental findings are beginning to attract a more careful examination in terms of whether such findings are culture specific and, if they are, to what extent social psychologists typically examine phenomena and develop and test theories that are peculiar to a specific population (Western Culture). This development constitutes one of the greatest challenges to social psychology.

See also: ETHOGENICS; SOCIAL COGNITION; SOCIAL CONSTRUCTIONISM.

BIBLIOGRAPHY

Cherry, C. (1967). "But there is nothing I have is essential to me" (Or "The human race is not a club"). In To honor Roman Jacobson (Vol. I, pp. 132–158). The Hague: Mouton.

Hallowell, A. I. (1971). Culture and experience (2nd ed.). Philadelphia, PA: University of Pennsylvania Press.

Hofstede, G. (1980) Culture's consequences: International differences in work-related values. Beverly Hills, CA: Sage.

Markus, H. R., & Kitayama, S. (1991). Culture and the self: Implications for cognition, emotion and motivation. Psychological Review, 98, 224–53.

Miller, J. (1984). Culture and the development of everyday social explanation. Journal of Personality and Social Psychology, 46, 961–78.

Mühlhäuser, P., & Harré, R. (1991). Identity and pronouns. Oxford: Blackwell Publishers.

Semin, G. R., & Manstead, A. S. R. (1983). The epistemological foundations of accountability of conduct. In G. R. Semin & A. S. R. Manstead, The accountability of conduct (pp. 156–85). London: Academic Press.

Shweder, R. A., & Bourne, E. J. (1982). Does the concept of person vary cross-culturally? In A. J. Marsella & G. M. White (Eds.), Cultural conceptions of mental health and therapy (pp. 97–137) Boston, MA: Reidel.

Smith, P. B., & Bond, M. H. (1993). Social psychology across cultures. Hemel Hempstead: Harvester Wheatsheaf.

Triandis, H. C. (1988). Collectivism vs. individualism: A reconceptualization of a basic concept of cross-cultural psychology. In G.

K. Verma & C. Bagley (Eds.), Cross-cultural studies of personality, attitudes and cognition (pp. 60–95). London: Macmillan

GÜN R. SEMIN

inference A term which refers to the use of available information to derive conclusions about a specific problem or task. Inference is extensively studied in the context of inductive REASONING. For instance, when do people infer stable personal characteristics from a specific behavior (see ATTRIBUTION THEORIES)? Another research area of relevance concerns statistical inference. Overall, the quality of statistical inference when making decisions and predictions tends to vary widely. Both experts and lay people tend to rely on HEURISTICS. BASE RATE information or prior probabilities are often ignored (see also BAYES" THEOREM) as compared to more concrete evidence that is easily accessed in memory. The use of intuitive inferential strategies is often compared with formal strategies. The latter tend to have greater dividends and often the costs are lower. For example, the mechanical application of simple linear models to infer or predict student performance seems to achieve better results than costly intuitive strategies based on extensive interviewing. Especially for recurrent judgment tasks such as personnel selection and (some) diagnostic tasks, formal approaches could greatly improve DECISION MAKING and choice. Improving statistical inference can also be achieved by training. Effects of training (e.g., in the context of diagnostic reasoning) tend to be mixed, however (see Fiske & Taylor, 1991).

See also: ATTRIBUTION THEORIES; DECISION MAKING; HEURISTICS; REASONING.

BIBLIOGRAPHY

Fiske, S. T., & Taylor, S. E. (1991). Social Cognition (2nd ed.). New York: McGraw-Hill.

JOOP VAN DER PLIGT

informational influence A major process of SOCIAL INFLUENCE. It is influence to accept information from (similar, expert, credible) others as (trustworthy) evidence about reality, leads to private ATTITUDE CHANGE rather than merely public COMPLIANCE, and is motivated by the desire to be correct and reduce one's uncertainty.

*See also*: ATTITUDE CHANGE; SOCIAL IN-FLUENCE.

JOHN C. TURNER

**innovation** The successful implementation of creative ideas by an organization or group. Although CREATIVITY (the production of novel and appropriate ideas) is possible without ultimately successful innovation, innovation is not possible without creative ideas. Some cognitive style researchers use the term "innovation" to describe an orientation toward breaking cognitive set.

*See also*: CREATIVITY.

TERESA M. AMABILE

**integration** A social policy one of whose objectives is the achievement of numerical group representation in schools, housing schemes, and workplaces roughly equivalent to the representation of those groups in the wider society. Another objective of integration is the mutual recognition of group differences, which distinguishes it from assimilation in which minority groups lose their separate identities in the dominant group culture. Its ultimate goal is the elimination of barriers and impediments which are based on ethnicity, gender, and disability. It is seen by the World Health Organization as a basic human right particularly for those minority groups who historically have not been accorded equal access in a number of important areas: e.g., education, housing, and sport. Of these, one of the most significant from both a political and a social psychological standpoint is education.

Over the past four decades there have been a number of policies in industrialized countries specifically aimed at redressing the balance in respect of children from minority ethnic groups and children with disabilities. One of the explicit rationales for these policies has been that the increased amounts of social interaction between groups arising from integration will result in more positive attitudes towards the previously excluded groups. In the United States an important stimulus for educational integration was the 1954 Supreme Court ruling that segregated schools were unconstitutional. Subsequent legislation at both national and state level required school systems to implement desegregation policies. Following these judicial rulings, attempts were made to change the ethnic composition of schools in areas characterized by ethnic diversity, albeit unwillingly in some cases. The hope of the instigators of these integration policies was that they would raise achievement and SELF-ESTEEM levels of previously disadvantaged groups and improve relationships between them and dominant groups. However, such hopes have not always been realized. While it is true that some commentators have concluded that desegregation did have the expected positive effects in raising minority group achievement, others have been more cautious (Stephan, 1978). Indeed, some studies reported negative consequences of integration – for example, lowered Black self-esteem or ethnic resegregation within the school (Gerard & Miller, 1975; Schofield, 1982). In other domains – for example, the integration of children with learning or physical disabilities – less evidence is available. What evidence there is suggests that integration can have positive benefits (e.g., Brinker, 1985).

Much of the ambiguity surrounding the social and educational effects of integration policies can be attributed to the way such policies have actually been implemented in schools. For integration to be successful in promoting more favorable intergroup relations it should satisfy the optimal conditions of intergroup contact as hypothesized by the CONTACT HYPOTHESIS. Of these, equal status interaction over cooperative goals in an institution which actively supports the goals of integration are probably the most important. However, many attempts to desegregate school systems have failed to meet one or more of these criteria. For example, preexisting status differences are often perpetuated inside the school in the form of different academic ability groupings which are usually correlated with ethnic or class origin. Typical class-room teaching practices may encourage competition between students – e.g., for grades or for the teacher's attention – rather than cooperation. Finally, some schools may have introduced integration unwillingly under the threat of legal sanction and hence may foster a climate unfavourable to its acceptance. Thus the outcomes of school integration have not always matched expectations (Stephan, 1978).

A further difficulty encountered in the implementation of school integration policies derives from the implied assimilation of minority groups into the dominant culture (Schofield, 1982). This can give rise to two problems. The first is that the curriculum may be devised, delivered, and assessed only from the dominant group's perspective which, if minority groups happen to endorse different value systems or adopt different cognitive, linguistic, or interactional styles, can put children coming from such groups at an academic disadvantage. The second is that minority groups may resist the integration policy because of fears that their cultural identity will be absorbed and lost in the dominant group. The desire to preserve their language or their religion are often particularly contentious issues.

One promising avenue to counter these problems is the wider use of cooperative learning groups, particularly when employed in the microcontext of the classroom. In a cooperative learning exercise the class is typically broken down into small ethnically mixed groups. Each group is given some task to undertake which requires the collaborative efforts of all its members for successful achievement. Assessment is based partly or wholly on the basis of the collective result. One advantage of this technique is that it satisfies several of the criteria for optimizing the effects of intergroup contact since participants enjoy equal status and are dependent on each other for the achievement of jointly desired goals. Moreover, learning tasks can sometimes be devised which capitalize on rather than eliminate the ethnic diversity of the group. The evidence suggests that the use of cooperative learning groups can raise the performance and self-esteem of minority group children, increase the number of cross-ethnic friendships, and improve the educational achievement and social acceptability of children with learning disabilities (Slavin, 1983).

*See also*: CONTACT HYPOTHESIS; SELF- ESTEEM.

BIBLIOGRAPHY
Brinker, R. P. (1985). Interactions between severely mentally retarded students and other students in integrated and segregated public school settings *American Association of Mental Deficiency*, 89, 587–94.
Gerard, H., & Miller, N. (1975). *School desegregation*. New York: Plenum.
Schofield, J. W. (1982). *Black and white in school: Trust, tension or tolerance?* New York: Praeger.
Slavin, R. E. (1983). *Cooperative learning*. New York: Longman.
Stephan, W. G. (1978). School desegregation: An evaluation of predictions made in *Brown* vs. *Board of Education*, *Psychological Bulletin*, 85, 217–38.

RUPERT BROWN
PAM MARAS

**integrative complexity** The capacity and willingness to:

(1) acknowledge the legitimacy of contradictory perspectives on a problem; and
(2) integrate those contradictory considerations into an overall judgment.

This construct was originally conceived as an effort to capture INDIVIDUAL DIFFERENCES in styles of social thinking (Schroder, Driver, & Streufert, 1978, Streufert & Streufert; 1978). Some people, it was posited, dislike ambiguity and dissonance and seek rapid cognitive closure in judging others and in making decisions. They form dichotomous (good versus bad) impressions of people, events, and issues. Other people, it was posited, adopt more flexible, open-minded, and multidimensional stances toward the social world. These people recognize that life abounds with inconsistencies and contradictions. In this view, the intentions underlying behavior often consist of complex mixtures of motives (some good, some bad); making decisions often requires balancing conflicting goals; and life itself is a process of continual change that requires frequent updating of basic assumptions and beliefs. The earliest efforts to assess individual differences in integrative complexity relied heavily on the semiprojective Paragraph Completion Test. This test presented subjects with sentence stems that focused on issues of interpersonal conflict, societal authority, and decisional ambiguity. Subjects were asked to complete each stem and to write at least one additional sentence. Trained coders then assessed responses on a seven-point complexity scale that was defined by two cognitive stylistic indicators: evaluative differentiation (the capacity and willingness to tolerate different points of view) and conceptual integration (the capacity and willingness to generate linkages between points of view, to understand why different people look at the same event in different ways, to confront trade-offs, and to appreciate interactive patterns of causation).

Low scores indicated low differentiation and integration (denial of ambiguity and shades of gray); moderate scores reflected moderate differentiation but no integration (recognition of divergent viewpoints but no means of synthesizing or tying perspectives together); high scores reflected high differentiation and high integration (explicit attempts to grapple with contradictions, to understand their sources, and to cope with their consequences). Research on individual differences in integrative complexity proved moderately fruitful. Persons classified as dispositionally complex were more tolerant of incongruous trait combinations in impression formation tasks, more likely to use a variety of information in making decisions, and more likely to reach mutually beneficial compromises in mixed motive games. The static TRAIT model of integrative complexity did, however, prove too confining. Later research branched out in a number of directions. One line of research focused on the impact of environmental stressors (time pressure, information load, threat) on the complexity of thinking. A second line of work focused on the impact of value conflict and demonstrated replicable ideology-by-issue interactions in integrative complexity.

A third line of work focused on the impact of ACCOUNTABILITY.

Since the mid-1970s, integrative complexity research has no longer been confined to laboratory settings (Suedfeld & Rank, 1976). Researchers have applied the integrative complexity coding system to a wide range of archival documents, including political speeches, letters and diaries, newspaper editorials, Supreme Court opinions, and diplomatic communications. This line of work has shown that it is possible to replicate many functional relationships observed in laboratory settings, in complex historical settings. Researchers have shown, for example, that integratively complex thinkers are less likely to resort to coercive tactics in conflicts of interest than are integratively simple thinkers and that integratively complex bargainers are more likely to reach mutually beneficial agreements than are integratively simple bargainers.

A major source of contention concerns the conditions under which integrative simplicity or complexity should be viewed as adaptive or maladaptive. This debate underscores the somewhat ironic point that in thinking about integrative complexity, it is useful to be integratively complex. It is too simple to conclude that people are always well advised to be integratively complex.

At first glance, the normative case for integrative complexity appears to be overwhelming. Integratively complex subjects have been found in several experiments to be more resistant to a number of judgmental biases. Complex thinkers are less likely, for example, to jump to strong conclusions about the personalities of others when there are plausible situational explanations for their behavior (the FUNDAMENTAL ATTRIBUTION ERROR), less likely to persist with their first impressions of an event in the face of contradictory evidence, and less likely to display overconfidence in their factual judgments and predictions. Integratively complex thinkers are also less likely to fall prey to GROUPTHINK and are more likely to acknowledge value trade-offs in policy debates (*see* Tetlock, 1986, 1992). Finally, integratively complex thinkers are better equipped to identify viable compromises in mixed motive games that leave everyone at least somewhat better off.

Additional research has, however, revealed that for every judgmental bias and shortcoming that integrative complexity reduces, there is a mirror image bias or shortcoming that integrative complexity may exacerbate. For example, complex thinkers are more prone to the dilution effect (the tendency to lose confidence in a genuinely diagnostic cue when that cue is accompanied by irrelevant evidence). Complex thinkers are more likely to procrastinate and buckpass in the face of difficult cost–benefit decisions concerning the admissibility of drugs into the US pharmaceuticals market. Although complex bargainers are better able to reach integrative agreements with reasonable adversaries in mixed motive games, they are also more vulnerable to exploitation by unreasonable adversaries in those same games. Finally, although awareness of trade-offs is often an adaptive attribute in decision making, there are occasions in which trade-off reasoning looks foolish and even immoral to many observers. Consider, for example, the finding that integratively complex thinkers are over-represented among centrists in mid-nineteenth century America who struggled unsuccessfully to find a trade-off formula that would permit but restrict slavery and thereby mollify both Northern critics of the practice and Southerners who threatened to secede unless slaves were regarded as property. Few contemporary observers would applaud integrative complexity in this context.

In brief, integrative complexity research has evolved in a variety of directions. Key issues have included the status of integrative complexity as a personality as opposed to situational variable, the usefulness of both experimental and nonexperimental methods in studying integrative complexity, and the conditions under which integrative simplicity–complexity is adaptive or maladaptive.

See also: ACCOUNTABILITY; GROUPTHINK.

BIBLIOGRAPHY

Schroder, H. M., Driver, M. J., & Streufert, S. (1967). *Human information processing*. New York: Holt, Rinehart & Winston.

Streufert, S., & Streufert, S. (1978). *Behavior in a complex environment*. Washington, DC: Winston & Sons.

Suedfeld, P., & Rank, A. D. (1976). Revolutionary leaders: Long-term success as a function of changes in conceptual complexity. *Journal of Personality and Social Psychology, 34*, 169–78.

Tetlock, P. E. (1986). A value pluralism model of ideological reasoning. *Journal of Personality and Social Psychology: Personality Processes and Individual Differences, 50*, 819–27.

——(1992). The impact of accountability on judgment and choice: Toward a social contingency model. In M. Zanna (Ed.), *Advances in experimental social psychology* (Vol. 25, pp. 331–76). New York: Academic Press.

PHILIP E. TETLOCK

**interaction process analysis**   A method devised by Bales (1950, 1970) for the continuous observation of communication patterns in interactive groups (*see also* GROUP PROCESSES, GROUP STRUCTURE). Based on the assumption that group success depends on both how well the group can solve its tasks (task function) and how satisfied it can keep its members (socio-emotional function), Bales identified 12 interactional "moves" in four categories:

(1) socio-emotional positive (shows solidarity, tension reduction, agreement);
(2) socio-emotional negative (shows antagonism, tension, disagreement);
(3) task-related attempted solutions (gives suggestions, opinions, orientation); and
(4) task-related questions (asks for suggestions, opinions, orientation).

At least one rater observes each group member, and scores occurrences of each interactional "move."

This method has been used in a variety of settings, and is a reliable and useful way to analyze group interactions. For instance, it reveals that different people tend to occupy the roles of socio-emotional specialist and task specialist in a group, and has led to the idea that there are two distinct styles of LEADERSHIP behavior. Interaction process analysis has been criticized for overemphasizing spoken communication, and failing to consider the important role of NONVERBAL COMMUNICATION.

*See also*: GROUP PROCESSES; GROUP STRUCTURE; LEADERSHIP; NONVERBAL COMMUNICATION.

BIBLIOGRAPHY

Bales, R. F. (1950). *Interaction process analysis: A method for the study of small groups.* Reading, MA: Addison-Wesley.

——(1970). *Personality and interpersonal behavior.* New York: Holt, Rinehart & Winston.

MICHAEL A. HOGG

**interdependence theory** Human experience is inherently social. Much of life unfolds in the context of dyadic or group interactions, many human traits have their origins in interpersonal experience, and the source of many powerful norms can be identified in the interdependent situations for which those norms provide good adaptations. To fully comprehend human behavior it is necessary that we understand the nature and meaning of interpersonal interdependence. This entry delineates the primary features of interpersonal phenomena using interdependence theory, a comprehensive model of interpersonal processes. (For an in-depth discussion, readers should consult original interdependence theory references (Kelley, 1979; Kelley & Thibaut, 1969, 1978; Thibaut & Kelley, 1959), as well as several recent extensions of the theory (Kelley, 1983, 1984a, b; Kelley & Thibaut, 1985).)

Thibaut and Kelley (1959) developed interdependence theory toward the goal of extending and clarifying Lewinian field theory propositions, particularly the life-space representation of human motivation. The theory presents a taxonomy of patterns of interdependence – a conceptual framework in which all possible forms of interdependence can be analyzed in terms of four critical properties: degree of dependence, mutuality of dependence, correspondence of outcomes, and basis for dependence. The theory also proffers methods for evaluating the major properties of interdependence, and discusses the ways in which perceived patterns of interdependence become transformed by personal values and dispositions. A variety of social-cognitive phenomena, affective experiences, and behavioral tendencies are said to be importantly shaped by the interdependent situations from which they emerge.

Interdependence theory focuses on *interaction* as the core of all social psychological phenomena. That is, individuals communicate with other persons, they create products for one another, or they emit behaviors that affect one another. As such, interaction involves the potential for unilateral or bilateral influence – the possibility that one individual's behavior will affect the behavior or experiences of one or more interaction partners. In new social situations and new relationships, the full range of potential joint behaviors and outcomes will not immediately be evident to interacting individuals – partners sample their behavioral repertoires through the course of extended interaction in ongoing relationships.

TRANSFORMATION OF MOTIVATION:
GIVEN VERSUS EFFECTIVE MATRIX
PREFERENCES

The options and outcomes of interaction are formally represented through the use of a simple conceptual tool – the *outcome matrix*. (The matrix is a theoretical tool, and is not intended to stand as a literal depiction of lay cognition, emotion, or MOTIVATION – it is unlikely that individuals conceptualize or experience interaction in terms of numerical values arrayed in matrices.) The simplest form of interaction can be described by a 2 × 2 matrix – as an interaction situation in which each of two individuals (Partners A and B) can enact either of two behaviors (Behavior 1 or 2). Each of the four cells in the 2 × 2 matrix represents the joint occurence of the respective behaviors emitted by the two interacting persons (see figure 1). Each cell in the matrix is associated with two outcome values, representing the impact of the interaction on each person (A's outcomes are above the diagonal; B's outcomes are below the diagonal).

Of course, interaction in ongoing relationships is more complex than a symmetrical

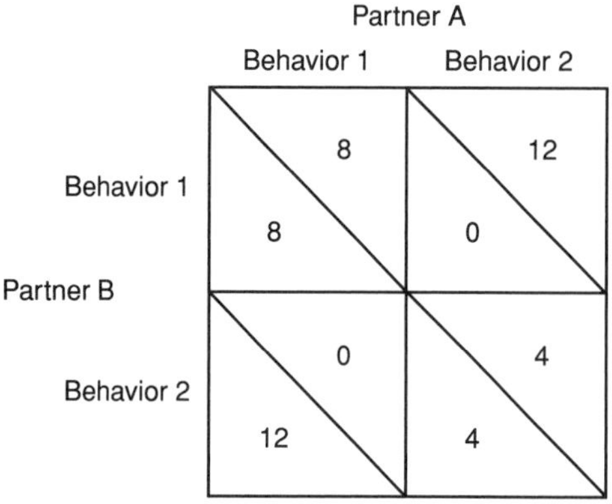

Partner A

Behavior 1        Behavior 2

Figure 1. 2 × 2 outcome matrix.

2 × 2 matrix: Extended relationships typically involve a large number of possible behaviors, the behavioral repertoires of the interacting persons may differ (i.e., the matrix may not be symmetrical), and the repertoires of the involved parties may change. Moreover, many interactions involve more than two individuals. But irrespective of the complexity of the full matrix representing a given relationship, specific interactions yield consequences for both persons – outcomes that can be delineated in terms of rewards and costs.

The individual's subjective experience of a specific interaction outcome is partly shaped by the direct, hedonistic effects of the interaction itself, or the direct, concrete outcomes of a given interaction. Immediate, self-centered preferences based upon direct self-interest are termed *given matrix* preferences. Such outcomes are "given" in that "the behavioral choices and outcomes are strongly under the control of factors external to the interdependence relationship itself. The outcome in each cell of the matrix – each intersecting or joint behavior – is *given* for the relationship by virtue of the specifications of the social and physical environment and the relevant properties of the two persons' (Kelley & Thibaut, 1978, pp. 16–17).

However, experienced outcomes, preferences, and behavioral choices frequently reflect more than the direct pursuit of primitive, immediate self-interest. Preferences are also shaped by broader concerns, such as strategic

considerations, long-term interaction goals, or desire to influence both one's own and a partner's outcomes. Movement away from "gut level," given matrix preferences is said to result from *transformation of motivation* – a process which often leads individuals to relinquish immediate self-interest and act on the basis of broader goals. For example, individuals may behave in ways that yield relatively poor personal outcomes because in so doing they can promote the well-being of an interaction partner. Also, individuals may forego immediate self-interest so as to obtain exceptionally desirable outcomes in future interactions.

By responding on the basis of broader issues of interdependence, individuals essentially transform the given matrix into a new set of behavioral preferences termed the *effective matrix* – a redefined set of preferences which is closely linked to actual behavior. The transformation concept stands as a means of describing important social psychological causes of behavior, including temporal organization, social VALUES, or broader norms and roles. Many types of transformation are possible. For example, Max Joint transformation represents motivation to maximize the goodness of both one's own and an interaction partner's outcomes; Max Rel transformation represents motivation to maximize the goodness of one's own outcomes relative to the outcomes of an interaction partner.

COMPARISON LEVEL AND COMPARISON LEVEL FOR ALTERNATIVES

Outcomes are not experienced in a vacuum. Above and beyond actual outcomes, individuals' evaluations of interactions and relationships are influenced by internal standards which to some degree are socially defined – the comparison level and the comparison level for alternatives. *Comparison level* (CL) is an internal standard representing the quality of outcomes an individual expects to obtain in a relationship. (CL) is affected not only by the individual's own previous experiences but also by SOCIAL COMPARISON. In contrast, the *comparison level for alternatives* (CL-alt) is an internal standard representing the quality of outcomes an individual perceives to be available outside of the current relationship. CL-alt is influenced not only by the specific alternative relationships that are available to an individual, but also by the broader field of alternatives and the desirability (or undesirability) of noninvolvement.

The positions of CL and CL-alt relative to actual obtained outcomes define two key variables – satisfaction and dependence. *Satisfaction level* refers to the degree to which a relationship fulfills important needs, or is experienced as gratifying. When obtained outcomes exceed an individual's CL the individual will feel satisfied; outcomes below CL are experienced as dissatisfying. *Dependence level* refers to the degree to which an individual relies on a given partner and relationship for the fulfillment of important needs, or the extent to which an individual "needs" a relationship. When outcomes exceed CL-alt the individual is dependent upon a relationship (i.e., experiences stronger COMMITMENT); when CL-alt is greater than actual obtained outcomes, the individual is more independent. This distinction between satisfaction and dependence is important in that it separates the evaluation of a relationship from the stability of that relationship – for example, it becomes clear why individuals sometimes remain involved in relationships that are not very satisfying.

## FUNDAMENTAL PROPERTIES OF INTERDEPENDENCE

According to interdependence theory, the *structure of outcome interdependence* is the key to understanding the course of interaction. That is, by examining the pattern of interdependence between interacting partners, it is possible to learn a great deal about their possibilities for coordination versus conflict, or to assess the likelihood that one or both individuals will come to need the partner and rely on the relationship for important outcomes. Several types of interdependence analysis can illuminate the fabric of interaction processes. For example, it may be instructive to examine the sources of CONTROL over each interacting individual's outcomes, or the degree to which:

(1) individuals have direct control over the quality of their outcomes (*reflexive control*, or RC);

(2) individuals' outcomes are directly influenced by the actions of their interaction partners (*fate control*, or FC); and

(3) individuals' outcomes are jointly influenced by the actions of themselves and their interaction partners (*behavior control*, or BC).

To the extent that individuals have greater control over their outcomes – and to the extent that interaction partners have little control over the individual's outcomes (high RC, low FC and BC) – individuals are more *independent*. To the extent that individuals have little control over their outcomes – and to the extent that interaction partners have greater control over the individual's outcomes (low RC, high FC and BC) – individuals are more *dependent*. It should be intuitively clear that this definition of dependence parallels the earlier definition based on CL-alt: Individuals are more dependent to the extent that they cannot unilaterally guarantee themselves good outcomes – either in the context of an alternative relationship or through the option of noninvolvement – and accordingly rely on the actions of a partner for the fulfillment of important needs. Indeed, dependence can be construed as the converse of POWER. Individuals are dependent to the degree that their partners possess the power to move them through a wide range of outcomes – a power which is limited by the individual's ability to obtain good outcomes elsewhere.

Interdependence theory identifies four critical properties of interdependent relationships. *Degree of dependence* is one such feature – in obtaining good versus poor outcomes, to what degree is each individual dependent on the partner and on their joint activities? A second property concerns *mutuality of dependence*, or the degree to which partners are mutually rather than unilaterally dependent (i.e., the degree to which partners need their relationship to the same degree). A third property centers on *correspondence of outcomes*, defined in terms of the extent to which interacting partners' preferences for various joint outcomes correspond versus conflict (i.e., do partners similarly evaluate the many joint "cells" in their matrix of possible behaviors, whether the joint outcomes involve similar or different behaviors?). The fourth property concerns *basis for dependence* – the degree to which dependence involves joint versus individual control (i.e., FC versus BC, or exchange versus coordination).

## ATTRIBUTIONAL ANALYSIS, EMOTIONAL REACTIONS, AND SELF-PRESENTATION PROCESSES

Interdependence involves some degree of uncertainty regarding important outcomes that are influenced by a partner's actions. Accordingly, behaving in an effective manner – and achieving gratifying long-term relationships – depends in part on the interacting partners' abilities to "read" one another's preferences and intentions. Individuals engage in *attributional activity* in the course of attempts to uncover the direct meaning and broader implications of a partner's actions (*see* ATTRIBUTION THEORY). Attribution resides at the heart of interaction in at least two respects. First, the essential information for attributional activity lies in the disparity between given matrix and effective matrix preferences. For example, "if the choice of a particular behavior departs from what would best suit one's personal, self-serving interests, then [the individual] will be providing evidence of [his or her] feelings and attitudes toward [a] partner" (Holmes, 1981, p. 262). Second, individuals can engage in "informed" transformation of motivation to the extent that they can predict interaction partners' preferences, motives, and probable behavior – prediction which rests on attributional inferences. Thus, attributional activity involves interpreting the partner's given matrix and effective matrix preferences, inferring the implications of these data for understanding a partner's intentions and motives.

AFFECT also plays an important role in interaction. Kelley (1984a) presents a functional analysis of the role of *emotional reactions* in guiding interaction, suggesting that along with attributional activity, affect plays a key role in summarizing and orienting interaction processes. Retrospectively, affect flags specific patterns of interdependence,

marking the causal factors that are relevant to a given interaction (e.g., feeling angry when a partner ignores one's needs and preferences). Prospectively, affect stimulates and directs behavior with respect to the causal structure of a given situation (e.g., fear-induced escape from potentially costly interdependent situations). Thus, both attributions and emotions "summarize" the gist of a given interaction, embodying the meaning of a partner's actions (e.g., blame, righteous indignation), encapsulating preferences for one's own and a partner's outcomes (e.g., desire for revenge), shaping motivation (e.g., Max Rel motivation), and directing actual behavior (e.g., vengeful acts).

Moreover, individuals engage in SELF-PRESENTATION as a means of communicating their own goals, values, and motivations to interaction partners. Just as individuals engage in attributional activity to interpret and predict a partner's preferences and behavior, they engage in self-presentational activities to influence the partner's interpretations of their own preferences, motives, and behavior. Sometimes self-presentation is oriented toward the goal of making one's true motives and preferences evident to an interaction partner, and sometimes individuals engage in deceptive self-presentation to disguise their true motives and preferences. In either event, self-presentation has the goal of shaping or controlling the partner's emotions, attributional interpretations, preferences, or behavior.

## HABITUAL TRANSFORMATIONAL TENDENCIES: DISPOSITIONS, MACROMOTIVES, AND NORMS

When an individual initially encounters a specific pattern of interdependence with a given partner, the pattern may be experienced as a unique situation, or a set of "problems and opportunities" to which the individual must react. The individual may experience a mix of cognitions and emotions, consider the surrounding circumstances, review the available options, and decide how to behave. Alternatively, the individual may react impulsively, being guided by the predominant emotional tone accompanying the interaction. In either event experience has been acquired, and such experience may give rise to a habitual response pattern. If the reaction yields undesirable outcomes, the individual is likely to behave differently in future experiences with similar patterns of interdependence. If the reaction yields desirable outcomes, the individual is likely to react similarly on encountering similar patterns in the future. Thus, individuals develop "solutions" for repeatedly encountered patterns of interdependence – solutions that on average yield desirable outcomes.

What do these habitual solutions – or transformational tendencies – "look like" in interaction? Such "human tendencies" can shape the course of interaction in at least three ways. First, some habitual tendencies operate as *interpersonal dispositions* (*see* INDIVIDUAL DIFFERENCES). Through the course of development individuals may take on transformational tendencies or social orientations (e.g., behaving selfishly versus cooperatively; seeking versus avoiding intimacy; *see* SOCIAL VALUES; *see* Messick & McClintock, 1968). Such tendencies presumably reflect one's social experiences – we undergo different experiences with parents and peers, are presented with different opportunities and constraints, and in short have different histories of interdependence. Accordingly, individuals acquire transformational tendencies, reflected in the probability of approaching certain classes of interdependent situation in one manner rather than another – tendencies to apply particular transformations to particular situations with greater or lesser probability.

A second type of transformational tendency exists at a relatively more interpersonal, or dyadic, level. *Macromotives* are relationship-specific solutions that can regulate behavior across a fairly wide range of specific interdependence problems (*see* Holmes, 1981). For example, COMMITMENT and TRUST can be construed as long-term orientations that lead individuals to engage in Max Joint transformation of motivation in situations of moderate to low correspondence. That is, the committed and trusting individual may fairly automatically accommodate rather than retaliate when a partner engages in a potentially destructive act, or may fairly unthinkingly exhibit willingness to sacrifice desirable outcomes for the good of a partner or relationship.

A third type of transformational tendency exists at a more global group or societal level. *Social* NORMS *and roles* are broad rules for dealing with specific problems and opportunities of interdependence. For example, most societies develop rules regarding acceptable sexual behavior (e.g., rules against adultery), perhaps as a means of avoiding the conflicts that might otherwise ensue. Likewise, everyday rules of civility and decency regulate interpersonal behavior so as to yield less conflictual, more harmonious interaction for all involved parties.

## TRANSITION LISTS AND INTERDEPENDENCE

A recent extension expands the analysis of interaction by representing interdependence using *transition lists* – a "set of lists, each of which specifies each person's options . . . and the consequences for each person of each combination of their respective selections among their options" (Kelley, 1984b, p. 960). That is, interdependence is understood not only in terms of the immediate outcomes associated with specific joint behaviors, but also in terms of the future interdependent situations and outcomes that are made available – or eliminated – as a consequence of specific joint behaviors. The transition list approach solves several problems inherent in the matrix representation, such as its omission of the sequential and temporal aspects of interdependence.

## SUMMARY AND CONCLUSIONS

Interdependence theory provides a taxonomy of interdependent situations and relationships, and assumes that social-cognitive phenomena (e.g., attribution, self-presentation), affective experiences (e.g., emotional reactions), and social behavior can best be understood through an analysis of the structure of the interdependent situations that give rise to such phenomena. Social behavior is mediated by transformation of motivation, the process by which individuals reconceptualize specific patterns of interdependence and act on the basis of broader interaction goals. Such transformational tendencies take the form of habitual response tendencies, manifested in interpersonal dispositions, relationship-specific macromotives, or internalized social norms. The utility of this orientation is underlined by the fact that interdependence theory can be – and has been – applied to a wide variety of social psychological content areas (e.g., cooperative and competitive behavior, interindividual versus intergroup interaction, organizational behavior, behavior in close relationships). Thus, through its formal analysis of the structure and functions of interdependence, interdependence theory stands as one of the most comprehensive models of interpersonal phenomena.

*See also:* ATTRIBUTION THEORIES; BARGAINING; CONFLICT; CONTROL; COOPERATION AND COMPETITION; EXPERIMENTAL GAMES; INTERGROUP RELATIONS; MOTIVATION; NORMS; POWER; SOCIAL COMPARISON; SOCIAL DILEMMAS; SOCIAL JUSTICE; SOCIAL VALUES; TRUST; VALUES; WORK.

BIBLIOGRAPHY

Holmes, J. G. (1981). The exchange process in close relationships: Microbehavior and macromotives. In M. Lerner & S. Lerner (Eds.), *The justice motive in social behavior: Adapting to times of scarcity and change* (pp. 261–84). New York: Plenum.

Kelley, H. H. (1979). *Personal relationships: Their structures and processes.* Hillsdale, NJ: Lawrence Erlbaum.

—— (1983). The situational origins of human tendencies: A further reason for the formal analysis of structures. *Personality and Social Psychology Bulletin, 9,* 8–30.

—— (1984a). Affect in interpersonal relations. In P. Shaver (Ed.), *Review of personality and social psychology* (Vol. 5, pp. 89–115). Newbury Park, CA: Sage.

—— (1984b). The theoretical description of interdependence by means of transition lists. *Journal of Personality and Social Psychology, 47,* 956–82.

—— & Thibaut, J. W. (1969). Group problem solving. In G. Lindzey & E. Aronson (Eds.), *Handbook of social psychology* (2nd ed., Vol. 4, pp. 1–101). Reading, MA: Addison-Wesley.

—— (1978). *Interpersonal relations: A theory of interdependence.* New York: Wiley.

—— (1985). Self-interest, science, and cynicism. *Journal of Social and Clinical Psychology, 3,* 26–32.

Messick, D. M., & McClintock, C. G. (1968). Motivational bases of choice in experimental games. *Journal of Experimental Social Psychology, 4,* 1–25.

Thibaut, J. W., & Kelley, H. H. (1959). *The social psychology of groups.* New York: Wiley.

CARYL E. RUSBULT
PAUL A. M. VAN LANGE

**intergroup relations** The social psychology of intergroup relations generally concerns the nature, causes, and consequences of individual's representations of relationships between their own and other groups. There have been two competing metatheoretical orientations, those which focus on personal or individual processes and those which focus on collective processes. All, however, aim to explain prejudice, discrimination and BIAS in intergroup perceptions.

EARLY APPROACHES
Theorists dating back to Gustav Le Bon have tried to account for the AGGRESSION and antinormative behavior of rioting crowds (*see* CROWD PSYCHOLOGY). Increased anonymity and nonidentifiability in the crowd produce DEINDIVIDUATION and a reduction in self-regulation (*see* SELF-AWARENESS) among crowd members. However, recent research has indicated that when the crowd has a common collective enemy (e.g., authorities, the police, or an ethnic outgroup) the behavior of its members is often well organized and conforms to NORMS established within the group or context (*see* Hogg & Abrams, 1988).

A related branch of theory concentrates on psychodynamic processes to account for the outgroups targeted for group aggression. Following Freudian theory, it was thought that when group members are frustrated because a goal is blocked, their aggressive response is displaced onto an outgroup which is sufficiently weak and dissimilar to the ingroup that the normal inhibitions on aggressive behavior do not operate. This FRUSTRATION-AGGRESSION analysis of intergroup relations was a precursor to more recent approaches such as RELATIVE DEPRIVATION and EQUITY THEORY.

Adorno and his colleagues explained the rise of fascism during World War II in terms of PERSONALITY dynamics. An authoritarian personality syndrome arises from suppressed hostility to parents and other unacceptable impulses which are then projected onto outgroups such as ethnic minorities. The problem with both of these psychodynamic approaches is that they cannot explain the consistency and specificity of intergroup hostility (*see* Hogg & Abrams, 1988).

The frustration–aggression model was expanded to include other moderating variables including situational cues and relative deprivation. Early versions of relative deprivation theory accounted for societal turmoil and unrest in terms of discrepancies between what individuals have and what they feel entitled to. Later models added variables such as the feasibility of attaining a desired outcome, and the sense of responsibility of not having attained it. Equity theory has also been applied to intergroup relations. Recent reviews emphasize a distinction between perceptions of inequality and affective reactions to those perceptions (Hogg & Abrams, 1993). An important distinction is made (following Runciman) between "egoistic" (or individual) and "fraternal" (or collective) deprivation. Intergroup attitudes and behavior are primarily affected by affective reactions to perceived deprivation of one's group vis à vis other groups, rather than egoistic deprivation. The situation is complicated by the fact that people actually make comparisons with different groups depending on whether they want to evaluate their situation or bolster their own position (in which case they are likely to select groups of lower status or wealth than their own). Thus the emphasis of this branch of theory has moved from the individual to the collective level.

Structural approaches to intergroup relations start with an analysis of the functional relationship (or type of interdependence) existing between groups. Perhaps the best known work is that by Sherif (1962), who defined intergroup relations as: "relations between two or more groups and their respective members. Whenever individuals belonging to one group interact, collectively or individually, with another group or its members *in terms of their group identifications* we have an instance of intergroup behaviour" (p. 5, my emphasis).

The behaviors and attitudes of group members are seen as a product of the intergroup relationship. Intragroup interaction defines norms, VALUES, and rules, along with outgroup STEREOTYPES, the content of which depends on the actual or perceived relations between the groups. If the groups are seen as being in competition for resources, the outgroup stereotypes are likely to be negative.

Sherif developed a REALISTIC CONFLICT THEORY. Through a series of field studies conducted in boys' summer camps, Sherif demonstrated that competitively interdependent conditions are sufficient to cause intergroup hostility. Equally important was the demonstration that personality or individual characteristics were not responsible for changes in intergroup relations. Equal status contact (*see* CONTACT HYPOTHESIS) was not sufficient to produce a positive intergroup relationship. The cumulative imposition of SUPERORDINATE GOALS seemed to be sufficient to improve intergroup relations. Recent research demonstrates that intergroup interdependence (whether competitive or not) can be sufficient to generate ingroup bias in an intergroup situation (Hogg & Abrams, 1988).

CATEGORIZATION
The equity/relative deprivation approaches and the structural approaches do not address the questions of how our own and other social categories are represented psychologically, and why individuals attach importance to collective outcomes. Tajfel and Turner (1986) developed an important distinction between objective competition and social competition; the latter referring to competition to improve a group's relative position regardless of objective gains or losses. Research

using the MINIMAL GROUP PARADIGM has indicated that individuals will compete to make their own group more advantaged than an outgroup regardless of personal gain, degree of acquaintance with individual group members, and whether they are distributing money or points. Moreover it seems that simple CATEGORIZATION into relatively meaningless categories is sufficient to produce ingroup bias.

The cognitive approach highlights the effects of categorization processes on intergroup judgments and perceptions. Tajfel demonstrated that categorization of a variable stimulus array tends to accentuate perceived intercategory differences and attenuate perceived intracategory differences. Doise developed a categorization model of intergroup behavior, proposing that differences in the behavioral domain (into ingroup and outgroup) produce corresponding differences in other (e.g., evaluative) domains. Common category membership does seem to produce perceptions of common fate.

Categorization may be imposed by an external agent or may emerge perceptually through differences in subgroup sizes. Minority group category membership tends to be more salient, and information about their members is processed more on the basis of prototypes than exemplars relative to majority group members. Among both real and minimal groups, minorities and outgroups tend to be perceived as more homogeneous (see OUTGROUP HOMOGENEITY) than majorities and ingroups. One basis for negative stereotypes of minority groups is distinctiveness-based ILLUSORY CORRELATION; people psychologically overrepresent the co-occurrence of infrequently occurring group members with infrequently occurring (often negative) behaviors or characteristics. Category-based expectancies can also influence judgments of ambiguous information. Attributes which are relevant to group stereotypes are more easily recalled and recognized than non-relevant attributes, and category-based processing of iniividuals seems to be a default (Fiske & Neuberg, 1990).

The content of representations of societal groups has been studied using a variety of dependent variables. Early studies simply asked respondents to indicate which attributes were associated with various groups. Increasingly, research participants are unwilling to be overt in making racist or ethnocentric judgements. Researchers have turned to indirect techniques to explore symbolic racism, or aversive racism (see PREJUDICE). SOCIAL COGNITION research using response times to primes (see PRIMING) such as "black," and "white" indicate that White respondents associate more positive attributes with Whites than with Blacks, and that stereotypic and biased judgments are increasingly likely when made under pressure of time or competing tasks. There is also evidence that anxiety, whether caused by ignorance, uncertainty, or other factors can increase stereotype-based judgments of and reactions to outgroups (Messick & Mackie, 1989). Moreover, even the subliminally primed abstract label "we" is associated with more positive evaluations than the category "they," indicating an unconscious basis for ingroup bias.

Multilevel categorization has been the focus of research into the cognitive basis of intergroup relations. It has been argued that intermediate level categories carry most socially useful information (see UNIQUENESS) and that these subtypes are easily activated, generated, and used for organizing information in memory. There are problems with simple vertical categorization systems because the relative location of a category (e.g., female senior academic) can be at different levels of generality within several different category systems. Given that social targets initially activate quite generic simple categories (e.g., race, gender), research has focused extensively on the conditions which encourage activation of subtypes and processing of individuating information. In general, the existence of category-inconsistent features, particularly if concentrated among a few category members, increases the likelihood of recategorization or subtyping. This, in turn, is seen as one means of changing intergroup relations based on general stereotypes. When people anticipate interacting with, or are dependent upon, the outgroup they are more likely to differentiate among outgroup members, reducing perceived outgroup homogeneity. However, the fact that the SELF is always available as an ingroup exemplar tends to ensure greater differentiation within the ingroup than the outgroup (Messick & Mackie, 1989).

SELF-CATEGORIZATION THEORY (Turner, Hogg, Oakes, Reicher, & Wetherell, 1987) holds that people categorize one another according to the comparative and normative fit of the categories within a context. The level of SOCIAL CATEGORIZATION which maximizes within-category similarities and between-category differences will tend to be used within any particular context. The perceiver's goals and motivation play an important part in determining which categorizations will be applied, and hence in constructing an intergroup relationship. Therefore, changes in the social frame of reference for judging a group can affect whether individuals include themselves in that group (self-stereotype) and are influenced by that or other groups (see SOCIAL INFLUENCE).

## SOCIAL STRUCTURE AND MOTIVATION

An important framework unifying the structural and cognitive approaches has been provided by SOCIAL IDENTITY THEORY (Tajfel & Turner, 1986). This assumes that categorization of people into groups involves the self-concept. Ingroup bias is a result of the motivation to maintain or enhance one's self-image, or SELF-ESTEEM, through social comparisons (see SOCIAL COMPARISON). This is achieved by making the ingroup positively distinctive from the outgroup on valued dimensions. Evidence concerning the role of self-esteem is mixed but does support the involvement of the self-concept in intergroup relations.

The question of why intergroup bias typifies intergroup relations continues to challenge researchers. Minimal group experiments indicate that ingroup bias can be generated easily in the laboratory but provide mixed support for the contention that it is associated with identification with the ingroup. This only appears to be true if the normative context and individual orientations and perceptions of relations between the groups are appropriate (see INDIVIDUALISM-COLLECTIVISM). In addition to seeking to maximize the difference between ingroup and outgroup profit, participants in minimal group experiments may adopt a combination of strategies including maximizing ingroup profit, joint profit, and fairness. Research using the PRISONERS' DILEMMA game indicates that people are more likely to be competitive in intergroup than in interpersonal encounters unless a superordinate group goal is made salient.

There is debate over the particular dependent variables appropriate for measuring intergroup relations. Some studies use allocation measures, others use performance evaluations, trait ratings, or attributions. Ingroup bias is likely to be greater when the ingroup and outgroup are evaluated on dimensions which are valued more highly for ingroup members.

Theorists emphasizing a cognitive basis for ingroup bias have proposed different consequences of crossed categorizations (e.g. $A/B$ and $X/Y$). Evidence suggests that group members are generally most biased against others who share neither category with themselves and most favorable toward others who share both categories with themselves. If group members share one, but not both, categories, intergroup bias may be reduced or even eliminated. Crossing of categories may reduce the SALIENCE of membership of both categories, and may also affect the motivation of individuals to differentiate in favor of a particular category. However, some categories are more subjectively dominant than others, depending on the relative meaningfulness and importance of the categories concerned. Intergroup differentiation and bias is more likely for a dominant than a nondominant categorization.

Social identity theory's macrosocial, or structural, analysis of intergroup relations, proposes that the actions engaged in by subordinate groups will depend on the perceived stability and legitimacy of their position. Depending on individuals' beliefs about the permeability of intergroup boundaries and their perceptions of cognitive alternatives, they may respond to subordinacy either by challenging the status quo, by creatively reevaluating the ingroup (social change belief system), or by trying to improve their personal situation (social mobility belief system) (Hogg & Abrams, 1988).

Taylor and Moghaddam (1987) propose a 5-stage model of intergroup relations which assumes that members of low status disadvantaged groups will first attempt to improve their situation by individual mobility. Only if this strategy is unsucccessful will people coordinate with other disadvantaged group members to challenge the advantaged group. There is now considerable evidence supporting the primacy of individual over collective action, but this is predominantly based on laboratory studies, conducted in individualistic cultures which may strongly inhibit the organization of collective strategies. Generally, there is a SELF-SERVING BIAS which manifests itself as ethnocentrism at the group level. Individuals seek membership of high status groups either by elevating the status of their existing group or by moving to join a higher status group. Direct competition with a higher status outgroup is likely when:

(1) ingroup status is seen as both illegitimate and unstable; and
(2) the boundary between groups is relatively impermeable.

High status groups which are secure in their position tend to elicit less identification than those whose position is open to change, while the reverse tends to be true of low status groups (see Hogg & Abrams, 1993).

Apart from self-esteem maintenance and enhancement, a variety of alternative motivations for intergroup behavior have been proposed. These include individual differences in social orientations (competitive, individualistic, cooperative), the need for optimal levels of distinctiveness, defense against negative self-perceptions, uncertainty reduction, and intragroup commitment. A further factor which has only recently been explored is that of POWER. In minimal group experiments, those with low power over allocations tend to show reduced ingroup favouritism.

## LANGUAGE
Intergroup relations are often manifested through LANGUAGE differences. For example, in many multicultural societies the language of the dominant group prevails while the languages of subordinate groups are ridiculed. The ability of a group to sustain its language may reflect its ethnolinguistic vitality, which is in turn dependent on the status, demography, and institutional support available to the group (see Hogg & Abrams, 1993). The language actually used by individuals denotes their group membership and their attitudes to or perceptions of the group memberships of those with whom they are communicating. Research using the "matched guise technique" (in which respondents judge recordings of a piece of text read in accents purportedly representing different speakers but which are actually generated by a single speaker) show that accents can produce stereotypical judgments and evaluations. Accents constitute a social marker of status and group membership. Speech accommodation (divergence or convergence of accents) reflects intergroup belief structures of social mobility or social change.

## IMPROVING INTERGROUP RELATIONS
Several possible techniques for improving intergroup relations have been proposed and tested, derived largely from work on the contact hypothesis. Categorization-based approaches tend to favor recategorization of groups using a superordinate category, or decategorization into individuals. Recategorization and decategorization can be achieved using tasks which promote cooperative interdependence between groups or by other techniques designed to increase the salience of common group memberships or reduce the salience of different group memberships. Both strategies make it harder for group members to respond to one another in terms of preexisting intergroup stereotypes. However, the success of both strategies is dependent on the formation of positive interpersonal relationships across intergroup boundaries. This in turn is dependent on interpersonal similarity and attraction (see SIMILARITY and ATTRACTION) between different groups. It is assumed that these positive relationships will then be generalized to the groups. There is some evidence that intergroup similarity can be threatening and promote further intergroup differentiation. Hewstone and Brown

(1986) propose that intergroup contact in which different positive features of the two groups are emphasized will maintain positive distinctiveness but enhance intergroup attitudes.

Other strategies for improving intergroup relations, identified by Messick and Mackie (1989), include institutional and legislative change, negotiation and BARGAINING to resolve conflicts, providing better information to counteract outgroup stereotypes, and diminishing the emotional ties with the ingroup. The concern with intergroup outcomes reflects an appreciation that while the cognitive processes involved in categorizing people may be neutral, the content of stereotypes and attributions are sometimes desirable and often undesirable, but generally serve social functions (Turner et al, 1987). For example, multiculturalism is strongly endorsed in some countries (stereotypical differences between cultures become matters of pride rather than conflict) whereas "ethnic cleansing" is pursued in others. The important point is that these stereotypes, and the evaluations associated with them, are culturally shared and agreed upon, not pure products of cognitive processes. Similarly, attributions made about groups (see ATTRIBUTIONAL BIAS) are more complex than those made about individuals because an external attribution can be external to the self or to the self and ingroup. In the latter case, some element of intragroup consensus is likely to be necessary, particularly as intergroup attributions, blame, and accusation are an important feature of hostile intergroup relationships.

CONCLUSIONS

The field of intergroup relations has developed its own set of theories and methods which have become highly influential in other areas of social psychology. These include bargaining, social influence, COMMUNICATION, GROUP COHESIVENESS and the self. The dominant concerns are with the nature of social categorization, the role of the self, and the psychological response to social structural variables.

See also: AGGRESSION; ATTRACTION; ATTRIBUTIONAL BIAS; BARGAINING; CATEGORIZATION; COMMUNICATION; CONFLICT; CONTACT HYPOTHESIS; CROWD PSYCHOLOGY; DEINDIVIDUATION; GROUP COHESIVENESS; GROUP PROCESSES; INDIVIDUALISM–COLLECTIVISM; LANGUAGE; NORMS; OUTGROUP HOMOGENEITY; PERSONALITY; POWER; PREJUDICE; RELATIVE DEPRIVATION; SELF; SELF-AWARENESS; SELF-CATEGORIZATION THEORY; SELF-ESTEEM; SOCIAL CATEGORIZATION; SOCIAL COGNITION; SOCIAL COMPARISON; SOCIAL IDENTITY THEORY; SOCIAL INFLUENCE; STEREOTYPING; UNIQUENESS; VALUES.

BIBLIOGRAPHY

Fiske S. T., & Neuberg, S. L. (1990). A continuum of impression formation from category-based to individuating processes; Influences of information and motivation on attention and interpretation. In M. P. Zanna (Ed.), *Advances in experimental social psychology* (Vol. 23, pp. 1–74). Orlando, FL: Academic Press.

Hewstone, M., & Brown, R. (Eds.) (1986). *Contact and conflict in intergroup encounters.* Oxford: Basil Blackwell.

Hogg, M. A., & Abrams, D. (1988). *Social identifications: A social psychology of intergroup relations and group processes.* London: Routledge.

——(1993). *Group motivation: Social psychological perspectives.* Hemel Hempstead: Harvester Wheatsheaf.

Messick, D. M., & Mackie, D. M. (1989). Intergroup relations. *Annual Review of Psychology, 40,* 45–81.

Sherif, M. (Ed.) (1962). *Intergroup relations and leadership.* New York: Wiley.

Tajfel, H., & Turner, J. C. (1986). The social identity theory of intergroup behaviour. In S. Worchel & W.G. Austin (Eds.), *Psychology of intergroup relations* (2nd ed., pp. 7–24). Chicago, IL: Nelson-Hall.

Taylor, D. M., & Moghaddam, F. M. (1987). *Theories of intergroup relations: International social psychological perspectives.* New York: Praeger.

Turner, J. C., Hogg, M. A., Oakes, P. J., Reicher, S. D., & Wetherell, M. (1987). *Rediscovering the social group: A self-categorization theory.* Oxford: Basil Blackwell.

DOMINIC ABRAMS

intimacy Researchers, clinicians, and the lay public share a great interest in the concept of intimacy. It is widely believed that intimate RELATIONSHIPS are an essential component of human well-being, and that their absence causes distress. Because the processes, states, and phenomena studied under the rubric of intimacy are diverse, any single definition is likely to omit a substantial part of the literature. For example, intimacy has been used to describe the process of revealing one's inner SELF to others; to refer to relatively intense nonverbal engagement; or to characterize the stage of life in which the primary developmental task is to establish an emotionally close, trusting, and sexual relationship with another person. In somewhat more liberal applications, the word "intimate" is often used in one of its lexical senses, as a synonym for closeness, sexuality, or MARRIAGE. The variability of these usages has sometimes created conceptual ambiguity, making it difficult to compare and integrate research conducted within different traditions, or with different empirical paradigms. But this diversity has also provided an enriching, multifaceted view of a complex phenomenon.

The most popular approach to intimacy began with Altman and Taylor's (1973) social penetration theory and Jourard's (1971) self-disclosure research. They defined intimacy as the depth and breadth of one person's disclosure of nominally private facts and feelings to another person. This extensive literature has supported two general conclusions: that self-disclosure moves from superficial to intimate topics as partners become acquainted, and vice versa; and that partners tend to reciprocate levels of self-disclosure. (In other words, too little or too much disclosure, in comparison to personal standards and situational NORMS, tends to hamper relationship development.) Studies of SEX DIFFERENCES in self-disclosure have also been plentiful. A recent META-ANALYSIS of 205 studies established that females generally self-disclose more intimately than men do, and that females are more often the target of self-disclosure than men are (Dindia & Allen, 1992).

More recent process models have attempted to broaden this conceptualization. Chelune, Robison, and Kommor (1984) proposed that true intimacy involves a high level of metacognition, in which partners share reciprocal understanding of each other's innermost selves. This is an important advance because it embeds self-disclosure within a relational framework. Reis and Shaver (1988) argued that intimacy is an interactive process that depends not only on emotional self-expression, but also on partners' responses to each other. Thus, they posited that feelings of intimacy arise when partners feel understood, validated, and cared for by each other. Their model is helpful in focusing attention on the functions served by SELF-DISCLOSURE, as well as on the fundamentally interactive nature of intimate experiences.

Spoken messages are not the only means of communicating intimacy. NONVERBAL COMMUNICATION has also been studied, in two ways: how intimacy-related affect is communicated nonverbally (e.g., through facial expressions, eye contact, and paralanguage), and how nonverbal behaviors regulate social interaction (e.g., eye contact and distance). Originally, nonverbal behaviors were considered to be direct indications of intimacy. More recent models propose that nonverbal behaviors are used to control levels of interpersonal engagement, such as maintaining, enhancing, or diminishing intimacy. Such models are promising, in that they can readily be integrated with the disclosure-based models discussed above.

Another line of research derives from Erikson's model of lifespan development. In his view, young adults must resolve the crisis of intimacy versus isolation. Intimacy is achieved if a primary relationship has several characteristics: mutual trust and openness; coordination of work, procreation, and recreation; mutually satisfying sexuality; and feelings of LOVE. One benefit of Erikson's approach is its close correspondence with lay accounts of intimacy, which commonly cite characteristics such as affection, expressiveness, cohesion, and sexuality. Research in the Eriksonian tradition typically uses an interview procedure to determine intimacy status; i.e., whether it has been achieved, and if not, the nature of its absence. Key questions in this literature concern the link between intimacy status and the resolution of earlier (identity versus role confusion) and later (generativity versus stagnation) developmental crises. Other research has examined the nature and correlates of achieved and non-achieved intimacy status. Generally speaking, people who have attained intimacy, or are moving productively toward it, are better off with respect to various markers of psychological development.

INDIVIDUAL DIFFERENCES in intimacy motivation have also been studied. People vary in the degree to which they prefer open, close and warm relationships with others, and McAdams (1989) developed a projective method for assessing this difference from free responses to standardized pictures. His research has shown how the intimacy motive relates to other motives, such as POWER and affiliation, and to the nature of ongoing social interaction. There is a close connection between the intimacy motive and tendencies to interact intimately, although several factors may moderate this link.

Although these varied research traditions have remained largely independent, they share several concepts and assumptions. Most models include processes by which individuals reveal their private selves to each other. Most incorporate interactional components whereby partners express mutual support and understanding. And most consider intimacy to be a deeply interdependent process involving TRUST, openness, and shared experience. Researchers also concur that intimate relationships are fundamental to human well-being. For example, it has often been demonstrated that people desire intimate relationships, starting around early ADOLESCENCE, and find them more satisfying than other types of relationships. Similarly, the presence of intimate ties is associated with higher social and psychological development, and better mental and physical health (see SOCIAL SUPPORT).

Thus, despite differences in methods and focus, consensus about the essential nature and importance of intimacy is apparent.

See also: ADOLESCENCE; MARRIAGE; META-ANALYSIS; NONVERBAL COMMUNICATION; NORMS; POWER; RELATIONSHIPS; SELF; SEX DIFFERENCES; SOCIAL SUPPORT; TRUST.

BIBLIOGRAPHY

Altman, I., & Taylor, D. A. (1973). *Social penetration: The development of interpersonal relationships*. New York: Holt, Rinehart & Winston.

Chelune, G. J., Robison, J. T., & Kommor, M. J. (1984). A cognitive interactional model of intimate relationships. In V. J. Derlega (Ed.), *Communication, intimacy and close relationships* (pp. 11–40). New York: Academic Press.

Dindia, K., & Allen, M. (1992). Sex differences in self-disclosure: A meta-analysis. *Psychological Bulletin, 112*, 106–24.

Jourard, S. M. (1971). *The transparent self*. New York: Van Nostrand.

McAdams, D. P. (1989). *Intimacy: The need to be close*. New York: Doubleday.

Reis, H. T., & Shaver, P. (1988). Intimacy as an interpersonal process. In S. Duck (Ed.), *Handbook of personal relationships* (pp. 367–89). Chichester: J. Wiley.

HARRY T. REIS

**intrinsic motivation** Intrinsically motivated behaviors are performed out of interest and do not require external reward; the enjoyment with which they are accompanied is sufficient to produce the behavior. This form of motivation, most often applied to the determinants of learning, is produced by the experience of free choice and autonomy.

BERNARD WEINER

# J

jealousy and envy  Related negative emotional states deriving from interpersonal
situations often involving SOCIAL COMPAR-
ISON. Although the word *jealousy* is often used
generically in common parlance, the distinct
nature of jealousy and envy must be realized;
the two emotions are based upon different
cognitive appraisals and motivate alternative
behaviors.

Jealousy is typically an aversive emotional
experience characterized by feelings of anger,
sadness, and fear, induced by the threat or
actual loss of a relationship with another
person to a real or imagined rival. A threatened relationship loss is the defining feature
of jealousy; it differentiates jealousy from the
kindred emotional experience of envy. Envy
is the term reserved for the begrudging of
another's possession of an attribute or relationship that one would like to have for
oneself; envy implies no threat of relationship
loss, only a desire to possess what another has
and thereby deprive him or her of it. This
begrudging of the other's possession is what
distinguishes envy from mere coveting, the
desire to have what another has without also
depriving him or her of it. The distinctions
between jealousy and envy are mirrored in
the etymologies of the two words. The derivation of the word *jealous* is from the same
Greek root (*zelos*) as *zealous*. Zealousness
connotes a strong devotion to the promotion
of a specific person or object; jealousy refers
to the suspicion that the prized person or
object may be lost. *Envy*, on the other hand,
stems from the Latin verb *invidere*, to look
upon another with malice.

The differences between jealousy and envy
can be conceptualized graphically by using
P–O–X triads (*see* figure 1). Here, P represents the person experiencing the emotion
(i.e., jealousy or envy), O represents another

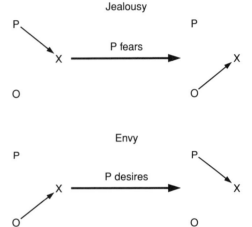

Figure 1. Jealousy and envy triads (Adapted from
Salovey & Rodin, 1989).

person, and X represents a desired person,
object, or attribute. Based on Bryson (1977),
Salovey and Rodin (1989) note that the re-
quisite factor in discriminating between the
jealousy and envy triads is the nature of the
subjectively important, previously established
relationship among members of the triad. In
the jealousy triad, P has a relationship with X
that P fears will be terminated because of the
possibility that X will begin a relationship
with O (i.e., the rival). If the loss of a
relationship to a rival is not likely, jealousy
cannot occur. Relationship dissolution not
caused by the desire to form a relationship
with another is likely to produce sadness, but
not jealousy. It is important to note that
although the rival is usually thought to be
another person, this is not always the case.
For example, a man may be jealous of his
wife's new career. She may devote great
amounts of time and energy to it while

consequently reducing the attention given to and time spent with her husband. He may view this as a weakening of or threat to their relationship. It is this threat of loss, not necessarily the features of the rival, that is the defining characteristic of jealousy. The envy triad, however, shows that O, not P, has a relationship with or possesses X; P is envious of O if P desires the relationship or possession at O's expense and begrudges O his or her possession of X.

Many different theories have been proposed to explain the causes and psychological mechanisms involved in jealousy. EVOLUTIONARY PSYCHOLOGISTS conceive of jealousy as a response that increases one's probability of propagating. PERSONALITY researchers have found some evidence suggesting that jealousy is a dispositional tendency that varies across individuals. SOCIAL PSYCHOLOGICAL theories of jealousy view it as a response to threats to SELF-ESTEEM. Other theorists view jealousy as an emotion that is SOCIALLY CONSTRUCTED; they posit that jealousy-evoking situations are culturally determined (for reviews of these literatures, *see* Salovey, 1991, and White & Mullen, 1989).

The causes and psychological mechanisms of envy derive mainly from social comparison processes (Salovey, 1990). Envy may result from situations where an individual feels that her or his status or self-evaluation in an important domain has been diminished by the achievements or possessions of another; the negative emotional state and disparaging thoughts or behaviors toward the other that may result are manifestations of envy. It is important to note that only social comparisons in domains important to an individual's self-esteem may result in envy; people care less when others excel in areas they consider tangential to self-definition.

*See also*: PERSONALITY; SELF-ESTEEM; SOCIAL COMPARISON; SOCIAL CONSTRUCTIONISM; SOCIAL PSYCHOLOGY.

BIBLIOGRAPHY

Bryson, J. B. (1977, September). *Situational determinants of the expression of jealousy*. Paper presented at the annual meeting of the American Psychological Association, San Francisco, CA.

Salovey, P. (1990). Social comparison processes in envy and jealousy. In J. Suls & T. Wills (Eds.), *Social comparison: Contemporary theory and research* (pp. 261–85). Hillsdale, NJ: Lawrence Erlbaum.

—— (1991). *The psychology of jealousy and envy*. New York: Guilford Press

—— & Rodin, J. (1989). Envy and jealousy in close relationships. *Review of Personality and Social Psychology, 10*, 221–46.

White, G. L. & Mullen, P. E. (1989). *Jealousy: Theory, research, and clinical strategies*. New York: Guilford Press.

DAVID A. DESTENO
PETER SALOVEY

**juries**  Groups of laypersons whose primary task is to decide culpability in criminal trials or liability in civil trials. Although the use of the jury is limited (predominantly to cultures with English common law traditions and to cases unresolved through plea bargaining), jury behavior has attracted increasing attention of social psychologists over the last quarter of a century. Part of the fascination with juries stems from familiar motivations for APPLIED SOCIAL PSYCHOLOGY. Juries often make momentous, even life-or-death decisions. The operation of the jury system (like many other legal institutions) is also based on a number of testable behavioral assumptions (e.g., that jury consensus is reached through PERSUASION and not coercion). For a variety of reasons (*see* LAW), most social psychological inquiry has focused upon the criminal trial jury and employed an experimental, trial-simulation methodology. The intrinsic interest value and behavioral richness of the juror's task has also made the latter paradigm quite popular for basic social psychological research on topics as varied as detection of DECEPTION to the power of STEREOTYPES.

Juries engage in GROUP DECISION MAKING, but prior to any jury deliberation, individual jurors must independently consider trial evidence and testimony and reach tentative, individual verdicts. Research clearly indicates that the prescribed evidence plays a crucial role in determining juror verdict preferences. But like cognitive psychologists, social psychologists have been even more fascinated by systematic BIAS in juror judgment. Under appropriate conditions (e.g., equivocal evidence), proscribed, extra-legal information has repeatedly been shown to influence juror judgment. Prominent among the many established sources of such bias are defendant and victim characteristics (e.g., PHYSICAL ATTRACTIVENESS, race, similarity to juror), inadmissible evidence (e.g., prior criminal record, pretrial publicity), purportedly irrelevant procedural factors (e.g., joining multiple charges at a single trial, the order of considering charges), and the prescribed penalty (see Hans & Vidmar, 1986). Practically no studies indicate that judicial admonitions or instructions to disregard such proscribed information eliminate its effect; in fact, a number of studies suggest that such admonitions can actually enhance such effects. Another well-established variety of juror bias is overreliance on inconclusive or unreliable evidence, particularly EYEWITNESS TESTIMONY. Even though eyewitness testimony is demonstrably unreliable, jurors appear to weigh it heavily, particularly when eyewitness identifications are asserted confidently; unfortunately, such eyewitness confidence is minimally associated with eyewitness accuracy.

Besides this concern with jurors' valuation of information, scholars have also begun to examine individual jurors' integration of information. Early attempts at modeling juror decision making employed familiar algebraic (e.g., information integration) and probabilistic (e.g., BAYES' THEOREM) models which envision a piecemeal evaluation and combination of each new piece of evidence along some guilt or culpability dimension (see Hastie, 1993). The most recent and promising approach draws on cognitive models of narrative production and comprehension. The *story model* of juror decision making suggests that jurors evaluate and integrate evidence by actively constructing plausible stories (interconnected "causal chains" of events, not dissimilar to the narrative accounts featured in many attorneys' closing statements) (see Hastie, 1993). Such stories are based not just on evidence, but also on generic world knowledge (e.g., stereotypes). They routinely include inferences to "fill in the gaps." Jurors

learn elements of possible verdicts (e.g., premeditation for first degree murder) from the judge's instructions and then try to match their "best" story to verdict criteria, settling on a verdict if the fit is good. Still other models have focused on how jurors decide that there is enough evidence of guilt to overcome the presumption of innocence. Such models have shown that a variety of prescribed (e.g., judge's definitions of reasonable doubt) and proscribed (e.g., victim attractiveness) factors can affect where jurors draw the line between sufficient and insufficient evidence of guilt (see Hastie, 1993).

The jury deliberation process itself has been analyzed both by CONTENT ANALYSIS of deliberation and through formal models of the group decision-making process (Stasser et al., 1982). The former approach has established several clear patterns: e.g., personal characteristics indicative of status (e.g., occupational status, gender) are associated with LEADERSHIP (viz. being selected foreperson) and with the amount and kind of verbal participation; deliberation is dominated by a few jurors, with substantial minorities of jurors (especially in larger juries) participating minimally in deliberation; juries move through qualitative stages, from orientation to open conflict to conflict resolution, like many other problem-solving groups; much of the conflict of deliberation reflects different judgments about which story best accounts for the trial evidence (Hastie et al., 1983).

In most criminal juries, such content analysis is unnecessary for predicting the outcome of jury deliberation. Initial, predeliberation majorities nearly always ultimately prevail in criminal juries (Kalven & Zeisel, 1966). This consistent pattern has two important consequences:

(1) juries, like most other groups, exhibit GROUP POLARIZATION – the more popular verdict among jurors is even more popular among juries; and

(2) with a few interesting exceptions, bias in juror judgment (e.g., attending to pretrial publicity) tends to be accentuated by deliberating juries.

On the other hand, in certain respects, juries outperform individual jurors; for example, recall of trial information is superior in the jury. The power of majorities, along with other evidence, indicates that jury deliberation involves more than simple persuasion or INFORMATIONAL INFLUENCE; several NORMATIVE INFLUENCE processes are also clearly involved (e.g., CONFORMITY, SOCIAL COMPARISON).

When there is no strong initial majority in the jury, advocates of acquittal are, *ceteris paribus*, relatively more likely to prevail; this asymmetry in the deliberation process results from common law principles (e.g., presumption of innocence; the reasonable doubt standard) designed to protect a defendant from false conviction. One consequence of the latter pattern is that disagreements between juries and individual triers of facts (e.g., judges) should be predominantly instances where the jury is more likely to acquit, and indeed, this is observed to be the case (Kalven & Zeisel, 1966).

Contemporary jury research continues to explore these and related questions, but with increasingly sophisticated theories and methodologies. Many interesting new questions are also being raised by research on the civil jury (e.g., are lay juries competent to try extremely complex cases?; how do juries decide on damage awards?).

*See also*: APPLIED SOCIAL PSYCHOLOGY; CONTENT ANALYSIS; DECEPTION; EYEWITNESS TESTIMONY; GROUP DECISION MAKING; LAW; LEADERSHIP; RAPE; SOCIAL COMPARISON; STEREOTYPING.

BIBLIOGRAPHY

Hans, V. P., & Vidmar, N. (1986). *Judging the jury*. New York: Plenum.

Hastie, R. (1993). *Inside the juror*. New York: Cambridge University Press.

——Penrod, S., & Pennington, N. (1983). *Inside the jury*. Cambridge, MA: Harvard University Press.

Kalven, H., & Zeisel, H. (1966). *The American jury*. Boston, MA: Little, Brown.

Stasser, G., Kerr, N. L., & Bray, R. M. (1982). The social psychology of jury deliberations: Structure, process, and product. In N. Kerr & R. Bray (Eds.), *The psychology of the courtroom*. New York: Academic Press.

NORBERT L. KERR

**just world phenomenon** People are motivated to see the world as a just place. This leads them to distort their judgments about events, making them consistent with the belief that people receive the outcomes they deserve.

TOM R. TYLER

# K

**kinesics** This term refers to the broad range of movement behaviors, including facial expressions, gestures, and posture, that are involved in NONVERBAL COMMUNICATION. Literally thousands of distinct kinesic patterns reflect differences in culture, gender, and personality. Kinesic behaviors are also critical in shaping the specific meaning of verbal messages.

*See also*: NONVERBAL COMMUNICATION.

MILES L. PATTERSON

# L

**labeling** Labeling theorists argue that the explicit, public attribution of deviant identities to individuals or groups by a community or social institution acts as a SELF-FULFILLING PROPHECY. It amplifies the DEVIANCE of those so labeled and justifies their stigmatization by others (*see* STIGMA). This approach treats deviance as a process of interaction rather than as an objective property of behavior.

*See also:* DEVIANCE; SELF-FULFILLING PROPHECIES; STIGMA.

NICHOLAS EMLER

**language** Language is undoubtedly the constitutive element of our everyday reality. It is the means by which we do our shopping; conduct or communicate our science; the medium by which we express our political opinions or preferences for soccer clubs; it is the device we employ in declaring our love and pronouncing our sorrow. One could easily go as far as saying that through language we express, explore, and find our identities as well as manage our way through the complex reality of our culture.

Knowledge about the world and social reality are generated, articulated and communicated through the medium of language. It is simply impossible to visualise how one could maintain systematic and coherent communication by non-verbal means. Language not only contains the distilled and crystallised knowledge of generations before us; it also enables us to structure our present by bringing the past to bear upon it, and also furnishes a medium by which bridges to the future may be built. (Semin & Fiedler, 1992, p. 2)

Thus, language has the remarkable quality of not being a closed system but an open-ended one that allows us to be creative, or generative, that permits, as a medium, the possibility of effecting change and undergoing it at the same time.

The pervasive quality of language also means that it is involved in all facets of social psychological phenomena, such as intraindividual, interindividual, intragroup and intergroup processes, which together constitute the global focus of social psychology (cf. Giles & Robinson, 1990). There is no doubt that all these phenomena are mediated by language. It is also involved in the diverse activities by which the social psychological investigation of these phenomena is carried out, namely in the construction of instructions, manipulations, independent variables, dependent variables, scales, etc. With very few exceptions all social psychological phenomena are investigated by the help of language. Despite some influential work in recent years (e.g., Giles & Coupland, 1991) language has not as yet claimed a position in our research programs that corresponds to the role it plays in the phenomena that are examined by social psychology. This is in part due to the fact that, until recently, language as a scientific object in social psychology had yet not undergone the necessary transformation to make it amenable to systematic research.

Current research that can be clearly identified as the "social psychology of language" falls, broadly speaking, into three groups, as can be seen from figure 1 below.

The first type of work examines how people speak and how such speech styles influence listeners' classifications and the types of inferences that they make about such target persons. Thus, in this particular approach language is treated very much as any other distinctive feature (e.g., gender race,

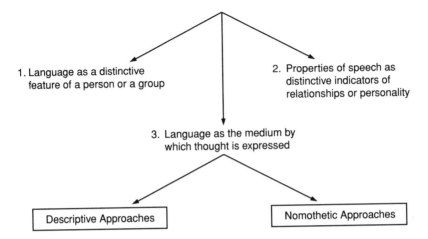

Figure 1. The domains in the social psychology of language.

etc.) that may lead one to go "beyond the information given" and to make inferences about other characteristics of the speaker.

The second social psychological approach to language has focused on the properties of speech and has a well-established tradition. The focus here is how speech styles in actual or manipulated social interactions are influenced by the properties of the interactants (e.g., their group membership, status relations, etc.) as well as the types of communicative behavior strategies that interactants adopt in the course of their communication.

Finally, the third stream of work focuses on the interface between properties of language (e.g., morphological, syntactical, or otherwise) and cognition, affect, and behavior. This is work concerned with disentangling the type and nature of influence exerted by cognitive and affective processes upon language and vice versa. Thus, we have here a concern with the hidden or implicit qualities of language and their use for specific psychological purposes as well as their influence on psychological conditions. This work is anchored in an old intellectual tradition which attempts to disentangle the intricate relationship between language and thinking. Within this last research orientation one can distinguish between two fundamentally distinctive approaches. One, which is more recent in social psychology, can be termed *descriptive* (or interpretative) *approaches* and builds upon

the fluid elements in communication and the situated constitution of meanings as a negotiated activity. Since these approaches are represented elsewhere in this volume (*see* DISCOURSE ANALYSIS, RHETORIC, inter alia) we shall focus here on the second, nomothetic approach, which is built on the assumption that although language and its use is fluid there must be some semantic invariances − since otherwise all communication would collapse. The focus in this second approach is to examine the properties of such invariances in the context of the interplay between language and thinking.

LANGUAGE AS A DISTINCTIVE FEATURE
The first and earliest work in what is known today as the social psychology of language derived from research conducted by Lambert and his colleagues (1960) in which the objective was to discover interethnic attitudes by examining whether specific speech styles (e.g., dialect, accent) elicit systematic and stereotyped trait inferences about the speaker (cf. Bourhis & Giles, 1977). The technique developed to test this, the *matched guise technique*, requires considerable care in developing stimulus material. This means, for instance, having Canadian bilinguals read the same prose passage in both English and French − thus allowing one to develop stimu-

lus materials which appears to have been produced by either an English Canadian or French Canadian. This material is then interspersed among other stimuli and subjects have to judge the speakers on a variety of trait terms (e.g., ambition, sincerity, intelligence, etc.). In this particular study English Canadian subjects rated their own ethnic group more favorably on 50 percent of the traits and French Canadians rated the "outgroup" more favorably on 71 percent of the traits. Also known as the "speaker evaluation paradigm" (Giles & Coupland, 1991), the focus of research is essentially on treating speech as a distinctive feature of a speaker and examining how it influences not only the types of inferences listeners make, and their attitudes, but also their behavioral intentions. In that sense speech is treated similarly to other potentially distinctive features such as race and gender (see. CATEGORIZATION). This approach can be seen as one which focuses on the surface properties of language, since it is not any specific property of language per se that is central here but speech style. Nevertheless, the importance of this area can be seen in the bridges it established between social psychology and socio-linguistics, as well as different domains within social psychology (e.g., language attitudes, INTERGROUP RELATIONS, inter alia).

## PROPERTIES OF SPEECH AS DISTINCTIVE INDICATORS OF RELATIONSHIPS OR PERSONALITY

The classic social psychological paradigm for communication research is *speech accommodation theory* developed by Giles (Giles & Coupland, 1991). This attends to the social consequences of interaction, such as attitudinal, attributional, behavioral, and communicative consequences; intergroup variables and processes; and discursive practices in naturalistic settings. The theory was originally developed to account for the way in which interactants converge or diverge with respect to their speech. It suggested that speakers are motivated under certain circumstances to adjust their speech style in order to fulfill identity concerns. Thus, one finds that the more effort in convergence a speaker was

perceived to make (for example, the more French used by English Canadians when speaking to French Canadians) the more favorably the person was evaluated, and the more listeners would converge in return.

Convergence is defined as "a strategy whereby individuals adapt to each other's communicative behaviors in terms of a wide range of linguistic/prosodic/nonvocal features including speech rate, pausal phenomena and utterance length, phonological variants, smiling, gaze, and so on" (Giles and Coupland, 1991, p. 35). Divergence refers to " . . . the way in which speakers accentuate speech and non-verbal differences between themselves and others" (Giles & Coupland, 1991, p. 36). One of the early natural niches for the theory has been in the field of intergroup relations. Here, adjustment in speech is regarded as fulfilling the function of identity maintenance. Convergence is seen as expressing a desire for social integration, and divergence was regarded as serving the function of promoting social distance. These accommodation processes are seen as motivated linguistic strategies that give rise to specific types of linguistic markers in communication that make salient either ingroup or outgroup identity.

An illustration of this is provided in studies which showed that Welsh people use accent divergence in an interethnic context (see Giles & Coupland, 1991). Welsh subjects were asked to participate in a survey of second language learning techniques by a very English-sounding speaker. This speaker at one point arrogantly challenged their reasons for what he termed "a dying language with a dismal future." This question, assumed to threaten the ethnic identity of the subjects, resulted in a broadening of their Welsh accents in their responses, as compared to previously asked, emotionally neutral questions. There was even an increase in the use of Welsh words and phrases.

While the original aim of the theory was to illustrate the cognitive and affective processes underlying speech convergence and divergence, more recently other speech and interaction strategies have been recognized, such as complementarity, and over- and under-accommodation. The theory has also moved in a more interdisciplinary direction, from a concern with specific linguistic variables to a greater focus on nonverbal and discursive dimensions of social interaction. For this reason, in more recent work the name of the theory has been changed to *communication accommodation theory* (Giles & Coupland, 1991).

## THE LANGUAGE-COGNITION INTERFACE

The issue here is whether linguistic differences observed between unrelated languages *determine* one's thinking or whether these differences are the *result* from differences in thinking. The general assumption is that language and thinking are related, but disentangling the nature of this relation is a complicated matter. The best-known hypothesis concerning the relation between language and cognition is the Sapir–Whorf hypothesis. There are two variants of this hypothesis. The weaker one is about *linguistic relativity* and suggests that structural differences between languages will have parallel nonlinguistic cognitive differences for the speakers of the respective languages. The stronger version is that of *linguistic determinism* which presupposes that the structure of a language fully determines the way people perceive their world. The issue has not been whether cognitive structures covary with language structures, but whether structures of language form or influence cognitive structures. The ensuing research has focused on tests of the first hypothesis and most of this work has been in the domain of classification of color terms and counterfactuals (*see* Brown, 1986).

There is also a tradition of research which is emerging within social psychology and which has a direct bearing on this issue. One particularly salient subject has been the type of causal inferences subjects are led to draw from sentences such as "John phoned Walter because he wanted sympathy" versus "John disliked Walter because he wanted sympathy." When subjects are asked to identify who "he" refers to in these sentences, they choose John in the first example and Walter in the second. There are no distinctive differences between these sentences in any respect except the verbs "to phone" and "to dislike," a verb referring to action in the first case and to a state in the second. A common finding is that verbs of action predominantly lead to inferences which identify the sentence subject as the causal agent (i.e., John) while state verbs lead to inferences which identify the sentence object (Walter) as the causal agent. This phenomenon, termed the "causality implicit in interpersonal verbs" (Brown & Fish, 1983) has led to different interpretations which, together with correlations evidence suggest that explanations in terms of both a linguistic relativity and cognitive universality may be possible, although the issue has yet to be resolved.

Other examinations of interpersonal verbs have focused on inferential properties other than the implicit causality that these verbs systematically mediate, such as the amount of information these verbs convey about a person, the type of information that they imply about the duration of an interpersonal event, the ease with which statements with such verbs can be verified, disputed, and so on. In examining these additional qualities, Semin and Fiedler (1991) have provided a more differentiated classification of interpersonal verbs and shown that these vary on a dimension of abstraction–concreteness. In their approach, termed the Linguistic Category Model, these authors suggest that the systematic inferential properties of interpersonal verbs are akin to the properties of tools that people use. Specific tools are suitable for specific purposes. The point is that people choose to use linguistic devices such as interpersonal verbs according to their suitability for particular contexts of discourse. The implication, however, is that once the distinctive properties of such tools are known (such as the abstractness–concreteness of interpersonal verbs), then it is also possible to examine what types of information the speakers/writers wish to transmit by examining the types of linguistic categories they use in their communication.

This research allows one to elucidate how social psychological phenomena such as the ACTOR–OBSERVER DIFFERENCE or egocentric bias are linguistically mediated. The interesting complexion that this approach adds to the language-thinking issue is that it does not attempt to map a direct-linguistic-property-to-thinking interface as most approaches have done, but rather suggests that:

(1) the terms (or devices) in the interpersonal domain have specific features which consistently elicit certain inferences; and

(2) how people use these devices depends upon how they *think* they are most appropriately employed as a function of the contexts in which they find themselves and the communicative intentions they wish to convey.

Thus, the devices are treated as consensually established and agreed upon conventions which turn out to be invariant across linguistic communities (European languages as well as Chinese, Japanese, inter alia). However, how they are used interindividually and interculturally is very much a function of individual and cultural "preferences." This approach attempts to move the language-cognition interface away from a one-to-one correspondence mapping to a richer "tool-use" approach and gives more scope for individual and cultural variation on a manifest level – i.e., which tools are used when by whom.

One of the most interesting applications of this approach is to be found in work done by Maass and her colleagues (Maass et al., 1989) on how stereotypes are transformed and sustained. These researchers examined how socially desirable and undesirable ingroup and outgroup behaviors are explained. They were able to show that socially desirable ingroup behavior and socially undesirable outgroup behaviors are described in terms of an abstract language that gives rise to the impression that such behaviors are expected, typical, and enduring. In contrast, socially undesirable ingroup behaviors and socially desirable outgroup behaviors are described in terms of concrete linguistic devices which particularize the event and convey the impression that the behaviors in question are due to specific and incidental circumstances and therefore do not have any permanence. This has been termed the linguistic intergroup bias. Maass (*see* Semin & Fiedler, 1992) has extended this approach to a number of ap-

plied contexts, in particular the analysis of the media. In numerous studies examining the reporting of intergroup conflicts in newspapers, ranging from reports on serious anti-semitic outbursts in Italy, to clashes between ecologists and antiecologists to victories and defeats of the Italian National soccer team, she has demonstrated that the linguistic intergroup bias is a stable phenomenon. More importantly, she has shown that the phenomenon emerges as a function of the media allegiance in relation to the target group. The important point is that this bias is an unconscious and unintended propensity, which can be detected by merely examining the properties of the language used by the authors. This approach to studying language focuses on the practices of subjects with regard to their intended consequences. In this perspective the relevance of language in facilitating communicative intent is fundamental.

The three typically social psychological approaches outlined here provide an overview of the language-based work typically conducted by social psychologists. This should not detract from the extensive work done in psycholinguistics and sociolinguistics, which obviously is of relevance, or from creative frameworks developed within social psychology such as the COMMUNICATION GAME which is concerned with the rules and roles of communicative practices and their influences on social cognition.

*See also*: CATEGORIZATION; COMMUNICATION GAME; DISCOURSE ANALYSIS; INTERGROUP RELATIONS; RHETORIC.

BIBLIOGRAPHY

Bourhis, R. H., & Giles, H. (1977). The language of intergroup distinctiveness. In H. Giles (Ed.), *Language, ethnicity and intergroup relations* (pp. 119–35). London: Academic Press.

Brown, R. (1986). Linguistic relativity. In S. H. Hulse & B. F. Green (Eds.), *One hundred years of psychological research in America: G. Stanley Hall and the John Hopkins tradition* (pp. 239–76). Baltimore, MD: Johns Hopkins University Press.

——& Fish, D. (1983). The psychological causality implicit in language. *Cognition*, *14*, 237–73.

Giles, H., & Coupland, N. (1991). *Language: Contexts and consequences.* Oxford: Open University Press.

—— & Robinson, W. P. (Eds.) (1990). *Handbook of language and social psychology.* Chichester: J. Wiley.

Lambert, W. E., Hodgson, R., Gardner, R. C., & Fillenbaum, S. (1960). Evaluational reactions to spoken languages. *Journal of Abnormal and Social Psychology, 60,* 44–51.

Maass, A., Salvi, D. Arcuri, L., & Semin, G. R. (1989). Language use in intergroup contexts: The linguistic intergroup bias. *Journal of Personality and Social Psychology, 57,* 981–93.

Semin, G. R., & Fiedler, K. (1991). The linguistic category model: Its bases, applications and range. In W. Stroebe & M. Hewstone (Eds.), *European Review of Social Psychology* (Vol. 2, pp. 1–30). Chichester: J. Wiley.

—— (Eds.) (1992). *Language, interaction and social cognition.* London: Sage.

GÜN R. SEMIN

**law** The scope of the law is variously defined, but a social psychological definition might identify the law as a set of formal behavioral NORMS along with institutions (e.g., police, courts) and procedures whose function it is to shape compliance to those norms. Viewed in this light, the law is fundamentally psychological. Its activities are based on many psychological assumptions (e.g., that the threat of legal sanction will deter violation of legal norms; that jurors can understand and follow the rules of evidence). Moreover, the effectiveness of the law is largely determined by the behavior of the many humans (police, attorneys, judges, jurors) who staff its institutions.

On the other hand, there is also an inherent tension and incompatibility between the outlooks of the law and of scientific psychology. For example, the law accepts legal precedent as authoritative; in psychology, new data routinely supersede old verities. The law is explicitly value-laden and prescriptive; psychology strives to be value-free and descriptive; and so forth. As a consequence, although it is hard to deny the relevance of psychological

knowledge for the law, the interface between the two disciplines is often fractious.

There are several distinct legal institutions. Legislatures enact laws. Police and prosecutors strive to enforce the laws. Trial courts adjudicate potential violations of the law and civil disputes. Appellate courts make case law. And correctional institutions sanction (and, decreasingly, attempt to rehabilitate) those who have violated the law. Although social psychology has contributed to knowledge and application in all of these areas, its primary contributions have been in the study of criminal trial courts. Other disciplines and psychological subdisciplines have concentrated on other institutions (e.g., political science for legislatures; criminal justice studies for law enforcement and corrections; psychiatry, clinical psychology, and developmental psychology for the etiology and rehabilitation of criminal behavior). And even within the criminal justice system, social psychology has concentrated its attention on a few topics (notably decision making by juries and EYEWITNESS TESTIMONY), leaving many other psychological issues (e.g., competency to stand trial, the prediction of future dangerousness) to sister disciplines.

Psychologists interested in the law have taken on several different roles, including basic researcher, applied researcher, trial consultant/expert witness, policy evaluator, and advocate (for a litigant or for a legal policy). By and large, social psychologists have tended to emphasize (and combine) the roles of basic and applied researcher. This emphasis has encouraged a focus on legal questions for which both social psychological theory is relevant *and* prevalent research methods (the laboratory experimental method, in particular) can be applied. The dominant topics and professional roles are emphasized below. However, as we shall see, social psychologists are steadily expanding the range of roles they take on and topics they investigate.

THE SOCIAL PSYCHOLOGY OF THE CRIMINAL TRIAL

*Pretrial*

A crucial gatekeeper for initiating and sustaining criminal investigation is the crime victim. Social psychological research (Greenberg & Ruback, 1992) has confirmed that stable individual difference variables are less predictive of victims' decisions to report and prosecute crimes than are aspects of the crime (e.g., severity of harm, emotional response to the crime) and situational factors. And one (if not the) crucial situational factor for such decisions is the advice others give the victim.

One area of pretrial investigation which has received considerable research attention is eyewitness testimony. Apart from data on the general unreliability of such testimony, key moderating variables for eyewitness accuracy have been identified (e.g., race of witness and target; stress levels; presence of a weapon). Typical investigatory procedures for obtaining identifications (e.g., line-ups) have been shown to introduce systematic sources of error. Wells and others have identified a number of ways of revising line-up procedures to help reduce such sources of error (e.g., giving an eyewitness practice and feedback with a line-up of innocent foils; having investigators explicitly acknowledge that the perpetrator may not be in the line-up) (Wells & Luus, 1990). Classic research by E. Loftus (e.g., 1991) and others has demonstrated how suggestible eyewitness recall is; for example, subtle variations in wording of questions to eyewitnesses can alter immediate and future recall.

The risk of suggestibility has more recently been examined in particular detail in two other areas. The first is the veracity of child eyewitnesses, particularly in cases where the child is the victim of crime (e.g., sexual assault) and must ultimately testify publicly on very traumatic experiences. On the whole, this research indicates that even young children are capable of recalling much that is forensically relevant, but also that age is inversely related to overall suggestibility (Ceci & Bruck, 1993). The second area concerns the use of hypnosis as an aid to eyewitness memory. Although this practice has gained in popularity as an investigatory tool, the potential for suggestion and confabulation under hypnosis has contributed to a trend in law to limit or prohibit hypnotically refreshed testimony as trial evidence.

Most of the other key stages between arrest and trial (indictment, setting bail, plea bargaining) have been studied only sporadically by social psychologists. This is largely due to ethical and practical limitations on observation and to the implausibility of modeling the decision-making processes of the key actors (e.g., grand jurors, prosecutors, judges) with lay subjects.

*The Trial*

In some countries, citizens are chosen for jury duty by officials or by lot. In the United States, a criminal jury trial begins with the *voir dire* or jury selection process. Usually a more or less random sample of potential jurors is drawn from a distinctive (e.g., older, more affluent) subpopulation of the adult population (most typically, those who have registered to vote). In addition to having jurors excused due to clear bias (e.g., acquaintance with the defendant), opposing counsel may excuse a number of potential jurors without explanation. This practice has stimulated much research to identify detectable juror individual difference variables that might be reliably related to juror verdicts. By and large, this research has mirrored the analogous findings for personality and attitude predictors – individual traits and demographics tend to predict specific behaviors (e.g., a juror's verdict) only weakly and inconsistently, although a few reliable but isolated effects have been identified (e.g., juror sex in RAPE trials; jurors' attitude toward the death penalty).

Before any evidence is presented to the seated jury, prosecutors and defense attorneys may summarize their versions of what will follow in opening statements. Jurors are cautioned that such statements are not evidence. Nevertheless, several studies (*see* Wrightsman, 1991) indicate that the presence and content of such statements are reliably associated with juror verdict preferences. This finding illustrates a recurrent theme in research on juries – that juror judgment is vulnerable to systematic BIAS. Jurors can be influenced by a variety of factors which the law holds to be completely irrelevant to the guilt of a defendant. These include characteristics and in-court behavior of the defendant, victim, and even the attorneys and judges (e.g., attractiveness, race, similarity to the juror, nonverbal behavior); inadmissible evidence or testimony (e.g., pretrial publicity, prior criminal record); and legally irrelevant features of the trial (e.g., joined charges, a defendant's decision not to testify, the prescribed penalty) (Hans & Vidmar, 1986). Another well-established variety of juror bias is overreliance on eyewitness testimony. Even though, as noted earlier, eyewitness testimony is demonstrably unreliable, jurors appear to weigh it very heavily, to the point of continuing to utilize it even when it has been discredited. Jurors are especially likely to credit a highly confident eyewitness, a tendency reinforced by judicial instructions on witness credibility. Yet experimental studies of eyewitness performance suggest that confidence and accuracy are correlated only weakly, if at all.

After all evidence has been presented, the trial judge instructs the jury. Such instructions convey the applicable law and distinguish what is evidence (and thus may be considered by jurors) from extra-legal, non-evidentiary information (e.g., defendant race). Such instructions are often quite long and full of complex legal terminology. Research has identified problems with comprehensibility of such instructions and explored means of clarifying them (e.g., explaining what a reasonable doubt is in terms of a quantitative level of certainty required to convict). Courts rely upon such posttrial instructions to eliminate the kind of juror biases alluded to above. But, by and large, the research evidence suggests that such instructions are ineffectual. For example, simply telling jurors to disregard information which appears quite relevant has little effect; in fact, a number of studies suggest that such instructions can even enhance juror biases.

The integration of trial information by jurors appears to be best described as an exercise in story construction (see JURIES). The distribution of verdict preferences with which jurors enter deliberation turns out to be highly predictive of juries' ultimate verdict. Initial majorities usually prevail. When there is no strong initial majority, hung juries become more likely, and those juries that can

reach a decision are relatively more likely to acquit than to convict, all other things being equal (Stasser et al., 1982).

## CONTRIBUTIONS OF PSYCHOLOGY TO LEGAL INNOVATION

Much of the legally relevant social psychological research has suggested or evaluated innovations in law or legal procedures. Proposed changes in the ways police stage lineups and question eyewitnesses have already been mentioned. Many other innovations involve courtroom procedure, such as rewording judicial instructions to increase comprehensibility. Another example is the timing of judicial instructions. These are typically delivered at the end of the trial. This means that the requirements for proof of guilt are generally not known to jurors at the time they are hearing the evidence. Kassin and Wrightsman (1979) have demonstrated that jurors are significantly less likely to convict when they were instructed about such requirements of proof (e.g., the need to prove each element of the crime beyond a reasonable doubt) *before* rather than after they heard the evidence. Heuer and Penrod's (1988) field experiment on juror questioning and note-taking is another noteworthy example. Most jurors are not allowed to pose questions or to take notes during a trail. However, Heuer and Penrod found no evidence for the usual rationales for prohibiting note taking (e.g., note takers would be inordinately influential in the jury). Furthermore, permitting jurors to ask questions helped alleviate their doubts about trial testimony.

Other potential legal innovations stem from technological innovations. For example, considerable research attention has been devoted to examining the validity of polygraph examinations and exploring the weight that jurors are likely to place on polygraph evidence. The ready availability of inexpensive and unobtrusive video technology has spurred not only greater interest in media coverage of courtroom trials, but also the use of such technology to overcome a number of problems such as obtaining testimony from inaccessible witnesses or the deletion of material ruled inadmissible by a judge. By and large, research comparing the impact of videotaped and live trials or testimony refutes fears that too much information is lost with video presentation.

Still other innovation research is targeted at influencing legislation. For example, research has examined the effect of revising the range of verdict options in cases employing an insanity defense (e.g., including a "guilty but mentally ill" verdict option). Much research has focused on the crime of rape. For example, some research has examined the net impact on jurors of "rape shield laws" which prohibit extensive inquiry into a rape victim's prior sexual history. Other research, exploring the links between exposure to violent and pornographic materials and aggressive attitudes and behaviors toward women, has been influential in the debate on "anti-PORNOGRAPHY laws."

## PSYCHOLOGY AND THE PSYCHOLOGIST IN LEGAL SETTINGS

As noted earlier, the modal role of social psychologists interested in the law has been that of basic/applied researcher. The fruits of their work have begun to appear in the deliberations of legislatures and appellate courts. And along with the incursion of psychological research knowledge into legal settings, nonclinical psychologists have begun to take on new and more active roles in such settings.

One illustration is psychologists functioning as paid consultants for litigants. The range of services that such consultants offer is wide, ranging from documenting intense pretrial publicity in order to bolster a motion for a change of venue to mounting practice trials to permit detailed analyses of mock juries' deliberations. Another common service is assisting in jury selection. This could include in-court observation of potential jurors' behavior or conducting surveys in order to identify the profile of the ideal juror (so-called "scientific jury selection" techniques). Although such jury selection services are becoming more widespread, there is practically no good evidence concerning their real utility.

Psychiatrists and clinical psychologists have long participated in trials as expert witnesses on such mental health issues as competency to stand trial, the insanity defense, etc. But many more nonclinical psychologists are beginning to serve as expert witnesses on a variety of topics (e.g., statistical evidence, effects of pretrial publicity). Noteworthy in this regard is expert testimony on eyewitness identifications (Loftus, 1991). Whether such testimony meets the legal and scientific criteria for utility to the triers of fact (e.g., the jury) remains a controversial question.

Judicial decisions do not hinge exclusively on matters of law; they also hinge on matters of fact, including psychological fact. So, for example, statistical summaries of behavioral data have increasingly been considered by courts and regulatory agencies (e.g., on such issues as employment discrimination). At times, important legal policies have hinged on social psychological questions for which the courts have had little good data. Two such instances have stimulated considerable research. The first is the US Supreme Court's explicit assumptions in the early 1970s that jury decisions would not be affected by jury size or the operative decision rule (i.e., whether unanimity is required for a verdict). Research has subsequently shown that these behavioral assumptions are false in many regards. For example, compared to the traditional unanimous 12-person jury, smaller, nonunanimous juries are less representative of the community, less likely to "hang" (i.e., to fail to reach a verdict), and more likely to produce dissatisfaction with a verdict. The second notable instance is the Supreme Court's assumption that juries which excluded those who opposed the death penalty (so-called "death-qualified juries") would not be more likely to convict a defendant. Considerable research has subsequently shown that, compared to those who oppose the death penalty, death-qualified jurors are reliably more likely to convict, and that this stems, in part, from their reduced concern with false convictions.

Unfortunately, refutation of erroneous behavioral assumptions by the courts through systematic research does not always mean reversal of the legal policy which was based upon those assumptions. For example, although research had shown that 12- and 6-person juries differed in many important ways, the conclusion that the Supreme Court came to in 1978 in *Ballew* v. *Georgia* after seeing all the research evidence was that states can still use 6-person juries for serious criminal cases, but cannot use juries with fewer than 6 persons. The disregard of clear empirical evidence was even more dramatic and disturbing in the *Lockhart* v. *McCree* ruling. The Court upheld the practice of excluding jurors who oppose the death penalty from capital trials. In so doing, they dismissed years of completely consistent research on death-qualified jurors. Thus, in the United States, verdicts which can carry the death penalty continue to be made by juries which are especially likely to convict (Thompson, 1989). Such rulings reillustrate a point made earlier, namely that the methods and standards for scientific reasoning and for legal reasoning can differ dramatically.

The study of social behavior in legal institutions stands as one of APPLIED SOCIAL PSYCHOLOGY's primary accomplishments. Future research promises to extend this research tradition to new substantive problems, to greater focus on field research, and to greater involvement in the evaluation of legal policy and procedures.

*See also*: APPLIED SOCIAL PSYCHOLOGY; EYE-WITNESS TESTIMONY; JURIES; NORMS; PORNOGRAPHY; RAPE.

BIBLIOGRAPHY
Ceci, S. J., & Bruck, M. (1993). Suggestibility of the child witness: A historical review and synthesis. *Psychological Bulletin, 113*, 403–39.
Greenberg, M. S., & Ruback, R. B. (1992). *After the crime: Victim decision making.* New York: Plenum.
Hans, V. P., & Vidmar, N. (1986). *Judging the jury.* New York: Plenum.
Heuer, L., & Penrod, S. (1988). Increasing jurors' participation in trials: A field experiment with jury notetaking and question asking. *Law and Human Behavior, 12*, 231–62.
Kassin, S. M., & Wrightsman, L. S. (1979). On the requirements of proof: The timing of judicial instructions and mock juror verdicts. *Journal of Personality and Social Psychology, 37*, 1877–87.
Loftus, E. F. (1991). *Witness for the defense: The accused, the eyewitness, and the expert who puts memory on trial.* New York: St Martin's Press.
Stasser, G., Kerr, N. L., & Bray, R. M. (1982). The social psychology of jury deliberations: Structure, process, and product. In N. Kerr & R. Bray (Eds.), *The psychology of the courtroom* (pp. 221–56). New York: Academic Press.
Thompson, W. C. (1989). Death qualification after *Wainwright* v. *Witt* and *Lockhart* v. *McCree*. *Law and Human Behavior, 13*, 185–216.
Wells, G. L., & Luus, C. (1990). Police lineups as experiments: Social methodology as a framework for properly conducted lineups. *Personality and Social Psychology Bulletin, 16*, 106–17.
Wrightsman, L. S. (1991). *Psychology and the legal system* (2nd ed.). Pacific Grove, CA: Brooks/Cole.

NORBERT L. KERR

**law of small numbers** A tendency to ignore the normative "Law of Large Numbers," according to which statistical inferences are more reliable when based on large rather than small data sets. This tendency involves overconfidence in the informativeness of individual cases and small samples; closely related to the REPRESENTATIVENESS HEURISTIC.

J. RICHARD EISER

**lay epistemics** This term applies to the process whereby lay persons and scientists alike acquire their knowledge. A theory of this process has been proposed by Kruglanski (1989, 1990). It depicts the cognitive and motivational factors involved in the formation and change of human knowledge on various topics. In this framework, knowledge is defined in terms of propositions (or bodies of propositions) in which a person has a given degree of confidence. Such definition imposes two requirements on a model of knowledge-formation: the contents of the knowledge have to be produced by the individual, implying a phase of *hypothesis generation*; also, those contents have to be assessed to see how much confidence (if any) they inspire – implying a phase of *hypothesis validation*.

The theory of lay epistemics holds that hypotheses are validated on the basis of relevant evidence. Relevance is determined by preexisting inference rules that, in the knower's mind, link together the "evidence" and the "conclusion" in an if–then fashion, e.g., "if everyone in the situation felt happy (the evidence) – the cause would have resided in the external context (the conclusion)." Occasionally, competing inference rules may be invoked, e.g., "if everyone in the situation felt happy – the cause would have resided in an internal state of alcoholic intoxication common to all the participants." Choice between plausible competing alternatives is accomplished via further inference rules incorporating diagnostic evidence, e.g., "if sober persons too would feel happy in this context, the cause of the happiness would reside in the external situation and not a common internal state."

In principle, the knower may continue generating further and further linkages in which the same category of evidence is tied to various competing conclusions. Given that at most times, we do possess firm subjective knowledge on various topics, such generation of alternatives must come to a halt. The lay epistemic model identifies two categories of conditions affecting the cessation (and/or conversely, initiation) of hypothesis generation: cognitive capability and epistemic motivation. Long-term capability relates to the availability of constructs in memory and short-term capability relates to their momentary accessibility.

Epistemic motivations are conceptualized in terms of the cognitive state the knower wishes to attain. Two issues are deemed critical:

(1) whether the knower desires or desires to avoid the state of cognitive closure, defined as a firm judgment on a topic and contrasted with confusion or ambiguity; and

(2) whether such desired or undesired judgment has specific (appealing or unappealing) contents, or is nonspecific – its desired or undesired nature stemming from its constituting a judgment versus the absence of judgment.

This analysis yields a typology of four motivational orientations, labeled needs for:

(1) specific closure;
(2) avoidance of specific closure;
(3) nonspecific closure; and
(4) avoidance of nonspecific closure.

Each motivational orientation is assumed to depend on the perceived benefits of attaining, or costs of failing to attain the correspondent epistemic state. Such costs and benefits can vary situationally and according to individual differences. This suggests a broad range of conditions potentially giving rise to the various epistemic motivations. For example, the potential benefits of nonspecific cognitive closure are that it affords predictability and guidance for action. In situations where predictability and guidance are deemed important (i.e., are considered as benefits) the need for nonspecific closure will be aroused. A costs of failing to attain closure could be the inability to make a timely decision and meet an important deadline. Hence, time pressures may elevate the need for nonspecific closure. Other costs of lacking closure relate to effortfulness of information processing that having closure would have obviated, personal reluctance to engage in such labors (e.g., because of fatigue), and task-based aversiveness of information processing (e.g., when the task is dull and boring). Similar cost/benefits analysis may be applied to derive the conditions under which the remaining epistemic motivations may be heightened.

## CONTRIBUTIONS OF THE LAY-EPISTEMIC FRAMEWORK

The lay epistemic framework has contributed to the understanding of social psychological processes in two distinct ways:

(1) by generating novel testable predictions to be explored in empirical research; and

(2) by affording a conceptual integration of numerous, heretofore separate, topics in social-cognition.

In the realm of empirical research, intensive effort has been applied to understanding epistemic motivations, in particular the need for (nonspecific) cognitive closure. In the context of knowledge formation, need for closure was shown to affect the extent of information seeking, type of information sought, judgmental confidence, and the tendency to overutilize early cues in the formation of judgments. In knowledge utilization contexts, heightened need for closure was shown to increase the tendency to retrieve from memory or base judgments on general categories or stereotypes rather than case-specific information. Finally, in social interaction contexts, need for closure has been shown to affect social comparison tendencies, group members' reactions to deviants and conformists (Kruglanski & Webster, 1991) and to influence persons' reactions to persuasion (Kruglanski, Webster, & Klem, 1993).

Its broad, content-free, nature allows the lay epistemic framework to integrate numerous domains of social psychological inquiry. Specific such integrative analyses have included a lay-epistemic conception of attitudes, of judgmental biases and errors, of attribution and cognitive-consistency models, of minority and majority influence, and of social comparison processes (Kruglanski, 1989).

BIBLIOGRAPHY

Kruglanski, A. W. (1989). *Lay epistemics and human knowledge: Cognitive and motivational bases.* New York: Plenum.

—— (1990). Lay epistemic theory in social-cognitive psychology. *Psychological Inquiry, 1,* 181–97.

—— & Webster, D. M. (1991). Group members' reactions to opinion deviates and conformists under varying degrees of proximity to decision deadline and environmental noise. *Journal of Personality and Social Psychology, 61,* 212–25.

—— & Klem, A. (1993). Motivated resistance and openness to persuasion in the presence or absence of prior information. *Journal of Personality and Social Psychology, 65,* 861–76.

ARIE W. KRUGLANSKI

**leadership** This term can be defined as having and being seen to have positive motivational influence on the thoughts, feelings, and actions of group members that are relevant to group objectives. Influence is the key word, although influence that is irrelevant or antithetical to group goals is not consistent with leadership, hence the need for the qualification, positive motivational influence . . . relevant to group objectives.

This definition is explicitly social and behavioral, implying that leadership is not inherent in people, the positions that they occupy, or the role scripts attached to these positions. It is, rather, a quality attributed to people as a result of their interrelations with others; the things that they think, say and do, and the way they are perceived by others. Personal qualities, titles of office, and specifications of their rights and duties may potentiate or inhibit the expression of leadership, but they are neither necessary nor sufficient for it.

Furthermore, leaders and leadership should not be confused: people named or known as "leaders" *may* be more positively influential than other group members, but the qualities and behaviors that make people influential are usually widely distributed in varying degrees among group members. The conditions under which people in the named position of "leader" (and terms denoting similar positions) attract the highest attributions of leadership, and are most influential, are matters for discovery, as are the conditions under which they fail to do so.

Leadership should also be distinguished from coercive POWER. Leadership usually implies power, but individuals who rely on coercion or force as a means of influence will not generally be seen as leaders, *unless* force is recognized by other group members as a legitimate means of exerting beneficial influence on the group. We would not ordinarily associate leadership with dictatorship or tyranny, for example, unless the tyrant had popular or charismatic appeal above and beyond the ability to wield force.

The quest for the origins, correlates, and consequences of leadership is an ancient and venerable one, and pithy observations on the topic can be found in the writings of most sages and social philosophers through the ages. Additionally, biographical and autobiographical accounts of contemporary figures will always inspire the dreams and schemes of would-be leaders. However, the modern study of leaders and leadership is heavily informed by the attitudes and methods of science: the requirement to define terms in observable, measurable ways; the need for objective evidence to support theories; and the desire to find general principles that transcend particular individuals and circumstances.

## THE LEADER CHARACTERISTICS OR TRAIT APPROACH

Early social scientific interest (mainly pre-1950s) centered on trying to find a set of personal characteristics (often PERSONALITY traits, hence the application of the label, the *trait approach*) that might reliably distinguish famous public figures and other "named" leaders from nonleaders. While perhaps an intuitively appealing starting-point, results appeared inconsistent, although in retrospect it seems that the research on individual differences may have produced more consistent findings than was apparent at the time. An analysis of the pooled results of many studies of emergent leaders in groups with no formal leader indicates that leaders tend to be more intelligent, masculine, dominant, extrovert, conservative, and well adjusted than nonleaders (Lord, DeVader, & Alliger, 1986).

However, the trait approach is still problematic on theoretical grounds. First, many such studies fall prey to the so-called *nominal fallacy*, assuming that people in formal or named positions of leadership are *in fact* the primary source of positive, relevant group influence. To the extent that they are not always, and that "leaders" are sometimes ignored but tolerated, or even manipulated by others behind the scenes, their personal qualities are at best epiphenomenal, not causal. For example, Lord, DeVader, and Aliger (1986) emphasize the role of followers' *implicit leadership theories* in explaining their findings regarding the personality traits of emergent leaders. These implicit theories, possibly shaped by social and cultural conditions, might serve as templates against which individual qualities are compared when people select and support leaders. Second, the study of individual differences, narrowly conceived, is not sensitive to variations in leader effectiveness either within or between leaders, or to the demands of different situations, or to the role of followers in leader selection and evaluation.

## LEADERSHIP BEHAVIOR

Throughout the 1950s and 1960s, research centered on descriptions of leader behavior or *style*, and its effect on the attitudes and behavior of other group members. Questionnaires and other instruments were developed to gauge the leader's and followers' perceptions of leader behavior, and these in turn were related to measures of group perception, attitude, and performance. For example, the Leader Behavior Description Questionnaire (LBDQ) asks people to indicate the frequency with which the leader engages in several dozen different behaviors, and scores are then related to job satisfaction, group productivity, superiors' appraisals of the leader, and so on (*see* Bass, 1990).

Within this enormous body of research, bipolar and two-dimensional models of leader behavior are numerous. Some of the more influential bipolar models, which are based on the idea of a continuum of leadership styles running between two antagonistic poles, contrast democratic with autocratic, participative with directive, Theory X with Theory Y, and relations-oriented with task-oriented leadership. In spite of differences among these models in terms of origins and emphases, they all capitalize on the distinction between "follower-focused" or group-maintenance-oriented behavior, on the one hand, and "task-focused" or goal-achievement-oriented behavior, on the other.

Whereas in the bipolar models these are mutually exclusive "styles," in other models they are conceived of as independent "dimensions" of leadership that can be manifest in various combinations. The most influential of these, based largely on studies using the LBDQ, is the distinction between the degree of concern shown by a leader for the welfare of group members (Consideration), and the degree to which a leader initiates, organizes, and directs goal-oriented activity (Initiation of Structure).

The study of leadership style explicitly recognizes the social, behavioral nature of leadership. But insofar as the subjects of study tend to be named or designated "leaders," the emergent, dynamic qualities of leadership may be ignored, as may the effect of different situations on leader behavior and the perceptions of followers.

## SITUATIONAL FACTORS

The importance of situational factors has been amply demonstrated. Bass (1990), for example, reviews a mass of evidence from which the following are just a few of the many conclusions that can be drawn: autocratic leadership is more effective in authoritarian environments with authoritarian personnel; participative leadership is more successful when the acceptance of the decision by followers is required for its implementation and when time is not in short supply; task-oriented leadership is more effective when circumstances affecting the leader's confidence that the task will be completed are either very favorable or very unfavorable, rather than moderately favorable; the relations between Consideration and Initiation of Structure, on one hand, and follower satisfaction and productivity, on the other, depend on subordinates' need for information, job level, and expectations about leader behavior, among other things.

## CONTINGENCY THEORIES

Such findings remind us that the contingencies that moderate perceptions of and reactions to leadership behaviors are undoubtedly very complex. There is no grand unified theory that enables us to say what elements of situations are most critical in determining the effectiveness of leadership or when they will be influential, although several minitheories have been proposed.

Fiedler and colleagues (e.g., Fiedler & Garcia, 1987) concentrate on three factors that affect the leader's ability to influence subordinates, namely the structure of the task, leader–member relations and the inherent power of the leader's position, and how these variables interact to produce environments which are more or less conducive to task-oriented or relationship-oriented leadership. Although based on controversial assumptions and measurements, the evidence overall suggests that relationship-oriented leadership is more successful in situations moderately favorable to the leader, than in very favorable or unfavorable situations.

Vroom and colleagues (e.g., Vroom & Jago, 1988) have developed a model of effective leadership style in short-term problem-solving situations that is based on the extent to which there is an objectively "good" task outcome, and subordinate acceptance is required. They define a continuum of styles ranging from autocratic, through consultative, to fully group decision-making, and prescribe a set of questions to ask about the requirements of the task that will help to determine what subset of styles is most appropriate in the situation.

A third model, associated mainly with House (e.g., House & Mitchell, 1974) aims to articulate the conditions under which different leadership styles clarify for subordinates the path between performance and reward, on the assumption that the clearer the path, the higher will be motivation. Such factors as the personal characteristics of the subordinates and the ambiguity of the task are proposed as determining whether directive or participative styles of leadership are more effective.

The basic message of these and numerous other contingency models is that leaders must be prepared to cope with differing and changing circumstances, or risk losing their influential status. However, coping does not necessarily mean accepting the situation or conforming to expectations. Burns (1978), for example, distinguished between *transactional* leadership that is based primarily on COMPLIANCE to group NORMS recognized through leader–follower exchanges of something valued (e.g., reward and praise for good performance), and *transforming* leadership based on changing the BELIEFS, VALUES, and needs of followers. Known more widely today as *transformational* leadership, several authors have built on this concept. Indeed modern writers on the subject of leadership increasingly tend to reserve the term to refer to behaviors and activities that cause the group to transcend the present and redefine its objectives in relation to changing circumstances. This explicitly strategic, causative view implies a degree of nonconformity with existing group views and practices. By contrast, activities and behaviors that are aimed at accommodating to and maintaining the *status quo*, however beneficially motivational, are designated "management." From this point of view, it could be suggested that much of what is traditionally reviewed under the rubric of "leadership" is really about "management style," or at best about a limited aspect of leadership (e.g., Kotter, 1990).

However, Bryman (1992) argues that this view represents a backward step, inasmuch as discussions of transactional leadership are generally insensitive to situational factors. This preempts the question of whether and when transactional visionaries, heroes, and magicians are superfluous or even detrimental to group objectives. One faces the irony here that nonconformists and visionaries whose exhortations are ignored or result in disaster are unlikely to be represented, retrospectively, as "Leaders," and may elude analysis. Thus we return to the point that effective leadership has to cope with differing and changing circumstances, sometimes requiring adaptation to circumstances and sometimes requiring altering these.

An integrative framework is suggested by Smith and Fritz (1987), who propose that one of the fundamental determinants of leader selection, performance, and evaluation is the salience of group membership. They start from the position, often neglected in this field, that no group or ORGANIZATION stands alone. Many kinds of groups, especially occupational organizations, convene and function almost *exclusively* in an explicitly comparative, intergroup environment. Tajfel and Turner (1979) employed the concept of an *interpersonal–intergroup continuum* to describe the effects of variations in the psychological prominence of group membership. At the interpersonal extreme, interaction among people within and between groups is determined entirely by their individual characteristics, likes, and preferences, while interaction at the intergroup extreme is fully determined by their respective group memberships.

Transitions between states of accentuated and attenuated intergroup comparison exert profound effects on almost every facet of social conduct. Most generally, factors that contribute to group salience such as competition, discrimination, loss of group status, etc., seem to cause people to think of themselves and others increasingly in terms of qualities and attributes that are relevant to group objectives, and less in terms of individuating personal interests, a process that has been termed *depersonalization*.

When group salience is low, Smith and Fritz (1987) argue, leader choice and evaluation of leader performance will tend to be based on personal tastes and the prospect of relative *personal* welfare (e.g., reward, status, recognition) in the group or organization. Leaders will be expected to be adept at "follower-focused," group-maintenance activity. This model could be expanded by suggesting that this activity can take either a *transactional* form (as in the optimization of individual terms and conditions of belonging, or performance-related reward systems), or a *transformational* form (as in bilateral or multilateral mentoring, personal, and career development). Both facets are concerned with the *internal management* of the group.

When group salience is high, depersonalization reorients attention away from concerns related exclusively to individual welfare, towards factors affecting the welfare of the group as a whole. Hence the role requirements of *group* success, and intuitions about how well group members in different positions can fulfill these, will dominate leader choice and evaluation. Leaders will be expected to show "task-oriented" strength in executive and strategic skills related to group goal-achievement. Again, adding to the Smith & Fritz (1987) model, this can take either a *transactional* form (as in the issue of orders or commands, or the establishment of organizational structure) or a *transformational* form (as in the development of an inspirational vision, or the reinterpretation of past and current affairs). Under such circumstances, both facets are concerned with *the management of the group or organization vis-à-vis the external world.*

From this point of view, the transactional–transformational distinction is subordinate to the interpersonal–intergroup continuum, with its implications for follower-focused and task-focused leadership. While such an approach does not address the issue of how depersonalization comes about, it does draw attention to the generic psychological underpinnings of group formation and functioning in a manner that distinguishes them from the specific conditions and variables that characterize particular groups. It also avoids the problem of nominalism by casting the research role of leaders and leadership as those of criterion rather than predictor variables. Finally it reminds us that leadership is about more than executive success in cut-throat commercial environments, however positive and motivational an impact such emphases have had on the field as a whole.

*See also*: NORMS; ORGANIZATIONS; PERSONALITY; POWER; VALUES.

BIBLIOGRAPHY

Bass, B. M. (1990). *Bass and Stogdill's handbook of leadership: Theory, research and managerial applications* (3rd ed.). New York: Free Press.

Bryman, A. (1992). *Charisma and leadership in organizations.* London: Sage.

Burns, J. M. (1978). *Leadership.* New York: Harper & Row.

Fiedler, F. E., & Garcia, J. E. (1987). *New approaches to effective leadership: Cognitive resources and organizational performance.* New York: Wiley.

House, R. J., & Mitchell, T. R. (1974). Path-goal theory of leadership. *Journal of Contemporary Business, 3,* 81–97.

Kotter, J. P. (1990). *A force for change: How leadership differs from management.* New York: Free Press.

Lord, R. G., DeVader, C. L., & Alliger, G. M. (1986). A meta-analysis of the relation between personality traits and leadership perceptions: An application of validity generalization procedures. *Journal of Applied Psychology, 71,* 402–10.

Smith, P. M., & Fritz, A. S. (1987). A person-niche theory of depersonalization: Implications for leader selection, performance and evaluation. In C. Hendrick (Ed.), *Review of personality and social psychology: Group processes* (Vol. 8). Newbury Park, CA: Sage.

Tajfel, H., & Turner, J. C. (1979). An integrative theory of intergroup conflict. In W.G. Austin & S. Worchel (Eds.), *The social psychology of intergroup relations.* Monterey, CA: Brooks/Cole.

Vroom, V. H., & Jago, A. G. (1988). *The new leadership: Managing participation in organizations.* Englewood Cliffs, NJ: Prentice Hall.

PHILIP M. SMITH

**lens model**   Views social perception as an inferential process with "distal," target attributes probabilistically related to "proximal" cues perceived. Given no one-to-one connection between proximal and distal stimuli, perceivers must integrate the variable cues in proximal stimulation and make inferences about the target attributes giving rise to them.

LESLIE A. ZEBROWITZ

**level of aspiration**   The level of future performance in a task that an individual explicitly undertakes to reach. Aspiration level thus refers to the difficulty of the goal for which one is striving. Aspirations are influenced by individual differences, prior performance, task characteristics, group standards, and cultural norms.

*See also:* ACHIEVEMENT MOTIVATION.

BERNARD WEINER

**life satisfaction**   Research on life satisfaction has focused on both *static* and *dynamic* determinants of subjective well-being (Diener, 1984; Strack, Argyle, & Schwarz, 1991).

From a sociological perspective, researchers have typically investigated the influence of *objective circumstances.* Surprisingly, most relationships have been weak or inconsistent. Even "income" or the experience of "stressful events" were not unequivocal predictors of life satisfaction. Most consistently, "MARRIAGE," "social RELATIONSHIPS," and "good health" were moderately associated with high satisfaction.

Psychological investigators have set out to discover the *traits* that might cause satisfaction with life. More than other stable PERSONALITY characteristics, extraversion and neuroticism have repeatedly been found to be correlates. Also, the tendency to distort reality in a positive direction has been revealed as a determinant.

Most recent psychological research has concentrated on the *dynamic* aspects of subjective well-being. For example, it was found that extraverted people were predisposed to have positive experiences. Pitting the frequency against the intensity of such events, it turned out that repeated experiences of moderately positive valence contribute more to a person's general satisfaction than do a few experiences of extremely positive valence. Moreover, few extremely positive experiences may eventually diminish the satisfaction that follows from moderately positive events, because people tend to adapt to their current state. As a consequence, extremely positive (and negative) events will gradually cease to be sources of satisfaction or dissatisfaction. Thus, with the passage of time, lottery winners' and accident victims' subjective well-being was found to differ less from one another than one would assume, even given the extremity of "disruptive" events in their lives (Brickman, Coates, & Janoff-Bulman, 1978).

These findings are consistent with approaches that view *judgmental* processes as an important aspect of life satisfaction (*see* SOCIAL JUDGMENT). In this perspective, the outcome of comparisons with other people and with one's own situation in the past were found to be better predictors of general satisfaction than the objective state (*see* SOCIAL COMPARISON).

Schwarz and Strack (1991) have proposed a judgment model of subjective well-being that specifies both the information that enters into judgments of happiness and satisfaction and the conditions under which judgments occur. Specifically, assessments of global life satisfaction may be based either on information about specific life domains or on the quality of one's AFFECT at the time satisfaction judgments are made. Thus, persons in a positive MOOD may use their transient affect when they describe themselves as satisfied with their lives as a whole. Alternatively, they may use information about specific experiences. This information, however, may either serve as a basis for judgment or as a standard of comparison. How these different determinants interact was investigated in a series of experiments, in which subjects considered positive or negative experiences. If these events were part of their present life, subjects reported higher satisfaction for positive than for negative experiences. In contrast, if the event was recalled from the past, the opposite influence was observed. That is, the information about one's past served as a comparison standard. Under specific circumstances, however, thinking about one's past may not only activate information but may also elicit affect that may influence satisfaction judgments congruently. This was the case when subjects were instructed to imagine the course of a positive or negative experience and to relive it in their mind's eye.

Of course, what enters into people's judgments depends on what comes to mind. This, in turn, hinges on what one happens to think about before making judgments. In surveys of satisfaction, prior questions about relevant specific life domains have been found to determine subsequent judgments of satisfaction with life as a whole (*see* SURVEY METHODS).

Social context influences people's reports of happiness and satisfaction. Typically, people report higher levels of subjective well-being when they provide responses in social communication such as interviews than they report in anonymous contexts such as self-administered questionnaires. However, considering the fate of a person who is considerably worse off, judges may edit their open responses in a negative direction.

Another dynamic aspect of subjective well-being is absorption in a particular task. It has been argued by Csikszentmihalyi (1990) that both in work and leisure, intrinsic satisfaction will be achieved if people experience "flow" as a function of being entirely absorbed by the particular activity and oblivious to their environment and aspects of their self (e.g., surgeons or mountain climbers). Finally, striving for goals may be a source of satisfaction. This is particularly true if the goals are important and striving for them does not lead to conflict.

*See also.* MARRIAGE; MOOD: IMPACT ON COGNITION AND BEHAVIOR; PERSONALITY; RELATIONSHIPS; SOCIAL COMPARISON; SOCIAL JUDGMENT; SURVEY METHODS.

BIBLIOGRAPHY
Brickman, P., Coates, D., & Janoff-Bulman, R. (1978). Lottery winners and accident victims: Is happiness relative? *Journal of Personality and Social Psychology*, 36, 917–27.
Csikszentmihalyi, M. (1990). *Flow: The psychology of optimal experience*. New York: Harper & Row.
Diener, E. (1984). Subjective well-being. *Psychological Bulletin*, 235, 542–75.
Schwarz, N., & Strack, F. (1991). Evaluating one's life: A judgment model of subjective well-being. In F. Strack, M. Argyle, & N. Schwarz (Eds.), *Subjective well-being. An interdisciplinary perspective* (pp. 27–47). Oxford: Pergamon.
Strack, F., Argyle, M., & Schwarz, N. (Eds.) (1991). *Subjective well-being. An interdisciplinary perspective* (pp. 77–100). Oxford: Pergamon.

FRITZ STRACK

**LISREL** A computer program developed by Karl Jöreskog and Dag Sörbom that estimates the coefficients of STRUCTURAL EQUATION MODELS. Typically maximum likelihood estimates are provided. Competitive programs, such as EQS developed by Peter Bentler, provide identical estimates.

*See also*: STRUCTURAL EQUATION MODELING.

CHARLES M. JUDD

**locus of control** An individual's generalized expectancies regarding the forces that deter-

mine rewards and punishments. Individuals with an internal locus of control view events as resulting from their own actions. Persons with an external locus of control view events as under the CONTROL of external factors such as luck. *See also*: CONTROL.

KERRY L. MARSH
GIFFORD WEARY

**loneliness** A state that has been defined as the unpleasant experience that occurs when a person's network of social relationships is deficient in some important way, either quantitatively or qualitatively (Peplau & Perlman, 1982, p. 4). Loneliness stems from a discrepancy between the level of social contact a person needs or desires and the amount s/he has. It is a subjective experience – people can be alone without being lonely, or lonely in a crowd.

Various types of loneliness have been suggested. Some scholars have distinguished between chronic and temporary loneliness. Others have discussed an existential or spiritual form of loneliness. Mikulincer and Segal (1990) recently identified four subtypes of loneliness via cluster analysis: self-concerned, paranoid, depressive, and socially estranged. In an influential older formulation, Weiss (1973) distinguished between emotional and social loneliness. Emotional loneliness stems from the absence of close emotional attachments (such as those provided by a spouse); social loneliness stems from the absence of an adequate social network. The affective sequelae of emotional loneliness (e.g., anxiety and apprehension) are generally more intense and unpleasant than the sequelae of social loneliness (e.g., boredom and feelings of exclusion).

Social scientists have focused increasing attention on loneliness during the past 15 years. A multidisciplinary search of the *Psychological Abstracts* and other sources for the 50-year period 1932–81 produced a bibliography of under 300 items (Peplau & Perlman, 1982). A more limited keyword search of just the *Psychological Abstracts* for the period 1980 to March 1993 produced over 525 publications with loneliness in their title. One building-block contributing to the increase in loneliness research has been the development of psychometrically sound instruments for measuring loneliness (e.g., the UCLA Loneliness Scale) (Shaver & Brennan, 1991). Another underpinning of this interest is the increasing body of evidence linking loneliness to various social problems and indices of well-being. These include: alcohol use, aggressive behavior, poor academic performance, neuroticism, running away from home in adolescence, suicide, less effective immune system functioning, and high age-adjusted mortality.

## THE DEMOGRAPHICS OF LONELINESS

In a representative sampling of United States citizens, 26 percent said they had felt "very lonely or remote from other people" in the past few weeks. British, Canadian, and Scandinavian surveys show similar results. Women are more likely than men to say they are lonely. Experimental evidence shows that the social censure for being lonely is less for women than for men, which may partially explain the greater willingness of women than men to admit being lonely.

Loneliness also varies as a function of other demographic variables. People with lower incomes, for example, are more likely to be lonely. With regard to age, loneliness is especially prevalent in late adolescence and young adulthood. It tapers off during the rest of the working years. Despite widespread stereotypes and concerns about loneliness being a problem for seniors, the prevalence of loneliness is not unusually high among seniors aged 65 to 80. An increased likelihood of being lonely has been found in some studies for respondents aged over 80. This may be due in part to the high proportion of the very elderly who are incapacitated and/or widowed.

Loneliness is less common among married than nonmarried individuals, but when the unmarried are divided into categories, the results vary somewhat by study. The general tendency appears to be for single people to be less lonely than the divorced or widowed. Loneliness is, of course, a common experience during BEREAVEMENT. Within MARRIAGE, loneliness is associated with marital happiness

so that unhappily married individuals are vulnerable to being lonely.

## THE ANTECEDENTS OF LONELINESS

Being socially isolated is an obvious antecedent of loneliness. Research suggests that the quality and provisions of RELATIONSHIPS are more crucial than quantitative aspects of a person's social network (Kraus, Davis, Bazzini, Church, & Kirchman, 1993).

One way of conceptualizing the determinants of loneliness is to start with predisposing and precipitating factors which lead to desired and actual levels of social contact. When predisposing and/or precipitating events produce a mismatch between desired and actual levels of social contact, then the person will normally experience loneliness. The intensity of the loneliness experienced may be moderated by cognitive factors.

Predisposing factors are persisting forces such as PERSONALITY traits and cultural VALUES which make people vulnerable to loneliness. Psychologists have empirically demonstrated links between loneliness and several personality characteristics: low SELF-ESTEEM, trait ANXIETY, DEPRESSION, SHYNESS, self-consciousness, the lack of SOCIAL SKILLS needed for making new friends, introversion, lack of assertiveness, and external LOCUS OF CONTROL. Sociological theorists such as David Riesman and Philip Slater have argued that North American culture in the mid-twentieth century had a paradoxical system of values: North Americans were simultaneously expected to be cooperative team players and competitive individualists. These inconsistent demands fostered loneliness.

Specific events such as moving to a new community, the breakup of a close relationship, or the death of a spouse can precipitate loneliness. While many such events undermine the attained level of social contact, other events (e.g., high-school dances) can trigger loneliness by raising people's expectations or desires for social contacts.

When deficiencies in social provisions occur, the resulting experience of loneliness is influenced by SOCIAL COMPARISON, attributions, and perceptions of personal control. For example, students who believe they have fewer friends than their peers are likely to become lonely. People who attribute their loneliness to internal, stable causes (i.e., their personality), are likely to experience depression and pessimism with their loneliness. When partners terminate a relationship, both lose their relationship. Yet the person terminating the relationship typically experiences less loneliness than the person being "dumped."

REACTIONS TO LONELINESS
Four patterns of reacting to loneliness are: Sad Passivity (e.g., sleeping, crying, doing nothing); Active Solitude (e.g., working, listening to music, exercising), Spending Money, and Social Contact. Many more people report having recently felt lonely than describe themselves as a lonely person. Most experiences of loneliness appear transitory; longitudinal studies of first-year university students consistently show that their loneliness declines over time. Treatment outcome studies provide encouraging evidence that therapy can, if pursued, help people overcome loneliness.
See also: DEPRESSION; MARRIAGE; PERSONALITY; RELATIONSHIPS; SELF-ESTEEM; SHYNESS; SOCIAL COMPARISON; SOCIAL SKILLS; VALUES.

BIBLIOGRAPHY
Kraus, L. A., Davis, M. H., Bazzini, D., Church, M. B., & Kirchman, C. M. (1993). Personal and social influences on loneliness: The mediating effect of social provisions. *Social Psychology Quarterly, 56,* 37–53.
Mikulincer, M., & Segal, J. (1990). A multidimensional analysis of the experience of loneliness. *Journal of Social and Personal Relationships, 7,* 209–30.
Peplau, L. A., & Perlman, D. (Eds.). (1982). *Loneliness: A sourcebook of current theory, research, and therapy.* New York: Wiley–Interscience.
Shaver, P. R., & Brennan, K. A. (1991). Measures of depression and loneliness. In J. P. Robinson, P. R. Shaver, & L. S. Wrightsman (Eds.), *Measures of personality and social psychological attitudes* (Vol. 1, pp. 195–289). San Diego, CA: Academic Press.
Weiss, R. S. (1973). *Loneliness: The experience of emotional and social isolation.* Cambridge, MA: MIT Press.

DANIEL PERLMAN

**love** A multifaceted experience with psychological, physiological, and behavioral components (*see* Hatfield & Rapson, 1993). Social psychologists generally distinguish between two types of love. Passionate love is a state of intense AROUSAL, characterized by strong emotions and high levels of psychological involvement with the other. In contrast, companionate love refers to feelings of TRUST, affection, respect, and closeness. Although these two types may co-occur in a given relationship, such as MARRIAGE, they are generally considered independent processes, each with its own antecedents, consequences, and underlying mechanisms.

Existing research on love is primarily concerned with the nature and dynamics of love experiences. Many of these studies seek to develop a more extensive, descriptively richer taxonomy than that mentioned above. One goal of this research is to identify INDIVIDUAL DIFFERENCES (including GENDER differences) in the emotional and behavioral manifestations of love. Other studies take a more process-oriented approach, describing the dynamic properties and functions of love. For example, ATTACHMENT-based theories are concerned with how adult romantic love is affected by beliefs about relationships, the self-concept, and early attachment experiences (*see* ATTRACTION; RELATIONSHIPS).
See also: AROUSAL; ATTRACTION; GENDER; MARRIAGE; TRUST.

BIBLIOGRAPHY
Hatfield, E., & Rapson, R. L. (1993). *Love, sex, and intimacy: Their psychology, biology, and history.* New York: Harper Collins.
Hendrick, S. S., & Hendrick, C. (1992). *Romantic love.* Newbury Park, CA: Sage.

HARRY T. REIS

**lowballing** A SOCIAL INFLUENCE strategy by which COMPLIANCE to an initial request is followed by a more costly and less beneficial version of the same request (Cialdini, Cacioppo, Bassett, & Miller, 1978). Individuals tend to maintain their commitment and still comply with the request though it has become more costly. It was originally thought that this technique worked because individuals were reluctant to change their commitment, despite the fact that the conditions had changed. However, Burger and Petty (1981) demonstrated that the underlying mechanism seems to be an unfulfilled obligation to the person requesting the behavior. Lowballing is different from the FOOT IN THE DOOR technique in which the initial behavior that is requested is related, but not identical to, the larger subsequently requested behavior. In lowballing, the initial behavior requested is the desired behavior, followed by a second request for that same behavior, the only change being that it is now costlier to engage in that behavior.

*See also*: SOCIAL INFLUENCE.

BIBLIOGRAPHY

Burger, J. M., & Petty, R. E. (1981). The low-ball compliance technique: Task or person commitment? *Journal of Personality and Social Psychology*, *40*, 492–500.

Cialdini, R. B., Cacioppo, J. T., Bassett, R., & Miller, J. A. (1978). The low ball procedure for producing compliance: Commitment then cost. *Journal of Personality and Social Psychology 36*, 463–76.

MICHAEL MIGDAL
BRIAN MULLEN

# M

majority social influence This is form of SOCIAL INFLUENCE in which a majority of group members influence a deviant person or minority to abandon their discrepant position and conform to the norm embodied in the position of the majority. It can be largely equated with CONFORMITY and works to maintain established group NORMS. In classic theory, the POWER of the majority to influence was seen as reflecting the social reality testing and group locomotion functions of the group. The more an individual is dependent on the group for information to reduce uncertainty and to achieve desired ends, the more likely is conformity to the majority position on relevant issues. Research (Allen, 1965; Asch, 1956) confirms that conformity to the majority is more likely when the discrepant person is uncertain; the stimulus is ambiguous; person and majority are cohesive, similar, and interdependent members of a relevant reference group; the majority is unanimous and the person without a partner; the person responds in public rather than private (under the surveillance of the majority); and the majority shows itself to be relatively more certain, competent, and successful. In CONVERSION theory, unlike the classic view, majority influence is assumed to produce largely COMPLIANCE without private acceptance.

See also: NORMS; POWER; SOCIAL INFLUENCE.

BIBLIOGRAPHY
Allen, V. L. (1965). Situational factors in conformity. In L. Berkowitz (Ed.), *Advances in experimental social psychology* (Vol. 2, pp. 133–75). New York: Academic Press.
Asch, S. E. (1956). Studies of independence and conformity: A minority of one against a unanimous majority. *Psychological Monographs: General and Applied, 70* (whole no. 416) 1–70.

JOHN C. TURNER

marriage Changing economic and social conditions at the turn of the century called public attention to disrupted FAMILY RELATIONS and stimulated the scientific study of marriage. Social scientists have focused most of their research on two phenomena, marital satisfaction and marital success or stability, and have investigated their behavioral, cognitive, and emotional correlates (*see* Fincham & Bradbury, 1990).

## BEHAVIOR

Although psychologists made contributions to early work on marriage, it was conducted mainly by sociologists. Reacting to the sociological tradition of large scale surveys, clinical psychologists began the systematic study of marriage in the 1970s by observing spouse behavior during marital COMMUNICATION. Contrary to the prevailing lore that marital satisfaction depends on the exchange of positive behaviors, they documented that dissatisfied couples differ reliably from satisfied couples in three respects: their interactions showed greater stereotypy or structure, higher rates of negative behavior, and greater reciprocation of negative behavior.

Two important but independent developments laid the groundwork for systematic social psychological research on marriage. First, recognition of the limits of a purely behavioral account of marriage led marital researchers to focus on cognition and emotion in the 1980s. Second, social psychologists became dissatisfied with research on

RELATIONSHIPS that involved people who were "personally irrelevant" to each other and the field of CLOSE RELATIONSHIPS emerged in social psychology (*see* Kelley et al., 1983). Although a founding father of modern social psychology had offered an analysis of CONFLICT in marriage (Lewin, 1948), the marital relationship did not assume center stage in this new area. Indeed, many of the topics addressed by social psychologists (e.g., LOVE, INTIMACY, commitment) are not yet well represented in research on marriage, a circumstance that may reflect the strong applied and interdisciplinary roots of marital research. Other topics such as SOCIAL EXCHANGE and interdependence have helped bridge the two areas.

COGNITION

Because the cognitive perspective has historically dominated social psychology in terms of the level at which problems are formulated, methodology, and theorizing, it is not surprising that the most complete integration of marital and social psychological research has occurred in the study of cognition in marriage. This is most evident in research on attributions. Informed by ATTRIBUTION THEORIES, work on LEARNED HELPLESSNESS, and analyses of ATTRIBUTION OF RESPONSIBILITY, most of the research has investigated whether spouses' attributions for marital events are related to their marital satisfaction. A considerable body of research shows that spouses assign responsibility and make causal attributions for partner behavior and marital difficulties that are likely to maintain their current levels of satisfaction. Longitudinal data also suggest that attributions may initiate changes in marital satisfaction. Such findings are not due to the relation between marital dissatisfaction and DEPRESSION, the nature of the stimuli used to elicit attributions, or the solicited versus unsolicited nature of the attributions studied.

A second focus of research was stimulated by the desire to understand the determinants of behaviors that distinguish distressed and nondistressed spouses, as well as the widespread belief among attribution theorists that attributions influence behavior. Although far fewer studies exist on this topic, there is evidence that attributions are related to observed behaviors and sequences of behaviors and suggestive evidence that attributions may even cause such behavior (Bradbury & Fincham, 1990). Recently, bodies of research have emerged on attributions for marital AGGRESSION and VIOLENCE and on ACCOUNTS of courtship, early years of marriage, and divorce.

Existing research on other cognitive contents (e.g., beliefs) and structures (e.g., cognitive complexity) has not been as obviously influenced by a social psychological perspective but the potential for integration is great. This potential is currently being explored in research on knowledge structures such as mental models and SCHEMAS in close relationships. Particularly promising is the extension of basic research on SOCIAL COGNITION to illuminate cognitive processes in marriage (*see* Fletcher & Fincham, 1991).

EMOTION

Similarly promising for understanding marriage is the explosion of research on emotion in social psychology. Early work on NONVERBAL COMMUNICATION was instrumental in advancing understanding of emotion in observational studies of marital communication. However, more recent research on emotion in marriage focuses on physiology and makes little contact with the social psychological literature. Although it has provided some dramatic findings, it remains a promissory note in the absence of replication.

CONCEPTUAL AND METHODOLOGICAL ISSUES

An urgent question that requires attention is the extent to which the findings of research on romantic relationships, such as the dating relationships that dominate the close relationships literature in social psychology, can be generalized to marriage. Does the socially sanctioned nature of marriage confer unique properties that require a categorical approach to studying marriage vis-à-vis other relationships or is the marital relationship best conceptualized as one that falls on a continuous dimension that can be used to characterize all relationships? Under what conditions are these two viewpoints differentially useful? Such questions are critical to integrating more fully marital and social psychological literatures.

Equally important is the unit of analysis. Although numerous marital studies reflect an *inter*personal level of analysis, most research on marriage examines questions regarding *intra*personal processes. Notable advances have been made in methodologies and analytic techniques to capture relationship properties (*see* STATISTICS) that will continue to redress this imbalance.

Methodological advances notwithstanding, complete understanding of marriage at both intra- and interpersonal levels requires theoretically informed research. Early sociological research on marriage tended to be atheoretical and the behavioral research that arose in reaction to this tradition eschewed theory. Despite recent attempts to address this theoretical vacuum, social psychological theory may represent the greatest potential contribution to understanding marriage. Such a contribution to the applied concerns of marital research would once again instantiate Lewin's profound insight that there is nothing as practical as a good theory.

*See also*: ACCOUNTS; AGGRESSION; ATTRIBUTION OF RESPONSIBILITY; ATTRIBUTION THEORIES; COMMUNICATION; CONFLICT; DEPRESSION; FAMILY RELATIONS; INTIMACY; NONVERBAL COMMUNICATION; RELATIONSHIPS; SCHEMAS; SOCIAL COGNITION; STATISTICS.

BIBLIOGRAPHY

Bradbury, T. N., & Fincham, F. D. (1990). Attributions in marriage: Review and critique. *Psychological Bulletin, 107*, 3–33.

Fincham, F. D., & Bradbury, T. N. (Eds.) (1990). *The psychology of marriage: Basic issues and applications*. New York: Guilford Press.

Fletcher, G. J., & Fincham, F. D. (Eds.) (1991). *Cognition in close relationships*. Hillsdale, NJ: Lawrence Erlbaum.

Kelley, H. H., Berscheid, E., Christensen, A., Harvey, J. H., Huston, T. L., Levinger, G., McClintock, E., Peplau, L. A., & Peterson, D. R. (1983). *Close relationships*. San Francisco; CA: Freeman.

Lewin, K. (1948). The background of conflict in marriage. *Resolving social conflicts: Selected papers on group dynamics*. New York: Harper & Row.

FRANK D. FINCHAM

**masculinity/femininity** Originally masculinity and femininity were conceived of as representing ends of a single continuum. Recent research suggests that masculinity and femininity are independent dimensions, each being broadly defined by multiple domains including appearance, behavior, personality, and interests. Many instruments exist to measure masculinity and femininity, but most ask individuals only about their personality characteristics. Individuals who claim both masculine and feminine characteristics are considered to be psychologically androgynous (*see* ANDROGYNY). A central issue has been how strongly the domains considered to be masculine and feminine relate to one another. Bem (1974) has argued that the domains are highly related, and that masculinity and femininity relate to many other aspects of GENDER-related behavior. In contrast, Spence and Helmreich (1980) have argued that the domains are not strongly related, and that measures of masculinity typically assess instrumentality, whereas measures of femininity typically assess expressiveness. As such, each should predict within this more narrow range. Thus far, the narrower approach has stronger empirical support than the broader approach.

*See also*: GENDER.

BIBLIOGRAPHY

Bem, S. L. (1974). The measurement of psychological androgyny. *Journal of Consulting and Clinical Psychology, 42*, 155–62.

Spence, J. T., & Helmreich, R. L. (1980). Masculine instrumentality and feminine expressiveness: Their relationships with sex role attitudes and behaviors. *Psychology of Women Quarterly, 5*, 147–63.

CAROL LYNN MARTIN

**mass media** In order to understand what we mean by the mass media, and in particular the major focus of social psychologists, mainly mass media effects, we first need to define the broader concept of mass communication. In the general field of COMMUNICATION, DeFleur and Dennis (1988) offer a useful definition: "Mass communication is a process in which professional communicators use media to disseminate messages widely, rapidly, and continuously to arouse intended meanings in large and diverse audiences in attempts to influence them in a variety of ways" (p. 12).

DeFleur and Dennis consider mass communication to be an ongoing process with *five distinct stages*. In the first stage, professional communicators first create various types of *messages* for presentation to assorted individuals for diverse purposes. These messages are disseminated in the second stage in a *quick and continuous* manner through some form of mechanical media (e.g., film, television). In stage 3, this message eventually reaches a *vast and diverse* (i.e., mass) audience. In the fourth stage the audience somehow *interprets* these messages and gives them a meaning. This response from the audience is considered by Harris (1989) to be the *communication* part of the definition, since it implies some form of reciprocity between sender and receiver. Lastly, as a result of all the above, the audience is influenced or changed in some manner. In other words, there is a mass media effect.

How an audience is changed or influenced by the mass media, the fifth of the above stages, has been the focus of social psychological research for decades. In fact, most research on mass communication has been the study of *effects* (Roberts & Maccoby, 1985). This is not to say that social psychologists have not been interested in other aspects of the mass media, such as studying the characteristics of the vast and diverse audiences attracted to mass media, or the cognitive and emotional processes that may influence how we interpret mass media messages and give them a meaning. It is the process giving rise to effects, however, that will be central to our current definition.

In thinking of mass media effects, we should be cognizant of what have been termed *intended and unintended influences*. According to McGuire (1986), the major social function of the mass media is "to influence the receiver's cognitions, attitudes, or behaviors in some desired direction" (p. 178). Most often the world of mass media is comprised of intended effects, deliberate attempts on the part of the communicator to influence the recipient in some way. While there are many potential types of intended effects, six have been most frequently studied by mass communication scholars. The two most widely acknowledged are *commercial advertising* and *political campaigns*. In addition there are *public service announcements* and *multimedia campaigns to change life-styles*, such as in the areas of AIDS awareness, smoking, drug use, and other soically relevant issues. A fifth intended effect has been termed *massive, monolithic, indoctrination effects on ideology*. It is possible for some totalitarian governments to control nearly all aspects of the mass media. Government officials believe that by controlling the media the government can ensure loyalty of its people to the government ideology. Lastly, there has been the study of *mass mediated rituals* in social control. Such mass media events as the *World Series*, the *Superbowl*, and *Wimbledon* are said to have particular affects on a region because of the community's symbolic participation in a ritualistic event. The large street demonstrations, parades, friendly drinking with strangers, and other festivities accompanying these sports media extravaganzas would imply some form of media influence. Likewise, *media events* like the showing of the mini-series *The Day After*, about the aftermath of a nuclear war, have been examined by media scholars as a means of determining whether the unified viewing of certain mass media presentations can affect viewers' attitudes and perceptions (Huston et al., 1992).

There are often media events which are not planned by broadcasters, like the assassinations of President John Kennedy and Martin Luther King, or natural disasters which result in mass viewer reactions. These unexpected viewer reactions represent the second kind of media effect discussed by McGuire. When we consider unintended media effects we are referring to what McGuire defines as media presentations which were "designed for purposes other than to exert social influence, usually to entertain" (p. 182). While the eventual reaction from the audience may be one approaching antisocial behavior, the original creator of the media presentation never intended viewers to react in that fashion. Like research on intended media effects, McGuire cites six areas of research attention given to these *unintended* media influences.

The first is *televised violence and viewers' aggression*. Perhaps no other area has received as much research attention as the effects of televised violence (*see* Linz & Donnerstein, 1989). For decades, media scholars, concerned citizens, congressional panels and others have debated whether exposure to violence in the media leads viewers to later aggressive behavior (*see* AGGRESSION). A second major area has been *underrepresentation and social invisibility*. How many women over 65 years old are there in England? What are the percentages of Hispanic or Native Americans in the United States? It is quite likely that those of us who are heavy television viewers would underestimate the percentage of individuals in these categories (Huston et al., 1990). A possible reason for these inaccurate perceptions is the infrequency with which these social groups appear on television. Even worse than simply believing that there are fewer older women than actually exist is the possibility that some viewers may come to STEREOTYPE older woman in a certain manner. This is an example of the third kind of unintended effect, *misrepresentation effects on viewer stereotypes*. Rather than not being portrayed in the media, some groups are misportrayed.

A fourth area of considerable research has been *effects of erotica and PORNOGRAPHY on sexual thoughts, feelings, and behaviors*. Can the viewing of sexually explicit movies and magazines, particularly those fused with violence, lead to rape and other forms of sexual violence? As with the subject of televised nonsexual violence and its possible effects, researchers and policy makers have been concerned with the potential effects of viewing sexually explicit materials for many years.

More recently research inquiry into unintended effects has focused on *media styles affecting cognitive processes*. Is the message different depending on the medium (McLuan, 1964)? Is there something about television's fast pace and visual coverage, for example, that affects us differently than other media? Is it possible that just the form of television presentation (e.g., fades, zooms, pans, special effects) have more of an effect on how we process the message than the message itself? These questions have been the subject of recent research by media scholars (e.g., Huston & Wright, 1989).

Lastly, there is the *effect of new forms of mass media on thought processes*. For some of us, it might be hard to visualize a community without television. But, such communities do exist. Williams (1986), along with other researchers in Canada, found such a community and were able to examine what changes occurred to individuals and their community as a whole *after* the introduction of television. To what degree did the introduction of television change behaviors, cognitive development, and leisure activities in the community? Two years after the introduction of television, children who previously had no access to this type of mass media showed reductions in cognitive skills like reading and creativity, as well as reduced leisure activities with the family. Furthermore, there was evidence for an increase in aggressive behaviors.

Intended or unintended, there is a general agreement among media researchers that the media do have an influence on its viewers. However, these effects undoubtedly differ from person to person. Just as importantly, effects can differ within each individual. There are four major categories of influences that have been extensively studied by mass media researchers (e.g., Harris, 1989) – *behavioral, attitudinal, cognitive*, and *physiological* effects.

For some reason when we think about how the media influence people, we tend to do so most often in terms of observable behavior. For many, and in particular policy makers, behavioral markers are thought of as the most powerful of media effects. After all, if we are concerned about televised violence shouldn't our concern be with changes in actual aggressive behavior? However, there are other avenues by which the media can impart its influence. The changing or reinforcing of one's attitude to violence is also a mass media influence. Likewise we can think of cognitive effects. Learning a fact from the mass media is the most straightforward type of cognitive effect. Obviously, television programs devoted to informing and educating viewers, such as many of the programs on Public Broadcasting, provide us with new facts we never would have known had we not tuned in. Less obvious, and considerably more complicated, is the way that different forms of mass media stimulate different cognitive *processes*. Mass media researchers have often borrowed heavily from psychology in explaining the cognitive effects produced by television or radio.

Lastly, there are emotional reactions, often accompanied by some physiological reaction, which are also media effects. Some effects (like crying during a sad scene) we are readily aware of but others (like an increase in blood pressure) might not be accessible at a conscious level. For some mass media theorists, excitement and its accompanying physiological AROUSAL is an indispensable component in explaining the relationship between media exposure and behavior (e.g., Zillmann, 1984). To understand mass media effects we often need to consider all four of these responses – *behavioral, attitudinal, cognitive,* and *physiological* – either separately or in combination with one other. The media has a multifaceted influence on us.

Historically there has been an assumption that the mass media's influence was so powerful that the media automatically altered the ideas, attitudes, and behaviors of anyone who came into contact with them. Today, we recognize what we should have known all along – that human behavior is a complex matter. It is difficult to change people's attitudes and actions under most circumstances. The mass media is but one, albeit important, social influence on a person's thoughts, attitudes, emotions, and behavior. Even here, however the type of influence varies.

*New* attitudes, cognitions, and behaviors may be formed as the result of exposure to messages in the mass media. Most often, however, messages in the mass media probably *reinforce* or strengthen attitudes that already exist or behavioral patterns that are already established. There are times when mass media messages *change* existing attitudes, cognitions, and behaviors. For most people exposure to mass media messages changes attitudes and behaviors in a subtle way. For a smaller number of people, however, the effect may be dramatic.

There remain several important questions that we need to raise in order to refine our understanding of mass media effects. These are questions that have often puzzled policy makers, academics, and students of mass media effects for decades. First, how long does it take for the mass media to have an effect? For some effects, like physiological or emotional changes in a viewer or listener after exposure to a mass media depiction, we might expect almost immediate results. For other media influences the time interval will increase from minutes, to days, to months, and even years.

Another temporal question that arises frequently concerns the *duration of the effect*. How long does physiological arousal last after exposure to a frightening or sexual film? Do most effects wax and wane over time and in constant need of a new infusion of new media exposure? For physiological arousal, the answer would be that the effect may last for only a few minutes and additional media exposure would be required to keep arousal high. For behaviors like aggression, however, the effect can last a lifetime. We should keep in mind that although it might appear that a particular media effect has vanished, or is short lived, it can appear sometime in the future. Media messages can be stored in memory for long periods of time and be reactivated later when conditions are suitable.

A second question often raised is what type of content, shown in what context, produces effects? The content of most mass media messages is complex. All types of violent materials do not facilitate aggressive behavior. Violent content which is gratuitous, arousing, or sexual in nature is more likely to affect the viewer than other types of violent content. The context in which the message is received is also important. There are several contextual variables that may alter mass media exposure outcomes. One such context variable concerns the number of times people are exposed to a given message. For example we may ask of many study outcomes: Does the effect occur after a single exposure or does the effect depend on multiple exposures?

Finally, there is the issue of exactly *who* is affected by the mass media. We can conceive of influences ranging from individuals to whole societies. Just as individuals will react differently to the mass media, as noted above, various subgroups within the population will also vary (e.g., children, elderly, the well educated).

In summary, the mass media can be thought of as *process* that includes program conception, production, transmission, and reception by the audience. It is this last step of mass media *effects* in which researchers are most interested. Mass media messages may be divided into those *intended* to influence viewers and listeners, or they may be *unintentional*. The mass media may influence our *behaviors, attitudes, cognitions*, or our *physiological arousal*. Researchers have been concerned with each of these outcomes. It is possible for the mass media to *form new* attitudes, beliefs, or behaviors, *reinforce* already existing ones, or *change* those attitudes and behaviors which we already possess. But, the media does not act alone. Other agents of socialization, like parents, schools, and peers, interact with the mass media to produce effects. Research within the social science community has moved through three stages with regard to the impact of the media. At first, there was the *magic-bullet theory* which advocated a powerful and direct effect from mass media exposure. With continued research, there developed a period of time in which there was a belief in a *limited* influence from the mass media. Today we see the media as having *indirect but powerful* influences on particular individuals under certain conditions.

*See also:* AGGRESSION; AROUSAL; COMMUNICATION; PORNOGRAPHY; STEREOTYPING.

BIBLIOGRAPHY

DeFleur, M. L., & Dennis, E. E. (1988). *Understanding mass communication*. Boston, MA: Houghton Mifflin.

Harris, R. J. (1989). *A cognitive psychology of mass communication*. Hillsdale, NJ: Lawrence Erlbaum.

Huston A. C., & Wright, J. C. (1989). Television forms and children. In G. Comstock (Ed.), *Public communication and behavior* (Vol. 2, pp. 103–59). New York: Academic Press.

Huston, A., Donnerstein, E., Fairchild, H., Feshbach, N., Katz, P., Murray, J., Rubinstein, E., & Zuckerman, D. (1992). *Big world, small screen: The role of television in American society*. Lincoln, NE: University of Nebraska Press.

Linz, D., & Donnerstein, E. (1989). The effects of violent messages in the mass media: Contemporary theory and research. In J. E. Bradac (Ed.), *Messages in communication science* (pp. 263–92). Newbury Park, CA: Sage.

McGuire, W. J. (1986). The myth of mass media impact. In G. Comstock (Ed.), *Public communication and behavior* (Vol. 1, pp. 175–259). New York: Academic Press.

McLuan, H. M. (1964). *Understanding media: The extensions of man*. New York: McGraw-Hill.

Roberts, D. F., & Maccoby, N. (1985). The effects of mass communication. In G. Lindzey and E. Aronson (Eds.), *Handbook of social psychology* (pp. 539–89). New York: Random House.

Williams, T. M. (Ed.) (1986). *Impact of television: A natural experiment in three countries*. New York: Academic Press.

Zillmann, D. (1984). *Connections between sex and aggression*. Hillsdale, NJ: Lawrence Erlbaum.

EDWARD DONNERSTEIN

**memory** Mechanisms by which people store and retrieve the knowledge they have encoded. The study of person memory by social psychologists addresses questions such as how social memory is stored in the mind, what codes are used for memories about people, whether traits or people are basic units of memory, and how memory influences people's judgments about others. Memory research in social cognition draws heavily on the progress made by cognitive psychologists, but unique insights also derive from the social context (*see* Fiske & Taylor, 1991, for a review).

## ASSOCIATIVE NETWORK MODELS OF MEMORY

The most common and well-developed model of memory is the associative network model. In this model, memory for an event or a person consists of concepts and connections between concepts. As the number of connections between a concept and other concepts increases, retrieval of that concept is easier, because there are many alternative routes to locate it in memory.

In the associative network model, concepts can be stored under a variety of memory codes (to be discussed later), but one common code is called a *proposition*. Propositions are made up of ideas, called nodes, and links between nodes. "Lucy attended the concert" is one example of a proposition, where the nouns and verbs (e.g., Lucy, attended) are nodes, and relations between them are links (e.g., "Lucy" is linked to "attended"). Under this model, ideas in a proposition cluster together and will be recalled together because of their links (*see* Anderson, 1990; Norman, 1976).

A feature of the associative model is that the links are labeled. If asked "Who attended the concert?" the person will use the memory of the link to provide the answer. Further, the more often a proposition is accessed, the stronger its links become. This feature of the model is called "spreading activation." If a node is activated in memory, the activation of the node spreads to its links and to other items, strengthening the links. Therefore, the more a person thinks about a proposition, the stronger its links become, and the greater the likelihood that it will be remembered. A related feature is that the more links there are between propositions, the more likely it is that one of those propositions will be recalled. Many links create alternative routes to retrieving the proposition, increasing the probability of a successful search.

Associative network models distinguish two kinds of memory: long term and short term. Long-term memory contains the store of knowledge that a person can potentially retrieve. It is thought to be practically limitless in capacity; the problem is finding and retrieving ideas if they are needed. In contrast, short-term memory refers to information that is occupying attention or consciousness at a particular time. Unlike long-term memory, short-term memory has very limited capacity; it can only store a few ideas simultaneously.

## ASSOCIATIVE NETWORKS FOR SOCIAL MEMORY

Two models of people's memory for other people have been based on associative networks. One, the Hastie model (Hastie, 1988), predicts that in forming an impression of another person, people pay most attention to information that is nonredundant with what they already know. Thus, people spend more time processing information that is inconsistent with their expectancies about the person, because this information is nonredundant. The increased processing time makes links with inconsistent information stronger and therefore makes it more memorable.

Another model of person memory based on associative networks is the Srull–Wyer model (Srull & Wyer, 1989), building on the Hastie model. According to this model, people organize their memory for people differently when they have a trait label than when they do not. When people do not have a trait label, they store each behavior separately, creating links when behaviors seem to cluster together. For example, given only the behaviors: "donates money to charity," "gives friend a ride home," and "forgets own phone number," people store each behavior separately. If people are asked to evaluate this person on a trait (such as generosity), they review the different stored behaviors for an answer. The evaluation process strengthens links between the behaviors, according to associative network principles.

In this model, when people have a trait expectancy about a person, their person memory is organized differently. If they expect that a person is generous, each generous behavior they subsequently store (e.g., donating money and giving a friend a ride home) will be connected to a preestablished node labeled "generous." People develop a network of associations around the trait label. In addition, people develop a second network around a global impression of the person. This global impression network contains the same behaviors related to generosity, but in addition, it contains behaviors irrelevant to generosity (e.g., forgets own phone number) and behaviors inconsistent with generosity (e.g., ignores a panhandler). Within the global impression network, the Srull–Wyer model assumes, like the Hastie model, that people pay attention to inconsistent information, creating more and stronger links that make it more memorable. Therefore, the Srull–Wyer model also predicts that people will have better memory for inconsistent information under many circumstances.

When people have a trait expectancy, judgments about the person take advantage of the two networks. When asked if the target woman is generous, when a trait-based network exists for that trait, people quickly retrieve the judgment. If no trait network exists for it, people use their global evaluative impression to inform their judgment. Thus, when asked if the woman is kind, people refer to the global impression, and if it is likable, they infer that she is kind. In both of these judgments, people use the top level of the network; they do not consider the actual behaviors that make up the labels.

Both the Hastie and Srull–Wyer models predict that people remember inconsistent information better, and much of the related research bears this out. But the findings seem to contradict other work based on SCHEMA theories, which predict that people gloss over inconsistent information so they can maintain congruent impressions. This paradox has been addressed by research that defines exactly when people rely more on categories or more on data. Basically, inconsistent information has an advantage in ENCODING, especially when people's expectations are weak and they are motivated to be accurate. Memory for consistent information has an advantage at retrieval, when people want to present a coherent impression, and when they are motivated to maintain a strong expectancy (Stangor & McMillan, 1992).

OTHER MODELS OF PERSON MEMORY
One model of memory adds a store of procedural knowledge to people's associative networks of declarative knowledge. Declarative knowledge consists of propositions and content knowledge. Procedural knowledge contains if–then action statements, such as "if phone rings, then pick up the receiver." A feature of the procedural model is that if people regularly use their declarative knowledge in a certain sequence, they may begin accessing the sequence as a single, efficient unit. These units develop with practice and are said to become proceduralized. Through this process, declarative knowledge can become procedural knowledge (see AUTOMATICITY for more discussion of proceduralization).

Parallel distributed processing is a much different memory model, at the time of this writing as yet undeveloped in SOCIAL COGNITION. It posits that memory does not contain separate ideas or nodes, but rather consists of content-free units with links among them. A remembered idea creates a pattern of facilitative and inhibitory links among these units. The patterns of links can be strengthened with use, creating stronger or weaker memory for ideas.

CONTENTS OF PERSON MEMORY
People's knowledge about others varies along a continuum from observable to inferred, including appearance, behavior, and traits. As people become acquainted, they rely more on inferred traits and less on observable behaviors or on appearance. Each of these three types of information may be stored within a different code (see Fiske & Taylor, 1991).

First, *traits* are stored in memory in propositions, like much nonsocial information. Often people's trait knowledge is inferred from several instances of relevant behavior. Therefore, traits are more abstract than behaviors, and as such, they form economical units in memory. People appear to organize trait information along two orthogonal dimensions: sociability and competence. People map traits on these two axes, so the traits "warm, sociable, and pleasant" cluster together and in a different location from the trait cluster of "intelligent, industrious, and determined."

Because *behaviors* occur in time, a temporal code may accompany memory for behavior sequences. Although sequence is preserved, people do not have to recall temporal sequences in their chronological order. They can work backwards in time to recall a behavior or event just as easily as they can work forwards. People's goals are also likely to organize memory for behaviors. A sequence of behaviors can be hierarchically organized by goals and subgoals, which can facilitate memory. For example, a person's goal of passing a class could include the subgoals of studying for a test and writing a paper.

People's memories for *appearance* may be stored in analog images. Analog representations preserve the relative relationships among features, so a visual analog code would retain the spatial arrangement of a stimulus. When people retrieve information about another's appearance, they seem to scan a stored image of the person. In general, people's memory for faces is extremely accurate, at least in laboratory studies and for people of their own race (*see* CROSS-RACIAL FACIAL IDENTIFICATION). A bias toward visual cues may be responsible for this accuracy. However, in high-arousal, disruptive settings, such as in eyewitness accounts of crimes, memories for people tend to be less accurate (*see* EYEWITNESS TESTIMONY).

Besides the propositional code for traits, the temporal code for behaviors, and the analog code for appearance, people may store an affective code for social memories. People store positive and negative social stimuli separately, and an affective tag can accompany virtually any piece of social information.

CONCRETE AND ABSTRACT
INFORMATION IN MEMORY
Social psychologists have found meaningful a distinction between specific (previously called episodic) and general (previously called semantic) contents of memory. People's specific memories for experiences (e.g., another person's behaviors) are stored as isolated instances, but their general memories (e.g., a person's traits) are usually embedded in an elaborate associative network. The process of inferring traits from specific experiences and forming links between the traits requires effort and attention, so people remember traits better. People access their general and specific memories differently when they make

judgments about a remembered person. If a question (e.g., "Is your friend honest?") matches a remembered trait (e.g., honesty), then the judgment is easy. If there is no matching trait in memory, then people review individual episodes of behavior that might be relevant, a more time-consuming process.

Another feature of general and specific memories is that once a trait is inferred from a series of behaviors, the behaviors and the trait become somewhat independent in memory. The trait label can be used instead of the behaviors. Finally, temporary contextual factors (e.g., a particular audience) that may have influenced the trait judgment at encoding will persist when the trait is stored, even after the context changes.

ORGANIZATION OF MEMORY
People normally use the person as the unit of organization in memory. For example, if told that David likes to dance and read, and that Nancy likes to ski and read, people usually organize their knowledge around David and Nancy, rather than around "readers," "skiers," and "dancers." This organization is especially likely when people know their targets well. However, people sometimes organize their memories of people around a situation they all share (friends at the ski club). And when they are overloaded, people may be too distracted to organize memory by person, and may default to noticeable social groups (e.g., age, sex).

When meeting new people, people first organize their knowledge by physically salient characteristics such as race, age, and sex. As they get to know people as individuals, the organization adds lower levels based on the person as a unit. But the organization by social group remains an important, higher-level structure, which may be one reason for the prevalence of stereotypes (*see* Srull & Wyer, 1989).

MEMORY, JUDGMENT, AND GOALS
People's judgments of a person may not be related to what they remember about the person. Although intuitively it seems that people would use their memories to guide

their judgments, in much research, people's judgments of a target are often not based on the information they remember about the target. The distinction appears to be that when people make their judgments on-line, as they receive the information, the judgments are independent of the actual information they later recall. But when people have to make their judgments from memory, after they receive the information (e.g., when the judgment is unexpected), the judgments are based more on recalled information (Hastie & Park, 1986).

People's goals in an interaction can determine how much information they remember about a person. Some goals cause people to process information more thoroughly, so their recall is better. For example, when people's goal is merely to comprehend information or to judge a communication's coherence and grammar, they recall less information because the information is processed in a relatively superficial way.

When people's goal is to memorize information about a target, they remember less than when their goal is to form an impression. When forming impressions, people forge links to create a coherent impression, so they process more thoroughly. Additionally, people group relevant behaviors into traits, which organize behaviors and make them easier to recall. Thus, people forming an impression remember information about others better. However, if people who are instructed to memorize happen to use people's goals as an organization structure, they outperform people with an impression goal. Goals, even more than traits, are especially good organizers for remembering behaviors. For example, the target behaviors: buys a balloon, smiles, gets candy from her pocket, are more easily remembered when grouped by the goal to befriend a young child.

People whose goal is to empathize with a target have better memories for the target's behavior than people who are detached. People are more empathic when they share the target's mood, when their personalities are similar, or when they are cooperating with the target. People who take another person's psychological or physical perspective are also more empathic, and they recall more. The improved recall of empathic people may be because they are more aware of a target's goals, one of the best organizers of information in memory (Kihlstrom, et al., 1988) (*see also* EMPATHY).

When people's goal is to compare a target to themselves, they also process information more carefully and remember it well. They create more links among items, and may apply their already well-organized cognitive structures (such as their SELF-SCHEMAS) to the target.

Finally, people who expect to interact with a target remember a great deal. Anticipating interactions motivates people to make a coherent impression, which creates more links among behaviors. This more elaborated processing enhances recall. However, being in an actual interaction with a target can be distracting, and can use up cognitive capacity for encoding the information. Therefore, recall for an actual interaction may be decreased.

In summary, goals that lead people to process information more thoroughly tend to produce better memory. This work is sometimes explained by depth of processing. However, critics of the depth-of-processing explanation contend that tasks do not inherently require different depths of processing. People can make impressions, yet still process on a shallow level, and people can memorize, yet process deeply. Depth of processing, then, may not be the only factor influencing recall.

ACCURACY AND EFFICIENCY
IN MEMORY
In memory, accuracy refers to whether or not information is remembered correctly. Efficiency refers to how quickly and easily information can be remembered. Often efficiency can inhibit accuracy, so people trade off accuracy for efficiency in memory, depending on their purpose.

Accuracy in memory has a limited meaning because there are no clear criteria for judging accuracy in person perception. Accuracy is especially hard to judge in multifaceted, real-world stimuli, as opposed to simplified stimuli used in laboratory research. In addition, people's previously held beliefs and cognitive structures cause them to bias information about targets at encoding. Thus, inaccurate memories may actually reflect biased encoding.

Efficiency in memory might be defined by three criteria. First, efficiency can include how easy memories are to access, how long they take to retrieve. In general, the faster people attempt to remember information, the less accurate they are. As a second criterion, efficiency could refer to the amount of wasted effort, measured as the ratio of inaccurate to accurate memory. In a recognition task, this ratio compares hits (correct "yes" answers) to false alarms (incorrect "yes" answers). A third efficiency criterion is how focused the search is. If related items are clustered together, and in a way that is relevant to the task, the memory search will be more efficient. This criterion relates efficiency to the specific task; different organizations in memory will be efficient for different tasks.

*See also*: AUTOMATICITY; EMPATHY; EYE-WITNESS TESTIMONY; SCHEMAS; SOCIAL COGNITION.

SUSAN T. FISKE
BETH A. MORLING

BIBLIOGRAPHY

Anderson, J. R. (1990). *Cognitive psychology and its implications* (3rd ed.). New York: W. H. Freeman.

Fiske, S. T., & Taylor, S. E. (1991). *Social cognition* (2nd ed., Chapter 8). New York: Wiley.

Hastie, R. (1988). A computer simulation model of person memory. *Journal of Experimental Social Psychology, 24*, 423–47.

—— & Park, B. (1986). The relationship between memory and judgment depends on whether the judgment task is memory-based or on-line. *Psychological Review, 93*, 258–68.

Kihlstrom, J. F., Cantor, N., Albright, J. S., Chew, B. R., Klein, S. B., & Neidenthal, P. M. (1988). Information processing and the study of the self. In L. Berkowitz (Ed.), *Advances in experimental social psychology* (Vol. 21, pp. 145–80). New York: Academic Press.

Norman, D. A. (1976). *Memory and attention: An introduction to human information processing*. New York: Wiley.

Srull, T. K., & Wyer, R. S., Jr. (1989). Person memory and judgment. *Psychological Review, 96*, 58–83.

Stangor, C., & McMillan, D. (1992). Memory for expectancy-congruent and expectancy-incongruent information: A review of the social and social developmental literatures. *Psychological Bulletin, 1*, 42–61.

**mental control** The motivated attempt to influence one's own psychological contents and processes, particularly through the activation and deactivation of attentional mechanisms according to priorities reflected in conscious thoughts (Wegner & Pennebaker, 1993). From the desire to suppress thoughts of a traumatic event to the concern with improving one's mood on a dreary afternoon, the motivations behind mental control are various and numerous. However, the objectives of such efforts are generally framed in terms of keeping something in mind or keeping something out of mind – concentration and suppression.

Recent studies of mental control have focused on the suppression of unwanted thoughts. Wegner, Schneider, Carter, and White (1987), for example, asked subjects to think aloud for five minutes as the subjects tried not to think of a white bear. Although most subjects tried to distract themselves with other thoughts, this was generally unsuccessful. They mentioned or signaled the occurrence of the unwanted thought more than once per minute. Subsequent research using techniques less intrusive than the requirement to report the thought has yielded similar conclusions (Wegner, 1992). When people are asked to suppress an emotional thought, for example, their psychophysiological responses show levels of agitation identical to those of people who are explicitly asked to concentrate on the emotional thought. Measures of cognitive accessibility such as word associations under time pressure also indicate that during suppression the unwanted thought is very easily brought to mind.

It appears that during the attempt to suppress a thought, the person consciously and effortfully seeks out potential distracters – but at the same time remains watchful at some level for the return of the unwanted thought (Wegner, 1992). These two tendencies can be portrayed as cognitive search processes – a controlled search for distracters, and an automatic search for the target. The controlled search for distracters is what most people consciously report as they attempt suppression, whereas the automatic search for the target is not consciously experienced. The automatic target search is initiated with the intention to suppress, however, because it sensitizes the person to the recurrence of the unwanted thought and so prompts renewed vigilance in the attempt to search for distracters. The automatic target search ironically increases the likelihood that the thought will be accessed. When the controlled search process is taxed (e.g., by fatigue or cognitive load), the automatic process becomes more dominant, such that the individual becomes uniquely sensitive to the very thought that is unwanted.

In addition to exploring the incidence of to-be-suppressed thoughts during distraction attempts, research has examined the incidence of such thoughts *following* distraction attempts, with subjects being told *to* think of white bears for a time immediately after a suppression period. During this opportunity for expression of the thought, subjects showed more thoughts of white bears than control subjects instructed to think of white bears with no preceding suppression period. This "rebound effect" appears to indicate an increase in preoccupation with thoughts previously suppressed. Research attempting to explain this effect has focused on the possibility that during suppression, associative links are formed between the unwanted thought and the various distracters that are enlisted in the attempt to avoid it, and that subsequently these distracters serve as reminders to increase the likelihood that the thought will return.

Unfortunately, then, due to the potentially ironic effect of the automatic process, and due to the inevitable attachment of distracter thoughts to unwanted thoughts, suppression, as a mental control strategy, may be more of a problem than a solution. When people opt to suppress thoughts as a way of avoiding unwanted emotions or as a way of inhibiting unwanted social behaviors, they may unwittingly fuel the very problems they are hoping to undermine. This approach suggests, for example, that individuals suffering from depression may actually be inviting the problem through their attempts to avoid unhappy thoughts and emotions. Similarly, people hoping to escape worries or fears may develop unique sensitivities to them, even to the point of preoccupation, obsession, or phobia, by virtue of their attempts to attain mental control.

Related research has moved beyond the basic cognitive processes of suppression to examine how and with what effect people may control their beliefs and emotions. In the case of belief, Gilbert (1991) has postulated that comprehension of a proposition entails simultaneous acceptance of that proposition. In order not to believe a proposition, then, either the individual must not comprehend it, or the individual must "unbelieve" the proposition; this unbelieving is not a passive process but requires active mental control – "cognitive work," in Gilbert's terms – to deny or falsify the proposition. Attitudes and beliefs, in this light, are often determined by the factors that impinge on the individual's inclination to invest work in disbelief.

Mental control also has important emotional and health implications. Pennebaker (1990) has conducted research indicating that chronic suppression of painful or traumatic experiences yields a range of negative psychological and physical consequences. He has found that the disclosure of emotional experiences reduces rumination about those experiences and enhances a number of indicators of physical health. In addition, recent research on the mental control of emotion indicates that attempting to suppress thoughts of a lost love inhibits one's ability to get past the heartache and move on with one's life; contrary to intuition, the best way to cope with a failed relationship may be to wallow in memory and misery.

*See also*: AUTOMATICITY; MINDFULNESS/MINDLESSNESS; STRESS AND COPING.

BIBLIOGRAPHY

Gilbert, D. T. (1991). How mental systems believe. *American Psychologist*, 46, 107–19.

Pennebaker, J. W. (1990). *Opening up: The healing power of confiding in others*. New York: Morrow.

Wegner, D. M. (1992). You can't always think what you want: Problems in the suppression of unwanted thoughts. In M. Zanna (Ed.), *Advances in experimental social psychology* (Vol. 25, pp. 193–225). San Diego, CA: Academic Press.

—— & Pennebaker, J. W. (Eds.) (1993). *Handbook of mental control*. Englewood Cliffs, NJ: Prentice Hall.

—— Schneider, D. J., Carter, S., & White, T. (1987). Paradoxical effects of thought suppression. *Journal of Personality and Social Psychology*, 53, 5–13.

CHRISTOPHER E. HOUSTON<br>DANIEL M. WEGNER

**mere exposure effect** Psychologists have long observed that repeated, unreinforced exposure to a stimulus results in increased liking for that stimulus. Zajonc (1968) termed this phenomenon the "mere exposure effect," and since the publication of Zajonc's seminal monograph there have been more than 200 published experiments examining parameters and properties of the mere exposure effect. The basic design of most exposure effect experiments is straightforward: Subjects are exposed to varying numbers of exposures of neutral stimuli (e.g., line drawings, nonsense words, musical selections), after which some dependent measure of *affect* regarding each merely exposed stimulus is collected. Both laboratory and field studies of the mere exposure effect typically utilize within-subjects designs, with each subject providing *affect* ratings of a number of stimuli that differ in amount of previous exposure or familiarity.

Detailed reviews of the literature on mere exposure effects are provided by Bornstein (1989) and Harrison (1977). The general pattern of results that has been obtained in this area during the past two decades may be summarized as follows.

MERE EXPOSURE EFFECTS ARE OBTAINED WITH A WIDE RANGE OF STIMULI AND OUTCOME MEASURES

An impressive variety of stimuli have been employed in mere exposure experiments, including nonsense words, meaningful words, idiographs, photographs, abstract drawings, paintings, common objects, actual people, auditory stimuli, olfactory stimuli, and gustatory stimuli. In general, these different types of stimuli produce comparable mere exposure effects, although it appears that abstract paintings and drawings produce somewhat weaker exposure effects than do other types of stimuli (*see* Bornstein, 1989). Similarly, a variety of *affect* measures have been used in mere exposure effect studies, including Likert-type ratings, forced-choice preference judgments, and behavioral measures. Research conducted to date indicates that these different outcome measures produce comparable exposure effects.

BOREDOM IS A LIMITING CONDITION ON THE MERE EXPOSURE EFFECT

Several sets of findings support this contention. For example, heterogeneous (i.e., random) stimulus presentations produce stronger mere exposure effects than do homogeneous (i.e., massed) stimulus presentations. In addition, brief exposure durations typically result in a stronger mere exposure effect than do longer exposure durations. Along slightly different lines, complex, interesting stimuli produce significantly stronger mere exposure effects than do simple, relatively uninteresting stimuli. Finally, when a large number of stimulus exposures are used researchers typically find a downturn in the exposure – *affect* curve at high exposure frequencies. A detailed discussion of boredom as a limiting condition on the mere exposure effect is provided by Harrison (1977).

A PERIOD OF DELAY BETWEEN STIMULUS EXPOSURES AND RATINGS RESULTS IN A STRONGER MERE EXPOSURE EFFECT

In general, those studies that introduce a period of delay between stimulus exposures and ratings produce stronger exposure effects than do studies wherein liking ratings are collected immediately following stimulus exposures (*see* Harrison, 1977). It is not clear how great a period of delay between stimulus exposures and ratings may be introduced while still retaining a robust mere exposure effect, since most mere exposure experiments utilize delays of less than thirty minutes. However, some recent investigations have found that the exposure effect can last up to one week following stimulus exposures (Bornstein, 1992).

## CHILDREN DO NOT PRODUCE TYPICAL MERE EXPOSURE EFFECTS

Bornstein's (1989) meta-analysis of research on the exposure effect revealed that although adults almost invariably show increases in liking toward a merely exposed stimulus with increasing exposure frequency, this effect is not obtained with children under age 12. It is not clear why typical mere exposure effects are not obtained with child subjects, but recent theoretical models of the exposure effect suggest that children may not show robust mere exposure effects because they become bored more easily than do adults following repeated, unreinforced stimulus exposures. When complex, interesting stimuli are used, children produce exposure effects comparable to those produced by adults.

## SUBLIMINAL STIMULI PRODUCE SIGNIFICANTLY STRONGER MERE EXPOSURE EFFECTS THAN DO STIMULI THAT ARE CLEARLY RECOGNIZED

This is one of the more striking (and counterintuitive) findings that has been obtained in this research domain. However, it appears to be a robust result: To date at least 14 separate experiments have obtained strong mere exposure effects for briefly presented stimuli that cannot be recalled, recognized or discriminated from other briefly presented stimuli at better-than-chance levels (*see* Bornstein, 1992 for a review and discussion of these experiments). The finding that subliminal stimuli produce particularly strong mere exposure effects has renewed researchers' interest in this phenomenon. Moreover, these findings have stimulated a great deal of interest in revising and updating extant theoretical models of the exposure effect.

Recent research on the exposure effect has focused on examining the affective and cognitive processes that underly this phenomenon. Although some researchers (e.g., Zajonc, 1980) have argued that exposure effects represent a "pure" affective response to a stimulus that occurs with little or no intervening cognitive activity, other researchers (e.g., Bornstein, 1992) have taken the opposite position, contending that considerable cognitive activity is involved in the production of mere exposure effects. Elucidating the ways in which affective and cognitive processes interact to produce mere exposure effects will likely be one of the most important challenges facing researchers who study this topic during the coming years.

*See also*: AFFECT.

BIBLIOGRAPHY

Bornstein, R. F. (1989). Exposure and affect: Overview and meta-analysis of research, 1968–87. *Psychological Bulletin, 106*, 265–89.

Bornstein, R. F. (1992). Subliminal mere exposure effects. In R. F. Bornstein & T. S. Pittman (Eds.), *Perception without awareness: Cognitive, clinical and social perspectives* (pp. 191–210). New York: Guilford Press.

Harrison, A. A. (1977). Mere exposure. In L. Berkowitz (Ed.), *Advances in experimental social psychology* (Vol. 10, pp. 39–83). New York: Academic Press.

Zajonc, R. B. (1968). Attitudinal effects of mere exposure. *Journal of Personality and Social Psychology Monograph, 9* (2, Pt. 2), 1–27.

—— (1980). Feeling and thinking: Preferences need no inferences. *American Psychologist, 35*, 151–75.

ROBERT F. BORNSTEIN

**meta-analysis** The statistical integration of the results of independent studies in a specific area of research. In a sense, meta-analysis involves methods of statistical analysis where the units of analysis are the results of independent studies rather than the responses of individual subjects.

Like traditional narrative reviews of research, meta-analysis is based upon the assumption that the summary and integration of the results of previous studies can further our understanding of a phenomenon beyond the level of understanding achieved by any single study. However, meta-analysis differs from traditional narrative review in terms of its concern with precision. The specific strategies and techniques for taking the statistical results of independent studies, converting these results to common metrics, and then integrating these statistical results are designed to be rigorously precise.

In addition, meta-analysis aspires to be more objective than traditional narrative review. The rules and standards for including studies in the review process, abstracting results from them, and weighing them in the final integration are never made explicit in the traditional narrative review, whereas these rules and standards must be made explicit in any meta-analytic review.

Finally, meta-analyses are characterized by a higher degree of replicability than traditional narrative reviews. Unlike the divergence of opinion that characterizes some narrative reviews of the same research literature, the conclusions derived from a meta-analytic review of a given research domain are the same conclusions which anyone would have arrived at if they had included the same studies and followed the same rules for integrating study outcomes.

Procedures for combining and comparing the results of independent studies have been around for quite some time (e.g., Fisher, 1932). However, it was not until Glass's labeling of this perspective as "meta-analysis" that this approach received the currency that it enjoys today. As Glass (1977, p. 352) noted. "The accumulated findings of hundreds of studies should be regarded as complex data points, no more comprehensible without statistical analysis than hundreds of data points in a single study."

Procedurally, there are several distinct steps in the development of an informative meta-analytic integration. First, the hypothesis test to be examined must be carefully and precisely defined. The specific operationalizations of the independent variable and the dependent variable must be clearly articulated.

Several distinct strategies can be followed in an effort to locate and retrieve the relevant studies. Meta-analysts regularly use the reference sections of studies which have already been retrieved to locate earlier studies, as well as indexing sources to locate subsequent studies which have cited earlier studies. Abstracting services like *Psychological Abstracts* allow the user to locate studies associated with keywords. In the "invisible college" approach, the meta-analyst asks researchers most active in a research domain about new, unpublished studies which might be "in the works."

Once the relevant studies have been retrieved, the appropriate tests of the well-defined hypothesis must be derived from each study. Sometimes this is perfectly straightforward. However, very often a more specific or more precise test than those reported in the published article may be needed. For example, sometimes researchers will identify the difference between two means as being simply "significantly different," without reporting a statistical test of the difference. Similarly, researchers will sometimes report an imprecise $F$-test based on more than 1 degree of freedom in the numerator, which actually tests the diffuse hypothesis of whether there are any differences of any kind among three or more conditions. In these instances of improperly reported hypothesis tests, the precise test of the well-defined hypothesis must be reconstructed from reported means and standard deviations, from reported means and $MS_{error}$s, and/or from related-but-different $F$-tests.

Of course, one study may report a $t$-test, a second study may report a chi-square, a third study may report a correlation coefficient, and so on. Because these different statistics are on different metrics, they must be transduced to more standard, common metrics. The two common metrics for statistical results are significance levels ($Z$ and one-tailed $p$) and effect size ($Z_{Fisher}$, $r$, $r^2$, and $d$).

Once placed on these common metrics, the results of separate hypothesis tests can be combined, compared, and examined for the fit of predictive models. Meta-analytic combinations of significance levels and effect sizes give us a gauge of the overall combined probability and strength of the effects. These combination statistics reveal something about the central tendency in the research domain. Meta-analytic diffuse comparisons give us a gauge of the overall heterogeneity of effects. These diffuse comparison statistics reveal something about the variability in the research domain. Meta-analytic focused comparisons give us a gauge of the extent to which the effects increase or decrease as a function of some theoretically relevant or practically important moderators. These focused comparison statistics reveal something about prediction of variability in the research domain.

For example, Mullen, Brown, and Smith (1992) have reported a meta-analysis of the research literature examining the ingroup bias effect. Ingroup bias refers to the tendency to evaluate the ingroup more positively than the outgroup. This meta-analysis (integrating the results of 137 separate hypothesis tests, and representing the behavior of 5,476 subjects) revealed that the ingroup bias effect was highly significant, $Z = 56.281$, $p < 0.00000001$ and of moderate magnitude, mean $Z_{Fisher} = 0.361$, mean $r = 0.346$, mean $r^2 = 0.120$. There was a significant amount of heterogeneity in these effects, $\chi^2_{(136)} = 915.226$, $p < 0.00000001$, indicating that these ingroup bias effects were quite variable. And, these ingroup bias effects were stronger when the ingroup and outgroup were real groups (mean $r = 0.395$) than when they were artificial groups created in the lab (mean $r = 0.264$), $Z = 2.171$, $p = 0.0150$.
*See also*: INGROUP BIAS.

BIBLIOGRAPHY
Fisher, R. A. (1932). *Statistical methods for research workers*, London: Oliver & Boyd.
Glass, G. (1977). Integrating findings: The meta-analysis of research. *Review of Research in Education*, 5, 351–79.
Mullen, B., Brown, R., & Smith, C. (1992). Ingroup bias as a function of salience, relevance, and status: An integration. *European Journal of Social Psychology*, 22, 103–22.

CRAIG JOHNSON
BRIAN MULLEN

**methodology** This term refers to the methods and procedures used in social psychology to gather and interpret empirical data in order to construct and evaluate theoretical hypotheses concerning social behavior. Ultimately, the methodology of social psychology is in service of the theoretical goals of the discipline. Methods of data colletion, analysis, and interpretation are useful to the extent that they help social psychologists construct theories of social behavior that have the ability to explain and predict such behavior.

The quality of any set of empirical data in constructing and evaluating social psychological theories is a function of the validity of both the data themselves and the research design used to collect those data. Three types of research validity have been defined. Data and research designs that maximize these three types of validity are data that are most useful in theory construction and evaluation.

RESEARCH VALIDITIES
*Construct validity* concerns the extent to which the measured variables accurately capture the constructs or phenomena of theoretical interest. Clearly, if the variables measured in some piece of research do not represent the constructs discussed by a theory or hypothesis, then the resulting data are not useful in evaluating that hypothesis. Procedures to maximize construct validity, i.e., to measure successfully the theoretical phenomena of interest, are a part of social psychological methodology (Cronbach & Meehl, 1955).

*Internal validity* concerns the extent to which the research permits causal inferences about the effects of one variable upon another. Most social psychological hypotheses concern the ways in which social behaviors and judgments are influenced by the social forces that act upon an individual. Thus, the issue of establishing CAUSALITY is central to methodology in social psychology. In general, the internal validity of research is determined by the type of research design employed.

*External validity* concerns the extent to which one can generalize from a particular set of data or piece of research to the intended populations and settings of interest. Social psychologists wish to construct theories with known, and hopefully broad, limits of generalizability. Research that permits conclusions about generalizability has high external validity. In general, wise sampling procedures and appropriate use of STATISTICS contribute to external validity.

## MEASUREMENT

Data in social psychology are most typically gathered from individual subjects or research participants who fill out questionnaires, respond to various tasks and social situations, or provide verbal interviews and protocols. Most usually, these participants are aware that they are providing data for purposes of research since they are explicitly asked to fill out a questionnaire or complete an interview. In addition, OBSERVATIONAL METHODS are used in social psychology. In such cases, data are gathered in such a way that those providing them may not be aware of doing so. Such collection procedures avoid the threat of presentational biases, i.e., subjects providing responses that they believe are normatively appropriate.

Regardless of whether data are collected via questionnaires, interviews, or observation, issues of measurement adequacy (or construct validity) are inevitable. In fact, most criticisms of individual social psychological studies concern the extent to which the researchers really measured what they believed they measured.

The goal of measuring a variable is to locate subjects along a continuum so that subjects who are closer to one another on that continuum (i.e., have similar scores on the variable) share some attribute or are similar to each other on the construct that is being measured. Inevitably, however, variables measure more than a single construct. They also measure things that the researcher would rather not measure, i.e., things that are irrele-

vant to the construct of research interest. To illustrate, consider scores on a final exam in some subject. Such scores are certainly likely to measure, to some extent, the construct of theoretical interest, i.e., how much learning took place concerning the course's subject-matter. But they probably also measure other things as well, such as the student's general level of motivation and attention the day the test was given. Finally, they also probably reflect some error, error in grading, or errors in communication by the student (e.g., circling the wrong multiple choice answer accidentally).

Any variable thus captures much more than the construct of interest. It captures in addition constructs of disinterest (things the researcher would like to avoid measuring), and random errors of measurement. The convergent validity of a variable concerns the extent to which it captures the construct of interest. The discriminant validity of a variable concerns the extent to which it avoids measuring constructs of disinterest. And the reliability of a variable concerns the extent to which it does not contain random error. A variable's construct validity is made up of all three components. Thus, a well-measured variable is one that has high convergent validity, high discriminant validity, and high reliability.

Since a reliable variable is one that contains little random error, scores on that variable ought to be reproducible if the variable is measured again. Errors of measurement, if they are truly random, ought to affect individual scores on the variable in a random manner and, hence, they should not be reproducible. Accordingly, to assess the reliability of a variable, one wishes to measure that same variable more than once and then see whether the orderings of individuals on the variable are the same in both cases. Standard procedures for doing this include test–retest measures of reliability, split-half measures of reliability, and other ways of assessing the consistency of scores across multiple forms of measurement of the same variable.

To assess the convergent validity of a variable, we want to measure other variables that also capture the construct of interest but that are as dissimilar in all other ways as possible. If two variables give the same ordering of individual scores when the only thing they are thought to have in common is the construct of interest, then both can be judged to have relatively high convergent validity.

Finally, to assess the discriminant validity of a variable against some particular construct of disinterest, one needs to measure a second variable that is thought to capture that construct of disinterest. If one can then show that different orderings of individual subjects occur on the two variables, then discriminant validity is demonstrated.

A matrix of correlations between multiple measures of two or more constructs, each measured in different ways, is frequently recommended to simultaneously establish convergent and discriminant validity. Such a matrix is known as a multitrait–multimethod matrix (Campbell & Fiske, 1959).

## RESEARCH DESIGN

As stated earlier, most social psychological hypotheses concern the causal effect of one construct upon another. Thus, for instance, social psychologists hypothesize that attitude similarity affects interpersonal attraction or that intergroup competition leads to outgroup derogation. In order to collect data that permit one to evaluate such hypotheses, variables that represent both the causal construct and the affected construct must be measured. The former is known as the independent variable and the latter as the dependent variable. To illustrate, to collect data relevant to the first of the above two hypotheses, one would need to measure both attitude similarity and interpersonal attraction. The measure of similarity is the independent variable; the measure of attraction, the dependent one.

Internal validity is maximized when a randomized experimental design is employed. This means that claims of causality, concerning the impact of the independent variable on the dependent one, can only be made in the context of EXPERIMENTATION. A randomized experimental design is one in which subjects are randomly assigned to levels of the independent variable. Thus, the independent variable cannot be simply a measured characteristic of subjects. Rather, the experimenter must manipulate it and actively assign subjects to its different levels. And the rule that the experimenter uses to accomplish this assignment must be a random one. This means that every subject has the same chance as every other subject of being assigned to each level of the independent variable. Assuming that subjects who differ on the independent variable are subsequently found to differ on the dependent one, one is in a position to make assertions about the causal impact of the independent variable on the dependent one. Since subjects have been randomly assigned to levels of the independent variable, on average subjects having different scores on that variable do not differ in any other way. Hence differences on the dependent variable are attributable to differences on the independent one (Campbell & Stanley, 1963; Judd & Kenny, 1981).

For both practical and ethical reasons, it is often impossible to conduct randomized experiments. Assume, for instance, that one wanted to examine the effects of living in a racially integrated neighborhood on racial prejudice. It is quite implausible that a researcher would ever be in a position to conduct a randomized experiment in this case. Randomly assigning some individuals to live in an integrated neighborhood and others to live in a segregated one is neither feasible nor desirable. In such cases, where random assignment is not possible, it is sometimes practical to employ what are called QUASI-EXPERIMENTAL DESIGNS. A quasi-experimental research design is one in which subjects are repeatedly measured on the dependent variable, both before and after they have been exposed to the independent variable, but subjects are not randomly assigned to the levels of the independent variable. Thus, in the neighborhood example, one would want to follow subjects over some long time period, measuring their levels of prejudice, and seeing what happened to those levels as they moved into or out of segregated and integrated neighborhoods. The two requirements for a quasi-experimental design are thus that subjects are measured repeatedly on the dependent variable at different points in time and that they change status or levels on the independent variable at some of those time points. The researcher then assesses the extent to which changes on the dependent variable over time are found to coincide with changes in status on the independent variable. Although quasi-experimental designs are clearly preferable, from the point of view of internal validity, to correlational or cross-sectional designs (discussed next) when experimental control is not feasible, threats to internal validity always persist with such designs. Regardless of the sophistication of the analysis of the resulting data, clear causal inference remains very difficult (Cook & Campbell, 1979; Judd & Kenny, 1981).

In many cases, data can only be collected cross-sectionally, measuring both the independent variable (rather than manipulating it) and the dependent variable at the same point in time. Data gathered in such a manner come from what is called a correlational research design. Although data from such a design can be examined to determine whether differences on the independent variable are predictive of differences on the dependent one, no claims about causality can be made. Consider, as an example, a researcher who is interested in whether more religious individuals show more or less racial prejudice than less religious individuals. Assuming this researcher measures both how religious and how prejudiced his subjects are at one point in time, he has used a correlational research design. Suppose further that he finds that subjects who profess to being more religious manifest more prejudice than subjects who profess to being less religious. There are three competing causal explanations for this observed relationship. One is that religiousness affects prejudice. A second is that prejudice affects religiousness. And a third, perhaps the most likely in this case, is that the two variables are related because they both derive from or are caused by some other common variable. If this is the case (perhaps the two variables are related because a certain personality style leads some individuals to be both highly religious and somewhat prejudiced), then the relationship between the two variables is said to be a spurious one.

The above classification of research designs into three types, randomized experiments, quasi-experiments, and correlational designs represents a continuum in terms of internal validity. At one extreme, randomized experiments are most useful in terms of making causal claims about the effect of the independent variable on the dependent one. At the other extreme, causal claims based solely on correlational data are virtually impossible. This is not to suggest, however, that correlational data are of no use. In many situations, one must be content with purely cross-sectional correlational data because it is simply not feasible to use any other design. In addition, the finding of a relationship between the independent and dependent variables is certainly consistent with a claim of causality. The research certainly could have found no relationship and such a result would have been inconsistent with causal claims. Thus, the demonstration that one variable is predictive of another is a necessary but far from sufficient condition for conclusions about the causal impact of the first on the second. Finally, it is important to realize that internal validity is not the only quality of useful research. There are many times when claims about causality are relatively unimportant. In such cases, correlational designs are likely to be entirely adequate.

## GENERALIZATION

We would like to have confidence that the results of any particular piece of research are reproducible or obtainable again if one were to collect similar data from similar subjects in similar circumstances. Such confidence comes only if one can specify the limits of generalization of the research and if one is able to rule out the conclusion that the obtained results are simply due to chance variations in the data. Establishing the limits of generalizability comes through the use of sampling procedures. Confidence that the results are not due to chance and that they would be obtained again comes from statistical inference.

Issues of generalization need to be considered prior to the collection of data. If generalization to some known population is of interest, say, all voting age citizens of a given country, then that population needs to be identified prior to the conduct of the research and the sample of subjects from whom data are actually collected needs to be representative of the population.

Representativeness of a sample is accomplished by randomly sampling from that population. Various random sampling schemes can be used (e.g., simple random sampling, stratified random sampling), and the efficiency of each for generalization can be calculated (Cochran, 1963).

The importance of engaging in random sampling and establishing the known limits of generalization to the population of interest depends on the sort of research question that is being asked. Thus, just as internal validity (i.e., establishing causality) may be more important in some cases than others, so too the importance of external validity to the research enterprise may also vary. In general, the claims of external validity tend to be more important in research where the goal is to describe a phenomenon or characterize some behavior than in research where the goal is to develop theoretical explanations for the phenomenon or behavior. In the former case, for instance when one wishes to characterize the sentiments of the voting age citizens of a country, sampling issues are of paramount importance. On the other hand, if the goal is to develop a potential explanation for a given observed behavior, greater emphasis is likely to be placed on the internal validity of the demonstration than on establishing the known limits of generalizability. Given the complexity of the research enterprise and the multiple claims of the research validities, trade-offs between these claims are unavoidable.

Statistical inference in research is used to estimate the probability that an observed result was not simply produced by chance variation in the data and would not be observed again if similar data were again collected. As such, statistical inference permits the researcher to calibrate the confidence in the obtained results and is a primary mechanism of generalization. Assuming that one has in fact engaged in random sampling, statistical inference yields confidence estimates of replicating an effect in repeated samples from the population (see STATISTICS for further information).

CONCLUSION

It is important to realize that there are diverse methods and procedures in behavioral and psychological research and that there is no single "correct" way of conducting research. The goal of all research is to help us critically evaluate theories and hypotheses concerning human behavior. A diverse set of tools are useful in accomplishing this goal, with different tools appropriate for different parts or subtasks of the theory construction process.

*See also*: CONTENT ANALYSIS; EXPERIMENTATION; OBSERVATIONAL METHODS; STATISTICS; STRUCTURAL EQUATION MODELING; SURVEY METHODS.

BIBLIOGRAPHY

Campbell, D. T., & Fiske, D. W. (1959). Convergent and discriminant validity by the multitrait–multimethod matrix. *Psychological Bulletin*, 56, 81–105.

—— & Stanley, J.C. (1963). *Experimental and quasi-experimental designs for research*. Chicago, IL: Rand McNally.

Cochran, W. G. (1963). *Sampling techniques* (2nd ed.). New York: Wiley.

Cook, T. D., & Campbell, D. T. (1979). *Quasi-experimentation: Design and analysis issues for field settings*. Chicago, IL: Rand McNally.

Cronbach, L. J., & Meehl, P. E. (1955). Construct validity in psychological tests *Psychological Bulletin*, 52, 281–302.

Judd, C. M., & Kenny, D. A. (1981). *Estimating the effects of social interventions*. Cambridge: Cambridge University Press.

CHARLES M. JUDD

**mindfulness/mindlessness**  Often people are not engaged in any kind of active thinking. This question of when people are or are not cognitively engaged is important in understanding human behavior and is the essence of the study of mindfulness/mindlessness.

Mindfulness may be characterized as a state of mind in which the individual is actively drawing distinctions and creating categories. As such the individual is open to novelty, aware of multiple perspectives, and sensitive to context. This context sensitivity keeps the individual situated in the present. Mindlessness, in contrast, is a state of mind overdetermined by the past, where the individual relies on distinctions and categories created in the past and is oblivious to novel (or simply other) aspects of the target information. Behavior, when mindless, is unmodulated by context, encouraging the person unwittingly to act like an automaton. When mindless there is no uncertainty and hence there are no choices to be made. This single-mindedness occurs and is maintained by default and not by design.

The central element of mindfulness is novelty. Noticing or creating distinctions implicitly makes one aware of novelty, perspective and context and vice versa. Each of these leads to the others. When one is trapped in a single perspective, on the other hand, one is insensitive to how things look different depending on context or perspective and as such one is unaware of new or different views or uses to which the information could be put. Instead, information is understood and used rigidly.

Mindlessness is similar to concepts like habit, inattention, and automatic processing but also quite distinct from them. While habits are built up over time and are typically enacted mindlessly, mindlessness also may come about on a single exposure to information. When one accepts information uncritically even on a single exposure to it, one unwittingly makes a cognitive commitment to that information and mindlessness ensues. Even if it becomes to the individual's advantage to reconsider the information, such reconsideration will not occur. Essentially the person becomes trapped by the premature commitment to a particular way of viewing the information.

Attention is necessary but not sufficient for mindfulness. When mindful, one actively draws distinctions. When mindless, one may be attentive to a stimulus, but the stimulus is understood in a single-minded way so that new things about it will go unnoticed.

Automatic and controlled processing (Schneider & Shiffrin, 1977) are also concepts similar to mindlessness and mindfulness but still differ from them. For example, memorizing a list would be an example of mindless but controlled processing. An awareness that "l" is both a number and a letter, depending on context, would be an instance of mindful but automatic processing.

Over the past twenty years a good deal of research has been conducted that reveals the benefits of mindfulness (*see* Langer, 1989 for a review of this work). These findings include an increase in competence, CREATIVITY, memory, perceived CONTROL, and health.

Consider Chanowitz and Langer (1981) as an example of this research. Subjects were exposed to information about a perceptual disorder in a manner that either encouraged them to think mindfully about the information or not. With no reason to examine the information to see how its truth might depend on circumstances, it was hypothesized and found that subjects would process the information uncritically and freeze its meaning. Later when that information became relevant, it did not occur to these subjects to reconsider it even though to do so would have resulted in better performance. When we make a cognitive commitment to one meaning of information it becomes frozen in that single way, and it is only available in that way in the future.

In another study, Langer and Piper (1987) introduced subjects to objects in an absolute way (e.g., "This is a dog's chew toy") or in a conditional way (e.g., "This could be a dog's chew toy"). When a need arose for an eraser, only those subjects introduced to the dog's toy in a conditional way thought to use it in this novel manner; for the others it "was" a dog's toy.

When information is given by an authority, initially appears irrelevant, or is given in absolute language, there is little apparent reason to consider it mindfully. Instead, we often freeze the meaning of the information and remain unaware that it could be used in novel ways. We do this even when such mindlessness may be costly because it simply doesn't occur to us that it could be otherwise. When we think about how much in our past we seemingly had no reason to question, we can get a glimpse of how pervasive mindlessness may be.

One may be mindless of some information while mindfully considering other information. One also, however, may not be mindfully considering very much of anything. In several nursing home studies, we intervened and provided an opportunity for subjects to consider novel information mindfully (*see* Rodin & Langer, 1977). Results of these studies and several others were dramatic. They revealed that an increase in mindfulness resulted in an increase in longevity, an increase in Immunoglobulin A (important to immunocompetence) and a decrease in Immunoglobulin E (important in combating allergies). A mindfulness intervention also resulted in improved functioning for those suffering from arthritis (*see* Langer, 1989).

Over fifty studies have been conducted that look at the negative effects of mindlessness and the positive effects of mindfulness. The results of this work suggest that mindfulness may indeed be important for effective human functioning.

*See also*: CONTROL; CREATIVITY.

BIBLIOGRAPHY

Chanowitz, B., & Langer, E. (1981). Premature cognitive commitment. *Journal of Personality and Social Psychology*, *41*, 1051–63.

Langer, E. (1989). *Mindfulness*. Reading, MA: Addison-Wesley.

——— & Piper, P. (1987). The prevention of mindlessness. *Journal of Personality and Social Psychology*, *53*, 280–7.

Rodin, J., & Langer, E. (1977). Long-term effects of a control-relevant intervention among the institutionalized aged. *Journal of Personality and Social Psychology*, *35*, 897–902.

Schneider, W., & Shiffrin, R. (1977). Controlled and automatic human information processing: I. Detection, search and attention. *Psychological Review*, *84*, 1–66.

ELLEN J. LANGER

**minimal group paradigm** In the minimal group paradigm, anonymous participants are experimentally classified as members of ad hoc, arbitrary, or minimally meaningful categories (e.g., X *versus* Y, Red *versus* Blue). Participants respond to nonidentifiable members of their own and other categories, often using reward allocation matrices to measure ingroup BIAS.

*See also*: INTERGROUP RELATIONS; SOCIAL CATEGORIZATION; SOCIAL IDENTITY THEORY.

DOMINIC ABRAMS

**minority social influence** This is a form of SOCIAL INFLUENCE in which a deviant subgroup rejects the established norm of the majority of group members and induces the majority to move to the position of the minority, a form by which group NORMS are changed. Moscovici (1976) argues that minorities exert influence by creating conflict and that they are a force for INNOVATION. The main factor in their success is "behavioral style," the "rhetoric" of their behavior, especially consistency. A consistent minority disrupts the existing norm and creates uncertainty in the majority; makes itself the center of attention; demonstrates certainty, confidence, and commitment; shows it has an alternative position from which it will not move; and signals that the majority must move to the minority to restore social stability, agreement, and cognitive coherence. Research (e.g., Mugny, 1982) confirms that a consistent, consensual minority, which is flexible rather than rigid, ingroup rather than outgroup, and in line with the Zeitgeist and the basic VALUES of the majority can influence the majority. The effect of minorities on COMPLIANCE is not large and seems to be less than the effect of majorities, but they may produce more CONVERSION than majorities.

*See also*: NORMS; SOCIAL INFLUENCE; VALUES.

BIBLIOGRAPHY

Moscovici, S. (1976). *Social influence and social change*. London: Academic Press.

Mugny, G. (1982). *The power of minorities*. London: Academic Press.

JOHN C. TURNER

**misattribution of arousal** The incorrect attribution of AROUSAL to a cause other than the actual one. Arousal that is thus misattributed may cause the experience of emotion that is relevant to the (falsely) attributed cause rather than to the appropriate cause.
*See also*: AROUSAL; EMOTIONAL EXPERIENCE.

RUSSELL G. GEEN

**modeling** A process in which human thought, affect, and action are altered by observing the behavior of others and the outcomes they experience. Modeling operates as a major mechanism of SOCIAL LEARNING (*see* Bandura, 1986). In learning from example, individuals extract the rules and standards embodied in the actions of others and then use this information to generate courses of action to suit particular purposes. With the enormous advances in the technology of COMMUNICATION, observational learning from the symbolic environment is playing an increasingly influential role in shaping thought patterns, attitudes, and styles of behavior.

Modeled influences can also strengthen or weaken restraints over preexisting behavior patterns. The impact of modeling on behavioral restraints depends on observers' judgments of their ability to perform the modeled behavior, their perceptions of the outcomes it produces, and their beliefs that similar rewarding or punishing consequences would result if they, themselves, behaved in similar ways. People develop attitudes, values, and emotional proclivities toward persons, places, or things through observation of modeled emotional experiences. In addition, the portrayal of human relations in the symbolic world shapes viewers' beliefs and conceptions of reality.
*See also*: COMMUNICATION; SOCIAL LEARNING.

BIBLIOGRAPHY
Bandura, A. (1986). *Social foundations of thought and action: A social cognitive theory.* Englewood Cliffs, NJ: Prentice Hall.

ALBERT BANDURA

**mood: its impact on cognition and behavior** Moods may be defined as generalized positive or negative feeling states. They differ from emotions in several ways. Most important, emotions have a specific referent; e.g., we are "happy about" something, "angry about" something, and so on. In contrast, moods lack a specific referent and are of a more diffuse nature. Thus, our anger about something may leave us in a diffuse negative mood once the anger-inducing event is no longer the focus of attention. Moreover, numerous minor events, none of which is sufficient to induce a specific emotion, may elicit diffuse moods. Finally, moods are less intense than emotions and do not usually attract the individual's attention. As an important consequence, mood states may function in the background of other cognitive activities. Their frequency and their undifferentiated and unfocused nature render them influential for a wide range of cognitive processes and overt behaviors (for a more detailed discussion, *see* Morris, 1989). Whereas moods and emotions are often subsumed under the general term "affective states," the differences between them require separate analyses.

That we may think and behave differently when we are in an elated rather than a depressed mood is a familiar experience. Nevertheless, cognitive (social) psychology had largely ignored the impact of moods and emotions until the late 1970s. Since then, this state of affairs has changed dramatically and a large body of experimental research has documented pervasive influences of affective states on cognitive processes. Below, key theoretical approaches and empirical findings are reviewed. Whereas one may differentiate moods along a variety of dimensions (*see* Morris, 1989), most researchers have focused on globally defined elated or depressed moods and the present review reflects this focus.

MOOD AND MEMORY
One of the most prominent assumptions about the interplay of affect and cognition holds that affective states may influence what comes to mind. For example, we are more

likely to recall positive material from memory when we are in an elated rather than a depressed mood. The most influential conceptualization of these influences has been provided by Bower's (1981) associative network model of human MEMORY. According to the model, mood states function as central nodes in an ASSOCIATIVE NETWORK, which are linked to related ideas, events of corresponding valence, autonomic activity, and muscular and expressive patterns. When new material is learned, it is associated with the nodes that are active at the time of learning. Accordingly, material that is learned in a particular affective state is linked to the respective affect node. When an affect node is stimulated, activation spreads along the pathways, increasing the activation of other nodes connected to it. The activation of a node above a certain threshold brings the represented material into consciousness.

Bower's model makes two key predictions: First, memory is enhanced when the affective state at the time of encoding matches the affective state at the time of retrieval (*state-dependent recall*). Thus, we are more likely to recall material that we learned while in a particular mood when we are in the same, rather than a different, mood at the time of recall. Second, information is more likely to be retrieved when the individual's mood at the time of recall matches the affective tone of the to-be-recalled material (*mood congruent recall*). Thus, information of a positive valence is more likely to come to mind when we are in an elated rather than a depressed mood. Note, that the first hypothesis focuses on a match of moods at encoding and retrieval, independent of the valence of the to-be-retrieved material. In contrast, the second hypothesis focuses on a match of mood at retrieval and the affective tone of the information, independent of the mood at the time of encoding.

Whereas experimental as well as clinical research has provided empirical support for both hypotheses, it has also revealed a number of empirical and conceptual complications (for a review, *see* Clore, Schwarz, & Conway, 1994; Morris, 1989). First, the impact of elated and depressed moods on recall is asymmetrical. Relative to neutral moods, happy

moods reliably facilitate the recall of happy memories and inhibit the recall of sad memories. Sad moods, however, rarely facilitate the recall of sad memories, although they inhibit the recall of happy memories. To account for this asymmetry, Isen (e.g., 1987) suggested that individuals in a sad mood may attempt to "repair" their mood by actively avoiding further negative memories. These controlled processes may override the automatic impact of sad moods on the ACCESSIBILITY of mood congruent material (*see* Morris, 1989, for a critical review).

Second, although state-dependency and mood congruency may be distinguished conceptually. they are difficult to separate empirically. In fact, mood effects on recall have been most reliably obtained for autobiographical memories. That is, people are more likely to recall happy events from their life when they are in a happy mood. Note, however, that happy events are not only of a positive valence, but also elicited a happy mood when they occurred. Hence, they satisfy the criteria for state-dependent as well as mood congruent recall, suggesting that mood effects on recall may be most reliable when both processes operate simultaneously.

Third, some of the initial findings have been difficult to replicate, suggesting that mood effects on memory are relatively fragile (*see* Clore et al., 1994). The available findings suggest that mood congruency may be limited to relatively unstructured material and that any structure that may facilitate recall may override the impact of mood states.

Finally, a competing line of research has demonstrated that depressed moods may restrict individuals' attentional resources and may hence interfere with learning and recall (Ellis & Ashbrook, 1988). This presumably reflects the fact that depressed moods bring self-referential thoughts to mind that may interfere with other tasks. At present, it is difficult to reconcile the findings generated by Ellis and Ashbrook's resource allocation model with the research reviewed above, or with the impact of moods on reasoning strategies, an issue that is addressed below (*see* Clore et al., 1994).

## MOOD AND JUDGMENT

Individuals in a positive mood have been found to evaluate a wide variety of targets, ranging from consumer goods to the quality of their life, more favorably than individuals in a negative mood (*see* Forgas, 1992; Morris, 1989; Schwarz & Clore, 1983). Two accounts for this phenomenon have been offered. On the one hand, Bower's (1981) memory model suggests that individuals in a happy mood may selectively recall positive information about the target, resulting in a more positive judgment (*see* Forgas, 1992). On the other hand, Schwarz and Clore (*see* Clore et al., 1994; Schwarz & Clore, 1983) suggested that our feelings may themselves serve as relevant information in making a judgment. Specifically, individuals may simplify complex judgmental tasks by asking themselves, "How-do-I-feel-about-it?", turning to their apparent affective reaction to the target as a basis of judgment. In fact, some evaluative judgments refer, by definition, to one's affective reaction to the stimulus (e.g., judgments of liking) and the current affective state may indeed be elicited by the target. However, due to the unfocused character of mood states, it is often difficult to distinguish between one's affective reaction to the object of judgment and one's preexisting mood state. Accordingly, individuals may misread their preexisting feelings as a reaction to the target, resulting in more favorable evaluations under elated than under depressed moods.

This feelings-as-information hypothesis generates a number of predictions that cannot be derived from the assumption that mood effects on evaluative judgments are mediated by mood congruent recall or encoding. Most importantly, individuals should only use their feelings as a basis of judgment if their informational value has not been called into question. In line with this prediction, the impact of mood on judgment was found to be eliminated if individuals attributed their feelings (either correctly or incorrectly) to a source that rendered them irrelevant to the judgment at hand. For example, subjects reported lower life-satisfaction when they were in a bad mood due to lousy weather; but this effect was eliminated when their attention was drawn to the weather, thus rendering it uninformative with regard to the quality of their life in general (*see* Schwarz & Clore, 1983). Such a DISCOUNTING effect would not be expected if the impact of mood were mediated by mood congruent recall. According to this latter account, subjects in a depressed mood would report lower life-satisfaction because they recall negative information about their life from memory. The implications of this information, however, would not be called into question by drawing their attention to the weather; rather, what is called into question is simply the informational value of one's current feelings themselves.

These and related findings (*see* Schwarz & Clore, 1983) indicate that our feelings may themselves serve as a basis of judgment, according to a "How-do-I-feel-about-it?" HEURISTIC. Accordingly, moods may influence evaluative judgments either *directly*, by serving as a basis of judgment, or *indirectly*, by influencing what comes to mind. Given the robustness of mood effects on evaluative judgments on the one hand, and the fragility of mood congruent recall on the other hand, the former process seems more likely than the latter.

## MOODS AND PROCESSING STRATEGIES

In addition to influencing memory and judgment, our moods may also influence our performance on a wide variety of cognitive tasks (*see* Clore et al., 1994; Forgas, 1992; Isen, 1987; Schwarz, Bless, & Bohner, 1991, for reviews). Whereas early research emphasized the disruptive nature of affective states, the accumulating evidence suggests a considerably more complicated picture. Apparently, feeling good, or feeling bad, may both facilitate and impair cognitive performance, depending on the nature of the task. We first review some of the available findings and subsequently turn to different theoretical accounts.

Being in a positive mood has been found to influence cognitive processes in ways that suggest greater reliance on heuristic strategies and preexisting knowledge structures. For example, when confronted with a persuasive message, individuals in a positive mood are less likely to engage in systematic elaboration of the arguments and more likely to rely on peripheral cues associated with the message. As a result, they are less influenced by strong arguments, and more influenced by weak arguments, than individuals in a neutral or a depressed mood. Similarly, in the person perception domain, positive mood seems to increase reliance on stereotypes at the expense of individuating information. Moreover, individuals in a positive mood store information about other persons in broader categories. Whereas such findings suggest a simplification of thought processes under elated mood, happy moods have also been found to improve performance on creativity tasks that require playful thinking, reflecting a higher degree of processing flexibility.

In contrast, the available evidence suggests that being in a negative mood may result in increased as well as decreased systematic information processing. In general, the processing style under negative mood is characterized by a narrower focus of attention, more attention to detail, and narrower categorization. For example, individuals in a mildly depressed mood pay more attention to the quality of persuasive arguments, rely less on stereotypes, and show fewer halo–effects in social judgments. However, being in a negative mood has also been found to decrease information use in some task domains, such as logical problem solving, relative to neutral mood conditions. Reviewing the available evidence, Clore et al. (1994) concluded that negative moods may increase information use in the domain of social judgment, but may decrease information use for nonsocial tasks, for reasons discussed below.

Different theoretical accounts have been offered for this mixed set of findings, focusing either on the impact of moods on processing capacity or on processing motivation. With regard to processing capacity, it has been suggested that both positive and negative moods may limit attentional resources. Positive moods may do so because positive material is more extensive and interconnected in memory than negative material. As a consequence, positive affect may potentially cue a wide range of thoughts. However, as more,

and more diverse, material is brought to mind, it may limit the resources available for other tasks (see Isen, 1987). Other researchers suggested that negative moods may be more likely to limit attentional resources because they may evoke intrusive thoughts, considerable rumination, and attempts to change one's mood (Ellis & Ashbrook, 1988). Unfortunately, direct evidence bearing on the hypothesized impact of moods on attentional resources is largely missing and the available evidence may also be accounted for by motivational assumptions.

In this regard, several models suggest that individuals in a positive mood may be motivated to maintain their current mood state. Assuming that intense cognitive processing is aversive, individuals in a positive mood may try to avoid it, resulting in a more heuristic processing style. On the other hand, individuals in a negative mood may attempt to distract themselves from negative thoughts by concentrating on the task at hand, thus resulting in more effortful processing (see Isen, 1987; Schaller & Cialdini, 1990).

A more complex perspective is suggested by the assumption that feelings may serve informative functions (Schwarz et al., 1991). We typically feel good in situations that do not threaten our goals, but feel bad in situations that do so. Assuming that the relationship between psychological situations and feelings is bidirectional, our feelings may inform us about the nature of the situation we are in, as has long been implied by the hypothesis that specific emotions, such as fear, serve a signaling function. Accordingly, negative affective states may inform the individual that the current situation is problematic, and is characterized either by a lack of positive outcomes or a threat of negative outcomes. Coping with these situations, however, requires causal analysis and attention to relevant details. It would hence be highly adaptive if negative feelings increased the cognitive accessibility of relevant procedural knowledge. Any increased accessibility of relevant procedural knowledge (e.g., by PRIMING), however, would also increase the likelihood that these procedures are applied to tasks on which the individual works. This would result in increased performance on tasks to which the primed procedures are applicable, but in decreased performance on tasks to which they are not. Hence, learning more about the nature of the procedural knowledge primed by different affective states may allow us to account for the inconsistent findings noted above (*see* Clore et al., 1994). Moreover, individuals may be unlikely to take risks in a situation that is already considered problematic, and may therefore avoid simple heuristics as well as novel solutions, resulting in a detail-oriented, analytic, and conservative processing strategy under negative affect.

In contrast, positive affective states may inform the individual that the world is currently a safe place. Accordingly, individuals in a good mood may see little need to engage in elaborate processing, unless required by other currently active goals, and may hence be more likely to use simple heuristics. Moreover, no specific procedural knowledge may be primed, resulting in equal access to a wider variety of procedures. As a result, one would observe a less systematic but more flexible processing style under elated mood, consistent with the findings reviewed above.

## MOOD AND BEHAVIOR

Investigations of the impact of mood on overt behavior have been largely limited to the domain of HELPING BEHAVIOR. In most studies, being in a positive mood has been found to increase helping, whereas being in a negative mood may increase as well as decrease helping (*see* Schaller & Cialdini, 1990, for a review). This mixed pattern of findings is not surprising if we assume that behavior is guided by cognitive processing. If so, the relationship between mood and behavior will be as complex as the relationship between mood and social cognition, requiring close attention to mediating variables.

For example, research on mood and persuasion suggests that the impact of mood on individuals' willingness to donate money should depend on the quality of the persuasive appeal. Consistent with this hypothesis, individuals in a good mood were found to be more likely to comply with a collector's request than individuals in a bad mood – but only if the collector used weak arguments. If the arguments were strong, individuals in a sad mood were more likely to comply, paralleling other findings on mood and persuasion (*see* Schwarz et al., 1991). Hence, predicting the impact of moods on behavior requires careful analyses of the underlying cognitive processes.

## SUMMARY

In summary, our moods may themselves serve as information, may influence what comes to mind, may determine our strategy of information processing, and may distract us from the task we work on. Given that most of these processes are not mutually exclusive, it is not surprising that they result in a rich array of diverse findings, for which a unifying theoretical account is currently not available (*see* Clore et al., 1994).

*See also*: HELPING BEHAVIOR; HEURISTICS; MEMORY.

BIBLIOGRAPHY

Bower, G. H. (1981). Mood and memory. *American Psychologist*, *36*, 129–48.

Clore, G. L., Schwarz, N., & Conway, M. (1994). Cognitive causes and consequences of emotion. In R. S. Wyer & T. K. Srull (Eds.), *Handbook of social cognition* (2nd ed., Vol. 1, pp. 323–418). Hillsdale, NJ: Lawrence Erlbaum.

Ellis, H. C., & Ashbrook, P. W. (1988). Resource allocation model of the effects of depressed mood states on memory. In K. Fiedler & J. Forgas (Eds.), *Affect, cognition, and social behavior* (pp. 25–43). Toronto: Hogrefe.

Forgas, J. P. (1992). Affect in social judgments and decisions: A multi-process model. In M. P. Zanna (Ed.), *Advances in experimental social psychology* (Vol. 25, pp. 227–75). San Diego, CA: Academic Press.

Isen, A. M. (1987). Positive affect, cognitive processes, and social behavior. In L. Berkowitz (Ed.), *Advances in experimental social psychology* (Vol. 20, pp. 203–53). San Diego, CA: Academic Press.

Morris, W. N. (1989). *Mood: The frame of mind*. New York: Springer–Verlag.

Schaller, M., & Cialdini, R. B. (1990). Happiness, sadness, and helping: A motivational integration. In E.T. Higgins & R. M. Sorrentino (Eds.), *Handbook of motivation and cognition: Foundations of social behavior* (Vol. 2; pp. 265–96). New York: Guilford Press.

Schwarz, N., & Clore, G. L. (1983). Mood, misattribution, and judgments of well-being: Informative and directive functions of affective states. *Journal of Personality and Social Psychology*, *45*, 513–23.

—— Bless, H., & Bohner, G. (1991). Mood and persuasion: Affective states influence the processing of persuasive communications. In M. Zanna (Ed.), *Advances in experimental social psychology* (Vol. 24, pp. 161–97). New York: Academic Press.

HERBERT BLESS
NORBERT SCHWARZ

**moral development** The process of acquiring the social rules that differentiate right from wrong. Unfortunately, although this definition appears straightforward, there is considerable disagreement as to what is right and wrong, and how the rules are learned.

Theoretical debate about the developmental origins of morality tends to revolve around the traditional dispute between relativists and universalists. Relativists point to the variety of moral codes across different societies and different eras, and argue that what is "right" is essentially a function of prevailing local VALUES. Universalists, in contrast, hold that there is a set of moral principles which transcend particular cultures and are acquired in the same way – if not always honored – by most individuals in most societies.

The most influential representation of the relativist tradition within psychology is SOCIAL LEARNING theory (Bandura, 1977). Social learning theorists regard morality as the outcome of learning the forms of behavior deemed acceptable within one's community. The principal mechanisms of development are held to be reinforcement, punishment, and observational learning, mediated by the learner's cognitive processing. Bandura holds that children strive to integrate information from diverse external sources and experiences, generating standards against which to monitor their own behavior. Individual differences in the extent to which learners conform to moral NORMS are explained chiefly in terms of variations in reinforcements, the amount of exposure to powerful models, and the extent to which the consequences of the models' actions can be seen to be reinforcing. One advantage of social learning theory is that it can account for the varieties of moral BELIEFS that are acquired by children growing up in different environments.

Since the 1930s, the dominant psychological theory of moral development has been a universalistic one, namely the cognitive-developmental theory, introduced by Piaget (1932) and elaborated by Kohlberg (1976). Piaget saw the central theoretical challenge posed by moral development as to explain on what basis the child comes to distinguish right from wrong. Soliciting children's reasoning about the nature and origins of rules, he characterized development as proceeding through three main stages: amoral (minimal understanding of rules), heteronomous (aware of rules as emanating from more powerful figures), and autonomous (recognizing the necessity for rules as a basis for organized and fair social relations).

Kohlberg's theory follows the Piagetian emphasis on the cognitive-developmental basis of morality, and also offers a universalistic, stage-sequence account of progress in moral reasoning. However, Kohlberg's model is more elaborate, in that he postulates several stages, and more encompassing, in that it aims to account for developments beyond childhood. Diagnosis of an individual's stage of development is also more systematic in this framework, based on responses to a set of "moral dilemmas" which are submitted to a standardized (if controversial) coding procedure.

In a Kohlbergian moral dilemma, the interviewee is required to articulate a choice between different courses of action. For example, should a man steal a drug that he cannot afford but which would save his wife's life? Should one turn in to the law a person who escaped prison many years ago but who is now a model citizen? Which option the subject prefers is of less interest than the *reasons* he or she advances to justify the decision. The quality of reasoning is taken to reflect the individual's moral stage.

In early formulations of his theory, Kohlberg (1976) postulated six stages, grouped into three major levels: Preconventional, Conventional, and Postconventional. The Preconventional thinker regards rules as external to the self and sees the main reason for obeying them as either to avoid punishment (Stage 1) or to further self-interest (Stage 2). The Conventional thinker is aware of the need for rules, and regards "good behavior" as desirable to meet social expectations (Stage 3) or to maintain the social system (Stage 4). The Postconventional thinker reasons at a more principled level, believing that the individual has a social contract to respect the rules and laws which serve to protect the rights of all (Stage 5), or that there is a set of universal ethical principals against which one can assess the validity of particular social practices and even laws (Stage 6).

Not all individuals are expected to reach the highest stages, but the normal (universal) course of development is predicted to follow the sequence outlined. In general, research has supported the broad claims of the theory that moral reasoning scores increase with age, although there is disagreement concerning how common is regression to lower stages, and respondents from nonindustrialised societies appear to progress at a slower pace and less frequently attain Postconventional scores (*see* Durkin, 1995).

The influence of the Kohlbergian model in contemporary research is reflected in the extent and breadth of challenges it has inspired. These come from both universalistic and relativistic corners. In the former, Turiel (1983) has proposed an alternative cognitive-developmental theory which proposes a distinction between moral prescriptions (concerned with the value of life, individual welfare) and social conventions (arbitrary regulations about social behavior, such as dress code, modes of greeting), and maintains that development in the different domains proceeds independently. Others have objected that the theory and the instruments show a bias towards male perspectives, particularly in the focus on detached issues of justice, while female SO-CIALIZATION fosters a greater emphasis on the morality of care and interpersonal dependencies. Cultural psychologists hold that moral development is the outcome of everyday social practices through which the child comes to reproduce the collective understandings of his or her community (*see* Durkin, 1995). While debate will certainly continue, one common theme of much current work is a return to prominence of the relationship between moral reasoning and moral behavior.

*See also*: NORMS; SOCIAL LEARNING; SOCIALIZATION; VALUES.

REFERENCES

Bandura, A. (1977). *Social learning theory*. Englewood Cliffs, NJ: Prentice Hall.

Durkin, K. (1995). *Developmental social psychology: from Infancy to old age*. Oxford: Blackwell Publishers.

Kohlberg, L. (1976). Moral stages and moralization: The cognitive-developmental approach. In T. Lickona (Ed.), *Moral development and behavior* (pp. 31–69). New York: Holt, Rinehart & Winston.

Piaget, J. (1932). *The moral judgment of the child*. London: Routledge & Kegan Paul.

Turiel, E. (1983). *The development of social knowledge. Morality and convention*. Cambridge: Cambridge University Press.

KEVIN DURKIN

**motivation** Three sets of phenomena have traditionally been of concern in the field of human motivation:

(1) the choice or selection of a certain course of action;
(2) the energization of the implied behaviors; and
(3) the regulation of these behaviors.

Accordingly, research on motivation focuses on the determinants of what type of goals people choose, and how they go about implementing them (i.e., when and how goal-directed behavior gets started, is energized, sustained, and stopped). Taking this broad and comprehensive perspective, it is evident that any field in social psychology (e.g., HELPING BEHAVIOR, AGGRESSION, INTERGROUP RELATIONS) may potentially be analyzed from a motivational point of view, and this extends not only to how people behave in social situations, but also to their social thoughts and feelings.

The layperson's understanding of the concept of motivation reflects an important insight. People are referred to as unmotivated when they do not live up to their potential, because they fail to exert respective efforts. Issues of what people *can* do, that is, their cognitive capabilities and limitations (*see* SOCIAL COGNITION) are just the starting point of a motivational analysis, which commonly attempts to discover the determinants and processes that underlie a person's willingness to use his/her potential.

The history of motivational theorizing can be summarized in terms of an evolving conception of the basic nature of human functioning and development. Early theories portrayed the human as a machine-like, reactive organism driven by internal and/or external forces that are beyond people's control (e.g., instincts, needs, drives, incentives, reinforces, and so forth). According to Weiner (1992) the following theories embrace the machine metaphor:

(1) the biological theories of Freud, Tinbergen, Lorenz, and Wilson;
(2) Hull's learning theory; and
(3) Lewin's field-theoretical approach.

It is implied that if one could just push or pull the right buttons, motivation would result. There is no room for conscious reflection and free will on the part of the individual. Instead, the proposed motivational forces are assumed to transmit their energy by establishing a state of balance or equilibrium (referred to as arousal reduction, self-preservation, or need satisfaction).

More modern theories of motivation construe the human as Godlike (Weiner, 1992). Accordingly, people are understood as the all-just and all-knowing final judges of their actions. Expectancy-value theories (e.g., Atkinson, 1957) and ATTRIBUTION THEORIES (e.g., Weiner) are based on this metaphor. Expectancy-value theories assume that people choose goals rationally, based on their comprehensive knowledge about the expected value and the probability of goal attainment. Attribution theories propose that the motivational determinants of a person's behavior are the causal explanations of prior action outcomes. The layperson is seen as an amateur scientist who systematically explores the causes of his or her past behaviors. The type of causes discovered are expected to affect the person's readiness to engage in these or related behaviors by influencing affects and expectations.

Present day theorizing on motivation portrays the human as a flexible strategist. The focus lies on the different kinds of tasks a person has to solve when transforming wishes into actions (Gollwitzer, 1990). Accordingly, humans are conceived of as highly flexible organisms that readily adjust to the demands of the task at hand. When it comes to choosing goals, people apparently try to live up to the ideals of being all-knowing and all-just (God-like) by processing a vast amount of the available information and weighing it impartially. However, when the implementation of an already chosen goal is at issue, people are determined to achieve the desired ends. As a consequence, the human becomes partial, favoring the implementation of the chosen goal. The desirability and feasibility of the chosen goal are seen in the most positive light, and the attentional focus is limited to the chosen goal. Although this determination to achieve the chosen goal invokes the machine metaphor, recent research contradicts this image of the goal-driven human. Goal achievement turns out to be a highly strategic undertaking that demands the flexible use of self-regulatory skills.

In the following paragraphs a select list of issues is presented that characterize present-day research on motivation in social psychology. We will address research on:

(1) motives and needs;
(2) expectations, control beliefs, and goals; and
(3) the willful and skillful regulation of goal-directed actions.

## MOTIVES AND NEEDS

Research on motives highlights the relation between motivation and AFFECT. It is assumed that motivated behavior is pulled by the anticipated affect associated with so-called natural incentives. Such incentives are attached to situations and actions that are important for the survival of the species (e.g., to affiliate with others, influence others, master intellectual problems). Accordingly, it is proposed that there is only a limited number of natural incentives, each of which shows an inborn relation to a specific cluster of emotions. The individual preference for certain classes of incentives is defined as the individual's motive disposition.

SOCIALIZATION is said to teach the individual which type of situations are associated with what kind of natural incentives and their respective affective experiences. In addition, people are assumed to acquire the skills which allow them to successfully approach desired incentives. David McClelland distinguishes three basic groups of motives: the achievement motive, the power motive, and the affiliative motives (i.e., the sexual motive, the need for affiliation, and the intimacy motive). Just as having food is the reward or incentive for the hunger drive, so is having improved one's performance on a given task the incentive for the achievement motive (*see* ACHIEVEMENT MOTIVATION). The incentive of the power motive is having impact, control, or influence over another person, group, or the world at large. How this impact or influence is established depends on the individual's socialization. There are the crude ways of attacking others physically, but also the more sophisticated routes of persuading or teaching others (*see* POWER, SOCIAL INFLUENCE). Finally, the incentives for the affiliative motives extend to sexual pleasures (sexual motive), being together with people (affiliative motive), and experiencing harmony, concern and commitment with respect to another person or a group of people (intimacy motive; *see* INTIMACY, RELATIONSHIPS, SEXUAL BEHAVIOR). It is recognized that all of the outlined motives may entail a fear or avoidance component. Trying to meet a standard of excellence may not solely be motivated by hope for success, but also by fear of failure, and spending one's spare time affiliating with others may not solely be determined by the anticipated positive feelings of togetherness, but also by a high fear of rejection.

In principle, all humans are seen as possessing the various motives described. There are vast differences, however, in terms of motive strength, which can be assessed by exploring both the array of situations a person interprets in terms of a given motive (e.g., a person high in need for power manages to interpret all kinds of different situations as power related) and the intensity of the anticipated affect associated with having acquired respective incentives. Commonly this is done by employing a Thematic Apperception Test (TAT) which contains pictures of scenes that are loosely related to the motive measured. In the Achievement TAT, for instance, one picture shows an employee knocking at his boss's door. Subjects who take the test are instructed to give free reign to fantasy, talking about what happens in the picture, how the depicted scenario came about, what the depicted persons think, and what will happen next. This procedure (often referred to as operant assessment procedure) is based on the idea that the presented pictures will trigger motive-related thoughts which will then find uninhibited expression in a person's free fantasy. Respondent assessment procedures (i.e., the standard self-report questionnaires) are not appropriate, because they obtain the reflected values people hold with respect to a certain motive. Most people know that achievement, for instance, is highly valued in our society, and many have learned to highly value achievement personally. But when it comes to actually behaving in an achievement-oriented manner in a given situation, a person who highly values achievement may spontaneously pick up the affiliative cues present in this situation, and opt towards enjoying togetherness in favor of achieving. A person's spontaneous fantasy production as stimulated by TAT pictures should reflect such preferences, and therefore provide a more valid assessment of a person's motive disposition than self-report questionnaires.

Being high with respect to a certain motive implies a recurrent concern for acquiring certain types of incentives, but does this concern select, energize, and guide respective behaviors? The predictions most clearly supported by research findings are those concerning frequency and intensity of behaviors, as well as life-span personality development. More specifically, people high on the affiliation motive perform affiliative acts frequently and energetically, they readily perceive affiliative cues in the environment and quickly detect affiliative networks. Also, predictions concerning the professional success of managers are strikingly accurate, particularly if one considers the motive dispositions in achievement (high), power (high), and affiliation (low) in concert. Finally, attempts to predict behaviors from motives commonly fail when engaging in these behaviors is based on conscious reflections. When it comes to choosing between different courses of action, tasks of different difficulty levels, persisting on a given task or leaving the field, people deliberate on the feasibility and desirability of the alternative courses of action. As it turns out, people do not determine the feasibility and desirability of an action solely on the basis of their motive dispositions, but also by thinking about their skills, the intricacies of the situation at hand, and the expected value of the respective course of action.

EXPECTATIONS, CONTROL BELIEFS,
AND GOALS

One of the first attempts to integrate these aspects was made by Atkinson (1957) in his risk-taking model that laid the foundation for expectancy-value theories. He proposed that the subjective probability of success and the task's incentive value conjointly affect task choice, both variables being influenced by the perceived difficulty of the task. Whereas easy tasks lead to a high subjective probability of success (direct function), they also possess low incentive value (inverse function), because the anticipated affect associated with success (pride) is lowest for easy tasks. The reverse is assumed for difficult tasks. Atkinson suggested that multiplying probability of success and incentive value will give a good estimate of whether a person will choose to work on a task, especially when the obtained score is weighted by the person's approach and avoidance component of his/her achievement motive (hope for success and fear of failure, respectively). The prediction is that primarily success-motivated individuals will choose tasks of medium difficulty, whereas failure-motivated people prefer easy or very difficult tasks. Research testing the model is supportive for predictions on task choice, but fails to account for the quantity and quality of task performance once people start working on the chosen tasks.

Elaborations of the model (Heckhausen, 1977) added further expectation-related concepts and differentiated various aspects of the incentive value of task performance. It is suggested that the incentive value of task performance is not simply determined by anticipated pride and shame. Positive self-evaluations, being praised by significant others (e.g., teachers, parents), the instrumentality of task performance to attain superordinate long-term goals, and extrinsic side-effects (e.g., when an achievement task has affiliative benefits) also have to be considered.

In addition, Heckhausen points out that even if there are many potential positive incentives to look forward to, one will only be motivated to strive for them if:

(1) one expects that the behaviors one is capable of performing will lead to successful task performance; and
(2) that successful task performance will lead to these positive incentives (i.e., high instrumentality).

Atkinson's model has also been elaborated by attribution theorists (see Weiner, 1992) who attempted to understand changes in expectations and incentive value in terms of the causal attributions made for past performances. Success and failure may be interpreted as caused by internal (e.g., ability, effort) or external factors (e.g., task difficulty, luck), whereby ability and task difficulty are more stable causal factors than effort and luck. Weiner shows that the stability of success or failure attributions affects people's expectations relating to successful task performance (stable attributions lead to high or low expectations, respectively), whereas the internality of performance outcome attributions relates to affect (internal attributions produce more pride or shame, respectively).

Weiner discovered that the approach component of the achievement motive (hope for success) is associated with attributing failure to luck or lack of effort and success to ability, whereas the avoidance component is linked to attributing failure to lack of ability and success to luck. Research on aggression also points to the importance of attributions for people's readiness to retaliate. Our experienced ANGER and the intended retaliation in response to hostile aggression are less related to the damage that was done to us, but rather depend on the interpretation of the aggressive act as intentional. Similarly, attributions also affect whether we help people in need. Interpreting the plight of victims as caused by their own irresponsible behaviors leads to less helping as compared to causal interpretations of their plight in terms of uncontrollable, external factors.

This recognition of the motivational importance of expectations and attributions provided the starting point of the cognitive revolution in the psychology of motivation. But this revolution has progressed and introduced further important cognitive concepts, such as control beliefs and goals. The most prominent theoretical explication of control beliefs is Bandura's self-efficacy theory (Bandura, 1986). Self-efficacious individuals are characterized by holding the firm belief that they possess the potential to execute the kinds of behaviors that performing a given task demands. People acquire this belief by reflecting on their own relevant past behaviors, observing the behaviors of similar others, and being evaluated by significant others (e.g., teachers). As it turns out, high self-efficacy beliefs are associated with choosing aspiring goals, exerting strong efforts to attain these goals, and high persistence in the face of obstacles and hindrances.

The other cognitive concept that has received much recent attention is that of goals (see Pervin, 1989). Goals define a standard or point of reference for assessing progress to the goal. Because falling short of a goal is associated with negative affect, goal discrepancies stimulate efforts that are geared towards goal attainment. Such efforts can be expected to be more pronounced when the goal state is defined in specific rather than vague terms (such as "I'll attempt to do my best"), is highly rather than mildly challenging, and is to be achieved in the proximal rather than the distal future. Also, efforts to reduce goal discrepancies are observed more frequently when the individual entertains high self-efficacy beliefs with respect to the implied behaviors, people receive frequent feedback on their actual standing, and there is high commitment to the goal at hand.

However, it is not only setting oneself concrete and proximal goals that has motivational benefits; so, too, does committing oneself to abstract, distal goals. Abstract, distal self-defining goals (such as being a good parent, achieving or retaining self-worth) give the individual direction and they keep the individual on track in the face of setbacks or obstacles. After all, there are many different, alternative ways of attaining such goals. If one has failed in one way or discovered that a certain route to goal achievement is out of reach, one can always compensate by taking an alternative route. As it turns out, people who have set themselves such self-defining goals and still feel committed to attaining them are likely to respond to experiences of falling short by engaging in compensatory efforts.

Finally, one should not ignore the content of goals. For instance, people may approach an achievement test with the goal of demonstrating their intelligence or with the goal of developing their cognitive skills. It is the latter goal that allows people to respond to failure experiences with persistence and greater effort, whereas the former goal makes people respond to failure by feeling helplessness and wanting to give up.

## WILLFUL REGULATION OF GOAL-DIRECTED ACTION

Research on motivation in the 1980s has witnessed a shift in interest from issues of choosing tasks or goals to the willful and skillful implementation of chosen goals (Heckhausen, 1991). The pivotal work on the latter issue was done by Mischel (1974), who studied how children manage to delay gratification (e.g., not eating a pretzel placed in front of them) in exchange for some bigger reward. Most importantly, the children's way of thinking about the pretzel (e.g., in abstract instead of concrete terms) turned out to strongly affect whether they achieved the goal of not eating the pretzel.

Kuhl (1984), who regards the major challenge to successful goal pursuit as arising from competing action tendencies, postulates various control strategies that offer effective protection from such competing tendencies (e.g., attention control or emotion control). People are expected to employ these strategies actively and passively when they are in an action-oriented mode of action control, but fail to do so in a state-oriented mode. This latter control mode is characterized by ruminative thoughts about past, present, or future events (action outcomes, emotional states, etc.). It can be triggered by the experience of repeated failures, but also by a big surprise. Moreover, the two control modes are also conceptualized as PERSONALITY attributes, such that people can be classified into state- versus action-oriented individuals. Indeed, action-oriented individuals are found to use the various control strategies more effectively than state-oriented individuals and as a result are comparatively more successful in their goal pursuits.

Another problem with implementing one's goals is getting started. Part of the reason for this is that people often hesitate to specify when, where and how they intend to implement their goals. If such implementation intentions are formed, however, the chances of goal achievement increase drastically (Gollwitzer, 1993). This is due to psychological processes that operate outside of the person's awareness (see AUTOMATICITY): First, the cognitive representation of the intended opportunity to act becomes highly activated. As a result, the specified opportunity is easily detected, attended to, and retrieved from memory. Second, the initiation of the intended action becomes automated. In the presence of the intended opportunity, action initiation is rather swift and effortless, and it does not need a further conscious intent.

## CONCLUSION

The recent advances in research on self-regulatory strategies of goal achievement have delivered many new insights. However, there should be further effective strategies that have yet to be discovered. In any case, future research in this realm should also attempt to relate these strategies to the classic motivational variables of motives and expectations.

*See also:* ACHIEVEMENT MOTIVATION; AGGRESSION; ATTRIBUTION THEORIES; AUTOMATICITY; HELPING BEHAVIOR; INTERGROUP RELATIONS; INTIMACY; PERSONALITY; POWER; RELATIONSHIPS; SEXUAL BEHAVIOR; SOCIAL COGNITION; SOCIAL INFLUENCE; SOCIALIZATION.

BIBLIOGRAPHY

Atkinson, J. W. (1957). Motivational determinants of risk-taking behavior. *Psychological Review, 64,* 359–72.

Bandura, A. (1986). *Social foundations of thought and action: A social cognitive theory.* Englewood Cliffs, NJ: Prentice Hall.

Gollwitzer, P. M. (1990). Action phases and mind-sets. In E. T. Higgins and R. M. Sorrentino (Eds.), *Handbook of motivation and cognition: Foundations of social behavior* (Vol. 2, pp. 53–92). New York: Guilford Press.

——(1993). Goal achievement: The role of intentions. In W. Stroebe & M. Hewstone (Eds.), *European review of social psychology* (Vol. 4, pp. 141–85). Chichester: J. Wiley.

Heckhausen, H. (1977). Achievement motivation and its constructs: A cognitive model. *Motivation and Emotion, 1,* 283–329.

——(1991). *Motivation and action.* Berlin: Springer-Verlag.

Kuhl, J. (1984). Volitional aspects of achievement motivation and learned helplessness: Toward a comprehensive theory of action control. In B. A. Maher & W. B. Maher (Eds.), *Progress in experimental personality research* (Vol. 13, pp. 99–171). New York: Academic Press.

Mischel, W. (1974). Processes in the delay of gratification. In L. Berkowitz (Ed.), *Advances in experimental social psychology* (Vol. 7, pp. 249–92). New York: Academic Press.

Pervin, L. A. (1989). *Goal concepts in personality and social psychology.* Hillsdale, NJ: Lawrence Erlbaum.

Weiner, B. (1992). *Human motivation.* Newbury Park, CA: Sage Publications.

PETER M. GOLLWITZER
VERONIKA BRANDSTÄTTER

**multidimensional scaling** A set of procedures that derive a spatial representation of a pairwise similarity matrix among a set of psychological objects. Typically, subjects are asked to judge the similarity between all pairs of objects in some domain. A spatial representation of the resulting similarity matrix is then obtained in some small number of dimensions, such that the distance between two objects in the representation (typically a euclidean distance) is a monotonic function of the judged similarity. Goodness of fit statistics provide a measure of the success with which the spatial representation captures the similarity data in varying numbers of dimensions. The representation is assumed to inform the researcher about the perceptual distinctions that underlie subjects' similarity judgments. The most readily available program for multidimensional scaling is ALSCAL (Young, 1984).

BIBLIOGRAPHY
Young, F. W. (1984). Scaling. *Annual Review of Psychology*, *35*, 55–81.

CHARLES M. JUDD

# N

**negativity effects** The study of negativity effects assesses the asymmetric impact of negative and positive events on human functioning. Evidence for asymmetric effects has been obtained in a variety of research domains. Many of these domains are of central interest to social psychologists (*see also* IMPRESSION FORMATION, SOCIAL COGNITION, MOOD, SELF). A brief review of some of this research will illustrate the variety and scope of the asymmetry effects obtained, and recent theoretical interpretations of these effects will be highlighted.

It is certainly true that negative and positive events have differing effects on social information processing. For example, negative information generally (but not always) has greater impact on person impressions than positive information, and evidence suggests that this effect cannot be accounted for by information extremity or atypicality. Instead, the theoretical debate concerning these effects centers around whether the enhanced impact of negative information is due to motivation or cognition. Although there are a number of possible motivational and cognitive explanations, two have been the topic of recent debate. Proponents of a motivational cause for negativity biases in impressions have recently speculated that these biases reflect the fact that it is more important to avoid negative outcomes than to approach positive outcomes, and that this tendency to avoid the negative causes greater weight to be given to negative characteristics in impression formation. Proponents of a cognitive cause have recently argued that negative information is often perceived to be more informative than positive information, and that this informativeness difference is produced by people's beliefs about the implications of positive and negative characteristics for membership in positive and negative categories (*see* Peeters & Czapinski, 1990; Skowronski & Carlston, 1989).

Other researchers investigating the impact of negative and positive events on person perception have found that negative information heightens attributional activity, and may lead to more complex cognitive representations of others than positive information (*see* Peeters & Czapinski, 1990). One implication of these findings is that negative information about others receives heightened attention and elaboration at encoding, a fact that should lead to enhanced memory for others' negative attributes relative to others' positive attributes. Although this appears to characterize short-term recall (Skowronski & Carlston, 1987), over the long term there may be no negative–positive recall difference. Furthermore, for autobiographical memory, positive events may be better recalled than negative events, and may be more precisely dated, as well (Skowronski, Betz, Thompson, & Shannon, 1991).

The apparent contradiction between the memory and impression results is mirrored in other research domains. In a recent attempt at theoretical integration, Taylor (1991) explained such paradoxical effects by suggesting that negative events heighten short-term activation, but that over the long term, there is a general tendency to minimize the effects of the negative information. This mobilization/minimization idea can be used to explain the results of the memory research described above. Negative information may heighten initial processing, leading to short-term enhancement of negative event recall. However, across time, the stored negative information might not be frequently rehearsed relative to positive information. Hence, over the long term, one might expect a decrease in long-term recall for negative events relative to positive events.

Taylor's hypothesis is a framework that can integrate the varied domains in which positive/negative asymmetry has been observed. For example, evidence suggestive of short-term mobilization processes appears frequently. People in negative moods are attentionally focused and cognitively active, processing information thoroughly, while those in positive moods are attentionally unfocused, processing information in passive, superficial ways. Furthermore, people are more inclined to search for the causes of events when the events are negative than when they are positive. Social behaviors are affected, as well: nonembarrassing negative events are particularly likely to cause people to be behaviorally active, seeking the company of others.

Evidence for long-term minimization is also abundant. People attribute performance or gambling setbacks to temporary external factors, such as bad luck, but attribute successes to stable internal factors, such as ability (*see also* MINDFULNESS/MINDLESSNESS). People in negative moods are more likely to misattribute their mood to external factors (thus eliminating the mood) than people in positive moods. Furthermore, negative moods seem generally to be more difficult to induce than positive moods. Finally, the affiliation that is prompted by nonembarrassing negative events often results in social support, a factor that significantly reduces the impact of the negative events on health-related outcome variables (*see* Taylor, 1991, for more information about short-term and long-term asymmetry effects).

Although the Taylor mobilization/minimization hypothesis is useful for understanding positive/negative asymmetry effects, there are clearly additional issues that need to be addressed. Even if negative events or negative moods activate cognitive processing or behaviors, the exact nature of the cognitive processes induced, or the behaviors activated, and how those vary across persons and situations, are still poorly understood. In addition, the mechanisms by which the impact of negative behaviors are minimized across time are still highly speculative. Nonetheless, the data clearly indicate that negativity and positivity do have differing effects on human cognition and behavior. The combination of motivation and cognition embedded in the mobilization/minimization hypothesis makes these effects more understandable, and sets a research agenda for the future.

*See also*: IMPRESSION FORMATION; MINDLESSNESS; MOOD; IMPACT ON COGNITION AND BEHAVIOR; SELF; SOCIAL COGNITION.

BIBLIOGRAPHY
Betz, A. D., Thompson, C. P., & Shannon, L. (1991). Social memory in everyday life: Recall of self-events and other-events. *Journal of Personality and Social Psychology*, *60*, 831–43.

Peeters, G., & Czapinski, J. (1990). Positive-negative asymmetry in evaluations: The distinction between affective and informational negativity effects. In W. Stroebe & M. Hewstone (Eds.), *European review of social psychology* (Vol. 1, pp. 33–60). Chichester: J. Wiley.

Skowronski, J. J., & Carlston, D. E. (1987). Social judgment and social memory: The role of cue diagnosticity in negativity, positivity, and extremity biases. *Journal of Personality and Social Psychology*, *52*, 689–99.

—— (1989). Negativity and extremity biases in impression formation: A review of explanations. *Psychological Bulletin*, *105*, 131–42.

Taylor, S. E. (1991). Asymmetrical effects of positive and negative events: The mobilization–minimization hypothesis. *Psychological Bulletin*, *110*, 67–85.

JOHN J. SKOWRONSKI

**nonreactive measures** *See* unobtrusive measures.

**nonverbal communication** In general, nonverbal communication refers to the transmission of information and influence by an individual's physical and behavioral cues. Some definitions, however, restrict "communicative" behavior only to cues that are intentional or goal oriented in nature and/or to cues that possess relatively universal meaning. In order to address the wide range of interpersonal processes affected by nonverbal behavior, the broader definition of nonverbal communication will be assumed in this article. An understanding of nonverbal communication necessitates attention to a variety of cues affecting both the encoding (sending) and decoding (receiving) sides of this process.

OVERVIEW OF CUES

In face-to-face encounters, the first cues noticed are usually *appearance characteristics*. For example, physically attractive individuals are typically viewed more favorably (e.g., happier, more intelligent) than are less attractive individuals. Other important appearance cues include height, body type, facial dominance or facial babyishness, grooming, and clothing style. Impressions based on appearance often develop outside of awareness. These first impressions are particularly important because they set the tone for the interaction and can lead to SELF-FULFILLING PROPHECIES about the partner.

Next, the *distance* between individuals and their *arrangement* relative to one another (*see* PROXEMICS) are important because these features set limits on other communicative behaviors. For example, people have to be relatively close in order to whisper to or touch a partner. Closer distances and more direct orientations also provide an opportunity for more detailed visual scrutiny of a partner. *Body movement* behaviors (*see* KINESICS) include especially rich and varied sources of information in the form of facial expressions, posture and postural change, and hand and gestural movements. *Touch* is a critical behavior in relationships and one that is important in nurturance, friendships, competition and dominance, greeting, comforting, and sexual behavior.

Next, *visual behavior* toward a partner is important because it is the means by which we gather a wide variety of appearance and behavioral information. In addition, gazing at another person is an important component in signaling interest and affection, as well as in signaling competition and threat. *Vocal cues*, in the form of pitch, loudness, tempo, intonation, and pauses can literally modify the

meaning of the spoken word and, in some cases, reverse it, as in sarcasm. Like appearance cues, vocal characteristics often have a considerable effect on first impressions. Finally, *olfaction* is important not only because most people are concerned about controlling body odor, but also because different scents (e.g., perfumes and colognes) can affect an individual's attractiveness. Particular scents can also affect mood and, in the process, make people more susceptible to influence.

Although it is convenient to describe specific cues in isolation, appearance and behavioral information occur as integrated patterns. Consequently, the impact of any given cue is qualified by the context provided by other behaviors. For example, comparable gazes toward a partner take on different meanings depending on the accompanying behavior, especially facial expression. One way of dimensionalizing overall patterns is in terms of the cumulative involvement indicated by different patterns. For example, a closer approach, touch, gaze, and greater expressiveness reflect higher nonverbal involvement with a partner than the contrasting behaviors. It is helpful to consider not only what individuals do in interactions (i.e., nonverbal involvement), but also how they do it (i.e., coordination of behaviors). For example, people who have similar interaction tempos and whose behavior patterns match one another tend to "get along" better than those who are dissimilar in tempo and style.

DETERMINANTS OF NONVERBAL COMMUNICATION

A number of different factors affect how nonverbal behaviors are encoded and decoded (Patterson, 1983, 1991). At the most basic level, GENETIC INFLUENCES apparently contribute to universal tendencies in:

(1) encoding and decoding expressive reactions;
(2) attention to and nurturance of infants;
(3) visual monitoring of conspecifics; and
(4) gender differences in decoding sensitivity.

That is, such patterns were probably selected over the course of evolution because of their survival value. The considerable research showing universality in the encoding and decoding of basic emotional reactions has generally been interpreted as reflecting a biologically based link between specific emotions and their respective facial expressions (*see* FACIAL EXPRESSION OF EMOTION). More recently, however, Fridlund (1991) has suggested that facial expressions are not manifestations of underlying emotions, but are signals reflecting intentions for action. According to this view, an "angry" face is primarily a threat signal, not an outward expression of covert anger.

CULTURE is a second determinant that affects patterns of nonverbal behavior. A major difference across culture is apparent in the form and meaning of gestures that typically accompany speech. Because similar gestures sometimes carry different meanings across culture, the inappropriate use of gestures in a foreign culture can lead to confusion and even insult. People in different cultures can also have contrasting preferences for involvement with their partners. E. T. Hall (1966) noted that people in southern Mediterranean, Latin American, and Semitic cultures typically prefer closer, more animated interactions than those from Britain and northern Europe.

A third important determinant is GENDER. In general, females tend to be better encoders (i.e., more expressive) and better decoders of nonverbal behavior than are males ( J. A. Hall, 1984). It is likely that both biological and social influences contribute to these differences. In addition, in Western cultures, females are typically more comfortable with higher levels of nonverbal involvement (closer distances, touch, and gaze) with other females than are males with other males (*see also* SEX DIFFERENCES).

An individual's style of interacting with others is also related to PERSONALITY. People who are socially anxious, introverted, or low in affiliative motivation typically prefer lower levels of nonverbal involvement with others than those who are nonanxious, extroverted, and high in affiliative motivation. More extreme differences in nonverbal behavior can be seen in the avoidant and/or inappropriate behavior of schizophrenic and depressed individuals compared to that of normals.

Finally, each of these determinants can moderate the influence of the others. Furthermore, factors proximate to interactions – the nature of the situation and the relationship to the partner – also shape specific patterns of nonverbal communication. In some cases, situational constraints and relationship expectancies lead people to manage and monitor carefully their nonverbal behavior, e.g., in an important interview. The contrast between behavior patterns that are more deliberate and those that are more spontaneous ones is one means of distinguishing among different functions of nonverbal behavior.

## FUNCTIONS OF NONVERBAL COMMUNICATION

A consideration of the functions served by nonverbal communication provides a useful means for understanding the pervasive influence of nonverbal behavior in social situations. Nonverbal communication serves a number of differnt functions including:

(1) providing information;
(2) regulating interaction;
(3) expressing intimacy;
(4) exercising influence;
(5) managing affect; and
(6) facilitating service and task goals (Patterson, 1991).

*Providing information* is the most basic and obvious function of nonverbal behavior. Appearance and almost any aspect of nonverbal behavior are potentially important in forming impressions of an individual. But not all cues are noticed and, among those that are noticed, some are weighted more heavily than others.

Generally, people pay more attention to facial expressions than to other cues, but a discrete behavior, like a touch or a prolonged gaze, often demands attention. Furthermore, behavior patterns that are more unexpected are more likely to gain our attention than are common patterns. For example, a close approach by a stranger or gaze avoidance by a good friend would typically be noticeable and may lead to an adaptive response (e.g., a question, confrontation, or perhaps avoidance).

Nonverbal communication can also serve to qualify the meaning of the verbal comments. Vocal cues, facial expressions, and gestures, for example, can intensify or dampen the impact of a verbal message.

Nonverbal behavior may also provide *intrapersonal* information. Facial feedback theory proposes that neural feedback from spontaneous changes in facial musculature (e.g., initiating a smile) determine the affect or emotion an individual experiences. SELF-PERCEPTION theory suggests that when people become aware of their own behavior, they use this information to make an attribution about the cause of their own behavior. For example, if you notice that you spend more time looking and smiling at Mary than at Sue, you might then conclude that you like Mary more than Sue. Thus facial feedback and self-perception theories propose that specific patterns of behavior determine feelings and beliefs, rather than feelings and beliefs determining behavior.

A second function, *regulating interaction*, identifies the role of nonverbal behavior in facilitating the orderly give-and-take of interactions. In most interactions, individuals position themselves in relatively facing arrangements that permit easy visual monitoring between them. In conversations, vocal cues (e.g., a change in pitch, a drawl on the last syllable, and a longer pause) and behavioral changes (e.g., relaxation of gestures and an increased partner-directed gaze) help to signal the end of a speaker's turn and thereby facilitate smooth turn-taking in conversations (Duncan & Fiske, 1977). Within a speaker's turn, listeners often signal agreement and encourage the speaker to continue by nodding, smiling, or offering brief vocalizations (e.g., "uh huh" or "yeh"). Furthermore, these listener responses predictably occur in the very brief intervals between small chunks of speech known as phonemic clauses.

Generally, listeners tend to gaze more at speakers than speakers do at listeners because fully appreciating the speaker's message often requires attention to the speaker's nonverbal behavior, especially facial expressions. In contrast, speakers gaze less at listeners because a steady gaze at the listener can interfere with the effective encoding of verbal

comments, especially more complicated ones. These regulating behaviors typically operate outside of awareness, as long as conversations proceed in a predictable manner.

Nonverbal behaviors also serve to control privacy in situations in which people share a common setting, but have no intention of conversing, like waiting rooms, libraries, or airport lounges. People who wish to maintain some privacy in such public settings may take more remote positions, avoid visual scrutiny by not sitting opposite other people, and claim neighboring seats with personal possessions.

Much of the early research and theory on nonverbal communication assumed that nonverbal behavior spontaneously reflected underlying interpersonal affect (e.g., a liking–disliking dimension). Consequently, this work emphasized the role of nonverbal behavior in *expressing intimacy*. That is, nonverbal involvement spontaneously reflected one's INTIMACY with or affective attachment to another person. Typically, people do initiate higher levels of involvement with close friends or loved ones than with strangers or disliked others, but such patterns are also affected by the constraints of the setting and by cultural and gender differences. For example, a man and a woman holding hands or sharing a brief hug in public is socially acceptable in North America and Western Europe, but such a display is not acceptable in some other cultures.

Interpersonal intimacy may also be reflected in the coordination of behavior patterns between interactants. In particular, increased rapport between individuals is related to behavior matching (e.g., adopting similar postures and gestures) and to greater synchrony in their behavior patterns (Bernieri & Rosenthal, 1991).

In contrast to the more spontaneous and affect-based intimacy behavior, *exercising influence* is characterized by more purposeful behavior patterns. This does not mean that an individual has to be aware of using a particular behavior pattern to affect a partner but, rather, that there is some recognition of the goal of the influence attempt (e.g., selling a product or making a good impression). In fact, the more effective routines are likely to be overlearned or scripted sequences that require little or no attention to the behavioral components.

Nonverbal behaviors may be especially effective in influencing others in circumstances of COMPLIANCE and PERSUASION. For example, gaining compliance to simple requests can be facilitated by an appropriately timed touch, gaze, or facial expression. The same high level of involvement that can be effective for behavioral compliance may be too intense and/or distracting for effective persuasion or ATTITUDE CHANGE. The impact and comprehension of messages can, however, be improved by a speaker's skillful use of gestures.

A second category of influence is that of IMPRESSION MANAGEMENT. Across a variety of situations where people are concerned about making a particular impression on others, managing nonverbal displays may be as important as managing the content of a message (see DePaulo, 1991). Obviously, the specific behavioral presentations depend on the goals of the actor, cultural norms, the setting, and the relationship to the partner. For example, moderately high levels of nonverbal involvement may be judged most positively in an initial interaction between peers, but not in the more formal, initial interaction with a new employer. Sometimes impression management patterns are the result of partners' collaborative efforts to project a specific couple identity or image to others in a social setting. For example, at a party, a normally quarrelsome couple might attempt to present an image of being happily married by holding hands and smiling at one another.

Nonverbal influence plays an especially important role in DECEPTION. Lies involve transmitting deliberately false information as true, while simultaneously trying to present a pattern of nonverbal behavior that supports the deception. In general, liars direct more attention to managing their facial expressions than to managing other behaviors, just as the targets of lies direct more attention toward the faces of liars. Research suggests that deception is typically detected at rates only slightly above chance for most people, although various situational factors (e.g., the increased importance of the lie, a closer relationship between the liar and target, and the availab-

ility of comparative instances of truth telling) can increase accuracy in detecting deception.

Next, nonverbal behavior is important in *managing affect*, especially in situations where affective reactions are strong. For example, intense ANXIETY or EMBARRASSMENT often leads to avoidance behaviors, such as decreased gaze toward others and even moving away from them. In contrast, GRIEF and fear are likely to result in increased contact with others. In both instances, the nonverbal adjustments serve to minimize the negative affect experienced by the individual. In the case of positive affect, celebrating accomplishments or good fortune often includes increased tactile involvement (e.g., hugs or kisses) and shared smiling and laughing.

A final function of nonverbal behavior is that of *facilitating service and task goals*. In this case, nonverbal patterns are a product of the service or task constraints in various professions and work settings. For example, the professional services of physicians, dentists, tailors, and hair stylists typically require close distances, touch, and careful visual scrutiny that would be inappropriate under other circumstances. To maintain the propriety of such potentially intimate exchanges and to minimize the discomfort of patients and clients, the professional's routine in providing a service may be more formal and stylized than is actually required by the nature of the service. On the task side, different activities (e.g., studying at the library versus working on an assembly line) often require varying degrees of privacy or separation from others. For both service and task goals, interpersonal behavior is substantially determined by "impersonal" requirements of the activity.

Most interactions reflect a mix of two or more functions. Casual interactions with friends, for example, may primarily reflect an intimacy function, but imbedded in such exchanges are attempts at influencing the friend. In general, as partners share more similar behavioral styles and preferences and common expectancies about the interaction, patterns of nonverbal exchange will tend to be more stable and predictable. When behavioral styles and interaction expectancies are not complementary and predictable, individuals usually feel uncomfortable and make behavioral adjustments to resolve the discomfort in the interaction.

## NONVERBAL COMMUNICATION IN PERSPECTIVE

It is convenient to distinguish between nonverbal and verbal communication, just as it is to distinguish between decoding and encoding processes, but such distinctions can be misleading. COMMUNICATION is a system, simultaneously engaging encoding and decoding processes. In social settings, we only occasionally speak, but we cannot "not behave." To understand nonverbal communication it is necessary to appreciate the interdependence of the verbal and nonverbal components of simultaneous encoding and decoding processes. An example of this interdependence may be seen in the cognitive processes directing verbal and nonverbal behavior.

Both encoding and decoding can vary from being automatic to being reflective and deliberate, but verbal communication is typically more deliberate and cognitively demanding than is nonverbal communication. Furthermore, if we assume that there are limited cognitive resources available for encoding and decoding verbal and nonverbal components, then changing the cognitive demands on any one process can affect other processes and the course of communication.

In general, to the extent that nonverbal processes require fewer cognitive resources than do verbal processes, nonverbal communication is more resilient than is verbal communication. Nevertheless, specific interpersonal goals can make the encoding of nonverbal behavior (e.g., a difficult impression management task) and the decoding of nonverbal behavior (e.g., looking for evidence of deception) less automatic and more cognitively demanding. Understanding the dynamic relationships between encoding and decoding aspects of verbal and nonverbal behavior is a critical step in understanding the broader communicative process.

*See also*: ATTITUDE CHANGE; COMMUNICATION; CULTURE; DECEPTION; EMBARRASSMENT; FACIAL EXPRESSION OF EMOTION; GENDER; GENETIC INFLUENCES; GRIEF; IMPRESSION MANAGEMENT; INTIMACY; PERSONALITY; SELF-FULFILLING PROPHECIES; SELF-PERCEPTION THEORY; SEX DIFFERENCES.

BIBLIOGRAPHY

Bernieri, F. J., & Rosenthal, R. (1991). Interpersonal coordination: Behavior matching and interactional synchrony. In R. S. Feldman & B. Rimé (Eds.), *Fundamentals of nonverbal behavior* (pp. 401–32). Cambridge: Cambridge University Press.

DePaulo, B. M. (1991). Nonverbal behavior and self-presentation. *Psychological Bulletin, 111*, 203–43.

Duncan, S. D., Jr, & Fiske, D. W. (1977). *Face to face interaction: Research, methods, and theory*. Hillsdale, NJ: Lawrence Erlbaum.

Fridlund, A. J. (1991). Evolution and facial action in reflex, social motive, and paralanguage. *Biological Psychology, 32*, 3–100.

Hall, E. T. (1966). *The hidden dimension*. New York: Doubleday.

Hall, J. A. (1984). *Nonverbal sex differences: Communication accuracy and expressive style*. Baltimore, MD: Johns Hopkins University Press.

Patterson, M. L. (1983). *Nonverbal behavior: A functional perspective*. New York: Springer-Verlag.

——(1991). A functional approach to nonverbal exchange. In R. S. Feldman & B. Rimé (Eds.), *Fundamentals of nonverbal behavior* (pp. 458–95). Cambridge: Cambridge University Press.

MILES L. PATTERSON

**norm theory** Postulates that every experience brings its own frame of reference or norm into being either by guiding memory retrieval or by constraining mental simulation (*see* Kahneman & Tversky, 1982; Miller, Turnbull, & McFarland, 1991). The assumption that the norms used in making inferences, predictions, and comparative judgments are evoked by the event itself, and hence are most appropriately viewed as "postcomputed" representations, contrasts with the more traditional assumption that norms consist of "precomputed" structures (e.g., SCHEMAS and expectancies) that the perceiver brings to the experience. According to the precomputed view, each member of a category (e.g., dogs) is evaluated with reference to the same norm (e.g., a schema for dogs); according to the postcomputed view no two members of the category will evoke exactly the same norm. The sight of a dog will bring to mind schematic information about dogs, but it will also bring to mind exemplars of specific other dogs, such as ones that the perceiver has seen recently.

One of the most important determinants of norm formation is similarity. The counterfactual images that an event retrieves from memory or generates in imagination will tend to resemble closely the actual event (*see* COUNTERFACTUAL THINKING). But the evoked norms will never match the observed event in all respects: If they did there would never be any surprise or contrast. Various rules guide which aspects of a stimulus are presupposed in the evoked norm and which aspects are not. One such rule is that causes are more likely to be presupposed in the evoked norm than are effects. Consider a perceiver who meets a 3-year-old girl and exclaims, "She's very tall for her age." The phrasing of this comparative judgment suggests that the norm evoked in the perceiver was one based on retrieved instances of other girls who shared the observed girl's age (a cause) but not her height (an effect). If it were as natural to think of other children sharing the girl's height but not her age, then it would be as natural for a perceiver to exclaim, "She's very young for her height."

The fact that not all aspects of experience are equally likely to be imagined differently is also important for an understanding of those norms that are constructed in imagination rather than retrieved from memory. Our imaginations can generate many counterfactual alternatives to any particular experience, but some of these will seem more natural or come to mind more readily than will others (*see* SIMULATION HEURISTIC). Various factors determine how likely it is that an aspect of an experience will be imagined differently in the counterfactual alternatives evoked by the experience. One relevant factor is its order in the event sequence. Early events in a sequence, especially an inconsistent or unexpected sequence, are less mutable and hence more easily imagined otherwise than are later events. Consider two inconsistent sequences in exam performances (grades of A and C and of C and A). Each of these sequences is likely to evoke both thoughts of a more consistent sequence and puzzlement as to why the sequence of the student's exam performances did not take the more consistent pattern. But which of the two more consistent patterns will come to mind and serve as the norm for evaluating the actual sequences: A, A or C, C? Consistent with norm theory's prediction that early events in a sequence are less mutable than later events, research demonstrates that the alternative sequence (norm) evoked by an inconsistent grade sequence will tend to presuppose the first grade but not the second. Thus, people will be puzzled not as to why the grade sequence for the first student was not A, A but why the grade sequence for the second student was not C, C (*see* PRIMACY-RECENCY EFFECTS).

Norm theory and the concept of mutability also helps explain why two events which yield identical consequences and which are equally probable can evoke different affective reactions. Consider the fate of an individual who is killed in the crash of a commercial airliner after switching from another flight only minutes before takeoff. Contrast this person's fate with the death of a passenger who had been booked on the fatal flight for some weeks. The fate of the first person elicits a stronger affective reaction from observers than does the fate of the second person. But why? The fates of the two passenger are identical and precomputed expectancies do not differ in the two cases: Switching flights is neither perceived to increase nor decrease one's probability of crashing. According to norm theory, the reason that the first passenger's fate evokes stronger AFFECT is because it is more mutable or abnormal. People do not routinely switch flights and so the act of switching will readily evoke thoughts of more normal actions, "If only she had not switched flights. . . ." Imagining an alternative reality in which the second person was saved is much more difficult because it involves imagining an alternative to the *status quo* (not switching) rather than to the exception (switching). One would not expect to hear someone say of this victim, "If only she had switched flights. . . ."

In summary, norm theory has two main postulates:

(1) an experience evokes its own frame of reference or norm; and
(2) the norm that an experience evokes will share some elements of the experience but not others.

The theory also identifies a number of factors that determine the ease with which different aspects of experience can be imagined otherwise. Finally, the theory links the concept of postcomputed norms to diverse psychological processes such as the attribution of CAUSALITY (*see* ATTRIBUTION THEORIES) and the generation of affect.

*See also*: ATTRIBUTION THEORIES; SCHEMAS/SCHEMATA.

BIBLIOGRAPHY

Kahneman, D., & Tversky, A. (1982). The simulation heuristic. In D. Kahneman, P. Slovic, & A. Tversky (Eds.), *Judgment under uncertainty: Heuristics and biases.* (pp. 201–8). New York: Cambridge University Press.

Miller, D. T., Turnbull, W., & McFarland, C. (1991). Counterfactual thinking and social perception: Thinking about what might have been. In M. Zanna (Ed.), *Advances in experimental social psychology* (Vol. 23, pp. 305–31). San Diego, CA: Academic Press.

DALE T. MILLER

**normative influence** A major process of SOCIAL INFLUENCE. It is CONFORMITY to the positive expectations of others, motivated by the desire for approval and to avoid rejection. It leads only to COMPLIANCE and is increased by group interdependence, surveillance, and the absence of prior commitment to an alternative position.

*See also*: SOCIAL INFLUENCE.

JOHN C. TURNER

**norms** Consensual standards that describe what behaviors should and should not be performed in a given context are called social norms. They prescribe the socially appropriate way to respond in the situation – the "normal" course of action – as well as proscribing actions to avoid if at all possible. Social norms, in contrast to statistical norms or general expectations based on intuitive BASE RATES for behavior, include an evaluative component. People who do not comply with the norms of a situation and cannot provide an acceptable explanation for their violation are evaluated negatively. This condemnation can include hostility, pressure to change, negative sanctions, and punishment, but the reaction depends on the magnitude of the discrepancy, the importance of the norm, and the characteristics of the person who violates the norm. Wearing too colorful a tie, not bowing properly when introduced, or talking about overly intimate matters with a new acquaintance may violate situational norms of propriety, but they will rarely earn public rejection. Small violations that reflect personal idiosyncrasies, if kept private, are often overlooked, as are violations committed by prestigious or powerful individuals. Violations of moral norms prohibiting theft or prescribing duties, in contrast, will be roundly condemned (Sabini & Silver, 1978). This evaluative reaction is, however, asymmetric. Whereas violating a norm often generates negative responses, merely complying with a norm will rarely earn one praise. A norm often becomes salient to interactants only after it is violated (Forsyth, 1990).

Some norms, such as taboos regarding incest and cannibalism, structure actions in a wide variety of contexts and cultures. Most norms, however, are more limited in their domain of application. Norms that regulate greetings and nonverbal behavior, for example, tend to vary from culture to culture or even within subgroups in a particular culture. A smile may be universally recognized as an expression of happiness, but *when* that smile can be displayed depends upon the display norms of the particular culture. These variations in content aside, normative processes affect all manner of social situations, from the informal and intimate to the ceremonious and public. Spouses splitting up household chores, friends greeting on the street, executives discussing business strategies, and strangers in queues all recognize and respond in ways that are consistent with the norms governing that particular situation. Norms also structure action in situations that range from the commonplace to the consequential. Simple behaviors such as choice of clothing ("Wear shoes in public"), manners ("Say thank-you"), and conventions of address ("Call adult men 'Mr' ") reflect social norms, but so do general societal principles of fairness ("Do unto others as they do unto you"), morality ("Do not lie and break promises"), and value ("Avoid laziness").

## NORMATIVE THEORIES OF SOCIAL PROCESSES

Norms are a fundamental element of social structure; they are the "cement of society" (Elster, 1989, p. 251). They simplify behavioral choices, provide direction and motivation, organize social interactions, and make other people's responses predictable and meaningful. Each person in society is restrained to a degree by norms, but each person also benefits from the order that norms provide. Moreover, although in some cases people may obey norms merely to avoid sanctions or to seem agreeable, when they internalize a norm it becomes a part of their total value system; hence people often follow norms not because of external pressure but because normative action is personally satisfying. Conversely, the violation of norms does not only carry sanctions from others. Individuals who violate norms that they accept condemn themselves as well, and experience a range of negative emotional consequences such as extreme self-consciousness, embarrassment, guilt, and shame (Elster, 1989).

Many theoretical explanations of social processes draw, either explicit or implicitly, on the concept of norms. Why, for example, do people who are part of social movements or large crowds sometimes engage in aberrant behavior (see DEINDIVIDUATION)? In some instances people can become so aroused by the experience that the norms that typically govern their conduct no longer constrain them.

Hence, they act in odd ways. In other cases atypical norms emerge within the collective, and these emergent norms prompt people to act in uncommon ways. Emergent norms in urban gangs, for example, often emphasize toughness and physical strength, so when conflicts among members occur violence is the preferred means of settling the dispute.

Why do people help needy others (see HELPING BEHAVIOR)? Because the norm of social responsibility prompts individuals to aid people who can't help themselves. Why are people kind to those who treat them with consideration but aggressive towards those who treat them harshly? Because the norm of RECIPROCITY enjoins them to pay back, in kind, what others give to them: analyses of interpersonal conflict ranging from interpersonal disputes to global warfare suggest that violence escalates when the norm of reciprocity requires that aggressive actions must be countered with a more aggressive action. Why do people respond negatively when they are underpaid or they feel that they are putting more time and effort into a relationship than their partner is (see EQUITY THEORY)? Because the norm of equity defines a relationship as fair only if those involved receive an amount in return that is proportional to the amount they have invested. The relationship becomes inequitable when what is given does not match what is received. Why do people fall in LOVE? Analyses suggest that love is, to a large extent, defined by societal norms. Most Western societies condone long-term, exclusive relationships based on passion and commitment but negatively sanctioning short-term relationships between people who lack commitment. As these examples suggest, the explanatory power of the concept of norms is exceptional.

## THE DEVELOPMENT AND TRANSMISSION OF NORMS

Norms, if written down, become formal rules of proper conduct, but in most instances norms are adopted implicitly as people align their behaviors until consensus in actions emerges. Sherif's classic analysis of this process suggests that this gradual alignment of action reflects the development of frames of reference for behaviors and perceptions (Sherif, 1936). Individuals, once they join with others, rapidly structure their experiences until they conform to a general standard. This standard can be pressed upon the group by an outside authority or a group leader, but Sherif notes that in most instances norms develop through reciprocal influence. Individuals do not actively try to conform to the judgments of others, but instead use the group consensus to revise their own opinions and beliefs. Sherif examined this process by taking advantage of naturally occurring perceptual illusion called the autokinetic effect. People, when shown a dot of light in an otherwise dark room, will think the light is moving because the visual system lacks a frame of reference. Sherif arranged for men to state aloud their estimates of the distance the light moved when alone and in groups. He found that individuals making judgments by themselves establish their own idiosyncratic average estimates, which varied from 1 inch to 10 inches. When people made their judgments with other people, however, their personal estimates blended with those of other group members until a consensus was reached. By the final session, the men accepted a standard estimate in place of their own idiosyncratic judgments. Moreover, in subsequent individual sessions subjects still relied on the group norm, suggesting that they had internalized the norm.

Subsequent studies found evidence of both change in the individual and change in the group when a single individual who made extreme judgments was placed in each group. This individual deflected the rest of the group members' judgments so that a more extreme norm guided the group members' judgments. Once this arbitrary standard had been created, the individual was removed from the group and replaced by a fresh member. The remaining group members retained the large distance norm, however, and the newest group member gradually adapted to the higher standard. Old members were removed from the group and replaced with naive subjects, but the new initiates continued to shift their estimates in the direction of the group norm. The arbitrary group norm eventually disappeared, but not before the group memberships had been changed five or six times (*see* Forsyth, 1990, for detailed references).

This process of SOCIALIZATION explains how norms, once they are established, can become part of the group's stable structure. Even though the individuals who originally fostered the norms are no longer present, their normative innovations remain a part of the organization's traditions and newcomers must change to adopt that tradition.

Socialization accounts for continuity in religious, economic, moral, political, and interpersonal beliefs across generations. Whenever children learn norms of appropriate behavior in their culture, new employees learn the boss's secret list of "dos and don'ts," or newcomers to a club discover the group's standards and expectations they are experiencing socialization. In most instances it is the individual who assimilates the group's norms, values, and perspectives (Moreland & Levine, 1982). At times, however, socialization can generate changes in norms as the group accommodates to fit the newcomer's needs. Moscovici's (1985) theory of minority influence similarly suggests that staunch, unyielding individuals can shift the group's norms provided they maintain the appearance of consistency and objectivity.

Newcomb demonstrated the intergenerational longevity of norms in his 1943 study of political attitudes. Newcomb noted that even though most of the students who entered the college where he taught came from politically conservative families, the upperclassmen tended to express more liberal attitudes. Newcomb, after examining students attitudes over a 4-year period, concluded that students' attitudes changed as they left the family group and joined the new group composed of classmates and faculty at the college. While the family's norms supported conservative attitudes, the college community supported only liberal attitudes, and many women shifted their political attitudes to better match the norm of liberality. Indeed, the shift towards liberalism was most pronounced among the popular students, those who were more deeply embedded in the university community, and those who were members of the most liberal subgroup within the overall social organization. Individuals who did not become more liberal tended to be isolated from the college's social life or to be very family-oriented. The impact of this socializing experience was considerable, for the more liberal attitudes created by the group remained a part of the beliefs of many of the graduates some 25 years later (*see* Forsyth, 1990, for detailed references).

Many other researchers have documented this norm-transmission process. Crandall (1988) describes how bulimia – a cycle of binge eating followed by self-induced vomiting or other forms of purging – can be sustained by group norms. Bulimia is considered by society-at-large to be an abnormal behavior, yet it is prevalent in certain groups, such as cheerleading squads, dance troupes, teams, and sororities. Crandall suggests that such groups, rather than viewing these actions as a threat to health, accept purging as a normal means of controlling one's weight. In the sororities he studied he found that the women who were popular in the group were the ones who binged at the rate established by the group's norms. Also, as time passed, those who did not binge began to binge. Thus, even norms that counter to society's general traditions can establish a life of their own in small subgroups within that society.

## THE POWER OF NORMS

Norms exert such a powerful influence on behavior that even individuals who privately reject their society's norms usually follow these standards nonetheless. Asch (1955) documented the too-human tendency to conform experimentally to norms by placing individuals into groups that were making incorrect judgments about the length of lines. All the group members save one were trained confederates who deliberately made errors to see if the subject would conform to a unanimous majority's judgments. Each group member stated his judgment aloud, so when the subject's time to speak came he could either report his own opinion – and disagree with the group – or conform to the group's opinion. Asch found that people conformed about 35 percent of the time – a surprisingly high rate

considering the simplicity of the judgment. He noted, however, that people who conformed did so for two different reasons. First, in some cases the individual's private position changed to match the norms of the group. They simply concluded "I am wrong, and the group is right." This form of social response to norms is termed CONVERSION or private acceptance. Others, in contrast, never accepted the norm of the group but they went along because they did not want to seem out of step with the others, anger the experimenter, or appear stupid. This type of conformity is usually labeled COMPLIANCE: a change in public behavior to match the norm paired with private rejection of the norm itself. But whether the individual was converted or merely complying, the result was the same: Conformity to the situational norm.

Why do we tend to feel, think, and act in ways that are consistent with social norms? Analyses of NORMATIVE INFLUENCE trace the source of a norm's power back to both interpersonal and personal factors. At an interpersonal level, people feel compelled to act in accordance with norms because a variety of negative consequences could result from nonconformity. Indeed, the interpersonal consequences suffered by people who violate society's norms are both commonplace and varied. Those who violate norms of civility are often reminded of their duty and told to change their ways. People who violate the norms and regulations of their groups are disliked, assigned lower status jobs, pressured to conform, and in some cases excluded from membership (as shown by the early research of Schachter, 1951; *see* Forsyth; 1990). Those who adopt alternative life styles or occupations are reminded that they should be ashamed for their variance from the normal path. The individual who publicly flaunts a moral norm, by acting in ways that society condemns, will likely meet with moral reproach: others respond by "telling him that he is doing something wrong, and exactly what it is that is wrong about what he is doing, and what it is that his wrong doing makes him – a cad, creep, or moral leper – or more simply just call him a creep for short" (Sabini & Silver, 1978, p. 103). And those who break society's laws – its legal norms – and are caught in the violation meet with more formal sanctions: incarceration, monetary fines, public degradation, and even death.

Normative influence, however, also has a personal component, for people also obey norms in order to fulfill their own expectations about proper behavior. Norms are not simply external constraints but internalized standards; people feel duty bound to adhere to norms since, as responsible members of society, they accept the legitimacy of the established norms and recognize the importance of supporting these norms. General norms such as "Do not tell lies" and "Help other people when they are in need" correspond to such personal norms as "I don't tell lies to other people" and "I help people whenever I can." Thus, people comply with the dictates of situational norms not only because they fear the negative interpersonal consequences – ostracism, ridicule, punishment – that their nonconformity may produce, but also because they feel personally compelled to live up to their own expectations.

Milgram's (1992) studies of encounters between people in urban settings document both the interpersonal and personal consequences of counternormative actions. He sought to explain the high degree of social order that characterizes encounters between complete strangers in public places. Although these encounters are fleeting and relatively inconsequential, Milgram noted that they are for the most part ordered and predictable. Consider, for example, the waiting line or queue. Even though this group is comprised of individuals who are strangers to one another and who will likely not meet again, interaction within the queue is ordered by commonly recognized norms: do not break line; do not talk to the stranger next to you; face the front; move forward to fill spaces; and so on. These norms of civility are implicitly obeyed, and when they are broken members of the queue are ready to challenge those who try to violate the norm.

Milgram studied this process by arranging for men and women to break into queues waiting outside of ticket offices and the like in New York City. Working either alone or in pairs, the accomplices would simply say, "Excuse me, I'd like to get in here." and then insert themselves in the line. The individuals in the queue defended the norms of the situation in nearly half of the lines studied. In a few cases they used physical action, such as a tap on the shoulder or a push. In some lines the reaction was verbal and ranged from the polite, "Excuse me, but I'm already in line here." to impolite, "Hey you SOB! The line's back there." In other cases the reaction was primarily nonverbal: the people in line used dirty looks, stares, and hostile, threatening gestures to vent their objections. More people challenged the intrusion into the queue by two individuals than by one, although hostility was partly tempered by location. Far more of the complaints came from people standing behind the point of intrusion rather than from people standing in front of the intrusion. Self-interest, as well as the normative force of the queues' rules, partly motivated people's reactions to the queue-breakers' actions.

Milgram also documented the personal consequences of violating norms. In one investigation he had men and women board a New York City subway and perform a simple counternormative behavior: asking someone for their seat. In this situation, all interactants recognize and accept the rule "all seats are filled on a first-come, first-served basis," so asking for someone to give up their seat is a norm violation. Still, many people gave up their seats, apparently because the request took them by surprise, they wanted to avoid interaction, or because they normalized the situation by concluding that the requestor was ill. Milgram was particularly intrigued, however, by the reactions displayed by the norm-violators. Even though they were volunteers who were deliberately breaking the situational norms in the name of research, all experienced severe emotional turmoil as they approached the situation. They "reported that when standing in front of a subject, they felt anxious, tense, and embarrassed. Frequently, they were unable to vocalize the request for a seat and had to withdraw" (Milgram, 1992, p. 42). Milgram, who also performed the norm-violation task, described the experience as wrenching, and concluded that there is an "enormous inhibitory anxiety that ordinarily prevents us from breaching social norms' (p. xxiv).

Norms, then, are not merely external forces that require certain kinds of actions in certain kinds of situations. Rather, they are a fundamental component of social structure that links each individual member of society to the larger social order. Individuals sometimes obey norms to avoid the sanctions that violations would provoke, but in most instances normative behavior is consistent with personal preferences, beliefs, and values. Norms exist independently of single individuals, but norms are nonetheless created by individuals in order to bring regularity to their social encounters. *See also*: SOCIALIZATION; DEINDIVIDUATION; HELPING BEHAVIOR; EQUITY THEORY.

BIBLIOGRAPHY

Asch, S. E. (1955). Opinions and social pressures. *Scientific American*, *193(5)*, 31–5.

Crandall, C. S. (1988). Social contagion of binge eating. *Journal of Personality and Social Psychology*, *55*, 588–98.

Elster, J. (1989). *The cement of society: A study of social order*. Cambridge: Cambridge University Press.

Forsyth, D. R. (1990). *Group dynamics*. Pacific Grove, CA: Brooks/Cole.

Milgram, S. (1992). *The individual in a social world: Essays and experiments* (2nd ed.). J. Sabini & M. Silver (Eds.). New York: McGraw-Hill.

Moreland, R. L., & Levine, J. M. (1982). Socialization in small groups: Temporal changes in individual–group relations. In L. Berkowitz (Ed.), *Advances in experimental social psychology* (Vol. 15, 137–92). New York: Academic Press.

Moscovici, S. (1985). Social influence and conformity. In G. Lindzey & E. Aronson (Eds.), *Handbook of social psychology* (3rd ed., Vol. 2, pp. 347–412). New York: Random House.

Newcomb, T. M. (1943). *Personality and social change*. New York: Dryden.

Sabini, J. P., & Silver, M. (1978). Moral reproach and moral action. *Journal for the Theory of Social Behavior*, *8*, 103–23).

Sherif, M. (1936). *The psychology of social norms*. New York: Harper & Row.

DONELSON R. FORSYTH

# O

obedience  A major theme of social psychology concerns the extraordinary degree to which people are responsive to SOCIAL INFLUENCE. The most explicit form of such influence is *obedience to authority*, that is, complying with orders from a person of higher social status within a defined hierarchical system or chain of command (e.g., family, military, government, corporation). The motives for obedience are diverse, from respecting the expertise of authority (e.g., physician) to fearing the consequences of disobedience (e.g., arrest for a speeding violation). This entry focuses upon the power of authority to evoke destructive behavior. We consider empirical data and theoretical issues in the experimental analysis of obedience as well as more general implications of a social–psychological perspective of this phenomenon.

## MILGRAM'S OBEDIENCE STUDIES: PARADIGM AND VARIATIONS

In what many regard as the most significant research in the history of social science, Stanley Milgram posed this question: "If X tells Y to hurt Z, under what conditions will Y carry out the command of X and under what conditions will he refuse?" (Milgram, 1965, p. 57). Upon arrival at Milgram's laboratory, participants, who had volunteered for a study on memory and learning, learned that the experiment was to examine the effects of punishment on learning. Two individuals (one an experimental accomplice) were assigned by what appeared to be random draw to be either "teacher" (the true subject) or "learner" who was then "wired" to receive shocks. The learner made errors on a memory task for which punishment was to be administered by means of a "shock generator" con-

sisting of 30 levers at 15-Volt increments. Subjects who remained in the experiment to its completion ultimately were ordered to inflict the most intense punishment (450 Volts). No shocks were in fact administered, although the learner went through a series of simulated (on tape) vocalizations of distress and demands to be released.

The experimenter (authority) ignored the plight of the learner (other than assuring the subject that no permanent harm would be caused) and ordered that all punishments be administered. Resistance from subjects was met by increasingly strident prods, including "you have no other choice, you must continue." (From this perspective, a critical but subtle feature of Milgram's experimental procedure was a temporal shift in the moral legitimacy of the experimenter's authority – initially legitimate, but ultimately *illegitimate*). Subjects refusing to continue beyond this point were excused. If directly asked, the experimenter agreed to take responsibility for what happened to the learner. Evidence suggests that this scenario was highly credible for a clear majority of subjects (Milgram, 1974; Miller, 1986, Chap. 4). A thorough debriefing was conducted following each experimental session.

Milgram conducted a series of experimental variations. In the *baseline condition*, the learner was situated in an adjoining room. No vocal protests were used, but at the 300-Volt level, the learner was heard pounding on the wall. In further experiments, various parameters of the situation were changed (*see* description below). *Obedience* was defined as administering *all* of the required 30 shocks. Subjects were thus confronted with a task which, although initially benign, quickly escalated into an extraordinarily intense conflict – incessant demands from the experimenter to continue shocking the learner and mounting pleas (screams, pounding, and ultimately silence) from the learner to be released.

## OBEDIENCE, EMOTIONAL RESPONSES, AND SITUATIONAL VARIATIONS

An unexpectedly high rate of obedience (65 percent) was observed in the initial study (26 of 40 subjects). This contrasts sharply with the extremely low predictions of obedience made when people are given a description of Milgram's experiment (Miller, 1986, Chap. 2). Only those who are extremely submissive or violent are expected to shock the learner to 450 Volts. This intuitive (mis)understanding of destructive obedience reflects a pervasive tendency to attribute dispositional causes for behavior controlled by powerful situational constraints, a judgmental bias known as the FUNDAMENTAL ATTRIBUTION ERROR. Milgram's findings suggest, however, that destructive obedience is well within the behavioral repertoire of *most* people regardless of their PERSONALITY or moral virtue. This is a disturbing message but one with potentially crucial implications. Holding to the intuitively compelling dispositional account might lead one to be more susceptible to the undesirable influences of authority and less vigilant to the power of situations to induce destructive behavior in good people. Many subjects expressed intense emotional conflict:

I observed a mature and initially poised businessman enter the laboratory smiling and confident. Within 20 minutes, he was reduced to a twitching, stuttering wreck, who was rapidly approaching a point of nervous collapse. He constantly pulled on his earlobe, and twisted his hands. At one point, he pushed his fist into his forehead and muttered: "Oh God, let's stop it." And yet he continued to respond to every word of the experimenter, and obeyed to the end. (Milgram, 1963, p. 377)

Obedience was thus hardly automatic or "blind," but rather the resolution of an excruciating struggle. In this context, the Milgram experiments have been the center of an ethical controversy regarding the emotional stress imposed upon subjects (Miller, 1986, Chap. 5).

Changes in the experimental situation produced powerful effects on obedience. When subjects were allowed freedom in choosing their own preferred shock level, only the most minimal shock levels were administered. However, when placed in the role of a bystander to another person's obedience, almost every subject (93 percent) remained in the situation, taking no action to prevent the peer's total obedience to authority. Increasing the physical proximity between the subject and learner reduced obedience. Similarly, obedience dropped sharply when the experimenter was not physically present but issued orders by phone from another location. The importance of the status (and manner) of authority was revealed when the experimenter (on a pretext) left the laboratory and the role of authority was assumed by a peer (in fact an accomplice). Obedience was substantially reduced. However, the most significant reduction of obedience (10 percent) occurred when two peers (in fact accomplices) defied the experimenter early in the experiment. Witnessing defiance was thus a powerful inducement to disobedience.

Relocating the study to an urban office building (instead of Yale University) had no significant impact on obedience. Women serving as subjects produced a 65 percent obedience rate, identical to the baseline. Obedience was only minimally reduced when a prior agreement was made assuring the learner of immediate release upon his request, only to have this contract subsequently ignored by the experimenter. In a series of variations (one consisting of the learner "demanding" that shocks continue to prove that he could "take it"), the experimenter ordered subjects to *stop* shocking the victim. All subjects obeyed instantly, suggesting that the basic dynamics in fact involved obedience to authority rather than merely taking advantage of an opportunity to harm another person under legitimate circumstances.

Obedience is thus shown to be strongly determined by specific, at times subtle, elements of the situation. The same individual who would likely be obedient in the baseline condition or who would be a nonintervening bystander to the total obedience of a peer, would likely disobey the experimenter in the presence of other defiant peers and would use only the weakest shocks in the absence of orders to increase their voltage.

Milgram's basic findings have been observed in a variety of other research contexts. Harmful obedience has been observed with children as well as women in the "teacher" role, and in a hospital context with nurses as (unsuspecting) subjects (Miller, 1986, Chap. 4). An informative study was conducted in The Netherlands in which subjects were ordered to inflict *verbal* harassment (instead of physical punishment) upon a peer (accomplice) working on an employment-interview exam. High rates of obedience were observed, replicating Milgram's baseline result, but also the sharply reduced obedience in the "rebellious peers" and "experimenter absent" variations. Recent evidence indicates that regardless of personal VALUES, people may conform to the preferences of an authority in the context of ethical decision making (e.g., a management decision to market a potentially dangerous drug), whereas without such constraints, decisions are based on personal values (Brief et al., 1991).

From an *objective* point of view, the most rational response would seem to have been for subjects to simply get up and walk out, for there were no obligations to obey nor harmful consequences of disobedience. Nevertheless many participants obeyed all instructions and administered what they perceived to be extremely painful (perhaps fatal) shocks to a protesting individual. It was thus *the situation as construed by the participants* that was the operative reality. Given the behavior observed in the relatively temporary conditions of Milgram's setting, one begins to appreciate the vastly stronger pressures for destructive obedience in contexts where the constraints upon subordinates are much greater (Darley, 1992).

A THEORETICAL ANALYSIS
OF OBEDIENCE

Milgram identified three major dynamics. A *sociocultural* perspective suggests that we learn to obey authority – parents, teachers, the police, the clergy, doctors – and expect to encounter legitimate, trustworthy authority

in innumerable contexts. This is particularly true with respect to institutions with powerful cultural or symbolic value – religion, education, science, medicine, military, government. The subjects who volunteered to participate in Milgram's scientific study thus entered the laboratory with a long history of rewarded obedience and a presumption that a trustworthy, credible authority would meet them.

Once participants are situated in the experiment, *binding factors* become operative. Diverse cues and perceptions create psychological barriers to disobedience – the experimenter's austere manner, his uniform, the learner's (apparent) willingness to receive punishment, the subject's having volunteered to be in the study. The *gradual* increase in punishment levels ordered by the experimenter is of particular interest. SELF-PERCEPTION THEORY can explain relatively powerful behavioral consequences, including highly undesirable actions, if an individual can initially be induced to perform seemingly inconsequential acts that virtually anyone would agree to perform. COGNITIVE DISSONANCE THEORY also suggests that disobedience might be particularly difficult if it is viewed as inconsistent with the individual's previous behavior and emotional investment. Milgram also suggested the importance of a seemingly trivial norm of "etiquette" – that some individuals might find it embarrassing or impolite to challenge authority, to "make a scene" (*see* NORMS). Many persons have never disobeyed authorities in any context similar to the Milgram laboratory.

The concept of binding factors has been instructive in linking Milgram's observations to destructive obedience in other real-world contexts. Individuals become enmeshed in bureaucratic scenarios in which unethical and immoral – perhaps genocidal – policies are set into motion by authorities, policies which are invariably preceded by a number of intermediate, seemingly minor violations. It is the slow, often subtle *progression* toward destructive obedience that is crucial in helping to understand how ordinary individuals, without initial malice, can ultimately commit actions of undeniable evil (Darley, 1992; Kelman & Hamilton, 1989). Thus, although the experimenter's explicit orders to shock the learner are the most critically important inducement to obedience, they are part of a larger mosaic of binding factors. Ultimate defiance of authority will necessitate the disruption of *all* of these factors.

Finally, the issue of *responsibility* is given a central role in Milgram's theoretical analysis, specifically his concept of the *agentic shift*. The subordinate in a hierarchical system does not accept personal responsibility for his or her actions but allocates this responsibility to an individual higher in the organization. One prototype for the agentic shift is the military chain of command. This was seen in the Nuremberg trials where many high-ranking Nazi defendants disclaimed personal responsibility in the context of following orders. The agentic shift was also observed in Colonel Oliver North's testimony in the "Iran–Contra" trials in the USA. When asked why he had never inquired into Admiral Poindexter's failure to inquire from President Reagan about the diversion of funds, he replied: "I'm not in the habit of questioning my superiors. If he deemed it not to be necessary to ask the President, I saluted smartly and charged up the hill" (Kelman & Hamilton, 1989, p. 41). The denial of personal responsibility for actions committed under authority does not, of course, necessarily absolve subordinates of responsibility for the consequences of their actions. Military law, for example, requires the disobedience of immoral orders (Kelman & Hamilton, 1989). Nevertheless, an important psychological consequence of being in a subordinate role is that people can justify or rationalize (perhaps unconsciously) their destructive actions by attributing responsibility to superiors.

Recognizing that obedience is under powerful situational control, one should not overlook the *disobedience to authority* observed in Milgram's research. In the baseline study, 35 percent of the subjects defied the experimenter at some point. Two conclusions are warranted. First, one should not completely minimize the role of personality factors in destructive obedience. A number of such variables – perhaps related to SELF-ESTEEM, AUTHORITARIANISM, political orientation – may play a role (Kelman & Hamilton,

1989), although the evidence for this is not particularly compelling. Second, under certain conditions, the major elements of Milgram's model – binding factors, agentic shift – are likely to be relatively fragile. As an illustration, witnessing defiance on the part of two peers was sufficient to override all of the binding and agentic-shift dynamics referred to above. Of course, the Milgram study is an extremely contained scenario with no history and no future with respect to the individual subjects involved. Settings for obedience in the ordinary lives of people may well be more protracted and involve stronger pressures and consequences for the individual. There is, in this context, research on the phenomenon of "whistle-blowing," documenting the extraordinary costs paid by individuals who challenge authority within the context of their organization and disclose corrupt or immoral practices to outside sources (Miceli & Near, 1992).

## OBEDIENCE TO AUTHORITY: MAJOR LESSONS OF THE MILGRAM STUDIES

Clearly, many individuals are capable of committing destructive acts under authorization, behaviors which they would never commit (nor think themselves capable of committing) without such influence. Furthermore, we are unlikely to recognize our susceptibility to such influence. Rather, we attribute the actions of those we observe in such situations to their defective moral character – not realizing that we, too, would likely engage in similar actions in the same circumstances. These circumstances need not require the massive trappings of military or governmental authority. The seemingly benign context of a university laboratory is shown to contain more than sufficient social–psychological force for the occurrence of destructive obedience. A particularly significant implication of Milgram's research is that obedience occurs despite the powerful evidence of emotional distress and conflict in the obedient subject. Authority, in many contexts, thus supersedes matters of conscience, EMPATHY, and ALTRUISM. It should also be noted that the power of authority is intricately linked to psychological transitions occurring over time in terms of the progressively more intense harm ultimately committed, and in terms of the difficulty people have in defining malevolent authority as truly illegitimate and taking decisive action in defying that authority.

## THE BANALITY OF EVIL

An analysis of destructive obedience must inevitably include the genocidal policy involved in the Nazi Holocaust (Miller, 1986, Chap. 7). Milgram made an explicit reference to this in the first paragraph of his initial article:

Gas chambers were built, death camps were guarded, daily quotas of corpses were produced with the same efficiency as the manufacture of appliances. These inhumane policies may have originated in the mind of a single person, but they could only be carried out on a massive scale if a very large number of persons obeyed orders. (1963, p. 371)

Prior to Milgram's research, it was traditional for social science to explain genocide primarily in terms of pathological or deviant personality characteristics, the authoritarian personality being the most familiar example. Upon the publication of Milgram's initial findings, however, a personality-based analysis of obedience became increasingly suspect. The current view – unquestionably the central legacy of Milgram's analysis – is that destructive obedience may be evoked from a very large number of people because of situational pressures and the manner in which these forces are interpreted by *most people* – not only from those who are deviant, unusually weak, or sadistic (Browning, 1992). Recent analyses focus in particular upon the *social organization of evil*, with the realization that the capacity for moral DECISION MAKING is powerfully constrained when an individual is embedded in subtle but powerful hierarchical structures within social systems (Darley, 1992).

After observing the trial of the high-ranking Nazi bureaucrat Adolf Eichmann in Jerusalem (1961), the philosopher Hannah Arendt used the phrase "the banality of evil" to characterize what she perceived to be the remarkable "ordinariness" of Eichmann. She reported an astonishing absence of what she had expected in terms of raging antisemitic attitudes and other manifestations of mental disturbance. Arendt's (1963) report on Eichmann was instantly controversial. The assertion that actions of unparalleled evil could be performed by individuals without obvious pathology was unacceptable and Arendt was widely discredited. Reactions to her thesis were very similar in fact to those directed against Milgram, which is understandable given that her message was, in crucial respects, identical to that of Milgram.

There is an important difference in the accounts of Arendt and Milgram, however. Arendt's analysis, although eloquently articulated, was speculative. Milgram went beyond speculation. It was (and remains) the undeniable reality of what large numbers of people actually did in Milgram's laboratory that explains the unprecedented interest generated by his research and, more generally, the power of a social psychological perspective. The experiments cast a shadow. They warn against relegating the potential for Holocaust-like events to the past. They signify that destructive obedience, in a variety of contexts, may be a disaster "waiting to happen." *See also*: AUTHORITARIANISM; COGNITIVE DISSONANCE THEORY; DECISION MAKING; - EMPATHY; NORMS; PERSONALITY; SELF-ESTEEM; SELF-PERCEPTION THEORY; SOCIAL INFLUENCE; VALUES.

BIBLIOGRAPHY

Arendt, H. (1963). *Eichmann in Jerusalem: A report on the banality of evil.* New York: Viking Press.

Brief, A. P., Dukerich, J. M., & Doran, L. I. (1991). Resolving ethical dilemmas in management: Experimental investigations of values, accountability, and choice. *Journal of Applied Social Psychology, 21,* 380–96.

Browning, C. R. (1992). *Ordinary men: Reserve Police Battalion 101 and the final solution in Poland.* New York: Harper Collins.

Darley, J. M. (1992). Social organization for the production of evil. *Psychological Inquiry, 3,* 199–218.

Kelman, H. C., & Hamilton, V. L. (1989). *Crimes of obedience: Toward a social psycho-*

logy of authority and responsibility. New Haven, CT: Yale University Press.

Miceli, M. P., & Near, J. P. (1992). Blowing the whistle: The organizational and legal implications for companies and employees. New York: Lexington Books.

Milgram, S. (1963). Behavioral study of obedience. Journal of Abnormal and Social Psychology, 67, 371–8.

—— (1965). Some conditions of obedience and disobedience to authority. Human Relations, 18, 57–76.

—— (1974). Obedience to authority: An experimental view. New York: Harper & Row.

Miller, A. G. (1986). The obedience experiments: A case study of controversy in social science. New York: Praeger.

ARTHUR G. MILLER

**observational methods** Social psychology is not just the study of socially relevant thoughts and feelings; it is the study of social behavior as well. For this reason, observational methods must be used to complement self-report methods by providing reliable data about the specific behavior(s) that subjects display.

The range of behaviors that can be observed and recorded is impressively large. According to Weick (1968), researchers can study:

(1) nonverbal behaviors such as facial expression, directed gazes, and body movements (see FACIAL EXPRESSION OF EMOTION, NONVERBAL COMMUNICATION and KINESICS);
(2) extralinguistic behaviors such as the pitch, amplitude, and rate of speech; and
(3) linguistic behaviors such as giving suggestions, expressing agreement, and asking for an opinion or evaluation (see INTERACTION PROCESS ANALYSIS).

According to Funder and Colvin (1991), researchers can also study more contextualized and psychologically meaningful units of behavior that require at least some subjective inference by the raters who code the behavior. Depending on the purposes of the study, researchers may examine only a single behavior, a set of behaviors, or the temporally patterned contingencies that relate the behavior of one interactant to that of another.

As Ickes and Tooke (1988) have noted, many observational studies are conducted in psychological laboratories. However, to enhance their ECOLOGICAL VALIDITY, observational studies are also conducted in real-world settings as diverse as an auction, a party, a playground, a police station, a subway train, and the United Nations building. And because observational research can be used to study the social behavior of subjects who are not capable of speech, as well as those who are, it may be the most broadly applicable METHODOLOGY in the field of social psychology. It has been used not only to study the social behavior of human children, adolescents, and adults, but that of human infants and a range of infrahuman (i.e., animal) species as well (see ETHOLOGY).

Traditionally, observational studies have required that summary judgments or behavioral records be made by trained raters whose independent judgments are later compared by means of reliability STATISTICS (Rosenthal, 1982). These statistics are used to estimate the degree of consensus or agreement in the raters' judgments. In most observational studies, the raters are unacquainted with the subjects in the research and have as little direct contact with them as possible. In fact, a common methodological ideal has been to use concealed raters or recording devices, and to collect the relevant data in the form of unobtrusive measures of the subjects' behavior. These unobtrusive measures are assumed to be nonreactive in the sense that subjects do not know that they are being studied and are therefore not motivated to alter their usual, naturally occurring behavior.

It should be noted, however, that some types of observational methods may encourage, or even require, substantial contact between the researchers and their subjects in order to permit a detailed exploration of the phenomena of interest. A prototypical example is the participant observation research that was pioneered by anthropologists and sociologists. And other, more recent types of observational research may require that the subjects be fully informed about the nature and purpose of the study – in many cases also requiring that the subjects be recruited to serve as self-raters who monitor and systematically record their own behavior.

These self-observation studies, which are increasingly used to sample people's day-to-day social relations and other activities, may be event-contingent, interval-contingent, or signal-contingent (Wheeler & Reis, 1991). Event-contingent studies require subjects to report their experience each time an appropriate event (e.g., a social interaction at least 10 minutes long) has occurred. In contrast, interval-contingent studies require the subjects to report at regular, predetermined intervals (e.g., by completing an interaction record at the end of each day), whereas signal-contingent studies require the subjects to report whenever signaled by the researcher (e.g., via telephone or electronic pager). Although self-observation studies can be criticized on the grounds that their data may be of questionable reliability and susceptible to various self-report biases, such studies do enable researchers to learn about events that could not easily (or ethically) be studied using direct observation by trained raters.

Recently, more integrative methods have emerged that seek to combine the best features of traditional observational studies (the reliable and nonreactive measurement of naturally occurring behavior) with the best features of self-observation studies (access to otherwise private events, including subjective thoughts and feelings). One such method – the unstructured interaction paradigm (Ickes & Tooke, 1988) – uses videotaping to capture the subjects' spontaneous interaction behavior for later analysis by trained raters. The same videotapes are also shown to the subjects themselves, as part of a stimulated recall procedure that occurs immediately after their interaction. This procedure facilitates the subjects' recall of the specific thoughts and feelings they had during the interaction itself and also enables them to make inferences about the thoughts and feelings of their interaction partners.

Despite the many advantages of observational methods, their use has been limited by their cost in terms of the time, labor, and other resources required. In most cases, the subjects' behavior must be monitored either by trained raters, electronic recording equipment, or some combination of the two. Coding the resulting data is often a laborious and time-consuming process, and the data analysis itself may be complicated by interdependence in the responses of interacting subjects. Finally, observational methods may require that the subjects' privacy be invaded, and may raise other ethical questions as well. *See also*: ETHOLOGY; FACIAL EXPRESSION OF EMOTION; METHODOLOGY; NONVERBAL COMMUNICATION; STATISTICS.

BIBLIOGRAPHY

Funder, D. C., & Colvin, C. R. (1991). Explorations of behavioral consistency: Properties of persons, situations, and behaviors. *Journal of Personality and Social Psychology*, *60*, 773–94.

Ickes, W., & Tooke, W. (1988). The observational method: Studying the interaction of minds and bodies. In S. Duck (Ed.), *Handbook of personal relationships: Theory, research and interventions* (pp. 79–97). Chichester: J. Wiley.

Rosenthal, R. (1982). Conducting judgment studies. In K. R. Scherer & P. Ekman (Eds.), *Handbook of methods in behavior research* (pp. 287–361). New York: Cambridge University Press.

Weick, K. (1968). Systematic observational methods. In G. Lindzey & E. Aronson (Eds.), *The handbook of social psychology* (2nd ed., Vol. 2, pp. 357–451). Reading, MA: Addison-Wesley.

Wheeler, L., & Reis, H. T. (1991). Self-recording of everyday life events: Origins, types, and uses. *Journal of Personality*, *59*, 339–54.

WILLIAM ICKES

**organizations** A commonsense definition of organizations would probably look something like this: "collective action in pursuit of a common mission, a fancy way of saying that a bunch of people have come together under an identifiable label . . . to produce some product or service" (Mintzberg, 1989, p. 2). For many people, especially in relation to their occupational organizations, this would suffice. Certainly most people do not spend a lot of time agonizing over the definition of organizations; their experience of them is immediate and direct.

For social scientists, however, the problem of definition is more important. If we want to describe and understand the effects of organizations on people's behavior, we need to know where to look. Even if we were only interested in "typical" organizations, we would still have to have some criteria for deciding which ones to include, and then we would risk missing some important phenomena that are characteristic only of "nontypical" organizations.

Part of the problem is in the way that terms like "organization" are used in everyday language, which tends to be less inclusive and technically precise than the way in which social scientists use them. Yet social scientists must be careful not to lose sight of the fact that it is everyday phenomena, and the experiences of ordinary people, that motivate their inquiries. So our definition must be capable of accounting for the ordinary usage and application of the term "organization." On the other hand, it must be capable of going beyond common usage, to indicate boundaries or limiting conditions.

The study of organizations is not uniquely within the domain of SOCIAL PSYCHOLOGY. Organizations, their structures, dynamics, outputs, artifacts, participants, and interrelations with the rest of society are also subject matter for sociology, anthropology, economics, politics, history, and business studies. Social psychology, however, has a distinctive contribution to make to the understanding of organizations, particularly in the field of *organizational behavior*.

ATTRIBUTES OF ORGANIZATIONS
There is probably no single feature or attribute, nor indeed a fixed point on any continuum, that unequivocally demarcates organizations from nonorganizations. Instead the attribution of "organization-hood" likely depends on a number of criteria, most of

which are continuously distributed rather than categorical in nature. From the social psychological point of view, we would like to be able to specify the features and attributes of "prototypical" organizations as construed by people in society.

In the absence of any systematic study of the way that the term *is* commonly used, we will begin with the observation that organizations are special kinds of social groups; i.e., all organizations are examples of social groups, but not all groups are examples of organizations. At minimum, members of organizations must be self-consciously aware of their inclusion in an organizational category, usually denoted by a name or title, although this does not require that they all have identical mental images of the group or its niche in society.

Awareness of membership, or SELF-CATE-GORIZATION, is critical in that we cannot, from a psychological point of view, attribute the effects of organizational life on behavior to the organization unless we can be sure that the organization is psychologically "real" to the subject in some way. However this alone does not distinguish organizations from other kinds of groups.

Mintzberg's (1989) commonsense definition, cited earlier, implies a deliberate association among people for the accomplishment of specific ends; that is, *intentional goal-directed interaction*. Organizational groups would not exist unless the people in them *chose* to affiliate for some purpose, and consequently organizations have higher goal-specificity than primary groups such as families or communities. Occupational organizations, for example, frequently articulate "mission statements" of their principal purposes and goals, both as a way of influencing staff, and as a means of defining accountabilities that are general enough to apply to *anyone* in the organization.

To this, we should add that most "typical" organizations also display a relatively high degree of *formal structure* compared with informal or casual groups, or with purposeful but unstructured groups like social movements. *Structure* is present to the degree that there are actual or perceived differences in group members' roles, status, rights, and so on, and that these are represented in members' expectations about themselves and others. People commonly speak in terms of "levels" or "grades" of vertical organizational structure, with strategic power and status concentrated at senior levels (e.g., the Board of Directors and possibly very senior managers), day-to-day responsibility for organizing people's work concentrated at middle levels (e.g., managers and supervisors), and responsiblity for actual operation and production concentrated at relatively low levels (e.g., line staff, operatives, shop-floor workers).

Horizontal structure is very often also present, in the form of specialized functions usually called Departments, with overlapping but distinct responsibilities within the organization. For example, the activities of civil servants working in the Treasury will be very different from those working in the Home Office or the Health Service, even though they may be on the same grade in the vertical hierarchy.

*Formality* is the extent to which structure is formally enshrined in some way (e.g., written documents, ceremonies) that transcends the personalities of specific individuals. In most occupational, military, and political organizations for example, there are formal charts depicting levels of responsibility and lines of authority, and written descriptions of the roles and responsibilities of each position on the chart. These templates serve as abstract representations of the "official" organization and its structure, independent of the specific personnel who fill the positions at a particular time.

Both structure and formality, like goal-specificity, are matters of degree. So too is a criterion proposed by Katz and Kahn (1978), building on the earlier work of Allport (1967). They conceive of organizations as systems of deliberate, interdependent social events, arranged to transform inputs into outputs. Furthermore these events are *cyclical*; that is, the organization repeatedly cycles through the input – transformation – output cycle. To survive, the output from the cycle must in some way replenish the energy and resources that are required to undertake another cycle. The labor of factory workers, for example, is arranged to transform energy and

raw materials into manufactured products, and these are sold or used to generate new inputs. Political organizations transform people's ideas, energy, and skills into policy, action, and influence, and thrive or fail on the basis of their ability to find the resources that enable this cycle to continue. The extent to which this cyclical aspect of organizational life figures prominently in ordinary thinking about organizations is unknown, but it seems likely that a group convened for a one-off input–output cycle (e.g., an experimental group in a laboratory experiment) would not earn the reputation of an "organization," no matter how self-aware, goal-directed, and formally structured it was.

The distinctive group qualities that we have described so far – goal-specificity, structure, formality, and cyclical input–output cycles – are independent of each other, and would seem capable of being combined in various ways to embrace commonsense definitions of organizations, as well as indicating possible limiting conditions. Additional criteria may be required. For example, the *size* of the organization, and the degree of *centralization* of its mechanisms of coordination and control, may play a role, although research on these matters is virtually absent. This is unfortunate since we are at risk of generating spurious or incorrect conclusions about organizational behavior if we examine only a subset of the subject matter.

CHALLENGES TO RESEARCH ON
ORGANIZATIONAL BEHAVIOR

Apart from the matter of definition, we face a number of other serious challenges to the discovery of general principles of behavior in organizations. Consider first, organizations as a whole. It will be clear from the foregoing that the subject matter is not contained by clear, crisp boundaries. Organizations are extremely diverse in form and function, and we do not at present have a unified or generative theory that enables us to describe this diversity within a single coherent framework, in spite of some useful attempts (Etzioni, 1975; Mintzberg, 1989; Scott, 1981). As society changes and evolves, it is also possible that new forms of social arrangements evolve, and our contemporary understanding of "organizations" changes, thus affecting the phenomena we study.

For example, a new model of corporate structure, consisting of temporary networks of companies coming together to exploit transient and changing markets, has been termed the "virtual corporation" (Byrne, 1993). While virtual corporations may not at the outset be the subject of self-categorization among the workforces of the individual companies that comprise them, there is no reason why they could not become so, thus creating a "superordinate" category within which their original organization fits. Another example is the Japanese *keiretsu* system of mutual investment and reciprocal trading relationships among huge networks of customers, suppliers, and shareholders. The financial interdependencies that underpin such networks inevitably exert an influence on the decisions and behavior of business people who hold a direct stake in the welfare of the network, as well as on the management and staff of member companies.

Furthermore, organizations are constantly adapting to shifting internal and external circumstances and their characteristics can change dramatically in a short time, as anyone who has tried to do research in organizations will attest. In the United Kingdom, for example, many state-owned industries were privatized in the 1980s, including water and electricity supply, the national airline, and the national telecommunication company. Privatization affected almost every aspect of organizational structure, function, and behavior in these industries, to the point of causing company directors in some cases to spend millions on programs aimed deliberately at changing staff and management practices, attitudes, and behavior.

Consider, next, individual members. Organizations exert only a *fractional* influence on the lives of their members. This is true with respect to the regulation of life both inside and outside the organization. Internally, even so-called *total institutions* (Goffman, 1961), such a prisons, asylums, and cults, rarely succeed in their ambitions completely to determine the thoughts, feelings, and actions of their constituents, however extreme the measures taken. Ordinarily, people have varying mental representations of an organization's purpose, structure, rules and so on, and of course only some of them can be "right" in relation to the mental images that organizational authorities would *wish* them to have. Furthermore, peoples' *activities* do not necessarily correspond to what they think they *should* be doing, no matter how accurate their understanding. Finally, unlike the parts of biological organisms or machines whose activities and fates are totally invested within the context of the whole, few people's lives are totally subsumed by organizations.

## ORGANIZATIONS AS RATIONAL SYSTEMS

Thus people's behavior is influenced and conditioned by many factors that can obscure regularities in organizational behavior. These difficulties are not insurmountable but they do require an approach which explicitly acknowledges that there are multiple vantage points, even within social psychology from which organizational behavior can be viewed and studied. Scott (1981), a sociologist, enumerates three. The first he labels the *rational system* perspective, which takes the organization as an abstract, formal, self-contained entity as a point of departure. Here the subject is the "official" organization, its "espoused theories," its formal structure, and how these are realized in behavior. This perspective has most in common with the present approach to the definition of "organization," which argues that the starting point for such a definition is to study the abstract conceptual structure of people's everyday application of the term.

## ORGANIZATIONS AS NATURAL SYSTEMS

Scott (1981) calls the second perspective the *natural system*, the actual behavior, perceptions, expectations, and feelings of members, and the extent to which these overlap or not with the formal organization and its abstract representation. The perspective shifts from organizations as entities, to the processes and actions of organizing. While this does not form part of the social psychological *definition* of organizations, it is the area of greatest activity in psychological research on organizational behavior: once we know where to look, this is what we must study.

As a branch of APPLIED SOCIAL PSYCHOLOGY, the study of organizational behavior has twin objectives: to attempt to understand and predict what people will think and do under different organizational conditions, and to attempt to improve organizational and individual life.

The general approach is to investigate the causes of variations in organizational behavior that are due to individual, group, and organization-level factors. Since true EXPERIMENTATION is often very difficult in organizations, field studies are the preferred methodology, although experimental methods are sometimes used. The range of specific topics covered in contemporary textbooks is similar to that found in general social psychology, and one will find sections devoted to SOCIAL COGNITION, COMMUNICATION, SOCIAL INFLUENCE, DECISION MAKING, MOTIVATION, GROUP DYNAMICS, CONFLICT, and so on (e.g., Jewell & Siegall, 1990; Szilagyi & Wallace, 1990).

At the individual level of analysis, topics often include theories of employee motivation, personality in relation to work, job design, and the implications of these for personnel assessment and selection, training, and the appraisal of work performance. An example of much current interest is investigation into the effects of individual involvement in goal setting and participation in decision making on organizational commitment, job satisfaction and productivity.

Topics at the group level of analysis commonly include group and team formation and development, work group dynamics, organizational communication and exchange processes, LEADERSHIP, intergroup relations, and group influences on decision making. The concept of cross-functional teamwork and communication, and its implications for customer satisfaction and organizational responsiveness, are topics currently commanding much attention.

At the organizational level of analysis, one finds discussions of organizational structure, design and administration, policy-making, change and development, health and safety, and industrial relations. Research on the design and implementation of employee performance appraisal systems, and the effects of centralized versus decentralized administration, performance-related pay and various kinds of measures of employee effectiveness, are topics that have commanded attention over the years.

ORGANIZATIONS AS OPEN SYSTEMS
The third of Scott's three perspectives is termed the *open system*, which explicitly considers the organization in relation to its external environment, as a "coalition of shifting interest groups that develop goals by negotiation ... (and is) strongly influenced by environmental factors" (Scott, 1981). This perspective underpins Katz and Kahn's (1978) influential text, *The social psychology of organizations*, in which they explicitly consider the implications of cycles of input–throughput–output activity, and interdependencies with environmental circumstances, for social behavior. Weick (1979) takes a more radical view, seeing "organizations" as the post-hoc inventions of bands of loosely-associated people whose activities are aimed at reducing uncertainty in the environment. The organization, its rules and ultimately, its self-conscious goals, are social constructions that arise as a consequence of organized activity, rather than being the rational precursors of organizational behavior.

The open system perspective, while widely acknowledged as useful, has not had the impact on theory and research that it could have been expected to. Thus for example, we know that events in people's private lives often influence behavior at work, but again there is no unifying or generative theory by means of which to organize specific detailed findings.

CONCLUSION
To summarize, we have argued for an approach to the definition of organizations that, while susceptible to quantification and operationalization, is based on ordinary use of the term, its scope and limits as a category of

social experience. Definitions which are purely technical, or those which are insightful but intuitive or speculative, are not necessarily wrong, but they threaten to bypass the interests of social psychology unless there is a mechanism for checking their relevance and completeness against ordinary social experience. We have indicated some of the parameters that might contribute to the attribution of "organization-hood" to some kinds of social groups, and we have sketched in barest outline the agenda of work for social psychologists and others that follows. Part of it consists in discovering more about the objective characteristics of organizations, their subjective interpretation, and their impact on individual and social behavior, with the proviso that we remain sensitive to change and variation in the social concept, "organizations." Another part consists of more systematic understanding of how to characterize organizations in relation to their environments, and the mutual influence of intraorganizational and extraorganizational factors on organizational behaviour.

See also: APPLIED SOCIAL PSYCHOLOGY; COMMUNICATION; CONFLICT; DECISION MAKING; EXPERIMENTATION; LEADERSHIP; MOTIVATION; SELF-CATEGORIZATION THEORY; SOCIAL COGNITION; SOCIAL INFLUENCE; SOCIAL PSYCHOLOGY.

BIBLIOGRAPHY

Allport, F. H. (1967). A theory of enestruence (event structure theory): Report of progress. *American Psychologist*, 22, 1–24.

Byrne, J. A. (1993). The virtual corporation. *International Business Week*, Feb. 8. New York: McGraw-Hill.

Etzioni, A. (1975). *A comparative analysis of complex organizations*. New York: Free Press.

Goffman, E. (1961). *Asylums*. Garden City, NY: Doubleday.

Jewell, L. N., & Siegall, M. (1990). *Contemporary industrial/organizational psychology* (2nd ed.). St Paul, MN: West.

Katz, D., & Kahn, R. L. (1978). *The social psychology of organizations* (2nd ed.). New York: Wiley.

Mintzberg, H. (1989). *Mintzberg on management*. New York: Free Press.

Scott, W. R. (1981). *Organizations: Rational, natural and open systems*. Englewood Cliffs, NJ: Prentice Hall.

Szilagyi, A. D., & Wallace, M. J. (1990). *Organizational behavior and performance* (5th ed.). Glenview, IL: Scott-Foresman.

Weick, K. E. (1979). *The social psychology of organizing*. Reading, MA: Addison-Wesley.

PHILIP M. SMITH

**other-total ratio** This is the number of people in the Other group (or outgroup) divided by the sum of the number of people in the Other group and the number of people in the Self group (or ingroup). For example, the Other-Total Ratio for a teacher in a class with nine students would be 0.90. The Other-Total Ratio quantifies the SALIENCE of the smaller group. As an individual's group gets larger, the Other-Total Ratio decreases and the individual experiences DEINDIVIDUATION. As an individual's group gets smaller, the Other-Total Ratio increases and the individual experiences SELF-AWARENESS. This Other-Total Ratio has been found to be a potent predictor of group behavior across a wide variety of contexts, including lynch mob atrocity (Mullen, 1986) and the self-focus of President Nixon in the *Watergate Transcripts* (Mullen, Chapman, & Peaugh, 1989).

See also: DEINDIVIDUATION; SELF-AWARENESS.

BIBLIOGRAPHY

Mullen, B. (1986). Atrocity as a function of lynch mob composition: A self-attention perspective. *Personality and Social Psychology Bulletin*, 12, 187–97.

——Chapman, J., & Peaugh, S. (1989). Focus of attention in groups: A self-attention perspective. *Journal of Social Psychology*, 129, 807–17.

BIRGIT KAUFMANN–BRYANT
BRIAN MULLEN

**outgroup homogeneity** Members of a group are seen as more homogeneous and similar to one another by an outgroup, relative to ingroup members' perceptions. For example, women are seen as more homogenously nurturant by males than by females. The effect has been shown to exist independently of ethnocentrism (the tendency to view ingroups more positively than outgroups). To measure the effect properly, it is necessary to obtain judgments from both ingroup and outgroup members of both target groups. The effect is defined as the interaction between subject group and target group in ratings of variability. Although main effects may exist (as when one group is seen as more variable, on average, by everyone), outgroup homogeneity can be identified over and above these. It is not possible to identify outgroup homogeneity if only one subject group (or one target group) is used. For example, if only male professionals are asked to judge what male professionals are like and what male plumbers are like, differences may be due either to group differences (plumbers are seen as less variable than professionals by everyone), or to outgroup homogeneity (plumbers are seen as particularly homogeneous by professionals, relative to plumbers' perceptions). It is impossible to tell which is the case in this "partial" design.

Two components of perceived variability have been identified, and at least under some conditions, the two are relatively orthogonal to one another (Park & Judd, 1990). The first component is the *perceived stereotypicality of the group*, which is assessed by the extremity of judgments of where the group stands on average on stereotypic and counterstereotypic attributes. Thus, males and females are both asked to judge how nurturant women are on average (or to estimate what percentage of women are nurturant), and how aggressive women are on average. Outgroup homogeneity predicts that males will see women as more nurturant than females see them, and as less aggressive than females see them. That is, the difference between the stereotypic and counterstereotypic estimates will be greater for male subjects than for female subjects. Thus the group is seen in a more stereotypic fashion by the outgroup relative to the ingroup. The second component is *perceived dispersion*, which is assessed by judgments of the spread of the group about the mean on

various attributes. Thus, males and females are both asked to estimate either the range or the standard deviation of women on the attributes nurturant and aggressive. Outgroup homogeneity predicts that males will judge women to have a smaller range and standard deviation on both attribute dimensions relative to the judgments of females. Thus the group is seen as less dispersed or diverse with respect to both stereotypic and counterstereotypic attributes by outgroup relative to ingroup members.

The cause, or best explanation, for the effect remains somewhat controversial. Some have argued that the effect derives primarily from differences in familiarity with ingroups and outgroups (Linville, Fischer, & Salovey, 1989). But the majority of the research examining the relationship between differences in familiarity and differences in perceived variability has resulted in null findings. Although individuals are typically more familiar with ingroups than outgroups, greater familiarity in and of itself does not appear to produce greater perceived variability. Moreover, at the level of individual subjects, differences in familiarity are not correlated with differences in perceived variability. Some research suggests that organizational properties of the knowledge structure are related to perceived variability. Specifically, the tendency to organize knowledge about a group at a subordinate level produces greater perceived variability. Moreover, information is more likely to be organized at the subordinate level by ingroup members than by outgroup members (Park, Ryan, & Judd, 1992). The mediational issue at this point, however, requires additional research and thought.

A number of moderators of outgroup homogeneity have also been proposed. There is some evidence that familiarity may moderate the magnitude of the effect across different groups. Thus, although at the individual subject level, differences in familiarity do not seem to predict differences in perceived variability, it may be that for pairs of groups, those with less familiarity will show the largest outgroup homogeneity effects. Thus men and women should produce a relatively small outgroup homogeneity effect, whereas white Americans and white South Africans should produce a relatively large effect. Competition also appears to moderate the effect, with heightened competition leading to larger outgroup homogeneity effects. Group size may also moderate the effect. There is some evidence that when the ingroup is a numerical minority, it is judged as more homogeneous than the outgroup (Simon, 1992). This may be due to processes suggested by SOCIAL IDENTITY THEORY, such that due to the numerical minority status, group members have a need to see themselves as unified and strong in the face of the outgroup. A similar effect may occur in the face of threats to the self-esteem of group members, independent of group size. (*See also* Ostrom & Sedikides, 1993.)

*See also*: SOCIAL IDENTITY THEORY.

BIBLIOGRAPHY

Linville, P. W., Fischer, G. W., & Salovey, P. (1989). Perceived distributions of characteristics of ingroup and outgroup members: Empirical evidence and a computer simulation. *Journal of Personality and Social Psychology*, *57*, 165–88.

Ostrom, T. M., & Sedikides, C. (Eds.) (1993). *Perceptions of group variability* [Special issue] *Social Cognition*, *11*.

Park, B., & Judd, C. M. (1990). Measures and models of perceived group variability. *Journal of Personality and Social Psychology*, *59*, 173–91.

——Ryan, C. S., & Judd, C. M. (1992). The role of meaningful subgroups in explaining differences in perceived variability for ingroups and out-groups. *Journal of Personality and Social Psychology*, *63*, 553–67.

Simon, B. (1992). The perception of ingroup and outgroup homogeneity: Reintroducing the social context. In M. Hewstone & W. Stroebe (Eds.), *European review of social psychology* (Vol. 3, pp. 1–30). New York: Wiley.

BERNADETTE PARK

# P

**pain** This is often described as a challenge or a mystery and indeed it is if one expects the subjective experience of pain to be directly proportional to the extent of the noxious stimulation and/or physical injury which is its source. This expectation of psychophysical parallelism is a natural product of our perceptual systems which are designed to generate veridical representations of external reality. Perceptions refer to the external world, and for pain this world consists of the injured surfaces and the aching muscles and joints of our bodies.

Pain, however, is more than a perceptual representation of an injurious event; it is an experience generated by a complex system that fuses sensory/perceptual experience with emotional reactions and with a variety of behavioral coping responses (*see* EMOTIONAL EXPERIENCE, STRESS AND COPING). There are two reasons why the complexity of the pain system makes its study of special value for psychological theory. First, the system embodies the properties of all complex motivational systems. Pain motivates behavior and learning, e.g., escape and avoidance learning in the rat, medical care seeking in humans, and chronic illness behavior which can be sustained by chronic pain in the absence of signs of injury in humans (Leventhal & Leventhal, 1993).

Second, the neurophysiological components of the system are reasonably well known, and provide both constraints and guides for psychological theories of the pain experience. For example, neuroanatomical studies reveal parallel conducting systems for the informational and emotional/motivational properties of noxious stimulation. Large $A$ fibers signal location and duration of noxious stimulation, while smaller $c$ fibers create generalized neural and autonomic arousal. The two systems are in constant interaction: the large $A$ fibers can gate the signals of the slower $c$ fibers

(Melzack & Wall, 1983), and endogenous opioids generated in the brain and spinal cord can modulate activity in the emotion/motivational tracks. It is clear, therefore, that the experience of pain involves the integration of complex interactions among a multicomponent physiological system. Pain includes locational, durational, qualitative (sharp, burning), and intensive attributes, combined with emotional and behavioral reactions.

The mystery and challenge of pain emerges for two simple, yet readily ignored reasons. First, the neurophysiological components of the pain system (e.g., endorphin production) respond to a wide range of psychological and social events, as well as to noxious stimuli. Second, emotional reactions, as well as covert and overt thoughts and instrumental coping responses elicited during a pain episode, feed back into the underlying system and become part of the unfolding episode. The result is substantial individual and situational differences in pain response to seemingly identical noxious stimulation, producing findings such as the differences in pain response among ethnic groups, athletes in contact versus noncontact sports, and cultures whose ideas about GENDER leaves women at work in the fields till the moment of labor while their husbands lie abed displaying the outward, emotional distress of childbirth.

A psychological model of the information processing system underlying pain experience is essential if we are to understand these individual and cultural differences and connect them to the neurophysiological description of the pain system. The input side of this system consists of attentional and interpretive mechanisms for processing or representing noxious stimuli. One view of the attentional mechanisms underlying pain experience is revealed in studies of hypnotic analgesia:

subjects given an analgesic instruction while in an hypnotic trance feel little or no pain when exposed to ice water: the combination (trance and analgesic instruction) immediately gates or blocks the pain experience from consciousness (Hilgard, 1975). In seeming contrast, pain can be reduced by monitoring the sensory features of a noxious stimulus as long as these sensations are not given a threatening interpretation. Monitoring, however, leads to a gradual and lasting reduction in pain due to the habituation of the emotional reaction to pain or to the enhancement of active efforts to cope with and manage pain, e.g., as in breathing and pushing during the latter stages of childbirth.

By altering the nature of the input, monitoring sensations appear to affect the output side of the system, i.e., the emotional and coping behavior elicited by pain. Therapies for pain management (Turk, Meichenbaum, & Genest, 1983) combine attentional, interpretive and behavioral skills training for the control and reduction of pain in a variety of clinical settings, e.g., dental pain, cancer pain, and pain of arthritis (see Special issue on pain, 1994). The success of these therapies may be partially due to the development of a sense of self-efficacy in controlling pain. Use of these procedures may produce endogenous opioids that are effective in reducing pain.

An important feature of the pain processing system is the formation of MEMORY structures capable of sustaining pain beyond the removal of the noxious stimulation. The precise mechanisms for the formation of chronic pain are unclear. Studies of phantom pain, i.e., pain in missing body parts (see Special Issue on Pain, 1994), suggest the presence of two types of memory systems: a conceptual memory that allows one to think and talk about pain episode, and a somatosensory (analogue) code of the region of the body that has been in pain. The somatosensory code, along with other perceptual and cognitive processes, can serve as a stimulus to the activation of emotional behaviors long after the disappearance of an offending stimulus. The presence of high levels of emotional distress, particularly DEPRESSION, at the time of an injury, may concentrate attention on an injured body part

and facilitate the formation of these somatosensory memories.

It is likely that many of the well-learned motor adjustments that are made to adapt to painful stimuli, e.g., automatic withdrawal reactions and expressive grimaces, can be elicited by external social cues which activate somatosensory codes. Questioning and expressing sympathy about pain by family, friends and medical practitioners, can both activate and reinforce behavioral and emotional components of the pain system, and these reactions may activate the somatosensory codes and the pain experience itself. In summary, the mystery and management of pain is clearly a social as well as a psychophysiological process. A full understanding of the production and reduction of pain awaits the further elaboration of the information processing system that underlies the pain experience.

See also: DEPRESSION; EMOTIONAL EXPERIENCE; GENDER; MEMORY; STRESS AND COPING.

BIBLIOGRAPHY

Hilgard, E. R. (1975). The alleviation of pain by hypnosis. Pain, 1, 213–31.

Leventhal, H., & Leventhal, E. A. (1993). Affect, cognition and symptom reporting. In C. R. Chapman & K. M. Foley (Eds.), Current and emerging issues in cancer pain: Research & practice, (pp. 158–173). New York: Raven Press.

Melzack, R., and Wall, P. D. (1983). The Challenge of Pain. New York: Basic Books.

Special Issue on Pain. (1994). Emotion and Motivation, 18.

Turk, D. C., Meichenbaum, D., and Genest, M. (1983), Pain and Behavioral Medicine. New York: Guilford Press.

HOWARD LEVENTHAL

**path analysis** The analysis of data, normally through ordinary least squares regression techniques, to estimate the coefficients of a class of hypothesized causal models. A path analytic model is a type of STRUCTURAL EQUATION MODEL in which all variables are assumed to be perfectly measured and standardized coefficients are estimated.

*See also*: STRUCTURAL EQUATION MODELING.
CHARLES M. JUDD

**peer popularity**  The general degree of liking that a person attracts in his or her peer network; this overlaps with but is distinct from FRIENDSHIP, since it is possible to be popular in the peer group but have few close friends, or to be relatively unpopular but have some close friends (*see* Berndt, 1984). Peer popularity is usually measured by sociometric techniques such as peer nomination (members of a group are asked to identify two to three liked individuals in that group) or peer rating (each member rates the likeability of each other member). Peer popularity is associated with psychosocial advantages, including well-being and social and educational attainment. It is also associated with certain characteristics, including SOCIAL SKILLS, above average intelligence, low aggressiveness, supportiveness, and attractive physical appearance. As with all correlational findings, these relationships could be interpreted in different ways: positive personal attributes could promote popularity or be enhanced by it. Developmental research indicates a continuing interaction, in that the quality of children's primary relationships (*see* ATTACHMENT) predicts their popularity in peer contexts, and experience of peer popularity in turn leads to more confident social behavior, which leads to further popularity (Erwin, 1993).

*See also*: FRIENDSHIP; SOCIAL SKILLS.

BIBLIOGRAPHY

Berndt, T. J. (1989). Friendships in childhood and adolescence. In W. Damon (Ed.), *Child development today and tomorrow* (pp. 308–31). San Francisco, CA: Jossey-Bass.

Erwin, P. (1993). *Friendship and peer relations in children*. Chichester: J. Wiley.

KEVIN DURKIN

**peer pressure**  An expression referring to overt or covert inducements from persons of comparable social status to adopt attitudes, behavior, or appearance in ways that one might not otherwise favor. The phenomenon is popularly associated with children and adolescents although, throughout life, most social organizations generate expectancies and standards which are supported by peer pressure. One of the principal social psychological mechanisms involved is SOCIAL COMPARISON, a process whereby individuals assess the extent to which they and their peers conform to group NORMS and criteria (*see* SOCIAL INFLUENCE). Peer pressure increases through childhood and peaks in early adolescence, but continues thereafter (*see* Durkin, 1995; Erwin, 1993). Developmentally, peer pressure is not monolithic: it does not apply to every aspect of behavior, and it is by no means the sole influence upon young people. In general, peer conformity is most pronounced with respect to matters of style, tastes, and appearance; with respect to substantive matters, such as IDEOLOGY and VALUES, stronger relations are found with parental measures. Finally, while peer pressure upon the young is often regarded as a negative process, at odds with adult priorities, this opposition is not found invariably and in some cases adolescents report pressure from peers to desist from negative behaviors (such as substance abuse; *see* ADDICTION).

*See also*: ADDICTION; IDEOLOGY; NORMS; SOCIAL COMPARISON; SOCIAL INFLUENCE; VALUES.

BIBLIOGRAPHY

Durkin, K. (1995). *Developmental social psychology: From infancy to old age*. Oxford: Blackwell Publishers.

Erwin, P. (1993). *Friendship and peer relations in children*. Chichester: J. Wiley.

KEVIN DURKIN

**perceived self-efficacy**  This is concerned with people's beliefs about their capabilities to produce performances that influence events affecting their lives. Self-efficacy beliefs regulate human functioning through four major processes. They include cognitive, motivational, emotional, and selection processes (*see* Bandura, 1986; Schwarzer, 1992).

A strong sense of efficacy enhances human accomplishment and personal well-being in diverse ways. People with high assurance in their capabilities approach difficult tasks as challenges to be mastered rather than as threats to be avoided. Such an efficacious outlook fosters intrinsic interest and deep engrossment in activities. They set themselves challenging goals and maintain strong commitment to them. They maintain a task diagnostic focus that guides effective performance. They heighten and sustain their efforts in the face of failure. They attribute failure to insufficient effort or deficient knowledge and skills which are acquirable. They quickly recover their sense of efficacy after failures or setbacks. They approach threatening situations with assurance that they can exercise control over them. Such an efficacious outlook produces personal accomplishments, reduces STRESS and lowers vulnerability to DEPRESSION.

In contrast, people who doubt their capabilities shy away from difficult tasks which they view as personal threats. They have low aspirations and weak commitment to the goals they choose to pursue. When faced with difficult tasks, they dwell on their personal deficiencies, on the obstacles they will encounter, and all kinds of adverse outcomes rather than concentrate on how to perform successfully. They slacken their efforts and give up quickly in the face of difficulties. They are slow to recover their sense of efficacy following failure or setbacks. Because they view insufficient performance as deficient aptitude it does not require much failure for them to lose faith in their capabilities. They fall easy victim to stress and depression.

People's beliefs about their efficacy can be developed by four main sources of influence. The most effective way of creating a strong sense of efficacy is through *mastery experiences* because they provide the most authentic evidence that one can muster what it takes to succeed. Successes build a robust belief in one's personal efficacy. Failures undermine it, especially if failures occur before a sense of efficacy is firmly established. The second way of creating and strengthening self-beliefs of efficacy is through the vicarious experi-ences provided by social models. Seeing people similar to oneself succeed by sustained effort raises observers' beliefs in their capabilities; observing others fail despite high effort lowers observers' judgments of their own efficacy and undermines their motivation. The impact of MODELING on perceived self-efficacy is strongly influenced by perceived similarity to the models. By their behavior and expressed ways of thinking, competent models also transmit knowledge and teach observers effective skills and strategies for managing environmental demands. Acquisition of better means raises perceived self-efficacy.

Social PERSUASION is a third way of strengthening people's beliefs that they have what it takes to succeed. Those who are persuaded verbally that they possess the capabilities to master given activities are likely to mobilize and sustain higher effort than if they harbor self-doubts and dwell on personal deficiencies when problems arise. To the extent that persuasive boosts in perceived self-efficacy lead people to try hard enough to succeed, they promote development of competencies and strengthen self-beliefs of efficacy.

People also rely partly on their somatic and emotional states in judging their capabilities. They interpret their stress reactions and tension as signs of vulnerability to poor performance. In activities involving strength and stamina, people judge their fatigue, aches, and pains as signs of physical debility. MOOD also affects people's judgments of their personal efficacy. Positive mood enhances perceived self-efficacy, despondent mood diminishes it. The fourth way of modifying self-beliefs of efficacy is to reduce people's stress reactions and alter their negative emotional proclivities and misinterpretations of their physical states.

A growing body of evidence indicates that human accomplishments and positive well-being require an optimistic sense of personal efficacy. This is because ordinary social realities are strewn with difficulties. They are full of impediments, adversities, setbacks, frustrations, and inequities. People must have a resilient sense of personal efficacy to sustain the perseverant effort needed to succeed. When people err in their self-appraisal they tend to overestimate their capabilities. This is a benefit rather than a cognitive failing to be eradicated. If efficacy beliefs always reflected only what people can do routinely they would rarely fail but they would not set aspirations beyond their immediate reach nor mount the extra effort needed to surpass their ordinary performances. Thus, the successful, the venturesome, the sociable, the nonanxious, the nondespondent, the social reformers, and the innovators take an optimistic view of their personal capabilities to exercise influence over events that affect their lives.

Many of the problems and challenges of life are not only individual but institutional, requiring collective effort to produce significant change. The strength of groups, organizations, and even nations lies partly in people's sense of collective efficacy that they can solve the problems they face and improve their lives through unified effort. People's beliefs in their collective efficacy influence what they choose to do as a group, how much effort they put into it, their endurance when collective efforts fail to produce quick results and their likelihood of success.

Many factors impede the development and exercise of collective efficacy. Modern life is increasingly regulated by complex technologies that most people do not believe they can do much to influence. Mazy bureaucratic structures in social systems create impediments to bringing desired changes to successful fruition. Effective action for social change requires merging diverse self-interests in support of common goals. Growing social fragmentation into separate interest groups, each exercising its factional power, gridlock collective efforts at change. To complicate matters further, life in the societies of today is increasingly affected by transnational interdependencies. The social mechanisms by which people can exercise reciprocal influence on transnational systems that affect their everyday lives are more intricate. Human influence, whether individual or collective, is a two-way process rather than flowing unidirectionally. People who have a strong sense of collective efficacy mobilize the efforts and resources needed to surmount obstacles to the social changes they seek.

See also: DEPRESSION; MOOD: IMPACT ON COGNITION AND BEHAVIOR; STRESS AND COPING.

BIBLIOGRAPHY
Bandura, A. (1986). *Social foundations of thought and action: A social cognitive theory*. Englewood Cliffs, NJ: Prentice Hall.
Schwarzer, R. (Ed.) (1992). *Self-efficacy: Thought control of action*. Washington, DC: Hemisphere.

ALBERT BANDURA

**person memory** This refers to knowledge people store about other people. Memories for people share some qualities with memories for objects: according to dominant current theories, they are stored in ASSOCIATIVE NETWORKS, are more retrievable after elaborate processing, are available in long-term memory, and are accessible in short-term memory (Fiske & Taylor, 1991) (*see* MEMORY).

Because people tend to be more involved when they encode information about others and because they apparently tolerate inconsistency less in people, person memory differs from memory for things. People try to form coherent impressions of other people, so they integrate others' behaviors more carefully. They abstract traits from related behaviors and link traits to each other in order to form a general impression (Srull & Wyer, 1989). People often attend more to behaviors that are inconsistent with their impressions, explaining them in terms of the overall impression. The elaborated processing of people's inconsistent behaviors can lead to better recall for this kind of information.

See also: MEMORY.

BIBLIOGRAPHY
Fiske, S. T., & Taylor, S. E. (1991). *Social cognition* (2nd ed., chap. 8). New York: McGraw-Hill.
Srull, T. K., & Wyer, R. S., Jr (1989). Person memory and judgment. *Psychological Review*, *96*, 58–83.

SUSAN T. FISKE
BETH A. MORLING

**person perception** A major component of SOCIAL PERCEPTION, person perception concerns the detection of people's "internal," psychological qualities, such as abilities, affordances, beliefs, emotions, goals, intentions, roles, personality traits, and veracity. Some theories focus on "external" stimulus cues specifying these qualities, and others focus on their construction by the perceiver. *See also*: SOCIAL PERCEPTION THEORY.

LESLIE A. ZEBROWITZ

**personal space** The distances and angles of orientation that people maintain from one another as they interact. Personal space is typically measured as the distance between individuals ("interpersonal distance"). Equating personal space to an invisible "bubble" is appealing but has been criticized because it implies that personal space has one distinct boundary and exists even when people are alone.

Because interpersonal cues change with increasing distances, personal spacing is one of several "boundary regulation" mechanisms that allow individuals to achieve and communicate desired levels of contact and intimacy (e.g., touch, visual, auditory, olfactory, and warmth cues vary in intensity; *see* NONVERBAL COMMUNICATION). E. T. Hall described four personal space zones that reflect varying degrees of cue exchange: intimate distance (0 cm–15 cm); personal distance (45 cm – 120 cm); social distance (1.2 m–3.5 m); and public distance ( 3.5 m). Research on personal space investigates varied phenomena, including liking/ATTRACTION, intrusions, cultural factors, PERSONALITY, and SEX DIFFERENCES (Aiello, 1987).
*See also*: ATTRACTION; NONVERBAL COMMUNICATION; PERSONALITY; SEX DIFFERENCES.

BIBLIOGRAPHY
Aiello, J. R. (1987). Human spatial behavior. In D. Stokols & I. Altman (Eds.), *Handbook of environmental psychology* (Vol. 1, pp. 389–504). New York: Wiley.

CAROL M. WERNER<br>IRWIN ALTMAN

**personality** The study of personality, known as personality psychology, is concerned with the intrinsic human qualities that lead to differences among individuals in their characteristic patterns of behavior. The scope of personality psychology is broader than the study of individual differences because it encompasses the whole person and the interface between the person and the world. As a result, personality is arguably one of the broadest fields within psychology in terms of the range of phenomena to be studied and the number of guiding theories from which to choose.

Personality is one of many words in psychology that has popular, nontechnical meanings that are close but not identical to its scientific definition. For example, in everyday language we may describe someone as having "A lot of personality," or "A strong personality." Such a description would lead one to expect a person who is more likely to shape the environment than be shaped by it. Indeed, the nontechnical use of the term personality often simplifies the concept to its most essential element: Personality is seen as an explanation for an individual's behavior that emphasizes the person as opposed to the situation (*see also* ATTRIBUTION THEORIES).

THE DIVERSITY OF PERSONALITY
THEORIES
Within the field of personality psychology there is a tremendous diversity of theoretical conceptions (Pervin, 1990). Personality theories are concerned with structure, process, and development: What is personality (structure), how does personality affect behavior (process), and why does this person have this particular personality (development)? These questions form the basis for distinguishing among the four broad classes of personality theory: Psychodynamic, humanistic, cogitive–behavioral, and trait theories. These approaches differ so fundamentally that they amount to distinct and sometimes conflicting paradigms within the field of personality psychology (Peterson, 1992).

*Psychodynamic Approaches*
This approach has its roots in medicine and psychiatry and illustrates the strong ties with

clinical psychology that characterize many approaches to personality. Freud originated the psychodynamic approach, which was subsequently developed in distinct ways by others such as Adler and Jung, and later by the neo-Freudians such as Horney, Fromm, and Erikson, who have incorporated a more social emphasis in their theorizing. According to the psychodynamic paradigm, people are complex energy systems whose behavior is ultimately determined by drives over which they have little conscious control. The psychodynamic approach is primarily concerned with explaining existing neurotic behavior patterns rather than predicting future behavior. It tends to be unsystematic and nonquantitative, and has therefore been criticized by personality psychologists of a more scientific persuasion.

### Humanistic Approaches

Humanistic personality theories such as those of Rogers, Maslow, May, and Laing are concerned with the uniqueness of individuals. Whereas psychodynamic theories are focused on past events, humanistic theories tend to look to the future – to what a person will become rather than what he or she has been. People are seen as existing in a state of flux in which there is capacity for personal growth leading ultimately to self-actualization. Behavior is conscious and purposive, but unpredictable because of constant personality change. Like psychodynamic approaches, humanistic ones are nonquantitative and nonscientific. Indeed, the notion of laws or generalizations that may be applied to all or most people is anathema to those who espouse a humanistic approach.

### Cognitive–Behavioral Approaches

In contrast to the psychodynamic and humanistic paradigms, the cognitive–behavioral paradigm incorporates many of the advances in the science of psychology. This approach is cognitive in the sense that it is recognized that reality is a subjective experience dependent on people's perceptions. Accordingly, people's thoughts about themselves and their worlds play an important role in determining their behavior. Kelly's construct theory is an extreme example of this cognitive position.

He defined personality as the set of constructs a person uses to understand and predict the world. Principles of human learning are incorporated in many cognitive–behavioral theories. For example, the idea that humans learn by modeling is an important element of Bandura's social learning theory. Rotter's social learning theory includes the concept that people develop a generalized expectancy about their degree of control over the relation between their behaviors and reinforcement. A common thread running through these theories is the emphasis on the interplay between the internal and the external, or the person and the situation.

### Trait Approaches

Trait theories adopt a quantitative approach to personality. It is assumed that individuals can be placed at points along dimensions that distinguish among people in much the same way that people can be classified on the basis of their physical dimensions such as height or weight (see TRAIT). Theories within the trait paradigm differ in their identification of the pertinent dimensions on which to classify people. However, they share the assumption that personality should be studied at the level of traits, which contrasts these approaches with more psychodynamic or humanistic ones where the emphasis is on studying the whole person rather than breaking people down into distinct constituents. In his influential personality text, Allport (1937) advocated traits as the elements of personality, and his definition of traits as structures within the individual that guide consistent behavior remains essentially unchanged today.

Much of social psychology is concerned with questions about external variables that affect people's behavior. For example, under what circumstances will people help, or fail to help, one another (HELPING BEHAVIOR), or follow orders to inflict pain on another (OBEDIENCE)? However, social psychologists have long recognized that individuals differ in their response to external variables, thus moderating the effects of social psychological manipulations (see INDIVIDUAL DIFFERENCES). Some people are more likely to help others regardless of the circumstances, and some people refuse to obey orders. Trait approaches have predominated when social psychologists have been concerned with personality variables because, via personality assessment, they provide the means to quantify the role of personality variables in social phenomena.

## ISSUES IN PERSONALITY PSYCHOLOGY

Below, is a summary of discussions concerning important issues that have dominated recent personality theorizing and research. Because of the dominance of the trait paradigm, most of these discussions have been conducted in the context of that approach.

### Is Personality Consistent?

Personality assessment depends upon the principle of behavioral consistency. Assessment techniques such as questionnaires or ratings provide a measure of supposedly stable traits that underlie consistent patterns of behavior. If behavior proved to be inconsistent, then personality assessment would be a pointless exercise. By the 1960s, evidence for the inconsistency of behavior appeared to have reached such proportions that a number of influential personality psychologists became disillusioned with personality and assessment. The arguments against personality assessment were presented most cogently by Walter Mischel. His influential review indicated that personality test scores were not good predictors of subsequent behaviors, and he coined the derisory term "personality coefficient" for the correlation of around 0.30 that was typically found between a trait measure and a behavioral measure (Mischel, 1968).

Despite, or because of, such criticism, personality psychology has flourished and faith in trait assessment has been restored. Personality psychology is richer theoretically and more sophisticated methodologically as a result of the innovations stimulated by its near demise. Impressive evidence of the stability of personality was discovered in longitudinal studies, and estimates of behavioral consistency doubled or tripled in size as a result of using more reliable, aggregated measures of behavior. More consistency and stability appear to be associated with broader units of analysis. Personality psychologists are experimenting with alternative units to traits, such

as goals, life tasks, and personal strivings, and also attend to the range of breadth encompassed by traits alone (Buss & Cantor, 1989). Stability of personality is no longer defined as consistency of specific behaviors across situations or over time but instead as coherent patterns of behavior reflecting consistent goals and values. It may even be necessary to define coherence afresh for each individual in order to take account of each person's understanding of the situation and the personal meaning of particular behaviors.

### What are the Major Personality Traits?

The trait approach is concerned with identifying the key dimensions along which individual differences in personality may be described. Within the trait approach, there have been two types of endeavors:

(1) the search for the overall structure of traits; and
(2) the investigation of particular traits.

The former, or multitrait, approach is concerned with identifying the precise number and nature of the key dimensions of personality, and has been the focus of considerable controversy. However, a consensus is gradually emerging that personality can be conceptualized in terms of five relatively distinct groups of traits (Digman, 1990; Goldberg, 1993):

(1) extroversion or surgency (e.g., talkative versus silent, dominant versus submissive);
(2) agreeableness (e.g., kind versus unkind, generous versus stingy);
(3) conscientiousness (e.g., hardworking versus lazy, reliable versus unreliable);
(4) emotional stability (e.g., relaxed versus tense, calm versus temperamental); and
(5) intellect (intelligent versus unintelligent, creative versus uncreative).

This structure has been obtained in both self-report and rating data, and for both adults and children. There are now questionnaires available that have been developed specifically to assess these five broad domains of personality.

The alternative approach to the investigation of personality traits, the single-trait approach, has been to focus on a particular trait by developing a reliable and valid measure and by exploring its origins and correlates. The popularity of this approach resulted in a proliferation of single-trait theories and numerous single-trait measures. The single-trait approach is useful for social psychology because it permits the investigation of the moderating effect of a particularly relevant aspect of personality on the behavior in question. For example, are individuals who have high levels of internal LOCUS OF CONTROL more likely to engage in political activities than those with external locus of control? Ultimately, it should be possible to unite single and multitrait approaches by locating single traits within the broader multitrait framework. Such a framework is valuable because it provides a starting point for investigations of the functional significance of personality. Having established the identity of the major dimensions of personality, it is possible to proceed to questions such as how they develop, and to what extent they determine behavior.

*To What Extent is Personality Inherited?*
As a result of several large-scale twin, adoption and family studies, and the application of sophisticated statistical techniques, it is now widely concluded that about 50 percent of the variance in self-report personality measures may be accounted for by heredity (Loehlin, Willerman, & Horn, 1988). This conclusion is not limited to particular aspects of personality but probably applies to all of the five broad personality domains. The evidence that personality is only partially determined by GENETIC INFLUENCES confirms that personality is also partially determined by experience. However, identifying the environmental determinants of personality is challenging. For example, intuitively, one would expect that family influences experienced by children raised in the same family would result in similarities among siblings' personalities. However, the evidence from studies of genetically unrelated adopted siblings suggests otherwise: the common experience of being raised in the same family appears to have little if any effect on personality (Loehlin et al., 1988). The influences of school and peer groups may be more important than the family in shaping personality.

Given that personality has a significant genetic component, some personality psychologists have begun to consider personality from an evolutionary perspective (Buss & Cantor, 1989). From the perspective of SOCIOBIOLOGY, it is possible to speculate about the natural selection of personality traits that would have been adaptive in ancestral environments. However, evolutionary accounts provide a distal explanation of human characteristics, at the expense of more proximal factors. Whether or not personality evolved in the Stone Age, people must adapt to their contemporary environment. In the study of personality, a major issue has been the importance of enduring personality traits versus more transient and immediate situational determinants of behavior.

*Is Behavior a Function of the Person,*
*or the Situation, or Both?*
This question is of particular interest to social psychologists, who are primarily concerned with the role of situational determinants of behavior. Social psychologists examine external variables in the environment that affect the behavior of individuals and groups. Because of individual differences, it is often necessary to examine also how the main effects of such manipulations are modified by, or interact with, personality variables. As a result of Mischel's critique, which emphasized the importance of situational over personality determinants of behavior, personality psychologists began to develop ways of investigating the combination of personality and situation, and the interaction between the two kinds of variables. Initially, interactionism was studied within an analysis-of-variance framework. However, person and situational variables are usually not strictly independent, which is a requirement for analysis of variance. In real life, people choose many of the situations in which they find themselves, and their presence will change those situations. Moreover, situations are typically defined in terms of the kinds of people and behaviors they attract and facilitate. Thus, persons and situations are inextricably linked.

While many social psychologists readily acknowledge that behavior is the result of complex interactions between person and situational variables that are themselves interdependent, for some the debate continues. Recently, Ross and Nisbett (1991) made a case for the power of situations, and claimed that much of the stability and predictability of social life is erroneously attributed to person variables as a result of the biases and heuristics of human judgment. Supposedly, one of the most pervasive of such biases, to which lay persons and psychologists alike are susceptible, is the FUNDAMENTAL ATTRIBUTION ERROR: the inflated belief in the importance of personality traits and dispositions.

### Is Personality a Construction?

The prevailing assumption in personality psychology has been that personalities, however conceived by any particular theorist, are located within individuals. Is this, however, yet another example of the fundamental attribution error? A contrasting position, derived from SOCIAL CONSTRUCTIONISM, is that personalities are created collectively by social processes and therefore exist interpersonally, not intrapersonally. The most extreme form of such a position would grant personality only a linguistic reality with no basis in actual behavior.

In a more moderate form, personality may be viewed as a social construction with a basis in reality (Hampson, 1988). According to this view, personality is composed of three elements: the actor, the observer, and the self-observer. The actor represents a combination of heredity and environmental influences, including a cumulative history of past experiences. Typically, the study of personality has been the study of the actor. The observer is another person or persons, actually present or imagined by the actor, who construes the actor's personality on the basis of information available, such as the actor's behavior, appearance, and possessions. The third element is the self-observer, or the capacity for self-awareness. This capacity permits the actor to imagine, and attempt to control, the personality that observers see. The three components function together to result in the construction of personality. The process of personality construction is complicated by the fact that actors and observers are really interpersonal roles that may be exchanged during the course of interaction or over the course of a relationship, and both roles can be conducted while one is also self-observing. Consequently, the process of personality construction is one of continuous negotiation between actors and observers.

One benefit of viewing personality as a construction is that it provides a framework within which to integrate topics that traditionally have been studied independently in personality and social psychology (Hampson, 1988). For example, PERSON PERCEPTION, attribution theories, and IMPRESSION FORMATION are all traditional topics in social psychology that are relevant to the construction of personality because they are studies of the observer's perspective. Similarly, issues in the study of the SELF, such as unitary versus multiple selves, and the public versus private aspects of self consciousness, become part of the construction of personality because they are studies of the self-observer. The study of IMPRESSION MANAGEMENT provides insights into the dynamics of personality construction.

### CONCLUSIONS

This overview has emphasized the links between personality and social psychology. However, many approaches to the study of personality are more closely allied with clinical than social psychology. The issues presented have been primarily concerned with personality structure and function within the normal range, and have emphasized cognitive–behavioral and trait approaches to personality. In contrast, psychodynamic and humanistic personality theories dwell on the more remarkable manifestations of personality. Whether abnormal personality can be understood with the same concepts and models that are applied to normal personality is a matter of debate, and depends in part on how personality abnormality, or DEVIANCE, is defined.

There are as many definitions of personality as there are theories of personality, and personality theories reflect the diversity of approaches to human behavior that are accommodated within psychology. Nevertheless, most approaches to personality share a common emphasis on the significance of the individual as the unit of analysis for both descriptive and explanatory purposes. Consequently, personality and social psychology have been viewed as contrasting approaches to the explanation of behavior, the former emphasizing the person, the latter the situation. However, this distinction has proved too simplistic, and the two disciplines are now recognized as being closely allied in the effort to understand social phenomena.

*See also*: ATTRIBUTION THEORIES; DEVIANCE; GENETIC INFLUENCES; HELPING BEHAVIOR; IMPRESSION FORMATION; IMPRESSION MANAGEMENT; OBEDIENCE; SELF; SOCIAL CONSTRUCTIONISM; SOCIOBIOLOGY.

BIBLIOGRAPHY

Allport, G. W. (1937). *Personality: A psychological interpretation.* New York: Holt, Rinehart & Winston.

Buss, D. M., & Cantor, N. (1989). *Personality psychology: Recent trends and emerging directions.* New York: Springer-Verlag.

Digman, J. M. (1990). Personality structure: Emergence of the five-factor model. *Annual Review of Psychology, 41,* 417–40.

Goldberg, L. R. (1993). The structure of phenotypic personality traits (or the magical number five, plus or minus zero). *American Psychologist, 48,* 26–34.

Hampson, S. E. (1988). *The construction of personality: An introduction.* London: Routledge.

Loehlin, J. C., Willerman, L., & Horn, J. M. (1988). Human behavior genetics. *Annual Review of Psychology, 39,* 101–33.

Mischel, W. (1968). *Personality and assessment.* New York: Wiley.

Pervin, L. A. (Ed.) (1990). *Handbook of personality: Theory and research.* New York: Guilford Press.

Peterson, C. (1992). *Personality.* New York: Harcourt Brace Jovanovich.

Ross, L., & Nisbett, R. E. (1991). *The person and the situation: Perspectives of social psychology.* New York: McGraw-Hill.

SARAH E. HAMPSON

**persuasion** Any COMMUNICATION intended to change the BELIEFS, attitudes, or behaviors of others is an instance of persuasion, an obvious example from everyday life being ADVERTISING. Social psychological research on persuasion typically examines the factors that determine the effectiveness of some form of communication in changing attitudes (*see* ATTITUDE CHANGE).

*See also*: ADVERTISING; ATTITUDE CHANGE; COMMUNICATION.

ANTONY S. R. MANSTEAD

**persuasive arguments theory** This theory was proposed to explain GROUP POLARIZATION. People become more convinced of their views by hearing novel arguments in support of their position. Through discussion, groups that already tend in a particular direction generate a pool of such arguments. Hence members' views become more extreme.

MICHAEL A. HOGG

**physical attractiveness** It is not certain what qualities comprise physical attractiveness, although it is positively related to facial prototypicality, perceived fertility, and approachability, as signaled by babyfaceness and facial expression. Attractiveness is typically defined by consensual judgments, and high interrater agreement is shown in judging facial attractiveness, regardless of the sex, age, or race of the judges or the judged. Even infants seem to concur with adults, preferentially looking at faces adults rate as attractive. Although this implicates a biological basis for physical attractiveness, there are also cultural contributions, evidenced by more agreement among judges from the same ethnic group.

Physical attractiveness produces ATTRACTION and a HALO EFFECT. Specifically, attractive people create more positive impressions, particularly of their social competence but also their adjustment, dominance, and intellectual competence. Impressions induced by attractiveness may influence SELF-FULFILLING PROPHECY effects, employment decisions, and

criminal justice outcomes. Effects may be stronger for females than males, and for those below than above average in attractiveness (Alley, 1988; Herman et al., 1986).
*See also*: ATTRACTION; SELF-FULFILLING PROPHECIES.

BIBLIOGRAPHY
Alley, T. R. (Ed.) (1988). *Social and applied aspects of perceiving faces*. Hillsdale, NJ: Lawrence Erlbaum.
Herman, C., Zanna, M., & Higgins, E. (Eds.) (1986). *Physical appearance, stigma, and social behavior: The Ontario symposium* (Vol. 3). Hillsdale, NJ: Lawrence Erlbaum.

LESLIE A. ZEBROWITZ

**political psychology** This field covers a broad interdisciplinary range of topics, including the study of public opinion, political leadership, political decision making, conflict and cooperation among groups, and judgments of fairness and justice. Political psychologists work within a variety of frameworks, including psychodynamic theory, behavioral decision theory, social cognition, attitude theory, game theory, and role theory. Some political psychologists make strongly reductionist assumptions about the possibility of explaining macrophenomena (such as war and peace) by invoking psychological attributes of individual participants. Other political psychologists view psychological constructs less as independent variables than as dependent variables (how people think and feel is a function of the macropolitical context). Most political psychologists, however, take a moderate interactionist position that recognizes feedback loops between psychological and political levels of analysis and assigns causal primacy to psychological processes in some situations and causal primacy to political processes in others.

Political psychology is not only theoretically pluralistic, it is methodologically pluralistic. In the study of groupthink in political leadership, for example, researchers have used case studies, comparative case studies, laboratory experiments and simulations, content analyses of both internal deliberations and public rhetoric, and expert observer $Q$-sort assessments (Tetlock, Peterson, McGuire, Feld, & Chang, 1992). In the study of intergroup conflict and bargaining and negotiation tactics, researchers have employed an equally broad range of methods plus computer simulations (Tetlock, McGuire, & Mitchell, 1991). There is a general consensus in political psychology that theory-derived hypotheses that can pass multiple methodological tests merit greater confidence than do hypotheses that receive support from only one methodological approach. There is less consensus, however, over how to handle mixed multimethod patterns of evidence in which one hypothesis receives support from one set of methods and a rival hypothesis receives support from another set of methods. Sharp disagreements lurk within the field over the usefulness of particular research methods. Some political psychologists defend qualitative interview and case study methods (a viewpoint especially influential among psychodynamic theorists and psychobiographers); others defend orthodox experimental techniques (a viewpoint especially influential among political cognition researchers); others defend mass surveys (especially influential among political scientists), and still others try to improvise compromise methodologies such as CONTENT ANALYSIS and systematic observer ratings that combine the advantages of both qualitative and quantitative approaches.

Political psychology is an inherently controversial field. Routine methodological and inferential decisions in other branches of social psychology can become the source of sharp debate in political psychology. Consider, for example, the well-known trade-off between Type 1 errors (rejecting the null hypothesis when it is true) and Type 2 errors (failing to reject the null hypothesis when it is false). Setting tolerance for Type 1 and Type 2 errors in research on symbolic racism (*see* PREJUDICE) or on the efficacy of deterrence becomes a consequential political act in itself. By operationalizing variables in particular ways, by selecting a particular sample, and by employing certain statistics and inferential procedures, the researcher in effect takes a stand on the relative importance of minimizing Type 1 versus Type 2 errors. In the context of work on symbolic racism, this stand requires weighing the risk of concluding that symbolic racism drives public policy preferences when it does not versus the risk of concluding that symbolic racism is a weak or irrelevant causal force when it is a potent variable. In the context of work on deterrence in international relations, this stand requires weighing the risk of concluding that deterrent threats work when they don't or do not work when they do (Tetlock, McGuire, & Mitchell, 1991). Political psychology can be easily politicized (Suedfeld & Tetlock, 1991).

Current areas of particularly active political psychological research include:

(1) the content, structure, and dynamics of public opinion;
(2) judgment and choice processes in leadership settings; and
(3) bargaining and negotiation processes.

## PUBLIC OPINION

Since the 1960s, this research area has been dominated by the thesis of minimalism (Converse, 1964). In this view, the average citizen's knowledge of politics hovers somewhere between nonexistent and fragmentary. People know remarkably little about both political candidates and issues. Indeed, survey researchers find that substantial segments of the public are often willing to express strong opinions on completely fictitious issues and unwilling to take stands on issues that are topics of actual controversy. Minimalism also maintains that only a small proportion of the general public relies on political abstractions like liberalism and conservatism in organizing their policy preferences. Positions on logically interrelated issues are frequently uncorrelated with each other. Finally, minimalism maintains that there is little longitudinal consistency in the views many people express on political issues. Opinions expressed a year ago are often weak predictors of the opinions expressed today.

A major trend in the past decade has been a systematic counterattack on minimalism (see Sniderman, Brody, & Tetlock, 1991). The critics maintain that people know more and have more well-articulated views than they

have been given credit for. The critics have also shown that it is deeply misleading to talk about the general public as an undifferentiated whole. People vary dramatically not only in how attentive they are to politics, but also in the particular political issues that engage them.

In addition to shifting emphases in the characterizations of mass publics, the last decade has seen important methodological innovations in research on public opinion. The traditional distinction between correlational survey studies and experimental laboratory studies has become increasingly arbitrary. As a result of computer-assisted telephone interviewing, survey researchers now frequently build complex factorial experiments into telephone interviews of representative national samples (see SURVEY METHODS). These experiments make it possible to assess the effects of question wording on support for particular policies, the power of various arguments and counterarguments to sway opinion on issues, and the role of prejudice and racism in driving particular policy preferences. The importance of these methodological innovations should not be understated. Researchers can now combine the internal validity advantages of experimental control and random assignment to experimental conditions with the external validity advantages of representative samples of the population. Political psychological questions that were once profoundly problematic to answer (e.g., Does the post-civil rights generation in American politics treat claims to government assistance differentially as a function of the race of the beneficiary?) can now be readily answered.

## JUDGMENT AND CHOICE PROCESSES IN LEADERSHIP SETTINGS

The study of political decision making, especially in international politics, has long been dominated by the rational actor model. In this view, policy makers are expected utility maximizers who are very skillful in sizing up the sources and distribution of power in a situation, dispassionately assessing their own strengths and weaknesses, and then fashioning a strategy that maximizes their influence within the power constraints of the situation.

The last 20 years of political psychological research have raised numerous challenges to this rational actor portrait of political decision making. Drawing heavily from research in cognitive and social psychology, researchers have depicted political decision makers as creatures of bounded rationality who rely on a variety of inferential shortcuts or HEURISTICS in appraising situations and choosing among options. These heuristics greatly simplify the decision making process and allow policy makers to make up their minds relatively quickly, easily, and confidently. The price of cognitive economy is, however, often steep. The political psychological literature now abounds with empirical reports of biases and errors in elite decision making. The following list conveys the general tenor of this literature:

(1) In assessing new situations, policy makers often look for relevant historical analogies or precedents. In this search, they use the AVAILABILITY and REPRESENTATIVENESS heuristics and are often content with the first analogy that comes to mind and resembles the case at hand reasonably well. Once they have identified an analogy, policy makers often use a confirmatory hypothesis-testing strategy and focus solely on the similarities between the preferred precedent and the current situation (downplaying or even ignoring important differences). The result is far too much faith in the diagnostic usefulness of simplistic analogies such as "Korea is like Munich"; "the Vietnam war is just like the Korean war"; "Afghanistan is a Soviet Vietnam"; "Nicaragua is a prospective American Vietnam"; "Lebanon is Israel's Vietnam"; "Angola is Cuba's Vietnam"; "Kampuchea is Vietnam's Vietnam"; and "Saddam Hussein is Hitler" (see George, 1980; Jervis, 1976).

(2) Students of political cognition not only claim that policy makers are too quick to jump to facile analogical conclusions, they also claim that policy makers are too slow to change their minds in response to contradictory evidence. Again, there is now a large literature that purports to demonstrate belief perseverance effects among elite decision makers: from British and French generals in World War I who were astonishingly slow to adapt to the realities of trench warfare, to American intelligence officers who were slow to recognize the significance of the Sino–Soviet split in the late 1950s and the Gorbechevian reforms in the Soviet Union of the late 1980s.

There are indeed intriguing parallels between the experimental literature on social cognition and many well-documented historical episodes of defective decision making. Social psychologists can take heart from the number of laboratory findings that appear to have real-world analogues. The critics of the rational actor model do, however, have their own critics. The skeptics note that we need to be careful in drawing inferences about how policy makers think from what they merely say. Policy makers may claim to believe a simplistic historical analogy because they believe it is politically advantageous to do so. In the late 1940s, for example, top American decision makers did not expect the Soviet Union to launch a Nazi-style blitzkrieg into Western Europe, but they often spoke in public as though they did hold such a belief (Breslauer & Tetlock, 1991). Such rhetoric was considered politically useful in mobilizing American public opinion behind NATO as well as in rallying support in Western Europe. The critics also note that it is problematic in international politics to label many judgments and decisions erroneous or biased. It is easy for academic observers – with the benefit of certainty of hindsight – to find fault with decision makers who had to work in real time and to cope with complex, contradictory, and ambiguous information. Unlike laboratory experiments where there are often well-defined right and wrong responses, we can rarely look back at history and say conclusively that policy makers should have changed their mind at one juncture rather than at another.

BARGAINING AND NEGOTIATION PROCESSES

In the post World War II period, deterrence theory has exerted enormous influence in

American academic and policy-making circles. The guiding notion here is that the most effective way to prevent war is by convincing would-be adversaries that one possesses the military strength necessary to counter aggression and the political will to deploy that military strength. Variants of this theory underlie doctrines of both nuclear and conventional deterrence.

Political psychologists have arrayed a variety of logical and empirical challenges to deterrence theory in the last 15 years. The most extreme critics have argued for replacing deterrence theory with some form of conflict spiral model which depicts the primary dangers to world peace arising not from appearing too weak and unthreatening, but rather from appearing too strong and threatening and, as a result, motivating the other side to arm and prepare itself politically and psychologically for war.

The more moderate critics have argued that both deterrence theory and conflict spiral theory capture important truths but are too simplistic. The most successful international negotiators rely on a broad range of influence tactics that include both threats and various forms of reassurance (Lebow & Stein, 1987). There is now a substantial research literature (including computer simulations, historical case studies, and laboratory experiments) that is consistent with the hypothesis that mixed-strategy negotiators (who rely on tit-for-tat, or fair-but-firm strategies) are indeed more successful than single-strategy negotiators in reaching mutually advantageous agreements (Downs, 1991).

Although a strong case can be made for blending deterrence and reassurance in a fairly wide range of bargaining and negotiation settings, the critics are themselves vulnerable to criticism. One problem is that some critics treat failures of deterrence in particular historical settings as automatic evidence of failures of deterrence theory (Lebow & Stein, 1987). Defenders of deterrence can argue, sometimes quite plausibly, that deterrence failed not because deterrence theory was wrong, but rather because policy makers poorly implemented the idea of deterrence. A second problem is that critics sometimes focus solely on deterrence failures. What social science theory would pass muster if we focused on only the disconfirming evidence? We need more balanced empirical treatments that attempt to identify the successes and failures of both deterrence and reassurance. A third problem is that critics of deterrence must often resort to highly speculative counterfactual reenactments of history to make their case that deterrence did indeed fail in particular cases. Political psychologists need to be candid about the limits of our current understanding. It is often unclear how historical conflicts such as World War I or the American–Soviet rivalry between 1945 and 1990 would have unfolded if policy makers had relied more on deterrence or reassurance at various times. The tendency to postulate counterfactual historical scenarios that unfold exactly as one's theoretical analysis would have predicted is epistemologically (if not ethically) analogous to doing laboratory experiments in which one observes what happens when the treatment effect is present, but one doesn't bother to run the no-treatment control condition and instead just makes up the data. The field will advance more rapidly if we acknowledge gaps in our understanding than if we try to conceal gaps with pseudo-evidence.

SUMMARY

Political psychologists tend to tackle problems of undeniable importance: the dynamics of public opinion (and, by implication, of democracy), the quality of decision making (and, by implication, the concept of political rationality), and the processes of intergroup conflict and conflict resolution (and, by implication, the causes of war and peace). The critical question, however, concerns not the importance of the questions, but rather the quality of the answers that political psychologists can provide. Here we see grounds for both pessimism (the frequent politicization of scientific debates) and optimism (the synthesis of survey and experimental methods, growing signs of multimethod convergence on key propositions).

*See also*: CONTENT ANALYSIS; HEURISTICS; PREJUDICE; SURVEY METHODS.

BIBLIOGRAPHY

Breslauer, G., & Tetlock, P. E. (Eds.) (1991). *Learning in U.S. and Soviet foreign policy*. Boulder, CO: Westview.

Converse, P. (1964). The nature of belief systems in mass publics. In D. E. Apter (Ed.), *Ideology and discontent* (pp. 206–61). New York: Free Press.

Downs, G. W. (1991). Arms races and war. In P. E. Tetlock, R. Jervis, P. Stern, J. L. Husbands, & C. Tilly (Eds.), *Behavior, Society, and Nuclear War* (Vol. 3, pp. 137–85). Washington, DC: Oxford University Press.

George, A. L. (1980). *Presidential decision-making in foreign policy: On the effective use of information and advice*. Boulder, CO: Westview.

Jervis, R. (1976). *Perception and misperception in international politics*. Princeton, NJ: Princeton University Press.

Lebow, R. N., & Stein, J. G. (1987). Beyond deterrence. *Journal of Social Issues, 43*, 5–71.

Sniderman, P. M., Brody, R., & Tetlock, P. E. (1991). *Reasoning about politics: Explorations in political psychology*. Cambridge: Cambridge University Press.

Suedfeld, P. & Tetlock, P. E. (Eds.) (1991). *Psychology and social advocacy*. Washington, DC: Hemisphere.

Tetlock, P. E., McGuire, C., & Mitchell, P. G. (1991). Psychological perspectives on nuclear deterrence. *Annual Review of Psychology* (Vol. 42, pp. 239–76) Palo Alto, CA: Annual Reviews.

—— Peterson, R., McGuire, C., Feld, P., & Chang, S. (1992). Assessing political group dynamics: A test of the groupthink model. *Journal of Personality and Social Psychology, 63*, 402–23.

PHILIP E. TETLOCK

**pornography** The term was originally used to refer to various descriptions of the lives of prostitutes. The term is derived from the Greek *pornographos*, which means "writing of harlots." Within and outside the legal community, the term pornography and obscenity have often been confused. The term *obscenity* has mainly referred to filthy and disgusting acts or depictions that offended people's sense of decency. Pornography was traditionally not viewed as obscene in the sense of shame and filth. Catholic canon law initiated a confusion of the two terms. For the most part, Victorian morality reinforced the confusion, and it seems unlikely that in the near future the two terms will become untangled even in the work of psychologists.

Unfortunately, even today the term "pornography" has been loosely applied to many forms of explicit (and even nonexplicit) depictions of SEXUAL BEHAVIOR. What depictions are considered pornographic depends to a large extent on the political and religious orientation of those who use these descriptions. For some, pornography is defined as depictions that elicit or are intended to elicit sexual AROUSAL. Others have suggested that the label should apply only to materials which include degrading and dehumanizing images of women, not simply if they are sexually arousing. And for still others the term refers only to those depictions which are violent in nature. Many individuals have stressed the idea that the dehumanizing aspect of pornography distinguishes it from material that may be termed "erotic."

When psychologists and others have studied the effects of pornography upon the viewer these definitional problems have also surfaced. As an aid in understanding the large amount of research in this area, researchers have recently grouped the variety of materials used in their research into a number of different categories. Rather than employing the term pornography directly, the research community tends to use the following categories in their discussions.

First, there is nonviolent, low-degradation sexually explicit stimuli. This material is most consistent with the definition of erotica (e.g., nonviolent, noncoercive, and nondegrading, but sexually explicit). Research by social psychologists, as well as reports by national commissions in both Great Britain and the United States, have concluded that exposure to this type of material has no antisocial impact on the viewer (e.g., increased AGGRESSION).

A second category is nonviolent, high-degradation sexually explicit stimuli. These materials are considered demeaning and degrading to women. Social psychological research investigating this type of material has generally concluded that there are limited effects from exposure. Linz (1989), after examining all the laboratory and correlational studies conducted with this type of material, concluded that individuals exposed to this form of pornography do not show any changes in antisocial attitudes or behavior. Other researchers, however, have found evidence for some negative attitudes towards women (*see Attorney General's Commission on Pornography*, 1986). This still remains one area where continued social psychological research, as well as theoretical processes to account for any findings, is needed.

The final category is violent pornography: This material depicts sexual coercion in a sexually explicit context. Research within the social psychological community has generally concluded that exposure to this form of pornography can lead to:

(1) increased aggression against women;
(2) calloused attitudes about rape; and
(3) heightened sexual arousal in individuals most prone to sexually aggressive behavior (*see* Malamuth & Donnerstein, 1984 and Donnerstein, Linz, & Penrod, 1987).

These categories do not completely classify the materials into mutually exclusive categories. They have, however, allowed researchers to understand better the influence which pornography has upon the viewer. It should be noted that in many research studies materials depicting similar themes and messages have also been employed. For example, research with graphically violent scenes of aggression against women which are not sexually explicit have been employed in many studies. This research has shown that individuals exposed to this form of MASS MEDIA can become desensitized to real violence against women. While some have considered these materials to fall under the heading of pornography, this has only led to further interpretational problems in the literature.

When policy makers who use this research (as well as other evidence) attempt to answer the question "does pornography have any positive or negative effects on individuals?",

the conclusion is no more straightforward than the definition of pornography. In the United States the 1970 *Commission on Obscenity and Pornography* basically concluded that pornography was not harmful to individuals. In 1986 the *Attorney General's Commission on Pornography* declared that most forms of pornography are directly related to crimes of sexual VIOLENCE. During the same year, the Surgeon General of the United States issued a report indicating that only violent or child pornography could be considered harmful. Reports in other countries (e.g., Great Britain, New Zealand, Canada) have also yielded mixed results. It is important to note that all these reports have been criticized in one way or the other for their findings, methodology, and recommendations.

The resolution of this conflict over the harmful effects of pornography may never be resolved, as both the term pornography and its potential effects are tied up in moral, ethical, emotional, and political debates. The issue, however, has become one of public discussion and continues to generate a great deal of research which should go a long way to resolving many of the issues.

*See also*: AGGRESSION; AROUSAL; MASS MEDIA; SEXUAL BEHAVIOR.

BIBLIOGRAPHY

*Attorney General's Commission on Pornography* (1986). Final report. Washington, DC: US Department of Justice, Government Printing Office.

Donnerstein, E., Linz, D., & Penrod, S. (1987). *The question of pornography: Research findings and policy implications*. New York: Free Press.

Linz, D. (1989). Exposure to sexually explicit materials and attitudes toward rape: A comparison of study results. *Journal of Sex Research*, 26, 50–84.

Malamuth, N., & Donnerstein, E. (Eds.) (1984). *Pornography and sexual aggression*. New York: Academic Press.

*Report of the Surgeon General's workshop on pornography and public health* (1986). E. P. Mulvey & J. L. Haugaard (Eds.). Washington, DC: US Department of Health & Human Services.

EDWARD DONNERSTEIN

**positive–negative asymmetry** Differences in information processing and judgments concerning evaluative positive and negative events. Thus, positive events may be judged as more frequent and normal, negative events as more distinctive, diagnostic and/or requiring explanation. Under conditions of uncertainty, potential losses may influence DECISION MAKING more than potential gains. *See also*: DECISION MAKING.

J. RICHARD EISER

**power** This can be defined from the perspective of the influencing agent, the target person, or third parties. From the perspective of the agent (who may be more or less powerful than the target person or the third party) power is the *production of intended effects* or, more generally, what he/she *can cause*. Behavior modification is typically framed from this perspective, as are most studies on compliance, SOCIAL INFLUENCE, and strategic SELF-PRESENTATION. The successful or unsuccessful experience of exercising power affects the agent's own SELF-ESTEEM, LOCUS OF CONTROL, sense of effectance or helplessness, and perception of the target person.

Kurt Lewin separated power from its effects by restricting power to the *possibility* of inducing forces, and by stressing the target person's *resistance*. Thus the influencing agent's power over the target person is the maximum force that the agent can induce on the target person relative to the latter's maximum resistance. When the agent is able to induce forces but unable to change the target person's behavior, he/she is said to have power over but does not actually influence or CONTROL the latter.

Forces can be induced on the basis of reward, coercion, referent, legitimate, or expert power. The first two power bases originate from the *agent's* ability to mediate respectively positive and negative outcomes for the target person. The others are derived from particular psychological states of the *target person*. When a person identifies with the influencing agent, this enables the agent to wield referent power over him/her. Legitimate power is based on the target person's internalized values regarding the rightfulness of the agent's position, and expert power is based on his/her respect for the agent's credibility. Informational power was later included in the typology to refer to the potential for influence based on the persuasive *content* of the agent's communication, as distinct from perceived communicator expertise. Changes resulting from information (as compared to the other five power bases) are socially independent and more stable; those resulting from reward or coercion are least stable because these two power bases require surveillance in order to be effective. The typology has been applied extensively in studies of power and LEADERSHIP in family and work settings, and now forms the basis of a power/interaction model of interpersonal influence (Raven, 1992).

Resistance to influence may also stem from *third parties*. In attempting to change the behaviour (e.g., food preference, productivity level) of members of a group, it is often more effective to involve the group in making decisions that modify the relevant group norm, rather than influencing individuals. This insight has been closely related to the notions of "ecological" manipulation and "group" pressure toward uniformity in group dynamics research.

SOCIAL EXCHANGE theory regards social interaction as an ongoing exchange of outcomes between interdependent participants. By controlling person Y's outcomes person X is able to alter Y's behavior. This ability (power) is proportional to the range of Y's outcomes that X can affect. After this point in their analysis of power, social exchange theorists who are psychologically oriented (but not sociologically oriented theorists – see below) drop the word power in favor of control. Three forms of outcome control have been distinguished and related to *dependence*: X's fate control over Y = Y's total dependence on X; X's behavior control over Y = Y's contingent dependence on X; X's contact control over Y = Y's relational dependence on X (i.e., Y is better off by remaining in the relationship with X than by opting for an alternative relationship). As in the case of Lewinian field theory and group dynamics, dependence analysis broadens the locus of power from the agent to the target person and third parties. It highlights the roles of human values, the awareness or freedom of alternative association, as well as their manipulation by influencing agents for keeping individuals in a state of emotional, ideological and social dependence (Ng, 1980).

Emerson (1962) deduced four mechanisms of *power change* from his sociological analysis of dependence in power relationships. In a husband–wife relationship, for example, a wife's (or husband's) dependence on her husband is positively related to her motivational investment in goals (outcomes) mediated by him, and negatively related to the availability of goals from alternative sources outside the relationship. From this analysis four mechanisms of power change are theoretically available to both partners. The wife, for example, may change the power relation by withdrawal (decreases motivational investment in him), power networking (searches for alternative relationships), status giving (increases his investment in her), or coalition formation (cuts off his alternative relationships). Power change in a supervisor–worker hierarchy is affected by the size of the existing power distance and by the bureaucratic principle of leader succession. Hierarchical and social structural aspects of power, as distinct from social status, have been much neglected in social psychology (Dépret & Fiske, 1993).

Power in social interaction is changeable and sequentially enacted between two or more parties. Research that establishes static relationships between power and other variables, but skips social interaction, is inadequate for tracking sequential enactment. Transition lists and sequential analysis are also needed, as are communication and discourse analyses for examining how the use of language may reflect, reproduce, constitute, or otherwise subvert power relationships (Ng & Bradac, 1993).

*See also*: CONTROL; LEADERSHIP; SELF-ESTEEM; SOCIAL INFLUENCE.

BIBLIOGRAPHY

Dépret, E. F., & Fiske, S. T. (1993). Social cognition and power: Some cognitive consequences of social structure as a source of control deprivation. In G. Weary, F. Gleicher, & K. Marsh (Eds.), *Control motivation and social cognition* (pp. 176–202). New York: Springer-Verlag.

Emerson, R. H. (1962). Power-dependence relations. *American Sociological Review*, 27, 31–41.

Ng, S. H. (1980). *The social psychology of power*. London: Academic Press.

—— & Bradac, J. J. (1993). *Power in language*. Newbury Park, CA: Sage.

Raven, B. H. (1992). A power/interaction model of interpersonal influence: French and Raven thirty years later. *Journal of Social Behavior and Personality*, 7, 217–44.

SIK HUNG NG

**prejudice**  This can be defined as the holding of derogatory *attitudes or beliefs*, the expression of *negative affect* or the display of hostile or *discriminatory behavior* toward members of a group on account of their membership in that group. In this light sexism, racism, homophobia, and ageism can all be considered as special cases of prejudice. Moreover, this definition does not confine prejudice to a cognitive or attitudinal domain, but acknowledges that it affects emotions and behaviors as well.

It is useful to conceive of prejudice as originating from three sources: sociopsychological motivations, cognitive processes, and sociocultural influences on individuals and their ingroups.

MOTIVATIONAL ORIGINS

Historically one of the first psychological explanations of prejudice was the FRUSTRATION-AGGRESSION (F–A) theory. This proposed that prejudice was a form of aggression resulting from the frustrations endemic in social life. Because it was thought that the true sources of those frustrations were either not easily identifiable or were powerful agencies capable of punishing direct aggression (e.g., the parents, the State) it was hypothesized that the resulting aggression was often displaced on to substitute and weaker targets, e.g., minority groups or "outsiders." For this reason the theory is often referred to as a "scapegoat" theory of prejudice. Much research has borne out the link between frustration and prejudice although not always unambiguously. Furthermore, it may not be plausible to assume that widespread levels of prejudice in a society can be attributable to the coincidentally high levels of frustration in thousands of individuals.

A related explanation is RELATIVE DEPRIVATION (RD) theory. In contrast to F–A theory which emphasizes *absolute* levels of frustration, RD theory holds that it is the discrepancy between what is expected and current experience which generates feelings of dissatisfaction or hostility. Translated to a group level, if the ingroup is perceived to be worse off than some outgroup it would normally expect to surpass, then a negative attitude (or prejudice) towards that outgroup is expected. Although the link between RD and ethnic prejudice has not been extensively researched, some supportive evidence exists.

Another theory which places much emphasis on the outcome of intergroup SOCIAL COMPARISONS is SOCIAL IDENTITY (SI) theory (Tajfel, 1981). According to SI theory people are motivated to perceive and attempt to achieve positive distinctiveness for their ingroup in relation to outgroups. The reason for this is that people's identity is thought to be implicated in the groups they belong to and it is assumed that they generally prefer a positive to a negative identity. Within the SI framework prejudice is most often manifested as biased attitudes or behaviors which have the effect of favoring the ingroup, and the conditions under which such ingroup bias is manifested have been extensively studied. Some of the most historically significant research both for the development of SI theory and for the understanding of intergroup discrimination were the MINIMAL GROUP experiments (Tajfel, 1981). These showed that the mere assignment of a person to an arbitrary social category was enough to generate behavioral discrimination in favor of that category, usually in the form of greater monetary rewards to fellow ingroup members than to those in the outgroup. Furthermore, such ingroup favoritism is found even when the self cannot benefit from the reward allocations. SI theory is now one of the most

influential perspectives for the understanding of intergroup relations and is currently the subject of much theoretical and empirical analysis and criticism.

The motivational approaches discussed thus far postulate social psychological processes underlying prejudice which are thought to be *generally* applicable. In contrast to these, one of the most well-known theories of prejudice holds that prejudice is especially characteristic of a certain personality syndrome – those individuals especially high in AUTHORITARIANISM. According to this psychodynamic view, authoritarian personalities are generated by a particularly harsh disciplinary regime in childhood, a result of which is an overdeferential orientation towards authority figures and a hostile and derogatory attitude toward minority or "foreign" groups. A further characteristic of authoritarianism is a cognitive style marked by the use of clearly demarcated categories and an intolerance of any overlap between them. Such a style was thought to facilitate the adoption and use of rigid group stereotypes in social judgments. Although this theory initially proved enormously popular, it is no longer widely regarded as providing, by itself, an adequate explanation of prejudice.

COGNITIVE FACTORS

An alternative approach concentrates on how the operation of normal human cognitive processes can account for prejudice. The focus of this approach has not strictly speaking been prejudice, but stereotypes. Prejudice, then, is implicitly equated to the consequences of holding negative stereotypes.

According to the cognitive perspective, biased perceptions of groups spring directly from mechanisms of information processing (*see* SOCIAL COGNITION, STEREOTYPING). People categorize and form stereotypes to simplify and reduce the amount of information to be dealt with. Processing strategies like those to select and categorize information and shortcuts like stereotypes economize on limited cognitive resources in complex tasks like social judgments and inferences. This view of the person has been termed the "cognitive miser" (Fiske & Taylor, 1991) and can be traced back to Allport (1954), whose definition of prejudice emphasized the faulty and inflexible generalizations which are often associated with the normal cognitive process of categorization. Tajfel (1981) later clarified the role of categorization, showing how these generalizations (stereotypes) are functional because they provide a well-differentiated, ordered, and predictable social environment. In particular, it was demonstrated that the categorization of stimuli leads to a perceptual enhancement of the similarities within categories and an exaggeration of the differences between them (Tajfel, 1981). These effects occur not just at a perceptual and attitudinal level but can also be observed in behavior.

*Consequences of Categorization*
Any process leading to the formation of a perception of attributes, beliefs, and expectancies differentially associated with two or more groups is a potential basis for stereotypes. Categorization is one such process because it involves a classification of the social world into groups along one or more criteria. These criteria, and other characteristics correlated with them, provide the starting content for group stereotypes. Some stereotypes may initially stem from veridical aspects of social reality, as in the case of the unequal distribution of different ethnic and gender groups in various social and economic roles. In their full-blown prejudiced form, however, such tiny "grains of truth" quickly become distorted beyond all recognition.

When people are themselves implicated in one of the categories a division into ingroup and outgroup occurs, and several effects follow. Ingroup members will be perceived as more similar to oneself than outgroup members, a form of ingroup stereotype (*see* SELF-CATEGORIZATION THEORY). Moreover, the perceiver sees him/herself and the ingroup as different from the outgroup. People also tend to prefer ingroup categories (containing the self) over outgroup categories. They are thus likely to show ingroup favoritism, even when the groups have been created on a fictitious basis (as in the minimal group experiments described above). This effect can be mitigated in cases of crossed categorization where

people share certain category memberships (e.g., white and black women). In this case, the simultaneous processes of within group assimilation and between group differentiation can cancel each other out, unless one of the category dimensions is particularly dominant (Vanbeselaere, 1991). A further effect of categorization is on people's attributions for social events. Negative outgroup behaviors tend to be attributed to internal causes more than negative ingroup behaviors; in contrast, positive outcomes or behaviors are attributed to internal causes less for the outgroup than for the ingroup (Hewstone, 1989).

Outgroup members are also perceived as similar to one another and as more homogeneous than one's own group. This is known as the OUTGROUP HOMOGENEITY effect. Outgroup members are thus more easily confused with one another than ingroup members and conceptualizations of the outgroup are usually less complex than those of the ingroup, so it is not difficult to see the outgroup as more extreme than the ingroup.

*Consequences of Distinctiveness*
What draws the attention of the perceiver can also create differential perception of groups. The SALIENCE of a person or group can result from properties of those stimuli in themselves (e.g., novelty, relevance for the task at hand), from aspects of the perceiver (e.g., his/her goals, moods, beliefs, or habitual category usage), or from features of the context (e.g., numerical properties of different groups) (Fiske & Taylor, 1991). Of particular interest for stereotype formation is the case of stimulus distinctiveness due to infrequency of occurrence. In the phenomenon of ILLUSORY CORRELATION the combination of two kinds of infrequency, membership in a minority group and performance of undesirable behaviors, becomes particularly distinctive and leads to the overestimation of the number of times minority group members engage in undesirable behaviors. This overestimation is called illusory correlation because the association between group membership and behavior desirability is perceived, but not real (Hamilton & Trolier, 1986). As a result the minority group is perceived in unfavorable terms, a typical manifestation of prejudice. Such

distinctiveness-based illusory correlations may not always be formed, however. They may be overridden when they run counter to other motives or to countervailing stereotypic expectancies.

*Stereotype Operation*
In the attempt to simplify the social world, the information to be sought out, attended to, processed, and recalled is selected by the perceiver, although not necessarily intentionally. Once formed, a category and its associated stereotypical traits can be activated by salient properties of the stimulus, perceiver, or situation. This can happen consciously when guided by the person's particular goals or needs of the moment. On the other hand, it can also happen automatically, as in priming, where cognitive structures activated frequently or recently affect encoding, interpretation, and storage of relevant stimuli (Fiske & Taylor, 1991). In addition, certain categories can become chronically accessible due to frequency of activation in one's social context, thus accounting for individual differences in the ease with which they are used. However produced, category activation determines what information is attended to. After this encoding, information is elaborated by means of interpretations, inferences, and attributions which will be recalled and retrieved to guide judgments and behaviors (Hamilton & Trolier, 1986).

What characterizes all of these effects is a tendency to confirm stereotypic expectancies. Thus, a news broadcast covering some event in which members of different groups are involved will tend to be interpreted or remembered in ways that are consistent with prior beliefs about those groups. Such a tendency can give rise to further prejudice if those prior beliefs are at all negative. Such expectancy-confirming strategies mean that prejudiced beliefs are often rather stable and resistant to change. Information inconsistent with existing stereotypes may be ignored or forgotten whilst consistent information is generally readily attended to, processed, and remembered, especially if those stereotypes are well established. A further compounding factor is the tendency for group members to recall selectively more negative information

and events associated with the outgroup than similarly negative aspects of the ingroup (Hamilton & Trolier, 1986).

Judgments of individuals – for example, in a job interview situation – can also be affected by stereotypic expectancies. The latter are most likely to be used when the unique information about a person is ambiguous, uninformative, or where the perceiver simply has too much information to deal with. On the other hand, on other occasions people are also motivated to form accurate impressions of others, especially when they have sufficient time and cognitive resources to do so, or when the individuating information is especially noticeable (Stangor & Ford, 1992). In the latter case, when the specific information available about the person is particularly diagnostic for the judgment being made then this can override the inference that might otherwise be drawn from the stereotype associated with that person's category membership.

A further important feature of prejudiced stereotypes is their ability to generate self-fulfilling prophecies. The perceiver's behavior is guided by his/her expectancies about the person to be encountered. In turn, this person may act in ways that confirm the original expectation. Thus, teachers in a school may label some children as less able than others. Their behavior towards those students may then be influenced by that label and, in turn, the students respond in ways consistent with their teachers' expectations, thus reinforcing the apparent validity of the initial classification. Such cyclical effects have been observed in a variety of domains including ethnicity and gender (*see* EXPECTANCY EFFECTS, BEHAVIORAL CONFIRMATION/DISCONFIRMATION, SELF-FULFILLING PROPHECIES).

*Covert Operation of Prejudice*
An additional reason for the popularity of the cognitive approach has been the difficulty in measuring prejudice in conventional overt ways in the light of new norms rejecting blatant discrimination. Thus, it is possible that prejudice as such has not decreased, but has simply become more subtle in its expression. New theories have emerged – particularly

in the USA – to account for the persistence of prejudice in this subtle way, variously labeled theories of "aversive," "modern," or "symbolic" racism (Dovidio & Gaertner, 1986). They have in common the assumption that prejudice stems from a conflict between an egalitarian ideology, the institutional inequality of most modern industrialized societies and anti-Black affect. In all three theories racist attitudes are justified on apparently nonracial grounds which allows Whites to maintain a nonprejudicial image, and the coexistence of different beliefs and feelings leads to ambivalence. To measure this more subtle orientation new scales have been developed and unobtrusive methodologies to study prejudice have gained in popularity (Dovidio & Fazio, 1992). Such techniques include subconscious priming of social categories, reaction times to measure the "fit" of conventional stereotypes with their categories, and paralinguistic cues in intergroup interactions.

SOCIOCULTURAL FACTORS

The approaches considered above locate the source of prejudice in processes within the individual. A third set of perspectives places more emphasis on the cultural context within which individuals and groups live. One such theory seeks to account for the origins of prejudice in the transmission of values and norms through the normal SOCIALIZATION agencies – e.g., family, media (Allport, 1954). On this view people become prejudiced by conforming to the attitudes and behaviors of those around them. Evidence for this perspective comes mainly from studies which find substantial regional or social class differences in prejudice, variations which seem readily attributable to variations in sociocultural norms. A second class of sociocultural theories locate the cause of prejudice between groups in the real interests or goals of those groups at particular moments in history (Sherif, 1966). Where these conflict – that is, where the groups feel they are competing for the same scarce resources such as employment or housing – relationships between the groups are likely to be negative. On the other hand, where groups' interests coincide, especially if they depend on each other for the satisfaction of joint goals, then prejudice should diminish (see CONTACT HYPOTHESIS). From this perspective intergroup attitudes are seen to reflect objective relations between groups, presumably motivated by instrumental considerations. Considerable empirical support for this approach has been forthcoming, although few studies have actually investigated relationships between different ethnic groups. Nevertheless, convincing analyses of interethnic attitudes from this realistic group conflict perspective do exist.

*Current Perspectives on Prejudice*

The study of cognitive processes in prejudice has emphasized the "automatic" operation of categorization and stereotyping, focusing on the capability of people's cognitive structures to control attention, encoding, storage, and retrieval of information. From this perspective little room is left for the "freedom" of the perceiver, who seems to be guided by stimuli in the environment interacting with cognitive structures. The most recent analyses, however, have qualified this view. In these there is renewed emphasis on the person's intentions in mediating the seemingly "automatic" processes underlying prejudice. Thus, the "cognitive miser" has become the "motivated tactician" who adopts cognitive strategies on the basis of goals, needs, and motives (Fiske & Taylor, 1991). As noted earlier, such motives could include the desire to form an accurate impression of others, the positive or negative interdependence between the person's group and others in a given sociocultural context, the need to maintain a positive ethnic group identity, and a concern with the entitlements of that group in relation to other groups. A complete understanding of prejudice therefore requires an integration of the motivational, cognitive, and sociocultural levels of explanation.

*See also*: AUTHORITARIANISM; BEHAVIORAL CONFIRMATION/DISCONFIRMATION; CONTACT HYPOTHESIS; HOMOGENEITY; RELATIVE DEPRIVATION; SELF-CATEGORIZATION THEORY; SELF-FULFILLING PROPHECIES; SOCIAL COGNITION; SOCIAL COMPARISON; SOCIAL IDENTITY; SOCIALIZATION; STEREOTYPING.

BIBLIOGRAPHY

Allport, G. W. (1954). *The nature of prejudice.* Reading, MA: Addison-Wesley.

Dovidio, J. F., & Fazio, R. H. (1992). New technologies for the direct and indirect assessment of attitudes. In J. M. Tanur (Ed.), *Questions about questions: Inquiries into the cognitive bases of surveys.* New York: Sage.

—— & Gaertner, S. L. (Eds.) (1986). *Prejudice, discrimination, and racism.* Orlando, FL: Academic Press.

Fiske, S. T., & Taylor, S. E. (1991). *Social Cognition* (2nd ed.). New York: McGraw-Hill.

Hamilton, D. L., & Trolier, T. K. (1986). Stereotypes and stereotyping: An overview of the cognitive approach. In J. F. Dovidio & S. L. Gaertner (Eds.), *Prejudice, discrimination and racism* (pp. 127–63). Orlando, FL: Academic Press.

Hewstone, M. (1989). *Causal attribution: From cognitive process to collective beliefs.* Oxford: Basil Blackwell.

Sherif, M. (1966). *Group conflict and cooperation.* London: Routledge.

Stangor, C., & Ford, T. E. (1992). Accuracy and expectancy-confirming processing orientations and the development of stereotypes and prejudice. In W. Stroebe & M. Hewstone (Eds.), *European review of social psychology* (Vol. 3, 57–90). Chichester: J. Wiley.

Tajfel, H. (1981). *Human groups and social categories: Studies in social psychology.* Cambridge: Cambridge University Press.

Vanbeselaere, N. (1991). The different effects of simple and crossed categorizations: A result of the category differentiation process or of differential category salience. In W. Stroebe & M. Hewstone (Eds.), *European review of social psychology* (Vol. 2, pp. 247–78). Chichester: J.Wiley.

RUPERT BROWN
LORELLA LEPORE

**primacy–recency effects** IMPRESSION FORMATION primacy effects occur when impressions are influenced more by early than later information about a person. The reverse, less common, recency effects can occur when later information supplants early information, when the impression concerns an unstable attribute, or when attention is focused on later information.

*See also*: IMPRESSION FORMATION.

LESLIE A. ZEBROWITZ

**priming** This explains how recently and frequently activated knowledge comes to mind easily. Priming occurs when an idea or category is both activated and applicable to a current situation. For example, people primed with hostile adjectives can interpret an ambiguous situation that follows in hostile terms. Priming only occurs when people are unaware that the prime is related to the way they interpret the situation. Priming can affect people's judgments, moods, and long-term interpretations of stimuli (Srull & Wyer, 1980).

Priming especially biases ENCODING rather than retrieval of information, so primes have the most impact if they precede the relevant stimulus. Priming occurs either because of the recency or the frequency of the category primed, depending on the decay of the prime and how often it was activated (Higgins, Bargh, & Lombardi, 1985) (*see also* ACCESSIBILITY).

REFERENCES

Higgins, E. T., Bargh, J. S., & Lombardi, W. (1985). The nature of priming effects on categorization. *Journal of Experimental Psychology: Learning, Memory, and Cognition, 11*, 59–69.

Srull, T. K., & Wyer, R. S., Jr (1980). Category accessibility and social perception: Some implications for the study of person memory and interpersonal judgments. *Journal of Personality and Social Psychology, 38*, 841–56.

SUSAN T. FISKE
BETH A. MORLING

**prisoner's dilemma** A mixed-motive reward structure in which each of two or more parties must choose between cooperation and noncooperation. The incentives are such that the parties are better off deciding not to cooperate; but, paradoxically, they are also better off if everybody cooperates than if nobody cooperates. Research on this phenomenon usually involves EXPERIMENTAL GAMES methodology.

*See also*: EXPERIMENTAL GAMES.

DEAN G. PRUITT

**procedural justice** When evaluating their outcomes in interactions with others people judge the fairness of the procedures by which those outcomes were determined. Procedural concerns are found to be distinct from outcome judgments. They have an especially strong impact on evaluations of authorities and institutions.

*See also*: SOCIAL JUSTICE.

TOM R. TYLER

**process-tracing** Methods used to investigate what information subjects seek before making a choice or decision, how this information is structured to form a cognitive representation of the decision problem, and how the information is used or processed in order to reach a decision or make a choice (*see* DECISION MAKING; Montgomery & Svenson, 1989). Three major methods of process tracing are the collection of verbal protocols, the use of information boards and the recording of eye movements.

Verbal protocols are either collected "on-line," while the subject is working on the task, or retrospectively. In the latter case subjects are asked about cognitive processes that took place in the past. Generally, on-line or concurrent verbal responses more accurately reflect individual information processing during the task (*see also* VERBAL REPORTS ON MENTAL PROCESSES). The protocols are interpreted to assess information use and information processing. The other two methods focus primarily on information search and the acquisition of information. Information boards require the decision maker to search explicitly for information about the available options. Typically, the subject is presented with a matrix containing information about the various alternatives in terms of the relevant attributes. The scores of each alternative are hidden, and the subject is asked to specify what information (s)he wants. The method assumes that information requested is attended to, encoded, and processed. This method is frequently used in applied areas such as consumer decision making. The third method, recording of eye movements, can be used in a variety of ways (e.g. fixation density, duration, and sequence of fixations) to assess information search and use. An essential requirement is that the items of information are limited and spaced far enough apart to allow precise measurement.

*See also*: DECISION MAKING; VERBAL REPORTS ON MENTAL PROCESSES.

BIBLIOGRAPHY
Montgomery, H., & Svenson, O. (1989). *Process and structure in human decision making*. Chichester: J. Wiley.

JOOP VAN DER PLIGT

**program evaluation** This seeks to describe and explain the implementation and consequences of social programs and their constituent parts. Evaluators nearly always follow some version of Scriven's (1980) general decision-theoretic logic that we apply below to social programs. His theory specifies that:

(1) a program should be clearly identified;
(2) criteria should be specified for determining its merit;
(3) competing programs should be identified with which the program under evaluation can be compared;
(4) data should be collected from each alternative for each criterion of merit; and
(5) the resulting data should be summarized to pronounce verdicts about the quality of program implementation, of program achievements, and of program standing relative to alternatives.

Scriven denies that evaluation should have anything to do with results being used to modify a program or otherwise influence social policy. Few evaluation theorists agree with him, and providing results that are more likely to be used is often added to Scriven's list of evaluation requirements (Cronbach, 1982).

Evaluation theorists differ in the emphasis placed on different aspects of a social program. Wholey (1983) stresses the need to analyze the *program plan* to:

(1) probe the adequacy of any substantive theory undergirding program design; and
(2) check whether the human, financial, and technical resources required for high-quality program implementation are on hand.

Patton (1980) emphasizes analysis of the program *as it is implemented*, judging it by whatever criteria are valued at local sites where a treatment is delivered rather than by the criteria that policy makers or officials at the central program headquarters favor. Local personnel usually want to describe what happens in their program to help improve it; they are usually less interested in pronouncing how good or bad it is or in learning about its standing relative to alternatives. Their knowledge needs lead Patton to prefer qualitative over quantitative methods, especially those methods that provide in-depth knowledge of a few sites under the assumption that such knowledge is particularly likely to be used because local staff have had a major role in setting the evaluation questions and because they enjoy constant contact with the evaluators.

Local program officials are usually less interested in assessing how successful their program is. Yet describing *how a program impacts on those who receive its services* is central in many evaluations (Reicken et al., 1974). Some impact evaluations assess how well a program has met its goals. But program goals are often unclear or contradictory; and anyway, unintended effects often occur. Hence, greater value is usually placed on describing program results rather than estimating how well goals have been met, though the former will often include the latter.

Describing program impacts is often linked to the advocacy of social experiments in one of two forms. The first involves assigning individuals *at random* to one treatment or another, including no-treatment control status (*see* EXPERIMENTATION). Such studies often examine promising ideas for new programs or promising modifications to existing ones as opposed to existing programs in their entirety. This is because random assignment is most feasible when the demand for program services exceeds the supply – or can be made to do so – and when it is both feasible and legal to withhold services from control groups. The results from such experiments are most interpretable in causal terms when the program has been well implemented, there are no differences in attrition between the various groups being contrasted, and there is no leakage of program details from one experimental group to another.

*QUASI-EXPERIMENTS* are like experiments in that one or more treatment groups are being contrasted, there is measurement of one or more outcomes, researchers know the time of treatment onset, and some form of a causal counterfactual baseline is available. But quasi-experiments do not have random assignment; instead, assignment to treatment is by self-selection or administrator choice. For evaluating existing programs as a whole, interrupted time-series designs are sometimes used if effects are likely to be produced quickly, there is a clear program starting point, and good quality archived data are on hand. Regression discontinuity designs are also used, but less often. These involve making a program available to everyone scoring above or below a program eligibility score – as happens when a financial means test is used for welfare eligibility or a score on a knowledge test is used for obtaining an academic scholarship. There is considerable pessimism about the quality of other quasi-experimental methods, particularly those that depend primarily on statistical techniques to adjust away all the initial group differences that routinely occur when individuals or communities self-select themselves into programs or when administrators judge who needs or deserves a program. The best advice then is to increase the number and specificity of causal implications indicating program effectiveness – e.g., by introducing more comparison groups and conducting data analyses under many different assumptions about how program participants differ from nonparticipants.

Cronbach (1982) asserts that the predominant need in evaluation is for *explanations of why a program has performed as it has* because such explanatory knowledge is relevant to many other programs, sites, and populations than those already studied. He believes such extrapolation is best achieved by identifying the forces a program sets in motion that are causally responsible for observed results. This presumes that program effectiveness (or lack thereof) has already been demonstrated. But Cronbach asserts that scholar-evaluators place so high a value on reducing uncertainty about program effectiveness that causal explanation is slighted, even though nonscholars in the policy-shaping community mostly want to know about the transfer of evaluation results to new sites, persons, and programs as opposed to reducing even more uncertainty about whether a program is effective. To identify causal mediating processes Cronbach prefers formal causal modeling or the qualitative methods used by ethnographers, journalists, and historians.

Perhaps the key question practising evaluators face is how to combine Wholey's pre-evaluative work, Patton's focus on program implementation, Reicken et al.'s primacy on descriptions of a program's impacts, and Cronbach's call for better causal explanation. All these types of questions should be asked if an evaluation is to be truly comprehensive (Rossi & Freeman, 1989). But budgets, time lines, and program maturity levels do not always permit this; nor do the priorities of particular evaluation funders or the parochial method preferences of some evaluators. Consequently, evaluation theorists now struggle to be explicit about the conditions under which each of the emphases and preferences noted above deserves priority (Shadish, Cook, & Leviton, 1991).

A related issue is how evaluations can be conducted so as to increase the likelihood that results will be used to modify programs and otherwise inform policy debates. Instrumental usage occurs when results are used as direct inputs into creating new programs or reconfiguring existing ones. This is sometimes found at the central program level, but is not widespread. Enlightenment usage occurs when evaluation results change the conceptual frameworks of members of the policy-shaping community, such as when evaluation findings help policy makers to see that a particular social problem is more or less serious than they thought, or to see that a particular type of program design is often better than some other type. Enlightenment usage is more common. But since it is an unintended byproduct of evaluation activities and does not depend on evaluation alone, it is difficult to design evaluations with enlightenment in mind. In a pragmatic field like evaluation, the dilemma is that the more common form of usage based on enlightenment is less easily planned for, while the less common form based on instrumental usage is more easily built into evaluation goals.

*See also*: EXPERIMENTATION.

BIBLIOGRAPHY

Cronbach, L. J. (1982). *Designing evaluations of educational and social programs*. San Francisco, CA: Jossey-Bass.

Patton, M. Q. (1980). *Qualitative evaluation methods*. Beverlly Hills, CA: Sage.

Reicken, H. W., Boruch, R. F., Campbell, D. T., Caplan N., Glennan, T. K., Pratt, J. W., Rees, A., & Williams, W. (1974). *Social experimentation: A method for planning and evaluating social intervention*. New York: Academic Press.

Rossi, P. H., & Freeman, H. E. (1989). *Evaluation: A systematic approach* (4th ed.). Beverly Hills, CA: Sage.

Scriven, M. S. (1980). *The Logic of Evaluation*. Inverness, CA: Edgepress.

Shadish, W. R., Cook, T. C., & Leviton, L. C. (1991). *Foundations of program evaluation: Theories of practice*. Newbury Park, CA: Sage.

Wholey, J. S. (1983). *Evaluation and effective public management*. Boston, MA: Little, Brown.

THOMAS D. COOK

**propaganda** The term refers to oversimplified or distorted messages, which advocate a partisan political or doctrinal position. The term generally has a pejorative connotation, for propaganda denotes messages which aim to persuade recipients without opening up debate or encouraging independent thinking. Thus, propaganda is often contrasted with messages which seek to inform or educate. Conventionally, propaganda is distinguished from commercial ADVERTISING by virtue of its political or doctrinal content. However, social psychologists tend to assume that propaganda and advertising operate according to similar principles of persuasion.

Concerns about the effectiveness of propaganda echo earlier fears about RHETORIC. From classical times, it was feared that skilled speakers would be able to use "base rhetoric" to make weak arguments appear more persuasive than stronger ones. Throughout the twentieth century there have been similar fears that political leaders, who have mastered the arts of propaganda, will possess unlimited powers over audiences. Two factors have contributed to the growth of these fears. First, the development of mass communication enables today's political figures to transmit their messages more directly and to greater audiences than ever before (see MASS MEDIA). Second, there have been fears that the sciences of persuasion, including psychology, have developed to such a degree of sophistication that mass audiences could be helplessly manipulated by unscrupulous politicians, skillfully adopting the principles of persuasion for their own purposes. The successes of Nazi propagandists, using radio, film, and photography to spread patent untruths, fueled such fears. Theodor Adorno (1978), having witnessed the effectiveness of Nazi propaganda in prewar Germany, speculated that Hitler may have beaten Freud to discovering the secrets of the unconscious mind.

Some of the early experimental work in the social psychology of PERSUASION arose directly from the efforts by the United States government to produce propaganda. During World War II, Kurt Lewin was commissioned by the Department of Agriculture to discover how to persuade people to eat offal. Carl Hovland, working for the War Department's Division of Education and Information, conducted a series of experiments investigating how to present propaganda to raise the morale of troops. After the war, Hovland continued his research program at Yale University, systematically seeking to discover the most persuasive ways of presenting information.

The Yale studies, and the hundreds of experiments which they spawned, demonstrated that there was no single technique of presentation which would guarantee successful persuasion. Much depended on the content of the message, the perceived credibility of the speaker and the characteristics of the audience (see ATTITUDE CHANGE). Hovland had addressed the question whether simple, one-sided propaganda would be more effective than two-sided propaganda: i.e., whether it was better only to mention the position which was being propounded, or whether opposing arguments should be mentioned, in order to be criticized. The results were inconclusive: sometimes one-sided propaganda was more effective, especially when directed at ill-informed audiences, but at other times two-sided propaganda could be more persuasive. One finding, which has been confirmed in many circumstances, is that audiences who suspect that they are being manipulated by propagandists tend to react against the message (see REACTANCE). Accordingly, successful propagandists are likely to deny that their own messages are "propaganda" and will try to dismiss rival messages as "mere propaganda."

Recently, the ELABORATION LIKELIHOOD model, propounded by Petty and Cacioppo (1986), has tried to make sense of the early, disparate findings. This model proposes that there are two ways in which persuasion tends to occur. When people are directly concerned in an issue they are likely to pay attention to the content of messages. In these circumstances, crude, one-sided propaganda may even be counterproductive, if informed audiences are spurred into thinking of counterarguments. However, when people are less interested, they may be swayed by peripheral factors rather than by the message itself. In these circumstances, the attractiveness of the presenter and, more generally, the attractiveness of the style of presentation, may be more crucial than the informational content of the message (for reviews, see Pratkanis and Aronson, 1991).

During the Korean War, fears that communists were successfully "brain-washing" captured American prisoners of war prompted the US War Department to sponsor research, aiming to discover how to withstand enemy propaganda. Perhaps the most notable social psychological theory to emerge from the desire to discover the principles of resisting propaganda was McGuire's Inoculation Theory. McGuire (1964) claimed that people were at their most vulnerable if they did not possess "counterarguments" to repel the messages of propaganda. If exposed to "enemy propaganda" in small doses, they could build up the necessary counterarguments which would later equip them to resist a concentrated onslaught of propaganda.

Much early research in the social psychology of propaganda assumed that the content of a message could be distinguished from its style of presentation. Indeed, classical rhetorical theory made the same assumption. However, a number of contemporary theorists have claimed that in the era of electronic communication such a distinction cannot be maintained. In much contemporary advertising – whether commercial or political – the style has become the message. Jamieson (1988) has suggested that political campaigns today, especially US presidential elections, are about the character of the candidates. Thus "communicator credibility" does not refer to ability of the speaker to deliver a distinct message in a trustworthy way: instead, credibility is the message itself which the candidates are seeking to convey. Certainly, much political propaganda, especially that which uses the visual media, resembles commercial advertising, in that it aims to transmit an image or a style, rather than a particular argument in the traditional sense.

This points to an important issue in the social psychology of propaganda. One should not expect universal laws of persuasion, because the techniques of propaganda are related to their sociohistorical contexts and to the media of transmission. Techniques which might have been effective in the early part of this century may appear crudely dated, even obvious, in the postmodern age of electronic communication.

*See also*: ADVERTISING; ATTITUDE CHANGE; IDEOLOGY; MASS MEDIA; REACTANCE; RHETORIC.

BIBLIOGRAPHY
Adorno, T. W. (1978). Freudian theory and the pattern of fascist propaganda. In A. Arato & E. Gebhardt (Eds.), *The essential Frankfurt School reader* (pp. 118–37).
Jamieson, K. H. (1988). *Eloquence in an electronic age*. Oxford: Oxford University Press.
McGuire, W. J. (1964). Inducing resistance to persuasion. In L. Berkowitz (Ed.), *Advances in experimental social psychology* (Vol. 1, pp. 1–46). New York: Academic Press.
Petty, R.E., & Cacioppo, J.T. (1986). *Persuasion and communication*. New York: Springer-Verlag.
Pratkanis, A., & Aronson, E. (1991). *The age of propaganda*. New York: W. H. Freeman.

MICHAEL BILLIG

**prosocial behavior** This represents a broad category of interpersonal actions that are positively evaluated with reference to cultural or social standards. It is defined by one's REFERENCE GROUP as behavior that is generally beneficial to other people and the ongoing social system. HELPING BEHAVIOR, ALTRUISM, and COOPERATION are normally examples of prosocial behavior.
*See also*: COOPERATION AND COMPETITION; HELPING BEHAVIOR.

JOHN F. DOVIDIO

**prospect theory** Kahnemann and Tversky (1979) developed this theory to remedy the descriptive failures of SUBJECTIVELY EXPECTED UTILITY (SEU) theories of DECISION MAKING. Prospect theory attempts to describe decisions under uncertainty, and has also been applied to the field of social psychology. Applications tend to focus on phenomena such as persuasion, negotiation, and bargaining. Most of these applications concern the effects of "framing" (the way decision alternatives are presented) on preference and choice (*see* e.g., Neale & Bazerman, 1991; Tversky & Kahneman, 1986). Like SEU theories, prospect theory assumes that the value $V$ of an option or alternative is calculated as the summed products over specified outcomes $x$. Each product consists of a utility $v(x)$ and a weight $\pi(p)$ attached to the objective probability $p$ of obtaining $x$. Thus the value $V$ of an option is $\Sigma_i \pi(P_i)v(x_i)$. Both the value function $v$ and the probability weighting function $\pi$ are nonlinear. The two functions are not given in closed mathematical form but have a number of important features. The decision weight $\pi(p)$ is a monotonic function of $p$ but is not a probability. Small probabilities are overweighted, and large probabilities are underweighted. To give an example of the latter; an objective probability of 0.50 receives less weight than 0.50 (*see* figure 1). Although $\pi(0) = 0$ and $\pi(1) = 1$, the probability weighting function is not well behaved near the end points. Extremely low probability outcomes can be exaggerated or ignored entirely. Similarly, differences between high probability and certainty is either neglected or accentuated. According to Kahneman and Tversky, this is so because people find it difficult to comprehend and evaluate extreme probabilities.

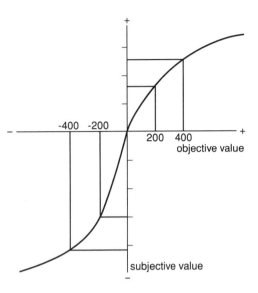

Figure 2. Prospect theory: hypothetical value function.

The value $v$ is defined in terms of gains and losses relative to a psychologically neutral reference point. The value function $v(x)$ is S-shaped: concave in the region of gains above the reference point, convex in the region of losses (*see* figure 2). Thus, each unit increase in gain has less and less value as gain increases; the subjective difference between gaining nothing and gaining £200 is greater than the difference between gaining £200 and gaining £400. Finally, the value function is steeper for losses than for gains. This implies that losing £200 is more unpleasant than gaining £200 is pleasant. In other words, a given change in the status quo hurts more as a loss than it pleases as a gain. A later, extended version of prospect theory employs cumulative rather than separable decision weights (Tversky & Kahneman, 1992).

Two phenomena played an important role in the formulation of prospect theory: the certainty effect and the reflection effect. The first refers to the tendency to give excessive weight to outcomes that are considered certain, as compared to outcomes that are "merely" probable. Thus, most people would prefer a certain win of £300 as compared to

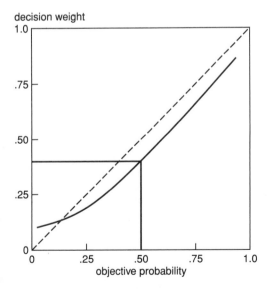

Figure 1. Prospect theory: hypothetical probability weighting-function.

an 80 percent chance to win £400, although the latter has a higher expected utility. The reflection effect is the tendency to reverse the preference order between two alternatives depending on their sign (losses or gains). For instance, if presented with a choice between a sure loss of £200, or a 50 percent chance of a loss of £400 and a 50 percent chance of no loss at all, most subjects will prefer the uncertain alternative. This risk-seeking preference is in sharp contrast with preferences when the choice is between a sure gain of £200, or a 50 percent chance of a gain of £400 and a 50 percent choice of no gain at all. In this case most subjects will prefer the certain, risk-avoiding alternative. Both the above results violate expected utility theory.

An important aspect of prospect theory is the so-called "editing phase" preceding the evaluation of options and the final choice. The function of this stage is to organize and reformulate or "frame" the options in order to simplify the subsequent stages (evaluation and choice). The frame that a person adopts is partly determined by the external formulation of the problem, and partly by other factors such as experience, habits, and norms. The most frequently studied framing effect concerns the reflection effect discussed earlier. Inducing subjects to adopt a gain frame when choosing between a gamble and a sure thing tends to result in a risk-avoiding preference. Inducing subjects to adopt a loss frame, on the other hand, tends to result in a risk-seeking preference. In a classic example of this effect subjects are asked to imagine that the United States is threatened with an unusual disease, expected to kill 600 people. A choice has to be made between two alternative interventions with different consequences:

If Program A is adopted, 200 people will be saved,

If Program B is adopted, there is 1/3 probability that 600 people will be saved, and 2/3 probability that no people will be saved.

Most subjects (72 percent) opted for "Program A" in the gain frame. Another group was presented with the same problem in a loss frame:

If Program C is adopted, 400 people will die,

If Program D is adopted, there is 1/3 probability that nobody will die, and 2/3 probability that 600 people will die.

In this group, the majority (78 percent) chose "Program D." This effect is most pronounced when subjects are presented with a gamble and a sure thing (when both the value function and the probability weighting function predict the described changes in preference). A further test of the reflection effect is to investigate whether subjects actually *adopt* the frame that corresponds with their preference (i.e., a gain frame when preferring the certain option, a loss frame when preferring the uncertain option). Research on this issue has obtained mixed findings, leading Slovic, Lichtenstein, and Fischhoff (1988) to conclude:

(1) that people seem to have considerable difficulties in introspecting the judgmental processes involved in framing; and

(2) that some natural frames (usually those concerning more familiar decision problems) may be so robust that it is difficult to lead subjects to adopt a different frame.

A more substantive theory focusing on how framing works in particular situations is needed to provide the answer to this question. Social psychological research in this area tends to focus on the effects of framing on attitudes and choice. Research in this area deals with issues such as medical decisions, preventive health behavior, and consumer behavior (*see* e.g., Plous, 1993).

*See also*: DECISION MAKING.

BIBLIOGRAPHY

Kahneman, D., & Tversky, A. (1979). Prospect theory: Analysis of decision under risk. *Econometrica*, 47, 263–91.

Neale, M., & Bazerman, M. H. (1991). *Rationality and cognition in negotiation*. New York: Free Press.

Plous, C. (1993). *The psychology of judgment and decision making*. New York: McGraw-Hill.

Slovic, P., Lichtenstein, S., & Fischhoff, B. (1988). Decision making. In R. D. Atkinson, R. J. Herrnstein, G. Lindzey, & R. D.

Luce (Eds.), *Stevens' handbook of experimental psychology* (Vol. 2): *Learning and Cognition* (pp. 673–738). New York: Wiley.

Tversky, A., & Kahneman, D. (1986). Rational choice and the framing of decisions. *Journal of Business, 59,* S251–78

——(1992). Advances in prospect theory: Cumulative representation of uncertainty. *Journal of Risk and Uncertainty, 5,* 297–323.

JOOP VAN DER PLIGT

**prototypes** A prototype is an abstract mental representation of the central tendency of members of a category (Cantor & Mischel, 1979; Mervis & Rosch, 1981). Category members vary in typicality, with the prototype being the most typical instance of a category. A prototype abstracts many members of a category; people may never actually encounter an instance identical to their prototypes.

Prototype models of CATEGORIZATION hold that categories do not require particular necessary and sufficient attributes for membership. Membership in a category is determined by family resemblance, which increases as an instance shares more features with other category members.

Prototype models contrast with exemplar models, which hold that people remember concrete instances of category members and that they assess category membership by comparing a new instance to a sample of remembered exemplars.

Prototypes resemble SCHEMAS but differ from them in important ways. In theory, a prototype fills in all known attributes, whereas schemas omit irrelevant features. And unlike prototypes, schemas have internal organization specifying links between features.

*See also*: CATEGORIZATION; SCHEMAS/SCHEMATA.

BIBLIOGRAPHY

Cantor, N., & Mischel, W. (1979). Prototypes in person perception. In L. Berkowitz (Ed.), *Advances in experimental social psychology* (Vol. 12, pp. 3–52). New York: Academic Press.

Mervis, C. B., & Rosch, E. (1981). Categorization of natural objects. *Annual Review of Psychology, 21,* 480–500.

SUSAN T. FISKE
BETH A. MORLING

**proxemics** This term was coined by the anthropologist E. T. Hall to refer to the human use of space as a specialized extension of culture. More commonly, proxemics has been equated with the study of interpersonal distance and arrangement cues as basic components of social behavior.

*See also*: NONVERBAL COMMUNICATION.

MILES L. PATTERSON

# Q

**quasi-experimental designs** Research designs that mimic true EXPERIMENTATION, but that do not employ random assignment of subjects, or involve treatments whose application is not under the control of the researcher, are labeled quasi-experimental. Owing to these limitations, causal interpretation of results is problematic. Such designs provide useful information, however, and are commonly employed in applied field settings (Cook & Campbell, 1979). Common quasi-experimental approaches involve time-series analyses, and the study of nonequivalent groups. In time series experiments, repeated measurements are interrupted by an external event (e.g., yearly convictions for murder may be studied before and after imposition of the death penalty). Variations in trends describing the data before and after the interruption are the focus of study. In nonequivalent groups designs, treatment and control subjects are generally constituted from intact groups (e.g., school classes). Differences cannot be attributed unambiguously to the treatment in the absence of randomized assignment. Initial differences attributable to selection, or differences in treatment susceptibility, may be responsible for results. In quasi-experimentation, controls specific to the peculiarities of the context are developed to facilitate interpretation.

*See also*: EXPERIMENTATION.

BIBLIOGRAPHY

Cook, T. D., & Campbell, D. T. (1979). *Quasi-experimentation: Design and analysis issues for field settings*. Chicago: Rand-McNally.

WILLIAM D. CRANO

# R

rape   As a criminal offense, rape is typically defined in Western countries as unlawful, i.e., extramarital sexual intercourse with a woman, forcibly and against her will. The problem of rape and other forms of sexual VIOLENCE against women has received growing attention over the last two decades, both in public awareness and by psychologists of different disciplines. While clinical psychologists have been concerned primarily with the immediate and long-term effects of sexual violence on the victim and with the development of appropriate intervention strategies (Koss & Harvey, 1991), social psychologists have concentrated on the antecedents and consequences of sexual violence in the context of social norms and practices.

In trying to identify *antecedents*, i.e., factors that facilitate the occurrence of sexual violence, the majority of research has focused on the *offender*. A variety of interlocking causes has been suggested that induce men to commit sexually violent acts against women, such as emotional deficits in early SOCIALIZATION, biological processes including the operation of evolutionary principles, exposure to PORNOGRAPHY, and exposure to a social environment which accepts interpersonal violence (Marshall et al., 1990). Moreover, aspects of social climate, such as widely shared GENDER stereotypes and the portrayal of sexual violence in the media have been shown to contribute to the problem of sexual violence. To avoid sampling biases, studies of convicted rapists have been complemented by large-scale investigations seeking to identify self-confessed, nonincarcerated sexual attackers.

In studying the *consequences* of sexual violence, the emphasis has been on the *victim* and on *others* who learn about and react to her plight. Two major issues have been explored as part of a social psychological perspective on rape. The first refers to the reactions to victims of rape by members of the police, the legal system, and the medical profession. This concern arose out of widespread public dissatisfaction with the way these institutions responded to the needs of victims of sexual violence. Systematic investigations demonstrating biased perceptions and unfavourable evaluations of rape victims by police officers, judges, and jurors have played a significant role in prompting institutional changes to achieve a more sympathetic treatment of victims. The second line of inquiry refers to the SOCIAL PERCEPTION of rape victims in society at large. This research has its roots in the conceptual framework of ATTRIBUTION THEORY where the question of when and why there is a tendency to attribute responsibility to victims of rape has generated a large body of evidence (Krahé, 1991). It was shown that certain victim characteristics, such as low social status, higher number of sexual partners, prerape behavior that is at odds with female role prescriptions, are linked with higher ATTRIBUTIONS OF RESPONSIBILITY to the victim (and often correspondingly lower responsibility attributed to the attacker). At the same time, individual differences between observers have been found in the sense that individuals with a more traditional sex-role orientation or with a greater readiness to accept "rape myth" as true tend to assign more responsibility to victims of rape. SEX DIFFERENCES, with men attributing more responsibility to victims than did women, were found regularly, but not pervasively in the literature. Both institutional and individual responses to victims of rape frequently amount to the experience of "secondary victimization" which can seriously impair the process of coping with sexual assault.

Recent years have also seen a rapid increase in research on a particular type of sexual assault occurring in dating or acquaintance relationships (Parrot & Bechhofer, 1991). Prevalance studies revealing that *date rape* is a large scale problem in adolescents' and young adults' sexual relationships have been complemented by evidence on predictors of date rape (e.g., PEER PRESSURE) as well as perceptions of responsibility for date rape (e.g., as a function of who paid for the dating expenses). A related issue refers to the problem of marital rape which most countries still do not assign the status of a criminal offense (Russell, 1990).

Altogether, social psychological research has illuminated important aspects of the social causes and consequences of sexual violence which can contribute to a more sympathetic treatment of rape victims, both at an institutional and an interpersonal level. However, a review of the social psychological research on rape would be incomplete without mentioning an important restriction: The evidence available to date has been collected almost exclusively by North American researchers. In an area so sensitive to the norms, values, and social practices of a particular society, there is an urgent need for more widespread investigations in other parts of the world.

*See also*: ATTRIBUTION OF RESPONSIBILITY; ATTRIBUTION THEORIES; GENDER; PORNOGRAPHY; SEX DIFFERENCES; SOCIAL PERCEPTION; SOCIALIZATION.

BIBLIOGRAPHY

Koss, M. P., & Harvey, M. R. (1991). *The rape victim: Clinical and community interventions*. Newbury Park, CA: Sage.

Krahé, B. (1991). Social psychological issues in the study of rape. In W. Stroebe & M. Hewstone (Eds.), *European review of social psychology* (Vol. 2, pp. 279–309). Chichester: J. Wiley.

Marshall, W. L., Laws, D. R., & Barbaree, H. E. (Eds.) (1990). *Handbook of sexual assault*. New York: Plenum.

Parrot, A., & Bechhofer, L. (Eds.) (1991). *Acquaintance rape: The hidden crime*. New York: Wiley.

Russell, D. H. (1990). *Rape in marriage*. Bloomington, IN: Indiana University Press.

BARBARA KRAHÉ

**reactance**  Psychological reactance is a motivational state directed toward the reestablishment of one or more behavioral freedoms (Brehm, 1966; Brehm & Brehm, 1981; Wicklund, 1974). Reactance theory assumes that people believe themselves to have specific behavioral freedoms – e.g., to read *War and Peace*, to eat beef, to be against taxation. When the freedom to engage in behavior X is threatened or taken away, the person experiences psychological reactance, which urges attempts to regain the threatened or lost freedom. Because the most direct form of reestablishing a freedom is to exercise it, reactance will frequently result in an intensified form of the behavior whose freedom has been threatened. However, whether or not one engages in the behavior, reactance will add to the motivation to engage in the behavior and thereby increase its attractiveness to the individual.

What constitutes a threat to, or elimination of, a freedom is perceived pressure not to exercise it. Typically, threats or eliminations of freedom occur through SOCIAL INFLUENCE attempts. For example, a parent tells a child not to drink alcohol, a supervisor tells a worker to stop talking on the job, or a law is passed that prohibits smoking in public places. How much of a threat each of these attempted influences is depends on the targets' perceptions of pressure. The child may comply completely, indicating that the freedom has been eliminated, but nevertheless see alcohol consumption as highly attractive, reflecting reactance; the worker may see a lot of pressure and because of the resulting reactance talk even more; and smokers may see no threat in the new law, believing that it cannot be enforced, feel no reactance, and show no change in behavior. Considerable research has shown that intensified behavior or increased preference for the behavior whose freedom has been threatened is directly proportional to the magnitude of the pressure to comply (*see* Brehm & Brehm, 1981).

The magnitude of reactance and its effects are also a direct function of the importance of the freedoms threatened or eliminated. What makes a freedom important is its unique instrumental value for the satisfaction of important motives. If a person has a great desire to be an oncologist and the only way to do so is go to medical school, then the freedom to go to medical school will be very important. The effect of importance has been demonstrated in several experimental projects (Brehm & Brehm, 1981).

Reactance will increase not only with importance of the freedoms but also with the number or proportion threatened or eliminated. One may go to a Chinese restaurant, for example, with the belief that one can eat beef with peapods, Szechuan pork, chicken with hoisin sauce, and stir-fried vegetables. To learn that two or more of these dishes were not available would create more reactance than to learn that only one was unavailable. Similarly, if one wanted a Szechuan dish and one of three on the menu was unavailable, more reactance would occur than if one of six was unavailable. Research has clearly demonstrated that reactance effects increase with the number of freedoms threatened; however, support for the proposition that reactance varies with the proportion of freedoms threatened is mixed (Brehm & Brehm, 1981).

Because choice alternatives constitute freedoms, when a choice requires a person to give up one or more alternatives in order to obtain another, the contemplation of choosing one alternative over others will threaten one or more freedoms and the actual choice will eliminate one or more freedoms. The resulting reactance should make choice difficult because the threat would enhance the relative attractiveness of the alternatives to be forsaken, and similarly, once the choice has been made, reactance will produce regret – the feeling that one should have chosen a different alternative. This analysis is supported by some evidence, though other evidence suggests that the effects are a function of their public nature and may not be due to reactance (*see* IMPRESSION MANAGEMENT).

Finally, freedoms can be threatened by implication, causing increases in the magnitude of reactance, and freedoms can be restored by implication, decreasing the magnitude of reactance. Research has shown that boomerang ATTITUDE CHANGE to a social influence attempt is stronger if there are a number of future opportunities for similar influence at-

tempts. Other research has shown that preference for a discussion topic decreases if there is an implied attempt by someone to push that topic, and this effect is eliminated if a third party acts in a way to imply that the freedom to reject the topic is restored (Brehm & Brehm, 1981). An important point made by this research is that reactance can be reduced by events whose cause is independent of the person experiencing the reactance.

Among the experimentally demonstrated causes of reactance are sales or promotional pitches, censorship, requests for help or donations, bureaucratic foul-ups, one-sided prosecutorial presentations for a trial, a new prohibition of a consumer product, and even the introduction of a new, attractive choice alternative. The introduction of a new and attractive choice alternative can threaten one's freedoms to choose prior alternatives, increasing the attractiveness of the latter. Reactance has also been suggested as an effect of the induction of learned HELPLESSNESS, and there is evidence to support this suggestion, although the nature of motivational effects from helplessness treatments appears to be complex (Brehm, 1993).

Reactance theory is applicable in all cultures though what behaviors are free and which are important varies from one culture to another. Whether humans are born with freedoms is not clear; research has shown reactance effects in 2-year-old males, but not females. The question is whether the infant begins life feeling all powerful or helpless, and learns, respectively, that there are constraints or capabilities. New developments have included individual difference measures of reactance proneness (Dowd, Milne, & Wise, 1991; Shoham-Salomon, Avner, & Neeman, 1988).

*See also*: ATTITUDE CHANGE; CONTROL; CONTROL MOTIVATION; IMPRESSION MANAGEMENT; SOCIAL INFLUENCE.

BIBLIOGRAPHY

Brehm, J. W. (1966). *A theory of psychological reactance*. New York: Academic Press.

—— (1993). Control, its loss, and psychological reactance. In G. Weary, F. H. Gleicher, & K. L. Marsh (Eds.), *Control motivation and social cognition* (pp. 3–30). New York: Springer-Verlag.

Brehm, S. S., & Brehm, J. W. (1981). *Psychological reactance: A theory of freedom and control*. New York: Academic Press.

Dowd, E. T., Milne, C. R., & Wise, S. L. (1991). The Therapeutic Reactance Scale: A measure of psychological reactance. *Journal of Counseling and Development, 69*, 541–5.

Shoham-Salomon, V., Avner, R., & Neeman, R. (1988). You"re changed if you do and changed if you don't: Mechanisms underlying paradoxical interventions. *Journal of Consulting and Clinical Psychology, 57*, 590–8.

Wicklund, R. A. (1974). *Freedom and reactance*. Hillsdale, NJ: Lawrence Erlbaum.

JACK W. BREHM

**realistic conflict theory**   This theory holds that hostility between groups is a result of direct competition (*see* COOPERATION AND COMPETITION) for limited and valued resources. Sherif (1966) proposed that intergroup relations reflect the functional relations between groups. If the outcomes of two groups are competitively interdependent (gains for one group depend on losses for the other) intergroup hostility will be maximized; competition gives rise to unfavorable stereotypes, increased ingroup solidarity and cohesiveness (*see* GROUP COHESIVENESS), and thus to ingroup biases in evaluations of the two groups. If the groups are cooperatively interdependent (e.g., there is a SUPERORDINATE GOAL), intergroup hostility will be reduced, cumulatively improving intergroup relations. These propositions were tested, and generally supported, in a series of classic field experiments conducted in boys' summer camps. Sherif manipulated the intergroup goal relations and demonstrated dramatic effects on intra- and inter-group relations. The theory marked an important step away from individualistic theories such as FRUSTRATION–AGGRESSION theory or the authoritarian personality. Subsequent research has indicated that intergroup competitiveness could arise even when no competitive interdependence exists (Tajfer & Turner, 1986).

*See also*: COOPERATION AND COMPETITION GROUP COHESIVENESS; INTERGROUP RELATIONS.

BIBLIOGRAPHY

Sherif, M. (1966). *Common predicament social psychology of intergroup conflict and cooperation*. Boston; MA: Houghton Mifflin.

Tajfel, H., & Turner, J. C. (1986). The social identity theory of intergroup behavior. In S. Worchel & W. G. Austin (Eds.), *Psychology of intergroup relations*. (2nd ed., pp. 7–24), Chicago, IL: Nelson-Hall.

DOMINIC ABRAMS

**reasoning**   This denotes a rule-governed thought process aimed at the solution of a problem or the inference of new information, as opposed to merely intuitive or HEURISTIC information processing. In cognitive social psychology, reasoning processes play essential roles in causal ATTRIBUTION, behavior-TRAIT inferences, in social judgment and decision tasks (e.g., RISK assessment), as well as in many social learning and observation tasks. It is convenient to distinguish between deductive and inductive reasoning, dependent on whether reasoning proceeds from abstract categories to concrete cases or from specific data to inferences of abstract principles.

DEDUCTIVE REASONING

The classical paradigm for studying deductive (or purely analytical) reasoning is the syllogism, where the logical correctness (or viability) of a conclusion (e.g., "Some car drivers are dangerous") has to be judged given two or more premises (e.g., "Some car drivers are drunk"; "Some drunk people are dangerous"). Early research has shown that syllogisms differ systematically in difficulty; the number of logically correct responses depends, among other factors, on the occurrence of negations and quantifiers. The so-called "atmospheric effect" refers to the fact that syllogistic inferences tend to be considered true if the conclusion resembles the premises superficially in terms of quantifiers (some, many, all) or the occurrence of negations, regardless of whether the conclusion is logically valid. The insight from these early studies, that human reasoning relies on other than strictly logical principles, received even more support from research on Wason's (1966) selection task which has attained the status of a leading paradigm. Given a display of four cards showing the symbols *a, 2, 1, b* and the additional information that a letter is on one side and a number on the other side of each card, subjects have to select those cards that have to be turned over to provide a logically appropriate test of an if–then rule like "If there is a vowel on one side, then there is an even number on the other side." While the correct solution would be to select the *a* and *1* in this case, the modal response is *a, 2*; the vast majority of even very intelligent subjects would select the positive examples named in the rule rather than engage in genuine logical reasoning. Later research has shown that performance on this task, which has obvious implications for scientific reasoning, depends on the problem contents, with greatly enhanced performance for certain concrete rules as compared with the above abstract rule. In search for a theory to describe this content dependency, recent research has demonstrated the important role of social variables. If the rule to be tested takes the form of a social contract (Cosmides, 1989) that encourages the detection of cheaters (e.g., "If a letter is sealed, it must have a 1-Deutsch-Mark stamp"), the majority of subjects would select the appropriate rule tests (i.e., *p* and *non-q* to test the rule *If p, then q*). In general, psychological research on deductive reasoning indicates that although people do not lack the intelligence or cognitive devices to solve many logical puzzles, they are often misled by heuristic thinking and their belief in the plausibility of a conclusion rather than its logical deducibility.

## INDUCTIVE REASONING

Inductive reasoning refers to the extraction or abstraction of rules from a set or sequence of observations. In the context of causal attribution (Kelley, 1967), for instance, the causes of behavior can be inferred from an analysis of how many subjects show the same behavior (consensus), to what extent the same behavior is elicited by different stimuli (distinctiveness), and whether the behavior varies over time and occasions (consistency). Causal at-

tribution is quite sensitive to all three sources of variation, although consensus information is sometimes neglected. If information about multiple behaviors (varying across subjects, stimuli, and time) is not available, causality may also be inferred from violations of expectations.

An essential prerequisite for inductive reasoning in attribution, social learning, and decision making is the human ability to detect and assess the covariation or contingency of two or more stimulus attributes (e.g., between prices and product quality). While the evidence from multiple-cue learning studies within Brunswik's (1956) LENS MODEL testifies to a remarkable human ability to extract (at least linear) relations among multiple cues simultaneously, the performance on explicit covariation assessment tasks (e.g., when subjects have to attend to and extract the correlation between a symptom and a disease from a series of relevant observations) is characterized by violations of basic statistical norms. In general, they tend to ignore the importance of negative information (e.g., the occurrence of a disease when the symptom is *absent*) and they tend to be misled by prior expectancies or stereotypes. Thus, the demonstration of ILLUSORY CORRELATIONS (i.e., the illusory detection of some contingency, for instance, beten social groups and desirability of behaviors, when in fact there is no such correlation) is of particular importance for the study of social stereotypes (Hamilton, 1981). Illusory correlations may either stem from prior knowledge or expectancies or they may reflect the selective processing of information that confirms or disconfirms the correlation between two attributes.

*See also*: ATTRIBUTION THEORIES; HEURISTICS; RISK.

BIBLIOGRAPHY
Brunswik, E. (1956). *Perception and the representative design of psychological experiments*. Berkeley, CA: University of California Press.
Cosmides, L. (1989). The logic of social exchange: Has natural selection shaped how humans reason? *Cognition, 31*, 187–276.
Hamilton, D. L. (1981). Illusory correlations as a basis for stereotyping. In D. L. Hamilton (Ed.), *Cognitive processes in stereotyping*

*and intergroup behavior* (pp. 115–44). Hillsdale, NJ: Lawrence Erlbaum.

Kelley, H. H. (1967). Attribution theory in social psychology. In D. Levine (Ed.), *Nebraska symposium on motivation* (pp. 192–238). Lincoln, NE: University of Nebraska Press.

Wason, P. C. (1966). Reasoning. In B. M. Foss (Ed.), *New horizons in psychology* (pp. 135-51). Harmondsworth: Penguin.

KLAUS FIEDLER
JEANNETTE SCHMID

**reciprocity**   This is the mutual exchange of similar-in-kind responses among interactants. Reciprocity of attraction occurs when liking is met with liking and disliking is met with disliking. Prosocial reciprocity occurs when people help in return for having been helped. It has been argued that reciprocity is a fundamental principle governing human behavior. Positive reciprocity encourages people to treat others positively when they themselves are treated fairly, but it can also lead to interpersonal conflict. Reciprocity calls for positive responses to favorable treatment but negative responses to unfavorable treatment.

DONELSON R. FORSYTH

**reference group**   Any group, including general social groupings based on demographic similarities (e.g., race or culture), that individuals use as a basis for SOCIAL COMPARISON. People determine their own social worth by comparing their personal qualities and accomplishments to the characteristics and achievements of the typical member of the identified group.

*See also*: SOCIAL COMPARISON.

DONELSON R. FORSYTH

**relationships**   Any ongoing association between two or more individuals is considered a relationship. Relationships take diverse forms, and have varied roots, such as affection (as among friends and lovers), kinship, role requirements (e.g., teachers and students, employers and employees), or common circumstances (e.g., neighbors, classmates). Regardless of their particular form, the existence of a relationship indicates that two or more persons have established an ongoing connection with each other; that their bond has special properties, including a sense of history and some awareness of the nature of the relationship; that they exert influence on each other's thoughts, feelings, and behavior; and that they expect to interact in the future. Relationships are best understood not in terms of isolated properties but rather as gestalt-like wholes – i.e., as global representations of a multidimensional and somewhat idiosyncratic bond between individuals. It might also be said that relationships play an essential role in underpinning human action; i.e., that they provide a context for most human goal-directed activity. The way in which this context affects behavior is one of the prime interests of social psychological research on relationships.

Although relationships have interested scholars and laypersons alike from time immemorial, only recently have they become the central focus of systematic empirical research (Duck, 1988). This development is highlighted by the launch during the 1980s and 1990s of two interdisciplinary organizations and two scientific journals devoted to the study of relationships. From the beginning, relationship researchers have been confronted with the question of levels of analysis. Existing social science paradigms were designed to study individuals or groups, but relationships, which are usually dyadic, pose special challenges. Some investigators study relationships from the perspective of individuals. This approach considers relationships from the vantage point of the individual partners' attributes. In contrast, the relationship perspective assumes that relationships are more than the sum of their parts; that is, that every relationship represents a unique synthesis of attitudes, goals, and personal dispositions that individuals bring to the relationship. It has been particularly important, in the emergence of this field, for researchers to develop new conceptual and statistical models for distinguishing individual-level and relationship-level constructs.

## WHAT IS A RELATIONSHIP?

The term relationship refers to an enduring association between two persons. As such, it is distinguished from the study of social interaction, which may occur between unrelated individuals. A key principle is that interaction between related persons will differ from interaction between unrelated persons, and that the nature of these differences is informative about the qualities of the relationship. This is not to imply that relationships stand apart from social interaction. Rather, relationships possess special properties that make comprehension of their meaning and structure considerably more complex than simple social events. As Hinde (1981, p. 3) noted, ". . . just as interactions involve emergent properties not relevant to the behavior of individuals in isolation, so also do relationships involve properties not relevant to their component interactions." Full understanding of relationship phenomena necessarily involves features distinct from those that apply to analysis of interactions. Among these special features are the following:

(1) Relationships exist within a temporal framework, including a past history and an imagined future. Past events may influence current behavior by fostering expectations and a context within which present experiences are evaluated. (For example, a critical comment is likely to be interpreted differently within a loving than a hostile relationship.) Similarly, expectations, goals, and fantasies about the future often affect partners' behavior toward each other. Generally, the closer two partners are, and the greater their commitment to the relationship, the stronger such influence will be.

(2) Relationships typically, but not always, involve mutual influence. That is, each partner affects the other in ongoing, and often complexly intertwined, "chains" of causal influence. The nature of these patterns is viewed by some researchers to hold the key to understanding the special properties of relationships (see INTERDEPENDENCE THEORY). Mutual influence is complex, and may not be evident in a single interactive episode. In ongoing relationships, RECIPROCITY may occur only across multiple, temporally spaced, events. For example, close friends might devote an entire conversation to one partner's problems, with the other assuming the role of confidant. In a future conversation these roles might be reversed.

(3) Relationships have enduring prototypical characteristics about which partners develop "relationship awareness" – i.e., a set of understandings about the nature of the relationship, and what each partner can expect from the other. These beliefs may be conscious and consensual, or they may be implicit and idiosyncratic. Relationship awareness is a broad concept, including feelings and beliefs about partners, as well as metaperspectives (which refer to each partner's understanding of the other's feelings about oneself and the relationship). To many researchers, these higher-order cognitions embody the essence of a relationship.

(4) Personal relationships are usually embedded within wider social networks. Partners must therefore balance the needs of one relationship with other relationships. For example, spouses are sometimes also parents, and must coordinate the demands of these relationships. Also, people often participate in social networks as members of a relationship. For example, spouses might be invited to dinner parties or community events as a couple; they are often judged as individuals on the basis of their relationship, or their partner's characteristics; and they are sometimes perceived to possess some of their partner's knowledge qualities or attributes. The extent of such embeddedness varies greatly, depending on such factors as closeness, privacy, and the nature of the relationship. Dyadic relationships may also affect the manner and degree to which partners socialize with other network members.

(5) Relationships vary in the degree to which they are unidimensional or multifaceted. Some relationships are limited to one domain of activity, whereas others are more diverse. MARRIAGE is usually a good example of the latter, in which family and

household maintenance activities, recreation, friendship, emotional confiding, and sexuality are typically consolidated. Generally speaking, the more multifaceted the relationship, the more difficult it is to characterize the relationship from single observations or with unidimensional principles. Diversity of interdependence is considered by some researchers to be an important criterion for understanding the meaning and impact of a relationship on the individual.

WHY DO HUMAN BEINGS VALUE
RELATIONSHIPS?
Few would argue with the time-honored maxim that human nature is fundamentally social. Nearly all theories of human motivation and activity incorporate notions about the role of social relations in the organization and development of behavior. (Social relations also figure prominently in the behavior of all but the lowest animal species.) However, considerably less consensus exists about the mechanisms underlying this propensity. Although prevailing explanations tend to emphasize nature or nurture, it seems incontrovertible that both sorts of mechanisms are not only involved, but must in fact complement each other. That is, a culture's SOCIAL-IZATION practices must expressly account for innate human relational abilities and aspirations, and develop practices that shape these predispositions in desired directions. Similarly, genetically determined tendencies by themselves seem unlikely to explain the immense variety and complexity that human relationships display (Hinde, 1987).

Theories rooted in evolutionary processes are currently popular. The most compelling applications of evolutionary thinking to human sociality appears in two lines of research: studies of human social attachments, and studies of cross-cultural similarities in mating preferences. ATTACHMENT theory applies principles of evolution and ethology to children's emotional and social development. According to this theory, infants who maintained proximity with an adult caregiver, and who exhibited appropriate protest behaviors when separated or threatened, were more

likely to survive into adulthood. Thus, natural selection may have endowed human beings with an innate tendency to seek security in close relationships. Although the logic behind attachment may be evolutionary, it is important to note that its proximal mechanisms involve AFFECT. That is, infants experience strong negative emotions like ANGER and distress when separted or threatened, and positive emotions like contentment, joy, and relief when safe and protected (either because caregivers are nearby or because secure mental representations have been established).

Genetically based predispositions to seek proximity to caregivers, and their derivative tendencies to experience strong emotions in the context of close relaionships, may help explain the importance of relationships in human motivation. Although Bowlby (1969) postulated attachment theory primarily from his observations of infants and young children, it was intended to apply "from the cradle to the grave"; that is, across the life span. This is evident in two ways. First, attachment-related processes have been implicated in such diverse phenomena as romantic LOVE; personal beliefs about close relationships; parental behavior; coping with divorce, death anxiety, BEREAVEMENT, and extreme stress; SELF-ESTEEM and mental health; and orientations toward work (Shaver & Hazan, 1993). Second, Bowlby predicated attachment as one of several interlocking behavioral systems, all of which derived from evolutionary forces. These systems include caregiving, affiliation, and sexual mating. Although attachment has received the lion's share of attention, these other drives may also underlie various relationship behaviors.

The importance of evolutionary theorizing is also evident in models of many other relationship phenomena (see EVOLUTIONARY PSYCHOLOGY). Many specific propositions have been offered, for example, describing the adaptive significance of cooperation, group living, pair-bonding, ALTRUISM, affective communication, and social coordination. Also, notions of sexual selection have been invaluable in accounting for the striking universality of SEX DIFFERENCES in mating preferences shown by men and women from widely differing cultures (Buss & Schmitt,

1993). Although specific phenomena and processes are still very much a matter of debate, one general principle is widely agreed upon: that social relationships provided significant survival and reproductive advantages during our evolutionary past, and that as a consequence, these tendencies came to be encoded in our genetic heritage. As such, the evolutionary basis of sociality seems unassailable.

Acknowledging the importance of evolutionary considerations does not contravene an equally significant role for socialization. Although the *raison d'être* for sociality may be its adaptive value, relationships vary greatly, and much of this diversity can be attributed to nurture. For example, although a genetically determined drive for proximity may underlie infants' attachment strivings, the actual quality of the infant–caregiver relationship is believed to influence the nature of later-life relationships. Among the relevant relationship qualities are warmth, responsiveness, accessibility, and encouragement of autonomy. In attachment theory, internal working (or representational) models provide the mechanism by which early social experience affects later relationships. These models are extensive and complex, incorporating one's view of SELF and others, and expectations about relationships. The concept of internal working models demonstrates just how important socialization experiences are, even in theories that root social drives in genetic forces. In fact, all relationship theories include constructs based on prior experience that are analogous in the most general sense to working models (e.g., attitudes, SCHEMAS, expectations, goals, and self- and object-models). Unquestionably, mental representations of self, others, and relationships play a significant role in social interaction (Berscheid, 1994; see SOCIAL COGNITION).

More generally, socialization practices must reflect human predispositions. A basic principle of CULTURE is that human action and well-being is facilitated by voluntary interdependent activity toward common goals, and it is apparent that such activities occur more readily within stable relationships. Thus, from birth, humans are encouraged to participate in relationships, and discouraged from "antirelational" behavior (such as disloyalty, shirking, and cheating). Successful relationship activity typically produces positive emotions, whereas unsuccessful activity begets negative emotions. In fact, some emotion theorists view relationships as the primary font of affect. Note, however, that socialization practices need not mirror genetic drives. Some practices are designed to channel human predispositions into productive, satisfying activity, but others are intended to inhibit or control undesired behaviors. Thus, while the drive to be social may have evolutionary origins, the specific characteristics of relationships are more likely to be determined by cultural forces and individual experiences.

## HOW DO RELATIONSHIPS FUNCTION?

One of the most daunting problems facing relationship researchers is the question of relationship type. Human relationships are diverse, and large literatures have emerged specializing in several of the more prominent varieties (e.g., marriage; courtship; friendship during childhood, ADOLESCENCE, and adulthood; parent–child and sibling relationships; therapist–client relationships; and employer–employee and co-worker relationships). Because these relationships differ inherently, often in multiple and complex ways, comparison and integration across types is often difficult. Social psychologists have generally addressed this complexity by focusing their attention on processes that affect the course and conduct of social behavior across varied relationships and settings. In other words, they seek to understand how and why people relate to one another, irrespective of the particulars of a given relationship.

Some of the resulting theories are broad and comprehensive, offering general principles that characterize most, if not all, relationships. Chief among them are theories of interdependence and SOCIAL EXCHANGE, discussed shortly. Other theories describe more specific processes that are present to varying extents in different relationships. Among these processes are INTIMACY, TRUST, emotion, love, commitment, SOCIAL COMPARISON, support, self-esteem maintenance, jealousy, POWER, and COOPERATION AND COMPETITION. Relationships can be characterized, then, not only descriptively but also in terms of the degree to which they involve these and other processes.

Interdependence theory is arguably the most comprehensive account of interaction patterns (Kelley, 1979; Kelley & Thibaut, 1978). Indeed, to many researchers, the very term interdependence is synonymous with relationship, inasmuch as both imply mutual reliance and contingent activity. Interdependence theory posits that social behavior is best understood by examining the manner in which partners influence each other's actions and outcomes. Thus, the theory considers how partners reconcile personal priorities and interests with the intrinsically social need to coordinate action. Kelley and Thibaut describe this reconciliation as a transformation process, in which personal desires and goals (the "given matrix") are, through characteristic patterns of responding to the other's interests, transformed into behavioral tendencies (the "effective matrix"). The essence of a relationship, according to interdependence theory, may be found in its typical transformation tendencies, and in the patterns of outcome interdependence that result. For example, one partner might regularly impose his/her will on the other; partners might take turns satisfying their personal preferences; or they might seek integrative solutions that maximize joint outcomes.

A major advantage of the interdependence approach is its attention to precise, clearly articulated patterns of preferences and coordination. Propositions derived from interdependence theory are content-free, in the sense that they are intended to apply to all shared activities (e.g., from division of household labor to emotional SELF-DISCLOSURE). Thus, the theory describes cooperation as the attempt to maximize joint outcomes, and competition as the desire to enhance own outcomes relative to the other, regardless of whether the activity is child care, sailing, or political deal-making. Sometimes, interdependence theory is subsumed under the heading of social exchange theory, in large part because these theories share the device of conceptualizing interaction events in terms of rewards and costs. The social exchange approach, derived from behaviorism, gave rise to much work on interpersonal attraction,

which focuses on the "rewards others provide" (see ATTRACTION). But as the above indicates, interdependence theory captures the dynamic and interactive nature of relationship behavior better than traditional reward/cost notions do.

Other approaches to interdependence have a more taxonomic flavor, seeking to distinguish relationships by their normative patterns of exchange and interaction. Such patterns, sometimes described as rules or expectations, are shaped by many factors: cultural and social roles, past experience, or personal predispositions. Regardless, their defining feature is that interaction tends to follow distinguishable, characteristic, and consensual patterns.

Various taxonomies have been proposed, of which Fiske's (1990) is prototypical. He proposes four distinct (and universal) forms of social interdependence:

*communal sharing*, which stresses group identity, caretaking, and solidarity;
*authority ranking*, in which social organization and privilege are hierarchical and status-based;
*equality matching*, in which reciprocity and equal status predominate; and
*market pricing*, in which social relations are dictated by evaluations of value along universal metrics (e.g., money).

This taxonomy, like its peers, assumes that each type of interdependence has conceptual integrity of its own, and that the rules of interaction differ fundamentally but systematically from one type to another. Moreover, it is very much a theory of relationships, since all human relationships are presumed to embody one of the four basic patterns (or in some instances, a blend of them).

Relationship processes have also been studied in terms of the social and psychological functions that they are intended to satisfy. In general terms, this approach concerns the goals, needs, and motives that a relationship fulfills; i.e., the outcomes that participants desire from their association. Functions are said to channel relational behavior: how and which partners are chosen, and how they perceive and respond to each other. Even a casual reading of this literature makes plain the enormous number of different functions operative in relationship behavior. Using a scheme borrowed from the functional theory of attitudes, relationship functions might be grouped into four categories:

*instrumentality* (how relationships help people attain desired goals);

*knowledge* (how relationships facilitate self-understanding and comprehension of one's environment);

*expression* (how relationships provide a context for expressing unique personal identities); and

*ego-defense* (how behavior in relationships helps people preserve their self-conceptions).

For each function, an extensive literature exists, demonstrating that interpersonal behavior can be understood by considering people's psychological and social goals within that relationship.

CONCLUSION

Relationships are a vital element of human activity, as is evident in their impact on mental health and physical well-being (*see* SOCIAL SUPPORT), and in the enormous expenditure of time, energy, and attention they receive in everyday life. Although the social psychological study of relationship processes has only begun, it is clear that this literature has the potential to contribute significantly to human self-understanding and welfare.

*See also*: ADOLESCENCE; ATTRACTION; COOPERATION AND COMPETITION; CULTURE; FRIENDSHIP; INTERDEPENDENCE THEORY; INTIMACY; MARRIAGE; POWER; SCHEMAS/SCHEMATA; SELF; SELF-ESTEEM; SEX DIFFERENCES; SOCIAL COGNITION; SOCIAL COMPARISON; SOCIAL SUPPORT; SOCIALIZATION; TRUST.

BIBLIOGRAPHY

Berscheid, E. (1994). Interpersonal relationships. *Annual Review of Psychology, 45,* 79–129.

Bowlby, J. (1969). *Attachment.* New York: Basic Books.

Buss, D. M., & Schmitt, D. P. (1993). Sexual strategies theory: An evolutionary perspective on human mating. *Psychological Review 100,* 204–32.

Duck, S. (Ed.). (1988). *Handbook of personal relationships.* Chichester: J. Wiley.

Fiske, A. P. (1990). *Structures of social life: The four elementary forms of human relations.* New York: Free Press.

Hinde, R. A. (1981). The bases of a science of interpersonal relationships. In S. Duck & R. Gilmour (Eds.), *Personal relationships: Studying personal relationships* (pp. 1–22). London: Academic Press.

——— (1987). *Individuals, relationships and culture: Links between ethology and the social sciences.* New York: Cambridge University Press.

Kelley, H. H. (1979). *Personal relationships: Their structure and processes.* Hillsdale, NJ: Lawrence Erlbaum.

——— & Thibaut, J. (1978). *Interpersonal relations: A theory of interdependence.* New York: Wiley.

Shaver, P. R., & Hazan, C. (1993). Adult romantic attachment: Theory and evidence. In D. Perlman & W. Jones (Eds.), *Advances in personal relationships* (Vol. 4, pp. 29–70). London: Jessica Kingsley.

HARRY T. REIS

**relative deprivation (RD)** A psychological state in which there is a perceived negative discrepancy between a current economic position or other material outcome and that which was expected. The state of relative deprivation is commonly thought to be associated with feelings of dissatisfaction and, if extreme enough, ANGER. It is important to distinguish it from conditions of absolute deprivation (e.g., objective levels of poverty) although in practice the two may be correlated.

The term relative deprivation originated in some World War II research into the morale and social attitudes of American soldiers. One surprising finding was that the morale of some sections of the military whose conditions appeared to be rather favorable, since the chances of promotion were good, was actually *lower* than the morale in other sections where the likelihood of promotion was less. This phenomenon, which has since been confirmed in other studies, can be understood if one assumes that in the more favorable situation people's expectations were higher, thus increasing the probability that they would fail to be fulfilled. This would give rise to relative deprivation and hence dissatisfaction.

The concept of relative deprivation has undergone considerable subsequent analysis. One of the first developments was the recognition that not all discrepancies between expectations and attainments would generate feelings of deprivation; some sense of entitlement should also be present to create a perception of injustice about the size of the discrepancy. A second, and still controversial, idea was that expectations should be feasible and not unrealistic daydreams (Runciman, 1966; see Gurr, 1970). Runciman also introduced another important distinction between deprivation that is experienced on an *individual* level – a discrepancy between a person's own expectations and current position – and *group* level deprivation – a perceived gap between the ingroup's current position and where it should be. These two types of relative deprivation are called egoistic and fraternalistic, respectively. Finally, a person's perception of the degree of control which they have over their life may affect the way feelings of relative deprivation are translated into behaviors designed to reduce that deprivation (Crosby, 1976).

The concept of relative deprivation has been used to explain the incidence of civil disorder at a societal level. Based on survey and archival data from 13 different countries, Gurr (1970) found a clear positive association between measured relative deprivation (RD) and the amount of reported social unrest. Analyses within countries have provided similar supportive evidence (Crosby, 1976).

There are several sources of RD. One may be past experience. Davies (1962) proposed that people's experience of a rising standard of living generates expectations for increasing affluence in the future. If actual economic standards level off or decline, RD may be expected. Drawing on historical evidence, Davies shows that revolutions are more likely to occur not after a period of prolonged absolute deprivation but after a period of prosperity followed by a sudden downturn.

A more potent source of RD are SOCIAL COMPARISONS, particularly with similar others. If other individuals or groups appear to be enjoying greater advantages than ourselves or our own group, this unfavourable comparison can generate thwarted expectations leading to RD. At an egoistic level there is extensive evidence which supports this idea; individuals' levels of personal satisfaction are strongly related to their position relative to other individuals (Crosby, 1976). Fraternalistic RD also appears to be largely determined by social comparisons. Runciman (1966) found that some British nonmanual workers, despite being objectively better off than manual workers, actually expressed lower feelings of satisfaction apparently because they compared themselves unfavorably to those same manual workers. In the United States, among White voters, support for conservative political candidates and racist attitudes has been found to be related to those Whites' perception of a negative discrepancy between themselves and Blacks.

In the political domain it becomes especially important to distinguish between egoistic and fraternalistic RD for they may have quite different outcomes. Egoistic RD is often found to be correlated with symptoms of individual stress and illness whilst fraternalistic RD is more usually related to support for political change or collective protest activities of various kinds. Despite the success of relative deprivation theory in explaining both individual and group dissatisfaction, some problems remain. Chief amongst these concerns the choice of the person or group with whom to compare. Crosby (1982) noted how the working women in her survey, despite being objectively worse off than male workers, seldom compared themselves to men. Even when such cross-sex comparisons were made by women (predominantly by those in more professional roles) the outcome of those comparisons was not noticeably more negative than those made by women in lower status occupations. As yet, the factors governing the actual reference other or the dimension of comparison are still not well understood. A second unresolved question concerns the translation of feelings of RD into actual behaviors. Most research examining this link between the experience of deprivation and action has done so either only indirectly or retrospectively. Attempts to study this more directly through experimental methods have not always found RD to lead to collective action.

*See also*: SOCIAL COMPARISON.

BIBLIOGRAPHY

Crosby, F. (1976). A model of egoistical relative deprivation, *Psychological Review*, *83*, 85–113.

——(1982). *Relative deprivation and working women*. New York: Oxford University Press.

Davies, J. C. (1962). Towards a Theory of Revolution. *Sociological Review*, *27*, 5–19.

Gurr, T. R. (1970). *Why men rebel*. Princeton, NJ: Princeton University Press.

Runciman, W.G. (1966). *Relative deprivation and social justice*. London: Routledge & Kegan Paul.

RUPERT BROWN

**religion** Substantive definitions identify religion by its unique content: attitudes toward or belief in God, conversion or mystical experiences, prayer, attending church or temple, and the like. Functional definitions identify religion by its unique process: whatever the individual does to address ultimate or existential questions about the meaning and purpose of one's life given death, about how one should relate to others, and the like. Each definition has led to its own research tradition (*see* Dittes, 1969; Wulff, 1991).

THE SUBSTANTIVE TRADITION

The dominant research strategy within the substantive tradition has been to correlate one or more measures of religion with some personal or social indicator. Early researchers like Coe, Leuba, and Starbuck, for example, examined the relationship between conversion experiences and age. More recently, measures of belief in God or an afterlife, positivity of religious attitudes, degree of orthodoxy, frequency of prayer, attendance at worship, or denominational affiliation have been correlated with age, sex, race, LIFE SATISFACTION, neuroticism, SELF-ESTEEM, LOCUS OF CONTROL, DOGMATISM, ethnocentrism,

PREJUDICE, racism, or HELPING BEHAVIOR (*see* Batson, Schoenrade, & Ventis, 1993).

Within the substantive tradition, measurement issues have been central. Galton initiated attempts to measure personal religion in the 1870s. In 1929, Thurstone and Chave used attitudes toward God and the church as primary examples in their pioneering work on ATTITUDE MEASUREMENT and scaling. In the 1960s and 1970s Scott as well as Fishbein and Ajzen used religion as a primary example of attitude–behavior consistency.

Psychometric research indicates that religion is best regarded as a multidimensional construct. In Western society, the most frequently found dimension has been commitment to traditional religious orthodoxy. Other frequently found dimensions are liberalism–conservativism, utilitarianism, and individualism–institutionalism. Current multiple-item scales for measuring primary dimensions of personal religion have good reliabilities and validities, matching or exceeding those of other attitude–belief measures used by social psychologists (*see* Gorsuch, 1988).

Many social–psychological theories have been used to interpret correlations within the substantive tradition. ROLE THEORY, various SOCIAL INFLUENCE theories, and SOCIAL LEARNING theory have been useful in understanding the social sources of religious NORMS, attitudes, BELIEFS, and behaviors. ATTRIBUTION THEORY has been used to examine the relation between religious beliefs, especially belief in God, and explanation of negative life events. Theories of cognitive development, notably the theories of Piaget and Kohlberg, have been used to understand the child's comprehension of religious concepts and MORAL DEVELOPMENT.

THE FUNCTIONAL TRADITION

Measurement precision and the array of correlations produced notwithstanding, research in the substantive tradition has been criticized for failure to provide any comprehensive explanation of the role of religion in individuals' lives (*see* Deconchy, 1980). Research in the functional tradition has sought to do precisely this; it has been less concerned with correlates of religious attitudes, beliefs, and behaviors and more concerned with why religion exists in human life and what effect it has.

Perhaps the most common answer, classically expressed by Freud, is that religion exists because it meets human needs for meaning and security. Such a view has a long history in Western thought and continues today, for example, in research on death anxiety and religion. Within the general view that devout religious beliefs serve to provide meaning and a sense of self-esteem, COGNITIVE DISSONANCE THEORY has proved useful in explaining why a person might maintain, even intensify, religious beliefs in the face of disconfirming evidence.

Gordon Allport agreed with Freud's view regarding religion's self-protective origins, but Allport painted a more complex picture. He distinguished between two different ways of being religious, extrinsic and intrinsic. Allport's concern was to separate those whose religion functions to meet self-serving ends from those for whom religion is an end in itself – a final, not an instrumental, good. Subsequent research has shown that these two ways of being religious, at least as measured by Allport's Extrinsic and Intrinsic scales, are independent dimensions, one reflecting a utilitarian approach to religion, the other reflecting devout religious commitment. Whether intrinsic religion transcends the self-protective concerns that underlie extrinsic religion, as Allport claimed, remains a matter of controversy.

Allport's extrinsic–intrinsic distinction has been widely used in research and has proved important in understanding the effect of religion on mental health, prejudice, and helping behavior. In recent years, a third independent dimension – the degree to which the individual's religion is an open-ended quest rather than a set of clear answers – has also proved important (see Batson et al., 1993).

Erik Erikson's sequence of conflicts faced in psychosocial development has provided a useful framework for examining psychodynamic functions of religion. Erikson himself traced the religious implications of his developmental scheme in psycho-histories of Luther and Gandhi. Recent empirical studies of the relation between ATTACHMENT styles and personal religion can be interpreted in the context of Erikson's work, as can Fowler's description of stages of faith development.

Perhaps the greatest challenge for any functional analysis of religion is to explain the life-changing and integrating role played by religious experience. William James long ago placed this challenge before psychologists interested in religion in *The Varieties of Religious Experience*, providing a rich array of dramatic examples. The challenge has rarely been taken up by psychologists since, even though its ability to transform a person's outlook and life would seem to be one of the most intriguing psychological puzzles that religion poses. Promising efforts have attempted to understand religious experience by comparing it to other dramatic, reality-transforming experiences such as creative insight (*see* CREATIVITY) or therapeutic change, but work on the nature and function of religious experience remains largely speculative.

*See also*: ATTITUDE MEASUREMENT AND QUESTIONNAIRE DESIGN; ATTRIBUTION THEORIES; COGNITIVE DISSONANCE THEORY; CREATIVITY; DOGMATISM; HELPING BEHAVIOR; LIFE SATISFACTION; MORAL DEVELOPMENT; NORMS; PREJUDICE; ROLE THEORY; SELF-ESTEEM; SOCIAL INFLUENCE; SOCIAL LEARNING.

BIBLIOGRAPHY
Batson, C. D., Schoenrade, P., & Ventis, W. L. (1993). *Religion and the individual: A social-psychological perspective*. New York: Oxford University Press.
Deconchy, J.-P. (1980). *Orthodoxie religieuse et sciences humaines* [Religious orthodoxy, rationality, and scientific knowledge]. The Hague: Mouton.
Dittes, J. E. (1969). Psychology of religion. In G. Lindzey & E. Aronson (Eds.), *The handbook of social psychology* (2nd ed., Vol. 5, pp. 602–59). Reading, MA: Addison-Wesley.
Gorsuch, R. L. (1988). Psychology of religion. *Annual Review of Psychology*, 39, 201–21.
Wulff, D. M. (1991). *Psychology of religion: Classic and contemporary views*. New York: Wiley.

C. DANIEL BATSON
CHRISTOPHER T. BURRIS

**representativeness** The representativeness HEURISTIC provides a rapid but sometimes

fallible method of judging the belongingness of an instance to a category on the basis of superficial or stereotypical similarity, often ignoring the logically appropriate criteria and the category BASE RATES. Several judgment BIASES can be explained in terms of representativeness.
*See also*: HEURISTICS.

KLAUS FIEDLER

**responsibility** Liability of a person for praise or (more typically) condemnation; a social judgment rendered by a perceiver who considers the actor's intentions, behavior, and possible excuses.
*See also*: ATTRIBUTION OF RESPONSIBILITY.

K. G. SHAVER

**responsiveness** Behaviors that interaction partners enact in reaction to their partner's real or imagined behavior constitute responsiveness. Responses perceived as appropriate and supportive tend to enhance relatedness, whereas inattention or inappropriate responses tend to produce distance. Responsiveness is communicated through both verbal content and nonverbal signals.
*See also*: INTIMACY; NONVERBAL COMMUNICATION; RELATIONSHIPS.

HARRY T. REIS

**rhetoric** This term refers both to the long-established discipline of studying oratory and also, more generally, to the persuasive content of discourse. The discipline of classical rhetoric developed in ancient Greece and it continued as a major component of Western education until the nineteenth century. In terms of its scope and topics it was the forerunner of modern social psychology. Recently, there has been a revival of interest in rhetoric. The "new rhetoricians" are claiming that social psychology itself is a rhetorical, or persuasive, enterprise, and they advocate that the study of attitudes and cognition should be reoriented around rhetorical insights.

CLASSICAL RHETORIC
Rhetoric originated in Athens during the fifth century B.C. as a practical instruction for public speakers. The rhetoricians taught how arguments should be constructed and presented in public. From this, rhetoric developed as an intellectual inquiry into the nature of effective communication. Aristotle, whose book *Rhetorica* was to have a major influence on the discipline, defined rhetoric as "the study of the available means of persuasion." As such, rhetoric covered many of the same areas as modern social psychology, especially in relation to ATTITUDE CHANGE and PERSUASION.

For instance, Aristotle's *Rhetorica* discussed how communicators could make themselves appear more credible, how they should project their characters, whether appeals to fear were more effective than appeals to reason, whether strong arguments should best be placed at the end of a communication. In short, many of the specific topics which form the basis of modern social psychology were discussed by classical rhetorical writers such as Cicero, Quintilian, and Aristotle. However, there are differences between classical rhetoric and modern social psychology. Rhetoric had a much stronger emphasis on analyzing language, especially the language of argument. Throughout the ages, rhetoricians have paid particular attention to the persuasive properties of metaphors and other figures of speech.

For over two thousand years, rhetoric occupied a central place in the Western educational curriculum. In the Middle Ages, rhetoric was one of the three basic subjects to be taught in schools, and the discipline maintained its importance until the nineteenth century. Then, the new human and social sciences, such as psychology, linguistics, and sociology, took over from classical studies in schools and universities. In consequence, rhetoric was displaced as the main discipline investigating communication.

The decline of rhetoric seemed to be confirmed when social psychologists applied the techniques of experimentation to answer the very questions which the rhetoricians had previously addressed. For instance, the Yale Studies of Communication, conducted in the United States during the 1940s and 1950s under the direction of Carl Hovland and Muzafer Sherif, produced a series of laboratory experiments investigating the relative effectiveness of different ways of presenting information. The variables which were investigated included many which had been specifically discussed by Aristotle in *Rhetorica*. Amongst other things, Hovland and Sherif examined the ordering of arguments, the credibility of the communicator and the effect of citing the counter-viewpoint. However, clear-cut results about the effectiveness of such variables were hard to obtain. If anything, the Yale experiments, not to mention countless subsequent studies, confirmed something which Aristotle and Cicero had claimed: there is no single way of presenting information that guarantees persuasion. Much depends on the relations between communicator, audience, the nature of the communication, and the particular circumstances of the communication.

THE NEW RHETORIC

In the past 15 years, there has been a revival of interest in rhetoric, producing what some analysts are calling "the new rhetoric" (Simons, 1990). This new rhetoric is not merely a revival of an older tradition, but it seeks to take rhetoric, and indeed social psychology, in new directions. Principally, the new rhetoricians urge researchers to pay close attention to the persuasive aspects of language, particularly in relation to:

(1) the language of psychology itself; and
(2) the language with which people formulate their views on social issues.

Foremost among the "new rhetoricians" are those who study the "rhetoric of inquiry" (Nelson et al., 1987). These rhetoricians claim that scientific writing is itself inherently rhetorical. Scientific texts are not neutral descriptions of "reality," but they are designed to persuade an audience of readers. Thus, they are constructed with particular rhetorical features, and, in consequence, the rhetoric of social psychological reports becomes a topic for investigation. This sort of rhetorical inquiry has been an important feature of recent CRITICAL SOCIAL PSYCHOLOGY, for it questions the conventions by which orthodox empirical investigations are written. By examining the rhetoric of social psychology, critical analysts seek to reveal theoretical assumptions, which orthodox psychologists tend to take for granted.

Some of the new rhetoricians emphasize that human thinking is an inherently rhetorical activity and, thus, they seek to create a rhetorical social psychology (Billig, 1987). This perspective shares the assumption of DISCOURSE ANALYSIS that many of the phenomena which have been studied by social psychologists are constituted in language. The rhetorical psychologists place particular attention upon argumentative language. It is claimed that social psychologists can study thinking by closely analyzing the language of discussion groups, in which people are arguing about issues.

This rhetorical orientation has theoretical and methodological implications for the study of attitudes. According to rhetorical theorists, attitudes are not primarily outward expressions of inner emotional states, but are rhetorical stances in matters of public controversy. Thus, an attitude in favor of a position is also a stance against a counterposition. The psychological meaning of the attitude depends on this rhetorical context of argumentation. Methodologically, this would imply that researchers should pay close attention to the argumentative language in which views and counterviews are put forward. Thus, rhetorical psychologists, investigating "attitudes," tend to use qualitative methods, in order to study actual discursive interaction (Billig, 1992). In this way, rhetorical psychology, through its stress on argumentation and language, claims to offer new perspectives on the topics of attitudes and persuasion.

*See also*: ATTITUDE CHANGE; CRITICAL SOCIAL PSYCHOLOGY; DISCOURSE ANALYSIS; PROPAGANDA; SOCIAL CONSTRUCTIONISM.

BIBLIOGRAPHY
Aristotle (1909). *Rhetorica*. Cambridge: Cambridge University Press.
Billig, M. (1987). *Arguing and thinking: A rhetorical approach to social psychology*. Cambridge: Cambridge University Press.
——(1992). *Talking of the royal family*. London: Routledge.

Nelson, J. S., Megill, A., & McCloskey, D. N. (Eds.) (1987). *The rhetoric of the human sciences*, Madison, WI: University of Wisconsin Press.

Simons, H. (Ed.) (1990). *The rhetorical turn*. Chicago, IL: Chicago University Press.

MICHAEL BILLIG

**risk**   The perception of risk and the acceptability of risks have been studied extensively in psychology. A formal definition of risk is the likelihood or probability $p$ of the negative event or consequence $i$ multiplied by the negative value or utility of that event or consequence $u_i$. If a negative event is characterized by multiple negative consequences, risk could be defined as $\Sigma_i p_i u_i$.

This definition more or less coincides with dictionary definitions of risk; "the possibility or chance of loss" is a frequently given definition. Other examples are: "hazard or danger" and "exposure to mischance or peril." Although there is quite some disagreement about the precise definition of risk among scientists, the many different risk definitions are clearly related to the above general meaning of risk. In medicine and epidemiology, risk is the chance of a specific adverse outcome such as death or the contraction of a particular disease. The risks of technological developments such as the use of nuclear power for generating electricity are often defined in terms of the chance of excess deaths per reactor–year. In the literature on economics opportunities whose returns are not guaranteed are commonly described as "risk."

Potential negative outcomes are sometimes quantified (e.g., financial loss, number of possible victims). However, quantification of outcomes is often difficult and uncertain. Risk also implies that there is uncertainty about the outcomes of actions. There are different ways in which uncertainty can affect risk (*see* Yates, 1992). Sometimes risk is said to exist whenever the (negative) outcomes of an action are not assured. Second, quite often decision makers are unable to foresee every significant consequence or outcome of their decision. This uncertainty concerns the relevant attributes or consequences that should be taken into account. Third, even if one accepts that specific negative consequences can occur, there is still uncertainty about whether these consequences will occur. Fourth, it is necessary to distinguish different "levels of uncertainty"; i.e., the firmness of the basis on which the probability of the negative consequence is estimated. The continuum of uncertainty levels ranges from ignorance (no basis whatsoever for estimating probabilities) via frequentistic probabilities (previous experience as the basis for estimating probabilities) to objective probabilities (e.g., if one decides that out of a group of five, one person will be selected by lot to be the spokesperson, the chance of any one of the group being selected is 1/5). The quality of the database for frequentistic probabilities can vary substantially (e.g., a handful of experiences versus epidemiological findings based on large samples). Yates (1992) argues that there is considerable (often implicit) agreement about a fundamental conception of risk. He mentions three essential risk elements:

(1) negative consequences or losses;
(2) the value or significance of these losses; and
(3) uncertainty associated with these losses or consequences.

Individual risk behavior has been studied in the area of DECISION MAKING. As a part of this area PROSPECT THEORY describes the effects of framing on preference for risky versus cautious alternatives in choice situations. Two themes have dominated social psychological research on risk. First, perceived risk and the acceptability of risk have been studied extensively in the context of large scale hazards such as nuclear power, environmental pollution, and a variety of technological developments with possible adverse consequences for the environment and public health. A second theme concerns individual risk-taking behavior. Research on these more personal risks often concerns risks for one's health. Thus, the second theme of this section will focus on the perception of health risks and its relation to risk-taking behavior.

PERCEIVED RISK AND ACCEPTABILITY
Generally, people have difficulties in understanding probabilistic processes. Sometimes

uncertainty is simply denied, sometimes it is misjudged and often one is overconfident about one's judgment. Interestingly, experts appear to be prone to many of the same biases as lay people, especially when they cannot rely upon solid data. Initially, research on risk perception attempted to develop a taxonomy of hazards in order to understand public responses to risks and why some hazards led to extreme aversion and others to indifference. Furthermore, it was hoped that the findings would also help to explain the discrepancies between public reactions and the opinions of experts. One of the major conclusions of this research is that the public is much more likely to accept risks from *voluntary* activities as compared to *involuntary* activities. Voluntary risks which are up to 1,000 times greater than involuntary risks with the same level of benefits, tend to be seen as equally acceptable. Another paradigm in this research is to ask subjects to give their subjective estimates of the frequency of death from a variety of sources or activities (e.g., nuclear power, hang-gliding, different illnesses and accidents) for which objective estimates are available. This research defined risk as annual deaths per activity.

Results show that people are approximately accurate, but that their judgments are systematically distorted (*see* Fischhoff et al., 1981). Overall, data suggested that people have a relatively consistent subjective scale of frequency. Furthermore, their judgments correlate fairly well with available statistical estimates. Responses also indicate a number of shortcomings. One is that differences between the (subjective) judged frequencies of the most and least frequent sources or events are considerably smaller than the corresponding differences in the objective, statistical estimates; i.e., larger risks are underestimated and smaller risks are overestimated. A second bias, AVAILABILITY, results in large differences in the estimated frequency of events with similar statistical frequencies. People who use this HEURISTIC judge an event as likely or common if instances of it are relatively easy to imagine or recall. Frequently occurring events generally come to mind more readily than rare events. Thus, quite often availability is an appropriate cue. However, it is

also affected by numerous factors unrelated to frequency of occurrence. For example, a recent aircrash or train disaster can have substantial distorting effects upon risk judgments. Generally, overestimated frequencies tend to be dramatic and sensational whereas underestimated risks are related to less spectacular events that claim one or a few victims at a time and are also common in nonfatal form. Not surprisingly, overestimated hazards also tend to be disproportionately mentioned in newsmedia. To summarize, lay people can assess annual fatalities if they are asked to, and generally produce estimates with the same general rank ordering as the existing statistical estimates. It seems, however, that their judgments of "risk" are related to other characteristics, such as dramatic impact and newsworthiness which results in increased psychological availability of the risk.

Experts' judgments of risk differ systematically from those of nonexperts. Experts' risk perceptions correlate quite highly with technical estimates of annual number of fatalities; their perceptions also reflect the complete range, from high to low risk. Lay people's perceptions of risk, however, are compressed into a smaller range and do not correlate as highly with annual mortality statistics.

A further line of research attempted to relate perceived risk to other characteristics such as familiarity, perceived control, catastrophic potential, equity, and level of knowledge (*see* Fischhoff et al., 1981). In these studies subjects were asked to judge a large number of technologies and risk-bearing activities on dimensions such as "voluntary–involuntary," "chronic–catastrophic," "common–dread," "not fatal–fatal," "known to exposed–not known to exposed," "immediate–delayed," "known to science–not known to science," "uncontrollable–controllable," and "new–old." The "risk profiles" derived from this research showed that a technological hazard such as nuclear power scored at or near the extreme high-risk end for most of the characteristics. Its risks were seen as involuntary, unknown to those exposed or to science, uncontrollable, unfamiliar, potentially catastrophic, severe, and dreaded. These characteristics can be condensed into a small set of higher-order characteristics. The ratings can largely be explained by two higher-order factors. The first being primarily determined by the characteristics "unknown to exposed" and "unknown to science," and to a lesser extent, by "newness," "involuntariness," and "delay of effect," while the second is defined by severity of consequences, dread, and catastrophic potential. Controllability contributes to both factors.

This research has helped to clarify structural aspects of the perception of technological risks and helps us to understand public reactions and predict future acceptance and rejection of specific technologies. An obvious case in point is nuclear power. The public's view about nuclear power risks is that these are *unknown, dreaded, uncontrollable, inequitable, catastrophic*, and *likely to affect future generations*. People's strong fears about nuclear power seem logical consequences of their concerns about these considerations. Furthermore, it seems likely that accidents occurring with unknown and potentially catastrophic technologies will be seen as indicative of our loss of control over this technology (*see also* Van der Pligt, 1992).

## PERCEIVED RISK AND RISK-TAKING BEHAVIOR

Increased knowledge of the possible health consequences of behavioral practices has led to a situation in which a wide range of behaviors have been labeled as risky. As morbidity and mortality have come to be related more to chronic conditions which are tied to lifestyle and behavior, there has been a significant increase in research attempting to understand these behaviors and to help design behavioral intervention programs.

Several theoretical models have been proposed to examine health-related behaviors; these theories are generally based on more general theories of decision making and risk taking. Another source of these models is the THEORY OF REASONED ACTION. These models all incorporate the concept of perceived risk. For instance, the Health Belief Model (Janz & Becker, 1984) states that an individual would be prepared to undertake preventive behavior(s) as a function of his or her perception of the severity of the threat, the perceived benefits of the recommended health action, and the perceived barriers to taking the action. Protection Motivation Theory (Rogers, 1975, 1983) focuses on cognitive appraisal processes in response to messages about health risks that induce fear. This theory also includes factors such as the perceived severity of the health threat and perceived vulnerability or susceptibility.

Both models deal with perceived risk. Unfortunately, individuals are not always accurate judges of their risk. One pervasive bias in people's judgments regarding their own risks, or susceptibility to negative health effects, is called unrealistic optimism (Weinstein, 1988). This optimism could reduce the effectiveness of health education programs that are intended to warn people about specific health risks and to persuade them to change risky behaviors or lifestyles. Weinstein argued that people tend to think they are "invulnerable"; others are more likely to experience negative health consequences than oneself. Each individual could be right in assuming that his or her risks are smaller than those of comparable others. However, if most people in a specific group rate their risk below average, a substantial part of them must be wrong or "unrealistic."

Six possible causes have been mentioned in the literature on unrealistic optimism. A first factor is *perceived control*: When rating one's own risk status as compared to others, optimism tends to be greater for those risks judged to be under personal control. Findings also indicate that for any specific health risk those who rate its controllability higher are more optimistic. This relation between perceived controllability and optimism is confirmed by research on risk appraisals in a wide variety of health-related domains.

A second factor that could be related to optimism is the so-called *egocentric bias*. When people are asked to assess their risks and those of others, they are bound to have more knowledge about their own protective actions than those of others. It seems that people tend to focus on risk-reducing actions while they tend to forget personal actions or circumstances that increase their risks. Moreover, one's own actions are more available than those of others; i.e. one simply forgets that most other people also take protective action. This bias is also related to cognitive availability. We simply have more knowledge about our own precautionary actions than those of others.

Third, lack of previous *personal experience* tends to increase unrealistic optimism. Personal experience tends to be relatively vivid (*see* VIVIDNESS) as compared to statistical information about risks, and enhances both availability and recall. Possible negative consequences for health and well-being that have been experienced more directly tend to result in less optimistic risk appraisals.

A fourth factor that could produce unrealistic optimism is related to *stereotypical* or *prototypical judgment*. People might have a relatively extreme image of those suffering from specific diseases. This extreme prototype is unlikely to fit one's self-image, hence it is concluded that the risk does not apply to oneself but primarily to others.

A fifth factor is SELF-ESTEEM *maintenance* or enhancement. Generally, people seem to think that their own actions, lifestyle, and personality are more advantageous than those of their peers. This mechanism would explain the fact that people are generally not optimistic about hereditary and environmental health-risks, for the latter do not constitute a threat to one's self-esteem. In contrast, a high-risk lifestyle could be seen to imply that we are ignorant of what we ought to do or are simply unable to exercise self-control. These factors concern a person's ability to cope effectively with life demands and have clear links to self-esteem.

The sixth and final factor is related to *coping strategies*. Under conditions of high stress or threat, denial is a response often used to protect against anxiety or worry. Denial can reduce emotional distress but can also reduce the likelihood of direct behavioral actions, which may be necessary to reduce one's risks. Unrealistic optimism is an illusion that can help the individual to adapt to threatening events. The issue of how people cope with risks which are seen as a threat and which induce anxiety and stress is addressed in more detail in the following section.

## RISK, THREAT, AND COPING

Information about risks to one's health can be threatening and relatively stressful. Janis and Mann's (1977) conflict theory provides a model of how stress caused by decisional conflict can affect decision making. The heart of their theory is an analysis of basic COPING patterns which are used to deal with intraindividual conflict and stress. These five patterns are unconflicted inertia, unconflicted change to a new course of action, defensive avoidance, hypervigilance, and vigilance. Conflict theory uses the term "risk" in its common, everyday meaning of "exposure to the chance of negative outcomes." Conflict is expected to be aroused whenever the person recognizes that there are serious risks arising from existing and/or new behaviors. This elicits feelings of anxiety and emotional stress. The three coping patterns commonly associated with decisional conflict and stress are defensive avoidance (which is generally assumed to take three forms: procrastination, shifting decision responsibility to others, and rationalization); hypervigilance (immediate and impulsive choice which is unstable and characterized by a high rate of vacillation); and vigilance (which refers to relatively careful, deliberate choice). Each of these three coping styles is associated with a distinctive level of stress. Defensive avoidance is related to variable stress levels as a function of the salience of the threat, hypervigilance is associated with extremely high levels of stress; while vigilance is generally associated with moderate levels of stress. Conflict theory relates levels of stress to the quality of information processing and decision making, with less adequate decision making being associated with maladaptive coping styles such as defensive avoidance and hypervigilance. Protection motivation theory also distinguishes between adaptive (e.g., rational problem solving) and maladaptive coping styles (e.g., avoidance, wishful thinking, fatalism, hopelessness). These distinctions are of importance in the context of risk communication and health education programs aiming to encourage people to change risky behavior. It seems essential that such programs increase people's awareness of specific risks but within certain limits. Programs that induce fear (*see* FEAR APPEALS) could induce high levels of stress which in turn could hinder behavioral change due to maladaptive coping styles such as defensive avoidance and hypervigilance.

Stress can also play a role in the context of technological risks. Information about technological risks can be threatening and lead to anxiety and stress. This is especially the case with large-scale disasters such as nuclear and chemical accidents. A major nuclear accident at Three Mile Island (USA) in 1979 resulted in a series of longitudinal studies. This research showed that the uncertainty about health risks and the economic future of the region resulted in increased stress levels for local residents. This research also showed the relevance of coping styles. Emotionally focused coping was associated with less stress than problem-focused coping and denial. In other words, local residents who chose to attend to their emotional response (focus inward and attempt to control fears and related responses) experienced less stress than people who focused on the source of stress in order to reduce or remove the threat that was posed. In extreme circumstances such as large-scale disasters, the situation is difficult for individuals to change and the realization of the necessary changes by the responsible agents (e.g., a local authority, national government or a specific firm) usually takes a long time. Due to the low controllability of the possible negative consequences, problem-oriented coping styles (such as vigilance) seem to be less effective in these circumstances.

CONCLUSIONS

Risk plays an important role in our lives. Research on the perception of risk has shown that people are reasonably adequate judges of many risks. Their perception is also biased, however. The availability heuristic is one of the distorting factors. Acceptability of large-scale technological risks seems to be primarily determined by qualitative characteristics of these risks such as the severity of the consequences, catastrophic potential, the novelty of the risks and low perceived controllability. People's perception of personal risks of their own behavioral practices follows a different

pattern. Generally, people seem rather optimistic about personal risks, an illusion that could reduce the need to take preventive action. Finally, approaches that incorporate stress and coping responses to risks that pose a serious threat could help to improve our understanding of public reactions to these risks.

*See also*: DECISION MAKING; HEURISTICS; PROSPECT THEORY; SELF-ESTEEM; STRESS AND COPING.

BIBLIOGRAPHY

Fischhoff, B., Lichtenstein, S., Slovic, P., Derby, S. L., & Keeney, R. L. (1981). *Acceptable risk*. Cambridge: Cambridge University Press.

Janis, I. L., & Mann, L. (1977). *Decision making*. New York: Free Press.

Janz, N. K., & Becker, M. H. (1984). The health belief model: A decade later. *Health Education Quarterly*, *11*, 1–47.

Rogers, R. W. (1975). A protection motivation theory of fear appeals and attitude change. *Journal of Psychology*, *91*, 93–114.

——— (1983). Cognitive and physiological processes in fear appeals and attitude change: A revised theory of protection-motivation. In J. T. Cacioppo & R. E. Petty (Eds.), *Social psychophysiology, a sourcebook* (pp. 153–76). New York: Guildford Press.

Van der Pligt, J. (1992). *Nuclear energy and the public*. Oxford: Blackwell Publisher.

Weinstein, N. H. (Ed.) (1988). *Taking care: Understanding and encouraging self-protective behavior*. Cambridge: Cambridge University Press.

Yates, J. F. (Ed.) (1992). *Risk-taking behavior*. Chichester: J. Wiley.

JOOP VAN DER PLIGT

**role theory** This theory builds on ideas rooted in a theatrical metaphor: Social life proceeds as performances by actors in a drama. There are various role theories. All hold that persons occupy different locations in organized social life; particular NORMS, BELIEFS, and ATTITUDES attach to varying social locations, for both persons in those locations and others not themselves in the locations; and persons' behavior reflects their social locations and consequent differences in norms, beliefs, and attitudes. More succinctly, conventionally, and controversially: Social behavior reflects persons' positions in organized structures of relationships and expectations for behavior attached to those positions. For some (e.g., Biddle, 1986), role refers to actors' performances and requires explanation; for others (e.g., Stryker & Statham, 1986), role means expectations linked to positions and helps explain social behavior. Using the language of role performance and role expectations avoids this ambiguity.

Role theory is not a theory: Its ideas constitute a conceptual frame for social structural, interactional, or behavioral analyses, from which explanatory theories may develop. The ideas fall into disparate subsets. Biddle (1986) distinguishes functional role theory, used primarily to analyze stability in social systems; symbolic interactionist role theory, oriented to analyses of persons and interaction; structural role theory, devoted to analyzing social networks and exchanges; organizational role theory, focusing on role conflict in formal organizations; and cognitive role theory, interested in role expectation–behavior relations. This classification fails to capture the most important distinguishing characteristics of work within role theory; doing so is the distinction between "structural role theory" and "interactional role theory" (see Stryker & Statham, 1986, for extended discussions).

### STRUCTURAL ROLE THEORY

Structural role theory (SRT) derives from classical sociological and anthropological theory and provides conceptual bases for the analysis of stability in persons and social structures. For SRT, actors play assigned parts in scripts written by culture and shaped by evolutionary adaptation. Persons play parts with minimal improvisation; the parts themselves are designed to restore scripts to their original forms should improvisation threaten the basic structure of the plays. More formally, social structures are differentiated and actors are expected to behave in varying, interrelated ways in carrying out functions of those structures. Social groups as organizations of positions and roles provide interfaces between individuals and larger social systems. Role expectations are located in the cultures of larger societies and in group contexts in which interaction occurs. They are grounded in widely shared values which are institutionalized prior to interaction. Expectations become moral imperatives, because persons have stakes in the predictability and regularity of role performances; complementarity of expectations and performances underlies conformity to those imperatives and social stability.

Links between expectations and performances and pressures toward CONFORMITY constitute major research foci of those working within an SRT frame. So too socialization processes – imitation, instruction, altercasting – for SOCIALIZATION is taken as the primary way persons internalize roles, and internalization is believed to be a key ingredient in efficiently achieving social stability. Recognition that persons may occupy multiple positions with potentially incompatible roles, relate to others whose expectations of them are internally inconsistent, or face role expectations from multiple others calling for conflicting role performances, has led to considerable research on role conflict, its personal and organizational consequences, and its resolution.

### INTERACTIONAL ROLE THEORY

Interactional role theory (IRT) partly derives from the same intellectual sources as, and tends to merge with, SYMBOLIC INTERACTIONISM. It is critical of SRT for its one-sided emphases on social stability, conformity, and complementarity of roles, its failure to consider seriously variable interests of differentiated groups within societies and individuals within groups, and its neglect of human agency. As these criticisms imply, the intellectual issues for IRT concern social processes more than social structures, social change more than social stability, conflict more than consensus, deviance, and creativity more than conformity. Not surprisingly, the theatrical imagery of IRT differs from that of SRT. Rather than being solidly in place prior to casting a play, scripts are developed, elaborated and changed in the course of performances. Scripts only broadly constrain what actors do; actors constantly ad lib as they and their co-actors construct the play. Performances are developed to achieve solutions to immediate problems posed in the play, which solutions merely are start-points for solutions to subsequent problems. Again more formally, for IRT persons do not simply play out roles as given by expectations linked to positions they occupy. Indeed, positions tend to be viewed broadly as kinds of persons it is possible to be in society rather than as parts of highly organized structures of relationships. Even in the context of organized structures, persons engage in role making (Turner, 1962), thus to some extent creating their roles. Human agency and creativity in shaping social structures are as much facts of social life as social constraint and conformity.

IRT research focuses on much the same topics as does SRT, but its emphases differ in ways consistent with the respective theatrical imageries recounted above. For example, it examines role conflicts as opportunities for creative solutions as well as bases of social and personal instability; and it examines socialization as source of novelty and change as well as conformity.

CONCLUDING OBSERVATION
Contemporary social psychology regards cognitive structures as products of persons' cumulative experience. Role theory of whatever variety reminds the field that personal experience is socially organized, not random. Consequently, persons will develop cognitive structures reflecting differential social locations and accompanying role expectations. The relative import of structure versus interaction in this process is a matter of debate.
See also: ATTITUDE THEORY AND RESEARCH; NORMS; SOCIALIZATION; SYMBOLIC INTERACTIONISM.

BIBLIOGRAPHY
Biddle, B. J. (1986). Recent developments in role theory. In R. H. Turner (Ed.), *Annual review of sociology* (Vol. 12, pp. 67–92). Palo Alto; CA: Annual Reviews.
Stryker, S., & Statham, A. (1986). Symbolic interaction and role theory. In G. Lindzey & E. Aronson (Eds.), *The handbook of social psychology*. (3rd ed., Vol. 1, pp. 311–78). New York: Random House.
Turner, R. H. (1962). Role-taking: Process vs. conformity. In A. M. Rose (Ed.), *Human behavior and social process*. Boston; MA: Houghton Mifflin.

SHELDON STRYKER

**rumor** Allport and Postman (1947), usually credited with the first systematic experimental studies of rumor transmission, specified two factors favorable to their spread, namely the subjective importance of events, and the absence or ambiguity of reliable news or information about the events concerned. However, their research dealt only with the manner in which the process of rumor transmission introduces errors into the story transmitted. This work drew upon Frederick Barlett's ideas about remembering, particularly the notion that, over time, recollection of the features of a story become simplified. It confirmed that, with successive retellings, stories do become shorter, more concise and less detailed, rather than elaborated (*see* MEMORY, SCHEMAS/ SCHEMATA).

Rosnow (1991) provides a meta-analysis of experimental studies of four factors favorable to rumor transmission: personal ANXIETY, general uncertainty, credulity, and outcome-relevant involvement. This reveals anxiety to have the strongest effect, and uncertainty the smallest effect.

Case studies of naturally occurring rumors highlight the phenomenon of recurring themes in rumors about outgroups, one of the most extensively documented of which is that of ritual child murder. This is consistent with a hypothesis first introduced by Festinger (*see* COGNITIVE DISSONANCE, THEORY), that rumors serve not to reduce the anxieties of a group or community but to justify the fears expressed by group members about, for example, ethnic minorities.
See also: COGNITIVE DISSONANCE THEORY; MEMORY; SCHEMAS/SCHEMATA.

BIBLIOGRAPHY

Allport, G. W., & Postman, L. (1947). *The psychology of rumor*. New York: Holt.

Rosnow, R. (1991). Inside rumor: A personal journey. *American Psychologist*, *46*, 484–96.

NICHOLAS EMLER

# S

**salience** This is a property of a stimulus that causes it to stand out and attract ATTENTION in its context. People can be salient in the context of their immediate environment: for example, as the only person of that ethnicity in a group or the person dominating one's visual field in a given context. People's expectations set up broader contexts for salience, such as a person acting in ways that are unusual for people in general (i.e., negative or extreme behavior), unusual for that person's role, or unusual for that particular person. People relevant to a perceiver's goals are also salient (Taylor & Fiske, 1978).

Salient people are perceived to have disproportionate impact on their group, their salient behavior is often attributed to underlying dispositions (*see* ATTRIBUTION THEORIES), and they are judged in extreme, polarized terms (McArthur, 1981).

*See also*: ATTENTION; ATTRIBUTION THEORIES.

BIBLIOGRAPHY

McArthur, L. Z. (1981). What grabs you? The role of attention in impression formation and causal attribution. In E. T. Higgins, C. P. Herman, & M. P. Zanna (Eds.), *Social cognition: The Ontario symposium* (Vol. 1, pp. 201–46). Hillsdale, NJ: Lawrence Erlbaum.

Taylor, S. E., & Fiske, S. T. (1978). Salience, attention, and attribution: Top of the head phenomena. In L. Berkowitz (Ed.), *Advances in experimental social psychology* (Vol. 11, pp. 249–88). New York: Academic Press.

SUSAN T. FISKE<br>BETH A. MORLING

**schemas/schemata** Cognitive structures that represent a person's knowledge about an object, person, or situation, including knowledge about attributes and relationships among those attributes. People's schemas are abstract concepts that represent a general case, emphasizing what is similar among a number of instances. As such, they help people simplify reality. Importantly, they guide processing of new information. Schemas set up expectations about what kind of information will follow, help to relate details about a stimulus to a general concept, and fill in missing information (*see* Fiske & Taylor, 1991, for a review of schema literature).

Schema-driven processing contrasts with data-driven processing. Whereas schemas use organized previous knowledge to facilitate information processing, data-driven processing facilitates conclusions that go beyond the information at hand. People use both schemas and data-driven strategies to perceive new information, depending on the situation and their personal motivations. As a consequence, much social-cognitive research has focused on identifying the circumstances under which people rely more on their schemas or more on the information given.

## ORIGINS OF THE SCHEMA CONCEPT

The schema concept shares some principles with early Gestalt theories of perception. According to Gestalt psychologists, perceptions of individual elements depend on how people interpret the context in which they are embedded. Schemas resemble Gestalt configurations in that they shape the perception of individual pieces of information by putting them in a single context.

In Gestalt-inspired person perception research, current schema theories grew out of Asch's configural model (Asch, 1946) and Heider's balance theory (Heider, 1958).

Given a list of traits about a new person, Asch's model predicts that people form a unified impression and then bring individual traits in line with it (*see* IMPRESSION FORMATION). Like schemas, configurations are made up of traits and their relationships, and can influence the perception of individual traits, bringing them in line with the overall impression.

Heider's balance theory is another framework that predates schema theories. Balance theory predicts that given a perceiver (P), another person (O), and an object (X), people prefer triads whose internal relationships are logically consistent. Like schema theory, balance theory specifies both the members of a triad and the relationships among the elements (*see* BALANCE THEORY).

The social schema concept also has origins in cognitive psychology, more specifically in research demonstrating how people can use patterns and their prior knowledge to help make sense of new information. For example, if people are told what a passage is about before they read it, they better comprehend, attend, and remember its details. Cognitive psychology also provided theories describing how people categorize information. Categorization is important because before people can use their schemas, they must first classify the instance as a member of a category to which schematic knowledge then applies (*see* CATEGORIZATION).

## TYPES OF SOCIAL SCHEMAS

All social schemas share the ability to describe relationships among attributes contained in the schema, to influence the understanding of new information, to remember schema-relevant facts, and to fill in missing details. Here we describe five primary types of social schemas (Taylor & Crocker, 1981).

### Person Schemas

People have schemas containing knowledge about different types of people, which include their personality traits and goals. For example, a person may have a schema for a "tennis pro," containing information about the person's appearance (dresses in white), traits (hard working, aggressive) and goals (to win tournaments). Often people's person schemas contain information about the situations in which the schematic person is usually found (e.g., at a country club).

### Self-Schemas

People also have schemas that organize their knowledge about themselves in particular domains. People are usually self-schematic on traits that are important to them and about which they have a store of knowledge. Self-schemas suggest that people organize knowledge about themselves in some of the same ways in which they store information about other people.

### Role Schemas

Social roles are sets of behaviors that are expected of people in a particular social position. Role schemas organize people's knowledge about social roles. Some social roles (e.g., doctor) are *achieved* – people earn them through deliberate effort. Other roles (e.g., age, race, gender) are *ascribed*, acquired automatically. Role schemas from ascribed roles are one way to explain stereotyping. Perceivers applying ascribed role schemas expect people to behave or to be treated according to their social position.

### Event Schemas or Scripts

These schemas contain information about the appropriate sequence of events in common situations. For example, a restaurant script may involve the sequence of being seated, reading the menu, ordering, eating, and tipping the waiter. Scripts include details about props (menus), roles (the hostess) and rules for the sequence of events (*see* SCRIPTS).

### Content-Free Schemas

A content-free schema contains information about a processing rule. It indicates links among elements but not the content of the elements themselves. For example, linear-ordering schemas are content-free schemas that specify transitive, hierarchical relationships. For example, if Alex is shorter than Bob, who is shorter than Carol, then we can conclude that Alex is shorter than Carol. The schema only specifies the rule (transitivity) not the content (the particular people or the dimension).

## THE EFFECTS OF SOCIAL SCHEMAS

Once activated, a schema can change people's encoding of schema-related events, so that what is noticed, remembered, and assumed is consistent with the activated schema. Age and gender schemas are likely to be universal dimensions that are activated quickly and consistently because of their visual salience (Brewer, 1988). Being told about a new person's race, job, or personality traits also serves to activate related schemas. Once cued, schemas immediately influence people's attention. People more often notice information that is consistent with their schemas, and may reinterpret inconsistent information to bring it in line with the schema. Once identified as a member of a schema category (such as a racial group), a person may appear to be like other category members, even if, in truth, the person has little in common with them. Schemas thus reduce the perceived variability of category members by stressing consistency among them. In general, people perceive more variance in their own group, whereas they assume that members of other groups are all the same (see OUTGROUP HOMOGENEITY, INTERGROUP RELATIONS).

Schemas also affect the retrieval of information from MEMORY. Although activating a schema before information is processed produces stronger effects, schemas do have significant influence on how information is retrieved. In general, people tend to remember schema-relevant information and forget schema-irrelevant information (e.g., Hastie, 1981). Within schema-relevant information, people remember schema-inconsistent information or schema-consistent information, depending on a host of factors (Fiske, 1993).

One factor that affects attention to and memory for schema-inconsistent information is schema strength. Schemas that are relatively less well developed make people more open to inconsistent information (see Fiske & Neuberg, 1990). Another factor is motivation. Because processing schema-inconsistent information requires effort, people notice it more when they are especially motivated by particular goals (such as the goal of forming an accurate impression).

Other factors make attention to and memory for schema-inconsistent information *less* likely. Given the chance to think about their impressions, people are more likely to remember schema-consistent information. Attention to consistent information is also more likely in complex situations (Srull & Wyer, 1989).

In addition to attention and memory effects, an activated schema can also influence people's evaluation of a person or group. Schemas may trigger particular affective reactions, such as fear or hatred, as well as influence a person's evaluation of a person. General schemas of "us" versus "them" can activate ingroup favoritism, which causes people to evaluate members of their own group more highly, even if the groups are arbitrary. People's schema-activated evaluations of others are often independent of whether or not they notice and remember schema-inconsistent information. People may have noticed inconsistencies about a person, but they may still use the original schema to evaluate him or her.

Although people use schemas initially and fairly automatically, people can abandon them when information contradicts the schema, especially if they are sufficiently motivated (e.g., the Continuum Model of impression formation and the Dual Process Model). Thus, people do not blindly use a schema if it does not apply; if motivated, they pay attention to the data, and modify their impressions accordingly.

## SPECIFICS OF SCHEMA USE

Given a particular person, what factors determine which particular schemas will be applied? Numerous conditions can affect schema use (see Fiske & Taylor, 1991, for a review). First, schemas based on social roles (e.g., politician) are used more often than those based on traits (e.g., extraversion). Role schemas are apparently richer in detail than traits are, so they are more informative. Second, people use schemas at an intermediate level more than they use either general or lower-level schemas. For example, people are more likely to think in terms of a "career woman," instead of the more general "woman" or more specific "female accountant." Third, people more often use schemas that are activated by physical, visual cues, such as age, race, gender, and attractiveness.

A fourth factor that influences schema use is primacy. Because schemas influence the way information is encoded, initial schemas show greater effects than schemas activated afterwards. Fifth, salient cues readily activate schemas. Features that stand out in a crowd are more likely to activate relevant schemas (*see* SALIENCE). Sixth, accessibility affects schema use. People are more likely to use schemas that they have used regularly or recently in the past. Next, people often use schemas that match their MOOD. People in a good mood are more likely to notice positive things about someone, and people in a bad mood may notice more negative things. Finally, people tend to pay more attention to people who have power over their outcomes, and therefore they have well-developed schemas for people in power. These dimensions, then, help predict which schemas will be activated for any particular person.

## SCHEMA DEVELOPMENT

People can develop schemas by direct experience or by hearing others talk about schema-related information. Schemas develop and change as people encounter more schema-related instances. For instance, people's schemas become more abstract; as people have more experience with different instances, they generalize about the commonalities among them. Schemas also become more complex as they develop, again because people have more experiences from which to draw details. Developing schemas also become more tightly organized, so that the information they contain is not only more complex, but also more usable. As they develop, schemas also may become more unitized. They start to be accessed and used as single (and thus, efficient) units of information. Schemas might also become more accurate as they develop.

As they develop, schemas also change in their ability to incorporate inconsistent in-

formation. People who are first forming schemas try to make sense of any inconsistent information. At an intermediate level of schema development, people focus all of their attention on consistencies. Finally, as people's schemas become more abstract, complex, organized, and compact, they can assimilate exceptions more easily (*see* Fiske & Neuberg, 1990; Higgins & Bargh, 1987; Ruble, 1993).

## SCHEMA STABILITY VERSUS CHANGE

Much of schema research has focused on how schemas remain stable and resilient to change. Stable schemas confer predictability, structure, and order. As a consequence, people may be motivated to maintain their schemas, even in the face of contrary evidence. For example, people may ignore or discredit information that threatens their schemas, or they may interpret such information in a way that supports the schema. Besides transforming any inconsistent information, another factor that leads to schema stability is mere thought. Just thinking about schemas makes them more stable, and polarizes judgments related to the schema. Thinking seems to induce people to gather new evidence in favor of their schemas and to make existing evidence more coherent.

While people's schemas often resist change, under certain circumstances they may be more open to change. Theoretically, the best supported model for schema change is the subtyping model, which suggests that people develop subcategories of their schemas in response to disconfirming evidence (*see* STEREOTYPING).

Some kinds of schemas are more likely to change than others, depending on how easily disconfirmed they are. Some schemas (e.g., honesty) permit only a narrow range of behavior, so they are easily disconfirmed, whereas others permit a wide range of behavior, so they are harder to disconfirm. For example, people would have a difficult time disconfirming the label "mental patient," because of the wide range of behaviors considered typical of mental patients.

One of the conditions that facilitates schema change is activating two opposing schemas for a single instance. For example, schemas for race may not be activated if another significant group membership cuts across racial categories. In this example, in-group status might be primary. Another factor that can influence schema change is the effort to see others as individuals with unique personal attributes. Finally, schemas are more likely to change if a wide range of otherwise typical category members behave in schema-inconsistent ways. If the counter-stereotypic behavior comes from members who are otherwise typical, simple subtyping will be less likely.

## GOALS AND SCHEMA USE

Depending on their specific goals, people can rely more on their schemas or more on the data at hand (*see* Fiske, 1993). When interactions increase the costs of being wrong, people are more motivated to be accurate. One such instance is outcome dependency. When people's rewards or punishments are contingent on another person (when they are interdependent), they pay more attention to the other person (Fiske & Neuberg, 1990). People also tend to be more complex and attentive when they know they will be held accountable for their decisions. However, accountability only makes people's impressions more complex; it doesn't necessarily make them more accurate (*see* ACCOUNTABILITY). Another factor that motivates accuracy is the target's self-concept. When targets appear very sure of their self-concepts, then perceivers are less likely to impose their schemas on them. People are also motivated to be accurate when they feel more responsible and when they are reminded to be accurate.

Other situations increase the costs of being indecisive, so people are more motivated to process social information efficiently, making fast, good-enough impressions. For instance, when people are under pressure to reach closure, they spend less time searching for additional information. When people's individual or group SELF-ESTEEM is threatened, they also rely more on category-based judgments. Narrating an event or explaining something to others also makes people more schema-dependent. In these instances, schemas may lend coherence to a smooth story or explanation.

Thus, to a great extent, people's relative reliance on schemas or data depends on their intentions. What people consider appropriate in a situation can influence their choices of schema-driven or individuating processes.

## INDIVIDUAL DIFFERENCES IN SCHEMA USE

People differ in the ways they characteristically process information about others. For example, when people are self-schematic on a trait (*see* SELF-SCHEMAS), they tend to be more sensitive to that trait in other people as well. People also have dimensions that they habitually use to describe people (*see* ACCESSIBILITY). These traits are typically more accessible and are termed "chronic." People who are chronic on a trait recognize it faster in others and are usually more accurate in applying the trait label.

Some more ways that people may differ in schema use are domain specific: People differ in masculinity and femininity, political expertise, and levels of interpersonal dominance or dependence. When a situation draws on one of these sensitivities, people use relevant schemas more efficiently than other people do.

## CRITIQUES OF THE SCHEMA CONCEPT

Criticisms of the schema concept have mainly faulted the research for focusing too much on the stable and biasing nature of schemas. Schema research has perhaps overemphasized how stable schemas are, and discouraged the study of schema change. Related to issues of stability, some have criticized the schema research as implying that "people can't help it," and are thus excused from responsibility for schema-related negative effects (such as stereotyping). However, some research emphasizes that people do have control over their use of schema-driven and individuating processes.

Schema research has recently changed its focus from the biases and inaccuracies of schemas to their relative usefulness and accuracy in the real world. Schemas are definitely useful tools for recognizing patterns of behavior, and they are often more adaptive than they are normally believed to be. In this light, people's reliance on schemas appears economical and wise. The functional nature of schemas has been interpreted from an evolutionary perspective: fast processing of information about others can have survival or reproductive benefits. In addition, schemas presumably help individuals feel that the world is a knowable, predictable place, giving people a sense of control.

*See also*: ACCOUNTABILITY; CATEGORIZATION; IMPRESSION FORMATION; INTERGROUP RELATIONS; MEMORY; MOOD; OUTGROUP HOMOGENEITY; SCRIPTS; SELF-ESTEEM; STEREOTYPING.

BIBLIOGRAPHY

Asch, S. E. (1946). Forming impressions of personality. *Journal of Abnormal and Social Psychology, 41,* 1230–40.

Brewer, M. B. (1988). A dual process model of impression formation. In T. K. Srull & R. S. Wyer, Jr (Eds.), *Advances in social cognition* (Vol. 1, pp. 1–36). Hillsdale, NJ: Lawrence Erlbaum.

Fiske, S. T. (1993). Social cognition and social perception. *Annual Review of Psychology, 44,* 155–94.

—— & Neuberg, S. L. (1990). A continuum of impression formation, from category-based to individuating processes: Influences of information and motivation on attention and interpretation. In M.P. Zanna (Ed.), *Advances in experimental social psychology* (Vol. 23, pp. 1–74). New York: Academic Press.

—— & Taylor, S. E. (1991). *Social cognition* (2nd ed., Chaps 4 & 5). New York: McGraw-Hill.

Hastie, R. (1981). Schematic principles in human memory. In E. T. Higgins, C. P. Herman, & M. P. Zanna (Eds.), *Social cognition: The Ontario symposium* (Vol. 1, pp. 39–88). Hillsdale, NJ: Lawrence Erlbaum.

Heider, F. (1958). *The psychology of interpersonal relations.* New York: Wiley.

Higgins, E. T., & Bargh, J. A. (1987). Social cognition and social perception. *Annual Review of Psychology, 38,* 369–425.

Ruble, D. N. (1993). A phase model of transitions: Cognitive and motivational consequences. In M. Zanna (Ed.), *Advances in experimental social psychology* (Vol. 26, pp. 163–214).

Srull, T. K., & Wyer, R. S., Jr (1989). Person memory and judgment. *Psychological Review, 96,* 58–83.

Taylor, S. E., & Crocker, J. (1981). Schematic bases of social information processing. In E. T. Higgins, C. P. Herman, & M. P. Zanna (Eds.), *Social cognition: The Ontario symposium* (Vol. 1, pp. 89–134). Hillsdale, NJ: Lawrence Erlbaum.

SUSAN T. FISKE
BETH A. MORLING

**scripts (also event schemas or event sequences)** These are SCHEMAS (knowledge structures) that describe the typical sequence of events in common situations. People have scripts for such varied social situations as eating in a restaurant, attending a lecture, or being ill. Scripts include behaviors (e.g., being seated), roles (e.g., waiters), and props (e.g., menus).

As schemas, scripts help people use prior knowledge to set up expectations about what kinds of behaviors will follow, relate details to a general pattern, and fill in missing information (Schank & Abelson, 1977). Scripts, like schemas, favor coherence, so information inconsistent with a script is surprising and often elaborated by the perceiver. The unique feature of scripts is that they are temporal, often including causal statements. Scripts also specify enabling conditions that precede a script (e.g., being hungry and having money) or occur within it (e.g., contacting the waiter to get the menu), as well as outcomes that follow (e.g., being less hungry and having less money).

ORGANIZATION OF SCRIPT KNOWLEDGE

Scripts and event sequences can be organized by scenes, subgoals, or causal links (for a review, *see* Wyer & Gordon, 1984). First, scenes specify shorter temporal clusters; for example, a script for food shopping may include smaller scenes, such as standing in the checkout line. Second, scripts can be organized by their goals and subgoals. A person's goal to buy food includes the subgoals of choosing the food and paying for it. Third, event sequences can be organized more linearly, by causal relationships. The causal sequence "Jayne thanked the employee for helping her carry the bags" is an example.

The organizational structure of scripts appears to include a hierarchy and a temporal label. Scenes are stored under a script label, and people can access a scene directly, without starting from the beginning of the script. The hierarchy apparently also contains temporal information, so people know whether a scene is nearer the beginning, middle, or end of a script.

## SCRIPT MEMORY AND DEVELOPMENT

When people experience an actual event, their script knowledge influences what they remember (for a review, *see* Bower, Black, & Turner, 1979). For example, if people hear a story in an unusual order, they later tend to recall the events in a script-consistent order. Scenes may contain events that are consistent with script knowledge (e.g., "Mark ordered from the menu" for a restaurant script), scenes that are inconsistent (e.g., "Mark left without paying"), and scenes that are irrelevant (e.g., "He was wearing a blue suit"). After a short delay, people remember inconsistent events best, followed by consistent and irrelevant events. But after a long delay, recall favors consistent information. One explanation for these results suggests that at encoding, people fit consistent behavior into an activated script structure and "tag" inconsistencies. While people's attention to inconsistencies means they are processed more thoroughly (facilitating better recall after a short delay), the tags are stored independently of the script knowledge and may not be recalled with the script when it is retrieved much later.

Scripts are developed through direct experience or communication. Cultural norms are also a source of script development. Cultures have different requirements for a good story or explanation (e.g., differences in folktales). Of course, the subjects and content of scripts can vary cross-culturally.

## SCRIPTS AND SOCIAL INFORMATION PROCESSING

People's scripts help them to link related events together and decide the importance of different behaviors. The goal structure of scripts helps especially here. For example, if people know that an actor in a scene would like to lose weight, they decide that the behaviors of stepping on a scale and smiling are both important and causally linked. The goal also gives meaning to certain ambiguous events (e.g., eating a salad on a cold day), and fills in details, such as whether or not the person will turn down dessert.

People's knowledge of scripts helps them plan their own behavior. Scripts specify the behavioral steps that lead to an abstract goal.

Script knowledge influences how people process ongoing events. As people witness others' actions, they group behaviors into meaningful chunks according to script knowledge. The groups of behaviors are not separated by beginning and ending breakpoints; rather, they are summarized as scenes. For example, the behaviors of walking to the kitchen and opening the refrigerator can be summarized in the scene, "getting a snack."

People's use of event schemas is important in their understanding of a wide variety of social information (Lalljee, Lamb, & Abelson, 1992). People store prototypical explanations that are causal sequences for particular events (e.g., theft). Narratives also help people make diverse information coherent. People are likely to use narrative explanations to understand unusual combinations of traits (such as a hostile yet nurturing person). People believe future events to be more likely to the extent that they can imagine a plausible scenario including them. And past events that are perceived as easy to undo (i.e., do not fit the usual script) elicit stronger emotional reactions (e.g., more regret or relief).

Narrative may also play a role in JURY decision making (Hastie & Pennington, 1991). If people can construct a good story to cover a lot of evidence, the causal relationships in the story are more believable and harder to disconfirm with contrary evidence. People also use narrative explanation to give meaning to traumatic life events. Constructing stories appears to help victims cope. People use active narratives, not just static categories, to understand the social world.

*See also*: CATEGORIZATION; JURIES; SCHEMAS/ SCHEMATA.

BIBLIOGRAPHY

Bower, G. H., Black, J. B., & Turner T. J. (1979). Scripts in memory for text. *Cognitive Psychology, 11*, 177–220.

Hastie, R., & Pennington, N. (1991). Cognitive and social processes in decision making. In L. Resnick, J. Levine, & S. Teasley (Eds.), *Perspectives on socially shared cognition* (pp. 308–27). Washington, DC: American Psychological Association.

Lalljee, M., Lamb, R., & Abelson, R. P. (1992). The role of event prototypes in categorization and explanation. In W. Stroebe & M. Hewstone (Eds.), *European Review of Social Psychology* (Vol. 3, pp. 153–82). Chichester: J. Wiley.

Schank, R. C., & Abelson, R. P. (1977). *Scripts, plans, goals, and understanding: An inquiry into human knowledge structures.* Hillsdale, NJ: Lawrence Erlbaum.

Wyer, R. S., Jr, & Gordon, S. E. (1984). The cognitive representation of social information. In R. S. Wyer, Jr, & T. K. Srull (Eds.), *Handbook of social cognition* (Vol. 2, pp. 73–150). Hillsdale, NJ: Lawrence Erlbaum.

SUSAN T. FISKE<br>BETH A. MORLING

**self** The study of the nature of self has been of great interest not only to social psychologists but also to the general public. Research on the self does not fall into one neatly integrated system but rather exists in a loose collection of overlapping subtopics.

DEFINITIONS

Despite frequent and colloquial usage, the term "self" is not easy to define. A full understanding of self must encompass the physical body, the socially defined identity (including roles and relationships), the personality, and the person's knowledge about self (i.e., the self-concept). Self is also understood as the active agent who makes decisions and initiates actions.

Although the term "self-concept" is popular, theorists generally agree now that it is misleading and probably wrong to assume that self-knowledge is uniform, constant, fully consistent, or unitary. Instead, researchers refer to multiple conceptions about how the self is (and how the self may become). Each time people reflect on themselves, only one small subset of this knowledge is brought to mind, and so self-awareness may have quite different contents on different occasions.

Still, this multiplicity should not be overstated. The very definition of self entails unity and continuity over time. Attributes, roles, motivations, and subjective states may change frequently, but they are all understood as belonging to one and the same self. The notion of self is thus best understood as embodying a fundamental unity with a diverse aggregate of attributes and facets.

CULTURAL AND HISTORICAL FACTORS

Although the roots of selfhood in the physical body are presumably constant across time and place, the meanings of selfhood have varied substantially. Different cultures place different emphasis on public, private, and collective aspects of self (*see* CROSS-CULTURAL SOCIAL PSYCHOLOGY, INDIVIDUALISM–COLLECTIVISM). The private self involves how the individual human being regards himself or herself; the public self refers to how other people perceive the person; and the collective self refers to memberships in social groups. Social psychology as created by North American and Western European psychologists is likely to share those cultures' emphasis on private and public selves, while neglecting the collective self and its phenomena of interdependence.

The Western sense of individual identity has evolved through recent centuries (*see* Baumeister, 1986). These changes can be summarized briefly as follows. First, the modern identity is composed of more facets that are more changeable than those of the identities of bygone eras. Whereas medieval identity and life course were heavily determined by immutable factors such as gender, social rank, and geographical home, modern identity is subject to an almost endless stream of choices and contingencies and is therefore frequently subject to renegotiation.

Second, the increasingly changeable and undefined nature of identity has led to a perception of the self as a focus of problems, conflicts, and uncertainties, as reflected in current terms such as identity crisis. Common speech and intellectual discourse have both developed broad vocabularies surrounding the problems of selfhood, such as the need to find oneself. ADOLESCENCE has become the age in which the self is particularly burdened with the paradoxical demand for creating itself, and so adolescence has become the prototypical age of identity crisis.

Third, the belief in an inner self has expanded dramatically over recent centuries, as people have ascribed more and more traits and characteristics to this hidden part of the self. Issues of hypocrisy, self-deception, inner search, self-actualization, and knowing oneself have gained in perceived importance with the expansion of the inner self. People have begun to believe that many pragmatic and personal issues can be resolved by searching inside themselves for answers supposedly contained there. Thus, people expect the inner self to contain the basis for selecting "personal" VALUES and morals, the wellsprings of creativity, personality TRAITS (even ones that contradict one's overt behavior), the keys to fulfillment, criteria for making major life decisions, and more. These inflated expectations have both fuelled the fascination with selfhood and contributed to the sense of endlessly unresolved struggle for self.

Fourth, social, political, and economic changes have placed ever more emphasis on the autonomous, unique individual. This rampant individualism is a defining feature of the modern Western self and distinguishes it from the more interdependent sense of self in earlier times and other cultures. Individualism offers various rewards, including an enhanced sense of personal freedom, a gratifying sense of personal specialness, and an enhanced egotistical satisfaction over one's own achievements. It also has costs, which include a growing vulnerability to alienation and a heightened feeling of pressure to maintain a public and private image of self that lives up to inflated expectations. These pressures have led some to conclude that the modern self is a potent source of stress. Many escapist and even self-destructive actions, such as suicide, sexual masochism, spiritual detachment, pathological eating patterns, and alcohol and drug abuse, represent attempts to cope with various stresses and vulnerabilities focused on the self (Baumeister, 1991).

Fifth, the disintegration of the social consensus regarding fundamental values has created a "value gap" that many people have turned inward to the self to resolve. The alleged needs, wants, and potentialities of the self are increasingly used to guide moral choices and justify actions that might well have been condemned in earlier times or other, less self-oriented cultures. Invoking the self to resolve fundamental questions of life's meaning is yet another way in which modern life places substantial, arguably excessive demands on the self. In many cases, therefore, what people describe as a problem of selfhood can be understood as a problem with finding a meaningful life.

SELF-KNOWLEDGE

People have a great deal of information about themselves. This is stored in a loosely organized fashion in memory. Rather than discussing a single, unitary self-concept, many social psychologists prefer to speak in terms of various particular beliefs about the self, which may be called self-schemas. The self-concept may be considered a loose aggregate of self-schemas (see SELF-SCHEMAS).

Each person has many self-schemas, and it is not possible to think of them all at the same time. Accordingly, only a small part of the totality of self-knowledge can be present in awareness at any moment. The part that is present in awareness has been called the phenomenal self, the SPONTANEOUS SELF-CONCEPT, or the working self-concept. Clearly, the contents of the phenomenal self change much more rapidly than the totality of self-knowledge changes, as people reflect on different aspects of themselves.

Where does self-knowledge come from? The standard answer, dating back at least to

SYMBOLIC INTERACTIONISM, is that people learn about themselves from other people. Although to some extent this is certainly true, a literature review by Shrauger and Schoeneman (1979) found that self-appraisals were only weakly correlated with how the person was perceived by others. On the other hand, strong correlations were found between self-appraisals and how people believed that others perceived them. The implication is that information about the self is indeed gained through social interaction, but the communication introduces significant inaccuracies. Some of these may arise from the fact that people do not always express their true appraisals of other people; for example, they may refrain from telling a person what they think his faults are. Other inaccuracies may arise from biases in the perceiver; for example, a person may disregard what others tell him/her if he/she does not like it.

The existence of inaccuracies in interpersonal communication raises the broader issue of whether self-knowledge is accurate. Although most self-knowledge must certainly have some basis in reality, there is ample evidence that several biases, distortions, and misconceptions make self-knowledge unreliable. In general, it appears that people seriously overestimate their powers of introspection, and that in fact people often have little or no access to their own mental processes (see VERBAL REPORTS ON MENTAL PROCESSES). This weakness of introspection leaves ample room for false assumptions and biased perceptions of the self to develop. Greenwald (1980) compared the self to a totalitarian government that indulges in propaganda and rewrites history to suit itself. Greenwald proposed that people distort their memories so as to exaggerate their own morally good qualities and intentions, to exaggerate their self-perceived efficacy, and to put themselves at the center of events. A literature review by Taylor and Brown (1988) found broad support for three general patterns of self-deception or, in their term, positive illusions. First, people overestimate their positive qualities, including abilities, achievements, and successes. Second, people exaggerate their degree of CONTROL. Third, they tend to be unrealistically optimistic, relatively

underestimating the probability that bad things will happen to them and overestimating the likelihood of positive outcomes.

Taken together, these works indicate that self-knowledge is systematically distorted. There may be factors and processes that keep self-deception from becoming too extreme; thus, people commonly tend to make slight exaggerations in their self-perceived abilities and virtues, but extreme overestimations are rare, possibly because they are maladaptive or vulnerable to disconfirmation. Self-knowledge is based in reality but generally altered in a positive direction. Put another way, the average person manages to regard himself or herself as above average.

Issues of stability and change in self-knowledge have also been of interest to social psychologists. There is a strong tendency for self-knowledge to remain stable; that is, people resist changing their views of themselves (e.g., Swann, 1987). Thus, once some belief about the self is formed, it is unlikely to change.

On the other hand, it is clear that people do sometimes alter their views of themselves. One mechanism for this is the internalization of behavior. When people behave in a certain way, they sometimes come to regard themselves as the sort of person who behaves in that way, possibly because these recent actions stand out in memory and exert an undue influence on self-perception (see SELF-PERCEPTION THEORY). Another factor appears to be sweeping change in one's social environment; self-concepts change most readily and thoroughly when people move to a new city, enter or leave a university, enter or leave a powerful religious or political movement, or undergo a similar change that simultaneously alters the majority of social relationships. Apparently, ongoing social relationships help stabilize and anchor self-perceptions. Understanding how self-concepts can evolve and change is an important challenge for current research.

## MOTIVATIONS ASSOCIATED WITH SELF
Although the self is the focus of knowledge, it is also the focus of motivation. Several sets of motivations have been identified.

A first set of motivations has to do with favorability. People want to regard themselves favorably and have others regard them favorably. According to Steele (1988), people have a strong need for self-affirmation, that is, a need to think about and express some positive features of themselves. A loss of esteem in one sphere can be compensated by an increase in esteem in another, so many people tend to find their good points and emphasize them.

There are several ways to satisfy this need to regard the self favorably. One has already been covered in this article, namely the tendency for people to distort the information they receive and remember about themselves so as to exaggerate their good points. Another is to alter behavior so as to make oneself conform to one's high standards and ideals. This process has been discussed by Markus and Nurius (1986) under the rubric of *possible selves*; that is, people have many possible conceptions of self and they are motivated to become the desirable ones and to avoid turning into the undesirable ones. Of particular importance is the concept of an undesired self, that is, the conception of the person one could become but does not want to become, leading to systematic efforts to avoid becoming that person. More generally, Wicklund and Gollwitzer (1982) have analyzed and studied people's efforts at self-completion, that is, their efforts to convince themselves and others that they are the person that they want to be. These efforts to claim desired identities often include the use of identity symbols (e.g., styles of clothing, tools, insignia) as well as behavioral efforts such as teaching others (whereby one's expertise is implicitly affirmed).

Interpersonal relations offer another sphere in which people can pursue favorable views of self. Tesser's (e.g., 1988) *self-evaluation maintenance* model holds that self-evaluation depends on three variables in relation to other people: performance, closeness, and relevance. Performance is a matter of how well the other person does in comparison with how well the self performs. Closeness refers to the relationship between oneself and the other person, and relevance refers to the importance of the particular performance dimension

to one's SELF-ESTEEM and self-concept. People desire to be closely linked to others who perform exceptionally well on dimensions that are irrelevant to their own self-concepts. In contrast, close links to people who do well on highly relevant dimensions are threatening (because the self feels inadequate by comparison) (*see also* SOCIAL COMPARISON).

These interpersonal factors reflect the far-reaching importance of the public self (*see* IMPRESSION MANAGEMENT). It appears that other people provide an important set of constraints on what people are able to believe about themselves, and so many efforts at constructing and enhancing one's self-image are directed toward other people. People seem to act as if the best way to claim some desired identity or self-conception is to persuade other people to view one in the desired fashion, which presumably then legitimates perceiving oneself in that fashion. In Wicklund and Gollwitzer's (1982) term, the perception of others confers *social reality* that validates one's self-perceptions.

The motivation to regard oneself favorably is sometimes opposed by the desire to maintain a stable, consistent view of self. Swann's (1987) work on SELF-VERIFICATION indicates that people resist feedback that will alter their views of themselves, including even flattering feedback that tells them they are better than they thought. Others have emphasized the broad tendency of people to seek positive, flattering feedback and to try to make optimally positive impressions on others.

Theorists have made several efforts to integrate these two competing motivational forces into an adequate account of self motivations. One is that people strive for the best out of the plausible views of self. That is, people desire favorability, but only up to the limits of what can plausibly be sustained, and so they resist both unfavorable and excessively favorable implications about the self. Another integrative hypothesis is that the preference for positivity is chiefly an emotional one, whereas the preference for consistency is a cognitive one. People thus may feel best after receiving a highly positive evaluation, but they may be more likely to believe and accept a less positive evaluation that fits what they already believe about themselves. Another is that because most people hold fairly positive views of themselves, there ceases to be any significant basis for distinguishing between accurate and positive feedback.

## SELF-REGULATION

In recent years, many researchers interested in self have been drawn to study issues of self-regulation. The self is not only a knowledge structure, a locus of motivations, and an interpersonal tool; it is also a mechanism for controlling itself.

It would be premature to offer any summary of self-regulation now, in view of the recency of widespread interest in the topic and the rapid pace at which new findings emerge. As an overview of the topic, however, it can be said that people variously seek to control their thoughts, actions, feelings, and appetites. Self-regulation of thought involves directing attention to and away from particular topics, suppressing unwanted thoughts, and guiding one's judgment processes toward preordained or preferred conclusions. Self-regulation of action includes maintaining persistence despite discouragement and boredom, maximizing performance, and controlling what one might reveal to others. Affect regulation includes the effort to move into or out of various emotional states, as well as efforts to prolong emotional states that arise naturally. Lastly, appetite regulation includes issues of impulse and addiction, such as people's efforts to control their eating (e.g., in dieting), smoking, drug and alcohol use, and sexual behavior.

Although self-regulation may be one of the prominent and fundamental functions of the self, it appears that people are far from broadly successful at it. The multiplicity of techniques for self-regulation in even one sphere is often staggering. Thus, a broad sample of people can easily furnish two or three dozen techniques for regulating their emotional states or even just for coping with sadness and depression, and there seems to be an almost endless array of methods for dieting. Because modern Western societies see themselves as pervasively struggling with self-control issues (manifested in concerns with obesity, alcoholism, drug addiction, smoking,

anger control, and the like; *see* ADDICTION), the topic of self-regulation goes beyond a theoretical preoccupation to encompass broad societal concerns, and therefore it seems likely to be one of the central topics in the study of self in the coming decades.

## CONCLUSION

Although social psychology has seemingly shown a steady, persistently high interest in studying the self over the past several decades, this interest has actually shifted among various subtopics. The study of the self is not a homogeneous or unitary enterprise but rather an aggregate of multiple, sometimes competing processes and phenomena. In this, the study of the self resembles its object of study, because the self is itself less a single phenomenon than an aggregate of bits of information, motivations, interpersonal patterns, and control processes. This complex diversity is sufficiently large and sufficiently important that it is safe to predict that research on the self will continue to be a major focus of social psychologists well into the twenty-first century.

*See also*: ADDICTION; ADOLESCENCE; CONTROL; CROSS-CULTURAL SOCIAL PSYCHOLOGY; IMPRESSION MANAGEMENT; INDIVIDUALISM-COLLECTIVISM; SELF-ESTEEM; SELF-PERCEPTION THEORY; SOCIAL COMPARISON; SYMBOLIC INTERACTIONISM; VALUES; VERBAL REPORTS ON MENTAL PROCESSES.

BIBLIOGRAPHY

Baumeister, R. F. (1986). *Identity: Cultural change and the struggle for self.* New York: Oxford University Press.

—— (1991). *Escaping the self: Alcoholism, spirituality, masochism, and other flights from the burden of selfhood.* New York: Basic Books.

Greenwald, A. G. (1980). The totalitarian ego: Fabrication and revision of personal history. *American Psychologist, 35,* 603–18.

Markus, H., & Nurius, P. S. (1986). Possible selves. *American Psychologist, 41,* 954–69.

Shrauger, J. S., & Schoeneman, T. J. (1979). Symbolic interactionist view of self-concept: Through the looking glass darkly. *Psychological Bulletin, 86,* 549–73.

Steele, C. M. (1988). The psychology of self-affirmation: Sustaining the integrity of the self. In L. Berkowitz (Ed.), *Advances in experimental social psychology* (Vol. 21, pp. 261–302). New York: Academic Press.

Swann, W. B. (1987). Identity negotiation: Where two roads meet. *Journal of Personality and Social Psychology, 53,* 1038–51.

Taylor, S. E., & Brown, J. D. (1988). Illusion and well-being: A social psychological perspective on mental health. *Psychological Bulletin, 103,* 193–210.

Tesser, A. (1988). Toward a self-evaluation maintenance model of social behavior. In L. Berkowitz (Ed.), *Advances in experimental social psychology* (Vol. 21, pp. 181–227). San Diego, CA: Academic Press.

Wicklund, R. A., & Gollwitzer, P. M. (1982). *Symbolic self-completion.* Hillsdale, NJ: Lawrence Erlbaum.

ROY F. BAUMEISTER

**self-awareness** As a central variable underlying moral behavior and attitude-consistent behavior this has its historical roots in Wolff (1932) and Mead (1934). The term "self-consciousness" has also been used in these contexts and may be regarded as interchangeable with "self-awareness," "self-directed attention," and "self-focus." Duval and Wicklund (1972) formulated a theory of self-awareness, also called "objective" self-awareness, in that the process entails a person's becoming the *object* of one's own attention. It is assumed that ATTENTION can focus on the self, thus on one's internalized attitudes, VALUES, morals, physical being as well as on the somewhat more vague causal agent SELF.

When attention comes to be directed to a self-aspect, such as one's own voice or face (*see* the techniques developed by Wolff, 1932), that self-focus will in turn come to settle upon whatever self-facets are at the moment salient. For example, should a person be in the midst of a CONFLICT regarding a moral issue (*see* Diener & Wallbom, in Gibbons, 1990), then self-focus that has been set off via attention to one's body will come to settle on one's own moral conflict. In turn, the person will then be sensitive to discrepancies between the relevant internalized moral and possible behavioral options. If the person can then act, behavior will be in accord with that moral (e.g., not cheating, as in Diener and Wallbom) to the extent that self-focus is high.

Alternatively, if the person has already behaved immorally and then becomes self-focused, the resulting negative AFFECT will force an avoidance response, in the sense of trying to avoid the stimuli that make for self-awareness. This can mean avoiding one's mirror image (*see* Duval & Wicklund, 1972; Greenberg & Musham, 1981, in Gibbons, 1990), avoiding a playback of one's own voice and the like.

For the most part, relevant research has examined the above postulates – namely, that subjects will act more in accord with their own standards when self-aware, that they will describe themselves more in line with their usual behaviors when self-aware, and that they will avoid self-awareness when an acute, within-self discrepancy (such as a hypocrisy) is salient (*see* Wicklund, 1975, and Gibbons, 1990 for reviews).

While the original formulation drew on GESTALT principles for analyzing the environmental forces that bring forth, or prevent, self-awareness, it is also possible to speak of relatively chronic individual differences with respect to self-awareness. A "private" self-consciousness scale (Fenigstein, Scheier, & Buss, 1975, in Wicklund, 1975), has been implemented in order to treat self-awareness as an individual difference, and the results associated with this measure are closely in accord with those for the self-awareness inductions. While a "public" self-consciousness measure also exists, there is little evidence that the scale bears on self-directed attention (*see* Wicklund & Gollwitzer, 1987, in Gibbons, 1990).

It has been contended that the child's coming out of the egocentric period was closely bound up with having a sense of the separateness of one's self, i.e., with self-awareness. It follows that perspective-taking (the contrary of Piaget's egocentrism) will develop, and will show itself acutely in proportion to the person's extent of self-focus. Using standard perspective-taking measures from developmental psychology, Hass (1984, in Gibbons,

1990) has shown such a relationship. These findings are also in accord with the more fundamental thoughts of SYMBOLIC INTERACTIONISM (Mead) that conformity is tied up with self-focused attention (see Duval & Wicklund, 1972).

In summary: The self-awareness mechanisms serve to bring the self – as a system of behavioral potentials – into play. The self-focused individual acts more on internalized attitudes and moral standards; internal discrepancies between such standards and relevant behaviors are acted upon to the extent that a person's thoughts are self-directed. If immobilized, thus unable to act on the standards, the self-aware person will then avoid the self-aware state, this tendency being reflected in an aversion to self-awareness-provoking settings.

See also: ATTENTION; CONFLICT; SELF; SYMBOLIC INTERACTIONISM; VALUES.

BIBLIOGRAPHY

Duval, S., & Wicklund, R. A. (1972). *A theory of objective self-awareness*. New York: Academic Press.

Gibbons, F. X. (1990). Self-attention and behavior: A review and theoretical update. In M. P. Zanna (Ed.), *Advances in experimental social psychology* (Vol. 23, pp. 249–303). New York: Academic Press.

Mead, G. H. (1934). *Mind, self, and society*. Chicago, IL: University of Chicago Press.

Wicklund, R. A. (1975). Objective self-awareness. In L. Berkowitz (Ed.), *Advances in experimental social psychology* (Vol. 8, pp. 233–75). New York: Academic Press.

Wolff, W. (1932). Selbstbeurteilung und Fremdbeurteilung im wissentlichen und unwissentlichen Versuch [Judgement of self and others under naive and informed conditions.] *Psychologische Forschung, 16,* 251–328.

ROBERT A. WICKLUND


**self-categorization theory** This is a theory of the SELF, GROUP PROCESSES, and SOCIAL COGNITION (Turner, 1985; Turner et al., 1987) which emerged from research on SOCIAL IDENTITY THEORY. It is concerned with variation in self-categorization (in the level, content and meaning of self-categories) and with the antecedents and consequences of such variation. It focuses on the distinction between personal and social identity. Where social identity theory seeks to explain intergroup discrimination in terms of the need for a positive social identity, self-categorization theory seeks to show how the emergent, higher-order processes of group behaviour can be explained in terms of a shift in self-perception from self-categorization in terms of personal identity to self-categorization in terms of social identity.

Personal identity refers to self-categories which define the individual as a unique person in terms of his or her individual differences from other (ingroup) persons. Social identity refers to SOCIAL CATEGORIZATIONS of self and others, self-categories which define the individual in terms of his or her shared similarities with members of certain social categories in contrast to other social categories. Social identity refers to the social categorical self (e.g., "us" versus "them," ingroup versus outgroup, us women, us men, etc.).

The theory was initially developed to explain group behavior. It hypothesizes that as shared social identity becomes salient, individual self-perception tends to become *depersonalized*. That is, individuals tend to define and see themselves less as differing individual persons and more as the interchangeable representatives of some shared social category membership. For example, when an individual man tends to categorize himself as a man in contrast to women, then he (subjectively "we") tends to accentuate perceptually his similarities to other men (and reduce his personal differences from other men) and enhance perceptually his stereotypical differences from women. His self changes in level and content and his self-perception and behavior becomes depersonalized. Depersonalization of the self is the subjective STEREOTYPING of the self in terms of the relevant social categorization and is considered to be the cognitive basis of group behavior.

During the 1980s researchers studied the conditions under which social categorizations of self and others become salient in social perception, and developed and tested derivative subtheories of group phenomena in terms of self-categorization and depersonalization. Much work was done (and continues to be done) on GROUP COHESIVENESS, COOPERATION, social CONFORMITY, GROUP POLARIZATION, MINORITY SOCIAL INFLUENCE, social stereotyping, and CROWD behavior (e.g., Hogg, 1992; Oakes, Haslam, & Turner, 1994; Turner, 1991; Turner et al., 1987). The aim has been to show that the hypothesis of the social categorical self was necessary to provide a satisfactory and heuristic explanation of the major group phenomena and that traditional theories assuming a dominant role for personal self-interest had reached the end of their useful life.

The varying "salience" of particular self-categories in self-perception is explained as a function of an interaction between the *relative accessibility* of a particular self-category (or "perceiver readiness," the readiness of a perceiver to use a particular categorization) and the *fit* between category specifications and the stimulus reality to be represented (the match between category meaning and reality).

Relative accessibility reflects a person's past experience, present expectations and current motives, VALUES, goals, and needs. It reflects the active selectivity of the perceiver in being ready to use categories which are relevant, useful, and likely to be confirmed by the evidence of reality.

Fit has two aspects: comparative fit and normative fit. Comparative fit is defined by the principle of *meta-contrast*, which states that a collection of stimuli is more likely to be categorized as a (higher-order) entity to the degree that the average differences perceived between them are less than the average differences perceived between them and the remaining stimuli which comprise the frame of reference. Thus a collection of individuals is more likely to be perceived at the level of a social categorization where the differences between the social categories are perceived as greater than the differences within the categories.

Normative fit refers to the content aspect of the match between category specifications and the instances being represented. For example, to categorize a group of people as Catholics as opposed to Protestants, they must not only differ (in attitudes, actions, etc.) from Protestants more than from each other (comparative fit), but must also do so in the *right direction* on *specific content dimensions* of comparison. Their similarities and differences must be consistent with our normative beliefs about the substantive social meaning of the social category.

The fit hypothesis predicts that self-categorizing is inherently comparative, variable, fluid, and relative to a frame of reference. It is always context-dependent. Self-categories do not reflect (fit) fixed, absolute properties of the perceiver, but relative, varying, context-dependent properties. This hypothesis has become the basis of much current work on the theory, in which the self and sterotypical ingroup–outgroup representations are seen as outcomes of a dynamic process of SOCIAL JUDGMENT rather than as fixed mental structures (Oakes et al., 1994). The emphasis in recent work has been on using the idea of the social contextual basis of self-categorization as a means of understanding how society shapes and interacts with cognition through the medium of the self-process.

*See also*: COOPERATION AND COMPETITION; CROWD PSYCHOLOGY; GROUP COHESIVENESS; GROUP PROCESSES; SELF; SOCIAL CATEGORIZATION; SOCIAL COGNITION; SOCIAL IDENTITY THEORY; SOCIAL JUDGMENT; STEREOTYPING; VALUES.

BIBLIOGRAPHY

Hogg, M. A. (1992). *The social psychology of group cohesiveness: From attraction to social identity*. New York: Harvester Wheatsheaf.

Oakes, P. J., Haslam, S.A., & Turner, J. C. (1994). *Stereotyping and social reality*. Oxford, UK, & Cambridge MA: Blackwell.

Turner, J. C. (1985). Social categorization and the self-concept: A social cognitive theory of group behaviour. In E. J. Lawler (Ed.), *Advances in Group Processes* (Vol. 2, pp. 77–122). Greenwich, CT: JAI Press.

——(1991). *Social influence*. Buckingham: Open University Press; Pacific Grove, CA: Brooks/Cole.

——Hogg, M. A., Oakes, P. J., Reicher, S. D., & Wetherell, M. S. (1987). *Rediscovering the social group: A self-categorization theory.* Oxford & New York: Basil Blackwell.

JOHN C. TURNER

Jourard, S. (1968). *Disclosing man to himself.* New York: Van Nostrand.

HARRY T. REIS

**self-disclosure** The process by which individuals reveal their innermost feelings and experiences to interaction partners is termed self-disclosure. Research on self-disclosure began in earnest in the 1960s, following the seminal writings of Jourard (1968). He proposed that self-revelation was the key to mental health and satisfying RELATIONSHIPS, a contention that has been supported by subsequent research. In early studies, self-disclosure was operationalized primarily in terms of revelation of normatively private information. More recent definitions are broader, so that the most intimate disclosures are thought to concern personal emotions and self-perceptions (e.g., feelings, fears, desires, and needs). According to some accounts, feelings about relationships may be particularly self-revealing.

Self-disclosure is a central part of the acquaintance process. A common metaphor invokes the peeling of an onion: People become acquainted by divulging successively more personal material, one layer at a time, until they have revealed their innermost selves to each other. As disclosure approaches the core SELF, intimacy deepens. Typically, but not always, this process is mutual, with partners reciprocating levels of disclosure (*see* INTIMACY).

Much research has examined contextual, relational, and individual difference variables that affect self-disclosure tendencies. Studies of NORMS that govern self-disclosure in different settings, relationships, and cultures have been particularly popular. In addition, the implications of varying levels of self-disclosure for relationship development, maintenance, and dissolution have been investigated extensively (*see* Derlega, Metts, Petronio, & Margulis, 1993).

*See also:* INTIMACY; NORMS; RELATIONSHIPS; SELF.

BIBLIOGRAPHY
Derlega, V. J., Metts, S., Petronio, S., & Margulis, S. T. (1993). *Self-disclosure.* Newbury Park, CA: Sage.

**self-discrepancy** A person possesses a self-discrepancy when the represented attributes in one self-state do not match those in another self-state (*see* Higgins, 1987). Self-discrepancies produce both emotional and motivational predispositions because each type of self-discrepancy reflects a distinct type of psychological situation. For example, a discrepancy between people's "actual" self-representation and their own or a significant other's hopes and wishes for them (their "ideal" self-representation) reflects the psychological situation of the "absence of positive outcomes," producing sadness and disappointment. In contrast, a discrepancy between people's actual self and their own or a significant other's beliefs about their duties and responsibilities (their "ought" self-representation) reflects the psychological situation of the "presence of negative outcomes," producing fear and worry. It is the psychological situations experienced in interpersonal interactions that underlie both the motivational significance of self-discrepancies and the construction of distinct regulatory systems – focusing on either regulating positive outcomes (presence or absence) or regulating negative outcomes (absence or presence). A self-discrepancy involving a person's own standpoint versus the standpoint of a significant other also produces different motives and behaviors.

*See also:* EMOTIONAL EXPERIENCE; MOOD; SELF.

BIBLIOGRAPHY
Higgins, E. T. (1987). Self-discrepancy: A theory relating self and affect. *Psychological Review, 94,* 319–40.

E. TORY HIGGINS

**self-enhancement** This term refers to the tendency of individuals to interpret and explain outcomes and seek information in ways that have favorable or flattering implications for the self. Self-enhancement typically involves favorable interpretations of ambiguous self-relevant information, rather than outright distortion of facts. For example, people may self-enhance by attributing positive outcomes to their abilities, rather than to luck or the ease of the task (*see also* SELF-SERVING BIAS). Several psychologists have suggested that self-enhancement is an important and universal human motivation (*see* Taylor & Brown, 1988).

Self-enhancement may be distinguished from the related phenomenon of self-protection, which refers to the tendency of individuals to interpret and explain outcomes and seek information in ways that avoid unflattering or unfavorable implications for the self. The motive to self-enhance has been contrasted with sometimes competing motives, such as the desire for self-consistency or SELF-VERIFICATION, and the desire for accurate or diagnostic information about the self. These motives are particularly likely to come into conflict in people who have negative self-concepts (*see also* SELF; SELF-SCHEMAS; SELF-ESTEEM). *See also*: SELF; SELF-ESTEEM.

BIBLIOGRAPHY

Taylor, S. E., & Brown, J. D. (1988). Illusion and well-being: A social psychological perspective on mental health. *Psychological Bulletin, 103*, 193–210.

JENNIFER CROCKER

**self-esteem** An evaluation of the SELF, or feelings of self-worth and self-respect (Rosenberg, 1979). Self-esteem may be either global (referring to the self as a whole, or in general) or specific (referring to some particular aspect of the self, such as one's athletic prowess, or physical appearance); it may also be a stable trait or a temporary state. Self-esteem is more stable (i.e., less variable over time) for some individuals than others. Global self-esteem and specific self-evaluations have been of interest to psychologists since William James (1890). Some of the major questions regarding self-esteem concern where it comes from (i.e., how people arrive at self-evaluations); how the self-concepts of high and low

self-esteem people differ; how self-esteem is maintained, enhanced, or protected; what other variables (e.g., behaviors, adjustment variables) self-esteem is related to; and how to measure self-esteem.

The vast majority of people in Western cultures tend to have high self-esteem (i.e., they score above the midpoint of the scale on most measures of self-esteem). Both classic and contemporary writings about the self assume that people have a need for self-esteem and are thereby motivated to maintain a positive self-view. High self-esteem may contribute to overall psychological well-being and functioning because the optimism, feelings of control over events, and positive self-views that typically accompany high self-regard enable individuals to continue to strive even in the face of daily setbacks or negative life events (Taylor & Brown, 1988). According to terror management theory (Solomon, Greenberg, & Pyszczynski, 1991), self-esteem protects individuals from existential anxiety that results from the knowledge of one's own mortality, and the potential meaninglessness and vulnerability of existence. This view suggests that self-esteem can be maintained, and anxiety lessened, by subscribing to a cultural worldview (e.g., a system of religious beliefs) and by believing that one lives up to the standards and values prescribed by that worldview.

SOURCES OF SELF-EVALUATION

Many factors contribute to feelings of self-worth and self-respect, including beliefs about one's individual attributes, competencies, and accomplishments in specific domains (e.g., career, academics, athletics). But how do people evaluate their attributes and their competence? Research and theory have focused on three sources of self-knowledge and self-evaluation. One source of self-evaluation is reflected appraisals. Individuals may evaluate themselves based on their knowledge or imagination of how others evaluate them, a process referred to as a "looking-glass self" because others are used as a mirror in which one sees the self. Research shows that people's self-evaluations are strongly related to how they believe others view them, but only weakly related to how others actually view them. Second, people may evaluate themselves through SOCIAL COMPARISONS with similar or significant others (Wood, 1989). Hence, self-evaluations may depend in large part on those with whom one compares oneself. People are both more interested in, and their self-evaluations are more influenced by, comparisons with others who are similar, rather than dissimilar, on some relevant characteristic such as age or sex. They are also more interested in and more influenced by comparisons with others who are close, rather than distant, in their relationship or connection to the self. Third, people may evaluate aspects of the self by simply observing and interpreting their own behavior, a process called SELF-PERCEPTION. For example, one may conclude that one is a terrible mechanic after repeatedly failing in attempts to repair a car. In this instance, the person evaluates the self by reflecting on her or his own achievements, or experiences with self-efficacy.

In addition to individual attributes and competencies, self-esteem may also depend on one's evaluation of social or collective aspects of the self. Based on group memberships such as race, gender, and occupation, individuals develop a social or collective identity. According to SOCIAL IDENTITY THEORY, one's social identity, and hence one's self-esteem, will be more positive if one's social group compares favorably to other groups.

Although little research has addressed this issue, people may differ in the sources of self-evaluation toward which they are oriented. For example, individuals high in SELF-MONITORING or public self-consciousness may rely heavily on the opinions of others to evaluate the self, whereas individuals low in these attributes may rely more on self-perception. Members of racial and ethnic minorities may base their self-esteem more on collective aspects of the self, and less on evaluation of specific attributes than do members of dominant or majority groups. Furthermore, cultures may differ in the sources of self-knowledge regarded as important. For example, many Asian cultures stress the importance of the opinions of others. Situations may also constrain the availability or viability of a particular source of self-evaluative knowledge, and thus affect the sources on which people base their self-esteem.

SELF-ESTEEM AND THE SELF-CONCEPT
One issue that has received a great deal of attention historically, and is currently receiving renewed attention from researchers, concerns how the self-concepts, or SELF-SCHEMAS of people who are high in self-esteem differ from those of low self-esteem people (*see* Baumeister, 1993).

*Positivity*
Not surprisingly, people who are high in self-esteem tend to rate positive traits and abilities as more true of themselves and negative traits as less true of themselves than do people who are low in self-esteem. Self-esteem differences are found on a wide variety of positive and negative traits. However, the relatively positive self-concepts of high self-esteem people do not mean that all people who are low in self-esteem have negative self-views. Rather, their self-views are simply less positive than are those of high self-esteem people.

Are the more positive self-concepts of high self-esteem individuals simply an accurate reflection of reality? Some evidence suggests that people who are high in self-esteem may, in fact, have somewhat more positive attributes and outcomes than do people who are low in self-esteem. For example, in a review of the literature, Wylie (1979) concluded that global self-esteem is weakly related to academic ability and achievement, with correlations ranging from .00 to .30. Apart from the academic achievement area, there is little evidence that high self-esteem people actually perform better or have more positive characteristics than do low self-esteem people. When differences in the outcomes or characteristics of high and low self-esteem people have been documented, they do not seem to be sufficient to explain the powerful differences in the self-concepts of high and low self-esteem people.

*Certainty*
People who are high in self-esteem have self-concepts that are more clear, well articulated,

certain, and internally consistent than do people who are low in self-esteem. High self-esteem people appear to be particularly certain about their positive attributes. Low self-esteem individuals tend to be relatively uncertain about both their positive and negative attributes. The less certain individuals are of their self-concepts, whether positive or negative, the more susceptible they should be to evaluative, self-relevant information.

## Self-discrepancies

People who are high in self-esteem also have self-concepts that more nearly match their standards or goals for themselves than do those of low self-esteem people. Higher self-esteem is associated with smaller discrepancies between an individual's actual self-conception (what one believes is true of the self) and her ideal (desired or hoped for) self (Moretti & Higgins, 1990; *see also* SELF-DISCREPANCY).

## Importance

Both high and low self-esteem individuals think it is important to have positive attributes, and not to have negative attributes. However, high self-esteem people tend to devalue or regard as less important the negative attributes they possess, and the positive attributes they do not possess. Low self-esteem people do not seem to devalue their negative attributes, or the positive attributes they do not possess. Self-relevant information on important dimensions should have a greater effect on mood and state self-esteem than information on less important dimensions.

## Expectations for the Future

High self-esteem people have positive expectations and low self-esteem people relatively negative expectations for their efforts and their future outcomes. High self-esteem people are higher in self-efficacy than are low self-esteem people. Expectancies may be conceptualized as *possible selves*, or conceptions of the self that could be realized in the future. Low self-esteem people have more negative and fewer positive possible selves, or selves they think might describe them in the future, than do high self-esteem people.

Because studies of the self-concepts of high and low self-esteem individuals are mainly correlational, it is not clear whether having positive and certain self-concepts with few self-discrepancies on dimensions that are important to the self *cause* one to be high in self-esteem, or whether people who are high in self-esteem interpret or distort self-relevant information by evaluating themselves more positively and certainly, and placing more importance on those dimensions they think are self-descriptive. It is likely that the causal relationship between the self-concept and self-esteem goes in both directions.

## MAINTAINING, PROTECTING, AND ENHANCING SELF-ESTEEM

Research has explored the effects of self-esteem on attempts to maintain, repair, enhance, and protect self-esteem from self-threats such as failure experiences or rejections (*see* Baumeister, 1993 for review). In anticipation of evaluation, high self-esteem people are less anxious, take more risks, and are more likely to SELF-HANDICAP to increase the credit they can take for success, whereas low self-esteem people are more anxious, tend to avoid risk, and self-handicap to avoid responsibility for failure. When positive or negative events occur, people who are high in self-esteem find positive information about the self to be more valid than negative information, and show more ATTRIBUTIONAL BIAS in that they are more likely to take credit for their successes and deny responsibility for their failures than are low self-esteem people. However, high and low self-esteem people tend to be equally disappointed or dissatisfied with negative outcomes. High self-esteem people are more likely to believe that they are superior to others and are more likely to seek upward social comparisons (i.e., comparisons with others who are better off ) than are low self-esteem people. The SELF-PRESENTATIONS of high self-esteem people also tend to be more positive than those of low self-esteem people.

The causes of these differences between high and low self-esteem people in the use of self-serving biases have been a matter of considerable debate. They may be due to cognitive differences in the way that high and low self-esteem people process or interpret self-relevant information, and they may be due to differences in the motivations of high and low self-esteem people. High self-esteem people appear to be motivated to engage in SELF-ENHANCEMENT, whereas low self-esteem people appear to be motivated to protect themselves against failure or disappointment (Baumeister, Tice, & Hutton, 1989).

## CORRELATES OF SELF-ESTEEM

### Affect and Psychological Well-being

In general, people who are high in self-esteem tend to be happier, more satisfied with their lives, and better adjusted than people with low self-esteem. People who are high in self-esteem tend to experience more positive emotion, less negative emotion, and less anxiety (both social anxiety and test anxiety). Self-esteem also is the best known predictor of life satisfaction in Western cultures, with high self-esteem people reporting greater life satisfaction than low self-esteem people. People who are low in self-esteem are vulnerable to psychological disorders such as depression and hopelessness, and are more likely to have suicidal thoughts, and actually to attempt suicide.

### Behavior

The more positive expectations of high self-esteem people lead them to persist more at tasks than do low self-esteem people. This greater persistence may lead to better performance among high self-esteem people when problems are solvable, especially after initial failure. When success is actually impossible (e.g., when problems are unsolvable), greater persistence by high self-esteem people may actually be detrimental. However, in some cases high self-esteem people may be faster to recognize that a task is unsolvable and to abandon it than are low self-esteem people.

## MEASUREMENT ISSUES

Self-esteem is most commonly measured using self-report questionnaires. A wide variety of reliable inventories exist to assess chronic, temporary, domain-specific, and global self-esteem (Blascovich & Tomaka, 1991). While convenient, the pervasive use of self-report measures contributes to several prob-

lems that plague self-esteem research. First, socially desirable responding is a particular concern given the content of most self-esteem questionnaires. Many individuals may not want to report that they feel negatively about themselves. As a result, reported self-esteem may be overly positive. Indeed, some researchers have argued that self-report measures of self-esteem measure styles of self-presentation, rather than intrapsychic differences among individuals (Baumeister et al., 1989). One consequence of this positivity bias is that it is difficult to identify and study individuals with truly low self-esteem.

Second, self-reported self-esteem is correlated with other self-report measures of mood, affect, and well-being. It is unclear to what extent these relationships are due to common method variance, or actual conceptual overlap. In any event, given the apparent relationship between self-esteem and other variables, it is often reasonable to question whether effects attributed to self-esteem are actually due to other, related variables.

Third, the use of self-reports to categorize people as high or low in self-esteem contributes to the difficulty of establishing the direction of causality in the relationships between self-esteem and other variables. Because self-esteem is typically measured simultaneously with other variables, it is often unclear whether self-esteem is a cause or a consequence of a particular phenomenon. Research that manipulates self-esteem addresses this problem, although such manipulations are more likely to affect domain-specific or state self-esteem than trait global self-regard. Research on self-esteem would benefit from the development and use of more subtle, nonreactive measures.

See also: ATTRIBUTIONAL BIAS; SELF; SELF-MONITORING; SELF-PERCEPTION THEORY; SOCIAL COMPARISON; SOCIAL IDENTITY THEORY.

BIBLIOGRAPHY

Baumeister, R. F. (Ed.) (1993). *Self-esteem: The puzzle of low self-regard.* Hillsdale, NJ: Lawrence Erlbaum.

——Tice, D. M., & Hutton, D. G. (1989). Self-presentational motivations and personality differences in self-esteem. *Journal of Personality, 57,* 547–79.

Blascovich, J., & Tomaka, J. (1991). Measures of self-esteem. In J. P. Robinson, P. R. Shaver, & L. S. Wrightsman (Eds.), *Measures of personality and social psychological attitudes* (pp. 115–60). San Diego, CA: Academic Press.

James, W. (1950). *The principles of psychology.* New York: Dover. (Original work published 1890.)

Moretti, M. M., & Higgins, E. T. (1990). Relating self-discrepancy to self-esteem: The contribution of discrepancy beyond actual self-ratings. *Journal of Experimental Social Psychology, 26,* 108–23.

Rosenberg, M. (1979). *Conceiving the self.* New York: Basic Books.

Solomon, S., Greenberg, J., & Pyszczynski, T. (1991). A terror management theory of social behavior: The psychological functions of self-esteem and cultural worldviews. In M. P. Zanna (Ed.), *Advances in experimental social psychology* (Vol. 24, pp. 93–159). San Diego; CA: Academic Press.

Taylor, S. E., & Brown, J. D. (1988). Illusion and well-being: A social psychological perspective on mental health. *Psychological Bulletin, 103,* 193–210.

Wood, J. V. (1989). Theory and research concerning social comparisons of personal attributes. *Psychological Bulletin, 106,* 231–48.

Wylie, R. C. (1979). *The self-concept* (Vol. 2): *Theory and research on selected topics.* Lincoln, NE: University of Nebraska Press.

JENNIFER CROCKER
WAYNE H. BYLSMA

**self-fulfilling prophecies** These occur when an originally false social BELIEF leads to its own fulfillment. Social belief refers to people's (typically referred to as "perceivers") expectations, IMPLICIT PERSONALITY THEORIES, PERSON PERCEPTIONS, and STEREOTYPES regarding another person or group of people (typically referred to as "targets"). Self-fulfilling prophecies differ from purely cognitive EXPECTANCY EFFECTS, which involve people *interpreting* others' behavior as supporting their own beliefs. In contrast, when a self-fulfilling prophecy occurs, perceivers' initially erroneous social beliefs cause targets to act in ways that *objectively* confirm those beliefs.

HISTORICAL BACKGROUND
The self-fulfilling prophecy was first described by sociologist Robert Merton in 1948, who applied it to phenomena as diverse as test anxiety and bank failures. However, most of the article focused on the role of self-fulfilling prophecies in social problems, such as discrimination against Jews and African–Americans.

Self-fulfilling prophecies did not receive much attention until Rosenthal's pioneering work on EXPERIMENTER EFFECTS. Rosenthal showed that researchers sometimes acted in ways that evoked behavior from research subjects (animal and human) that confirmed the researchers' hypotheses. However, it was Rosenthal and Jacobson's (1968) seminal Pygmalion study that launched self-fulfilling prophecies as a major empirical focus in psychology and education. Rosenthal and Jacobson led teachers to believe that some students in their classes were "late bloomers" – destined to show dramatic increases in IQ over the school year. In fact, these students had been selected at random. Results showed that, especially in the earlier grade levels, the "late bloomers" gained more in IQ than other students.

Several branches of research sprang from this seminal study:

(1) controversy, replication, and meta-analysis;
(2) process studies; and
(3) the self-fulfilling nature of stereotypes.

CONTROVERSY, REPLICATION, AND META-ANALYSIS
Rosenthal and Jacobson's study (1968) received considerable attention in the popular press because it seemed to provide a powerful explanation for the low achievement of "disadvantaged" students. However, it was also criticized by educational psychologists on conceptual, methodological, and statistical grounds. A controversy over the existence of the phenomenon continued over the next

10 years, which included numerous attempts to replicate in classrooms and other contexts (work settings, job training programs, laboratories, etc.).

Consistently, only about one-third of the studies attempting to demonstrate a self-fulfilling prophecy succeeded (Rosenthal & Rubin, 1978). This pattern was often interpreted by critics as demonstrating that the phenomenon did not exist because support was unreliable. It was interpreted by proponents as demonstrating the existence of self-fulfilling prophecies because, if only chance differences were occurring, replications would only succeed about 5 percent of the time.

This controversy was to have an effect that went well beyond self-fulfilling prophecies. In his attempt to refute critics, Rosenthal developed META-ANALYSIS (Harris, 1989) – statistical techniques for summarizing the results of multiple studies. Although meta-analysis, too, was greeted with considerable skepticism by Rosenthal's critics (*see* the commentaries on Rosenthal and Rubin's, 1978 meta-analysis in *Behavioral and Brain Sciences*), it has subsequently become the dominant method within psychology for summarizing the results of large literatures and resolving controversies about the existence and size of effects.

Rosenthal and Rubin's (1978) meta-analysis of the first 345 studies of interpersonal expectancy effects conclusively demonstrated the existence of self-fulfilling prophecies. The 345 studies were divided into eight categories. Z-scores representing the combined expectancy effect for all studies in each category were computed. The median of the eight combined Z-scores was 6.62, indicating that the probability of finding the observed expectancy effects, if the phenomenon did not exist, was essentially zero.

PROCESS
A second branch of research focused on identifying the social and psychological processes mediating self-fulfilling prophecies. Researchers generally agreed that three broad steps were necessary for an expectancy to become self-fulfilling:

(1) perceivers must develop erroneous expectations;
(2) perceivers' expectations must influence how they act toward targets; and
(3) the target must react to the perceiver's behavior in a manner that confirms the originally false expectation.

Accordingly, two branches of self-fulfilling prophecy research addressed:

(1) how perceivers (mainly teachers) develop expectations; and
(2) how perceivers acted on their expectations (*see* Harris, 1989; Jussim, 1986 for reviews of the research discussed below).

*Development of Expectations*
In many studies, how subjects developed expectations was obvious – they were induced by experimental manipulation (unless the manipulation failed – *see* Harris, 1989). The information that people normally used as a basis for their expectations, however, was less clear. One major focus was identifying how much teachers used past performance information versus social stereotypes. Dozens of experiments manipulated information about students' race, gender, social class, physical attractiveness, family background, and/or previous achievement. This research showed that:

(1) students' gender had virtually no influence on teachers' expectations;
(2) students' race and physical attractiveness had relatively modest influences on teachers' expectations;
(3) students' social class had a somewhat larger influence on teachers' expectations; and
(4) the major influence on teacher expectations was students' previous performance – its effect size was nearly twice as large as that of the strongest stereotype effect.

*Perceiver Behavior*
Influences of perceivers' expectations on their treatment of targets can be grouped into four broad categories. In comparison to when they hold low expectations for targets, when perceivers hold positive expectations they provide more:

(1) emotional support (warmer communication style);

(2) input (time and attention);

(3) output (opportunities for targets to perform and learn difficult material); and

(4) feedback (clearer and more favorable information about performance).

Self-fulfilling prophecies are most strongly mediated by emotional support, least strongly by feedback, and input and output have intermediate roles.

## STEREOTYPES

In the 1970s, a third branch of self-fulfilling prophecy research began focusing on the self-fulfilling effects of social stereotypes. Experimental laboratory research showed that:

(1) White interviewers' racial stereotypes could undermine the performance of Black interviewees;

(2) males acted more warmly toward, and evoked warmer behavior from, female interaction partners erroneously believed to be more physically attractive;

(3) when interacting with a sexist male who was either physically attractive or who was interviewing them for a job, women altered their behavior to appear more consistent with traditional sex stereotypes; and

(4) teachers used social class as a major basis for expectations, and treated students from middle-class backgrounds more favorably than students from lower-class backgrounds (*see* reviews by Darley & Fazio, 1980; Jussim, 1986; Snyder, 1984; and BEHAVIOURAL CONFIRMATION/DISCONFIRMATION and STEREOTYPING).

## WIDESPREAD ACCEPTANCE AND MORE QUESTIONS

By the 1980s, Rosenthal and Rubin's (1978) meta-analysis and the 1970s work on stereotypes led to widespread agreement among social psychologists that self-fulfilling prophecies do occur and that they were theoretically and practically important (Darley & Fazio, 1980; Jussim, 1986). Nonetheless, since the 1970s, many educational psycholog-

ists had expressed strong reservations about the ECOLOGICAL VALIDITY of many experimental studies of self-fulfilling prophecies. Toward the end of the 1980s, these concerns began to influence social psychological perspectives on self-fulfilling prophecies.

## STRENGTHS AND WEAKNESSES OF THE EARLY EXPERIMENTS

The experimental research was extremely well suited for demonstrating the potential existence of self-fulfilling prophecies. Typically, such studies provided perceivers with information about targets (e.g., that they are attractive or unattractive, that they are "late bloomers," etc.), and then obtained objective assessments' of targets' behavior. Because this information was provided regarding targets who were selected at random, the researchers insured that perceivers' expectations were unrelated to targets' previous behavior or achievement. If targets' future behavior confirmed perceivers' expectations, self-fulfilling prophecy was the only viable explanation.

These early studies were often interpreted as demonstrating that:

(1) self-fulfilling prophecies are a powerful and pervasive phenomenon; and

(2) the influence of social beliefs on social reality equaled or exceeded the influence of social reality on social beliefs.

For several reasons, however, the experimental studies did not directly support these conclusions.

First, conclusions regarding pervasiveness in daily life required evidence of naturally occurring self-fulfilling prophecies, rather than experimentally induced ones. Second, experiments that required perceivers to develop erroneous expectations did not (and were never intended to) assess the extent to which expectations might be accurate. Thus, they provided no basis for comparing the extent of self-fulfilling prophecies (influence of social beliefs on social reality) to the extent of accuracy (influence of social reality on social beliefs).

Third, in most experiments, if the expectancy manipulation was successful, perceivers developed erroneous expectations. However, under naturalistic conditions perceivers may often develop more accurate expectations than in experiments, where they are exposed to false information about targets as part of an expectancy–induction manipulation. Accurate expectations do not create self-fulfilling prophecies (which, by definition, begin with an initially false belief). These differences between experimentally induced and naturally developed expectations represented a major limitation to the ecological validity of experimental demonstrations of self-fulfilling prophecies. Overall, therefore, the experiments (even experiments conducted in field settings) did not provide a strong empirical basis for concluding that self-fulfilling prophecies were powerful and pervasive under naturalistic conditions.

NATURALISTIC RESEARCH

These difficulties with generalizing from experiments led some researchers to investigate naturally occurring interpersonal expectancies in order to address several broad questions:

(1) do naturally developed expectations also create self-fulfilling prophecies?;
(2) if so, are they large and powerful?; and
(3) do targets behave in ways consistent with perceivers' expectations mainly because those expectations created self-fulfilling prophecies, or mainly because the expectations were accurate?

In comparison to experiments, however, it is much more difficult for naturalistic research to determine whether self-fulfilling prophecies occur. Doing so requires meeting at least three conditions:

(1) perceivers' expectations must predict changes in targets' behavior;
(2) accuracy must be ruled out as an alternative explanation; and
(3) either objective assessments (such as standardized achievement tests) or independent observers (as opposed to perceivers judgments) must be used to evaluate targets' behavioral outcomes.

Beginning in the mid-1970s, and continuing to the present, studies have used longitudinal designs and PATH ANALYSIS to meet

these three conditions. There were several fundamental similarities among these studies. First, they all assessed relations between teacher expectations and students' past and future achievement. In general, if teacher expectations predicted future achievement beyond effects accounted for by students' past achievement, results were interpreted as providing evidence of self-fulfilling prophecies. Second, these studies also provided data capable of addressing two related questions:

(1) How large are naturally occurring teacher expectation effects?; and
(2) Do teacher expectations predict students' achievement more because they create self-fulfilling prophecies or more because they are accurate?

Despite spanning about twenty years, involving different samples, and employing different operationalizations of both student achievement and teacher expectations, the results from these studies were highly consistent:

(1) in terms of standardized regression coefficients, the self-fulfilling effects of teacher expectations were about 0.1–0.2 (because of the relatively large sample sizes, these effects were usually statistically significant);
(2) students' achievement influenced teachers' expectations to a much greater extent than teachers' expectations influenced students' achievement; and
(3) teachers' expectations predicted students' achievement more because they were accurate than because they led to self-fulfilling prophecies (see Jussim, 1991, for a review).

THE SEARCH FOR MODERATORS

Throughout the 1970s and 1980s, evidence from experimental laboratory and field studies, and from naturalistic studies, documented considerable limitations to self-fulfilling prophecies. Even the meta-analyses that conclusively demonstrated the existence of the phenomenon (e.g., Rosenthal & Rubin, 1978) showed that about two-thirds of the studies failed to find significant expectancy effects. Other research showed that even when perceivers developed erroneous expectations, they did not always treat high and low expectancy targets differently. Sometimes, rather than perceivers' erroneous expectations influencing targets' behavior, targets' behavior leads perceivers to change their expectations. Similarly, some low-expectancy students perform well anyway; and some high-expectancy students perform poorly anyway (Jussim, 1986). These findings prompted some researchers to begin searching for moderators – factors that inhibit or facilitate the occurrence of self-fulfilling prophecies (see Harris, 1989; Jussim, 1986, 1990; and Snyder, 1992 for reviews of factors moderating self-fulfilling prophecies that are discussed below).

## PERCEIVER CHARACTERISTICS

### Goals

When perceivers' main goal is to get along in a friendly manner with targets, and when perceivers are motivated to develop an accurate impression of targets, perceivers are less likely to produce self-fulfilling prophecies. When perceivers are offered an incentive for confirming a belief about a target, or when their main goal is to arrive at a stable and predictable impression of the target, self-fulfilling prophecies are more likely.

### Cognitive Rigidity and Belief Certainty

Cognitive rigidity, which is usually construed as an individual difference factor, and belief certainty, which is usually construed as a situational factor, are similar in that both identify people who may be unlikely to alter their beliefs when confronted with disconfirming evidence. People who do not readily change their beliefs about others are more likely to create self-fulfilling prophecies, especially if they are in high-power or high-status positions (teacher, employer, parent, etc.).

## TARGET CHARACTERISTICS

### Self-concept

Unclear self-perceptions lead people to become more vulnerable to social influences

in general, including self-fulfilling prophecies. In contrast, when targets have clear self-perceptions, they are not only less likely to fulfill others' expectations, they often convince perceivers to view them much as they view themselves.

### Goals

Targets may become more or less susceptible to self-fulfilling prophecies, depending upon their goals. When perceivers have something targets want (such as a job), and when targets are aware of the perceiver's beliefs, they often confirm those beliefs in order to create a favorable impression. Similarly, when targets desire to facilitate smooth social interactions, they are also more likely to confirm perceivers' expectations.

In contrast, when targets believe that perceivers hold a negative belief about them, they often act to disconfirm that belief. Similarly, when their main goal is to defend a threatened identity, or express their personal attributes, they are also likely to disconfirm perceivers' expectations.

### Age

Self-fulfilling prophecies were strongest among the youngest students in the original Rosenthal and Jacobson (1968) study. If younger children have less clear self-conceptions than older children and adults, they may generally be more susceptible to self-fulfilling prophecies. However, subsequent research has shown that the strongest teacher expectation effects occurred in first, second, and seventh grade. Further, the largest self-fulfilling prophecy effects yet reported were obtained in a study of adult Israeli military trainees (Eden & Shani, 1982). Although these findings do not deny a moderating role for age, they do suggest that situational factors may also influence targets' susceptibility to self-fulfilling prophecies.

## SITUATIONAL FACTORS

### New Situations

People may be more susceptible to confirming others' expectations when they enter new situations. Whenever people engage in major life transitions, such as entering a new school or starting a new job, they may be less clear and confident in their self-perceptions, which may render them more susceptible to confirming perceivers' expectations.

This analysis may help explain the seemingly inconsistent findings regarding age. Students in first, second, and seventh grade, and new military inductees, are all in relatively unfamiliar situations. Therefore, all may be more susceptible to self-fulfilling prophecies than are other students or adults in more familiar surroundings.

### Timing of Expectancy Induction

Many of the early attempts to replicate Rosenthal and Jacobson (1968) failed. The main factor differentiating the failures from the successes was the timing of the expectancy induction. Many studies attempted to manipulate teacher expectations several months into the school year. By then, however, teachers had already formed clear perceptions regarding their students, and they largely ignored the information provided by experimenters. However, when researchers presented the information early in the school year, before teachers' own impressions had crystallized, self-fulfilling prophecy effects were usually found.

### FUTURE DIRECTIONS AND UNDER-EXPLORED ISSUES

### Moderators

Research on factors that moderate self-fulfilling prophecies is relatively recent, and will likely continue to prove informative. Research on the role of targets' and perceivers' goals in producing self-fulfilling prophecies seems especially likely to continue. However, despite social psychology's traditional emphasis on situational factors, there has not been much research on situational moderators. Understanding whether factors such as schools that do versus do not track students by ability levels, ethnically integrated versus segregated schools, new versus familiar situations, being hired under an affirmative action program versus an equal opportunity program, etc., affect self-fulfilling prophecies would seem to be important areas for future research.

### Accumulation

Even small self-fulfilling prophecy effects, if they accumulate over time, might lead to large differences between the characteristics and achievements of targets of high versus low expectations. The idea that self-fulfilling prophecy effects accumulate over time lies at the heart of claims emphasizing the power of social beliefs to create social reality. Unfortunately, however, only a few studies have addressed this issue, and they have yielded mixed results. Systematic research on the accumulation of expectancy effects is greatly needed.

### Naturalistic Studies outside of Classrooms

Except for teacher expectations, there have been very few studies of the self-fulfilling effects of naturally occurring expectations. Such research can provide direct evidence regarding the prevalence of self-fulfilling prophecies, their extent relative to accuracy, and the accumulation of expectancy effects over time (with longitudinal data). The expectations that parents, employers, therapists, coaches, etc., develop regarding their children, employees, clients, athletes, etc., are all potentially rich areas for future research.

### CONCLUSION

Self-fulfilling prophecies occur under a wide variety of laboratory conditions, and in public school classrooms. They also may occur in many other types of social interactions. Consequently, self-fulfilling prophecies are a major phenomenon linking SOCIAL PERCEPTION to social behavior.

See also: BEHAVIORAL CONFIRMATION/DISCONFIRMATION; EXPERIMENTER EFFECTS; META-ANALYSIS; SOCIAL PERCEPTION; STEREOTYPING.

BIBLIOGRAPHY
Darley, J. M., & Fazio, R. H. (1980). Expectancy-confirmation processes arising in the social interaction sequence. *American Psychologist*, *35*, 867–81.

Eden, D., & Shani, A. B. (1982). Pygmalion goes to boot camp: Expectancy, leadership, and trainee performance. *Journal of Applied Psychology*, *67*, 194–9.

Harris, M. J. (1989). Controversy and cumulation: Meta-analysis and research on interpersonal expectancy effects. *Personality and Social Psychology Bulletin*, *17*, 316–22.

Jussim, L. (1986). Self-fulfilling prophecies: A theoretical and integrative review. *Psychological Review*, *93*, 429–45.

——(1990). Social reality and social problems: The role of expectancies. *Journal of Social Issues*, *46*, 9–34.

——(1991). Social perception and social reality: A reflection-construction model. *Psychological Review*, *98*, 54–73.

Rosenthal, R., & Jacobson, L. (1968). *Pygmalion in the classroom: Teacher expectations and student intellectual development*. New York: Holt, Rinehart & Winston.

——& Rubin, D.B. (1978). Interpersonal expectancy effects: The first 345 studies. *The Behavioral and Brain Sciences*, *3*, 377–86.

Snyder, M. (1984). When belief creates reality. In L. Berkowitz (Ed.), *Advances in Experimental Social Psychology* (Vol. 18, pp. 247–305). New York: Academic Press.

——(1992). Motivational foundations of behavioral confirmation. In M. P. Zanna (Ed.), *Advances in experimental social psychology* (Vol. 25, pp. 67–114). San Diego, CA: Academic Press.

LEE JUSSIM

**self-handicapping** The act of creating an obstacle to one's task success in order to obscure the evaluative implications of a performance (*see* Jones & Berglas, 1978). Subsequent failures then can be discounted by attributing them to the obstacle instead of central components of one's identity (e.g., low task ability); whereas task successes seem more impressive because they occurred despite the obstacle, thereby augmenting attributions to central components of one's identity (e.g., high task ability). Self-handicapping is more likely to occur when people are uncertain how they will perform on a task that is relevant to central components of their self-conceptions. Self-reporting the existence of obstacles prior to task performance also has been viewed by some researchers as a type of self-handicapping. A variety of handicaps have been studied, including alcohol, debilitating drugs, distracting music, anxiety, bad moods, illness, reduced effort, sleeplessness, childhood traumas, and recent adversities. The concept has stimulated considerable research because of its clinical applications and the seemingly paradoxical way in which failure-inducing behavior functions to preserve self-esteem (*see* Higgins, Snyder, & Berglas, 1990).

*See also*: ACCOUNTS.

BIBLIOGRAPHY

Higgins, R. L., Snyder, C. R., & Berglas, S. (Eds.) (1990). *Self-handicapping: The paradox that isn't*. New York: Plenum.

Jones, E. E., & Berglas, S. (1978). Control of attributions about the self through self-handicapping strategies: The appeal of alcohol and the role of underachievement. *Personality and Social Psychology Bulletin*, *4*, 200–6.

BARRY R. SCHLENKER

**self-monitoring** According to this theory, people differ in the extent to which they monitor (i.e., observe and control) their expressive behavior and self-presentation (Snyder, 1974, 1979, 1987). Individuals high in self-monitoring are thought to regulate their expressive SELF-PRESENTATION for the sake of public appearances, and thus be highly responsive to social and interpersonal cues to situationally appropriate performances. Individuals low in self-monitoring are thought to lack the ability or the motivation to regulate their expressive self-presentations for such purposes. Their expressive behaviors are thought to reflect their own inner states and dispositions, including their attitudes, emotions, self-conceptions, and personalities.

Research on self-monitoring typically has employed multi-item, self-report measures to identify people high and low in self-monitoring. The two most frequently employed measuring instruments are the 25 true–false items of the original Self-Monitoring Scale (Snyder, 1974) and an 18-item refinement of this measure (Snyder & Gangestad, 1986).

Empirical investigations of testable hypotheses spawned by self-monitoring theory have accumulated into a sizable published literature. Among others, it includes studies of the relation of self-monitoring to expressive control, SOCIAL PERCEPTION, correspondence between private belief and public action, tendencies to be influenced by interpersonal expectations, propensities to tailor behavior to specific situations and roles, susceptibility to advertising, and orientations toward friendship and romantic relationships (for a review, *see* Snyder, 1987).

## MAJOR THEMES OF SELF-MONITORING THEORY AND RESEARCH

Soon after its inception, self-monitoring was offered as a partial resolution of the "TRAITS versus situations" and "ATTITUDES AND BEHAVIOR" controversies in PERSONALITY and social psychology. The propositions of self-monitoring theory clearly suggested that the behavior of low self-monitors ought to be readily predicted from measures of their attitudes, traits, and dispositions whereas that of high self-monitors ought to be best predicted from knowledge of features of the situations in which they operate. Self-monitoring promised a "moderator variable" resolution to debates concerning the relative roles of person and situation in determining behavior. These issues set the agenda for the first wave of research on self-monitoring (for a review, *see* Snyder, 1979).

In its second decade, research on self-monitoring moved beyond issues of dispositional and situational determination of behavior to examinations of the linkages between self-monitoring and interpersonal orientations. Central themes have been the propositions that high self-monitors live in a world of public appearances created by strategic use of IMPRESSION MANAGEMENT, and that low self-monitors live in a world revolving around the private realities of their personal identities and the coherent expression of these across diverse life domains. Research on interpersonal orientations has

revealed that high self-monitors choose friends for their instrumental value in facilitating social performances; in selecting romantic partners, high self-monitors particularly value their PHYSICAL ATTRACTIVENESS. By contrast, the friendship choices of low self-monitors tend to revolve around considerations of similar identities and shared values; their romantic relationships tend to be characterized by closeness, commitment prior to sexual relations, and greater long-term levels of intimacy.

## THE NATURE OF SELF-MONITORING

Over the years, the self-monitoring construct has been the subject of considerable controversy over how it ought to be interpreted and measured. The roots of this controversy are factor analyses which clearly reveal that the items of the Self-Monitoring Scale are multifactorial, with the emergence of three factors being the most familiar product of factor analyses (Snyder & Gangestad, 1986). These factor analyses prompted a critical question: Is self-monitoring truly a unitary phenomenon?

Although there is widespread agreement about the multifactorial nature of the self-monitoring items, there exist diverging viewpoints on the interpretation of this state of affairs. One interpretation is that some criterion variables represented in the literature might relate to one factor, other criterion variables to a second independent factor, and yet others to still a third factor – an interpretation which holds that self-monitoring is not a unitary phenomenon.

Without disputing the multifactorial nature of the self-monitoring items, it is nevertheless possible to construe self-monitoring as a unitary psychological construct. Taxonomic analyses have revealed that the self-monitoring subscales all tap, to varying degrees, a common latent variable that may reflect two discrete or quasi-discrete self-monitoring classes (Gangestad & Snyder, 1985). In addition, the Self-Monitoring Scale itself taps a large common factor accounting for variance in its items and correlating, to varying degrees, with its subscales; this general factor approximates the Self-Monitoring Scale's first unrotated factor (Snyder & Gangestad, 1986). Thus, the Self-Monitoring Scale may "work" to predict diverse phenomena of individual and social functioning because it taps this general factor, an interpretation congruent with self-monitoring as a unitary, conceptually meaningful psychological construct.

CONCLUSIONS
To some extent, the productivity of the self-monitoring construct may derive from the fact that it appears to capture one of the fundamental dichotomies of psychology – whether behavior is a product of forces that operate from without (exemplified by the "situational" orientation of the high self-monitor) or whether it is governed by influences that guide from within (typified by the "dispositional" orientation of the low self-monitor). In theory and research, self-monitoring has served as a focal point for issues in assessment, in the role of scale construction in theory building, and in examining fundamental questions about personality and social behavior.
*See also*: ATTITUDES AND BEHAVIOR; IMPRESSION MANAGEMENT; PERSONALITY; SOCIAL PERCEPTION.

BIBLIOGRAPHY
Gangestad, S., & Snyder, M. (1985). "To carve nature at its joints": On the existence of discrete classes in personality. *Psychological Review*, 92, 317–49.
Snyder, M. (1974). Self-monitoring of expressive behavior. *Journal of Personality and Social Psychology*, 30, 526–37.
—— (1979). Self-monitoring processes. In L. Berkowitz (Ed.), *Advances in experimental social psychology* (Vol. 12, pp. 85–128). New York: Academic Press.
—— (1987). *Public appearances/public realities: The psychology of self-monitoring*. New York: W. H. Freeman.
—— & Gangestad, S. (1986). On the nature of self-monitoring: Matters of assessment, matters of validity. *Journal of Personality and Social Psychology*, 51, 125–39.

MARK SNYDER

**self-perception theory** Originally proposed by Bem (*see* Bem, 1972, for a review), self-perception theory offers a view of the way people come to know their internal states. In Bem's terms, people come to know their internal states "partially by inferring them from observations of their own overt behavior and/or the circumstances in which this behavior occurs" (Bem, 1972, p. 5). In this view, people often do not know their attitudes by direct introspection, but rather examine their own behavior. A person who is crying may infer that he or she is sad. A person who attends a rally for a particular political candidate may infer that he or she has a positive attitude toward that candidate.

Environmental circumstances also play a role. If the person who is crying knows that he was peeling an onion, he may deduce that his behavior is not relevant to a conclusion about his emotions. Similarly, a person who attends a political rally but knows that the professor in her Government class instructed all of the students to attend, may not conclude that her participation in the rally is evidence about her political attitudes.

Bem, using the language promoted by behaviorists in their analysis of human speech, differentiated between manded and tacted behavior. Manded behaviors are those that are under the control of environmental stimuli. They are thus are not useful in inferring a person's internal state. Being commanded to attend a rally is one such behavior. Tacted behaviors, on the other hand, are those that are not environmentally caused and are useful in describing an individual's internal state.

Curiously, the inference procedure is precisely what an observer would use in making a guess about an actor's behavior, determine whether the behavior was manded or tacted, and make an inference about internal states. Bem's second postulate makes this similarity specific: "To the extent that internal cues are weak, ambiguous or uninterpretable, the individual is functionally in the same state as an outside observer, an observer who must necessarily rely upon those same external cues to infer the individual's inner states" (Bem, 1972, p. 5).

This postulate is perhaps self-perception theory's most fundamental and controversial contribution. Although it is often the case that we detect strong and unambiguous cues about our internal states, such as when we are furious or elated, it is also true that many times our internal cues are weak, ambiguous, and uncertain. At these times, we are forced to draw inferences about the true nature of these states based on self-observation. This claim is important because it has been used to reinterpret many experimental findings which theretofore had been explained in ways which assumed unerring self-knowledge on the part of the individual participant. The most notable of these, and the area that created the largest theoretical controversy was self-perception's alternative explanation of COGNITIVE DISSONANCE findings.

Festinger's (1957) dissonance theory proposed that an individual experiences a state of cognitive dissonance when he or she holds two cognitions that are inconsistent with each other. The inconsistency is experienced as an aversive internal state and motivates a person to alleviate the inconsistency. A classic approach to studying dissonance is FORCED COMPLIANCE in which a person makes a counterattitudinal statement for either a high or low inducement. Dissonance theory predicts that people will experience more tension from a counterattitudinal statement made for a low inducement. A large inducement serves as a cognition consonant with the counterattitudinal behavior and reduces the magnitude of dissonance. Self-perception theory argues that the same prediction can be made from the observation of behavior and does not need the intervening process of aversive, internal states. For example, a person with liberal ideology who says that (s)he favors a conservative political candidate would be seen by an observer as having conservative attitudes – unless that behavior was manded by the environment. A large inducement is a manding stimulus and renders the behavior irrelevant in inferring the person's attitude, whereas the behavior of the individual who made a proconservative speech for a low inducement would be seen as tacted and serve as the basis for inferring a proconservative attitude.

Bem conducted a series of "interpersonal simulations" in which he demonstrated that observers who read about participants in forced compliance studies predicted precisely the same attitudes as the involved participants who, in terms of dissonance theory, should be experiencing arousal. Self-perception theory therefore questioned the parsimony or accuracy of positing internal states as a mediating mechanism.

Subsequent research has demonstrated that, despite its compelling logic, self-perception does not account accurately for forced compliance research because, consistent with dissonance theory, arousal is a necessary condition for the involved participants. However, self-perception seems to work well as a way of accounting for inferences one makes about the SELF when the self is relatively uninvested or when behavior is not inconsistent with prior attitudes.

Self-perception theory served as a precursor to more general theories of causal attribution (see also ATTRIBUTION THEORIES; for review, Jones, 1990). Although it began with the language of behaviorism, self-perception became a general perspective for understanding the various circumstances in which people make inferences about themselves. Kelley (1967) adopted self-perception's central point of view and used it to illustrate how individuals apply the rules of causal attribution to the self in the same way that they apply them to others. The scope of self-perception theory was expanded by Nisbett and Valins (1972), who argued that our perceptions of our behavior, its causes, and its consequences are all interrelated. The end result is that self-perception theory is well enough established that it is now a routine assumption in social psychology that there are occasions in which people set about a rule-based process to infer their attitudes, emotions, and other internal states.

See also: ATTRIBUTION THEORIES; COGNITIVE DISSONANCE THEORY; SELF.

BIBLIOGRAPHY

Bem, D. J. (1972). Self-perception theory. In L. Berkowitz (Ed.), *Advances in experimental social psychology* (Vol. 6, pp. 1–62). New York: Academic Press.

Festinger, L. (1957). *A theory of cognitive dissonance*. Palo Alto, CA: Stanford University Press.

Jones, E. E. (1990). *Interpersonal Perception*. New York: W. H. Freeman.

Kelley, H. H. (1967). Attribution theory in social psychology. In D. Levine (Ed.), *Nebraska symposium on motivation*, Nebraska: University of Nebraska Press (Vol. 15, pp. 192–238).

Nisbett, R. E., & Valins, S. (1972). Perceiving the causes of one's own behavior. In E. E. Jones, E. E. Kanouse, H. H. Kelley, R. E. Nisbett, S. Valins, & B. Weiner (Eds.), *Attribution: Perceiving the causes of behavior* (pp. 63–78). Morristown, NJ: General Learning Press.

JOEL COOPER
HART BLANTON

**self-presentation** This is the conscious or nonconscious attempt to control images of self that are conveyed to audiences during social interactions. Self-presentation is a subcategory of IMPRESSION MANAGEMENT, which deals more broadly with how people try to control and regulate information about people, objects, and events.

*See also*: IMPRESSION MANAGEMENT.

BARRY R. SCHLENKER

**self-schemas** Mental structures that represent one's self-knowledge in a particular domain (e.g., generosity). They organize and help process domain-relevant information about oneself. People with well-developed self-schemas in a domain are termed schematic on it. People are self-schematic on dimensions that are important to them, on which they consider themselves extreme, and on which they feel the opposite does not apply (Markus, 1977).

People's self-schemas affect processing of schema-relevant information. People judge themselves faster on, and think in more depth about, information related to self-schemas. People easily remember many instances of behavior relevant to their self-schemas, and they predict future behavior that is consistent with them (Markus & Sentis, 1982).

The working self-concept contains both a core set of self-knowledge and a more changeable set of self-knowledge activated by particular situations. Self-schemas make up the stable, chronically accessible set of self-knowledge (Markus & Wurf, 1987).

*See also*: SCHEMAS/SCHEMATA; SELF.

REFERENCES

Markus, H. (1977). Self-schemata and processing information about the self. *Journal of Personality and Social Psychology*, *35*, 63–78.

——& Wurf, E. (1987). The dynamic self-concept: A social psychological perspective. *Annual Review of Psychology*, *38*, 299–337.

SUSAN T. FISKE
BETH A. MORLING

**self-serving bias** Research on ATTRIBUTIONAL BIAS has shown that people are more likely to attribute their successes to internal causes such as ability, whereas they tend to attribute failures to external causes such as task difficulty. This bias appears due to cognitive and motivational factors, varying across public and private settings.

*See also*: ATTRIBUTIONAL BIAS.

MILES HEWSTONE

**self-verification** This is a SELF-PRESENTATION strategy designed to produce feedback from others which confirms our self-conceptions. According to Swann (1984, 1957) people are motivated to maintain consistency in their self-conceptions. Self-verification is particularly likely when others are believed to hold disconfirming information about the SELF, and in relation to aspects of the self which are subjectively important. Different forms of self-verification include: selective attention to confirmatory information; selective interaction with people who confirm the self-conception, and behaviour designed to elicit confirmatory, or avoid disconfirmatory, feedback from others. The self-concept may undergo temporary changes when people are unable to rebut disconfirming feedback, but enduring changes only occur if social interaction with significant others validates and legitimizes the initial change (e.g., when a person changes roles). The cognitive need to verify our self-concept sometimes overrides our affective need to enhance it (to improve SELF-ESTEEM); it can be more important to ensure that audiences have an impression which is consistent with one's own, than one which is positive.

See also: ROLE THEORY; SELF-ESTEEM.

BIBLIOGRAPHY

Swann, W. B. Jr (1984). Quest for accuracy in person perception: A matter of pragmatics. *Psychological Review, 91*, 457–47

Swann, W. B. Jr (1987). Identity negotiation: Where two roads meet. *Journal of Personality and Social Psychology, 53*, 1038–51.

DOMINIC ABRAMS

**sex differences** Differences between samples of males and females in the mean values of physical, behavioral, or psychological features. In psychology, the study of sex differences originated in individual differences research, through the unintentional discovery of statistically significant sex differences on specific mental tests (for example in mathematical and in linguistic performance). Such findings were later assembled by those interested in sex differences *per se*, notably by Maccoby and Jacklin (1974), and the field of research expanded to include differences in social behavior and related attributes (*see* Eagly, 1987).

In recent times, the term sex differences has been widely replaced in the social sciences and psychology by GENDER differences to indicate that these attributes arise from social rather than biological processes. In doing so, a false dichotomy between environmental and hereditary sources of influence is perpetuated, as many so-called gender differences are clearly the result of both. Physical AGGRESSION provides a good example: its predominance in males can be viewed as the result of past

evolutionary processes (*see* SOCIOBIOLOGY), current physiological sex differences, male cultural values, and power relations between and within the sexes. It is therefore preferable to distinguish between the terms "sex" and "gender" in the following way. Sex refers to the categories male and female; gender refers to the categories masculine and feminine, which are the attributes associated to a greater or lesser extent with the two sexes: hence "sex differences" but "gender role" (*see* ROLE THEORY) and gender stereotype (Archer, 1992). Note that sex is a categorical distinction, whereas gender refers to "fuzzy" categories.

A sex difference can be any difference between mean values for the two sexes on a measured variable. It can therefore range from an absolute distinction to greatly overlapping distributions. The first possibility would include the physical attributes that define sex, such as the occurrence of two X chromosomes in females, and penises in males. In the social domain, the distribution of the sexes in certain occupations, such as priests and midwives, would (until recently) have also constituted a categorical distinction completely coinciding with sex.

Most psychological attributes are not of this sort: instead, they form overlapping distributions with consistent differences in mean values between males and females. For this reason some researchers have referred to them as "sex-related differences," to distinguish them from non-overlapping sex differences.

The perceived need for such a term can be traced to the way psychologists identify differences between experimental conditions or social categories. The defining feature has traditionally been statistical significance. If a mean difference between two comparison groups had an associated probability level of 0.05 or less, it was viewed as a "real" difference. Applying this reasoning to an extensive review of sex differences led Maccoby and Jacklin (1974) to conclude that certain differences were reliable because studies had repeatedly produced significant differences in a consistent direction. Spatial performance, linguistic performance and aggression were three such attributes. Others, such as as SELF-ESTEEM, dependency and SOCIAL INFLUENCE, which produced less consistent findings in terms of reaching significance levels in individual studies, were not.

However, statistical significance is a measure of the reliability of a finding in a specific study. Its use as an informal method for reaching conclusions from a number of such studies is problematic. As was realized by several critics of their review, it made Maccoby and Jacklin's conclusions unreliable.

The use of a single criterion – in this case significance level – to define what is an acceptable sex difference and what is not masks their continuity from total separation to total overlap. It presents a more definite picture of differences between males and females than is warranted. The bias in psychology journals towards reporting statistically significant differences, and the consequent underreporting of null results, could in theory further contribute to distorting conclusions based on counting up significant findings among published studies. If many nonsignificant findings have remained unreported, some at least of the published findings are likely to be type 1 errors, i.e., false positives (for an argument against this view, see Eagly & Wood, 1991).

An alternative, and altogether more satisfactory, way of viewing sex differences, came from the application of a different set of statistical procedures. These are the techniques of META-ANALYSIS, used primarily in quantitative reviews of empirical studies. The important measures for evaluating sex differences were estimates of the relative magnitude of effects (as opposed to their reliability). Such "effect size" measures can in the first instance be applied to single studies to express the magnitude of difference obtained. A simple and standard measure – generalizable across studies, sample sizes, and particular measures – involves the difference between the two mean scores ($d$) expressed in units of their average standard deviation. This can be simply converted into $r$, the point biserial correlation between the independent variable (i.e., sex) and the specific measure. Using such measures, comparisons

can readily be made between the magnitude of the sex differences obtained in studies involving one psychological attribute and another.

More importantly, meta-analysis can be used to draw general conclusions from a large number of studies. This is particularly appropriate in the case of sex differences, where the comparison groups are categories – male or female – which are the same across different studies, rather than some imposed experimental or intervention condition which varies from study to study. Consequently, meta-analytic techniques which combine and compare research findings have been widely applied to sex differences research in cognitive and social psychology. This began in a limited way shortly after Maccoby and Jacklin's review, when their data were reanalyzed by meta-analysis to show that sex differences were more widespread. Other researchers drew attention to the importance of estimating the magnitude of overlap when studying sex differences. There soon followed more detailed reevaluations of specific attributes using meta-analytic techniques (see Eagly, 1987; Eagly & Wood, 1991).

It has typically been found that sex differences in cognitive abilities are relatively small, leading to the conclusion that they are of little significance compared to other categories of individual difference such as age and social class. In contrast, some sex differences in social behavior are of a greater magnitude, notably those in nonverbal communication (summarized by Hall, 1984). Aggression, when it is measured in laboratory and questionnaire studies, shows a smaller difference (Eagly & Steffen, 1986). HELPING BEHAVIOR, and social influence, show even smaller differences when measured in laboratory studies (Eagly, 1987).

Conceptualization of sex differences in social behavior involves a broader perspective than that applied to cognitive sex differences. Sex differences are seen as the outcome of people's interactions within the contexts of social situations, rather than as properties of individuals. Researchers have therefore recognized the importance of wider gender-related processes, such as ROLE

THEORY, the POWER relations of men and women, gender stereotyping, and situational influences. For example, Deaux and Major (1987) described a model of sex differences in social behavior which viewed them as the outcome of interactions between people, to which are brought gender-related BELIEFS about the other and oneself, some of which may be activated by the situation, and affect behavior. The emphasis here has shifted from sex differences as a concept in itself, to processes such as gender-related STEREOTYPING and beliefs, SELF SCHEMATAS, SELF-PRESENTATION and SELF-VERIFICATION, and the SALIENCE of gender for those people in that situation. This produces a view of sex differences as flexible and context-dependent.

Bearing in mind the fluid nature of sex differences in social behavior, two examples can be used to indicate their extent and magnitude. Hall (1984) analysed 125 studies of NONVERBAL COMMUNICATION, and found comparatively large differences between men and women. Thus men were more expansive in bodily movements, used more filled pauses and interrupted more in conversations. The point biserial correlations ($r$) for these differences were between 0.46 and 0.51, with effect sizes ($d$) of between 1.0 and 1.2. For the behavioral sciences generally, these are very large differences. They can be contrasted with the smaller values found for cognitive abilities (Hyde, 1981): for spatial performance, r was approximately 0.22 ($d = 0.46$), a medium-sized effect, and for verbal ability, it was approximately 0.1 ($d = 0.2$), a small effect. Other sex differences in nonverbal communication are equally large, or nearly so, in the other direction, women using more facial expressions ($r = 0.45$), being approached more closely by others ($r = 0.43$), and smiling more ($r = 0.30$).

In other cases, smaller sex differences have been found. North American social psychological studies of helping behavior have generally involved a staged emergency situation or a request for help, involving a stranger. For 99 such studies where the effect size was known (Eagly, 1987), the mean value for $d$ (weighted for study reliability) was 0.34, men showing more helping. Eagly remarked that such studies involve an agentic form of helping which is consistent with masculine role norms. However, this sex difference is smaller than any of those listed above for nonverbal behavior: the biserial correlation is 0.167.

In explaining sex differences in the social domain, Eagly (1987) adopted what she referred to as a structural approach, arguing that the differences directly follow from the societal positions of men and women (*see also* Henley, 1973). Before elaborating it, it is useful to clarify how it differs from other types of explanation for psychological sex differences. Such explanations can be classified into three broad categories (Archer, 1992). Biological explanations involve processes controlled by heredity, such as brain development and neuroendocrine action, ultimately being the product of past selection pressures. SOCIALIZATION, or cultural explanations involve the impact and internalization of CULTURE, particularly during childhood: in psychology a large amount of research has concentrated on applying a SOCIAL LEARNING or cognitive developmental framework to the acquisition of sex-typed behavior and beliefs. Structural explanations also concern the impact of the wider society, but emphasize its direct impact on people's behavior or dispositions, rather than the slow acquisition and accumulation of habits and beliefs.

For example, Henley (1973) explained sex differences in nonverbal communication as the direct manifestation of the POWER relations between the sexes. Women's behavior is comparable to that of low-status individuals generally: they can be approached more closely than men when speaking, they defer to men more (both in speech and in terms of moving out of the way), and they look more at the other person. Men feel more free to touch women, and to exercise a more familiar manner generally. The important points about this type of explanation are first that it arises directly from the implicit feelings of power associated with societal positions, and secondly that it is reversible over relatively short periods of time by reversing the position of the actors (in contrast to a socialization explanation, which implies that a long period of social learning and internalization of values would be necessary).

Eagly (1987) offered a similar explanation for several domains in which men and women differ. In general such sex differences arise from the different social positions occupied by men and women, which differ in terms of normative expectations about behavior, and in terms of relative power. Social influence provides an example. In natural settings, men are found to exert more influence on others, whereas women are more subject to influence by others. Eagly argued that these differences stem from men having more formal status and feelings of power than women: within limits, those of lower status are expected to defer to those of higher status. In laboratory studies, small sex differences in the same direction are found in small group settings where men and women have equal formal status. These are regarded as residual influences of the expectancies resulting from the unequal experiences of men and women in the outside world. Although the structural explanation predicts changes in behavior to follow changes in status, it would nevertheless hold that these have to be fully accepted by the people concerned. In the case of laboratory groups, there will be an air of artificiality about the equal status.

This leads to a final point about sex differences in social behavior. Most of the existing meta-analyses rely heavily on laboratory (and in some cases questionnaire) research. Where we are are dealing with behavior that can be reproduced in the laboratory, as is the case for nonverbal communication, this is not so important. But in other cases, the sex differences found under laboratory conditions represent at best residual psychological dispositions from much more extensive differences occurring in the outside world. We saw that this was to some extent the case for social influence. Aggression provides a much more clear-cut case.

In laboratory studies involving experimentally induced provocations, and in questionnaire studies, sex differences on aggression are moderate in magnitude. Eagly and Steffen (1986) analyzed such studies of aggressive behavior involving North American adolescents or adults, the majority of whom were undergraduates. For the 50 studies where sufficient information was provided for an

effect size to be calculated, $d$ was 0.4, a value which is reduced to 0.29 when weightings are introduced to take into account the reliability of various findings. Clearly, this represents only a small difference between the sexes (*see* meta-analysis). However, this overall figure has limited value for two reasons: first, there was considerable variability in the findings from the various studies; secondly, laboratory studies of aggression have doubtful ECOLOGICAL VALIDITY, i.e. they may not be related to the sorts of aggression that occur in the outside world.

When studying aggression in the laboratory, the experimenter is first taking out of social context something that can only be fully understood in context, and secondly is constrained by ethical considerations from making it anything like a real simulation of an aggressive act. At present, attempts to assess the real extent and magnitude of sex differences in aggression – and related attributes – in the outside world rely on a variety of incomplete and indirect sources of evidence. Many of these are summarized by Daly and Wilson (1988) in their book on homicide viewed from the perspective of EVOLUTIONARY PSYCHOLOGY. Such evidence indicates that most serious physical aggression is carried out by males, and that this conclusion transcends wide variations in culture. Although this pattern can be understood in terms of the social roles of men and women, Daly and Wilson's analysis indicates that ultimately it is derived from the evolutionary consequences of conflicting reproductive strategies by males and females.

In conclusion, sex differences in social behavior vary in magnitude from large to small and cover a range of different types of behavior. At the immediate level, they can be viewed as the outcome of social situations, to which people bring different gender-related beliefs, which influence behavior to different extents according to the situation. At a broader level, they can be viewed as the consequence of the different social positions or roles of men and women, which can have immediate effects on behavior via social beliefs. Ultimately, some aspects of role-related behavior are understandable in terms of evolutionary biology.

*See also*: AGGRESSION; CULTURE; GENDER; HELP-
ING BEHAVIOR; META-ANALYSIS; NONVERBAL
COMMUNICATION; POWER; ROLE THEORY; SELF-
ESTEEM; SOCIAL INFLUENCE; SOCIAL LEARNING;
SOCIALIZATION; SOCIOBIOLOGY.

BIBLIOGRAPHY

Archer, J. (1992). Childhood gender roles:
Social context and organisation. In H.
McGurk (Ed.), *Childhood social development: Contemporary perspectives* (pp. 31–
61). Hillsdale, NJ: Lawrence Erlbaum.
Daly, M., & Wilson, M. (1988). *Homicide*.
New York: Aldine de Gruyter.
Deaux, K., & Major, B. (1987). Putting gender into context: An interactive model of
gender-related behavior. *Psychological Review, 94*, 369–89.
Eagly, A. (1987). *Sex differences in social
behavior: A social role interpretation*. Hillsdale, NJ: Lawrence Erlbaum.
—— & Steffen, V. J. (1986). Gender and
aggressive behavior: A meta-analytic review. *Psychological Bulletin, 100*, 309–30.
—— & Wood, W. (1991). Explaining sex differences in social behavior: A meta-analytic
perspective. *Personality and Social Psychology Bulletin, 17*, 306–15.
Hall, J. A. (1984). *Non-verbal sex differences*.
Baltimore, MD: Johns Hopkins University
Press.
Henley, N. M. (1973). Power, sex and nonverbal communication. *Berkeley Journal of
Sociology, 18*, 1–26.
Hyde, J. S. (1981). How large are cognitive
gender differences? A meta-analysis using
$w^2$ and *d*. *American Psychologist, 36*, 892–
901.
Maccoby, E. E., & Jacklin, E. E. (1974) *The
psychology of sex differences*. Stanford, CA:
Stanford University Press.

JOHN ARCHER

**sexual behavior** The field encompasses biological and behavioral substrates of genitally
oriented arousal and reproduction, which
among humans includes the study of GENDER,
CLOSE RELATIONSHIPS, sexual orientation, DE-
VIANCE, antisocial behavior, and dysfunction.
Theories applied to findings in this field

range from SOCIAL LEARNING and SOCIALIZA-
TION to SOCIAL COGNITION and ROLE THEORY.

The contribution of two major components
of contemporary social psychology to sexual
behavior will be examined. Attribution
underlies a wide range of responses found
within human sexuality, as well as being a
cornerstone of social cognition (*see* ATTRIBU-
TION THEORIES). The second component, affect, also plays an important role in social
behavior, by mediating situational and individual difference variables. Thus attribution
and affect will be jointly used to review many
of the topics considered within human sexuality, as summarized by Kelley and Byrne
(1992) and Baron and Byrne (1991).

DEVELOPMENT OF SEXUALITY
With regard to sexual development, children
tend to proceed from a state of relative
unawareness of sexual labels through a gradual recognition of the sexual connotations of
thought, action, and feeling. The self-attribution that one is a sexual being occurs as a
developmental process. Feelings of anticipation of the physical changes associated with
puberty and a greater awareness of sexual
meanings are learned as ADOLESCENCE approaches. The pace of these changes can
influence the youngster's SELF-ESTEEM, in a
social context in response to SOCIAL COMPARI-
SON processes. Theories of sexual development, primarily Freudian psychoanalytic and
Simon/Gagnon's sexual script explanations,
focus on qualitative changes and role theory,
respectively. These theories have not yet integrated developmental change with its attributional and affective components.

SEXUAL INTERACTIONS
Because of the inherently social nature of
sexual behavior, much of its study focuses on
interpersonal interactions that involve themes
of sexual arousal and reproduction, and this
discussion is confined to those aspects of
relationships. At the beginning stages of relationships, individual variables such as PHYS-
ICAL ATTRACTIVENESS and SIMILARITY act to
increase positive affect. Attributions toward
attractive individuals tend to be more positive

than toward the unattractive. Childlike qualities in appearance and voice produce negative attributions about the adult possessor's personality (e.g., Montepare & Zebrowitz-McArthur, 1987). Similar examples include feminine nonverbal behavior among men, which produces attributions about atypical sexual orientation, and sexy clothing worn by women, which heightens attributions of sexual interest and receptivity among male but not female observers. The theory of SOCIOBIOLOGY, widely criticized and not generally accepted by many sexologists, attempts to explain such results through their effects on inclusive fitness for reproduction. Through strategies of SELF-PRESENTATION and IMPRESSION MANAGEMENT, individuals seek to appear interpersonally attractive to potential partners.

One's affective state also affects attraction toward an individual, and the source of this feeling state can be situationally or interpersonally dependent. An enjoyable experience, a success, or interpersonal imbalance can all lead to like or dislike.

When attraction develops into love, several aspects of attribution and affect appear to be important. One theory of passionate LOVE proposed by Hatfield and colleagues describes the MISATTRIBUTION OF AROUSAL and cultural acceptance of love as the primary reasons for its occurrence in the presence of an appropriate love object. In Sternberg's triangular model of love, positive affect underlies its major bases of INTIMACY, passion, and commitment.

Problems in developing close relationships include deficits in social skills and conflict. Varying degrees of negative affect are associated with LONELINESS, and attribution about the frequency of its occurrence relates to the FALSE CONSENSUS effect. Cognitive therapy attempts to modify this attributional style. Among more socially skilled individuals, variable gender differences occur cross-culturally in dating competence, which also depends on other individual differences including self-monitoring. High self-monitors express less commitment toward their partners, and lows desire to interact with their partners for many more types of activities (Snyder & Simpson, 1984). CONFLICT can arise in a dating rela-

tionship, and JEALOUSY can produce difficulties by contributing to its deterioration. Strategies for inducing jealousy in a partner may originate from a desire to bolster one's own self-esteem or to provide evidence that the partner would react as expected. Jealousy involves a negative emotional state and is associated with negative evaluations of the rival's personality.

Relationships can progress through five stages: initial attraction, building, continuation, deterioration, and ending. The last two stages commence when partners attribute sufficient dissatisfaction toward their relationship, particularly when they differ in marriage-relevant beliefs; low self-esteem increases the likelihood that a partner will neglect or exit from the coupling instead of working or waiting for improvement (Rusbult, Verette, Whitney, Slovik, & Lipkus, 1991).

Attributions about the reasons for divorce can influence recovery. Ex-wives who blamed their former spouses experienced more unhappiness than those less concerned with blame, especially when the husband initiated the divorce. Numerous studies describe the negative affect, self-blame, and behavioral changes that can occur among some children of divorce.

SEXUAL AROUSAL AND ATTRACTION
Sexual attraction depends on the factors that enhance friendships, such as physical attractiveness and similarity, as well as certain attributional features. Conclusions about a person's sexual interests arise from attributions about his or her appearance, assumed experience level, and other personal characteristics. In Western societies, women identify emotional involvement as a prerequisite for sexual activity more often than men. The SEX (gender) DIFFERENCE in preoccupation with closeness versus sexual arousal also occurs in ratings of desired behaviors in close relationships. Upon becoming sexually active, two of the most common reactions involve enjoyment and attributions of love, again with the expected sex difference. At the beginning stages of sexual interactions, both

affect and attributions influence how the relationship proceeds. The most compatible, satisfied couples tend to maintain their relationships longer than mismatched, dissatisfied couples.

The decision to become sexually active has been studied from the perspective of theories of MORAL DEVELOPMENT. For example, individuals engaging in the same sexual behavior could do so for entirely different reasons that reflect Kohlberg's stages of moral reasoning. Thus the persons are attributing different reasons for their identical behaviors. At the conventional level described as law and order, sexual acts elicit relatively high levels of guilt in oneself and intolerance for others' sexual variance.

The SELF-SERVING BIAS affects the methods for attributing the reasons for sexual experiences varying in satisfaction level. Specifically, men tend to use external attributions for their own unsatisfying experiences, while women adopt internal attributions for them.

In a potentially arousing situation, both cognitive and affective factors can enhance or interfere with sexual arousal. Interference occurs when subjects attempt to process complex, nonsexual information in a dichotic listening task, compared to a less complex task. Subjects experience higher levels of sexual arousal if imagery is presented in the context of information that similar others find it highly arousing. Sexual arousal produced by exposure to erotic imagery persists in the presence of the individual's efforts to prevent it (Wegner, Shortt, Blake, & Page, 1990). However, sexual arousal is one of the responses incompatible with anger as a potentiator to aggression.

ANTISOCIAL ASPECTS OF SEXUALITY

The effects of violent and nonviolent sexual explicitness, harassment, and coercion are three of the topics with antisocial themes studied in sexology. With regard to the first, a wealth of evidence shows that exposure of males to explicit imagery heightens laboratory aggression, mediated by affect and arousal. When combined with violence such as RAPE, explicitness can also influence viewers' appraisals of their current relationships, typically in the negative direction because of the impersonality and brutality portrayed in such images. The validity of these findings for application remains controversial, but their aggressive content seems to interact with the sexual theme to produce effects including misattribution of arousal.

Sexual harassment evokes different perceptions depending on the individual's sex, and males express more leniency and acceptance about this and other types of coercion. The person's motivation for participating in a romantic affair in the workplace partially determines its effects (Dillard & Broetzman, 1989). Sexual pressure on dates also reflects attributional patterns, in the sense that the victim, usually female, is considered responsible for its occurrence. Similarly, rape continues this pattern as demonstrated among victims, rapists, and observers such as jurors, given widespread beliefs in rape myths and the victim's responsibility, and the aftereffect known as the rape trauma syndrome. In the latter the victim progresses through phases of denial, blame, anger, and possible acceptance and recovery. When considering the guilt or innocence of an accused rapist, mitigating circumstances work in favor of the defendant – whether the victim drank alcohol or the accused is attractive, for example.

SEXUAL VARIATION

As an instance of sexual variation, homosexuality involves both attributional and affective variables. The current definition of homosexuality includes not only sexual activity but also interpersonal affection and sexual fantasy. During the process of coming out, awareness – the initial self-attribution – of homosexual interest evolves into acceptance as a firmer self-attribution. Public communication, the third stage of coming out, encourages others to complete the process of assigning the label of homosexuality to an individual. Negative, stereotypic attitudes toward homosexuals, known as homophobia or the less extreme homosexual bias, are based on negative affect engendered by the social stigma of this sexual orientation.

The history of defining sexual deviance reveals an interesting exercise in changing attributions toward sexual variance – demonology, the medical model, statistical definition, and the sociological approach have all been used. For some variations, the individual's belief embodies the category, as in transsexualism. For others, strongly held attitudes affect sexuality in the absence of behavioral validation. Old age and disability are two examples of variation in which STEREOTYPING produces limitations on individual's sexuality.

## ATTITUDES RELATED TO SEXUALITY

One of the most powerful predictors of sexual responses is the general class of attitudes about sexuality. Sexual attitudes predict a wide range of related behaviors, including domains as disparate as use of sexually explicit imagery known as PORNOGRAPHY, contraceptive behavior, effects of sex education, and personal health care. A portion of the general concept of sexual attitudes is contributed by the attitude known as sex guilt, developed by Mosher (e.g., Mosher & Vonderheide, 1985).

Certain constellations of attitudes and PERSONALITY variables also relate to sexuality (see ATTITUDES AND BEHAVIOR). Regarding abortion, a false consensus effect occurs among college students; and medical professionals who disapprove abortion also evaluate abortion patients more negatively than other patient types, suggesting an instance of affect generalization.

Other examples of the utility of attitudes and personality include: the use of sexual components on scales of stressful experiences, and the role of close relationships as social support buffering stress and resultant strain; self-efficacy as explained by protection–motivation theory, in relation to the maintenance of breast self-examination; perceived control and hardiness as factors in adolescent contraception; and changes in sexual activity depending on perceived vulnerability to acquired immune deficiency syndrome (AIDS). These examples combine affective and attributional processes to produce effects on sexuality and related behaviors.

Similar sets of variables influence reproductive aspects of sexuality. The premenstrual syndrome has been studied cross-culturally, and some mood-related and physical symptoms occur in women regardless of their beliefs about it. However, stronger belief systems result in more symptom reporting on a retrospective basis, indicating the involvement of an attributional process (McFarland, Ross, & DeCourville, 1989).

Childbearing patterns partly depend on the individual's beliefs about the utility and value of increasing family size. Even aspects of labor and delivery relate to personality factors such as sexual attitudes, and the popular methods of drug-free birth rely on self-control processes developed by the prospective mother. Negative feelings about breastfeeding influence its occurrence and persistence, and the concept of postpartum depression certainly involves some affective, attributional components in addition to hormonal and experiential factors.

## SEXUAL DISSATISFACTION AND DYSFUNCTION

Within marriages sex differences occur in the sources identified for sexual dissatisfaction. That is, spouses agree that dissatisfaction exists, but often disagree about the reasons for it. Sexually dissatisfied couples make internal attributions about this topic more commonly than do satisfied couples, a pattern which also applies to marital satisfaction.

One common type of sexual dysfunction, inhibited sexual desire, may according to the theorist Kaplan be based on rejecting the self-attribution of sexual interest. Often this occurs because of extremely negative socialization, or traumatic experiences like rape or sexual abuse. Another dysfunction affecting the desire phase of the sexual response cycle, sexual aversion, can have similar roots. Accuracy in recognizing the signs of sexual arousal can be involved; men whose erections were covered by a sheet experienced less arousal than uncovered men (Sakheim, Barlow, Beck, & Abrahamson, 1985). Two dysfunctions of the excitement phase, sexual anxiety (typically appearing among women) and performance anxiety (typically appearing among men), can stem from anticipation of negative sexual experiences. Several types of therapy combine behavioral and cognitive treatment applied to sexual dysfunction, such as rational – emotive therapy, systematic desensitization, and orgasmic reconditioning.

BRIEF SUMMARY
Several lines of evidence about sexual behavior indicate the importance of two factors commonly found in social psychological literature. The roles of affect and attributional processes were outlined in regard to sexual development, close relationships, antisocial behavior, and sexual variance, attitudes, and dysfunction. *See also*: ADOLESCENCE; ATTRIBUTION THEORIES; CONFLICT; DEVIANCE; GENDER; JEALOUSY AND ENVY; IMPRESSION MANAGEMENT; INTIMACY; LONELINESS; MORAL DEVELOPMENT; PERSONALITY; PORNOGRAPHY; RAPE; ROLE THEORY; SELF-ESTEEM; SEX DIFFERENCES; SOCIAL COGNITION; SOCIAL COMPARISON; SOCIAL LEARNING; SOCIALIZATION; SOCIOBIOLOGY; STEREOTYPING.

BIBLIOGRAPHY
Baron, R. A., & Byrne, D. (1991). *Social psychology: Understanding human interaction* (6th ed.). Boston, MA: Allyn & Bacon.
Dillard, J. P., & Broetzman, S. M. (1989). Romantic relationships at work: Perceived changes in job-related behaviors as a function of participant's motive, partner's motive, and gender. *Journal of Applied Psychology, 19*, 93–110.
Kelley, K., & Byrne, D. (1992). *Exploring human sexuality*. Englewood Cliffs, NJ: Prentice Hall.
McFarland, C., Ross, M., & DeCourville, N. (1989). Women's theories of menstruation and biases in recall of menstrual symptoms. *Journal of Personality and Social Psychology, 57*, 522–31.
Montepare, J. M., & Zebrowitz-McArthur, L. (1987). Perceptions of adults with child-like voices in two cultures. *Journal of Experimental Social Psychology, 23*, 331–49.
Mosher, D. L., & Vonderheide, S. G. (1985). Contributions of sex guilt and masturbation guilt to women's contraceptive attitudes and use. *Journal of Sex Research, 21*, 24–39.
Rusbult, C. E., Verette, J., Whitney, G. A., Slovik, L.F., & Lipkus, I. (1991). Accommodation processes in close relationships: Theory and preliminary empirical evidence. *Journal of Personality and Social Psychology, 60*, 53–76.
Sakheim, D. K., Barlow, D. H., Beck, J. G., & Abrahamson, D. J. (1985). A comparison of male heterosexual and male homosexual patterns of sexual arousal. *Journal of Sex Research, 21*, 183–98.
Snyder, M., & Simpson, J. A. (1984). Self-monitoring and dating relationships. *Journal of Personality and Social Psychology, 47*, 1281–91.
Wegner, D. M., Shortt, J. W., Blake, A. W., & Page, M. S. (1990). The suppression of exciting thoughts. *Journal of Personality and Social Psychology, 58*, 409–18.

KATHRYN KELLEY
ANDREA HARVAN

**shyness** This term connotes timidity and awkward, inhibited, or withdrawn behavior. Psychologists use the term in two ways. It describes an experience of discomfort in social situations that is characterized by intense self-consciousness and is frequently accompanied by symptoms like blushing, perspiring, and increased heart rate. It is commonly, but not necessarily expressed as gaze avoidance, reticence, and a reluctance to initiate conversation or to break silences in conversation. In its second sense, it refers to a personality trait or predisposition to respond in a shy way. Impetus to research in shyness was provided by large scale surveys carried out by Pilkonis and Zimbardo in the 1970s (*see* Jones et al., 1986, Chap. 2) which reported that the experience of shyness was widespread and that some 40 percent of respondents identified their shyness as dispositional. This and subsequent research (*see* Jones et al., 1986; Crozier, 1990), has established that shyness produces largely negative outcomes, in that it restricts social life, leads to being misunderstood by others, and results in failure to realize one's potential. Shy people tend to be anxious, low in SELF-ESTEEM, and to underestimate their SOCIAL SKILLS. They are prone to LONELINESS. They experience a conflict over participation in social encounters, in that they are motivated to be sociable but lack confidence in their ability to cope with the situation or to make a good impression on others. Their resolution of this conflict is a passive one, characterized by lack of assertiveness, minimal or hesitant participation, or even avoidance of social encounters. These tendencies may have effects upon major life events. Caspi et al. (1988) found that, at least among the men in their study, shyness assessed in childhood was correlated with delay in marriage and in entry to a stable career, the latter being associated with subsequent lower occupational achievement. For some, shyness can be a serious personal problem, and several approaches have been taken to help people overcome it, the differences among programs reflecting in large part the absence of a theoretical consensus on the causes of shyness. The most common methods are designed to bring about improvements in one or more of the following: enhancing social skills, reducing ANXIETY, increasing self-confidence, and developing the client's understanding of shyness.

Despite its pervasiveness in everyday accounts of social life and the coherence of findings in psychological research, particularly from the perspective of individual differences, shyness has eluded any simple explanation. Different theoretical positions may be classified in terms of:

(1) the emphasis that they place upon the SELF; and
(2) the stance that they take on the emotional component of shyness, in particular whether it should be regarded as a form of social anxiety or of shame.

Kagan has argued that shyness is a manifestation of inhibition, a temperament that is characterized by a tendency towards fear, wariness, and inhibited behavior in response to novel stimulation and that can be detected in children as young as four months old (*see* Jones et al., 1986, Chap. 7). The nature and the age of first appearance of these reactions implies that no very sophisticated concept of self is required. An alternative perspective proposes that shyness is a form of anxiety over SELF-PRESENTATION concerns, where the individual is motivated to create a favorable impression but lacks confidence in the ability

to do so (Schlenker & Leary, 1982). In another version of this approach Arkin construes shyness as a protective presentation strategy intended to forestall disapproval (*see* Crozier, 1990, Chap. 10). Self-presentation concerns have been combined with SELF-AWARENESS theory to offer an explanation of the self-consciousness inherent in shyness. This hypothesizes that attention is focused on the self when attention centred on engagement in social interaction is disrupted by the assessment that one lacks the ability to produce satisfactory outcomes.

The self-presentation approach clearly makes strong assumptions about the person's capacity for taking different perspectives on the self and this casts doubt on the claim that shyness may appear very early in life. It also brings the experience of shyness close to those of shame and EMBARRASSMENT in that it treats all of these as forms of social anxiety. Yet there are many reasons why it is important to distinguish between shame-related emotions and anxiety. Embarrassment that is vicarious or that is a response to being praised seems closer to shyness and to modesty than to anxiety. Blushing seems characteristic of shame, shyness, and embarrassment but not of fear or anxiety. There are also arguments against identifying shyness with embarrassment. Immunity to shyness could be regarded as a positive attribute, but an inability to experience embarrassment (or shame) would surely be regarded as pathological.

A possible resolution of these issues is offered by Buss's proposal that there may be two forms of shyness, one form related to fear and inhibition and the other to self-consciousness (*see* Jones et al., 1986, Chap. 4). Some empirical support is provided by Asendorpf (1989) who distinguishes between inhibition in response to strangers and inhibition in anticipation of social evaluation, and his findings suggest that these may be expressed differently in behavior, in that closed body posture is associated with the first, and blushing with the second. Further research is needed to confirm this distinction and to elucidate the many aspects of shyness that remain problematic.

*See also*: ANXIETY; EMBARRASSMENT; LONELINESS; SELF; SELF-AWARENESS; SELF-ESTEEM; SELF PRESENTATION; SOCIAL SKILLS.

BIBLIOGRAPHY

Asendorpf, J. (1989). Shyness as a final common pathway for two different kinds of inhibition. *Journal of Personality and Social Psychology*, *57*, 481–92.

Caspi, A., Elder. G. H., & Bem, D. J. (1988). Moving away from the world: Life-course patterns of shy children. *Developmental Psychology*, *24*, 824–31.

Crozier, W. R. (Ed.) (1990). *Shyness and embarrassment: Perspectives from social psychology*. Cambridge: Cambridge University Press.

Jones, W. H., Cheek, J. M., & Briggs, S. R. (Eds.) (1986). *Shyness: Perspectives on research and treatment*. New York: Plenum.

Schlenker, M. R., & Leary, M. R. (1982). Social anxiety and self-presentation: A conceptualization and model. *Psychological Bulletin*, *92*, 641–69.

W. RAY CROZIER

**similarity** Social psychologists have long been interested in the degree of similarity in the attitudes and traits of relationship partners. With regard to attitudes and physical attractiveness, an extensive literature shows that friends and romantic partners tend to be similar to each other. However, the role of similarity of personality traits is less clear.

*See also*: ATTRACTION.

HARRY T. REIS

**simulation heuristic** Subjective probability judgments may not always follow the AVAILABILITY of relevant examples in memory but may sometimes be based on the ease with which fictitious examples can be mentally simulated or imagined. Such a HEURISTIC can account for several cognitive fallacies and BIASES, such as the overestimation of causally plausible event combinations or the enhanced regret experienced when it is easy to mentally undo an unfortunate event (e.g., an accident).

*See also*: HEURISTICS.

KLAUS FIEDLER

**smoking** A major cause of illness and premature death. It is a highly intractable behavior maintained by social, psychological, and pharmacological factors related to the DRUG nicotine. Social psychologists have paid most attention to the initiation stage and have emphasized the role of SOCIAL INFLUENCE and PEER PRESSURE.

*See also*: ADDICTION; SOCIAL INFLUENCE.

STEPHEN SUTTON

**social categorization** This process cuts to the very heart of social psychology, bringing together the social with the psychological, reality and representation. Within psychology it is a widely held view that how we see and understand the world is a function of the categories we use to interpret it, and (sometimes less commonly acknowledged) that this depends on the categories the world imposes on us. The problem of how we can know an external world and avoid the twin perils of Kantian idealism on the one hand, and mechanical materialism on the other, has arguably been one of the major problems of epistemology. Fortunately perhaps, such questions do not seem to have impeded the activity of social psychologists, with the result that it has variously fallen prey to the problems of both camps.

THEORETICAL APPROACHES AND ELEMENTS

Theoretical approaches differ as to how they conceive of the process of social categorization, and in their view of the epistemological and ontological status of social categories. They vary in the role they accord to reality and cognition, but also with respect to the additional mediating role of language, communication, and action (if these are recognized at all). At one pole, some radical social constructionist and discourse analytic approaches are antirealist in denying the ontological status of social categories as such but see these as social constructions of discourse, created and disputed in negotiation (i.e., at most a form of linguistic realism; *see* SOCIAL CONSTRUCTIONISM, DISCOURSE ANALYSIS). It is important to distinguish constructionism from the more cognitive tradition of "constructivism" which regards (social) categories as primarily mental constructs (e.g., knowledge structures, SCHEMAS) which filter information processing, their relation to the social realm (of reality and its construction) being often secondary or unacknowledged. This cognitivism has arguably tended to preserve a dualism between individual cognition and the social world outside, although despite this mentalistic metatheory, it has been more likely to build bridges with more materialist/realist accounts than has the constructionist tradition. Materialist approaches have borrowed from Gibson's ecological perspective, such that the perception of social categories might be regarded as direct and unmediated reflections of "social reality," that do not even have to be cognitively mediated. Philosophical difficulties aside, elements of constructionism, constructivism, and realism do not have to be mutually exclusive. More interactionist approaches to social categorization which theorize the relations between cognition, language, social activity, and "reality" are feasible if not always evident in mainstream accounts. Rather than getting side-tracked into taxonomic details, it is more fruitful to examine the various ways that writing and research has dealt with the issue of social categorization in practice and provide some historical perspective on developments. Within mainstream social psychology there has tended to be an emphasis on the cognitive and perceptual aspects of social categorization, reflecting the influence of both "constructivist" and "ecological" themes.

## HISTORICAL ROOTS: COGNITIVE BASIS OR BIAS?

The importance of both cognition and reality are recognized in the pioneering work of Bruner (1957) who stressed the dynamic relation between the cognitive "accessibility" of categories and their correspondence or "fit" to real invariances in the environment, a central theme being the idea that perception and cognition could be influenced by the perceiver's goals and motivations (the "New Look"). However, it was Tajfel (see, e.g.,

Tajfel, 1981) who developed these ideas and applied them most fully to the realm of social categorization and its effects, building on earlier work on the cognitive determinants of STEREOTYPING and PREJUDICE by Allport, Campbell, and others. Tajfel's insight was to translate the findings of accentuation effects from the perception of physical objects to the social domain. The finding that people tended to accentuate differences between and similarities within classes of physical stimuli categorized according to some criterion (e.g., length) was used to help to account for the stereotyping of social categories, in which such "accentuation" effects could be further enhanced by the value or emotional significance attached to the categories. Social categorization and its effects formed an important cognitive foundation of SOCIAL IDENTITY THEORY, the broader theory of intergroup relations which grew out of this work.

Like Bruner, Tajfel viewed (social) CATEGORIZATION as a generally adaptive and functional process used to organize and simplify the essentially overwhelming complexity of the stimulus environment. The cognitive revolution in social psychology which took off in the 1970s meant that Tajfel's work was formative in signaling the cognitive/perceptual emphasis in research on social categorization and stereotyping just as his own theorizing was developing along more sociomotivational and integrative lines. The idea that we perceive social categories just as we might other categories of objects brought social categorization and social stereotyping into the mainstream of cognitive analysis. The assumption that people are optimal information processors swiftly gave way to the "cognitive miser" model of SOCIAL COGNITION according to which perceivers use simplifying strategies or HEURISTICS to render the contents of cognition and the process of judgment manageable. Like the earlier work then, this approach emphasized the role of social categorization in simplifying the complex stimulus input coming from the social world, although this focus on simplification tended to dominate other aspects of the process. The role of categorization as a functional way of organizing the world and ascribing meaning in relation to the evaluative dimension, motivation, and goals became less central. Viewed within the heuristics tradition it was possible to conceive of social categorization and its effects more explicitly as a cognitive or perceptual BIAS.

In line with the heuristics approach much of this research tended to see the use of social categories as relatively automatic or "top of the head" compared with the processing of individuating or individual level information. Some models regarded SALIENCE of certain categories (e.g., "race", GENDER) as virtually perceptually prepotent. Indeed, definitions of salience in terms of (contextual) stimulus properties of such categories provides a good example of the ecological approach to categorization coexisting with and even reinforcing more top-down constructivist approaches to the process within social cognition research. Thus social categories are both pregiven in the environment, but also cognitive constructs which tend to bias the processing of information contained within them. The idea that social categorization and its associated stereotyping effects result from "everyday" but biased information processing gave an impetus for much experimental research into the underlying cognitive processes and mechanisms involved. Research focused not just on perceptual judgment effects, but on the role of MEMORY (the encoding, storage, and retrieval of information) as enhancing or explaining categorization and stereotyping effects. The cognitive revolution in the field inspired many to investigate to what extent stereotyping and even ethnocentrism could be explained by cognitive information processing biases alone (see, e.g., ILLUSORY CORRELATION), or at least to see how far it was possible to push this level of explanation (see, e.g., Hamilton, 1981).

A paradigmatic case for the study of social categorization as an organizing and simplifying principle in social perception is provided by the "who said what" paradigm developed by Taylor et al. (1978). In this paradigm subjects are presented with a video or slides of people from two social categories (for example "race" or gender), engaged in a group discussion. Perceivers who are subsequently asked to remember who said what typically make more within- than between-category recall errors, indicating that people use the social categories as ways of organizing or simplifying perception and the storage of social information in memory. Attempts to suppress the use of such categories (e.g., by using cross-cutting categorizations) have had limited success, suggesting that categories such as "race" or gender may indeed be quite powerful. On the other hand, there has been surprisingly little evidence for the prediction that increasing information load increases the proportion of intra to intercategory errors, as is implied by the cognitive miser explanation of category use.

Another way in which the cognitive tradition has influenced the way social categories are conceived is through models of category structure or category–instance relations. An important example is Rosch's work on the categorization of physical objects, in which categories are defined in terms of a taxonomic hierarchy of inclusion, with exemplars defined in terms of their prototypicality for the particular category level (e.g., Rosch, 1978). This approach also suggests that there are "natural" categories which maximize the informativeness and thus the appropriateness of a particular level of categorization. Again, the direct translation from the physical (and cognitive) to the social domain has led some in the cognitive tradition to speculate whether social categories such as gender and "race" are themselves "natural" social categories, a view which concurs with the apparent power and perceptual prepotency of these categories. Such hierarchical inclusion models of categorization also implicitly supported the notion that categorization involves information loss and thus implies bias.

## THE SOCIAL IDENTITY TRADITION

The power of social categorization is not restricted to "natural" or real-life social categories, however. Research on "minimal" groups demonstrates that the pure fact of social categorization can have quite dramatic effects on perception and behavior, without their having any history or meaning beyond the laboratory (see MINIMAL GROUP PARADIGM). In this paradigm, groups are categorized according to a trivial or even arbitrary criterion (e.g., on the basis of a preference for a particular painter, or a coin toss). So categorized, subjects tend to allocate more points or rewards to other (anonymous) ingroup members and to maximize this difference even at the expense of absolute gains. This paradigm provided an important empirical demonstration that intergroup relations were not just mediated by objective conflicts of interests over scarce resources as implied in the earlier REALISTIC CONFLICT THEORY of Sherif and Campbell. Rather, another level of explanation was needed to explain such effects. This was provided by social identity theory, as developed by Tajfel and his co-workers (e.g., Tajfel & Turner, 1979). This approach makes a distinction between personal and social identity, suggesting that behavior can be ordered along a theoretical continuum from interpersonal relations to intergroup behavior. In intergroup contexts, the social identity corresponding to that group is likely to be made salient, producing behavior appropriate to identity and context. Social identity theory stresses the "value" attached to being a member of a group or category, asserting that people strive to attain a positive social identity through favorable social comparisons with other outgroups, as a means of enhancing esteem. In other words social psychological conflicts are not just reflections of the material base (although this aspect is not denied), but also reflect "social competition," a search for positive group distinctiveness on important dimensions of comparison. Although some have interpreted the minimal group studies as evidence for a basic or universal tendency for groups to be discriminatory or ethnocentric, social identity theory argues more broadly that groups seek positive *differentiation* from others (although discrimination is the only form of differentiation possible in the minimal group paradigm). Studies where other dimensions of comparison are possible, and with real-life groups, demonstrate that social differentiation is specified by the contents of group identity and can take more benign and even concessionary forms (Spears & Manstead, 1989).

The social identity tradition has inspired a long line of both empirical research and theoretical development. Despite the centrality of the cognitive process of social categoriza-tion in the theory, it is important to contrast this tradition with the more purely cognitive approach to categorization and stereotyping. First, the theory stresses the importance of motivational elements in social perception and attempts to integrate these with cognitive and perceptual processes. Second, the theory aims at a social level of analysis and explanation of cognition and behavior, in contrast to the individualism inherent in many cognitive information processing approaches. This critique of individualism is also maintained in SELF-CATEGORIZATION THEORY (e.g., Turner et al., 1987), a development of the social identity tradition that emphasizes the importance of social categorization in most classic domains of social psychology (the SELF, group formation, GROUP COHESIVENESS, SOCIAL INFLUENCE, social stereotyping, crowd behavior). In this approach the interpersonal–intergroup continuum is replaced by a hierarchy of levels of self-categorization (e.g., person, group member, human). As well as this nested hierarchical structure, another similarity with Rosch's work can be detected in how social categories become defined and made salient. This is explained by the principle of metacontrast, which also has its roots in the earlier work on accentuation effects in categorization as well as affinities with Bruner's concept of "fit." In other words, categorization is determined by the reality of the stimulus, as well as by the accessibility of cognitive categories. Perhaps more explicitly than social identity theory, self-categorization theory argues that categorization does not primarily result from a need to cut down on overwhelming stimulus input, but is a meaningful way of organizing reality in ways relevant, appropriate, and valid for stimuli and the operative level of self. In these terms social categories can be seen as units of meaning as much as means of unifying.

Self-categorization theory has been important in raising concerns about the "categorization as bias" emphasis in theory and research. The information processing emphasis of the cognitive tradition has tended to encourage a quantitative and stimulus-driven understanding of information, such that the quantity and detail of information rather than its meaning or relevance are regarded as critical.

Because information lower down the category hierarchy is more detailed, it is typically assumed that it is more accurate, and therefore more real, than information at higher levels of abstraction. Indeed, categories are themselves often viewed as merely cognitive "abstractions"; the category exemplar is the stimulus object so that the relation of category to exemplar is almost one of representation to reality. Again, the implication is that the more abstract or inclusive the category, the further removed it is from detail and from reality, so that categories in themselves are not real. The hierarchical or inclusion approach to categorization further encourages a conceptual "container" metaphor, in which categories are treated as (in principle) independent of their content, as things that are filled rather than things in themselves or entities which define what they contain. Such cognitivism has arguably helped to sustain the individualistic metatheory which implies that the individual is the appropriate level of analysis for both perceiver and perceived. The emphasis here is on individual differences rather than category similarities, whereas these are arguably interdependent and a matter of focus (Turner et al., 1987). By no means least significant in the emphasis on bias is the relation of social categorization to its negative correlates (negative stereotyping, ethnocentrism, and prejudice). The understandably critical evaluation of such phenomena has reinforced the tendency to define the cognitive processes themselves as faulty or as producing the bias, rather than looking elsewhere.

More realist approaches to categorization such as self-categorization theory reject the ontological priority of individual over group. In these terms social categories are no less real than individuals as the objects of perception or as causal agents. The fact that individuals can function as category members is the theoretical means of challenging the primacy of the individual and the dualism of individual and social category, whilst also explaining the difference between individual and group behavior. If group identity is salient in an intergroup situation, it may be appropriate to focus perception on common group similarities rather than individual differences.

Moreover, this is not just a matter of perspective or of being tuned in to relevant AFFORDANCES. Moving to the social level of identity also implies a transformation of identity or nature. Although a chair will always remain a piece of furniture in the Roschian scheme (and perhaps most appropriately so), the variable nature of the self, and thus one's perspective on the social world, as well as the actual nature of that world, make the attempt to define "natural" social categories problematic in anything but a static descriptive sense. If the self is not fixed, but a function of social context, there is no absolute or a priori way of defining which level or basis of social categorization is most appropriate. Thus it is possible to argue for a more realist position which is also "relativist", in the specific sense that reality is relative to self, where the self is itself a product of social circumstances. In these terms, the reality of social categories is not pregiven but is continually being reproduced or transformed by those that use, occupy, or resist them (Bhaskar, 1989). It is arguably the possibility for social activity in defining the nature of the social world that rescues this line of theorizing from the dangers of a passive and uncritical "mechanical realism" in which the nature and content of categories, and thus potentially ethnocentrism and prejudice, become justified by their very existence. Alternative categories and identities to those which promulgate prejudice or racism can not only be conceived, they can become real through use. Negative stereotypes and prejudice may be meaningful and real in their own terms of reference but the appropriate response may be to tackle these forms of self-definition, and the conditions that sustain them (economic, systemic, historical, etc.) rather than psychologizing their products as the result of generic information processing biases.

According to this line of analysis social categorization is not simply a matter of emphasizing the important perceptual and cognitive processes involved, but also of theorizing the relation of these to identity, communication, and social interaction. Although recent research has been very successful in specifying the mechanisms and products of the categorization process, this emphasis has sometimes deflected attention from how these categories come about, and are used – how social categories are naturalized, as opposed to being natural. Part of the answer to the dilemma between idealism and mechanical materialism posed earlier may therefore be an interactionism, which includes the social activity in-between, so to speak, and which thus makes social categories meaningful and real. In these terms social categorization is not just mental activity, and not just a reflection of material reality; it is also a product of social activity and social relations.

*See also*: CATEGORIZATION; DISCOURSE ANALYSIS; GENDER; GROUP COHESIVENESS; HEURISTICS; MEMORY; PREJUDICE, SCHEMA/SCHEMATA; SELF; SELF-CATEGORIZATION THEORY; SOCIAL COGNITION; SOCIAL CONSTRUCTIONISM; SOCIAL IDENTITY THEORY; SOCIAL INFLUENCE; STEREOTYPING.

BIBLIOGRAPHY

Bhaskar, R. (1989). *Reclaiming reality: A critical introduction to contemporary philosophy*. London: Verso.

Bruner, J. S. (1957). On perceptual readiness. *Psychological Review, 64*, 123–51.

Hamilton, D. L. (Ed.) (1981). *Cognitive processes in stereotyping and intergroup behavior*, Hillsdale, NJ: Lawrence Erlbaum.

Rosch, E. (1978). Principles of categorization. In E. Rosch & B. B. Lloyd (Eds.), *Cognition and categorization* (pp. 27–48). Hillsdale, NJ: Lawrence Erlbaum.

Spears, R., & Manstead, A. S. R. (1989). The social context of stereotyping and differentiation. *European Journal of Social Psychology, 19*, 101–21.

Tajfel, H. (1981). *Human groups and social categories*. Cambridge: Cambridge University Press.

—— & Turner, J. C. (1979). The social identity theory of intergroup behaviour. In W.G. Austin & S. Worchel (Eds.), *The social psychology of intergroup relations* (pp. 7–24). Chicago, IL: Nelson-Hall.

Taylor, S. E., Fiske, S. T., Etcoff, N. L., & Ruderman, A. J. (1978). Categorical and contextual bases of person memory and stereotyping. *Journal of Personality and Social psychology, 36*, 778–93.

Turner, J. C. Hogg, M. A., Oakes, P. J., Reicher, S. D., & Wetherell, M. (1987). *Rediscovering the social group: A self-categorization theory.* Oxford: Basil Blackwell.

RUSSELL SPEARS

**social cognition** The study of social knowledge (its content and structure) and cognitive processes (including acquisition, representation, and retrieval of information) provides a key to understanding social behavior and its mediating factors (*see* Fiske & Taylor, 1991; Wyer & Srull, 1994). Social cognition leans heavily on the theory and methodology of cognitive psychology to provide precise and detailed models of social information processing. In this pursuit, memorial processes (i.e., encoding, representation, and retrieval) are assumed to play a particularly prominent role in the mediation of a range of social judgments.

While SOCIAL PSYCHOLOGY has experienced something of a cognitive revolution in recent years (*see* Fiske and Taylor, 1991), this approach has a long and noble history. Indeed, it owes much to the input of Gestalt ideas into American social psychology by Europeans such as Kurt Lewin and Fritz Heider. The vast majority of social–psychological data are about thoughts – as judgments, opinions, recollections, attitudes, or attributions. Furthermore, cognition pervades social psychology at three levels – the level at which the problem is formulated, the level of methodology, and the level of theorizing (*see* Markus & Zajonc, 1985). By nature, social cognition is more complex and multifaceted than cognition in general. First, perceivers typically go beyond the information given in any social encounter. Second, the objects of social cognition (e.g., beliefs, judgments, desires) are malleable and can be changed by being the focus of information processing. Third, nearly all social cognition is evaluative in implication (i.e., there is an affective involvement between perceivers and persons perceived).

Three fundamental questions (all based around MEMORY) drive much of contemporary research and theorizing in social cognition: first, what type of information is stored and how is it organized in memory?; second, how does information stored in memory affect subsequent information processing, decision making, and behavior?; and, third, how and when is stored information changed, both by new information and by cognitive processes (Sherman, Judd, & Park, 1989)?

For much of the 1980s, the prominent metatheory in this domain characterized the social perceiver as a *cognitive miser*. This approach asserted that perceivers are capacity-limited processors who can deal with only a restricted range of information at any time. Given these limitations, people were seen as using economical strategies (i.e., HEURISTICS) to simplify complex problems of judgment, decision, and attribution. These heuristics typically produce fast and quite adequate, rather than slow, normatively correct, solutions – as illustrated by the three heuristics governing intuitive prediction and judgment. According to the REPRE-SENTATIVENESS heuristic, an object is assigned to a conceptual category by virtue of the extent to which its main features represent or resemble one category more than another. The ADJUSTMENT AND ANCHORING heuristic refers to people's general failure to adjust their initial judgments in the light of subsequent evidence. The AVAILABILITY heuristic refers to the general tendency to judge events as frequent, probable, or causally efficacious to the extent that they are readily available in memory. These heuristics provide a general understanding of human judgment, although it remains difficult to evaluate them in a truly competitive and rigorous manner.

As social perceivers, we are rarely afforded the luxury of interacting with others in isolation from our current concerns and preconceptions. Instead, we possess an assortment of mental constructs (e.g., prejudices, stereotypes, goals, desires) which, ultimately, direct information processing and behavior (*see* Fiske & Taylor, 1991). Reflecting this state of affairs, research and theorizing in social cognition is currently experiencing something of a metamorphosis (Fiske, 1992, 1993). Following an era in which motivational and affective influences on social cognition were, at best, largely neglected (at worst, ignored), researchers are once again acknow-

ledging the pivotal role occupied by goals and motives in mental life. Thus, while in the service of cognitive expedience we may at times appear to operate as cognitive misers, at other times, if so motivated, we do possess the capacity to be considerably more diligent and systematic in our information processing (*see* MOTIVATION).

Recognizing the role motivational and affective factors play in mental life, a more recent metatheoretical perspective, that of the *motivated tactician*, has emerged (Fiske & Taylor, 1991). This approach characterizes the social perceiver as a fully engaged thinker who chooses between alternative information processing strategies on the basis of currently active goals, motives, and needs. This view develops and extends the earlier cognitive miser approach because it implies that the social perceiver processes information in a more or less careful manner, depending upon the particular information-processing goal which is operative. This perspective, accordingly, lays emphasis upon social perceivers' pragmatic concerns and how goal-directed cognitive processes help disambiguate a complex stimulus world (*see* Fiske, 1992, 1993).

## SOCIAL CATEGORIZATION

Social categorization is a central tool perceivers deploy to help make sense of a dauntingly complex social world (*see* CATEGORIZATION, SELF-CATEGORIZATION THEORY, SOCIAL CATEGORIZATION). Essentially, the process of social categorization involves matching a target person to an existing social category and it is instigated when information sufficient to activate a relevant category has been encountered. The information necessary to cue an appropriate category can take several forms. It may, for instance, take the form of an observable feature such as race, gender, or age. Alternatively, and more commonly in social psychological research, it may comprise a written category label or cluster of category-cuing attributes. Rather than try to process all the stimulus information available, social perceivers simplify matters by assigning individuals to social categories on the basis of their shared or common characteristics.

To the extent that social categories capture and reflect real differences and similarities between people, social categorization can be considered a useful cognitive tool. A number of studies have demonstrated, however, pernicious judgmental biases which derive from the process of social categorization itself. For example, once a person has been classified into a particular social group, it may be assumed that he or she possesses all the attributes that characterize the group as a whole. That is, the person is deemed to possess a range of category-relevant attributes, despite the fact that none of these attributes may have served as the basis of the initial categorization. Moreover, once we have classified two people into different categories, we tend to ignore their similarities and exaggerate their differences. Correspondingly, once individuals have been assigned to the same category, we exaggerate their similarities and ignore their differences. These effects are accentuated if the social perceiver belongs to one of the groups in question (i.e., ingroup or outgroup; *see* INTERGROUP RELATIONS). In general, the perceiver demonstrates greater differentiation between ingroup members, with representations of ingroup members generally more complex than those of outgroup members. Consequently, ingroups and outgroups reflect an asymmetrical relationship, with perceived ingroup heterogeneity contrasted with OUTGROUP HOMOGENEITY.

## SCHEMAS

The process of social categorization is central to both research and theorizing in social cognition. This is because once a social category has been activated, it plays a prominent part in subsequent information processing. The activated or primed category affects the encoding, representation, and retrieval of social information. A central tenet of social cognition is that people assimilate what they observe to preexisting cognitive structures or SCHEMAS. These abstract knowledge structures, represented in long-term memory, specify both the attributes associated with a particular stimulus domain and the interrelations among those attributes. Five main types

of schema have been identified (person, self, role, event, and procedural), each of which can influence three main types of information processing: perception and encoding of new information; memory for old information; and inferences that extend beyond the information available in a stimulus array (*see* Fiske & Taylor, 1991).

The impact of schemas on social information processing can be interpreted in terms of both functions and liabilities. These preexisting knowledge structures tend to aid memory for schema-consistent information, increase confidence in schema-consistent recognition, enhance memory for schema-consistent information that, in fact, was never presented, and guide inferences and predictions. Further, it appears that under certain conditions perceivers will tend to remember different types of information. For example, when forming impressions of others, perceivers tend to show preferential recall of schema-inconsistent information. This is consistent with a range of studies that suggest that the presentation of relatively infrequent, novel, or salient behaviors will result in increased ATTENTION during impression formation which, as a consequence, increases the accessibility of this information in memory. Schema-inconsistent information also experiences a memorial advantage when activated expectancies are relatively weak and perceivers are motivated to understand the presented information. In contrast, consistent information is more readily recalled when manipulated expectancies are strong and when information-processing unfolds in suboptimal (i.e., resource-depleting) task environments (Fiske, 1993).

## ILLUSTRATIONS OF THE 'SOCIAL COGNITION' APPROACH

Driven to a large extent by the schema concept, the social cognition perspective has been usefully applied to an impressive range of substantive domains of social psychology, of which two – stereotyping and attitudes – are perhaps most obvious and impressive.

### Stereotyping

Stereotypes, as social categories, may be formed and represented in memory much like any other object category. Thus, they may be organized around a prototypical representation, with exemplar or specific instance information also represented in long-term memory. Social cognition research is currently evaluating prototypic and exemplar-based models of category representation (*see* Sherman et al., 1989). As cognitive schemas, stereotypes have been shown to influence all stages of information processing. This approach has been particularly fruitful in clarifying how social stereotypes are formed, how they are maintained, and how, ultimately, they might be changed (*see* STEREOTYPING; and Hamilton & Sherman, 1994).

A range of cognitive mechanisms are implicated in the formation of stereotype-based expectancies. These include SALIENCE (differential attention to salient stimuli) and ILLUSORY CORRELATION (the inference of a relationship between two variables when, in reality, none actually exists). At the stereotype-maintenance stage, researchers have demonstrated persistent biases in patterns of causal attribution and in memory retrieval which enable perceivers' erroneous stereotype-based beliefs to persevere in the face of potentially disconfirming information. In particular, perceivers tend to attribute stereotype-confirming behavior to internal, stable, causes, and stereotype-disconfirming behavior to external, unstable causes. This attributional tendency enables perceivers to explain away stereotype-discrepant behavior. Similarly, the preferential recall of stereotype-confirming behavior, together with the tendency to select only confirmatory information when testing stereotypical beliefs, further perpetuates social stereotypes.

Finally, schematic models have investigated how stereotypes might change in response to the amount and distribution of any disconfirming information which is presented in relation to the stereotyped group. This work reveals that it is better to disperse disconfirming information across several outgroup members than to concentrate it in only a few, highly atypical members. Interest here centers on when subcategories may be formed as a result of encountering new group members who are divergent from a category proto-

type or central tendency. A social cognition approach to intergroup contact therefore emphasizes that successful contact (i.e., positive contact that generalizes to other outgroup members) depends upon the typicality of the outgroup member with whom contact occurs (*see* CONTACT HYPOTHESIS).

*Attitudes*

Attitudes also appear to function like schemas, as illustrated by selective attention to, and encoding, retention, and retrieval of, attitude-relevant information. For example, attitudes facilitate recall of attitude statements that are strongly agreed or disagreed with, compared with statements that elicit more moderate responses on the agreement scale. Accordingly, the social cognition approach has led to a major shift in the way attitudes are conceptualized, defined, and assessed. In many situations, evaluations seem to be formed spontaneously and stored in long-term memory for future retrieval and use. Other information stored with the evaluation may include information about the attributes of an attitude object, affective responses elicited by the object, past behavior toward the object, and the evaluations of significant others. This conception of attitudes yields a new, mediational (rather than methodological) approach to ATTITUDES AND BEHAVIOR. According to Fazio's (1990) work on attitude ACCESSIBILITY, the strength of the association between an object and an evaluation determines the degree to which the attitude is activated upon exposure to an object (attitude strength may be measured by response time to evaluative questions about the attitude object). From this view, we need to study *how* the relative activation of an attitude, or of particular elements of it (cognitions, feelings), at the time attitudes are expressed or behaviors performed, affects attitude–behavior relationships. If an object does not activate an associated attitude, then the attitude will be unlikely to influence behavior towards the object.

The social cognition approach has contributed enormously to the study of ATTITUDE CHANGE, via process theories of persuasion (*see* Eagly & Chaiken, 1993). According to the ELABORATION LIKELIHOOD

MODEL, persuasion is determined by the extent and direction of cognitive responses to persuasive messages. Persuasion via a "central" route requires active processing of the message, which itself requires cognitive capacity and effort. Persuasion via a "peripheral" route involves minimal cognitive elaboration of the message, and is influenced by a multitude of nonmessage factors (e.g., source credibility). The HEURISTIC-SYSTEMATIC MODEL offers a rather different process model of attitude change. According to this view, attitude change is determined by two *parallel* modes of information processing, whose differences are qualitative and not merely quantitative (Eagly & Chaiken, 1993). "Heuristic" processing refers to the mediation of persuasion by simple decision rules, whereas "systematic" processing refers to a comprehensive, analytic mode of information processing involving detailed scrutiny of available information. While debate continues about the relative merits of these two models, they agree that cognitive processes play a central role in attitude change.

## METHODOLOGY

As social psychologists have explored the metaphor of information processing, so they have used a wider array of cognitive measures: visual attention, self-reports, requests for information, recall (quantity, errors, sequence, clustering), recognition, resource allocation, and chronometric analyses (inspection time, decision time). These measures all attempt to sidestep a major methodological problem – the fact that we can never tap directly what is going on inside the heads of our research subjects.

More ambitious still are attempts to use these different measures to build process models of mental life. A process model is, simply, the description of everything that goes on inside the subjects' head from start to finish of an experimental task. It is a statement of the presumed stages through which information is processed, such as encoding, storage, retrieval, and judgement. The aim of process analysis is to provide methodological precision, to specify the stages in social information processing, and to identify the stages

in social cognition at which specific effects occur (*see* PROCESS TRACING). Process models have been used to explore a number of topics in social cognition, including dispositional inference, IMPRESSION FORMATION, and control of MENTAL PROCESSES. One valuable aspect of these models is that they enable researchers to deconstruct mental life and identify the contribution that automatic and controlled cognitive processes make to our everyday inferential functioning (*see* AUTOMATICITY). Theories about process are potentially more general than theories about content because the same procedure may operate over a wide range of stimuli. By definition, however, any attempt to measure cognitive processes necessarily interferes with normal thinking, hence it is conceivable that process analysis may not be informative about social information processing occurring outside the rarefied atmosphere of the laboratory.

## CONCLUSIONS

Social cognition represents an approach or set of assumptions guiding research in social psychology, rather than a separate theory or domain of enquiry within the discipline. Among the most important assumptions (*see* Schneider, 1991), are that:

(1) *process* is general (i.e., detached from the content of social domains);
(2) processing of information follows a defined *sequence of information-processing stages* (with memory and response times seen as critical measures of underlying process);
(3) *knowledge structures* have a decisive impact on encoding and storage (typically transforming social knowledge via top-down processing); and
(4) our information-processing is prone to BIAS (we condense information, apply heuristics, lose details, and are inclined to preserve, rather than change, existing knowledge structures).

This approach has had an enormous impact on a wide variety of traditional substantive domains of social psychology; we have mentioned explicitly stereotyping and attitudes (other areas include ATTRIBUTION THEORIES, intergroup relations, the SELF, SURVEY

METHODS, and SOCIAL INFLUENCE). Despite, or perhaps because of, this impact, the contribution of the social cognition perspective is not without its critics. At its best, it is driven by the desire to understand the processes underlying important social phenomena (e.g., PREJUDICE), including their affective and motivational components. At its worst, critics view it as ignoring motivation and affect, obsessed with testing overly precise models of epiphenomena, and divorced from the richness of the everyday social world. We believe the former view gives a more accurate picture of the continuing legacy of this perspective to the field of social psychology as a whole.

*See also*: ATTENTION; ATTITUDE CHANGE; ATTITUDES AND BEHAVIOR; ATTRIBUTION THEORIES; AUTOMATICITY; CATEGORIZATION; CONTACT HYPOTHESIS; HEURISTICS; IMPRESSION FORMATION; INTERGROUP RELATIONS; MEMORY; MOTIVATION; OUTGROUP HOMOGENEITY; PREJUDICE; SCHEMAS/SCHEMATA; SELF; SELF-CAGEGORIZATION THEORY; SOCIAL CATEGORIZATION; SOCIAL INFLUENCE; SOCIAL PSYCHOLOGY; STEREOTYPING; SURVEY METHODS.

BIBLIOGRAPHY

Eagly, A. H., & Chaiken, S. (1993). *The psychology of attitudes*. Fort Worth, TX: Harcourt Brace Jovanovich.

Fazio, R. H. (1990). Multiple processes by which attitudes guide behaviour. The MODE model as an integrative framework. In M. P. Zanna (Ed.), *Advances in experimental social psychology* (Vol. 23, pp. 75–110). San Diego, CA: Academic Press.

Fiske, S. T. (1992). Thinking is for doing: Portraits of social cognition from daguerrotype to laserphoto. *Journal of Personality and Social Psychology*, 63, 877–89.

—— (1993). Social cognition and social perception. *Annual Review of Psychology*, 44, 155–94.

—— & Taylor, S. E. (1991). *Social cognition* (2nd ed.). New York: McGraw-Hill.

Hamilton, D., & Sherman, J. W. (1994). Stereotypes. In R. S. Wyer & T. K. Srull (Eds.), *Handbook of social cognition* (2nd ed., Vol. 2, pp. 1–68). Hillsdale, NJ: Lawrence Erlbaum.

Markus, H., & Zajonc, R. B. (1985). The cognitive perspective in social psychology. In G. Lindzey & E. Aronson (Eds.), *The handbook of social psychology* (3rd ed., Vol. 1, pp. 137–230). New York: Random House.

Schneider, D. J. (1991). Social cognition. *Annual Review of Psychology*, 42, 527–61.

Sherman, S .J., Judd, C. M., & Park, B. (1989). Social cognition. *Annual Review of Psychology*, 40, 281–326.

Wyer, R. S., & Srull, T. K. (Eds.) (1994). *Handbook of social cognition* (2 Vols., 2nd ed.). Hillsdale, NJ: Lawrence Erlbaum.

NEIL MACRAE<br>MILES HEWSTONE

**social comparison** Speaking generically, when social psychologists refer to social comparison, they are referring to comparisons with other people and the effects of those comparisons on cognitions, affect, and behavior. Though not always recognized, social comparison research and theory actually represent two parallel bodies of thought and empirical investigation. The first line, which began in the 1950s, refers to the process by which people strive to obtain correct or accurate assessments of their abilities and opinions; we refer to this as self-evaluation. The second line of work, which did not emerge systematically until the 1980s, focuses on the way people use comparison information to maintain or enhance their evaluations of self. According to this second perspective, people strive to feel good about themselves rather than for accuracy. We refer to this later use or form of social comparison as SELF-ENHANCEMENT.

SELF-EVALUATION

Although early social psychologists, such as Asch and Newcomb, considered social comparison important, Leon Festinger (1954) formally introduced the concept in a paper that has since come to be considered a classic, despite containing several ambiguous elements. The central tenet of Festinger's model was that individuals are motivated to obtain accurate assessments of their opinions and abilities. Festinger noted, however, that in some cases (perhaps the majority), there are no objective standards by which to evaluate how well one is doing, whether one's opinions or beliefs are correct, or predict what one can do in the future. If one wishes to know whether it is freezing outside, one could perform a simple reality test by placing a container of water outside and observing it to see if ice forms. It is less straightforward, however, to predict with confidence if one can scale a mountain, obtain a college degree, or if one's opinions regarding the presidential race are appropriate. Festinger observed that, when objective standards of measurement are unavailable, one's abilities or opinions can be evaluated by comparing oneself to other individuals.

The goal of social comparison, according to Festinger, was to define one's ability/opinion standing in objective terms. The critical question in self-evaluative social comparison is "How good am I?" Festinger predicted that comparison with a similar other would yield maximal information and be most effective in addressing self-evaluative concerns; consequently, the comparer should experience the greatest feeling of subjective confidence in his self-evaluation after comparison with a similar other. Festinger additionally suggested that, in the case of abilities, there was a unidirectional drive upward, i.e., striving to improve or excel. Because the need for accuracy, served by comparison with a similar other, is at odds with the pressure to excel, Festinger predicted that this would lead to comparisons with others who are similar, but slightly more skilled than oneself.

The similarity hypothesis generated considerable empirical investigation. Studies undertaken primarily at the University of Minnesota in the 1960s used a rank-order procedure to provide early explorations into the choice of similar versus dissimilar comparison others. In rank-order studies the subject was provided with a bogus numerical achievement score for some domain under evaluation, the maximum score in the distribution, and finally with a rank-ordered list of other participants. The subject was then asked to indicate, by rank, the one individual whose score they would like to view. Selection of a rank adjacent to one's own was interpreted as support for Festinger's similarity hypothesis. Wheeler (in Latané, 1966), utilized such a rank-order design, providing subjects with test scores supposedly to be used for selection for a special psychology seminar. Wheeler found support for both the similarity hypothesis and the unidirectional drive upward; his subjects consistently preferred to compare with individuals from the rank immediately above and closest to their own. The tendency to select a rank above one's own was interpreted as the subject's attempts to establish similarity with a somewhat superior other. Along related lines, Radloff (in Latané, 1966) found that when subjects were deprived of a similar comparison other (i.e., they were told that they were either markedly inferior or superior to their peers), their ratings of personal performance on a pursuit rotor task tended to be inaccurate and unstable over time.

Stanley Schachter (1959) generated further support for social comparison processes and the similarity hypothesis. In what came to be known as the fear-affiliation effect, Schachter found that subjects threatened with electric shock preferred to wait with other similarly frightened participants. Schachter suggested two possible explanations for this phenomenon: first, that the physical presence of others reduced anxiety and second, that subjects wished to evaluate the appropriateness of their alarmed emotional reactions by comparing themselves to other individuals. Comparison with similar others thus seemed to apply not only to abilities and opinions, but also to emotional states.

Other evidence, however, followed which indicated that subjects sometimes selected dissimilar comparison others. The original rank-order paradigm studies provided subjects with information regarding the highest score in the distribution. Wheeler and associates (Wheeler et al., 1969) found, however, that when subjects were not informed of the high and low scores, they first sought to define the field by requesting these scores. Once the range of scores was clear, subjects then resumed selection of similar comparison others. In this instance, dissimilar comparison others apparently offered important information that could not be deduced from a similar other comparison (*see* Mettee & Smith in Suls & Miller, 1977).

This evidence, apparently inconsistent with the original interpretation of the 1954 theory, led social psychologists to look more closely at the theory, and to observe that several aspects of similarity, one of the building blocks of the theory, were ambiguous. How can one know that a comparison other is in fact similar (and hence an appropriate comparison candidate) unless some sort of comparative process has already occurred? It was also unclear from Festinger's original statements whether similarity should be operationalized in terms of performance similarity, or if similarity on related elements was relevant. That is, in evaluating my running ability, would I learn the most from a comparison other who ran as far and as fast as me (performance similarity), or would I gain the most information from a comparison with someone sharing characteristics presumably related to running performance, like gender, age, and physical size (similarity on related attributes)?

Goethals and Darley's (in Suls & Miller, 1977) reformulation of social comparison theory using an attributional perspective, was thought to resolve these questions (*see* ATTRIBUTION THEORIES). Previous researchers had operationalized similarity in terms of performance outcome measures; Goethals and Darley shifted the focus to similarity on related attributes. Related attributes influence performance, but are distinct from performance itself. Ability level can be inferred from one's standing on related attributes. For example, height, speed, and amount of time spent practising are related attributes pertinent to basketball performance. If a comparison other outperforms me, I might be inclined to discount the implications of that comparison for my ability level if I realize that that individual is eight inches taller than me or practiced twice as much. Studies inspired by this analysis showed that subjects preferred to compare with individuals similar on related attributes and also were more confident of their judgments when they received information that comparison others shared similar related attribute characteristics (*see*, review by, Wood, 1989).

In the case of opinions, Goethals and Darley (in Suls & Miller, 1977) contended that the distinction between belief and values was of importance. Beliefs represent information that is potentially verifiable, while values represent subjective states of like or dislike. For beliefs, learning that someone with a different perspective (i.e., someone dissimilar on related attributes) agrees with us should increase our confidence in that belief. In this instance, we would be inclined to discount the beliefs of a similar comparison other because that person would share our personal biases. If, however, I am attempting to predict if I would like a particular movie or book (a value judgment), for example, I would place the most weight on information coming from someone similar to me on related attributes. In this instance, the shared biases of a similar other operate as an asset rather than a liability. Although there is some evidence supportive of the attributional analysis of opinion comparison (*see* Goethals & Darley in Suls & Miller, 1977), it has not been as thoroughly researched as the ability reinterpretation.

The similarity hypothesis remains controversial for researchers. Individuals sometimes prefer dissimilar comparison others. In addition, people sometimes compare on related attributes that are irrelevant to performance (*see* review by Wood, 1989). Finally, social comparisons are frequently forced upon the individual by others in her environment, so the supposed selectivity (whether for comparison others similar on related attributes or on performance) may be difficult to muster (Wood, 1989). These considerations prompted some scholars to propose that neither similarity of performance or similarity on related attributes is central to the ability evaluation process (Kruglanski & Mayseless, 1990). Critics have, in fact, argued that there is nothing inherently more informative about comparison with similar others.

We propose that this criticism represents a misunderstanding of the actual meaning of ability evaluation as Festinger originally conceived it. When social comparison processes are used to predict future performance (i.e., "What *can* I do?"), then comparison to a similar other provides maximal information.

If I perform at the same level as another person, and if the comparison other performed at his or her maximum level, then I can confidently predict that I, too, can match their subsequent performance. Under circumstances where it is impossible to determine whether or not the comparison other's performance was maximal, then their similarity to me on related attributes would allow me to make confident predictions about my future performance potential. This latest perspective on the similarity hypothesis is promising, but has not yet received extensive empirical investigation (Wheeler, Suls, & Martin, 1993).

SELF-ENHANCEMENT

Though strivings for predictability and ability to choose appropriate goals etc. require accurate self-assessments, there are times when self-enhancement may be a more important consideration than self-evaluation. For example, a student receiving a "C" on an important exam might find it more important to bolster her spirits by comparing her score to that of a class member who failed the exam than to focus on details of accurate status. The goal of social comparison in this scenario is to maintain or improve self-esteem or well being. The critical question addressed in self-enhancement social comparisons is not "How good am I?", but "How can I feel good about what I am or what I have attained?"

Hakmiller (*see* Latané, 1966) first provided evidence since interpreted as supportive of self-enhancement in an experiment where subjects were provided with bogus personal feedback regarding hostility toward one's parents. This trait was presented as highly negative for some participants; these threatened subjects subsequently demonstrated a strong preference for downward social comparisons. That is, they chose to compare themselves with someone who had an even more extreme score on the dimension of hostility toward parents. Hakmiller suggested that such downward comparisons reduce the affective discomfort associated with learning negative information about oneself (*see* Wills, 1981).

Goethals and Darley (in Suls & Miller, 1977) indicated that social comparison could be motivated by either objective, evaluative concerns or by the need for self-enhancement (which they referred to as "self-validation"). Self-validation was oriented toward the protection of self-esteem, and reassured the comparer that his opinions or abilities were appropriate or good (rather than defining one's status in the opinion/ability domain). Concurrent needs for evaluation and enhancement necessitate different, and sometimes conflicting, comparison strategies. For example, comparison with a similar other would provide the most appropriate information for objective self-evaluation, while a relatively disadvantaged dissimilar other would facilitate social comparisons that enhance self-esteem.

Brickman and Bulman (*see* Suls & Miller, 1977) elaborated on the themes of self-esteem and the comparer's active contribution to social comparison, observing that the affective consequences of social comparison might lead the individual to selectively restrict comparison targets or even to avoid comparison altogether. If, for example, one's older sibling is a particularly talented athlete, one might invest one's effort instead in cultivating excellence in music or academics – a comparison strategy that protects both individuals' self-esteem.

Wills' (1981) theory of downward social comparison integrated a diffuse body of empirical findings and brought self-enhancement to the forefront of social comparison research. Will's central premise was that under threat or compromised self-esteem individuals seek downward social comparisons with less fortunate others to improve subjective well-being. Downward comparisons could involve either active or passive processes. In passive downward comparison, the individual simply capitalizes on comparison opportunities with disadvantaged targets spontaneously encountered in daily life. Active downward comparison, by contrast, involves the intentional derogation or harm of another person, essentially creating a less fortunate other for comparison purposes.

Downward comparison has enjoyed considerable popularity among researchers in recent years. Some empirical evidence supports Wills' model; for example, people under threat such as breast cancer and infertility patients report predominantly downward social comparisons that appear to reassure them that they were coping effectively with their illness (Wood, 1989).

Recent refinements of social comparison processes under threat is provided by Buunk, Collins, Taylor, VanYperen, and Dakof (1990). This perspective emphasized the role of selectivity in social comparison and proposed that, under threatening circumstances, social comparison processes diverge, leading the comparer to seek both advantaged and disadvantaged comparison targets simultaneously. Downward comparison provides information that the individual is superior and consequently bolsters self-esteem. Comparison and contact with more fortunate others provides role-models and inspirations for future coping. Wood (1989) similarly noted that social comparisons motivated by the desire for self-improvement provided comparer with inspiration and learning opportunities. Buunk and his associates found that individuals can use either upward or downward comparison to manipulate affect, the direction of comparison being less important than the interpretation and meaning placed on the comparison by the individual. For example, a cancer patient comparing downward to someone even more ill than themselves could either feel reassured that they are doing well, or troubled that their own health status could decline further. The effective use of self-enhancing social comparisons may be moderated by personality factors such as self-esteem. High self-esteem individuals seem able to make positive use of social comparisons regardless of whom they compare themselves to, while low self-esteem individuals are less adept at manipulating comparison information. This unfortunately suggests that the individuals most in need of enhancing social comparisons are least likely to utilize social comparison to their advantage.

The dynamics of social comparison via self-enhancement have not been fully delineated. Most of the supportive data for the various positions (Wills' downward prediction and Buunk et al.'s multidirectional prediction) comes from correlational studies. Experimental research in the next few years should bring closure on these issues.

*See also*: ATTRIBUTION THEORIES.

REFERENCES

Buunk, B. P., Collins, R. L., Taylor, S. E., VanYperen, N. W., & Dakof, G. A. (1990). The affective consequences of social comparison: Either direction has its ups and downs. *Journal of Personality and Social Psychology, 59*, 1238–49.

Festinger, L. (1954). A theory of social comparison processes. *Human Relations, 7*, 117–40.

Kruglanski, A. W., & Mayseless, O. (1990). Classic and current social comparison research: Expanding the perspective. *Psychological Bulletin, 108*, 195–208.

Latané, B. (1966). Studies in social comparison. *Journal of Experimental Social Psychology* [Suppl.].

Schachter, S. (1959). *The psychology of affiliation*. Stanford, CA: Stanford University Press.

Suls, J., & Miller, R. L. (Eds.) (1977). *Social comparison processes: Theoretical and empirical perspectives*. Washington, DC: Hemisphere.

Wheeler, L., Shaver, K. G., Jones, R. A., Goethals, G. R., Cooper, J., Robinson, J. E., Gruder, C.L., & Butzine, K.W. (1969). Factors determining the choice of a comparison other. *Journal of Experimental Psychology, 5*, 219–32.

—— Suls, J., & Martin, R. (1993). *On the accurate self-assessment of ability through social comparison*. Unpublished manuscript. Rochester, NY: University of Rochester.

Wills, T. A. (1981). Downward comparison principles in social psychology. *Psychological Bulletin, 90*, 245–71.

Wood, J. V. (1989). Theory and research concerning social comparisons of personal attributes. *Psychological Bulletin, 106*, 231–48.

JERRY SULS
RENÉ MARTIN

**social constructionism** A research orientation which regards the social world in general and specific aspects of it, such as psychological phenomena, as the products of socially and historically situated practices (*see* Gergen, 1985; Harré & Secord, 1972). It does not constitute a unitary doctrine or general theory about, for instance, emotions, persons, or other aspects of social reality. Social constructionism as a movement has emerged as a result of a combination of developments in the philosophy of science, in ordinary language analysis, in cognitive sociology, and aspects of SYMBOLIC INTERACTIONISM and Goffman's dramaturgical approach.

The chief criticism arising from this orientation is directed at the traditional view of scientific theory upon which mainstream social psychology is based. This critique questions the positivist–empiricist conception of science and its reliance on observational language (facts and data) as objective indicators of truth. The traditional view of science rests on the assumption that data as such are *theory neutral* and therefore can be regarded as containing genuine references to the properties of the "real world." This assumption of *intersubjective* observational knowledge is criticized by social constructionists. In their view, there are no such things as pure observations. All observations require a prior viewpoint, irrespective of whether these stem from a theoretical perspective, or are due to learning or acculturation. Thus data are socially "manufactured," irrespective of which form these data take.

From this fundamental objection a number of more specific critiques have been derived and directed at mainstream social psychology. These follow from the type of empirical method adopted in mainstream social psychology. One of the most frequently articulated criticisms has been that of the mechanistic account of human beings that is implied by the application of this view of science. This, it is argued, disregards the active, creative, and intentional aspects of human beings, and therefore their agency and constructive potential. A second criticism which has been initiated by Gergen and which has caused considerable debate (e.g., Schlenker, 1974; Semin & Manstead, 1983) is leveled at the assumption that the scientific enterprise is in itself a historical. The social constructionist argument is that social psychology, as a discipline, is in need of a view that recognizes the historical embeddedness of social phenomena and, by implication, of its theories. Third,

the so-called objectivity of the "scientist," disengaged from the cultural and historical circumstances, although now regarded as a myth, has come under renewed attack. The demand here is for a conceptualization of social psychology which clearly positions the scientist in the active role that s/he plays in the research process and which locates the scientist in the relevant sociohistorical context. Other criticisms that have been leveled at mainstream social psychology from this perspective concern the adherence to Humean causality in explanations; the reliance on the experiment for the arbitration between theories; and the artificiality of the experimental laboratory situation (Harré & Secord, 1972).

Although the social constructionist movement in social psychology originated in systematic critique, it has begun to develop specific research strands. However, since social constructionism is in the main a general orientation one would not expect it to yield a systematic body of theory or methodology. Indeed, it explicitly eschews this possibility (Gergen, 1985) and embraces methodological pluralism. As a consequence, a number of diverse developments in social psychology such as DISCOURSE ANALYSIS, RHETORIC, and ETHOGENICS can be regarded as rooted in social constructionism. In addition, other approaches, which are not explicitly rooted in social constructionism, such as SOCIAL REPRESENTATIONS, can be seen to share some common properties with it. These approaches have attempted to identify broader frameworks by which psychological realities can be understood by examining specific types of social practices, such as conversation, the devices used in persuasive conversations, or simply by analyzing the strategic use of rules in social interaction. Common to these research developments is their acknowledgement that language and its strategic use is fundamental to the understanding of how social reality is created, maintained, transformed, and transmitted. However, the way in which they approach and examine language varies radically.

In contrast to these broader approaches there are also social constructionist approaches which focus on specific psychological domains with a view to understanding the social practices by which they are constituted, such as Averill's (1982) analyses of emotions. Such research attempts to understand an emotion (e.g., anger) as a socially constructed role rather than resorting to different analytic levels such as the psychophysiological.

The problems that social constructionism faces are at least two fold. On the one hand, the assumption that all knowledge is socially constructed, and historically and culturally bounded, leads to an internal logical paradox within social constructionism, namely, social constructionism is also bounded and therefore a temporary appearance in the kaleidoscope of human sciences. More importantly, the argument that all research activities are reflexive and socially constructed means in essence that all investigative activity turns out to be the social practice of groups that share the same metaphors, rules, and thus language. The argument that all activity (including research) is situated and thus to be understood specifically with reference to its social and historical context denies any possibility of transhistorical and transcultural knowledge. Yet, it is undoubtedly the case that we are able to communicate across the situated practices of research groups and this suggests that there may be aspects to the social psychological enterprise that supersede the merely situated features of knowledge.

*See also*: DISCOURSE ANALYSIS; ETHOGENICS; RHETORIC; SOCIAL REPRESENTATIONS; SYMBOLIC INTERACTIONISM.

REFERENCES

Averill, J. R. (1982). *Anger and aggression: An essay on emotion*. New York: Springer-Verlag.

Gergen, K. J. (1985). Social constructionist inquiry: Context and implications. In K. J. Gergen & K. E. Davis (Eds.), *The social construction of the person* (pp. 3–18). New York: Springer-Verlag.

Harré, R., & Secord, P. (1972). *The explanation of social behavior*. Oxford: Basil Blackwell.

Schlenker, B. R. (1974). Social psychology and science. *Journal of Personality and Social Psychology, 29*, 1–15.

Semin, R. R., & Manstead, A. S. R. (1983). The epistemological foundations of accountability of conduct. In G. R. Semin & A. S. R. Manstead (1983), *The accountability of conduct* (pp. 156–85). London: Academic Press.

GÜN R. SEMIN

**social dilemmas** "There should be a law against social dilemmas." This summarizes a famous statement made by Luce and Raiffa (1957) that underlines the potential destructiveness of social dilemmas. Social dilemmas are characterized as situations in which private interests are at odds with the collective interests. They arise because we often tend to let our own short-term interest determine what we are going to do, without sufficient consideration of the associated longer-term consequences to all of the persons involved. As a consequence we might face a situation in which we regret having acted the way we have.

There are numerous social problems which can be viewed from the perspective of social dilemmas. Overpopulation, one of the most critical problems of our age, is easily understood as such a situation. Problems of overuse of resources and underuse of strategies to protect the environment also seem to be natural examples. Failure to vote in democratic elections has been explained in such a way, as have productivity declines in collective workplaces. People's reluctance to take collective actions that could be collectively beneficial (joining labor unions, going out on strike) but personally costly, at least in the short run, are easily understood from the perspective of social dilemmas.

These examples of social dilemmas are in conflict with Adam Smith's famous notion of the beneficent "invisible hand" which assumes that our self-interests correspond to collective interests. In contrast, in social dilemmas the "rational" pursuit of immediate self-interest by most of us ultimately leads to collectively irrational solutions.

Research on social dilemmas has attracted social and behavioral scientists mainly for two reasons. First, there is the desire to understand the conditions under which people are tempted to behave either egoistically or cooperatively. Second, there is of course the need to offer recommendations for the solution of man-created societal problems.

## EXPERIMENTAL GAMES

Prior research on factors that enhance cooperative choices in situations of CONFLICT is strongly dominated by game theory and EXPERIMENTAL GAMES, which provided researchers in the social sciences with a promising new methodology for analyzing DECISION MAKING in situations of interdependence and conflict.

An experimental game is a situation in which each of the participants has to choose one of several well-defined alternatives. All choices have consequences for the actor as well as for the other persons involved, while everybody is aware of these consequences. Experimental games are generally presented to the participants in the form of an "outcome matrix." Choices in experimental games are very simple actions like pressing a key or checking a letter which corresponds to a choice-alternative. Outcomes in experimental games have a value for the participants like, for example, money or lottery tickets. A famous and important example is the PRISONER'S DILEMMA Game (PDG) for two persons. This game constitutes the prototypical social dilemma (figure 1). Suppose you are taking part

in this PDG. You have to choose between option C or option D. So has the other person. You are not allowed to communicate with the other person, and the choices are made privately. The outcome matrix in figure 1 represents the amounts of money which you and the other person gain as a consequence of the choices both of you make. Your rewards are encircled, those for the other are displayed in boxes.

The dilemma is obvious. Whatever the other does, it is better to choose D. Choosing D, the *defecting* option, always yields the highest possible rewards for self, that is D dominates C. However, a mutual D choice results in the second worst outcome cell for both persons whereas each could have got more by choosing C, the *cooperative* option.

From a game-theoretical standpoint, the generalization of this 2-person PDG to an N-person PDG is quite straightforward. Some researchers define social dilemmas as an N-person PDG: A situation in which:

(1) each person has available a dominating strategy, i.e. one which yields the person the best payoff in *all* circumstances; and in which,
(2) the collective choice of dominating strategies results in a deficient outcome – a result that is less preferred by all persons than the result which would have occurred if all had not chosen their dominating strategy.

Other researchers, however, point out that the requirement of having a dominating strategy is not crucial for considering a situation a social dilemma. What is critical is that a strategy can be chosen which ultimately results in an outcome which is deficient for all persons involved, and which nonetheless can be attractive since in *some* circumstances that strategy yields the best payoff for the person choosing that strategy. It can be shown that under these conditions there exist three and only three N-person generalizations of basic 2-person games: the N-person PDG, the N-person Chicken Game and the N-person Trust Game.

At least partly because of the perceived conceptual and methodological advantages of

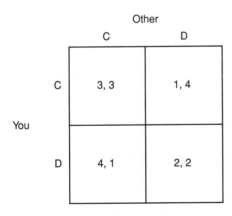

Figure 1. Outcome matrix for a prisoner's dilemma for two persons. The first number in each box denotes rewards for you, the second denotes rewards for the other person.

using experimental games, the 1960s witnessed a veritable flood of experimental gaming studies. Although the research effort had great potential, some social scientists have been critical of the accomplishments (Pruitt & Kimmel, 1977). According to these researchers, the two most important problems of the two-person experimental game tradition were the lack of a theoretical basis for generating research questions and the low external validity of the abstract two-person PDG.

The lack of external validity still remains a problem, and will probably always be so to the extent that experimental social dilemmas are evaluated as imitations of those that exist in the world outside the laboratory. However, to enhance the representativeness of experimental situations, recent experimental dilemmas have been patterned more closely on real problems than was previously the case. Take for instance, tasks which are designed to simulate the shared use of replenishable resources. In these resource dilemmas, subjects take resources from a common pool and try to maintain that public good over a series of trials. The social dilemma structure is reflected by the fact that it is in each person's interest to accumulate as much as possible from the pool, but if each tries to do that the pool will be destroyed.

Another class of games is called public good or free-rider games. These games simulate situations in which members of a group benefit when a member makes a personally costly act. For example, others benefit when I join a union or when I pay my taxes. It costs me to do so, but in the long run we are all better off if we all pay the cost and resist the temptation to free-ride on the contributions of others. While public goods games have the same structure as resource dilemmas at a high level of abstraction, the external validity of the research is enhanced to the extent that the experimental paradigm provides a better way of simulating specific "real life" social dilemmas.

Another type of social dilemma with high external validity is the so-called communications dilemma. This situation occurs when it is in an organization's best interest for people to share information that they have, but when it is also in the individuals' best interest to hoard information. Organizational inefficiency will result when information needed by one person or unit is withheld.

PRIOR RESEARCH FINDINGS

In both 2-person and *N*-person social dilemmas a variety of factors promoting CO-OPERATION have been identified (for reviews, *see* Dawes, 1980; Messick & Brewer, 1983; Van Lange, Liebrand, Messick, & Wilke, 1992). One of the most robust factors concerns the monetary payoff structure. Cooperation can be enhanced by both decreasing the incentive associated with noncooperative behavior and increasing the incentive associated with cooperative behavior. Research has also demonstrated that people are much more likely to cooperate to the extent that interdependent others can benefit more from it.

Generally, the influence of payoff structure has been shown to be strong not only in experimental work on social dilemmas, but also in field studies. For example, it has been found that monetary reward for electricity conservation was one of the most effective means of attaining electricity conservation.

A second factor concerns the possibility of COMMUNICATION. Indeed, one interesting and potentially important way to escape from massive noncooperation is to coordinate the social dilemma in a manner such that people feel committed, or actually promise to contribute to the collective welfare. As mentioned before, there is a collective basis for rational behavior, and communication opportunities help individuals to find such collectively rational solutions.

Third, collectively rational solutions to social dilemmas are attainable only if a sufficient number of others are willing to choose cooperatively as well. From this perspective, it is not surprising that there are stronger tendencies for individuals to cooperate to the extent that they think that more others will also cooperate. However, it is not altogether clear how precisely this relationship should be understood: EXPECTANCY EFFECTS may influence cooperative choices, but it may also be that choices affect expectations through post-hoc justification or assumed consensus.

Because there is evidence for both causal directions, the relationship can best be understood by assuming that expectations influence own choices as well as the reverse.

A fourth factor is group size, as prior research has indicated that individuals are more likely to cooperate in relatively small groups than in larger groups. However, in reality things are more complex: cooperation typically declines as group size increases up to about seven or eight persons; if groups become larger than seven or eight persons then the level of cooperation is not strongly influenced by a further increase in group size.

Finally, behavior in social dilemmas is influenced not only by situational factors, such as the ones described above, but also by preexisting individual differences such as SOCIAL VALUES and personality variables such as TRUST.

In addition to the above findings, there is also evidence that for $N$-person social dilemmas, cooperation is greater to the extent that:

(1) perceived efficacy of cooperation is higher;
(2) individuals are less anonymous, and can be better identified;
(3) feelings of personal responsibility are greater; and
(4) group identity is more salient and stronger.

Factors that are particularly relevant in the context of two-person social dilemmas are:

(1) other's behavioral strategy; and
(2) the perceived characteristics of interdependent others.

The highest levels of cooperation can be observed when the other follows a Tit-for-Tat (TFT) strategy – a strategy which starts with a cooperative choice, and subsequently mimics the other's prior choice. TFT is more effective than 100 percent cooperation which, in turn, is more effective than 100 percent COMPETITION. TFT is assumed to be effective because it is pleasant, reciprocal, forgiving, and clear. Individuals tend also to exhibit more cooperation to the extent that the interdependent other is viewed as moral, trustworthy, intelligent and to the extent that individuals believe that the other holds similar attitudes and beliefs. It is interesting to note that there is in fact very little evidence that perceptions of others' gender influence cooperation, either for men or women.

The above summarizes findings directly relevant to the question "what factors promote cooperation?" Additionally, some of these studies (as well as others) have examined how individuals construe social dilemma situations and evaluate their own and others' behavior in these situations (see SOCIAL VALUES). Generally, these studies reveal that cooperative individuals interpret social dilemmas primarily in terms of morality and fairness, whereas noncooperative individuals are more likely to make interpretations in terms of rationality and power. These findings contribute to our understanding of how interpretations of social dilemmas may differ from those of other decision situations, and how such interpretations may mediate choice behavior. Below, we provide a brief overview of theoretical issues and contemporary lines of research that are related to different construals of social dilemmas.

CONTEMPORARY RESEARCH
In order to highlight some of the theoretical threads running through contemporary work on social dilemmas, we next discuss the developments in the context of the following categories: payoffs and frames; risk and uncertainty; and finally, intergroup processes and larger scale dilemmas. A more extensive discussion of the topics listed below, can be found in Liebrand, Messick, and Wilke (1992).

*Payoffs and Frames*
A central problem in the study of social dilemmas has been to understand the effects of payoffs and, especially, the possible discrepancies between the experimenter's specification of a situation and the interpretation of that situation by the persons involved. These discrepancies could arise from individual differences in social value orientations or from situational factors that lead people to frame outcomes in different ways.

There is indeed increasing evidence that behavior is a function not only of payoffs but of how those payoffs are framed.

There may be important differences between a decision to contribute part of your own possessions in the hope of receiving more than the original contribution (a give-some situation), and a decision to take some collective shared resources (a take-some situation) even if the objective payoffs in the two situations are identical. Greater levels of cooperation may be obtained in give-some dilemmas than in take-some dilemmas because the former situations may evoke more strongly feelings of trust and norms of helping. However, there is also evidence supporting Kahneman and Tversky's PROSPECT THEORY regarding the appraisal of gains and losses. In their terminology, give-some games might be perceived in terms of losses, which would lead to risk-seeking behavior and hence to lower cooperation rates than in take-some games. In this case, we clearly see the need for subsequent research to settle this debate.

### Risk and Uncertainty

One central topic in judgment and decision making is the question of how people think about and respond to risk and uncertainty. This problem includes the study of the ways in which people make judgments about frequencies, relative frequencies, or probabilities; the understanding of people's perception of RISK; and the analysis of people's willingness to engage in behavior with uncertain outcomes. It is hardly surprising, therefore, that these concerns are emerging as important research questions in the study of social dilemmas. It has also been shown that people's attitudes toward risk may be very different in social and nonsocial domains owing to the differences between social and nonsocial preferences. The processes involved in making judgments about social and nonsocial uncertainty may be quite different as well. We can use our own behavior as a basis for predicting what others may do but it is less easy to rely on this source of information for estimating next year's rainfall. Furthermore, we believe that we can influence or control the former more than we can the other.

People avoid futile actions, especially if those actions are costly. How can one estimate the impact that one's decision is going to have in achieving a collective goal? Perceived efficacy, the probability that one will make a difference, has been proposed as a crucial factor in determining one's willingness to contribute to a public good. Related to this perceived efficacy is the observation that for public persuasion campaigns to be effective, one goal they must accomplish is to convince people that enough others will participate in the collective action to make it successful. In this regard, successful campaigns have a certain self-fulfilling quality: if people believe that enough others will participate to make a collective action successful, enough people will participate to make it successful.

### Intergroup Structure and Larger-scale Social Dilemmas

Consistent with a large body of research on ingroup–outgroup biases and social categorization effects it has been demonstrated that cooperation can be promoted by greater levels of common group membership or group identity. However, as argued by several researchers intergroup and intragroup interdependence structures are often perceived as conflicting. Cooperative intragroup behavior may be called for in the service of intergroup competition. The side with the most cooperators wins! But it is wasteful to have more cooperators than is necessary to win. Related to this, there is research on INTERGROUP RELATIONS that has established strong differences between individuals and groups, such that groups approach each other less cooperatively, less trustfully, and more competitively than do individuals.

One of the features that makes the study of social dilemmas so important is the prospect of finding solutions to real social problems. This holds especially for the question of how a government, agency, or organization can elicit cooperative, socially responsible behavior from multitudes of people. Social dilemmas are, after all, collective problems and their solutions must be on a collective scale. A solution to a social dilemma may penalize violators. However, unless the population to whom the sanction is going to apply accepts the necessity of having the sanction, it may not only be ineffective, it may boomerang.

## CONCLUSIONS

Social dilemmas are situations in which private interests are at odds with collective interests, to such a level that when the majority of the persons involved massively decide to act in their own interest, they ultimately would have been better off had they decided to act differently. Prior social psychological research has relied heavily upon game theory and experimental games to find solutions for these social dilemmas. More recently, researchers have extended their methodology to incorporate more ecologically valid laboratory settings in their research paradigms. Also, there has been a shift from simply demonstrating that factors enhance cooperation to focusing on the possible mediators and moderators of these factors, thereby contributing to a stronger theoretical basis for decision making in social dilemmas. As a consequence, we currently witness some very promising lines of research that help us to understand why and how individuals may forego their immediate self-interest, and how the potential destructiveness of social dilemmas can be limited or prevented.

See also: COMMUNICATION; CONFLICT; COOPERATION AND COMPETITION; DECISION MAKING; EXPERIMENTAL GAMES; GROUP STRUCTURE; INTERGROUP RELATIONS; PROSPECT THEORY; RISK; SOCIAL VALUES; TRUST.

BIBLIOGRAPHY

Dawes, R. M. (1980). Social dilemmas. *Annual Review of Psychology*, *31*, 169–193.

Liebrand, W. B. G., Messick, D. M., & Wilke, H. A. M. (1992). *Social dilemmas; Theoretical issues and research findings*. Oxford: Pergamon.

Luce, R. D. & Raiffa, H. (1957). *Games and decisions: Introduction and critical survey*. Chichester: J. Wiley.

Messick, D. M. & Brewer, M. B. (1983). Solving social dilemmas: A review. In L. Wheeler & P. Shaver (Eds.), *Review of personality and social psychology* (Vol. 4, pp. 11–44). Beverly Hills, CA: Sage.

Pruitt, D. G., & Kimmel, M. J. (1977). Twenty years of experimental gaming: Critique, synthesis, and suggestions for the future. *Annual Review of Psychology*, *28*, 363–92.

Van Lange, P. A. M., Liebrand, W. B. G., Messick, D. M., & Wilke, H. A. M. (1992). Social dilemmas: The state of the art; introduction and literature review. In W. B. G. Liebrand, D. M. Messick, & H. A. M. Wilke (Eds.), *Social dilemmas; Theoretical issues and research findings* (pp. 3–28). Oxford: Pergamon.

WIM B.G. LIEBRAND
PAUL A.M. VAN LANGE
DAVID M. MESSICK

**social exchange theories** Exchange theorists (e.g., P. M. Blau and G. C. Homans) use principles from learning theory and economics to analyze the structure and functions of interaction. Individuals are characterized as thoughtful and goal-directed, seeking to maximize interaction outcomes. Individuals are likely to apply exchange rules that have more frequently or powerfully been reinforced in past interactions.

CARYL E. RUSBULT
PAUL A. M. VAN LANGE

**social facilitation** One of the earliest discoveries of experimental social psychology was that an individual's performance may be facilitated or impaired by the presence of either passive audiences or other persons performing the same task (coactors). During the years 1900–60, facilitating and inhibiting effects were reported about equally often, in both audience and coactor settings. One common finding was that social facilitation of performance was usually found on easy or well-learned tasks and social inhibition was the typical outcome of difficult or novel ones. In a pioneering set of studies utilizing the coaction paradigm, Allport (*see* Cottrell, 1972) found that performance on such tasks as crossing out vowels from printed text and simple word association was facilitated by the presence of co-workers, whereas performance on a task involving thought and reasoning was inhibited by the same conditions.

## NONDIRECTIVE INFLUENCES OF SOCIAL PRESENCE

Findings such as these remained unexplained until the appearance of a major theoretical paper by Zajonc (1965), who proposed that both the facilitating and inhibitory effects are mediated by increased general AROUSAL elicited by the presence of others. Arousal activates dominant habits according to the formula $E = D \times H$ from DRIVE theory. Zajonc assumed that on an easy task the dominant response is likely to be correct, so that drive energizes the behavior necessary for good performance. On a difficult task the dominant response is more likely to be incorrect, so that increased drive energizes behavior that inhibits good performance.

The drive-theoretical hypothesis of social facilitation and inhibition proposed by Zajonc rested on the postulate that the mere presence of other members of the same species has an arousing effect on the individual. Most of the evidence adduced for this proposition by Zajonc (1965) came from studies of subhuman species, and the early research on the drive theory of social facilitation included studies of lower organisms. Because social facilitation in lower animals (e.g., insects) is less likely to reflect higher cognitive processes than it is in humans, data from animals studies is sometimes cited in support of the contention that arousal is produced by the presence of others and not by complex inferences of the meaning of that presence. In addition, studies designed to test for the "mere presence" effect in humans have yielded some support for that position (Geen, 1989).

Despite these findings, however, numerous investigators have sought additional variables that mediate socially engendered arousal. Evidence indicating that more than the mere presence of others is required for social facilitation and inhibition comes from several sources. The effect of the presence of others is usually reduced or eliminated when these people are not aware of what the performer is doing, and exacerbated when the others are specifically described as judges and evaluators. The socially facilitating/inhibiting effect of audiences is also a function of the perceived expertise of the members, with audiences of high expertise eliciting the effect to a greater extent than those of low expertise. This finding is usually interpreted as showing that audiences arouse individuals through their power to elicit evaluation apprehension, with highly expert audiences seen as more likely to evaluate the performer critically than those of lower capability.

Several variables have been proposed as mediators of the effects of audiences and coactors. Cottrell (1972) proposed that the person being evaluated becomes aroused by the expectation that the outcome of his or her performance will be either a social reward or punishment. Anticipation of punishment produces secondary drive, whereas anticipation of reward elicits incentive; drive and incentive both energize responses, and their effects are additive. However, subsequent theorizing and research showed that anticipation of reward is not a strong predictor of the social facilitation effect.

Anticipation of being evaluated elicits arousal by introducing the threat of failure. In the audience setting this effect is direct: the audience is perceived to be the evaluating agent. In a series of studies designed to test the hypothesis that the evaluation apprehension experienced in the audience setting is anxiety, Geen (1976b) showed that when audience evaluation is described as a prelude to the actor's being helped by the audience, social facilitation effects are significantly attenuated relative to those found among subjects who are merely evaluated. Other studies have shown that when observation by an audience is preceded by a successful task experience, subjects do not exhibit the effects of socially generated arousal. Still further evidence that socially generated arousal is related to anxiety is found in studies showing that the social facilitation/inhibition effect is moderated by individual differences in trait test anxiety (Geen, 1976b).

In the coaction setting the basis for socially engendered anxiety is less direct and is assumed to involve feelings of competition among the performers. The experimenter, or some other purveyor of social punishment, is regarded as the evaluator and the judge of who succeeds and who fails in the competition. Some evidence indicates that social arousal is engendered by coaction only when an audience is also present, suggesting that the coaction effect may be a special case of the audience effect (Geen, 1989).

Another variable that mediates the effects of audiences and coactors on arousal is an attentional conflict caused by competing demands on the actor. Other persons in the situation may attract attention that would otherwise be directed toward the task, producing the conflict. Research by Baron and his associates (Baron, 1986) has shown that the presence of observers has approximately the same physiological and behavioral effects on someone performing a task as does a nonsocial distractor like flashing light. Subjects who work before an audience also describe themselves as being less attentive to their task than do subjects working alone. Separating the effects of attentional conflict from those evoked by evaluation apprehension is often difficult in practice, however, and it is usually assumed that both occur (Geen, 1989).

A third antecedent of arousal in audience or coaction settings is uncertainty regarding what the other persons in the situation are likely to do. The actor is motivated to reduce arousal by watching the others in order to ascertain and predict their actions, a process called social monitoring. The social facilitation/inhibition effect is therefore stronger in situations in which such social monitoring is ruled out than in situations in which it is permitted. This effect has been reported in numerous studies (Guerin, 1986).

We may conclude that distraction, uncertainty, and evaluation apprehension may all be consequences of the presence of others and therefore that all may lead to increased arousal. It is also possible that these antecedent conditions are not independent of each other. Distraction from a task in which one is being evaluated may lead to anxiety, as may uncertainty about what others are doing.

## EVIDENCE FOR SOCIALLY INDUCED AROUSAL

Evidence of socially induced arousal comes from two sources: behavioral and psychophysiological studies. Social arousal is inferred when behavioral outcomes that are known to be produced by arousal from non-social sources are also elicited by the presence of others. Audiences have been shown to energize dominant responses at the expense of subordinate ones, a finding consistent with the drive-theoretical postulate of the multiplicative effect of drive and habit strength ($E = D \times H$) noted above. Several research paradigms have been used. Audience-produced arousal is associated with relatively poor learning of difficult word lists whereas it enhances the learning of less difficult lists. Acquisition of complex motor responses is slower among subjects working in coacting groups than among subjects performing alone. The presence of an audience leads to increased emission of common word associations and to a reduction in the emission of uncommon associates. Observation by an audience also hinders the breaking of perceptual "sets" and the assimilation of new information that contradicts the set (for reviews, *see* Geen, 1989).

In contrast to the amount of behavioral evidence supporting the drive theory of social facilitation/inhibition, the evidence from studies of psychophysiological correlates of arousal has been weak and inconclusive. The measure that has been reported most often to vary with the presence versus absence of others has been palmar sweat, but what this measure indicates is not clear. Other common measures of autonomic activity have shown little or no variability as a function of the presence of audiences or coactors (Geen & Bushman, 1989).

## DIRECTIVE INFLUENCES OF SOCIAL PRESENCE

A major alternative to the drive theory of social facilitation is that the presence of others has a *directive* influence, i.e., that it creates either explicit or implicit demands on the person to behave in some specific way. The person is enjoined to present the best possible appearance to others, either by attempting to perform up to some standard or to refrain from actions that might invite social censure. Social presence may enhance the performer's sense of SELF-AWARENESS, which in turn motivates the performer to bring performance into line with internalized standards. It may also elicit a motive for optimal SELF-PRESENTATION. This possibility is raised by findings that both performance and task motivation are facilitated by an audience after a prior success experience but not following a failure. These findings suggest that previous success leads to the hope of further successful self-presentation. Other studies have shown that persons who perform while being observed by others inhibit socially undesirable behaviors that could affect performance, such as using the fingers while counting and reading aloud. To the extent that such inhibited actions are helpful in task performance, social presence should have a negative effect on the latter.

## ATTENTIONAL EFFECTS OF SOCIAL PRESENCE

A third theoretical approach to the effects of the presence of others is based on contemporary theories of cognition and attention. The effect of audiences and coactors is mediated by a temporary stimulus overload (Baron, 1986). It is assumed that the human being has a finite amount of attentional capacity and that as demands are increased, the less spare capacity exists for task-relevant activities. To refer back to the antecedents of arousal listed above, any of the hypothesized effects of social presence – evaluation apprehension, distraction, and uncertainty – can place such demands on attentional capacity.

One immediate consequence of an overtaxed attentional system is a selective narrowing of attention to a relatively small range of central stimuli (Easterbrook, 1959). A set of attentional priorities is created in order to limit the degree of overload on the system. Reduction in the range of stimuli to which the person attends has effects on the performance of easy and difficult tasks similar to those hitherto attributed to increased drive. Easy tasks require attention to only a few central stimuli, whereas complex tasks demand attention to a wider range of cues. Stimulus overload should therefore terminate attention to irrelevant distractors when the task is easy, but cause interference with more important task-relevant stimuli when the problem is more complex. The consequences for performance are social facilitation on easy problems, through elimination of distractors, but impairment of performance on difficult tasks, caused by diminished attention to relevant cues (Geen, 1976a,b). This is, of course, the same outcome predicted by drive theory (Zajonc, 1965).

A related viewpoint (Manstead & Semin, 1980) is that the demands on attention caused by the presence of others impairs controlled cognitive processing and, as a consequence, hinders performance on complex and demanding tasks. Performance of easier tasks, which are handled through automatic processing, is not hampered by social presence, and may instead be facilitated through a focusing of attention.

## CONCLUSION

The changing approaches that characterize the study of social facilitation and inhibition of performance since 1965 reflect the general demise of energy theories of motivation and the corresponding ascendancy of cognitive explanations in psychology over that period. The two major changes in emphasis that have taken place are:

(1) the conceptualization of the presence of others as either a cause of stimulus overload or a cue for self-presentational behavior; and
(2) an increasing emphasis on the directional, rather than energizing, influence of others on behavior.

As a consequence, the theory of social facilitation, once cast in terms of drive and motivation, is now a more complex theory involving both motivational and cognitive elements. *See also:* AROUSAL; DRIVE; SELF-AWARENESS.

BIBLIOGRAPHY
Baron, R. S. (1986). Distraction/conflict theory: Progress and problems. In L. Berkowitz (Ed.), *Advances in experimental social psychology* (Vol. 19, pp. 1–40). New York: Academic Press.
Cottrell, N. B. (1972). Social facilitation. In C. G. McClintock (Ed.), *Experimental social psychology* (pp. 185–236). New York: Holt, Rinehart & Winston.

Easterbrook, J. A. (1959). The effect of emotion on cue utilization and organization of behavior. *Psychological Review*, 66, 187–201.

Geen, R. G. (1976a). Test anxiety, observation, and range of cue utilization. *British Journal of Social and Clinical Psychology*, 15, 253–9.

—— (1976b). The role of the social environment in the induction and reduction of anxiety. In C. D. Spielberger & I. G. Sarason (Eds.), *Stress and anxiety* (Vol. 3, pp. 105–26). Washington, DC: Hemisphere.

—— (1989). Alternative conceptions of social facilitation. In P. B. Paulus (Ed.), *Psychology of group influence* (2nd ed., pp. 15–51). Hillsdale, NJ: Lawrence Erlbaum.

—— & Bushman, B. J. (1989). The arousing effects of social presence. In H. Wagner & A. S. R. Manstead (Eds.), *Handbook of social psychophysiology* (pp. 261–81). Chichester: J. Wiley.

Guerin, B. (1986). Mere presence effects in humans: A review. *Journal of Experimental Social Psychology*, 22, 38–77.

Manstead, A. S. R., & Semin, G. R. (1980). Social facilitation effects: Mere enhancement of dominant processes? *British Journal of Social and Clinical Psychology*, 19, 119–36.

Zajonc, R. B. (1965). Social facilitation. *Science*, 149, 269–74.

RUSSELL G. GEEN

**social identity theory** A social psychological theory of group membership, GROUP PROCESSES, and INTERGROUP RELATIONS. It contributes to our understanding of a wide variety of topics including PREJUDICE, discrimination, STEREOTYPING, ethnocentrism, CONFORMITY, GROUP COHESIVENESS, collective behavior (*see* CROWD PSYCHOLOGY), GROUP POLARIZATION, GROUP DECISION MAKING, and the social psychology of language. A conceptual distinction is drawn between, on the one hand, group (and intergroup) relations, processes, representations, and behavior, and on the other, interpersonal relations, processes, representations, and behavior. The former are associated with social identity – a prescriptive and evaluative self-definition in terms of the properties of a specific ingroup. The latter are associated with personal identity – a self-defintion derived from close personal relationships and idosyncratic personality attributes. Social identity theory maintains that social identity phenomena (i.e., group and intergroup phenomena) cannot be reduced to or explained in terms of personal identity. Social identity is associated with group behavior due to the operation of individual cognitive and motivational processes (CATEGORIZATION and SOCIAL COMPARISON/SELF-ESTEEM) and their articulation with people's cognitive representations of, or beliefs about, the nature of intergroup relations. These "social beliefs" derive, in turn, from the real nature of the relations between groups.

CONTEXT AND ORIGINS OF THE THEORY.
Social identity theory arose as part of the self-conscious development of a distinctively European social psychology, whose agenda was to address the "lost" social dimension of human behavior by, among other things, constructing nonreductionist explanations of group phenomena. The theory was originally developed in the mid- to late 1970s by Henri Tajfel and Turner, and their associates, at the University of Bristol (*see* Tajfel, 1978; Tajfel & Turner, 1979; Turner & Giles, 1981). However, the wider implications of the theory for social psychology were soon recognized, and it quickly gained ground and support. This has ensured its high profile and continuing popularity in contemporary social psychology (e.g., Abrams & Hogg, 1990; Hogg, 1992; Hogg & Abrams, 1988).

Social identity theory is framed by an assumption that society is hierarchically structured into different social groups that stand in POWER and status relations to one another (e.g. men and women, Blacks and Whites in South Africa, Catholics and Protestants in Northern Ireland, Malays and Chinese in Malaysia). Power and status differentials also mark the relations between smaller and more transient groups such as classes in a school. The basic premise is that social categories (large groups like a nation or church, or smaller groups like an organization or club) provide members with a social identity: a definition of who one is and a description and evaluation of what this entails. Social identities not only describe members but prescribe appropriate behavior (i.e., NORMS) for members. For example, being a member of the social category "gypsy" means not only that one defines and evaluates oneself and one is defined and evaluated by others as a gypsy, but that one thinks and behaves in characteristically gypsy ways.

## SOCIAL IDENTITY

Social identity is that part of the self-concept that derives from group membership. It is quite separate from personal identity, which is that part of the self-concept that derives from PERSONALITY traits and idiosyncratic personal RELATIONSHIPS one has with other people (Turner, 1982). People have a repertoire of as many social and personal identities as they have groups with which they identify, or close relationships in terms of which they define themselves. These identities continually vary in their overall importance (or SALIENCE) in the self-concept, and they become the relevant basis of self-perception and behavior as a function of contextual factors. For example, talking with a close friend about a mutual acquaintance would most likely render a particular personal identity salient and cause one to consider oneself and one's partner in terms of that identity. Talking with the same close friend about the outcome of a sporting contest in which you support opposing teams would very likely render the interaction an intergroup one based on definition of self and other in terms of opposing supporters' groups.

Social identity theory distinguishes social from personal identity as part of a self-conscious attempt to avoid explaining group and intergroup processes in terms of personality attributes or interpersonal relations. Social identity theorists believe that a significant problem with many social psychological theories of group processes and intergroup relations is that they do not provide a complete answer because they try to explain the phenomena by simply combining the effects of personality predispositions or interpersonal relations – the authoritarian personality theory (see AUTHORITARIANISM) and the FRUSTRATION-AGGRESSION hypothesis are examples of this type of explanation of prejudice and discrimination, and traditional approaches to group cohesiveness are an example of this approach to group processes. To illustrate, if a social psychologist asks why people stick their arms out of car windows to indicate a turn, the question would remain unanswered by an explanation in terms of the biochemistry of muscle action. An explanation in terms of adherence to social norms would be more appropriate (though, of course, inappropriate to a biochemist asking the same question). It is the problem of *reductionism* that prompts social identity theory to distinguish between social and personal identity.

## CATEGORIZATION

Social identity is associated with group behavior, which has some notable general characteristics: ethnocentrism, ingroup favoritism, intergroup differentiation, conformity to ingroup norms, ingroup attraction, and perception of self, outgroupers, and fellow ingroupers in terms of relevant group stereotypes. Social identification produces these effects because it is associated with SOCIAL CATEGORIZATION. The categorization of both nonsocial and social stimuli has been shown to produce a perceptual accentuation effect in which people accentuate similarities among stimuli (e.g., people) falling within the same category and differences between stimuli from different categories. The accentuation effect occurs on attitudinal, behavioral, and emotional dimensions that are believed to be associated with the categorization – i.e., stereotypical dimensions. Social categorization thus accentuates the perceived stereotypic distinctiveness of social groups–the process of categorization is responsible for stereotyping. Accentuation is considered to be an inevitable consequence of categorization, which in turn is considered a basic human cognitive process that serves the important function for people of simplifying in meaningful ways the potentially limitless array of discernible stimuli in our environment.

The categorization process can also include self as a social stimulus. Minimal group studies (*see* MINIMAL GROUP PARADIGM) in which people, including self, are merely categorized on a random basis into noninteractive groups (often simply labeled "X-group" and "Y-group") reveal that categorization per se reliably produces a competitive intergroup orientation in which people discriminate in favor of their own group, and evaluate their own group and its members more favorably than the outgroup and its members.

Categorization of oneself is believed to be responsible for assigning the group's identity to oneself – i.e., for identifying with the group. Self-categorization also accentuates stereotypic similarity between self and fellow ingroupers, and differences between self and outgroup members – where stereotypic dimensions can be attitudinal, emotional, or behavioral. This idea has recently been taken a great deal further by SELF-CATEGORIZATION THEORY (Turner, Hogg, Oakes, Reicher, & Wetherell, 1987) which is an extension of social identity theory that focuses upon the role of self-categorization in group behavior. An important feature of this extension is that it elaborates in some detail the way in which people in intergroup contexts construct representations of the defining features of the ingroup in terms of shared PROTOTYPES.

## CATEGORIZATION AND GROUP INFLUENCE

The categorization process is used by social identity theorists to explain the SOCIAL INFLUENCE process in groups that produces behavioral and attitudinal conformity – called *referent informational influence*. When social identity is a salient basis for self-definition people construct a contextually appropriate and identity-consistent ingroup norm from available information (e.g., the behavior of ingroup members). Self-categorization theory extends this analysis and provides further detail about precisely how this happens, and about the sorts of properties the norm may have (Turner, 1991). One important feature of such a norm is that it balances a minimization of differences among ingroup members with a maximization of differences between in- and outgroup. One implication of this is that the ingroup norm does not necessarily have to be the mean of ingroup members' behaviors – on the contrary the norm may be polarized from the ingroup mean in a direction away from an outgroup.

The accentuation effect, when applied to self, simply brings one's own behavior into line with the norm – that is, it produces individual conformity to the norm. To the extent that most people in a particular group context are exposed to similar information and thus construct a very similar contextual ingroup norm, the overall effect is that group members' behavior becomes more homogenous. Uniformity of conduct is one of the principal features of group behavior. The social identity analysis of social influence in groups has been applied to a number of phenomena: e.g., conformity, group polarization, crowd behavior (*see* crowd psychology), GROUPTHINK.

## SOCIAL COMPARISON AND SELF-ESTEEM

The categorization process is believed to operate in tandem with a SELF-ENHANCEMENT or self-esteem motive. Drawing on social comparison theory, it is assumed that people have a need to obtain, through comparison between themselves and others, a relatively positive evaluation of their attitudes and behaviors, and thus of themselves. People strive for self-enhancement by obtaining or maintaining relatively positive self-esteem. In intergroup contexts, when social identity is the salient basis of self-evaluation, this need manifests itself as a need to maintain or secure a relatively positive social identity for the ingroup. For this reason, the accentuation of intergroup differences produced by social categorization has two further features:

(1) it occurs only on dimensions which favor the ingroup (hence it is ethnocentric – ingroup favoring); and

(2) it is amplified under conditions embodying a strong need to differentiate the groups (e.g., when intergroup boundaries are becoming unclear, in times of conflict, or among individuals with low self-esteem or for whom the ingroup is extremely important).

Experimental studies of specific details of how self-esteem motivates intergroup behavior or how self-esteem is influenced by intergroup behavior have tended to produce rather inconsistent findings. However, the role of positive social identity in large-scale intergroup relations is better understood. The self-esteem hypothesis was originally elaborated to address large-scale intergroup relations, and, in particular, social change. The categorization process operating alone was seen as a conservative force that reflected and recreated existing status relations. Self-esteem gave direction to categorization effects and allowed one to see how people might strive to change existing intergroup relations in order ultimately to address self-evaluation concerns.

## INTERGROUP RELATIONS AND SOCIAL BELIEFS

In pursuit of positive social identity, groups and individuals can adopt an array of different behavioral strategies, the choice of which is determined by people's beliefs about the nature of relations between their own and other groups (e.g., Tajfel & Turner, 1979). These beliefs, which may or may not accord with the reality of intergroup relations, hinge firstly on whether it is possible, as an individual, to "pass" from a lower status group and gain acceptance in a higher status group. This belief, called *social mobility*, inhibits group action on the part of subordinate groups, and instead encourages individuals to dissociate themselves from the group and try to gain acceptance for themselves and their immediate family in the dominant group. The belief in social mobility is enshrined in Western democratic political systems, and an example of the use of a strategy of individual mobility is the "nouveau riche" phenomenon.

Where individuals believe that intergroup boundaries are impermeable to "passing," a *social change* belief system exists – e.g., Blacks in South Africa. Under these circumstances positive social identity can only be achieved by forms of group action, and the sort of action taken is influenced by whether the status quo (the existing status and power hierarchy) is perceived to be secure or insecure. If the status quo is perceived to be stable, legitimate, and thus secure, it is difficult to conceive of an alternative social structure (i.e., no *cognitive alternatives* exist), let alone a path to real social change. Groups tend to adopt *social creativity* strategies:

(1) They can engage in intergroup comparisons on novel or unorthodox dimensions which tend to favor the subordinate group. For example, in one study, children engaged in an intergroup competition to build the best hut, but were provided with poor building materials and thus no possibility of winning – these children went on to emphasize what a good garden they had made.

(2) Groups can attempt to change the consensual value attached to ingroup characteristics – e.g., the slogan "Black is beautiful."

(3) Groups can compare themselves with other low- or lower-status groups – e.g., "poor White racism."

Where social change is associated with a recognition that the status quo is illegitimate, unstable, and thus insecure, and where cognitive alternatives (i.e., conceivable and attainable alternative social orders) exist, then direct *social competition* occurs – that is, direct intergroup conflict (e.g., political action, terrorism, revolutions, war). Social movements typically emerge in these circumstances.

The macrosocial aspect of social identity theory has been tested fairly successfully in a range of laboratory and naturalistic contexts, and has been elaborated and extended in many areas of social psychology. For instance the social psychology of language has employed and applied social identity theory with a great deal of success to explain the circumstances under which ethnolinguistic groups (i.e., ethnic groups that are defined by their language) lose their language (it withers away and the group assimilates to the majority culture) or undergo a language revival (*see* LANGUAGE).

Social identity theory attributes the general form of intergroup behavior (e.g., ethnocentric and stereotypic intergroup attitudes, intergroup differentiation) to social categorization and self-esteem processes, and the specific manifestation (e.g., whether there is conflict, and in what form, or relative harmony between groups) to people's beliefs about the nature of intergroup relations. As such, it is a theory that articulates individual psychological processes with socially elaborated representations, in order to account in noninterpersonal terms for the general form and specific content of group behavior.

## CRITICAL COMMENTS

Social identity theory has not gone unchallenged (*see* Abrams & Hogg, 1990). As alluded to above, although the notion of positive distinctiveness has been very useful in explaining macrosocial intergroup relations, the self-esteem assumption upon which this idea ultimately rests does not have consistent empirical support. A number of explanations has been proposed, one of which is that self-esteem and positive distinctiveness are conceptually incompatible because they derive from different levels of analysis (the former is at the individual level, and the latter at the group level). Groups may be able to achieve positive distinctiveness in all sorts of ways that are not mechanically reflected in individual self-esteem.

Another problem is the question of salience. It is relatively easy to specify general rules that govern the conditions under which social or personal identity may be salient, or under which specific social identities may be salient (Turner et al., 1987). It is also easy, with hindsight, to account very plausibly for the salience of specific identities. However, it is still difficult with any certainty to predict identity salience in any but the most simple contexts.

Some critics have felt that social identity theory reifies social identities as static clusters of characteristics that suddenly leap into operation when the right context comes along. This is actually a misreading of the theory – social identification is a dynamic and constructive process in which sociostructural and specific situational factors, and individual processes and motives operate to produce identity-consistent and context-specific behaviors that have certain unique forms associated with groups that are quite distinct from

interpersonal behavior. This dynamic aspect is taken further by self-categorization theory.

A related criticism is that because social identity theory invokes the operation of cognitive and individual motivational processes it is a reductionist theory. Again this may be a misreading. Social identity theory sees cognitive processes (which of course are individual in the trivial sense that they occur in the head of the individual) as lending some distinct from to group behavior, while socially constructed representations provide content and more context-dependent aspects of form.

## RECENT DEVELOPMENTS

The most significant recent development in social identity theory is self-categorization theory (Turner et al., 1987). It is both an extension of, and a development within the broader scope of, social identity theory. Social identity regulates behavior in the way it does because the underlying process is self-categorization. In intergroup contexts people call up from memory, or construct from the range of ingroup and outgroup people present, a contextually appropriate cognitive representation of the defining features of each group. These "prototypes" are fuzzy sets of features that define each group and describe appropriate behavior for members of each group – prototypes are the way in which we represent social categories. Prototypes tend both to minimize intragroup differences and to exaggerate intergroup differences. When we categorize others as ingroup or outgroup members we accentuate their similarity to the relevant prototype – thus perceiving them stereotypically and ethnocentrically. When we categorize ourselves, we define, perceive, and evaluate ourselves in terms of our ingroup prototype, and behave in accordance with that prototype. Self-categorization produces ingroup normative behavior and self-stereotyping, and is thus the process underlying group behavior. Self-categorization theorists believe that self-categorization *depersonalizes* perception and behavior such that people, including ourselves, are perceived and behave not as unique individuals but as group members. Depersonalization is not the same thing as "dehumanization" – though it can produce dehumanization if the outgroup is deeply hated, and is stereotyped in terms that deny its members any respect or human dignity. Self-categorization theory has provided some important insights into the operation of social influence processes such as conformity and group polarization, and it has also been applied to help understand group cohesiveness, stereotyping, and the process of salience (Hogg, 1992; Oakes, Haslam, & Turner, 1993; Turner, 1991).

*Also see*: AUTHORITARIANISM; CATEGORIZATION; CROWD PSYCHOLOGY; GROUP COHESIVENESS; GROUP DECISION MAKING; GROUP PROCESSES; GROUPTHINK; INTERGROUP RELATIONS; LANGUAGE; NORMS; PERSONALITY; POWER; PREJUDICE; RELATIONSHIPS; SELF-CATEGORIZATION THEORY; SELF-ENHANCEMENT; SELF-ESTEEM; SOCIAL CATEGORIZATION; SOCIAL COMPARISON; SOCIAL INFLUENCE; STEREOTYPING.

BIBLIOGRAPHY

Abrams, D., & Hogg, M. A. (Eds.) (1990). *Social identity theory: Constructive and critical advances*. Hemel Hempstead: Harvester Wheatsheaf; New York: Springer-Verlag.

Hogg, M. A. (1992). *The social psychology of group cohesiveness: From attraction to social identity*. Hemel Hempstead: Harvester Wheatsheaf; New York: New York University Press.

——— & Abrams, D. (1988). *Social identifications: A social psychology of intergroup relations and group processes*. London & New York: Routledge.

Oakes, P. J., Haslam, S. A., & Turner, J. C. (1993). *Stereotyping and social reality*. Oxford: Blackwell Publishers.

Tajfel, H. (Ed.) (1978). *Differentiation between social groups*. London: Academic Press.

——— & Turner, J. C. (1979). An integrative theory of intergroup conflict. In W. G. Austin & S. Worchel (Eds.), *The social psychology of intergroup relations* (pp. 33–47). Monterey, CA: Brooks/Cole.

Turner, J. C. (1982). Towards a cognitive redefinition of the social group. In H. Tajfel (Ed.), *Social identity and intergroup relations* (pp. 15–40). Cambridge: Cambridge University Press.

——— (1991). *Social influence*. Milton Keynes: Open University Press; Monterey, CA: Brooks/Cole.

——— & Giles, H. (Eds.) (1981). *Intergroup behaviour*. Oxford: Basil Blackwell.

——— Hogg, M. A., Oakes, P. J., Reicher, S. D., & Wetherell, M. S. (1987). *Rediscovering the social group: A self-categorization theory*. Oxford: Basil Blackwell.

MICHAEL A. HOGG

**social impact theory** A general theory claiming that all forms of SOCIAL INFLUENCE, whatever the specific social process, will be proportional to a multiplicative function of the strength, immediacy, and number of people who are the sources of influence, and inversely proportional to the strength, immediacy, and number of people being influenced. In addition to its direct utility in making quantitative predictions about a wide variety of social phenomena, it forms the basis for dynamic social impact theory, which predicts the group-level consequences of individual influence processes in spatially distributed populations of people interacting with each other.

Social impact theory was introduced in 1981 by Latané, who defined social impact as "any of the great variety of changes in physiological states and subjective feelings, motives and emotions, cognitions and beliefs, values and behavior, that occur in an individual, human or animal, as a result of the real, implied, or imagined presence or actions of other individuals" (Latané, 1981, p. 343).

The basic metaphor underlying social impact theory is the social force field. Social impact is seen as resulting from social forces (like the physical forces of light, sound, gravity, and magnetism) operating in a spatio-temporal social force field or structure. Social impact theory is a metatheory, rather than a theory of specific social processes. It does not attempt to explain why people get nervous in front of audiences, obey an authority, or imitate the clothing styles of their co-workers. It does attempt to integrate specific theories developed to account for these phenomena and provide general principles under which they work.

In its static form, social impact theory consists of three principles. According to Principle 1, when some number of social sources are influencing a target person, the amount of impact (î) experienced by the target should be a multiplicative function of the strength (s), immediacy (i), and number (n) of those people: $î = f(sin)$. Strength can be taken as the net salience, power, importance, or intensity of a given source to the target, and results from such factors as age, socio-economic status, ability, or motivation. Immediacy represents closeness in space and time, and the absence of intervening filters and barriers. Number means simply how many people there are. These factors are assumed to combine multiplicatively, rather than additively. In an additive combination, simply making one factor very large would make the total large also, while in a multiplicative combination, if any one value is small, so too will be the total.

The second principle of social impact theory, known as the Psychosocial Law after S. S. Stevens' power law of psychophysics, states that there is a marginally decreasing effect of additional sources of impact, such that $î = sN^t$, $t < 1$ where impact will equal some power, $t$, of the number of sources, $N$, times a scaling constant, $s$. According to the theory, the value of the exponent $t$ should be less than one, and exponents from a variety of experiments seem to cluster around 0.5 – it seems that social influence grows only as the square root of the number of sources of influence.

The third principle of social impact theory attempts to capture the concept of "diffusion of RESPONSIBILITY" introduced by Latané and Darley (1970) as one explanation for the social inhibition of bystander intervention in emergencies (see HELPING BEHAVIOR). When others are present, they share the onus of responsibility and each feels less impetus to act. More generally, when N people stand together as the target of influence, the amount of impact experienced by each will be an inverse function of the strength, immediacy, and number of people being influenced: $î = f(1/sin)$.

Numerous experiments have provided empirical support for the theory. For example,

Latané and Harkins (1976) asked volunteers to adjust the brightness of a light or the loudness of a tone to match how tense and nervous they would be reciting a poem in front of audiences varying in size and status. Anticipated stage fright increased in proportion to the square root of the size of the audience, high status audiences produced more EMBARRASSMENT than low status audiences, and these effects combined multiplicatively. Further studies have shown that although increasing audience size increases nervousness, increasing the number of coperformers *decreases* it as an inverse power function of the number of coperformers. Other research supporting social impact theory involves such phenomena as CONFORMITY and imitation, CROWDING, the interest value of news events, MAJORITY and MINORITY SOCIAL INFLUENCE (Latané & Wolf, 1981), OBEDIENCE, tipping in restaurants, and SOCIAL LOAFING.

Social impact theory as stated in 1981 is a static theory, dealing with how a single individual is affected by his or her social environment. Recently, Latané, Nowak, and others have begun to explore the ways in which these individual effects feed back into a complex dynamic system, using computer simulations and actual social groups to discover the group-level consequences of allowing a spatially distributed population of interacting individuals to influence each other (Nowak, Szamrej, & Latané, 1990). When applied to public opinion, dynamic social impact theory predicts the emergence of spatial clusters of like-minded people with minorities reduced in number. In other words, social systems can organize themselves through individual ATTITUDE CHANGE processes so that everybody finds themselves in agreement with their neighbors, albeit at some cost to the minority. Dynamic social impact theory thus provides a way of bridging the micro–macro interface linking the individual to society.

Social impact theory is a general theory, drawing on basic laws, predicting to many domains, and encompassing a variety of processes. It is also specific in that it is quantifiable, deals with parametric variations, and makes precise predictions about observable aspects of the real world. Thus it is falsifiable

– if relationships turn out to be nonmonotonic or if exponents are greater than one, the theory will be disconfirmed. Perhaps its greatest advantage is that, by attempting to represent the net sum of all factors affecting social impact, it can be used as the basis for predicting the dynamic outcomes of GROUP PROCESSES.

*See also*: ATTITUDE CHANGE; CROWDING; EMBARRASSMENT; GROUP PROCESSES; HELPING BEHAVIOR; OBEDIENCE; SOCIAL INFLUENCE; SOCIAL LOAFING.

BIBLIOGRAPHY

Latané, B. (1981). The psychology of social impact. *American Psychologist, 36*, 343–56.

—— & Darley, J. M. (1970). *The unresponsive bystander: Why doesn't he help?* New York: Appleton-Century-Crofts.

—— & Harkins, S. (1976). Cross-modality matches suggest anticipated stage fright a multiplicative power function of audience size and status. *Perception and Psychophysics, 20*, 482–8.

—— & Wolf, S. (1981). The social impact of majorities and minorities. *Psychological Review, 88*, 438–53.

Nowak, A. Szamrej, J., & Latané, B. (1990). From private attitude to public opinion: A dynamic theory of social impact. *Psychological Review, 7*, 362–76.

BIBB LATANÉ
STEPHEN DRIGOTAS

**social influence**    A large and important field of research concerned with processes whereby people's BELIEFS, opinions, attitudes, VALUES, and behavior are changed or controlled through social communication and interaction as a function of social relationships between the recipient(s) and source(s) of influence. Areas of study and major phenomena include:

(1) the formation of social NORMS;
(2) social CONFORMITY;
(3) ATTITUDE CHANGE and PERSUASION;
(4) POWER and COMPLIANCE;
(5) MINORITY SOCIAL INFLUENCE;
(6) GROUP POLARIZATION; and
(7) OBEDIENCE to authority.

Given that any and all social modifications of individual psychology can be described as effects of social influence, another sense of the term summarizes the whole field of SOCIAL PSYCHOLOGY (e.g., as an attempt to understand how the thoughts, feelings, and behavior of individuals are influenced by the actual, imagined, or implied presence of others). However, the more restricted meaning exemplified in the areas listed above is more usual. These areas study the functioning of social-normative processes in social interaction and the related problem of the subjective validation of own and others' beliefs about appropriate behavior. Influence relates to the processes whereby people agree or disagree about appropriate behavior; form, maintain, or change social norms; and the social conditions that give rise to, and the effects of, such norms.

SOCIAL NORMS
A social norm is a generally accepted way of thinking, feeling or behaving that is endorsed and expected because it is perceived as the right and proper thing to do. It is a rule, value or standard shared by the members of a social group and anchored in that group membership that defines correct, appropriate, valued conduct. It implies that members *should* or *ought* to think, see or act in a certain way in relevant circumstances, not merely prefer to do so. *Subjective validity* is the subjective aspect of a normative belief: it is one's subjective confidence that some idea, judgment, or action is right (correct, proper, etc.). Where, for example, an institution such as the Catholic Church adheres to the normative belief that abortion is wrong and immoral, an individual Catholic who shares the belief will not only reject abortion but is likely to do so with moral certainty, with confidence in the correctness of his or her position on the issue. Belonging to a group of like-minded others and sharing their views establishes a group norm, provides members with subjective validity, and reduces uncertainty about the correct belief. The opposite of subjective validity is uncertainty. The desire to reduce uncertainty is widely assumed to be one of the two fundamental motives for

accepting social influence (the other being the desire to maintain membership in the group and avoid social rejection).

Early work on group interaction showed that where members made public judgments, they tended gradually to move towards agreement. Sherif (1936) explicitly equated the movement of group members towards an agreement with the *formation of social norms*. Subjects in his "autokinetic paradigm" were placed in a perceptually ambiguous situation with nonavailable external frames of reference. Over trials in group settings they tended to converge towards each other in their judgments of the apparent movement of a point of light. The gradual mutual convergence in judgments to a modal range of judgment was interpreted by Sherif as an expression of the formation of a social norm, defined as an internalized and shared frame of reference which stabilized judgment and reduced uncertainty.

In classic theory (e.g., Festinger, 1950), both norm formation and conformity were seen as an outcome of pressures towards uniformity in task-oriented groups with face-to-face communication. Uniformity served the "social reality testing" and "group locomotion" functions of group membership: that is, agreement within the group provided members with subjective validity for beliefs which could not be tested directly against physical reality (social reality testing is the consensual validation of beliefs through SOCIAL COMPARISON) and was perceived as instrumentally necessary for the group to reach desired goals. These separate sources of uniformity pressure functioned in combination and increased as a function of GROUP COHESIVENESS, the degree of discrepancy within the group and the relevance of the disagreement to the goals and values of the group. Implicitly, too, the more uncertainty in the group (the less physical reality testing available for beliefs) and the more that uniformity is perceived to facilitate a desired outcome, the greater is the pressure exerted on a deviant to conform through communication from other group members. Where neither the deviant nor the majority will move toward each other, the deviant is likely to be excluded from the group.

CONFORMITY

Where a social group has a well-established norm specifying correct behavior, pressures tend to arise in the group to maintain that norm. Pressures tend to be exerted upon and experienced by deviants to bring them back into line or upon the majority to hold the line. All things being equal, it can be assumed that one or more deviants will be more likely to move towards the majority than will the majority to move towards the minority. Social conformity (MAJORITY SOCIAL INFLUENCE) is defined as movement on the part of one or more deviants towards the group norm as a function of explicit or implicit social pressure from the majority of group members. The opposite of conformity may be defined as independence (the deviant is uninfluenced by the majority) or anticonformity (the deviant moves away from the majority).

The Asch paradigm (Asch, 1952) provides a powerful experimental illustration of conformity pressures. Faced with a group of ostensible peers (in fact confederates of the researcher) making unanimously incorrect judgments about the lengths of lines, a lone, naive subject tends to conform on average on approximately 33 percent of critical trials. In control conditions, without the group, almost no errors are made. There are large individual differences, but one-third of subjects conform on 50 percent or more of the critical trials – this where the judgment is simple and unambiguous and the significance of the group membership seems minimal.

Deutsch and Gerard (1955) suggest that conformity pressures are of two kinds. INFORMATIONAL INFLUENCE is influence to accept information from another as valid evidence about objective reality. In this process conformity is motivated by the desire to form an accurate view of reality and to act correctly. It is increased by one's uncertainty and reduced by the perceived uncertainty of others. NORMATIVE INFLUENCE is influence to conform to the positive expectations of others (or oneself): one conforms to others' expectations to elicit a positive reaction. In this process, conformity is motivated by a desire to please others, to gain social approval and avoid rejection. It is increased by ATTRACTION to the group, responding publicly rather than privately, and reduced by a prior commitment to one's own beliefs. Deutsch and Gerard see normative influence as the process specifically associated with groups. They showed that both kinds of influence are at work in the Asch paradigm.

In fact, research and theory in the conformity area point to a major distinction between two types of process and outcome: an informational, cognitive process leading to *private acceptance*, and a normative, social process leading to *public compliance*. Influence that leads to private attitude change but may or may not be directly expressed in overt words or deeds is termed private acceptance. Influence that changes overt or public behavior in the intended direction but may or may not lead to private attitude change is termed public compliance. The idea that acceptance or compliance are produced by two distinct processes is a pervasive one in the field and can be referred to as the *dual-process model*.

## PERSUASION AND POWER

The informational/acceptance versus normative/compliance dichotomy is reflected in the distinction between the attitude change/persuasion and power/compliance areas of research. In forming, maintaining, and changing social norms, people seek to *persuade* each other to change their private attitudes. In persuasion research one studies features of the source, message, and recipient of the message that induce private attitude change in the recipient in the direction intended by the source. Classic source variables are perceived prestige, credibility, expertness, attractiveness, and trustworthiness. Message variables include the degree to which the presented arguments are perceived as strong or weak, the discrepancy between the message and the position of the recipient, the emotions the message arouses and whether it presents one or both sides of the issue. Recipient variables include the recipient's existing attitudes and his or her ego-involvement in them.

Several major theories of attitude change have been employed to explain persuasion (e.g., reinforcement, COGNITIVE DISSONANCE, SELF-PERCEPTION, social comparison and ATTRIBUTION THEORIES). Current work examines the cognitive responses which recipients make to the message. The ELABORATION LIKELIHOOD MODEL and the HEURISTIC/SYSTEMATIC PROCESSING model, for example, specify when messages will lead to persuasion via cognitive elaboration and information processing of message content and when factors other than rational processing of message content will come into play. Persuasion research, therefore, can be seen as an elucidation of the informational process of influence in its focus on the social, motivational, and cognitive responses which facilitate or impede systematic information processing of the message.

Similarly, power and compliance mirror the normative process of influence and focus on the conditions under which people's actions may be controlled by those with power (to reward and punish) even where persuasion has not or may not have taken place. Classic theory (*see* Turner, 1991) conceptualizes all influence as reflecting a power relationship in the sense that the target (typically a deviant) is by definition dependent upon the source (typically the group) for information and/or positive outcomes. Thus "power" was used as a generic term for the capacity to exercise influence and influence was seen as power in action. French and Raven (1959) formalized in detail the types of power that functioned as distinct bases of influence (reward, coercive, referent, informational, expert, and legitimate power). Within their framework, reward and coercive power (control over the recipient's positive and negative outcomes) were the specific bases of compliance in the narrow sense. Similarly, Kelman (1958) distinguished public *compliance* based on power in the sense of outcome control from *internalization* and *identification* as more enduring forms of private acceptance. Nevertheless, there has been a general tendency to conceptualize all conformity as a slavish process of submission to social pressure, of seeking to meet the tacit expectations of powerful others because of a deep-rooted need for social approval. This picture is at odds with evidence and sits uneasily with the seminal theories of social reality testing and uncertainty-reduction. It is a view which has been given new life, however, by Moscovici's theories of minority influence (1976, 1980).

## MINORITY INFLUENCE

Moscovici defines power and influence as alternatives. If one can persuade through influence, then, in his view, one has no need of power (i.e., domination and coercion leading to compliance); one resorts to power only when one does not have influence. Indeed, he proposes that true influence is the prerogative of the *powerless*, the social minorities who lack resources and access to information. In his (1980) CONVERSION theory conformity to the group is a purely power-based process of compliance in which *comparison* with and conformity to the majority prevent any genuine processing of their message. Only minorities can free influence targets from concerns with why they disagree with the source and enable them to concentrate on validating the message, leading to conversion. The stark suggestion that only minorities can change people's minds (which is surely *real* power) has produced a surge of interest in the characteristics of majority and minority influence.

Minority influence research was launched by Moscovici and colleagues as a rejection of what they saw as the "conformity bias" in classic influence research. It was argued that influence is not a one-way process from the powerful to the dependent, from majorities to minorities, but that minorities can also exert influence upon majorities. In a clever reversal of the Asch paradigm, early studies using judgments of the color of slides showed that a consensual and consistent minority of two persons responding incorrectly ("green" to blue slides) over a series of trials was able to influence the judgments of a naive majority. The majority significantly increased its number of "green" judgments compared to control conditions or to conditions in which the majority was faced with an inconsistent minority. Minority influence was still not as large as majority influence at the manifest level (i.e., on public, direct, or immediate measures), but there was some evidence, subsequently confirmed for specific conditions, that minorities were having a larger impact at the latent level (i.e., on private, indirect, or delayed measures).

Moscovici argues that minority influence produces social change and INNOVATION, that it is based on the power of minorities to create CONFLICT and uncertainty in the group, and that it depends on the "rhetoric" of minority behavior, the way it is organized and patterned, its style. Minorities do not have power in the sense of resources, but nevertheless they can influence through behavioral style. Moscovici's original (1976) "genetic" theory of influence was modified in 1980 (as described above) to suggest that majorities tend to produce compliance and minorities conversion. As well as testing the conversion theory, other important work in this tradition examines the implications of minority influence for creative, divergent thinking and information processing, and the role of social identity and ingroup–outgroup membership in mediating influence reactions.

## GROUP POLARIZATION

Group polarization is an area (initially referred to as "risky shift" research) that developed to make sense of a property of norm formation that is problematic for classic theory. It is found that group interaction or some related manipulation tends to *polarize* the prevailing response tendency within a group. Where group members, for example, are seeking to reach consensus on an issue, the mean response of members (and group consensus) tends to become more extreme after interaction than the mean individual response before interaction, but in the same direction. Members do not – except under very specific conditions – simply converge on their average individual position, as one might have expected on the basis of conformity theories. The phenomenon is theoretically important and there are several contending theories (most notably, social comparison/ value theory, PERSUASIVE ARGUMENTS THEORY, and SELF-CATEGORIZATION THEORY; *see* Turner, 1991).

## OBEDIENCE TO AUTHORITY

Authority may be defined as the power to influence (or control) based on social norms, traditions, values, and rules (generally the social structure) that prescribe that one has the right to such power. Social norms not only arise from influence processes but also specify that certain persons or positions in a social hierarchy (such as elected or formally designated leaders) should have influence, be obeyed, and even believed. Obedience to authority is an example of the functioning of *legitimate power*: an internalized institutional or group framework of norms, values, customs, or procedures, which specify that such influence is appropriate, and legitimate the exercise of influence and its acceptance.

Milgram's (1974) work provides the best-known example of research on obedience to authority. In these studies, solely as a function of the instructions of the experimenter, the legitimate authority in this situation, a naive subject is induced to mete out what appears to be extreme punishment to an innocent "learner" for failing to perform a task successfully. At what point, the research asks, will the subject act to stop the obvious and increasing distress of his/her fellow participant (distress supposedly resulting from receiving electric shocks of increasing intensity) by defying authority? Other than where authority is undermined in some way, the answer seems to be much too late, if at all.

THE NATURE OF THE INFLUENCE
PROCESS
Classic and much contemporary work on influence largely adheres to the dual-process model typified by the informational versus normative distinction. Influence is supposed *either* to reflect private, informational, cognitive change *or* a largely superficial submission to group-based norms and social pressure, as if information were not socially mediated and social norms were not the product of individual reality-testing and thought.

A different view is provided by self-categorization theory (Turner, 1991). This theory proposes that there is one unified process which is both informational and normative and that shared social identity is a precondition of influence. It is assumed that people expect to agree with others socially categorized as similar to themselves (i.e., ingroup members) and that consensus amongst ingroup members implies that their behavior

is a function of the shared objective world rather than personal biases. Thus the behavior of ingroup members tends to be perceived as objectively appropriate (as providing valid information about reality) to the degree that it is consensual (i.e., normative). It is agreement with ingroup members that validates one's beliefs and disagreement (rather than the difficulty of physical reality testing) that creates uncertainty and makes mutual influence possible. This conception has been elaborated to generate novel explanations of conformity, polarization, and minority influence.

Self-categorization theory illustrates that while research on cognitive, information-processing models of persuasion, polarization, creativity and minority influence has been pursued vigorously in recent years, it has been matched, both within the influence field and elsewhere, by a resurgence of interest in GROUP PROCESSES, social identity, and intergroup relations. The challenge for the future of the field (and for social psychology as a whole) is to reunite productively the cognitive and social perspectives, to explore the interdependence of social influences and individual cognition.

*See also*: ATTITUDE CHANGE; ATTRACTION; ATTRIBUTION THEORIES; COGNITIVE DISSONANCE THEORY; CONFLICT; GROUP COHESIVENESS; GROUP PROCESSES; NORMS; OBEDIENCE; POWER; SELF-CATEGORIZATION THEORY; SELF-PERCEPTION THEORY; SOCIAL COMPARISON; SOCIAL PSYCHOLOGY; VALUES.

BIBLIOGRAPHY
Asch, S. E. (1952). *Social psychology*. Englewood Cliffs, NJ: Prentice Hall.
Deutsch, M., & Gerard, H. B. (1955). A study of normative and informational social influences upon individual judgment. *Journal of Abnormal and Social Psychology, 51,* 629–36.
Festinger, L. (1950). Informal social communication. *Psychological Review, 57,* 271–82.
French, J. R. P., & Raven, B. H. (1959). The bases of social power. In D. Cartwright (Ed.), *Studies in social power* (pp. 118–49). Ann Arbor, MI: Institute of Social Research.

Kelman, H. C. (1958). Compliance, identification, and internalization: Three processes of attitude change. *Journal of Conflict Resolution*, 2, 51–60.

Milgram, S. (1974). *Obedience to authority*. London: Tavistock.

Moscovici, S. (1976). *Social influence and social change*. London: Academic Press.

—— (1980). Towards a theory of conversion behaviour. In L. Berkowitz (Ed.), *Advances in experimental social psychology* (Vol. 13, pp. 209–39). New York: Academic Press.

Sherif, M. (1936). *The psychology of social norms*. New York: Harper.

Turner, J. C. (1991). *Social influence*. Buckingham: Open University Press; Pacific Grove, CA: Brooks/Cole.

JOHN C. TURNER

**social intelligence** To respond expertly to the problems of social life, it is necessary to be well endowed with social intelligence. As with intellectual problem solving, social problem solving requires knowledge, strategies, and plans. Social knowledge includes information about people and situations; strategies and plans include the ways in which social judgments and inferences are made, and the ways in which intentions are translated into a series of actions (*see* Cantor & Kihlstrom, 1987).

Social intelligence incorporates many of the concepts, strategies, and plans that are the subject matter of SOCIAL COGNITION. Indeed, social intelligence may be thought of as the cognitive basis of PERSONALITY. Unlike intellectual intelligence, social intelligence cannot be reduced to a few key abilities. Instead, it is multidimensional, domain or task-specific in content, and dynamic in the sense that new expertise is generated in response to changing situations. Deficits in social intelligence result in dysfunctional patterns of social interaction, and maladjustment or DEVIANCE can be conceptualized as maladaptive social intelligence. From this perspective, personality change involves changing a person's concepts, strategies, and plans.

*See also*: DEVIANCE; PERSONALITY; SOCIAL COGNITION.

BIBLIOGRAPHY
Cantor, N., & Kihlstrom, J. F. (1987). *Personality and social intelligence*. Englewood Cliffs, NJ: Prentice Hall.

SARAH E. HAMPSON

**social judgment** Stated in broad terms, social judgment is the study of how we make judgments of objects, people, or events which derive their meaning from their social context. More narrowly, it is concerned with the relevance to social psychology of processes of psychological judgment. Different views of such processes have historically directed attention to different research questions. Early psychophysical research viewed judgment as related to the measurement of perceptual sensations. Such measurement depended on inferences from observable responses, such as verbal *judgments* of the heaviness of a weight or loudness of a tone. Two main questions were distinguished: how do differences in physical stimulus intensity predict differences in judgment, and how do differences in judgment relate to differences in sensation or feeling ("psychological magnitude")?

These questions were given a new twist by Thurstone (1928). He proposed that attitudes, as a subclass of feeling, could be measured in much the same way as perceptual sensations, specifically by determining the kinds of statements on an issue with which they agree or disagree. Someone who agrees mainly with statements expressing a favorable attitude will have a more pro attitude score than someone who agrees mainly with unfavorable or anti statements. The calculation of such scores depends in turn on determining the "scale value" of each statement, i.e., how unfavorable or favorable is the attitude it expresses. Such scale values can be calculated from the ratings given by groups of independent "judges" who have the task of saying, *not* whether they themselves agree with each statement, but how anti or pro on the issue was the attitude it expresses. Conventionally, such ratings are in terms of a continuum from 1 = extremely anti to 11 = extremely pro. More controversially, Thurstone proposed that such ratings should be *unaffected by judges' own attitudes* (e.g., both pacifist and militarists would judge a statement like "No war is ever justified" as equally antiwar) (see ATTITUDE MEASUREMENT).

It was disquiet with Thurstone's assumption which really got social judgment started. Hovland and Sherif (1952) took a Thurstone scale constructed 20 years earlier to measure attitudes "toward the social position of the Negro" and reported that the ratings given by Blacks, and by Whites with pro-Black attitudes, differed substantially from those given by Whites with more segregationist opinions. In particular, the former groups rated many more statements as very unfavorable towards Black people. They related this finding to two contemporary theoretical concerns: first, to perceptual research on ADAPTATION-LEVEL which showed that stimuli were rated differently depending on the context of other stimuli with which they are presented; and second, to the so-called "New Look" research claiming that "basic" psychological processes such as MEMORY and perception would be biased by personal motives and attitudes, especially if people showed strong EGO-INVOLVEMENT in an issue.

These notions became formalized into the ASSIMILATION-CONTRAST model of social judgment. According to this model, when judges rate an attitude statement, they use their own position or viewpoint on the issue as an "anchor" or subjective reference point. That is, the judges implicitly turn the task into one of comparative judgment. What Sherif and Hovland predict is that judges with more extreme attitudes and high ego-involvement in an issue will "assimilate" statements that are close to their own opinion (more specifically, ones that fall within the "latitude" of positions they would still accept), but will "contrast" statements which are further away. In other words, more extreme judges (whether pro or anti) should show in their ratings a bilateral displacement or "polarization" towards *both* extremes of the scale.

The claim that such effects reflect anchoring processes is problematic. In psychophysics, there is considerable evidence that judgments are influenced by the value of any "anchor" or standard comparison stimulus. Commonly, a standard stimulus is presented alternately with the variable stimuli that the subjects must judge. Generally, the higher the magnitude or intensity of this anchor, the lower are the judged magnitudes of the variable stimuli. For instance a series of varied weights will all be judged as "lighter" in the presence of a heavy, as opposed to a light, anchor. This is termed a *contrast* effect. This could account for the tendency (in Hovland and Sherif, 1952) for pro-Black judges to judge more statements as anti-Black, since they would be using a more extremely pro comparison standard than other judges. Sherif and Hovland report that the opposite effect – *assimilation* – can occur when the anchor is very close in magnitude to the most extreme stimulus in the series. This involves stimuli being judged as, say, heavier in the presence of a heavy anchor. This is not a robust effect, and is sensitive to experimental instructions. Once the anchor is noticeably more extreme than any of the other stimuli, contrast is found. Such assimilation and contrast effects are *unilateral*. If an anchor weight is somewhat heavy, either *all* the other weights will be judged lighter (contrast) or *all* will be judged heavier (assimilation). These effects are quite different from the *bilateral* shifts of judgment Sherif and Hovland predict for attitude statements.

Sherif and Hovland's model fails on another account: it does not adequately explain observed findings, even their own. As predicted, judges with more pro-Black opinions seem to show greater polarization than neutral judges (i.e., assimilate some pro statements closer the favorable extreme while contrasting more anti statements towards the unfavorable end). However, the model should also predict comparable polarization for those with extremely anti opinions, and this does not happen. This asymmetry between the observed effects for extremely pro and anti judges was replicated in other studies using the same issue of attitudes towards Black people (e.g., Upshaw, 1962): all showed that more pro judges polarized most and anti judges least.

Responding to these inadequacies, Upshaw (1962) proposed his *variable perspective* model. This states that judges do not use a single anchor, but instead think of a *range of* positions they may need to take into account. If one holds the number of response categories constant, any manipulation that extends this subjective range (or "perspective") in one direction should cause a contrast effect. For instance, if someone's own attitude is more extremely pro than any of the statements presented for judgment, his or her perspective should be extended towards the pro extreme and so the statements on average should be judged as more anti. Upshaw (1962) offers evidence of such an effect, but cannot explain why judges' attitudes can still influence judgment when they are less extreme and so do not require an extension of perspective beyond the range of statements presented. Differences in polarization can also be interpreted as reflecting differences in perspective. If judges only think of a narrow range (or "perspective"), their judgments will be more polarized since more statements will fall near the extremes of this perspective. However, Upshaw offers no explanation of why judges with extremely pro-Black attitudes should have narrower perspectives than those with anti-Black attitudes. His model should be viewed more as an application of broader notions of scaling and measurement to the social judgment area than as a set of predictions concerning attitude–judgment relationships.

A wider range of social judgment phenomena is explained by *accentuation theory* (Eiser, 1990). Although originating from work on perceptual judgment, this approach emphasizes the more cognitive process of CATEGORIZATION. A considerable literature shows that judgments of stimuli are influenced by their perceived class-membership. Frequently, this influence takes the form of different categories of stimuli being judged as more separate from one another, in other words an accentuation of interclass differences. Eiser (1971) found an accentuation of the judged differences between prodrug and antidrug attitude statements in a condition where the different statements were attributed to different sources.

Turning to the influence of judges' own opinions, Eiser (1971) proposed that assimilation–contrast effects result, not from any anchoring process, but from judges categorizing statements into those acceptable and less acceptable to themselves and then *accentuating the differences* between these subjective categories. This leaves unexplained the case of anti-Black judges in Hovland and Sherif (1952) and subsequent studies. To account for this, a further principle is added: accentuation effects depend on the nature of the response scale. Specifically, it is argued that the adjectives used to label the extremes of the scale frequently differ in implied value. When the value connotations of the response scale are deliberately manipulated (so that sometimes the pro end is evaluatively positive, and sometimes the anti end), this strongly mediates the influence of judges' own attitudes on polarization of ratings. Basically, judges polarize on response scales where their "own end" is labeled by an evaluative positive term, but not on scales where they would have to apply a "bad" label to statements of which they approve.

It seems that judges try to avoid making judgments that misrepresent their *own* approval/disapproval of the statements. For instance, when asked to judge statements concerning adult authority over young people, proauthority teenagers gave more polarized ratings on scales such as "disobedient–obedient," whereas those with antiauthority attitudes polarized more on scales like "bold–timid." Likewise, opponents of nuclear power prefer not to label antinuclear statements as "alarmist," just as supporters of nuclear power prefer not to label pronuclear statements as "complacent" (*see* Eiser, 1990, for a review).

Can this explain the asymmetry in the studies using attitudes to Black people? Perhaps so, if we assume that even (some of) those with anti-Black opinions do not wish to *declare* themselves to be "unfavorable" towards Black people; they might therefore not show accentuation effects because the rating scale is evaluatively incongruent with their own acceptance/rejection of the statements. However, Romer (1983) has suggested a more banal explanation – some judges may fail to follow the instructions attentively, and simply rate as "favorable" statements they are *in favor of* (i.e., agree with) while rating as "unfavorable" any they find unacceptable. Such misinterpretation (for which Romer

finds direct evidence) would remain unde-
tected in the case of pro judges, but could
lead to anti judges reversing the direction of
their ratings from that intended by the experimenter, thus artificially reducing the polarization of the (average) scale values of the
anti group. This underlines the danger of
assuming that subjects always share the researcher's interpretation of their task.

More recent work has extended the categorization notion to consider comparisons
*within* categories. In particular, it has been
suggested that, along with sorting items into
classes, people form subjective standards of
what is "normal" or "prototypical" for that
class (*see* NORM THEORY), and judge individual
items relative to the appropriate standards for
their class. (As an everyday example, a "big"
book is considerably smaller than a "small"
house, because there are very different norms
for the sizes of books and houses). Such
norms reflect *expectations*, acquired through
learning, and these can vary considerably
between contexts. Building on these ideas,
Manis, Paskewitz, and Cutler (1986) conducted an experiment in which subjects were
presented with diagnostic test responses supposedly provided by psychiatric patients at
two hospitals. Contrasting norms were first
established for the two groups of patients, so
that one hospital appeared to have many more
disturbed patients than the other. Later, subjects had to compare pairs of patients, one
from each hospital, and rate which was the
more disturbed. The results suggest that each
patient was judged in relation to the norm for
the relevant hospital. If the hospital contained very disturbed patients, a moderately
disturbed patient was seen as *less* disturbed
than a comparable patient from a hospital
where few patients were disturbed.

Although it seems reasonable to suppose
that we make distinctions between and within
classes of objects at the same time, the evidence is not yet conclusive on how this
influences judgment. Category NORMS may
provide relevant standards for comparison,
and hence contrast, or expectations to which
category exemplars can be assimilated. This
leads into broader issues addressed by social
cognition research concerning the influence
of memory on information processing.

The term "social judgment" is also used in
DECISION MAKING research to refer to work
concerned mainly with preferences among
multiattribute objects or options. Hammond's
(1966) "social judgment theory" is essentially
a set of procedures for determining which
attributes of an object contribute most to its
perceived value. This can be an aid to policy
makers aiming to choose optimal or most
widely acceptable solutions. Questions for
research concern how different cues or pieces
of information combine to form a composite
expression.

A considerable amount of other research on
decision making could also be regarded as
part of "social judgment" although it is
usually not classified in this way. Among the
most important issues considered are those
relating to judgments of probability and inferences based on the use and misuse of
statistical information. It is well known that,
in a wide variety of cases, such judgments do
not conform to "correct" statistical principles, but instead reflect the use of informal
rules-of-thumb or cognitive HEURISTICS.
Closely related is the issue of judgment under
uncertainty, which typically means expressing preferences between options involving
combinations of outcomes of different probabilities and levels of benefits and costs. Here
again there is ample evidence that people do
not obey the axiom of normative models of
economic decision making. The "feel" of
much of this work is not especially social–
psychological, being concerned with abstract
or mathematical decision problems, but many
of the theoretical issues have application
to real-world problems such as medical
diagnosis and assessment of environmental
hazards.

Many other fields of work lie within sight
of social judgment's conventional borders.
The largest, but most diffuse, of these is that
of how we form impressions of other people
(*see* IMPRESSION FORMATION). Except insofar
as this brings in questions of STEREOTYPING,
this has made little contact with the mainstream social judgment literature here described. The most enduring question has
been that of the manner in which different
items of information are combined to form a
composite impression. More recent research

has concentrated on how interpersonal judgments are affected by the ACCESSIBILITY of information stored in memory, and by the congruency or incongruency of information with expectancies, including those based on group stereotypes.

More closely tied to social judgment's traditional concerns with scaling and measurement is research on methodological biases in various kinds of opinion surveys and self-report measures of behavior (*see* SURVEY RESEARCH METHODS). Work by Schwarz and colleagues demonstrates that responses can be strongly influenced by the range of categories in terms of which people have to express their judgments. For instance, if people are asked how much television they (or people on average) watch each day in terms of categories from "up to half an hour" to "more than two-and-a-half hours," they report less viewing than if responding in terms of categories from "up to two-and-a-half hours" to "more than four-and-a-half hours" (Schwarz et al., 1985). The response scale can thus provide expectations about what responses would be "normal". A variety of other biasing factors have been investigated, for instance concerning the order in which people are asked questions concerning their happiness and quality of life (*see* LIFE SATISFACTION). Judgments of mood and happiness generally appear to be susceptible to contextual influences. Parducci (1984) has proposed that happiness ratings reflect the range (or perspective) as well as the skewness of previous life-events in a manner directly comparable to psychophysical judgments. More general support can be found for the view that accessible memories can both prime present MOOD states, and provide standards with which new experiences are compared.

Judgmental processes are now seen to be involved in many different areas of social psychological research. As a consequence, the field of social judgment is much more diffuse than when the primary question was that of how ratings of the favorability of attitude statements are affected by judges' own opinions. However, most of the classic questions – such as the influence of subjective categories and comparison standards – still have relevance and are being thrown into sharper focus by recent advances in the study of cognitive processes.

*See also*: ATTITUDE MEASUREMENT AND QUESTIONNAIRE DESIGN; CATEGORIZATION; DECISION MAKING; HEURISTICS; IMPRESSION FORMATION; LIFE SATISFACTION; MOOD; MEMORY; NORM THEORY; NORMS; STEREOTYPING; SURVEY METHODS.

BIBLIOGRAPHY

Eiser, J. R. (1971). Enhancement of contrast in the absolute judgment of attitude statements. *Journal of Personality and Social Psychology*, *17*, 1–10.

——(1990). *Social judgment*. Buckingham: Open University Press.

Hammond, K. R. (Ed.) (1966). *The psychology of Egon Brunswik*. New York: Holt, Rinehart & Winston.

Hovland, C. I. & Sherif, M. (1952). Judgmental phenomena and scales of attitude measurement: Item displacement in Thurstone scales. *Journal of Abnormal and Social Psychology*, *47*, 822–32.

Manis, M., Paskewitz, J. R. & Cotler, S. (1986). Stereotypes and social judgment. *Journal of Personality and Social Psychology*, *50*, 461–73.

Parducci, A. (1984). Value judgments: Toward a relational theory of happiness. In J. R. Eiser (Ed.), *Attitudinal judgment* (pp. 3–21) New York: Springer-Verlag.

Romer, D. (1983). Effects of own attitude on polarization of judgment. *Journal of Personality and Social Psychology*, *44*, 273–84.

Schwarz, N., Hippler, H. J., Deutsch, S., & Strack, F. (1985). Response scales: Effects of category range on reported behavior and comparative judgments. *Public Opinion Quarterly*, *49*, 388–95.

Thurstone, L. L. (1928). Attitudes can be measured. *American Journal of Sociology*, *33*, 529–54.

Upshaw, H. S. (1962). Own attitude as an anchor in equal-appearing intervals. *Journal of Abnormal and Social Psychology*, *64*, 85–96.

J. RICHARD EISER

**social justice** This study explores how people's evaluations and behaviors are influenced by their judgments about what is fair. Social psychologists have a long history of interest in the basis of people's reactions to their experiences with others. This interest includes a concern with: the factors shaping people's behavioral choices about entering into or leaving social relationships, groups, and organizations; the basis of people's behavioral choices when dealing with others while in relationships; and the origin of feelings of satisfaction and dissatisfaction about outcomes, about groups, and about authorities and rules when people are involved in relationships with others.

Social justice theories have helped social psychologists to understand how people react to their experiences with other people. They suggest that people's subjective satisfaction with outcomes, authorities, and rules and their behavioral choices are not only affected by concerns about maximizing personal gain. They are also independently influenced by people's judgments about what is "fair" or "just."

One of the major contributions of the social science research which was conducted during World War II was the development of the theory of RELATIVE DEPRIVATION. That theory suggests that subjective satisfaction is not a simple reaction to the objective quality of a person's outcomes when dealing with others (Merton & Kitt, 1950). Rather, people evaluate the quality of their outcomes by comparing them to the outcomes received by others. Implicit in such comparisons is a model of what they "deserve" relative to others, that people use to decide how their outcomes ought to compare to those received by others.

The theory of relative deprivation is an important development within social psychology. It suggests that subjective feelings will not necessarily mirror objective conditions. On the contrary, people can potentially be very satisfied with objectively poor, unfavorable, conditions, or they can be dissatisfied with more favorable outcomes. What is important is how people interpret their experiences. This recognition of the importance of interpreting experience moved social psychology away from models of human feeling that link subjective feelings closely to objective

conditions. It anticipates the more complex cognitive models of subjective judgments about social interaction which developed later in the context of theories of SOCIAL COGNITION.

Relative deprivation theories have had an important influence on efforts to understand the occurrence of riots and other types of collective disorder. One seeming paradox, explained by relative deprivation theory, is when civil disorders occur. For example, a period of racially motivated riots occurred in the United States after the occurrence of the civil rights movement, when the objective conditions of African Americans had been dramatically improved. Theories of relative deprivation suggested that dissatisfaction occurred when people's expectations differed from what they obtained. Following a period of improvement, people expected continued improvement. Riots occurred when the rate of improvements slowed, creating a discrepancy between expectations and reality. Paradoxically, discontent was greater following a period of improvement than it was after a period of steady levels of outcomes, even if the level of those outcomes was low.

Relative deprivation theories also explained who rioted. The people who participated in riots were not found to be those who were the least well off. Rather, more advantaged African Americans were found to riot. Studies found that those African Americans who were better educated and had better jobs were more likely to compare themselves to Whites than were less advantaged African Americans. Hence, although they were objectively better off, their experience was of greater deprivation relative to their "comparison" others (*see* SOCIAL COMPARISON).

An important conceptual distinction in relative deprivation theory, introduced by Runciman (1966), is between individual egoistic deprivation and group-based fraternal deprivation. A person might judge, for example, that they were personally deprived and/or that a social group to which they belonged (e.g., due to their gender, racial/ethnic background, age, etc.) was deprived. Subsequent studies have suggested that feelings of fraternal deprivation were especially likely to lead to collective behavior.

Studies examining the distinction between feelings of personal and group-based deprivation have found that people separate these judgments, with the result that they may feel personally deprived without feeling fraternal deprivation and they may feel that their group is deprived, but that they are not. Studies of disadvantaged groups suggest that the latter pattern is more common. For example, studies of working women find that most believe that women in general were discriminated against, but that their own pay was fair.

Studies of relative deprivation have been hampered by an inability to specify in advance to whom people will compare themselves, a topic addressed by theories of social comparison. Relative deprivation theory also lacks a theory explaining how people know to what they are entitled. For example, do they deserve the same as others, and, if not, what justifies discrepancies among people?

An important advance in theories of social justice was the development of a model of DISTRIBUTIVE JUSTICE to explain the principles underlying people's judgments that their outcomes were or were not fair. That model was EQUITY THEORY (Adams, 1965). It was originally developed in the context of work organizations to explain workers' reactions to their wages, and subsequently developed as a general theory of justice (see Walster, Walster, & Berscheid, 1978). Equity theory was important because it articulated a criterion against which individuals were suggested to judge the fairness of their wages – that relative wages (outputs) should equal relative work contributions (inputs). Equity theory hypothesized that both satisfaction and behavior were linked not to objective outcome levels, but to outcomes received relative to those judged to be equitable.

Equity theory inspired a large number of studies of wage satisfaction, studies which generally supported the equity theory model. In particular, people were found to be more satisfied when they received equitable outcomes than they were when they received larger or smaller outcomes which they viewed as unfair. These feelings were found to have a behavioral effect, with workers leaving organizations characterized by inequity to join organizations in which wages were more fairly distributed, even if such a move led them to be less highly paid.

An important contribution of equity theory was the development of the distinction between actual and psychological equity. It was recognized that people receiving inequitable levels of outcomes could restore equity in two ways. One is to adjust their work effort, restoring actual equity between their work inputs and their wages. Another is to adjust their evaluations of work difficulty, justifying the existing work effort/wage ratio, and restoring psychological equity. Those unjustly advantaged benefit by restoring psychological equity, those unjustly disadvantaged by restoring actual equity.

In exchange relationships the tension between the restoration of actual and psychological equity can lead to conflicts between the advantaged and the disadvantaged. The advantaged may add insult to injury by first gaining material advantages and then justifying those advantages by enhancing their evaluations of their own virtues and/or derogating the characteristics of those receiving lesser outcomes. Equity theory research suggests that the disadvantaged can increase the likelihood of restoring actual equity by indicating to the advantaged exactly what type and amount of compensation will restore equity. Harmdoers are more likely to attempt to restore actual equity if they can do so completely.

Equity theory emphasizes the centrality of judgments about principles of justice or deservingness to people's reactions to the outcomes they receive in groups. It further links those judgments to the application of the principle of equity. In an important qualification of equity theory, Deutsch (1975) distinguished these two questions. He suggested that people might evaluate their outcomes using judgments of justice or deservingness, but might use different principles. He suggested that people might also use the principles of equality and need. Subsequent research has suggested that under different circumstances people utilize a wide variety of principles of distributive justice, including equity, equality, need, and many others.

Distributive justice research has generally focused on issues of individual deserving, rather than the issues of group deserving represented by the concept of fraternal deprivation. However, it has been recognized that microjustice concerns are distinct from judgments about justice on the level of groups and/or society. These principles of distributive justice differ from those used to make macrojustice evaluations. On the microlevel, people strongly endorsed the use of equity. However, on the macrolevel they regarded the outcome distributions that developed in equity-based systems as unfair, feeling that they were too unequal.

Justice theories also recognize that people are concerned with the way outcomes are distributed in groups. In addition to evaluating the fairness of outcomes, people evaluate the fairness of the procedures by which those outcomes are arrived at. Such fairness judgments have been labeled judgments of PROCEDURAL JUSTICE.

Although many justice researchers have noted the importance of procedural issues (see Leventhal, 1980), Thibaut and Walker (1975) first formalized the idea of "procedural" justice as a distinct social justice concern. They hypothesized that people's evaluations of the fairness of decision-making procedures have an influence on their reactions to the outcomes of those procedures which is distinct from their reactions to outcomes themselves. They demonstrated the occurrence of such procedural justice effects in a series of studies comparing the adversarial and the inquisitorial procedures for dispute resolution.

Since the publication of Thibaut and Walker's book *Procedural justice* (Thibaut & Walker, 1975), a substantial body of research has been conducted on procedural justice issues. Subsequent studies have demonstrated that people react to procedures in a wide variety of settings, including legal trial procedures, studies of plea bargaining and mediation, and studies of police–citizen interactions. Procedural justice effects have also been found in organizational, interpersonal, political, and educational settings (see Lind & Tyler, 1988, for a complete review).

In studies of personal satisfaction both procedural and distributive justice are typically found to be important. However, the evaluation of group authorities, institutions, and rules has been found to be primarily influenced by procedural justice judgments. This has been found in studies of legal, political, and managerial authorities. Similarly, procedural justice considerations have been found to be central to the willingness to accept third-party decisions and to follow group rules. These findings suggest that procedural justice is especially important when people are dealing with third parties, like managers, judges, parents, and political leaders.

The literatures outlined suggest that people care about issues of social justice. However, social psychologists have not agreed about the nature of the motive which leads to concerns about justice. One approach flows from SOCIAL EXCHANGE models, which suggest that justice concerns develop from people's interest in maximizing their attainment of desired outcomes from others. To do so in social interactions, people collectively develop mutually accepted systems for allocating resources, systems whose rules are codified in terms of fairness. People expect others to follow these rules, and expect to follow the same rules themselves (Walster, Walster, & Berscheid, 1978). Hence, justice concerns arise out of the motivation to gain personally from social interactions. People follow justice rules as long as it is in their interest to do so.

Thibaut and Walker's control theory of procedural justice is also based on social exchange motives (Thibaut & Walker, 1975). Thibaut and Walker suggest that people normally prefer to control decisions which influence their own outcomes when they are in negotiation with others (see BARGAINING). Hence, they resist third-party intervention in conflicts with others. However, people sometimes feel that they cannot resolve conflicts in bilateral negotiation, so they reluctantly give some amount of the control over decisions to a third party. When they do so, people try to keep indirect control over outcomes by maintaining their opportunities to influence the third party through evidence presentation (i.e., voice or process control). People view procedures as fair if those procedures allow them to control the presentation of evidence to third parties. In other words, as with distributive justice, people's justice judgments are linked to considerations of self-interest.

It has also been argued that people value evidence that they are receiving justice as an indicator of the quality of their relationship to the group and its authorities (Lind & Tyler, 1988; Tyler & Lind, 1992). Because of such relational concerns people in organized groups do not focus on the number of resources they receive from others, but on their status within the group. High status has positive implications for SELF-ESTEEM and feelings of self-worth. When people are treated rudely and without respect and concern, in other words without procedural fairness, by authorities in a group, that communicates information about their low social status. Conversely, when people are treated with respect by honest, competent authorities, who listen to them, care about their problems, and try to treat them fairly, that communicates information about their high social status. High status is not only an issue of self-esteem and self-worth. High-status group members also believe that the authorities involved will treat them fairly, so they will not be disadvantaged by group membership.

The models of justice outlined suggest that there may be limits to the scope of justice concerns. Deutsch, for example, elaborates the implications of the instrumental view. He suggests that people may only care about treating people fairly if they have a productive exchange relationship with them. Outside of the scope of such relationships, people may not care if they are treating others fairly. The relational perspective also suggests that justice may only be an issue in some relationships. However, it links justice concerns to the scope of people's identification with others.

Other social psychologists have argued that people are intrinsically motivated to behave fairly. Lerner (1980) suggests that people have a basic desire to behave fairly and to believe that justice exists in the world (the JUST WORLD PHENOMENON). In addition to noting the previously outlined evidence that fairness shapes how people feel and what they do, Lerner points out that people engage in cognitive distortions to maintain the belief that the world is a "just place." If people see someone else suffer, for example, they distort their judgments to decide that they deserved to suffer even if given evidence that the

suffering is actually randomly determined. This suggests that people are motivated to distort their judgments to support the belief that people get what they "deserve" in life. Lerner's argument is supported by other findings demonstrating that, even when people have power over others and can do to them whatever they desire, as in wars, they typically engage in considerable cognitive effort to justify their actions and make them seem "just." If people's desire to see justice done is intrinsic, it should extend to all dealings with others, not just to productive exchange relations or to people linked by social bonds.

*See also*: BARGAINING; RELATIVE DEPRIVATION; SELF-ESTEEM; SOCIAL COGNITION; SOCIAL COMPARISON.

BIBLIOGRAPHY

Adams, J. S. (1965). Inequity in social exchange. In L. Berkowitz (Ed.), *Advances in experimental social psychology* (Vol. 2, pp. 267–99). New York: Academic Press.

Deutsch, M. (1975). Equity, equality, and need: What determines which value will be used as the basis for distributive justice? *Journal of Social Issues, 31*, 137–49.

Lerner, M. J. (1980). *The belief in a just world*. New York: Plenum.

Leventhal, G. S. (1980). What should be done with equity theory? New approaches to the study of fairness in social relationships. In K. Gergen, M. Greenberg, & R. Willis (Eds.), *Social exchange* (pp. 27–55). New York: Plenum.

Lind, E. A., & Tyler, T. R. (1988). *The social psychology of procedural justice*. New York: Plenum.

Merton, R. K., & Kitt, A. S. (1950). Contributions to the theory of reference group behavior. In R. K. Merton & P. F. Lazarsfeld (Eds.), *Continuities in social research: Studies in the scope and method of "The American Soldier"* (pp. 40–105). Glencoe, IL: Free Press.

Runciman, W. G. (1966). *Relative deprivation and social justice: A study of attitudes to social inequality in twentieth-century England*. Berkeley, CA: University of California Press.

Thibaut, J., & Walker, L. (1975). *Procedural justice: A psychological analysis*. Hillsdale, NJ: Lawrence Erlbaum.

Tyler, T. R., & Lind, E. A. (1992). A relational model of authority in groups. In M. Zanna (Ed.), *Advances in experimental social psychology* (Vol. 25, pp. 115–91). San Diego, CA: Academic Press.

Walster, E., Walster, G. W., & Berscheid, E. (1978). *Equity: Theory and research*. Boston, MA: Allyn & Bacon.

TOM R. TYLER

**social learning** This is concerned with the processes by which social influences alter human thought, affect, and action. The early theories of social learning relied heavily on principles of reinforcement to explain how human behavior is acquired and modified (*see* Dollard & Miller, 1950; Rotter, 1954). In the conception of social learning through response consequences, rewards strengthen behavior, punishments weaken or suppress it. The more contemporary view of social learning is founded on a theory that assigns a central role to cognitive, vicarious, self-regulative, and self-reflective processes in human functioning (Bandura, 1986). Sociocognitive theory addresses the three major aspects of human adaptation and change: the origins of human behavior, the mechanisms governing its activation and direction; and its long-term regulation.

Social learning theory is based on a causal model involving triadic reciprocal causation. In this model environmental influences, behavior, and cognitive, biological, and other personal factors operate as interacting determinants that affect each other bidirectionally. Reciprocality does not mean that the different sources of influences are of equal strength. Some may be stronger than others. Nor do the reciprocal influences all occur simultaneously. It takes time for a causal factor to exert its influence and activate reciprocal influences. Reciprocal causation provides people with opportunities to exercise some control over events in their lives, as well as setting limits of self-direction. Because of the bidirectionality of influence, people are both producers and products of their environment. People are characterized in terms of a number of basic capabilities. These include the capability for symbolization, forethought, vicarious learning, self-regulation, and self-reflection.

SYMBOLIZING CAPABILITY
The advanced capacity for symbolization provides humans with a powerful tool for comprehending their environment and for creating and altering environmental conditions that touch virtually every aspect of their lives. Most environmental influences operate through cognitive processes (*see* Cantor & Kihlstrom, 1987). Cognitive factors partly determine which environmental events will be observed, what meaning will be conferred on them, whether they leave any lasting effects, what emotional impact and motivating power they will have, and how the information they convey will be organized for future use. It is with symbols that people process and transform transient experiences into cognitive models that serve as guides for reasoning and action. With the aid of symbols, people give structure, meaning, and continuity to their experiences.

People gain understanding and expand their knowledge by operating symbolically on the information derived from direct and vicarious experiences. The remarkable flexibility of symbolization enables people to create ideas that transcend their sensory experiences. Through the medium of symbols they can communicate with others at any distance in time and space. However, in keeping with the interactional perspective, social learning theory devotes much attention to the social origins of thought and the mechanisms through which sociostructural factors exert their influence on cognitive functioning.

VICARIOUS CAPABILITY
Psychological theories have traditionally emphasized learning through the effects of one's exploratory actions. Human behavior is, indeed, extensively regulated by its effects. Patterns of behavior that produce positive outcomes are readily adopted and used, whereas those that bring unrewarding or punishing outcomes are generally discarded (*see* Rotter, 1954). However, external consequences

are not the only kind of outcomes that influence human behavior. People profit from the successes and mistakes of others as well as from their own direct experiences. As a general rule, they do things they have seen succeed and avoid those they have seen fail. Observed outcomes exert their influence through perceived similarity that one is likely to experience analogous outcomes for similar courses of action and that one possesses the capabilities to produce the required performances (*see* Bandura, 1986). People also influence their own motivation and behavior by the positive and negative consequences they create for themselves. Self-regulation of behavior through anticipatory self-evaluative reactions will be addressed later.

Because outcomes exert their influence mainly through forethought, they have little or no impact until people discover how outcomes are linked to actions in one's environment (*see* Brewer, 1974). This is no easy matter. In everyday life, courses of action usually produce mixed effects, they may occur immediately or far removed in time, the same behavior may produce different effects depending on where, when, and toward whom it is performed, and many situational factors influence how actions affect the environment. Such causal ambiguity provides a fertile ground for misjudgment. When belief about the effects of actions differs from actuality, behavior is weakly controlled by its actual consequences until repeated experience instills realistic beliefs. But it is not always one's beliefs that change in the direction of social reality. Acting on erroneous beliefs can alter how others behave, thus shaping the social reality in the direction of the misbeliefs (*see* Snyder, 1981).

If knowledge and skills could be acquired only by direct experience, human development would be greatly retarded, not to mention exceedingly tedious and hazardous. A culture could never transmit its language, mores, social practices, and adaptive competencies if they had to be shaped tediously in each new member by response consequences without the benefit of models who exemplify the cultural patterns. The abbreviation of the acquisition process through MODELING is vital for survival as well as for human development. This is because natural endowment provides few inborn skills and errors can produce costly or even fatal consequences. Moreover, the constraints of time, resources, and mobility impose severe limits on the situations and activities that can be directly explored for the acquisition of new knowledge and competencies.

PRIMACY AND SCOPE OF
MODELING INFLUENCES

Humans have evolved an advanced capacity for observational learning that enables them to expand rapidly their knowledge and competencies that have stood the test of time on the basis of information conveyed by modeling influences. Indeed, virtually all behavioral, cognitive, and affective learning resulting from direct experience can occur vicariously by observing people's behavior and its consequences for them (*see* Bandura, 1986; Rosenthal & Zimmerman, 1978).

Much learning occurs either deliberately or inadvertently by observing those around one. However, a vast amount of information about human values, thinking skills, and styles of behavior is gained from models in the MASS MEDIA. A major significance of symbolic modeling lies in its wide-reaching influence. Unlike learning by doing, which requires shaping the actions of each individual through repeated trial-and-error experiences, in observational learning a single model can transmit new ways of thinking and behaving simultaneously to large groups of people in widely dispersed places. There is another aspect of symbolic modeling that magnifies its psychological and social impact. During the course of their daily lives, people have direct contact with only a small sector of the physical and social environment. Consequently, their conceptions of social reality are greatly influenced by vicarious experiences – by what they see and hear – without direct experiential correctives. The more people's images of reality depend upon the media's symbolic environment, the greater is its social impact.

Most psychological theories were formulated long before the advent of enormous advances in the technology of COMMUNICATION. As a result, they give insufficient attention to the increasingly powerful role that the symbolic environment plays in present-day human lives. The video system feeding off satellites has become the dominant vehicle for disseminating symbolic environments both within and across societies. New ideas and social practices are now being rapidly diffused by symbolic modeling within a society and from one society to another (*see* Bandura, 1986; Rogers & Kincaid, 1981).

## DIVERSE EFFECTS OF MODELING

Modeling influences can have diverse psychological effects. First, they foster acquisition of new competencies, cognitive skills, and behavior patterns. Observational learning is governed by four subfunctions. *Attentional processes* determine what is observed and extracted from the profusion of modeling influences. Cognitive *representational processes* facilitate memory of what has been observed. Symbolic conceptions are translated into appropriate courses of action through a *behavioral production process*. People do not perform everything they learn. Performance of observationally learned behavior is governed by *motivational processes* based on three major types of incentive motivators – the consequences people experience directly, those they see happening to others, and those they create for themselves.

In addition to cultivating new competencies, modeling influences can strengthen or weaken restraints over behavior patterns by the information they convey about the probable rewarding or punishing consequences of modeled courses of action. People are easily aroused by the emotional expressions of others. What gives significance to vicarious emotional arousal is that observers can acquire lasting attitudes, and emotional proclivities toward persons, places, or things that have been associated with modeled positive or negative emotional experiences. The actions of models can also serve as social prompts that activate, channel, and support previously learned behavior. Thus, the types of models that prevail within a social milieu partly determine which human qualities, from among many alternatives, are selectively encouraged.

In sum, modeling influences serve diverse functions – as tutors, inhibitors, disinhibitors, social prompters, emotion arousers, and shapers of values and conceptions of reality.

## SELF-REGULATORY CAPABILITY

People are not simply reactors to their immediate environment nor are they steered by their past. They are self-reactors with a capacity for self-direction. Most human behavior, being purposive, is regulated by forethought. People motivate themselves and guide their actions by setting goals for themselves and anticipating the likely consequences of prospective actions. Future events cannot be causes of current motivation and action because they have no actual existence. However, by being represented cognitively in the present, foreseeable future events are converted into current motivators and regulators of behavior.

The self-regulation of motivation, affect and action operates partly through internal standards and evaluative reactions to one's own behavior (*see* Bandura, 1991a). Goals and behavioral standards motivate by enlisting self-evaluative involvement in the activity. People seek self-satisfactions from fulfilling valued goals, and are prompted to intensify their efforts by discontent with substandard performances. Perceived self-efficacy is another cognitive factor that plays an influential role in the exercise of personal control over motivation. Whether negative discrepancies between internal standards and attainments are motivating or discouraging is partly determined by people's beliefs that they can attain the goals they set for themselves. Those who harbor self-doubts about their capabilities are easily dissuaded by failure. Those who are assured of their capabilities intensify their efforts when they fail to achieve what they seek and they persist until they succeed.

Most theories of self-regulation are founded on a negative feedback system. In this view, negative discrepancy between one's perceived performance and an adopted standard motivates action to reduce the disparity. However, self-regulation by negative discrepancy tells only half the story and not necessarily the more interesting half. In fact, people are proactive, aspiring organisms. Human self-regulation relies on *discrepancy production* as well as *discrepancy reduction*. People motivate and guide their actions by setting themselves challenging goals and then mobilizing their skills and effort to reach them. After people attain the goal they have been pursuing, those with a strong sense of efficacy set higher goals for themselves. Adopting further challenges creates new motivating discrepancies to be mastered.

## SOCIAL AND MORAL
## SELF-REGULATORY STANDARDS

In areas of functioning involving achievement strivings and cultivation of competencies, the internal standards that are selected as a mark of adequacy are progressively raised as knowledge and skills are acquired and challenges are met. However, in many areas of social and moral behavior the internal standards that serve as the basis for regulating one's conduct have greater stability. People do not change from week to week what they regard as right or wrong or good or bad. After they adopt a standard of morality, their evaluative self-sanctions for actions that match or violate their personal standards serve as the regulatory influences. People do things that give them self-satisfaction and a sense of self-worth. They refrain from behaving in ways that violate their moral standards because it will bring self-disapproval. Self-sanctions thus keep conduct in line with internal standards.

Moral standards do not function as fixed internal regulators of conduct. Self-regulatory mechanisms do not operate unless they are activated, and there are many psychosocial processes by which moral reactions can be disengaged from inhumane conduct (*see* Bandura, 1991b). Selective activation and disengagement of internal control permits different types of conduct with the same moral standards. One set of mechanisms disengages moral control by *moral justification*. What is culpable is made personally and socially acceptable by portraying it in the service of moral purposes. Self-deplored acts can also be made righteous by *advantageous comparison* with more flagrant inhumanities.

*Euphemistic language* provides another convenient device for masking reprehensible activities or even conferring a respectable status upon them.

Self-sanctions are activated most strongly when personal causation of detrimental outcomes is apparent. Another set of disengagement practices operates by obscuring or distorting the relationship between actions and the effects they cause. This is achieved by *displacement of responsibility* for detrimental conduct to others, or by *diffusing responsibility* through division of labor, GROUP DECISION MAKING, and group action. Additional ways of weakening deterring self-sanctions operate through *disregard or distortion of the consequences of action*. As long as the detrimental results of one's conduct are ignored, minimized, distorted, or disbelieved there is little reason for self-censure to be activated.

The final set of disengagement practices operates on how perpetrators view the people they harm. Self-sanctions against cruel conduct can be disengaged or blunted by *dehumanization*, which divests people of human qualities or invests them with bestial qualities. *Attribution of blame* to victims is still another expedient that can serve self-exonerative purposes. By blaming victims or circumstances, not only are one's own actions excusable but one can even feel self-righteous in the process. Because internalized controls can be selectively activated and disengaged, marked changes in moral conduct can be achieved without altering people's personality structures, moral principles, or self-evaluative systems.

The self-regulation of conduct is not entirely an intrapsychic affair, nor do people operate as autonomous moral agents impervious to the social realities in which they are enmeshed. In the interactionist perspective of social cognitive theory, moral conduct is regulated by an interplay between thought, conduct, self-sanctions, and a network of social influences.

## SELF-REFLECTIVE CAPABILITY

If there is any characteristic that is distinctively human, it is the capability for reflective self-consciousness. This enables people to analyze their experiences and to think about their own thought processes. By reflecting on their varied experiences and on what they know, they can derive generic knowledge about themselves and the world around them. People not only gain understanding through reflection, they evaluate and alter their own thinking by this means. In verifying thought by self-reflective means, people monitor their ideas, act on them or predict occurrences from them, then judge from the results the adequacy of their thoughts, and change them accordingly. Judgments concerning the validity and functional value of one's thinking are formed by comparing how well thoughts match some indicator of reality. Four different modes of thought verification can be distinguished. They include *enactive, vicarious, persuasory*, and *logical* forms.

Enactive verification relies on the adequacy of the fit between one's regulative thoughts and the results of one's actions. Good matches verify their reasoning; mismatches tend to refute it. In the vicarious mode of thought verification, observing other people's behavior and its effects serves as a way of checking the correctness of one's own thinking about what leads to what. A related way of evaluating the soundness of thinking relies on comparing one's thoughts to the judgments of others. This mode is used heavily when verification by direct experience is either difficult or impossible. In the course of development, people acquire rules of inference. By reasoning from what is already known, they can derive knowledge about things that extend beyond their experience and check the validity of their reasoning.

Self-reflectivity entails shifting the perspective of the same agent rather than reifying different internal agents or selves regulating each other. Thus, in their daily lives people act on their thoughts and later analyze how well their thoughts have served them in managing events. But it is one and the same person who is doing the thinking and later evaluating the adequacy of one's knowledge, thinking skills, and action strategies. The shift in perspective does not transform one from an agent to an object. One is just as much an agent reflecting on one's experiences as in executing the original courses of action.

## SELF-EFFICACY APPRAISAL

Among the types of thoughts that affect human development and functioning, none is more central or pervasive than people's judgments of their capabilities to exercise control over their own functioning and over events that affect their lives. The self-efficacy mechanism plays a central role in human agency (*see* Bandura, 1986). People's beliefs in their efficacy influence how they think, feel, act, and motivate themselves. Such beliefs influence what people choose to do, how much effort they invest in activities, how long they persevere in the face of obstacles and failure experiences, whether their thought patterns are self-hindering or self-enhancing, and how much stress and despondency they experience during anticipatory and actual transactions with the environment. A high sense of self-efficacy pays off in performance accomplishments and personal well-being.

Viewed from the social learning perspective, human nature is characterized by a vast potentiality that can be developed by direct and vicarious experience into a variety of forms within biological limits. To say that a major distinguishing mark of humans is their endowed plasticity is not to say that they have no nature or that they come structureless. The plasticity, which is intrinsic to the nature of humans, depends upon specialized neurophysiological mechanisms and structures that have evolved over time. These advanced neural systems, which are specialized for processing, retaining, and using coded information, provide the capacity for the very characteristics that are distinctly human – generative symbolization, forethought, symbolic communication, evaluative self-regulation, and reflective self-consciousness.

## THE NATURE OF HUMAN NATURE

Most patterns of human behavior are organized by individual experience and retained in neural codes, rather than being provided readymade by extensive inborn programming. Although human thought and conduct may be developed largely through experience, innate endowments enter into every form of behavior to some degree. Genetic factors and neural systems affect behavioral potentialities and place constraints on capabilities (*see* GENETIC INFLUENCES). Even in behavior formed almost entirely through experience, rudimentary elements are present as part of the natural endowment. Similarly, action patterns that draw heavily on inborn elements require appropriate experience to be developed. Sensory systems and brain structures are alterable by environmental influences. Because behavior contains mixtures of inborn elements and learned patterns, dichotomous thinking, which separates activities into innate and acquired categories, is seriously inaccurate.

*See also*: COMMUNICATION; GENETIC INFLUENCE; GROUP DECISION MAKING; MASS MEDIA; MODELING.

BIBLIOGRAPHY

Bandura, A. (1986). *Social foundations of thought and action: A social cognitive theory*. Englewood Cliffs, NJ: Prentice Hall.

—— (1991a). Self-regulation of motivation through anticipatory and self-reactive mechanisms. In R. A. Dienstbier (Ed.), *Perspectives on motivation: Nebraska symposium on motivation* (Vol. 38, pp. 69–164). Lincoln, NE: University of Nebraska Press.

—— (1991b). Social cognitive theory of moral thought and action. In W. M. Kurtines & J. L. Gewirtz (Eds.), *Handbook of moral behavior and development* (Vol. 1, pp. 71–129). Hillsdale, NJ: Lawrence Erlbaum.

Brewer, W. F. (1974). There is no convincing evidence for operant or classical conditioning in adult humans. In W. B. Weimer & D. S. Palermo (Eds.), *Cognition and the symbolic processes* (pp. 1–42). Hillsdale, NJ: Lawrence Erlbaum.

Cantor, N., & Kihlstrom, J. F. (1987). *Personality and social intelligence*. Englewood Cliffs, NJ: Prentice Hall.

Dollard, J., & Miller, N. E. (1950). *Personality and psychotherapy*. New York: McGraw-Hill.

Rogers, E. M., & Kincaid, D. L. (1981). *Communication networks: Toward a new paradigm for research*. New York: Free Press.

Rosenthal, T. L., & Zimmerman, B. J. (1978). *Social learning and cognition*. New York: Academic Press.

Rotter, J. B. (1954). *Social learning and clinical psychology*. Englewood Cliffs, NJ: Prentice Hall.

Snyder, M. (1981). On the self-perpetuating nature of social stereotypes. In D. L. Hamilton (Ed.), *Cognitive processes in stereotyping and intergroup behavior* (pp. 182–212). Hillsdale, NJ: Lawrence Erlbaum.

ALBERT BANDURA

**social loafing** Described as the tendency for individuals to exert less effort on a task when working for a group than when working for themselves, social loafing has been demonstrated across a variety of tasks and cultures, and can be dramatically reduced by making individual efforts identifiable within the group.

In the mid-1880s Max Ringelmann, a French agricultural engineer interested in determining the relative work efficiency of horses, oxen, men, and machines, completed perhaps the world's first social psychological experiment, although it was not published for almost thirty years and then only in an obscure (to psychologists, at least) outlet (Kravitz & Martin, 1986). Ringelmann's procedure was simple; he asked students at the agricultural school of Grand-Jouan to pull as hard as they could on a rope, alone and in groups of two, three, and eight. One would expect three workers pulling together to exert three times as much force as one person, and eight people to exert eight times as much. Ringelmann's results defied these expectations: groups of three averaged only two and a half times, and groups of eight less than four times the rate of an isolated worker.

Ringelmann's results are important not only because they violate a common stereotype that team cohesiveness can lead to increased effort, but because they seem to contradict Zajonc's popular theory of SOCIAL FACILITATION, which states that the mere presence of either coperformers or an audience should enhance the performance of individuals engaged in simple tasks such as rope-pulling. Steiner's (1972) resolution of this conflict was to suggest that group performance was reduced by coordination losses from the $N(N-1)/2$ links among the $N$ individuals working together in a group.

In 1979, Latané, Williams, and Harkins, intrigued with the similarity of Ringelmann's results to the social inhibition of bystander intervention, wondered whether SOCIAL IMPACT THEORY could account for both. Participants in their initial experiment came to the laboratory in groups of six, were seated in a semicircle, and asked to yell or clap as loudly as they could, either alone, in pairs, in groups of four, or all together. Performance on this simple and well-learned task was measured with a sound-level meter. Group members influenced each other in two ways: First, they seemed to adapt or conform their individual efforts to those of their teammates. Second, as with Ringelmann's students, the total amount of noise produced was not proportional to the number of people producing it: pairs made 1.4, foursomes 2.0, and groups of six only 2.4 times as much noise as single individuals. As in the case of rope pulling, however, much of this reduction could be attributed to coordination losses, especially since sound cancellation is a well-known physical phenomenon.

Inspired by an ingenious technique developed by Ingham et al., Latané and his colleagues asked participants to wear blindfolds and listen to masking noises over earphones to reduce CONFORMITY, while measuring sound production in "pseudogroups" in which participants were told they were shouting in groups when actually shouting alone. Participants made only 82 percent as much noise when they thought they clapped or yelled with one other person, and only 74 percent when they thought five others worked with them as when they worked alone, providing strong evidence for reduced effort in groups. Latané et al. coined the term "social loafing" to describe this phenomenon, which they regarded as a kind of social disease – a disease in that it results in a reduction in human efficiency, social in

that it results from the presence or actions of other people. Social loafing has now been shown with a variety of meaningful and trivial tasks involving both physical and mental effort in both face-to-face and computer-mediated e-mail groups. It seems to be a very robust phenomenon, occurring in swimming squads, production teams, BRAINSTORMING groups, and evaluation committees.

What causes social loafing? Can it be cured? Considerable evidence now suggests that *identifiability* is the key (*see*, e.g., Williams, Harkins, & Latané, 1981). Making individual efforts identifiable, even when people are working in groups, can eliminate loafing. For example, swim team members swim faster in individual than relay races where their efforts are not identifiable. When individual efforts in relays are made identifiable in these highly cohesive groups, however, performance is enhanced even in comparison to individual events (Williams, Nida, Baca, & Latané, 1989).

Is social loafing a universal biological/economic given, or does it result from cultural forces such as the emphasis on individual achievement in Western society? The first interpretation would explain loafing as resulting from the fact that effort is fatiguing, and, when there is an opportunity to free ride in groups, will be conserved. The second would suggest that social loafing is culturally learned. Iowa kindergarten children show no evidence of social loafing, while second graders exhibit a limited amount and sixth graders as much as college students, consistent with the idea that SOCIAL LEARNING may influence social loafing. On the other hand, sixth grade children in Japan, Taiwan, Malaysia, Thailand, and India, all societies with strong emphases on collectivism, all show significant social loafing, suggesting that social loafing is a universal phenomenon that can be modified by cultural values.

*See also*: BRAINSTORMING; SOCIAL FACILITATION; SOCIAL IMPACT THEORY; SOCIAL LEARNING.

BIBLIOGRAPHY

Kravitz, D., & Martin, B. (1986). Ringelmann rediscovered: The original article. *Journal of Personality and Social Psychology*, *50*, 936–41.

Latané, B., Williams, K., & Harkins, S. (1979). Many hands make light the work: Causes and consequences of social loafing. *Journal of Personality and Social Psychology*, *37*, 822–32.

Steiner, I. D. (1972). *Group process and productivity*. New York: Academic Press.

Williams, K., Harkins, S., & Latané, B. (1981). Identifiability as a deterrent to social loafing: Two cheering experiments. *Journal of Experimental Social Psychology*, *40*, 303–11.

——Nida, S., Baca, L. D., & Latané, B. (1989). Social loafing and swimming: Effects of identifiability on individual and relay performance of intercollegiate swimmers. *Basic and Applied Social Psychology*, *10*, 73–81.

BIBB LATANÉ
STEPHEN DRIGOTAS

**social perception**   This subject concerns the qualities that people perceive in others and the factors within the perceiver and the target person that contribute to these perceptions (*see* Fiske & Taylor, 1991; Zebrowitz, 1990). Fundamental goals in the study of social perception are to explicate general conceptions of human attributes, group stereotypes, evaluations of individuals and impressions of their attributes, perceptions of people's emotions and veracity, and causal attributions for their behavior. The accuracy of perceptions is a focus of inquiry in each of these domains as is the impact of perceptions on social interactions and on the target of perception (*see* SELF-FULFILLING PROPHECIES). The theoretical approaches represented in social perception research include a structuralist approach, which emphasizes the impact of the target person's attributes upon perceptions; a constructivist approach, which emphasizes the impact of the perceiver's cognitive structures and cognitive and motivational processes upon perceptions; and mixed approaches, which consider contributions of the perceiver and the target person (*see* McArthur & Baron, 1983).

CONCEPTIONS OF HUMAN ATTRIBUTES
Linguistic analyses and free-response person descriptions have revealed that the categories of social perception include demographic attributes, social roles, physical appearance, nonsocial behaviors, interpersonal interactions, traits and abilities, intentions, causes, motives, emotions, and AFFORDANCES, which are the behavioral opportunities that others provide. This research has further shown that the perceiver's cultural background and age exert a significant impact on the frequency with which the various categories of description are employed. The most frequent categories in adult US samples are abstract dispositions – i.e., personality traits and abilities – and behaviors. Contextual characteristics, such as social roles, specific social interactions, and social origins appear with much lower frequencies. The relative frequency of the various descriptors is reversed in some non-Western cultures, such as Ethiopia, India, and Japan (*see* Markus & Kitayama, 1991).

Age differences paralleling these cultural differences have been documented in the United States. The parallel between the person descriptions favored by children and non-Western adults suggested to some early researchers that adults from "traditional" societies may have a less well-developed capacity to make abstract trait inferences. However, the evidence does not support this interpretation. While Americans use more trait descriptors with increasing age, there is no such trend for Hindus, who use more contextual descriptors with increasing age. The developmental increase in attention to contextual factors among non-Westerners reflects an increase in the degree to which behavior is recognized as conditional upon certain situational, temporal, or internal states. The developmental trend for Westerners, on the other hand, reflects an increase in the degree to which concrete behaviors are recognized as reflecting abstract, global traits. These cultural differences parallel cultural differences in the construal of the SELF.

Considerable research has investigated the specific contents of one particular category of social perception – personality traits. Linguistic analyses and free response person descriptions have revealed that intelligence, affiliation, and conscientiousness are the most frequent trait descriptors, at least in English.

Research using a variety of methods has consistently organized perceived traits along a small number of dimensions which, while not identical from method to method, do show some convergent validity. The IMPLICIT PERSONALITY THEORY reflected in one recurrent set of dimensions, is dubbed the "Big Five" and consists of Extraversion, Agreeableness, Conscientiousness, Emotional Stability, and Culture/Openness to Experience (*see* John, 1990). Research shows considerable pancultural similarity in the dimensions of implicit personality, although the similarities are weaker for ratings on culturally indigenous trait dimensions than for ratings on the same set of traits.

According to the *accurate reflection* hypothesis, intuitions about personality structure are derived from observations of co-occurrences among behaviors and traits in the real world. In contrast, the *systematic distortion* hypothesis argues that the pattern of correlations among retrospective trait ratings can be explained by the semantic similarity of the trait terms. Research provides some support for both positions. People can acquire implicit personality theories from observing actual behavioral co-occurrences. At the same time, those theories, once acquired, may operate as conceptual structures that can systematically distort *recalled* relationships among subsequently observed behaviors.

## GROUP STEREOTYPES

Whereas the "Big Five" places the targets of perception on a graded set of trait scales, targets may also be differentiated by their goals or by their membership in discrete categories – person types – that reflect distinct personality traits, appearance qualities, and social and demographic roles. The constellation of physical characteristics that define a person's gender, age, and race may serve as a basis for the person types that we commonly call stereotypes (*see* STEREOTYPING). Group stereotypes have a variety of effects on person perception. They may influence impressions of a specific person, such that behavior is assimilated to the stereotype when it is not incongruent or contrasted with the stereotype when it is directly contradictory (*see* ASSIMI-LATION-CONTRAST). Perceivers also show an *ingroup favoritism* effect, such that more positive qualities are perceived among ingroup than outgroup members, and an OUTGROUP HOMO-GENEITY effect, such that outgroup members are perceived as being more homogeneous in their traits and behavior than ingroup members. Finally, there tends to be more *evaluative extremity* in judgments of the outgroup than the ingroup, an effect that may reflect the impact of AFFECT or affective ambivalence on judgments of outgroup members, the SA-LIENCE of outgroup members, and/or the simplicity of outgroup representation.

## IMPRESSION FORMATION

According to constructivist models, cognitive and affective characteristics of perceivers other than their group stereotypes may influence evaluative and descriptive impressions of a specific target person (*see* ATTRACTION and IMPRESSION FORMATION). Structuralist models, in contrast, assume that impressions are data-driven and that the individual elements in the information we have about a person will be linearly combined to "build up" an overall judgment.

Support for constructivist theories is provided by evidence that impressions of a target person are influenced by the perceiver's short-term mental states, such as expectations and trait descriptor accessibility (*see* EXPECTANCY EFFECTS); stable mental structures, such as personal constructs and SELF-SCHEMAS; and various information processing strategies, such as AVAILABILITY and REPRESENTATIVENESS. Impressions are also influenced by the perceiver's affect and goals (*see* MOOD: ITS IMPACT ON COGNITION AND BEHAVIOR). These perceiver characteristics may impact impressions by influencing what information about others is registered, what is recalled, how it is weighted, and/or what meaning it has for the perceiver (*see* Eiser, 1990).

Research in the structuralist tradition has supported an AVERAGING MODEL of impression formation. When people are given lists of person descriptors, the positivity of their overall impression reflects the average *scale value* of the individual traits – i.e., how positively each trait is evaluated – weighted according to the trait's importance to the perceiver. To accurately predict impressions from the weighted average model further requires factoring in the perceiver's initial impression. Thus, this data-driven model also incorporates attributes of the perceiver.

The effect on impressions of target person characteristics other than trait labels provides additional evidence consistent with the assumption that impression formation is data-driven. The influence of the target's behavior is reflected in PRIMACY – RECENCY EFFECTS, salience effects, and impressions based on NONVERBAL COMMUNICATION. The joint effect of salient target qualities and salient behaviors is reflected in the ILLUSORY CORRELATION effect. The influence of the target's appearance is reflected in the effects of familiarity, which induces liking (*see* MERE EXPOSURE EFFECT), PHYSICAL ATTRACTIVENESS, which creates a positive HALO EFFECT, and a babyface, which creates the impression of childlike traits regardless of the target's age. A person's voice, body build, and gait also elicit distinct impressions. For example, a higher-pitched voice increases impressions of extroversion and decreases impressions of dominance, whereas loud, fast, or highly inflected voices are perceived as both extroverted and dominant. Such voices are also perceived as more competent, although the positive effect of speed may be limited to Western cultures, indicating the joint effects on impressions of perceiver and target characteristics. Finally, research demonstrating ACCURACY IN IMPRESSION FORMATION also supports data-driven models, since accuracy presumes agreement between impressions of a person and the data provided by that person's actual qualities.

## EMOTION PERCEPTION

People have implicit theories of emotions, analogous to their implicit theories of personality. As with trait terms, researchers have reduced the universe of emotion descriptors to a manageable and representative set. Cluster analyses on emotion names sorted according to similarity have revealed six basic categories: love, happiness (joy), surprise, anger, sadness, and fear. These categories have been replicated across diverse cultures as well as across age groups, and some have concluded that the central tendencies named by basic emotional terms are universal. Other researchers have taken a multidimensional approach to the representation of emotions, arguing that emotions are better conceptualized as points located on a small set of continuous dimensions than as separate, distinct, categories. Multidimensional scaling analyses have revealed that emotion terms can indeed be represented along two dimensions – evaluation (pleasure–displeasure) and a combination of potency and activity (arousal–sleep).

Descriptions of various emotions reveal that the prototypical representation of an emotion incorporates a set of antecedent event appraisals in addition to a set of physiological, cognitive, expressive, and behavioral responses (e.g., Roseman, 1984). Research has also shown pancultural similarities in the perceived antecedents of the basic emotions as well as the emotional responses (*see* EMOTIONAL EXPERIENCE). Each of the facets included in the representation of an emotion may affect its perception. For example, the display of a prototypical fear response may increase the likelihood of perceiving fear as may the presence of an antecedent condition for the prototypical fear emotion. Most research on emotion perception has focused on the influence exerted by expressive and behavioral responses.

There is strong evidence that the emotions of joy, anger, sadness, surprise, fear, disgust, and contempt, are universally and accurately perceived in both still and dynamic posed facial expressions (Ekman, 1982). The same emotions may also be universally perceived in posed vocal expressions and bodily movements, although there is less research on these modalities. Whereas positive emotions are more accurately identified from facial expressions than negative ones, the reverse seems to be true for vocal expressions. There has been relatively little research investigating the combined effects of face, voice, and/or body on emotion perception. Facial cues appear to dominate vocal ones in the perception of happiness whereas vocal cues dominate in the perception of fear. Facial cues may also dominate contextual ones when these two sources of information are discordant.

Whereas research has identified specific FACIAL EXPRESSIONS OF EMOTION, it has not yet determined the constellation of vocal or movement qualities that communicate the basic emotions. There is also relatively little research investigating spontaneous expressions of emotion. The existing evidence is confined largely to spontaneous *facial* expressions, which can be accurately identified, albeit less reliably than posed ones.

The ability to read facial expressions of emotion develops at a very early age, and it may be innate. Nevertheless, socialization does seem to have an impact on judgment accuracy. Females, whose socialization stresses social sensitivity, outperform males, and perceivers from cultures that suppress the expression of negative emotions are relatively inept in the recognition of these emotions, at least when expressed in the face. Familiarity with particular targets may also augment the ability to judge their emotions accurately.

Some targets are easier to "read" than others, even when emotional expressions are posed. The facial expressions of Western males, who are socialized to hide their emotions, are harder to read than females, a gender difference that emerges in late childhood and grows larger through adolescence. Japanese targets, who are socialized to suppress negative emotions, are harder to read than targets from other cultures when expressing such emotions visually. And, elderly adults are harder to read than younger ones, perhaps because the aging face provides more ambiguous stimulus information.

## DECEPTION DETECTION

Whereas people are able to accurately perceive others' emotions, the ability to detect DECEPTION is more limited (*see* Ekman, 1985; Zuckerman et al., 1981). When untrained people are asked to judge whether videotaped individuals are lying or telling the truth, they rarely do better than chance. Indeed, they sometimes do even worse than chance, which indicates that false positives and false negatives outnumber correct judgments. This results from the fact that naive assumptions about cues to deception, such as shifty eyes and a nervous smile, are wrong. The fact is that liars tend to show more eye contact and less smiling than truthtellers. Even trained professionals, such as customs officials and police officers may do no better than chance at detecting which videotaped individuals are lying, although members of the US Secret Service do show better than chance accuracy.

The accurate perceiver of deception is more likely to attend to nonverbal cues and to detect facial expressions that last only microseconds. These cues to deception may reflect "leakage" of the hidden, true message, evidence of anxiety about the deception, or cues to the falsity of the overt message, such as nongenuine smiles. The low detection accuracy when people judge the veracity of videotaped individuals reflects, in part, the fact that liars are very good at falsifying their facial expressions. Lie detection is often more accurate when people attend to vocal and body cues which are less controllable and therefore more apt to "leak" deception.

## CAUSAL ATTRIBUTIONS

People perceive social CAUSALITY, and they make a variety of attributions for social events which vary in causal locus – internal to the actor versus external – and in descriptive correspondence with the actor's overt behavior (*see* CORRESPONDENT INFERENCES). A number of other causal dimensions have also been identified, including stability and controllability, and the specific causal distinctions that people make may vary across behavior domains and across cultures.

Consistent with a constructivist view of social perception, a number of perceiver characteristics influence causal attributions. These include the perceivers' expectations, their affective reactions to the event to be explained, their causal schemas, and their perspective – i.e., whether they are explaining their own or another person's behavior (*see* ACTOR–OBSERVER DIFFERENCES).

Characteristics of the actor and the behavior to be explained also influence causal attributions, as predicted by "data-driven" theories of social perception. An actor's physical SALIENCE, the nature of an actor's behavior, the distinctiveness of its effects, its CONSISTENCY over time and its DISTINCTIVENESS across targets all influence causal attributions. The social context in which a behavior occurs is also a significant factor. Explicit social pressures, implicit social norms, and the behavior of others (*see* CONSENSUS) all have an effect on attributions for an actor's behavior. The influence of these data on attributions may depend upon how they are incorporated into the perceiver's causal SCHEMAS.

ATTRIBUTION THEORIES assume that people operate as naive scientists in their efforts to understand the causes of behavior. Although research has affirmed the application of logical principles such as temporal order, contiguity, COVARIATION, and DISCOUNTING, ATTRIBUTIONAL BIAS has been a recurrent theme. Biases include:

(1) the FUNDAMENTAL ATTRIBUTION ERROR, whereby people tend to underestimate the causal impact of situational factors and overestimate the role of dispositional factors;

(2) victim blaming (*see* JUST WORLD PHENOMENON and ATTRIBUTION OF RESPONSIBILITY);

(3) sex-stereotyped attributions, whereby differential assumptions about the abilities of males and females influence performance attributions;

(4) salience effects, whereby people tend to attribute causality to physically salient actors;

(5) egocentric attributions, whereby people take more than their share of credit or blame for a jointly produced outcome; and

(6) the FALSE CONSENSUS effect, whereby people tend to assume high consensus for their own past or expected behaviors.

Whether these biases are construed as reflecting motivational or cognitive influences, their existence has been taken as evidence that the attributor does not fare too well as a "naive scientist" searching for true causes of behavior. However, *bias* need not imply error. For example, the FUNDAMENTAL ATTRIBUTION ERROR may reflect an efficient, automatic process of dispositional inference from behavior that, on the average, yields accurate perceptions by perceivers who are too cognitively busy to make conscious corrections based on situational causes.

## CONCLUSIONS

There is a wealth of theory and data pertaining to the conceptualization of human attributes, group stereotypes, impression formation, emotion perception, deception detection, and causal attribution. Despite the obvious interrelations among these domains of social perception, there is little integrative research. For example, whereas perceivers' trait impressions have been linked to their causal attributions for a person's behavior, it remains for future research to link perceivers' impressions to their implicit personality theories and/or to their perceptions of the targets' recurrent emotional states.

*See also*: ATTRACTION; ATTRIBUTION OF RESPONSIBILITY; ATTRIBUTION THEORIES; ATTRIBUTIONAL BIAS; DECEPTION; EMOTIONAL EXPERIENCE; FACIAL EXPRESSIONS OF EMOTION; IMPRESSION FORMATION; MERE EXPOSURE MOOD: ITS IMPACT ON COGNITION AND BEHAVIOR; NONVERBAL COMMUNICATION; OUTGROUP HOMOGENEITY; SELF; SELF-FULFILLING PROPHECIES; SCHEMAS/SCHEMATA; STEREOTYPING.

BIBLIOGRAPHY

Eiser, J. R. (1990). *Social judgment*. Buckingham: Open University Press.

Ekman, P. (Ed.) (1982). *Emotion in the human face* (2nd ed.). Cambridge: Cambridge University Press.

——(1985). *Telling lies*. New York: Norton.

Fiske, S. T., & Taylor, S. E. (1991). *Social cognition*. New York: McGraw-Hill.

John, O. P. (1990). The "big five" factor taxonomy: dimensions of personality in the natural language and in questionnaires. In L. Pervin (Ed.). *Handbook of personality: Theory and research* (pp. 66–100). New York: Guilford Press.

Markus, H. R., & Kitayama, S. (1991). Culture and the self: Implications for cognition, emotion, and motivation. *Psychological Review*, 98, 224–54.

McArthur, L. Z., & Baron, R. (1983). Toward an ecological theory of social perception. *Psychological Review*, 90, 215–47.

Roseman, I. J. (1984). Cognitive determinants of emotions: A structural theory. In P. Shaver (Ed.), *Review of personality and social psychology* (Vol. 5, pp. 11–36). Beverly Hills, CA: Sage.

Zebrowitz, L. A. (1990). *Social perception.* Buckingham: Open University Press.

Zuckerman, M., DePaulo, B. M., & Rosenthal, R. (1981). Verbal and non-verbal communication of deception. In L. Berkowitz (Ed.), *Advances in experimental social psychology* (Vol. 14, pp 1–59). Orlando, FL: Academic Press.

LESLIE A. ZEBROWITZ

**social psychology** The scientific study of the reciprocal influence of the individual and his or her social context. Through the behavioral expression of his or her thoughts and feelings, the individual can have an impact on the social environment. The social environment, in turn, contains many factors that serve to encourage or constrain the individual's behavior. Within this general concern with the interface between the individual and his or her social context, the topics studied by social psychologists range from intrapersonal processes (e.g., how we perceive, feel and think about other people; *see* PERSON PERCEPTION; ATTITUDE THEORY AND RESEARCH; SOCIAL COGNITION), and interpersonal relations (e.g., AGGRESSION; ATTRACTION; HELPING BEHAVIOR; INTERDEPENDENCE; FRIENDSHIP; MARRIAGE), to intergroup behavior (e.g., INTERGROUP RELATIONS; STEREOTYPING), and societal analyses (e.g., the BELIEFS shared by large numbers of people within a society; *see* SOCIAL REPRESENTATIONS).

ORIGINS OF SOCIAL PSYCHOLOGY

Studying the origins and development of social psychology is a topic of research in its own right (*see* HISTORY OF SOCIAL PSYCHOLOGY). The "history" of the discipline has normally been regarded as beginning in 1908, and the "past" as extending as far back as Plato and Aristotle. The discipline as we now know it developed mainly in the social and scientific climate of the United States, after the First and (particularly) the Second World War.

It was after World War I that social psychology became a "science of the individual," the individualist conception coinciding with an experimental–behavioral methodological orientation. This combination of individualism, behaviorism, and experimentalism was intended to make social psychology a scientifically respectable discipline. According to Cartwright (1979), this effort preoccupied the field for the first three or four decades of its new existence; it relied heavily on studying the effect of a manipulable social environment upon individual behavior under laboratory conditions. It has since been argued that this scientific credibility was purchased at the cost of a discipline that became increasingly less relevant and further removed from the study of social issues until, under the weight of economic and political crises (such as the Great Depression and World War II), laboratory purists turned their attention to pressing social problems. The Society for the Psychological Study of Social Issues was founded in the 1930s, but it was the threat of Fascist domination in World War II that galvanized social psychologists into action, as they tried, first, to help win the war and, later, to plan for a better world of democratic societies. Thus Cartwright (1979) argued that World War II was the most important single influence on the development of social psychology.

Notwithstanding the achievements of American social psychologists during this period, their role in the history of the discipline has sometimes been exaggerated. Both Americans and Europeans contributed enormously to the development of social psychology. As Cartwight (1979) argued, it is hard to imagine what the field would look like today, had scholars such as Lewin and Heider (to name perhaps the two most influential) not fled Europe for the United States. This net loss from Europe left postwar social psychology on the continent of Europe almost nonexistent and it was left to Americans to reestablish the discipline, which they did in their own image. It was only later that a distinctive brand of "European" social psychology emerged.

VARIETIES OF SOCIAL PSYCHOLOGY

There are several ways in which one might attempt to characterize variation in social psychology. Here we limit ourselves to two significant classifications within the community of social psychologists.

### Psychological and Sociological Social Psychology

Jones (1985) argued that although social psychology was "an excellent candidate for an interdisciplinary field" (p. 47), it had in fact evolved as a subdiscipline of psychology, albeit with some areas of overlap with sociology. He reported a number of failed interdisciplinary administrative arrangements in American universities that are reflected in the emergence of two distinct types of social psychology – "psychological social psychology" (PSP) and "sociological social psychology" (SSP) (*see* Stephan, Stephan, & Pettigrew, 1991).

PSP focuses on psychological processes of, and seeks to understand the impact of social stimuli on, individuals, and adopts a primarily experimental methodology. It is the "mainstream of social psychology" (House, 1977, p. 161) and is the field predominantly represented in this volume. PSP is the dominant field, in terms of impact, the amount of work published, graduate students trained, and control over publications. Of the major social psychology journals (see below), all are sponsored and edited by psychological organizations, with the exception of *Social Psychology Quarterly* (sponsored by the American Sociological Association); but even this journal publishes many articles by psychologists.

SSP concentrates on the reciprocity of society and the individual, sees its fundamental task as the explanation of social interaction, and relies methodologically on naturalistic observation and surveys. Stryker (1977) has pointed specifically to developments in SYMBOLIC INTERACTIONISM, identity theory and ethnomethodology as exemplary of the SSP tradition. House (1977) has proposed that there are, in fact, "three faces" of social psychology, arguing for a second variant of SSP: "psychological sociology," which relates macrosocial phenomena (e.g., organizations, societies) to individuals' psychological attributes and behavior, usually using quantitative but nonexperimental techniques, such as SURVEY METHODS.

Both Stryker and House argue for more cross-fertilization and interchange between the two social psychologies, but the "emergent commonality" identified by Stryker (p. 156) has not been borne out by subsequent developments. Although there is virtually no hostility between proponents of the two orientations, they have not been integrated into a comprehensive theoretical framework for the discipline as a whole (Cartwright, 1979). It would be wrong, however, to state that there is no overlap or borrowing. As Jones (1985) pointed out, work on symbolic interactionism, for example, has had an impact on psychological theorizing about SELF-PRESENTATION. Nevertheless, as Jones concluded: "the literatures of the social aspects of psychology and the psychological aspects of sociology are remarkably sealed off from each other. . . . such mutual isolation and disciplinary inbreeding is not entirely irrational, however, because the central foci and traditions of the two disciplines are quite divergent. Thus much of the overlap is quite superficial, reflecting superficial similarities that gloss over distinct analytic differences" (1985, p. 50).

These differences between the two orientations are now entrenched and seem likely to remain so. Disciples of the two approaches tend to take different curricula, study, teach or research in different departments, and read and write for different books and journals. After some generations of this cleavage, affiliates of PSP and SSP have learned different histories, with different "pioneers" and "heroes": F. H. & G. W. Allport, Asch, Campbell, Festinger, Lewin, and Schachter for PSP; Bales, French, Goffman, Homans, and Mead for SSP (Wilson & Schafer, 1978). There is remarkably little cross-citation between PSP and SSP journals.

Just how serious is this divide was identified by a survey carried out on the research and professional activities of social psychologists identified with each of these two camps. Little or no overlap was found in research methods; textbooks; journals read, cited, or published in; and academic department in which doctorates were awarded (Wilson & Schafer, 1978). Clearly, there are two worlds, but there is also enough overlap to suggest that effort may be wasted, and knowledge not effectively shared, by the present division.

### North American and European Social Psychology

The second important classification of social psychologists is that between North American and European approaches. This distinction is nothing like as clear as the previous one, but it contrasts the predominantly individualistic American approach with a more social European one. The European perspective is most evident in what Tajfel (1981) called "the social dimension"; he argued that "social psychology can and must include in its theoretical and research preoccupations a direct concern with the relationship between human psychological functioning and the large-scale social processes and events which shape this functioning and are shaped by it" (p. 7).

The contrast between American and European approaches is clarified by Doise's (1986) distinction between four kinds of explanation or "levels of analysis" in social–psychological research:

(1) The *intraindividual* level focuses on the mechanisms by which people organize their perception and evaluation of the social environment (Level I).
(2) The *interindividual* and *situational* level concerns interindividual processes as they occur in a given situation; the different positions that persons occupy outside the situation are not taken into account (Level II).
(3) The *social–positional* level is concerned with extrasituational differences in social position, such as the different group or categorical memberships of participants (Level III).
(4) The *ideological* level refers to systems of beliefs, representations, evaluations and norms that subjects carry with them into an experimental situation (Level IV).

Doise used this scheme to analyze published work and he identified a dominant tendency in social psychological research, both American and European, to limit the analysis to Levels I and II. He noted, however, that European

social psychology did attempt, more than its American counterpart, to introduce Level III and IV analyses into both theory and research.

An integration of American and European approaches will surely yield a more complete understanding of phenomena than either perspective can achieve alone. This can readily be seen, for example, in research on ATTRIBUTION THEORIES, SOCIAL INFLUENCE and intergroup relations. In each case, American researchers have tended to work at levels I and II, whereas at least some Europeans have worked at levels III and IV. Increasingly, however, researchers are "crossing the divide," often back and forth, so that in future this distinction should become less important.

### THE CULTURE OF THE DISCIPLINE

There are four core aspects of what may be called the "culture of the discipline": the level of theorizing characteristic of social psychology; its dominant methodology and associated issues; its primary modes of communication and publication; and its relationship to wider societal issues.

### Theory

A general, and philosophical, question concerns the level of theory adopted in most social–psychological explanations. One underlying aspect of this theorizing is the concept of individualism. The notion of the individual lies at the heart of North American social psychology, but European scholars have argued for a clear distinction between individualistic theories and theories concerned with socially shared patterns of individual behavior. In the latter case, however, measurement is still at the level of the individual (even in group research where, for example, individual responses to questionnaire items may be averaged to yield a group mean) which is characteristic of the social psychological approach.

A second fundamental aspect of social psychological theorizing is the absence of "generic theory." Pettigrew (in Stephan et al., 1991) has contended that, to date, the field has provided only narrow to middle-range theories that are almost impossible to falsify. These theories, he claims, lack boldness and hold the discipline back from uncovering new and unexpected facts and problems. Many scholars might challenge the assertion that social psychological theories are unfalsifiable, but they would probably share the worry that social psychological ideas seem to have become obsessed with specifying the mediating processes of particular and limited phenomena. Notwithstanding this profusion of "mini-theories," surveys of the field (e.g., Jones, 1985) show that it is not as fragmented as one might fear. It remains true, however, that social psychologists need to adopt a more ecumenical stance toward theory which, as an issue, has lagged behind METHODOLOGY.

*Methodology*
Social psychologists employ a wide range of methodological techniques, depending on the topic studied. Methods include attitude measurement, surveys, interviews, systematic observational methods, field studies, field experiments and, most prominently, laboratory experiments (*see* ATTITUDE MEASUREMENT AND QUESTIONNAIRE DESIGN, EXPERIMENTATION, OBSERVATIONAL METHODS, survey methods).

The laboratory experiment has become "the core research method in social psychology" (Aronson, Brewer, & Carlsmith, 1985), because it is the method best suited to testing theory rather than merely describing the world as it is. It permits experimenters a great degree of control over possible random variation and, even more advantageous, allows them to assign research subjects at random to experimental conditions. To its proponents, laboratory experimentation, allied to probabilistic STATISTICS, has led to the discovery of reliable, counterintuitive effects, often specified in the form of an interaction between manipulated variables. It has been described as the "royal road" to causal inference (Aronson et al., 1985) and it is no accident that the term "experimental" appears in the names of the major professional organizations of social psychologists in both the United States (the Society for Experimental Social Psychology) and Europe (the European Association of Experimental Social Psychology). But the use, abuse and overuse of laboratory experiments has also fueled a long-running controversy in the discipline.

*Laboratory experimentation and its discontents.*
According to its critics, social psychology in the 1960s and 1970s stumbled into a "crisis" about its goals, methods and accomplishments. Jones (1985) referred to the discipline's "tendency toward self-flagellation" (p. 97), but it should be acknowledged that many of the critiques originated outside social psychology. Whatever their source, these evaluations centered on three areas: the ethics involved in, the artifacts undermining, and the doubtful relevance of laboratory experimentation. In fact, none of these critiques is peculiar to laboratory experimentation, but it more than any other method came to be the whipping boy. In each case, it will be argued, the way social psychologists have responded to the challenge illustrates their willingness to learn from critics and improve their discipline wherever possible.

Ethical concerns arise in experimentation whenever deception is used and, more generally, whenever anxiety, pain, embarrassment, guilt, or other intense feelings are aroused in subjects (*see* Schlenker & Forsyth, 1977). Aronson et al. (1985) suggest that these issues arise in any procedure that enables subjects to confront some aspect of themselves that may not be pleasant or positive. Jones (1985) referred to this as a kind of "entrapment" of subjects, who later have to deal with the implications of their experimental behavior for their self-concept.

The purpose served by deception is to eliminate or weaken contaminating artifactual variables, often by means of a "cover story" which provides the subject with a sensible rationale for the research. Alternatives to deception have been suggested, but the ethical issues involved are more general. Partly as a result of the furore surrounding Milgram's studies of OBEDIENCE (which both deceived and distressed subjects), weaker forms of deception now tend to be used. There has also been a public debate on the pros and cons of deception in social psychological research and a rapid growth of professional and governmental regulations on the protection of human subjects (*see* relevant guidelines issued by, e.g., American Psychological Association or British Psychological Society). Most universities, where the vast majority of social–psychological research is conducted, have established human subjects or ethics committees that must approve the ethics of a specific procedure before an experiment may be conducted.

Aronson et al. (1985) argued that the field of social psychology is "constructed on an ethical dilemma" (p. 466), the conflict between "a belief in the value of free scientific inquiry" and "a belief in the dignity of humans and their right to privacy." Social psychologists will, in the future, need to maintain their concern about the ethics of research, but this is neither specific to them among scientists, nor to the laboratory experiment as a method.

By its very nature the placement of a "subject," under the control of an "experimenter," in an experimental setting can result in behavior that may not occur in other settings. The term "demand characteristics" refers to cues in the experimental setting that convey to the subject the nature of the experimenter's hypothesis and thus vitiate the results of social–psychological research. It is possible that the experimenter's own behavior may provide cues that influence the responses of subjects. This inadvertent influence of the experimenter, via verbal and nonverbal cues, can suggest covertly to the subject the experimenter's own expectations concerning the outcomes of an experiment (*see* EXPECTANCY EFFECTS). One solution to this problem is to eliminate the human experimenter and use mechanical instruction and recording devices. This practice is now frequently employed in experiments; alternatively, the "researcher" and the "experimenter" are different persons, with the latter remaining "blind" to the researcher's hypotheses.

The tendency of social psychologists slavishly to emulate natural science techniques has led to the charge of irrelevance, based on three claims: the supposed artificiality of the laboratory experiment; the asocial nature of much social psychology; and limitations of social psychology as a transhistorical enterprise. The claim that laboratory experiments are "artificial" tends to confuse two ways in which an experiment can be said to be realistic: an experiment has "experimental realism" if the situation is involving to subjects and has "impact"; it has "mundane realism" if the events occurring in the research setting are

likely to occur in the normal course of a subject's life (Aronson et al., 1985). The successful laboratory experiment depends only on the establishment of experimental realism, thus side-stepping some of its critics who tend to ignore the fact that the artificiality of laboratory experiments is a common characteristic of any science.

Experiments may also be seen as artificial in terms of their unrepresentative samples of subjects, who are often volunteers and/or undergraduate students. Certainly, these samples are not representative of the general population, but critics sometimes fail to recognize that social psychologists typically do not attempt to generalize findings from their laboratory experiments with student subjects to the general population in other settings.

The view that much social psychology is rather asocial was neatly captured by Tajfel's observation that too many experiments were conducted "in a social vacuum" (*see* Tajfel, 1981). Instead of advocating the abandonment of experimental methods, Tajfel argued that social psychologists should be more inventive in bringing society into the laboratory. This inventiveness, he argued, should include more attention to the "intergroup" aspects of social life, and not merely the "interpersonal" ones. Once again, the positive response to criticism is apparent in the burgeoning research on social influence and intergroup relations.

The third strand to the argument about the discipline's relevance equates social psychology with history. Gergen (1973) proposed that human behavior is culturally and historically relative, at best characterizing a particular sample, in a particular setting, at a particular time. He argued, moreover, that social psychological findings enlighten the public, thus making the observed behavior less likely in the future. This historical nature of social psychology means, according to Gergen, that no general laws can be, or have been, established by the discipline. However, this view tends to ignore the heterogeneity of research approaches and objectives within the field which increase the generalizability of social–psychological research.

*The generalizability of social–psychological research.* All these criticisms of experimentation converge on the questions of whether social–psychological research has provided generalizable results, and how to achieve, or improve progress toward, that goal. As Aronson et al. (1985) argued, all experiments should be conducted in a variety of settings, and hypotheses should be tested in both the laboratory and the field. These authors refer to the interplay between laboratory and field experimentation as "programmatic research," a research program that capitalizes on the advantages of each approach. This solution is best understood in terms of the distinction between internal and external validity. Internal validity refers to the confidence with which one can draw cause and effect conclusions from research results; external validity refers to the extent to which a causal relationship, once identified in a particular setting with particular subjects, can be generalized to other times, places, and people. Aronson et al. proposed that many different experimental procedures should be used to explore the same conceptual relationship, thus replacing the profusion of single, isolated studies with systematic, conceptual replications.

It should be clear that neither laboratory nor field studies should be preferred: both are necessary. Hypothesis tests carried out under artificial, laboratory conditions are best at telling us whether or not $x$ can cause $y$ under favorable circumstances; they can thereby promote theoretical progress. Once this relation is established, the criterion of successful research should shift to the validity of the proposition in everyday life. It should, furthermore, be realized that it is theories, not empirical findings, that should be generalized to realistic settings. Thus, for example, SOCIAL IDENTITY THEORY, which gained initial insights from artificial, laboratory research, has since been successfully applied to a number of highly realistic intergroup contexts. An adequate social psychology should, then, continually move back and forth between the laboratory and the field.

### Primary Modes of Communication and Publication

Like psychology in general, the publication hierarchy of social psychology accords higher status to articles in refereed journals than to chapters in edited books or even research monographs, although the variation in quality within each category is high and there are national differences in rankings. Bibliometric indices of journals' "citation impact" are used by some institutions and hiring/promotion committees, but challenged by others. It is probably safest simply to refer to the major international journals of social psychology in alphabetical order: *Basic and Applied Social Psychology, British Journal of Social Psychology, European Journal of Social Psychology, Journal of Applied Social Psychology, Journal of Experimental Social Psychology, Journal of Personality and Social Psychology, Journal of Social Issues, Journal of Social and Clinical Psychology, Journal of Social Psychology, Journal of Social and Personal Relationships, Personality and Social Psychology Bulletin, Social Cognition*, and *Social Psychology Quarterly* (formerly *Social Psychology*, formerly *Sociometry*). Other major publications in the field are the *Handbook of Social Psychology* (Lindzey & Aronson, 1985), the social psychological contributions to the *Annual Review of Psychology*, and the annual volumes of *Advances in Experimental Social Psychology* and *European Review of Social Psychology*.

The impact of the "crisis literature" on these publications has been minimal. Surveys have reported the continuing popularity (sometimes even an increase in the number) of published laboratory studies in relation to other forms of empirical inquiry (*see* Greenwood, 1989). Other surveys report a continued reliance on the conjunction of laboratory experimentation and the use of undergraduate subjects. If these data can be interpreted as a "backlash," then it is explicable on two counts. First, as Greenwood (1989) has noted, many of the more radical critiques have come from professional philosophers rather than psychologists. Second, the cure suggested is so drastic that it would kill the patient; it would effectively abandon a scientific social psychology and eliminate experimentation as a legitimate research strategy.

### Social Psychology and Society

The extent to which social psychology is influenced, if not determined, by external factors has been recognized in two influential historical retrospectives (Cartwright, 1979; Jones, 1985). This view is reinforced by a historical analysis of the topics thrown out to social psychology by World War II, or by a contemporary analysis of issues such as ethnic relations or health. Social psychology has worked closely with government bodies and, judged by the frequency with which it is asked to do so, it is held in quite high esteem. This is particularly evident in the contribution of social psychologists to PROGRAM EVALUATION, where the unique disciplinary blend of testable theory and sophisticated methodology has proved attractive and effective.

Despite this positive track record, government funding has been and continues to be cut in many countries and social psychologists may be increasingly forced to accommodate their research interests to those of a funding body or sponsor. At worst, this could lead to an abandonment of laboratory experimentation, and a consequent lack of theoretical progress. At best, however, it could encourage social psychologists to think more deeply about the external validity and applicability of their theories. An interesting paradox concerning basic versus applied research is that basic research enjoys a higher status within the discipline, while applied research seems to be held in higher esteem outside social psychology. This state of affairs is certainly unsatisfactory, not least because it carries the implications that basic work is "useless," and applied work "atheoretical", neither of which is true. Social psychology needs both types of research and it is to be hoped that its future environmental relations will allow it to develop on both fronts.

CONCLUSIONS

Any statements concerning the future of social psychology are bound to be speculative. In addition, social psychology has shown itself to be highly vulnerable to fads and fashions in research, which Jones (1985) colorfully described in terms of "band wagons and sinking ships." One can, at least, predict that social psychology will remain an empirical, primarily experimental, discipline, notwithstanding new challenges to its hard-earned scientific respectability. It will also apply itself to the major social issues of the day, be they ethnic relations, health issues, or the evaluation of new government programs. What social psychology must not lose is its unique perspective on and contribution to the behavioral sciences, the subjective view of the individual in a social context.

*See also*: AGGRESSION; ATTITUDE MEASUREMENT AND QUESTIONNAIRE DESIGN; ATTITUDE THEORY AND RESEARCH; ATTRACTION; ATTRIBUTION THEORIES; EXPERIMENTATION; FRIENDSHIP; HELPING BEHAVIOR; HISTORY OF SOCIAL PSYCHOLOGY; INTERDEPENDENCE THEORY; INTERGROUP RELATIONS; MARRIAGE; METHODOLOGY; OBEDIENCE; OBSERVATIONAL METHODS; PROGRAM EVALUATION; SOCIAL COGNITION; SOCIAL IDENTITY THEORY; SOCIAL INFLUENCE; SOCIAL REPRESENTATIONS; STATISTICS; STEREOTYPING; SURVEY METHODS; SYMBOLIC INTERACTIONISM.

BIBLIOGRAPHY

Aronson, E., Brewer, M. B., & Carlsmith, J. M. (1985). Experimentation in social psychology. In G. Lindzey & E. Aronson (Eds.), *Handbook of social psychology* (3rd ed., Vol. 1, pp. 441–86) New York: Random House.

Cartwright, D. (1979). Contemporary social psychology in historical perspective. *Social Psychology Quarterly*, 42, 82–93.

Doise, W. (1986). *Levels of explanation in social psychology*. Cambridge: Cambridge University Press.

Gergen, K. J. (1973). Social psychology as history. *Journal of Personality and Social Psychology*, 26, 309–20.

Greenwood, J. D. (1989). *Explanation and experiment in social psychological science: Realism and the social constitution of action*. New York: Springer-Verlag.

House, J. S. (1977). The three faces of social psychology. *Sociometry*, 40, 161–77.

Jones, E. E. (1985). Major developments in social psychology during the past four decades. In G. Lindzey & E. Aronson (Eds.), *Handbook of social psychology* (3rd ed., Vol. 1, pp. 47–108) New York: Random House.

Lindzey, G., & Aronson, E. (Eds.) (1985). *Handbook of social psychology* (2 vols, 3rd ed.). New York: Random House.

Schlenker, B. R., & Forsyth, D. R. (1977). On the ethics of psychological research. *Journal of Experimental Social Psychology*, *13*, 369–96.

Stephan, C. W., Stephan, W. G., & Pettigrew, T. F. (Eds.) (1991). *The future of social psychology*. New York: Springer-Verlag.

Stryker, S. (1977). Developments in "two social psychologies": Toward an appreciation of mutual relevance. *Sociometry*, *40*, 145–60.

Tajfel, H. (1981). *Human groups and social categories: Studies in social psychology*. Cambridge: Cambridge University Press.

Wilson, D. W., & Schafer, R. B. (1978). Is social psychology interdisciplinary? *Personality and Social Psychology Bulletin*, *4*, 548–52.

MILES HEWSTONE
ANTONY S. R. MANSTEAD

**social psychophysiology** The scientific study of the physiological, cognitive, emotional, and behavioral effects of human association. The assumptions underlying a social psychophysiological approach are that:

(1) neurophysiological processes underlie social psychological phenomena;
(2) developmental, environmental, and sociocultural factors influence these neurophysiological processes; and
(3) attempting to study these influences solely as neurophysiological transactions results in unnecessary costs and conundrums.

Research in social psychophysiology has historically emphasized the concomitants of social processes, and social psychophysiology represents a multilevel integrative analysis of social phenomena rather than reductionism per se.

HISTORY

The possibility that important aspects of human nature and human problems might be illuminated by focusing on the interaction between an information-processing organism and social and environmental stimuli was recognized more than 2,000 years ago, when a young son of one of Alexander the Great's leading generals named Antiochus had the misfortune of falling in love with his father's young and beautiful bride. Recognizing that his love for his stepmother would never be realized, Antiochus tried to control his demeanor when in her presence. A mysterious malady soon befell Antiochus; he occasionally suffered profuse sweating, stammering speech, pallor, uneven heartbeat, and weakened muscles. Several physicians had tried unsuccessfully to diagnose the young man's ailment when Erasistratos, a well-known Greek physician, attended to Antiochus. To establish what particular condition triggered Antiochus' attacks, Erasistratos observed the young man's physiological signs (e.g., pulse rate) in response to various people and events. He observed that Antiochus' attacks covaried with his stepmother's visits to wish him well. Erasistratos concluded that the young man's disruptive physiological reactions were attributable to a social condition: lovesickness.

Articles bearing the imprint of a social psychophysiological perspective began appearing in the psychological literature in the 1920s with reports about the changes in the breathing of poker players when they were bluffing and about the galvanic skin responses (GSRs) of students on learning their attitudes were shared by few peers. The first summary of empirical research in social psychophysiology was published by Kaplan and Bloom in 1960. The review dealt with the physiological concomitants of social status, social sanction, definition of the situation, and empathy. An optimism was expressed that the field of social psychophysiology had come of age: "In recent years sociological and social psychological concepts have been applied in physiological studies at an ever increasing rate. The acceptance and utilization of such concepts have been said to form the basis for a relatively new field of inquiry." (Kaplan & Bloom, 1960, p. 133). This review appeared in the *Journal of Nervous and Mental Disorders* rather than a social science journal, perhaps because most of the research surveyed dealt with assessing therapeutic effectiveness rather then psychological processes. At about the same time, Lacey (1959) published a critical and cogent review wherein he argued there was little consistency in the literature upon which to build bridges between psychophysiological data and psychological constructs. He noted that an individual's physiological responses could be described as arising from:

(1) the demands of stimuli or stressors, or what is termed *stimulus response specificity*; and
(2) an individual's predisposition to respond in a particular fashion across stimuli or stressors, or what is termed *individual response specificity*.

He went on to argue that the phenomena of individual response specificity and stimulus response specificity were largely responsible for the apparent inconsistency in the literature, and that these stereotypes were so pervasive that they, rather than complex therapeutic factors, should be the focus of research in the coming decade. The frequency of studies of psychophysiological measures during social interaction in therapeutic settings did indeed decline during the 1960s (*but see* the update by Cacioppo, Berntson, & Andersen, 1991).

Nevertheless, investigations of the reciprocal influence of social and physiological systems began to broaden in scope and increase in number. In 1962, Schachter and Singer published their influential paper, "Cognitive, social, and physiological determinants of emotional state." The thrust of their two-factor theory of emotions was that the sensations derived from a large and unexpected increase in physiological arousal could be experienced as widely different emotions, depending upon the circumstances covarying with these sensations. Two years later, Leiderman and Shapiro published a small edited book on *Psychobiological approaches to social behavior* that represented a different vein of research: Evidence was presented for the dramatic impact that social factors such as conformity pressures have on physiological responding.

By the turn of the next decade, psychophysiological recording had become relatively standardized. The discipline of psychophysiology had its first textbook, journal, and handbook. The second edition of the *Handbook of social psychology*, published in 1969, contained a chapter by Shapiro and Crider on

"Psychophysiological approaches to social psychology" and a chapter entitled "Psychophysiological contributions to social psychology" by Shapiro and Schwartz appeared in the *Annual Review of Psychology* a year later. This coverage of social psychophysiological research was not directed solely to social psychologists either, as a review by Schwartz and Shapiro entitled "Social psychophysiology" appeared in 1973 in a book on electrodermal activity compiled primarily for psychophysiologists.

The attractiveness of psychophysiological procedures was tempered, however, by three formidable barriers:

(1) the paucity of conceptual links between the psychophysiological data and social psychological constructs;
(2) the technical sophistication and expensive instrumentation required to collect, analyze, and interpret psychophysiological data in social psychological paradigms; and
(3) the inevitable pitting of social psychological and psychophysiological procedures against one another in studies of construct validation.

Three distinct strategies developed for dealing with these barriers. One strategy was simply to dismiss physiological factors as irrelevant to the study of social cognition and behavior, and to dismiss social factors as too molar to contribute to an understanding of psychophysiological relationships. This strategy led to findings such as the fact that the simple belief by a person that a change in physiological arousal occurs is sufficient to stimulate the cognitive search for an emotional label. However, the fact that a person's expectations are sufficient to influence information processing does not imply that actual physiological events or sensations of physiological changes are unrelated to information processing, emotion, and behavior.

A second strategy was to view *the* physiological factor important in the study of social processes as being diffuse, perceptible changes in physiological arousal. This view provided the rationale for conducting research with little or no psychophysiological recording equipment and expertise, since it followed from this reasoning that any single physiological response, or even sensitive measures of interoceptive sensations, reflected a person's physiological arousal at any given moment. Hence, psychophysiological procedures as simple as occasionally palpating the radial artery in a subject's wrist to measure heart rate or monitoring any one of a number of measures of electrodermal activity (e.g., GSR, palmar sweating) were employed in various studies as if they were equivalent measures of physiological functioning.

The third approach typically narrowed the breadth of the social issue under investigation, emphasized the theoretical rationale for the variables that were manipulated or measured, and spanned multiple levels of analysis. For instance, rather than viewing physiological arousal as the *sine qua non* of organismic influences on social cognition and behavior, specific patterns of physiological responses were conceived as reflecting and/or influencing specific individual differences and social processes. Social psychophysiology blossomed as social psychologists and psychophysiologists began to converge in their use of this approach. For instance, advanced texts covering social psychophysiology in just the past decade include Cacioppo and Petty's (1983) *Social psychophysiology*, Gale and Edwards' (1983) *Physiological correlates of human behaviour*, Waid's (1984) *Sociophysiology*, Wagner's (1988) *Social psychophysiology and emotion*, Wagner and Manstead's (1989) *Handbook of social psychophysiology*, and Cacioppo and Tassinary's (1990) *Principles of psychophysiology*.

## SOCIAL PSYCHOPHYSIOLOGICAL PRINCIPLES

The hallmark of social psychophysiology has become its emphasis on multilevel, integrative analyses of phenomena that manifest at a social psychological level of analysis. The importance of multilevel analyses is exemplified by three general principles: multiple determinism, nonadditive determinism, and reciprocal determinism (Cacioppo & Berntson, 1992).

The *principle of multiple determinism* states that a target event at one level of organization

(e.g., a neuroeffector response, an emotional percept) may have multiple antecedents within or across levels of organization. An example of the principle of multiple determinism can be found in the extensive literature on drug abuse. It now seems clear that endogenous brain opiod receptor systems constitute ultimate bases for the physiological, cognitive and affective actions of opiate drugs of abuse. Studies of these systems have illuminated, and will continue to clarify, the underlying dynamics and physiological consequences of drug self-administration. Central opiod systems are present across individuals, however, only some of whom will succumb to drug abuse. Hence, central opiates merely constitute permissive substrates for substance abuse. The proximate and powerful determinants of drug abuse include the social factors of economics, opportunity, peer group influences, and family dynamics. These determinants will not be understood through exclusively neuroscientific analysis. Rather, the interactions between social processes and the neural processes underlying addiction represent some of the most important issues currently facing society. As is so often the case, it was the molar features of a phenomenon that prompted and guided inquiry into underlying mechanisms. Indeed, it was the profound psychological effects of the opiates, and their abuse potential, that stimulated research leading to the discovery of central opioid systems.

A corollary of the principle of multiple determinism is the *corollary of proximity*, which states that the mapping between elements across levels of organization becomes more complex (e.g., many-to-many) as the number of intervening levels of organization increases. This is because an event at one level of organization (e.g., depressive behavior) can have a multiplicity of determinants at an adjacent level of organization (e.g., psychological), which in turn may have a multiplicity of implementations at the next level of organization (e.g., physiological), and so forth. The implication is not to avoid venturing across the abyss separating physiological and behavioral levels of organization, but to proceed incrementally across levels of analysis.

A second principle, the *principle of nonadditive (emergent) determinism*, also implies that the understanding of complex mental processes and behavior can be advanced by multilevel integrative analyses. According to this principle, properties of the collective whole are not always predictable from the properties of the parts until the properties of the whole have been clearly documented and studied across levels. Analyses have traditionally focused on a given level of organization (e.g., behavioral, molecular) with generally good success. Theories of emotion within social psychology, for instance, have been derived largely from verbal analyses, and the resulting knowledge regarding people's conceptual organization of emotion has contributed to our understanding of the cognitive antecedents and consequences of emotion (e.g., priming, mood congruence effects). Analyses limited to phenomena within a given level of organization can also mask the underlying order in data, however. In an illustrative study, investigators studying the effect of amphetamine on primate behavior found that the administration of amphetamine had no reliable effect until the primate's position in the social hierarchy was considered: Amphetamine administration increased dominant behaviors in primates high in the social hierarchy but increased submissive behaviors in primates low in the social hierarchy. This result is especially interesting because it demonstrates how the effects of the physiological changes on behavior can *appear* unreliable (or chaotic) until analysis is extended to include higher (e.g., social) levels of organization. Armed with this knowledge, underlying neurobiological bases can be investigated. A physiological analysis, regardless of the sophistication of the measurement technology, may not have unraveled the orderly relationship that existed between the physiological manipulation and behavior. Thus, a multilevel (social psychophysiological) analysis that includes social factors may not only illuminate organization in apparently chaotic data, but it can also stimulate and guide research on the physiological mechanisms underlying these phenomena. In this way, the identification of the physiological substrates of behavior, particularly complex behavior, are often better served by systematic investigations within and across multiple levels of organization rather than by a reductionistic focus alone.

Finally, the *principle of reciprocal determinism* specifies that there can be mutual influences between microscopic (e.g., biological) and macroscopic (e.g., social) factors in determining brain, behavioral, and social processes. Research in behavior genetics has revealed that there are a wide variety of genetic influences that are repressed unless or until certain environmental factors are introduced – that is, brain and behavioral processes are a function of particular genetic factors, which in turn are governed by environmental agents. Within social psychology, Dolf Zillmann and his colleagues have demonstrated that violent and erotic material influences the level of physiological arousal in males, and that the level of physiological arousal has a reciprocal influence on the perceptions of and tendencies toward sex and aggression. Research on hormonal influences in primate behavior has shown that testosterone in male primates promotes sexual behavior, and the availability of sexually receptive females in the colony influences testosterone levels in male primates. These reciprocal influences between biological and social factors cannot be mapped if either level of organization is regarded as irrelevant.

The predictable yield from isolated research on discrete determinants of a multiply determined psychological outcome is a portfolio of fact lists and disparate microtheories. These microtheories each provides a limited account for the phenomenon of interest, however, and are at best pieces of a larger conceptual puzzle. Even determinants of a phenomenon that account for a modicum of variance are noteworthy if the goal is to achieve a comprehensive theory of the psychological phenomenon rather than a microtheory of the determinant.

Knowledge of the body and brain can usefully constrain and inspire concepts and theories of psychological function and behavioral organization. However, knowledge about the functional organization of ordered and disordered mental activities and behavior must also guide the study of the underlying brain processes because these are the phenomena of primary interest, and because they set constraints on the probable neurophysiological substrates. Moreover, the nature of the particular physiological mechanisms and events could be suggested by the observed cognitive activity, behavior, or interaction. Furthermore, there are neurophysiological processes that are affected, for instance, by human association and which underlie the associated psychological and social phenomena, but these phenomena shape physiological events in ways that may not be evident from studies of the physiological isolated from the social or environmental context in which they manifest. Hence, without attention to basic social psychological factors and processes, reductionistic research may yield spectacular images and experimental effects but rather limited answers to the problems of mental processes and the determinism of social behavior.

In sum, reductionism has contributed to the solution of some of the most perplexing scientific problems in human history and has much to contribute to our understanding of social and psychological phenomena. However, it is counterproductive to presume that reductionism will convert the abstractions of the psychological sciences to "real" science in the coming millennium, just as it is counterproductive to presume that reductionism produces insights that are irrelevant to theories of social processes and phenomena. To do either ignores:

(1) the distinction between levels of explanation;
(2) the scientific breakthroughs that can result from research at each of the levels of explanation and/or the relationships among variables that can be derived from descriptions of phenomena from multiple scales or perspectives; and
(3) the economy of thought to be reaped by capitalizing on the form of representation most appropriate for the task.

Social psychophysiological analyses, therefore, will likely play an important role in providing the empirical data and theoretical insight needed for a comprehensive understanding of the myriad interesting phenomena that manifest (though are not entirely explicable) at a social psychological level of analysis.

BIBLIOGRAPHY
Cacioppo, J. T., & Berntson, G. G. (1992). Social psychological contributions to the decade of the brain: The doctrine of multilevel analysis. *American Psychologist*, *47*, 1019–28.
—— & Petty, R. E. (1983). *Social psychophysiology: A sourcebook*. New York: Guilford Press.
—— & Tassinary, L. G. (1990). *Principles of psychophysiology: Physical, social, and inferential elements*. New York: Cambridge University Press.
—— Berntson, G. G., & Andersen, B. L. (1991). Psychophysiological approaches to the evaluation of psychotherapeutic process and outcome: Contributions from social psychophysiology. *Psychological Assessment: A Journal of Consulting and Clinical Psychology*, *3*, 321–36.
Gale, A., & Edwards, J. A. (1983). *Physiological correlates of human behaviour* (Vol. 1); *Basic issues*, London: Academic Press.
Kaplan, H. B., & Bloom, S. W. (1960). The use of sociological and social–psychological concepts in physiological research: A review of selected experimental studies. *Journal of Nervous and Mental Disorders*, *131*, 128–34.
Lacey, J. I. (1959). Psychophysiological approaches to the evaluation of psychotherapeutic process and outcome. In E. A. Rubinstein & M. B. Parloff (Eds.), *Research in psychotherapy* (Vol. 1, pp. 160–208). Washington, DC: American Psychological Association.
Wagner, H. L. (1988). *Social psychophysiology and emotion: Theory and clinical applications*. Chichester: J. Wiley.
—— & Manstead, A. S. R. (1989). *Handbook of social psychophysiology*. Chichester: J. Wiley.
Waid, W. M. (1984). *Sociophysiology*. New York: Springer-Verlag.

JOHN T. CACIOPPO
GARY G. BERNTSON

**social remembering** Recall by or on behalf of groups. There are two main approaches to the topic, the first of which emphasizes the group basis of individual memory, while the second studies memory as a group process.

## GROUP BASIS OF INDIVIDUAL MEMORY

Durkheim and Halbwachs from Sociology, and Sir Frederick Bartlett from Psychology emphasized in different ways that (individual) MEMORY is socially determined. For Durkheim, collective memories were seen to coerce individuals into common ways of perceiving and thinking. More interestingly, Halbwachs (1950/1980) saw that remembering functions to sustain the groups in which we live and work, and that the validation of our memories by others in the group constitutes an important social process. The sociological concepts of collective memory should be carefully distinguished from C. G. Jung's unverifiable concept of the collective unconscious embodying archetypal themes and images, a notion that has exerted little influence on social psychology.

Bartlett (1932), an experimental psychologist, argued that although conventionally studied as an interpersonal phenomenon, remembering both embodies and facilitates group processes. He saw, in addition, that group membership exerts its influence most clearly when individuals speak for the group in both intra- and intergroup contexts. He suggested that social appropriateness rather than accuracy is the fundamental principle of recall, and he illustrated by means of simple experiments the role that language itself plays in recall. More recently, research in this tradition has illustrated the role that culturally determined SCRIPTS exert in human remembering.

What has been termed a "communitarian" tradition may also be discerned in Soviet Psychology which emphasizes the role of recall in sustaining networks of social relationships (Middleton & Edwards, 1990). In this tradition, collaborative activity systems are perceived to be the central unit of analysis in human psychology, and memory is to be studied as a key component of such systems. Children *learn* to remember in social settings as a means of participating more fully in the activities appropriate to those settings, for example, in family gatherings. It is in this sense that memory has an inherently social basis, and must be studied as a process of social and symbolic communication.

## COLLABORATIVE OR GROUP REMEMBERING

This is the process by which a number of people come to agree on a given version of one or more events. Collaborative testimony is a form of group remembering and has been studied in formal settings by anthropologists and social psychologists (Clark & Stephenson, 1989). In group remembering, a descriptive framework and principles of selection and interpretation of events are negotiated by the group. This may enhance learning in some contexts, but quantitative studies of recall indicate that groups do not maximize the potential recall of their individual numbers (*see* GROUP PRODUCTIVITY), and show also that groups distinguish less effectively than do individuals between accurate and inaccurate components of their accounts. Compared with individual recall, group remembering is also more complete, homogeneous and focused on actions rather than descriptive detail. All of these effects are directly linked to increases in group size. Despite their differences, there are essential similarities between collaborative and individual accounts of events. The preexisting cognitive scripts and SCHEMAS of individuals serve to structure collaborative remembering in essentially the same ways – albeit more completely in group than in individual remembering (Clark & Stephenson, 1989).

Intergroup processes play an important role in remembering and in group remembering in particular. The structure and content of what is recalled by groups is influenced by the salience of SOCIAL IDENTITY. When acting as representatives of groups, individuals will be more likely to fill in gaps in accounts of events, and to deny error in ways that are apparently consistent with group goals. Stephenson, Kniveton, and Wagner (1991) suggest that the collaborative effects on remembering may be analyzed in terms of their cognitive, affiliative, and intergroup components: enhanced intellectual resources improve performance, affiliative loyalties enhance confidence, and social competition introduces exaggeration, error, and misplaced confidence.

The study of social remembering is emerging as a topic of major interest in social psychology. This is happening because memory is now being studied in more naturalistic contexts than hitherto. Members of established groups and organizations are frequently called upon to remember on behalf of groups, in both intra- and intergroup settings, and decision making in groups and organizations cannot be fully understood without an understanding of how this is accomplished (see GROUP DECISION MAKING). Different group members (e.g., in a family) may come to divide necessary tasks of memory between themselves in a process known as TRANSACTIVE MEMORY. The respective contributions to organizational functioning of formal record-keeping and of informal remembering of the history of the interaction of its members, is now being explored. Joining a group entails learning its history, entering into the process of co-constructing and reconstructing a common memory system within which narratives are rehearsed which justify the present and facilitate the future. What is recalled in groups will be judged by others in terms of a given group's model of reality and its established or emerging value systems. Active participation in the creation and development of the common memory system may even be viewed as an index of identification with that group. In these and other ways (Middleton & Edwards, 1990) a broad conception of social remembering is emerging which will properly enrich the study of SOCIAL COGNITION and GROUP PROCESSES alike.

See also: GROUP DECISION MAKING; GROUP PROCESSES; GROUP PRODUCTIVITY; MEMORY; SCHEMAS/SCHEMATA; SCRIPTS; SOCIAL COGNITION; SOCIAL IDENTITY THEORY; TRANSACTIVE MEMORY.

BIBLIOGRAPHY

Bartlett, F. C. (1932). *Remembering: A study in experimental and social psychology*. Cambridge: Cambridge University Press.

Clark, N. K., & Stephenson, G. M. (1989). Group remembering. In P. B. Paulus (Ed.), *Psychology of group influence* (2nd ed., pp. 357–91). Hillsdale, NJ: Lawrence Erlbaum.

Halbwachs, M. (1950/1980). *La Mémoire collective/ The collective memory* (F. J. Ditter & V. Y. Ditter Trans.). New York: Harper & Row.

Middleton, D., & Edwards, D. (Eds.) (1990). *Collective remembering*. London: Sage.

Stephenson, G. M., Kniveton, B. H., & Wagner, W. (1991). Social influences on remembering: Intellectual, interpersonal and intergroup components. *European Journal of Social Psychology*, *21*, 163–475.

GEOFFREY M. STEPHENSON

**social representations** This term refers to the manner in which values, ideas, and practices are structured in and by ordinary communication, allowing people to both communicate and to order their world. The "social representations" approach embraces a conceptual framework which is not cast in the mould of mainstream thinking in social psychology. It does not consist of a coherent theoretical perspective, with a set of specific and systematic assumptions from which precise and testable ideas or hypotheses can be derived. In contrast, the aim of this approach can be best described as involving an attempt to legitimize and enable the social psychological analysis of everyday social phenomena as they dynamically unfold by trying to capture general features of daily discourse (see other related approaches, DISCOURSE ANALYSIS, ETHOGENICS, SOCIAL CONSTRUCTIONISM, SYMBOLIC INTERACTIONISM).

Daily discourse is to be understood in the broadest possible manner, ranging from immediate conversation (at a dinner table, in cafés or pubs) to mediated conversation (i.e. mass media). The particular focus of social representations is on the *content* of such discourse and in particular what happens to this content in the process of daily discourse: representation is regarded as a special category of knowledge and beliefs. It is essentially knowledge that is to be found in ordinary communication. Furthermore, the structure of this knowledge is assumed to correspond to that found in ordinary communication (*see* Moscovici, 1984b). The word social is used to indicate explicitly that representations (both internal and external) are the outcome of permanent dialogue and that representations are adapted to the flow of interactions between people (Moscovici, 1961, 1984b).

Serge Moscovici, who is the originator of this approach, defines social representations as "systems of values, ideas, and practices with a two-fold function: first to establish an order which will enable individuals to orient themselves in and master their material world, and second, to facilitate communication among members of a community by providing them with a code for naming and classifying the various aspects of their world and their individual and group history" (Moscovici, 1973, p. xiii). Thus, social representations are first of all reference points. They provide a position or perspective from which an individual or a group can observe and interpret events, situations, etc. More importantly, they provide reference points in terms of which a person communicates with others, by allowing her to situate things concerning herself and her world. A single word or sentence (e.g., she says: "I am a Scorpio") is sufficient to evoke social representations in the listener (e.g., he says: "Women born in October are too much of a pepperpot for my love diet; I might end up as a victim of chronic heartburn, etc."), assuming that the participants share the same knowledge base (e.g., astrology). The classic examples employed to illustrate how a single word or sentence establishes a reference point that locates the interactants and the subject of their communication are words such as psychoanalysis (Moscovici, 1961), Marxism, race, charisma, madness ( Jodelet, 1991), illness (Herzlich, 1973), etc. These topics illustrate some of the substantive research efforts within this tradition. As reference points social representations enable orientation by furnishing specific interpretative views of the social and physical world. They are therefore content-bound, in as much as they entail specific domains of knowledge about our social existence. To narrow the meaning of social representations further we need to dis-

cuss the substance of social representations, namely socially shared knowledge (i.e., content) and its distinctive features as they are identified by this approach.

To the extent that the focus is on the dynamic processes by which social representations are formed and transformed the orientation of this tradition can be seen as unfolding in three steps:

HOW IS A SOCIAL DOMAIN DEFINED?
WHAT IS THE ROLE OF CONTENT?
To continue with the example of astrological signs, our first task would be to chart people's knowledge of astrology, along with all its ramifications, nuances, propensities, etc. What is of interest then is an ethnography of the socially shared knowledge of astrology as it is distributed in the particular community or society. This would also involve documenting the knowledge of those who do not share these beliefs, i.e., the socially shared knowledge concerning the lack of credibility of astrology. "(T)he unifying factor and the specific nature of this tradition in contrast to other traditions of social psychology is its predominant interest in the contents of the 'mind.' These contents make up the raw material of our thoughts and communications, a raw material consisting of 'theories,' 'stories,' 'legends,' etc. It is only by taking a specific content in all its wealth of nuances as our starting point that we can hope to derive general principles or mechanisms" (Moscovici, 1984b, 946). Indeed, Moscovici himself draws a parallel between his type of social psychology and anthropology (1984b).

WHAT ARE THE IMPLICATIONS
OF THE FOCUS UPON "CONTENT"?
This emphasis on socially shared knowledge as content, or the ethnographic dimension of this approach, is made in contrast to the emphasis on (underlying) process in most of modern cognitive social psychology. Commonly, in social psychology process is distinguished from content in order to separate universal and transhistorical properties of human social behavior (process) from historically and culturally situated aspects of it

(content). For instance in mainstream SOCIAL COGNITION an explicit distinction is made between the content of what is being processed (i.e., information about persons, events, situations, etc.) and the processes by which this information is encoded, stored, and retrieved. This content–process distinction enables a differentiation between culturally relative propositions or "cultural artefacts," that are subject to change over time, and psychologically universal properties. This distinction is regarded by many social and cognitive psychologists as an essential proposition for any "scientific" research.

In Moscovici's approach (1972, p. 72; 1984a, b) this distinction is explicitly rejected. Such a critique is not new and has been articulated in the literature for some time (e.g., SOCIAL CONSTRUCTIONISM, ETHNOGENICS). The driving idea behind this critique is that content furnishes the answer to both the formal elements that are activated. Further, these formal elements are assumed to exert an influence only through their social content (Moscovici, 1984b). In this perspective then, content *is* process. This is a view that is beginning to gain currency in cognitive social psychology within a cross-cultural perspective (*see* INDIVIDUALISM-COLLECTIVISM). The notion that content is process can be illustrated with an example of the social representations concerning the Zodiac. Given a request such as "Think about a person born on October 25!" people can respond in two possible manners. Some people will simply draw a blank: nothing to visualize, no inferences, no responses, nothing. We are dealing with somebody who cannot meaningfully deal with the request. The absence of meaning is due to the absence of relevant social representations, namely socially shared information about the meaning of birthdays in the context of the Zodiac. If, however, the person in question is a knowledgeable Taurean a number of inference processes are evoked covering the qualities of someone born on October 25, his or her behavioral inclinations, the manner in which dynamic interpersonal relationships are likely to be shaped in the future, and so on.

Thus, the "formal elements" by which all these cognitive processes are evoked is to be found in the specific content-based propositions of astrology. No abstract, decontextualized, content-free process is going to be able to capture the wealth of the cognitive processes involved. Thus, the argument from the social representations approach is that there are no content-free mechanisms and cognitions.

## WHAT ARE THE PROCESSES BY WHICH SOCIAL REPRESENTATIONS ARE FORMED AND TRANSFORMED?

The central question for any theory that tries to examine the dynamic by which social representations are acquired and transformed is the question of change. The theory of social representations postulates a process of the *familiarization of the unfamiliar*, or how the "unknown" from the "outside" becomes transferred into the "inside." The assumption is that available consensually shared world knowledge serves as a framework into which additional or new knowledge is "assimilated" or "familiarized." The unfamiliar is generally regarded as coming primarily from scientific sources and as presenting knowledge that is novel and incompatible with existing social representations. Two processes are assumed to be centrally involved in the familiarizing the unfamiliar or the conversion of new knowledge into the habitual. The first process is *anchoring* and refers to the integration of new knowledge into categories and images that are already known and that present readily identifiable reference points. Thus, the analogy between therapy in psychoanalysis and the confessional within Catholic practices (Moscovici, 1961) provides a "mechanism" by which the unfamiliar is made familiar. As can be seen from such an example, anchoring proceeds by means of *classification* and *naming processes*. By classifying and naming a new object it becomes possible to integrate it into an already existing order and to generate further inferences about the object. More commonly, this process is known in social psychology as CATEGORIZATION.

The second general process that is postulated is *objectification*. This refers to how the unusual becomes part of general discourse, not so much as an object of discourse, but as an integral element in discourse. Take the case of psychoanalysis, originally an object of discourse. Once it had been objectified it became an integral interpretative tool within discourse. It was no longer the unfamiliar that had to be talked about, but the familiar in terms of which persons, events and behaviors could be explained. From being an object of discourse, psychoanalysis, through the processes of anchoring and objectification, has become transformed into a shared representation.

The final question that needs to be addressed in an overview of social representations is:

## WHAT ARE THE AMBIGUITIES IN THIS APPROACH AND THE IMPLICATIONS OF THESE?

Although the social representation approach has captured the imagination of many European social psychologists it has also given rise to considerable criticism (e.g., Jahoda, 1988) as a result of its lack of specificity and conceptual clarity. Such critiques stem primarily from the difficulty of specifying what is meant by the qualifier "social" in social representations. As Harré (1984) has pointed out the social representations approach refers to the social in a variety of different and contradictory ways, and this is reflected in the diversity of contradictory empirical work that is conducted under the social representations rubric. There are a number of distinct ways in which "social" can be used to qualify "representations." First, the representation may be *of* something social. Alternatively, it may indicate that the representation is *itself* something social. Research conducted in these two senses is, in principle, no different from the research done in mainstream social cognition. A further possibility is that social is considered to be a "property" that each member of a group has. Thus the reference is to an individual property but since the property is distributively realized, as in the group, it is "social." But this is not distinctive from work that is conducted within mainstream social psychology, for example, social identity theory (*see* INTERGROUP RELATIONS). A final possibility is

to consider the social as a property that is only collectively realized, as in communication or conversation and therefore requiring a level of analysis that goes beyond the individual level of analysis.

It is difficult to identify what distinguishes social representation research from mainstream work in social psychology to the extent that the social in social representations is used in the first three senses specified above. There are also ambiguities in the social representation approach some of which are theoretical, as in the case of the processes of anchoring and objectification by which the assumed transformation of the unfamiliar takes place. These processes are not specified with respect to the level at which they operate. Do they refer to intraindividual processes, or are they processes that take place on the interindividual plane? Furthermore, the postulated mechanisms appear to be somewhat conservative, in that they seem to be largely responsible for transforming the novel or the unfamiliar into the familiar or reassuring. Amongst the major sources of novel phenomena in social representations appears to be the "re-presentation" or transliteration of aspects of the scientific discourse into the conceptual vocabulary of everyday life. This involves a process of active assimilation in order to accomplish the translation, but implicitly presupposes a passive and nondialectical relationship between science and the society within which it operates. This passivity is necessarily entailed by the distinction between the two discourses that Moscovici postulated in order to establish the domain of social representations.

The ambiguity of the level of analysis is evidenced by the diversity of research activities classified as social representation research (*see* Jodelet, 1984). At one extreme, there is research focusing on the individual cognitive processes by which representations are regarded as emerging. Here, the "social" is defined in terms of the group membership of the subject, the situation in which these processes occur and the object of cognition. In effect, this is what one would regard as social cognition in mainstream social psychology. Other types of social representations research treat representations as a form of discourse and analyze their characteristics from the practical discourse of socially shared situations. Still other studies examine the influence of group membership on the dynamics of representations. The latter approaches imply a social which is "collectively realized," although how the diverse processes (anchoring, classification) that are postulated within this framework relate to such collective realizations remains unspecified. A related ambiguity is seen in Moscovici's identification of the important role played by language and the relationship between representations and memory and his suggestion that "language has been welded to representation" (1981, p. 184). Similar to the problems mentioned in the specification of the level of analysis, there is no specification of how language, which requires a social level of analysis, can be empirically approached. As a consequence of this problem, which is not only peculiar to this approach (*see* SO-CIAL CONSTRUCTIONISM), the methodological tools that suit this orientation remain unclear.

Paradoxically, it is the distinctively social level of analysis which distinguishes this approach from mainstream social psychology that is also the aspect which is in most need of further specification. This is required not only for an improved understanding of the analytic perspective that social representations offer, but also to clarify the feasibility of the methodology(ies) best suited for this approach.

*See also*: CATEGORIZATION; DISCOURSE ANALYSIS; ETHOGENICS; INDIVIDUALISM-COLLECTIVISM; INTERGROUP RELATIONS; SOCIAL COGNITION; SOCIAL CONSTRUCTIONISM; SYMBOLIC INTERACTIONISM.

BIBLIOGRAPHY
Herzlich, C. (1973). *Health and illness: A social psychological analysis*. London: Academic Press.
Jahoda, G. (1988). Critical notes and reflections on "social representations". *European Journal of Social Psychology, 18*, 195–221.
Jodelet, D. (1984). Représentations sociales: Phénomènes, concept et théorie [Social representations: Phenomena, concepts and theory.]. In S. Moscovici (Ed.), *Psychologie sociale* (pp. 12–34). Paris: Presses Universitaires de France.
——(1991). *Madness and social representations*. Hemel Hempstead: Harvester Wheatsheaf.
Moscovici, S. (1961/1976). La Psychanalyse: Son image et son public [Psychoanalysis: Its image and public.]. Paris: Presses Universitaires de France.
——(1981). On social representations. In J. P. Forgas (Ed.), *Social Cognition* (pp. 181–210). London: Academic Press.
——(1984a). The phenomenon of social representations. In R. Farr & S. Moscovici (Eds.), *Social representations* (pp. 1–35). Cambridge: Cambridge University Press.
——(1984b). The myth of the lonely paradigm. *Social Research, 51*, 940–67.

GÜN R. SEMIN

**social skills** Despite the great growth of social skills training (sometimes called interactional or interpersonal skills) there remains no consensus as to the history, definition, or theory underlying social skills training (Ellis & Whittington, 1981; Furnham, 1985). Social skills can be defined as "a set of goal-directed, interrelated social behaviors which can be learned and which are under the control of the individual." It seems that social skills research is "influenced" by rather different models or paradigms: the *conditioning* model derived from learning theory according to which social deficits are the results of poor learning; the *cybernetic* model which sees social behavior modified by feedback and deficits due to negligible or inaccurate feedback; the *experiential* model which sees skills deficit as due to lack of correct or sufficient exposure to salient everyday experiences; and the *teleological* model which believes that an analysis of, and commitment to, the goals of everyday interaction provide the necessary skills to perform it.

Because social skills trainers initially saw social interaction as a skill akin to playing the piano or flying a helicopter they relied too heavily on motor skills models which they attempted to adapt for social behavior. This led to an underemphasis on both affect and cognition. More recently the roles of cognition (in the form of knowing social rules, appropriate schemas) and affect (particularly social anxiety) have been stressed in social skills training.

Social skills (note both the use of the plural in skills and its nonpejorative tone as opposed to terms like inadequacy, or deficiency) is assessed by one of three measures: self-report (usually questionnaires), behavioral techniques (content-analyzed video-tapes of role plays), and physiological measures such as electrodermal activity. These measures have serious psychometric shortcomings, particularly with regard to evidence of validity, and do not intercorrelate very highly. This assessment problem renders both research and therapy problematic but it has continued apace. There have been various epidemiological studies looking at demographic correlates of social skills. There have also been various attempts to evaluate the efficacy of social skills training which are based on three principles: demonstration (instruction, guidance, analysis), practice (role play, natural behavior massed or spaced) and feedback (descriptive rather than judgmental).

Training has been enthusiastically applied to various groups of people including professionals who work with people (doctors, lawyers, teachers), mental patients (neurotics and psychotics, both in- and out-patient), addicts (particularly drugs but also alcohol and food), recidivists (prisoners, delinquents, rapists, arsonists), handicapped people (both mental and physical), and adolescents (both "normal" and those with special problems).

Whereas many British (and some American) researchers have agonized over the theoretical problems in social skills training, many American (and some British) researchers have been more concerned with the pragmatic question of "Does it work?" Researchers have been particularly interested in methodological critiques of the studies done, whereas therapists have been particularly interested in a careful evaluation of the outcomes of treatment.

Methodological and research criticisms have revolved around a number of issues. Many researchers have lamented the poor psychometric quality of assessment techniques, particularly self-report inventories (Hersen & Bellack, 1976). Few techniques have good reliability or validity figures; they are often multidimensional, culture- and situation-specific, and poor predictors of performance. A second, related problem is the ecological validity of the training situation – that is, how representative the training situation is of real life. Often, experiments are run and training is done in environments that bear only a slim resemblance to those in the real world, and hence generalizability becomes a problem. Another problem in both research and therapy is the selection of subjects. They are often self-selecting, highly heterogeneous, and of higher intelligence than average patients. Curran (1980) suggested that multiple screening procedures be used to attempt to delineate specific skills deficits in subjects before onset of training so that the full and specific effects of training may be measured. Few studies have attempted a careful, extended follow-up assessment to test the generalizability of findings across time, situations, and skills. The problem of generalization has been extensively discussed; yet it still appears to be the Achilles' heel of social skills training. Finally, from a methodological point of view, the analysis of multivariate data has, for the most part, been crude and often inappropriate. The fact that many dependent measures are highly correlated suggests descriptive analysis as well as such techniques as multivariate analysis of variance and discriminant analysis rather than simple nonparametric analysis on each dependent variable.

It is not only the methodology of research that has received criticism (Curran, 1980; Hersen & Bellack, 1976), but also the therapy. Marzillier (1978) has offered a critique of various aspects of social skills therapy. In essence, these criticisms refer to four aspects of therapy;

(1) the type of social skills therapy offered;
(2) therapist effects;
(3) the neglect of individual differences; and
(4) measures of the significance of change.

As regards the exact type of social skills training programs offered, there are a number of problems. First, courses differ radically according to their content, length, and emphasis on various training methods, and therefore to compare different methods or do a meta-analysis of different studies is fraught with problems. Thus, in order to assess the effectiveness of different training programs, it is important that all groups should have equivalent amounts and types of treatments. Another problem concerns the fact that with nearly all inpatients and also with a number of outpatients, additional therapies (drug relaxation, psychoanalysis, etc.) are conducted alongside social skills training. It therefore becomes very difficult to establish the cause of the change (or lack of change) over time because it could be the social skills training, the other therapy, or the particular combination of the two. A related problem is the amount of spillover or leakage between patients of the different therapies they are receiving. Therefore, it is important to ensure that patient groups are not undergoing some alternative equivalent treatment.

Second, it has been shown in all forms of therapies that certain characteristics or attributes of the therapist (age, sex, personality, enthusiasm) can greatly effect the behavior of the patients. This can mean that if one treatment shows poorer effects than another, the cause lies in the personality of the therapist rather than in the treatment received. Similarly effects due to the therapist may also occur in the rating of patients before and after therapy. Only carefully balanced therapy programs and carefully trained raters can overcome this problem.

Third, many effectiveness and assessment studies have neglected individual differences. However, because there is such variation between patients, it is important to look more closely at individual differences both in the planning of individual treatment and in conducting evaluative research. Furthermore, thorough analysis of individual differences before treatment would allow for comparison of patients who persevere with, or drop out of treatment.

Finally, there is the criticism associated with the measurement of change. It is problematic to decide who evaluates change – the patient, her/his peers, the therapist – and according to what criteria – namely global rating scales of warmth, assertiveness, happiness, or detailed fine-grained measures of eye contact and the like. Furthermore, as skills are not culture free, inflexible, or stable over time, it is difficult to determine absolutely the nature of the change. Statistical significance in the form of changes in social behavior before and after treatment may not in itself be a very good measure of change.

These criticisms of social skills training on both sides of the Atlantic are important but not damning. Indeed, recent reviewers, both in America and in Britain seem optimistic about the future of social skills training. Furnham (1985) offers three reasons for guarded optimism:

(1) the awareness on the part of social skills theorists and researchers of the deficiencies in social skills research;
(2) the advantages of social skills training over other types of psychotherapy; and
(3) finally, the encouraging evidence regarding the effectiveness of social skills training with a wide range of population groups.

*See also*: META-ANALYSIS.

BIBLIOGRAPHY

Curran, J. (1980). Social skills: Methodological issues and future directions. In A. Bellack & M. Hersen (Eds.), *Research and practice in social skills training* (pp. 319–54). New York: Plenum.

Ellis, R., & Whittington, D. (1981). *A guide to social skills training*. London: Croom Helm.

Furnham, A. (1985). Social skills training: A European perspective. In L. Abate & M. Milan (Eds.), *Handbook of social skills training and research* (pp. 555–80). New York: Wiley.

Hersen, M., & Bellack, A. (1976). Assessment of social skills. In A. Ciminero, K. Calhoun, & H. Adams (Eds.), *Handbook of behavioural assessment* (pp. 392–414). New York: Wiley.

Marzillier, J. (1978). Outcome studies of skills training: A review. In P. Trower, B. Bryant, & M. Argyle (Eds.), *Social skills and mental health* (pp. 103–30). London: Methuen.

ADRIAN F. FURNHAM

**social support** This term delimits a diverse literature demonstrating that the existence of positive social RELATIONSHIPS may help maintain or advance the health and well-being of organisms. Although the folk wisdom that "friends can be good medicine" predates biblical times, it was only in the 1970s, with the advent of large epidemiological studies of mortality rates, that systematic empirical evidence for a link between social relationships and health began to emerge. Since then, hundreds of studies have been published, spanning disciplines as distinct as social, clinical, and community psychology; sociology; epidemiology; and psychophysiology. The widespread appeal of this subject can be attributed in part to the intellectual excitement and therapeutic prospects inherent in a well-articulated (and potentially modifiable) connection between people's social circumstances and their physical and psychological well-being.

The benefits of social support may be substantial. House, Landis, and Umberson (1988) noted that the age-adjusted mortality risk of social isolation exceeded the comparable risk ratio for cigarette smoking. Despite the enthusiasm of the research community, however, the mechanisms underlying social support effects have remained elusive. To date, there is little agreement among researchers as to the means by which social support prevents or ameliorates illness, or the conditions under which social support has more or less impact.

The central phenomenon in this literature is well established: The presence of social support (however this variable is defined) is associated with better health, less illness, and lower mortality rates. This correlation has been demonstrated with widely differing health indicators, ranging from general (e.g., illness symptoms, general well-being, visits to treatment sites) to specific (e.g., immune system changes, markers of coronary artery disease or cancer). Although some of the most dramatic findings have been obtained in studies of physical health, psychological health has been investigated more extensively (e.g., mood disturbances, psychiatric symptomatology). By far the majority of existing studies rely on self-reported indications of healthfulness, leading to the occasional criticism that existing results may be artifacts of PERSONALITY traits (e.g., neuroticism) and other response-biasing tendencies. However, the many available studies that use objective or independent assessments of health help to refute, or at least minimize, this alternative explanation.

Two general models characterize the existing literature. *Main effects models* propose a positive, monotonic relationship between social support and well-being: The more social support one perceives, the better one's health. *Stress-buffering models* posit that social support attenuates the debilitating effects of stress (*see* BUFFERING THEORY; STRESS AND COPING). Thus, social support would have little value when stress is low, but would become increasingly beneficial to the extent that stress exceeds some threshold. Stress-buffering models focus attention on the need for a match, or "fit," between the specific nature of stress and the type of support received, an important theoretical consideration. Main effects models, on the other hand, tend to focus somewhat less precisely on the role of social support in fulfilling important human needs and goals, including needs related to social integration and ATTACHMENT.

Readers are often daunted by the many diverse conceptual and operational definitions of social support that different investigators use. To date, no consensus appears on the horizon, and it seems likely that social support will turn out to involve a complex combination of multiple processes. In its most general sense, social support refers to the existence of positive, caring and helpful, relationships with others. Closer examination reveals considerable diversity around this general theme, however.

One key distinction differentiates *structural* and *functional* measures (Cohen & Syme, 1985). Structural measures refer to social network characteristics such as density, social integration, network size, marital status, and frequency of social contact. Functional measures, on the other hand, describe the psychological functions fulfilled by social relationships. Numerous functional taxonomies have been offered, differing in certain respects but embracing several common themes (Reis, 1984): tangible (material) assistance;

information (i.e., advice and guidance); emotional support (especially in primary love relationships); SELF-ESTEEM boosting; and group belonging. Within the functional view of social support, an additional distinction contrasts the perceived availability of support with its actual receipt. Studies of the former are more common. Interestingly, however, in some instances the latter has produced *negative* correlations with health, presumably because receiving support indicates that a person's problems may have exceeded personal coping resources. Another important question now being addressed concerns the link between the perception that support is available and relationship and personality characteristics (Sarason, Sarason, & Pierce, 1990). Attachment and INTIMACY are two processes that have been implicated.

Despite popular consensus that social support is indeed beneficial, the question of causal mechanism remains vexing: By what means do social relations come to have health-promoting effects? Because the vast majority of studies use correlational designs, causal inferences have been precluded. (Helpful in this regard are several prospective longitudinal studies, however.) Many possible mechanisms have been offered, some of which show promise. Consideration of these possibilities illustrates the broad conceptual span that social support processes encompass. For example, social support may enhance disease-resistance by improving immune function, neuroendocrine response, or cardiovascular reactivity; perceived social support may enhance self-esteem, thereby encouraging adoption of more healthful life styles and practices; and the absence of valued relationships may produce harmful negative emotions such as ANXIETY and despair. Perceiving social support may also reduce feelings of learned helplessness by maximizing perceptions of CONTROL. Many other mechanisms are also plausible. The key point is that current knowledge about how social states are transformed into physical symptoms is at best rudimentary. As a result, many researchers feel that the rush to intervention, not only by individuals but especially in large-scale public health programs, may be premature (Vaux, 1988).

*See also*: CONTROL; INTIMACY; PERSONALITY; RELATIONSHIPS; SELF-ESTEEM; STRESS AND COPING.

BIBLIOGRAPHY
Cohen, S., & Syme, S. L. (1985). *Social support and health*. New York: Academic Press.
House, J. S., Landis, K. R., & Umberson, D. (1988). Social relationships and health. *Science, 241*, 540–5.
Reis, H. T. (1984). Social interaction and well-being. In S. Duck (Ed.), *Personal relationships V: Repairing personal relationships* (pp. 21–45). London: Academic Press.
Sarason, B. R., Sarason, I. G., & Pierce, G. R. (1990). *Social support: A transactional view*. New York: Wiley.
Vaux, A. (1988). *Social support: Theory, research, and intervention*. New York: Praeger.
HARRY T. REIS

**social values** An important class of human decision making takes place in situations of outcome interdependency where the decisions have reciprocal consequences for the well-being of all the individuals involved. The preference of an individual for a particular distribution of outcomes for self and the other person involved in situations of outcome interdependency, define his or her SOCIAL VALUE. An extreme but well-known example of outcome interdependency can be found in situations in which private interest can be at odds with public interest, that is in SOCIAL DILEMMAS.

Starting with Deutsch (1958), it has been recognized by several researchers that individuals systematically differ in the kind of decisions they make in settings of outcome interdependency. Deutsch reasoned that decisions are guided by interpersonal orientations, or certain rules people use to evaluate own and other's outcomes, and distinguished three different interpersonal orientations. COOPERATION refers to valuing joint outcomes for both self and other, COMPETITION to valuing relatively higher outcomes for self than for the other, and individualism to valuing own outcomes independent of the outcomes for the other.

Not choosing the alternative which affords oneself the maximum of the available outcomes is considered irrational behavior from the so-called "dollar maximizing" perspective. In contrast, one can consider it to be rational if one assumes that in defining the utility of the available outcome alternatives, individuals evaluate and take into account other's outcomes as well as their own. They select the behavioral option which affords them the greatest perceived utility, based on own and other's outcomes. In this perspective, the subject's utility function can be defined as a linear combination of

$$W_1 \text{ (Outcomes for self)}$$
$$+ W_2 \text{ (Outcomes for other)}.$$

For individuals with a cooperative orientation $W_1 = 1$ and $W_2 = 1$, for those with an individualistic orientation $W_1 = 1$ and $W_2 = 0$, and for those with a competitive orientation $W_1 = 1$ and $W_2 = -1$.

By differentially weighting own and other's outcomes, theoretically a variety, or even an infinite number of utilities can be constructed. Each of these utilities refer to a different social value. A well-known set of social values is shown in figure 1. Even more differentiation in social values is proposed by assuming nonlinear utility functions. However, research

using different methods to assess social values demonstrated that only three categories are needed to capture the utility functions most subjects actually employ in settings of outcome interdependency. Those are the above mentioned social values of cooperation, individualism, and competition.

## ASSESSING SOCIAL VALUES

In the EXPERIMENTAL GAMES employed in most of the research investigating behavior in interdependency situations, individuals are provided with alternative outcome distributions with outcomes for self and for the other, and are asked to select their most preferred one. The final outcomes each individual will receive depend upon the choices made by one's partner(s) as well as by oneself. That is, the individuals have *mutual fate control*.

The available outcome distributions in experimental games can be presented in a two-alternative two-person matrix format. This format, however, limits the identification of individuals' social values. By presenting own as well as other's available outcome distributions, the game does not differentiate between social goals and strategy, because choices may be governed by motivational as well as strategic determinants. Moreover, most of these games do not differentiate between various social values. For example, the two-alternative two-person PRISONER'S DILEMMA game, one of the most thoroughly studied experimental games, distinguishes a cooperative from a noncooperative choice, but a noncooperative choice may be based on an individualistic as well as on a competitive social value.

To overcome these problems, *decomposed games* were developed to assess the individual's social value (Messick & McClintock, 1968). In decomposed games the traditional matrix format is decomposed in such a way that it explicitly specifies the consequences of the choice for one of the two alternatives in terms of the outcome for self and separately, that for the other person. In an assessment procedure, subjects are provided with a series of decomposed games. In each decomposed game they are asked to select the alternative they most prefer, and are told that the other

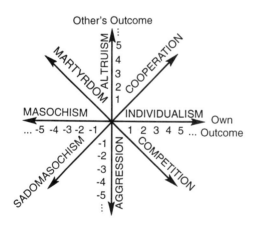

Figure 1. A geometric taxonomy of eight different social values, the *x*-axis representing outcomes for self, and the *y*-axis representing outcomes for the other.

person is facing exactly the same decision problem. An example of a decomposed game is given in table 1.

*Table 1.* An example of a decomposed game.

|        | A   | B   | C   |
|--------|-----|-----|-----|
| Self   | 490 | 560 | 500 |
| Other  | 90  | 300 | 500 |

Kelley and Thibaut (1978) propose that in these interdependency situations, individuals do not generally respond to the outcomes as specified in the externally defined outcome distribution, but instead transform the outcomes into subjective outcomes. That is, before making a choice, individuals psychologically transform the "given" outcomes, which are generally beyond the subject's control and dictated by the environment, into "effective" outcomes by assigning weights to own and other's outcomes. The effective outcomes are supposed to be the basis for the individual's choice and to reflect their SUBJECTIVE EXPECTED UTILITY, defined here as social values.

The example in table 1 is a Triple Dominance Game, in which each social value leads to a unique choice (Kuhlman & Marshello, 1975). After transforming each available outcome distribution, a cooperative value prescribes a choice for Alternative C, a competitive value a choice for Alternative A, and an individualistic value a choice for Alternative B.

The decomposed games technique is a particularly useful method for assessing social values. Although the subject is told that the other person is facing the same decision problem, only his or her own available outcome distributions are presented. Therefore, decision makers seem to have unilateral rather than mutual fate control over own and other's outcomes, which makes it likely that the strategic determinants of a choice are suppressed and the motivational determinants are released. That is, in contrast with the games representing outcomes in a two-alternative two-person matrix format, subjects' choices in decomposed games are more likely to represent their most preferred distribution of outcomes for self and the other, rather than to

represent their methods they employ in order to receive their most preferred outcomes. Moreover, with this technique it is possible to differentiate between various social values, because they easily allow one to include some additional outcome distributions in order to assess additional social values.

Several other methods using decomposed games have been developed to assess social values. Examples are the judgmental procedure in which subjects are asked to judge the desirability of the various outcome distributions, and the rank-order procedure in which subjects are asked to rank-order the various outcome distributions in terms of their preference. In the pair-comparison procedure, $N$ own/other outcome distributions are paired with each other and subjects indicate their preference for one alternative of the pair. Different methods for representing the outcomes in decomposed games have also been developed, for example, numbers and rectangles of various sizes representing the amount of money involved and various facial expressions representing the overall satisfaction.

The Ring Measure of Social Values (Liebrand & McClintock, 1988) is a computerized geometric procedure assessing choice behavior in decomposed games, as well as subject's response latencies. Mathematically, like the geometric taxonomy of social value, the own/other outcome distributions in the Ring Measure can be represented as points in the own/other outcome space depicted in figure 1.

The agreement between different measurement procedures is reasonably high. The Ring Measure and the Triple Dominance Game were found to agree with respect to the classification of 73 percent of the subject pool. The ranking and pair comparison methods revealed an agreement of 76 percent.

## VALIDITY OF THE SOCIAL VALUE CONCEPT

The validity of the social value concept has been thoroughly examined in previous research and the relationship between subject's social value and their behavior in social dilemmas is a well-established finding (for an overview, *see* Liebrand et al., 1992).

Numerous studies have shown that the base-rate level of cooperation in both formal game settings and in nonlaboratory field settings is highest among individuals classified as cooperators, lowest among those classified as competitive, and in between among those classified as individualists.

For example, it has been demonstrated that cooperatively oriented subjects make more cooperative choices in two-person experimental games, and also expect more cooperative choice behavior of others than either competitively oriented subjects or individualists.

In N-person games, in which every person during several rounds can take resources for him or herself from a commonly owned pool, the degree to which subjects economized on their takes was shown to depend on their social values.

Evidence concerning the predictive validity of social values has also been provided in a study that examined choice behavior in social dilemmas as a function of social value, the task's outcome contingency structure, and other's choice strategy.

The stability of social values and their influence in formal game settings was demonstrated by assessing social values four to six weeks before a social dilemma study. Support for the stability and the ecological validity of social values has also been obtained. Social values were measured using simple, noncomputerized, decomposed games several weeks before subjects were asked to volunteer for psychological research. The mean number of hours subjects were willing to contribute varied as a function of their social values. Further support for the ecological validity of the social value construct has been provided by using roommates' personality descriptions of cooperators, individualists, and competitors.

Several other studies on PERSONALITY have demonstrated a relationship with responses in settings of outcome interdependency. AUTHORITARIANISM is found to be related to social values, competitors having a higher level of authoritarianism than individualists and cooperators in a Prisoner's Dilemma game and in decomposed games. Also, subjects who were classified as cooperators on the basis of their choices in decomposed games, scored higher on an affiliation scale but lower on an aggression scale, relative to individualists and competitors.

Although research on social values has repeatedly shown that social values strongly influence behavior and judgment in interdependent situations, the construct validity of the social value concept would be strengthened substantially if it could be demonstrated that variations in social values not only influence the nature of judgments and/or decisions, but also the cognitive processing of information associated with SOCIAL JUDGMENTS and/or decisions. As will be discussed below, recent research efforts are addressing this issue.

COGNITIVE PROCESSES AND
SOCIAL VALUES
While much research concerning DECISION MAKING in interdependency situations concentrates on the existence of social value-related differences in behavior, relatively few studies have paid attention to the cognitive processes associated with the expression of these social values.

The "Might over Morality" hypothesis (Liebrand, Jansen, Rijke, & Suhre, 1986) predicts that cooperatively oriented subjects will attempt to establish relationships characterized by fairness, honesty, and TRUST. Cooperators are expected to bring a cooperative orientation to an interaction and would judge other's behaviors in evaluative terms of "good" and "bad." Individuals who evaluate relationships in terms of power or potency, on the other hand, would be most likely to establish relationships in which they could exercise dominance over others. These competitors are then expected to evaluate other's behavior in terms of "strong" and "weak."

Sattler and Kerr (1991) pointed out that the Might over Morality hypothesis has both a motivational and a cognitive component. The motivational model suggests that differences in social values reflect differences in goals, cooperators striving for morality and individualists striving for POWER and might. The cognitive interpretation or schema-model, on the other hand, suggests that differences in social values reflect differences in cognitive knowledge structures, or SCHEMAS, cooperators having an evaluation-related schema and individualists having a power-related schema. Until now, evidence for both interpretations has been reported.

Response Latencies (RLs) constitute a different domain in which the relation between social values and cognitive processes is currently being investigated.

The critical distinction between "given" and "effective" outcomes in the transformation model of Kelley and Thibaut (1978) suggests that individuals carry out different mental processes before making a decision. These mental processes would be reflected in the time needed to make a choice in outcome interdependency situations. The given outcomes constitute the information given to individuals, and the effective outcomes, on which the actual decisions are based, carry the information inferred from these given outcomes. Because the effective outcomes should be social value dependent, the amount of information necessary to generate the effective outcomes should also be social value-dependent.

According to this transformation model, it is obvious that both cooperators and competitors have to carry out more complex cognitive transformations than individualists or altruists, who are supposed to be concerned with either their own or the others' outcomes only. Liebrand and McClintock (1988) indeed found that altruists and individualists were faster in making decisions than cooperators and competitors. Furthermore, an interaction between the social value of the decision maker and the type of own/other outcomes was found. Cooperators' RLs turned out to be relatively long for those outcome distributions in which outcomes for both persons were negative, whereas for competitors an increase in RLs was found where own outcomes were negative and other's outcomes were positive. This finding is consistent with the assumption that negative outcomes for both persons should be aversive for cooperators, while outcome distributions in which one is put at a disadvantage should be especially aversive for competitors. However, besides this motivational explanation, the interaction between social value and outcome quadrant can also be explained on a cognitive basis. It is conceivable that RLs

may be influenced by arithmetic computations. More specifically, the social value-related patterns of RLs may demonstrate that comparing two negative numbers takes longer than comparing two positive numbers, that adding two negative numbers takes longer than adding two positive numbers, and that subtracting a positive from a negative number takes longer than subtracting a negative number from a positive one. In fact, this purely cognitive explanation would also support the transformation analysis. The most recent research findings indicate that both the motivational and the pure cognitive explanation accounts for part of the research findings on response lantencies related to choices in situations of outcome interdependency.

CONCLUSIONS

Social values can be defined as a more-or-less consistent system of orientations that influences both the manner in which an outcome-interdependent relationship is perceived and evaluated and the decisions that are made in these situations.

See also: AUTHORITARIANISM; COOPERATION AND COMPETITION; DECISION MAKING; EXPERIMENTAL GAMES; PERSONALITY; POWER; SCHEMAS/SCHEMATA SOCIAL DILEMMAS; SOCIAL JUDGEMENT; SOCIAL VALUES; TRUST.

BIBLIOGRAPHY

Deutsch, M. (1958). Trust and suspicion. *Journal of Conflict Resolution, 2*, 265–79.

Kelley, H. H., & Thibaut, J. (1978). *Interpersonal relations: A theory of interdependence.* New York: Wiley.

Kuhlman, D. M., & Marshello, A. (1975). Individual differences in game motivation as moderators of preprogrammed strategic effects in prisoner's dilemma. *Journal of Personality and Social Psychology, 32*, 922–31.

Liebrand, W. B. G., Jansen, R. W. T. L., Rijken, V. M., & Suhre, C. J. M. (1986). Might over morality: Social values and the perception of other players in experimental games. *Journal of Experimental Social Psychology, 22*, 203–15.

——— & McClintock, C. G. (1988). The ring measure of social values: A computerized procedure for assessing individual differences in information processing and social value orientation. *European Journal of Personality*, *2*, 217–30.

——Messick, D. M., & Wilke, H. A. M. (1992). *Social dilemmas: Theoretical issues and research findings*. Oxford: Pergamon.

Messick, D. M., & McClintock, C. G. (1968). Motivational bases of choice in experimental games. *Journal of Experimental Social Psychology*, *4*, 1–25.

Sattler, N. D., & Kerr, N. L. (1991). Might versus morality: Motivational and cognitive bases for social motives. *Journal of Personality and Social Psychology*, *60*, 756–65.

WIM B. G. LIEBRAND<br>F. M. J. DEHUE

**socialization** The process whereby people acquire the rules of behavior and the systems of BELIEFS and attitudes that equip a person to function effectively as a member of a particular society. Although socialization is a familiar and seemingly straightforward concept, it proves remarkably difficult to determine exactly how it occurs since it can never be observed directly. It is possible to monitor how people attempt to socialize others (e.g., how parents teach, guide, or correct their children) but the ways in which the recipients of such attentions develop their understanding and learn to regulate their own behavior can only be inferred from their observable responses. What is observable may provide only a partial insight into what is occurring within the organism. As a result, explaining how socialization comes about has been a fundamental source of controversy among theories of human social development.

The sheer scope of socialization also poses challenges to the investigator. The rules of behavior and the value systems of a society cover an enormous range of phenomena, from the daily domestic practices of an individual's family and personal network, through the public expectations of the community concerning the behaviors appropriate to age, class, GENDER, and other social categories, to the understanding of societal structures and elaboration of moral systems. Learning to operate effectively in respect of each of these involves not only building a massive information base but also changing one's personal responsibilities and capacities for action (for example, shifting through childhood from dependency to autonomy). Furthermore, many parties and institutions may be involved – including parents, siblings, peers, church, school, MASS MEDIA – and the contributions of any one may complement or conflict with the contributions of others.

Socialization – although typically studied in the young – never ceases, since progress through life involves learning new roles, entering new RELATIONSHIPS or institutions, adjusting to new developments in one's community and myriad other accommodations to a continually changing social environment. Hence, the study of socialization is not only controversial but also multifaceted, and part of the reason why there is a proliferation of theories of socialization is that there is so much to account for.

HISTORICAL INFLUENCES ON
CONCEPTS OF SOCIALIZATION
Much of the controversy revolves around the presumed contributions of the individual who is undergoing socialization. Traditionally, theories have divided broadly around the nature–nurture debate. At the "nature" end of the continuum, the child has been represented variously as innately "good" (or pure) and innately "bad" (or selfish). Hobbes depicted children as inherently selfish and competitive, driven by egoistic, pleasure-seeking motives and with little initial care for the interests of others. According to Hobbes, society's task was to control these bestial impulses and to instill in the young a sense of social responsibility.

A quite different representation of human nature was favored subsequently by Rousseau. Rousseau gained considerable influence over eighteenth-century European thought when he advanced the doctrine of innate purity, the thesis that all things are good at the point of creation but that they may be spoiled by the degenerative influences of society. It followed from Rousseau's position that the optimal conditions for child development would be those which impinged least upon the natural course of healthy personal development, and he placed great emphasis on the virtues of self-directed discovery in environments which allowed for the child's natural inquisitiveness and sense of moral equity.

Hence, different nature theorists have divergent views of the child but similar views of the origins of social behavior. For Hobbes the child was an inherently nasty brute, while for Rousseau, the child was a noble savage; but both saw these attributes as endowed by nature and socialization as resulting from intervention in natural development.

"Nurture" theorists, in contrast, represent the child as bringing very little to the process of socialization and instead regard him or her as a "blank slate" upon which society writes its message. The principal early exponent of this view was Locke, who described the infant as a *tabula rasa* who was innately neither good nor bad, but was shaped by the influences of whichever social environment he or she happened to join. In this empiricist view, nature makes minimal contributions, and socialization is essentially a process of moulding the newcomer and transmitting the accumulated learning of earlier generations.

NATURE AND NURTURE
IN PSYCHOLOGICAL THEORIES
OF SOCIALIZATION

Although some of the terminology has changed and the religious overtones of early doctrines were discarded with the advent of a discipline which regarded itself as a scientific enterprise, echoes of the early nature–nurture theories survive in recent and contemporary psychology. Freud, for example, viewed young children as naturally impulsive, with easily aroused emotions and little ability to restrain or delay gratification. For him, socialization came about as society (primarily represented by the parents) repressed and disciplined the reluctant newcomer into publicly accepted conventions. Problems incurred in the early periods of this process would be manifest in psychoses later in life, reflecting a tension between the needs and

drives of the developing organism and the constraints and goals of the surrounding society.

More recently, ethological and sociobiological theories have placed emphasis on the adaptive significance of the biological preparedness of both child and parent for regulated social behavior (*see* ETHOLOGY, SOCIOBIOLOGY). These approaches, too, regard socialization as constrained by nature, though both acknowledge the potential for society to disrupt or modify naturally emerging behaviors.

Learning theories dominant in North American psychology through the early part of the twentieth century maintained the nurture view of socialization, insisting that most behaviors are transmitted and maintained by learning. Influential behaviorists such as Watson and Skinner argued that the child knows very little at birth and that his or her behavior can be directed by environmental contingencies. Classical and operant conditioning were held by these theorists and their many followers to explain how children are guided to accept the rules of their family and broader social environment. Thus, the child discovers an association between a particular behavior and a particular outcome (e.g., between saying "please" and receiving a desired object, or between swearing and being sent to one's room), and learns to repeat actions which lead to a positive return and to reduce or abandon behaviors which result in negative consequences.

Bandura (1977) led a major advance on these early accounts with the development of SOCIAL LEARNING theory. Social learning theory accepts the importance of environmental feedback for modifying behavior, but places emphasis on two other components of the relationship between the child and the context: observation and cognition. Observation is important because it provides a swifter and more economical means of learning about socially approved modes of behavior than simply waiting for reinforcement of spontaneous behaviors. By watching the deeds of other people, the child can acquire new skills and can learn vicariously about the outcomes of particular actions. Hence, social learning theorists stress the importance of MODELING and observational learning in socialization, and much of their work has been concerned with the influence of sources such as parents or the mass media upon children's social behavior. Among other things, observational learning processes help to explain why children growing up in different societies come to adopt the social practices favoured in their particular environment.

Cognition is another key component of the socialization process, according to social learning theorists, because it mediates the ways in which children attend to the environment, how they represent the relationships among social events, how they store and retrieve information about behavior and its consequences, and how they elect to behave in a particular context. Children have to distinguish among behaviors and represent their meanings if they are to organize their own behavior accordingly. One benefit of a cognitive representation of modeled behavior is that the child can enact it subsequently in the absence of the original source. In this way, others' actions become internalized and available for reproduction (depending upon the child's capabilities).

Many psychological formulations of both nature and nurture theories represent socialization as a largely *unidirectional* process, in that society is seen as doing something to the newcomer which ensures that he or she fits in to the existing order. However, Bandura's exposition of social learning theory stresses the importance of *reciprocal* influences between the individual's behavior and events in his or her social environment. For example, a child who behaves aggressively might well elicit aggressive responses from her peers; this may result in her becoming still more aggressive as she finds this response the most efficacious means of dealing with the problems that her own behavior provokes.

SOCIALIZATION IN SOCIAL AND
DEVELOPMENTAL CONTEXTS
Recent thinking about socialization has been influenced substantially by two major thrusts in developmental psychology. The first has been the dominant influence of cognitive-developmental psychology, especially in the Piagetian tradition, during the middle part of

the twentieth century, and the second has been the advent, in the latter part of the century, of new technologies for the study of the very earliest stages of social interaction. These two developments have not proceeded hand-in-hand but each has affected how psychologists conceive of social developmental processes and each contributes to a revised understanding of the nature of socialization which goes beyond theories of inheritance or social shaping.

COGNITIVE-DEVELOPMENTAL THEORY
Cognitive-developmentalists stress the active role of the child in constructing an understanding of the world and his or her relation to it. In standard Piagetian theory, intellectual development is held to progress in a predictable, universal sequence of stages of increasing sophistication. At any one stage, the child's thinking in any domain is constrained by his or her current level of reasoning. In broad terms, the infant is focused on his or her sensorimotor capacities and the tangible characteristics of the external world, the preschooler is learning to represent the world symbolically but tends to see things largely from his or her own perspective, the middle school-aged child is coming to understand more complex causal relationships but performs best with tasks that be can handled directly, while the adolescent is developing newly emerging capacities for abstract, hypothetical reasoning.

According to Piaget, the child's stage of development determines how she or he will deal with data encountered in the environment. Most of Piaget's work was concerned with the child's understanding of the spatio-temporal environment, but in a seminal text (1932) he applied the general paradigm to the study of MORAL DEVELOPMENT, and more recent followers have attempted to extend it to other areas of social understanding such as the child's concepts of society, laws, domestic and occupational roles. The gist of this complex account is that the infant is largely oblivious to social regulations, while the preschooler is becoming aware that adults can direct behavior; the school-aged child grasps the need for rules, and the adolescent assesses the basis for the rules, imagines different rules, challenges the rules, and so on. In short, the environment does not simply impinge upon the child, but the child's stage of development determines what he or she assimilates from it. Much research confirms that children's cognitions of social phenomena do undergo qualitative changes in the course of development (Durkin, 1995).

In respect of socialization, the central premise of Piagetian-inspired studies is that the child is engaged in *self-socialization* (Ruble, 1987), embarking upon an active search for information that will guide his or her social behavior. For example, Ruble reviews work on gender role socialization which indicates that as children discover the significance of their own gender label (*boy* or *girl*) they attend selectively to the actions of particular people (men or women, as appropriate) who can provide them with clues as to what is expected of members of their social category. As the child organizes this information, he or she builds an increasingly sophisticated theory of the regularities of the social world.

## MUTUALITY IN PARENT–CHILD INTERACTION

On the basis of traditional nature or nurture theories, it might be expected that the infant would come into the world with either a rigidly preprogrammed repertoire of behaviors endowed by biology or an open receptivity to any sort of external actions the environment happened to afford. However, as researchers began to study the behavior of infants and caregivers in fine detail via microanalytic study of videorecorded interactions, neither image was confirmed.

Instead, it became clear that from very early in the infant's life, parent and child are engaged in reciprocal behavior (Kaye, 1982; Schaffer, 1984; Stern, 1985). Kaye showed that even in the simplest burst-pause patterns of early feeding, mother and infant begin to establish a mutual, rhythmic interchange in which each party influences responses of the other; Schaffer demonstrated that the mother–baby dyad evolves patterns of vocal and gestural alternation which bear marked

similarities to the turn-taking of later conversation; Stern concludes that the infant is socially responsive and involved in a developing relationship with the caregiver. While there is dispute about the relative contributions of each partner to the smoothness of the interaction, it is certainly established that from the beginnings of social life the infant plays an active role and that this enables him or her to participate in joint behavior. Many developmentalists maintain that the origins of a great deal of the child's later social, linguistic, and cognitive skills are to be found in this joint activity (*see* Durkin, 1995, for fuller discussion).

Hence, applications of cognitive-developmental frameworks to the study of social knowledge have led to a greater emphasis on the active role of the child in constructing an understanding of the social order. Research into the dynamics of parent–infant interaction provides another perspective on the active contributions of the child but highlights also the joint nature of social behavior. These theoretical developments have contributed to a general rejection among psychologists of accounts which attribute socialization to the unfolding of inherited behaviors or to the impact of external forces. However, asserting the active role of the child does not in itself address the question of how a particular way of social life is sustained and reproduced.

## DIVERSITY OF SOCIALIZATION PRACTICES AND OUTCOMES

Studies of socialization are circumscribed by the fact that the outcomes are so variable across cultures. Different societies maintain radically different value systems and behavioral practices, even in respect of such seemingly fundamental matters as morality, tolerance of aggression, the roles of the genders, the status of different age groups, collective and personal goals (*see* CROSS-CULTURAL SOCIAL PSYCHOLOGY, CULTURE, VALUES). The shift in psychology away from earlier "clay moulding" theories of socialization has led to some neglect of this environmental diversity. Critics of constructivist theories argue that they fail to take adequate account of the *content* of socialization, and press the need to address more fully the processes which ensure that the child acquires the particular values and practices of a particular community.

These objections have led in turn to new directions in socialization theory. Drawing substantially upon cross-cultural data, researchers are investigating the ways in which the young acquire the SOCIAL REPRESENTATIONS that are shared in their society (Emler, Ohana, & Dickinson, 1990). Shweder (1991) maintains that children acquire local moral orders as a result of recurrent involvement in moral discourse with members of their community who trace for them "the boundaries of a normative reality and assist [them] in stepping into the frame" (p. 191). Goodnow (1990) argues similarly that children become socialized through participation in daily routines, which immerse them directly in the values of their community. To take a simple but telling example, if most people in the community wear and consult watches, this is likely to lead to the child discovering the salience of time; in their absence, the child's understanding of the structures of daily life may be markedly different to that assumed in industrialized nations.

These emphases upon social representations and practices do not necessarily refute concepts of the active child and of cognitive constraints upon the assimilation of social information, although there is much dispute about the validity of purportedly universal stage theories (*see* Emler et al., 1990; Shweder, 1991, for critiques). The active involvement of a cognitive being is presupposed, but greater attention is paid to the ways in which specific routines and beliefs are incorporated into developing social understanding and reflected in actual social behavior.

While the breadth of the processes is such that a great deal remains to be investigated, the evolution of the concept of socialization is continuing. It is manifest in a shift from early notions of unidirectional transmission or control, to an emphasis on construction and reciprocity, followed by a greater awareness of the participatory social activities through which a community's value system is enacted and reproduced.

*See also*: CROSS-CULTURAL SOCIAL PSYCHOLOGY; CULTURE; ETHOLOGY; GENDER; MASS MEDIA; MORAL DEVELOPMENT; RELATIONSHIPS; SOCIAL LEARNING; SOCIAL REPRESENTATIONS; SOCIOBIOLOGY; VALUES.

BIBLIOGRAPHY

Bandura, A. (1977). *Social learning theory.* Englewood Cliffs, NJ: Prentice Hall.

Durkin, K. (1995). *Developmental social psychology: From infancy to old age.* Oxford: Blackwell Publishers.

Emler, N. P., Ohana, J., & Dickinson, J. (1990). Children's representations of social relations. In G. Duveen and B. Lloyd (Eds.), *Social representations and the development of knowledge* (pp. 161–83). Cambridge: Cambridge University Press.

Goodnow, J. J. (1990). The socialization of cognition: What's involved? In J. W. Stigler, R. A. Shweder, & G. Herdt (Eds.), *Cultural psychology. Essays on comparative human development* (pp. 259–86). Cambridge: Cambridge University Press.

Kaye, K. (1982). *The mental and social life of babies.* Brighton: Harvester.

Piaget, J. (1932). *The moral judgment of the child.* Harmondsworth: Penguin.

Ruble, D. N. (1987). The acquisition of self-knowledge: A self-socialization perspective. In N. Eisenberg (Ed.), *Contemporary topics in developmental psychology* (pp. 281–312). New York: Wiley.

Schaffer, H. R. (1984). Parental control techniques in the context of socialization theory. In W. Doise and A. Palmonari (Eds.), *Social interaction in individual development* (pp. 65–77). Cambridge: Cambridge University Press.

Shweder, R. A. (1991). *Thinking through cultures. Expeditions in cultural psychology.* Cambridge, MA: Harvard University Press.

Stern, D. (1985). *The interpersonal world of the infant.* New York: Basic Books.

KEVIN DURKIN

**sociobiology**  This is the application of Darwin's principle of natural selection to explaining the origins and maintenance of social behavior. It became identifiable as a specific approach with the publication of the book *Sociobiology: The new synthesis,* by E. O. Wilson (1975), in which he sought to provide a theoretical framework, based on natural selection, for both the biological and social sciences. Although mostly concerned with animal societies, it was Wilson's recommendations that the human social sciences be swallowed up by Darwinian biology, together with his single chapter on human behavior, that provoked controversy and in some cases outrage.

The term sociobiology therefore covers both animal and human societies. In the former case (where it is often replaced by, or overlaps with, the term behavioral ecology), it has provided the impetus for a large body of theory and research on the adaptive significance of behavior, arising from a synthesis of social ETHOLOGY, ecology, and population biology (see Archer, 1992).

Applying the principle of natural selection to human behavior raises a number of problems (outlined at the end of this entry). These have been ignored by enthusiastic advocates of sociobiology and used by critics to deny that the enterprise has any merit at all. Sociobiology has now come to exert a wide influence on the social sciences, notably in anthropology and (more recently) in social psychology. In anthropology, the principal issue is whether human social organization can be viewed in terms of a series of adaptations to the ecological conditions in which different peoples live; the alternative perspective is to regard variations in social organization as following cultural beliefs which are unrelated to questions of biological fitness.

The impact of sociobiology on social psychology has been to place the following premise on the research agenda: that the social dispositions of human beings can be understood as the results of the past workings of natural selection, rather than the learning of cultural values and beliefs which are unconnected with biological fitness (see SOCIAL LEARNING; SOCIALIZATION). There is, therefore, a parallel between the central issue dividing those who work within a sociobiological framework and those who reject it, in both anthropology and social psychology. However, the two disciplines differ in the level at which they study social behavior.

The starting-point that human social dispositions can be understood in terms of nat-ural selection leads the researcher to frame hypotheses in terms of ultimate or functional explanations rather than the causal mechanisms which are the usual concern of psychologists. The two types of explanation may, however, be linked if the results of natural selection can be detected in the way people act, and the way their minds work, today. The functional evolutionary approach may therefore explain both the original reason for human beings behaving as they do, *and* the types of thinking patterns and dispositions that this background has left them with today. Many of those who concentrate on this second question prefer to call themselves EVOLUTIONARY PSYCHOLOGISTS rather than sociobiologists.

Although Darwin clearly regarded behavior, like morphology, as resulting from natural selection, the exact implications of this conclusion were, with a few exceptions, not fully realized until the 1960s. Two interrelated general issues needed to be tackled in order to pave the way for the sociobiological theorizing that followed. These concerned the unit of selection and HELPING BEHAVIOR (or ALTRUISM).

Darwin viewed natural selection as involving a struggle for survival at the individual level. However, a number of those who later studied behavior within psychology and ethology referred to traits as evolving for the good of the group or the species (even if they might handicap the individual). The central flaw in this argument is as follows. Any individual which behaves so as to benefit the whole group more than itself will be vulnerable to being replaced in future generations by individuals that behave so as to benefit themselves irrespective of the effect on the group. This point was clearly demonstrated by Maynard Smith, Williams, and others, leading to a consensus that selection operated on the individual. Yet this posed an apparent problem in accounting for the origin of behavior which seemed to benefit others more than the individual displaying it. Such behavior (sometimes called altruism) can be observed widely among animals: e.g., a soldier ant fighting to defend its colony; parental behavior which puts the parent at risk from predation; an animal sharing food.

The existence of most cases of "altruism" in animals can be understood when it is realized that the gene is the true unit of selection (although in practice groups of genes are selected together). A donor can therefore indirectly increase its own fitness (i.e., the representation of its genes in future generations) by helping other individuals who are genetically related to it, and the tendency to do so will increase with the degree of relatedness. The term "inclusive fitness" is used to refer to the way fitness is affected by such interactions with relatives.

In practice, most cases of so-called altruism in the animal world can be explained in these terms. For advanced social animals, Trivers (1971) demonstrated that there would also be circumstances in which altruistic behavior would occur between unrelated individuals, provided that the acts cost little to the donor, were of considerable benefit to the recipient, and there was likely to be RECIPROCITY in the future. This was termed "reciprocal altruism."

In practice, the principles of kin selection and reciprocal altruism go a long way to explaining human altruism, particularly in an anthropological context. Thompson (1980) examined the conditions under which people helped one another, as found in experimental psychological studies, and found a close fit with the variables identified by Trivers; Vine (1983) also explored the implications for social psychology of sociobiological explanations of altruism, including the extent to which being conscious agents enables humans to act outside this evolved framework.

This analysis of the conditions under which altruism has evolved demonstrates the way in which specific models have to be carefully derived from the principle of individual selection. In this sense sociobiology provides a predictive approach. However, there has also been a tendency – particularly in the initial sociobiological accounts of human behavior – to seek post hoc "explanations" which were not so carefully derived.

There is now a large body of theory about the outcomes of natural selection for specific types of behavior under particular conditions. Some of this began with R. A. Fisher in the 1930s, but most dates from the late 1960s onwards. Some has involved intuitive reasoning aided by graphical representations, as in the influential work of Robert Trivers (see above); however, these were soon succeeded by mathematical models and computer simulations of the evolutionary process.

One important theoretical advance for understanding the evolution of social behavior in animals was the use of game theory (see EXPERIMENTAL GAMES). It has been applied extensively to animal fighting (Archer, 1988), and has also been used to depict mating strategies, and parental behavior. The relative fitness consequences of different behavioral strategies are depicted in a pay-off matrix showing their costs and benefits in relation to one another. This provides a way of calculating the fitness of different forms of behavior when they depend on the nature and frequency of other strategies. Maynard Smith also introduced the important concept of evolutionarily stable strategy (ESS): this refers to a specific strategy or combination of strategies which cannot be replaced by alternatives under the current fitness costs and benefits operating in that population. The game theory approach is important for demonstrating the *relative* nature of fitness where social interactions are concerned. It has, however, seldom been applied to humans.

Social psychology has used only a restricted range of sociobiological concepts compared to those applied to animals. These are inclusive fitness (see above), reproductive value (see below) and extensions of Darwin's theory of sexual selection. However, the topics to which they have been applied are more numerous, including altruism (see above), ATTACHMENT, ATTRACTION, BEREAVEMENT, child abuse, friendship, GENDER roles, homicide (see VIOLENCE), JEALOUSY, PERSONALITY, and RAPE.

Reproductive value is an age-dependent measure of an individual's potential contribution to future generations: typically, it increases from the beginning of life as life expectancy increases, and then decreases from the time the first offspring is produced, reaching zero at the end of reproductive life. Daly and Wilson (1988) derived hypotheses about infanticide and parricide from the relative changes in reproductive value with age for parents and offspring. They tested these by examining cross-cultural, historical, and criminological data, which were generally consistent with their predictions. For example, infanticide (which was viewed as occurring when the survival prospects for that offspring were poor) decreased with the age of the mother (as her reproductive value declined); it also decreased with the child's age (as its reproductive value increased). Parricide, on the other hand, increased with parental age (since the parents' reproductive value for themselves and for their offspring – via inclusive fitness – declined).

Crawford, Salter, and Jang (1989) used the same concept to derive hypotheses about the grief experienced by parents losing different-aged children in an automobile accident. Participants rated the relative grief they expected parents to experience following the death of a series of two differently aged children. A correlation of 0.64 was found between the grief ratings and reproductive value calculated from census data for Canada (the location of the study); however, this was raised to 0.94 when the curve for reproductive value against age for !Kung hunter-gatherers was used. Since the !Kung curve is likely to be nearer to that for evolving hominids, this finding suggests that the social judgments of modern humans are informed by an intuitive appreciation of the reproductive values of children as they were throughout most of human evolution and history.

Darwin realized that natural selection based on differential access to fertile members of the opposite sex involves some specialized features, which he termed "sexual selection." He observed that it usually took the form of intermale competition and female choice of suitable mates. Trivers (1972) identified the origin of these different reproductive strategies as the imbalance between female and male in the investment of time and energy needed to produce eggs or sperm. Other things being equal, this enables the male but not the female to adopt the strategy of leaving the other with the fertilized eggs, to fertilize further eggs elsewhere. However, this pattern can often be reversed by environmental circumstances, and by the requirements of parenting, particularly where fertilization is external and where both sexes can feed the offspring. In mammals, however, neither is the case, thus making departures from the typical pattern less likely. Internal fertilization also introduces uncertainty of paternity, which becomes a particularly important factor where there is paternal care.

Mammals vary in mating patterns from monogamous pairs (where the male is similar in size to the female and is involved in paternal care) to extreme polygyny (where a larger male defends and herds a number of females, but provides little paternal care). Behavioral differences, particularly in aggression, accompany these mating patterns and size differences. In the human case, there is a moderate size difference between the sexes, indicating at least some tendency towards different male and female strategies: this will produce not only a conflict of interest between the sexes which will have implications for their interactions and relationships with one another, but also different dispositions and inclinations in males and females.

This analysis has been applied to research in a number of areas of human behavior, for example mate selection (*see* attraction), the training of boys and girls, behavior in CLOSE RELATIONSHIPS, AGGRESSION and violence, RISK taking, and jealousy. The following two examples illustrate the contrasting methods which have been brought to bear in assessing sociobiological hypotheses.

Sexual selection predicts greater variability in male than female reproductive success, and as a consequence greater intermale competition. A game theory simulation of competition where the fitness prospects were poor for the losers (Daly & Wilson, 1988) showed that selection would favor risky strategies despite their having high mortality costs for individuals. Daly and Wilson found that homicide data showed such reckless behavior in young males, notably those with few resources. Homicides arose from escalated disputes which involved status or face-saving or from sexual rivalry or resistance encountered in the course of a robbery.

Internal fertilization brings with it uncertainty of paternity, yet complete certainty of maternity. If a male rears another male's offspring, he will not only have wasted that mating opportunity but, more importantly, he will have expended parental aid and protection to an unrelated individual. Such behavior will have severe fitness costs, and where it is a possibility, various male counter-strategies have evolved, including infanticide, sperm competition, and mate guarding. All three are likely to occur in humans, where paternal involvement is relatively high. Buss et al. (1992) view the emotion of jealousy as reflecting this concern with sexual access in males, but not in females (where it should be more related to withdrawal of male interest and support to another female). They tested this hypothesis by presenting undergraduates with scenarios depicting their partner engaged in sexual activities with someone else or forming a romantic attachment to them. Men showed a stronger reaction when sexual infidelity was depicted whereas women showed more in the case of emotional attachment, supporting the hypothesis. The authors do, however, recognize the limitations of the sample in terms of age and cultural background, a point which has led to other researchers abandoning social psychological methods, in favor of examining crosscultural and archival material.

Finally, it is important to note a number of potential limitations to the sociobiological approach. First, we should recognize that selection acts on existing organisms, so that many adaptive avenues are ruled out (constrained) by the existing form that an organism takes. Evolving hominids were therefore unlikely to evolve wings or asexual reproduction from their ancestral form. Other adaptations are possible, but involve compromises producing less than optimum designs in other bodily systems: bipedalism and large brains were both crucial changes in human evolution, but they have been achieved at the expense of back and birth problems respectively. In terms of behavior, attachment is clearly adaptive for parenting and for offspring survival, but it has as its cost the EMOTIONAL EXPERIENCE of GRIEF, which is maladaptive. These examples show that although the overall effects of adaptations are likely to increase fitness in the evolutionary environment, individual behavioral reactions may not necessarily do so.

Secondly, it is important to recognize that it is not necessarily specific acts of behavior which have been subject to selection but dispositions to act in particular ways. Some of these are very simple responses to stimuli, so that when the environment is changed (as it has to a large extent for humans) they readily become maladaptive: a liking for sugar might be considered an example of such a feature. Other reactions are mediated by emotions such as ANGER or jealousy or LOVE, which are not themselves adaptive but produce a tendency to act in an adaptive way in the evolutionary environment. Under present conditions, which include the availability of guns, anger associated with jealousy may prove a fitness-reducing activity for the person who acts it out in a violent way (Daly & Wilson, 1988).

This leads to a third point, that a sociobiological explanation does not necessarily inform us about the mechanisms controlling behavior: these may simply have worked (i.e., aided fitness) in the evolutionary environment, but not in other circumstances. Alternatively, they may have been designed so as to respond in a variable way to maximize fitness in a range of environments. It is these sorts of mechanisms which are of interest to evolutionary psychologists (*see above*).

The value of the sociobiological approach is that it can provide a broad integrating framework linking many phenomena hitherto studied separately, thus enabling old issues or problems to be viewed in different ways. It is now beginning to generate novel hypotheses about human behavior, which can be tested against existing data from the social sciences, and against novel data specifically collected for this purpose.

*See also*: AGGRESSION; ATTRACTION; EMOTIONAL EXPERIENCE; ETHOLOGY; EXPERIMENTAL GAMES; GENDER; GRIEF; HELPING BEHAVIOR; JEALOUSY AND ENVY; PERSONALITY; RAPE; RISK; SOCIAL LEARNING; SOCIALIZATION.

BIBLIOGRAPHY

Archer, J. (1988). *The behavioral biology of aggression*. Cambridge: Cambridge University Press.

—— (1992). *Ethology and human development*. Hemel Hempstead: Harvester; Savage, MD: Barnes & Noble.

Buss, B. M., Larsen, R. J., Westen, D., & Semmelroth, J. (1992). Sex differences in jealousy: Evolution, physiology and psychology. *Psychological Science*, *3*, 251–5.

Crawford, C. B., Salter, B. E., & Jang, K. L. (1989). Human grief: Is its intensity related to the reproductive value of the deceased? *Ethology and Sociobiology*, *10*, 297–307.

Daly, M., & Wilson, M. (1988). *Homicide*. New York: Aldine de Gruyter.

Thompson, P. R. (1980). And who is my neighbour? An answer from evolutionary genetics. *Social Science Information*, *19*, 341–84.

Trivers, R. L. (1971). The evolution of reciprocal altruism. *Quarterly Review of Biology*, *46*, 35–57.

—— (1972). Parental investment and sexual selection. In B. Campbell (Ed.), *Sexual selection and the descent of man* (pp. 136–79). Chicago, IL: Aldine.

Vine, I. (1983). Sociobiology and social psychology – rivalry or symbiosis? The explanation of altruism. *British Journal of Social Psychology*, *22*, 1–11.

Wilson, E.O. (1975). *Sociobiology: The new synthesis*. Cambridge, MA: Belknap Press.

JOHN ARCHER

**spontaneous self-concept** The spontaneous self-concept is the SELF as spontaneously described when a person is asked "Tell us about yourself." This technique of questioning is primarily used by sociologically oriented social psychologists. The aim is to provide a nonreactive measure of the self-concept. Earlier and well-established techniques include the "Twenty Statements Test," which asks respondents to write twenty sentences answering the question "Who am I?". Responses are content-analyzed (*see* CONTENT ANALYSIS). McGuire and McGuire (1988) conducted a major research program testing Distinctiveness Theory using the "Tell us about yourself" method (*see also* McGuire, McGuire, & Cheever, 1986). Their studies show that the spontaneous self-concepts of children typically consist of attributes which are distinctive (uncommon) in their social environment. For example, ethnicity is more salient for minority groups within a school. This finding is consistent with other research demonstrating the

SALIENCE of minority features. It is also possible to explore the importance of other people (such as parents or friends) to the self-concept using these techniques.

*See also*: CONTENT ANALYSIS; SELF.

BIBLIOGRAPHY

McGuire, W. J., & McGuire, C. (1988). Content and process in the experience of self. In L. Berkowitz (Ed.), *Advances in experimental social psychology* (Vol 20, pp. 92–144). New York: Academic Press.

—— & Cheever, J. (1986). The self in society: Effects of social contexts on the sense of self. *British Journal of Social Psychology*, *25*, 259–70.

DOMINIC ABRAMS

**statistics** Numbers that are computed from a batch or sample of data that have been collected by a researcher. These numbers summarize or describe the shapes of the distributions of the data in the sample. Most frequently, researchers are interested not only in describing the sample of data they have collected but also in describing the distributions of data in the full population from which they have sampled. Statistics computed in a sample are thus useful in part because they provide the researcher with estimates of the population parameters (i.e., the numbers that would summarize or describe the shapes of the distributions in the entire population if all such data were available). Statistical inference is the process of estimating the population parameters from the sample statistics and quantifying the uncertainty of those estimates. As such, statistical inference is used by researchers in social psychology to draw conclusions from data about the replicability of empirical results if repeated samples of data were drawn from the same population.

DESCRIPTIONS OF A SAMPLE OF DATA
Assume that a researcher has measured some variable $X$ in a sample of subjects. Assume further that scores on variable $X$ are numeric and vary more or less continuously. (S)he

now wants to describe what the set of $X$ scores looks like or to summarize the resulting distribution of data. (S)he can draw pictures of the data to do this. Frequency distributions, frequency polygons or histograms, box plots, stem and leaf diagrams, and other graphic displays of data are useful ways to draw pictures of data (Tukey, 1977).

Drawing such pictures of data makes clear that distributions differ in a variety of ways. First of all, distributions differ in their central tendency. The central tendency of a distribution of data is the middle of the distribution or the typical score of the distribution. Some distributions have scores that have higher typical scores than other distributions. Thus, to describe a distribution, statistics that measure the distribution's central tendency are useful.

Distributions of data also differ in how spread out or variable the scores in the distributions are. Some distributions contain scores that are all very similar to each other. Other distributions contain scores that are highly variable or where there are big differences from one score to the next. Statistics that describe the variability of a distribution of data are thus also useful in summarizing a sample of data.

Other characteristics of data distributions may also be useful for describing their shape in addition to their central tendency and variability. One might be interested in whether a distribution of data seems relatively symmetric around the central tendency or whether the outlying or unusual scores seem more abundant in one tail of the distribution than the other. This feature of data is known as the skewness of the data and appropriate statistics exist for summarizing the skewness of a distribution. For most purposes, statistics that assess the central tendency and variability of a distribution are sufficient and those will be described in greater detail below. But other statistics exist that summarize additional characteristics of data distributions.

Measures of central tendency include, most usefully, the mean and the median. The mean is the number that is the average of all the scores in the distribution of data. The median is the fiftieth percentile score in a distribution of data, meaning that half of the scores lie below it and half above it. The two statistics, the mean and the median, will not equal each other unless the distribution is perfectly symmetric.

Measures of variability include the range, the interquartile range, and the variance. The range is simply the difference between the highest and lowest scores in the distribution. The interquartile range is the difference between 25th and 75th percentile scores. The variance is the average squared distance of each individual score from the mean of the distribution. The standard deviation is simply the square root of the variance and hence redundant with it as a measure of variability.

Descriptive statistics also exist to describe the joint distributions of two or more variables. Assuming a linear relationship between two variables, the slope or regression coefficient gives the best prediction of changes in one variable, given changes in the other. The correlation coefficient or Pearson $r$ indicates the magnitude of the linear relationship between the two variables and is simply the standardized form of the slope. With multiple predictor variables, partial slopes or regression coefficients tell us about predicted changes in the dependent variable, given changes in the predictor, holding other predictor variables constant. The multiple $R$ indicates how well the set of predictors does in generating predictions of the dependent variable.

Formulas for the computation of all of these descriptive statistics are readily available in statistics textbooks (e.g., Glenberg, 1988; Kenny, 1987, Judd & McClelland, 1989). They are also computed routinely by statistics software packages available for both personal and mainframe computers (e.g., SAS, 1990; SPSS, 1990).

## STATISTICS AS ESTIMATES OF POPULATION PARAMETERS

Inferences about the value of a population parameter, based on sample data, are typically conducted by testing what is called a null hypothesis about a particular value of that parameter. Alternatively, researchers can estimate an interval within which they believe the value of population parameter lies, with known confidence. This confidence interval, as it is called, turns out to be equivalent to the test of any null hypothesis about any particular value of the parameter.

Statistical inference is based on the idea that statistics themselves have distributions, if one were to repeatedly sample from the population and compute the sample statistic in those repeated samples. Such distributions are known as sampling distributions. Making assumptions about the distribution of scores on the relevant variables in the population, mathematical statisticians have given us exact derivations of many of these sampling distributions. The assumptions that underlie these derivations are typically that the variable's scores in the population have a normal distribution, are independent of each other, and have a constant variance.

Such sampling distributions permit the researcher to test particular values of population parameters, formulated as a null hypothesis, using the following logic. One starts by assuming that the population parameter equals the value specified in the null hypothesis. If this is true, then one can derive the probability of all possible values for the corresponding sample statistic, given the appropriate sampling distribution. One then defines a decision rule for deciding whether or not one will reject the null hypothesis. That decision rule takes the form of specifying a probability limit for observing given values of the sample statistic. Typically, that probability limit, also known as alpha or the probability of a Type I error, is set at 0.05. If the observed sample statistic in the data collected would occur under the null hypothesis with probability less than 0.05, then one rejects the null hypothesis.

This logic makes clear that one can only decide about unlikely values for population parameters. One can never reach a decision that a parameter equals some particular value; one can simply reject a given value or a set of given values. The confidence interval for the values of a parameter is the set of values that one would not reject if one tested each one as a null hypothesis.

The width of the confidence interval is in part affected by the size of the sample from which data have been collected. Larger sam-ples tend to yield smaller confidence intervals. Smaller confidence intervals mean greater statistical precision or power, since there is then a narrower range of possible values for the parameter and a wider range of rejected values. All too often, researchers commit the error of designing research with insufficient statistical power. (*See* Cohen, 1988, for a full discussion of statistical power.)

The logic underlying statistical inference can be applied not only to tests of individual parameter values but also to tests of differences between parameter values and more complicated questions. Some of the most frequently used statistical inferential tests are described below.

## SPECIFIC INFERENTIAL TESTS

*t*-test for independent samples: Used to ask whether the means from two independent samples, such as subjects in an experimental and control groups, differ from each other.

*t*-test for dependent samples: Asks the same question as the independent test but allows for links between observations in the two groups, e.g., when each subject is observed twice, once in the control group and once in the experimental one.

One way analysis of variance: Permits a test of whether there exist any differences among a set of means, where those means come from independent groups who differ in value on a single independent variable.

Higher order analysis of variance: Asks whether multiple independent groups have different means when those groups differ on more than a single independent variable. Permits tests both of differences in means as a function of each independent variable separately as well as differences due to interactions among two or more independent variables. An interaction implies that differences in means as a function of one independent variable depend on the level of one or more of the other independent variables.

Repeated measures or within-subjects analysis of variance: Asks about mean differences as a function of multiple independent

variables when there are linked or noninde-
pendent observations in the different levels
of the independent factors. If observations
are independent of each other across some
factors but linked across others, then the
analysis is call a mixed model analysis of
variance.

Analysis of covariance: Asks whether there are
mean differences between multiple groups,
as a function of one or more independent
variables, when controlling for or holding
constant some concomitant variable.

Test of a correlation coefficient: Asks whether
two variables are reliably related to each
other. Equivalent to a test that the slope
differs from zero.

Test of partial regression coefficients: Asks
whether one predictor variable is predictive
of the dependent variable when controlling
for or holding constant other predictor
variables. Equivalent to a test of a partial
correlation coefficient.

Test of the multiple correlation coefficient:
Asks whether a set of predictor variables are
useful in predicting a dependent variable.

Although the above tests are listed as discrete questions that statistical inference permits the researcher to ask of his or her data,
there are strong links and even equivalences
among these tests. Thus, for instance, a test
for the difference between two group means
can be equivalently conducted as a test that a
correlation coefficient departs from zero.
Similarly, a higher-order analysis of variance
can be equivalently conducted as tests of
partial regression coefficients (Judd &
McClelland, 1989).

Many additional tests exist for particular
questions that are more rarely of interest. In
addition, multivariate equivalences of all of
the above tests exist. Multivariate tests are
simply tests of the same hypotheses as those
listed above when there are multiple dependent variables that are analyzed simultaneously
(Dillon & Goldstein, 1984).

LIMITS OF STATISTICAL INFERENCE:
DATA EXPLORATION

All of the above inferential tests make certain
"parametric" assumptions about the data in
the population. These assumptions, briefly
mentioned earlier, are that the data are normally distributed, that they come from one
distribution having a single variance, and that
they come from independent observations unless the statistical test specifically deals with
nonindependence (e.g., repeated measures
analysis of variance). There are many times
when these assumptions are very unlikely.
Certainly, for instance, the assumption that a
variable is normally distributed will be violated when the variable can take on only two
values (e.g., subjects respond either with a
yes or a no). In such cases, researchers rely
on what are known as nonparametric statistical tests (Siegal & Castellan, 1988). Such
methods are frequently equivalent to the
usual parametric methods applied to data that
has been subject to a rank-order transformation. In general, transformations of non-
normal data or data with different variances
can help alleviate assumption violations (Judd
& McClelland, 1989).

The two assumptions of normality and constant variance are known as "robust" assumptions. This means that small violations of
them generally do not lead to major biases in
hypothesis testing or parameter estimation.
This is not true, however, for the assumption
of independence. If observations are linked
in ways that are not taken into account in
the analyses, major mistakes of statistical
inference are likely. Consider a case where
a researcher is interested in social developmental issues. Suppose children from ten
classrooms in a school served as subjects,
with those from five of the classrooms being
assigned to one experimental condition and
those from the other five classrooms being
assigned to another condition. If individual
children are treated as the unit of analysis,
then the statistical conclusions are likely to be
biased since children within classrooms are
likely to be more similar to each other than
children in different classrooms. Hence classrooms induce nonindependence in observations and must be taken into account in the
analysis, preferably by treating classrooms as
the unit of analysis.

Another situation where nonindependence
is frequently encountered in social psychological research is when dyadic or group

behavior is the subject of study. In fact, in this case, the nonindependence of the dyadic data that creates statistical difficulties, unless it is taken into account in the analysis, is the very phenomenon likely to be of theoretical interest to the social psychologist. Dyadic nonindependence, i.e., how the behaviors of two individuals are affected by each other, is the essence of social psychology. Procedures for the analysis of such data, recognizing the nonindependence problems, have been the subject of much recent research (e.g., Kenny & LaVoie, 1984).

The final problem that can lead to serious biases in parameter estimation and statistical inference occurs when there are very unusual or "outlying" observations in a set of data. Such outliers in fact mean that one is sampling observations from different distributions, having different variances, and hence the presence of outliers in a set of data constitutes a violation of the constant variance assumption. As discussed by Judd and McClelland (1989), outliers can lead to serious estimation errors. Procedures to detect and deal with outliers are also discussed by these authors.

An appropriate conclusion from the above list of potential problems in statistical inference is that researchers should not rely exclusively on inferential tests of null hypotheses. Researchers should be encouraged to look at raw data and to report parameter estimates rather than only their associated inferential statistics. And they should be wary about the presence of outliers, data that are clearly not normally distributed, and hidden sources of nonindependence. Only a close look at data permits the researcher to identify these and other problems. In this regard, recent advances in computer software for analyzing data are somewhat of a mixed blessing for the researcher. On the one hand, the availability of very efficient technology for analyzing data has meant that it is very easy simply to let the computer do the work and never look closely at the data. On the other hand, recent advances in statistical software include some very sophisticated new ways of looking at data graphically. The social psychologist who is seriously interested in what his or her data have to say, and wishes to

avoid the pitfalls that arise from exclusive reliance on significance testing, is well advised to make use of the these graphic capabilities.

*See also*: METHODOLOGY.

BIBLIOGRAPHY

Cohen, J. (1988). *Statistical power analysis for the behavioral sciences* (2nd ed.). Hillsdale, NJ: Lawrence Erlbaum.

Dillon, W.R., & Goldstein, M. (1984). *Multivariate analysis: Methods and applications.* New York: Wiley.

Glenberg, A. M. (1988). *Learning from data.* San Diego, CA: Harcourt Brace Jovanovich.

Judd, C. M., & McClelland, G.H. (1989). *Data analysis: A model comparison approach.* San Diego, CA: Harcourt Brace Jovanovich.

Kenny, D. A. (1987). *Statistics for the social and behavioral sciences.* Boston, MA: Little, Brown.

——& LaVoie, L. (1984). The social relations model. In L. Berkowitz (Ed.), *Advances in experimental social psychology* (Vol. 18, pp. 141–82). New York: Academic Press.

*SAS language: Reference* (1990). Version 6. Carey, NC: SAS Institute.

*SPSS base system user's guide.* (1990). Chicago, IL: SPSS

Siegel, S., & Castellan, N.J. (1988). *Nonparametric statistics for the behavioral sciences* (2nd ed.). New York: McGraw-Hill.

Tukey, J. W. (1977). *Exploratory data analysis.* Reading, MA: Addison-Wesley.

CHARLES M. JUDD

**status-expectation states theory** This theory holds that individuals make judgments about each other on the basis of status characteristics (ability, age, gender, race). This gives rise to expectations about the other's performance capabilities. These performance expectations in turn influence behavior in the interaction (Berger & Conner, 1969). This perspective is different from SOCIOBIOLOGY perspectives that argue that responses to status cues reflect inherited behavior patterns, and that status cues elicit behavior directly with no mediation by expectations. Driskell and Mullen (1990) integrated the results of previous research examining these two possibilities, and found evidence in support of status-expectation states theory. Status exerts strong effects on expectations but relatively weak effects on behavior. Expectations are a strong independent predictor of behavior. These findings support the argument that status exerts its effects on behavior indirectly, through its effects on expectations. *See also*: SOCIOBIOLOGY.

BIBLIOGRAPHY
Berger, J., & Conner, T. L. (1969). Performance expectations and behavior in small groups. *Acta Sociologica, 12,* 186–97.
Driskell, J. E., & Mullen, B. (1990). Status, expectations, and behavior: A meta-analytic review and test of the theory. *Personality and Social Psychology Bulletin, 16,* 541–53.

MICHAEL MIGDAL
BRIAN MULLEN

**stereotyping**   The use of stereotypes when judging others. Stereotypes are societally shared BELIEFS about the characteristics (such as personality TRAITS, expected behaviors, or personal VALUES) that are perceived to be true of social groups and their members. The term stereotype was first used in this sense by Lippmann (1922). The beliefs that Italians are romantic, that women are poor drivers, and that homosexuals have liberal political views are stereotypes. Stereotyping is of interest to social psychologists because stereotypes are frequently and easily activated upon contact with members of disliked groups and this activation influences how people respond to group members. People often use their stereotypes as HEURISTICS or short-cuts, rather than going though more effortful PERSON PERCEPTION processes in which each individual is judged on his or her own merits (Fiske & Neuberg, 1990). Stereotyping thus frequently results in unfair and generalized reactions to individuals that do not take into consideration the possibility that the stereotype may be inaccurate or that the individual may not conform to the stereotype held about the group.

The most commonly studied stereotypes concern broad social categories, such as GENDER, race, nationality, age, and PHYSICAL ATTRACTIVENESS. Many stereotypes are also held about lower-level social categories such as homemakers, beatniks, and librarians, and these stereotypes may be used even more frequently than are stereotypes about larger social groups.

Stereotypes are generally considered as abstract mental representations of social groups – group SCHEMAS or group PROTOTYPES. A group representation consists of the stereotypical beliefs (e.g., "romantic"), which are associated in long-term MEMORY with the group label (e.g., "Italians"). The activation of stereotypes is determined by principles of ACCESSIBILITY. When the mental representation of the social group is activated (through contact with group members, for instance) the associated stereotypes are activated from memory through spreading activation and become available for use in judgment. In addition to being stored in such abstract representations, some stereotypes may be associated with memories of specific individual group members who have previously been encountered. These exemplars, and the associated stereotypes, are activated upon encounters with similar individuals.

STEREOTYPE ASSESSMENT
Stereotypes have been measured using standard assessment techniques, each of which has been shown to have some validity. Most traditional is the Katz and Braly (1933) checklist technique in which subjects are asked to check off which of a preselected list of traits they perceive to be descriptive of the group. In the percentage estimate approach the judgment concerns the percentage of people in the group who are believed to possess the trait. An extension of the percentage approach is to construct a diagnostic ratio that indicates the extent to which the perception of a trait in a given group differs from that in the population more generally. The percentage-estimate approach is conducive to conceptualizing stereotypes in terms of population BASE RATES.

Because expression of stereotypes is influenced by SELF-PRESENTATION goals, nonreactive measures of stereotyping such as the BOGUS PIPELINE have been employed to gain more direct access to group beliefs.

Stereotypes may also be measured using PRIMING paradigms. In these techniques the category label is activated through the presentation of a lexical label or a photograph, and the subject is then immediately presented with a stereotypical word. Reaction time to make a judgment about the word is measured to assess whether the stereotypical term has been activated by the presentation of the category label. These procedures can be used to test whether stereotypes are automatically activated upon exposure to category members (see AUTOMATICITY). Another popular measurement device is a free-response approach in which subjects indicate the thoughts that come to mind when they think about the group. It is also possible to construct MULTIDIMENSIONAL SCALING maps of the stereotypes of social groups.

As cognitive beliefs about social groups, stereotypes are related to other social constructs, including prejudice, racism, and discrimination. Stereotypes are often considered to represent the cognitive or belief "component" of PREJUDICE (see ATTITUDE THEORY AND RESEARCH). Prejudiced individuals tend to express more negative stereotypes than do those who are less prejudiced. The tendency to hold and use stereotypes is also related to PERSONALITY characteristics, including AUTHORITARIANISM. Stereotypes are also linked in memory to EMOTIONAL EXPERIENCES that have occurred in previous encounters with social groups. Although some theorists have argued that stereotypes may exist at the individual level (one's own group beliefs), most definitions of stereotyping propose that beliefs are only stereotypical if they are consensually held among the members of a given society or culture (see Katz & Braly, 1933).

One of the goals of stereotype measurement has been to assess the accuracy of group beliefs. This is a difficult problem, exacerbated by self-presentation biases and the difficulty of generating an appropriate criterion. In early conceptualizations, stereotypes were considered to consist of "inaccurate," "overgeneralized," or "inflexible" beliefs about social groups, and holding stereotypes, as was being prejudiced, was considered to be the mark of a deficient or irrational personality.

However, not all stereotypes are entirely inaccurate. It has been demonstrated that there is a "kernel of truth" to many stereotypes, although these real differences may frequently be perceptually exaggerated. People are indeed very good at perceiving real differences between groups when they do exist, such as those associated with physical appearance. Many stereotypes are found to correspond to the typical roles of social groups in society. For instance, women as a group are perceived as "nurturant" at least partially because of their roles as mothers and caretakers. Although there may never be a satisfactory answer to the accuracy of most stereotypes, it is safe to assume that their use in judging others may frequently produce unfair reactions to individuals who are members of disliked social groups.

FUNCTIONS OF STEREOTYPES

It is commonly assumed that stereotypes are developed and maintained because they serve a functional value, helping the individual meet important psychological needs. Needs for acceptance by parents and valued peers may lead people to internalize stereotypes through CONFORMITY to the attitudes of these individuals (see MODELING). Stereotypes may also result from needs for individual SELF-ENHANCEMENT or for obtaining positive social identity. As a result, stereotypes about ingroups (groups of which the perceiver is a member) tend to be positive and stereotypes about outgroups (groups of which the perceiver is not a member) tend to be negative. Stereotypes may also be the result of attempts to satisfy psychodynamic needs, such as when negative beliefs about the self are projected onto less powerful social groups or when hostility is displaced onto members of such groups (see FRUSTRATION–AGGRESSION hypothesis). Stereotypes may also facilitate needs to justify or rationalize existing negative attitudes toward social groups, social conditions in which one group is systematically treated more favorably than another, or previous discriminatory behaviors. As a result of these processes stereotypes may be incorporated into the ideology of a social group, and may be reflected in the LANGUAGE of the culture.

Stereotypes are frequently determined by the social relationship among social groups. Negative stereotypes are particularly likely to develop in contexts characterized by competition between groups (Sherif et al., 1961; *see* REALISTIC CONFLICT THEORY). Stereotypes change as the functional relation between groups changes. For instance, when SUPERORDINATE GOALS are invoked in relationships that were previously adversarial, group stereotypes quickly change.

Stereotypes also serve the basic function of disambiguating, simplifying, informing, and enriching perception of the social environment through the process of SOCIAL CATEGORIZATION (Allport, 1954). Stereotypes develop to the extent that they differentiate groups among each other on dimensions that are valued by the perceiver (Tajfel, 1978). Stereotypes are more useful in terms of a knowledge function when they are perceived to be highly descriptive of the social groups, have low variability within each group and highly differentiate groups from each other. Real group differences may frequently be accentuated in the direction of magnifying such differences.

## STEREOTYPE FORMATION AND MAINTENANCE

Stereotypes tend to develop more strongly about outgroups than about ingroups, due to the fact that interactions with outgroup members are frequently at an intergroup (rather than an individual) level. Thus stereotypes about outgroups are generally more negative and more extreme than those about ingroups. One result is the OUTGROUP HOMOGENEITY effect in which outgroup members are perceived as being more similar to each other in comparison to ingroup members.

Stereotypes may also be formed in some cases as a result of perceptual SALIENCE. Targets that are highly salient are more likely to be stereotyped in comparison to less salient targets. This may be why stereotypes about race and sex (which are immediately perceptually visible) are more strongly developed than are stereotypes about less visible social categories. Salience effects contribute to the perceptions of ILLUSORY CORRELATION (S) in which negative behaviors performed by minority groups become salient and have a disproportionate impact on judgment.

Once developed, stereotypes are maintained through expectancy effects that lead people to encode and process information in a manner that preferentially supports existing beliefs. Stereotypes lead people to seek out information that supports their stereotypes rather than information that disconfirms their beliefs (*see* BEHAVIORAL CONFIRMATION/DISCONFIRMATION). Existing expectations may also result in preferential ATTENTION to stereotype-consistent information. Information that supports existing stereotypes about social groups is better incorporated into the group representation, and thus better remembered (Stangor & Lange, 1993). Stereotypes may also be maintained because behaviors that conflict with existing stereotypical beliefs are attributed to external causes whereas those that support existing beliefs are attributed to internal causes. Holding negative stereotypes about a group may also lead individuals to avoid situations in which those stereotypes might be disconfirmed.

In addition to cognitive processes that tend to perpetuate existing stereotypes (Hamilton, 1981), because stereotypes serve important functions for the individual, they are subject to consistency effects, such as proposed by COGNITIVE DISSONANCE THEORY. Individuals form group stereotypes to help them accomplish important goals and are reluctant to abandon them. The many cognitive and motivational processes that underlie stereotype development and maintenance make them highly resistant to change.

## THE EFFECTS OF STEREOTYPING

The process of stereotyping has wide impact upon responses to others. Stereotyping influences how information about others is interpreted such that ambiguous behaviors are perceptually distorted in the direction of existing stereotypical beliefs. When relevant information is unknown about an individual, the stereotype may be used to "fill in" the picture. When clearly stereotype-inconsistent behaviors are encountered, they are likely to be attributionally discounted and attributed to external factors rather than having an influence upon impression formation (see AT-TRIBUTION THEORIES). Stereotypes also bias information processing about ingroup and outgroup members and facilitate the creation of a SELF-FULFILLING PROPHECY such that stereotypical beliefs may lead people to act in ways that actually elicit the expected stereo-typical behavior from others. When stereo-types about groups are negative these influences of stereotypes upon judgments will have deleterious effects upon intergroup be-havior and attitudes (see INTERGROUP RELA-TIONS). That many of these processes occur entirely out of the awareness of the individual making the responses may exacerbate the harmful effects of stereotypes.

Stereotypes are not always used as a basis of judgment. In accord with their functional value in simplifying the social environment, stereotypes are capacity-conserving devices that are more likely to be employed in cognit-ively demanding situations. Stereotypes that promote group differentiation and thus which are highly diagnostic about personality are used more routinely than are stereotypes that do not promote this function. Stereotypes are more likely to be activated in situations that are perceived as "intergroup" than in "intragroup" situations, at least in part in the service of promoting positive ingroup identity (see SOCIAL IDENTITY THEORY; SELF-CATEGORIZATION THEORY). When perceivers are in extreme affective or emotional states their information-processing capacity is reduced and they are more likely to rely upon their stereotypes. A target individual is more likely to be stereotyped to the extent that he or she is a prototypical or "typical" example of a group member.

In short, unless perceivers are both motiv-ated and capable of making individuated judgments, stereotypes are likely to be the default form of social judgment. When per-ceivers are accountable for their perceptions or are motivated to make an accurate assess-ment of the other to accomplish important goals, stereotypes are less likely to be used as a basis of judgment (see ACCOUNTABILITY).

Low-prejudice perceivers may in some cases actively inhibit the use of their stereotypes in judgments of others, particularly when con-cerns about social equality are activated.

## STEREOTYPE CHANGE

Although some change in the content of stereotypes (e.g., toward Blacks, the Japanese, women) has been noted over the years, it is notoriously difficult to effect such changes through interventions. Indeed, the rigidity of stereotypes has been an important determin-ant of the interest in studying them. Stereo-type change is generally expected to occur either through direct encounters with indi-viduals from the stereotyped group which disconfirm existing beliefs (see CONTACT HY-POTHESIS, INTEGRATION) or through changes in the perceiver such that possessing or using stereotypes is no longer perceived as useful or desirable. Of course many processes work against this type of change. Individuals may actively avoid contact with disliked group members, and, as discussed above, expect-ancy confirmation processes tend to maintain stereotypes intact.

Individuals would be expected to change their beliefs about outgroups through contact with outgroup members if the encountered individuals are perceived to engage in beha-viors that contradict the stereotypical beliefs. The resulting change might be expected to be either gradual, through a process of "bookkeeping" of positive and negative infor-mation, or it may produce a sudden "conver-sion" in which the beliefs are quickly abandoned. Either type of change requires, however, that the intergroup contact provide opportunities for disconfirmation of the exist-ing beliefs, and many intergroup encounters do not. In many cases the contact does not allow the stereotyped group to engage in behaviors that would disconfirm the stereo-types. The contact may actually elicit stereo-type-confirming behavior, such as when the contact involves unequal status between the groups. Some stereotypes are difficult to change because behaviors which would dis-confirm them do not regularly occur in every-day social interaction, even among people who do not actually possess the trait.

Even when stereotype-disconfirming behaviors occur in intergroup encounters, they may not produce change. Frequently the contact with an individual is not perceived as relevant to group stereotypes. Thus although impressions of individuals may be changed through contact with them, the contacted individuals may not be perceived as "real" members of the stereotyped group and thus no change occurs at the group level (Hewstone & Brown, 1986). When observed disconfirming behavior is very extreme it is likely that the target will be "subtyped" or "refenced" (Allport, 1954; Rothbart & John, 1985). In this case the disconfirming individual is placed into a separate category, allowing the original stereotype to remain intact. In some cases contact may be effective in the long run, because even though it might not change the content of the stereotype, it may increase the perceived variability of the group on the trait dimension such that not all group members are perceived as having the trait. This change will have the positive result of making the stereotypes less useful in terms of the basic functions of perception and categorization, and thus may reduce their future use.

In addition to processes of stereotype change driven by intergroup contact, perceivers may also be motivated not to use their stereotypes. Although it has been argued that stereotypes may be activated automatically upon exposure to target group members, it is unlikely that all stereotypes about a target could simultaneously be activated. Individuals may be categorized in many different ways (as a woman; an Asian; a lawyer), and perceivers, when so motivated, can be flexible about which categories they activate in which situations. Thus individuals can "get beyond" their stereotypes, by using individuated information processing, by categorizing using other less deleterious categories, or by actively avoiding the use of stereotypes in judgment. Such techniques may be particularly useful for more egalitarian perceivers who are already convinced of the harmful nature of stereotyping, but who may not at first realize the extent to which their stereotypes influence their behavior. A potential negative outcome to avoiding the use of stereotypes is that suppressing their use on one occasion may produce greater stereotyping on subsequent occasions. Beliefs about social groups may also be changed through their connections to other aspects of personality, such as by increasing SELF-ESTEEM, reducing frustration, or through education.

CONCLUSION

Stereotyping involves the use of beliefs about the personality characteristics of social groups as a basis of judgments about individual group members. This process is sometimes unfair to the individuals who are so judged, because stereotypes are developed and maintained through motivational and cognitive biases which frequently cause them to be exaggerated or inaccurate. Although it is possible for people to avoid using their stereotypes, because it takes effort to do so stereotyping is often the default form of social judgment. Both cognitive and motivational factors contribute to making stereotypes highly resistant to change.

*See also*: ACCOUNTABILITY; ATTENTION; ATTITUDE THEORY AND RESEARCH; ATTRIBUTION THEORIES; AUTHORITARIANISM; AUTOMATICITY; BEHAVIORAL/CONFIRMATION; DISCONFIRMATION; COGNITIVE DISSONANCE THEORY; CONTACT HYPOTHESIS; EMOTIONAL EXPERIENCE; GENDER; HEURISTICS; INTEGRATION; INTERGROUP RELATIONS; LANGUAGE; MEMORY; OUTGROUP HOMOGENEITY; PERSONALITY; PREJUDICE; SCHEMAS/SCHEMATA; SELF-CATEGORIZATION THEORY; SELF-ESTEEM; SELF-FULFILLING PROPHECIES; SOCIAL CATEGORIZATION; SOCIAL IDENTITY THEORY; VALUES.

BIBLIOGRAPHY

Allport, G. (1954). *The nature of prejudice*. Reading, MA: Addison-Wesley.

Fiske, S. T., & Neuberg, S. L. (1990). A continuum of impression formation, from category-based to individuating processes: Influences of information and motivation on attention and interpretation. In M. P. Zanna (Ed.), *Advances in experimental social psychology* (Vol. 23, pp. 1–74). New York: Academic Press.

Hamilton, D. L. (Ed.) (1981). *Cognitive processes in stereotyping and intergroup behavior*. Hillsdale, NJ: Lawrence Erlbaum.

Hewstone, M., & Brown, R. J. (Eds.). (1986). *Contact and conflict in intergroup encounters.* Oxford: Basil Blackwell.

Katz, D., & Braly, K. W. (1933). Racial stereotypes of one hundred college students. *Journal of Abnormal and Social Psychology, 28,* 280–90.

Lippmann, W. (1922). *Public Opinion.* New York: Harcourt & Brace.

Rothbart, M., & John, O. P. (1985). Social categorization and behavioral episodes: A cognitive analysis of the effects of intergroup contact. *Journal of Social Issues, 41,* 81–104.

Sherif, M., Harvey, O. J., White, B. J., Hood, W. R., & Sherif, C. (1961). *Intergroup conflict and cooperation: The robbers' cave experiment.* Norman, OK: University of Oklahoma Press.

Stangor, C., & Lange, J. (1993). Cognitive representations of social groups: Advances in conceptualizating stereotypes and stereotyping. In M. P. Zanna (Ed.), *Advances in experimental social psychology* (Vol. 26, pp. 357–416). San Diego, CA: Academic Press.

Tajfel, H. (Ed.) (1978). *Differentiation between social groups: Studies in the social psychology of intergroup relations.* London: Academic Press.

CHARLES G. STANGOR

**stigma** Stigmatizing conditions lead to the rejection of individuals because those individuals have an attribute that compromises their humanity in the eyes of others (Jones et al., 1984). In Goffman's (1963) terms, the stigmatized have a "spoiled identity." The specific conditions that elicit negative reactions from others may change over time, as knowledge, tastes, and public acceptance of deviant conditions and behaviors change (*see* Archer, 1985). Thus, stigma resides not in the stigmatizing condition itself, but in others' reactions to that condition.

Goffman (1963) suggested that there are three major types of stigmatizing conditions: "tribal stigmas," such as membership in disadvantaged or despised racial, ethnic, or religious groups; "abominations of the body," including physical handicaps and disfiguring conditions; and "blemishes of individual character," such as substance abuse, juvenile delinquency, and homosexuality. Some conditions may be doubly stigmatizing. For example, obesity is often regarded as both an "abomination of the body" and a character flaw. As Goffman's analysis suggests, many conditions may be considered stigmatizing, in that people with those conditions are the targets of negative stereotypes, are devalued in the larger society, and receive disproportionately negative interpersonal and economic outcomes (*see also* PREJUDICE, STEREOTYPING).

DIMENSIONS OF STIGMA
Because of the wide variety of stigmatizing conditions, a number of efforts have been made to identify the crucial underlying dimensions of stigmas. According to several perspectives on stigma one important dimension is *visibility* or concealability. Visible stigmas, such as those associated with one's race or obesity, can be identified easily by others in face-to-face interactions. Concealable stigmas, such as stigmas associated with sexual orientation, or certain illnesses, need not be disclosed, leaving the decision whether to reveal or conceal the stigma up to the stigmatized individual.

The *controllability* of a stigma also appears to be a crucial dimension. Controllable stigmas are those that are judged to be due to lack of personal effort or will. Individuals with stigmatizing conditions that are controllable may be blamed both by themselves and by others for their condition, and its associated problems. Individuals with uncontrollable stigmas are less likely to be liked or pitied, and elicit more anger and less assistance than individuals with uncontrollable stigmas.

Other dimensions that are important to the stigmatizing process are the *centrality* of the stigma to the self-concept (i.e., its importance to one's identity), *time since acquisition* and the *course* of the stigma, the *disruptiveness* of the stigma in face-to-face interactions, the *aesthetic qualities* of the stigma (i.e., its repulsiveness), and the *degree of peril or danger* the stigma poses to others (*see* Crocker & Major, 1989; Goffman, 1963; Jones et al., 1984, for discussions). These dimensions may in-fluence both the subjective experience of stig-matized individuals and the reactions the stigma elicits from the nonstigmatized.

## AMBIVALENCE TOWARD THE STIGMATIZED

Attitudes toward the stigmatized are often ambivalent, rather than uniformly negative; the nonstigmatized may feel sympathy and concern, as well as repulsion and disgust, for the stigmatized (Katz, 1981). Furthermore, the stigmatized may provoke in the nonstig-matized a conflict between egalitarian values (e.g., equality of opportunity) and individual-istic values (e.g., belief in a meritocracy). This ambivalence may cause the nonstig-matized to be highly anxious and confused in their interactions with the nonstigmatized. Increased anxiety may, in turn, amplify or intensify the responses of the nonstigmatized. Hence, the nonstigmatized may behave in exaggerated ways – either positive or negative – toward the stigmatized (Katz, 1981).

## SELF-PRESENTATION ISSUES

Because stigmatizing conditions elicit strong reactions from others, people who have these conditions face important considerations re-garding the management of their public SELF-PRESENTATIONS (see Goffman's, 1963, essay). Goffman notes that stigmatized individuals face many decisions in their interactions with others. Among a few of those Goffman men-tions, the stigmatized must choose whether to avoid interactions with the nonstigmatized altogether, and if not whether to reveal or conceal the stigma from others, whether to attempt to "pass" as unstigmatized, whether to confront others with the stigma by raising it in conversation, and whether to treat it with humor. Each of these strategies may have associated advantages and disadvantages.

## CONSEQUENCES FOR THE SELF-CONCEPT

Several social psychological theories, includ-ing the SYMBOLIC INTERACTIONIST and SELF-FULFILLING PROPHECY perspectives, predict that prejudice and discrimination against members of stigmatized groups result in lowered SELF-ESTEEM and diminished self-concept for the stigmatized. Despite the strong theoretical support for such a prediction, empirical evidence suggests that members of many stigmatized groups have self-esteem that is equal to or higher than that of the nonstigmatized (see Crocker & Major, 1989, for a review). Yet, members of some stig-matized groups do appear to be vulnerable to low self-esteem. For example, people who are obese or overweight, those who are on wel-fare, and women who have been raped may suffer from low self-esteem.

Crocker and Major (1989) have suggested that the stigmatized may protect their self-esteem by:

(1) attributing negative outcomes they ex-perience to prejudice and discrimination;
(2) devaluing those domains in which their stigma makes it unlikely they will excel; and
(3) selectively comparing themselves and their outcomes to others who have their stigma, rather than nonstigmatized individuals.

Thus, self-esteem differences between stig-matized groups, as well as differences among individuals who share a stigma, may be ex-plained by their tendency to use these self-protective strategies. Of course, apart from self-esteem, stigma may have negative con-sequences for individuals' economic well-being, and aspects of psychological well-being such as DEPRESSION and hopelessness.

See also: DEPRESSION; PREJUDICE; SELF-ESTEEM; SELF-FULFILLING PROPHECIES; STEREOTYPING; SYMBOLIC INTERACTIONISM.

BIBLIOGRAPHY
Archer, D. (1985). Social deviance. In G. Lindzey & E. Aronson (Eds.), *Handbook of social psychology* (3rd ed., Vol. 2, pp. 743–804). New York: Random House.
Crocker, J., & Major, B. (1989). Social stigma and self-esteem: The self-protective properties of stigma. *Psychological Review*, 96, 608–30.
Goffman, E. (1963). *Stigma: Notes on the management of spoiled identity*. Englewood Cliffs, NJ: Prentice Hall.

Jones, E. E., Farina, A., Hastorf, A. H., Markus, H., Miller, D. T., & Scott, R. A. (1984). *Social stigma: The psychology of marked relationships*. New York: W. H. Freeman.

Katz, I. (1981). *Stigma: A social-psychological perspective*. Hillsdale, NJ: Lawrence Erlbaum.

JENNIFER CROCKER

**stress and coping** Stress has been conceptualized in different ways by different theorists, but definitions typically incorporate some variation on the idea that people who are under stress are attempting to meet demands from the environment that either approach or exceed their capacities to respond. The concept of coping refers to the various ways in which people try either to meet these demands or deal with the emotions that are created by the pressure of the demands (*see* Zeidner & Endler, 1995).

Interest in stress and coping has had several different focuses over the years. Some people have been most interested in the psychological processes that are involved in the experience of stress. People who have this focus of interest are usually concerned with issues bearing on either emotional reactions or task performances. For example, what sorts of coping responses can minimize the negative feelings that often arise when people are under stress? What variables influence the quality of task performances under conditions of stress? Can certain responses reduce the effects of stress, or serve as a buffer to stress (see BUFFERING HYPOTHESIS)?

The interest of others has been captured by the fact that the psychological processes of stress and coping have physiological concomitants. The physiological reactions are believed to play a role in the development of several sorts of illnesses and failures of the body (e.g., Selye, 1956/1976). Accordingly, many people have become interested in questions about how the body reacts to stress, the pathways by which these physical reactions come to influence the development of physical disorder, and how the adverse physical reactions can be diminished or prevented.

THEORY

Although several stress theories have been proposed, the one that is used most widely by people who study stress and coping is the theory developed by Lazarus (1966; Lazarus & Folkman, 1984). Lazarus holds that the experience of psychological stress consists of the occurrence of three processes. *Primary appraisal* is the process of perceiving a threat in the environment. *Secondary appraisal* is the process of deciding how to respond to the threat. *Coping* is the process of executing whatever responses have been selected during secondary appraisal. Taken together, these three elements constitute the experience of psychological stress.

This analysis of the stress experience is sometimes termed a transactional model. This reflects the idea that the experience of stress represents a transaction between the person and the situation – it depends on both rather than on just one or the other. To be more specific, the perception of threat depends partly on the situation that the person encounters, and partly on what the person brings to the situation. For example, the sight of a spider may pose no threat to one person, but the same sight may create a severe threat to another person. This is one point at which the Lazarus model of stress intersects the broad domain of SOCIAL COGNITION. That is, how a given person organizes and mentally represents knowledge about the world can be expected to influence the outcomes of the person's appraisals.

There is also a transactional quality to the secondary appraisal process. People do not always respond reflexively and automatically to the situations they confront (or even the situations as they are construed). Rather, secondary appraisal often involves weighing options and considering the consequences of responding in various ways, before deciding what to do. As is true of primary appraisal, these evaluating and decision-making processes also involve information from the person's MEMORY as well as information from the situation. As a result, the outcome of the secondary appraisal process also can be expected to differ from person to person, even if the people view the threat itself in the same way.

Two further elaborations on this model should be stated before going further. First, although these processes form a logical or conceptual sequence, they should not be assumed to operate in a strictly sequential way. Rather, the outcome of one process may reinvoke a preceding one. For example, realizing that an adequate coping response is readily available may cause the person to reappraise the situation as less threatening. As another example, if the use of a coping response turns out to be less effective than was expected, the person may reappraise the level of threat or reappraise what coping reaction is most appropriate to the situation.

A second elaboration stems from the fact that the preceding description was presented entirely in terms of threat appraisal. Lazarus actually holds that three different kinds of events can give rise to stress. *Threat* appraisal occurs when the person anticipates the possibility that something harmful or unpleasant will occur. *Challenge* appraisal occurs when the person anticipates the possibility of acquiring a good or desirable outcome, but also anticipates that doing so will not be easy. Many of the stressful situations in life involve combinations of threat and challenge. An intuitively obvious example is the experience of preparing for and taking an examination. This situation incorporates the possibility of an unpleasant outcome (a poor score), but it also holds out the possibility of a positive outcome (a good score). In contrast to threat and challenge, *loss* appraisal occurs when the person experiences a bad outcome that cannot be undone. The clearest examples of loss include such events as BEREAVEMENT or the ending of a RELATIONSHIP.

## WAYS OF COPING

It should be clear from the preceding paragraph that the concepts of stress and coping can be applied to a broad range of situations. It should also be clear that the stressful situations that people experience differ from one another in several ways. For example, in some stressful situations the person can do a great deal to change the situation for the better. This is often the case in situations where threat is mixed with challenge. In such situations (and in many other situations in which only threat is present), the person can mobilize efforts to do something about the threat (or the opportunity). In other situations there is little the person can do but endure the stressful experience. This is more likely to be the case when the stress derives from a loss experience than when it derives from threat or challenge.

Not only do situations vary in several important ways, but so do the coping responses that the situations elicit from people. Lazarus and Folkman (1984) have distinguished between two broad classes of coping reactions. What they call *problem focused coping* is any response that is aimed at doing something to alter the source of the stress, removing the threatening event or altering its impact. *Emotion focused coping* is any response aimed at reducing or managing the negative feelings that arise in response to the threat or loss.

Although these two categories are easy to distinguish from each other in principle, both typically occur to some degree during every given stressful transaction. Indeed, their effects can be difficult to disentangle. That is, emotion focused coping can make problem focused coping easier, by removing some of the distress that can interfere with problem focused efforts. Similarly, problem focused coping can render a threat less forbidding, thereby diminishing distress emotion. Moreover, certain kinds of coping reactions have both problem focused and emotion focused aspects. For example, people can make use of SOCIAL SUPPORT resources both for advice and instrumental aid (problem focused) and for reassurance and comfort (emotion focused).

There is a certain similarity between these two classes of coping reactions and the two classes of stressful situations described just beforehand. Although the match is far from perfect, it has often been noted that the balance between problem focused and emotion focused coping reactions is influenced by the kind of situation the person is confronting. When the situation is one in which something can be done to change it, problem focused coping tends to predominate. When the situation is one that must be endured, emotion focused coping tends to predominate.

The distinction between problem focused and emotion focused coping is an important one. By itself, however, it probably does not go far enough. For example, coping reactions that are emotion focused are extremely varied. They range from the use of social support, to positive reframing of the situation, to daydreaming, to wishful thinking and escapist fantasy, to making jokes about the stressful event, to heightened religious activity, to ALCOHOL and DRUG use, and beyond (*see*, e.g., Carver, Scheier, & Weintraub, 1989). It is important to recognize that such diverse ways of coping may also differ in the effects they have. One goal of research is to examine these coping reactions separately, to determine what their distinct effects are.

Studies that have done this have found that not all of these responses are effective in diminishing negative feelings. In fact, there is evidence that some kinds of coping responses actually make things *worse*. Some of the responses that seem to have this effect have been termed avoidance coping (e.g., Billings & Moos, 1984). Such reactions include wishful thinking, escapist fantasy, denial, turning to alcohol, and overeating. Another response that seems to intensify distress is self-blame. The idea that some kinds of coping reactions are dysfunctional rather than helpful is an important one. Although most people probably think of coping as responses that are somehow effective in dealing with a problem, research on the effects of coping provides just as much evidence – and maybe even more – that coping responses can also work against the person.

RESEARCH ISSUES
How do researchers determine what effects are caused by the various aspects of coping? Determining the effects of coping is somewhat more difficult than most people may realize. The research challenges are perhaps even greater in this area of study than in many other areas of psychology. Several different types of research have been conducted, but none of them is completely without problems.

There is a very large set of studies in which subjects report two things at the same time: the ways in which they are currently coping with some stressor, and their current EMO-

TIONAL EXPERIENCE. (Some of these studies ask people to think back and report on a stressor from the recent past.) These studies typically find that avoidance coping is related to higher distress, and they sometimes find that other aspects of coping are related to lower distress. The problem with these studies is that it is impossible to tell from them whether the coping reaction is influencing the emotional distress, or whether the emotional distress is influencing how people cope. This problem always exists when the researcher measures the coping and the emotions at the same time point.

The best way to get around this problem (and the best kind of research design for studying naturally occurring coping) requires measuring coping reactions and emotions at more than one time point during the period of stress (a "prospective" design). That way, coping at time 1 can be used as a predictor of emotions at the later time point, while controlling statistically for the emotions that were reported at time 1. In the same way, emotions at time 1 can be used to predict coping at time 2, controlling for coping at time 1. This is one way to disentangle which came first, the emotional responses or the coping.

This prospective design often has a problem of its own, though. Sometimes the situation changes enough between the two time points that the person's emotional responses at time 2 are more likely to reflect the change in situation than to reflect the effects of coping. This is especially likely to be true when the person is coping with a crisis of some sort, in which there is an anticipatory period, an event period, and a subsequent period of adjustment. Shifts in the psychological meaning of the situation from one phase to another can be dramatic and the person's feelings can also shift considerably from one phase to another. When the situation changes a lot between assessments, it can be hard to be sure that the influence of the coping responses on emotions has received a fair test.

Another problem in coping research is that most studies examine how people cope naturally with whatever stressor is under investigation. That is, subjects in these studies decide for themselves how to cope. Only rarely are coping responses experimentally manipulated. As a result, most of the research on coping examines INDIVIDUAL DIFFERENCES in coping and how these individual differences relate to emotional well-being (or to some other outcome). The problem here is the same problem as is always encountered in individual differences research: it is very hard to determine whether the coping response produced the effect in the study or whether the effect was caused by some other variable that also differed between persons and was not being directly examined. This is a limitation that is inherent in all correlational research, although this point is often ignored in discussions of the effects of coping.

## FURTHER ISSUES IN CONCEPTUALIZING COPING

Although the Lazarus model of stress and coping has had more influence on people's work in this area over the past two decades than any other model, other ideas have also been advanced by other theorists. For example, Hobfoll (1989) has proposed a model of stress that relies on a principle he calls "conservation of resources." His basic assumption is that people strive to build, retain, and protect resources of various types, and that the potential or actual loss of those resources is threatening and stress inducing. Resources, in this model, are anything the individual values. Resources may be objects (house, car), conditions (status, seniority), energies (time, knowledge), or personal characteristics (SELF-ESTEEM, optimism). People try to hold onto their resources and when they are under stress their goal is to minimize resource loss. One implication of this model is that actual or potential loss lies at the heart of all stress.

Hobfoll argues further that the experience of loss is followed by efforts to replace the resources, either directly or symbolically. Sometimes doing this requires the investment of further resources, which itself poses a risk to the person. If the person cannot spare the further resources that have to be invested, the result can be a "loss spiral," in which one loss leads to further losses. As an example, consider a person whose home is severely damaged in a hurricane and wants to restore it to its previous condition. To do this, the person must invest time and effort (either doing work on the house personally or making arrangement for others to do the work). If the person has little free time (another resource) to use on such activities, his or her WORK performance may suffer, which may have further adverse consequences. In an extreme case, the person might even lose the job because of the time taken away from work to restore the lost resource.

### Coping and Behavior

Finally, consider a somewhat broader point. Treatments of the concepts of stress and coping sometimes make the topic sound as though it stands separate from the rest of psychology. Stress can be made to seem an exotic event that occurs only under special circumstances; coping can seem to be a special class of actions that differs in important ways from other actions. Such a picture, however, would be far from accurate. Stress is part of almost everyone's everyday life (Selye, 1956/1976), and coping is in many ways the same as any other behavior.

It is arguable that the facets of experience and behavior that are emphasized in models of stress and coping are more or less the same as those that are assumed in broader models of behavior-in-general (for broader discussion, *see* Carver, Scheier, & Pozo, 1992). Today's models of behavior-in-general tend to rely on the assumption that behavior is goal directed, and they tend to assume that that people have somewhat idiosyncratic construals of the world and of the consequences of their behavior. Finally, such models typically assume that behavior becomes more variable when obstacles interfere with the attainment of (or even progress toward) desired goals. People who remain confident of eventual success continue their task directed efforts. Those who are more doubtful do a variety of things that reflect an avoidance of effort toward the the goal (*see also* HELPLESSNESS), and sometimes even a giving up of the goal. Giving up is often painful and difficult, however, and it sometimes takes a long time to occur.

A comparison with what came earlier in this entry will reveal that the conceptual points in the preceding paragraph are very similar to the elements in the Lazarus model of stress. One need add only one further link: the idea that threat occurs when there is interference with the attainability of some goal (and loss occurs when attainability has been prevented altogether). People sometimes respond to threats with renewed effort at goal attainment, and they sometimes respond with avoidance coping. Avoidance coping does not help the people move toward the goals, however, and it may actually interfere with such movement. For that reason it ultimately can have adverse rather than positive effects. When viewed from this angle, then, coping is simply a special label for what people do every time they encounter obstacles in life, whether temporary or permanent.

*See also*: EMOTIONAL EXPERIENCE; MEMORY; RELATIONSHIPS; SELF-ESTEEM; SOCIAL COGNITION; SOCIAL SUPPORT; WORK.

BIBLIOGRAPHY

Billings, A. G., & Moos, R. H. (1984). Coping, stress, and social resources among adults with unipolar depression. *Journal of Personality and Social Psychology*, 46, 877–91.

Carver, C. S., Scheier, M. F., & Pozo, C. (1992). Conceptualizing the process of coping with health problems. In H. S. Friedman (Ed.), *Hostility, coping, and health* (pp. 167–99). Washington, DC: American Psychological Association.

——& Weintraub, J. K. (1989). Assessing coping strategies: A theoretically based approach. *Journal of Personality and Social Psychology*, 56, 267–83.

Hobfoll, S. E. 1989. Conservation of resources: A new attempt at conceptualizing stress. *American Psychologist*, 44, 513–24.

Lazarus, R. S. (1966). *Psychological stress and the coping process*. New York: McGraw-Hill.

——& Folkman, S. (1984). *Stress, appraisal, and coping*. New York: Springer Publishing Company.

Selye, H. (1956/1976). *The stress of life*. New York: McGraw-Hill.

Zeidner, M., & Endler, N. S. (Eds.) (1995). *Handbook of coping: Theory, research, applications*. New York: Wiley.

CHARLES S. CARVER

**structural equation modeling** A set of procedures to estimate the parameters associated with a particular linear model from some set of data. In addition, these procedures allow, in some cases, the researcher to determine whether there are inconsistencies between the specified model and the data, thereby determining whether the data discredit the model (Bentler, 1980; Judd, Jessor, & Donovan, 1986; Kenny, 1979).

Structural equation modeling subsumes a variety of procedures designed to estimate the parameters of linear models. These procedures include PATH ANALYSIS and multiple regression, confirmatory factor analysis, and latent variable structural models. A variety of programs exist that provide parameter estimates for a very general class of linear models that subsume and include all of these procedures (e.g., LISREL: Jöreskog & Sörbom, 1989; EQS: Bentler, 1989). These programs derive parameter estimates by iterative algorithms that minimize weighted discrepancies between the observed variances and covariances of measured variables in some dataset and the variances and covariances predicted by the linear model whose parameters are estimated. Typically, the minimization results in maximum likelihood parameter estimates although a variety of more robust estimates can be derived as well.

The variety of linear models whose parameters can be estimated is very broad. Path analytic models involve linear structural effects of exogenous or independent measured variables on endogenous or dependent measured variables. Confirmatory factor analysis models involve one or more latent factors, which may or may not covary, that are hypothesized to be responsible for the observed variances and covariances of a set of measured variables. Latent variable structural models involve an integration of confirmatory factor analysis and a path analytic model, examining the linear effects of independent latent variables on other latent variables, each measured with a set of observed variables or indicators. The utility of this last class of models lies in the flexibility of the specifications that are possible. The latent variable approach permits one to overcome the biasing effects of both random and systematic error variance, assuming that sufficient information exists in the variance/covariance matrix of the observed indicators to estimate the model's parameters.

Estimation of the parameters of a model proceeds iteratively, by minimizing some weighted discrepancy between the observed variance/covariance matrix and that predicted by the model. In many cases, no single set of parameter estimates provide a unique "best" solution and the model is said to be "under-identified." This means that there is simply not enough information in the observed variance/covariance matrix to derive estimates of the entire set of model parameters. For "just identified" models, there is a unique set of parameter estimates and these are able to exactly reproduce the observed variance/covariance matrix. Finally, "overidentified" models are those in which more information exists in the observed variance/covariance matrix than is necessary for parameter estimation. As a result, a series of overidentifying restrictions must be satisfied if the model is said to be consistent with the sample data. In other words, multiple solutions to the parameter estimation problem exist, using only partial subsets of the full information available in the observed variance/covariance matrix. If the model and the data are said to be consistent, then these multiple solutions must be identical within the limits of sampling error. Under certain distributional assumptions, this consistency between model and observed data can be tested by a chi-square goodness of fit test, the chi-square being a function of the discrepancies between the observed variance/covariance matrix and that produced by the model's "best" parameter estimates. If the resulting chi-square statistic is not reliable, then the model is said to be consistent with the observed data, meaning that the predicted and observed variance/covariance matrices are equivalent, within the limits of sampling error.

Since the conclusion of consistency between a model and observed data depends on the failure to reject the null hypothesis of significant discrepancies between the predicted and observed matrices, one can never "accept" a model based on a structural equation modeling approach. All such an approach can do is estimate the "best" parameter estimates and provide an indica-

tion of inconsistencies between the model and the data. The demonstration that those inconsistencies are unreliable does not provide evidence that the model is the most appropriate one. A wide range of alternative models may provide an equal or better fit to the observed data. Since one is in the awkward position of attempting to verify the null hypothesis (assuming one wishes to demonstrate the validity of a chosen structural model), the usual power considerations in hypothesis testing are reversed. For instance, with very large sample sizes (over 1,000), one will almost never find a model that satisfactorily reproduces the observed variance/covariance matrix. Various indices of goodness-of-fit, less dependent on sample size than the usual chi-square test, have been developed to deal with this problem.

Although structural equation models have been used widely and fruitfully in social psychology, they have associated abuses. Claims of causality can be made only by the use of appropriate experimental designs. No matter how sophisticated the data analysis, no "causal" model can be used to confirm causal effects in the absence of an experimntal design. Additionally, it is very easy to forget that structural equation modeling can only establish the sufficiency of a model rather than its necessity. Finally, it is tempting to modify an ill-fitting model in light of empirical results with insufficient acknowledgment that in so doing one may profit from chance. Social psychologists need to use these powerful tools appropriately.

*See also*: EXPERIMENTATION.

BIBLIOGRAPHY

Bentler, P. M. (1980). Multivariate analysis with latent variables: Causal modeling. *Annual Review of Psychology*, *31*, 419–56.

Bentler, P. M. (1989). *EQS: Structural equations program manual*. Los Angeles, CA: BMDP Statistical Software.

Jöreskog, K. G., & Sörbom, D. (1989). *LISREL 7; A guide to the program and applications*. Chicago, IL: SPSS.

Judd, C. M., Jessor, R., & Donovan, J. E. (1986). Structural equation models and personality research. *Journal of Personality*, *54*, 149–98.

Kenny, D. A. (1979). *Correlation and causality*. New York: Wiley–Interscience.

CHARLES M. JUDD

ture; the latter emerge in studies of several cultures, are relevant to all cultures, and can be evaluated by using universal, theoretical, abstract criteria.

**subjective culture** "A cultural group's characteristic way of perceiving its social environment." (Triandis, 1972, p. 3). Culture is the human-made part of the environment (Herskovits, 1955). It is desirable to distinguish its objective (tools, roads, clothes, dwellings, etc.) and subjective (beliefs, attitudes, norms, roles, myths, values, etc.) aspects.

A cultural group consists of people who, through past and present intragroup communication, have arrived at shared understandings of how to perceive their social environment and how to solve the key problems of life. Such understandings are likely to have been adaptive or reinforcing at some point in time and to have been transmitted from one generation to the next as recommended ways of thinking and acting. In short, culture is to society what memory is to individuals.

Subjective culture can be decomposed into key elements, such as categories, associations, attitudes, BELIEFS, goals, attributions, expectations, NORMS, roles, rules, SELF definitions, STEREOTYPES, ideals, VALUES; aesthetic, economic, social, political, scientific, religious standards; theories, myths, ideologies, RELIGION, and approved behavior patterns.

Subjective culture includes both linguistic and SOCIAL REPRESENTATIONS (Moscovici, 1961/1976). It is convenient to distinguish linguistic representations, where each member of a culture has almost identical representations of a concept, e.g., mother, from social representations, where each member of a culture may have approximately similar representations of the concept, e.g., the meaning of "childhood," "psychoanalysis," or "Marxism." Whether an element of subjective culture is more like a linguistic or a social representation must be determined empirically.

It is especially important to distinguish elements of subjective culture that are emic (culture specific) from etic (universal). The former emerge in studies of a single culture, are relevant only to that culture, and can be evaluated using only criteria from that cul-

METHODS

The first step in analyses of subjective culture is to use focus groups to obtain the emic constructs and ways of thinking about the social environment used by members of that culture.

All social science methods can be used to study elements of subjective culture, but especially important are methods that examine the meanings of concepts, events, conceptions, and approved behaviors. The semantic, behavioral, and role differentials (Triandis, 1972), the antecedent–consequent method for the analysis of values, and several ethnoscience methods (Tyler, 1969) are especially important.

Specifically, categories are identified when it is determined that members of a culture respond to discriminably different stimuli as if they were identical. The researcher asks: "How do you call" particular entities in the social environment, and tests the limits of the category by establishing which apparently similar entities are not called by that name.

Associations are established by a free-association method, or by asking respondents to complete sentences that include a term, such as "*Rice* is __," "The more __, the more rice," "If you have __, then you have *rice*." "If you have *rice*, then you have __."

Attitudes include evaluations of a concept, e.g., a rating of *rice* on a good–bad semantic differential scale. Beliefs are tested with agreement/disagreement to statements of the form "If you have *rain*, then you have *rice*." Attributions may be studied by presenting scenarios of interpersonal behaviors and by asking the respondent to provide the causes of specific behaviors in the scenario or to select one attribution from a set of attributions obtained from focus groups. Roles may be examined by obtaining responses concerning whether particular social behaviors are appropriate in a relationship, such as that the actor (e.g., a mother) is likely to act in a certain way (e.g., admire the ideas of) toward the target of action (e.g., her son). Rules may be studied by asking if certain actions must occur in certain situations (e.g., tenants pay the rent monthly). Self definitions can be studied by asking respondents to complete sentences, such as "I am . . ." or to agree/disagree with statements such as "I am the kind of person who pays the rent before the first of the month." Stereotypes are most conveniently obtained by asking for a rating of a category (e.g., professors) on a scale (e.g., professors are "slightly" to "greatly" absentminded) or by asking for an estimate, on a 100-point scale, of the percentage of members of a category having a particular attribute. Ideals require agreement/disagreement with statements of the form "My ideal is to be $X$." Values can be obtained by ratings of the form: "*Equality* (equal opportunity for all) is an unimportant/most important guiding principle in my life." The remaining elements of subjective culture are more complex and require correspondingly more complex methods.

There is a tendency for elements of subjective culture to be consistent, and organized around a theme. That is, they form cultural syndromes, determined by the correlations among the elements of subjective culture. For example, many elements of subjective culture form a syndrome around the theme of individuals being autonomous entities (individualism) as opposed to being embedded in groups (collectivism) (*see* INDIVIDUALISM-COLLECTIVISM).

Subjective culture is relevant for the prediction of behavior (Triandis, 1972, 1980). Social behavior is a function of habits (automatic situation–behavior sequences) and intentions (self-instructions to act in a specified way), as well as facilitating conditions (appropriate physiological arousal, sufficient ability, relatively easy task, self-efficacy). Intentions are a function of self definitions, norms, roles, interpersonal agreements, the affect toward the behavior (do I enjoy or do I feel disgusted at the thought of this action?) and the perceived consequences of the action (if I do $X$ there is a high probability that $Y$ will happen, and I want $Y$).

*See also*: ATTITUDE THEORY AND RESEARCH; CATEGORIZATION; CULTURE; IDEOLOGY; INDIVIDUALISM–COLLECTIVISM; NORMS; RELIGION; ROLE THEORY; SELF; SOCIAL REPRESENTATIONS; STEREOTYPING; VALUES.

BIBLIOGRAPHY

Herskovits, M. (1955) *Cultural anthropology*. New York: Knopf.

Moscovici, S. (1961/1976) *La Psychanalyse: Son image et son public* (Psychoanalysis: Its image and public). Paris, France; Presses Universitaires de France.

Triandis, H. C. (1972) *The analysis of subjective culture*. New York: Wiley.

—— (1980) Values, attitudes, and interpersonal behavior. In H. E. Howe & M. M. Page (Eds.), *Nebraska Symposium on Motivation* (pp. 195–260). Lincoln, NE: University of Nebraska Press.

Tyler, S. A. (1969) *Cognitive anthropology*. New York: Holt, Rinehart & Winston.

HARRY C. TRIANDIS

**subjectively expected utility (SEU)** This principle can be expressed as $\Sigma_i\, p_i\, u(x_i)$, in which $p_i$ is the probability of outcome $i$ and $u(x_i)$ the utility of outcome $i$. The weight $p_i$ refers to a subjective or personal probability. SEU-theory assumes that in choice situations people prefer the option with the highest subjectively expected utility (*see* DECISION MAKING).

*See also*: DECISION MAKING.

JOOP VAN DER PLIGT

**superordinate goals** These are shared goals that can only be achieved by cooperation between individuals or groups. Superordinate goals establish positive INTERDEPENDENCE between parties (e.g., responding to threat from a common enemy, or solving a problem requiring expertise from both parties). Studies of INTERGROUP RELATIONS demonstrate that, cumulatively, superordinate goals can reduce intergroup conflict.

*See also*: BARGAINING; INTERDEPENDENCE THEORY; INTERGROUP RELATIONS.

DOMINIC ABRAMS

**survey methods** In its most general meaning, the term survey refers to systematic data collection about a sample drawn from a larger population. The best-known form of a survey is the opinion poll, in which information is gathered from a sample of individuals by asking questions. However, surveys may also be conducted of organizations or events (e.g., court sentences). Here we concentrate on polls, that is, surveys of individuals.

As any other research study, a survey must begin with a statement of its objectives: What does one want to study? The objectives determine the population of interest, from which the sample is to be drawn, as well as the questions that are to be asked. The questions may be asked in face-to-face or telephone interviews, or by means of a self-administered questionnaire, which may be mailed to respondents. Following data collection, the answers need to be coded for data analysis. Data analysis, interpretation of the results, and dissemination of the findings complete the research process. Bradburn and Sudman (1988) and Weisberg et al. (1989) provide highly recommended nontechnical introductions to survey research.

## POPULATIONS AND SAMPLES

The research objectives determine the population about which data are to be collected. If data can be gathered from all members of the population, the study is called a census. In most cases, however, this is unfeasible and a sample will be drawn from a well-defined population (for this reason, the population is also referred to as the sampling frame). Drawing inferences from the sample about the larger population of interest requires that the sample is representative, that is, that it replicates the population from which it was drawn. A biased sample, i.e., a sample which does not represent all parts of the sampling frame, will be devastating to the validity of the obtained survey results. Reflecting its crucial importance, survey sampling is a highly specialized field in its own right (*see* Kalton, 1983, for an introduction).

At a basic level, one can distinguish probability and nonprobability samples. A probability sample requires that each member of the population has a specified likelihood of being included in the sample. The two main types of probability sampling procedures are known as simple random sampling and stratified random sampling. In simple random sampling, each member of the population has an equal likelihood of being selected in the sample. In stratified random sampling, the population of interest is divided into different strata, that is, different groups based on some characteristic (e.g., socio-economic level or age). Each of these strata is then randomly sampled, ensuring that within each stratum each member has an equal likelihood of being selected. This procedure assures that characteristics of the population with a low frequency of occurrence (e.g., high age) will be represented in the sample. These same low-frequency characteristics may fail to be represented in a simple random sample. If the researcher knows in advance that some small segment of the population may be of special interest, this segment may be oversampled, i.e., represented by a number of respondents that is larger than its proportion in the population, to allow more detailed analysis. In drawing inferences about the population in general, this oversampling would then be corrected for. Either type of random sampling renders survey research expensive, in part because the interviewer needs to track down the specified respondents, which may involve numerous unsuccessful attempts.

The main type of nonprobability sampling procedure employed in surveys is quota sampling. In this case, a sample is selected based on a set of characteristics in the population. For example, if our population contains 40 percent married people, 18 percent black, and 35 percent over the age of 45, we can select a sample that will conform to these characteristics. To accomplish this, the interviewers are not given a specified list of respondents but are provided with the quota criteria and are free to select any respondent who fits these criteria. Although this method may seem similar to stratified random sampling, this similarity is quite misleading because each member in the quota specification group does *not* have an equal likelihood of being selected. Rather, the selection of respondents within those groups is left to the interviewer's discretion. Whereas this procedure reduces the cost of the study, it does not allow strong conclusions about the population, which require the calculation of sampling error. Sampling error, however, can only be calculated for probability samples.

Specifically, sampling error reflects the discrepancy between the results one obtains from a particular sample and the results one would have obtained from the entire population. Suppose that a survey based on simple random sampling (to be explained below) indicates that 70 percent of the sample would vote for candidate A. With a sample size of $N = 500$ and a desired confidence interval of 95 percent, sampling error would be around 4 percent. Hence, one may conclude that about 66 percent to 74 percent of the population would vote for candidate A. Sampling error decreases with increasing sampling size. For the above example, sampling error would be 9 percent for a sample of 100, but only 3 percent for a sample of 1,000. For the same reason, the error for any subgroup, e.g., 18–20 year olds, is larger than the error for the sample as a whole. Sampling error cannot be estimated with the use of nonprobability sampling techniques, because the likelihood of being selected is unknown for nonprobability samples.

Finally, some studies masquerade as surveys but do not deserve this term. These are studies based on convenience samples, that is, samples which are readily available or comprised solely of volunteers. Such samples, be they college students who voluntarily sign up for a study or readers who respond to a questionnaire printed in a magazine, do not allow any inferences about any population because their representativeness is unknown. Hence, such studies are useless if we are interested in learning about some specified population. Convenience samples are very useful, however, in experimental research designed to explore the impact of some experimental treatment. Because estimating the values of some larger population is not crucial to experimental research, it suffices that the experimental groups themselves are comparable. This can be guaranteed by random assignment of volunteers to experimental conditions (see EXPERIMENTATION).

## SOME COMMON SURVEY DESIGNS
If a given sample is interviewed only once, the survey is often called a cross-sectional survey; if the sample is followed over time and interviewed repeatedly, the resulting longitudinal study is called a panel survey. Cross-sectional surveys provide a snapshot of the population's opinion or behavior at a given point in time; their results can be compared with other snapshots and can be used to describe differences between subpopulations. However, cross-sectional surveys are limited in their ability to trace changes in opinion or behavior over time, which is the major advantage of panel surveys. Occasionally, survey researchers employ experimental elements in a survey, e.g., by using different question wordings or different question orders for parts of the sample. The resulting between-subjects design (see EXPERIMENTATION) is often called a split-ballot design in survey research.

## QUESTIONNAIRE CONSTRUCTION AND THE PROCESS OF QUESTION ANSWERING
In addition to specifying the population of interest, the research objectives also determine which questions are to be asked. The results of any survey are largely dependent on the specific wording of the questions asked and the context in which a given question is presented. For a long time, questionnaire construction has been considered an "art" that required extensive experience but lacked a strong theoretical basis. In recent years, however, collaborative research conducted by cognitive (social) psychologists and survey researchers has yielded useful theoretical insights into the cognitive and communicative processes underlying the question-answering process in surveys, which can guide questionnaire construction. Bradburn and Sudman (1983) provide an excellent "how-to-do-it" introduction to question wording; below, we summarize the key psychological issues (see Strack & Martin, 1987; Tourangeau & Rasinski, 1988, for more detail).

From a psychological perspective, answering a survey question requires that respondents solve several tasks. As a first step, respondents have to interpret the question to understand what is meant. If the wording of the question is ambiguous, they may turn to the content of preceding questions to determine its meaning; for example, the term "drug" may be interpreted quite differently in the context of crime-related questions than in the context of medical questions. If the question is an opinion question, respondents may either recall a previously formed opinion from memory, or they may form an opinion on the spot. To do so, they need to retrieve relevant information from memory to form a judgment. In forming a judgment, however, people are unlikely to retrieve all information that may potentially be relevant. Rather, they truncate the search process as soon as enough information has come to mind to make a judgment with sufficient subjective certainty. As a result, the judgment is based primarily on the information that comes to mind most easily. This is typically the information that has been used most recently, e.g., for answering a preceding question. For example, if a question that requires an evaluation of the government's performance has been preceded by questions about economic issues, these issues are more likely to come to mind than other aspects of the government's performance, and will hence receive more weight in the overall evaluation. The impact of preceding questions on the cognitive accessibility of relevant information is one of the primary source of context effects in survey measurement (see the contributions to Schwarz & Sudman, 1992).

Once respondents have formed a "private" judgment in their mind, they have to communicate it to the researcher. If the question follows a so-called open response format, they may simply tell the interviewer their opinion. Because open-ended answers are expensive to analyze, however, survey questions typically use a closed response format. In this case, respondents have to select one of several response alternatives offered to them, e.g., the statement that best describes their opinion or a number along a rating scale. The specific alternatives provided can strongly affect the obtained results (see Schwarz & Hippler, 1991 for a review). For example, opinions that are omitted from a question asked in a closed format are unlikely to be reported at all, and some response alternatives may remind respondents of options they may otherwise not have thought of. Finally, respondents may in some cases hesitate to disclose their opinion to the interviewer and may hence edit their judgment prior to reporting it, due to influences of social desirability and situational adequacy (see SELF-PRESENTATION).

Similar considerations apply to behavioral questions (see the contributions to Schwarz & Sudman, 1994), e.g., questions that ask respondents how often they have bought something. Again, respondents first need to understand which behavior they are supposed to report. Next, they have to recall or reconstruct relevant instances of this behavior from memory. If the question specifies a reference period (e.g., "during the last month"), they must also determine whether or not these instances occurred during this reference period. Similarly, if the question refers to their "usual" behavior, respondents have to determine whether the recalled instances are reasonably representative or whether they reflect a deviation from their usual behavior. If they cannot recall or reconstruct specific instances of the behavior, or are not sufficiently motivated to engage in this effort, respondents may rely on their general knowledge, or other salient information that may bear on their task, to compute an estimate. This is particularly likely for frequent and mundane behaviors, which are not well represented in memory.

Accordingly, interpreting the question, generating an opinion or a representation of the relevant behavior, formatting the response, and editing the answer are the main psychological components of a process that starts with respondents' exposure to a survey question and ends with their overt report. Each of these aspects is strongly influenced by the specific wording of the question, the response alternatives offered to respondents, and the content of preceding questions. Pretests that involve experimental variations of these aspects of the questionnaire provide an opportunity to identify major problems and highly sophisticated methods of pretesting have been developed in recent years, employing methodological tools borrowed from cognitive psychology.

## MODES OF DATA COLLECTION

Questions can be asked in face-to-face interviews, on the telephone, or in self-administered questionnaires, which may be mailed to respondents (Weisberg et al., 1989). Because face-to-face interviews require trained field staff at all interviewing locations, involving considerable administrative effort and travel cost, they are more expensive to conduct than telephone interviews. The latter may be completed by a smaller number of interviewers at a centralized telephone facility, which also facilitates interviewer supervision and quality control. Nowadays, telephone interviewing is usually conducted with the help of a computer system (called CATI, for computer assisted telephone interviewing) that displays the question to the interviewer who types in the respondent's answer, a procedure that reduces coding efforts and transcription errors. Telephone interviews are only feasible, however, if the sampled respondents can be reached on the phone, which may depend on the population of interest. Mail surveys are the least expensive to conduct, but typically show rather low response rates, unless a considerable number of reminder letters is used. Moreover, individuals who are particularly interested in the topic are more likely to return the questionnaire, introducing some risk of topic related self-selection. This risk is less pronounced for face-to-face or telephone surveys, where respondents are unaware of the specific questions to be asked by the time they agree to be interviewed. On the other hand, the responses obtained in face-to-face or telephone surveys are susceptible to interviewer influences, which are largely absent in mail surveys.

Not surprisingly, the different modes of data collection also differ in the tasks that they pose to respondents. Most importantly, telephone interviews preclude the use of visual aids and put respondents under more time pressure, because periods of silence during which respondents think about their answer are experienced as more unpleasant on the phone. Accordingly, the intended mode of data collection must be kept in mind at the questionnaire construction stage and some of the influences of questionnaire design vary as a function of the data collection procedure used (see Schwarz et al., 1991, for a review).

## EVALUATING SURVEYS

Mass media reports of survey results do not typically provide the information that would be necessary for a reasonable evaluation of the survey. A serious report should allow readers to answer the following questions (see Weisberg et al., 1989, for a fuller discussion): Who sponsored the survey and who conducted it? When and how (mode of data collection) were the interviews taken? Was a probability or a nonprobability sample used? If the data are based on a convenience sample, as is always the case for call-in polls of radio stations or reader polls of magazines, the study is largely useless. What was the sample size and the response rate? How high is the sampling error? What was the exact wording of the question and which response alternatives were offered to respondents? If this information is not provided, there is no way to tell what the answers actually referred to. Are the reported percentages based on the sample as a whole or only on respondents who gave an answer to the question? If a large proportion of respondents say they do not have an opinion, calculating the percentages on the basis of those who reported an opinion may be quite misleading. If the report claims that opinions or behaviors changed over time, is there sufficient evidence to indicate that the different surveys are comparable? If different questions or different sampling frames were used, nothing but the features of the survey may have changed. Whereas a well-conducted survey can provide highly accurate and useful information, not everything presented as a survey is well conducted. Hence, suspicion is justified if the report does not provide sufficient detail.

*See also*: EXPERIMENTATION.

BIBLIOGRAPHY

Bradburn, N. M., & Sudman, S. (1983). *Asking questions: A practical guide to questionnaire design*. San Francisco, CA: Jossey-Bass.

——(1988). *Polls and surveys: Understanding what they tell us*. San Francisco, CA: Jossey-Bass.

Kalton, G. (1983). *Introduction to survey sampling*. Beverly Hills, CA: Sage.

Schwarz, N., & Hippler, H. J. (1991). Response alternatives: The impact of their choice and ordering. In P. Biemer, R. Groves, N. Mathiowetz, & S. Sudman

(Eds.), *Measurement error in surveys* (pp. 41–56). Chichester: J. Wiley.

——Strack, F., Hippler, H. J., & Bishop, G. (1991). The impact of administration mode on response effects in survey measurement. *Applied Cognitive Psychology, 5,* 193–212.

——& Sudman, S. (Eds.) (1992). *Context effects in social and psychological research.* New York: Springer-Verlag.

————(Eds.) (1994). *Autobiographical memory and the validity of retrospective reports.* New York: Springer-Verlag.

Strack, F., & Martin, L. L. (1987). Thinking, judging, and communicating: A process account of context effects in attitude surveys. In H. J. Hippler, N. Schwarz, & S. Sudman (Eds.), *Social information and survey methodology* (pp. 123–48). New York: Springer-Verlag.

Tourangeau, R., & Rasinski, K. A. (1988). Cognitive processes underlying context effects in attitude measurement. *Psychological Bulletin, 103,* 299–314.

Weisberg, H. F., Krosnick, J. A., & Bowen, B. D. (1989). *An introduction to survey research and data analysis* (2nd ed.). Glenview, IL: Scott, Foresman.

NORBERT SCHWARZ
TRACY R. WELLENS

**symbolic interactionism** Although stemming in important part from the seminal thinking of a philosopher–psychologist, George Herbert Mead, symbolic interactionism is the major framework for the analysis of social psychological phenomena developed by sociologists. The defining emphases of the framework include: Social interaction as the source from which social persons and social structures derive; human agency; indeterminacy as an important feature of social life; the symbolic character and social construction of the physical and social environments of human activity; the significance of subjective experience in mediating the relation between those environments and behavior; and SELF as a subjective experience of particular import in that relation. Given these emphases, when behaviorism reigned relatively supreme in general psychology, social psychologists trained in psychology (if they were aware of symbolic interactionism and with some notable exceptions – e.g., Sherif, Newcomb) tended to dismiss symbolic interactionist ideas as subjectivist and phenomenological, so unscientific. Today's virtual hegemony of SOCIAL COGNITION as a guiding framework for the social psychological theorizing and research of psychologists, and the prominence of the concept of self within that theory and research, has opened this audience to symbolic interactionism. Consequently, substantial cross-disciplinary communication has developed where little existed earlier. This communication provides the opportunity for cognitive social psychologists to appreciate better the ways in which cognitions are influenced by persons' locations in social structures and participation in social processes, and so the limitations of a purely cognitive emphasis in predicting and explaining social behavior. It also provides the opportunity for symbolic interactionists to appreciate better the significance of individual differences in experience and in cognitive structures in modifying the impact of social location on self, and of self on subsequent behavior.

THE BASIC SYMBOLIC
INTERACTIONIST FRAMEWORK
The term symbolic interactionism was invented by Herbert Blumer to refer to ideas whose immediate source was Mead (1934). The frame both antedates and resembles a variety of contemporary currents in social psychological thinking – currents suggested by the language of action theory, phenomenology, ethogeny, hermeneutics, ethnomethodology, constructivism, interpretive social science, structuration, sociorationalism – without necessarily sharing the senses of social psychology as an intellectual enterprise associated with those currents. Mead and Blumer are part of a tradition of thought in which the Scottish moral philosophers (e.g., Adam Smith, Adam Ferguson, Francis Hutcheson, David Hume) link the more remote past to the American pragmatic philosophers (e.g., Charles Pierce, William James, John Dewey) who link to Mead and early American sociology (especially Charles Horton

Cooley, William Isaac Thomas) who link through Blumer to more contemporary interactionists (e.g., Erving Goffman, Howard Becker, John Lofland, Anselm Strauss, Ralph Turner, Arlene Daniels, Arlie Hochschild, David Snow, Gary Fine, Peter Burke, George McCall, John Hewitt). Cooley's dictum that person and society are two sides of the same coin and Thomas's dictum that if persons define situations as real, they are real in their consequences together assert much of the core of symbolic interactionism.

That core can be expressed as three fundamental premises:

(1) adequate accounts of human social behavior cannot rest on the perspective of observers of that behavior but must take into account the points of view of the behaving actors;
(2) self, or persons' reflexive responses to themselves, intervenes in relating larger social structures and processes to the social interaction of those persons; and
(3) processes of social interaction are ontologically and experientially prior to self and social organization, which emerge from social interaction.

These premises undergird ideas and concepts that together comprise an elaborated symbolic interactionist frame. The proposition that self reflects society and organizes behavior is a convenient starting point in describing the ideas. Society is a web of communication. Alternatively, society is interaction, reciprocal influence of persons who take into account one another's characteristics and actions; and interaction is communication. Society is a label aggregating and summarizing interaction; it is created and recreated as persons interact. Interaction is symbolic: It proceeds through participants using meanings they develop in the process of interacting; and it is conducted in a symbolically defined and interpreted social and physical environment. The symbolic environment is context for interaction; at the same time it shapes and is the object of interaction.

Thus, persons create society through their interaction. However, society creates social beings. That the interaction creating social beings is symbolic implicitly asserts that the capacity of human beings for manipulating symbols in thought is critical to accounts of their behavior. Thought takes place as internal conversation using symbols developed in the social process; in that sense, thinking is an internalized social process. Persons have minds, and their minds have the potential of reflexivity; they are subjects who can take themselves as objects of their own reflection. When they do so, they create selves; self exists in reflexive responses to self. The selves created are inherently social products, for persons reflect on themselves from the standpoint of others with whom they interact. Mind emerges in an evolutionary as well as individual sense in response to problems, interrupted activities, and entails formulating and selecting among alternative courses of action oriented to the resolution of those problems. Since social life is inherently problematic, choice is an ever-present possibility in social interaction.

It follows that human beings, individually and collectively, are active and creative in responding to circumstances impinging on them; they are actors as well as reactors. It also follows that social interaction can be constructed in the course of interaction itself. There is, then, indeterminacy in human behavior, in that as a matter of principle interaction cannot be completely predicted from conditions existing prior to that interaction.

The ideas described are central to the framework of symbolic interactionism, as are concepts implicated in those ideas. Fundamental is the meaning of "meaning." Social interactions takes place over time and so permit the appearance of *gestures*, parts of acts that come to indicate the future courses of those acts. Words or other sounds, physical movements, clothing, etc., can serve as gestures; when they do so, they have meaning which lies in the parts of acts, the behaviors, that follow after them. Gestures having common meaning – that is, that predict the same future behaviors – to persons who provide them and persons who observe them are *significant symbols*.

Social reality is constituted by objects (including things, ideas, and relationships among things and ideas) whose meanings are anchored in and emerge from social interaction. Ongoing interaction and communication are made possible by significant symbols whose meanings, while they typically will not be identical among parties to the interaction and communication, are sufficiently shared to enable coherent interaction. Anticipating future behavior, significant symbols incorporate plans of action: they serve to organize behavior with respect to that which they symbolize.

In ongoing interaction, meanings must be assigned, at least on a tentative basis, to the situation of interaction and its constituent features if the behavior of participants is to be organized. That is, the situation and its most important features must be defined and interpreted; the products of this symbolization are *definitions of the situation*. Tentative definitions and interpretations, permitting preliminary organization of actions in the situation, are tested and if necessary reformulated as interaction unfolds.

From the point of view of the actors involved, it is who or what they are in a situation and who or what the others implicated in that situation are that particularly requires definition. Defining others and self in situations is largely a matter of locating both others and self as members of socially recognized categories of actors, as one or more of the kinds of persons it is possible to be in a society. Symbolizing self and others in this way provides expectations for, and so cues to, the behavior of others and permits organizing one's behavior with reference to those others. Expectations attached to social categories are *roles* (*see* ROLE THEORY), a term some symbolic interactionists object to as both imputing too much order to social life and as outside the experience of actors themselves. Often, situations permit locating self and others in multiple categories and open the possibility of conflicting role expectations for both self and others coming into play; when this happens there may be no clear means of organizing responses. Locating oneself in socially recognized categories is to respond reflexively to oneself and so is to have a *self*. Self, like any other significant symbol, derives from interaction and provides a plan for future action, a plan that takes into account expected responses of others.

What we can provisionally expect from others is learned in interaction through *role-taking*, a process of anticipating the future responses of those with whom we interact. On the bases of prior experience with others, knowledge of the social categories in which those others are located, and symbolic cues available in the situation of interaction and the interaction itself, we in effect put ourselves in the place of those others to see the world as they do. We formulate tentative expectations with respect to others' behavior that are validated or reshaped in interaction. Role-taking allows anticipating the consequences of one's own or others' plans of action, monitoring the results of those plans, and redirecting behavior accordingly. We also engage in *role-making*. That is, we sometimes find ourselves in situations in which existing roles lack consistency and clarity yet behavior must be organized as if they were unequivocal. Then, we create and modify our own roles through devising performances in response to roles we impute to others in the situations (Turner, 1962).

Organized systems of action – the model is a team engaging another team in a contest – provide settings for interactions that relate a given person to a large number of others who are themselves implicated in complex interrelationships. In such settings, role-taking and role-making occur with reference to a *generalized other*, a differentiated yet interrelated set of others to whom persons respond as a more or less coherent unit. The concept of *significant other* is invoked to recognize that when expectations impinging on a person from various others differ or are incompatible, not all others are given equal weight in arriving at a plan of action. Asserted here is that situations vary in the degree that meanings are shared, or shared in detail, by those involved in them; implied is that accuracy in role-taking or ease of role-making will vary across situations. Also implied is that accurate role taking does not necessarily produce cooperative interpersonal relations.

To this point, the discussion has proceeded as though symbolic interactionism is a singular framework accepted by all who invoke that label to describe their thinking. In fact, there is as much conceptual and methodological diversity within it as there is unity; some would say there is more. This suggests, correctly, that the three premises of symbolic interactionism reviewed earlier leave considerable room for differences in the objectives, methods, and content of what is done in its name. To simplify matters, the discussion will proceed by reviewing two ideal typical versions even while admitting that practice defies that simplification.

## TRADITIONAL SYMBOLIC INTERACTIONISM

What may be called traditional symbolic interactionism was defined in its essentials by Blumer (1969), who shaped the frame in opposition to a sociology developed around social structural and organizational concepts. Blumer viewed such a sociology, and the theoretical aims (e.g., search for general laws and general theories) and methodological means (e.g., reliance on statistical analyses of survey data) he believed were inextricably tied into it, with great suspicion; he did not think either those aims or those means could hold if we recognized the fundamental place of meanings in human action and interaction. For him, structural concepts, which refer to social arrangements that are presumably relatively fixed over time, deny the fundamentally open character of social life, and so are more likely to mislead than to enlighten the sociological analyst and audience. It is this version of the frame that defines its meaning for many of its most passionate adherents and most vociferous critics, that currently dominates the journal *Symbolic Interaction*, and that is most likely to come to the minds of social psychologists of whatever kind when the label is introduced. In this version, the emphasis is on social process, and the dominant theme is the openness and fluidity of that process. Consequently, definitions and interpretations are viewed as having a moment-to-moment, situationally specific character; and social order is viewed as continuously created anew in the fluid process of interaction.

It follows that self is also seen as a moment-to-moment, situationally specific phenomenon. Self is construed as acting in a relatively unconstrained way to organize social behavior, with the result that human behavior is characterized by creativity and novelty. Given its emphasis on social life as a continuously changing flow marked by creativity and novelty, this version of symbolic interactionism holds that there is little warrant for science as a predictive enterprise and there is little utility for analyses of that social life in conceptualizations and theory based on analyses of social life at some previous point in time. It tends to hold, relatedly, that introducing the point of view of the observer into analyses serves to contaminate reasonable accounts based on the points of view of participants engaged in the interaction observed. Since a priori conceptualizations and theory reflecting an investigator's point of view are necessary to the elaboration of an experimental or survey research design, such methods of data gathering and associated methods of analysis are abjured in favor of reliance on what has been called grounded theory (Glaser & Strauss, 1967) and on ethnographic methods, in particular on direct and participant observation. For those with this vision of symbolic interactionism, the development of general sociological or social psychological theory should not be the goal of research, for that goal cannot be achieved; rather, the goal must be after-the-fact interpretation, and understanding via interpretation, of the social behavior that has occurred. The logic of this version of symbolic interactionism means that research arising from it tends to be descriptive and its motivation tends to be found in substantive rather than theoretical issues.

## STRUCTURAL SYMBOLIC INTERACTIONISM

As might be expected, the alternative version of symbolic interactionism places distinctively greater emphasis on the import of social structure in shaping the course and product of social process; it thus tends to merge with interactionist role theory. This alternative version can be labeled structural symbolic interactionism. In part, it has come into existence in response to critiques of the traditional framework which assert among other things that minimizing the import of social structure itself denies and distorts social reality (*see* Stryker, 1980, and Stryker & Statham, 1986, for more complete accounts of these critiques). Epigrammatically and illustratively, the argument is that social class impacts the course and outcomes of social interaction whether or not implicated actors attach meanings to class. Accepting the fluidity and openness of social life as ever-present possibilities of human existence, it argues that social structures make some possibilities much more likely than others to actually occur (Stryker, 1980). Structures either enhance or limit possibilities by the opportunities they offer or fail to offer, and by bringing together or keeping apart particular kinds of people with particular symbolic or material resources for engagement in particular kinds of interaction oriented to the solution of particular kinds of problems. That is, social structures are viewed essentially as social boundaries linking or separating categories of persons, so facilitating or constraining the experiences those persons are likely to have, their opportunities to be involved in given interaction networks and engage in given behaviors, the content of symbols they are likely to learn, the aspirations they are likely to hold for themselves and for others to whom they relate, the kinds of persons it is possible for them to become, etc.

## CURRENT WORK IN SYMBOLIC INTERACTIONISM

Work in both the traditional and structural varieties of symbolic interactionism flourishes today, when concern with human agency is high, following a period – the 1950s into the 1970s, when first structural functionalist and later various forms of Marxist and European structuralist thought dominated sociology – in which interest waned. Newer work contains a focus on emotion in an effort to balance the cognitive bias of those analyses that follow Mead's lead. Work over recent decades, perhaps especially in the structural vein, draws more on William James than on Mead to introduce a multiple self, or multiple identity, perspective (Stryker, 1980) that promises rich conceptual and theoretical payoffs. The "new" stress on social structural constraints and facilitators has been an important source of the current vitalization of symbolic interactionism (Stryker, 1987).

Other sources of that vitalization are methodological. At least some work in the traditional frame has become increasingly rigorous; for example, Corsaro and Heise (1990) use ethnographic data systematically rather than anecdotally to elaborate the social organization of interaction processes. Work in the structural frame tends to be oriented to formulating explanatory theories and testing these theories empirically, and uses a full range of social science methods; instances include work on identity theory (Stryker, 1992) and on affect control theory (Heise, 1979).

*See also*: ROLE THEORY; SELF; SOCIAL COGNITION.

BIBLIOGRAPHY
Blumer, H. (1969). *Symbolic interactionism: Perspective and method.* Englewood Cliffs, NJ: Prentice Hall.
Corsaro, W. A., & Heise, D. R. (1990). Event structure models from ethnographic data. *Sociological Methodology, 20,* 1–57.
Glaser, B. G., & Strauss, A. L. (1967). *The discovery of grounded theory.* Chicago, IL: Aldine.
Heise, D. R. (1979). *Understanding events.* New York: Cambridge University Press.
Mead, G. H. (1934). *Mind, self, and society.* Chicago, IL: University of Chicago Press.
Stryker, S. (1980). *Symbolic interactionism: A social structural version.* Menlo Park, CA: Benjamin/Cummings.
—— (1987). The vitalization of symbolic interactionism. *Social Psychology Quarterly, 50,* 83–94.
—— (1992). Identity theory. In E. F. Borgatta and M. L. Borgatta (Eds.), *Encyclopedia of sociology* (pp. 871–6). New York: Macmillan.
—— & Statham, A. (1986). Symbolic interactionism and role theory. In G. Lindzey & E. Aronson (Eds.), *The handbook of social psychology* (3rd ed., Vol. 1, pp. 311–78). New York: Random House.
Turner, R. H. (1962). Role-taking: Process versus conformity. In A. M. Rose (Ed.), *Human behavior and social process* (pp. 20–40). Boston: Houghton-Mifflin.

SHELDON STRYKER

# T

territoriality  Territories are physical areas that are used, controlled, marked and/or defended by individuals and groups. They are one of several boundary regulation mechanisms (*see* PERSONAL SPACE) that allow individuals to maintain control over their possessions, thoughts, and behaviors. Territories are different from personal space in that they are physical areas, can be left and reclaimed, and have physical boundaries. Altman (1975) and Brown and Altman (1981) distinguished among primary, secondary, and public territories along the dimensions of psychological centrality, duration of occupancy, degree to which occupants intend to claim the territory, territorial markings, and how occupants respond to intrusions.

*Primary territories*, such as homes, are central to the individual's self-concept, under the individual's control, occupied for long durations, extensively marked, and well defended. *Secondary territories* are less psychologically central and occupied for shorter periods of time; they are often shared by a group of regular occupants who may mark and defend the area. *Public territories* are entered for shorter periods of time, little control is expected, they are not central to users' self-concepts, may be marked, and are not always defended. These three levels of territory are not separate and distinct, but rather are general areas along a continuum. Primary and secondary territories develop over time as people appropriate space, build memories, engage in patterns of activities and become bonded to the area.

Territorial behaviors are complex, as reflected in this description by Altman and Chemers (1980, pp. 121–2);

(1) There is control and ownership of a place or object on a temporary or permanent basis.

(2) The place or object may be small or large.
(3) Ownership may be by a person or group.
(4) Territoriality can serve any of several functions, including social functions (status, identity, family stability) and physical functions (child rearing, food regulation, food storage).
(5) Territories are often personalized or marked.
(6) Defense may occur when territorial boundaries are violated.

Early work on territorial behavior focused on animals who often establish and defend areas in order to maintain control over resources such as hunting/foraging and nesting opportunities. Animal territorial behavior is complicated, varying in form from one species to another; within a species, territoriality varies with time of year, relationship to intruder, availability of food, and other factors. Although territories may require extensive fighting and posturing initially, once established and recognized by conspecifics, territories support the social order, thereby reducing the frequency of aggressive behaviors.

Human territorial behavior has been documented for centuries and can be seen in broad political and local individual behaviors. Similar to animal territories, human territories involve boundary regulation, allow control over and protection of resources, and bring order to social relations. Human territories are usually protected by laws and social NORMS rather than by physical strength.

Most recent conceptualizations of human territoriality add the idea that territories support psychological goals; thus, people become attached to some territories as they invest the area with personal meaning (Brown, 1987). Indeed, for many primary and secondary territories, it is common for people to realize both "social regulation" and "identity" functions. Social regulation refers to the dialectic opposition of accessibility/inaccessibility. The home – a primary territory – serves as a semipermeable boundary between the owner family and others, selectively admitting and excluding visitors or intruders. Similar accessibility/inaccessibility regulation can occur in neighborhoods and public housing developments, especially if the designed environment encourages residents to get to know one another and protect the common areas from potentially threatening outsiders. In defensible settings, residents often protect their neighborhood as a primary or secondary territory, whereas in others there is little sense of neighborhood ownership, and the area outside the home moves quickly from primary to public territory. Urban renewal projects often replaced a system of small neighborhood blocks with large, undifferentiated housing developments where it was difficult to develop a sense of neighborhood cohesion. When residents know each other and think of the neighborhood as theirs, they engage in surveillance of the street, there is less disorder and fewer "incivilities" (abandoned cars, unkempt buildings), often a greater sense of safety, and a lower crime rate (Newman, 1972; Taylor, 1988).

The identity function of territories can also be seen as a dialectic in which the need to be unique and distinctive is opposed with the need to be part of a larger social group. Homes are often decorated in ways that reflect the unique identities of the residents; at the same time these decorations reflect the residents' membership in various collectives, such as religious, local neighborhood, and school or university affiliations. Often, these displays achieve a desired balance between individual and group identities. Secondary territories are also decorated in ways that reflect the group's or neighborhood's identity (e.g., name signs, gang graffiti), but they may also contain information about individual members or a even larger social group, reflecting the multiple identities of residents. Public territories may reflect group identity, such as religious, historical, or cultural shrines that draw group members together and make salient their common past and collective identity.

Current research continues to clarify how territorial bonds develop and are maintained and how they relate to family and neighborhood ties, safety, and viability.

*See also*: NORMS.

BIBLIOGRAPHY

Altman, I. (1975). *Environment and social behavior: Privacy, personal space, territory and crowding*. Monterey, CA: Brooks/Cole.
——& Chemers, M. M. (1980). *Culture and environment*. Belmont, CA: Wadsworth.
Brown, B. B. (1987). Territoriality. In D. Stokols & I. Altman (Eds.). *Handbook of Environmental Psychology* (Vol. 1, pp. 505–31). New York: Wiley.
Newman, O. (1972). *Defensible space*. New York: Macmillan.
Taylor, R. B. (1988). *Human territorial functioning: An empirical, evolutionary perspective on individual and small group territorial cognitions, behaviors, and consequences*. Cambridge: Cambridge University Press.

CAROL M. WERNER
IRWIN ALTMAN

**theory of planned behavior** An extension of the THEORY OF REASONED ACTION, the theory of planned behavior adds perceived behavioral control to ATTITUDES and subjective norms so that, together with behavioral intentions, it becomes possible to predict actions that are under incomplete volitional control.

ICEK AJZEN

**theory of reasoned action** The theory of reasoned action was developed in the context of research on the relation between ATTITUDES AND BEHAVIOR (Ajzen & Fishbein, 1980). Suitable for the prediction of volitional actions, the theory posits that intentions are the immediate antecedents of behavior and that these intentions are determined by attitudes toward the behavior and by subjective norms. The attitude is the tendency to evaluate performance of the behavior favorably or unfavorably and the subjective norm represents the perceived social pressure to engage in the behavior.

The theory of reasoned action has been used successfully to predict behaviors in a wide range of situations, and to develop programs of intervention designed to modify undesirable patterns of behavior. When dealing with activities that are largely under volitional control, intentions are predictive of actual behavior, and they correlate well with attitudes and subjective norms. Among the many behaviors studied are cigarette smoking, family planning, dental care, water conservation, condom use, recycling, charitable behavior, fat consumption, physical exercise, cancer self-examination, outdoor recreation, television viewing, living kidney donation, and seat-belt use.

See also: ATTITUDES AND BEHAVIOR.

BIBLIOGRAPHY

Ajzen, I., & Fishbein, M. (1980). Understanding attitudes and predicting social behavior. Englewood Cliffs, NJ: Prentice Hall.

ICEK AJZEN

**trait** A central concept in PERSONALITY. Traits refer to stable, internal properties that distinguish among individuals. They are psychological characteristics of individuals that are used to describe, explain, understand, and predict behavior. Traits form one class of the many INDIVIDUAL DIFFERENCES that moderate behavior. Like physical characteristics such as height and weight, traits provide information about a person's standing relative to others. However, unlike height or weight, traits cannot be assessed directly but must always be inferred from behavior.

Although there is agreement at the level of a general definition, there is a lack of consensus among personality theorists about the specifics of the trait concept, particularly with regard to the epistemological status of traits and their causal potency (see Alston, 1975). At one extreme, some theorists claim that traits exist as structures in the brain that determine behavior, whereas at the other extreme traits are viewed merely as linguistic devices that distort rather than reflect reality. Somewhere between these extremes is the view that traits have a social reality: traits refer to the variation among individuals in their consistent patterns of socially meaningful behaviors.

See also: PERSONALITY.

BIBLIOGRAPHY

Alston, W. P. (1975). Traits, consistency, and conceptual alternatives for personality theory. Journal for the Theory of Social Behavior, 5, 17–37.

SARAH E. HAMPSON

**transactive memory** A system shared among group members for encoding, storing, and retrieving information such that detailed memories are available to group members without actual physical possession (Wegner, 1986; Wegner, Giuliano, & Hertel, 1985). It is defined in terms of two components representing a structure-process distinction:

(1) an organized store of knowledge that is contained entirely in the individual memory systems of the group members; and
(2) a set of knowledge-relevant transactive processes that occur among group members.

These two components distinguish transactive memory from the group mind concept popular early in the century – first, because the thought processes of transactive memory are completely observable, and second, because previously ignored communication processes among group members are proposed as a key source in producing the distinction between the group mind and the minds of individual members.

Although transactive memory resides entirely in the individual memory systems of group members, it is transactive in the sense that group members can easily access information stored by other members. Three types of information in personal memory define the organization of transactive memory: lower-order information, higher-order information, and location information. Lower-order information consists of specific facts or details – for example, a recipe, mortgage amount, or phone number. Higher-order information is the topic or label for some set of items of lower-order information, such as cooking or bills. Location information is a directory associating higher-order topics with group members such that lower-order information can be found in the group.

To the extent that group members have mutual higher-order and location information, they maximize their access to the lower-order information available from individual members. In communicating and updating others about their areas of knowledge, each member cultivates the others as external memory aids and in so doing becomes part of a larger system. The less overlap of lower-order information among members, the more differentiated is the transactive structure. Differentiation typically increases the efficiency and amount of information available in the group as long as members have access to the location of that information. When groups use communication to tie different lower-order items under a common higher-order topic, the transactive structure becomes more integrated. Integration increases the likelihood groups will combine existing information in new and creative ways. A balance between differentiation and integration helps create an optimal transactive memory.

The organization of the transactive memory structure is likely to change over the course of the relationship. In early stages of a relationship, members may rely on stereotypes or social categorization as default indicators of the types of information the others are likely to know. As members become more familiar, they may establish their directories or location information through explicit negotiation (i.e., "if you remember this, I'll remember that"), or through more implicit means, such as perceptions of the relative expertise of group members in different knowledge domains, or knowledge of another's access to information. Ultimately, the organized structure becomes a critical basis for the group's interaction, facilitating its memory performance as compared to that of groups that do not have a structure in place (Wegner, Erber, & Raymond, 1991).

Equally as important as the transactive memory structure are the transactive processes that occur as a group encodes, stores,

or retrieves information. Transactive encoding occurs in group discussions about a memory topic as it is encountered. Individual perceptions will often differ, and the discussion will lead to a new understanding, or new memory, by one or more members. Even if perceptions are similar, discussion increases the likelihood that memories will become more elaborately encoded, and that they will therefore be more likely to be available for later retrieval. In these ways, the information that is stored by the individuals may differ as a result of group communication processes.

Transactive storage may produce still more modification of originally encoded information because of the iterative effects that occur in the process of communication. In discussing past events, for example, group members may simplify or elaborate originally stored information in an attempt to make their individual accounts more consistent or understandable to others. The resulting memory may be more or less accurate than the original, but it will almost certainly be different.

Finally, transactive processing may occur in retrieval. A group may retrieve some target item through interactive cuing, for instance, as members retrieve relevant items of information that serve as cues for others's retrieval of more relevant items, and eventually cue retrieval of the target. Context effects could account for another aspect of transactive retrieval. Information encoded in the presence of a group member would subsequently be retrieved more effectively in the presence of the group member. The participation or mere presence of group members, then, is likely to affect the retrieval process.

Transactive memory has applications in several domains, including intimate relationships, health behavior, instructional psychology, and organizational management (Wegner, 1986). In the case of intimate relationships, for example, the operation of transactive memory has important implications for the quality of a relationship. Although differentiation leads to efficiency, it can also lead to overconfidence about one's access to knowledge or a lack of common discussion topics. And the dependence on another for integration could result in complete devastation when the relationship comes to an end. Although a smoothly functioning transactive memory can infinitely benefit its members, problems with faulty information or miscommunication can have damaging impact. The notion of transactive memory is useful, in sum, for understanding how groups process and store information in structured ways that both depend upon and transcend individual memory.

*See also*: GROUP PROCESSES; INTIMACY; SOCIAL REMEMBERING.

BIBLIOGRAPHY

Wegner, D. M. (1986). Transactive memory: A contemporary analysis of the group mind. In B. Mullen & G. R. Goethals (Eds.), *Theories of group behavior* (pp. 185–208). New York: Springer-Verlag.

—— Giuliano, T., & Hertel, P. (1985). Cognitive interdependence in close relationships. In W. J. Ickes (Ed.), *Compatible and incompatible relationships* (pp. 253–76). New York: Springer-Verlag.

—— Erber, R., & Raymond, P. (1991). Transactive memory in close relationships. *Journal of Personality and Social Psychology*, *61*, 923–9.

TONI G. WEGNER
DANIEL M. WEGNER

**triangle hypothesis** This asserts that people with a primarily competitive orientation expect others to also be competitive, whereas cooperatively oriented people expect more variation in others. Its name is derived from the triangular relationship between one's own cooperative versus competitive tendencies and the range of expected behaviors on the part of others. It is based on the assumption that competitors induce competitive behavior in all others they interact with but they are unaware of their own role in the process. Cooperators, on the other hand, have mixed experiences (*see* COOPERATION AND COMPETITION).

*See also*: COOPERATION AND COMPETITION.

EDDY VAN AVERMAET

**trust** Although a consensus on a common definition of trust remains elusive (Webb & Worchel, 1986), social psychological treatments of trust have drawn a fundamental distinction between two conceptually independent but related aspects of this construct: trust viewed as a subjective state of being versus trust viewed as trusting behavior (*see* Kee & Knox, 1970). On the one hand, subjective trust is generally conceptualized as a readiness or predisposition to trust others – that is, to evaluate them as worthy of trust – given the appropriate circumstances (Holmes, 1991). It is variously described as a state of subjective certainty, confidence, or faith that some other, upon whom we must depend, will not act in ways that might occasion us painful consequences. Behavioral trust, in contrast, is defined in operational terms as subjective trust put into action, the observable behavioral manifestation of an individual's confident expectations regarding the benevolence of the other's motives and intentions. A central tenet of this operational perspective is that trusting behavior typically involves, at some level or other, placing one's self in a position of potential vulnerability relative to another. It is important to note that, although theorists might view these two faces of trust as *conceptually* distinct, it is assumed that they are intimately linked in people's real-life experiences. Accordingly, whether or not a person chooses to engage in trusting behavior in any particular situation is predicated upon his or her appraisal of the other's trustworthiness (Holmes, 1991), that is, his or her degree of certainty or faith that the other who is to be trusted is unselfishly and charitably motivated.

Despite this two-fold understanding of the nature of trust, investigations of trusting *behavior* have been the primary focus of social psychological inquiry on this topic within the past few decades. Adopting the stance that the situation governs the role and meaning of trust, a considerable body of research has accumulated delimiting the situational and contextual variables that determine when people will act in a trusting versus a suspicious manner. Much of the early work in this area employed paradigms based on applications of the PRISONER'S DILEMMA and similar non-zero-sum game scenarios in which participants' interests were in conflict and their outcomes interdependent. For example,

Deutsch's (1958) pioneering work on trust and suspicion revealed the potent influence of a variety of structural factors on people's willingness to cooperate in such situations (see also COOPERATION AND COMPETITION). Most notable among such influences were those features of a situation that impeded a person's ability to determine the opponent's motives and intentions, for example, simultaneity of choice and lack of mechanisms for effective communication among participants. In fact, trust (as measured by rate of cooperation) was reduced most significantly under conditions where few opportunities existed for appraisal of the opponent's motives and the structure of the situation underlined the existence of incentives for the opponent to act in a competitive, self-serving manner.

Deutsch's (1958) findings exemplify the kinds of results obtained from other studies of the situational variables that may affect the rate of cooperative or trusting behavior. The available evidence suggests that the crux of the matter for participants in these sorts of investigations rested in establishing the degree of RISK inherent in choosing to cooperate in any given situation. When features of the situation conspired to raise the spectre of being exploited if they chose to act in a trusting manner, rates of cooperation were correspondingly low. Consistent with this viewpoint, Kee and Knox (1970) note that "one of the distinguishing aspects of real-life situations involving trust and suspicion is that there's something at stake" (p. 362). Theorists have thus argued that, ultimately, information about another's motives is used to assess the degree of risk that may accompany a trusting course of action within the context of a particular situation. The outcome of this appraisal process is believed to determine whether a person will or will not engage in trusting behavior.

Considering also the flipside of trust – its subjective dimension – theory and research in the area of CLOSE RELATIONSHIPS have made a substantial contribution to our understanding of the process by which a sense of trust is developed and maintained (e.g., Holmes, 1991; Kelley & Thibaut, 1978). The heightened degree of INTERDEPENDENCE characteristic of such relationships provides a backdrop against which the dynamics of trust

are clearly exposed, particularly the role that risk plays in enabling the attribution of trustworthy motives. According to Kelley and Thibaut, for example, the growth of trust in a relationship is a conjunctive process of risk-taking in which both individuals allow themselves to be vulnerable by acting in ways that put the other's needs before their own. By doing so, by taking risks that expose them to potential disappointment and hurt, each partner is able to signal his or her own good intentions and thus furnish the other with the type of evidence needed to reduce his or her uncertainty regarding their motives. Intriguingly, as the cycle of reciprocal risk-taking escalates, a developing sense of reassurance or confidence in the partner's motives in turn serves to diminish psychologically the perception of the risk involved (Holmes, 1991; Kelley & Thibaut, 1978). Consequently, in a rather paradoxical manner, the evidence suggests that a sense of trust is borne of *trusting* acts – of first taking the risk of trusting.

See also: COOPERATION AND COMPETITION; INTERDEPENDENCE THEORY; RISK.

BIBLIOGRAPHY

Deutsch, M. (1958). Trust and suspicion. *Journal of Conflict Resolution, 2*, 265–79.

Holmes, J. G. (1991). *Trust and the appraisal process in close relationships*. In W. H. Jones & D. Perlman (Eds.), *Advances in personal relationships* (Vol. 2, pp. 57–104). London: Jessica Kingsley.

Kee, H. W., & Knox, R. E. (1970). Conceptual and methodological considerations in the study of trust and suspicion. *Journal of Conflict Resolution, 14*, 357–66.

Kelley, H. H., & Thibaut, J. W. (1978). *Interpersonal relations: A theory of interdependence*. New York: Wiley.

Webb, W. M., & Worchel, P. (1986). Trust and distrust. In S. Worchel & W. G. Austin (Eds.), *Psychology of intergroup relations* (pp. 213–28). Chicago, IL: Nelson-Hall.

SUSAN D. BOON

**type A behavior pattern** This pattern refers to behavioral attributes that appear to increase risk for coronary disease. These include achievement-striving, competitiveness, impatience, hostility, and vigorous speech. Type B refers to the relative absence of these characteristics.

Specific Type A behaviors are only modestly intercorrelated and are differentially reflected in scores on different measures. The preferred measure is a structured interview, which yields a global score primarily reflecting vigorous speech, and component scores reflecting specific speech and anger-related dimensions. Questionnaires include the Jenkins Activity Survey and Framingham Type A scale. The Cook–Medley scale, derived from the MMPI, has been used to measure hostility, which may be the most risk-enhancing Type A attribute.

Type A behaviors are thought to promote coronary disease primarily through their association with heightened physiological reactivity to psychological stress (*see* STRESS AND COPING). The mechanism probably involves enhanced sympathetic-adrenomedullary activity, which may contribute to the initiation and/or progression of atherosclerosis, and to the precipitation of ischemic disease. There is some evidence that modification of Type A behavior may reduce coronary risk (*see* Contrada, Leventhal, & O'Leary, 1990).

*See also*: HEALTH PSYCHOLOGY; STRESS AND COPING.

BIBLIOGRAPHY

Contrada, R. J., Leventhal, H., & O'Leary, A. (1990). Personality and health. In L. Pervin (Ed.), *Handbook of personality* (pp. 638–69). New York: Guilford Press.

RICHARD J. CONTRADA

# U

**unconscious processing** refers to mental content and processes that occur without awareness. Theoretical definitions range from stored information not currently in awareness, to any automatic procedures (*see* AUTO-MATICITY), to a nonlogical, experiential system, to emotionally aversive, repressed material. Unconscious processes demonstrably can detect stimuli or patterns presented too fast for conscious processing.

*See also*: AUTOMATICITY.

SUSAN T. FISKE
BETH A. MORLING

**unemployment** A state of involuntary joblessness. Although many adults have chosen not to be in paid employment, for instance being home makers or retired from the labor force, having a paid job is normal in developed societies. Individuals who wish to have a job but who have failed to obtain one are referred to as "unemployed," whereas those voluntarily out of the labor market may be described as "nonemployed"; *see also* WORK.

Although some short-term unemployment is often unavoidable, as people move between jobs, recent years have seen raised levels of long-term joblessness with substantial negative impacts upon those involved. Both cross-sectional studies (comparing people who are unemployed against those who are in jobs) and longitudinal research (following individuals as they move between the two conditions) have demonstrated that unemployment is a significant source of STRESS. It can give rise to greater ANXIETY, DEPRESSION, insomnia, and general distress, reduced SELF-ESTEEM and confidence, and sometimes disrupted FAMILY RELATIONS (*see* Fryer, 1992; Jahoda, 1982).

The financial and other constraints of unemployment also tend to create a generalized reduction in subjective autonomy and LEVEL OF ASPIRATION. In a foreword to the 1971 edition of a classic study by Jahoda, Lazarsfeld, and Zeisel (1933), Lazarsfeld emphasizes "the vicious cycle between reduced opportunities and reduced level of aspiration," in which "prolonged unemployment leads to a state of apathy in which the victims do not utilize any longer even the few opportunities left to them" (p. vii). Associated with those outcomes is a strong sense of STIGMA, through which unemployed people are aware of the process of negative STEREOTYPING which is applied to them.

In retrospective studies (asking unemployed individuals to describe what has happened since they lost their job), between 20 percent and 30 percent of unemployed men report a deterioration in their HEALTH since job loss. On the other hand, many report no such deterioration and up to 10 percent indicate an improvement. In some cases, that improvement is in respect of physical illnesses which had been exacerbated by working conditions (bronchitis, back problems, and so on), and for others the improvement is psychological, because they are now free from negative aspects of their jobs.

Prolonged unemployment is often associated with *physical* ill-health of many kinds, but it is difficult to pinpoint a precise causal link in that respect. Persons who are out of work for a long period are likely also to have experienced poverty and poor living conditions for several years, whether or not they held a job at the time of an investigation. The negative effect is thus likely to arise from a syndrome of environmental features, of which lack of a paid job at one point in time is only a single component.

Given that the experience of unemployment is not uniform, and that different people report different consequences, can we specify those factors which might moderate its impact? Important moderating features have been identified in the environment and also associated with personal characteristics.

It is clear that lack of money is a major cause of the problems arising from unemployment. Some unemployed people, for example those with substantial family demands, experience considerable poverty, whereas for others financial difficulties are less severe. Other environmental influences are through the magnitude of the decrement in an unemployed person's opportunity for CONTROL, opportunity for skill use, SOCIAL SUPPORT, and level of environmental clarity. Another factor is the customary level of unemployment in a region; it appears that the negative psychological consequences of involuntary joblessness are felt particularly strongly in those areas of the country in which unemployment is least endemic.

Unemployed people often have great difficulty filling time, as the deadlines and demands of a structured work-role are no longer present. Variations between people in the extent to which they can proactively set targets and achieve personal goals are positively associated with mental health during unemployment.

Personal characteristics such as age, employment commitment, and baseline mental health have also been shown to moderate the impact of enforced joblessness. Individuals aged in their thirties and forties (with family responsibilities) tend to display more anxiety and general distress than those who are younger or older; those unemployed people for whom having a paid job is especially important are likely to report greatest distress; and people who were more depressed before losing their job are also likely subsequently to report lower well-being.

With greater time since job loss, unemployed people exhibit increasing distress on average for about six months. Thereafter, some leveling-off occurs which may be followed by a small improvement in reported well-being. This adaptation may be either of two kinds. One is "constructive adaptation,"

where unemployed people take positive steps to develop interests and activities outside the labor market. Hobbies may be taken up, social networks expanded, and voluntary work for the community initiated and enjoyed.

Alternatively, "resigned adaptation" involves reduced aspirations and lower investment in the environment. In this case, people tend to withdraw from job-seeking, depend on limited routines of behavior, and protect themselves from threatening events by avoiding new situations and potentially stressful or expensive activities. Although such resigned adaptation may be accompanied by slight improvements in affective well-being, the severely constrained lifestyle impairs functioning and psychological development. By wanting less, long-term unemployed people achieve less, and they may become less (see Warr, 1987).

See also: CONTROL; DEPRESSION; FAMILY RELATIONS; SELF-ESTEEM; SOCIAL SUPPORT; STEREOTYPING; STIGMA; STRESS AND COPING; WORK.

BIBLIOGRAPHY

Fryer, D. F. (1992). Marienthal and beyond: Twentieth-century research on unemployment and mental health. [Special issue] *Journal of Occupational and Organizational Psychology*, 65(4).

Jahoda, M. (1982). *Employment and unemployment: A social psychological analysis.* Cambridge: Cambridge University Press.

——Lazarsfeld, P. F., & Zeisel, H. (1933). *Marienthal: The sociography of an unemployed community.* (English translation, 1971, New York: Aldine-Atherton.)

Warr, P. B. (1987). *Work, unemployment, and mental health.* Oxford: Oxford University Press.

PETER WARR

**uniqueness**  Gordon Allport considered that "the outstanding characteristic of man is his individuality" (1961, p. 4). Snyder and Fromkin (1980) proposed that people have an underlying need to perceive themselves as unique. They suggested that people are aware of the reality of similarities among people. However, people also devote considerable energy to resisting cultural and social forces that encourage CONFORMITY and to avoiding situations which bring about a state of DE-INDIVIDUATION.

Many theories hold that people will be attracted to others who share similar attributes to themselves (*see* ATTRACTION) and that, when people are uncertain of their own abilities or opinions, they seek similar others with whom to compare themselves (*see* SOCIAL COMPARISON). However, early research tended only to focus on similarity with respect to a limited set of attributes, leaving participants free to believe they retained a high degree of individuality. Snyder and Fromkin suggested that a very high degree of similarity across a wide set of attributes produces strong negative affect. In order to reduce negative affect, people seek additional individuating information. The typical research study by Fromkin used the "test feedback method," which provided participants with bogus feedback demonstrating that they were either very highly or slightly similar to 10,000 of their peers on a large number of comparison attributes (PERSONALITY, VALUES, attitudes, etc.). In response to high similarity participants show a decrease in SELF-ESTEEM, become more diverse in their ideas for uses for common objects, assume greater dissimilarity from an unknown other person, and show greater preferences for experiences which are unavailable to other research participants. They also seem to distort the feedback to reduce the apparent similarity between themselves and others. If the comparison other has negative attributes (e.g. is a member of an outgroup or is unpopular) people are likely to have a lower threshold of similarity at which they will try to establish uniqueness. If the comparison other has positive attributes (e.g. is an ingroup member) the threshold is raised.

Tesser (1988) has developed a model of self-evaluation maintenance which specifies the kinds of similarity people will seek and avoid. When a performance dimension is highly relevant to one's self-definition the self is threatened by comparisons with psychologically close others who perform well. If the dimension is nonrelevant the self is enhanced by basking in the reflected glory of the other's achievements.

There are also individual differences in need for uniqueness, measured using a scale developed by Snyder and Fromkin. High scorers on this scale are more likely to see themselves as different from comparison others, to use unusual word-associations, and to join groups emphasizing uniqueness. Moreover, people with a high need for uniqueness are more likely to have lowered self-esteem when they are given low uniqueness feedback. People who focus attention on their privately held attitudes (*see* SELF-AWARENESS) are more likely to resist conformity pressure and to assert their unique attitudes or BELIEFS (*see* ATTITUDE THEORY AND RESEARCH).

People may possess or acquire uniqueness attributes – features which distinguish them from others (names are an example). Not only are people more sensitive to their own name (the "cocktail party" effect), they also show greater preference for letters that are in their own than in other peoples' names (the "name letter" effect (Nuttin, 1987)). People with high need for uniqueness may highlight uniqueness attributes, for example having larger signatures than others. Attitudes and beliefs also serve as uniqueness attributes.

People often make false assumptions about their own uniqueness. In relation to people holding the opposite view to themselves, people tend to assume greater uniqueness for their desirable attitudes and greater consensus for their undesirable attitudes (*see* FALSE CONSENSUS). There is also a tendency for people to have an "illusion of unique invulnerability," and unrealistic optimism, particularly in relation to health outcomes, where they tend to believe they are less vulnerable than others. These false assumptions may arise from cognitive biases, but generally seem to reflect motivational SELF-ENHANCEMENT biases (Hoorens, 1993).

Uniqueness is partly conferred by distinctiveness within a social context (*see also* SPONTANEOUS SELF-CONCEPT). For example, children who are in a gender or ethnic minority in a particular context find that feature more salient in their self-concept. Uniqueness also changes over time; within the family context there is evidence that children see themselves as increasingly separate and different from their parents as they get older. It may also be that first-born children are more individuated.

Brewer (1983) has proposed an optimal distinctiveness model which combines uniqueness theory with SELF-CATEGORIZATION THEORY. Brewer proposes that social identity (*see* SOCIAL IDENTITY THEORY) is activated in order to meet competing needs for differentiation of the self from others and inclusion of the self into larger social collectives. Like Snyder and Fromkin, Brewer stresses that people avoid extremes of both uniqueness and similarity, but Brewer's model views these as interdependent opposing motives so that movement towards increased inclusion activates the opposing drive for greater differentiation, and vice versa. Thus, people seek an equilibrium or "optimal" level of distinctiveness. Social groups and categories, such as musical subcultures and political parties or interest groups, are most likely to satisfy these needs if they are at intermediate levels of generality. As group membership becomes more distinctive, intergroup biases increase. However, if a group becomes too salient, particularly if it has low status, members may seek to dissociate themselves from it.

*See also*: ATTITUDE THEORY AND RESEARCH; ATTRACTION; DEINDIVIDUATION; PERSONALITY; SELF-AWARENESS; SELF-CATEGORIZATION THEORY; SELF-ESTEEM; SOCIAL COMPARISON; SOCIAL IDENTITY THEORY; VALUES.

BIBLIOGRAPHY

Brewer, M. B. (1993). The role of distinctiveness in social identity and group behaviour. In M. A. Hogg & D. Abrams (Eds.), *Group motivation: Social psychological perspectives* (pp. 1–16). Hemel Hempstead: Harvester Wheatsheaf.

Hoorens, V. (1993). Self-enhancement and superiority biases in social comparison. *European Review of Social Psychology*, *4*, 113–39.

Nuttin, J. M. (Jr.) (1987). Affective consequences of mere ownership: The name letter effect in twelve European Languages. *European Journal of Social Psychology*, *17*, 381–402.

Snyder, C. R. & Fromkin, H. L. (1980). *Uniqueness: The pursuit of human difference*. New York: Plenum.

Tesser, A. (1988). Toward a theory of self-evaluation maintenance model of social behaviour. In L. Berkowitz (Ed.), *Advances in experimental social psychology* (Vol. 21, pp. 181–227). New York: Academic Press.

DOMINIC ABRAMS

**unobtrusive measures**   This term refers to "social science research data *not* obtained by interview or questionnaire" (Webb, Campbell, Schwartz, Sechrest, & Grove, 1981, p. 1). Unobtrusive measures include *observation* in natural settings (*see* OBSERVATIONAL METHODS), *physical traces* of behavior, and *archival records* (Webb et al., 1981). They are *nonreactive* in the sense that they do not require the cooperation of participants or contaminate responses in the process of measurement. The primary purpose of their use in social psychology is to avoid sources of invalidity associated with the reactive nature of most measures commonly employed.

THE REACTIVITY PROBLEM

The validity of verbal responses obtained by interview or questionnaire is threatened by *reactivity* effects, i.e., changes in the dependent variable merely due to the fact that a measurement has taken place (*see* Weick, 1985). These threats include potential influences of the measurement instrument (*see* SURVEY METHODS), the research situation (*see* EXPERIMENTAL DEMAND), the experimenter or interviewer (*see* EXPERIMENTER EFFECTS, EXPECTANCY EFFECTS), and the respondent (*see* IMPRESSION MANAGEMENT, SELF-PRESENTATION).

Researchers have devised various strategies to reduce potential bias due to reactivity. The proposed remedies range from temporarily misinforming subjects (*see* BOGUS PIPELINE) or withholding information from them, to asking subjects for their cooperation by emphasizing the importance of truthful responses (Aronson, Ellsworth, Carlsmith, & Gonzales, 1990). However, none of these approaches is likely to fully eliminate bias, because respondents must always interpret the meaning of information they are given and of questions they are asked, and bias may result from respondents' following the rules of natural conversation (*see* Bless, Strack, & Schwarz, 1993). *Unobtrusive measures* avoid these problems because they usually do not involve the cooperation of respondents.

TYPES OF UNOBTRUSIVE MEASURES
*Observation* of behavior or of exterior physical signs may supplement verbal measures of attitudes (*see* ATTITUDE MEASUREMENT; BEHAVIORAL CONFIRMATION/DISCONFIRMATION). Throwing away a flier, mailing a "lost" letter, being present at a meeting, even growing a beard are examples of behaviors open to unobtrusive observation and more or less directly related to attitudes. Technical equipment may support or replace the human observer (Webb et al., 1981, chaps. 7 and 8), and various aspects of behavior may be studied, such as frequency, speed, duration, intensity, etc. (Aronson et al., 1990). A special case of observational data are physiological responses (*see* SOCIAL PSYCHOPHYSIOLOGY, UNCONSCIOUS PROCESSING). Although, for obvious reasons, they cannot be gathered unobtrusively, these measures are nonreactive if they are outside of the respondent's voluntary control (see also the use of response times in SOCIAL COGNITION research).

Probably the least frequently employed unobtrusive measures are *physical traces* of behavior. Webb et al. (1981) distinguish between *erosion measures*, e.g., the wear on floor tiles in front of museum exhibits as an indicator of the exhibits' popularity, and *accretion measures*, e.g., amount of dust accumulated on machines as a measure of frequency of their use. Both unobtrusive observation and the study of physical traces may or may not involve active intervention of the researcher.

*Archival records* are another source of nonreactive data. A study by Archer, Iritani, Kimes, and Barrios (1983) illustrates how archival sampling may be fruitfully combined with experimentation. These researchers compared the relative size of the head (versus rest of body) in depictions of women and men, sampled from eleven cultures over six centuries, and found greater facial prominence for men than women. In a subsequent laboratory experiment, they discovered that greater facial prominence led to higher ratings of intelligence and other characteristics. Archival data may be collected from a variety of sources, e.g., legal records, the mass media, sales records or personal documents (*see* Webb et al., 1981, chaps. 4 and 6).

LIMITATIONS AND ETHICAL CONSIDERATIONS
Although unobtrusive measures are less prone to reactivity effects than standard verbal measures, they are susceptible to other biases and technical difficulties (*see* Webb et al., chap. 9). Among the typical problems are population and content restrictions, questionable construct validity (*see* METHODOLOGY), a low yield of useful data given the effort expended and difficulty of replication. Most importantly, data often come in "naturally" aggregated form and are impossible to disaggregate (e.g., how much did any single person contribute to the wear on the museum tiles?).

The most prominent *ethical issues* in unobtrusive measurement are subjects' right to privacy and difficulties in obtaining informed consent (Webb et al., 1981, chap. 5). With respect to privacy, one may think of a public–private continuum along which measures can be ordered. Studying phenomena at the public end of this continuum, such as the content of politicians' speeches or archival data, is considered ethically unproblematic by most people, whereas the unobtrusive study of phenomena at the private end of the continuum, like surreptitiously recording personal conversations, clearly violates ethical standards. For most situations between these two extremes, it is difficult to formulate general guidelines. In any case, confidentiality of personal data must be guaranteed.

Obtaining informed consent from participants is another problem in unobtrusive measurement. Informing subjects beforehand interferes with the aim of avoiding reactivity. Additionally, in field studies, it is often difficult to identify potential "participants." One solution consists of employing nonreactive measures within laboratory settings. This may be achieved by staging an event that is ostensibly unrelated to the study for which the subject was recruited. For example, in a study on helping behavior, an encounter with a confederate who needs help may be arranged while the subject is waiting in the hall. Studies of this kind allow for informed consent and, if well designed, combine a high degree of control with a minimum of reactivity in their dependent measure.

CONCLUSION

No single research instrument or method in social psychology will probably ever be free of systematic error. Because different methodologies have different weaknesses, however, it seems wise to use "multiple measures that are hypothesized to share in the theoretically relevant components but have different patterns of irrelevant components" (Webb et al., 1981, pp. 34–5). In this sense, unobtrusive measures provide a valuable supplement to the social researcher's methodological toolbox.

*See also*: ATTITUDE MEASUREMENT AND QUESTIONNAIRE DESIGN; BEHAVIORAL CONFIRMATION/DISCONFIRMATION; CONTENT ANALYSIS; EXPERIMENTER EFFECTS; IMPRESSION MANAGEMENT; METHODOLOGY; OBSERVATIONAL METHODS; SOCIAL COGNITION; SOCIAL PSYCHOPHYSIOLOGY; SURVEY METHODS.

BIBLIOGRAPHY

Archer, D., Iritani, B., Kimes, D. D., & Barrios, M. (1983). Face-ism: Five studies of sex differences in facial prominence. *Journal of Personality and Social Psychology, 45*, 725–35.

Aronson, E., Ellsworth, P. C., Carlsmith, J. M., & Gonzales, M. H. (1990). *Methods of research in social psychology*. New York: McGraw-Hill.

Bless, H., Strack, F., & Schwarz, N. (1993). The informative functions of research procedures: Bias and the logic of conversation. *European Journal of Social Psychology, 23*, 149–65.

Webb, E. J., Campbell, D. T., Schwartz, R. D., Sechrest, L., & Grove, J. B. (1981). *Nonreactive measures in the social sciences* (2nd ed.). Boston, MA: Houghton Mifflin.

Weick, K. E. (1985). Systematic observational methods. In G. Lindzey & E. Aronson (Eds.), *The Handbook of Social Psychology* (3rd ed., Vol. 1, pp. 567–634). New York: Random House.

GERD BOHNER

# V

values  Human values are trans-situational goals that serve as guiding principles in the life of a person or group (e.g., freedom, honesty). Values serve as standards of the desirable when judging behavior, events, and people (including the self), when forming and expressing attitudes, and when selecting and rationalizing actions. The hierarchical ordering of values according to their importance forms a relatively enduring value system (Rokeach, 1973; Schwartz, 1992). Any value may be instrumental to attaining more ultimate values, though some researches distinguish terminal (end-state) from instrumental (behavioral) values. Another conception of values, popular especially in economics, views values as qualities inherent in objects that give them worth.

Values share elements with other motivational concepts, in particular, attitudes and needs. (See ATTITUDES AND BEHAVIOR). Values differ from attitudes in that values transcend specific situations and objects, are ordered among themselves in a hierarchy of importance, serve as criteria of the desirable and not merely of the desired, and are less numerous and more central to personality. Values might be conceived loosely as attitudes toward abstract end-states of human existence.

Individual needs are represented cognitively – in socially accepted terms – as values. For example, sexual needs may be transformed into values concerning intimacy and love. When needs are transformed into values, their pursuit can be coordinated with others and justified to them and to the self more readily. The needs of groups and societal institutions also generate values. Through socialization, individuals internalize – as values – goals that foster the welfare of others and the survival and smooth functioning of groups (e.g., social order, obedience).

## VALUE CONTENTS AND STRUCTURE

The content of values is classifiable by the motivations they express. People in most cultures implicitly distinguish ten motivational types of values (Schwartz, 1992): Benevolence (preservation and enhancement of the welfare of close others); Tradition (commitment to cultural and religious customs and ideas); Conformity (restraint of socially disapproved impulses and actions); Security (safety and stability of society, relationships, and self); Power (control over people and resources); Achievement (demonstrated competence according to social standards); Hedonism (pleasure, sensuous gratification); Stimulation (excitement, novelty, challenge); Self-Direction (independent thought and action); Universalism (tolerance and protection of *all* people and nature).

Actions that express values have psychological and social consequences that may conflict or be compatible with actions that express other values. This yields a structure of relations among value types (*see* figure 1) found across cultures (Schwartz, 1992). Competing value types emanate in opposing directions from the center; complementary types are adjacent. Two bipolar dimensions organize values nearly universally: Openness to Change versus Conservation and Self-Transcendence versus Self-Enhancement (*see* figure 1).

Associations of value priorities with other variables (attitudes, behaviors, demographics) tend to reflect this structure. If any variable associates most positively with one value type (e.g., age with conformity), its associations with the others tend to be progressively less positive as one moves around the circle in either direction towards the diametrically opposing type (e.g., stimulation).

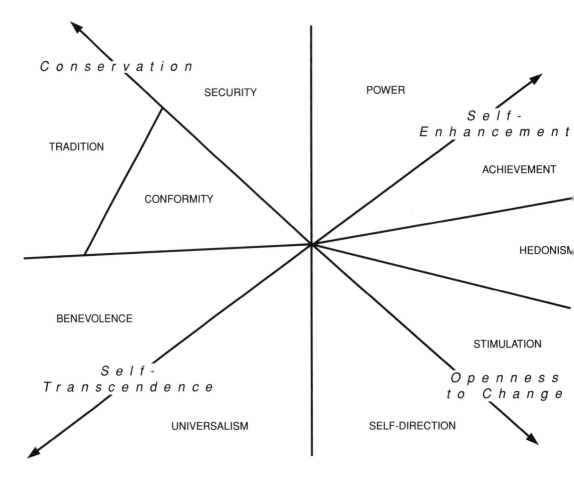

Figure 1.   Structure of value types and dimensions.

## RELATIONS TO BEHAVIOR AND ATTITUDES

Differences in value priorities have been associated with many behaviors (e.g., political, environmental, religious, educational, health, consumer, delinquent, occupational, friendship). The causal impact of values on behavior is demonstrated in experimental studies that inform people how the value priorities of positive reference groups may differ from their own (Ball-Rokeach, Rokeach, & Grube, 1984). This causes changes in own priorities for relevant values, in specific related attitudes, and in subsequent behavior.

Expectancy-value theory describes one process whereby values are linked to behavior (Feather, 1990). The attractiveness of a behavior and hence the likelihood of its enactment depend on the values that its consequences are expected to promote or undermine. Assume, for example, that interethnic contact is expected to promote tolerance but undermine certainty. Persons who attribute high priority to universalism and low priority to security values will find contact more attractive than persons with the opposite priorities. Value priorities may also influence behavior by attuning perception to particular actions or consequences. Only a subset of a person's values is activated in specific situations. The interplay among these, together with other variables, determine behavior.

Value priorities underlie, organize and predict people's attitudes (*see* Eagly & Chaiken,

1993). Forming or adopting attitudes consistent with one's value priorities serves a value-expressive function by affirming desired self-conceptions. This function is particularly important to these low in SELF-MONITORING. Asserting socially valued attitudes serves a self-presentational, social-adjustive function, particularly important to low self-monitors. Attitudinal issues elicit more integratively complex reasoning (awareness and synthesis of multiple perspectives) when they arouse conflict between highly and equally important values (see INTERACTIVE COMPLEXITY). Thus, attitudes toward censorship laws might be especially complex among people who attribute high priority both to self-direction and to tradition values.

Values also maintain and justify attitudes. The more value-relevant an attitude, the more resistant it is to change in the face of persuasion or adversity. Relevance to own values (i.e., ego-involvement) or to REFERENCE GROUP values presumably anchors an attitude, so that changing it entails broad and fundamental cognitive change. People justify attitudes by increasing the perceived relevance of values that support them. For example, people who favor nuclear weapons see security as a more relevant value to this attitude than peace, whereas opponents see peace as more relevant than security.

The most popular instruments for measuring values were designed by Rokeach (1973) and Schwartz (1992). In both, respondents report the importance of general values as guiding principles in their lives.

See also: ATTITUDES AND BEHAVIOR; INTEGRATIVE COMPLEXITY; SELF-MONITORING.

BIBLIOGRAPHY

Ball-Rokeach, S. J., Rokeach, M., & Grube, J. W. (1984). The great American values test. New York: Free Press.

Eagly, A. H., & Chaiken, S. (1993). The psychology of attitudes. New York: Harcourt Brace Jovanovich.

Feather, N. T. (1990). Bridging the gap between values and actions. In E. T. Higgins & R. Sorrentino (Eds.), Handbook of motivation and cognition (Vol. 2, pp. 151–92). New York: Guilford Press.

Rokeach, M. (1973). The nature of human values. New York: Free Press.

Schwartz, S. H. (1992). Universals in the content and structure of values. In M. Zanna (Ed.), Advances in experimental social psychology (Vol. 25, pp. 1–65). New York: Academic Press.

SHALOM H. SCHWARTZ

verbal reports on mental processes
Although in everyday social life people readily offer explanations for their own actions phrased in terms of the thought processes that supposedly led to the behavior in question, there is some dispute in contemporary social psychology about how accurate these causal explanations are. Debates about the value of introspection as a source of reliable knowledge predate the beginnings of psychology as a scientific discipline, but resurfaced more recently within the area of SOCIAL COGNITION research as a result of a provocative and influential paper by Nisbett and Wilson (1977). These authors argued that actors lack introspective access to the cognitive processes controlling behavior, and depend upon culturally supplied causal theories when constructing accounts of their actions.

Nisbett and Wilson's argument was developed for both theoretical and empirical reasons: In terms of theory, they pointed out that many of the explanatory mechanisms invoked in cognitive accounts of psychology were simply not the kinds of things to which an introspecting subject could in principle gain access. For example, many information-processing theories view consciousness as an end-product of nonconscious selective and constructive processes. To the extent that social psychological explanations rely on similar mechanisms, they necessarily diverge from commonsense accounts of action based on conscious experience.

In terms of research findings, Nisbett and Wilson marshaled together an impressive body of experimental evidence that people are often affected by stimuli without understanding how they have been influenced, or even realizing that they have been influenced in the first place. Correspondingly, stimuli that have no demonstrable effect on judgments or behavior may be considered influential to the extent that they are salient and plausible psychological causes (*see* SALIENCE). For example, participants in a study ostensibly concerning consumer preferences were susceptible to a powerful order effect in their selection of their favored brand of nylon stocking, choosing the first pair examined four times as often as the last pair. However, when asked whether sequence had affected their judgments, almost all participants strongly denied such an influence, referring instead to the impact of aspects such as the texture or feel of the material.

If Nisbett and Wilson's conclusions are correct, then it makes no sense for social psychological researchers to treat experimental participants' verbal reports as valid descriptions of the causal processes determining behavior. In other words, there is little point in asking people why they do what they do, because the answers they give are of no direct scientific value. Furthermore, Nisbett and Wilson's thesis implies that people are radically mistaken in their firmly held intuitive conviction that they have direct knowledge of the reasons for their behavior.

Clearly these implications are controversial from many points of view, and a series of responses to Nisbett and Wilson's original article have questioned their more extreme conclusions from several different angles (*see* White, 1988, for a review). Some of these critical commentaries offer alternative explanations for inaccuracy of verbal reports that do not depend on the hypothesized failures of introspective access. For example, Ericsson and Simon (1980) suggested that participants' mistaken explanations may often be due to their inability to remember the relevant processes rather than lack of awareness. Additional inaccuracies may enter into verbal reports at the stage of translation of memory content into linguistic representation.

Even if the relevant mental process is consciously registered, correctly remembered, and accurately rendered in words, it still may not offer a correct causal account of the relevant actions according to the criteria of social psychological explanation. This is because experimental participants typically try

to account only for their own individual actions, whereas social psychological researchers are in the business of explaining why different subject groups behaved differently (or why one group behaved differently under different conditions). This means that participants will focus on what made their own behavior distinctive in the experiment, while experimenters will focus on what was distinctive about the different experimental conditions. Even assuming that the investigator's account of the hypothetical process that explains group tendencies is generally valid, this does not necessarily imply that this process characterized the mental operations of all subjects within the group. In other words, subjects might be perfectly accurate about their own action in their own terms, yet incorrect about how people in general behave.

The above critical analysis assumes that participants in social psychological studies are motivated to explain their action accurately when answering questions set them by experimenters. However, it is possible that participants' verbal responses to these requests for information might serve conversational goals other than straightforward description. For example, subjects might simply have been reporting what they (mistakenly) believed that the investigators wanted to hear; they might have been performing a self-presentational act to avoid looking stupid (*see* SELF-PRESENTATION); they might have been trying to give an answer that would avert the necessity for further questioning and allow them to get out of the laboratory as quickly as possible; and so on. Indeed, an approach based on DISCOURSE ANALYSIS would suggest that the versions of psychological reality presented in conversation are always formulated to serve particular pragmatic functions and are never simply objective descriptions of what "actually" happened.

In conclusion, Nisbett and Wilson's thesis depends on the idea that there is one true scientific cause for any behavior, and furthermore that the experimental approach provides direct and valid information about this cause. A more realistic assessment is that a multitude of workable explanations for any effect are available (even assuming that there is initial agreement concerning the definition of the effect in question), and that different accounts are appropriate in different circumstances and for different purposes. When explaining why I have written this dictionary entry, for instance, the answer I give would depend on whether I was being asked by my bank manager, my Head of Department, my worst enemy, or my neglected spouse, although it is perfectly possible that my account might in some sense be true in every case. Correspondingly, my typing behavior could be validly explained in terms of physics, physiology, psychology, or economics. The implication of this plurality of practicable accounts for the present analysis is that participants in social psychology experiments may have different criteria from experimenters about what should count as an explanation, or indeed about what they are doing when they are answering questions about their actions, and their answers to postexperimental enquiries need to be interpreted accordingly and with all due care and attention.

*See also*: DISCOURSE ANALYSIS; SOCIAL COGNITION.

BIBLIOGRAPHY

Ericsson, K. A., & Simon, H. A. (1980). Verbal reports as data. *Psychological Review, 87*, 215–51.

Nisbett, R. E., & Wilson, T. D. (1977). Telling more than we can know: Verbal reports on mental processes. *Psychological Review, 84*, 231–59.

White, P. A. (1988). Knowing more about what we can tell: "Introspective access" and causal report accuracy 10 years later. *British Journal of Psychology, 79*, 13–45.

BRIAN PARKINSON

**violence** The infliction of intense force upon persons or property for the purposes of destruction, punishment, or control. Violence may be committed upon a personal scale, as in murder or assault, or on a larger one, as in warfare and riots. Some of the principles that apply to AGGRESSION also apply to violence, although the two terms are generally considered to refer to different degrees of interpersonal conflict.

Violence is often a product of CULTURE. Its causes may lie in beliefs that the goods and services of society are inequitably distributed, so that some groups exerience RELATIVE DEPRIVATION. At other times violence grows out of hostility of an ingroup toward members of an outgroup. Certain cultures and subcultures (e.g., juvenile gangs) may place high values on violent behavior, so that such acts are relatively more likely to occur within these subcultures of violence than in other cultures. Violence or the threat of violence may also be used systematically for the control of others both by individuals and by organizations. At the personal level, violent behavior can result from family conflict, social reinforcement, organic and neurologial disorders, or acculturation within violent groups.

*See also*: AGGRESSION; CULTURE; RELATIVE DEPRIVATION.

RUSSELL G. GEEN

**vividness** A property of some stimuli that causes them to attract ATTENTION. Unlike SALIENCE, where stimuli attract attention by virtue of contrasting with their context, vividness is inherent in the stimulus itself. Stimuli are defined as vivid to the extent they are emotionally interesting, imagery provoking, or sensorially prominent.

*See also*: ATTENTION.

SUSAN T. FISKE
BETH A. MORLING

**voting behavior** A great deal of research has explored the determinants of citizens' vote choices in elections and the psychological processes by which citizens make those choices. In fact, voting behavior has been one of the central topics of social science research on mass political behavior. Empirical research on voter decision making began in the late 1940s and has progressed through four stages of development, as we shall review below. During the first three phases, research focused primarily on identifying the determinants of citizens' vote choices. In the fourth stage, interest has shifted to understanding the psychological processes involved.

## SOCIAL STRUCTURE

During the first phase of voting research, studies focused on the impact of social structure on vote choices. This approach was best exemplified by the classic book, *The People's Choice*, by Lazarsfeld, Berelson, and Gaudet (1948). These researchers examined data from repeated survey interviews of a panel of citizens and found that their candidate preferences were a function of their memberships in various social groups. Specifically, three demographic variables were found to be particularly strong determinants of citizens' preferences: place of residence, social class, and religion. Living in a rural area, being middle-class, and being Protestant enhanced the likelihood of voting for Republicans, whereas living in urban areas, being working-class, and being Catholic enhanced the likelihood of voting for Democrats. Citizens who belonged to social groups with conflicting tendencies (e.g., an urban, working-class Protestant) were "cross-pressured" and were found to have unstable political preferences, selected a candidate late in the election, and frequently did not vote at all.

## PARTY IDENTIFICATION

During the second phase of voting research, the emphasis shifted from a sociological approach to a psychological approach that emphasized attitudes (*see also* ATTITUDE THEORY AND RESEARCH). This new perspective was advanced by University of Michigan researchers Campbell, Converse, Miller, and Stokes (1960) in *The American voter*. The Michigan approach acknowledged both long-term attitudinal influences on voting by party identification and political IDEOLOGY, as well as short-term influences of attitudes on specific policy issues and attitudes towards specific candidates.

The Michigan approach emphasized party identification as the key determinant of vote choice. A citizen's party identification was presumed to be a result of his or her place in the social structure as well as the interpersonal influence of family members, especially parents. Adopted early in life, party identification was hypothesized to be a highly stable orientation that directly influenced voting. Additionally, party identification was thought to function as a perceptual screen that shaped short-term influences on voting.

Although a great deal of research has consistently demonstrated that party identification is a stable and powerful predictor of vote choice, the relation between party identification and short-term influences on voting has turned out to be more complex than originally thought. Specifically, in addition to influencing short-term forces, party identification appears to be influenced by them as well. For example, although party identification has been found to influence citizens' perceptions of economic conditions and their preferences on policy issues, the latter seem to influence the former as well. Thus, the relation among party identification and short-term influences is reciprocal in nature. Consequently, it appears that party identification may reflect other determinants of vote choices rather than being the single, primary engine driving voters' decisions.

## ADDITIONAL DETERMINANTS OF VOTING

During the third phase of voting research, researchers maintained the psychological emphasis and expanded the list of vote determinants. One major body of work focused on the impact of attitudes on specific policy issues. In contrast to the *American voter*'s presumption that such attitudes play relatively peripheral roles in vote decisions, more recent work has shown that policy attitudes do indeed have significant impact when the issue is considered personally important by a voter. But when an issue is considered personally unimportant, it appears to have little or no impact on candidate preferences.

Other phase-three research has focused on retrospective judgments of the past performance of the candidates and parties in handling national problems. Judgments in domains such as the economy and foreign affairs have been shown to exert substantial influence on vote choices (e.g., Abramson, Aldrich, & Rohde, 1991).

Finally, voters' perceptions of candidates as people have been found to influence voting. Specifically, perceptions of candidates' personality traits (i.e., competence, integrity, leadership, and empathy), as well as the emotions candidates elicit (e.g., anger, pride), shape the impressions voters form of candidates and thereby determine voting in part (Kinder, 1986).

PSYCHOLOGICAL PROCESSES
Most recently, research has moved beyond specifying the determinants of voting and has focused on the processes by which these determinants are combined. It has been suggested that this is a relatively simple process, in which voters simply add up the number of things they like and dislike about each candidate and choose the candidate with the most positive net score. However, Lodge, McGraw, and Stroh (1989) have proposed a more complex psychological process model that distinguishes between on-line and memory-based decision making. Rather than waiting until the end of an election campaign to integrate information from memory about the candidates (as the memory-based perspective would suggest), voters appear to form evaluations of the candidates early on and continually update these attitudes on-line as new information is encountered. This sort of on-line updating seems especially prevalent among citizens who are political experts rather than political novices.

CONCLUSION
Voting researchers have done much to specify the determinants of who a citizen will vote for. Only recently has this work begun to examine carefully the processes by which individual determinants are combined into summary choices. Future research in this area is likely to cast further light on process models of voting with useful implications for an understanding of choice in general.
See also: ATTITUDE THEORY AND RESEARCH; IDEOLOGY.

BIBLIOGRAPHY
Abramson, P. R., Aldrich, J. H., & Rohde, D. W. (1991). *Change and continuity in the 1988 elections* (rev. ed.). Washington, DC: *Congressional Quarterly*.
Campbell, A., Converse, P. E., Miller, W. E., & Stokes, D. E. (1960). *The American voter*. New York: Wiley.
Kinder, D. R. (1986). *Presidential character revisited*. In R. Lau & D. Sears (Eds.), *Political cognition* (pp. 233–55). Hillsdale, NJ: Lawrence Erlbaum.
Lazarsfeld, P. F., Berelson, B., & Gaudet, H. (1948). *The people's choice* (2nd ed.). New York: Columbia University Press.
Lodge, M., McGraw, K. M., & Stroh, P. (1989). An impression-driven model of candidate evaluation. *American Political Science Review*, *83*, 401–19.

LEANDRE R. FABRIGAR
JON A. KROSNICK

# W

**work** An activity directed to valued goals beyond enjoyment of the activity itself. Although the term often refers to "a job" or "paid employment," work also takes many other forms, such as housework, voluntary work, and numerous other activities. Definitions have in common the assertion that work is *required* in some way; it is frequently seen as unavoidable. The term also connotes difficulty, a need to labor or exert oneself against the environment: the goal is to achieve something that is physically and/or psychologically difficult.

Work can vary from momentary exertion through to activity sustained over long periods of time. Sustained work almost always takes place within a network of social roles and institutions, for example, in paid jobs, in voluntary welfare groups, or in the family home. Themes which recur in discussions of the concept are the joint presence of obligation and choice and of benefit and cost. As with other salient parts of their lives, people are likely to have mixed feelings about their work: emotional ambivalence is very common.

This entry will focus upon social psychologists' contributions to the understanding of *paid* work. For most people, having a job means being an employee, although between 10 percent and 15 percent of the workforce in most developed countries are self-employed. Despite this focus on paid activities, many of the themes examined here are also relevant to work behavior outside a paid job.

THE OUTCOMES OF PAID WORK
An obvious outcome of having a job is that people earn money which is necessary to live. Other outcomes have been studied in terms of work attitudes, mental health, and productivity.

*Work Attitudes*
Particular attention has been paid to the notion of "job satisfaction", viewing that either in terms of overall satisfaction (with one's job as a whole) or in respect of satisfaction with specific aspects of a job (sometimes known as "facet satisfactions"). Principal attitudes of the second kind include satisfaction with one's pay, colleagues, supervisor, promotion prospects, actual work undertaken, and the organization in general. Facet satisfactions are usually found to be significantly intercorrelated with each other, each contributing to overall satisfaction, but they are differentially responsive to job and organizational characteristics.

A second set of studies has focused on organizational commitment. That is a general attitude to the organization, rather than a reaction to a particular job. High organizational commitment is defined in terms of three factors: a strong belief in, and acceptance of, the organization's goals and values; a readiness to exert considerable effort on behalf of the organization; and a strong desire to remain part of the organization.

Also studied are job involvement and employment commitment. The first of those concerns a person's attachment to his or her present job; and employment commitment is a broader attitude concerned with the personal salience of having a paid job at all (*see also* UNEMPLOYMENT).

*Mental Health*
Recognizing that a person's job can significantly influence his or her health and day-to-day effectiveness, much research has examined the impact of STRESS-creating job characteristics on different aspects of mental health. Most commonly studied is psychological well-being in terms of feelings of job-related

ANXIETY or DEPRESSION (e.g., Warr, 1991), but the influence of jobs on self-efficacy and SELF-ESTEEM has also been documented. Employees' generalized LEVEL OF ASPIRATION is also likely to be affected by the opportunities available in work for self-validation through successful goal-attainment.

PRODUCTIVITY

Occupational social psychologists have also examined the effectiveness of people working in jobs with particular characteristics and role requirements. Different measures of productivity are necessary in different settings, although in practice measurement of that complex concept is often less than ideal.

Investigations into work ATTITUDES AND BEHAVIOR have shown that more satisfied employees are not necessarily more productive. However, it is known that stress-induced job-related mental ill-health can impair work perfomance and give rise to increased absenteeism.

KEY CHARACTERISTICS OF WORK

Many investigations have identified features of jobs that are associated with high or low outcomes of the kinds illustrated above. Several so-called "psychosocial" job characteristics (distinguished from "physical" work conditions) are as follows. A job may be high or low in respect of each characteristic.

*Opportunity for Control*

The extent to which a person is able to exercise discretion in a job has repeatedly been shown to affect attitudes, mental health, and productivity. Many lower-level jobs provide very little discretion latitude of this kind, although it is increasingly needed for effective working in modern information-based jobs (e.g., Wall & Davids, 1992).

*Opportunity for Skill Use*

A related aspect of a job is the extent to which a person can utilize and develop skills. Jobs lacking opportunities for control (above) tend also to exclude skill use, and the absence of that feature is particularly associated with low mental health (e.g., Warr, 1987).

*Task Demands*

Many studies have pointed to the negative effects of both too few and too many demands on a worker. Excessively high demands are especially harmful when extended over a long period of time or when accompanied by limited opportunity for control over one's activities. Psychosomatic, psychiatric, and cardiovascular impairments have all been recorded in those circumstances (Karasek & Theorell, 1990).

*Environmental Clarity*

Lack of clarity of role demands or about future developments has also been examined as a potential stressor. For instance, high levels of role ambiguity in a job, such that a person is unsure what forms of behavior will be rewarded or punished, can lead to raised anxiety and low self-esteem.

*Interpersonal Support*

Another way in which jobs differ between themselves is in terms of the quantity and quality of support available from coworkers. As in other studies of SOCIAL SUPPORT, a significant positive effect of this variable on mental health is regularly found in job settings. Some researchers have also looked for a moderating or BUFFERING effect, through which social support is important in reducing the harmful effect of high levels of a job-related stressor but does not make a difference at lower levels of that stressor. Evidence about that possible buffering effect in job settings is inconsistent (Kahn & Byosiere, 1992).

OTHER THEMES IN OCCUPATIONAL SOCIAL PSYCHOLOGY

This field is known generically in the United Kingdom as "occupational" psychology, as "industrial and organizational psychology" in the United States of America, as "work and organizational psychology" in continental Europe, and as "organizational psychology" in Australia and New Zealand. Although some components of the subject (e.g., human–computer interaction, psychological testing for personnel selection) have only limited *social* psychological content, much of occupational psychology draws from and contributes to themes presented throughout this volume. (*See also* ORGANIZATIONS.) Six illustrative topics are as follows.

### Motivation

Occupational social psychologists have made substantial contributions to theories of motivation, with relevance outside as well as inside the workplace. Three main types of model have been developed.

Several theorists have built upon early need theories, to clarify the part played by motives and values. Desire for self-actualization, need for a developed sense of personal competence, and forms of ACHIEVEMENT MOTIVATION have all been examined in work settings. Currently important are theories in terms of the intrinsically motivating characteristics of personally challenging activities and the operation of motives for mastery and environmental control (e.g., Kanfer, 1990).

Other theories of work motivation have been constructed in terms of cognitive choices made on the basis of postulated calculations of SUBJECTIVE EXPECTED UTILITY. These theories emphasize two key determinants of action: subjective expectations about the consequences of different possible actions; and personal evaluations of each of those possible alternative consequences. Work behaviors have been analyzed in those terms, with considerable predictive success.

Third are models in terms of the processes and outcomes of goal-setting at work, both in respect of actual behavior and in terms of the allocation of attention to prioritized issues. Key themes in those models are processes of self-regulation in relation to established goals, and the nature and stability of commitment to a goal once that has been established.

### Work-groups

Group membership is of course an essential part of working, and there is increasing interest in the development and success of groups in work settings. Work-group effects on individuals can be of three kinds.

First, groups can convey information and knowledge: through direct instruction and feedback, by providing behavioral models, and by supplying standards against which to judge future work performance. Second are influences on affective state, through the provision of reward or punishment for particular work activities, or by altering beliefs and their associated consequences. Finally, work behavior is itself modified by group membership, through changes to knowledge and through group-mediated reward processes.

Early research focused upon relationships between GROUP COHESIVENESS, CONFORMITY and performance. It is clear that the more cohesive is a work-group, the more do members conform to perceived group NORMS. However, increased cohesiveness is not necessarily associated with better performance. The direction of that relationship depends upon the content of the norm. In cases where group pressure is toward restriction of output or limited expenditure of effort, increased cohesiveness is associated with particularly low performance. However, in the case of high-performance norms cohesiveness gives rise to more productive groups.

Other studies have examined the characteristics of work-groups that are associated with greater innovation and CREATIVITY (e.g., West & Farr, 1990). Features that have been identified as especially important are a clear vision of valued outcomes from group activity, and a climate of participative safety in which ideas can be pursued in an environment that is interpersonally nonthreatening. Associated group features encouraging innovation include explicit norms and support for new ways of working. (*See also* GROUP PRODUCTIVITY.)

### Managers' Style and Effectiveness

The key outcomes and characteristics of work are in part determined by the managers of an organization. The behavior of management has thus been much investigated.

One approach has been to seek to identify the personal characteristics of those managers who are more and less successful. It is of course difficult to examine a set of extremely unsuccessful managers in this way (since they are unlikely to collaborate), and it may be that research has failed to contrast sufficiently different degrees of success. For whatever reason, few characteristics have been found to be consistently associated with managerial success, apart from a general physical and mental robustness.

Other studies have investigated specific kinds of managerial behaviors. For instance, effectiveness has been examined in relation to defined managerial practices: planning, clarifying, monitoring, motivating, supporting, delegating, rewarding, etc. Two higher-level factors for the description of managers' behavior have been identified as "initiating structure" (concerned with defining subordinates' goals, roles, time schedules, etc.) and "consideration" (concerned with support and pleasantness in interactions with subordinates). It is known that managers' level of consideration is predictive of their subordinates' attitude toward them, but otherwise no general patterns of association between specific behaviors and managerial effectiveness have been identified.

More recent research has explored the bases of a manager's power to influence other people, both in terms of his or her own characteristics and habitual behavior and also in terms of the position granted within an organization's structure. There is thus an emphasis on situational factors which can determine the requirements for different managerial processes in different settings. However, many nonpsychological factors also influence organizational success (economic, technical, and multiply determined processes), and a focus upon purely psychological variables has so far not proved to be very productive. (*See also* LEADERSHIP.)

## The Design of Jobs

Given that certain job characteristics are known to have negative psychological and performance consequences (see above), it has become important for psychologists to develop theories and procedures for the better design of roles and tasks. For example, many lower-level jobs have been created through a process of simplification, such that very little opportunity exists for employee control or skill use; work can be repetitive, undemanding, and tedious.

Evidence is accumulating for the organizational as well as individual disadvantages of that kind of work, and managers and trade unions are increasingly interested in procedures for creating more psychologically appropriate work; in many cases that change is likely to be accompanied by raised productivity. One approach is through the "enlargement" of individual jobs, such that a job-holder is granted greater responsibility for decisions, fault identification, and fault rectification. That change may require training in respect of new procedures, and can create initial difficulties as employees find stressful the process of change and its associated uncertainty. There can also be problems for supervisory staff, whose own jobs are themselves made more simple as a result of the increased responsibility allocated to their subordinates (Wall & Martin, 1987).

Jobs may also be redesigned in a way which allocates responsibility to a group rather than only to individual workers. For instance, members of a work-group as a whole may be charged with carrying out necessary tasks, setting their own targets, allocating responsibilities among themselves, recording output, solving minor problems, and training new team members. Such "semi-autonomous group-working" provides a more psychologically rich environment than is normal for many lower-level employees, although its non-traditional nature ensures that the transition is not always easy.

## Organizational Culture

Overlapping interests of anthropologists, management theorists, and social psychologists have recently come together in studies of the CULTURE of work organizations. The size of the organization in question can vary, from a small department to an entire company, but the general rationale is that behavior and attitudes in any group depend in part on its overall culture.

That concept is usually defined in terms of widely shared basic assumptions, VALUES, norms, and artifacts. Shared understandings help members to make sense of the organization and its demands, and provide an interpretive scheme or way of perceiving, thinking, and feeling in relation to shared problems and activities. Furthermore, new members are expected to learn about key cultural features.

Within that definition, basic assumptions are beliefs (often unspoken) about appropriate goals and behavior; those are best investigated through qualitative research or detailed observation across a period of time. Values and norms are more accessible through quantitative procedures, and are often examined in research by means of questionnaires completed by a representative sample of organization members. Information gathered by those means is similar to that describing the "climate" of an organization (Schneider, 1990). Artifacts within organizational culture include the physical layout, the dress code, company records, statements of philosophy, and similar visible features.

Among the dimensions of culture that have been examined are: employee involvement in decision making, concern for high output, encouragement of creativity, customer orientation, degree of formalization, relationships between groups, and employees' awareness of overall goals. It is clear that organizations vary considerably in these terms, and that managers are able in some degree to influence the nature of their organization's culture.

*Organization Development*
Systematic attempts to modify culture are sometimes referred to as "organization development." This is a set of models and practices for determining and introducing planned change within an organization, based on the recognition that individual work effectiveness can often only be enhanced substantially through changes to the social system and culture. For instance, there is ample evidence that training individual employees on their own has limited impact on work effectiveness, without adequate concern for the goals and reward-processes which are salient within a work-group or wider organization.

Theories in this area are of two kinds. First are approaches of the type illustrated above, identifying those social and task structures which are most conducive to positive work attitudes, mental health, and organizational productivity. Second are theories of individual and group change and learning. Within those frameworks, organization development specialists are concerned with a range of tools and procedures through which to implement change.

Implementation is at one or more of the individual, interpersonal, or intergroup levels. In the first case, procedures may be improved in relation to personnel selection, individual payment, goal-setting, stress management, etc. At the interpersonal level, changes might be sought in respect of role development, SOCIAL SKILLS, team-building, and the creation of more effective GROUP PROCESSES. INTERGROUP RELATIONS issues include the interactions between different work teams, overall organization design, and matching more closely the activities of different sections to the broad strategy of the organization as a whole. The richness of organization development provides an excellent setting in which to develop and apply many aspects of social psychology.

*See also*: ACHIEVEMENT MOTIVATION; ATTITUDES AND BEHAVIOR; CONTROL; CREATIVITY; CULTURE; DEPRESSION; GROUP COHESIVENESS; GROUP PROCESSES; GROUP PRODUCTIVITY; INTERGROUP RELATIONS; LEADERSHIP; NORMS; ORGANIZATIONS; SELF-ESTEEM; SOCIAL SKILLS; SOCIAL SUPPORT; STRESS AND COPING; UNEMPLOYMENT; VALUES.

BIBLIOGRAPHY

Kahn, R. L., & Byosiere, P. (1992). Stress in organizations. In M. D. Dunnette & L. Heugh (Eds.), *Handbook of industrial and organizational psychology* (Vol. 3, pp. 571–650). Palo Alto, CA: Consulting Psychologists Press.

Kanfer, R. (1990). Motivation theory in industrial and organizational psychology. In M. D. Dunnette & L. Heugh (Eds.), *Handbook of industrial and organizational psychology* (Vol. 1, pp. 75–170). Palo Alto, CA: Consulting Psychologists Press.

Karasek, R. A., & Theorell, T. (1990). *Healthy work: Stress, productivity, and the reconstruction of working life*. New York: Basic Books.

Schneider, B. (Ed.). (1990). *Organizational climate and culture*. San Francisco, CA: Jossey-Bass.

Wall, T. D., & Davids, K. (1992). Shopfloor work organization and advanced manufacturing technology. In C. L. Cooper & I. T. Robertson (Eds.), *International review of industrial and organizational psychology* (Vol. 7, pp. 363–97). Chichester: J. Wiley.

——& Martin, R. (1987). Job and work design. In C. L. Cooper & I. T. Robertson (Eds.), *International review of industrial and organizational psychology* (Vol. 2, pp. 61–92). Chichester: J. Wiley.

Warr, P. B. (1987a). *Work, unemployment, and mental health*. Oxford: Oxford University Press.

——(Ed.) (1987b). *Psychology at work*. Harmondsworth: Penguin.

——(1991). Mental health, well-being and satisfaction. In B. Hesketh & A. Adams (Eds.), *Psychological perspectives on occupational health and rehabilitation* (pp. 143–65). New York: Harcourt Brace Jovanovich.

West, M. J., & Farr, J. L. (Eds.) (1990). *Innovation and creativity at work*. Chichester: J. Wiley.

PETER WARR

# Index

Note: page numbers in **bold** refer to key headings in the text.